THE ENCYCLOPEDIA OF
SCIENCE FICTION AND FANTASY

VOLUME THREE

THE ENCYCLOPEDIA OF SCIENCE FICTION AND FANTASY

Through 1968

Compiled by DONALD H. TUCK

A bibliographic survey of
the fields of science fiction, fantasy,
and weird fiction through 1968

Volume 3: MISCELLANEOUS

Advent:Publishers, Inc.

Chicago: 1982

For
AUDREY
and
MARCUS

Library of Congress Catalog Number: 73-91828

International Standard Book Numbers: 0-911682-20-1 (Volume 1)
0-911682-22-8 (Volume 2)
0-911682-26-0 (Volume 3)

FIRST EDITION, March 1974 (Volume 1)
January 1978 (Volume 2)
December 1982 (Volume 3)

Contents

Introduction

This volume culminates my project of the 1960's for *The Encyclopedia of Science Fiction and Fantasy* to appear in three volumes.

This particular volume collects my original supplementary material. In particular, I feel my sections on MAGAZINES and PAPERBACKS are of major reference importance for the period through 1968. The GENERAL section, now somewhat dated, nevertheless provides information not available elsewhere, including the coverage of science fiction in a number of countries, the book clubs, etc., as well as information now available in other reference works, such as the Hugo and Nebula Award winners.

One important aspect of the PSEUDONYM section is that, following the suggestion of Advent, it has been updated to cover the science fiction and fantasy fields through to the 1980's.

Advent has also indicated that it will continue publishing further volumes of my *Encyclopedia*. We are now assessing the form of material to be covered, with present thoughts being to provide *WHO'S WHO* listings as in Volumes 1 and 2, but with less emphasis on biographies of the foremost authors, as this area is now well covered by other reference works in the science fiction and associated fields.

Donald H. Tuck
P.O. Box 44
Lindisfarne, Tasmania, 7015
Australia

October 1982

Acknowledgments

I still wish to acknowledge the help of my friends as noted in Volumes 1 and 2. However, with the time lag in producing this volume, many sections were revised in the light of more recent information from these people and newer contacts. Considerable information has been added to my original MAGAZINE coverage through material provided by the late Ronald Graham of Sydney. Also, thanks are due to Bob Michelucci of Pittsburgh, U.S.A., for his *The Collectors Guide to Monster Magazines* (1977), which clarified many aspects of this particular group of magazines, and to R. Weinberg and L. McKinstry, whose *The Hero-Pulp Index* has been a major reference source on the magazine field.

I also thank R. Reginald and his comprehensive work *Science Fiction and Fantasy Literature* (1979) for clarifying the pseudonyms of a number of writers. This information has been used in both the PSEUDONYMS and PAPERBACKS sections. Similar informamation, especially covering the British paperback field of the early 1950's, has also been supplied by Michael Ashley of Chatham, England. Bob Gaines of Columbus, Ohio, provided much information on pseudonyms, and data from Marty Massoglia was very useful in checking paperbacks.

Donald H. Tuck

System and Abbreviations

Indexing throughout the *Encyclopedia* is alphabetical word by word. Abbreviations such as "Dr." and "Mr." occurring in titles are alphabetized as if they were spelled out.

ABBREVIATIONS

General

A	anthology
abr	abridged
Aust.	Australian
B.C.	Book Club
Brit.	British
C	collection(s)
¢	cents
ca.	*circa* (about; approximately)
cont.	continued
contd	continued
D'day	Doubleday
ed.	edition
ext.	extract
frontis.	frontispiece
fy	fantasy
h	house name
IFA	International Fantasy Award
illus.—	illustrated (by)
lib.	library edition
n	novel(s)
nd	not dated (or unknown)
nn	not numbered
np	not priced (or unknown)
n'te	novelette(s)
pa	paperback, papercovered)
pp.	pages (inclusive)
pseud.	pseudonym
rev.	revised
sf, s-f	science fiction
SF	Science Fiction (as part of title or name)
SFWA	Science Fiction Writers of America
S.J.	Sidgwick & Jackson
sr	serial (with number showing how many parts)

Magazines and Series published in English

AFR	*Avon Fantasy Reader*
Arg	*Argosy*
AS	*Amazing Stories*
ASF	*Analog Science Fiction / Science Fact*
	Astounding Science Fiction
	Astounding Stories
ASQ	*Amazing Stories Quarterly*
ASW	*All-Story Weekly* (including title changes)
BB	*Blue Book*
FA	*Fantastic Adventures*
Fan	*Fantastic* (including title changes)
F&SF	*The Magazine of Fantasy and Science Fiction*
FFM	*Famous Fantastic Mysteries*
FN	*Fantastic Novels*
FSM	*Fantastic Story Magazine*
FU	*Fantastic Universe*
Fut	*Future Science Fiction* (including title changes)
GSF	*Galaxy Magazine*
	Galaxy Science Fiction
NW	*New Worlds*
S&I	*Science and Invention*
SEP	*Saturday Evening Post*
SFA	*Science Fiction Adventures* (U.S. unless specified to be British)
SS	*Startling Stories*
SSS	*Super Science Stories*
2CSAB	*Two Complete Science Adventure Books*
TWS	*Thrilling Wonder Stories*
WOT	*Worlds of Tomorrow*
WS	*Wonder Stories*
WSQ	*Wonder Stories Quarterly*
WT	*Weird Tales*

General Note: The majority of the above abbreviations have come into use in the field gradually, and are therefore not entirely consistent. For most magazines other than the above, the first principal word of the title is given in full and the remainder omitted unless there would be ambiguity; for example, *Planet* means *Planet Stories*, but *Space SF* differs from *Space Stories*.

Foreign Language Publications (country of origin is always mentioned)

Danish:	F	Fremtidsromanen
	P	Planetbogerne
French:	A	Anticipation
	Classique SF	Les Classiques de la Science-Fiction
	Le RF	Le Rayon Fantastique
	PF	Presence du Futur
German:	AW	*Abenteuer in Weltenraum*
	L	*Luna-Weltall*

	T	*Terra*
	TE	*Terra Extra*
	TN	Terra Nova
	TS	*Terra Sonderband*
	UG	*Utopia-Grossband*
	UK	*Utopia-Kriminal*
	UTR	*Utopia-Taschenroman*
	UZ	*Utopia-Zukunftsroman*
	WF	*Der Weltraumfahrer*
Italian:	*Cosmo*	*I Romanzi di Cosmo Fantascienza*
	GRF	*Galassia Romanzi di Fantascienza*
	Urania	*I Romanzi di Urania* [later *Urania*—but do not confuse with original *Urania* magazine]
Swedish:	A	Atombóckerna (Lindqvists)
	JVM	*Jules Verne Magasinet*
	R	Rymdbóckerna

MAGAZINES

Introduction

This section outlines the science fiction, fantasy, and weird magazines of importance, as well as foreign titles and some general fiction magazines which have at times published material of direct interest in these fields. Some publishers' chains of magazines are also listed, as well as a number of still-born magazines.

Coverage is as complete as possible for the magazines catering directly to the science fiction, fantasy, and weird fields. A number of borderline publications in the weird mystery, terror, and similar fields are also covered.

Extensive use has been made of *The Complete Checklist of Science-Fiction Magazines*, by B. M. Day (published by B. M. Day, New York, 1961), to whom thanks are expressed. I also acknowledge use of *The Weird Menace*, by Bob Jones (Opar Press, 1962), and *The Shudder Pulps*, by R. K. Jones (1975), per kind favour of the author, and Fax Collector's Editions. The major reference for British magazines, including British editions of American magazines, was Graham Stone's *Index to the British Science Fiction Magazines 1934–1953*, published in sections in the 1970's.

Regular foreign magazine series are included, but regular paper-covered series in the English language are listed in the *Publishers* part of the *PAPERBACKS* section in this volume. Amateur magazines of note are covered in the *GENERAL* section in this volume.

Within each magazine entry an attempt has been made wherever possible to cover the magazine under appropriate subheadings, according to this layout:
MAGAZINE TITLE (generally used abbreviation)
(country of publication) (type: sf, fantasy, etc.)
Former titles (if any)
Number of issues (first to last; for magazines still current, the last 1968 issue; "ceased" indicates magazines which have died since 1968)
Size; number of pages; frequency; price (certain of these may be separately outlined)
Editor(s)
Publisher(s)
Format and price changes (as necessary)
Cover artists – interior artists
Review (general outline of the magazine's history, policy, etc.)
Notable Fiction (see below)
Issues (complete checklist table, or outline of dates and frequency of publication)

The "Notable Fiction" section is an attempt by the compiler to outline most of the noted stories, series, etc., published through the years by each magazine. These choices have been made through personal preference and through comments by noted authorities in the amateur field. Often the later reprinting of a story has been considered as reasonable basis for its mention. (However, this aspect has not been covered for reprintings since 1968.)

Italicized titles indicate a story that has seen book publication; further information may be obtained by checking under the appropriate author in the *WHO'S WHO* sections. Further information on series and sequels may be found in the *SERIES* section in this volume. Interpolated phrases (in brackets or parentheses) give the author's real name, or the later title of the story in book form, etc.

A title is understood to be a novel unless qualified as "short," "n'te" (novelette), or "art" (article). An exception is when a general qualification covers a set of stories.

A virgule (/) between month dates ("April/May") indicates a single issue bearing both dates.

A virgule is also used to connect volume number and issue number in the checklists of issues and elsewhere. Thus, "4/12" means Volume 4, Issue No. 12.

In the issues checklist tables, the last column, "W", gives the Whole Number, i.e., the cumulative number of issues to that point.

A. MERRITT'S FANTASY MAGAZINE [*AMF*] U.S. Fantasy
5 issues (Dec 1949—Oct 1950).
Pulp; 130 pp.; quarterly?; 25¢.
Editor: Mary Gnaedinger.
Publisher: Popular Publications, New York.
Cover artists: Lawrence [L. S. Stevens] (2); N. Saunders (3).
Interiors: Many by V. Finlay.
Review: This magazine was started because of the interest in Abraham Merritt's fiction; most issues featured one of his stories.
Notable fiction:
1949 Dec *Creep, Shadow!*, A. Merritt
1950 Feb "The Smoking Land," G. Challis [F. Faust]
    Apr *The Ninth Life*, J. Mann [C. Cannell]
    July "The Face in the Abyss," A. Merritt
    Oct "The Elixir of Hate," G. A. England
The never-published 6th issue was to have had "The Snake Mother," A. Merritt, and "The Lost Garden," M. Brand [F. Faust].
Issues:

	Jan	Feb	Mar	Apr	May	Jun	Jul	Aug	Sep	Oct	Nov	Dec	W
1949												1/1	1
1950		1/2		1/3		1/4			2/1				5

Canadian Edition
5 issues (Dec 1949—Oct 1950), as for the U.S. edition.
Pulp; 130 pp.; quarterly?; 25¢.
Publisher: Recreational Reading Inc., an affiliate of Popular Publications Inc., Toronto, Ontario, Canada.
   Entire contents, covers and dates are identical with the U.S. editions, except that the magazines are a half inch longer, enabling the panel at the bottom of the front cover to give the title of the secondary story as well as the main novel. Advertisements are the same as U.S. except that two Canadian beer firms have the outside back covers.

ABENTEUER IM WELTENRAUM [*AW*] German Science fiction
19 issues (*ca.* May 1948—May 1959), not dated (fortnightly).
6 in. x 9 in.; 96 pp., 1DM.
Publisher: A. Semrau-Verlag, Hamburg.
Review: Mainly printed translations of U.S. novels, beginning with *Mankind on the Run*, G. R. Dickson, and ending with *The Man With Absolute Motion*, N. Loomis. P. K. Dick and J. Vance each had two novels; other authors included H. B. Piper, A. Norton and G. O. Smith. The famous *Auf Zwei Planeten* by K. Lasswitz was reprinted in Nos. 5 and 6, 1958.

ACE MYSTERY U.S. Mystery weird
3 issues (May 1936, July 1936, Sep 1936).
Editor: Harry Widmer.
Publisher: Periodical House (subsidiary of A. A. Wyn's Magazine Publishers).
Review: One of the "shudder pulps." Frederick C. Davis led off each of the three issues ("The Destroying Angel" in No. 2); other writers included Hugh B. Cave, G. T. Fleming-Roberts and Paul Ernst. R. K. Jones in *The Shudder Pulps* feels that "Coyote Woman," by Charles M. Warren (July 1936) was one of the most effective stories.

ADVENTURE U.S. General fiction
   An American magazine, started Nov 1910 and ceased April 1971. Mostly monthly but at times twice monthly (and thrice monthly 1921 to 1926). It presented some fantastic fiction, mainly by Talbot Mundy.
Notable Fiction:
1920   Jan "The Green Splotches" (n'te), T. S. Stribling
1921 10 Nov "The Adventure of El-Karak," T. Mundy [first of "Jimgrim" series]
1922 10 Nov "The Gray Mahatma," T. Mundy [*The Caves of Terror*]
1923 20 Mar *The Nine Unknown* (sr5), T. Mundy
1924 10 Oct *Om: The Secret of Ahbor Valley* (sr6), T. Mundy

1925 10 Feb *Tros of Samothrace*, T. Mundy [first of 11 stories in the series, later appearing in books]
1926 8 Jun "Ramsden" (sr5), T. Mundy [*The Devil's Guard*]
1930 1 Jun "Mogglesby" (short), T. S. Stribling
    15 Nov "King of the World" (sr7), T. Mundy [*Jimgrim*]

ADVENTURES FUTURISTES, LES
                    Canadian (in French) Science fiction
10 issues (1 Mar 1949—Sep 1949).
Numbered, not dated; issues ran two per month 1 Mar to 1 June, then monthly. Published in Montreal, Canada.
   Printings were apparently small, as this is very rare. It retailed the exploits of two scientist heroes, in "The Spherical Men," "The Talking Plants," and others.

AIKAMME Finnish Science fiction
4 issues (late 1958—early 1959).
   An edition of *Galaxy Science Fiction*.

AIR WONDER STORIES [*Air Wonder*] U.S. Science fiction
11 issues (Jul 1929—May 1930).
Large size; 96 pp.; monthly; 25¢.
Editor: H. Gernsback.
Publisher: Stellar Pub. Corp., New York.
Artists: F. Paul for all covers and most interior work.
Review: One of the magazines founded by Gernsback when he was forced to leave *Amazing Stories*, his first science fiction magazine. *Air Wonder* catered to the then keen interest in aviation and its future possibilities. It featured future air stories, inventions, etc. The late J. B. Harris won a slogan competition with "Future Flying Fiction," but it was not used, as the magazine was combined with *Science Wonder Stories* to form *Wonder Stories*.
Notable Fiction:
1929 Jul *The Ark of the Covenant* (sr4), V. MacClure; "Men With Wings" (n'te), L. F. Stone [having later sequel]
    Aug "Beyond Gravity" (n'te), E. E. Repp
    Nov "Cities of the Air" (sr2), E. Hamilton
1930 Jan *The Flying Legion* (sr4), G. A. England
    Feb "The Vanishing Fleet" (n'te), H. D. Juve
    Mar "The Space Visitors" (short), E. Hamilton
    May "The Bat-Men of Mars" (sr3), W. Jackson
Issues:

	Jan	Feb	Mar	Apr	May	Jun	Jul	Aug	Sep	Oct	Nov	Dec	W
1929							1/1	1/2	1/3	1/4	1/5	1/6	6
1930	1/7	1/8	1/9	1/10	1/11 merging into *Wonder Stories*								11

ALDINE CHEERFUL LIBRARY
7-5/8 in. x 10-1/8 in.; 32 pp.; weekly; 1d.
   A boy's magazine apparently contemporary with *Aldine Invention, Travel and Adventure Library*. Issues sighted were Nos. 2, 5, 8 and 11, all dealing with the adventures of Jack Wright.

ALDINE INVENTION, TRAVEL AND ADVENTURE LIBRARY
                            British   Boy's magazine
272 issues (Mar 1899—Nov 1905).
8½ in. x 5½ in.; 36 pp., weekly, 1d.
Publisher: Aldine Publishing Co., London.
Review: This was the British reprint of the U.S. *Frank Reade Library*. Issue No. 1 contained "Frank Reade Jr. and His New Steam Man, or The Young Inventor's Trip to the Far West." In issue No. 189 came the first meeting of Frank Reade Jr. and Jack Wright—"Jack Wright and Frank Reade, or The Great 10,000 Dollar Wager." From then on the stories were indiscriminately about either or both of the two protagonists. The series ceased with No. 272, "Frank Read [sic] on the Wings of the Wind." The covers were the same as the American originals. The late Ron Graham of Sydney, N.S.W., collected over half the issues.

ALIEN WORLDS British Science Fiction
1 issue; No. 1, not dated (Aug 1966).
Digest size; 64 pp. including covers; saddle-stapled; 2/6.
Editor and Publisher: Charles Partington and Harry Nadler, Lancashire, England.

Review: Photolithographed, with some colour illustrations. The contents were fiction—"Contact Man," H. Harrison; "Not Human," K. Bulmer; "The Childish Fear," J. R. Campbell—plus articles on Flash Gordon, the film *1 Million B.C.*, and a mention of the film *2001* as being in production.

ALL AMERICAN FICTION   U.S.   General fiction
Publisher: Frank A. Munsey, New York.
Pulp size; 128 pp., 15¢.
Issues: From Nov 1937 as a monthly, bimonthly from Mar/Apr 1938 to Sep/Oct 1938, and then combined with *Argosy*.
Notable Fiction:
1938 Feb   "Beyond Time and Space" (short), J. T. Rogers [reprinted in *Super Science Stories*, Sep 1950)
      Mar/Apr   "Jane Brown's Body" (short), C. Woolrich [reprinted in *F&SF*, Oct 1951]
Of associational interest is that "Beat to Quarters," the first story of C. S. Forester's "Hornblower" series, appeared in Sep/Oct 1938 (2/2).

ALL-STORY MAGAZINE [*ASW*]   U.S.   General fiction
Title changes: Monthly Jan 1905—Mar 1914; *All-Story Weekly* 7 Mar 1914—9 May 1914; *All-Story-Cavalier Weekly* 16 May 1914—8 May 1915; *All-Story Weekly* 15 May 1915—17 Jul 1920. Then ceased, combining with *Argosy Weekly* to form *Argosy-All-Story Weekly* [check *Argosy*].
Editor: R. H. (Bob) Davis.
Publisher: Frank A. Munsey, New York.
  Published much of interest in the fantasy field, and was one of the sources of reprints for *Famous Fantastic Mysteries* and *Fantastic Novels*.
Notable Fiction:
1905 May *The Moon Metal*, G. P. Serviss
1908 Nov "The Planet Juggler" (short), J. G. Frederick
1909 Jan *A Columbus of Space* (sr6), G. P. Serviss
1911 Jan "A Place of Monsters" (short), T. P. Byron
1912 Feb "Under the Moons of Mars" (sr6), N. Bean [*A Princess of Mars*, E. R. Burroughs]
      Oct *Tarzan of the Apes*, E. R. Burroughs
1913 Jan *The Gods of Mars* (sr5), E. R. Burroughs
      Jul *The Cave Girl* (sr3), E. R. Burroughs
      Nov "A Man Without a Soul," E. R. Burroughs [*The Monster Men*]
      Dec "The 'V' Force" (short), F. Smale; *Warlord of Mars* (sr4), E. R. Burroughs
1914 7 Mar *The Eternal Lover*, E. R. Burroughs
      4 Apr *At the Earth's Core* (sr4), E. R. Burroughs
      16 May *The Beasts of Tarzan* (sr5), E. R. Burroughs
      14 Oct *The Mucker* (sr4), E. R. Burroughs
      14 Nov "The Empire in the Air" (sr4), G. A. England
1915 23 Jan "Sweethearts Primeval" (sr4), E. R. Burroughs [*The Eternal Lover*]
      13 Feb "The Methods of Morris Klaw"(n'te), S. Rohmer [began series of 4]
      1 May *Pellucidar* (sr3), E. R. Burroughs
      18 Sep "The God of the Invincibly Strong Arms" (sr5), A. Abdullah [*The Red Stain*]
      4 Dec *The Son of Tarzan* (sr6), E. R. Burroughs
      18 Dec *Polaris of the Snows* (sr3), C. B. Stilson [first of series]
1916 1 Jan *The Sea Demons* (sr4), V. Rousseau [V. R. Emanuel]
      25 Mar "The God of the Invincibly Strong Arms" (2nd series) (sr6), A. Abdullah [*The Blue-Eyed Manchu*]
      8 Apr *Thuvia, Maid of Mars* (sr3), E. R. Burroughs
      12 Aug *Minos of Sardanes*, C. B. Stilson [2nd of "Polaris" series]
      7 Oct "Almost Immortal" (n'te), A. Hall
      18 Nov "The God of the Invincibly Strong Arms" (3rd series) (sr4), A. Abdullah; *Tarzan and the Jewels of Opar* (sr5), E. R. Burroughs
1917 31 Mar "The Cave Man" (sr4), E. R. Burroughs [*The Cave Girl*]
      3 Jun *The Lad and the Lion* (sr3), E. R. Burroughs; "The Rebel Soul" (short), A. Hall
      14 Jul *The Terrible Three* (sr4), T. Robbins
      15 Sep "Polaris and the Goddess Glorian," C. B. Stilson [*Polaris and the Immortals*—last of "Polaris" trilogy]

      24 Nov "The Cosmic Courtship" (sr4), J. Hawthorne; "Through the Dragon Glass" (short), A. Merritt
1918 5 Jan "The People of the Pit" (n'te), A. Merritt
      9 Feb "The Diminishing Draft" (n'te), W. Kaempffert
      9 Mar "The Planeteer" (n'te), H. E. Flint
      1 Jun *The Draft of Eternity* (sr4), V. Rousseau [V. R. Emanuel]
      8 Jun "John Ovington Returns," M. Brand [F. Faust]
      22 Jun "The Moon Pool" (short), A. Merritt [with sequel, as *The Moon Pool*]
      13 Jul *Palos of the Dog Star Pack* (sr5), J. U. Giesy [first of "Palos" trilogy]; "Devil Ritter" (short), M. Brand [F. Faust]
      27 Jul "The Labyrinth" (sr3), F. Stevens [G. Bennett]
      21 Sep "Behind the Curtain" (short) F. Stevens [G. Bennett]
      12 Oct "The King of Conserve Island" (n'te), H. E. Flint
      21 Dec "Who Wants a Green Bottle?" (n'te), T. Robbins [title story of collection]
1919 11 Jan *Cursed* (sr6), G. A. England
      15 Feb "That Receding Brow" (n'te), M. Brand [F. Faust]
      15 Mar "The Girl in the Golden Atom" (n'te), R. Cummings [with sequel, as *The Girl in the Golden Atom*]
      5 Apr "The Living Portrait" (n'te), T. Robbins
      12 Apr *Into the Infinite* (sr6), A. Hall
      10 May *The Lord of Death* (n'te), H. E. Flint
      5 Jul *The Mouthpiece of Zitu*, J. U. Giesy [2nd of "Palos" trilogy]
      26 Jul "The Strange Case of Lemuel Jenkins" (short) P. M. Fisher
      9 Aug "Three Lines of Old French" (short), A. Merritt
      16 Aug "The Queen of Life" (n'te), H. E. Flint [as paperback, with *The Lord of Death*]
      18 Oct "The Other Man's Blood" (n'te), R. Cummings
      25 Oct "The Whimpus" (short), T. Robbins
      15 Nov *The Flying Legion* (sr6), G. A. England
      13 Dec "The Man Who Saved the Earth" (n'te), A. Hall
1920 3 Jan "The Ship of Silent Men" (n'te), P. M. Fisher; "The Lost Garden" (short), M. Brand [F. Faust]
      10 Jan "The Man Who Discovered Nothing" (short), R. Cummings [first of "Tubby" series]
      17 Jan "The Eye of Balamok" (sr3), V. Rousseau [V. R. Emanuel]
      14 Feb "Wild Wullie, the Waster" (n'te), T. Robbins
      20 Mar "Tarzan and the Valley of Luna" (sr5), E. R. Burroughs [see *Tarzan the Untamed*]

ALPHA   Swedish [projected]   Science fiction
Editor: Sam J. Lundwall.
Review: First issue was planned to be August 1958, with cover in three colors by Sven O. Emilsson and interior illustrations by Orban and V. Finlay. Stories were to have been "The Fog Horn" (short), R. Bradbury; "Feeding Time" (short), J. E. Gunn; "Aesop" (short) C. D. Simak; "Frankenstein" (as serial), M. W. Shelley. It was to have been 50 pp. and priced at 1.50 kr. After material had been collected, copyright holders contacted, and some printing plates made, the financier backed out.

AMAZING   U.S.   Science fiction
1 issue (August 1950); large size; 26 pp.; sold for 10¢ through the mail.
  It contained the story "Lullaby," by Peter Worth [R. P. Graham?]. In 1950 the editor of *Amazing Stories*, Howard Browne, considered turning it into a general fiction magazine such as *Blue Book* or the old *Argosy*. But the Korean War broke out in June of 1950 and the plans were cancelled. This item may be one signature from that "never-to-be" magazine. It is among the rarest of the rare.

AMAZING DETECTIVE TALES   U.S.   Science fiction/detective
Formerly *Scientific Detective Monthly* (Jan-May 1930)
10 issues (Jan 1930—Oct 1930).
Large size; 96 pp.; monthly; 25¢.
Editor: H. Gernsback. **Editorial Commissioner:** A. B. Reeve.
Publisher: Techni-Craft Pub. Co., New York.
Review: A sister magazine to *Air Wonder Stories* and *Science Wonder Stories*.
  [A slightly later magazine, *Amazing Detective Stories* (Fiction Publishers, Inc., New York; pulp size; 128 pp.; 20¢) *may* have been a con-

tinuation. It published little of fantasy interest, but serialized "The Feathered Serpent," E. Wallace. Issues sighted are 1931 Mar, May and Aug (2/2, 2/3, 2/4).]

Notable Fiction: Presented the "Craig Kennedy" series, by A. B. Reeve; also had E. Balmer/W. McHarg collaborations in most issues.

1930 Jan   "The Bishop Murder Case" (sr3), S. S. Van Dine

     Feb   "A Scientific Widowhood" (short), D. H. Keller

     Apr   "The Invisible Master" (n'te), E. Hamilton

     May   "The Murder in the Clinic" (n'te), E. Hamilton; "The Electrical Man" (n'te), N. R. Jones

     Jun   "Burning Water" (short), D. H. Keller

     Aug   "The Vanishing Man" (short), R. M. Farley [R. S. Hoar]

     Sep   "Menacing Claws" (short), D. H. Keller

     Oct   "Murder in the Fourth Dimension" (short), C. A. Smith

Issues:

	Jan	Feb	Mar	Apr	May	Jun	Jul	Aug	Sep	Oct	Nov	Dec	W
1930	1/1	1/2	1/3	1/4	1/5	1/6	1/7	1/8	1/9	1/10			10

AMAZING FACT AND SCIENCE FICTION STORIES See *AMAZING STORIES*

AMAZING SCIENCE FICTION (STORIES) See *AMAZING STORIES*

AMAZING SCIENCE STORIES   British   Science fiction
2 issues (#1, #2), not dated; about Mar and Apr 1951.
Large size; 66 pp.; monthly.
Publisher: Pembertons, Manchester, England.

Covers and most contents were reprinted from the Australian science fiction magazine *Thrills Incorporated*, but a few short stories of U.S. origin were also presented.

AMAZING STORIES [*AS*]   U.S.   Science fiction
Current (Apr 1926—).
436th issue—November 1968; digest size; 146 pp.; bimonthly; 50¢.
Title Changes: *Amazing Stories* through to Feb 1958; *Amazing Science Fiction* Mar and Apr 1958; *Amazing Science Fiction Stories* May 1958 to Sep 1960; *Amazing Stories* Oct 1960 to date (1968) (with cover subtitle "Fact and Science Fiction" to June 1965).
Editors: H. Gernsback, Apr 1926—Apr 1929; Arthur Lynch, May 1929—Oct 1929; T. O'Conor Sloane, Nov 1929—Apr 1938; R. A. Palmer, June 1938—Dec 1949; H. Browne, Jan 1950—Aug 1956; P. W. Fairman, Sep 1956—Nov 1958; C. Goldsmith (later married, name changed to Lalli, Dec 1958—June 1965 (N. Lobsenz as Editorial Director for this period); J. Ross, Aug 1965—Oct 1967; H. Harrison, Dec 1967—Sep 1968; B. Malzberg, Dec 1968— (Associate Editor, Sep 1968). Upon his purchase of this magazine Sol Cohen was listed as Editor and Publisher from Aug 1965, the editors above being listed as Managing Editor.
Publishers: Experimenter Pub. Co., Apr 1926—1929; Teck Pub. Corp., 1929—Apr 1938; Ziff-Davis Publishing Co., June 1938—June 1965; Sol Cohen, Aug 1965 to date (1968).
Size Changes: large size, Apr 1926—Aug/Sep 1933; pulp size, Oct 1933—Mar 1953; digest size, Apr/May 1953 to date.
Cover Artists: More notable include F. R. Paul, Apr 1926—June 1929; L. Morey, Feb 1930—Apr 1938 except for Sigmond, Jan 1933—July 1933 and several by H. Wesso. R. A. Palmer introduced Fuqua [J. W. Tillotson], H. McCauley, P. St. John and R. Jones. H. Browne introduced others, including E. Valigursky, who ran Mar 1955—Dec 1958, with some later. M. Hunter had two covers in 1954. A. Schomburg first appeared in 1960. Others in the early 1960's were E. Emsh(willer), L. Birmingham, R. Adragna and G. Morrow. Since Cohen became publisher many reprint covers have been used, including F. R. Paul's "Stories of the Stars" series, and some by J. B. Settles.
Review:

Gernsback first announced plans for this magazine under the title *Scientifiction* in a circular to subscribers of *Science and Invention* in 1925, but the response was so poor that he delayed it. Then, feeling this name lacked general appeal, he brought out the magazine under the title *Amazing Stories*. Initially it reprinted many stories by the old masters—J. Verne, H. G. Wells, E. A. Poe, etc.—until new writers gradually developed.

Under Gernsback, *Amazing* ran the first appearances of David H. Keller and Edward E. Smith, while writers such as G. P. Wertenbaker,

M. J. Breuer, Clare W. Harris and J. Williamson also were noteworthy.

The early circulation was around 100,000 (per editorial, Sep 1926). Several inducements were offered to build readership, such as the free booklet *The Vanguard to Venus*, L. Bartlett (to find where the readers lived), and various contests, including a story to be written around the Dec 1926 cover and also a symbol for scientifiction. In 1927 the companion magazine *Amazing Stories Annual* appeared; it was successful and evolved into *Amazing Stories Quarterly*.

In the early years of Sloane's editorship *Amazing* was quite high class. Then the magazine gradually deteriorated until by 1938, when it was sold to Ziff-Davis, it was but a shadow of its former self. During the early 1930's, however, John W. Campbell, Jr. and C. Cloukey first appeared in its pages, and there was much further fiction from such authors as D. Keller, E. E. Smith, J. Williamson, S. P. Meek and J. R. Fearn. An unusual venture in cover design was the group of seven Sigmond symbolic covers in 1933, which probably would have been better received many years later. A noted series starting in the period was N. R. Jones' "Professor Jameson" stories. Towards the end of the period writers of interest included W. K. Sonneman, A. K. Barnes, and the South African, Walter Rose.

The publisher Ziff-Davis of Chicago bought the magazine in 1938; Ralph M. Farley (pseudonym of R. S. Hoar) was instrumental in the appointment of R. A. Palmer as editor. Palmer began a policy of mass appeal, and soon the circulation of *Amazing Stories* rose until it peaked with the "Shaver Mystery" issues of 1945. One innovation was the introduction of colour back cover illustrations appearing in the series "Cities on Other Worlds" and "Life on Other Worlds"—both by Frank R. Paul, "Transportation on Other Worlds" (J. B. Settles), and "Stories of the Stars" (F. R. Paul). Palmer also initiated a Monthly Merit Award (monetary incentive to authors by reader vote) and started using cartoons. He continually increased the size of the magazine until it reached a peak of 274 pages in 1942. The Sep 1944 issue was entirely written and illustrated by authors and artists in the armed forces. The notable fan column *The Club House* began in Jan 1948 and was conducted for a number of years by Rog Phillips (pseudonym of R. P. Graham).

Under Brown the story policy improved somewhat. In Aug 1950 it was announced that *Amazing* was to go large size and slick with the Nov 1950 issue, priced at 35¢; this never eventuated, due to the Korean War. However, a new companion magazine (besides *Fantastic Adventures*, which had started in 1939), *Fantastic*, was begun in 1952; its success in digest size, coupled with the recession in the sf field, caused *Amazing* itself to become digest size from Apr/May 1953. Departments were revived to a certain extent from mid-1955—book reviews by Villiers Gerson (*New York Times* book reviewer) and fan magazine reviews by Roger De Soto. Particular issues of note were the Apr 1956 Thirtieth Anniversary Issue (50¢, 258 pp. in smaller type reprinting 14 stories from 1927-1942) and Oct 1957 (featuring flying saucer material). There seemed to be hardly any change of policy during Fairman's tenure.

The first years of editorship by Lobsenz and Goldsmith saw the magazine reach a quite high standard and become the least stereotyped in the science fiction field. The addition of "Fact" in the magazine title covered the printing of articles by such authors as Dr. A. Barron, L. del Rey, F. Tinsley, and B. Bova. From Dec 1960 classic reprints of quite some interest appeared, selected and introduced by S. Moskowitz, who also began a series of "profiles" on contemporary sf authors in alternate issues from June 1961 (he had covered H. Gernsback earlier, in Sep 1960). As a follow-on to the one-shot companion *Amazing Stories Science Novel*, for a period beginning Mar 1958 *Amazing* ran novels in small type as a sort of supplement; many of these later saw book editions. The format was "modernized" in Oct 1960. The 35th Anniversary Issue, Apr 1961 reprinted 7 stories (50¢, 196 pp.). The back cover was used for a black and white illustration (for a story inside) from May 1961 (except for June 1961).

By the mid-1960's sales were slipping badly, and both *Amazing* and *Fantastic* were offered for sale by Ziff-Davis. Both were purchased by Sol Cohen. Naturally wishing to make a small profit, Cohen used the magazines' only assets—the magazine reprint rights on all stories originally published in its pages. Thus about three quarters of the contents of each issue were reprints, with only one quarter being new material—often a serial installment. Both magazines were boycotted in some quarters for non-payment of authors of the reprints, but more recently it is understood that nominal payments have been made. A higher proportion of new material was also being used at the turn of the 1970's. The 40th Anniversary Issue, Apr 1966, was 192 pp.; it reprinted eight stories ranging from 1926 to 1951 and included a portfolio of F. R. Paul's illustrations of H. G. Wells's stories.

Notable Fiction: Early issues to 1928 had many reprints of E. A. Poe, J. Verne and H. G. Wells; only the longer stories by these authors are mentioned below.

1926   C. Fezandie's "Dr. Hackensaw's Secrets" series continued in June from *Science & Invention*.

Apr   *Off on a Comet* (sr2), J. Verne; "The Man From the Atom" (sr2), G. P. Wertenbaker; "The Man Who Saved the Earth" (n'te), A. Hall

May   *A Trip to the Center of the Earth* (sr3), J. Verne

Jun   "The Coming of the Ice" (n'te), G. P. Wertenbaker; "The Runaway Skyscraper" (short), M. Leinster [W. F. Jenkins]

Jul   *Station X* (sr3), G. M. Winsor; *The Moon Metal*, G. P. Serviss

Aug   *A Columbus of Space* (sr3), G. P. Serviss

Sep   *The Purchase of the North Pole* (sr2), J. Verne; "The Moon Hoax" (article from 1835), R. A. Locke

Oct   "Beyond the Pole" (sr2), A. H. Verrill; *The Island of Dr. Moreau* (sr2), H. G. Wells

Nov   *The Second Deluge* (sr4), G. P. Serviss; "The Mad Planet" (n'te), M. Leinster [W. F. Jenkins] [with later stories, as *The Forgotten Planet*]

Dec   *First Men in the Moon* (sr3), H. G. Wells; "The Diamond Lens" (short), F.-J. O'Brien

1927   E. Balmer & W. McHarg collaborations began in Feb; "Hick's Inventions With a Kick" series, H. H. Simmons, began in Apr; first appearances of Clare W. Harris and Bob Olsen in June.

Feb   *The Land That Time Forgot* (sr3), E. R. Burroughs

Mar   "The Green Splotches" (n'te), T. S. Stribling; "The People of the Pit" (short), A. Merritt

Apr   "John Jones's Dollar" (short), H. S. Keeler

May   *The Moon Pool* (sr3), A. Merritt; *The Time Machine*, H. G. Wells

Aug   *The War of the Worlds* (sr2), H. G. Wells; "The Tissue-Culture King" (short), J. Huxley

Sep   "The Colour out of Space" (short), H. P. Lovecraft

Oct   *Around the Universe*, R. Cummings; *The Treasures of Tantalus* (sr2), Garret Smith

Nov   "The Machine Man of Ardathia" (short), F. Flagg [had sequel]

Dec   *Robur the Conqueror* (sr2), J. Verne

1928   H. Gernsback's "Baron Munchausen's Scientific Adventures" series ran Feb to July.

Jan   "The Comet Doom" (n'te), E. Hamilton

Feb   *Master of the World* (sr2), J. Verne; "Revolt of the Pedestrians" (short), D. H. Keller

Mar   "Sub-Satellite" (short), C. Cloukey

Apr   "The Yeast Men" (short), D. H. Keller; "The Miracle of the Lily" (short), Clare W. Harris; "A Story of the Days to Come" (sr2), H. G. Wells

Jun   *The Invisible Man* (sr2), H. G. Wells; "The Golden Girl of Munan" (n'te), H. Vincent [had sequel]

Aug   *The Skylark of Space* (sr3), E. E. Smith; "Armageddon—2419," P. Nowlan [with sequel as book of same title]

Nov   "The World at Bay" (sr2), B. & G. C. Wallis

Dec   "The Appendix and the Spectacles" (short), M. J. Breuer; "The Metal Man" (short), J. Williamson

1929 Jan   "The Sixth Glacier" (sr2), Marius

Feb   "The Death of the Moon" (short), A. M. Phillips; "The Last Man" (short), W. West

Mar   "Into the Green Prism" (sr2), A. H. Verrill [had sequel]

Apr   "The Terror of the Street" (short), G. McLociard

May   *The English at the North Pole* (sr2), J. Verne

Jun   "The Radio Telescope" (short), S. A. Coblentz; *The Desert of Ice* (sr2), J. Verne

Jul   "The Book of Worlds" (short), M. J. Breuer; "Futility" (short), S. P. Meek

Aug   "Barton's Island" (n'te), H. Vincent; *Out of the Void* (sr2), L. F. Stone [had later sequel]

Oct   "The Secret Kingdom" (sr3), A. S. & O. A. Kline; "The Chamber of Life" (short), G. P. Wertenbaker

Nov   "The Undersea Tube" (short), L. T. Hansen

Dec   "A Baby on Neptune" (short), C. W. Harris & M. J. Breuer

1930   J. W. Campbell Jr. first appeared in Jan; his "Arcot" series began in June.

Jan   "The Hungry Guinea Pig" (short), M. J. Breuer

Mar   *The Green Girl* (sr2), J. Williamson; "The Gostak and the Doshes" (short), M. J. Breuer

May   "The Universe Wreckers" (sr3), E. Hamilton

Jul   "Paradox+" (short), C. Cloukey

Aug   *Skylark Three* (sr3), E. E. Smith

Oct   "The Man Who Saw the Future" (short), E. Hamilton; "Dynasty of the Blue-Black Rays" (short), M. R. Peril

Nov   *The Drums of Tapajos* (sr3), S. P. Meek; "The Cosmic Express" (short), J. Williamson

Dec   "The Second Missile" (short), E. E. Repp [in *The Stellar Missiles*]

1931   "Professor Jameson" series, N. R. Jones, began in July [published as paperback series 1967-1968].

Feb   "Television Hill" (sr2), G. McLociard

Apr   "The Ambidexter" (short), D. H. Keller; "The Laughing Death" (n'te), S. G. Hale [had sequel]

May   "Through the Vibrations" (short), P. S. Miller

Jun   "The Power Planet" (n'te), M. Leinster [W. F. Jenkins]

Jul   *Spacehounds of IPC* (sr3), E. E. Smith

Aug   "Submicroscopic" (n'te), S. P. Meek [had sequel]

Sep   "The Arrhenius Horror" (short), P. S. Miller

Oct   "The Stone From the Green Star" (sr2), J. Williamson

Nov   "Automaton" (short), A. J. Gelula; "Luvium" (n'te), A. R. Mackenzie [first of series]

Dec   "The Inevitable Conflict" (sr2), P. H. Lovering

1932   "Lemurian Documents" series, J. L. Burtt, began Jan; "Posi and Nega" series, J. W. Skidmore, began Sep.

Jan   "Tumithak of the Corridors" (n'te), C. R. Tanner [first of series]

Feb   *Troyana* (sr3), S. P. Meek

Mar   "The Light From Infinity" (short), L. A. Eshbach

Apr   "The Lost Machine" (short), J. B. Harris

May   "The Metal Doom" (sr3), D. H. Keller

Aug   "The Swordsman of Sarvon" (sr3), C. Cloukey; "The Last Evolution" (short), J. W. Campbell Jr.

Oct   "The Man Fought a Fly" (short), L. F. Stone; "The First Martian" (short), Eando Binder

Nov   "World of the Living Dead" (sr2), E. E. Repp

Dec   "No More Tomorrows" (short), D. H. Keller

1933 Jan   "The Treasure of the Golden God" (sr2), A. H. Verrill

Mar   "Beyond the End of Space" (sr2), J. W. Campbell Jr.; "In the Scarlet Star" (short), J. Williamson

May   "Martian and Troglodyte" (n'te), N. R. Jones

Jun   *The Intelligence Gigantic* (sr2), J. R. Fearn

Aug   "Essence of Life" (short), F. Pragnell

Oct   "When the Universe Shrank" (sr2), J. L. Burtt

Dec   "A Vision of Venus" (short), O. A. Kline

1934 Jan   *Triplanetary* (sr4), E. E. Smith; "Master of Dreams" (n'te), H. Vincent

Feb   "Terror out of Space" (sr4), H. H. Hill [J. M. Walsh]; "The Time Jumpers" (short), P. Nowlan

Mar   "Peril Among the Drivers" (n'te), B. Olsen

Apr   "Cat's Eye" (n'te), H. Vincent

May   "The Lost City" (sr3), M. R. Peril; "Dr. Grimshaw's Sanitarium" (short), F. Pratt; *Measuring a Meridian* (sr4), J. Verne

Jul   *Life Everlasting* (sr2), D. H. Keller [title story of collection]

Sep   "The Moon Pirates" (sr2), N. R. Jones; "The Plutonian Drug" (short), C. A. Smith; "Through the Andes" (sr3), A. H. Verrill; "Master Minds of Venus" (n'te), W. K. Sonneman

Issues:

	Jan	Feb	Mar	Apr	May	Jun	Jul	Aug	Sep	Oct	Nov	Dec	W
1926				1/1	1/2	1/3	1/4	1/5	1/6	1/7	1/8	1/9	9
1927	1/10	1/11	1/12	2/1	2/2	2/3	2/4	2/5	2/6	2/7	2/8	2/9	21
1928	2/10	2/11	2/12	3/1	3/2	3/3	3/4	3/5	3/6	3/7	3/8	3/9	33
1929	3/10	3/11	3/12	4/1	4/2	4/3	4/4	4/5	4/6	4/7	4/8	4/9	45
1930	4/10	4/11	4/12	5/1	5/2	5/3	5/4	5/5	5/6	5/7	5/8	5/9	57
1931	5/10	5/11	5/12	6/1	6/2	6/3	6/4	6/5	6/6	6/7	6/8	6/9	69
1932	6/10	6/11	6/12	7/1	7/2	7/3	7/4	7/5	7/6	7/7	7/8	7/9	81
1933	7/10	7/11	7/12	8/1	8/2	8/3	8/4		8/5	8/6	8/7	8/8	92
1934	8/9	8/10	8/11	8/12	9/1	9/2	9/3	9/4	9/5	9/6	9/7	9/8	104
1935	9/9	9/10	9/11	10/1	10/2	10/3	10/4	10/5		10/6		10/7	114
1936		10/8		10/9		10/10		10/11		10/12		10/13	120
1937		11/1		11/2		11/3		11/4		11/5		11/6	126
1938		12/1		12/2		12/3		12/4		12/5	12/6	12/7	133
1939	13/1	13/2	13/3	13/4	13/5	13/6	13/7	13/8	13/9	13/10	13/11	13/12	145
1940	14/1	14/2	14/3	14/4	14/5	14/6	14/7	14/8	14/9	14/10	14/11	14/12	157
1941	15/1	15/2	15/3	15/4	15/5	15/6	15/7	15/8	15/9	15/10	15/11	15/12	169
1942	16/1	16/2	16/3	16/4	16/5	16/6	16/7	16/8	16/9	16/10	16/11	16/12	181
1943	17/1	17/2	17/3	17/4	17/5	17/6	17/7	17/8	17/9		17/10		191
1944	18/1		18/2		18/3			18/4			18/5		196
1945		19/1			19/2			19/3			19/4		200
1946		20/1		20/2	20/3	20/4	20/5	20/6	20/7	20/8	20/9		209
1947	21/1	21/2	21/3	21/4	21/5	21/6	21/7	21/8	21/9	21/10	21/11	21/12	221
1948	22/1	22/2	22/3	22/4	22/5	22/6	22/7	22/8	22/9	22/10	22/11	22/12	233
1949	23/1	23/2	23/3	23/4	23/5	23/6	23/7	23/8	23/9	23/10	23/11	23/12	245
1950	24/1	24/2	24/3	24/4	24/5	24/6	24/7	24/8	24/9	24/10	24/11	24/12	257
1951	25/1	25/2	25/3	25/4	25/5	25/6	25/7	25/8	25/9	25/10	25/11	25/12	269
1952	26/1	26/2	26/3	26/4	26/5	26/6	26/7	26/8	26/9	26/10	26/11	26/12	281
1953	27/1	27/2	27/3	27/4		27/5		27/6		27/7		27/8*	289
1954	*		28/1		28/2		28/3		28/4		28/5		294
1955	29/1		29/2		29/3		29/4		29/5		29/6	29/7	301
1956	30/1	30/2	30/3	30/4	30/5	30/6	30/7	30/8	30/9	30/10	30/11	30/12	313
1957	31/1	31/2	31/3	31/4	31/5	31/6	31/7	31/8	31/9	31/10	31/11	31/12	325
1958	32/1	32/2	32/3	32/4	32/5	32/6	32/7	32/8	32/9	32/10	32/11	32/12	337
1959	33/1	33/2	33/3	33/4	33/5	33/6	33/7	33/8	33/9	33/10	33/11	33/12	349
1960	34/1	34/2	34/3	34/4	34/5	34/6	34/7	34/8	34/9	34/10	34/11	34/12	361
1961	35/1	35/2	35/3	35/4	35/5	35/6	35/7	35/8	35/9	35/10	35/11	35/12	373
1962	36/1	36/2	36/3	36/4	36/5	36/6	36/7	36/8	36/9	36/10	36/11	36/12	385
1963	37/1	37/2	37/3	37/4	37/5	37/6	37/7	37/8	37/9	37/10	37/11	37/12	397
1964	38/1	38/2	38/3	38/4	38/5	38/6	38/7	38/8	38/9	38/10	38/11	38/12	409
1965	39/1	39/2	39/3	39/4	39/5	39/6		40/1		40/2		40/3	418
1966		40/4		40/5		40/6		40/7		40/8		40/9	424
1967	40/10		41/1		41/2		41/3		41/4		41/5		430
1968	41/6		42/1**			42/2		42/3		42/4			435

* Vol. 27 No. 8 is dated Dec 1953/Jan 1954.

** Vol. 42 No. 1 is dated June on cover, April inside.

British Editions

(1) 1 issue; unnumbered, no date but *ca.* Nov 1946; 64 pp.; 2/-.

Publisher: Ziff-Davis, London.

Front and back covers were from the U.S. Feb 1939 issue; contents were the two novelettes from that issue, "Wanted: Seven Fearless Engineers," W. Van Lorne, "Valley of Lost Souls," E. Binder, plus two other stories. Included were several illustrations from the original stories.

(2) 32 issues; undated, mid-1950—early 1955.

Publisher: Thorpe & Porter, Leicester.

Pulp size: #1 to #24 (1953), numbered.

Digest size: 1/1 (late 1953) to 1/8.

The pulp-size issues used U.S. covers with stories identical to certain U.S. original issues, except sometimes omitting stories. The digest-size issues corresponded to the eight U.S. originals running from Aug/Sep 1953.

Issues (all undated):

	Jan	Feb	Mar	Apr	May	Jun	Jul	Aug	Sep	Oct	Nov	Dec	W
1946											nn		1
. . . .
1950					#1		#2		#3		#4		4
1951	#5		#6	#7							#8		8
1952		#9	#10	#11		#12	#13		#14		#15		15
1953	#16	#17		#18		#19	#20	#21	#22	#23	#24	1/1	25
1954		1/2		1/3		1/4		1/5		1/6		1/7	31
1955		1/8											32

Canadian Edition

24 issues (Sep 1933—Aug 1935).

Pulp size; 144 pp.; monthly; 25¢.

Publisher: Teck Pub., Inc., Toronto.

Identical to the U.S. editions except that the front covers had the overprint "Printed in Canada on Canadian Paper."

No postwar issues are known.

Issues:

Same volumes and numbers as the U.S. originals for the same period.

Japanese Edition

7 issues *ca.* Apr-Jul 1950, not dated; approx. 256 pp.; 100 yen.

Publisher: Seibun-dô Shinkô-sha, Tokyo.

The first Japanese attempt to introduce American science fiction postwar. Stories were selected principally from 1948-1950 *Amazing*, but also some from *Fantastic Adventures* as well as two stories from 1927 and 1929 Amazing. Each issue generally had four or five stories.

AMAZING STORIES ANNUAL   U.S.   Science fiction

1 issue (1927).

Large size; 128 pp.; 50¢.

Editor: H. Gernsback.

Publisher: Experimenter Pub. Co., New York.

Cover Artist: F. R. Paul, who also did most of the interior illustrations.

This collector's item featured *The Master Mind of Mars*, E. R. Burroughs; other stories of interest are "The Face in the Abyss" and "The People of the Pit," both by A. Merritt, and "The Man Who Saved the Earth," A. Hall.

The magazine was so successful that Gernsback started publishing *Amazing Stories Quarterly* in 1928.

AMAZING STORIES QUARTERLY [*ASQ*]   U.S.   Science fiction

22 issues (Win 1928—Fall 1934).

Large size; 144 pp. [last 2: 128 pp.]; quarterly; 50¢.

Editors: H. Gernsback, Win 1928—Win 1929; A. Lynch, Spr 1929—Sum 1929; T. O'C. Sloane, Fall 1929—Fall 1934.

Publishers: Experimenter Pub. Co., New York, to Sum 1930; Radio-Science Pubs., Fall 1930—Fall 1931; Teck Pub. Co., Win 1932—Fall 1934.

Cover Artists: F. R. Paul, Win 1928—Spr 1929; H. Wesso, Sum 1929—Fall 1929; L. Morey, Win 1930—Fall 1934. In the same periods these artists (and a few others) also did interiors.

Notable Fiction:

1928 Win *When the Sleeper Wakes*, H. G. Wells; "The Moon of Doom," E. L. Bell

     Spr "A Modern Atlantis," F. A. Hodge; "The Nth Man" (n'te), H. E. Flint

     Sum *The Sunken World*, S. A. Coblentz; 4 of "Taine" series, D. H. Keller

     Fall "World of the Giant Ants," A. H. Verrill; "Stenographer's Hands" (short), D. H. Keller

1929 Win *Ralph 124C 41+*, H. Gernsback; "The Beast Men of Ceres" (n'te), A. Septama

     Spr "Locked Worlds," E. Hamilton; *After 12,000 Years*, S. A. Coblentz

     Sum "Venus Liberated," H. Vincent; "Paradox"(short), C. Cloukey [had sequels]

     Fall *The Bridge of Light*, A. H. Verrill; "The Other Side of the Moon," E. Hamilton

1930 Win *White Lily*, J. Taine [E. T. Bell]; "Tani of Ekkis" (n'te), A. Septama

     Spr "Reclaimers of the Ice," S. A. Coblentz; "Dragons of Space" (n'te), A. Septama

     Sum "Paradise and Iron," M. J. Breuer; "A Princess of Arelli" (n'te), A. Septama

     Fall "A Modern Prometheus," C. G. Waters; *The Black Star Passes*, J. W. Campbell Jr.

1931 Win "The Birth of a New Republic," M. J. Breuer & J. Williamson; "Elaine's Tomb" (n'te), G. P. Wertenbaker; *When the Moon Ran Wild*, A. H. Verrill [pa as Ray Ainsbury]

     Spr *Islands of Space*, J. W. Campbell Jr.; "Extra-Galactic Invaders" (n'te), J. Schlossel

     Sum *The Blue Barbarians*, S. A. Coblentz

Fall *Seeds of Life*, J. Taine [E. T. Bell]; "The War of the Universe" (n'te), C. Constantinescu
1932 Win "A Voice Across the Years," F. Pratt & I. Stephens [*Alien Planet*]
Spr/Sum *Invaders From the Infinite*, J. W. Campbell Jr.; "The Ant With a Human Soul" (n'te), B. Olsen
Fall/Win "Faster Than Light," H. Vincent
1933 Spr/Sum "The Man From Tomorrow," S. A. Coblentz; "The Mother World" (n'te), B. & G. C. Wallis
Fall/Win *The Second Deluge*, G. P. Serviss; "A Winter Amid the Ice" (n'te), J. Verne
1934 Fall "Barton's Island" (n'te), H. Vincent; *The Sunken World*, S. A. Coblentz

Issues:

	Winter	Spring	Summer	Fall	W
1928	1/1	1/2	1/3	1/4	4
1929	2/1	2/2	2/3	2/4	8
1930	3/1	3/2	3/3	3/4	12
1931	4/1*	4/2	4/3	4/4	16
1932	5/1	5/2		5/3**	19
1933	**	6/4			21
1934	7/1			7/2	22

* Vol. 4 No. 1 dated Winter 1930.
** Vol. 5 No. 3 dated Fall-Winter 1932.

Canadian Edition
1 issue (Fall 1934).
Large size; 128 pp.; 50¢.
Publisher: Not known.
Identical to U.S. original of that date, with overprint on cover: "Printed in Canada on Canadian Paper."

AMAZING STORIES QUARTERLY (Re-issue)
Unsold monthly issues of *Amazing Stories* bound three in a volume with a new cover; sold at 50¢. First series appeared Fall 1940 to Win 1943, and second series Win 1947 to Win 1951 (missing two quarters).

AMAZING STORIES SCIENCE FICTION NOVEL
U.S.   Science fiction
1 issue, 1957 (*ca.* June).
Digest size; 130 pp.; 35¢.
Editor: P. W. Fairman.
Publisher: Ziff-Davis Pub. Co., New York.
Planned as a quarterly to present book-length novels. The only one to appear was a very poor choice, "200 Million Miles to Earth," by H. Slesar, based on the Columbia film of the same title. The issue also gave brief actor biographies.
The proposed long novels were then incorporated into *Amazing Stories* from Mar 1958.

AMERICAN FICTION   British   Weird science fiction
About 12 issues (1944–1946).
Publisher: Utopian Pubs., London (F. Herbert).
First two cost 9d, thereafter 1/6; usually 36 pp.
Review: W. Gillings was associated with the editing of many of these. Other publications not in this series are given in the publisher's entry (*PAPERBACK* section).
Material of U.S. origin was reprinted, frequently with changed titles. Some titles were not designated "American Fiction" but fit in with the series. The covers all had nudes. Most stories were shorts or novelettes. Cover-story titles are given first for each issue below. It is understood that No. 11 never appeared.
nn (Sep 1944) "Girl in Trouble," E. Frank Parker (original).
nn (Nov 1944) "Arctic Bride," S. P. Meek ("Gates of Light"); "Nasturtia," S. P. Meek.
nn (Feb 1945) "Sea-Kissed" ("Black Kiss"), "Lady in Wax," "Beetles," "The Totem Pole," all by Robert Bloch. A variant of this also has a further story, "Goper's Head," B. Herbert.
nn (Jul 1945) "Lady in Danger" ("Wizard's Isle"), J. Williamson; "Spanish Vampire," E. H. Price; "The Curse of the House," R. Bloch.
nn (Nov 1945) "Tiger Girl" ("Six Sleepers"), E. Hamilton; "Apprentice Magician," E. H. Price.

nn (Nov 1945) "Love in Time" ("Wanderers of Time"), Johnson Harris [J. B. Harris].
#7 (Jan 1946) "Murder in the Clinic," E. Hamilton; "The Island of Unreason," E. Hamilton.
#8 (Jan 1946) "Youth Madness," S. A. Coblentz; "The Secret of Sebek," R. Bloch.
#9 (Nov 1945) "The Sex Serum," H. O. Dickinson; "The Red Swimmer," R. Bloch; "The Man With X-Ray Eyes," E. Hamilton.
#10 (Jan 1946) "Strange Offspring," R. A. Palmer; "The Malignant Entity," O. A. Kline.
#12 (Jan 1946) "Master of Dreams," H. Vincent; "Ham on Rye," C. Marlowe (not fantasy).

AMERICAN SCIENCE FICTION   Australian   Science Fiction
41 issues (Jun 1952–Sep 1955), not numbered, not dated.
Publisher: Malian Press, Sydney.
Size 5¼ x 7¼ in.; 34 pp.; monthly; first 3 at 8d, then 9d.
Cover Artist: All covers painted by Stanley Pitt, with a few under his pseudonym Safone Jais.
This notable reprint series featured a novelette in each issue, with short stories to fill out as necessary. Two issues appeared in Aug 1954. Its later companion was *Selected Science Fiction Magazine*. No royalties were ever paid on the stories printed. The title became *American Science Fiction Magazine* from No. 24.
Issues: Dates and issue whole numbers are shown below, but are not on the magazines. The issues are generally known by the cover-story titles, which are:
1952 (June): "Red Death of Mars," R. M. Williams (#1); "Conquest of the Stars," M. Leinster (#2); "The Man Who Sold the Moon," R. A. Heinlein (#3); "The Soldato Ant," M. Leinster (#4); "The Thing From Another World," J. W. Campbell (#5); "Death of the Moon," A. M. Phillips (#6); "The Unknown," M. Leinster (#7).
1953: "Clash by Night," L. O'Donnell (#8); "The Monster," N. S. Bond (#9); "Refuge for Tonight," R. M. Williams (#10); "Adventure in Time," P. St. John (#11); "Fires of Forever," C. Oliver (#12); "Moonwalk," H. B. Fyfe (#13); "Moon-Blind," E. Van Lhin (#14); "The Dead World," C. W. Harris & M. J. Breuer (#15); "Dead Knowledge," J. W. Campbell (#16); "Elimination," J. W. Campbell (#17); "Danger Moon," J. MacCreigh (#18); "Veiled Knowledge," E. James (#19).
1954: "The Invaders," R. S. Carr (#20); "The Other Side," W. Kubilius (#21); "Men Against the Stars," M. W. Wellman (#22); "The Lonely Planet," M. Leinster (#23); "There Shall Be Darkness," C. L. Moore (#24); "Never Trust a Martian," P. W. Fairman (#25); "The Ark of Mars," L. Brackett (#26); "Double Identity," R. Z. Gallun (#27, Aug); "Way of the Gods," H. Kuttner (#28, Aug); "Remember Tomorrow," H. Kuttner (#29); "Derelict of Space," R. Garrett (#30); "The Moving Finger," B. Livingston (#31); "Meteor of Death," B. Livingston (#32).
1955: "Nine Worlds West," P. W. Fairman (#33); "Sword of Tomorrow," H. Kuttner (#34); "Common Time," J. Blish (#35); "Of Such as These," I. Cox (#36); "The Guthrie Method," R. Z. Gallun (#37); "As You Were," H. Kuttner (#38); "The Irrationals," M. Lesser (#39); "The Gift of the Gods," R. F. Jones (#40); "Stopwatch on the World," D. R. Gilgannon (#41).

ANALOG SCIENCE FICTION — SCIENCE FACT [*ASF*]
U.S.   Science fiction
[formerly *Astounding Science Fiction*, etc.]
Current (Jan 1930–)
457th issue–December 1968
Digest size; 178 pp.; monthly; 60¢.
Title Changes: *Astounding Stories of Super-Science*, Jan 1930 to Jan 1931; *Astounding Stories*, Feb 1931 to Nov 1932; *Astounding Stories of Super-Science*, Jan 1933 & Mar 1933; *Astounding Stories*, Oct 1933 to Feb 1938; *Astounding Science Fiction*, Mar 1938 to Jan 1960; *Analog Science Fiction–Science Fact*, Feb 1960–.
"Astounding" was less emphasized in the title from Aug 1946 to Jan 1953, then became prominent again. Much against fan preference, the title *Analog* was adopted and has slowly come into general use. The abbreviation *ASF* is still suitable.

Editors: H. Bates, Jan 1930 to Mar 1933; F. O. Tremaine, Oct 1933 to Oct 1937; J. W. Campbell, Nov. 1937—.

Publishers: Fiscal Corp. [W. M. Clayton], later Clayton Magazines Inc., New York, to Mar 1933; Street & Smith, Oct 1933 to Jan 1961; The Condé Nast Pubs., New York, Feb. 1961—Aug 1980 [taken over by Davis Publications, Nov 1980—].

Size Changes: Pulp, Jan 1930—Dec 1941; large, Jan 1942-Apr 1943; pulp, May 1943—Oct 1943; digest, Nov 1943—Feb 1963; large, Mar 1963—Mar 1965; digest, Apr 1965—.

Price Changes: 20¢, Jan 1930—Dec 1941; 25¢, Jan 1942—Jul 1951; 35¢, Aug 1951—Oct 1959; 50¢, Nov 1959—Jul 1966; 60¢, Aug 1966—.

Cover Artists: H. Wesso, Jan 1930—Mar 1933; H. Brown, Oct 1933—May 1937; Wesso and Brown each had a number of covers up to Nov 1938. H. Rogers made his first appearance Feb 1939 and did all the covers Apr 1940 to Jun 1942. Timmins painted Dec 1942 to Oct 1946, with several more later. Schneeman appeared May 1938, with several to Jan 1940; Alejandro [Canedo] had a number from Dec 1946; C. Bonestell's first was Oct 1947, with occasional appearances through the years to May 1968. Van Dongen appeared Aug 1951 and had many in the early 1950's. K. Freas first appeared Mar 1954 and had a number of covers until 1960, then returned to do most covers from Aug 1965 to Dec 1968. J. Schoenherr first appeared Jun 1960 and painted the majority of covers from Dec 1960 to Jul 1965, with several later. A feature of *ASF* has been a large number of astronomical covers by C. Bonestell and others. All the above artists except Bonestell also did interior illustrations; E. Cartier began with interiors in 1939 and later became a mainstay for *Unknown*.

Review:

Clayton *Astoundings* (as these were popularly called) were essentially science fiction adventure. In this regard they are noted for the appearances of the "John Hansen" series (S. P. Wright), most "Dr. Bird" stories (S. P. Meek), and all but the last of the "Hawk Carse" series (H. Bates). R. Cummings appeared frequently, while other regular authors included A. J. Burks, C. W. Diffin, V. Rousseau [V. R. Emanuel], and H. Vincent. Its companion magazine was the short-lived *Strange Tales*.

F. O. Tremaine became editor after the magazine's purchase by Street & Smith. After an inauspicious start he made *Astounding* very successful with a heavy-science type of story, although such space-opera serials as *The Legion of Space* (J. Williamson) naturally had their place. He was able to maintain a monthly schedule while the other science fiction magazines were hard put to remain in the field; at one stage in 1934, serious consideration was given to publishing two issues per month. He published the greatest of the "Skylark" series of E. E. Smith, as well as the first of Smith's "Lensman" series. Tremaine ran J. W. Campbell's *The Mightiest Machine*, and also Campbell's stories under the "Don A. Stuart" by-line. Other noted authors included J. R. Fearn (for his 'Magnificanzas'!), N. Schachner and S. G. Weinbaum.

J. W. Campbell's editorship brought *Astounding* to what some consider to be its heyday in the early 1940's. Nevertheless it is to his credit that he maintained the magazine in the forefront of the sf field for over 30 years.

In the early 1940's Campbell introduced such authors as R. A. Heinlein, L. del Rey, T. Sturgeon, A. E. van Vogt, H. Kuttner [as L. Padgett and L. O'Donnell, often in collaboration with his wife, C. L. Moore], and I. Asimov. Writers starting in the mid-1940's included H. Clement [H. C. Stubbs], R. F. Jones, G. O. Smith, and C. Davis. Among other writers of importance are P. Anderson, H. Harrison, M. Reynolds, J. H. Schmitz, C. D. Simak, and A. McCaffrey.

Since the inception of the Hugo Awards in 1953, the magazine has won the "Best Magazine" award in 1953 (shared with *Galaxy*), 1955, 1956, 1957, 1961, 1962, 1964, and 1965.

The magazine kept its leading position in the field despite strong criticism of Campbell on such matters as his sponsoring of Hubbard's "Dianetics" (later "Scientology") in the early 1950's when this alleged science was originated, his support of the "Dean Drive," and his continual bias toward publishing "psi" stories.

Through the years such high-class series as "City" (C. D. Simak), "Foundation" (I. Asimov), "Galloway Gallegher" (L. Padgett), and "Ole Doc Methuselah" (L. R. Hubbard) have appeared, while practically every serial novel has seen later hardcover or paperback publication. For many years the magazine was the most anthologised in the field, and still has a high proportion of stories selected for reprinting.

Campbell ran the "Probability Zero" department Apr 1942 to Dec 1944, presenting vignettes sent in by readers—tall stories violating some well-known scientific law. Technical articles have long been a feature, while Campbell's editorials were always quite thought-provoking—a number were edited by H. Harrison as *Collected Editorials From Analog* (Doubleday, 1966). Campbell also edited a number of anthologies directly from the magazine: *The Astounding Science Fiction Anthology* (1952); *Prologue to Analog* (1962), and the regular *Analog* series (Nos. 1-6, 1962-68).

Astounding's companion 1939-1943 was *Unknown (Worlds)*. A nostalgic chronicle of the development of *Astounding* up to its title change to *Analog* is the book *A Requiem for Astounding*, by A. Rogers (Advent, 1964).

Notable Fiction:

1930		"Dr. Bird" series, S. P. Meek, began in Jan; "John Hansen" series, S. P. Wright, began in July.
	Jan	"The Beetle Horde" (sr2), V. Rousseau [V. R. Emanuel]
	Mar	*Brigands of the Moon* (sr4), R. Cummings
	May	"Into the Ocean's Depths" (short), S. P. Wright; *Murder Madness* (sr4), M. Leinster [W. F. Jenkins]
	Jul	"Earth the Marauder" (sr3), A. J. Burks
	Sep	"Jetta of the Lowlands" (sr3), R. Cummings
	Nov	"The Pirate Planet" (sr4), C. W. Diffin
1931		"Hawk Carse" series, H. Bates, began in Nov.
	Jan	"Fifth Dimension Catapult," M. Leinster [W. F. Jenkins] [had sequel]
	Feb	"Phalanxes of Atlans" (sr2), F. V. W. Mason
	Mar	*Beyond the Vanishing Point*, R. Cummings
	Apr	*Exile of Time* (sr3), R. Cummings
	May	"Dark Moon" (n'te), C. W. Diffin (began series)
	Jun	"Manape the Mighty" (n'te), A. J. Burks [had sequel]
	Jul	"The Revolt of the Machines" (short), N. Schachner & A. L. Zagat
	Dec	"Giants on the Earth" (sr2), S. P. Meek
1932	Feb	"Pigmy Planet" (n'te), J. Williamson; *Wandl the Invader* (sr4), R. Cummings
	Apr	"The Einstein See-Saw" (short), M. J. Breuer
	May	"Pirates of the Gorm" (short), N. Schachner; "The Martian Cabal" (n'te), R. F. Starzl
	Jun	"2,000 Miles Below" (sr4), C. W. Diffin; "Hellhounds of the Cosmos" (short), C. D. Simak
1933	Dec	"Ancestral Voices" (n'te), N. Schachner; "Land of the Lost" (sr2), D. W. Diffin
1934	Jan	"Colossus" (n'te), D. Wandrei; "Redmask of the Outlands" (n'te), N. Schachner [both had sequels]
	Feb	*Rebirth* (sr2), T. C. McClary; "Short-Wave Castle," C. Peregoy [had sequel]
	Mar	"The Man Who Stopped the Dust" (n'te), J. R. Fearn
	Apr	*The Legion of Space* (sr6), J. Williamson; "A Matter of Size" (n'te), H. Bates; "He From Procyon," N. Schachner; "Lo!" (sr8), C. Fort
	May	"Blinding Shadows" (short), F. Wandrei; "Brain of Light," J. R. Fearn
	Jun	"Sidewise in Time," M. Leinster [W. F. Jenkins] [title story of collection]; "Crater 17, Near Tycho" (n'te), F. K. Kelly; "Rex" (short), H. Vincent
	Aug	*Skylark of Valeron* (sr7), E. E. Smith; "Warriors of Eternity" (n'te), C. Buchanan & C. Carr [had sequel]
	Sep	"The Living Equation" (n'te), N. Schachner; "Dragon's Teeth" (short), W. West
	Oct	"The Bright Illusion" (n'te), C. L. Moore
	Nov	"The Mole Pirate," M. Leinster [W. F. Jenkins]; "Twilight," D. A. Stuart [J. W. Campbell]
	Dec	*The Mightiest Machine* (sr5), J. W. Campbell; "Old Faithful" (short), R. Z. Gallun [first of series]
1935		Notable stories by S. G. Weinbaum, F. B. Long (on future man), and D. A. Stuart [J. W. Campbell], with "W62" series, C. B. Kruse, from Sep.
	Jan	"Star Ship Invincible," F. K. Kelly
	Feb	"The Ultimate Metal" (n'te), N. Schachner
	Mar	"Proxima Centauri," M. Leinster [W. F. Jenkins] [in *Sidewise in Time*]

Apr "The Einstein Express" (sr2), J. G. Frederick; "Prowler of the Wastelands" (short), H. Vincent [had sequel]

May "1287" (sr5), J. Taine [E. T. Bell]; "Earth's Mausoleum," J. R. Fearn

Jun "Alas, All Thinking!" H. Bates

Jul "The Accursed Galaxy" (short), E. Hamilton

Aug "The Galactic Circle," J. Williamson; "The Phantom Dictator" (short), W. West

Sep "Islands of the Sun" (sr2), J. Williamson; "Earth Minus" (n'te), D. Wandrei; "Greater Glories" (n'te), C. L. Moore

Oct "I Am Not God" (sr2), N. Schachner

Nov "The Red Peri" (n'te), S. G. Weinbaum; "Blue Magic" (sr4), C. W. Diffin; "The Adaptive Ultimate" (n'te), J. Jessel [Weinbaum]

1936   "Colbie & Deverel" series, R. Rocklynne, began in June; "Durna Rangue" series, N. R. Jones, in Sep.

Feb At the Mountains of Madness (sr3), H. P. Lovecraft; "Mathematica" (n'te), J. R. Fearn [had sequel]

Apr "Spawn of Eternal Thought" (sr2), E. Binder

May The Cometeers (sr4), J. Williamson

Jun "Reverse Universe" (n'te), N. Schachner; "The Shadow out of Time," H. P. Lovecraft

Aug "The Incredible Invasion" (sr5), M. Leinster [W. F. Jenkins] [The Other Side of Here]; "En Route to Pluto" (short), W. West [see The Bird of Time]

Nov "The Eternal Wanderer," N. Schachner; "Macklin's Little Friend" (short), H. W. Guernsey [H. Wandrei]

Dec "Tryst in Time" (n'te), C. L. Moore; "The Flame Midget" (short), F. B. Long

1937   "Past, Present and Future" series, N. Schachner, began Dec.

Jan "Beyond Infinity," C. Corbett; "The Blue Spot" (sr2), J. Williamson

Feb "The Saga of Pelican West" (n'te), E. F. Russell; "At the Perihelion," R. Willey [W. Ley]

Mar "Worlds Within," J. R. Fearn

Apr "Sands of Time," P. S. Miller [had sequel]

May "Nova in Messier 33," C. Corbett [had sequel in Jun]

Jun "Forgetfulness" (short), D. A. Stuart [J. W. Campbell]

Jul "Frontier of the Unknown" (sr2), N. L. Knight; "Seeker of Tomorrow," E. F. Russell & L. T. Johnson

Aug "Released Entropy" (sr2), J. Williamson

Sep Galactic Patrol (sr6), E. E. Smith

Oct "Out of Night" (n'te), D. A. Stuart [J. W. Campbell] [had sequel]

1938   "Von Theil" series, K. Casey, began Mar; "Kelton" series, K. Casey, began Jul; "Josh McNab" series, A. J. Burks, began Aug; "Johnny Black" series, L. S. de Camp, began Oct.

Jan "Dead Knowledge," D. A. Stuart [J. W. Campbell]

Mar "The Master Shall Not Die," R. D. Miller [The Man Who Lived Forever]; "Jason Sows Again" (sr2), A. J. Burks

Apr Three Thousand Years (sr3), T. C. McClary; "The Faithful" (short), L. del Rey

May The Legion of Time (sr3), J. Williamson; "Catastrophe!" (article), E. E. Smith

Jun "Men Against the Stars" (n'te), M. W. Wellman [title story of anthology]

Jul "Rule 18" (n'te), C. D. Simak

Aug "Who Goes There?" D. A. Stuart [J. W. Campbell] [title story of collection]

Sep "The Tramp" (sr3), L. R. Hubbard; "Orbit XXIII-H" (n'te), R. Willey [W. Ley]

Nov "Simultaneous Worlds" (sr2), N. Schachner

Dec "A Matter of Form," H. L. Gold; "Nuisance Value" (sr2), M. W. Wellman [The Dark Destroyers]; "Helen O'Loy" (short), L. del Rey

1939 Jan "Maiden Voyage" (n'te), V. Phillips

Feb "Crucible of Power" (n'te), J. Williamson; Cosmic Engineers (sr3), C. D. Simak

Mar "Cloak of Aesir," D. A. Stuart [J. W. Campbell]

Apr One Against the Legion (sr3), J. Williamson

May "Special Flight" (n'te), J. Berryman; "Design for Life" (article, 2), L. S. de Camp

Jul "Black Destroyer" (n'te), A. E. van Vogt [see Voyage of the Space Beagle]; "Trends" (short), I. Asimov; "Greater Than Gods" (n'te), C. L. Moore

Aug "The Luck of Ignatz" (n'te), L. del Rey; "General Swamp, C.I.C." (sr2), F. Engelhardt [L. R. Hubbard]; "Lifeline" (short), R. A. Heinlein

Sep "Ether Breather" (short), T. Sturgeon [had sequel]

Oct Gray Lensman (sr4), E. E. Smith

1940   "Kilkenny Cats" series, K. Von Rachen [L. R. Hubbard], began July; "Bullard" series, M. Jameson, began Apr [Bullard of the Space Patrol].

Jan "The Smallest God" (n'te), L. del Rey; "Requiem" (short), R. A. Heinlein

Feb "If This Goes On . . ." (sr2), R. A. Heinlein [see Revolt in 2100]

Mar "Cold" (n'te), N. Schachner

Apr Final Blackout (sr3), L. R. Hubbard

May "Space Guards" (n'te), P. Nowlan

Jun "The Roads Must Roll" (n'te), R. A. Heinlein

Jul "Crisis in Utopia" (sr2), N. L. Knight; "Coventry" (n'te), R. A. Heinlein

Aug "The Stars Look Down" (n'te), L. del Rey

Sep Slan (sr4), A. E. van Vogt; "Blowups Happen" (n'te), R. A. Heinlein

Oct "Farewell to the Master" (n'te), H. Bates

Dec "Old Man Mulligan" (n'te), P. S. Miller

1941   "Jay Score" series, E. F. Russell, began May; "Weapon Shop" series, A. E. van Vogt, began Jul.

Jan Sixth Column (sr3), A. MacDonald [R. A. Heinlein]

Feb "Magic City" (n'te), N. S. Bond; "And He Built a Crooked House . . ." (short), R. A. Heinlein

Mar "Logic of Empire" (n'te), R. A. Heinlein

Apr "The Stolen Dormouse" (sr2), L. S. de Camp [in Divide and Rule]; "Microcosmic God" (n'te), T. Sturgeon

May Universe (n'te), R. A. Heinlein; "Liar!" (short), I. Asimov

Jun "Old Fireball" (n'te), N. Schachner [with sequel, in Space Lawyer]

Jul Methuselah's Children (sr3), R. A. Heinlein

Sep "Nightfall" (n'te), I. Asimov; "Adam and No Eve" (short), A. Bester

Oct "By His Bootstraps" (n'te), A. MacDonald [R. A. Heinlein]

Nov Second Stage Lensmen (sr4), E. E. Smith

1942   "Foundation" series, I. Asimov, began May; "Seetee" series, W. Stewart [J. Williamson], began Jul; "Venus Equilateral" series, G. O. Smith, began Oct.

Feb "There Shall Be Darkness" (n'te), C. L. Moore; "The Sorcerer of Rhiannon" (short), L. Brackett

Mar "Recruiting Station" (n'te), A. E. van Vogt [Masters of Time, etc.]

Apr Beyond This Horizon (sr2), A. MacDonald [R. A. Heinlein]; "Cooperate or Else" (n'te), A. E. van Vogt [see The War Against the Rull]

May "Asylum" (n'te), A. E. van Vogt

Jun "Heritage" (n'te), R. Abernathy

Aug Waldo, A. MacDonald [R. A. Heinlein]

Sep "The Twonky" (short), L. Padgett [H. Kuttner]; Nerves, L. del Rey

Oct "The Wabbler" (short), M. Leinster [W. F. Jenkins]

1943   "Galloway Gallegher" series, L. Padgett [H. Kuttner], began Jan; "Artur Blord" series, E. M. Hull [& A. E. van Vogt], in Apr; "Dellian Robot" series, A. E. van Vogt, in Sep.

Feb "Mimsy Were the Borogoves" (n'te), L. Padgett [H. Kuttner]

Mar "Clash by Night" (n'te), L. O'Donnell [C. L. Moore]; "Q.U.R." (short), H. H. Holmes [A. Boucher]

May Gather, Darkness! (sr3), F. Leiber

Jul "Hunch" (n'te), C. D. Simak; "The Great Engine" (n'te), A. E. van Vogt

Aug *Judgment Night* (sr2), C. L. Moore

Sep "Attitude" (n'te), H. Clement [H. C. Stubbs]

Oct "Fifty Million Monkeys" (n'te), R. F. Jones

Dec "The Iron Standard" (n'te), L. Padgett [H. Kuttner]

1944   "City" series, C. D. Simak, began in May [later became book]

Jan "Technical Error" (n'te), H. Clement [H. C. Stubbs]; "Far Centaurus" (short), A. E. van Vogt

Mar "The Children's Hour" (n'te), L. O'Donnell [C. L. Moore]; "Deadline" (n'te), C. Cartmill

Apr *The Changeling*, A. E. van Vogt

May *The Winged Man* (sr2), E. M. Hull & A. E. van Vogt; "This Means War!" (short), A. B. Chandler

Jul *Renaissance* (sr4), R. F. Jones

Nov "Killdozer," T. Sturgeon; "When the Bough Breaks" (n'te), L. Padgett [H. Kuttner]

Dec *Nomad* (sr3), W. Long [G. O. Smith]; "No Woman Born" (n'te), C. L. Moore

1945   "Baldy" series, L. Padgett [H. Kuttner], began Feb [in book as *Mutant*]

Mar *Destiny Times Three* (sr2), F. Leiber

May "First Contact" (n'te), M. Leinster [W. F. Jenkins]

Jun "The Ethical Equations" (short), M. Leinster [W. F. Jenkins]

Aug *World of Ā* (sr3), A. E. van Vogt

Oct "Giant Killer" (n'te), A. B. Chandler

Nov "Line to Tomorrow" (short), L. Padgett [H. Kuttner]

1946   "Gods" series, A. E. van Vogt, began in May [later published as books]

Jan *The Fairy Chessmen* (sr2), L. Padgett [H. Kuttner] [in *Tomorrow and Tomorrow & The Fairy Chessmen*]

Feb "Special Knowledge" (n'te), A. B. Chandler [enlarged as *Deep Reaches of Space*]

Mar *Pattern for Conquest* (sr3), G. O. Smith; "A Logic Named Joe" (short), W. F. Jenkins

Apr "Loophole" (short), A. C. Clarke; "Memorial" (short), T. Sturgeon

May "Rescue Party" (n'te), A. C. Clarke; "Placet Is a Crazy Place" (short), F. Brown

Jun "The Chromium Helmet" (n'te), T. Sturgeon; "The Chronokinesis of Jonathan Hull" (short), A. Boucher

Sep "The Toymaker" (n'te), R. F. Jones [title story of collection]; "Vintage Season" (n'te), L. O'Donnell; "Meihem in Ce Klasrum" (article), D. Edwards

Oct "The Chronicler" (sr2), A. E. van Vogt [*Siege of the Unseen*]

Nov "Mewhu's Jet" (n'te), T. Sturgeon

Dec "Metamorphosite" (n'te), E. F. Russell

1947   "Doc Methuselah" series, R. Lafayette [L. R. Hubbard], began Oct.

Jan *Tomorrow and Tomorrow* (sr2), L. Padgett [H. Kuttner]

Feb "Maturity" (n'te), T. Sturgeon

Mar "Tomorrow's Children" (n'te), P. Anderson & F. Waldrop [see Anderson's *Twilight World*]; "Little Lost Robot" (short), I. Asimov

May *Fury* (sr3), L. O'Donnell [H. Kuttner]; "E for Effort" (short), T. L. Sherred

Jun "Centaurus II" (n'te), A. E. van Vogt

Jul "With Folded Hands . . ." (n'te), J. Williamson

Aug "The End Is Not Yet" (sr3), L. R. Hubbard

Nov *Children of the Lens* (sr4), E. E. Smith; "Thunder and Roses" (short), T. Sturgeon

1948   "Paratime" series, H. B. Piper, began Jul; "Bureau of Slick Tricks" series, H. B. Fyfe, in Dec.

Feb "There Is No Defense" (n'te), T. Sturgeon

Mar ". . . And Searching Mind" (sr3), J. Williamson [*The Humanoids*]; "The Endochronic Properties of Resublimated Thiotimoline" (article), I. Asimov

May "The Rull" (n'te) A. E. van Vogt [see *The War Against the Rull*]; "The Strange Case of John Kingman" (short), M. Leinster [W. F. Jenkins]

Jun *Dreadful Sanctuary* (sr3), E. F. Russell; "That Only a Mother" (short), J. Merril

Sep "Dreams Are Sacred" (short), P. Phillips

Oct *The Players of Ā* (sr3), A. E. van Vogt [also called *Pawns of Null-A*]; "School for the Stars" (short), J. D. MacDonald

Nov "In Hiding" (n'te), W. H. Shiras [first of series, published as *Children of the Atom*]

1949 Jan "Private Eye" (n'te), L. Padgett [H. Kuttner]

Feb *Seetee Shock* (sr3), W. Stewart [J. Williamson]

May *Needle* (sr2), H. Clement [H. C. Stubbs]; "Mother Earth" (n'te), I. Asimov

Jun "The Aphrodite Project" (article), P. Latham [R. S. Richardson]

Jul "Agent of Vega" (n'te), J. H. Schmitz [in book of same title]

Aug "The Queen of Zamba" (sr2), L. S. de Camp [*Cosmic Manhunt*]

Sep "The Double-Dyed Villains" (n'te), P. Anderson

Oct "Defense Mechanism" (short), K. MacLean

Nov "Gulf" (sr2), R. A. Heinlein [in *Assignment in Eternity*]

1950   "Okie" series, J. Blish, began in Apr.

Feb "To the Stars" (sr2), L. R. Hubbard [*Return to Tomorrow*]

Apr *The Wizard of Linn* (sr3), A. E. van Vogt [last of "Gods" series]

May "The Helping Hand" (n'te), P. Anderson; "Dianetics" (article), L. R. Hubbard

Jul "The Little Black Bag" (n'te), C. M. Kornbluth

Oct "The Hand of Zei" (sr4), L. S. de Camp [see *The Search for Zei*]

Nov "Tools of the Trade" (n'te), R. F. Jones

Dec "A Subway Named Mobius" (short), A. J. Deutsch

1951   "Philosophical Corps" series, E. B. Cole, began in Mar [later as book].

Mar "High Threshold" (short), A. E. Nourse

Apr "The Peddler's Nose" (short), J. Williamson

May "Izzard and the Membrane" (n'te), W. M. Miller Jr.

Jun "And Then There Were None" (n'te), E. F. Russell [part of *The Great Explosion*]; "Breeds There a Man" (n'te), I. Asimov

Aug "Courtesy" (short), C. D. Simak

Sep "Day of the Moron" (n'te), H. B. Piper

Oct *Iceworld* (sr3), H. Clement [H. C. Stubbs]; "Ultima Thule" (short), E. F. Russell

Nov "The Hunting Season" (n'te), F. M. Robinson

Dec "Dune Roller" (n'te), J. May

1952 Jan "That Share of Glory" (n'te), C. M. Kornbluth; "The Analogues" (short), D. Knight [see *Hell's Pavement*]

Feb "Firewater," W. Tenn [P. Klass]

Mar *Gunner Cade* (sr3), C. Judd [J. Merril & C. M. Kornbluth]; "Man Down" (n'te), J. Williamson [see *The Trial of Terra*]

Apr "Dumb Waiter" (n'te), W. M. Miller Jr.

May "Fast Falls the Eventide" (short), E. F. Russell

Jun "The Specter General" (n'te), T. R. Cogswell

Sep "Frontier of the Dark" (n'te), A. B. Chandler

Oct *The Currents of Space* (sr3), I. Asimov

Nov "Pax Galactica" (short), Ralph Williams

Dec "Noise Level" (n'te), R. F. Jones; "The Impacted Man" (short), R. Sheckley

   "Joey" series, M. Clifton, began in Aug.

1953 Jan *Un-Man*, P. Anderson

Feb "Null-ABC" (sr2), H. P. Piper & J. J. McGuire [*Crisis in 2140*]; "Crucifixus Etiam" (short), W. M. Miller

Apr *Mission of Gravity* (sr4), H. Clement [H. C. Stubbs]; "Settle to One" (n'te), C. Dye & A. Smith

Jun ". . . And a Star to Steer Her By" (n'te), L. Correy [G. H. Stine]

Jul "Solution Delayed" (short), M. Clifton & A. Apostolides

Aug "Sam Hall" (n'te), P. Anderson; "Commencement Night" (short), R. Ashby

Sep "What Thin Partitions" (n'te), M. Clifton [first of "Kennedy" series]; "Humpty Dumpty" (n'te), L. Padgett [H. Kuttner]

Oct "Belief" (n'te), I. Asimov

Nov "Trade Secret," R. F. Jones

1954 Feb "Sucker Bait" (sr2), I. Asimov [see *The Martian Way*]; "Run Away Home" (short), E. G. Von Wald

Mar "Immigrant," C. D. Simak

May "At Death's End" (n'te), J. Blish

Jun "Question and Answer" (sr2), P. Anderson [*Planet of No Return*]

Aug *They'd Rather Be Right* (sr4), M. Clifton & F. Riley [in "Joey" series]; "The Cold Equations" (n'te), T. Godwin

Sep *Martians, Go Home*, F. Brown

1955 Jan "The Darfsteller," W. M. Miller Jr.

Apr "The Long Way Home" (sr4), P. Anderson [*No World of Their Own*]

May "Allamagoosa" (short), E. F. Russell

Jun "The Guardians" (short), I. Cox

Jul "The Waitabits" (n'te), E. F. Russell

Aug "Call Him Dead" (sr3), E. F. Russell [*Three to Conquer*]

Sep "The Gift of Gab" (n'te), J. Vance

Nov "Under Pressure" (sr3), F. Herbert [*The Dragon in the Sea*]

Dec "Sand Doom" (n'te), M. Leinster [W. F. Jenkins] [see *Colonial Survey*]

1956 "Nidor" series, R. Randall [R. Silverberg & R. Garrett] began in June [later as books].

Feb *Double Star* (sr3), R. A. Heinlein; "The Last Thousand Miles" (short), D. McLaughlin [in *The Man Who Wanted Stars*]

Mar "Exploration Team" (n'te), M. Leinster [W. F. Jenkins] [see *Colonial Survey*]

Apr "The Dead Past" (n'te), I. Asimov; "Legwork" (n'te), E. F. Russell

Jun "Plus X" (n'te), E. F. Russell [see *Next of Kin*]

Sep "Margin of Profit" (short), P. Anderson [first of "Trader" series]

Oct *The Naked Sun* (sr3), I. Asimov

1957 "Med Service" series, M. Leinster [W. F. Jenkins], began Jun.

Jan *Get Out of My Sky* (sr2), J. Blish [title story of anthology]

Feb "Omnilingual" (n'te), H. B. Piper

Apr "Call Me Joe" (n'te), P. Anderson; "The Mile-Long Spaceship" (short), K. Wilhelm [title story of collection]

Jul "Hot Potato" (short), A. Budrys [see *The Falling Torch*]

Aug *The Stainless Steel Rat*, H. Harrison [n'te; book has sequels]

Sep *Citizen of the Galaxy* (sr4), R. A. Heinlein

1958 Jan "Unwillingly to School," P. Ashwell [had sequel]

Feb "The Man Who Counts" (sr3), P. Anderson [*War of the Wing-Men*]

Mar "The Man on the Bottom" (n'te), D. McLaughlin [see *Dome World*]; "Second Game" (n'te), C. De Vet & K. MacLean [see *Cosmic Checkmate*]

May *Close to Critical* (sr3), H. Clement [H. C. Stubbs]

Aug "We Have Fed Our Sea" (sr2), P. Anderson [*The Enemy Stars*]

Oct "The Big Front Yard" (n'te), C. D. Simak

Nov "A Bicycle Built for Brew" (sr2), P. Anderson [*The Makeshift Rocket*]

1959 Jan "To Run the Rim" (n'te), A. B. Chandler

Feb "The Pirates of Ersatz" (sr3), M. Leinster [W. F. Jenkins] [*The Pirates of Zan*]

May "Dorsai!" (sr3), G. R. Dickson [*The Genetic General*]

Jun "Cat and Mouse" (n'te), Ralph Williams

Aug "Familiar Pattern" (n'te), G. Whitley [A. B. Chandler] [enlarged to *The Ship From Outside*, Chandler]

Sep "That Sweet Little Old Lady" (sr2), M. Phillips [R. Garrett & L. M. Janifer] [see *Brain Twister*]

Nov "The Best Made Plans" (sr2), E. B. Cole

1960 Jan *Deathworld* (sr3), H. Harrison

Feb "The Calibrated Alligator" (n'te), C. M. Knox [R. Silverberg]

Apr "Out Like a Light" (sr3), M. Phillips [R. Garrett & L. M. Janifer] [*The Impossibles*]

Jul *The High Crusade* (sr3), P. Anderson; "Subspace Survi-

vors" (n'te), E. E. Smith [enlarged as *Subspace Explorers*]

Aug "Adaptation" (n'te), M. Reynolds [*The Rival Rigelians*]

Nov "Occasion for Disaster" (sr4), M. Phillips [R. Garrett & L. M. Janifer] [*Supermind*]

Dec "The Longest Voyage" (n'te), P. Anderson

1961 Mar "Ultima Thule" (n'te), M. Reynolds [part of *Planetary Agent X*]

Apr "The Fisherman" (sr4), C. D. Simak [*Time Is the Simplest Thing*]; "Still, Small Voice" (n'te), L. Biggle [see *The Still, Small Voice of Trumpets*]

May "Death and the Senator" (n'te), A. C. Clarke

Jul "A Spaceship Named McGuire" (n'te), R. Garrett [had sequel]

Aug "The Quaker Cannon" (n'te), F. Pohl & C. M. Kornbluth

Sep "Sense of Obligation" (sr3), H. Harrison [*Planet of the Damned*]

Oct "Lion Loose" (short novel), J. H. Schmitz

Dec "Black Man's Burden" (sr2), M. Reynolds

1962 Apr "Mercenary," M. Reynolds [*Mercenary From Tomorrow*]

May *Anything You Can Do . . .* (sr2), D. T. Langart [R. Garrett]

Jun "Novice" (n'te), J. H. Schmitz [first of "Telzey" series]

Jul *Listen! The Stars!*, J. Brunner; "Border, Breed Nor Birth" (sr2), M. Reynolds

Sep *A Life for the Stars* (sr2), J. Blish

Nov *Space Viking* (sr4), H. B. Piper

1963 Jan "The Hard Way" (n'te), G. R. Dickson [part of *The Alien Way*]

Feb "Code Three" (n'te), R. Raphael [see *Code Three*]

Mar "Frigid Fracas" (sr2), M. Reynolds [*The Earth War*]

May "The Dueling Machine," B. Bova & M. R. Lewis

Jul "The Ethical Engineer" (sr2), H. Harrison [*Deathworld*]

Sep "The Thirst Quenchers" (n'te), R. Raphael

Oct "Where I Wasn't Going" (sr2), W. & L. Richmond

Dec "Dune World" (sr3), F. Herbert [in *Dune*]

1964 Mar "Spaceman" (sr2), M. Leinster [W. F. Jenkins] [*The Other Side of Nowhere*]

Apr "Sunjammer" (n'te), W. P. Sanders [P. Anderson]

May "Undercurrents" (sr2), J. H. Schmitz [in *The Universe Against Her*]

Jul *Sleeping Planet* (sr3), W. R. Burkett

Sep "A Case of Identity" (n'te), R. Garrett [first of "Lord Darcy" series]

Oct "Sweet Dreams, Sweet Princes" (sr3), M. Reynolds [*Time Gladiator*]

Nov "Gunpowder God," H. B. Piper [see *Lord Kalvan of Otherwhen*]

1965 Jan "The Prophet of Dune" (sr5), F. Herbert [in *Dune*]

Feb "The Mailman Cometh" (n'te), R. Raphael

Apr "Goblin Night" (n'te), J. H. Schmitz

Jun "Glimpses of the Moon" (n'te), W. West

Jul "Trader Team" (sr2), P. Anderson [in *The Trouble Twisters*]

Sep *Space Pioneer* (sr3), M. Reynolds

Nov "Down Styphon!" (n'te), H. B. Piper [see *Lord Kalvan of Otherwhen*]

Dec "Beehive" (sr2), M. Reynolds [*Dawnman Planet*]; "Mission Red Clash" (n'te), J. Poyer

1966 Mar "Bookworm, Run!" (n'te), V. Vinge; "The Ship Who Mourned" (short), M. McCaffrey; "Operation Malacca" (n'te), J. Poyer [enlarged as book]

May "Moon Prospector" (n'te), W. B. Ellern

Jun "The Ancient Gods" (sr2), P. Anderson [*World Without Stars*]

Jul "An Ounce of Dissension" (short), M. Loran

Aug *Too Many Magicians* (sr4), R. Garrett

Dec "Amazon Planet" (sr3), M. Reynolds; "The Weathermakers" (n'te), B. Bova [enlarged as book]

1967 Feb "There Is a Crooked Man," J. Wodhams

Mar "The Time Machined Saga" (sr3), H. Harrison [*The Technicolor Time Machine*]

Jun *Computer War* (sr2), M. Reynolds

Jul "The Man From P.I.G." (n'te), H. Harrison [enlarged as book]

Sep "Fiesta Brava," M. Reynolds
Oct "Weyr Search," A. McCaffrey [with sequel: *Dragonflight*]
Dec "Dragonrider" (sr2), A. McCaffrey [in *Dragonflight*]
1968 Feb "The Horse Barbarians" (sr3), H. Harrison [*Deathworld 3*]
May "Satan's World" (sr4), P. Anderson
Jul "Hawk Among the Sparrows," D. McLaughlin
Sep "The Tuvela" (sr2), J. H. Schmitz [*The Demon Breed*]

Issues:

	Jan	Feb	Mar	Apr	May	Jun	Jul	Aug	Sep	Oct	Nov	Dec	W
1930	1/1	1/2	1/3	2/1	2/2	2/3	3/1	3/2	3/3	4/1	4/2	4/3	12
1931	5/1	5/2	5/3	6/1	6/2	6/3	7/1	7/2	7/3	8/1	8/2	8/3	24
1932	9/1	9/2	9/3	10/1	10/2	10/3			11/1		11/2		32
1933	11/3		12/1							12/2	12/3	12/4	37
1934	12/5	12/6	13/1	13/2	13/3	13/4	13/5	13/6	14/1	14/2	14/3	14/4	49
1935	14/5	14/6	15/1	15/2	15/3	15/4	15/5	15/6	16/1	16/2	16/3	16/4	61
1936	16/5	16/6	17/1	17/2	17/3	17/4	17/5	17/6	18/1	18/2	18/3	18/4	73
1937	18/5	18/6	19/1	19/2	19/3	19/4	19/5	19/6	20/1	20/2	20/3	20/4	85
1938	20/5	20/6	21/1	21/2	21/3	21/4	21/5	21/6	22/1	22/2	22/3	22/4	97
1939	22/5	22/6	23/1	23/2	23/3	23/4	23/5	23/6	24/1	24/2	24/3	24/4	109
1940	24/5	24/6	25/1	25/2	25/3	25/4	25/5	25/6	26/1	26/2	26/3	26/4	121
1941	26/5	26/6	27/1	27/2	27/3	27/4	27/5	27/6	28/1	28/2	28/3	28/4	133
1942	28/5	28/6	29/1	29/2	29/3	29/4	29/5	29/6	30/1	30/2	30/3	30/4	145
1943	30/5	30/6	31/1	31/2	31/3	31/4	31/5	31/6	32/1	32/2	32/3	32/4	157
1944	32/5	32/6	33/1	33/2	33/3	33/4	33/5	33/6	34/1	34/2	34/3	34/4	169
1945	34/5	34/6	35/1	35/2	35/3	35/4	35/5	35/6	36/1	36/2	36/3	36/4	181
1946	36/5	36/6	37/1	37/2	37/3	37/4	37/5	37/6	38/1	38/2	38/3	38/4	193
1947	38/5	38/6	39/1	39/2	39/3	39/4	39/5	39/6	40/1	40/2	40/3	40/4	205
1948	40/5	40/6	41/1	41/2	41/3	41/4	41/5	41/6	42/1	42/2	42/3	42/4	217
1949	42/5	42/6	43/1	43/2	43/3	43/4	43/5	43/6	44/1	44/2	44/3	44/4	229
1950	44/5	44/6	45/1	45/2	45/3	45/4	45/5	45/6	46/1	46/2	46/3	46/4	241
1951	46/5	46/6	47/1	47/2	47/3	47/4	47/5	47/6	48/1	48/2	48/3	48/4	253
1952	48/5	48/6	49/1	49/2	49/3	40/4	49/5	49/6	50/1	50/2	50/3	50/4	265
1953	50/5	50/6	51/1	51/2	51/3	51/4	51/5	51/6	52/1	52/2	52/3	52/4	277
1954	52/5	52/6	53/1	53/2	53/3	53/4	53/5	53/6	54/1	54/2	54/3	54/4	289
1955	54/5	54/6	55/1	55/2	55/3	55/4	55/5	55/6	56/1	56/2	56/3	56/4	301
1956	56/5	56/6	57/1	57/2	57/3	57/4	57/5	57/6	58/1	58/2	58/3	58/4	313
1957	58/5	58/6	59/1	59/2	59/3	59/4	59/5	59/6	60/1	60/2	60/3	60/4	325
1958	60/5	60/6	61/1	61/2	61/3	61/4	61/5	61/6	62/1	62/2	62/3	62/4	337
1959	62/5	62/6	63/1	63/2	63/3	63/4	63/5	63/6	64/1	64/2	64/3	64/4	349
1960	64/5	64/6	65/1	65/2	65/3	65/4	65/5	65/6	66/1	66/2	66/3	66/4	361
1961	66/5	66/6	67/1	67/2	67/3	67/4	67/5	67/6	68/1	68/2	68/3	68/4	373
1962	68/5	68/6	69/1	69/2	69/3	69/4	69/5	69/6	70/1	70/2	70/3	70/4	385
1963	70/5	70/6	71/1	71/2	71/3	71/4	71/5	71/6	72/1	72/2	72/3	72/4	397
1964	72/5	72/6	73/1	73/2	73/3	73/4	73/5	73/6	74/1	74/2	74/3	74/4	409
1965	74/5	74/6	75/1	75/2	75/3	75/4	75/5	75/6	76/1	76/2	76/3	76/4	421
1966	76/5	76/6	77/1	77/2	77/3	77/4	77/5	77/6	78/1	78/2	78/3	78/4	433
1967	78/5	78/6	79/1	79/2	79/3	79/4	79/5	79/6	80/1	80/2	80/3	80/4	445
1968	80/5	80/6	81/1	81/2	81/3	81/4	81/5	81/6	82/1	82/2	82/3	82/4	457

British Edition

Title Changes: *Astounding Science Fiction*, Aug 1939 — Jun 1960; *Analog Science Fiction — Science Fact*, Jul 1960 — Jun 1963.

220 issue (Aug 1939 — Jun 1963).

Publisher: Atlas Pub. Co., London.

Size Changes: Aug 1939 — Jul 1941, 6½ x 9⅛ in.; Aug 1941 — Jan 1943, 6 x 8¾ in.; Feb 1943 — Jun 1948, 6⅛ x 8⅞ in.; Aug 1948 — Oct 1953, 6⅝ x 9⅝ in.; Nov 1953 — Jul 1955, 5½ x 8¼ in.; Aug 1955 — Oct 1956, 5⅜ x 7½ in.; Nov 1956 — end, 5¼ x 8⅛ in.

Price Changes: 9d through to Oct 1953; 128 pp. at 1/6 to Feb 1961; 2/6 Mar 1961 on.

Review:

This publication played a most important role in the history of the British science fiction magazine field. It was the only regular science fiction to appear in Britain throughout World War II. It began as a wartime measure when U.S. magazines were banned from import, and then remained, competing with the original in the late 1950's. It ceased around the June 1963 issue and was replaced by the Sep 1963 U.S. original.

The early issues up to the 1950's printed only one serial (*Gray Lensman*, E. E. Smith) and were cut-downs from various U.S. originals. Covers were copies of the U.S. and usually were appropriate for a story contained in that issue.

Issues:
[First numbered corresponding to the U.S. edition, then not numbered (nn), then numbered as if the first British issue had been Vol. 1 No. 1.]

	Jan	Feb	Mar	Apr	May	Jun	Jul	Aug	Sep	Oct	Nov	Dec	W
1939								23/6	24/1	24/2	24/3	24/4	5
1940	24/5	24/6	25/1	25/2	25/3	25/4	25/5	25/6	26/1	26/2	26/3	26/4	17
1941	26/5	26/6	27/1	27/2		27/4	27/5	27/6	28/1		28/3	28/2*	27
1942	28/5		28/6		29/3			29/4		30/1			32
1943	30/2	30/4		31/1		nn	nn					nn	38
1944		nn		nn		nn		nn		nn		nn	44
1945		4/9			4/10		4/11		4/12		5/1		49
1946	5/2		5/3		5/4		5/5		5/6			5/7	55
1947	5/8			5/9		5/10		5/11		5/12		6/1	61
1948		6/2		6/3		6/4		6/5		6/6		6/7	67
1949		6/8		6/9		6/10			6/11	6/12			72
1950	7/1	7/2			7/3	7/4		7/5		7/6		7/7	79
1951		7/8		7/9		7/10		7/11		7/12		8/1	85
1952		8/2	8/3	8/4	8/5	8/6	8/7	8/8	8/9	8/10	8/11	8/12	96
1953	9/1	9/2	9/3	9/4	9/5	9/6	9/7	9/8	9/9	9/10	9/11	9/12	108
1954	10/1	10/2	10/3	10/4	10/5	10/6	10/7	10/8	10/9	10/10	10/11	10/12	120
1955	11/1	11/2	11/3	11/4	11/5	11/6	11/7	11/8	11/9	11/10	11/11	11/12	132
1956	12/1	12/2	12/3	12/4	12/5	12/6	12/7	12/8	12/9	12/10	12/11	12/12	144
1957	13/1	13/2	13/3	13/4	13/5	13/6	13/7	13/8	13/9	13/10	13/11	13/12	156
1958	14/1	14/2	14/3	14/4	14/5	14/6	14/7	14/8	14/9	14/10	14/11	14/12	168
1959	15/1	15/2	15/3	15/4	15/5	15/6	15/7	15/8		15/9	15/10		178
1960	15/11	15/12	16/1	16/2	16/2*	16/4	16/5	16/6	16/7	16/8	16/9	16/10	190
1961	17/1	17/2	17/3	17/4	17/5	17/6	17/7	17/8	17/9	17/10	17/11	17/12	202
1962	18/1	18/2	18/3	18/4	18/5	18/6	18/7	18/8	18/9	18/10	18/11	18/12	214
1963	19/1	19/2	19/3	19/4	19/5	19/6							220

* These are correct.

Danish Edition: See *PLANET-MAGASINET*
Spanish Edition: 1 issue, not dated, *ca.* 1948 [unauthorised edition].

ANTICIPATION   Spanish   Science fiction
At least 6 issues, not dated; digest size; 30 pesetas.
Publisher: Editorial Ferma, Barcelona, Spain, & Buenos Aires, Argentina.

Issues sighted have been Nos. 1,3,5,6. A Spanish magazine apparently intended for distribution in Spain and in Spanish-speaking America.

ANTICIPATIONS   Belgian [in French]   Science fiction
14 issues (No. 1, 25 Sep 1945 — No. 15, May 1946, with one double issue, No. 13-14). Printed in Brussels.

First 7 issues were titled "Collection Anticipations"; then "Collection" disappeared and was replaced by "Magazine" in small type after "Anticipations." Generally two issues appeared per month, omitting mid-March 1946. Price was 10 Belgian francs for Nos. 1-12, thereafter 20 francs.

This was the first attempt at presenting magazine science fiction in French. It mainly gave translations from *Tales of Wonder* (both originals and reprints that appeared there), as well as reprints from the pre-war U.S. field, many under pseudonyms and not identified as of U.S. origin.

A complete coverage is given in *Les Marges "A"* (Versins, Lausanne, Switzerland, 1960).

ANTOLOGIA DE CUENTOS FANTASTICOS, POLICIACOS Y DE MISTERIO   Mexican [in Spanish]   Science fiction/mystery
4 issues (Aug 1950 — Nov 1950), monthly.

APOLLO SCIENCE-FICTION   Dutch   Science   fiction
At least 3 issues, not dated.
7½ x 10⅞ in.; 50 pp.; 1.25 guilders (?)
Publisher: N.V. Uitg 'De Vrijbuiter,' Tilburg, and Uitg 'De Schorpiden,' Strombeek-Bove, Netherlands.

One issue, No. 3, has been sighted.

ARGOSY [*Arg*]   U.S.   General
Current (9 Dec 1882 —).
Title Changes: *The Golden Argosy* (weekly), 9 Dec 1882 — 24 Nov 1888; *The Argosy*, (weekly) 1 Dec 1888 — Mar 1895, (monthly) Apr 1894 — Sep 1917; *The Argosy Weekly*, 6 Oct 1917 — 17 July 1920; combined with *All-Story Weekly* to form *Argosy All-Story Weekly*, 24 July 1920-28 Sep 1929. As of 5 Oct 1929 it combined with *Munsey's Maga-*

zine to form two titles, *Munsey's All-Story Magazine* and *Argosy Weekly*; the latter gradually became *Argosy*. It was weekly to 4 Oct 1941, bimonthly 1 Nov 1941—May 1942, monthly from July 1942; it was called *New Argosy* Mar 1946—July 1946, and more recently *The New Golden Argosy* (from Jan 1961).

Editors: F. A. Munsey, 1882-1925; Matthew White Jr., 1925-1928; A. H. Bittner, 1928-1930; Don Moore, 1930-1931; Albert J. Gibney, 1931-1936; Chandler W. Whipple, 1937-1939; George W. Post, 1940-1942; Henry Steeger, 1942-1948; Jerry Mason, 1948-1953; Howard J. Lewis, 1953-1954; Ken W. Purdy, 1954-1955; Henry Steeger, 1955—. Alden H. Norton was an Executive Editor in the 1950's.

Publishers: E. G. Rideout & Co., 1882-1883; Frank A. Munsey, 1883-1925; William T. Dewart, 1926-1941; Henry Steeger (Popular Pubs.), 1942—.

Review:

Argosy, like *All-Story*, published much of interest in the fantasy field and was a frequent source of the reprints used in *Famous Fantastic Mysteries* and *Fantastic Novels*. A story policy change in Sep 1943 eliminated science fiction and fantasy. Since Sep 1943 the magazine has had a modern format, large size, and slick paper, with the emphasis shifting from fiction towards articles.

An interesting editorial, "The Story of Argosy," by W. T. Dewart, appeared in 10 Dec 1932. It tells of the difficulties Frank A. Munsey had in starting the magazine—he had no experience and no backing, but only an idea: publication of decent "red-blooded" fiction for the millions. *Argosy* began in 1882 as an 8-page newspaper-format weekly; it changed to pulp-size in 1894. Amongst its early contributors were Horatio Alger Jr., Oliver Optic, G. A. Henry, R. H. Titherington, and Matthew White Jr.

Two historic magazines were merged with *Argosy*—*Peterson's Magazine*, which began in 1842, was bought in 1898; *Godey's Lady's Book* (founded in 1839) was also incorporated into the Munsey magazines.

Around the turn of the century Upton Sinclair was writing adventure serials for *Argosy*. Other writers included Charles G. D. Roberts, William McLeod Raine, James Branch Cabell, Ellis P. Butler, William Sidney Porter (later writing as O. Henry), and Mary Roberts Rinehart. Among authors appearing somewhat later, prior to the merger with *All-Story Weekly* in 1920, were Elmer L. Reizenstein (Elmer Rice), P. G. Wodehouse, Achmed Abdullah, Edison Marshal, George F. Worts, Max Brand, and Carolyn Wells. The 10 Dec 1932 number marked the 50th Anniversary and was the 1,670th issue.

Notable Fiction:
1899 Feb *A Queen of Atlantis* (sr7), F. Aubrey [Hutchinson, 1899]
1903 Jul "A Round Trip to the Year 2000" (sr5), W. W. Cook [Street & Smith, 1903]
1904 Dec "Adrift in the Unknown" (sr5), W. W. Cook [Street & Smith, 1904-1905]
1905 Aug "Marooned in 1492" (sr5), W. W. Cook [Street & Smith, 1905]
1906 Nov "The Eighth Wonder" (sr4), W. W. Cook [Street & Smith, 1906-1907]
1910 Jan "On the Brink of 2000" (n'te), G. P. Serviss
1911 Oct "Castaways of the Year 2000" (sr5), W. W. Cook
1915 Jan *The Abyss of Wonders*, P. P. Sheehan
     May "The Moon Maiden" (n'te), G. P. Serviss
1916 Apr "Who Is Charles Avison?" (short), E. Marshall
1918 14 Sep *The Citadel of Fear* (sr7), F. Stevens [G. Bennett]
1919 18 Jan "After a Million Years" (sr6), Garret Smith
     22 Feb "The Runaway Skyscraper," M. Leinster [W. F. Jenkins]
     16 Aug "Avalon" (sr4), F. Stevens [G. Bennett]
     11 Oct *Between Worlds* (sr5), Garret Smith
1920 24 Jan *The Torch* (sr5), J. Bechdolt
     6 Mar *Claimed* (sr3), F. Stevens [G. Bennett]
     12 Jun "The Mad Planet," M. Leinster [W. F. Jenkins] [with sequels, as *Forgotten Planet*]
     19 Jun *Serapion* (sr4), F. Stevens [G. Bennett]
     7 Aug *The Metal Monster* (sr8), A. Merritt
     25 Sep "The Sky Woman" (short), C. B. Stilson
     11 Dec *The Treasures of Tantalus* (sr5), Garret Smith
1921 12 Feb *Tarzan the Terrible* (sr7), E. R. Burroughs
     16 Apr *Jason, Son of Jason* (sr6), J. U. Giesy [in "Palos" trilogy]
     14 May *The Blind Spot* (sr6), H. E. Flint & A. Hall
     23 Jul *The Devolutionist*, H. E. Flint

3 Sep "The Emancipatrix" (n'te), H. E. Flint [in *The Devolutionist & The Emancipatrix*]
1922 18 Feb *The Chessmen of Mars* (sr5), E. R. Burroughs
     5 Aug "The Devil of the Western Sea" (n'te), P. Fisher
     21 Oct "The Fire People" (sr5), R. Cummings [in "Matter, Space & Time" trilogy]
     9 Dec *Tarzan and the Golden Lion* (sr7), E. R. Burroughs
1923 5 May *The Moon Maid* (sr5), E. R. Burroughs
     8 Sep "The Face in the Abyss" (short), A. Merritt [see book of same title]
     27 Oct "Fungus Isle" (n'te), P. M. Fisher
1924 3 Feb *Tarzan and the Ant-Men* (sr7), E. R. Burroughs
     28 Jun *The Radio Man* (sr4), R. M. Farley [R. S. Hoar]
     12 Jul *The Man Who Mastered Time* (sr5),. R. Cummings
     8 Nov *The Ship of Ishtar* (sr6), A. Merritt
1925 21 Feb "The Moon Man" (sr4), E. R. Burroughs [see *The Moon Maid*]
     21 Mar *The Radio Beasts* (sr4), R. M. Farley [R. S. Hoar] [in "Radio Man" series]
     5 Sep "The Red Hawk" (sr3), E. R. Burroughs [see *The Moon Maid*]
     21 Nov "The Sun-Makers" (sr3), W. F. Morrow [had sequel]
1926 9 Jan *The Vanishing Professor* (sr4), F. MacIsaac [Waterson, 1927]
     26 Jun *The Radio Planet* (sr6), R. M. Farley [R. S. Hoar] [in "Radio Man" series]
1927 16 Apr "World in the Balance" (short), J. P. Marshall
     2 Jul *Seven Footprints to Satan* (sr5), A. Merritt
     15 Oct *The Return of George Washington* (sr6), G. F. Worts
     17 Dec "A World of Indexed Numbers" (short), W. F. McMorrow
1928 22 Dep *A Brand New World* (sr6), R. Cummings
     29 Dec *The Phantom in the Rainbow* (sr6), S. La Master [McClurg, 1929]
1929 2 Mar *The Sea Girl* (sr6), R. Cummings
     22 Jun *The Shadow Girl* (sr4), R. Cummings
     20 Jul *The Planet of Peril* (sr6), O. A. Kline
     14 Sep *Princess of the Atom* (sr6), R. Cummings
     30 Nov "The Darkness on Fifth Avenue" (n'te), M. Leinster [W. F. Jenkins] [first of "Master of Darkness" series]
     21 Dec *Maza of the Moon* (sr4), O. A. Kline
1930 2 Aug *The Prince of Peril* (sr6), O. A. Kline
     30 Sep "The Red Germ of Courage" (short), R. F. Starzl
     27 Sep "Spawn of the Comet" (n'te), O. A. Kline
     25 Oct "The Snake Mother" (sr7), A. Merritt [see *The Face in the Abyss*]
     13 Dec *Tama of the Light Country* (sr3), R. Cummings
1931 21 Feb "The Hothouse World" (sr6), F. MacIsaac
     18 Apr *Jan of the Jungle* (sr6), O. A. Kline [or *The Call of the Savage*]
     27 Jun *Tama, Princess of Mercury* (sr3), R. Cummings
     1 Aug "The Radio Pirates" (sr4), R. M. Farley [R. S. Hoar] [in "Radio Man" series]
     12 Sep "Red Twilight" (sr3), H. Vincent
1932 23 Jan *The Dwellers in the Mirage* (sr6), A. Merritt
     12 Mar *Tarzan and the City of Gold* (sr6), E. R. Burroughs
     16 Apr *The Insect Invasion* (sr5), R. Cummings
     2 Jul "The Radio War" (sr5), R. M. Farley [R. S. Hoar]
     13 Aug *The Spot of Life* (sr5), A. Hall
     17 Sep *Pirates of Venus* (sr6), E. R. Burroughs
     22 Oct *Burn, Witch, Burn!* (sr6), A. Merritt
1933 7 Jan *Swordsman of Mars* (sr6), O. A. Kline
     4 Mar *Lost on Venus* (sr7), E. R. Burroughs
     15 Apr "The Earth-Shaker" (sr4), M. Leinster [W. F. Jenkins]
     15 May "The Golden City" (sr6), R. M. Farley [R. S. Hoar]
     23 Sep "The Fire Planet" (sr3), R. Cummings
     25 Nov *Outlaws of Mars* (sr7), O. A. Kline
1934 24 Feb "War of the Purple Gas" (sr2), M. Leinster [W. F. Jenkins]
     5 May "The Prophet of Death," A. V. Elston
     8 Sep *Creep, Shadow!* (sr7), A. Merritt
     20 Oct "Earth-Mars Voyage 20" (n'te), R. Cummings
     17 Nov "The Immortals" (sr6), R. M. Farley [R. S. Hoar]
1935 12 Jan "Jan in India" (sr3), O. A. Kline

23 Feb *The Monster of the Lagoon* (sr6), G. F. Worts
10 Aug "The Morrison Monument" (short), M. Leinster [W. F. Jenkins]
23 Nov "The Monster From Nowhere" (short), D. Wandrei
1936 2 May "The Witch-Makers" (n'te), D. Wandrei
15 Aug "The Dead Remember" (short), R. E. Howard
19 Sep "Tarzan and the Magic Men" (sr3), E. R. Burroughs [*Tarzan the Magnificent*]
1937 9 Jan "Seven Worlds to Conquer," E. R. Burroughs [*Back to the Stone Age*]
29 May "The Smoking Land" (sr6), G. Challis [F. Faust]
31 Jul "Drink We Deep" (sr6), A. L. Zagat
1938 8 Jan *Carson of Venus*, E. R. Burroughs
19 Mar "The Red Star of Tarzan" (sr6), E. R. Burroughs [*Tarzan and the Forbidden City*]
2 Jul "Three Against the Stars" (sr5), E. North [B. Cronin]
29 Oct *The Ship of Ishtar* (sr6), A. Merritt
1939 7 Jan *Synthetic Men of Mars* (sr6), E. R. Burroughs
14 Jan "The Eye of Doom" (sr4), C. Woolrich [*The Doom Stone*]
25 Feb "Nonstop to Mars" (n'te), J. Williamson
11 Mar *Seven out of Time* (sr6), A. L. Zagat
25 Mar "Tomorrow" (n'te), A. L. Zagat [first of "Tomorrow" series]
22 Apr *Minions of the Moon* (sr3), W. G. Beyer [first of "Minions" series]
24 Jun *Seven Footprints to Satan* (sr5), A. Merritt [reprinted from 2 July 1927]
5 Aug *The Ninth Life* (sr4), J. Mann [E. C. Vivian]
23 Sep *Lords of Creation* (sr6), E. Binder
4 Nov "Let 'Em Eat Space" (short), W. G. Beyer
18 Nov "The Golden Boneyard" (n'te), D. V. Reed
9 Dec *Maker of Shadows* (sr5), J. Mann [E. C. Vivian]
1940 24 Feb "The Green Flame" (sr4), E. North [B. Cronin] [*Toad*]
15 Jun "Postmarked for Paradise," R. Arthur [in "Murchison Morks" series]
1941 5 Apr "To Heaven Standing Up" (n'te), P. Ernst
23 Aug "The Quest of Tarzan" (sr3), E. R. Burroughs [*Tarzan and the Castaways*]
1943 Apr *Earth's Last Citadel* (sr4), C. L. Moore & H. Kuttner
1954 Mar "Queen of the Deep," P. J. Farmer [as "Son" in *Strange Relations*]

ARGOSY (British) British General

This monthly British magazine has been published since the early 1940's (Vol. 7 No. 1 was Jan 1946). Since the 1950's it has featured a "Science Fiction Selection" in each issue. The magazine has published a considerable number of R. Bradbury's short stories, as well as many science fiction and fantasy stories by recognised authors in those fields and some by writers usually considered as mainstream. The Dec 1968 issue was Vol. 29 No. 12 (the 348th issue if the numbering is uniform).

ARKHAM SAMPLER U.S. Weird reference
8 issues (Winter 1948—Autumn 1949).
6 x 9 in; 100 pp. [last, 128 pp.]; quarterly; $1.00.
Editor: A. W. Derleth.
Publisher: Arkham House, Sauk City, Wisconsin.

Produced by Derleth as a scholarly and informative magazine for those seriously interested in all imaginative writing as a literary form. The magazine specialised in book reviews and general notes on writers, especially H. P. Lovecraft, but also published fiction and verse. It is generally recommended, but is now becoming a collector's item, as only 1,000 copies of each issue were published.

Notable Material:
1948 Win "History and Chronology of the Necronomicon," H. P. Lovecraft & A. Derleth; *The Dream Quest of Unknown Kadath* (sr4), H. P. Lovecraft
Sum "The Novels of M. P. Shiel," A. Reynolds Morse; "The Loved Dead" (short), C. M. Eddy [*WT*, May-Jun-Jul, 1924]
Aut "Nut Bush Farm" (n'te), Mrs. J. H. Riddell
1949 Win "A Basic Science-Fiction Library" (a symposium); "Dear Pen Pal" (short), A. E. van Vogt; "Time to Rest" (short), J. B. Harris

Spr "The Root of Ampoi" (short), C. A. Smith; "The Last American" (n'te), J. A. Mitchell
Sum "In the Year 2889," J. Verne; "Journey to the World Underground" (sr2), L. Holberg

Issues:

	Winter	Spring	Summer	Autumn	W
1948	1/1	1/2	1/3	1/4	4
1949	2/1	2/2	2/3	2/4	8

ASTONISHING STORIES U.S. Science fiction
16 issues (Feb 1940—Apr 1943).
Pulp size; 112 pp.; bimonthly/quarterly; 10¢.
Editors: F. Pohl, Feb 1940—Sep 1941; A. Norton, Nov 1941—Apr 1943.
Publishers: Fictioneers Inc., then Popular Pubs., New York.

Originally planned as *Incredible Stories*. Although the lowest priced magazine in the field when it appeared, it maintained quite a good standard. It had a number of departments, including film, book and fan magazine reviews, and also (from Mar 1942) "Fantasy Circle," which gave items of interest from the fan field.

Notable Fiction:
1940 Feb "Half Breed" (n'te), I. Asimov [had sequel]
Jun "Into the Darkness" (n'te), R. Rocklynne [first of "Darkness" series]
Aug "Cat-Men of Aemt" (n'te), N. R. Jones [continuation of "Jameson" series—included in pa series]
Oct "Quicksands of Youthwardness" (sr3), M. Jameson
1941 Feb "The Pet Nebula" (short), A. Bester
Apr "Heredity" (n'te), I. Asimov; "Beyond Doubt" (n'te), L. Monroe [R. A. Heinlein] & E. Wentz
Sep "Mars-Tube" (n'te), S. D. Gottesman
1942 Mar "Pied Piper" (short), L. Monroe [R. A. Heinlein]
Jun "Storm Cloud on Deka" (n'te), E. E. Smith [see *The Vortex Blaster*]
Oct "Thunder in the Void" (n'te), H. Kuttner; "The Vortex Blaster Makes War" (short), E. E. Smith
Dec "Mimic" (short), M. Pearson [D. A. Wollheim]
1943 Feb "The Halfling" (short), L. Brackett

Issues:

	Jan	Feb	Mar	Apr	May	Jun	Jul	Aug	Sep	Oct	Nov	Dec	W
1940		1/1		1/2		1/3		1/4		2/1		2/2	6
1941		2/3		2/4					3/1		3/2		10
1942			3/3			3/4				4/1		4/2	14
1943		4/3		4/4									16

Canadian Edition
3 issues (Jan, Mar, May 1942).
Publisher: Popular Pub., Inc., West Toronto, Ontario.
Pulp size; 96 pp.; bimonthly; 10¢.

This magazine reprinted from both the U.S. *Astonishing Stories* and *Super Science Stories*, but in no set order. All covers and interiors were by Canadian artists; the issues were the same size as the U.S. editions.

Jan 1942 (1/1)—entire contents, including editoral and fan departments, of the U.S. *Astonishing Stories* of Nov 1941; no U.S. illustrations, but three beautiful ones by an anonymous Canadian artist.

Mar 1942 (1/2)—entire contents except "Pendulum" (R. Bradbury & H. Hasse) of the U.S. *Super Science* of Nov 1941; three more fine illustrations as above.

May 1942 (1/3)—entire contents of U.S. *Astonishing* for Mar 1942. Cover copied from U.S. issue by a Canadian artist, while there were three fine illustrations by another artist.

ASTOUNDING SCIENCE FICTION See *Analog Science Fiction—Science Fact*

ASTOUNDING STORIES (OF SUPER-SCIENCE) See *Analog Science Fiction—Science Fact*

ATLANTA Belgian Science fiction
Current (Jan/Feb 1966—).
Size 12.5 x 17 cm.; 60-80 pp.; bimonthly; 40 Belgian francs.

This started as a duplicated amateur magazine; in 1966 it became printed and professional, still edited by Michael Grayn. The first two professional issues were published by Cercle d'Etudes Littéraires Française, with the succeeding ones by the Association Europeénne des Littératures Parallèles (AELP) (Michael Grayn as President).

The only Belgian professional sf and fantasy magazine, it has organized an annual story contents and gives a reward, the Prix du Conte Atlanta, of about 100 dollars to the best sf or fantasy short story written by a young author during the year. It publishes material by Belgian and other European writers, but nothing from the English or U.S. field.

AU DELA DU CIEL   Italian [in French]   Science fiction
40 issues (mid-Mar 1958—Feb 1961).
Published in Rome.

Derived from the Italian magazine *Oltre il cielo*, which is still continuing. This has published some original material as well as translations; the latter include *First Men in the Moon*, H. G. Wells, and (from No. 21) the "Troon" series, J. B. Wyndham [J. B. Harris].

Issues to Dec 1959 were covered in *Les Marges A* (Versins, Switzerland, 1960).

AUTHENTIC SCIENCE FICTION   British   Science fiction
85 issues (Jan 1951—Oct 1957)
Title changes: *Authentic Science Fiction Series*, No. 1; *Authentic* [small letters] *Science Fiction Fortnightly*, Nos. 2-8; *Authentic* [small letters] *Science Fiction Monthly*, Nos. 9-12; *Authentic Science Fiction*, Nos. 13-28; *Authentic Science Fiction Monthly*, Nos. 29-68; *Authentic Science Fiction*, Nos. 69-85.
Editors: L. G. Holmes, Nos. 1-27; H. J. Campbell [formerly Technical Editor], Nos. 28-65; E. C. Tubb, Nos. 66-85.
Publisher: Hamilton & Co. (Stafford) Ltd., London.
Size Changes: Pocket book size to No. 77, then digest.
Price Changes: 1/6 to No. 59, thereafter 2/-.
Cover Artists: Davis painted a number of fine covers, including a series on "Man's Trip to the Stars" for Nos. 35-48; various other cover artists were also used.
Review: This magazine began as a paperback book series with long novels only. A serial began in No. 26, and departments gradually appeared from No. 29. It is from No. 29 that the title can be considered as a magazine; some U.S. reprints were used early in its magazine career. Campbell emphasized science articles during his tenure, but Tubb brought fiction back into prominence. The magazine was considered to have achieved a good standard when it ceased.
Notable Fiction: All novels from Nos. 1 to 28 are listed in the Publishers section of the Paperbacks listing, under Hamilton & Co.; these included the "Old Growler" series by J. J. Deegan, while novels by H. J. Campbell, F. G. Rayer and E. C. Tubb were also of note.
1952 #26 "Frontier Legion" (sr6), S. J. Bounds
1953 #29 "Immortal's Playthings," W. F. Temple
     #30 "Lady of Flame," S. J. Byrne
     #31 *The Rose*, C. L. Harness [title story of collection]
     #36 "My Name Is Ozymandias," M. Jordan
     #38 "Old Man of the Stars," J. F. Burke
     #39 "Highway i" (short), C. E. Maine [D. McIlwaine] [*Timeliner*]
1954 #43 "Tomorrow Is Another Day," K. H. Brunner [J. Brunner]
     #52 "Star Haven," E. C. Tubb
1955 #57 "The Big Hop" (sr2), J. T. McIntosh [J. M. MacGregor]
     #61 "Private Satellite" (sr2), J. F. Burke
     #63 "The Lady and the Bull" (sr2), J. T. McIntosh [J. M. MacGregor]
1956 #66 "The Creep" (sr2), R. Presslie
1957 #78 "Dead Weight" (sr3), D. West
Issues:

	1 Jan	15 Jan	1 Feb	15 Feb	1 Mar	15 Mar	1 Apr	15 Apr	W
1951	#1	#2	#3	#4	#5	#6	#7	#8	8

	Jan	Feb	Mar	Apr	May	Jun	Jul	Aug	Sep	Oct	Nov	Dec	W
1951					#9	#10	#11	#12	#13	#14	#15	#16	16
1952	#17	#18	#19	#20	#21	#22	#23	#24	#25	#26	#27	#28	28
1953	#29	#30	#31	#32	#33	#34	#35	#36	#37	#38	#39	#40	40
1954	#41	#42	#43	#44	#45	#46	#47	#48	#49	#50	#51	#52	52
1955	#53	#54	#55	#56	#57	#58	#59	#60	#61	#62	#63	#64	64
1956	#65	#66	#67	#68	#69	#70	#71	#72	#73		#74*	#75	75
1957	#76	#77	#78	#79	#80	#81	#82	#83	#84	#85			85

* Dated 15th of each month through No. 73; by month from No. 74.

U.S. Edition
Some were issued for sale in the U.S.A. with U.S. price printed on the cover. (Copies are known from Nos. 39 to 42.)

AVENGER, THE   U.S.   Mystery science fiction
24 issues (Sep 1939—Sep 1942)
Pulp size; 128 pp. in 1939, then 114 pp. from Jan 1940; monthly to Jul 1940, then bimonthly (6 issues per volume); 10¢.
Publisher: Street and Smith, New York.

One of the pulp hero magazines (listed in *The Hero-Pulp Index*, McKinstry & Weinberg, 1970). An industrial engineer is transformed into an invincible crime fighter after his wife and daughter are murdered by thugs. The author was Paul Ernst under the house pseudonym "Kenneth Robeson." The series was continued by Emile C. Tepperman for a further five stories under the same pseudonym in the magazine *Clues-Detective* (Sep 1942—May 1943).

AVON FANTASY READER   [AFR]   U.S.   Fantasy & weird
18 issues (1947-1952), not dated.
Digest size, 5½ x 7¾ in., with first 4 standard glued binding and remainder saddle-stapled; 128 pp.; irregular; 35¢.
Editor: D. A. Wollheim.
Publisher: Avon Book Co., New York.

A quite unique magazine specializing in reprints from all sources and generally highly considered. It used small print and had no interior illustrations. It is now a collector's item.
Notable fiction: [All stories were shorts, and practically every story in each issue is of interest.]
1947 #1 "The Voice in the Night," W. H. Hodgson; "The Woman of the Wood," A. Merritt
     #2 "Stenographer's Hands," D. H. Keller; "The Mirrors of Tuzun Thune," R. E. Howard
     #3 "The Silver Key," H. P. Lovecraft; "Black Thirst," C. L. Moore
     #4 "Conqueror's Isle," N. S. Bond; "The Derelict," W. H. Hodgson
     #5 "Scarlet Dream," C. L. Moore; "The Miracle of the Lily," Clare W. Harris
1948 #6 "The Metal Man," J. Williamson; "The Thing in the Cellar," D. H. Keller
     #7 "The Curse of a Thousand Kisses," S. Rohmer; "The Slugly Beast," Lord Dunsany
     #8 "The Cat-Woman," M. E. Counselman; "Zero Hour," R. Bradbury
1949 #9 "The Flower-Woman," C. A. Smith; "Child's Play," A. M. Schnirring
     #10 "Bimini," B. Morgan; "The Gostak and the Doshes," M. J. Breuer
     #11 "The Golden Hour of Kwoh Fan," F. Owen; "Mogglesby," T. S. Stribling
1950 #12 "In the Valley of the Sorceress," S. Rohmer; "The Captured Cross-Section," M. J. Breuer
     #13 "Original Sin," S. F. Wright; "Raiders of the Universe," D. Wandrei
     #14 "The Three-Eyed Man," R. Cummings; "The Curse of Yig," Z. B. Bishop
1951 #15 "In Amundsen's Tent," J. M. Leahy; "Ubbo-Sathla," C. A. Smith
     #16 "The Black Kiss," R. Bloch; "The Water Ghost of Harrowby Hall," J. K. Bangs
     #17 "The Sapphire Siren," N. Dyalhis; "Through the Gates of the Silver Key," H. P. Lovecraft & E. H. Price
1952 #18 "Out of the Eons," H. Heald; "Amina," E. L. White
Issues (all undated):

	Jan	Feb	Mar	Apr	May	Jun	Jul	Aug	Sep	Oct	Nov	Dec	W
1947	#1			#2			#3			#4			4
1948		#5			#6				#7			#8	8
1949		#9					#10			#11			11
1950	#12			#13				#14					14
1951		#15			#16		#17						17
1952	#18												18

AVON SCIENCE FICTION AND FANTASY READER
                U.S.   Science fiction/fantasy
2 issues (Jan & Apr 1952).
Digest size; 128 pp.; quarterly; 35¢.
Editor: Sol Cohen.
Publisher: Avon Novels, Inc., New York.
   Avon's attempt to continue a combined sf and fantasy magazine after D. A. Wollheim left. Unlike its predecessors, *Avon Fantasy Reader* and *Avon Science Fiction Reader*, this had interior illustrations. It was generally quite well received.
Notable Fiction:
1953 Jan (1/1) "The Forgotten Enemy" (short), A. C. Clarke; "Mr. Kowtshook" (short), J. Christopher [C. S. Youd]; "One-Man God" (short), F. Owen
    Apr (1/2) "DP!" (n'te), J. Vance; "Survivor" (short), I. Cox; "Forever Is So Long" (short), J. Jakes; "The Parasite" (short), A. C. Clarke

AVON SCIENCE FICTION READER   U.S.   Science fiction
3 issues (1951-1952), not dated.
Digest size, saddle-stapled; 128 pp., irregular; 35¢.
Editor: D. A. Wollheim.
Publisher: Avon Novels, Inc., New York.
   This magazine was begun as a companion to *Avon Fantasy Reader* to cover science fiction, but was not nearly as successful.
Notable Fiction (short stories):
1951 #1, nd (Apr) "Green Glory," F. B. Long; "The Morrison Monument," M. Leinster [W. F. Jenkins]
    #2, nd (Jun) "The Whisperers," D. Wandrei; "The Book of Worlds," M. J. Breuer
1952 #3, nd (Jan) "The Master Ants," F. Flagg; "In the Walls of Eryx," K. Sterling & H. P. Lovecraft

B

BEST SCIENCE FICTION, THE   U.S.   Science fiction
2 issues, not dated [*ca.* May & Oct 1964].
Digest size; 162 pp.; 50¢.
Editor: F. Pohl.
Publisher: Galaxy Publishing Corp., New York.
   Subtitles indicated these were reprint magazines—No. 1: From *Worlds of If Magazine*; No. 2: From *Worlds of Tomorrow*. No. 1 had 12 stories, including "The Snowbank Orbit," F. Leiber, and "The Expendables," A. E. van Vogt; No. 2 had 10 stories, including "The Long Remembered Thunder" (n'te), K. Laumer, and "Little Dog Gone," R. F. Young. There were no illustrations; the covers carried small motifs plus an outline list of the authors presented.

BEYOND FANTASY FICTION See *BEYOND FICTION*

BEYOND FICTION   U.S.   Fantasy
10 issues (Jul 1953—No. 10, not dated, 1955).
Digest size; 160 pp. to Jul 1954, then 128 pp.; bimonthly/irregular; 35¢.
Title Changes: *Beyond Fantasy Fiction* Jul 1953—Sep 1954, then *Beyond Fiction*.
Editor: H. L. Gold.
Publisher: Galaxy Publishing Corp., New York.
   A companion to *Galaxy Science Fiction*, started by Gold in emulation of *Unknown (Worlds)*. Although it printed some very good material, it was never commercially successful, and the publication rate slowed down before the magazine ceased. A paperback selection from its pages was *Beyond* (9 stories, anonymously edited, Berkley: F712, 1963, 160 pp., 50¢).

Notable Fiction:
1953 Jul *...And My Fear Is Great*, T. Sturgeon; "Babel II" (n'te), D. Knight
   Sep "The Wall Around the World," T. R. Cogswell [title story of collection]; "Kid Stuff" (short), I. Asimov
   Nov "The Real People" (n'te), A. Budrys; "Sorry, Right Number" (short), R. Matheson
1954 Jan "Call Me Wizard" (n'te), Evelyn E. Smith; "Perforce to Dream" (short), J. Wyndham [J. B. Harris]
   Mar "The God Business" (n'te), P. J. Farmer; "The Watchful Poker Chip" (short), R. Bradbury
   May "Sine of the Magus" (n'te), J. Gunn
   Jul "No More Stars" (n'te), C. Satterfield [F. Pohl]
   Dec "The Green Magician," L. S. de Camp & F. Pratt [see *Wall of Serpents*]

Issues:

	Jan	Feb	Mar	Apr	May	Jun	Jul	Aug	Sep	Oct	Nov	Dec	W
1953							1/1		1/2		1/3		3
1954	1/4		1/5		1/6		2/1		2/2		#9 nd		9
1955		#10 nd											10

British Edition
Titled *Beyond Fantasy Fiction*.
4 issues, not dated (1954).
Digest size; 1/6.
Publisher: Strato Pubs., Leicester, for Thorpe & Porter Ltd.
   These covered the first four issues. They were one story shorter than the corresponding U.S. originals, but used the same covers.
Issues:

	Jan	Feb	Mar	Apr	May	Jun	Jul	Aug	Sep	Oct	Nov	Dec	W
1954	1/1		1/2		1/3		1/4						4

BEYOND INFINITY   U.S.   Science fiction/fantasy
1 issue (Nov-Dec 1967).
Digest size; 160 pp.; 50¢.
Editor: Doug Stapleton.
Publisher: I.D. Publications Inc., Hollywood, Calif.
   The only issue presented 12 stories; authors included B. Bova, J. Brunner, and J. Christopher. Blue or red was added to a number of interior illustrations.

BIZARRE! MYSTERY MAGAZINE   U.S.   Mystery weird
3 issues (Oct 1965; Nov 1965; Jan 1966).
Digest size; monthly (?); 144 pp.; 50¢.
Editor: John Poe (Associate: Sean Kelly; Art Director: Hilary Wilson).
Publisher: Pamar Enterprises Inc., Concord, New Hampshire (Gerald Levine).
   Subtitled "Murder—Black Magic—Suspense—Horror." Quite an interesting magazine. The first issue had 12 stories, including "One Drop of Blood," C. Woolrich and "The Horror at Red Hook," H. P. Lovecraft. *Planet of the Apes*, P. Boule (abridged), was the lead novel in the second issue. Other authors included R. Bloch, A. C. Clarke, A. Davidson, A. Derleth, T. M. Disch, J. Jakes and A. Porges.

BLACK CAT, THE   U.S.   General/weird
Oct 1895—Apr 1923(?); retitled *The Thriller* from Oct 1919.
Editors: H. D. Umbstaetter, 1895-1912; Theresea E. Dyer, 1913; T. H. Kelly, 1914; Harold E. Bessom, 1915-1920; William R. Kane, 1922-1923.
Publishers: Shortstory Pub. Co., Boston, Mass. [H. B. Umbstaetter, owner], 1895-1912; Shortstory Pub. Co., Salem, Mass. [Samuel E. Cassino, owner], 1913-1915; same [Herbert E. Cassino, owner], 1915-1919; Black Cat Pub. Co., New York, 1919-1920; Black Cat Magazine Inc., New York, Feb-Oct 1920; William R. Kane, Highland Falls, N.Y., 1922-1923.
Price Changes: Began at 5¢; financial crisis of 1907 forced rise to 10¢ in 1908; 15¢ in 1918; 20¢ in 1920.
Format Changes: 50-60 pp. most of its life, but the 1922 revived edition was only 36 pp.; used pulp paper from 1915. Two 1898 issues sighted were saddle-stapled, 6 x 9 in.; these featured the face of a black cat set in a design with a table of contents below; the usual type of cover around the turn of the century is unknown.

Frequency: Monthly, 1895-1920; semi-monthly, 1922-23. The volume numbering ran annually: Vol. 1, Oct 1895, through Vol. 25 ending Oct 1920; issues from Dec 1917 are not verified but may have missed one month; apparently suspended Nov 1920—Dec 1921; Vols. 26-27, 1922-1923.

Review: The issues sighted were not fantastic in content, but more of a mystery nature. It may be that a number of near-weird stories published through the years have caused the magazine's importance to the weird field to be over-emphasized, but it did encourage the detective type of story and also ran some ghost and Oriental stories. *Black Cat* apparently nurtured such writers as Jack London, and printed much by R. W. Chambers and M. P. Shiel.

Umbstaetter edited a collection of stories from the magazine under the title *The Red Hot Dollar* (1911).

BLACKWOOD'S MAGAZINE   British   General

The oldest magazine in continuous circulation—nearly 230 years. It caters to outdoor interests, with most of its contents at present being non-fiction adventure. Some fantasy has been published, including:
Late 1880's: *Aut Diabolus aut Nihil*, XL [pseud] [book, Methuen, 1894]
1899 Jan "No Man's Land," John Buchan
1901 Feb "The Captivity of the Professor,"A. L. Green
1924 Jun "An Affair of Some Gravity," T. B. Simpson
1935 Apr "The Power of Destruction," N. Martyr

BLUE BOOK MAGAZINE [*BB*]   U.S.   General

Current (May 1905—).
Title Changes: Began as *The Monthly Story Magazine*; from Sep 1906 became *The Monthly Story Blue Book Magazine*; in May 1907 became *Blue Book Magazine*; about Oct 1960 became *Bluebook for Men*, with a change in emphasis from fiction to fact-adventure.
Editors: Around 1920's, Karl Edwin Harriman; Donald Kennicott, 1929-1940's [Associate Editor of the group *Blue Book*, *Red Book* and *Green Book* 1910-1929; ca. 1960, Fredrick A. Birmingham.
Publishers: Story-Press Corp., Chicago; The Consolidated Magazines Corp., Chicago (at least in the 1920's); The McCall Co. (later Corp.) in 1930's; from 1960, H.S. Publications, New York.
Size Changes: Began pulp-size, then became large 1930-1931; changed back to pulp and then to large again in 1941.
Price Changes: Began at 15¢; had become 20¢ in 1922, then 25¢ by late 1925; lowered to 15¢ around Sep 1932; was 35¢ in early 1960's.
Format: Although it began blue, the spine and cover-frame were black in the 1920's. It was under Kennicott that the magazine assumed its distinctive blue spine and cover-frame which lasted until 1941. It was always monthly until the 1950's.
Review:

In its early years to 1915, *Blue Book* published much fantasy as well as other varied fiction, but from 1915 to 1928 practically the only fantasy was the few E. R. Burroughs serials. By the 1940's most fantasy material was short stories; noted series appeared from Nelson S. Bond and Bertram Atkey. The latter had a long series about "Mr. Honey," who was always visiting past eras; a number of these apparently were published as *The Escapes of Mr. Honey* (MacDonald, London, 1944). H. Bedford-Jones had a historical series detailing the story of "The Sphinx Emerald."

Among the cover illustrators, Herbert Morton Stoops was discovered in 1935 and later became *Blue Book*'s most popular artist. Kennicott experimented with interior illustrations early in his editorship, and the magazine achieved a higher quality than most others. One artist noted for interiors was John Richard Flanagan, an Australian who excelled at historical pageantry.

From Feb 1952 a greater emphasis was placed on fact-adventure.

Notable Fiction
1907 Nov "The Voice in the Night" (short), W. H. Hodgson [who had some stories earlier]
1911 Jun "The Strange Cases of Dr. Xavier Wycherly," M. Rittenberg [began a series of 12; the author had a further series of 6 from Feb 1913]
1914 Nov "The Bride of the Sun," G. Leroux [book, Nast, 1915]
1915 Feb *The Ivory Child* (sr8), H. R. Haggard
1916 Nov "New Stories of Tarzan" (sr10), E. R. Burroughs [see "Tarzan" series for this and later "Tarzan" works in *BB*]

1918 Aug *The Land That Time Forgot*, E. R. Burroughs [see book for novelette trilogy]
1929 Mar *Tanar of Pellucidar* (sr6), E. R. Burroughs
       Jul "Hercules" series, B. Atkey, began.
1930 Apr *A Fighting Man of Mars* (sr6), E. R. Burroughs
1931 May "The Land of Hidden Men" (sr5), E. R. Burroughs [*Jungle Girl*]
       Nov *The Phantom President* (sr6), G. F. Worts
1932 Jul "The Wall of Fire" (short), J. M. Kirkland [in *Editor's Choice in Science Fiction*, Moskowitz, 1954]
       Sep *When Worlds Collide* (sr6), E. Balmer & P. Wylie
1933 Nov *After Worlds Collide* (sr6), E. Balmer & P. Wylie
1934 Jun "The Day of the Dragon" (short), G. Endore
       Nov *Swords of Mars* (sr6), E. R. Burroughs
1935 Apr "Kioga" series, W. L. Chester, began [one published as book].
       Oct "Tarzan and the Immortal Man" (sr6), E. R. Burroughs
1937 Feb "The Treasure of Vanished Men" (sr4), J. F. Dwyer
1938 Nov "Trumpets From Oblivion," H. Bedford-Jones (first of series of 13 stories)
1940 May *Exiles of Time*, N. S. Bond
1942 Jan *Beyond the Farthest Star*, E. R. Burroughs
       Jul "Pat Pending" series, N. S. Bond, began.
1943 Mar "Squaredeal Sam McGhee" series, N. S. Bond, began (some not fantasy).
1945 ?   "The Paradise Crater" (n'te), P. Wylie
1949 Mar "Refuge for Tonight" (short), R. M. Williams [in *The Best Science-Fiction Stories 1950*, Bleiler]
       Jul "Star of Doom" (sr2), L. Sowden [*Tomorrow's Comet*]
       Dec "Delilah and the Space-Rigger" (short), R. A. Heinlein [in *The Green Hills of Earth*]
1950 Aug "The Laughter of the Stars," R. S. Carr [retitled in *Beyond Infinity*]
1951 Sep "Planets in Combat" (sr2), R. A. Heinlein [*Between Planets*]
1952 Jan "Second Genesis," E. F. Russell
1953 Jul "The Man With the Golden Hand" (short), R. Arthur
1954 Mar "Button, Button" (short), N. S. Bond
1956 Mar *The Power*, F. M. Robinson

BOOK OF TERROR, THE   U.S.   Weird horror

1 issue (Dec 1949).

Mentioned by M. Ashley in *Who's Who in Horror and Fantasy Fiction* (1977) as low-grade with the only notable story being one by E. Hoffmann Price.

BOOK OF WEIRD TALES, A   British   Weird

1 issue (#1, not dated, Aug 1960).
Digest size; 128 pp.; 2/6.
Editor: C. Lawton; **Associate Editor:** F. J Ackerman
Publishers: Veevers and Hensman Ltd., Burnley.

Appeared as a one-shot with a view to becoming regular if it sold well. All stories were selected by Ackerman, who also had an article on Bela Lugosi (from *Famous Monsters of Filmland*). Most stories were reprints, including "The Curse of Amen-Ra" (n'te), V. Rousseau, and "The Hunters From Beyond," C. A. Smith; one new story was "The Wild One," M. Z. Bradley.

It had a quite neat format, with a design-type cover; there were no interior illustrations, except that often the story title took up a whole page. The magazine was generally quite well received by weird-story enthusiasts.

BORDERLINE   U.S.   Mystery-fantasy

At least 8 issues (Sep 1964—Sep 1965); monthly to Nov 1964, then bimonthly; 128 pp.; 60¢.
Publisher: Sherbourne Press, Los Angeles.
No further information.

BOY'S FRIEND LIBRARY

A paper-covered series listed in *PAPERBACKS: PUBLISHERS (Ephemerals)*.

BOY'S STAR LIBRARY, THE   U.S.   Boys' magazine
Publisher: Frank Tousey, New York.
   Published in the 1880's and 1890's, this presented some sf stories, mainly about Jack Wright. An issue sighted was No. 341, 1893, "Jack Wright and His Electric Air Rocket"—7⅜ x 10⅝ in., 32 pp., 5¢, weekly.

BRITISH SCIENCE FICTION MAGAZINE   See *BRITISH SPACE FICTION MAGAZINE*

BRITISH SPACE FICTION MAGAZINE   British   Science fiction
19 issues (Jan 1954—Feb 1956); only first 2 issues dated.
Title Changes: *Vargo Statten Science Fiction Magazine*, 1/1—1/3; *Vargo Statten British Science Fiction Magazine*, 1/4—1/5 [same for Table of Contents of 1/6]; *British Science Fiction Magazine*, 1/6—1/12; *British Space Fiction Magazine*, 2/1-2/7.
Editor: Vargo Statten [J. R. Fearn]; **Associate Editor:** A. Paterson (for 1/1—1/5).
Publisher: Scion Ltd. (Distributors), London, 1/1—1/7; then Dragon Pubs., London.
Format changes: large, 1/1—1/3, 64 pp.; 5⅝ x 8½ in., 1/4, 1/6—1/9 (1/5 slightly smaller), 128 pp.; digest (5 x 7⅛ in.), 1/10—, 128 pp. Price, always 1/6. Supposedly a monthly.
General
   This magazine stemmed from the interest in the Vargo Statten paperbacks, and began reasonably well. It was slanted to the younger reader and had many departments. It was hit by the great sf slump of 1954-1955. Recognised authors other than E. C. Tubb did not submit much material, and Fearn was eventually forced to run many of his own stories of many years earlier, using many pen names.
Issues (not dated after first 2):

	Jan	Feb	Mar	Apr	May	Jun	Jul	Aug	Sep	Oct	Nov	Dec	W
1954	1/1	1/2		1/3	1/4		1/5			1/6		1/7	1/8	8
1955	1/9	1/10	1/11	1/12			2/1	2/2	2/3	2/4	2/5	2/6	10
1956		2/7											19

C

CAPTAIN FUTURE   U.S.   Science fiction
17 issues (Win 1940—Spr 1944).
Pulp size; 130 pp.; quarterly; 15¢.
Editor: Oscar J. Friend [Editorial Director: L. Margulies].
Publisher: Better Publications, New York.
   The best-known one-character magazine in the science fiction field, featuring novels about Curt Newton (Captain Future), with his companions Otho, Grag, and the Brain, plus supplementary love interest. These are mainly interplanetary space opera.
   When the magazine was planned, Edmond Hamilton was commissioned as writer, and he wrote all the novels except the 14th and 17th, which were by Joseph Samachson. The last four appeared under the house name Brett Sterling. (The series was then continued in *Startling Stories*.) The issues were filled out with short stories and serialised reprints. Earl K. Bergey painted all the covers except the first two, done by G. Pozen.
Notable Fiction [The "Captain Future" novels are listed under *SERIES* for E. Hamilton]:
1940 Win   "The Human Termites" (sr4), D. H. Keller
1941 Win   "Mutiny in Space" (sr2), G. Edwards
        Sum   "The Man Who Awoke" (sr3), L. Manning [first of series]
1942 Spr   "The Alien Intelligence" (sr3), J. Williamson
Issues:

	Winter	Spring	Summer	Fall	W
1940	1/1	1/2	1/3	2/1	4
1941	2/2	2/3	3/1	3/2	8
1942	3/3	4/1	4/2	4/3	12
1943	5/1	5/2	5/3		15
1944	6/1	6/2			17

CAPT. HAZZARD   U.S.   Science fiction
1 issue (May 1938).
Pulp size; 96 pp.; planned as bimonthly; 10¢.
Publisher: Magazine Publishers, Inc. (A. A. Wyn).
   A lesser-known magazine of sf interest. Lead novel: "Python Men of Lost City," Chester Hawks. This was to have been a "one-character" magazine with the hero, Captain Hazzard, of great mental powers, forming a group to fight crime. In his only adventure he travelled with a girl explorer to a lost city. Norman Saunders did the cover for the issue, which also contained three short stories.

CAPTAIN MORS   German   Science fiction
Over 180 issues (1908-1914).
Publisher: Verlag Moderner Lecture.
   This magazine was apparently monthly, then became fortnightly, and ceased during World War I. It printed complete stories about hero "Captain Mors" which were scientifically accurate according to the science of the day. [See W. Ley, *Fantasy Review*, Aut 1949.]

CAPTAIN SATAN   (U.S. magazine and series)   See *STRANGE DETECTIVE MYSTERIES*

CAPTAIN ZERO   U.S.   Science fiction and mystery
3 issues (Nov 1949—Mar 1950).
Pulp size; 130 pp.; bimonthly; 25¢.
Publisher: Recreational Reading Corp., Kokomo, Indiana.
   Each issue featured a novel by G. T. Fleming-Roberts about "Captain Zero," an invisible agent fighting the underworld. Short stories filled out the issues.
Issues:
1949 Nov (1/1) "City of Deadly Sleep"
1950 Jan (1/2) "The Mark of Zero"
        Mar (1/3) "The Golden Murder Syndicate"
Canadian Edition
3 issues (Nov 1949—Mar 1950), as for U.S. edition.
Pulp size; 130 pp.; 25¢.
Publisher: Recreational Reading inc., an affiliate of Popular Pub. Inc., Toronto.
   Identical to U.S. editions except a half inch longer and with advertisements on the outside back cover similar to those on *A. Merritt's Fantasy* (Canadian).

CASSELL'S MAGAZINE   British   General
   Began in 1853 as the weekly *Cassell's Illustrated Family Paper*, and changed its name in 1867 to *Cassell's Magazine*; in 1874 it became *Cassell's Family Magazine* and later *Cassell's Magazine of Fiction*. Among its distinguished editors were John Tillotson, Sir Max Pemberton and Newman Flower.
   It published some fantasy, including stories by J. S. Le Fanu. In the early 1910's its publication of S. Rohmer's "The Sins of Séverac Babylon" set this writer on his famous career. Another novel of interest was *The Ancient Allan* (sr8), H. R. Haggard, which began in Mar 1919.

CASTLE OF FRANKENSTEIN   U.S.   Movie monster
25 issues (Jan 1962—1974) plus yearbook 1967.
Editor: C. T. Beck.
Publisher: Gothic Castle Pub. Co., New Jersey.
   One of the movie magazines produced to emulate Ackerman's successful *Famous Monsters of Filmland*. It was one of the best of its kind. A precursor was *Journal of Frankenstein* (1 issue, 1959).
Issues: Jan 1962 (1/1); Mar 1962 (1/2); Apr 1963 (1/3); May 1964 (1/4); No. 5, May 1965; No. 6, Spr 1965; No. 7, Dec 1965; Nos. 8 to 10, dates not known; unnumbered "Annual," Jan. 1967; No. 11, Feb 1967; No. 12, Mar 1968.

CAVALIER   U.S.   General fiction
   Began Oct 1908 as a successor to the second section of *Scrap Book*. Following the Jan 1912 issue it became weekly, with the issue of 10 Jan 1912. It ceased with 9 May 1914, combining with *All-Story Weekly*.
Publisher: Frank A. Munsey, New York.
Notable Fiction:
1909 Nov *Morning Star* (sr8), H. R. Haggard

1911 Jul   *The Second Deluge* (sr11), G. P. Serviss
       Aug   *The Elixir of Hate* (sr4), G. A. England
1912 Jan   "Darkness and Dawn" (sr4), G. A. England [with sequels, as book]
1912 18 May   *The Golden Blight* (sr6), G. A. England
1913 11 Jan   "Fishhead" (short), I. S. Cobb

CHAMBERS' JOURNAL   British   General
Began as *Chambers' Edinburgh Journal* in 1832, and adopted the title *Chambers' Journal* from 1854. It was weekly for a long time—at least the late 1840's to 1935. It was founded by William and Robert Chambers (who also founded the famous publishing firm that bore their name). Covering popular literature, science and art, it published many works by renowned authors of the day.
Some fiction of interest:
1893 3 Jun   "The Sacred Beetle" (sr4), L. Graeme
1903 1 Dec   *The Closed Book* (sr40), W. LeQueux [book, 1904]
1908 1 Dec   "The House of Whispers" (sr39), W. LeQueux [book, 1910]
1922 Dec   "Spirit Island" (sr4), H. T. Munn
[The last was the only story recommended by a collector checking 1880-1932.]

CHILLING MONSTER TALES   U.S.   Movie monster
1 issue (Aug 1966).
Large size; 68 pp.; 50¢.
Publisher: M.M. Publishing Ltd., New York.
One of the short-lived monster magazines.

CIENCIA Y FANTASIA   Mexican [in Spanish]   Fantasy
14 issues (late 1956—Oct 1958).
Spanish edition of *The Magazine of Fantasy and Science Fiction*.
Publisher: Novaro-Mexico, S.A.
First 2 issues 2 pesos (*ca.* 20¢ U.S.), then price rose slightly. Size: 12½ x 19 cm.

Apparently selected stories from various issues of the U.S. original. The print order began at 15,000 and became 20,000 for later issues, but these sales apparently were not maintained.

CLACK BOOK, THE   U.S.   Weird
12 issues (Apr 1896—Jun 1897).
A magazine which apparently printed a number of stories of a weird flavour; all issues are now collector's items.

CLASSICS ILLUSTRATED   U.S.   Comic-book novel series
Publisher: Gilberton Co. Inc., New York. British edition published by Thorpe & Porter Ltd., London; there has also been a Swedish edition.

A series which ran around 1940 to 1970, printing in pictures (comic-book format) the stories of the world's greatest authors. Many novels by J. Verne and H. G. Wells have been published; others include M. Shelley's *Frankenstein*, H. R. Haggard's *King Solomon's Mines*, W. H. Hudson's *Green Mansions*, and J. Swift's *Gulliver's Travels*.

COLLIER'S   U.S.   General
First issue 28 Apr 1888, last issue 4 Jan 1957.
During its life this noted magazine presented some science fiction and fantasy but not as a regular practice.

An issue of interest was 27 Oct 1951, labeled "Preview of the War We Do Not Want—Russia's Defeat and Occupation 1952-60." It was devoted to "articles" about World War III as if it had already happened, plus fiction and cartoons in the same setting. Bonestell did a number of illustrations, including atomic bombing scenes. The 20 or so items included three stories: "Philadelphia Base," Philip Wylie, and others by John Savage and Kathryn Morgan-Ryan. The issue was reproduced in Australia, fairly complete, probably as an issue of *Australian Monthly*.

There were several issues with feature sections on the coming age of space travel: "Man Will Conquer Space *Soon*" (22 Mar 1952), with articles by Wernher von Braun, Willy Ley, Fred Whipple, and others; "Man on the Moon" (18 Oct & 23 Oct 1952), articles by von Braun, Ley, and Whipple; "Man's Survival in Space" (28 Feb, 7 Mar, 14 Mar 1953), ed. Cornelius Ryan with contributions by von Braun and others; "Baby Space Station" (27 Jun 1953), von Braun & Ryan; and "Can We

Get to Mars — Is There Life on Mars?" (30 Apr 1954), von Braun, Whipple, and Ryan. All were lavishly illustrated, including several cover paintings, by Chesley Bonestell, Rolf Klep, and Fred Freeman.
Notable Fiction:
1947 14 Jun   "Symbiosis" (short), W. F. Jenkins
1949   8 Jan   "Jizzle" (short), J. Wyndham [J. B. Harris] [title story of collection]
1951   6 Jan   *The Day of the Triffids* (sr5), J. Wyndham [J. B. Harris]
1954   2 Apr   *Dark Dominion* (sr4), D. Duncan
       10 Dec   *The Body Snatchers* (sr3), J. Finney
1955 11 Nov   "The Spaceman Cometh" (short), H. G. Felsen

COLUMBIA MAGAZINES
Columbia Publications, New York, has published the following science fiction magazines [disregarding slight changes in title]: *Science Fiction* (Mar 1939—Sep 1941); *Future Fiction* (Nov 1939—Jul 1943); *Future Science Fiction* (May 1950—Apr 1960); *Science Fiction Quarterly* (Sum 1940—Spr 1943; May 1951—Feb 1958); *(Original) Science Fiction Stories* (1953—May 1960); *Dynamic Science Fiction* (Dec 1952—Jan 1954).

COMET   U.S.   Science fiction
5 issues (Dec 1940—Jul 1941).
Pulp size; 128 pp.; bimonthly; 20¢.
Editor: F. O. Tremaine.
Publisher: H.K. Publications, Springfield, Mass.

This represented Tremaine's return to the field after leaving *Astounding* in 1937, and generally was considered to be quite good. Morey and Paul painted the covers on alternate issues, while interior artists included J. Binder and J. Giunta. A department was "The Spacean" (future interplanetary newspaper).
Issues and Notable Fiction:
1940 Dec (1/1)   "Equation for Time" (short), R. R. Winterbotham; "Primal City" (short), C. A. Smith
1941 Jan (1/2)   "The Twilight People" (n'te), F. E. Arnold; "The Way Back" (n'te), S. Moskowitz
       Mar (1/3)   "The Immortal" (n'te), R. Rocklynne; "The Star of Dreams" (n'te), J Williamson
       May (1/4)   "We Are One" (n'te), E. Binder; "The Ransom for Toledo" (n'te),. N. R. Jones
       Jul (1/5)   "The Vortex Blaster" (n'te), E. E. Smith [first of series, later in book]; "The Street That Wasn't There" (short), C. D. Simak & C. Jacobi

CONQUÊTES   French   General
A French magazine featuring some science fiction. Published by G. H. Gallet, only one experimental issue appeared, dated 24 Aug 1939, at 1 franc. This began serialising F. Pragnell's *Green Man of Graypec* and also had an apparent sf novel, *Le mystère de Radio-Zero*, by Commandant Cazal [pseudonym of Jean de la Hire].

CORNHILL MAGAZINE   British   General
Began in 1860, edited by W. M. Thackeray. Later editors included Frederick Greenwood (1862-1868), James Payn (1883-1896), and Leonard Huxley. It published several H. R. Haggard novels, including *Jess* (sr12, May 1886) and *Moon of Israel* (sr10, Jan 1918).

COSMIC: Selezione di Fantascienza   Italian   Science fiction
3 issues (June 1957—May 1958).
Digest size (5½ x 7½ in.); 128 pp., 150 lire.
Editor: Mario Todarello
Publisher: Irsa Muraro Editrice, Rome.

Very neatly produced, with four-colour covers. It included a number of original stories, as well as fact articles and a science fiction crossword puzzle.

COSMIC SCIENCE FICTION   See *COSMIC STORIES*

COSMIC SCIENCE STORIES   British   Science fiction
1 issue (not numbered, not dated—*ca.* Jun 1950).
Publisher: Popular Press Ltd., London.
A reprint of the U.S. *Super Science Stories* for Sep 1949, slightly abridged, and featuring "Minion of Chaos," J. D. MacDonald.

COSMIC STORIES   U.S.   Science fiction
Retitled *Cosmic Science Fiction* from May 1941.
3 issues (Mar, May, Jul 1941).
Pulp size; 130 pp.; bimonthly; 15¢.
Editor: D. A. Wollheim.
Publisher: Albing Pub., Holyoke, Mass.
    The companion of *Stirring Science Stories*, and of reasonable quality. Covers were by L. Morey, H. Bok and E. Dold. It printed many stories by C. M. Kornbluth under pseudonyms.
Issues and Notable Fiction:
1941 Mar (1/1) "Mecanica," F. E. Arnold; "The Reversible Revolutions" (n'te), C. Corwin [C. M. Kornbluth]
    May (1/2) "Phoenix Planet" (n'te), J. Blish; "What Sorghum Says" (n'te), C. Corwin
    Jul (1/3) "The Red Death," D. H. Keller; "The City in the Sofa" (short), C. Corwin

COSMOPOLITAN   U.S.   General
A noted U.S. magazine at the turn of the century.
Notable Fiction:
1893 Apr "Omega" (sr4), C. Flammarion
1897 May *The War of the Worlds* (sr8), H. G. Wells
1900 Nov *The First Men in the Moon* (sr8), H. G. Wells
1903 Nov *The Food of the Gods* (sr10), H. G. Wells
1906 Jan *In the Days of the Comet* (sr8), H. G. Wells

COSMOS SCIENCE FICTION AND FANTASY MAGAZINE
      U.S.   Science fiction
4 issues (Sep 1953—Jul 1954).
Digest size (5⅝ x 7⅞ in.); 128 pp.; irregular; 35¢.
Editor: L. B. Cole.
Publisher: Star Publications [J. A. Kramer], New York.
    One of the magazines published during the science fiction boom of the 1950's, and of moderate standard. It was first intended to be called *Star Science Fiction*.
Issues and Notable Fiction:
1953 Sep (1/1) "The Troublemakers," P. Anderson; "Gateway" (short), A. B. Chandler.
    Nov (1/2) "The Gentleman Is an EPWA" (short), C. Jacobi
1954 Mar (1/3) "Simpson," P. Latham [R. S. Richardson]; "Homecoming" (short), I. Cox
    Jul (No. 4) "Teucan" (n'te), P. Anderson

COUNT-DOWN!   U.S.   Nonfiction
Subtitled "The Rockets and Missiles Annual."
1 issue (12 May 1960).
Pulp size; 96 pp.; 50¢.
Publisher: Great American Publications, New York.
    This published mainly reprints, probably from previous Great American magazines such as *Space*. The "Complete Chart of Satellites and Space Probes" was by no means complete, omitting the Sputniks, mentioning some fallen vehicles as still being in orbit, and covering events only to Sep 1959.

CREEPY   U.S.   Weird
Current (Feb 1965—)
Large; 74 pp.; 75¢.
Bimonthly through Oct 1967 (No. 17), then: Jan 1968 (18), Mar (19), May (20), Jul (21), Aug (22), Oct (23), Dec (24). The 1969 Yearbook also appeared in 1968.
Publisher: Warren Publishing Co., New York.

CRONACHE DEL FUTURO [Chronicles of the Future]
      Italian   Science fiction
24 issues (15 Aug 1957—16-30 Aug 1958).
Size 4¾ x 8 in.; 128 pp.; fortnightly; 150 lire.
Editor: The three issues sighted all had different editors.
Publisher: Edizioni Kappa, Rome.
    Well printed, with four-colour covers. Slightly sexually slanted. Each issue had a long novel plus a serial of 2 or 3 pages. The novels were all apparently by Italian writers. This magazine was apparently succeeded by the item next below.

CRONACHE DEL FUTURO, LE   Italian   Science fiction
Apparently a continuation of *Cronache Del Futuro* (listed next above) by another publisher.
11 issues (30 Nov 1958—30 May 1959).
Size 5½ x 7½ in.; 128 pp.; fortnightly; 150 lire.
Publisher: Editrice Maya, Rome.
    Each issue had a long novel. Of three issues sighted (Nos. 4, 8, 9), a translation appeared in No. 8: *Assassinio sulle dune* [*The Witching Night*], C. S. Cody. This may indicate that other translations appeared, as well as original Italian novels. The magazine *I Romanzi del Futuro* is probably a continuation of this.

CUENTOS FANTASTICOS, LOS
      Mexican [in Spanish]   Science fiction
45 issues (July 1948—2nd Fortnight Apr 1954).
Mostly irregular, though fortnightly at times.
Price Changes: Nos. 1-3, 60¢; 4-14, 90¢; 15-31, $1.00; 32-45, $1.20.
Pages: #1-#8, 50 pp.; #9, 60 pp.; #10-#30, 50 pp.; #31, 52 pp.; #32-#38, 50 pp.; #39, 42 pp.; #40-#41, 50 pp.; #42-#44, 42 pp.; #45, 34 pp.
Editor: Edited anonymously at first. José Sotres noted as Editor from No. 27.
Covers: All were copies of U.S. magazine covers except one original by the late H. Eichner. The cover on No. 2 was also used on No. 43, and that for No. 5 was repeated on No. 42.
    This magazine used material from the U.S. science fiction magazines, and even amateur magazines, without acknowledgment.
Issues [1F = 1st fortnight of month; 2F = 2nd fortnight; some issues also dated]:

1948	#1, 8 Jul	#2, 15 Jul	#3, 31 Jul	#4, 2F Aug
	#5, 1F Sep	#6, 2F Sep	#7, 1F Oct	#8, 2F Oct
	#9, 30 Nov	#10, 1F Dec		
1949	#11, ?	#12, ?	#13, 2F Mar	#14, ?
	#15, 2F Jun	#16, 15 Jul	#17, 10 Aug	#18, 15 Aug
	#19, 15 Sep	#20, 15 Oct	#21, 1F Nov	#22, 2F Nov
	#23, 1F Dec			
1950	#24, Jan	#25, 15 May	#26, Jun	#27, Jul
	#28, Oct	#29, Nov		
1951	#30, not dated	#31, Mar	#32, Apr	#33, Aug
	#34, Oct	#35, Dec		
1952	#36, Feb	#37, 1F Mar	#38, ?	#39, not dated
	#40, Aug	#41, not dated		
1953	#42, Jan	#43, Apr	#44, May	
1954	#45, 2F Apr			

D

DIFFERENT   U.S.   Fantasy
Editors: L. Lorraine & S. A. Coblentz.
Publisher: Avalon Arts Academy.
    Issues sighted include Jan/Feb 1951 (Vol. 6 No. 6), Aut 1951 (7/3), and Fall 1953 (7/6). The last was 6 x 9 in., 32 pp., noted as quarterly, 50¢. The two early issues had verse by C. A. Smith; the magazine aimed to publish material of a "different" nature.

DIME MYSTERY   U.S.   Weird menace
159 issues (Dec 1932—Oct/Nov 1950); monthly to Jun 1940, then mainly bimonthly.
Title Changes: First issues titled *Dime Mystery Book*; then *Dime Mystery Magazine*; name addition in 1942: "combined with *Ten Story Mystery*"; retitled to *15 Mystery* in 1950.

Editor-in-Chief: Rogers Terril (with many sub-editors).
Publisher: Popular Publications, New York.
Review: One of the weird menace pulp magazines. The main period of terror stories was Oct 1933—Sep 1938 (60 issues); from May 1941 the policy changed from horror to detective fiction, though some fantasy still appeared. Some issues are listed in *The Macabre Index*, W. M. Austin (mimeo, 1952); issues are fully indexed in *The Weird Menace*, B. Jones (1972). An outline of the stories presented is given in *The Shudder Pulps*, R. K. Jones. Authors of interest included N. W. Page, H. B. Cave, C. M. Knox, A. L. Zagat, W. Blassingame, F. C. Davis, H. M. Appel, N. Schachner, P. Ernst, A. J. Burks, Stewart Sterling, Dale Clark, and R. Cummings.
Notable Fiction:
1932 Dec "Bride's House Horror," Nelson Duff; short by E. Wallace
1933 Nov "The Corpse Maker," H. B. Cave
1934 Jan "Dark Slaughter," H. B. Cave
1935 May "House of the Restless Dead," H. B. Cave
      Jul "Dark Melody of Madness" (n'te), C. Woolrich
      Oct "Mistress of the Dead," H. B. Cave
1936 Apr "Girls for the Torture God," A. L. Zagat
      May "Lash of the Living Dead" (n'te), N. Schachner
      Jun "Forest of the Damned" (n'te), P. Ernst
      Dec "Bride of the Dust Demon," P. Ernst
1937 Jan "Hell's Dancing Master," Dave Barnes
      Feb "Death Breaks Quarantine," A. L. Zagat
      Jul "The Mummy in My Arms" (n'te), R. Cummings
      Oct "Satan Calls a Strike," A. L. Zagat; "Children of Murder," N. Schachner
      Nov "Twelve Were Damned," P. Ernst
1938 Mar "Coming of the Faceless Killers," Francis James
      Aug "Beasts Who Once Were Men," Edith & Ejler Jacobson
1939 Jan "Plague of Invisible Flame," J. T. Fleming-Roberts
      Mar "The Case of the Tortured Corpses," R. Cummings
      Apr "The Dead Hand Horrors," Russell Gray
      Nov "The Red Eye of Rin-Po-Che," N. W. Page
1940 Apr "Brides for Murdered Men," Ray King
      Nov "The Red Hand of Kali," N. W. Page

DOC SAVAGE   U.S.   Borderline science fiction

181 issues (Mar 1933—Jun 1949).
Publisher: Street & Smith, New York.
    This is probably the most noted of the single-character magazines associated with the science fiction field. It is indexed in *The Hero-Pulp Index*, McKinstry & Weinberg (mimeo, 1970). All the novels were under the pseudonym "Kenneth Robeson"; most were by Lester Dent, with some by Norman A. Daniels and Alan Hathway. Since 1964 Bantam has been reprinting the novels in a paperback series, reaching No. 31 by the end of 1968. These are listed under DENT in *WHO'S WHO Vol. 1*. The magazine was monthly to Feb 1947, then bimonthly for six issues, then quarterly for its last three.
British Edition: It is understood that one appeared, but no data is known.
Spanish Edition: Some issues appeared until 1946.

DR. DEATH   U.S.   Weird mystery

3 issues (Feb 1935, Mar 1935, Apr 1935).
Pulp size; monthly; 15¢.
Editor: Probably Arthur Ward.
Publisher: Dell Publishing Co., New York.
    A character magazine continuing the exploits of a supreme villain, Dr. Death, which began running as short novels in *All-Detective Magazine* in 1934. Lead novels, written by Harold Ward, were "Twelve Must Die," "The Gray Creatures," and "The Shriveling Murders." Corinth Publishers reprinted these as paperbacks in 1966, with a fourth—*Stories From Doctor Death and Other Terror Tales*—a selection of the short stories used to fill out the magazine issues.

DR. YEN SIN   U.S.   Weird mystery

3 issues (May/Jun 1936—Sep/Oct 1936).
    Issued by Popular Publications in imitation of Sax Rohmer's "Fu Manchu" stories—Dr. Yen Sin being an Oriental genius plotting to become emperor of the world.

DOUBLE DETECTIVE   U.S.   Weird mystery

Before 1940—Mar 1943.
Publisher: Frank A. Munsey Co.
    The issues of interest run from Apr 1940 (5/5) to Mar 1943 (7/6), presenting novels by Richard Foster [pseud. of K. F. Crossen] about The Green Lama, one of the strangest of all crime fighters (an American who had lived in Tibet). Listed in *The Hero-Pulp Index*, McKinstry & Weinberg (mimeo, 1970).

DREAM WORLD   U.S.   Fantasy

3 issues (Feb 1957—Aug 1957).
Digest size; 130 pp.; quarterly; 35¢.
Editor: Paul W. Fairman.
Publisher: Ziff-Davis Pub. Co., New York.
    The magazine that was started because the "dream" issues of *Fantastic Science Fiction* sold well. It gave light, frothy, often slightly erotic material, none of which is of note.
Issues:
1957 Feb (1/1)   May (1/2)   Aug (1/3)

DUSTY AYRES AND HIS BATTLE BIRDS

                  U.S.   Science fiction
12 issues (July 1934 [5/4]—Jun 1935 [8/3]; 4 issues per volume.
A retitling of *Battle Birds Magazine*.
Pulp size; monthly; 128 pp.; 15¢.
Publisher: Popular Pubs., Chicago.
Review: Robert Sydney Bowen was commissioned to write a series of stories about a war in the air in the near future. Dusty Ayres keeps thwarting the Black Invaders, led by the mysterious Fire-Eyes, who have conquered the entire world except for the U.S. In a radical departure from the usual pulp novels, Bowen wrote the last novel to end the series with the killing of Fire-Eyes and the collapse of the Black Invasion; this was even noted in an editorial in the letter column.
    In 1966 Corinth Books reprinted the first three stories and the last one, plus a volume of short stories: *Black Lightning*; *Crimson Doom*; *Purple Tornado*; *The Telsa Raiders*; *Battle Birds Versus the Black Invaders* (collection).

DYNAMIC SCIENCE FICTION   U.S.   Science fiction

6 issues (Dec 1952—Jan 1954).
Pulp size (3rd, 5th & 6th with trimmed edges); 132 pp. to Aug 1953, then 98 pp.; quarterly/bimonthly; 25¢.
Editor: R. A. W. Lowndes.
Publisher: Columbia Pubs., New York.
    A short-lived companion to *Future Science Fiction* and *Science Fiction Quarterly*, and of the same standard. The department "Inside Science Fiction," run by R. Madle, became a feature from June 1953 (and was later continued in the companion magazines). The articles on science fiction by J. E. Gunn are of importance.
Issues and Notable Material:
1952 Dec (1/1) "I Am Tomorrow" (n'te), L. del Rey
1953 Mar (1/2) "Sea-Change" (n'te), Cyril Judd [C. M. Kornbluth & J. Merril]; "The Philosophy of Science Fiction" (article), J. E. Gunn [first of a series of 4]
      Jun (1/3) "Double Identity" (n'te), R. Z. Gallun
      Aug (1/4) *The Duplicated Man*, J. Blish & M. Sherman
      Oct (1/5) "The Plot-Forms of Science Fiction" (article), J. E. Gunn
1954 Jan (1/6) "The Chapter Ends" (n'te), P. Anderson
British Edition
3 issues (not dated): 1954, #1 (Jan), #2 (Jun), #3 (Nov).
Pulp size; 98 pp.; 1/-.
    No. 1 selected stories from the June 1953 U.S. issue, No. 2 from Dec 1952, and No. 3 from Jan 1954.

DYNAMIC SCIENCE STORIES   U.S.   Science fiction

2 issues (Feb 1939; Apr/May 1939).
Pulp size; 114 pp.; bimonthly; 15¢.
Editor: R. O. Erisman.
Publisher: Western Fiction Pub. Co.
    A short-lived companion to *Marvel Science Stories*; of fair quality. There were plans to reissue it in late 1950, but this never eventuated.

Notable Fiction:
1939 Feb (1/1)   *Lord of Tranerica*, S. A. Coblentz
      Apr/May (1/2)   "Prison of Time," E. Binder; "Ananias" (n'te),
              L. S. de Camp
British Edition: 1 issued, not dated, about Apr 1939; extremely scarce.

E

EERIE   U.S.   Weird [comic book]
Current (*ca.* Jan 1966—).
Large size; 60 pp.; 60¢.
Bimonthly through No. 12 (Nov 1967), then: 1968 Feb (13), Apr (14),
Jun (15), Jul (16), Sep (17), Nov (18), Dec (19).
Publisher: Warren Publishing Co., New York.

EERIE MYSTERIES   U.S.   Weird
4 issues (Aug 1938, Nov 1938, Feb 1939, Apr/May 1939).
Pulp size; 112 pp.; 15¢.
Editor: Harry Widmer.
Publisher: Magazine Publishers Inc., Springfield, Mass.
     A mixture of mystery, fantasy and weird of only fair quality. Feature
stories in the first three issues were by Ralph Powers: "City of Stone
Corpses," "When It Rained Corpses" (n'te), "Horror's Handshake."

EERIE STORIES   U.S.   Weird
1 issues (Aug 1937); was to have been bimonthly.
Pulp size; 128 pp.; 15¢.
Publisher: Magazine Publishers Inc., Springfield, Mass.
The one issue to appear had the novel "Virgins of the Stone Death,"
Gates Alexander, and 11 short stories. The cover was by Norman Saun-
ders and the cover story was "The Soul Searcher's Lair," Ronald Flagg.

EERIE TALES   Canadian   Weird
1 issue (Jul 1941).
Large size; 64 pp.; monthly; 15¢.
Publisher: C.K. Pub. Co., Toronto.
     Stories included "The Hound," T. P. Kelley and "A Dictator Dies,"
L. A. Crouch; "The Weird Queen," T. P. Kelley, was begun as a serial.

ELECTRICAL EXPERIMENTER, THE   U.S.   Popularised science
     One of the early Gernsback technical magazines which published
some science fiction. An indexed period, Jun 1914—Jul 1920 (Vol.
2/2—8/3) shows a serial, "At War With the Invisible" (sr2, Mar
1918), G. & R. Winthrop, and a "Baron Munchausen" series, H.
Gernsback. The index also shows 32 short stories, including "Whispering Ether," Charles S. Wolfe (Mar 1920), a number of others by Wolfe,
Charles M. Adams, and George F. Stratton, and a series by Thomas W.
Benson on the "Wireless Wiz."

ENIGMAS   Mexican [in Spanish]   Science fiction
16 issues (Aug 1955—early 1958)
Pulp size; 128 pp.; monthly; 3 pesos.
Editor: Bernardino Diaz.
Publisher: Editorial Proteo S.A., Mexico City.
     Reprints of U.S. material that had originally appeared in the Standard
sf magazines. For example, the first issue ran a Weinbaum novel; the
2nd had "Vulcan's Dolls," M. St. Clair; and the 3rd had "The Bird of
Time," W. West. It printed 8,000 copies per issue. Publication was on a
fairly regular monthly schedule, except that the last issue was delayed
some months.

ESPACIO, El Mundo Futuro   Spanish   Science fiction
     Space-opera magazine series (128 pp.) from Spain, with material by
Spanish pulp writers under English-sounding pseudonyms. By the end
of 1962 there were well over 200 issues.

EXPERIMENTER, THE   U.S.   Popularised science
     One of the Gernsback technical magazines. In an indexed period—
Nov 1924 (4/1) to Jan 1926 (5/3), it published only one serial of note:
The Ark of the Covenant (sr15, Nov 1924), V. MacClure.

EXPLORING THE UNKNOWN   U.S.   Nonfiction
Current (Jan 1960—) [ceased 1971].
Digest size; 130 pp.; generally quarterly; 35¢, then 50¢ in mid-1960's.
Editor: Stewart Robb for 1960, then R. A. W. Lowndes.
Publisher: Health Knowledge Inc., New York.
     Presented articles on psychic phenomena, the occult, etc.

F

FAMOUS FANTASTIC MYSTERIES [*FFM*]
               U.S.   Science fiction/fantasy
Pulp size; 128 pp. (varying); mainly bimonthly.
Price Changes: 15¢; 10¢ from Oct 1940; 15¢ from Jun 1941; 25¢ from
Apr 1942.
Editor: Mary Gnaedinger.
Publishers: Frank A. Munsey, New York, to Dec 1942; Popular Pubs.
(subsidiary of All-Fiction Field Inc.), New York.
Review:
     A magazine founded to reprint fantasy and sf material from the old
Frank A. Munsey magazines (*Argosy, All-Story*, etc.). It became popular
in its initial year. Some novels were serialised in the early issues, until
the companion *Fantastic Novels* was started and began publishing complete novels. (The latter, however, had only 5 issues at that time and
was combined back into *FFM*.) The covers were only coloured story
listings until Feb 1940, when paintings by F. Paul and V. Finlay began.
     After *FFM* was bought by Popular Pubs. in 1943 the fiction policy
changed to the reprinting of novels that had previously appeared only in
book form. Some quite good works were presented; these are covered
below. From Aug 1947 to Apr 1950 there was a section "Masters of
Fantasy" (drawings and a short appreciation) by N. Austin. The magazine became "streamlined" from Jan 1951—smaller in size and with no
advertisements—but soon returned to its older format. Lawrence was
the principal artist; in conjunction with *Fantastic Novels*, portfolios of
work by Lawrence and V. Finlay were published.
     Popular's *FFM* also had *Fantastic Novels* (2nd series) as a companion
for a period, as well as *A. Merritt's Fantasy* and *Super Science Stories* (2nd
series). The Munsey *FFM* was used as a source for the fiction in the
Canadian *Super Science* (Feb 1945—Dec 1945).
Notable Fiction:
1939 Sep/Oct   "The Moon Pool" (short), A. Merritt [see book]; "The
               Girl in the Golden Atom" (n'te), R. Cummings [see
               book]
      Nov   "The Conquest of the Moon Pool" (sr6), A. Merritt [see
               The Moon Pool]; *The Moon Metal*, G. P. Serviss; "Almost
               Immortal" (n'te), A. Hall
      Dec   *The Radio Man* (sr3), R. M. Farley [R. S. Hoar]; "The Lord
               of Death" (n'te), H. E. Flint
1940 Jan   "On the Brink of 2000" (short), Garret Smith
      Feb   "The Man Who Saved the Earth" (n'te), A. Hall
      Mar   *The Blind Spot* (sr3, not completed), A. Hall & H. E. Flint
      Apr   "The Devil of the Western Sea," P. M. Fisher
      May/Jun "Sunken Cities," D. Newton; "Three Lines of Old
               French" (short), A. Merritt
      Aug   "Darkness and Dawn," G. A. England [first of trilogy; see
               book]; "The Rebel Soul" (n'te), A. Hall
      Oct   *The Face in the Abyss*, A. Merritt; "Fungus Isle," P. M.
               Fisher
      Dec   "The Sun-Makers," W. McMorrow [had sequel]

1941 Feb	*The Spot of Life*, A. Hall; "The Ship of Silent Men," P. M. Fisher	
Apr	*Claimed*, F. Stevens [G. Bennett]	
Jun	"John Ovington Returns," M. Brand [F. Faust]	
Aug	*The Metal Monster*, A. Merritt	
Oct	"Palos of the Dog Star Pack," J. U. Giesy [first of "Palos" series]; "The Colour out of Space" (short), H. P. Lovecraft	
Dec	"The Lost Garden" (n'te), M. Brand [F. Faust]	
1942 Feb	*The Citadel of Fear*, F. Stevens [G. Bennett]	

1941 Feb *The Spot of Life*, A. Hall; "The Ship of Silent Men," P. M.
Fisher
Apr *Claimed*, F. Stevens [G. Bennett]
Jun "John Ovington Returns," M. Brand [F. Faust]
Aug *The Metal Monster*, A. Merritt
Oct "Palos of the Dog Star Pack," J. U. Giesy [first of "Palos"
series]; "The Colour out of Space" (short), H. P. Love-
craft
Dec "The Lost Garden" (n'te), M. Brand [F. Faust]
1942 Feb *The Citadel of Fear*, F. Stevens [G. Bennett]
Apr *The Radio Planet*, R. M. Farley [R. S. Hoar]
Jun *Burn, Witch, Burn!*, A. Merritt
Jul "Polaris—of the Snows," C. B. Stilson [first of "Polaris"
series]; *Serapion*, F. Stevens [G. Bennett]
Aug *Creep, Shadow!*, A. Merritt
Sep *A Brand New World*, R. Cummings; "Wild Wullie, the
Waster" (n'te), T. Robbins
Oct *The Elixir of Hate*, G. A. England; *Into the Infinite* (sr4), A.
Hall
Dec "The Golden City," R. M. Farley [R. S. Hoar]
1943 Mar "Ark of Fire," J. Hawkins
Sep *The Iron Star*, J. Taine [E. T. Bell]
Dec *Three Go Back*, J. L. Mitchell; "The Derelict" (short), W.
H. Hodgson
1944 Mar *The Man Who Was Thursday*, G. K. Chesterton; *The Ghost
Pirates*, W. H. Hodgson
Jun *The Greatest Adventure*, J. Taine [E. T. Bell]
Sep *The Day of the Brown Horde*, R. Tooker; "The Novel of the
White Powder" (n'te), A. Machen
Dec *The Lost Continent*, C. Hyne
1945 Mar *The Machine Stops*, Wayland Smith
Jun *The Boats of the Glen Carrig*, W. H. Hodgson
Sep *Phra the Phoenician*, E. L. Arnold
Dec *The Ancient Allan*, H. R. Haggard
1946 Feb *Before the Dawn*, J. Taine [E. T. Bell]; *The House of the
Secret*, C. Farrere
Apr *The Island of Captain Sparrow*, S. F. Wright
Jun *The Undying Monster*, J. D. Kerruish; "The Novel of the
Black Seal" (short), A. Machen
Aug *The Twenty-Fifth Hour*, H. Best; "The Secret of the Growing
Cold" (short), B. Stoker
Oct *The Island of Dr. Moreau*, H. G. Wells
Dec *Unthinkable*, F. Sibson
1947 Feb *The Star Rover*, J. London
Apr *Allan and the Ice Gods*, H. R. Haggard
Jun *The People of the Ruins*, E. Shanks
Aug *Minimum Man*, A. Marvel
Oct *The City of Wonder*, E. C. Vivian
Dec *The Man Who Went Back*, W. Deeping
1948 Feb *The Peacemaker*, C. S. Forester
Apr *City of the Dead*, A. Groner
Jun *The Devil's Spoon*, T. Du Bois
Aug *The Purple Sapphire*, J. Taine [E. T. Bell]
Oct *The Lion's Way*, C. T. Stoneham
Dec *Nordenholt's Million*, J. J. Connington [A. W. Stewart]
1949 Feb *Angel Island*, I. H. Gillmore; *The Scarlet Plague*, J. London
Apr *Dian of the Lost Land*, E. Marshall
Jun *The Purple Cloud*, M. P. Shiel
Aug *The Valley of Silent Men*, E. C. Vivian
Oct *The Starkenden Quest*, G. Collins
Dec *Ogden's Strange Story*, E. Marshall; "No-Man's Land"
(n'te), J. Buchan
1950 Feb *Morning Star*, H. R. Haggard
Apr *The Secret People*, J. Beynon [J. B. Harris]
Jun *The Adventure of Wyndham Smith*, S. F. Wright; "The Out-
sider" (short), H. P. Lovecraft
Aug *The Time Machine*, H. G. Wells; *Donovan's Brain*, C. D.
Siodmak
Oct *The Woman Who Couldn't Die*, A. Stringer; *The Weigher of
Souls*, A. Maurois
1951 Jan *Brood of the Witch-Queen*, S. Rohmer; "The Disintegration
Machine" (short), A. C. Doyle

Mar *The Threshold of Fear*, A. J. Rees; "The Music of Erich
Zann" (short), H. P. Lovecraft
May *The Slayer of Souls*, R. W. Chambers; "Lukundoo" (short),
E. L. White
Jul *The War of the Worlds*, H. G. Wells; "Tchériapin" (short),
S. Rohmer
Oct *Rebirth*, T. C. McClary
Dec *The Gray Mahatma*, T. Mundy; "And He Built a Crooked
House" (short), R. A. Heinlein
1952 Feb *The Valley of Eyes Unseen*, G. Collins
Apr *The Death Maker*, A. J. Small
Jun *Her Ways Are Death*, J. Mann [C. Cannell]
Aug *The White Wolf*, F. Gregory; "The Green Splotches" (n'te),
T. S. Stribling
Oct *The Bat Flies Low*, S. Rohmer; "Thus I Refute Beelzy"
(short), J. Collier
Dec *Skull-Face*, R. E. Howard; "Killdozer" (n'te), T. Sturgeon
1953 Feb *Full Moon*, T. Mundy
Apr *The Wanderer's Necklace*, H. R. Haggard
Jun *Anthem*, A. Rand; *The Metamorphosis*, F. Kafka; "Worms of
the Earth" (n'te), R. E. Howard

Issues:

	Jan	Feb	Mar	Apr	May	Jun	Jul	Aug	Sep	Oct	Nov	Dec	W
1939									1/1		1/2	1/3	3
1940	1/4	1/5	1/6	2/1	2/2		2/3		2/4		2/5		11
1941		2/6	3/1		3/2		3/3		3/4		3/5		17
1942		3/6		4/1		4/2	4/3	4/4	4/5	4/6	5/1	5/2	26
1943		5/3							5/4			5/5	29
1944		5/6				6/1			6/2			6/3	33
1945		6/4				6/5			6/6			7/1	37
1946		7/2		7/3		7/4		7/5		8/1		8/2	43
1947		8/3		8/4		8/5		8/6		9/1		9/2	49
1948		9/3		9/4		9/5		9/6		10/1		10/2	55
1949		10/3		10/4		10/5		10/6		11/1		11/2	61
1950		11/3		11/4		11/5		11/6		12/1			66
1951	12/2		12/3		12/4	12/5				12/6		13/1	72
1952		13/2		13/3		13/4		13/5		13/6		14/1	78
1953		14/2		14/3		14/4							81

Canadian Edition

27 issues (Feb 1948—Aug 1952)
Pulp size; 112-130 pp.; bimonthly; 25¢.

Publishers: All-Fiction Field Inc., Toronto, Feb 1948—Jul 1951; then
(merely name change) Popular Pub. Inc., Toronto, Oct 1951—Aug
1952.

Identical to U.S. edition except a half inch longer and the same adver-
tisements on the back cover as on the Canadian *A. Merritt's Fantasy*.
This edition also became "streamlined" (smaller, no advertisements)
Jan 1951 to July 1951, then returned to the older format.

FAMOUS FILMS SERIES   U.S.   Film reviews
3 issues (1964).

Films covered included: Vol. 1 No. 1, *The Horror of Party Beach*; 1/2,
The Mole People; 2/3, *Curse of Frankenstein* and *Horror of Dracula*.

FAMOUS MONSTERS OF FILMLAND   U.S.   Film reviews
Current (Jan 1958—)
Large size; 66 pp.; irregular; 35¢ (special issues 50¢).
Editor: F. J Ackerman.
Publisher: Central Publications, Philadelphia [J. A. Warren].
Review: The magazine that began the "monster" craze of the late
1950's. However, it was based on fact—the films produced in Hollywood and elsewhere. Although the text has been strained and sketchy,
the abundant still photographs from the Ackerman collection of over
four decades of cine-monstrosities are magnificent. This was especially
the case with the first issue, which is understood to have sold over
300,000 in the U.S., as well as a British edition of 20,000 or so.

It has since tapered off in standard but at times presents quite noteworthy material, and has formed its own cult of readers. The magazine
was banned in Australia and so were Ackerman's paperbacks derived
from its pages: *Best From Famous Monsters of Filmland* (1964), *Son of
Famous Monsters of Filmland* (1964), and *Famous Monsters of Filmland
Strike Back* (1965).

Issues:

	Jan	Feb	Mar	Apr	May	Jun	Jul	Aug	Sep	Oct	Nov	Dec	W
1958	#1 (nd)							2 (1/2)(nd)					2
1959			3 (1/3)			4 (1/4)			5 (1/5)				5
1960		6 (2/1)			7 (2/7)			8 (2/8)		9 (2/9)			9
1961	10 (3/1)		11 (3/2)		12 (3/3)		13 (3/4)		14 (3/5)				14
1962	15 (3/6)	16 (4/1)		17 (4/2)		18 (4/3)		19 (4/4)		20 (4/5)			20
1963		21 (4/6)		22 (5/1)		23 (5/2)		24 (5/3)		25 (5/4)			25
1964	26		27		28		29		30			31	31
1965			32		33			34		35		36	36
1966		37		38		39		40			41		41
1967	42		43		44		45		46		47		47
1968		48			49		50	51		52			52

Yearbooks: 1963, 1964, 1965, 1966, 1967, 1968.

FAMOUS SCIENCE FICTION   U.S.   Science fiction
9 issues (Win 1966/67 – Win 1968/69)
Digest size—saddle-stapled; 130 pp.; quarterly; 50¢.
Editor: R.A.W. Lowndes.
Publisher: Health Knowledge Inc., New York.

Although this magazine reprinted much old science fiction of interest and some new stories, it did not sell as well as its companion magazines (*The Magazine of Horror, Startling Mystery Stories,* etc.) and consequently was dropped.

Issues and Notable Fiction:
1966/1967 Win (1/1) "The Girl in the Golden Atom," R. Cummings [see novel of same title]; "Voice of Atlantis" (n'te), L. Manning; "The City of Singing Flame" (short), C. A. Smith [sequel "Beyond the Singing Flame" in Sum 1967]

Spr (1/2) "The Moon Menace" (n'te), E. Hamilton; "Seeds of Space" (n'te),L. Manning

Sum (1/3) "The Last American" (n'te), J. A. Mitchell; "The Man Who Awoke" (n'te), L. Manning [first of series, continuing 4 more issues]

Fall (1/4) "The Last Shrine" (n'te), C. D. Cuthbert
1967/1968 Win (1/5) "The Pygmy Planet" (n'te), J. Williamson

Spr (1/6) "The Hell Planet" (n'te), L. F. Stone; "The Invulnerable Scourge" (n'te), John Scott Campbell

Sum (2/1) "Men of the Dark Comet" (short novel), Festus Pragnell

Fall (2/2) "Dark Moon," C. W. Diffin
1969 Spr (2/3) "The Forgotten Planet" (short), S. P. Wright; "The Derelict of Space" (n'te), R. Cummings

FANCIFUL TALES   U.S.   Weird, sf , fantasy
1 issue (1/1, Fall 1936).
5⅝ in. x 8½ in.; 48 pp.; 20¢.
Editor: Donald A. Wollheim [Associate and Business Editor: Wilson Shepherd].
Publisher: W. Shepherd in Oakman, Alabama, & D. Wollheim in New York.
Review: This was intended as a professional magazine; it is now very scarce. It had a photolithographed cover in black and white by Clay Ferguson Jr. The story line-up was: "The Nameless City," H. P. Lovecraft; "Umbriel," D. A. Wollheim; "The Forbidden Room," Duane W. Rimel; "Solomon Kane's Homecoming," Robert E. Howard; "The Typewriter," David H. Keller; "The Man From Dark Valley," August Derleth; "The Globe," William S. Sykora; "The Electric World," Kenneth B. Pritchard.

The stories are probably minor ones by the particular writers but nevertheless are of interest. Stories planned for future issues included "Judgment of Netheris," J. Harvey Haggard; "The Psycho Traveller," Ralph M. Farley; "The Escape," Robert Bloch.

FANTASCIENZA   Italian   Science fiction
7 issues (Nov 1954 – May 1955).
Editor: Livio Garzanti.
Publisher: Aldo Garzanti Editore, Milan.
Digest size; 112 pp.
This was a translation of *The Magazine of Fantasy and Science Fiction.*

FANTASIA E FANTASCIENZA   Italian   Science fiction
10 issues (Dec 1962 – Oct 1963).
Monthly; 128 pp.; 250 lire.
Publisher: Editrice Minerva, Milan.
Further translations from *The Magazine of Fantasy and Science Fiction.*

FANTASIAS DEL FUTURO   Mexican (in Spanish)   Science Fiction
1 issue (26 Sep 1958)
Digest size; 128 pp.; $2.00 Mexican.
Publisher: Editora Sol. S.A. (ES) Mesones.
Translations from the U.S. magazines *Science Fiction Quarterly, Future Science Fiction, Science Fiction Stories, Super Science* and *Planet.*

FANTASIE EN WETENSCHAP   Dutch   Science fiction
4 issues (Dec 1948 – Mar 1949).
Digest; monthly.
Publisher: Ben Abbas.
Quite neat in general format; now a collector's item. A serial was "The Moon Mystery." The title translates as *Fantasy and Science.*

FANTASTIC   U.S.   Fantasy
Current (Sum 1952–); 148th issue, December 1968.
Digest size; bimonthly; 146 pp.,; 50¢.
Title changes: Merely varied phrasing of the main title: *Fantastic,* Sum 1952 – Feb 1955; *Fantastic Science Fiction,* Apr 1955 – Feb 1958; *Fantastic,* Mar 1958 – Aug 1959; *Fantastic Science Fiction Stories,* Sep 1959 – Sep 1960; *Fantastic Stories of Imagination,* Oct 1960 – June 1965; *Fantastic: Science Fiction · Fantasy,* Sep 1965 – . The spine was simply *Fantastic* to Dec 1959, then followed the magazine title to June 1965, and has since been *Fantastic Stories.*
Editors: H. Browne, Sum 1952 – Aug 1956; P. W. Fairman, Oct 1956 – Nov 1958; Cele Goldsmith (changed to Lalli by marriage), Dec 1958 – June 1965 [N. Lobsenz, Editorial Director for this period]; J. Ross, Sep 1965 – Nov 1967; H. Harrison, Jan 1968 – Oct 1968; B. Malzberg, Dec 1968 – [Associate Editor, Oct 1968]. Sol Cohen was listed as Editor and Publisher of *Fantastic* and *Amazing Stories* after their purchase, with the above editors listed as Managing Editors.
Publishers: Ziff-Davis Publishing Co., Sum 1952 – June 1965; Sol Cohen, Sep 1965 – .
Review:

This was the first Ziff-Davis digest-size magazine. It began as a companion to *Amazing Stories* and *Fantastic Adventures*; the latter soon ceased. Originally a quarterly, sales bolstered by a Mickey Spillane thriller soon enabled it to become bimonthly; it alternated with *Amazing* for a period until that magazine returned to a monthly schedule.

The first years presented little of note, but the early years of editorship by Lobsenz and Goldsmith saw constant improvement. A number of S. Moskowitz's profiles of fantasy authors were presented from May 1960 to Sep 1960; a notable fantasy story was reprinted in each issue from May 1961 to June 1964, usually with an introduction by Moskowitz. A number of these were from quite obscure sources. The back cover carried a black and white story illustration from May 1961 to Feb 1964 (except June 1961).

Like *Amazing,* the magazine fell into the doldrums in the mid-1960's and Ziff-Davis sold it. Cohen began reprinting so much that new fiction was less than a quarter of each issue [see last paragraph of *Amazing Stories* Review].

The reception of the Dec 1955 "dream issue" and a later similar one caused the short-lived *Dream World* to be launched. July 1958 saw the return of the Shaver Mystery with a novel and various articles for and against.

Notable Fiction:
1952 Sum "For Heaven's Sake" (short), S. Martinez; "Professor Bingo's Snuff," Raymond Chandler

Fall "The Sex Opposite" (short), T. Sturgeon; "Miriam" (short), T. Capote
1953 May "Sally" (short), , I. Asimov; "Johnny Pye and the Fool-Killer" (short), S. V. Benét

Jul "The Altar" (short), R. Sheckley; "The Man Who Liked Dickens" (short), E. Waugh

Sep "Mother by Protest" (n'te), R. Matheson

Nov "Let's Do It for Love" (short), R. Bloch

1954 Apr "The Young One" (n'te), J. Bixby
    Jun "Woman Driver," R. Garrett
    Dec "Water Cure," John Boland
1956 June "Dream Girl" (n'te), R. Silverberg
    Aug "The Long Forgotten" (short), H. Still
    Oct "The Pint-Size Genie" (short), Kate Wilhelm
1957 Apr "The Vengeance of Kyvor" (sr2), R. Garrett
    Sep "The Breeder" (short), P. F. Costello
1958 A series of articles by E. F. Russell, from his *The Great World Mysteries*, began in April. The "Troon" series by J. Wyndham (originally from *New Worlds*) began in November.
1959 May "The Hungry Eye" (n'te), R. Bloch
    Jun "The Fife of Bodidharma" (short), Cordwainer Smith
    Jul "The Four-Sided Triangle" (n'te), W. F. Temple [1939; later expanded as a book]
    Oct "Conquering Hero" (n'te), Marion Z. Bradley
    Nov All stories by F. Leiber, including one in the "Grey Mouser" series.
    Dec "A Message in Secret," P. Anderson [*Mayday Orbit*]; "The Clone" (short), T. L. Thomas [enlarged as a novel, with K. Wilhelm]
1960 Jan "Diplomat-at-Arms" (n'te), K. Laumer [first of "Retief" series]
    May "The Challenge From Beyond" (short, 1935), H. P. Lovecraft
    Jun "The Mirror" (n'te), A. E. Nourse
    Jul "The Covenant," round robin story by Anderson, Asimov, Sheckley, Leinster and Bloch; "The Crispin Affair" (sr2), J. Sharkey
    Dec "A Plague of Masters" (sr2), P. Anderson [*Earthman, Go Home*]
1961 Feb *Worlds of the Imperium* (sr3), K. Laumer
    May "Scylla's Daughter" (n'te), F. Leiber; "The Garden of Fear" (short, 1934), R. E. Howard
    Jun *Second Ending* (sr2), J. White; "The Cosmic Relic" (short), E. F. Russell
    Jul *The Creator* (1933), C. D. Simak
    Aug "The Root of Ampoi" (short, 1949), C. A. Smith
    Sep "Ship of Darkness" (n'te, 1947), A. E. van Vogt; "Magnanthropus" (sr2), M. Banister
    Oct "The Mother" (short, 1938), D. H. Keller
    Nov "To Heaven Standing Up" (short, 1941), P. Ernst
    Dec "The Dead Remember" (short), R. E. Howard
1962 Jan "The Human Zero" (n'te, 1931), Erle S. Gardner
    Feb "The Shadow out of Space" (short), H. P. Lovecraft & A. W. Derleth
    Mar *Joyleg* (sr2), W. Moore & A. Davidson; "The Darkness on Fifth Avenue" (n'te, 1929), M. Leinster [W. F. Jenkins] [first of "Master of Darkness" series]
    Apr "Nonstop to Mars" (n'te, 1939), J. Williamson
    Jun *Shield* (sr2), P. Anderson; "The Past Master" (n'te, 1954), R. Bloch
    Jul "The Dragon of Iskander" (n'te, 1934), N. Schachner
    Aug *The Titan* (n'te, 1933), P. Schuyler Miller
    Sep "New Worlds" (n'te, 1932), E. S. Gardner
    Oct "Presence of Mind" (short), M. Armstrong
    Nov "It's Magic, You Dope!" (sr2), J. Sharkey; *Planetoid 127* (1929), E. Wallace
    Dec "Heritage" (n'te, 1935), E. J. Derringer
1963 Jan "The Man Next Door" (n'te, 1939), P. Ernst
    Feb "Let 'Em Eat Space" (n'te, 1939), W. G. Beyer
    Mar "Physician to the Universe" (n'te), C. D. Simak
    Apr "Rain Magic" (n'te, 1928), E. S. Gardner
    May "Devils in the Walls" (short), J. Jakes; "Professor Jonkin's Cannibal Plant" (short, 1905), Howard R. Garis
    Jun "A Hoax in Time" (sr3), K. Laumer [*The Great Time Machine Hoax*]
    Jul "He That Hath Wings" (short, 1938), E. Hamilton
    Aug "The Devil in Hollywood" (short, 1936), Dale Clark
    Sep "The Singing Sands of Prester John" (short, 1939), H. Bedford-Jones
    Oct "The Wolf Woman" (short, 1939), H. Bedford-Jones

    Nov "Witch of the Four Winds" (sr2), J. Jakes
    Dec "Lilliput Revisited," A. Bradford [had sequels]
1964 Jan "The Lords of Quarmall" (sr2), F. Leiber
    Mar "The Coming of the Little People" (n'te, 1952), R. S. Carr
    Apr "The Devil Came to Our Valley" (n'te, 1937), F. T. Grant
    May "Adept's Gambit" (1947), F. Leiber
    Jun "Paingod" (short), H. Ellison [title story of collection]; "From the Beginning" (n'te, 1938), E. Binder
    Jul "The Kragen," J. Vance [*The Blue World*]
    Aug "When the Idols Walked" (sr2), J. Jakes
    Oct "Seed of Eloraspon" (sr2), M. Banister
    Dec *The Unteleported Man*, P. K. Dick
1965 Jan *The Repairmen of Cyclops* (sr2), J. Brunner
    Mar "102 H-Bombs" (n'te), T. M. Disch [title story of collection]
    Apr *The Other Side of Time* (sr3), K. Laumer
    Sep "Stardock," F. Leiber
    Nov "Axe and Dragon" (sr3), K. Laumer
1966 Mar "The People of the Pit" (short, 1927), A. Merritt
    May *The Phoenix and the Mirror*, A. Davidson
    Jul "Just Like a Man," Chad Oliver; "A Portfolio," V. Finlay
    Sep "For a Breath I Tarry" (n'te), R. Zelazny
1967 Jan "The People of the Black Circle" (1934), R. E. Howard
    Mar "Shifting Seas" (n'te, 1937), S. G. Weinbaum; "Battle in the Dawn" (n'te, 1938), M. W. Wellman
    May "The Ant With the Human Soul" (sr2, 1932), B. Olsen; "The Thinking Seat" (n'te), P. Tate
    Jul "The Narrow Band" (n'te), J. Vance
    Sep "The Green Splotches" (n'te, 1927), T. S. Stribling
    Nov "The Metal Doom" (sr2, 1932), D. H. Keller
1968 Jan "Undersea Guardians" (short, 1944), R. Bradbury
    Mar "Spartan Planet" (sr2), A. B. Chandler [*False Fatherland*]
    Aug "The Two Best Thieves in Lankhmar" (short), F. Leiber
    Dec "The Broken Stars" (n'te), E. Hamilton

Issues:

	Jan	Feb	Mar	Apr	May	Jun	Jul	Aug	Sep	Oct	Nov	Dec	W
1952					1/1 (Sum)		1/2 (Fall)			1/3			3
1953	2/1		2/2		2/3		2/4		2/5		2/6		9
1954	3/1		3/2		3/3		3/4		3/5		3/6		15
1955	4/1		4/2		4/3		4/4		4/5		4/6		21
1956	5/1		5/2		5/3		5/4		5/5		5/6		27
1957	6/1	6/2	6/3	6/4	6/5	6/6	6/7	6/8	6/9	6/10	6/11		38
1958	7/1	7/2	7/3	7/4	7/5	7/6	7/7	7/8	7/9	7/10	7/11	7/12	50
1959	8/1	8/2	8/3	8/4	8/5	8/6	8/7	8/8	8/9	8/10	8/11	8/12	62
1960	9/1	9/2	9/3	9/4	9/5	9/6	9/7	9/8	9/9	9/10	9/11	9/12	74
1961	10/1	10/2	10/3	10/4	10/5	10/6	10/7	10/8	10/9	10/10	10/11	10/12	86
1962	11/1	11/2	11/3	11/4	11/5	11/6	11/7	11/8	11/9	11/10	11/11	11/12	98
1963	12/1	12/2	12/3	12/4	12/5	12/6	12/7	12/8	12/9	12/10	12/11	12/12	110
1964	13/1	13/2	13/3	13/4	13/5	13/6	13/7	13/8	13/9	13/10	13/11	13/12	122
1965	14/1	14/2	14/3	14/4	14/5	14/6			15/1		15/2		130
1966	15/3		15/4		15/5		15/6		16/1		16/2		136
1967	16/3		16/4		16/5		16/6		17/1		17/2		142
1968	17/3		17/4		17/5			17/6		18/1		18/2	148

British Edition
8 issues (late 1953—early 1955), not dated.
Digest size.
Publisher: Strato Pubs. (Thorpe & Porter)
Issues correspond to the U.S. originals running from Sep/Oct 1953.
Issues:

	Jan	Feb	Mar	Apr	May	Jun	Jul	Aug	Sep	Oct	Nov	Dec	W
1953											1/1		1
1954	1/2		1/3		1/4		1/5		1/6		1/7		7
1955	1/8												8

FANTASTIC ADVENTURES [*FA*]   U.S.   Fantasy
129 issues (May 1939—Mar 1953)
Editors: R. A. Palmer, May 1939—Dec 1949; H. Browne, Jan 1950—Mar 1953.
Publisher: Ziff-Davis, Chicago.
Large size May 1939—May 1940, 98 pp.; pulp size from June 1940 with varying number of pages. Began as bimonthly, varied as monthly and quarterly, and was monthly from Sep 1947 on. Price 20¢ through April 1942, then 25¢.

Cover Artists: These included Fuqua (J. Tillotson), H. McCauley, J. A. St. John (mainly for stories by E. R. Burroughs), M. Smith, and R. G. Jones.

Review: This magazine was begun by Palmer as a companion to *Amazing Stories* and was large size to emulate the early *Amazing*; this did not last long. It published much light "frothy" fantasy in its early years, but by the late 1940's was printing much the same material as its companion, only more in a fantastic vein. At one stage in the very early 1940's it nearly ceased. Some novels around 1950-1951 were of importance, but the story standard dropped considerably in its last year. Its position as companion to *Amazing* was taken by *Fantastic*.

Notable Fiction:

1939 "Golden Amazon" series, T. Ayre [J. R. Fearn] began in July; "Lancelot Biggs" series, N. S. Bond, began in Nov.
   Jul   "The Scientists Revolt," E. R. Burroughs; "The Monster From Nowhere" (short), N. S. Bond
   Sep "Golden Girl of Kalendar," F. O. Tremaine [had sequel]

1940 "Oscar, Detective of Mars" series, J. Norman, began in Oct.
   Feb "The Prince of Mars Returns" (sr2), P. Nowlan
   Mar "The Little People" (n'te), E. Binder [had sequel]
   Apr "The Judging of the Priestess" (n'te), N. S. Bond [one of "Meg the Priestess" series]
   Oct "Jongor of Lost Land," R. M. Williams [had sequel]

1941 Published 4 novelettes in Burroughs "Venus" series, starting in March [see *Escape on Venus*]; "Tink" series, W. P. McGivern, began in Oct.
   Jul   "City of Lost Souls," R. M. Farley & A. P. Nelson [had sequel]
   Aug "The Return of Circe," N. Schachner
   Nov "Eight Came Back" (n'te), N. Schachner

1942 "Lefty Feep" series, R. Bloch, began in Apr.
   Feb "Doorway to Hell" (sr2), F. Patton [R. A. Palmer]
   Jun "Quest in Time," E. Hamilton
   Jul   "The Eagle Man," D. Wilcox

1943 Jan "The Man With Five Lives," C. Woodruff
   Mar "Enchanted Bookshelf" (n'te), W. P. McGivern [had sequels, some by other authors]
   Aug "The Star Shepherd" (n'te), W. Brengle

1945 "Toka" series, J. W. Pelkie [R. A. Palmer], began in Oct.

1946 Sep "Minions of the Tiger," C. S. Geier

1947 "Toffee" Series, C. F. Myers, began in Jan.
   Mar "Forever Is Too Long," C. S. Geier
   May "The Tale of the Red Dwarf" (short), R. S. Shaver [first of "Red Dwarf" series]
   Jul   "Largo" (short), T. Sturgeon
   Sep "The Children's Room" (short), R. F. Jones

1948 Mar "The Court of Kublai Khan" (n'te), D. V. Reed
   May "Forgotten Worlds," L. Chandler
   Aug "The Man From Yesterday," L. Francis
   Oct "This Way to Heaven," H. M. Sherman

1949 Jan "The Return of Sinbad," C. S. Geier
   Dec *The Involuntary Immortals*, R. Phillips [R. P. Graham]

1950 Jan "The Usurpers" (n'te), G. St. Reynard [R. W. Krepps] [had sequel]
   Feb *The Dreaming Jewels*, T. Sturgeon
   Jul   "You're All Alone," F. Leiber [*The Sinful Ones*]
   Oct "The Masters of Sleep," L. R. Hubbard [sequel to *Slaves of Sleep*]
   Nov "Mistress of the Djinn," G. St. Reynard [R. W. Krepps] [had sequel]
   Dec "When the World Tottered," L. del Rey [*Day of the Giants*]

1951 Jan "The Trouble With Ants" (short), C. D. Simak [in *City*]
   May "The Eye of Tandyla" (n'te), L. S. de Camp
   Aug "Excalibur and the Atom," T. Sturgeon
   Sep "The Terrible Puppets," P. W. Fairman; "Dark Benediction" (short), W. M. Miller
   Oct "Medusa Was a Lady," W. Tenn [P. Klass] [*A Lamp for Medusa*]

1952 Jan "When Greed Steps In" (short), F. G. Rayer
   Oct "Is This the Way Home?" L. Chandler

1953 Feb "Gods Under Glass" (short), G. Archette

Issues:

	Jan	Feb	Mar	Apr	May	Jun	Jul	Aug	Sep	Oct	Nov	Dec	W
1939					1/1		1/2		1/3		1/4		4
1940	2/1	2/2	2/3	2/4	2/5	2/6		2/7		2/8			12
1941	3/1		3/2		3/3	3/4	3/5	3/6	3/7	3/8	3/9	3/10	22
1942	4/1	4/2	4/3	4/4	4/5	4/6	4/7	4/8	4/9	4/10	4/11	4/12	34
1943	5/1	5/2	5/3	5/4	5/5	5/6	5/7	5/8		5/9		5/10	44
1944		6/1		6/2		6/3				6/4			48
1945	7/1			7/2			7/3			7/4		7/5	53
1946		8/1		8/2		8/3		8/4		8/5			58
1947	9/1		9/2		9/3	9/4			9/5	9/6	9/7	9/8	66
1948	10/1	10/2	10/3	10/4	10/5	10/6	10/7	10/8	10/9	10/10	10/11	10/12	78
1949	11/1	11/2	11/3	11/4	11/5	11/6	11/7	11/8	11/9	11/10	11/11	11/12	90
1950	12/1	12/2	12/3	12/4	12/5	12/6	12/7	12/8	12/9	12/10	12/11	12/12	102
1951	13/1	13/2	13/3	13/4	13/5	13/6	13/7	13/8	13/9	13/10	13/11	13/12	114
1952	14/1	14/2	14/3	14/4	14/5	14/6	14/7	14/8	14/9	14/10	14/11	14/12	126
1953	15/1	15/2	15/3										129

British Edition:

26 issues from two publishers: (1) 2 issues in 1947, #1, #2, not dated, from Ziff-Davis, London; (2) 24 issues, first 2 not numbered, remainder numbered, all not dated, from Thorpe & Porter Ltd., Leicester.

Coverage:

Ziff-Davis #1 contained "Cult of the Eagle," B. Livingston (July 1946) and stories from various issues. Back cover, "Antares," F. R. Paul. No. 2 contained "The Giant From Jupiter," G. Vance & B. Dennis (June 1942) and others. Back cover, "Aldebaran," F. R. Paul.

Thorpe & Porter issues were derived from the U.S. originals as follows: #1, nn, identical with Mar 1950; #2, nn, Apr 1950; #3, May 1950; #4, Sep 1950; #5, Oct 1950; #6, Aug 1950; #7, Feb 1951; #8, Jan 1951; #9, Feb 1950; #10, Nov 1950; #11, Dec 1950; #12, Mar 1951; #13, Apr 1951; #14, May 1951; #17, Sep 1951; #18, Oct 1951; #19, Apr 1952; #20, June 1952; #21, July 1950; #22, Jan 1953; #23, Dec 1951; #24, Dec 1952. One or two stories were omitted from each issue starting at No. 13.

Issues:

	Jan	Feb	Mar	Apr	May	Jun	Jul	Aug	Sep	Oct	Nov	Dec	W
1947					#1	2							2
1950					#1 nn			2 nn	3		4		6
1951	5		6	7						8			10
1952		9	10	11			12		13	14	15		17
1953	16	17		18		19	20	21	22	23			25
1954		24											26

FANTASTIC ADVENTURES QUARTERLY   U.S.   Fantasy [reissue]

Unsold monthly issues of *Fantastic Adventures* rebound three in a volume with a new cover, priced 25¢ for first series (Win 1941—Fall 1943), 50¢ for second series (Sum 1948—Spr 1951).

FANTASTIC MONSTERS OF THE FILMS   U.S.   Film reviews

One of several monster magazines apparently along the lines of *Famous Monsters of Filmland*. Published by Black Shield Pubs. Inc., Topanga, Calif., edited by Ron Haydock. There were seven issues—four in 1962 and three in 1963. Well edited, it presented in each issue a fold-out "Monster of the Month," usually in colour.

FANTASTIC NOVELS [FN]   U.S.   Fantasy & science fiction

25 issues in two series: 5 issues July 1940—Apr 1941; 20 issues Mar 1948—June 1951.

Editor: Mary Gnaedinger.

Publishers: First series, Frank A. Munsey, New York; second series, Popular Publications, New York.

Pulp size, 144 pp. varying to 132 pp.; bimonthly; first 2 issues 20¢, then 10¢ for next 3; second series all 25¢.

Review: Began as a companion to *Famous Fantastic Mysteries* to publish long novels without serialisation. The first five issues are now collector's items.

It was revived in 1948 to once again reprint old Munsey magazine material which did not fit *FFM*'s policy. Other companion magazines of this era were *A. Merritt's Fantasy* (begun in late 1949 because of the interest in A. Merritt shown by *FN* and *FFM* readers) and *Super Science Stories* (2nd Series). When *Fantastic Novels* folded it was a great loss to enthusiasts of the older fiction.

Notable Fiction [R. Dard, Perth, Australia, produced *Fantastic Novels: A Check List* (1957), a 12-page, 6 x 8½ in. printed brochure listing stories for all issues, with foreword by A. Derleth]:

1940 Jul   *The Blind Spot*, A. Hall & H. E. Flint
     Sep   "People of the Golden Atom," R. Cummings [see *The Girl in the Golden Atom*]
     Nov   "The Snake Mother," A. Merritt [see *The Face in the Abyss*]
1941 Jan   *The Radio Beasts*, R. M. Farley [in "Radio Man" series]
     Apr   *Dwellers in the Mirage*, A. Merritt
1948 Mar   *The Ship of Ishtar*, A. Merritt
     Mary "The Moon Pool" (n'te), A. Merritt [see book]; "Jason, Son of Jason," J. U. Giesy [last of the "Palos" trilogy]
     Jul   *The Second Deluge*, G. P. Serviss
     Sep   "Conquest of the Moon Pool," A. Merritt [see *The Moon Pool*]
     Nov   "The Terrible Three," T. Robbins [title story of collection]; "The Mad Planet" (n'te), M. Leinster [W. F. Jenkins] [see *The Forgotten Planet*]
1949 Jan   *Seven Footprints to Satan*, A. Merritt
     Mar   *The Golden Blight*, G. A. England; "The Toys of Fate" (n'te), T. Robbins
     May   "The Eye of Balamok," V. Rousseau [V. R. Emanuel]; "The Red Dust" (n'te), M. Leinster [W. F. Jenkins] [see *The Forgotten Planet*]
     Jul   *Between Worlds*, Garret Smith
     Sep   *Dwellers in the Mirage*, A. Merritt
     Nov   "Minos of Sardanes," C. B. Stilson [2nd of "Polaris" trilogy]; "The Living Portrait" (n'te), T. Robbins
1950 Jan   *The Flying Legion*, G. A. England
     Mar   *The Man Who Mastered Time*, R. Cummings
     May   *Three Against the Stars*, E. North [B. C. Cronin]
     Jul   *Earth's Last Citadel*, C. L. Moore & H. Kuttner
     Sep   "Polaris and the Goddess Glorian," C. B. Stilson [last of "Polaris" trilogy]
     Nov   *The Hothouse World*, F. MacIsaac
1951 Jan   *Drink We Deep*, A. L. Zagat
     Apr   *The Torch*, J. Bechdolt
     Jun   "Spawn of the Comet" (n'te), O. A. Kline; "The Girl in the Golden Atom" (n'te), R. Cummings [see book]; "The Song of the Sirens" (short), E. L. White

Issues:

	Jan	Feb	Mar	Apr	May	Jun	Jul	Aug	Sep	Oct	Nov	Dec	W
1940							1/1		1/2		1/3		3
1941	1/4			1/5									5
1948			1/6	2/1		2/2		2/3		2/4			10
1949	2/5	2/6	3/1		3/2		3/3		3/4				16
1950	3/5		3/6	4/1		4/2		4/3		4/4			22
1951	4/5		4/6	5/1									25

British Edition: 2 issues from different publishers: (1) Pembertons, Manchester, unnumbered and not dated, *ca.* Mar 1950, a reprint of Nov 1949; (2) Thorpe & Porter, Leicester, No. 1, not dated, *ca.* June 1951, a reprint of May 1949.

Canadian Edition:
17 issues (Sep 1948–June 1951).
Publisher: New Publications Inc., Toronto, a subsidiary of Popular Pub. Inc.
Pulp size; 130 pp.; bimonthly; 25¢.
   Identical to the U.S. edition except that pages were a half inch longer and the back covers had the same advertisements as on the Canadian edition of *A. Merritt's Fantasy*.

FANTASTIC SCIENCE FICTION   U.S.   Science fiction
2 issues (Aug & Dec 1952).
Large size; 50 pp.; 25¢.
Editor: Walter B. Gibson.
Publishers: Super Fiction Pub. for first issue; Capitol Stories for second.
   Very juvenile in content, with nothing presented of a lasting nature.

FANTASTIC SCIENCE FICTION (STORIES) See FANTASTIC

FANTASTIC SCIENCE THRILLER, THE   British   Science fiction
Publisher: Stanley Baker (Pub.) Ltd., Brighton, England.
Pocket book size; 1/6.
   A juvenile series of five novels, listed in *Publishers* section of *Paperbacks*.

FANTASTIC STORIES OF IMAGINATION See FANTASTIC

FANTASTIC STORY MAGAZINE [*FSM*]   U.S.   Science fiction
[First titled *Fantastic Story Quarterly*, Spr 1950–Win 1951.]
23 issues (Spr 1950–Spr 1955).
Pulp size; 162 to 114 pp.; quarterly and bimonthly; 25¢.
Editors: S. Merwin, Spr 1950–Fall 1951; S. Mines, Win 1952–Fall 1954; A. Samalman, Win & Spr 1955.
Publisher: Best Books, New York [a subsidiary of Standard Pubs.].
   This magazine began as a companion to *Thrilling Wonder Stories* and *Startling Stories*, taking over the role of reprinting material from the older *Wonder Stories*, etc. Such reprints had run regularly as "Hall of Fame" stories in *Startling* since its inception. *FSM* printed many original short stories. Most covers were painted by E. K. Bergey and A. Schomburg. At one time in the early 1950's it was the best selling of the Standard science fiction magazines. It ceased early in 1955 and was incorporated into *Startling Stories*.

Notable Fiction:

1950 Spr "The Hidden World," E. Hamilton
     Sum "The Exile of the Skies," R. Vaughan
     Fall "In Caverns Below," S. A. Coblentz [*Hidden World*]
1951 Win *Enslaved Brains*, E. Binder
     Spr *Vandals of the Void*, J. M. Walsh
     Sum "The Conquerors," D. H. Keller
     Fall "Beyond Pluto," John S. Campbell
1952 Win "The Evening Star," D. H. Keller
     Spr "Dawn of Flame," "The Black Flame," S. G. Weinbaum [see books]
     Sum *Slan*, A. E. van Vogt
     Sep "A Million Years to Conquer" H. Kuttner [*The Creature From Beyond Infinity*]
     Nov *The Gods Hate Kansas*, J. J. Millard
1953 Jan *A Yank at Valhalla*, E. Hamilton
     Mar *Shadow Over Mars*, L. Brackett
     May "Devils From Darkonia," J. Shelton
     Sep *Island in the Sky*, M. W. Wellman
1954 Win *The Dark World*, H. Kuttner
     Spr "The Laws of Chance," M. Leinster [W. F. Jenkins] [*Fight for Life*]
     Sum "A God Named Kroo," H. Kuttner
     Fall "Forgotten World," E. Hamilton
1955 Win "Things Pass By," M. Leinster [W. F. Jenkins]
     Spr "Fog Over Venus," A. K. Barnes

Issues:

	Jan	Feb	Mar	Apr	May	Jun	Jul	Aug	Sep	Oct	Nov	Dec	W
1950				1/1 (Spr)			1/2 (Sum)			1/3 (Fall)			3
1951	2/1 (Win)			2/2 (Spr)			2/3 (Sum)			3/1 (Fall)			7
1952	3/2 (Win)			3/3 (Spr)			4/1 (Sum)	4/2		4/3			12
1953	5/1		5/2		5/3		6/1		6/2				17
1954	6/3 (Win)			7/1 (Spr)			7/2 (Sum)			7/3 (Fall)			21
1955	8/1 (Win)			8/2 (Spr)									23

Canadian Edition:
Titled *Fantastic Story Quarterly*.
4 issues (Spr, Sum, Fall, 1950; Win 1951).
Publisher: Better Publications of Canada Ltd., Toronto.
Pulp size; 162 pp.; quarterly; 25¢.
   Identical to the U.S. edition except page size a half inch longer. It had the same advertisements as the U.S. edition.

FANTASTIC STORY QUARTERLY See FANTASTIC STORY MAGAZINE

FANTASTIC UNIVERSE SCIENCE FICTION [*FU*]   U.S.
Science fiction
69 issues (June/July 1953–Mar 1960).
Editors: S. Merwin, Jun/Jul 1953–Oct/Nov 1953; Beatrice Jones, Jan

& Mar 1954; L. Margulies [Editorial Director], May 1954—Aug 1956; H. Santesson, Sep 1956—Mar 1960.
Publishers: King-Size Pubs., New York [first L. Margulies & H. L. Herbert; from Sep 1956 Herbert only], to July 1959; Great American Publications, New York, Sep 1959—Mar 1960.
Format changes: First 3 issues, digest size, 192 pp., bimonthly, 50¢; changed to 160 pp. & 35¢ from Jan 1954; became 128 pp. & monthly from Sep 1954; bimonthly from Nov. 1958; became pulp size, 128 pp., 35¢ from Sep 1959 (except last issue 96 pp.).
Cover artists: Included A. Schomburg, M. Hunter, K. Freas, E. Emsh(willer), H. Bok, and V. Finlay (who did Mar 1957—Oct 1958 and others); F. B. Long wrote "The Story Behind the Cover" Oct 1954—Aug 1956. There were no interior illustrations until the Great American issues.
Review:

This magazine began as the first 50¢ sf magazine since the old quarterlies, but soon came down to 35¢. It was originally of quite reasonable standard but fell off considerably in its later years. From 1957 it featured many "flying saucer" articles, both pro and con. A series of articles by L. del Rey in 1958 are of note. Although the magazine had a broader story scope than the others in the science fiction field it published little of importance. Of Australian interest were a number of short stories by D. Stivens and by F. B. Bryning.

"Fannotations," a fan review column by Belle C. Dietz, began appearing in Nov 1959, following the change in publisher. The Detroit SF Convention was written up in Nov 1959. S. Moskowitz wrote two sf history articles which were well illustrated. Santesson compiled an anthology from the magazine—*The Fantastic Universe Omnibus* (1960, 1962 British paperback; 1968 U.S. paperback).
Notable Fiction:
1953 Jun "Nightmare Tower," J. J. Ferrat
     Oct "The Sane Man of Satan," J. J. Ferrat
1954 Jan "The Sensitive Man," P. Anderson; "The Gambling Ghost" (short), D. Stivens
     May "Rastignac the Devil," P. J. Farmer
     Sep "The Life Watch" (n'te), L. del Rey
1955 Two series by F. Brying began; some "Conan" stories of R. E. Howard completed by L. S. de Camp began in Oct. [see Series listing and *Tales of Conan*]
     Feb "The Unhappy Man" (short), J. E. Gunn
     Jun "In the Still Waters" (n'te), L. del Rey; "Hiding Place" (short), W. Morrison
     Jul "The Man From the Flying Saucer" (n'te), S. Merwin
1956 Aug "So Bright the Vision" (n'te), C. D. Simak
1957 Jan "The Martyr" (short), A. E. Nourse
     Feb "How To Be a Saucer Author" (article), D. McLaughlin
     Mar "Lone Star Planet," H. B. Piper & J. J. McGuire [*A Planet for Texans*]
     Sep "Conan the Victorious," B. Nyberg & L. S. de Camp [*The Return of Conan*]
1958 Jul "Road to Nightfall" (n'te), R. Silverberg
1960 Mar *The Mind Thing* (sr, first part only), F. Brown
Issues:

	Jan	Feb	Mar	Apr	May	Jun	Jul	Aug	Sep	Oct	Nov	Dec	W
1953						1/1			1/2		1/3		3
1954	1/4		1/5		1/6		2/1		2/2	2/3	2/4	2/5	11
1955	2/6	3/1	3/2	3/3	3/4	3/5	3/6	4/1	4/2	4/3	4/4	4/5	23
1956	4/6	5/1	5/2	5/3	5/4	5/5	5/6	6/1	6/2	6/3	6/4	6/5	35
1957	7/1	7/2	7/3	7/4	7/5	7/6	8/1	8/2	8/3	8/4	8/5	8/6	47
1958	9/1	9/2	9/3	9/4	9/5	9/6	10/1	10/2	10/3	10/4	10/5		58
1959	11/1		11/2		11/3		11/4		11/5	11/6	12/1	12/2	66
1960	12/3	12/4	12/5										69

FANTASTICA   Spanish   Science fiction
19 issues, not dated, in 1948.

Little is known about this magazine except that it printed original stories by Spanish authors.

FANTASY   British   Science fiction
3 issues (No. 1, 1938—No. 3, 1939).
Pulp size; 128 pp.; quarterly; 1/-.
Editor: T. Stanhope Sprigg.

Publisher: George Newnes Ltd., London.

Usually referred to as "Newnes *Fantasy*" to differentiate it from the later British magazine of the same name. It published fiction of moderate quality and an article by P. E. Cleator and two by W. Ley. The magazine ceased because of World War II.
Issues and Notable Fiction:
1938 #1 (Aug) "Beyond the Screen" (short), J. Beynon [J. B. Harris]; "The Red Magician" (n'te), J. R. Fearn
1939 #2 (Mar) "Winged Terror" (n'te), G. R. Malloch; "The Trojan Beam" (n'te), J. Beynon [J. B. Harris]; "Climatica" (short), J. R. Fearn
     #3 (Jun) "Child of Power" (short), W. Parkes [J. B. Harris]; "Whom the Rat Bites" (short), S. F. Wright

FANTASY   British   Science fiction
3 issues (Dec 1946—Aug 1947).
Digest size; 96 pp.; all saddle-stapled; 1/-.
Editor: W. Gillings.
Publisher: Temple Bar Pub. Co., London.

Subtitled "The Magazine of Science Fiction," this was W. Gillings' immediate postwar effort at producing a science fiction magazine. His earlier *Tales of Wonder* had folded during the war. *Fantasy* was short-lived mainly because of Britain's paper shortage.
Issues and Notable Fiction:
1946 Dec (1/1) "The Worlds of If" (short), S. G. Weinbaum; "Technical Error" (short), A. C. Clarke
1947 Apr (1/2) "Relic" (n'te), E. F. Russell; "Castaway" (short), C. Willis & A. C. Clarke
     Aug (1/3) "Time Trap" (n'te), S. A. Coblentz; "The Fire Within" (short), E. G. O'Brien [A. C. Clarke]

FANTASY AND SCIENCE FICTION See *MAGAZINE OF FANTASY AND SCIENCE FICTION*

FANTASY BOOK   U.S.   Fantasy and science fiction
8 issues (No. 1, 1947—No. 8, 1951).
Editor: Garret Ford [pseudonym for William Crawford with his wife Margaret, and one or two others].
Publisher: Fantasy Publishing Company, Inc., Los Angeles.
Format: First 2 large size, then various digest sizes; 42 to 114 pp.; irregular; 25¢. Some issues had three editions: subscribers, collectors (book paper, at 35¢), and newsstand, which appeared to be sold only in California.

Although the magazine has become a collector's item, its fiction was not highly considered. There were many stories by A. E. van Vogt and Basil Wells [some under pseudonym]. It also published the first stories by Alice [Andre] Norton, as "Andrew North." Lilith Lorraine ran "Songs of the Spaceways," a poetry section, from the third issue. Selections from the magazine appeared in 1953 as *Science and Sorcery*, G. Ford [see W. L. Crawford].
Notable Fiction:
1947 #1 "The People of the Crater" (n'te), A. North [Andre Norton]; "The Cataaaaa" (short), A. E. van Vogt
1948 #2 "The Ship of Darkness," A. E. van Vogt; "The Machine-God Laughs" (sr3), F. Pragnell
     #3 "The Great Judge" (n'te), A. E. van Vogt
     #4 "Black Goldfish" (sr2), J. Taine [E. T. Bell]
1949 #5 "Battle of the Wizards" (short), L. R. Hubbard
1950 #6 "Little Man on the Subway," I. Asimov & J. MacCreigh [F. Pohl]; "Scanners Live in Vain" (n'te), Cordwainer Smith [P. M. L. Linebarger]
     #7 "Journey to Barkut" (sr2, unfinished), M. Leinster [W. F. Jenkins] [*Gateway to Elsewhere*]
Issues:

	Jan	Feb	Mar	Apr	May	Jun	Jul	Aug	Sep	Oct	Nov	Dec	W
1947							1/1						1
1948		1/2					1/3				1/4		4
1949							1/5						5
1950	6 (1/6)									2/1			7
1951	8 (2/2)												8

FANTASY FICTION   U.S.   Fantasy

2 issues (May, Nov 1950), 2nd titled *Fantasy Stories.*
Digest size; 128 pp.; 25¢.
Editor: Curtis Mitchell.
Publisher: Magabooks Inc.

One of the lesser-known items in the fantasy field. Some stories were reprints; it also tried to introduce alleged 'true experience' articles.
Issues and Fiction:
1950 May (1/1) "Speak to Me of Death" (n'te), C. Woolrich
      Nov (1/2) "The Vengeful Pearls of Madame Podaire" (short), R. Arthur

FANTASY FICTION (MAGAZINE)   U.S.   Fantasy

4 issues (Feb—Nov 1953)
Digest; 160 pp.; bimonthly; 35¢.
Editors: L. del Rey, Feb—Aug 1953; Cameron Hall (pseud., first del Rey, then H. Harrison), Nov 1953. F. Pratt was to have been editor with the fifth issue; it was set up but never printed.
Publisher: Future Pubs., New York.
Title changes: First issue was titled *Fantasy Magazine* and the spine was dated Mar 1953; later issues were *Fantasy Fiction Magazine* on the spine but *Fantasy Fiction* on the cover and table of contents.

This magazine was a companion to *Space Science Fiction* and *Science Fiction Adventures*. It was originally to have been called *Fantasy Unlimited*. Many fantasy enthusiasts rated it the best fantasy magazine since *Unknown (Worlds)*. H. Bok painted all the covers.
Issues and Notable Fiction:
1953 Feb (1/1) "The Black Stranger," R. E. Howard [see *King Conan*]
      Jun (1/2) *Wall of Serpents*, L. S. de Camp & F. Pratt
      Aug (1/3) "So Sweet as Magic...," B. Elliott; "The Frost Giant's Daughter," R. E. Howard & L. S. de Camp [in *The Coming of Conan*]
      Nov (1/4) "Web of the Worlds," K. MacLean & H. Harrison

FANTASY MAGAZINE See *FANTASY FICTION (MAGAZINE)*

FANTASY STORIES See *FANTASY FICTION*

FATE   U.S.   Occult nonfiction

Current (Spr 1948—).
Editor: Robert N. Webster (R. A. Palmer); later Managing Editor: C. S. Geier; then Curtis Fuller in early 1960's.
Publisher: Clark Pub. Co., Evanston, Illinois.
Format: Digest, 128 pp.; 25¢; quarterly, then bimonthly, then monthly. Saddle-stapled to July 1951, then ordinary (side) stapled.

Features "true" experiences and articles on the strange and unknown. In the 1960's it tended more towards "Forteana"—sea serpents, flying saucers, surviving cavemen, and the like.
Issues:

	Jan	Feb	Mar	Apr	May	Jun	Jul	Aug	Sep	Oct	Nov	Dec	W
1948			1/1 (Spr)				1/2 (Sum)			1/3 (Fall)			3
1949	1/4 (Win)			2/1			2/2		2/3	2/4			8
1950	3/1		3/2		3/3		3/4	3/5	3/6		3/7	3/8	16
1951	4/1		4/2	4/3	4/4		4/5		4/6	4/7		4/8	24
1952	5/1	5/2		5/3	5/4		5/5		5/6	5/7	5/8	5/9	33
1953	6/1	6/2	6/3	6/4	6/5	6/6	6/7	6/8	6/9	6/10	6/11	6/12	45
1954	7/1	7/2	7/3	7/4	7/5	7/6	7/7	7/8	7/9	7/10	7/11	7/12	57
1955	8/1	8/2	8/3	8/4	8/5	8/6	8/7	8/8	8/9	8/10	8/11	8/12	69
1956	9/1	9/2	9/3	9/4	9/5	9/6	9/7	9/8	9/9	9/10	9/11	9/12	81
1957	10/1	10/2	10/3	10/4	10/5	10/6	10/7	10/8	10/9	10/10	10/11	10/12	93
1958	11/1	11/2	11/3	11/4	11/5	11/6	11/7	11/8	11/9	11/10	11/11	11/12	105
1959	12/1	12/2	12/3	12/4	12/5	12/6	12/7	12/8	12/9	12/10	12/11	12/12	117
1960	13/1	13/2	13/3	13/4	13/5	13/6	13/7	13/8	13/9	13/10	13/11	13/12	129
1961	14/1	14/2	14/3	14/4	14/5	14/6	14/7	14/8	14/9	14/10	14/11	14/12	141
1962	15/1	15/2	15/3	15/4	15/5	15/6	15/7	15/8	15/9	15/10	15/11	15/12	153
1963	16/1	16/2	16/3	16/4	16/5	16/6	16/7	16/8	16/9	16/10	16/11	16/12	165
1964	17/1	17/2	17/3	17/4	17/5	17/6	17/7	17/8	17/9	17/10	17/11	17/12	177
1965	18/1	18/2	18/3	18/4	18/5	18/6	18/7	18/8	18/9	18/10	18/11	18/12	189
1966	19/1	19/2	19/3	19/4	19/5	19/6	19/7	19/8	19/9	19/10	19/11	19/12	201
1967	20/1	20/2	20/3	20/4	20/5	20/6	20/7	20/8	20/9	20/10	20/11	20/12	213
1968	21/1	21/2	21/3	21/4	21/5	21/6	21/7	21/8	21/9	21/10	21/11	21/12	225

British Edition:
Current (No. 1, Nov 1954—); price 1/-; Nov 1966 was No. 144; an issue is understood to have been missed in 1959 because of a printer's strike.
Editor: James Leigh; Associate, R. N. Webster, etc.
Publisher: Press Books Ltd.

This series has included some original British material, and has colour covers from the original U.S. issues.

FEAR   U.S.   Weird-horror

2 issues (May, July 1960).
Format: Digest; 128 pp.; bimonthly; 35¢.
Editor: Joseph L. Marx.
Publisher: Great American Pubs., New York.

Generally well received, this magazine published mainly new stories and a few reprints.
Notable Fiction:
1960 May (1/1) "The Dream Woman" (n'te), W. Collins
      July (1/2) "How Love Came to Professor Guildea" (n'te), R. S. Hichens
British Edition: Thorpe & Porter distributed some copies in the United Kingdom stamped with district reference and price.

FICTION   French   Science fiction and fantasy

Current (15 Oct 1953—); 178th issue—Dec 1968.
Format: Digest size; monthly; in late 1962 was 176 pp..
Price & page changes: #1—#40, 100 Fr, 128 pp.; #41—50, 120 Fr, 144 pp.; #51—78, 140 Fr, 144 pp.; #79-107, 160 Fr, 144 pp.; #108, 250 Fr, 176 pp. Pages and prices since not known. Early special numbers, outside the regular series, were: #1 (May 1959), only French authors, 222 pp., 250 Fr; #2 (June 1960), only French authors, 222 pp., 280 Fr; #3 (June 1961), translation of *Star of Stars* [Pohl], 240 pp., 335 Fr.
Editor: Alan Dorémieux.
Publisher: Editions Opta, Paris [headed by Maurice Renault].

This is the French edition of *The Magazine of Fantasy and Science Fiction*, but has included many original stories by French writers. A number of these by such writers as C. Henneberg, Claude Veillot, and Claude F. Cheinisse were translated by Damon Knight and published in the U.S. *F&SF* and also in Knight's anthology *13 French Science-Fiction Stories* (Bantam, 1965, pa; Corgi, 1966, pa). The magazine is the most highly considered of those published in France.
Issues [first three issues dated 15th of the month]:

	Jan	Feb	Mar	Apr	May	Jun	Jul	Aug	Sep	Oct	Nov	Dec	W
1953										#1	2		2
1954		3	4	5	6	7	8	9	10	11	12	13	13
1955	14	15	16	17	18	19	20	21	22	23	24	25	25
1956	26	27	28	29	30	31	32	33	34	35	36	37	37
1957	38	39	40	41	42	43	44	45	46	47	48	49	49
1958	50	51	52	53	54	55	56	57	58	59	60	61	61
1959	62	63	64	65	66	67	68	69	70	71	72	73	73
1960	74	75	76	77	78	79	80	81	82	83	84	85	85
1961	86	87	88	89	90	91	92	93	94	95	96	97	97
1962	98	99	100	101	102	103	104	105	106	107	108	109	109
1963	110	111	112	113	114	115	116	117	118	119	120	121	121
1964	122	123	124	125	126	127	128	129	130	131	132	133	133
1965	134	135	136	137	138	139	140	141	142	143	144	145	145
1966	146	147	148	149	150	151	152	153	154	155	156	157	157
1967	158	159	160	161	162	163	164	165	166	167	168	169	169
1968	170	171	172	173	174	*	*	*	*	*	179	180	180

* One issue skipped, June—Oct 1968, but not known which.

FIRESIDE GHOST STORIES   British   Ghost

1 issue (not numbered, not dated, about 1938); probably 1/-.
Publisher: World's Work, England.

One of the Master Thriller series, featuring reprinted material by such authors as C. Dickens, H. Bolitho and R. Thurston Hopkins.

FLAME   U.S.   Fantastic verse

Editor: L. Lorraine.
Publisher: Avalon Arts Academy, U.S.
One issue sighted was Spr 1954: 6 x 9 in.; 16 pp.; quarterly; 50¢.

A magazine printing modern verse tending toward fantasy. [There was also an Australian magazine of this title which ran for about six issues around 1935. It had several borderline science fiction stories, including one about Japanese invading Australia and another about future revolution in Sydney.]

FLASH GORDON STRANGE ADVENTURE MAGAZINE

U.S.   Science fiction

1 issue (Dec 1936).
Format: 64 pp., saddle-stitched; 10¢.
Editor: H. Hersey.
Publisher: C.J.H. Publications.

Very juvenile in nature, but the first sf magazine to have colour interior illustrations. The single issue had as book-length novel "The Master of Mars," James E. Northfield. It was to have been monthly, and "The Sun Men of Saturn" was announced for the second issue. The magazine is now a collector's item.

FLYING SAUCER REVIEW

British   UFO review

Current? (May 1955—)
Quarterly, then bimonthly; 21/- per year.
Editors: Derek D. Dempster; later Charles Bowen.
Publisher: Flying Saucer Service, London.

A collecting medium for all reports on flying saucers and associated phenomena. (Issues have been sighted for 1969 and 1973.)

FLYING SAUCERS FROM OTHER WORLDS

U.S.   UFO's

At least 44 issues (June 1957—Oct 1965).
Pulp size.

Began as alternate issues of *Other Worlds Science Stories*, and continued independently.

Issues (*Other Worlds* issues of 1957 shown):

	Jan	Feb	Mar	Apr	May	Jun	Jul	Aug	Sep	Oct	Nov	Dec	W
1957	OW20		OW21		OW22	#1	OW24	2		OW26	3		3
1958		4		5		6				7		8	8
1959		9		10		11				12		13	13
1960		14			15		16			17			17
1961		18		19		20		21		22			22
1962	23		24	25		26		27		28			28
1963	29			30		31		32		33			33
1964		34	35		36		37		38		39		39
1965		40	41		42		43		44				44

Publication continued, but information is not known.

FORERUNNER

Australian   Science fiction

2 issues (Spr 1952; Aut 1953).
Editor: R. D. Nicholson, Sydney.

First issue duplicated with some pages photolith (quarto); 2nd photolith, 7 in. x 8 in., 5/-.

A meritorious attempt to produce Australian sf of a good standard. It published a serial by the late Vol Molesworth and also had fiction by F. Bryning, N. Hemming, and others.

FOR MONSTERS ONLY

U.S.   Monster magazine

9 issues (1965—1972).
Large size.
Editor: Lorraine Zuckerman
Publisher: Major Mags. Inc., Valley Stream, N.Y. 11580, U.S.A.

Issues sighted include 1/2, Sep 1966; 1/3, Nov 1966; 1/7, Apr 1969, and Annual 1967. June 1972 is known.

FRANK READE LIBRARY

U.S.   Sf adventure

191 issues (24 Sep 1892—? 1896).
Size 8¼ in. x 11¼ in.; 24 pp., later 32 pp.; weekly; 5¢.
Publisher: Frank Tousey.

This periodical featured the adventures of inventor Frank Reade Jr. and his friends. The first story was "Frank Reade Jr. and His New Steamman, or, The Young Inventor's Trip to the Far West." All stories were written by L. P. Senarens (under pseudonym). The magazine was revived as *Frank Reade Weekly* in 1902 and ran for 96 issues, using reprints from the original. Ron Graham of Sydney has the first 45 issues.
British Edition:

There have been a number of reprint editions; the main one was *Aldine Invention, Travel and Adventure Library.*

FUTURE combined with SCIENCE FICTION (STORIES) See *FUTURE SCIENCE FICTION*

FUTURE FANTASY AND SCIENCE FICTION See *FUTURE SCIENCE FICTION*

FUTURE FICTION See *FUTURE SCIENCE FICTION*

FUTURE SCIENCE FICTION

U.S.   Science fiction

First series, 17 issues (Nov 1939—July 1943); second series, 48 issues (May/June 1950—Apr 1960).
Title Changes: *Future Fiction*, Nov 1939—Aug 1941; *Future Combined With Science Fiction*, Oct 1941—Aug 1942; *Future Fantasy and Science Fiction*, Oct 1942—Feb 1943; *Science Fiction Stories*, Apr & Jul 1943; *Future Combined With Science Fiction Stories*, May 1950—Nov 1951; *Future Science Fiction Stories*, Jan & Mar 1952; *Future Science Fiction*, May 1952—Apr 1960.
Editors: C. D. Hornig, Nov 1939—Apr 1941; R. W. Lowndes, Aug 1941—Apr 1960.
Publisher: Blue Ribbon, New York; then Columbia Pubs., New York.
Format: Pulp size through to Mar 1954, digest size from June 1954. First series 114 pp., 15¢ except last issue 20¢; second series 100 pp., 15¢ (lowest in the field at the time), then 20¢ from Nov 1950, 25¢ from Jan 1953, 35¢ from June 1954.
Cover Artists: F. R. Paul, H. Bok and M. Luros painted a number of covers of the first series. E. K. Bergey began the new series; other artists included L. Morey and M. Luros. From the end of 1953 Schomburg did several covers, though Emsh(willer) was the most used, with occasional ones by K. Freas. From March 1959 there was much experimentation with cheaper colour covers.
Review:

C. D. Hornig began this magazine as a companion to *Science Fiction*. Because of World War II, both were combined into *Future*, which eventually ceased in July 1943 (the last two issues being titled *Science Fiction Stories*). Lowndes improved the magazine considerably after he became editor; he included a number of reprints of stories by R. Cummings.

In 1950 Lowndes was able to revive the magazine as one of the lowest-priced in the field; however, this meant cheap paper and low story payments. Thus the quality could not be high, but nevertheless it was always capably edited and of interest, as were its companions *Science Fiction Quarterly*, *Dynamic Science Fiction*, and the more recent *(Original) Science Fiction Stories.*

When the one-shot issue of *Science Fiction Stories* in digest size in 1953 was successful, *Future* changed to that size in June 1954. After some issues as a bimonthly in this form, its role was taken over by *SFS*, and *Future* appeared only occasionally until it was made regular again in 1958. It had some good articles at times, and interesting editorials on various phases of science fiction. The quality tapered off considerably before its demise, which was probably due to poor sales from the lack of a distributor. Reprints were used in most issues from June 1959.
Notable Fiction:

1940 Mar "Ring Around the Sun" (short), I. Asimov
1941 Oct *The Man on the Meteor*, R. Cummings; "Ajax Calkins" series, M. Pearson [D. Wollheim], began.
　　Dec *Around the Universe*, R. Cummings
1942 Feb "Beyond the Stars," R. Cummings
　　Apr "The Core," S. D. Gottesman [collaboration including C. M. Kornbluth]
　　Aug "Once in a Blue Moon," N. L. Knight
1950 May "Dynasty Lost," G. O. Smith
　　Sep "Wide-Open Planet," L. S. de Camp
1951 Jul "Ultrasonic God" (short), L. S. de Camp
　　Sep "If I Forget Thee, Oh Earth," A. C. Clarke
1952 "Great Legend" series, W. West [*Lords of Atlantis*], began in May.
　　Nov "Doomsday's Color-Press" (n'te), R. F. Jones
1953 Jan "Time Stops Today" (n'te), J. Wyndham; "Testament of Andros", (n'te), J. Blish
　　Mar "And the Truth Shall Make You Free" (short), C. D. Simak; "Courier of Chaos" (n'te), P. Anderson
　　May "Liberation of Earth" (short), W. Tenn
　　Jul "Where or When?" (short), K. MacLean

Nov "Countercheck" (n'te), C. V. De Vet
1954 Mar "The Wayward Course" (n'te), R. Garrett
Jun "Peace on Earth" (n'te), I. Cox
Aug "Cure, Guaranteed" (n'te), T. L. Sherred
Oct "Despite All Valor" (short), A. Budrys
1955 #28 "Decline" (n'te), W. L. Bade
1956 #29 *Vulcan's Hammer*, P. K. Dick
#30 "Heav'n, Heav'n" (short), E. F. Russell; "The Hills of Home" (short), A. Coppel
Win "Worlds Without End," C. D. Simak
1957 Sum "Mars Trail" (n'te), T. L. Thomas
Fall "The Lonely Stars" (short), S. Nichols
1958 Jun "A Yardstick for Science Fiction" (article), D. Knight
1959 Apr "The Renegade" (n'te), T. Scortia

Issues:

	Jan	Feb	Mar	Apr	May	Jun	Jul	Aug	Sep	Oct	Nov	Dec	W
1939											1/1		1
1940		1/2				1/3					1/4		4
1941			1/5				1/6	2/1			2/2		8
1942		2/3		2/4		2/5		2/6	3/1		3/2		14
1943		3/3		3/4			3/5						17
1950						1/1		1/2		1/3	1/4		4
1951	1/5		1/6		2/1		2/2		2/3		2/4		10
1952	2/5		2/6		3/1		3/2		3/3		3/4		16
1953	3/5		3/6		4/1		4/2		4/3		4/4		22
1954	4/5		4/6			5/1		5/2		5/3			27
1955		#28 (nd)											28
1956	29 (nd)								30 (nd)			31 (Win)	31
1957		32(Spr)			33(Sum)			34 (Fall)					34
1958	35		36		37		38		39		40		40
1959	41		42		43		44		45		46		46
1960	47		48										48

British Edition:
25 issues in two series, 1951—1960.
(1) 14 issues (1951-1954), not dated, pulp size; publisher: Thorpe & Porter. The titles of this series were *Future Combined With Science Fiction Stories*, #1 to 5, and 8; *Future Science Fiction* 6, 7, and 9 to 14. These were abridgements of the U.S. issues.
(2) 11 issues (Nos. 1-11, 1957—1960), not dated, digest size; publisher: Strato Pubs., London. These were practically complete copies of the U.S. originals; they corresponded as follows: #1 = Sum 1957; #2 = Fall 1957; #3 = Apr 1958; then are understood to be continuous to #11. The covers were the same except that #7's was that of the Spr 1957 U.S. issue.
Note: One of the Swan American Magazines—No. 11—had the prominent title "Future Fantasy and Science Fiction," and reprinted most of the Dec 1942 U.S. *Future*.

Issues:

	Jan	Feb	Mar	Apr	May	Jun	Jul	Aug	Sep	Oct	Nov	Dec	W
1951											1	2	2
1952	3				4	5		6			7		7
1953	8			9						10		11	11
1954		12		13		14							14
1957											1		15
1958		2				3			4			5	19
1959	6		7			8			9		10		24
1960	11												25

FUTURE SCIENCE FICTION Australian Science fiction
8 issues in two series 1953—1967.
(1) Nos. 1—6, not dated: July 1953—Mar 1956; 5¼ in. x 7½ in.; 64 pp.; irregular; price 1/3 first two, then 1/6; publisher: Frew Publications, Sydney.
(2) No. 1, Apr 1967, #2, Sep 1967, not dated; 5¼ in. x 7½ in.; 20¢; publisher: Page Pubs., Sydney, New South Wales.
The first series featured reprints of U.S. material, with some Australian authors in later issues. The adviser at first was Vol Molesworth and later Graham Stone. The companion was *Popular Science Fiction*, both paid their ways, but not enough for the publisher to keep them running. The second series was a complete reprint, with No. 1 reprinting first series No. 4, and No. 2 reprinting No. 6.

Issues and Feature Stories (approximate dating):
1953 #1 (Jul) "The Infinite Moment" (n'te), H. Kuttner
#2 (Nov) "The Faceless Men" (n'te), A. L. Zagat
1954 #3 (Mar) "No War Tomorrow" (short), W. West
#4 (Jul) "Martian Gesture" (short), A. M. Phillips
#5 (Dec) "As You Were" (short), N. Hemming; "The Immortal" (short), R. Rocklynne
1955 #6 (Mar) "Journey to the Hotlands" (n'te), J. L. Hensley

FUTURISTIC SCIENCE STORIES British Science fiction
16 issues (No. 1 [not numbered], Aug 1950—No. 16, June 1954), not dated.
Pocket book size; irregular; 1/6.
Editor: John S. Manning.
Publisher: John Spencer, London.
A publication of only minor interest; one of the four juvenile sf magazines published by Spencer. It is one of those listed in G. Stone's *Index to British Science Fiction Magazines 1934-53*, Part 6, 1974.
Issues:

	Jan	Feb	Mar	Apr	May	Jun	Jul	Aug	Sep	Oct	Nov	Dec	W
1950								1 (nn)		2		3	3
1951		4										5	5
1952			6			7			8				8
1953	9			10		11		12		13			13
1954	14			15		16							16

FUTURISTIC STORIES British Science fiction
2 issues (not dated, not numbered), *ca.* 1946—1947.
Publisher: Hamilton & Co. (Stafford) Ltd., London.
Both issues 7 in. x 9¾ in.; first *ca.* Dec 1946, 48 pp., 2/-, lead story "The Lords of Zorm," N. W. Firth; second, *ca.* Dec 1947, 32 pp., 1/-, lead and only story "Dark Asteroid," R. A. Ackman. A quite juvenile magazine. It is understood that all stories were by the same author, N. W. Firth, under various pseudonyms.

FUTURO, *Novelas de ciencia y fantasia* Spanish Science fiction
34 issues (1954).
Irregular; 160 pp.
All but two of the first 26 issues were practically translations of U.S. material, but did not mention the original titles or authors. For Nos. 27-32 the stories were written by pseudonymous Spanish authors and were of lower quality. The last two were of better quality: No. 33, "El planeta artificial" [*Wheel in the Sky*], R. Bernard; No. 34, "Nuestras son las estrellas" [*The Stars Are Ours*], K. Bulmer; with the copyrights being noted.

FUTURO, *Rassegna Italiana di Fantascienza* Italian Science fiction
8 issues (May/June 1963—15 Nov 1964).
Size: 5½ in. x 7⅝ in.; 80 pp.
This had various editors, and was published by Editoriale Futuro, Rome.

G

GALASSIA Italian Science fiction
Three series:
(1) 3 issues (Jan 1953—June 1953); digest size; 104-112 pp.
   Editor: O. G. Landini. **Publisher:** Collana "Galassia," Milan.
(2) 5 issues (1 Jan 1957—15 Apr 1957); digest size; 144-160 pp.
   Publisher: Casa Editrice Galassia, Udine.
(3) 90 issues (Jan 1961—), current.
   Digest size; 128-256 pp., monthly; 150 lire.
   Editors: R. Rambelli to No. 56; Rambelli with U. Malaguti to No. 59; Malaguti from No. 60.
   Publisher: Casa Editrice La Tribuna.

The last is a regular series specialising in translations of the better contemporary U.S. and British sf. An issue sighted was No. 8 (15 Aug-15 Sep 1961), which gave *L'Asso di Coppe* [*Jack of Eagles*], J. Blish. Other writers have included I. Asimov, H. Kuttner, C. D. Simak, and R. A. Heinlein.

GALAXIE   French   Science fiction
Two series:
(1) 65 issues (Dec 1953-Apr 1959); 128 pp.; 100 Fr.
   Publisher: Nuit et Jour, Paris.
(2) Current (May 1964—), No. 55 at Dec 1968; digest size; 3 Fr.
   Publisher: Editions Opta, 24 rue de Mogador, Paris.
   The French edition of *Galaxy Science Fiction*. The first series was not highly regarded because of poor translations.

GALAXIS SCIENCE FICTION   German   Science fiction
15 issues (Mar 1958—July 1959).
Digest size; 128 pp.; 1.50 DM.
Editor and Translator: Lothar Heinecke.
Publisher: Moewig, Munich.
   The German edition of *Galaxy Science Fiction*.

GALAXY MAGAZINE See *GALAXY SCIENCE FICTION*

GALAXY SCIENCE FICTION [*GSF*]   U.S.   Science fiction
Titled *Galaxy Magazine* Sep 1958—Dec 1965 [and *Magazine* continued to be used on the title page for some years].
Current (Oct 1950—); 161st issue, Dec 1968.
Digest size; 194 pp.; monthly; 60¢.
Editors: H. L. Gold, Oct 1950—Oct 1961; F. Pohl, Managing Editor, June 1961—Oct 1961, then Editor, Dec 1961—. Assistant or Associate Editors at times: P. W. Fairman, J. Bixby, S. Merwin, Judy-Lynn Benjamin, L. del Rey.
Publisher: World Editions to Sep 1951; Galaxy Pub. Corp., New York, Oct 1951—.
Format: Began at 25¢, then 35¢ May 1951 to Dec 1958, all monthly issues, 160—144 pp.; bimonthly at Feb 1959, 194 pp., 50¢; became 60¢ Dec 1964.
Cover Artists: Has had many, including M. Hunter, C. Bonestell, E. Emsh(willer) (well over 40 covers), J. Coggins, V. Finlay, Dember, and J. Gaughan. Many covers have used astronomical or space travel themes, or have shown some future "pertinent" scene. Some of Emsh's Christmas covers depict Christmas for alien beings. Art Directors were W. I. Van Der Poel to June 1960 and S. Rudivich Aug. 1960—Oct 1962, with brief periods for others; the position was absorbed in 1964.
Review:
   This is the magazine which became top-ranking with *Astounding Science Fiction* (now *Analog*) as soon as it appeared. It then followed a more variable policy. *Galaxy* tied for the magazine Hugo Award in 1953, but has since dropped in quality. It acquired its own flavour, with Gold's editorship becoming somewhat stereotyped and Pohl following in much the same vein. Nevertheless it has always been classed in the "Big Three" (with *ASF* and *F&SF*).
   The late Willy Ley as Science Editor continuously maintained a department of high standard, including the answering of technical questions. The book reviews were done by G. Conklin until Oct 1955, then by Floyd Gale until Oct 1963; since Feb 1965 A. Budrys has been in control and has made a name for himself with his searching and constructive reviews.
   Anthologies from the magazine in the *Galaxy Reader* series have been selected by H. L. Gold and F. Pohl. Gold also selected some volumes covering only "novellas." Most serials and novels published in *Galaxy* have seen book editions, while most single-author short story collections directly selected from the sf field have at least one story from its pages. A *Galaxy Checklist* index covering issues to Dec 1958 was published at 3/6 by the British Science Fiction Association. *Galaxy* is the only sf magazine to have had a Braille edition; this was published by the U.S. Library of Congress beginning in Oct 1960.
Notable Fiction:
1950 Oct   "Time Quarry" (sr3), C. D. Simak [*Time and Again*]; "Third From the Sun" (short), R. Matheson [title story of collection]

Nov   "Honeymoon in Hell" (n'te), F. Brown [title story of collection]; "To Serve Man" (short), D. Knight; "Misbegotten Missionary" (short), I. Asimov
Dec   "Second Night of Summer" (n'te), J. H. Schmitz [see *Agent of Vega*]
1951 Jan   "Tyrann" (sr3), I. Asimov [*The Stars, Like Dust*]
Feb   "The Fireman," R. Bradbury[enlarged as *Fahrenheit 451*]
Apr   "The Marching Morons" (short), C. M. Kornbluth [title story of collection]
May   "Mars Child" (sr3), C. Judd [J. Merril & C. M. Kornbluth] [*Outpost Mars*]
Jun   "Angel's Egg" (n'te), E. Pangborn
Jul   "Venus Is a Man's World" (n'te), W. Tenn [P. Klass]
Aug   "Beyond Bedlam" (short novel), W. Guin
Sep   *The Puppet Masters* (sr3), R. A. Heinlein; "Cabin Boy" (n'te), D. Knight
Oct   "The C-Chute" (n'te), I. Asimov
Nov   "Tiger by the Tail" (short), A. E. Nourse [title story of collection]
1952 Jan   *The Demolished Man* (sr3), A. Bester
Feb   "Conditionally Human" (n'te), W. M. Miller [title story of collection]
Mar   "The Year of the Jackpot" (n'te), R. A. Heinlein
Apr   "Accidental Flight," F. L. Wallace [see *Address: Centauri*]
May   "Category Phoenix" (short novel), B. Ellanby [L. & B. Boyd]
Jun   "Gravy Planet" (sr3), F. Pohl & C. M. Kornbluth [*The Space Merchants*]
Aug   "Surface Tension" (n'te), J. Blish [in *The Seedling Stars*]
Oct   "Baby Is Three," T. Sturgeon [part of *More Than Human*]
Nov   "The Martian Way," I. Asimov [title story of collection]
Dec   *Ring Around the Sun* (sr3), C. D. Simak
1953 Feb   "Four in One" (n'te), D. Knight; "Watchbird" (n'te), R. Sheckley
Mar   "The Old Die Rich," H. L. Gold [title story of collection]
Apr   "Made in U.S.A." (n'te), J. T. McIntosh; "Seventh Victim" (short), R. Sheckley
Jul   "Kindergarten" (n'te), C. D. Simak; "Home Is the Hunter" (n'te), C. L. Moore & H. Kuttner
Sep   "Far From the Warming Sun" (n'te), R. D. Nicholson
Oct   *The Caves of Steel* (sr3), I. Asimov
Nov   "Keep Your Shape" (n'te), R. Sheckley
1954 Jan   "Natural State," D. Knight [*Masters of Evolution*]
Mar   "Ironclad" (n'te), A. Budrys
Apr   "The Midas Plague" (short novel), F. Pohl
Jun   *Gladiator-at-Law* (sr3), F. Pohl & C. M. Kornbluth
Sep   "Dusty Zebra" (n'te), C. D. Simak; "AAA Ace" series, R. Sheckley, began.
Nov   "How-2" (n'te), C. D. Simak
1955 Jan   "The Tunnel Under the World" (n'te), F. Pohl
Mar   "Project Mastodon" (n'te), C. D. Simak
Apr   "The Servant Problem" (n'te), W. Tenn [P. Klass]
May   "Sam, This Is You" (n'te), M. Leinster [W. F. Jenkins]
Jun   *Preferred Risk* (sr4), E. McCann [F. Pohl & L. del Rey]; "The Princess and the Physicist" (n'te), Evelyn E. Smith
Oct   "A Ticket to Tranai" (short novel), R. Sheckley; "The Game of Rat and Dragon" (n'te), C. Smith [P. Linebarger] [first of "Instrumentality" series]
Nov   "The Ties of Earth" (sr2), J. H. Schmitz
1956 Feb   "Bodyguard" (short novel), C. Grimm [H. L. Gold] [title story of anthology]
Mar   "A Gun for Dinosaur" (n'te), L. S. de Camp [title story of collection]; *Slave Ship* (sr3), F. Pohl
Aug   "Time in Advance" (n'te), W. Tenn [P. Klass] [title story of collection]
Oct   *The Stars My Destination* (sr4), A. Bester
Nov   "The Man Who Ate the World" (n'te), F. Pohl [title story of collection]
Dec   "Of All Possible Worlds," W. Tenn [P. Klass] [title story of collection]
1957 Mar   "The Other Celia" (short), T. Sturgeon
Apr   "Operation Stinky" (n'te), C. D. Simak
Jul   "Help! I Am Dr. Morris Goldpepper" (n'te), A. Davidson

Aug "Time Waits for Winthrop" (short novel), W. Tenn [P. Klass] [title story of collection]

Sep "The Pod in the Barrier" (short novel), T. Sturgeon

Oct *Wolfbane* (sr2), F. Pohl & C. M. Kornbluth

Dec "Galley Slave" (n'te), I. Asimov [robot story not in *I, Robot*]

1958 Jan "The World That Couldn't Be" (n'te), C. D. Simak [title story of anthology, H. L. Gold]

Feb "The Rule of the Door" (n'te), L. Biggle [title story of collection]; "Graveyard of Dreams" (n'te), H. B. Piper [enlarged as *Junkyard Planet*]

Mar *The Big Time* (sr2), F. Leiber

May "Or All the Seas With Oysters" (short), A. Davidson [title story of collection]

Aug "To Marry Medusa" (short novel), T. Sturgeon [see *The Cosmic Rape*]

Sep "Lastborn" (short novel), I. Asimov

Oct "Time Killer" (sr4), R. Sheckley [*Immortality Delivered*]; "The Wizards of Pung's Corners" (n'te), F. Pohl

Dec "Nightmare With Zeppelins" (short), F. Pohl & C. M. Kornbluth

1959 Feb "I Plinglot—Who You?" (n'te), F. Pohl

Apr "The City of Force" (short novel), D. F. Galouye; "The Man in the Mailbag" (n'te), G. R. Dickson [enlarged as *Spacial Delivery*]

Jun "Whatever Counts" (short novel), F. Pohl

Oct "A Death in the House" (n'te), C. D. Simak

1960 Apr "The Lady Who Sailed the Soul" (n'te), C. Smith [P. Linebarger]

Jun *Drunkard's Walk* (sr2), F. Pohl

Aug "Mind Partner" (n'te), C. Anvil [H. C. Crosby]

1961 Apr "Tandy's Story" (n'te), T. Sturgeon

Aug "The Gatekeepers" (n'te), J. T. McIntosh [J. M. Mac-Gregor]

Oct "A Planet Named Shayol" (short novel), C. Smith [P. Line-barger]; "Jerry Norcriss" series, J. Sharkey, began.

Dec *The Day After Doomsday* (sr2), P. Anderson

1962 Feb "Critical Mass" (short novel), F. Pohl & C. M. Kornbluth

Apr "A Planet for Plundering" (short novel), J. Williamson [see *The Trial of Terra*]

Jun *The Seed of Earth*, R. Silverberg

Aug *The Dragon Masters*, J. Vance

Oct "The Ballad of Lost C'Mell" (n'te), C. Smith [P. Line-barger]; *A Plague of Pythons* (sr2), F. Pohl

1963 Apr "The Visitor at the Zoo," D. Knight [*Mind Switch*]

Jun "Here Gather the Stars" (sr2), C. D. Simak [*Way Station*]

Aug "Hot Planet" (n'te), H. Clement [H. C. Stubbs]

Oct "The Men in the Walls" (short novel), W. Tenn [P. Klass] [in *Of Men and Monsters*]; "On the Gem Planet" (n'te), C. Smith [P. Linebarger] [first of set published as *Quest of the Three Worlds*]

Dec *The Star King* (sr2), J. Vance; "No Great Magic" (short novel), F. Leiber

1964 Apr "The Boy Who Bought Old Earth," C. Smith [P. Linebarg-er] [*The Planet Buyer*]

Oct *Soldier, Ask Not*, G. R. Dickson

Dec "The Starsloggers," H. Harrison [*Bill, the Galactic Hero*]

1965 Apr "Death and Birth of the Angakok" (n'te), H. Howard [in *The Eskimo Invasion*]

Jun *Mindswap*, R. Sheckley; "Blue Fire" (n'te), R. Silverberg [with later stories in *To Open the Sky*]

Aug "Do I Wake or Dream?" F. Herbert [*Destination: Void*]

Oct *The Age of the Pussyfoot* (sr3), F. Pohl

Dec "'Repent, Harlequin!' Said the Ticktockman" (short), H. Ellison

1966 Feb "Under Old Earth" (n'te), C. Smith [P. Linebarger]

Apr *The Last Castle*, J. Vance

Jun "Heisenberg's Eyes" (sr2), F. Herbert [*The Eyes of Heisen-berg*]; "Eskimo Invasion" (n'te), H. Howard [see *The Eskimo Invasion*]

Oct *The Palace of Love* (sr3), J. Vance; "The Ship Who Killed" (n'te), A. McCaffrey

1967 Apr "Thunderhead" (n'te), K. Laumer [see *The Day Before Forever*]

Jun "To Outlive Eternity" (sr2), P. Anderson

Aug *Hawksbill Station*, R. Silverberg

Oct "Damnation Alley" (n'te), R. Zelazny

1968 Apr *The Goblin Reservation* (sr2), C. D. Simak; "The World and Thorinn" (n'te), D. Knight [first of "Thorinn" series]

Jun "The Beast That Shouted Love" (short), H. Ellison

Jul "A Specter Is Haunting Texas" (sr3), F. Leiber

Sep "Nightwings" (n'te), R. Silverberg

Issues:

	Jan	Feb	Mar	Apr	May	Jun	Jul	Aug	Sep	Oct	Nov	Dec	W
1950										1/1	1/2	1/3	3
1951	1/4	1/5	1/6	2/1	2/2	2/3	2/4	2/5	2/6	3/1	3/2	3/3	15
1952	3/4	3/5	3/6	4/1	4/2	4/3	4/4	4/5	4/6	5/1	5/2	5/3	27
1953	5/4	5/5	5/6	6/1	6/2	6/3	6/4	6/5	6/6	7/1	7/2	7/3	39
1954	7/5*	7/5*	7/6	8/1	8/2	8/3	8/4	8/5	8/6	9/1	9/2	9/3	51
1955	9/4	9/5	9/6	10/1	10/2	10/3	10/4	10/5	10/6	11/1	11/2		62
1956	11/3†	11/4	11/5	11/6	12/1	12/2	12/3	12/4	12/5	12/6	13/1	13/2	74
1957	13/3	13/4	13/5	13/6	14/1	14/2	14/3	14/4	14/5	14/6	15/1	15/2	86
1958	15/3	15/4	15/5	15/6	16/1	16/2	16/3	16/4	16/5	16/6	17/1	17/2	98
1959		17/3		17/4		17/5		17/6		18/1		18/2	104
1960		18/3		18/4		18/5		18/6		19/1		19/2	110
1961		19/3		19/4		19/5		19/6		20/1		20/2	116
1962		20/3		20/4		20/5		20/6		21/1		21/2	122
1963		21/3		21/4		21/5		21/6		22/1		22/2	128
1964		22/3		22/4		22/5		22/6		23/1		23/2	134
1965		23/3		23/4		23/5		23/6		24/1		24/2	140
1966		24/3		24/4		24/5		24/6		25/1		25/2	146
1967		25/3		25/4		25/5		25/6		26/1		26/2	152
1968		26/3		26/4		26/5	26/6	27/1	27/2	27/3	27/4	27/5	161

* Correct, numbers duplicated in magazine.

† Actually no time delay; updating because of change in distributor.

Argentine Edition:
Rumoured to exist.

British Edition:
Publisher: Thorpe & Porter, later Strato Pubs., London.
This began with an exact copy of the Oct 1952 U.S. issue, noted as Vol. 3 No. 1, for 1/6. Later the issues were only numbered and the pages were reduced slightly, omitting a story or department.

From No. 26 the price was raised to 2/-; with No. 72 it became bimonthly, 192 pp., and 3/6. From No. 80 no actual British edition was printed, but U.S. copies with open covers were imported and Thorpe & Porter added the appropriate information for British distribution (usually "British Edition," number, price, and T&P imprint). Because of a U.S. printing strike, No. 85 was not so prepared, but was overprinted. Dates first appeared in the table of contents of No. 72, and from No. 80 (June 1960) volume numbering, etc., inside each issue followed the U.S. edition. The number ceased being stamped on the cover after No. 94 (Oct 1962), when Thorpe & Porter issued the U.S. editions with a rubber-stamped circle on the cover giving the month (by figure) and the price (3/6); e.g., British July 1963 was the U.S. Apr (21/4) stamped "7" (July), and Sep was the U.S. June (21/5) stamped "9." Effective Mar-Apr 1967 the covers and title pages were again printed for British distribution. The Aug 1966 U.S. edition (24/6) became Mar-Apr 1967 in England, priced at 3/6; Oct 1966 U.S. became May-June 1967; the last one so printed was Sep-Oct 1967 (U.S. Feb 1967). The policy since is not known.

Issues:

	Jan	Feb	Mar	Apr	May	Jun	Jul	Aug	Sep	Oct	Nov	Dec	W
1953	3/1	3/2	3/3	3/4		3/5		3/6	3/7	3/8	3/9		9
1954	10	11	12	13	14	15	16	17	18	19	20	21	21
1955	22	23	24	25	26	27	28	29	30	31	32	33	33
1956	34	35	36	37	38	39	40	41	42	43	44	45	45
1957	46	47	48	49	50	51	52	53	54	55	56	57	57
1958	58	59	60	61	62	63	64	65	66	67	68	69	69
1959	70	71	72		73		74		75		76		76
1960	77		78		79		80		81		82		82
1961	83		84		85		86		87		88		88
1962		89		90		91		92	93	94	(95)		95
1963	(96)		(97)		(98)		(99)		(100)		(101)		101
1964	(102)		(103)		(104)		(105)		(106)		(107)		107

[*cont.*]	Jan	Feb	Mar	Apr	May	Jun	Jul	Aug	Sep	Oct	Nov	Dec	W
1965			(108)		(109)		(110)		(111)		(112)		(113)	113
1966			(114)		(115)		(116)		(117)		(118)		(119)	119
1967			(120)		(121)		(122)		(123)		(124)		(125)	125

Finnish Edition: See *AIKAMME*
French Edition: See *GALAXIE*
German Edition: See *GALAXIS*
Italian Editions:

Many selections presented in *Urania* (1952-1953).
72 issues (June 1958—May 1964) as *Galaxy.*

Edited by R. Valente, Mavi & R. Rambelli; 128 to 260 pp.; 150 lire; published by Editrice due Mondi, Milano, to No. 10, then Casa Editrice La Tribuna. It apparently used the same covers as the U.S. originals.
Norwegian Edition: No information.
Swedish Edition:
19 issues (Sep 1958—July 1960).

First 16 issues monthly, 132 pp., 2 kr; last 3 bimonthly, 196 pp., 3.50 kr.
Editor: Henrik Rabe. **Publisher:** Illusterade Klassiker, Stockholm.

This translated stories from the U.S. original, but also had some articles and short stories by Swedish authors, and a letter column. It serialised A. Bester's *Tiger! Tiger!* [*The Stars My Destination*].

GALAXY SCIENCE FICTION NOVELS   U.S.   Science fiction
46 issues (Sep 1950—mid-1961), not dated.
Editor: H. L. Gold.
Publisher: World Editions, New York, for first 7, then Galaxy Pub. Corp., New York.

This can be considered a paperback book series; all the novels are listed under Galaxy Pub. Corp. in the *Paperbacks—Publishers* section, and are also covered under specific authors in the *Who's Who* section.

It began in magazine format as a companion to *Galaxy Science Fiction.* At No. 32 it changed to small paperback book size; from No. 37 it was incorporated into Beacon Distributing Company with a different serial numbering system (though occasionally the Galaxy number was given). Many of the Beacon series were sexed-up versions of the originals (though relatively mild by later standards).

GAMMA   U.S.   Science fiction and fantasy
5 issues (mid-1963, not dated—Sep 1965).
Editor and Publisher: Charles E. Fritch (Star Press Inc., North Hollywood, Calif.); Executive Editor: Jack Matcha. Managing Editor (first 3 issues): W. F. Nolan. Fritch and Matcha noted as publishers from No. 3.
Format: digest size; 128 pp.; 50¢; last 3 saddle-stapled.
Cover Artists: M. S. Dollens for first 3, then John Healey.

A magazine of some interest. It was the first sf magazine from the West Coast of the U.S.A. since *Spaceway* (which more recently began a second series). Though somewhat irregular in frequency, it was quite well received.

It presented a number of stories by C. Beaumont, C. E. Fritch, W. F. Nolan, R. Matheson, R. Bradbury, and others. The last issue had a short novel, "Nesbit," by R. Goulart.
Issues:

	Jan	Feb	Mar	Apr	May	Jun	Jul	Aug	Sep	Oct	Nov	Dec	W
1963							1/1					1/2	2
1964			2/1										3
1965		2/2							2/5*				5

* Appeared as noted.

GAMMA Fantascienza   Italian   Science fiction
27 issues (Oct 1965—Mar 1968).
Monthly; digest size; 112 to 192 pp.
Editor: Valentino De Carlo; **Publisher:** Edizioni Gamma, Milan, to No. 5, then Edizioni Dello Scorpione.

GEORGE PAL'S TALES OF SPACE CONQUEST (projected)
    U.S.   Science fiction
The first issue was linotyped, interior cuts made, and page proofs pulled when poor market prospects (*ca.* 1954) and lack of financial backing stopped this magazine from appearing.

GHOST STORIES   U.S.   Ghost
64 issues (July 1926—Dec 1931/Jan 1932).
Monthly; 25¢. Apparently began as large size, 96 pp., to July 1928, then pulp size, 128 pp., to Mar 1929, then large size again Apr 1929 to Dec 1929, then finished as pulp size.
Editors: Editorials written by George W. Wilder to Aug 1927, then Robert Napier from Sep 1927. However, the semiannual Publisher's Statements show: Jan 1927, Editor, Harry A. Keller, Managing Editor, Joseph M. Roth; July 1927, same; Jan 1928, Ed., W. Adolphe Roberts, Man. Ed., Joseph M. Roth; July 1929, Ed., George Bond, Man. Ed., Edith L. Becker; July 1929, Ed., George Bond; Man. Ed., Camille MacAdams; Dec 1929, Ed., D. E. Wheeler, Man. Ed., Camille MacAdams; July 1930, Ed., Arthur B. Howland; Man. Ed., Edith L. Becker; Jan 1931, Ed. & Man. Ed., Harold Hersey; July 1931, same; Oct-Nov 1931, same.
Publishers: Constructive Pub. Corp., Dunellen, New Jersey (a Macfadden publication); from Apr 1930, Good Story Mag. Co., New York (H. Hersey, President).

This magazine was begun by Bernarr Macfadden as a companion to *True Detective Tales* and as a rival to H. Gernsback's *Amazing Stories.* R. W. Lowndes judged that the magazine missed the bus and should have appeared much earlier to cater to the interest in spiritualism which had already begun to wane (see editorial, *Mag. Horror,* Mar 1968). He comments on the attraction this magazine, with its 'roto' form and trick photography, had for the uninformed and impressionable young enthusiasts of the day; the journalistic "true story" approach of the stories was certainly convincing to the inexperienced.

The Hersey issues differed from their predecessors by presenting most stories as fiction rather than with the superficial veneer of "fact"—stories in the first person "by" so-and-so as told to a professional writer—which marked the original policy. Hersey also allowed a far broader choice of locale and historical period, where the earlier stories were almost exclusively contemporary.

The material presented included stories by Archie Binns, A. M. Burrage, Harold S. Corbin, Jack D'Arcy, A. C. Doyle, Guy Fowler, Edwin A. Goewey, Nell Kay, Lyon Mearson (many serials), Marl Mellen, Stuart Palmer (many articles also), Emil Raymond, W. Adolphe Roberts, V. Rousseau [V. R. Emanuel], Robert W. Sneddon, Wilbert Wadleigh (many serials), and H. G. Wells. There were articles by Hereward Carrington, Samri Frikell, Gordon M. Hillman, and Horace Leaf, among others.

More recently the magazine apparently had two one-shot reprint collections, *Prize Ghost Stories* and *True Twilight Tales.* It has also been indexed by James R. Sieger: *Ghost Stories* (Opar Press, 1973), a booklet having magazine outline coverage by S. Moskowitz.
Fiction of Possible Fantasy Interest:

1926 Jul   "The Phantom of the Fifteenth Floor" (sr6), F. Oursler; "The Girl Who Lived with the Dead" (sr4), Grant Hubbard; "The Transferred Ghost" (1882, short), F. R. Stockton

Oct   "Pawn of the Unseen" (sr7), Lyon Mearson

Nov   "The Woman Who Stole a Ghost" (short), Agatha Christie [later revised as "The Last Seance"]; "The Bold Dragoon" (short), W. Irving

1927 Jan   "The Black Spider," E. Snell [in *Gruesome Cargoes*, Thomson, 1928]; "They Hanged a Phantom for Murder" (short), 'Doctor Grey' as told to R. Cummings; "The Man Who Died Twice" (short), F. B. Long

Feb   "The Phantom Ace" (sr2), Edwin A. Goewy [Aden Ashton]

Mar   "The Ghost of the Red Cavalier" (short), V. Rousseau [V. R. Emanuel]

Aug   "The Story of the Late Mr. Elvesham" (short), H. G. Wells; "The Soul That Lost Its Way" (short), V. Rousseau [V. R. Emanuel]

Oct   "Conan Doyle's Museum of Psychic Wonders" (article), L. Crocombe

1928 Jan   "The House of Living Dead" (sr6), V. Rousseau [V. R. Emanuel]

Mar   "The Haunted Hotel" (sr3), Jack Grey

May   "When the Red Gods Call" (sr6), Edwin A. Goewey

Aug   "The Prisoner of Life" (sr6), V. Rousseau [V. R. Emanuel]

Dec   "The Spider" (sr8), Grace Oursler

1929 Jan "Phantom Lovers" (sr5), Grant Hubbard
     Mar "The Roll-Call of the Reef" (short), Sir A. T. Quiller-
         Couch
     Apr "The Witch in the Next Room" (short), Walter Gibson
     Nov "The Spirit in the Garden" (short), S. W. Ellis
1930 Jan "The Radio Mind" (sr2, article), Upton Sinclair
     Mar "The Screaming Skull" (sr2), F. Marion Crawford
     Dec "The Evil Three" (sr5), V. Rousseau [V. R. Emanuel]
1931 Jan "The House of the Fog" (sr6), H. Thompson Rich
Issues:

	Jan	Feb	Mar	Apr	May	Jun	Jul	Aug	Sep	Oct	Nov	Dec	W
1926							1/1	1/2	1/3	1/4	1/5	1/6	6
1927	2/1	2/2	2/3	2/4	2/5	2/6	3/1	3/2	3/3	3/4	3/5	3/6	18
1928	4/1	4/2	4/3	4/4	4/5	4/6	5/1	5/2	5/3	5/4	5/5	5/6	30
1929	6/1	6/2	6/3	6/4	6/5	6/6	7/1	7/2	7/3	7/4	7/5	7/6	42
1930	8/1	8/2	8/3	8/4	8/5	8/6	9/1	9/2	9/3	9/4	9/5	9/6	54
1931	10/1	10/2	10/3	10/4	10/5	10/6	11/1		11/2		11/3	11/4*	64

* Issue dated Dec 1931-Jan 1932.

GHOST SUPER-DETECTIVE, THE   U.S.   Mystery
7 issues (Jan 1940—Sum 1941).
Not fantastic. Detective novels by G. T. Fleming-Roberts; first four under pseudonym George Chance. Title changed from fifth issue to *The Green Ghost Detective.*

GHOSTS AND GOBLINS   British   Weird
1 issue (not numbered, not dated, *ca.* 1938). Probably 1/-.
Publisher: World's Work, Tadsworth, England.
One of the Master Thriller series, presenting fiction by R. Thurston Hopkins, H. Rawle, and G. Radcliffe, among others.

GOLDEN FLEECE   U.S.   Historical fantasy
9 issues (Oct 1938—June 1939).
Pulp size; 128 pp.; 20¢, monthly.
Associate Editors: A. J. Gontier & J. H. Bellamy (first issue), then C. G. Williams for remaining issues.
Publisher: Sun Publications Inc., Chicago.
Cover Artists: DeLay did the first six, and Brundage two of the remainder.
Of minor interest, this magazine is now a collector's item. It printed fantastic adventures based on history, and featured material by T. Mundy, H. Bedford-Jones, A. M. Rud, R. E. Howard, L. S. de Camp, S. Quinn, and E. H. Price. It is covered in T.G.L. Cockcroft's *Index to the Weird Fiction Magazines* (1962).

GREAT AMERICAN PUBLICATIONS. A publisher headed by Henry Scharf. It produced the following magazines in the early 1960's: *Fantastic Universe* [bought from King-Size Pubs.], Oct 1960—Mar 1961; *Fear*; *New Worlds* [U.S. edition]; *Countdown!*; *Space* [incorporating *Speed Age*].

GREAT SCIENCE FICTION   U.S.   Science fiction reprint
Current (No. 1, 1965—); 12th issue, Fall 1968.
Digest size; 130 pp.; quarterly?; 50¢.
Publisher: Ultimate Publishing Co., Flushing, New York.
One of Sol Cohen's reprint magazines using material from the early Ziff-Davis magazines. Issues 1 to 5 alternated as *Great Science Fiction From Amazing* and *Great Science Fiction From Fantastic*; with No. 6 it became simply *Great Science Fiction.* It is reported that the title changed to *Science Fiction Greats* after the period covered here (with No. 13) and publication ceased with Spr 1971. It is understood that at first no payment was made to authors for stories in the early issues, but nominal payments have since been made.
Issues (not dated until No. 9):

	Jan	Feb	Mar	Apr	May	Jun	Jul	Aug	Sep	Oct	Nov	Dec	W
1965											#1		1
1966		2		3				4			5		5
1967	6		7					8					8
1968	9 (Win)		10 (Spr)		11 (Sum)			12 (Fall)					12

GREAT SCIENCE FICTION STORIES See *TREASURY OF GREAT SCIENCE FICTION STORIES*

GREEN GHOST DETECTIVE, THE See *GHOST SUPER-DETECTIVE, THE*

GUNTER'S MAGAZINE   English   General
A general magazine which published H. R. Haggard's novels *The Ghost Kings* in 1907 and *Queen Sheba's Ring* in 1909.

H

HÄPNA   Swedish   Science fiction
125 issues (1 Mar 1954—1 Jan 1966)
Editor: Kjell Ekstrom.
Publisher: Grafiska Förlaget K & S, Jönköping.
Digest size; generally monthly except for a few combined issues, usually July/August; price 1.35 kr to start, up to 1.75 kr by 1958.
This was a fan-financed and excellently produced magazine created by the work of the brothers Kurt and Karl-Gustav Kindberg. It reprinted stories and articles from both the U.S. and British magazines. Covers were often bought from Nova Publications. Amateur magazine reviews were by Sigvard Ostlund (1954-56), Alvar Appeltofft (1956-59), and Sam Lundwall (1959-66). The book reviews were done by Roland Adlerberth.
Swedish authors published included Denis Lindbohm, S. J. Lundwall, and S. Lönnerstrand. A cover and a number of interior illustrations were by Swedish fan artist Sven O. Emilson.
Novels since inception were: *Slan,* A. E. van Vogt (1954: Jan—July); *The Legion of Space,* J. Williamson (1954:7—1955:6); "The Hunting Season," F. M. Robinson (1955:7/8—9); *Foundation,* I. Asimov (1955:9—1956:2); *Donovan's Brain,* C. Siodmak (1955:10—1956:4); *Foundation and Empire,* I. Asimov (1955:9—1956:9); *Spaceways,* C. E. Maine [C. McIlwain] (1956:11—1957:4); *The Caves of Steel,* I. Asimov (1957:10—1958:4); *The Secret Visitors,* J. White (1958:5—10); "The Other Side of the Sky," A. C. Clarke (1958:11—1959:4); *Second Foundation,* I. Asimov (1959:2—9); the remainder included in 1960 several of A. E. van Vogt's "Gods" series, in 1961 a Heinlein novel (original not known), and in 1964 "The Big Front Yard," C. D. Simak.
Issues:
1954 Mar (1/1) to Dec (1/9), with July/Aug as 1/5.
1955 Vol. 2, Jan (2/1) to Dec (2/12), with Jul/Aug as 2/7&8. Numbering continued along these lines for most years, with the 125th and final issue being Jan 1966.

HEALTH KNOWLEDGE INC., New York, N.Y. 10003.
U.S. publisher which issued the following magazines: *Exploring the Unknown*; *Magazine of Horror*; *Startling Mystery Stories*; *Famous Science Fiction.*

HIDDEN WORLD, THE   U.S.   Science fiction
At least 16 issues (Spr 1961—Win 1964); issues noted as A1—A16.
Pulp size; 192 pp.; quarterly; $1.50.
Editor: R. A. Palmer.
Most stories were by R. S. Shaver and many excerpts from his unfinished and unpublished novel *The Elder World* appeared. A 2-part serial began in A6: "Beyond the Verge," DeWitt C. Chifman (a "Hollow Earth" story). In most issues Palmer asked for material but gave the warning "No payment except by arrangement." The quality of the paper and printing was a credit to Palmer but it was unfortunate that the magazine appealed to only a small "crank" audience. Circulation figures were given in A5 and A8 as 3289 and 3006 respectively.

HORROR MONSTERS   U.S.   Monster magazine
10 issues (Jan 1961—Win 1964-67); usually 2 per year.
Large size; quarterly (?); 64 pp.; 35¢.
Publisher: Charlton Pubs., Inc., Derby, Connecticut.
Another of the monster magazines.

HORROR STORIES   U.S.   Weird menace
41 issues (Jan 1935—Apr/May 1941).
Pulp size; first monthly, then bimonthly.
Editor: Steve Farrelly, with Rogers Terrill as Editorial Director.

One of the weird menace pulp magazines. It is fully indexed in *The Weird Menace*, B. Jones (1972), and some issues are listed in *The Macabre Index*, W. M. Austin (mimeo, 1952). Outlines of many of the stories are presented in *The Shudder Pulps*, R. K. Jones (1978). Writers for the magazine included H. B. Cave, A. J. Burks, N. W. Page, N. Schachner, P. Ernst, R. Cummings, E. Hoffman Price, C. Woolrich, and many others.
British Edition: 3 issues, not numbered, not dated, 1948-1950.

HUGIN   Swedish   Science (fiction)
85 issues (7 Apr 1916—15 Jan 1920).
Editor & Publisher: Otto Witt.

Published in alternate weeks, with many double and triple issues. Price 1916-1918 was 5 kr/year, then 10 kr/year. It was sold only by subscription, with 15,000 copies printed at first, later down to 10,000. Issues usually ran 24 to 30 pages.

The covers were all the same, the ancient god Odin, and all in two colours. One illustrator was "Jonathan," 14 years old. Issues usually had two or three serials plus short stories and articles, including much material by O. Witt. No foreign translations were used. The magazine can be considered of sf nature, with much popular science. It was reportedly greatly enjoyed, and Nobel Prize winner Svante Arrhenius wrote some letters of comment to it. *Hugin* is now a collector's item; only one complete set is known to exist outside the Royal Library of Sweden.

I

IDLER, THE   British   General fiction
Feb 1892—Mar 1911.
Editors: Jerome K. Jerome, Richard Barr, and in latter days A. Lawrence, S. H. Sime.
Publisher: Chatto & Windus, London.

One of the most attractive and well-patronised magazines of its time. It always maintained a high literary standard and published much interesting fiction and nonfiction by notable authors of the day.

Some noted fantasy includes:
1892 Mar "De Profundis" (short), A. C. Doyle
     Nov "The Doom of London" (short), Richard Barr
1895 Jun "The Roll Call of the Reef" (short), 'Q' [A. T. Quiller-Couch]
1897 May Began series of 5 "Stories of the Stone Age," H. G. Wells.
1906 Apr *The Tracer of Lost Persons*, (sr7), R. W. Chambers
1910 Jan *Carnacki, the Ghost-Finder*, (sr5), W. H. Hodgson

Other authors included W. L. Auden, L. Housman, E. O'Donnell, and W. Irving. Fantasy in *The Idler* is listed in B. Day's *Index on the Weird and Fantastica*.

IF—Worlds of Science Fiction   U.S.   Science fiction
Mar 1952—Dec 1974; 133rd issue, Dec 1968.
Digest size; 160 pp. at first, to 120 pp. Nov 1952, to 130 pp. July 1959; monthly; began at 35¢, 40¢ Mar 1963, 50¢ Dec 1964, 60¢ Aug 1967.
Editors: P. W. Fairman, Mar 1952—Sep 1952; J. L. Quinn, Nov 1952—Aug 1958 [L. T. Shaw, Associate Editor May 1953—Mar 1954]; D. Knight, Oct 1958—Feb 1959; H. L. Gold, July 1959—Sep 1961; F. Pohl, Feature Editor, July 1959—Jan 1961, Managing Editor to July 1962, Editor Sep 1962—Dec 1968. Judy-Lynn Benjamin became Associate Editor June 1966 and L. del Rey became Managing Editor June 1968.
Publishers: Quinn Pub. Co., New York, to Feb 1959; then Digest Productions Corp., New York [Robert M. Guinn], becoming from July 1963 Galaxy Pub. Corp., New York. [Sold again in 1969.]
Art Editors: E. Valigursky, Mar 1953—Oct 1955; M. Hunter, Dec 1955—Dec 1957; then S. Rudivich and some others until the position was absorbed into other editors' duties.
Review:

If was always of quite good quality. Declining sales in 1958 forced J. L. Quinn to take on D. Knight as editor, but this was not enough to save the magazine from temporary suspension. At one stage L. T. Shaw was to have been editor, but he left and later edited another magazine, *Infinity*. Under H. L. Gold *If* was very similar in story material to its companion *Galaxy SF*, but was inclined to experiment more. The stories printed by F. Pohl were generally so good that the magazine won the Hugo for 1966, 1967 and 1968, after *F&SF* and *Analog* seemed to have monopolized this award for a number of years.

A Collegiate Science Fiction Contest was run in early 1954 for short stories with new ideas; the results were given in Nov 1954—the first prize ($1,000) was for "And Gone Tomorrow," Andy Offutt; other winners followed in later issues. For a time in early 1956 F. J Ackerman wrote Guest Editorials. The Dec 1958 issue presented a fictionalised "Short History of Space Travel."

Quinn published selections as the anthologies *First World of If* and *Second World of If*. More recently F. Pohl selected *The If Reader of Science Fiction* and *The Second If Reader of Science Fiction*.

The title *If* was originally used on an amateur magazine published by Con Pederson in 1948.
Notable Fiction:
1952 Jul "McIlvaine's Star" (short), A. Derleth
     Sep "The Beautiful People" (short), C. Beaumont
1953 Mar "Deadly City" (short novel), I. Jorgenson [P. W. Fairman] [filmed]; "The Sword" (short), F. Quattrocchi
     May "Jupiter Five" (n'te), A. C. Clarke
     Sep "A Case of Conscience," J. Blish [enlarged as book]
     Nov "Homo Inferior," M. Wolf; "The Custodian" (n'te), W. Tenn [P. Klass]
1954 Jan "Malice in Wonderland" (short novel), E. Hunter [see *Tomorrow's World*]
     Apr "The Golden Man" (n'te), P. K. Dick
     Jun "The Colonists" (n'te), R. F. Jones
     Jul "The Thing in the Attic" (n'te), J. Blish [in *The Seedling Stars*]
     Aug "The Unlearned" (n'te), R. F. Jones
     Nov "The Very Secret Agent" (short), M. Wolf
1955 Jan "The Earth Quarter," D. Knight [*The Sun Saboteurs*]
     Feb "The Odd Ones" (n'te), G. Dickson
     Mar "The Cyber and Justice Holmes" (short), F. Riley
     May "Snowball" (n'te), P. Anderson
     Aug "Franchise" (short), I. Asimov
     Oct "Last Rites" (short), C. Beaumont
1956 Feb "Avoidance Situation" (short novel), J. McConnell
     Apr "The Executioner" (short), F. Riley; "Life Hutch" (short), H. Ellison; "Chrome Pastures" (n'te), R. F. Young
1957 Feb "Ultimate Melody" (short), A. C. Clarke
     Apr "The Maze" (short), A. B. Chandler
     Aug "The Tunesmith" (n'te), L. Biggle
     Dec "Captain Peabody," R. Phillips [R. P. Graham]
1958 Feb "Assassin" (n'te), J. F. Bone
     Apr "A Question of Identity" (n'te), F. Riley
     Jun "The Songs of Distant Earth" (n'te), A. C. Clarke
     Dec "The Night of Hoggy Darn" (short), R. M. McKenna
1959 Feb "Pipe Dream" (short), F. Leiber
     Sep "Summer Guests" (short novel), J. H. Schmitz
1960 Jan "The Last Leap" (n'te), D. F. Galouye
     Mar "Gleaners" (short novel), C. D. Simak
     Sep "The Six Fingers of Time" (n'te), R. A. Lafferty
1961 Sep "The Frozen Planet" (n'te), K. Laumer
     Nov "Masters of Space" (sr2), Edward E. Smith & E. E. Evans
1962 Mar "Kings Must Die" (n'te), P. Anderson
     Jul "From Gustible's Planet" (short), C. Smith [P. M. A. Linebarger]
     Nov *Podkayne of Mars* (sr3), R. A. Heinlein
1963 Jan "Fortress Ship" (short), F. Saberhagen [first of "Berserker" series]

May "The Green World" (short novel), H. Clement [H. Stubbs]
Jul *The Reefs of Space* (sr3), F. Pohl & J. Williamson
Sep "The Expendables" (n'te), A. E. van Vogt
1964 Jan *Three Worlds to Conquer* (sr2), P. Anderson
May "The Imperial Stars" (short novel), Edward E. Smith; "The Store of Heart's Desire" (short novel), C. Smith [P. M. A. Linebarger] [*The Underpeople*]
Jul *Farnham's Freehold* (sr3), R. A. Heinlein; "The Silkie" (n'te), A. E. van Vogt
Aug "The Slaves of Gree" (n'te), C. C. MacApp [C. M. Capps] [first of "Gree" series]
Nov "The Hounds of Hell" (sr2), K. Laumer [*A Plague of Demons*]
1965 Jan *Starchild* (sr3), F. Pohl & J. Williamson
Apr *The Altar at Asconel* (sr2), J. Brunner; "White Fang Goes Dingo" (n'te), T. M. Disch [enlarged as *Mankind Under the Leash*]
Jun *Skylark DuQuesne* (sr5), Edward E. Smith
Jul "Research Alpha" (short novel), A. E. van Vogt & J. H. Schmitz
Oct *Retief's War* (sr3), K. Laumer
Nov *The Doomsday Men*, K. Bulmer
Dec *The Moon Is a Harsh Mistress* (sr5), R. A. Heinlein
1966 Feb "Prisoners of the Sky" (short novel), C. C. MacApp [C. M. Capps]; "Nine Hundred Grandmothers" (short), R. A. Lafferty
Mar "The Long Way to Earth," J. Brunner [*A Planet of Your Own*]
Apr *Earthblood* (sr4), K. Laumer & R. G. Brown
Jul "The Hour Before Earthrise" (sr3), J. Blish [*Welcome to Mars*]
Sep "Edge of Night" (sr2), A. B. Chandler [*Contraband From Otherspace*]
Oct "Neutron Star" (n'te), L. Niven [title story of collection]; *Snow White and the Giants* (sr4), J. T. McIntosh [J. M. MacGregor] [also titled *Time for a Change*]
1967 Jan "The Iron Thorn" (sr4), A. Budrys [*The Amsirs and the Iron Thorn*]
Mar "The Billiard Ball" (n'te), I. Asimov; "I Have No Mouth and I Must Scream" (short), H. Ellison [title story of collection]
Apr *The Road to the Rim* (sr2), A. B. Chandler
May "Spaceman" (sr3), K. Laumer [*Galactic Odyssey*]
Jun "Wizard's World" (short novel), Andre Norton [in "Witch World" series]
Jul "The Felled Star" (sr2), P. J. Farmer [in "River World" series]
Aug "Faust Aleph Null" (sr3), J. Blish [*Black Easter*]
Oct "Ocean on Top" (sr3), H. Clement [H. C. Stubbs]
Nov "Brother Berserker" (short novel), F. Saberhagen [in "Berserker" series]
Dec *All Judgment Fled* (sr3), J. White
1968 Jan "The Peacemakers" (n'te), J. Rankine
Feb "Slowboat Cargo" (sr3), L. Niven [*A Gift From Earth*]
Apr *The Man in the Maze* (sr2), R. Silverberg; "The Rim Gods" (n'te), A. B. Chandler [part of book, 1969]
Jun "Rogue Star" (sr3), F. Pohl & J. Williamson
Nov "The Computer Conspiracy" (sr2), M. Reynolds; "Creatures of Light" (short novel), R. Zelazny

Issues:

	Jan	Feb	Mar	Apr	May	Jun	Jul	Aug	Sep	Oct	Nov	Dec	W
1952		1/1		1/2		1/3		1/4		1/5			5
1953	1/6		2/1		2/2		2/3		2/4		2/5		11
1954	2/6		3/1	3/2	3/3	3/4	3/5	3/6	4/1	4/2	4/3	4/4	22
1955	4/5	4/6	5/1	5/2	5/3	5/4		5/5		5/6		6/1	31
1956		6/2		6/3		6/4		6/5		6/6		7/1	37
1957		7/2		7/3		7/4		7/5		7/6		7/6*	43
1958		8/2		8/3		8/4		8/5		8/6		9/1	49
1959		9/2					8/6*		9/4		9/5		53
1960	9/6		10/1		10/2		10/3		10/4		10/5		59
1961	10/6		11/1		11/2		11/3		11/4		11/5		65
1962	11/6		12/1		12/2		12/3		12/4		12/5		71
1963	12/6		13/1		13/2		13/3		13/4		13/5		77

[cont.]	Jan	Feb	Mar	Apr	May	Jun	Jul	Aug	Sep	Oct	Nov	Dec	W
1964	13/6		14/1		14/2		14/3	14/4		14/5	14/6	14/7	85
1965	15/1	15/2	15/3	15/4	15/5	15/6	15/7	15/8	15/9	15/10	15/11	15/12	97
1966	16/1	16/2	16/3	16/4	16/5	16/6	16/7	16/8	16/9	16/10	16/11	16/12	109
1967	17/1	17/2	17/3	17/4	17/5	17/6	17/7	17/8	17/9	17/10	17/11	17/12	121
1968	18/1	18/2	18/3	18/4	18/5	18/6	18/7	18/8	18/9	18/10	18/11	18/12	133

* As noted on contents page.

British Edition: Three series [fourth began Nov 1969—].
(1) 15 issues (1953—1955), not dated; digest size; 128 pp.; 1/6; publisher: Strato Pubs., for Thorpe & Porter.

These correspond to the U.S. issues from Mar 1953 for the first six; No. 7 was equivalent to Jan 1953; and the remainder ran through from Mar 1954 to Oct 1954.
(2) 18 issues (No. 1, 1959—No. 18, 1962), not dated; digest size; 130 pp.; bimonthly; 2/-; publisher: Strato Pubs., London.

Nos. 1 to 4 were printed in England and were identical to the U.S. edition from July 1959. With No. 5, however, U.S. copies with open covers were imported by Thorpe & Porter, who made appropriate changes (similar to *Galaxy*)—overprinting the no. and new price. This design began at July 1960.
(3) 9 issues (Feb 1967—Oct 1967), dated; digest size; 3/6.

This series used U.S. issues with a new title page with the caption "*Worlds of If Science Fiction* is distributed in Great Britain and the Irish Republic by Gold Star Publications Ltd., 42-44 Dock St., London E1." Covers were specially printed: the front was the same as the corresponding U.S. edition but with the new date and price and Gold Star logo at the top right corner; the inside front and back and outside back covers carried British advertisements. British issues corresponded to U.S. Apr 1966—Dec 1966 (monthly), with the same whole numbers and volume numbers.

Issues:

	Jan	Feb	Mar	Apr	May	Jun	Jul	Aug	Sep	Oct	Nov	Dec	W
1953											1	2	2
1954	3		4	5	6	7	8	9	10	11	12	13	14	14
1955	15												15
. . . . . .													
1959							1						1
1960	2		3		4		5		6		7		7
1961	8		9		10		11		12		13		13
1962	14		15		16		17		18				18
. . . . . .													
1967		101	102	103	104	105	106	107	108	109			9

(or, 16/4 through 16/12)

IF SCIENCE FICTION See *IF*

IMAGINATION   U.S.   Science fiction
63 issues (Oct 1950—Oct 1958).
Digest size; 162 pp. to Mar 1954, then 130 pp.; bimonthly to Feb 1953, monthly Apr 1953 to Jul 1955, then bimonthly; 35¢.
Title change: *Imagination Science Fiction* from Oct 1955.
Editors: R. A. Palmer, Oct & Dec 1950; then W. L. Hamling.
Publishers: Clarke Pub. Co.; then Greenleaf Pub. Co., Evanston, Illinois.
Art Editors: Malcolm Smith, Oct 1952—Dec 1954; W. E. Terry, Jan 1955—June 1958; Paul Quaiver.
Cover Artists: Mainly H. McCauley, M. Smith, W. E. Terry, and Rognan. Front covers were always flamboyantly colourful; some back covers were notable astronomical photographs.
General:

This magazine was begun by R. A. Palmer as a companion to *Other Worlds*, but was soon taken over by Hamling. Most issues included a long novel, but not many were noteworthy, most being in the interplanetary/space opera/adventure field.

A very good fan section was run by Mari Wolf, Apr 1951—Apr 1956, and then by R. Bloch until the magazine ceased. This was considered a great loss, as it was one of the few departments of its type in the magazines. From June 1958 space articles (by Henry Bott) were a feature.

A companion, *Imaginative Tales*, began in late 1954, changing its title to *Space Travel* before eventually ceasing in 1958. The title *Imagination* was originally suggested by F. J Ackerman and used for a high-class amateur magazine produced by the Los Angeles Science Fantasy Society for 13 issues (Oct 1937—1938).

Notable Fiction:
1951 Feb "Revolt of the Devil Star," R. Rocklynne [last of "Darkness" series]
1952 Jan *Special Delivery*, K. Neville [reprinted Aug 1958]
    May "Tonight the Sky Will Fall," D. Galouye
1953 Jul "Voyage to Eternity," M. Lesser [*Recruit for Andromeda*]
    Oct "The Time Armada" (sr2), F. B. Holden
    Nov "Sky Lift" (n'te), R. A. Heinlein; "Roll Out the Rolov!" (short), H. C. Crosby
1954 Jan *Peril of the Starmen*, K. Neville
1955 Jan "World of the Drone," R. Abernathy
    Mar *Highways in Hiding* (sr4), G. O. Smith
1956 Jun *Battle for the Stars*, A. Blade [house pseudonym; E. Hamilton in this case]
1957 Feb "Compete or Die!" M. Reinsberg
    Dec *Fugitive of the Stars*, E. Hamilton
1958 Oct "The Assassin," H. Ellison [*Doomsman*]

Issues:

	Jan	Feb	Mar	Apr	May	Jun	Jul	Aug	Sep	Oct	Nov	Dec	W
1950										1/1		1/2	2
1951		2/1		2/2		2/3			2/4		2/5		7
1952	3/1		3/2		3/3		3/4		3/5	3/6		3/7	14
1953	4/1	4/2		4/3	4/4	4/5	4/6	4/7	4/8	4/9	4/10	4/11	25
1954	5/1	5/2	5/3	5/4	5/5	5/6	5/7	5/8	5/9	5/10	5/11	5/12	37
1955	6/1	6/2	6/3	6/4	6/5	6/6	6/7			6/8		6/9	46
1956		7/1		7/2		7/3		7/4		7/5		7/6	52
1957		8/1		8/2		8/3		8/4		8/5		8/6	58
1958		9/1		9/2		9/3		9/4		9/5			63

IMAGINATION SCIENCE FICTION See *IMAGINATION*

IMAGINATIVE TALES   U.S.   Science fiction
Title change: *Space Travel* July—Nov 1958.
26 issues (Sep 1954—Nov 1958).
Digest size; 162 pp. first issue, then 130 pp.; bimonthly; 35¢.
Editor: W. L. Hamling.
Publisher: Greenleaf Pub. Co., Evanston, Illinois.

Companion to *Imagination*, printing long novels complete in one issue. After some reprints in the first few issues its story policy became the same as its companion's. The change in title for the last issues was an attempt by Hamling to find a name directly relating to the science fiction field and so increase sales; this was not successful.

F. J Ackerman ran a regular scientifilm column. Cover artists included H. W. McCauley, Rognan, and M. Smith.

Notable Fiction:
1954 First two issues reprinted novels in the "Toffee" series, C. F. Myers.
1955 First four issues published novels by R. Bloch, including "The Big Binge" (July). Some were reprints.
1956 From here on there were many novels by Dwight V. Swain and Edmond Hamilton (some under pseudonym), with Hamilton having a novel in each issue of *Space Travel*.
1957 Mar "Starship Saboteur" (short), R. Silverberg

Issues:

	Jan	Feb	Mar	Apr	May	Jun	Jul	Aug	Sep	Oct	Nov	Dec	W
1954									#1		2		2
1955	3		4		5		1/6		2/1		2/2		8
1956	3/1		3/2		3/3		3/4		3/5		3/6		14
1957	4/1		4/2		4/3		4/4		4/5		4/6		20
1958	5/1		5/2		5/3		5/4		5/5		5/6		26

IMPULSE   British   Science fantasy
12 issues (Mar 1966—Feb 1967).
Digest size; 160 pp.; monthly; 3/6.
Editors: K. Bonfiglioli, Mar 1966—Sep 1966, with Associate Editor K. Roberts; Editor in Chief H. Harrison, Oct 1966—Feb 1967, with Managing Editor K. Roberts.
Publisher: Roberts & Vinter Ltd., London.

Actually a continuation of *Science-Fantasy* (which ceased in Feb 1966 after 81 issues), this magazine published some quite notable material, much of which has since appeared in book form. Some original U.S. material also was used. Keith Roberts painted most covers.

Notable Fiction:
1966 Mar "You and Me and the Continuum" (short), J. G. Ballard; "Pavane" series, K. Roberts, began.
    Apr "Homecalling" (sr2), J. Merril
    May "Seventh Moon," John Rankine
    Jun "Hatchetman" (n'te), M. Reynolds
    Aug *Make Room! Make Room!* (sr3), H. Harrison
    Oct "Day Million" (short), F. Pohl
    Nov *The Ice Schooner* (sr3), M. Moorcock

Issues:

	Jan	Feb	Mar	Apr	May	Jun	Jul	Aug	Sep	Oct	Nov	Dec	W
1966			1/1	1/2	1/3	1/4	1/5	1/6	1/7	1/8	1/9	1/10	10
1967	1/11	1/12											12

INFINITY SCIENCE FICTION   U.S.   Science fiction
20 issues (Nov 1955—Nov 1958)
Digest size; 130 pp.; 9 per year; 35¢.
Editor: L. Shaw.
Publisher: Royal Publications, New York.

Shaw began this magazine after leaving J. L. Quinn at *If*. The fiction presented was at times quite thought-provoking and also of high quality. Each issue usually reprinted some noteworthy piece of fan writing. Most book reviews were done by D. Knight; the last three were by R. Silverberg. All covers except the first were painted by Emsh(willer). *Science Fiction Adventures* was a companion magazine with a more space-opera type of material.

Notable Fiction:
1955 Nov "The Star" (short), A. C. Clarke [Hugo winner]
1956 Feb "The Engineer" (short), F. Pohl & C. M. Kornbluth
    Jun "The Stilled Platter" (short), J. E. Gunn
    Dec "The Superstition-Seeders" (short novel), E. Wellen
1957 Jun "The Band Played On" (n'te), L. del Rey
    Sep "The Other Side of the Sky," A. C. Clarke [3 short stories, with 3 more in Oct]; "Dio," D. Knight
1958 Jan *And Then the Town Took Off* (sr2), R. Wilson
    Mar "The Leaf" (short), R. F. Young
    Apr "Leg. Forst." (n'te), C. D. Simak
    Jun *Recalled to Life* (sr2), R. Silverberg
    Oct *The Silent Invaders*, C. M. Knox [R. Silverberg]

Issues:

	Jan	Feb	Mar	Apr	May	Jun	Jul	Aug	Sep	Oct	Nov	Dec	W
1955											1/1		1
1956		1/2				1/3		1/4		1/5		1/6	6
1957		2/1		2/2		2/3	2/4		2/5	2/6	3/1		13
1958	3/2		3/3	3/4		3/5		3/6		4/1	4/2		20

INSIGHT   British   Macabre reviews
2 issues—No. 1 *ca.* 1964, No. 2 *ca.* 1965, not dated.
Size 7 x 9½ in.; 16 pp. including covers; 1/-.
Edited and published by Henry K. Simmonds and Jeremy Pender, from Battersea, London.

A very creditable attempt at reviewing macabre material and printing some current film stills. No. 2—biography of R. Matheson; "A Look at Vincent Price"; film reviews of *The Unearthly* and *The Masque of the Red Death*. No. 2—biography of Roger Corman; film reviews of *The Black Sleep* and *Shock Corridor*. Both issues also had book reviews.

INTERNATIONAL SCIENCE FICTION   U.S.   Science fiction
2 issues (1/1, Nov 1967; 1/2, June 1968).
Digest size; 130 pp.; 50¢.
Editor: F. Pohl.
Publisher: Galaxy Pub. Corp., New York.

An interestingly conceived magazine printing or reprinting fiction from many countries of the world.

No. 1—*U.S.S.R.*: 1 story by A. Strugatsky, 2 by I. Varshavsky, article by J. Kogarlitsky. *Germany*: 2 stories by H. W. Mommers & E. Vleck in collaboration, article by W. Ernsting. *Netherlands*: story by J. L. Mahe. *Italy*: story and article by L. Cozzi, story by F. C. Gozzini. *France*: story by M. Ehrwein. *Australia*: story by D. Broderick. *England*: story by R. Presslie, another by P. E. High.

No. 2—Only article is on I. Yefremov's *Andromeda*. Stories from: *U.S.S.R.*: E. Parnov & M. Yemtsew (collab.), by A. Dneprov (2), R. Yarov. *Netherlands*: G. Gils. *France*: J. Ruabe, N. Charles-Henneberg. *Italy*: A. Mussi. *Austria*: C. Feiber. *Poland*: G. Altow. *Chile*: H. Corre. *India*: B. S. Rao.

J,K,L

JEWEL [literal translation]   Japanese   General fiction
1 issue in 1956, 322 pp., publishing the following:

"Conqueror's Isle" (short), N. S. Bond; "Dr. M's Discovery," G. Aida; "The Lanson Screen" (n'te), A. L. Zagat; "Strange Playmate" (short), I. Asimov; "Farewell Earth!" U. Yumeza; "En Route to Pluto" (short), W. West; "The Time Machine," H. G. Wells; some articles.

JULES VERNE MAGASINET   Swedish   Science fiction/adventure
330 issues (16 Oct 1940—8th issue of 1947); weekly.
Title change: From Vol. 2 No. 28 the subtitle *Veckans Aventyr* ("Adventures of the Week") gradually supplanted the original title.

This started with mostly translations from contemporary U.S. sf magazines. It often used front and back covers from *Amazing Stories* as well as the interior illustrations accompanying the original story. It was juvenile in outlook and contained much non-sf. With the change in title westerns began to appear and take over the story content; late issues ran American comics such as *Superman* and *Jungle Jim*.
Notable Fiction:
1940 "Five Steps to Tomorrow," E. Binder (#1-#7); "Sons of the Deluge," N. S. Bond (#1-#7)
1941 "The Magician of Mars," E. Hamilton (#46/1941-#6/1942); "The Triumph of Captain Future," E. Hamilton (#32-#43)
1942 "The Water World," O. J. Friend (#28-#39); *The Kid From Mars*, O. J. Friend (#6-#19); "Captain Future and the Space Stones," E. Hamilton (#10-#25); "Outlaws of the Moon," E. Hamilton (#41/1942-#2/1943)
1943 *A Yank at Valhalla*, E. Hamilton (#19-#33); "The Lost World of Time," E. Hamilton (#5-#18); "The Comet Kings," E. Hamilton (#51/1943-#16/1944)
1944 "After an Age," E. Binder (#20-#46); *Warrior of the Dawn*, H. Browne (#18-#38); *City of Glass*, N. Loomis (#3-#18)
1945 "The Giant Atom," M. Jameson (#38-#47) [*Atomic Bomb*]; "The Magic Moon," B. Sterling [E. Hamilton] (#33-#45)
1946 "Murder in Space," D. V. Reed (#17-#35)

JUNGLE STORIES   U.S.   Adventure-fantasy
Two series:
(1) 3 issues (Aug, Oct, Dec 1931); 160 pp.; 25¢.
    Editor: H. A. McComas; **Publisher:** Clayton Magazines.
(2) 59 issues (Win 1939—Spr 1954); quarterly, occasionally missing issues.
    Publisher: Glen-Kel, U.S.
The first series are now collector's items. The second series was based around the character "Ki-Gor," a Tarzan-like inhabitant of Africa, with his mate Helen Vaughan and friend M'Gesso, chief of the pygmies. All stories in the second series, except the first, were by John Peter Drummond. All titles are listed in *The Hero-Pulp Index*, McKinstry & Weinberg (1970).
British Edition:
At least 5 issues *ca.* 1950.
Pulp size; No. 1 at 9d, remainder 1/-.
Publisher: Pembertons (of Manchester) Ltd.
Each issue contained several stories, with the main ones and date of U.S. original being:

No. 1 "The Mad Monster of Mu-Ungu"; "The Chained God" (Fall 1949)
No. 2 "The Sword of Sheba" (Win 1950)
No. 3 "Lost Princess of the Nile" (Spr 1950)
No. 4 "The Beast Gods of Atlantis" (Sum 1950)
No. 5 "Voodoo Slaves for the Devil's Daughter" (Fall 1950)
    No further issues are known.

KA-ZAR   U.S.   Adventure fantasy
3 issues (Oct 1936, Jan 1937, June 1937).
Size 10 x 7 in.; 128 pp. first two, then 112 pp.; all 10¢.
Publisher: Manvis Publications.
A one-character novel magazine detailing the adventures of Ka-Zar, a white man raised by lions in the African Congo. He had no mate, but could speak with animals. The last issue was titled *Ka-Zar the Great*. The stories, all by Robert Byrd, are listed in *The Hero-Pulp Index*, McKinstry & Weinberg (1970).

LONDON MYSTERY MAGAZINE   British   Mystery
A magazine of interest, this was founded and edited by Michael Hall—The London Mystery Magazine Ltd., London. It was a little larger than digest size. The first issue was labelled only Vol. 1 No. 1 (approx. Dec 1949); No. 2 was Mar 1950; Nos. 3 to 15 were dated Apr-May 1950, June-July 1950, etc. through to Apr-May 1952. It cost 2/6.
After a break in publication the magazine was bought by Norman Kark Publications Ltd., London, with Austen Kark; he was replaced from No. 20. Issue No. 16 was Mar 1953 and the magazine then became a regular quarterly dated Mar, June, Sep, Dec, except for a few strange variations such as No. 24 being Feb 1955, No. 41 Apr 1959, No. 49 May 1961, and No. 51 Nov 1961, though it was still regular overall. It is still current.
Notable authors have included Algernon Blackwood, John Collier, Edmund Cooper, L. P. Davies, Gerald Kersh, Arthur Porges, A. E. Murch, Rosemary Timperley, and Muriel Spark. These and others wrote some weird fiction. The cartoons were of note, especially in the early issues; many Mendoza cartoons were reprinted in early issues of *Fantastic Stories of Imagination*.
The volume *Mystery* (Hulton, London, 1952) is an anthology selected from this magazine; it was edited anonymously, with the initials A.L.G.C. at the end of the preface. The book gives over 30 stories and a number of Mendoza cartoons.

LUCHADORES DEL ESPACIO   Spanish   Science fiction
Presented much the same kind of material as *Espacio*.

LUNA-WELTALL (Luna-Utopia-Roman)   German   Science fiction
52 issues (*ca.* Aug 1956—early 1959); 66 pp.; 60 pfennigs.
Editor: M. Gollmer.
Publisher: Walter Lehning Verlag, Hanover.
Rather juvenile in nature, this reprinted original German space-opera by such authors as W. Coover, W. D. Rohr, J. E. Wells, and K. H. Scheer. Only two British works were reprinted: *The Echoing Worlds*, J. Burke (No. 7) and *From What Far Star?*, B. Berry (No. 47).

M

MACABRE   U.S.   Weird
At least 21 issues (June 1957—1970).
Various sizes; saddle-stapled; semiannual; 24 pp.; 40¢.
Editor and Publisher: J. P. Brennan, New Haven, Connecticut.
This is more of an amateur magazine. It presented fiction, poetry, and also magazine and book reviews. Authors included the editor, Robert F. Young, and Lee Priestley.

MAD   U.S.   Comic

This noted comic magazine began with the Oct-Nov 1952 issue. Published by Wm. Gaines (Educational Comics Inc.), it started as a bimonthly comic book at 10¢, became monthly with No. 9 (Mar 1954), and with No. 24 (July 1955) went to large size and 25¢. Harvey Kurtzman was Editor to 1955. It is noted for its satirisation and lampooning of noted comic strips, movies, ways of life etc., with take-offs on *Buck Rogers, Mandrake*, and the like. A companion, *Panic*, began around Dec 1953 but later ceased. Imitators have included *Cracked*.

The magazine is still current, has had regular annuals, and selections reprinted in paperback and hardcovers. The paperback series began with Ballantine's *The Mad Reader* in 1954; the series switched to Signet in 1959, where the first title was *The Bedside Mad*. A British edition of *Mad* ran to at least No. 86.

MAGAZINE OF FANTASY AND SCIENCE FICTION, THE [*F&SF*]
                    U.S.   Science fiction and fantasy
Current (Fall 1949—); 211th issue, Dec 1968.
Digest size; 130 pp.; monthly; 35¢ to 50¢ (see below).
Title change: First issue, Fall 1949, was titled *The Magazine of Fantasy*.
Editors: A. Boucher and J. F. McComas jointly, Fall 1949—Aug 1954; A. Boucher alone, Sep 1954—Aug 1958 (with R. P. Mills as Managing Editor); R. P. Mills, Sep 1958—Mar 1962; A. Davidson, Apr 1962—Nov 1964; J. W. Ferman, Dec 1964—Dec 1965; E. L. Ferman (formerly Managing Editor), Jan 1966—. Ted White was Assistant Editor and then Associate Editor from Nov 1963 to May 1968.
Publisher: Fantasy House Inc., New York [a subsidiary of Ellery Queen]; from Feb 1968, Mercury Press, New York [Joseph W. Ferman].
Frequency, etc.: Began as quarterly and moved through bimonthly to monthly from Aug 1952. Priced at 35¢ to Dec 1958 (except 40¢ for Oct 1958 Ninth Anniversary issue), 40¢ Jan 1959—Dec 1964 (except 50¢ and 162 pp. for Oct 1959 Tenth Anniversary issue), then 50¢.
Cover Artists: These have included C. Bonestell, E. Emsh(willer), J. Coggins, M. Hunter, K. Freas, and J. Gaughan. Nov 1963 had one of H. Bok's last covers. Many covers have been wrap-around. The space flight and astronomical covers have been considered the best in the field for their atmosphere of realism.
Review:

This magazine was rated one of the "Big Three" (with *Astounding* and *Galaxy*) as soon as it appeared. It had the widest story scope, printing both original material and out-of-the-normal reprints (though the latter have not been so dominant in the 1960's). It was runner-up for the magazine Hugo Award in 1956 and 1957, eventually winning it in 1958 and holding it for 1959 and 1960, and winning again in 1963. The quality has since tapered off, with the printing of much pointless fiction. There is usually an all-star (anniversary) issue in October.

The book reviews were first done by A. Boucher, to Jan 1959, then D. Knight Apr 1959—Sep 1960, A. Bester, Oct 1960—Aug 1962, A. Davidson Aug 1962—Aug 1963; J. Merril took over from Mar 1965. Some special "appreciation" issues for authors have appeared: T. Sturgeon, Sep 1962; R. Bradbury, May 1963; I. Asimov, Oct 1966.

A companion magazine *Venture Science Fiction* began in Jan 1957, and after it ceased this name was incorporated in the overall *F&SF* title from July 1959 [*Venture* since reappeared for a brief period from May 1969].

F&SF stories have been regularly anthologised in the *Best From Fantasy and Science Fiction* annuals, with the 17th series in 1968. [These are covered under compilers A. Boucher, R. P. Mills, A. Davidson, and E. L. Ferman.] Other anthologies directly selected from its pages are *No Limits* [J. W. Ferman], 1964; *Once and Future Tales From the Magazine of Fantasy and Science Fiction* [E. L. Ferman], 1968; *A Decade of Fantasy and Science Fiction* [R. P. Mills], 1960.

Notable Fiction:
1949 Fall "The Hurkle Is a Happy Beast" (short), T. Sturgeon
1950 Win "The Gnurrs Come From the Voodvork Out" (short), R. Bretnor; "Gavagan's Bar" series, L. S. de Camp & F. Pratt, began; reprint of a "Murchison Morks" series story, R. Arthur
       Sum "Huge Beast" (short), C. Cartmill; "Born of Man and Woman" (short), R. Matheson [title story of collection]
       Fall "The Silly Season" (short), C. M. Kornbluth; first of "C. P. Ransom" series, H. Nearing

Dec "The Listening Child" (short), Idris Seabright
1951 Feb "My Brother's Wife" (short), W. Tucker
    Apr "The Last Seance" (short, 1926), Agatha Christie
    Aug "John Thomas's Cube" (short, 1945), J. Leimert
    Oct "Of Time and Third Avenue" (short), A. Bester; "Jane Brown's Body," C. Woolrich
    Dec "John the Minstrel" series, M. W. Wellman, began [see *Who Fears the Devil*]; "The Earlier Service" (short, 1935), Marg. Irwin
1952 Feb "Jizzle" (short, *Collier's*, 1949), J. Wyndham [title story of collection]
    Apr "SRL Ad" (short), R. Matheson; "Sealskin Trousers" (n'te, 1947), E. Linklater
    Aug "Nine-Finger Jack" (short), A. Boucher
    Sep "The Fly" (short), A. Porges
    Oct First of "People" series, Z. Henderson [see *Pilgrimage*, etc.]; "The Third Level" (short, 1951), J. Finney [title story of collection]
    Nov "Bring the Jubilee", W. Moore [enlarged as book]
1953 Feb "One in Three Hundred" (n'te), J. T. McIntosh [J. M. MacGregor] [with sequels as *One in 300*]
    Apr "Beggars All" (n'te), J. T. McIntosh [J. M. MacGregor]
    May "Snulbug" (short), A. Boucher; "Lot" (n'te), W. Moore [had sequel]
    Jun "The Preserving Machine" (short), P. K. Dick
    Jul "The Hypnoglyph" (short), J. Anthony
    Sep *Three Hearts and Three Lions* (sr2), P. Anderson
    Oct "Father Carmody" series, P. J. Farmer, began; "The Ruum" (short), A. Porges
    Nov "The Silken-Swift" (n'te), T. Sturgeon
1954 Mar "5,271,009" (n'te), A. Bester
    May "Star Lummox" (sr3), R. A. Heinlein [*The Star Beast*]
    Jun "Heirs Apparent" (n'te), R. Abernathy
    Aug "Fondly Fahrenheit" (n'te), A. Bester
    Nov "Dead Center" (n'te), J. Merril
1955 Jan "The Singing Bell" (short), I. Asimov [first of "Wendell Urth" series]
    Feb "The Climbing Wave," M. Z. Bradley
    Mar "The Golem" (short), A. Davidson; story in "Hoka" series (continued from another magazine), P. Anderson & G. R. Dickson
    Apr "A Canticle for Leibowitz" (short), W. M. Miller (first of series, in book of same title)
    May "Time Patrol" series, P. Anderson, began [see *Guardians of Time*]
    Aug "Two-Handed Engine" (n'te), H. Kuttner & C. L. Moore
    Oct "Project Nursemaid" (short novel), J. Merril
    Nov "The (Widget), the (Wadget) and Boff" (sr2), T. Sturgeon [see *Aliens 4*]
1956 Jan "The Cosmic Charge Account" (n'te), C. M. Kornbluth; "The Jet-Propelled Couch" (article, 1954), R. Lindner [enlarged, in *The Fifty-Minute Hour*]
    Apr "Shock Treatment" (n'te), J. F. McComas
    Jun "The Asa Rule" (short), Jay Williams
    Sep "Operation Afreet" (n'te), P. Anderson [first of "Stephen Matuchek" series]
    Oct *The Door Into Summer* (sr3), R. A. Heinlein; "Anything Box" (short), Z. Henderson [title story of collection]
    Dec "Stranger Station" (n'te), D. Knight; "Venture to the Moon" (comprising 2 short-shorts, plus others in next 2 issues), A. C. Clarke
1957 Mar "Visit to a Small Planet" (play), G. Vidal
    Apr "Anthropological Note" (n'te), M. Leinster [W. F. Jenkins]
    Jun *Night of Light*, P. J. Farmer [in "Father Carmody" series]
    Jul "Ms. Found in a Chinese Fortune Cookie" (short), C. M. Kornbluth
    Aug "The Menace From Earth" (n'te), R. A. Heinlein [title story of collection]
    Sep "Goddess in Granite" (n'te), R. F. Young
    Oct "The Lamp of Alhazred" (1957), A. Derleth & H. P. Lovecraft

Nov "A for Anything" (n'te), D. Knight [see *The People Maker*]

Dec "Holdout" (short), R. Sheckley

1958 Jan "A Touch of Strange" (short), T. Sturgeon [title story of collection]

Apr "A Deskful of Girls" (n'te), F. Leiber; "Guardian Spirit" (n'te), C. Oliver

May "The Prize of Peril" (short), R. Sheckley

Jul "Gil Braltar" (short, 1887), J. Verne; "Theory of Rocketry" (short), C. M. Kornbluth

Aug *Have Space Suit— Will Travel* (sr3), R. A. Heinlein

Sep "Casey Agonistes" (short), R. M. McKenna; "That Hellbound Train" (short), R. Bloch

1959 Jan "The Silver Eggheads" (n'te), F. Leiber [enlarged as book]; "Ferdinand Feghoot" vignettes, G. Briarton [R. Bretnor], became a regular feature.

Feb "What Rough Beast?" (n'te), D. Knight

Mar " 'All You Zombies—' " (short), R. A. Heinlein; "The Sky People" (n'te), P. Anderson

Apr "Flowers for Algernon" (n'te), D. Keyes [enlarged as book]

Jun "The Alley Man" (n'te), P. J. Farmer [in *The Alley God*]

Jul "To Fell a Tree" (n'te), R. F. Young

Aug "The Walker-Through-Walls" (short, 1943), M. Aymé [title story of collection]

Oct "The Man Who Lost the Sea" (short), T. Sturgeon; "Starship Soldier" (sr2), R. A. Heinlein [*Starship Troopers*]

Nov "The Martian Shop" (n'te), H. Fast

1960 Jan "The Blind Pilot" (short), C. Henneberg

Mar "All the Traps of Earth" (short), C. D. Simak

Apr "Among the Dangs" (n'te, 1958), G. P. Elliott

May "Open to me, My Sister" (n'te), P. J. Farmer

Jul *To the Tombaugh Station*, W. Tucker

Oct "Inside the Comet" (short), A. C. Clarke

Dec "Rogue Moon" (short novel), A. Budrys [enlarged as book]

1961 Jan "The Sources of the Nile" (n'te), A. Davidson

Feb "Hothouse" series, B. Aldiss, began [*The Long Afternoon of Earth*]

Apr "The Ship Who Sang" (short), A. McCaffrey

Jun "Alpha Ralpha Boulevard" (n'te), C. Smith [P. Linebarger]

Oct "The World of Myrion Flowers" (short), F. Pohl & C. M. Kornbluth; *Naked to the Stars* (sr2), G. R. Dickson

1962 Feb "The Garden of Time" (short), J. G. Ballard; "Pirate Island" (short), J. Nesvadba (others later in the year)

Mar "Jonathan and the Space Whale" (n'te), R. F. Young

Apr "Moon Fishers" (short), C. Henneberg

Aug "The Secret Songs" (short), F. Leiber

Oct "The Journey of Joenes" (sr2), R. Sheckley [*Journey Beyond Tomorrow*]

1963 Feb "Satan Mekatrig" (n'te, 1899), I. Zangwill

Mar "Hunter, Come Home" (n'te), R. McKenna

Jun "No Truce With Kings," P. Anderson [in *Time and Stars*]

Jul *Glory Road* (sr3), R. A. Heinlein

Oct "They Don't Make Life Like They Used To" (n'te), A. Bester

Nov "A Rose for Ecclesiastes" (n'te), R. Zelazny

Dec "The Tree of Time" (sr2), D. Knight [*Beyond the Barrier*]; "What Strange Stars and Skies" (short), A. Davidson

1964 Feb "Burning Spear" (n'te), K. Denton

Mar "Automatic Tiger" (short), K. Reed

Jul "Cantata 140" (short novel), P. K. Dick [*The Crack in Space*]

Dec "The Fatal Eggs" (short novel), M. Bulgakov

1965 Feb "Marque and Reprisal," P. Anderson [see *The Star Fox*]

Mar "The Doors of His Face, the Lamps of His Mouth" (n'te), R. Zelazny

Jul *Rogue Dragon*, A. Davidson

Sep "The Saliva Tree" (n'te), B. W. Aldiss

Oct "And Call Me Conrad" (sr2), R. Zelazny [*This Immortal*]

Dec "Cugel" series, J. Vance, began [*The Eyes of the Overworld*]

1966 Jan "L'Arc de Jeanne" (short), R. F. Young

Apr "We Can Remember It for You Wholesale" (n'te), P. K. Dick

Aug *The Productions of Time* (sr2), J. Brunner

Oct "The Key" (n'te), I. Asimov

Nov "The Manor of Roses" (short novel), T. B. Swann

1967 Jan *The Little People*, J. Christopher [C. S. Youd]

Feb "The Hall of the Dead" (n'te), R. E. Howard & L. S. de Camp

Mar "Zoomen" (short), F. Hoyle

Jun "Death and the Executioner" (n'te), R. Zelazny; appreciation and bibliography of Charles Beaumont

Jul "The Day Before Forever" (short novel), K. Laumer

Oct "Home the Hard Way" (n'te), R. McKenna

Nov "The Sword Swallower" (n'te), R. Goulart [enlarged as book]

Dec "The Cloud Sculptors of Coral D" (short), J. G. Ballard

1968 Feb "Stranger in the House" (short novel), Kate Wilhelm; "The Veiled Feminists of Atlantis" (short, 1926), B. Tarkington

Mar "The Egg of the Glak" (n'te), H. Jacobs

Apr "Final War" (n'te), K. M. O'Donnell [B. Malzberg]

Jun "The People Trap" (short), R. Sheckley [title story of collection]

Jul *Sos the Rope* (sr3), P. Anthony [P. Jacob]; "Remote Projection" (short), G. Apollinaire

Dec "Gadget Man" (n'te), R. Goulart

Issues (semi-annual indexes in June and Dec issues):

	Jan	Feb	Mar	Apr	May	Jun	Jul	Aug	Sep	Oct	Nov	Dec	W
1949										1/1 (Fall)			1
1950	1/2 (Win-Spr)						1/3 (Sum)			1/4 (Fall)		1/5	5
1951		2/1		2/2		2/3		2/4		2/5		2/6	11
1952		3/1		3/2		3/3		3/4	3/5	3/6	3/7	3/8	19
1953	4/1	4/2	4/3	4/4	4/5	4/6	5/1	5/2	5/3	5/4	5/5	5/6	31
1954	6/1	6/2	6/3	6/4	6/5	6/6	7/1	7/2	7/3	7/4	7/5	7/6	43
1955	8/1	8/2	8/3	8/4	8/5	8/6	9/1	9/2	9/3	9/4	9/5	9/6	55
1956	10/1	10/2	10/3	10/4	10/5	10/6	11/1	11/2	11/3*	11/4	11/5	11/6	67
1957	12/1	12/2	12/3	12/4	12/5	12/6	13/1	13/2	13/3	13/4	13/5	13/6	79
1958	14/1	14/2	14/3	14/4	14/5	14/6	15/1	15/2	15/3	15/4	15/5	15/6	91
1959	16/1	16/2	16/3	16/4	16/5	16/6	17/1	17/2	17/3	17/4	17/5	17/6	103
1960	18/1	18/2	18/3	18/4	18/5	18/6	19/1	19/2	19/3	19/4	19/5	19/6	115
1961	20/1	20/2	20/3	20/4	20/5	20/6	21/1	21/2	21/3	21/4	21/5	21/6	127
1962	22/1	22/2	22/3	22/4	22/5	22/6	23/1	23/2	23/3	23/4	23/5	23/6	139
1963	24/1	24/2	24/3	24/4	24/5	24/6	25/1	25/2	25/3	25/4	25/5	25/6	151
1964	26/1	26/2	26/3	26/4	26/5	26/6	27/1	27/2	27/3	27/4	27/5	27/6	163
1965	28/1	28/2	28/3	28/4	28/5	28/6	29/1	29/2	29/3	29/4	29/5	29/6	175
1966	30/1	30/2	30/3	30/4	30/5	30/6	31/1	31/2	31/3	31/4	31/5	31/6	187
1967	32/1	32/2	32/3	32/4	32/5	32/6	33/1	33/2	33/3	33/4	33/5	33/6	199
1968	34/1	34/2	34/3	34/4	34/5	34/6	35/1	35/2	35/3	35/4	35/5	35/6	211

* Misdated 1955 on spine.

Australian Edition:

14 issues (1954—1958), numbered but not dated.

Publisher: Consolidated Press, Sydney, N.S.W.

Digest size; saddle-stapled; 128 pp. to No. 6, 112 pp. from No. 7, 96 pp. from No. 11; quarterly; 2/-.

This edition reprinted material from the U.S. originals, but only as selections, not complete issues. It serialised "Star Lummox" (from No. 4), gave the last two stories of the trilogy comprising *A Canticle for Leibowitz*, and only the first and last of the *One in 300* trilogy.

Issues:

	Jan	Feb	Mar	Apr	May	Jun	Jul	Aug	Sep	Oct	Nov	Dec	W
1954												#1	1
1955		2			3			4			5		5
1956		6			7			8			9		9
1957	10					11							11
1958	12			13			14						14

British Edition:

Two series:

(1) 12 issues (1953-54). Digest size; 1/6.

    Publisher: Mellifont Press, London.

    Contents selected from various U.S. originals.

(2) 56 issues (Dec 1959—June 1964). Digest size; start 128 pp.; from Jan 1961, 112 pp.; Dec 1961, 128 pp.; May 1962, 112 pp.; monthly; 2/-, later 2/6.

    Publisher: Atlas, London.

    Again, a general selection from various U.S. issues.

In 1965 J. L. Durie compiled and published an index to the British editions of *F&SF* with cross references to the original U.S. editions (quarto, duplicated, 44 pp., 6/-).

French Edition: See *FICTION*

German Edition:

This is a paperback series from Heyne, selected and mostly translated by W. Ernsting. It started in early 1960 and was at its 20th selection in early 1968.

Italian Edition: See *FANTASCIENZA* and *FANTASIA E FANTA-SCIENZA*

Japanese Edition: See *S-F MAGAZINE*

Mexican Edition (in Spanish): See *CIENCIA Y FANTASIA*

MAGAZINE OF HORROR, THE   U.S.   Weird

(Aug 1963 — Apr 1971); 24th issue, Nov 1968.

Digest size; 130 pp.; first issues side-stapled, then saddle-stapled from No. 4 (May 1964); 50¢.

Editor: R.A.W. Lowndes.

Publisher: Health Knowledge Inc., New York.

Up to No. 6 the contents page gave *The Magazine of Horror and Strange Stories*; from No. 7 the subtitle changed to *Strange Tales and Science Fiction*, and from No. 15 to *the Bizarre and the Unusual*.

A magazine for weird enthusiasts, this has mainly reprinted notable stories from *Weird Tales* and other old sources, with a few original short stories. It was very capably edited by Lowndes, with interesting and knowledgeable lead-ins to most stories, and did much to keep the classical (or near classic) weird stories in print. Book reviews have been presented at times, and the letter department "It Is Written" did much to build up a sense of comradeship within the magazine.

Notable Fiction [many reprints by H. G. Wells, A. Bierce, E. A. Poe, R. Kipling, and R. W. Chambers not covered]:

1963 Aug "The Man With a Thousand Legs" (n'te, 1927), F. B. Long
1964 Feb "The Seeds of Death" (n'te, 1964), D. H. Keller; "The Place of Pythons" (short, 1931), A. J. Burks
  May "The Dreams in the Witch-House" (n'te, 1933), H. P. Lovecraft
  Sep "Cassius" (n'te, 1931), H. S. Whitehead
  Nov "Caverns of Horror" (n'te, 1933), L. Manning [first of "Strange Club" series to appear; followed by others]
1965 Jan "The Phantom Farmhouse" (n'te, 1923), S. Quinn
  Apr "The Dead Who Walk" (n'te, 1931), R. Cummings
  Jun "The Night Wire" (short, 1926), H. F. Arnold; "Skulls in the Stars" (short, 1928), R. E. Howard
  Nov "The Devil's Pool" (n'te, 1932), Greye La Spina
  Win "The Black Beast" (n'te, 1931), H. S. Whitehead
1966 Sum "Almost Immortal" (n'te, 1916), A. Hall
  Win "The Monster-God of Mamurth" (n'te, 1926), E. Hamilton
1967 Spr "The Room of Shadows" (n'te, 1936), A. J. Burks
  Sum "Night and Silence" (short, 1932), M. Level; "The Dog That Laughed" (short, 1931), C. W. Diffin
  Fall "The Laughing Duke" (n'te, 1932), W. West; "Williamson" (short, ?), H. S. Whitehead; "The Curse of Amen-Ra" (n'te, 1932), V. Rousseau [V. R. Emanuel]
  Nov "In Amundsen's Tent" (short, 1928), J. M. Leahy; "Wolves of Darkness" (short novel, 1932), J. Williamson
1968 Jan "The Red Witch" (n'te, 1932), N. Dyalhis; "The Last of Placide's Wife" (n'te, 1932), K. Mashburn
  Mar "A Cry From Beyond" (n'te, 1931), V. Rousseau [E. R. Emanuel]; "The Monsters" (n'te, 1933), M. Leinster [W. F. Jenkins]
  May "Kings of the Night" (n'te, 1930), R. E. Howard; "The Dark Star" (n'te, 1937), G. G. Pendarves
  Jul "Worms of the Earth" (n'te, 1932), R. E. Howard
  Sep "The Abyss" (sr2, 1948), D. H. Keller; "The Leapers" (1942), R.A.W. Lowndes
  Nov "Once in a Thousand Years" (n'te, 1935), F. B. Middleton; "Four Prose-Poems," H. P. Lovecraft

Issues [always numbered as well as Vol. No.]:

	Jan	Feb	Mar	Apr	May	Jun	Jul	Aug	Sep	Oct	Nov	Dec	W
1963					1 (1/1)				2 (1/2)				2
1964	3 (1/3)			4 (1/4)				5 (1/5)		6 (1/6)			6

[*cont.*]

	Jan	Feb	Mar	Apr	May	Jun	Jul	Aug	Sep	Oct	Nov	Dec	W
1965	7 (2/1)			8 (2/2)		9 (2/3)	10 (2/4)			11 (2/5)			11
1966		2/6 (Win)*				3/1 (Sum)				3/2 (Win)			14
1967			3/3 (Spr)			3/4 (Sum)			3/5 (Fall)		3/6		18
1968	19 (4/1)		20 (4/2)		21 (4/3)		22 (4/4)		23 (4/5)		24 (4/6)		24

* Winter 1965/1966.

MAGIC CARPET, THE   See *ORIENTAL STORIES*

MARK POWERS, der Held des Weltalls   German   Science fiction

47 issues (early 1963 — 1964).

Size 8¾ x 6⅛ in.; 64 pp.; 70 pfennigs.

Publisher: Erich Pabel, Baden.

After the incredible success of *Perry Rhodan*, which had first been offered to Pabel by W. Ernsting and K. H. Scheer and rejected, Pabel looked for a rival. W. W. Shols (Winifried Shols) was commissioned as chief author of a team which included Alf Tjornsen, W. P. Hoffmans, Jeff Mescalero, Axel Nord, H. G. Francis, and M. Wegener, to produce "Mark Powers — The Hero of the Universe," adventure stories in the style of Flash Gordon.

The first 16 adventures of Mark Powers were printed in *Utopia Zukunftsroman*, the first in No. 320 and the 16th in No. 352. This new magazine was then launched to give his further adventures. *Mark Powers* was never much of a success with either readers or critics but rode for a period on the *Perry Rhodan* success wave.

MARVEL SCIENCE FICTION   See *MARVEL SCIENCE STORIES*

MARVEL SCIENCE STORIES   U.S.   Science fiction

Two series: 9 issues (Aug 1938 — Apr 1941); 6 issues (Nov 1950 — May 1952).

Title changes: *Marvel Science Stories*, Aug 1938 — Aug 1939; *Marvel Tales*, Dec 1939 — Nov 1940; *Marvel Stories*, Apr 1941; *Marvel Science Stories*, Nov 1950 — May 1951; *Marvel Science Fiction*, Aug 1951 — May 1952.

Editor: R. O. Erisman [with D. Keyes on some of 2nd series].

Publishers: First series, Postal Pub. for 2 issues, then Western Fiction. Second series, Stadium Corp.

Format: First series, pulp size; 130 pp.; bimonthly?; 15¢. Second series, pulp size first two and last, other three digest size; 130 pp.; quarterly; 25¢.

Review:

This was one of the earliest magazines to enter the science fiction field against the three established magazines of the late 1930's. It did not give serious opposition. Although it printed some good material in it is mainly remembered as the first magazine to bring sex into the field. This first series had *Dynamic Science Stories* as a companion.

The second series was of better quality, especially in the digest-size issues, but the last issue was only fair and the magazine ceased unmourned.

Notable Fiction:

1938 Aug "Survival," A. J. Burks[had sequel]
1939 Feb *After World's End*, J. Williamson
  Apr-May "Tomorrow," J. Taine [E. T. Bell]
1940 Nov "The Man Who" (short), A. Fedor & H. Hasse
1951 May "The Ones," Betsy Curtis; "Captain Wyxtphll's Flying Saucer" (short), A. C. Clarke
  Aug "Skag With the Queer Head" (n'te), M. Leinster [W. F. Jenkins]
  Nov "'Will You Walk a Little Faster?'" (short), W. Tenn [P. Klass]
1952 May "Time Was," F. G. Rayer [part of *The Star Seekers*]

Issues:

	Jan	Feb	Mar	Apr	May	Jun	Jul	Aug	Sep	Oct	Nov	Dec	W
1938								1/1		1/2			2
1939	1/3			1/4				1/5			1/6		6
1940			2/1							2/2			8
1941		2/3											9
1950											3/1		10
1951	3/2			3/3				3/4		3/5			14
1952			3/6										15

British Edition:
1 issue: No. 1, not dated (May 1951). Pulp size; 130 pp.
The one issue was a complete reproduction of the Feb 1951 *Marvel Science Stories.*

MARVEL STORIES See *MARVEL SCIENCE STORIES*

MARVEL TALES   U.S.   Science fiction
5 issues (May 1934—Sum 1935).
Digest size, except last issue large size; irregular; 15¢.
Editor: W. L. Crawford, also publisher as Fantasy Publications, Los Angeles.
One of the attempts of a private publisher to add a further sf magazine to the field in the 1930's. The format was quite amateurish; Crawford used his own small printery. It was available mainly by subscription, though the last issue had some newsstand distribution. Quite a few copies of the Spr 1935 (next to last) issue were available several years later in second-hand magazine stores. Only about a thousand copies of each issue appeared, and these are now collector's items. In some case two, three, or four variant covers were used on each issue, so it is nearly impossible to have a complete set. It had a companion, *Unusual Stories.*
Issues and Notable Fiction:
1934 May (1/1) "Celephais" (short), H. P. Lovecraft
     Jul-Aug (1/2) "The Garden of Fear" (n'te), R. E. Howard
     Win (1/3) "Lilies" (short), R. Bloch; *The Titan* (sr3—unfinished), P. S. Miller
1935 Spr (1/4) "The Creator" (n'te), C. D. Simak; "The Nebula of Death" (sr2—unfinished), G. England
     Sum (1/5) "Mars Colonizes" (n'te), M. Breuer

MARVEL TALES See also *MARVEL SCIENCE STORIES*

MÁS ALLÁ   Argentine (Spanish)   Science fiction
48 issues (June 1953—March 1957).
Digest size; monthly.
Published translations of U.S. and British science fiction, mostly from *Galaxy Magazine.* There were illustrations from the original stories, science articles, and a letter department.
Novels and nonfiction serialised included: *The Puppet Masters*, R. A. Heinlein; *The End of the World*, K. Heuer; *Pebble in the Sky*, I. Asimov; *The Space Merchants*, F. Pohl & C. M. Kornbluth; *The Conquest of the Moon*, W. Von Braun; *Costigan's Needle*, J. Sohl; *The Long Loud Silence*, W. Tucker; *The Duplicated Man*, J. Blish.

MASTER THRILLER SERIES   British   Various
A regular series from World's Work, Tadsworth, England, this included westerns, air stories, and some fantasy or weird. The first 19 (at least) were titled *Tales of . . .* ; these were: 1, *. . . the Foreign Legion* (No. 1); 2, *. . . the North West Mounted*; 3, *. . . the Seven Seas*; 4, *. . . Mystery and Detection*; 5, *. . . the Foreign Legion* (No. 2); 6, *. . . the Uncanny*; 7, *. . . African Adventure*; 8, *. . . the Orient*; 9, *. . . the Jungle*; 10, *. . . the Foreign Legion* (No. 3); 11, *. . . the Sea*; 12, *. . . Valour*; 13, *. . . the Levant*; 14, *. . . the Air*; 15, *. . . the Foreign Legion* (No. 4); 16, *. . . Adventure*; 17, *. . . Terror*; 18, *. . . the East and West*; 19, *. . . the Uncanny*. Others known are 26, *Tales of the Far Frontiers* (June 1939); 27, *Tales of the Underworld*; 32, *Ghosts and Haunted Houses* (Dec 1939).
Other titles in the series appear to have been *Fireside Ghost Stories* and *Ghosts and Goblins*, while offshoots were the apparently regular magazines *Mystery and Detection* and *Mystery Stories. Tales of Wonder* may have begun as part of the series but is usually never considered to be in it. Titles within the scope of this encyclopedia are covered separately. There was also a "Master Thriller Novels" series, but this was not science fiction.

MERRITT See *A. MERRITT'S FANTASY MAGAZINE* (in A's)

MIND MAGIC   U.S.   Occult
6 issues (June 1931—Dec 1931).
Title Change: Last two titled *My Self.*
Large size (7½ x 9½ in.); 64 pp.; 20¢.
Editors: August Derleth (Nos. 1 to 4); G. R. Bay (5, 6).

Publisher: Shade Publishing Co.
This published fiction with a strong occult slant and articles on reincarnation, spiritualism, possession, ESP, etc. It used fillers on all sorts of occult subjects. It was considered a poorly edited and arranged magazine with crude covers.

MINOTAURO   Argentine (Spanish)   Science fiction
At least 10 issues.
This Spanish-language edition of *The Magazine of Fantasy and Science Fiction* probably began in 1965; issues known are No. 8, May 1966; No. 9, July 1967; No. 10, June 1968.

MIRACLE SCIENCE AND FANTASY STORIES
                    U.S.   Science fiction
2 issues (Apr/May and June/July 1931).
Pulp size; 138 pp.; bimonthly; 20¢.
Editor: Douglas Dold.
Publisher: Good Story Magazine Co., New York (H. Hersey).
Readable science fiction adventure, now a collector's item. Elliot Dold did the covers and interior illustrations. V. Rousseau [V. R. Emanuel] had a story in each issue.

MODERN ELECTRICS   U.S.   Popularised science
One of the H. Gernsback early electrical magazines, started in 1908. It is of interest because it serialised Gernsback's noted *Ralph 124C 41+* (12 parts from Apr 1911). Jacques Morgan had five stories monthly from Oct 1912 (most later reprinted in Amazing Stories). In 1913 the title changed to *Electrical Experimenter* and in Aug 1920 to *Science and Invention.*

MONDI ASTRALI   Italian   Science fiction
4 issues (Jan—Apr 1955).
Editor: Eggardo Beltrametti.
Publisher: Ed. Gioggi, Rome.

MONSTER MAGAZINES
Following the success of F. J Ackerman's *Famous Monsters of Filmland*, a number of other magazines along these lines were started, but few have lasted.
These include (* = separate entry, *q.v.*):
* *Castle of Frankenstein*—25 issues (Jan 1962—1974).
* *Chilling Monster Tales*—1 issue (1/1, Aug 1966).
* *Famous Films Series*—3 issues (1964).
* *Fantastic Monsters of the Films*—At least 7 issues (1962—1963).
* *For Monsters Only*—9 issues (1965—1972).
* *Horror Monsters*—10 issues (Jan 1961—Win 1964/65), Charlton Publications.
Journal of Frankenstein—Apparently a trial issue, appearing in 1959, of the magazine which was later titled *Castle of Frankenstein.*
Mad Monsters—10 issues (1961—Win 1964), Charlton Publications.
Modern Monsters—4 issues (Apr 1966—Oct/Nov 1966), Prestige Pubs., Los Angeles.
Monster Howls—1 issue (Dec 1966); large, 66 pp., bimonthly?, 35¢; Humor-Vision Inc., New York.
Monster Mania—3 issues (Oct 1966, Jan 1967, Apr 1967); large, 66 pp.; Renaissance Prods., New York.
Monsters and Heroes—At least 7 issues (Jan 1967—May 1970); published by Larry Ivie, Ansonia, N.Y.
* *Monster Parade*—4 issues (late 1958—Mar 1959).
* *Monster World*—10 issues (Nov 1964—Sep 1966).
* *Monsters and Things*—About 5 issues (Jan 1959—?)
Monsters to Laugh With—3 issues (1964); 25¢; Non-Pareil Pub. Co., New York.
* *Screen Thrills and Macabre Stories*—1 issue (Jan 1958).
* *Shriek*—4 issues (1965—1967).
3-D Monsters—1 issue (1964).
* *Werewolves and Vampires*—1 issue (1962).
* *World Famous Creatures*—4 issues (Oct 1958—1959).
The sf magazine *Super-Science Fiction* adopted a monster theme from April 1959, but ceased shortly afterwards.

MONSTER PARADE   U.S.   Monster
6 issues (late 1958—Mar 1959).
Editor: M. J. Shapiro.
Publisher: Magnum Publications Inc., New York.
  Presented horror fiction.

MONSTER WORLD   U.S.   Monster films
10 issues (Nov 1964—Sep 1966).
Large size; 66 pp.; bimonthly; 35¢.
Editor: Forrest J Ackerman.
Publisher: Warren Pubs., New York.

MONSTERS AND THINGS   U.S.   Monster
Two issues (Jan 1959—Apr 1959).
Large size; 48 pp.; bimonthly; 25¢.
Editor: L. Shaw.
Publisher: Magnum Publications, New York.

MOST THRILLING SCIENCE FICTION EVER TOLD
      U.S.   Science fiction reprint
No. 1 (1966—); 11th issue Win 1968 (ceased as *Thrilling SF*, July 1975, 40 issues).
Digest size; first 2, 162 pp., then 130 pp.; quarterly; 50¢.
Publisher: Ultimate Publishing Co., Flushing, N.Y.
  Another magazine of the Cohen reprint chain, using material from the early Ziff-Davis magazines. Like *Great Science Fiction*, it is understood that no royalty was originally given to the authors, but later a nominal payment was made. The name has been changed since the period under review.
Notable Fiction:
1967 No. 6 "Tongues of the Moon," P. J. Farmer
     No. 7 "Thirteen to Centaurus," J. G. Ballard
1968 Fall   "Long Ago, Far Away," M. Leinster [W. F. Jenkins] [*Four From Planet Five*]
     Win   "Gold in the Sky," A. E. Nourse [*Scavengers in Space*]
Issues (not dated until No. 5):

	Jan	Feb	Mar	Apr	May	Jun	Jul	Aug	Sep	Oct	Nov	Dec	W
1966			1			2			3				3
1967	4			5			6 (Fall)			7 (Win)			7
1968		8 (Spr)				9 (Sum)			10 (Fall)		11 (Win)		11

MUNSEY MAGAZINES
  General term for the following titles (published by the Frank A. Munsey Co.): *Golden Argosy* (later *Argosy*), 1882—; *Munsey's Illustrated Weekly*, 1884; *Munsey's Weekly/Magazine*, 1889—1929; *The Puritan*, 1897—1901; *The Quaker*, 1897—1902 (*Junior Munsey*, 1900—); *All-Story Magazine*, 1905—(combined with *Argosy*, 1920); *Railroad Man's Magazine*, 1906—1919; *Scrap Book*, 1906—1907; *Ocean*, 1907—1908 (*Live Wire*, 1908); *Cavalier*, 1908—1914.
  At the end of 1939 there were: *Argosy*; *Detective Fiction Weekly*; *Love Tales*; *Railroad Magazine*; *Double Detective*; *Famous Fantastic Mysteries*. In 1940 were added: *Fantastic Novels*; *Red Star Adventures*; *Red Star Mystery*; *Red Star Western*; *Red Star Detective*; *Big Chief Western*; *Foreign Legion Adventures*; *Cavalier Classics*. By 1943 all had ceased or been sold.

MUNSEY'S MAGAZINE   U.S.   General fiction
2 Feb 1889—Oct 1929.
Title Changes: *Munsey's Weekly*, 1889-1891; then monthly as *Munsey's Magazine*, Oct 1891—1918; *Munsey*, 1918—1929.
Editors: Frank A. Munsey, 1889—1925; R. H. Davis, 1925—1929.
Publisher: Frank A. Munsey Co., New York.
  Like a number of other Munsey magazines, this published some material of interest to the science fiction field. After the Oct 1929 issue it and *Argosy All-Story Weekly* were reorganised to form *Argosy Weekly* and *Munsey's All-Story Magazine*; the latter title published no fantasy or science fiction.
Notable Fiction:
1919 Jan   *The Golden Scorpion* (sr5), S. Rohmer
1921 Jan   "Toys of Fate" (n'te), T. Robbins
1923 Oct   "Sunken Cities" (n'te), D. Newton
1924 May   "Beyond the Pole," P. M. Fisher

MY SELF See *MIND MAGIC*

MYSTERIOUS TRAVELER MAGAZINE, THE
      U.S.   Weird/fantasy
5 issues (four, Nov 1951—June 1952; fifth not dated).
Digest size; 160 pp.; bimonthly; 35¢.
Editor: R. Arthur.
Publisher: Grace Pub. Co., New York.
  Subtitled "Great Stories of Mystery, Detection and Suspense, Old and New." It was issued because of interest in the *Mysterious Traveler* radio programme. The magazine published some fantasy by such authors as Agatha Christie, R. Bradbury, and J. D. Carr. The fifth issue was titled *The Mysterious Traveler Mystery Reader*.

MYSTERY ADVENTURES   U.S.   Mystery/weird
Title Changes: First two issues (at least) titled *New Mystery Adventures*; changed in 1936 to *Mystery Adventure Magazine*; later issues *Mystery Adventures Magazine*.
  It apparently began Mar 1935 (1/1), with monthly issues through to Mar 1937 (5/3), except for May/June 1935 (so dated to bring the month up to date); Austin's *Macabre Index* notes a May 1937 issue as Vol. 5 No. 4, but no further ones are known.
  The first publisher was Pierre Publications Inc., 120 West 42nd St., New York, with A. A. Roberts as Editor (pulp size, 128 pp., monthly, 20¢). By 1936 this had changed to Fiction Magazines Inc., also 120 West 42nd St., New York, with Rev. W. W. Hubbard as Editor (still monthly, but 15¢). In a later issue Stanley Hubbard was listed as Business Manager, and by Jan 1937 Harold Hersey was Editor.
  Norman Saunders appeared to do all the covers (at least those on the issues sighted).
Issues and Stories of Interest (all issues sighted):
1935 Apr (1/2) "Eye of the Monster" (sr2), Richard Sale; "The Flame Fiend," Hugh B. Cave
1935 May/Jun (1/3) "The Cossack" (short), L. R. Hubbard
     Jul (1/4) "Smoked Heads Split" (n'te), R. Sale; "Hell's Legionnaire" (short), L. R. Hubbard
     Dec (2/3) "Master of the Space Ray," N. Schachner
1936 Feb (2/5) "Island of Fear," Richard R. Wallace
     Jun (3/4) "Zenith Rand, Planet Vigilante" (n'te), Richard Tooker (interplanetary)
     Oct (4/2) "Angels of Oorn" (n'te), R. Tooker [in "Zenith Rand" series]; "Flaming Arrows" (n'te), L. R. Hubbard
     Dec (4/4) —
1937 Jan (5/1) —
     Mar (5/3) "Tomb of the Living Dead" (lead n'te), William M. Rouse

MYSTERY AND DETECTION   British   Mystery/weird
At least 7 issues in 1935 [including Apr (1/3), May (1/4), Aug (2/1), Sep (2/2), Oct (2/3)]; 128 pp.; 1/-.
Publisher: World's Work Ltd., Tadsworth, England.
  This was an offshoot of the "Master Thriller" series, with its first issue being No. 4 of that group. It published some weird stories.

MYSTERY NOVELS   U.S.   Mystery/weird
  A mystery magazine for which a complete issue listing is not known. Austin's *Macabre Index* lists stories for Mar 1935 (2/6) and Feb 1936 (3/4), while D. B. Day lists July 1935 (3/2) and Sep 1935 (3/3). The novel in Mar 1935 was "Horror Island," J. W. Vandercock, while Leslie Charteris had a short story, "The Unblemished Bootlegger". For Feb 1936 the novel was "The Crystal Eye," W. R. Randall.

MYSTERY NOVELS AND SHORT STORIES   U.S.   Mystery/weird
  A mystery magazine which published some weird fiction. No complete issue listing is known, but Austin's *Macabre Index* covers issues as follows: Sep 1939 (1/4), 4 novelettes, plus short stories by H. Ward and A. J. Burks; Dec 1939 (1/5), 3 novelettes—one by A. J. Burks, with 4 short stories; Nov 1940 (2/1), 3 novelettes plus other fiction.

MYSTERY STORIES   British   Mystery/weird
At least 22 issues, 1937-38.
Publisher: World's Work, Tadsworth, England.

Apparently an offshoot of the "Master Thriller" series. Issues sighted have been No. 10, *ca.* Spr 1938, 128 pp., subtitled "Tales of Crime, Terror and Detection"; and No. 20, 80 pp., subtitled "Mainly About Ghosts." It was pulp size, 1/-, and gave occasional fantasy. No. 10 had as lead novelette "Wer' Wolf—the Mystery of Chateau Fontmarcelle," B. S. Henderson.

MYSTERY TALES   U.S.   Mystery/weird
About 17 issues (1937—July 1940).
Pulp size; 128 pp.; bimonthly; 15¢.
A 'Red Circle' magazine published by Western Fiction Pub. Co., Chicago.

Issues were generally subtitled either "Exciting Stories of Horror and Terror" or "10 Stories of Horror and Terror." Most issues contained 4 or 5 horror novelettes and 5 eerie short stories, all apparently sex-oriented.

Some Issues and Lead Novelettes:
1938 Mar (2/3) "Lucifer's Bride," Alan Hyde
     Jun (2/4) "Black Pool for Hell Maidens," Hal K. Wells; "Devil's Masquerade" (short), Henry Kuttner
     Nov (2/5) "Dweller in Darkness," Henry T. Sperry
1939 Feb (2/6) "The Devil's University," Donald Dale
     Jun (3/1) "Spawn of Satan's Scourge," A. J. Burks
     Sep (3/2) "Tonight I Sleep With Terror," A. J. Burks
     Dec (3/3) "School for Beasts," Gabriel Wilson
1940 Mar (3/4) "New Girls for Satan's Blood Ballet," Russell Gray
     May (3/4) "Betrothal of the Thing," Gabriel Wilson
     July?   A mooted issue which may not have appeared, with "Maidens Must Furnish the Flesh," Russell Gray, and "Souls for Sale," Allan K. Echols.

MYSTIC MAGAZINE   U.S.   Occult
At least 5 issues (Nov 1930—Apr 1931).
Large size; slick with trimmed edges; 98 pp.; monthly; 25¢.
Editor: Captain W. H. Fawcett.
Publisher: Fawcett Pubs., Minneapolis.

This presented mainly occult articles with some fiction, often illustrated by suggestive drawings as well as classical-type nudes. It presented no material of note, though the last issue, retitled *True Mystic Crimes*, had an article by T. Everett Harre and others by Tally Mason.

MYSTIC MAGAZINE See *SEARCH*

N

NARRACIONES TERRORIFICAS
           Argentine (Spanish)   Science fiction
72 issues (*ca.* 1939—Jan 1950); irregular.
This magazine used reprints from various sources.

NARRATORI DELL'ALPHA TAU, I   Italian   Science fiction
8 issues (12 Jan 1957—15 June 1957).
Size 4¾ x 6½ in. first 4 issues; 4⅜ x 6¾ in. last 4; fortnightly; 150 lire.
Editorial Director: Bernardino De Rugeriis.
Publisher: Editrice Irsa Muraro, Rome.

NEBULA SCIENCE FICTION   Scottish   Science fiction
41 issues (Aut 1952—June 1959).
Size 5½ x 8½ in.; 120 and 128 pp., then 112 pp. from #13; variable frequency; 2/- (last 2 at 2/6).
Editor: P. Hamilton.
Publisher: Crownpoint Pubs. (P. Hamilton).

This normally featured one short novel per issue with short stories and departments of interest, including film reviews by F. J Ackerman,

"Fanorama" by W. Willis, and book reviews by K. Slater. The covers were painted by various British artists and always had plenty of colour; from No. 10 the back cover presented a black and white illustration.

The magazine was generally quite entertaining, though few stories will become classics. Authors included most of the contemporary British writers, such as E. C. Tubb, K. Bulmer, E. F. Russell, and W. F. Temple. R. Silverberg made his first appearance in any magazine in *Nebula*. R. A. Heinlein was reprinted a number of times.
Issues:

	Jan	Feb	Mar	Apr	May	Jun	Jul	Aug	Sep	Oct	Nov	Dec	W
1952									1/1 (Aut)				1
1953	1/2 (Spr)		1/3 (Sum)			1/4 (Aut)			2/1		2/2		6
1954		2/3		2/4			9		10		11		11
1955			12					13		14			14
1956	15		16			17				18	19		19
1957		20		21		22	23	24	25				25
1958	26	27	28	29	30	31	32	33	34	35	36	37	37
1959	38	39		40	41								41

American Edition:
This was the British edition stamped at 35¢. It began at No. 30, dated Sep 1958 (not May) and ran monthly to No. 39 (dated June 1959).

NEUE ABENTEUER, DAS   German   Adventure
An adventure series which published some science fiction. In a poll of this magazine's readers in 1958 (when it had over 130 issues of which 6 or 7 could be termed sf), *Alarm Auf Station Einstein* (a space station thriller) placed first, with another sf story, *Kobalt 60*, as runner-up.

NEW FRONTIERS   British   Occult
2 issues (Jan 1947 & Apr/May 1947).
Editors: B. Herbert, Joyce Fairbairn, and C. S. Youd.
Publisher: Utopian Pubs., London.
Nonfiction, featuring articles on telepathy, Atlantis, and the like.

NEW MYSTERY ADVENTURES See *MYSTERY ADVENTURES*

NEW WORLDS   British   Science fiction
201 issues (3 issues 1946-1947; No. 4, 1949—Mar 1971).
Editors: E. J. Carnell to No. 141 (Apr 1964); M. Moorcock from No. 142 (J. Sallis, Associate Editor end of 1968, later Co-Editor).
Publishers: Pendulum Publications, London, first 3 issues; Nova Publications, London, 1949—Apr 1964; Roberts & Vinter Ltd., London, May/June 1964—Jan 1967; Gold Star Publications Ltd., London, Mar 1967—Apr 1967; then published (with the assistance of the Arts Council of Great Britain) by a consortium including M. Moorcock (Editor), Langdon Jones (Associate Editor), Charles Platt (Design), and Claire Walsh (Advertising).
Format: Size: Nos. 1 to 3, 7¼ x 9½ in.; 5½ x 8½ in. to No. 20; varied slightly, then became digest size from No. 23 (May 1954); became large size July 1967. Pages: 64 pp. Nos. 1 to 3; 96 pp., Nos. 4 to 22; 128 and 160 pp. in digest size; 64 pp. from July 1967 (large size). Price: Began at 2/-; 1/6 from No. 3; 2/- from No. 32; 2/6 from No. 89; 3/6 from No. 160 (at 160 pp.); 5/- from No. 177.
General:

E. J. Carnell originally started this magazine after World War II, but it ceased when the publisher failed. In order to revive it English fans formed and took shares in the company Nova Publications, and *New Worlds* reappeared in 1949 as a quarterly. It proved quite successful for a period, until sales slumped in the early 1960's.

For many years it was considered the best British sf magazine, presenting material with a typically British slant. For a time some U.S. novels were serialised, but later original British novels appeared (many of which later saw paperback editions in the U.S., mainly from Ace).

Cover artists for the Carnell period included Clothier, Quinn, Terry, and Lewis; to save costs, from 1962 to 1964 photographs with a one- or two-colour background were used. Interior illustrations ceased from No. 62. A number of cover illustrations were sold and used on the Swedish magazine *Hapna*. Guest editorials by prominent writers and others in the science fiction field appeared for a number of issues from Oct 1961 and created considerable interest. The Nova issues for many years printed up-to-date science articles by "Kenneth Johns" (J. Newman and K. Bulmer).

Overprinted issues for sale in Canada and New Zealand appeared for a while from late 1954, and later were done for the U.S. market (after an actual U.S. edition had appeared).

The editorial policy under Moorcock gradually changed from straight science fiction to experimental fiction. In 1968 the serialisation of N. Spinrad's *Bug Jack Barron* created quite a stir because of its graphic sex and language. By 1969 science fiction seemed to have dropped out of the magazine, so that in many quarters it was no longer considered science fiction.

Anthologies directly selected from the magazine are *The Best From New Worlds Science Fiction*, Carnell (1955); *The Best of New Worlds*, Moorcock (1965); *The Best SF Stories From New Worlds*, Moorcock (1967); *The Best SF Stories From New Worlds II* and *The Best SF Stories From New Worlds 3*, both Moorcock, 1968.

The title *New Worlds* had earlier been used on a pre-war British amateur magazine which had been a retitle of *Novae Terrae*. A British Science Fiction Assn. publication *A History and Checklist of New Worlds*, Brian Burgess (3/6, 2/6 to B.S.F.A. members) indexed the first 55 issues (to 1957).

Notable Fiction:

1946	#1	"The Three Pylons" (n'te), W. F. Temple
	#3	"Dragon's Teeth," J. K. Aiken [had sequel]
1949	#5	"Time to Rest" (short), J. Beynon [had sequel]
1950	Win	"Guardian Angel" (n'te), A. C. Clarke [see *Childhood's End*]; "Magnis Mensas" series, F. G. Rayer, began.
1951	Spr	"Max Larkin" series, J. Christopher [C. S. Youd] began.
	Win	"Time Was . . ." (n'te), F. G. Rayer [with sequel, as *The Star Seekers*]
1952	Jan	"Without Bugles" (short), E. C. Tubb [see *Alien Dust*]
	Mar	"Enchanted Village" (short), A. E. van Vogt
	Jul	"The ESP Worlds" (sr3), J. T. McIntosh [J. M. MacGregor]
	Nov	"Of Those Who Came" (short). G. Longdon
1953	Jan	"Assisted Passage" (short), J. White
	Mar	"Jetsam" (short), A. B. Chandler
1954	Apr	*Take-Off* (sr3), C. M. Kornbluth; "The Sentinel" (short), A. C. Clarke; "Jacko" series, A. Barclay, began.
	May	"Zoological Specimen" (short), A. B. Chandler
	Aug	*Wild Talent* (sr3), W. Tucker
	Dec	*Prisoner in the Skull* (sr3), C. Dye
1955	Jan	"Johnny Dawson" series, L. Wright, began.
	Feb	"Gomez" (short), C. M. Kornbluth
	Apr	"Star Ship" (sr3), E. C. Tubb [*The Space-Born*]
	Sep	*The Time Masters* (sr3), W. Tucker
1956	Feb	"The Solomon Plan" (n'te), J. T. McIntosh
	Mar	"Place of the Throwing Stick" (short), F. Bryning
	Apr	*Who Speaks of Conquest?* (sr4), L. Wright
	Oct	"Tourist Planet" (sr3), J. White [*The Secret Visitors*]
	Dec	J. G. Ballard's set on crowded city life began.
1957	Jan	"Royal Prerogative" (short), A. C. Clarke
	Mar	"Green Destiny" (sr3), K. Bulmer [*City Under the Sea*]
	Apr	"Oh, Ishrael!" (short), B. W. Aldiss
	Aug	*The Uninhibited* (sr3), D. Morgan
	Oct	"The Menace From Earth" (short), R. A. Heinlein
	Nov	"Sector General" series, J. White, began [*Hospital Station*].
	Dec	*Threshold of Eternity* (sr3), J. Brunner
1958	Mar	*Wasp* (sr3), E. F. Russell
	Apr	"Troon" series, J. Wyndham [J. B. Harris], began [*The Outward Urge*]
	Jul	"Segregation" (n'te), B. W. Aldiss
	Sep	"Equator" (sr2), B. Aldiss [*Vanguard From Alpha*]
	Dec	*A Man Called Destiny* (sr3), L. Wright
1959	Mar	*Count-Down* (sr3), C. E. Maine [D. McIlwain]
	Jul	"The Patient Dark" (sr3), K. Bulmer [*The Secret of ZI*]
	Oct	"The Railways up on Cannis" (short), C. Kapp
	Nov	"The Waiting Grounds" (n'te), J. G. Ballard
	Dec	*Time out of Joint* (sr3), P. K. Dick
1960	Mar	"X for Exploitation" (sr3), B. W. Aldiss [*Bow Down to Nul*]
	May	"Planetary Exploration" series, D. Malcolm, began.
	Jul	*The Fatal Fire* (sr3), K. Bulmer
	Oct	"The Voices of Time" (short), J. G. Ballard [title story of collection]
	Nov	100th issue—all stories of interest

1961	Jan	*Venus Plus X* (sr4), T. Sturgeon
	Jun	"Put Down This Earth" (sr3), J. Brunner [*The Dreaming Earth*]
	Sep	"Storm-Wind" (sr2), J. G. Ballard [*The Wind From Nowhere*]
	Nov	"The Golden Age" (sr2), R. Clinton
1962	Jan	*Field Hospital* (sr3), J. White [in "Sector General" series]
	Apr	"The Dawson Diaries" (sr2), J. Rackham; "Refuge" series, J. L. Green, began [*The Loafers of Refuge*].
	Jun	"Minor Operation" (sr3), B. W. Aldiss [*The Primal Urge*]
	Sep	"Crack of Doom" (sr2), K. Woodcott [J. Brunner] [*The Psionic Menace*]
	Nov	"Galactic Survey Team" series, R. Markham, began.
	Dec	"Lambda 1" (n'te), C. Kapp
1963	Jan	"Dawn's Left Hand" (sr3), L. Wright [*Exile From Xanadu*]
	Apr	"Window on the Moon" (sr3), E. C. Tubb[*Moon Base*]
	Aug	*To Conquer Chaos* (sr3), J. Brunner
	Nov	"The Dark Mind" (sr3), C. Kapp [*Transfinite Man*]
1964	Jan	"Toys" (short), J. Baxter
	Feb	*Open Prison* (sr3), J. White [also *The Escape Orbit*]
	Mar	"The Terminal Beach" (short), J. G. Ballard
	May	"Equinox" (sr2), J. G. Ballard [in *The Crystal World*]
	Sep/Oct	"The Shores of Death" (sr2), M. Moorcock [*The Twilight Man*]
1965	Jan	"The Power of Y" (sr2), A. Sellings [R. A. Ley]
	Mar	"Sunjammer" (short), A. C. Clarke
	Apr	"The Life Buyer" (sr3), E. C. Tubb
	Aug	*Bill, the Galactic Hero* (sr2), H. Harrison; "Jerry Cornelius" series, M. Moorcock, began [all as *Final Programme*].
	Nov	*The Wrecks of Time* (sr3), J. Colvin [M. Moorcock]
1966	Feb	"A Two-Timer" (n'te), D. I. Masson
	Mar	"The Evil That Men Do" (sr2), J. Brunner
	Apr	"The Assassination Weapon" (short), J. G. Ballard
	Jun	"The God Killers" (sr2), J. Baxter [*The Off-Worlders*]
	Sep	"Behold the Man" (short novel), M. Moorcock
	Oct	*The Garbage World* (sr2), C. Platt
	Nov	"Storm Bird, Storm Dreamer" (short), J. G. Ballard
	Dec	*Echo Round His Bones* (sr2), T. M. Disch
1967	Jan	"The Day of Forever" (short), J. G. Ballard
	Feb	*Report on Probability A*, B. W. Aldiss
	Apr	"Daughters of Earth" (short novel), J. Merril
	Jul	*Camp Concentration* (sr4), T. M. Disch
	Oct	*An Age* (sr3), B. W. Aldiss
	Nov	"Stand on Zanzibar" (extracts), J. Brunner
	Dec	*Bug Jack Barron* (sr6), N. Spinrad
1968	Dec	"Time Considered as a Helix of Semi-Precious Stones" (n'te), S. R. Delany

Issues:

	Jan	Feb	Mar	Apr	May	Jun	Jul	Aug	Sep	Oct	Nov	Dec	W
1946							1/1 (nd)		1/2 (nd)				2
1947									1/3 (nd)				3
1949			2/4 (nd)					2/5 (nd)					5
1950			2/6 (Spr)			3/7 (Sum)					3/8 (Win)		8
1951			3/9 (Spr)			3/10 (Sum)			4/11 (Aut)		12 (Win)		12
1952	13		14		15		16		17		18		18
1953	19		20		21								21
1954			22	23	24	25	26	27	28	29	30		30
1955	31	32	33	34	35	36	37	38	39	40	41	42	42
1956	43	44	45	46	47	48	49	50	51	52	53	54	54
1957	55	56	5⁷	58	59	60	61	62	63	64	65	66	66
1958	67	68	6_	70	71	72	73	74	75	76	77	78	78
1959	79	80	81	82	83	84	85	86		87	88	89	89
1960	90	91	92	93	94	95	96	97	98	99	100	101	101
1961	102	103	104	105	106	107	108	109	110	111	112	113	113
1962	114	115	116	117	118	119	120	121	122	123	124	125	125
1963	126	127	128	129	130	131	132	133	134	135	136	137	137
1964	138	139	140	141	142		143		144		145		145
1965	146	147	148	149	150	151	152	153	154	155	156	157	157
1966	158	159	160	161	162	163	164	165	166	167	168	169	169
1967	170		171	172			173	174	175	176	177	178*	178
1968		179	160	181			182			183	184	185	185

* Dated Dec 1967/Jan 1968.

U.S. Edition:
5 issues (March—July 1960).
Publisher: Great American Pubs., New York.

This magazine published stories as if new, with no credit anywhere to the British original magazine. It selected from various British issues, but did not publish any serials. It was monthly, numbered Vol. 1 No. 1 through Vol. 1 No. 5.

Later the British original went on sale in the U.S.A. with No. 99, dated November (the October issue in Britain). This issue had a special editorial to explain the long time lapse after British publication, compared with the reprint edition from Great American.

NUGGET LIBRARY   U.S.   Juvenile adventure
At least 134 issues (12 Jan 1889— ?).
Size 8¾ x 11⅜ in.; 16 pp.; 5¢; weekly.
Publisher: Street & Smith, New York.

About one quarter of this boy's paper appears to deal with sf, mainly covering the adventures of "Tom Edison Jr." Science fiction issues sighted include Nos. 2, 22, 102, 110, 115, 119, 124, 128, and 134.

O

OCTOPUS, THE   U.S.   Weird
1 issue, Feb 1938 (1/4).
Editor: Rogers Terrill.
Publisher: Popular Publications.

A misleading pulp in that the volume numbering implied earlier issues. A masked villain, the Octopus, leads the Purple Eyes, an assassin cult. The novel in this issue was "The City Condemned to Hell," Randolph Craig (pseud. of N. W. Page). The second story of the proposed series was rewritten for another character magazine, *The Scorpion.*

OLTRE IL CIELO   Italian   Science fiction
148 issues (Sep 1957—Feb 1967).
Editor: C. Falessi.
Publisher: Gruppo Editoriale "esse," Rome.

This ran 24 to 32 pp., large size (9⅝ x 13⅝ in.), with covers by Italian artists. For a period it had a French offshoot: *Au Dela du Ciel.*

OPERATOR #5   U.S.   Mystery/science fiction
48 issues (Apr 1934—Nov/Dec 1939). Monthly to Apr 1936, bimonthly June/July 1936 to Oct/Nov 1936, monthly Dec 1936 to Mar 1937, then bimonthly May/June 1937 to end.
Pulp size; 4 issues to volume (exactly 12 vols.).
Publisher: Popular Publications, New York.

This was one of the more successful one-character magazines; it is fully listed in *The Hero-Pulp Index*, McKinstry & Weinberg (1970). Each issue contained a "full-length" novel by Curtis Steele. (Popular Publications said "Steele" was a pseudonym of Emile Tepperman, though Frank Gruber in *The Pulp Jungle* stated that most were by Frederick Davis.) Other regular material included one or more short spy stories and the department "The Secret Sentinel," which also incorporated the club "The Secret Sentinels of America" with a distinctive badge for members.

Jimmy Christopher was Operator #5, a master of disguise, languages, etc. Various other characters appear. The stories usually dealt with some menace to the U.S.A. either from a foreign country or a group within. From June/July 1936 to March/April 1938 the "Purple Invasion" series (with the U.S.A. completely under conquest) was featured. Not strictly science fiction, the magazine was more in the fantastic mystery style.

Corinth Publications reprinted the following titles in paperback in 1966 (original magazine dates noted): *Legions of the Death Master* (July

1935); *The Army of the Dead* (Aug 1935); *The Invisible Empire* (May 1934); *Master of Broken Men* (Sep 1934); *Hosts of the Flaming Death* (Aug 1935); *Blood Reign of the Dictator* (May 1935); *March of the Flame Marauders* (Apr 1935); *Invasion of the Yellow Warlords* (June 1935).
British Edition:
Publisher: Thorpe & Porter, Leicester.
1 issue (early 1940); pulp size; 80 pp.; 1/6; reprint of Nov/Dec 1939 issue, "The Army From Underground."

ORBIT SCIENCE FICTION   U.S.   Science fiction
5 issues (1/1, 1953, not dated—Nov/Dec 1954).
Digest size; 130 pp.; bimonthly; 35¢.
Editor: Jules Saltman [General Editor for the Publisher; D. A. Wollheim actually selected the stories].
Publisher: Hanro Corp., New York.

After two "one-shot" issues this became a regular bimonthly magazine, but then ceased in the general slump in the sf field. It was originally to have been called *Dimension Science Fiction*. The internal format was very similar to *Galaxy Science Fiction*.

There was an Australian edition (see below); in addition, the fiction in Nos. 2, 4, and 5 was sold in Australia and used (with other material) in the "Satellite" series of 1958 [see *WHO'S WHO—Anonymous Anthologies—Satellite Series*].
Notable Fiction [each issue published a story in the "Tex Harrigan" series by A. Derleth]:
1953 No. 1   "D. P. From Tomorrow" (short), M. Reynolds; "Luena of the Gardens" (short), P. Brandts
1954 Sep/Oct "Last Night of Summer" (short), A. Coppel
      Nov/Dec "So Lovely, So Lost" (short), J. Causey
Issues:

	Jan	Feb	Mar	Apr	May	Jun	Jul	Aug	Sep	Oct	Nov	Dec	W
1953							1/1 (nd)						1
1954	1/2 (nd)						1/3		1/4		1/5		5

Australian Edition:
1 issue, published by Consolidated Press, Sydney.

This was a reprint of No. 1, but numbered No. 10; it appeared in April 1954 (not dated). It was 10¼ x 7½ in.; 64 pp.; 2/-; on semi-transparent paper; and glued, not stapled. Good editorial work was rendered abortive by the cheap newsprint paper which ruined the appearance.

ORIENTAL STORIES   U.S.   Weird
14 issues (Oct/Nov 1930—Jan 1934).
Title changed to *The Magic Carpet* from Mar 1933.
Editor: F. Wright.
Publisher: Popular Fiction Co., Indianapolis, Indiana.
Pulp size; 144 pp. to Sum 1932, then 128 pp.; 25¢, dropped to 15¢ for Jan—July 1933, then back to 25¢.

This was a sister magazine to *Weird Tales*, primarily presenting fantasy of the "Far East" or oriental type. The majority of the covers were done by Margaret Brundage.
Notable Fiction:
1930 Oct/Nov First of "Man Who Limped" series, O. A. Kline
      Dec/Jan "The Burning Sea" (short), Richard Kent
1931 Feb/Mar "Red Blades of Black Cathay" (n'te), T. C. Smith & R. E. Howard; "Della Wu, Chinese Courtezan" (short), F. Owen [R. Williams]
      Apr/May "Hawks of Outremer" (n'te), R. E. Howard
1932 Spr "Lords of Samarkand" (n'te), R. E. Howard
1933 Apr "Kaldar, World of Antares" (n'te), E. Hamilton
      Jul "The Lion of Tiberias" (short), R. E. Howard
      Oct "The Snake Men of Kaldar" (n'te), E. Hamilton
1934 Jan "The Shadow of the Vulture," R. E. Howard; "Five Merchants Who Met in a Tea-House," F. Owen [R. Williams]
Other authors included P. Ernst, G. G. Pendarves, E. H. Price, F. B. Long, A. Derleth, C. A. Smith, H. B. Cave, and S. Quinn; there was much verse by Hung Long Tom.
Issues:

	Jan	Feb	Mar	Apr	May	Jun	Jul	Aug	Sep	Oct	Nov	Dec	W
1930										1/1	1/2*		2
1931		1/3		1/4		1/5 (Sum)			1/6 (Fall)				6
1932	2/1 (Win)		2/2 (Spr)			2/3 (Sum)							9
1933	3/1		3/2			3/3			3/4				13
1934	4/1												14

* Dec 1930/Jan 1931.

ORIGINAL SCIENCE FICTION STORIES, THE See *SCIENCE FICTION STORIES*

OTHER WORLDS SCIENCE STORIES   U.S.   Science fiction
45 issues in two series (31 issues Nov 1949—July 1953; 14 issues May 1955—Oct 1957). [Some issues in 1957 are not included in the preceding, being titled *Flying Saucers From Other Worlds*, which see.]
Format: First series all digest size; 162 pp.; 35¢. Second series, 3 issues to Sep 1955, 130 pp., digest; then pulp size, 98 pp.; all 35¢.
Editor: R. A. Palmer.
Publisher: Clark Pub. Co., Evanston, Illinois, for first series; Palmer Pubs., Evanston, for second series.
General:
This is the magazine R. Palmer began when he left Ziff-Davis Publications (where he edited *AS* and *FA*) in 1949. It displayed his bent for showmanship. The first series had as companion *Imagination*, but this was soon sold to W. L. Hamling. In 1953 Palmer began *Science Stories* (as a name adaptation of *Other Worlds Science Stories*) and also purchased *Universe Science Fiction*. *Science Stories* soon ceased. He maintained *Universe* for a period and then returned to the *Other Worlds* title, but retained the *Universe* numbering.
From May 1957, in order to feature "flying saucer" material in alternate issues, Palmer used the title *Flying Saucers From Other Worlds* [see separate listing], many issues of which later had *OW* and *FS* numbering. However, *Other Worlds* is generally considered to have finished at Oct 1957.
Notable Fiction:
1950 May   "Dear Devil" (n'te), E. F. Russell; "War of Nerves" (short), A. E. van Vogt; first of "Colossus" novels by S. J. Byrne.
     Jul   "Enchanted Village" (short), A. E. van Vogt
1951 May   "Hoka" series, P. Anderson & G. R. Dickson, began.
     Dec   "Act of God" (sr2), R. Ashby
1952 Jan   "These Are My Children" (sr2), R. Phillips [R. P. Graham]
     Apr   "The Golden Guardsmen" (sr3), S. J. Byrne
     Jul   "The Sun Smiths" (sr3), R. S. Shaver
     Oct   "Lost Continents" article series, L. S. de Camp, began.
     Nov   "Beyond the Barrier" (sr4), R. S. Shaver
1953 Feb   "Field of Battle," W. F. Temple [*Battle on Venus*]
     Mar   "Tedric" (short), E. E. Smith [had sequel]
     May   "Power Metal" (sr3), S. J. Byrne
     Jul   "The Game of White" (n'te), J. McConnell
1955 May   "Gift of Zar," D. C. Reese
     Nov   "Reckoning From Eternity," H. Annas [first of 3 connected novels]
1956 Jun   "The Timeless Man" (sr2), R. Arcot
     Nov   "Reluctant Eve," Evelyn Martin
1957 Oct   "The Heart's Long Wait" (short), C. L. Fontenay
Issues:

	Jan	Feb	Mar	Apr	May	Jun	Jul	Aug	Sep	Oct	Nov	Dec	W
1949											1/1		1
1950	1/2		1/3		1/4		2/1		2/2	2/3	2/4		8
1951	3/1		3/2		3/3		3/4		3/5	3/6		3/7	15
1952	3/5*		4/2	4/3		4/4	4/5	4/6		4/7	4/8	4/9	24
1953	5/1	5/2	5/3	5/4	5/5	5/6	5/7						31

Continued as *Science Stories*, then as *Universe Science Fiction*, before resuming as *Other Worlds* with No. 11. Issues began alternating with *Flying Saucers From Other Worlds* [*FS*] with No. 23.

	Jan	Feb	Mar	Apr	May	Jun	Jul	Aug	Sep	Oct	Nov	Dec	W
1955					11		12		13		14		35
1956		15		16		17			18		19		40
1957	20		21		22 23(*FS*1) 24 25(*FS*2)		26 27(*FS*3)						45†

* As printed.
† Not counting *FS* issues.

OUT OF THIS WORLD   British   Weird
2 issues (Nov 1954, Jan 1955), not dated.
Pocket book size; 128 pp.; 1/6.
Editor: John S. Manning (pseudonym for Michael Nahum and Sol de Salle).
Publisher: John Spencer, London.

The material presented was original but not very high grade. After two issues the magazine ceased, though the companion *Supernatural Stories* was titled *Out of This World and Supernatural Stories* for several issues—Nos. 13, 15, 17, and 19.

OUT OF THIS WORLD ADVENTURES   U.S.   Science fiction/fantasy
2 issues (July, Dec 1950) [1/1, 1/2].
Pulp size; 130 pp.; 25¢.
Editor: D. A. Wollheim.
Publisher: Avon Periodicals, New York.
A short-lived effort which was somewhat unusual in that it ran a centre comic-book section. The fiction was only fair.
Canadian Edition:
2 issues (Nov 1950, Apr 1951).
Pulp size; 130 pp.; 25¢.
Publisher: American News Co. Ltd., Toronto.
The comic sections were the same in the first Canadian and first U.S. issues, but different in the second issues. Fiction content was identical. The Canadian issues had slightly longer pages, and had the same advertisements.

OUTLANDS   British   Occult, etc.
1 issue (Win 1946) [No. 1]
Size 5½ x 8⅜ in.; 40 pp.; 1/6.
Publisher: Outlands Pubs., Liverpool.
Subtitled "a magazine for adventurous minds," this ran material rated as "unusual." The only issue to appear had six short stories—including one each from J. R. Fearn and S. J. Bounds—and also verse and articles.

P

PAL See *GEORGE PAL*, etc. (in G's)

PALL MALL MAGAZINE   British   General
A noted magazine first co-edited by Lord Frederic Hamilton and Sir Douglas Strout, and later by Hamilton alone. It ran from May 1893 to Sep 1929 and then combined with *Nash's Magazine* (which had run Oct 1914 to Apr 1927); the amalgamation continued from Oct 1929.
Prior to 1900 it published some material of fantasy flavour, including some well-painted plates "Guesses at Futurity" printed between Oct 1894 and Apr 1895. Early authors of interest were Grant Allen, C.J.C. Hyne, A. C. Benson, R. March, A. T. Quiller-Couch, R. S. Hichens, F. Anstey, E. Jepson, G. Atherton, E. & H. Heron, J. S. Clouston, O. Onions, and H. G. Wells.
Notable Fiction:
1895 Apr   "Huguenin's Wife" (n'te), M. P. Shiel
1897 Apr   "A Volcanic Valve," W. L. Alden [in "Prof. W. von Wagener" series]
1898 Feb   "A Mysterious Fever," W. L. Alden [in "Prof. W. von Wagener" series]
1899 Apr   "The Haunted Island" (short), A. Blackwood
1900 Dec   "A Case of Eavesdropping," A. Blackwood

PASSING SHOW, THE   British   General
A prewar British weekly magazine of 40 pages, costing 2d. It is notable for printing the E. R. Burroughs novels *The Pirates of Venus* (sr9, 30 Sep 1933) and *Lost on Venus* (sr10, 2 Dec 1933), both very well illustrated by Fortunino Matania. These are collector's items. A further serial was *The Secret People*, J. Wyndham [J. B. Harris] (sr8, 20 July—14 Sep 1935).

PEARSON'S   British   General

One of the regular British magazines at the turn of the century, this ran from Jan 1896 to Nov 1939. It was edited by Sir Arthur Pearson and published by C. A. Pearson Ltd. Novels serialised included *The Ghost Kings*, H. R. Haggard (sr9, Oct 1907).

PERRY RHODAN German Science fiction

Current (late 1960—); to No. 386, weekly, by end of 1968.

Size 6¼ x 8⅞ in.; 64 pp.; 70 pfennigs to No. 182, 80 pf 183-385, 90 pf 386-405; 1 DM 406—.

Publisher: Moewig Verlag, Munich.

Initiated by C. Darlton [W. Ernsting], this is one of the most successful "one-character" magazine series ever to appear from any publisher in the world. It uses a completely integrated intergalactic background built up by the current German writers. The hero is a contemporary American who is contacted by an alien civilization in the first story. Of the first 400 issues, Clark Darlton wrote 102, Kurt Mahr 75, William Voltz 75, K. H. Scheer 50, H. G. Ewers 46, Kurt Brand 36, Hans Kneifel 9, W. W. Shols 4, and C. C. Shepherd 3.

The magazine presents only original German stories. There are also frequent reissues of earlier stories, a comic-book version, a paperback book edition (each 160 pp.; up to No. 53 by end of 1968), Perry Rhodan clubs, buttons, etc., and an offshoot magazine *Atlan*.

The late Ron Graham of Sydney, Australia (publisher of *Vision of Tomorrow*), tried to acquire British and Commonwealth rights, but instead Ace purchased the "English Language Rights" and began publishing English translations in 1969.

Paperback Edition: *Perry Rhodan: Planetenromane*

At least 81 issues starting in 1964.

Price 2.20 DM to No. 8; 2.40 DM from No. 9.

All original German sf stories by the Perry Rhodan team.

Comic-Book Edition: *Perry Rhodan im Bild*

Size 6¾ x 10 in.; 32 pp.; 1 DM.

Each issue carries three cartoon stories featuring Perry Rhodan, Gucky, and Atlan.

Dutch Edition: *Perry Rhodan*, published by Born N.V., Amsterdam.

The first 35 issues have been sighted; they have exactly the same stories and cover illustrations as their German originals, but are more substantially made and have a better appearance. A Dutch paperback book series from Born N.V. is also known; No. 1 to 4, 96 pp., appeared in 1967.

U.S. Edition: Began as Ace paperbacks in 1969; then became a regular Ace series. [A British paperback series has also appeared, after 1969.]

PHANTOM British Weird

16 issues (Apr 1957, not dated—July 1958).

Size 5½ x 9½ in.; 112 pp.; monthly; 2/-.

Editor: None listed at first; then from No. 9 Leslie Sydall so noted, with Cliff Lawton, Art Editor.

Publisher: Dalrow Pubs., Lancashire, to No. 12; then Pennine Pubs., Lancs.

The first issue purported to be "true stories"; this claim was soon dropped, and toward its finish it was subtitled "Weird Tales." The fiction was quite reasonable in quality, with some reprints from *Weird Tales*; these included three stories by E. Worrell and single works from F. Leiber, Mary Counselman, H. Lawlor, and A. Derleth. Many covers were by "R.W.S." From Sep 1957 the department "Phantom Forum" ran quite regularly.

Issues:

	Jan	Feb	Mar	Apr	May	Jun	Jul	Aug	Sep	Oct	Nov	Dec	W
1957				1 (nd)	2	3	4	5	6	7	8	9	9
1958	10	11	12	13	14	15	16						16

PHANTOM DETECTIVE U.S. Detective

170 issues (Feb 1933—Sum 1953).

A magazine of possible sf interest; a number of its novels were reprinted in 1966-1967 by Corinth Publishers (see *PAPERBACK* section).

PISTAS DEL ESPACIO Argentine (Spanish) Science fiction

At least 14 issues (early 1958—); 14th issue, Apr 1959.

Publisher: Acme Agency, Buenos Aires.

Spanish translations of U.S. and British sf novels. It cost 15 pesos, rising to 60 pesos (15¢) from No. 11. It was intended to become fortnightly. The title may be translated as "Spaceways."

PIU' GRANDI SCRITTORI DEL FUTURO, I Italian Science fiction

6 issues (June 1962—Nov 1962); monthly.

Publisher: I.L.E., Milan.

PLANEET SCIENCE FICTION—Avontuur en Technik Dutch Science fiction

1 issue (Jan 1953).

Digest size; 96 pp.; [95¢].

Editor: N. Osterbaan. **Publisher:** Drukkerijen CevaDo, The Hague.

The first issue featured "Ruimteschip 2213," J. J. Deegan ["Old Growler," *Authentic*, No. 4]. For the second issue the British paperback *Planet Fall*, G. Hunt, was announced.

PLANET-MAGASINET Danish Science fiction

5 issues (Apr 1958—Sep 1958).

100 pp.; monthly; 1.50 krone.

Publisher: Skrifola Pubs., Copenhagen.

This magazine gave translations of 3 or 4 stories from *Astounding Science Fiction* each issue. It had no inside illustrations, but presented original colour covers (not reprints). It published a chapter of A. C. Clarke's *Exploration of Space* in each issue.

PLANET STORIES U.S. Science fiction

71 issues (Win 1939—Sum 1955).

Pulp size; 128 pp., then 112 pp. from Sum 1949, 96 pp. from Sum 1954; quarterly/bimonthly; 20¢, then 25¢ from Mar 1951.

Editors: M. Reiss, Win 1939—Sum 1942; W. S. Peacock, Fall 1942—Fall 1945; C. Whitehorne, Win 1945—Sum 1946; P. L. Payne, Fall 1946—Spr 1950; J. Bixby, Sum 1950—July 1951; M. Reiss, Sep 1951-Jan 1952; J. O'Sullivan, Mar 1952—Sum 1955.

Publisher: Love Romances Pub. Co., New York City, then Stamford, Connecticut from Sep 1952.

This magazine always published "space-opera" and some of it was quite notable. It had very colourful covers by lesser-known artists, although its last issues had some by K. Freas. The more noted authors included P. Anderson, R. Bradbury (with many of the sf stories that made him famous), and L. Brackett (with many of her colourful adventures set on other planets).

Bixby began the companion magazine *Two Complete Science Adventure Books*, while O'Sullivan began the reprint magazine *Tops in Science Fiction*, selecting material from *Planet*'s early issues.

Notable Fiction:

1940 Fall "The Planet That Time Forgot" (short), D. A. Wollheim

1942 Spr "The Star-Mouse" (short), F. Brown [had sequel]

1943 Mar "Citadel of Lost Ships" (n'te), L. Brackett

1946 Sum "Lorelei of the Red Mist," L. Brackett & R. Bradbury; "The Million Year Picnic" (short), R. Bradbury

  Spr "Rocket Summer" (short), R. Bradbury

1947 Fall "Zero Hour" (short), R. Bradbury

1948 Sum "Pillar of Fire" (n'te), R. Bradbury

  Fall "Mars Is Heaven!" (short), R. Bradbury

  Win "The Beast-Jewel of Mars" (n'te), L. Brackett; "Asleep in Armageddon" (short), R. Bradbury

1950 Spr "The Rocketeers Have Shaggy Ears," K. Bennett

1951 Jan "Tiger by the Tail" (n'te), P. Anderson [first of "Dominic Flandry" series]

1953 Jan "Design for Great-Day," E. F. Russell

  Mar "Chicken Farm" (short), R. Rocklynne

  Sep "The Ark of Mars," L. Brackett

1954 Sum "Dawn of the Demi-Gods," R. Z. Gallun

  Win "Teleportress of Alpha C" (n'te), L. Brackett

Issues:

	Jan	Feb	Mar	Apr	May	Jun	Jul	Aug	Sep	Oct	Nov	Dec	W
1939											1/1 (Win)	1
1940	1/2 (Spr)		1/3 (Sum)		1/4 (Fall)			1/5 (Win)	5
1941	1/6 (Spr)		1/7 (Sum)		1/8 (Fall)			1/9 (Win)	9
1942	1/10 (Spr)		1/11 (Sum)		1/12 (Fall)			2/1 (Win)	13

[cont.]	Jan	Feb	Mar	Apr	May	Jun	Jul	Aug	Sep	Oct	Nov	Dec	W
1943		2/2		2/3					2/4 (Fall)		2/5 (Win)		17
1944		2/6 (Spr)			2/7 (Sum)				2/8 (Fall)		2/9 (Win)		21
1945		2/10 (Spr)			2/11 (Sum)				2/12 (Fall)		3/1 (Win)		25
1946		3/2 (Spr)			3/3 (Sum)				3/4 (Fall)		3/5 (Win)		29
1947		3/6 (Spr)			3/7 (Sum)				3/8 (Fall)		3/9 (Win)		33
1948		3/10 (Spr)			3/11 (Sum)				3/12 (Fall)		4/1 (Win)		37
1949		4/2 (Spr)			4/3 (Sum)				4/4 (Fall)		4/5 (Win)		41
1950		4/6 (Spr)			4/7 (Sum)				4/8 (Fall)		4/9		45
1951	4/10	4/11	4/12		5/1			5/2		5/3			51
1952	5/4	5/5	5/6		5/7			5/8		5/9			57
1953	5/10	5/11	5/12		6/1			6/2		6/3			63
1954	6/4	6/5	6/6		6/7 (Sum)			6/8 (Fall)		6/9 (Win)			69
1955		6/10 (Spr)			6/11 (Sum)								71

Note: 5/10 given as 5/8 on spine; 5/11 as 6/3; 6/11 as 6/12.

British Edition:
12 issues (1950–1954), not dated.
Size 6½ x 9½ in.; 68 pp. for No. 1, 64 pp. for Nos. 2 and 3, 66 pp. for Nos. 4 to 11, 68 pp. for No. 12; priced 9d for Nos. 1 and 2, 1/- for Nos. 3 to 7, 9d for No. 8, 1/- for Nos. 9 to 12.
Publishers: No. 1, Streamline Pubs. Ltd., London; Nos. 2 to 12, Pembertons (of Manchester) Ltd.

The magazine presented selections from the U.S. issues, with the last reprinting from March 1953.

Issues:

	Jan	Feb	Mar	Apr	May	Jun	Jul	Aug	Sep	Oct	Nov	Dec	W
1950		1				2							2
1951	3			4									4
1952													
1953						5		6		7		8	8
1954		9		10		11		12					12

Canadian Edition:
12 issues (Fall 1948–Mar 1951).
Publisher: The American News Co. Ltd., Toronto.
Pulp size; 128 pp., then 112 pp. from Sum 1949; quarterly & bimonthly; first 20¢, then 25¢ from Fall 1950.
Identical to the U.S. edition in dates and contents.

PLAYBOY
U.S. — Men's magazine
Current (1954–).
Editors: Ray Russell (after being Associate Editor was Executive Editor 1955–1960, then Consulting Editor to 1968), plus others.
Publisher: HMH Publishing Co. [Hugh Hefner], Chicago.

This magazine, like *Rogue*, has published in practically every issue short stories of sf/weird/fantasy nature, a number of which have been anthologised by such authorities as J. Merril. The selections *The Playboy Book of Science Fiction and Fantasy* (1966+) and *The Playboy Book of Horror and the Supernatural* are directly covered in the *WHO'S WHO* section under *Playboy Magazine*.

A nostalgic article, "The Bloody Pulps," C. Beaumont, appeared Sep 1962 and was illustrated with the covers of 20 magazines from the 1930's.

PLUCK AND LUCK
U.S. — Adventure
At least 174 issues (19 May 1898– ?).
Size 8½ x 11¼ in.; 22 pp.; weekly; 5¢.
Publisher: Frank Tousey, New York.

A boy's weekly which at times published sf issues; the ones known are: No. 76, "The Rocket"; Nos. 139 and 166, Jack Wright stories; No. 174, "Two Boys' Trip to an Unknown Planet."

POPULAR SCIENCE FICTION
Australian — Science fiction
Two series:
(1) 6 issues, Nos. 1 to 6, not dated: July 1953, Nov 1953, Mar 1954, July 1954, Dec 1954, Mar 1955.
Size 5¼ x 7½ in.; 64 pp.; irregular; price 1/3 first 2, then 1/6.
Publisher: Frew Publications, Sydney.
(1) 2 issues: No. 1, Apr 1967 & No. 2, Sep 1967, not dated.
Size 5¼ x 7½ in.; 20¢.
Publisher: Page Pubs., Sydney, N.S.W.
The first series featured reprints of U.S. material, with some Australian authors in later issues. The adviser at first was Vol Molesworth and

later Graham Stone (who had a "Fandom's Corner" in some issues). The companion was *Future Science Fiction*; both just paid their way but were not profitable enough for the publisher to keep them running.

The second series was a complete reprint from the first series—No. 1 duplicated No. 4 and No. 2 reprinted No. 6.

Feature Stories (and approximate dating):
1953 #1 (Jul) "Assignment on Pasik" (n'te), M. Leinster [W. F. Jenkins]
#2 (Nov) "The Shores of Tomorrow" (short), C. Oliver; "Stolen Centuries" (short), O. A. Kline
1954 #3 (Mar) "Colony in the Stars" (n'te), J. Gibson
#4 (Jul) "The Moonfire Gods" (n'te), L. Brackett
#5 (Dec) "The World Tube Murders" (n'te), R. F. Starzl; "Honorable Enemies" (short), P. Anderson
1955 #6 (Mar) "The Viscous Circle" (short), A. B. Chandler

POVESTIRI STIINTIFICO-FANTASTICE
Roumanian — Science fiction
Very little information available. Issue No. 89 appeared in 1959.

PRACTICAL ELECTRICS
U.S. — Popularised science
One of the Gernsback technical magazines which occasionally published some science fiction. In the main period, Feb 1924 (3/4) to Oct 1924 (3/12), 9 sf short stories appeared, some by George F. Stratton.

PRIZE GHOST STORIES
U.S. — Ghost
1 issue, not dated, not numbered, *ca.* Apr 1963.
Large size (8½ x 10¾ in.); 86 pp.; 50¢.
Publisher: League Publications, Inc., New York.

This had 17 items, of which 16 were reprinted from various 1927 issues of *Ghost Stories*. All stories were anonymous except "The Late Mr. Elvesham" by H. G. Wells, and were usually abridged, "revised," and retitled from their original appearances. The final story was a "book-length" feature, "The Tiger Woman"—originally "The Tiger Woman of the Punjab," Allen Van Hoesen (sr2, Oct 1927).

R

RADIO NEWS
U.S. — Popularised science
One of the Gernsback technical magazines which published quite an amount of science fiction. Between Nov 1919 (1/5) and Feb 1929 (10/8) it presented 112 short stories and 3 serials: "The Crystal" (sr2, Apr 1922), B. Greensfelder; "The Radio King" (sr2, Nov 1922), George B. Howard; "Echoing Silence" (sr2, Sep 1926), George B. Ludlam. The short stories included a number by C. Sterling Gleason, Marius Logan, Gerald A. Schive, Robert F. Smith, and Ellis P. Butler, whose "Solander's Radio Tomb" (Dec 1923) has been reprinted.

READE, FRANK See *FRANK READE LIBRARY*

REAL MYSTERY MAGAZINE
U.S. — Mystery weird
2 issues (Apr/May 1940, July/Aug 1940).
A mystery magazine which is covered in W. Austin's *Macabre Index*. No authors of note to the science fiction field appeared. The only novel was "Mates for Hell's Half-World Minions," Donald Graham, in the second issue.

RED STAR ADVENTURES
U.S. — Adventure fantasy
4 issues (June 1940–Jan 1941).
Pulp size; bimonthly.
Publisher: Frank A. Munsey Co., New York.
A "one character" magazine with a novel in each issue about the hero "Matalaa, the White Savage." The only survivor of a South Seas shipwreck, and raised by the natives, Matalaa fights for the rights of his

adopted islands. All stories by Martin McCall.
Issues and Novels:
1940 Jun (1/1) "The White Savage"
     Aug (1/2) "Cruise of the Savage"
     Oct (1/3) "Savage Jeopardy"
1941 Jan (1/4) "Treasure of the Savage"

RED STAR MAGAZINES
A magazine series published around 1940 by Frank A. Munsey Co. See separate entries above and below for *Red Star Adventures* and *Red Star Mystery*. Others were *Red Star Western* (with the character "The Silver Buck"), *Red Star Detective* ("Doc Harker"), and *Big Chief Western* ("White Eagle").

RED STAR MYSTERY   U.S.   Weird mystery
5 issues (June 1940—Feb 1941).
Pulp size; bimonthly; 10¢.
Publisher: Frank A. Munsey Co., New York.
A "special character" magazine with a novel in each issue about Don Diavolo, "The Scarlet Wizard." The hero was a stage magician who used his skills to expose supposedly supernatural crimes. All stories were by Stuart Towne (pseud. of Clayton Rawson).
Issues and Novels:
1940 Jun (1/1) "Ghost of the Undead"
     Aug (1/2) "Death out of Thin Air"
     Oct (1/3) "Claws of Satan"
     Dec (1/4) "The Enchanted Dagger"
1941 Feb (?) "Murder From the Grave"

REN DHARK—Weg ins Weltall   German   Science fiction series
At least 82 issues (*ca.* 1966—1968).
Size 6 x 8¾ in.; 66pp.; 70 pfennigs; first weekly, then fortnightly.
Publisher: Martin Kelter Verlag, Hamburg.
This magazine presented original German sf stories set in the year 2050 dealing with the adventures of Ren Dhark, a young officer in the "time-effect" spaceship *Galaxis*, who later becomes the commander of a colony planet in a nine-sun system.
This was an attempt by Kelter to produce a magazine along the lines of the very successful *Perry Rhodan*. Over half the stories were by Kurt Brand, and from No. 68 on he did all but two. The only other authors to have more than three stories in the series were Staff Caine, with ten, and Cal Canter, nine.
Omnibus volumes of three issues of the magazine were produced under the title *Sammelband* ["collected volume"]. These had the original covers but were set in a new binding with a new cover illustration. There at least 4 issues: No. 1 contained *Ren Dhark* Nos. 1-3; and Nos. 2, 3, and 4 each contained the next three issues in sequence.

REX CORDA—Der Retter der Erde   German   Science fiction series
At least 4 issues (1966).
Size 6 x 9 in.; 66 pp.; 80 pfennigs.
Publisher: Bastei Verlag, Gladbach.
Another contender for some of the *Perry Rhodan* success. This series written by H. G. Francis and M. Wegener dealt with the adventures of Rex Corda, Provisional President of the U.S.A. and saviour of the Earth.

RHODAN, PERRY See *PERRY RHODAN*

ROCKET—The First Space-Age Weekly
     British   Science fiction comic
32 issues (21 Apr 1956—24 Nov 1956).
Size 10½ x 13½ in.; 16 pp.; weekly; 4½d.
Editor: Douglas Bader.
Publisher: Eric Ambrose, Liverpool, for "News of the World."
A juvenile colour comic of good standard. The comic strips included *Flash Gordon, Captain Falcon*, etc., with some text fiction serials.

ROCKET STORIES   U.S.   Science fiction
3 issues: Apr 1953 (1/1), July (1/2), Sep 1953 (1/3).
Digest size; 160 pp.; bimonthly; 35¢.
Editor: Wade Kaempfert.
Publisher: Space Pubs., New York [J. Raymond].

A short-lived companion to *Space Science Fiction* and *Science Fiction Adventures*. It was of reasonable standard; probably the best story was "Apprentice of the Lamp," I. Cox (Sep 1953). H. Harrison was to have become the editor from the fourth issue.

ROMANZI DEL COSMO FANTASCIENZA, I
     Italian   Science fiction
Size 4¾ x 7¼ in.; 160 pp. to #10, then 144 pp.; monthly to #20, then mainly fortnightly; 150 lire.
Editors: Many, including F. Urbini (Nos. 86—141).
Publisher: Ponzoni Editore, Milan.
One of the better series, giving many translations of contemporary English-language sf, as well as some French and German novels. One issue sighted, No. 82 (31 Aug 1961), published *La Sfera Temporale*, F. R. Bessiere [French original: *Destination Moins J.-C.*].

ROMANZI DEL FUTURO, I   Italian   Science fiction
5 issues (20-25 Mar 1961—20-30 May 1961).
One issue sighted, No. 2 (15 Apr 1961): 5 x 7¼ in.; 128 pp.; 150 lire.
Publisher: Editrice P.E.N., Rome.
A well-produced magazine, with the novel sighted being an original Italian story. Probably the successor to *Le Cronache del Futuro*.

ROMANZI DI URANIA, I   Italian   Science fiction
Title change: To *Urania* at No. 153.
Current (10 Oct 1952—); 490 issues by the end of 1968.
Digest size, 5½ x 7⅞ in. to No. 272, 5⅛ x 7½ in. from No. 273; varying frequency; 128 to 256 pp.; price 150 lire Nos. 1 to 20, 130 lire Nos. 21 to 160, then 150 lire.
Editors: Giorgio Monicelli, Nos. 1 to 267; C. Fruttero, No. 281—; with F. Lucenti joining from No. 336.
Publisher: Arnoldo Mondadori, Milan.
The most important of the Italian sf magazine series, this has specialised in translations of contemporary U.S., British, French, and German science fiction, with some original Italian novels. It was said to have begun as the Italian edition of *Galaxy Science Fiction Novels*, but its frequent publishing schedule required other material also. It has presented occasional serials and cartoons.
The issues sighted—all early ones—were of pleasing format with a colourful cover on good board. The early companion was the magazine *Urania*; this ceased in Dec 1953 and the name was later adopted for this magazine with No. 153. Periodicity has varied from 2 per month, to 3 per month, then weekly for a time, and fortnightly since Mar 1956; any changes since then are not known. It had a supplement *I Capolavori di Urania* for 8 issues in 1967.

S

S-F [MAGAZINE]   Japanese   Science fiction
Current (Feb 1960—); 115th issue, Dec 1968.
Size 6 x 8¼ in.; 70 pp. generally, some special issues more; monthly, with a special extra issue each year from 1961.
Publisher: Hayakawa-Shobo Co., Tokyo.
Early issues were subtitled the "Japanese Edition of *The Magazine of Fantasy and Science Fiction*."
This is the only regular Japanese sf magazine. It began as an edition of *F&SF*, but with some original Japanese writers. By Jan 1962 the contract with Mercury Press was dissolved, and the magazine has since printed stories from various U.S. magazines as well as original Japanese material.
Issues (see extra issues, following table):

	Jan	Feb	Mar	Apr	May	Jun	Jul	Aug	Sep	Oct	Nov	Dec	W
1960		1	2	3	4	5	6	7	8	9	10	11	11
1961	12	13	14	15	16	17	18	19	20,21	22	23	24	24

[cont.]	Jan	Feb	Mar	Apr	May	Jun	Jul	Aug	Sep	Oct	Nov	Dec	W
1962	25	26	27	28	29	30	31	32	33,34	35	36	37	33
1963	38	39	40	41	42	43	44	45,46	47	48	49	50	50
1964	51	52	53	54	55	56	57	58,59	60	61	62	63	63
1965	64	65	66	67	68	69	70	71,72	73	74	75	76	76
1966	77	78	79	80	81	82	83	84,85	86	87	88	89	89
1967	90	91	92	93	94	95	96	97	98	99,100	101	102	102
1968	103	104	105	106	107	108	109	110	111,112	113	114	115	115

Extra issues: No. 20, weird; No. 33, weird; No. 46, "Sexology"; No. 59, "space novels"; No. 72, "pseudo-event novels by Japanese authors"; No. 85, "space-opera"; No. 100, "Introduction to SF"; No. 112, "space travel."

SATELLITE   French   Science fiction
47 issues (Jan 1958—Jan 1963).

Considered by P. Versins as one of the worst magazines he had ever seen. It had innumerable typographic errors; stories were translated twice and published under different titles; the staff and publishers changed quite often, and so did the size and the number of pages; and it had no regularity. Although it gave some good material, it was too much of a fan magazine professionally printed to be of interest to any except the completist.

Issues:

	Jan	Feb	Mar	Apr	May	Jun	Jul	Aug	Sep	Oct	Nov	Dec	W
1958	1	2	3	4	5	6	7	8	9	10	11	12	12
1959	13	14	15	16	17	18	19	20	21	22	23	24	24
1960	24	26	27	28	29								29
1961	30	31	32	33		34		35		37	38	39	40	40
1962	40*	41		42		43		44/45			46			46
1963	47												47

* Issue 40 bis.

SATELLITE SCIENCE FICTION   U.S.   Science fiction
18 issues (Oct 1956—May 1959).

Editors: S. Merwin, Oct & Dec 1956; Cylvia Kleinman, Feb 1957—May 1959 (with F. B. Long as Associate Editor from Feb 1959).

Publisher: Renown Pubs. [L. Margulies], New York.

Format: Began digest size, 128 pp., bimonthly, 35¢; Feb 1959 went to large size, 64 pp., monthly.

This was the magazine begun by L. Margulies when he left *Fantastic Universe*. It concentrated on long novels, and most of these are of interest. S. Moskowitz ran a book review column from the third issue, and in Oct 1957 began his "Profiles" on the older fantasy writers. (These were continued in other magazines and became the basis for several of his books.)

Although it was hoped the change to large size would save the magazine, it was unable to continue. There were distribution difficulties and it was generally felt that the size was against prominent display on the newsstands. An interesting innovation in the large issues was the "Department of Lost Stories," which published some old and unique stories. The fifth large issue was printed but never distributed; only four copies now remain, of which two are in the U.S. Library of Congress. The feature novel was "The Strange Birth," P. J. Farmer.

Feature Novels:

1956 Oct   "The Man From Earth," A. Budrys [*Man of Earth*]
     Dec   "A Glass of Darkness," P. K. Dick [*The Cosmic Puppets*]
1957 Feb   "Planet for Plunder," H. Clement [H. C. Stubbs] & S. Merwin
     Apr   "Operation: Square Peg," I. W. Lande & F. B. Long
     Jun   *Badge of Infamy*, L. del Rey
     Aug   *Year of the Comet*, J. Christopher [C. S. Youd]
     Oct   *Rocket to Limbo*, A. E. Nourse
     Dec   *The Languages of Pao*, J. Vance
1958 Feb   "Mission to a Distant Star," F. B. Long [*Mission to a Star*]
     Apr   "The Strange Invasion," M. Leinster [W. F. Jenkins] [*War With the Gizmos*]
     Jun   "Wall of Fire," C. E. Maine [D. McIlwain] [*Crisis 2000*]
     Aug   *The Million Cities*, J. T. McIntosh [J. M. MacGregor]
     Oct   *The Man With Absolute Motion*, N. Loomis
     Dec   *The Resurrected Man*, E. C. Tubb
[Short novels from here on]
1959 Feb   "Second Chance," J. F. Bone
     Mar   "A World of Slaves," J. Christopher

     Apr   "The Soloman Plan," J. T. McIntosh [J. M. MacGregor]
     May   "Sister Planet," P. Anderson

Issues:

	Jan	Feb	Mar	Apr	May	Jun	Jul	Aug	Sep	Oct	Nov	Dec	W
1956										1/1		1/2	2
1957	1/3		1/4		1/5				1/6	2/1		2/2	8
1958	2/3		2/4		2/5				2/6	3/1		3/2	14
1959		3/3	3/4	3/5	3/6								18

SATURDAY EVENING POST   U.S.   General

This magazine was derived from an earlier one founded by Benjamin Franklin. It was weekly until 1962, when biweekly issues began during the summer months; it ceased as of Feb 8, 1969. It was large size and saddle-stapled. The emphasis was mainly on articles rather than fiction, but nevertheless it presented occasional sf/fantasy in both short story and serial form.

The earliest known fantasy is "The Battle of the Monsters," Morgan Robertson, published just before 1900. Then a pioneering sf story, *The Man Who Rocked The Earth*, A. Train, appeared around 1915. In the 1920's the most important story was *The Maracot Deep*, by A. C. Doyle (sr4, 18 Oct 1927), while "Our Distant Cousins," Lord Dunsany, appeared 23 Nov 1929. In the 1930's S. V. Benét was the main fantasy writer to appear, with such stories as "The Devil and Daniel Webster" (24 Oct 1936) [for others see the author listing].

After a long hiatus without fantasy in the *Post*, R. A. Heinlein broke into the magazine with his short story "The Green Hills of Earth" (8 Feb 1947), and followed this with "Space Jockey" (26 Apr 1947) and "It's Great To Be Back" (26 July 1947). R. S. Carr's "Morning Star" appeared 18 Sep 1947. The year 1948 brought Heinlein's "The Black Pits of Luna" (10 Jan), "The Brighton Monster," G. Kersh (21 Feb), and "The Fascinating Stranger," M. Fessier (22 May). In 1949 there were "Easter Eggs," R. S. Carr (24 Sep) ("Those Men From Mars"), "Doomsday Deferred," W. F. Jenkins (24 Sep), and "The Outer Limit," Graham Doar (24 Dec).

The 1950's had Bradbury and several notable serials. For 1950 there were "The World the Children Made," R. Bradbury (23 Sep) ["The Veldt"], and "The Enemy Planet," D. V. Gallery (30 Sep). The only important 1951 short was Bradbury's "The Beast From 20,000 Fathoms" (23 June), while in 1952 his "The April Witch" (5 Apr) appeared. A serial in 1952 was "The Mystery of the Third Compartment" (sr5, 22 Nov) [*The Secret Masters*]. "The Little Terror," W. F. Jenkins (8 Apr 1953) was later televised as *Best of the Post*, while a further short that year was "The Day the Rocket Blew Up," L. Correy (15 Aug). In 1954 there were "The Second Trip to Mars," W. Moore (28 Aug) ["Dominions Beyond"], and the beginning of the famous novel "The Day New York Was Invaded," L. Wibberley (sr6, 25 Dec) [*The Mouse That Roared*]. Later short stories of note were "The Invisible Boy," Edmund Cooper (23 June 1956) ["Brain Child"], and "River of Riches," G. Kersh (8 Mar 1958). One of the *Post's* most controversial serials was John Christopher's *No Blade of Grass* (sr7, 24 Apr 1957). A later one was *Too Many Ghosts*, P. Gallico (sr7, 31 Oct 1959).

In the early 1960's much sf still appeared. Serials were the weak *Moon Pilot*, R. Buckner (sr3, 19 Mar 1960) [also called *Starfire*], and "If Hitler Had Invaded England," C. S. Forester (sr3, 16 Apr 1960)—a quiet and unsung story. A short novel of interest was "The Other Wife," J. Finney (30 Jan 1960) [enlarged as *The Woodrow Wilson Dime*]. Other stories included three by R. Bradbury: "The Forever Voyage" (9 Jan 1960), "The Drummer Boy of Shiloh" (30 Apr 1960), and "The Beggar on Dublin Bridge" (14 Jan 1961). There were also "The Talking Dog," Robert Standish (16 Apr 1960); "Nine Days to Die," William Sambrot (9 July 1960); "The Lost Continent," Geoffrey Household (3 Sep 1960); "Creature of the Snows," W. Sambrot (29 Oct 1960); and "The Girl Who Made Time Stop," Robert F. Young (22 Apr 1961). An article about John W. Campbell Jr. appeared in the 8 Oct 1960 issue.

Science fiction and fantasy then virtually ceased except for I. Asimov's novelisation of the film *Fantastic Voyage*, which appeared as a two-part serial from 20 Feb 1966.

Anthologies directly derived from the magazine were: *Saturday Evening Post Fantasy Stories*, B. Fles (1951) (9 stories), and *The Post Reader of Fantasy and Science Fiction*, SEP Editors (1964) (20 stories including the short novel *The Answer*, P. Wylie).

SATURN SCIENCE FICTION AND FANTASY U.S. Science fiction
5 issues (Mar 1957—Mar 1958).
Digest size; 128 pp.; bimonthly; 35¢.
Editor: D. A. Wollheim.
Publisher: Candar Pub. Co. [Robert Sproule], New York.

Subtitles varied: for the first, "the Magazine of Science Fiction," and "Magazine of Fantasy and Science Fiction" for the second issue. With the sixth issue the magazine changed to detective stories, becoming *Saturn Detective*; it then became *Web Detective Stories*, and by 1962 was *Web Terror Stories*, which ran at least to 1965.

Notable Fiction:
1957 Mar "Eternal Adam," J. Verne
    May "The Murky Glass" (short), H. P. Lovecraft & A. Derleth
    Jul "The Ordeal of Doctor Trifulgas" (short), J. Verne
    Oct "The Elephant Circuit" (short), R. A. Heinlein

Issues:

	Jan	Feb	Mar	Apr	May	Jun	Jul	Aug	Sep	Oct	Nov	Dec	W
1957			1/1		1/2		1/3			1/4			4
1958			1/5										5

SCIENCE AND INVENTION U.S. Popularised science
Editor: H. Gernsback.

Originally titled *Electrical Experimenter* to 1920. In this magazine Gernsback published much science fiction, though the quantity lessened considerably following the founding of *Amazing Stories* in Apr 1926. The noted sf issue was Aug 1923 (11/4). A survey by T.G.L. Cockcroft of New Zealand gives 7 serials and 86 short stories from Aug 1920 (8/4) to Aug 1929 (17/4). The magazine ceased during Gernsback's financial setback in 1929.

The serials were: "Around the Universe," R. Cummings (sr6, July 1923); "The Man on the Meteor," R. Cummings (sr9, Jan 1924); "The Living Death," J. M. Leahy (sr9, Oct 1924); "Tarrano the Conqueror," R. Cummings (sr14, July 1925); "Into the Fourth Dimension," R. Cummings (sr9, Sep 1926); "The Metal Emperor," A. Merritt (sr11, Oct 1927) [another version of *The Metal Monster*]. All were illustrated by F. Paul, who was also very prominent in covers for the magazine. The short stories included "The Vibrator of Death," Harold F. Richards (Jan 1922); "The Thing From . . . Outside," G. England (Apr 1923); and "The Man From the Atom," G. P. Wertenbaker (Aug 1923). There was also C. Fezandie's "Dr. Hackensaw's Secrets" series (43 stories).

SCIENCE-FANTASY British Science fiction / fantasy
81 issues (Sum 1950—Feb 1966)
Editors: W. Gillings, Sum & Win 1950; E. J. Carnell, Win 1951—Apr 1964; K. Bonfiglioli, June/July 1964—Feb 1966.
Publishers: Nova Publications, London, to Apr 1964, then Roberts & Vinter Ltd., London.
Format: First 2 issues 5½ x 7½ in., 1/6; Nos. 3 to 6, 5⅜ x 8⅜ in., 2/-; digest size from No. 7, and back to 1/6; from No. 11, 2/-; from No. 46, 2/6; from No. 61, 3/-; from No. 65 (Roberts & Vinter issues), 4½ x 7 in., still 128 pp.

This magazine began with the formation of the fan-financed Nova Publications. Initially it was meant to be a sort of continuation of W. Gillings' excellent amateur magazine *Fantasy Review*, and departments from that magazine were carried over. However, business commitments caused Gillings to leave, Carnell became editor, and this aspect was dropped, leaving no departments except occasional book reviews.

The fiction policy called for far more fantasy than in *New Worlds*, the companion magazine. This was generally a short novel, most of which were well received, plus short stories. For a time S. Moskowitz's biographical profiles of noted science fiction and fantasy authors were published (following a U.S. appearance). Quinn and Lewis did most of the cover artwork in the Carnell period; like *New Worlds*, no interior illustrations were used.

From No. 41 (June 1960) there was U.S. distribution. Following the drop in sales of the early 1960's, *Science-Fantasy* and *New Worlds* were forced to cut costs and were eventually taken over by the firm of Roberts & Vinter. Under the new editor several noteworthy stories appeared.

Notable Fiction:
1950 Sum "Time's Arrow" (short), A. C. Clarke
    Win "History Lesson" (short), A. C. Clarke
1951-52 Win "Pawley's Peepholes" (short), J. Wyndham [J. B. Harris]
1953 Spr "Mr. Kowtshook" (short), J. Christopher [C. S. Youd]
1954 #7 "Beggars All" (n'te), J. T. McIntosh [J. M. MacGregor]
    Sep "Five Into Four" (n'te), J. T. McIntosh [J. M. MacGregor]
1955 Sep "No Future In It" (short), J. Brunner [title story of collection]
1956 Feb "Non-Stop" (n'te), B. W. Aldiss [enlarged as book of same title, also as *Starship*]
    Dec "Prima Belladonna" (short), J. G. Ballard
1957 Feb "The Maze" (short), A. B. Chandler
    Dec "Hek Belov" series, E. Mackin, began.
1958 Apr "Web of the Norns," H. Harrison & K. MacLean
    Jun "Earth Is But a Star," J. Brunner [*The 100th Millennium*]
    Dec "City of the Tiger," J. Brunner [with sequel as *The Whole Man*]
1959 Feb "Super City," R. Wilson [*And Then the Town Took Off*]
    Jun *200 Years to Christmas*, J. T. McIntosh [J. M. MacGregor]
    Aug *Echo in the Skull*, J. Brunner
1960 Feb "The Sound Sweep" (n'te), J. G. Ballard
    Oct *Beyond the Silver Sky*, K. Bulmer
    Dec "The Black Cat's Paw" (n'te), J. Rackham [J. T. Phillifent] [with later story as *The Touch of Evil*]
1961 Feb "The Map Country," K. Bulmer [*Land Beyond the Map*]
    Apr "Need" (n'te), T. Sturgeon
    Jun "The Dreaming City" (n'te), M. Moorcock [first of "Elric" series, later as books]
1962 Apr *Father of Lies*, J. Brunner
    Jun "The Watch-Towers" (n'te), J. G. Ballard
    Aug "Beginner's Luck" (short), S. Hall [first of "Midnight Club" series]
1963 Feb "Some Lapse of Time" (n'te), J. Brunner [in *Now Then*]
    Aug "The Dolphin and the Deep" (n'te), T. B. Swann [title story of collection]
    Oct "Aspects of Fantasy" (article, sr4), M. Moorcock
    Dec "Skeleton Crew," B. W. Aldiss [enlarged as *Earthworks*]
1964 Feb "The Murex" (n'te), T. B. Swann [in *The Dolphin and the Deep*]
    Apr "The Deep Fix" (n'te), J. Colvin [M. Moorcock] [title story of collection]
    Sep/Oct "The Blue Monkeys" (sr3), T. B. Swann [*Day of the Minotaur*]; "Anita" series, K. Roberts, began.
1965 May "The Impossible Smile" (sr2), J. Cracken
    Jul *The Furies* (sr3), K. Roberts
    Sep "Coming-of-Age Day," A. K. Jorgensson
    Oct *The Weirwoods* (sr2), T. B. Swann
    Dec *Plague From Space* (sr3), H. Harrison
The magazine was continued as *Impulse*.

Issues:

	Jan	Feb	Mar	Apr	May	Jun	Jul	Aug	Sep	Oct	Nov	Dec	W
1950						1/1 (Sum)						1/2 (Win)	2
1951												1/3 (Win)	3
1952		2/4 (Spr)					2/5 (Aut)						5
1953		2/6 (Spr)											6
1954		7 (nd)		8		9		10			11		11
1955	12		13		14			15		16			16
1956	17			18			19				20		20
1957	21		22		23		24		25		26		26
1958	27		28		29		30		31		32		32
1959	33		34		35		36			37	38		38
1960	39		40		41		42		43		44		44
1961	45		46		47		48		49		50		50
1962	51		52		53		54		55		56		56
1963	57		58		59		60		61		62		62
1964	63		64		65	66		67			68*		68
1965	69	70	71	72	73	74	75	76	77	78	79		79
1966	80	81											81

* Dec 1964/Jan 1965.

SCIENCE FICTION   U.S.   Science fiction
12 issues (Mar 1939–Sep 1941)
Pulp size; 128 pp.; bimonthly?; 15¢.
Editor: C. Hornig.
Publisher: Columbia Pubs., New York.

This was Hornig's first effort after his experience with *Wonder Stories*, and the first issue was said by many to be one of the worst first issues ever published. A number of stories from the early issues were published as separate pamphlets in the Columbia "Science Fiction Classics" series [see *PAPERBACKS, Publishers*]. In the main the magazine gave fiction of only fair quality. R. Lowndes later combined it with the companion *Future Fiction* under that title.

Notable Fiction:
1939 Jun   "Where Eternity Ends," E. Binder [appeared also as Australian paperback]
     Oct   "Swordsmen of Saturn," N. R. Jones
     Dec   "Planet of the Knob Heads," S. A. Coblentz
1940 Jun   "The Man Who Was Millions," W. E. Hawkins
1941 Jan   "Space-Flight of Terror," R. Cummings
Issues:

	Jan	Feb	Mar	Apr	May	Jun	Jul	Aug	Sep	Oct	Nov	Dec	W
1939			1/1			1/2			1/3	1/4		1/5	5
1940			1/6		2/1				2/2				8
1941	2/3		2/4		2/5				2/6				12

British Edition:
2 issues (Oct, Dec 1939).
Publisher: Atlas Publications, London.
Slightly abridged from the corresponding U.S. editions.
Canadian Edition:
6 issues (Oct, Nov 1941; Jan, Feb, Mar, June 1942).
Large size (8½ x 11 in.); 64 pp.; 25¢.
Editor: Wm. Brown-Forbes.
Publisher: Superior Magazines Publishers, Toronto, for first 2; then Duchess Printing & Publishing Co. Ltd., Toronto.

This reprinted fiction from both the U.S. *Science Fiction* and the U.S. *Future Fiction* (yet some issues were prominently marked "written by Canadian authors"!). The rarest magazines in the Canadian field.

SCIENCE FICTION — 1/- LIBRARY   British   Science fiction
3 issues, not dated (No. 1 *ca.* June 1960, No. 2 *ca.* Aug 1960, No. 3 ? 1961).
Size: 4¾ x 7 in.; 64 pp.; 1/-.
Publisher: G. G. Swan, London.

This pocket-sized magazine had no title page or table of contents (stories in other issues were often listed on the back covers, and not always correctly). It used small type and poor-quality paper. The fiction was only fair, with some reprints from U.S. magazines of the 1940's. A companion was *Weird and Occult — 1/- Library*.

SCIENCE FICTION ADVENTURES   U.S.   Science fiction
Two series:
(1) 9 issues (Nov 1952–May 1954).
    Digest size; 160 pp.; varied, mostly bimonthly; 35¢.
    Editors: P. St. John [L. del Rey], Nov 1952–Sep 1953; H. Harrison, Dec 1953–May 1954.
    Publisher: Science Fiction Pubs. for first issue; then Future Pubs. [J. Raymond], New York [same address for both].
(2) 12 issues (Dec 1956–June 1958).
    Digest Size; 130 pp.; varied, mostly bimonthly; 35¢.
    Editor: L. Shaw.
    Publisher: Royal Pubs., New York.

The first series was quite high class; it began as a companion to *Space Science Fiction*. It had book reviews by D. Knight.

The second series was a companion to *Infinity Science Fiction* and printed good space-opera. Its British edition [see following entry] continued even after the U.S. original ceased.

Notable Fiction:
1952 Nov   "The Firest of Forever," C. Oliver
1953 Feb   "Farewell to the Lotus," A. B. Chandler
     Mar   *Police Your Planet* (sr4), E. van Lhin [L. del Rey]
     Jul   "Long Life to You, Albert" (short), W. Morrison
     Dec   *The Syndic* (sr2), C. M. Kornbluth

1954 Mar   "The Prodigy" (n'te), T. N. Scortia; "The Ride" (short), W. L. Kleine
     May   "Rain Check" (n'te), J. Merril; "Rule Golden," D. Knight
1956 Dec   "Hadj" (short), H. Ellison; "The Starcombers," E. Hamilton
1957 Jun   "Chalice of Death," C. M. Knox [R. Silverberg] [first of trilogy; see *Lest We Forget Thee, Earth*]
     Aug   "This World Must Die!" I. Jorgenson [R. Silverberg] [*The Planet Killers*]
     Sep   "The Slave," C. M. Kornbluth
     Oct   "Thunder Over Starhaven," I. Jorgenson [R. Silverberg] [*Starhaven*]
1958 Jan   *One Against Herculum*, J. Sohl; "Hunt the Space-Witch," R. Silverberg
     Apr   "Shadow on the Stars," R. Silverberg [*Stepsons of Terra*]
     Jun   "The Man From the Big Dark," J. Brunner; "The World Otalmi Made," H. Harrison
Issues:

	Jan	Feb	Mar	Apr	May	Jun	Jul	Aug	Sep	Oct	Nov	Dec	W
1952											1/1		1
1953		1/2		1/3		1/4		1/5		1/6		2/1	7
1954			2/2		2/3								9
1956												1/6*	1
1957		1/2		1/3		1/4		1/5	1/6	2/1		2/2	8
1958	2/3		2/4	2/5		2/6							12

* Sic (printer's error).

SCIENCE FICTION ADVENTURES   British   Science fiction
32 issues (Mar 1958–May 1963).
Digest size; 112 pp.; bimonthly; 2/6.
Editor: E. J. Carnell.
Publisher: Nova Publications, London.

This magazine originally began as the British Edition of L. Shaw's *Science Fiction Adventures*, giving a selection of U.S. stories in its first five issues (also noting Shaw as Editor). However, when the U.S. magazine ceased, the British one maintained publication with original stories, and these were generally of good standard. It was a companion to *New Worlds* and *Science-Fantasy*, slanted to space-opera.
Notable Fiction:
1958 Mar   "The Slave," C. M. Kornbluth; "Chalice of Death," C. M. Knox [see U.S. June 1957]
     May   *One Against Herculum*, J. Sohl
     Nov   "This World Must Die!" I. Jorgenson [see U.S. Aug 1957]
1959 Jan   "Shadow of the Sword," W. Whiteford [had sequel]
     Jul   "Children of the Stars," C. C. Reed [first of trilogy; see *Martian Enterprise*]
     Oct   "Galactic Destiny," E. C. Tubb
1960 Feb   "Deadly Litter" (n'te), J. White [title story of collection]
     May   "Of Earth Foretold," K. Bulmer [*The Earth Gods Are Coming*]
     Nov   "Earth's Long Shadow," K. Bulmer [*No Man's Land*]
1961 May   *Wind of Liberty*, K. Bulmer
     Jul   "A Trek to Na-Abiza," W. F. Temple [*The Three Suns of Amara*]
1962 Jan   *The Drowned World*, J. G. Ballard
     Mar   "Spoil of Yesterday," J. Brunner [first of trilogy; see *Times Without Number*]
     Nov   *The Sundered Worlds*, M. Moorcock
1963 May   "The Blood Red Game," M. Moorcock
Issues:

	Jan	Feb	Mar	Apr	May	Jun	Jul	Aug	Sep	Oct	Nov	Dec	W
1958			1		2		3		4		5		5
1959	6		7		8		9		10	11	12		12
1960		13		14		15		16		17			17
1961	18		19		20		21		22		23		23
1962	24		25		26		27		28		29		29
1963	30		31		32								32

SCIENCE FICTION CLASSICS   U.S.   Science fiction
Current (No. 1, not dated, *ca.* June 1967). [Apparently ceased as *Science Fiction Adventures*, Nov. 1974, after 34 issues.]

Digest size; quarterly; 130 pp.; 50¢.

Editor and Publisher: Jack Lester; first 3 by Magazine Productions, New York, then apparently became part of the Ultimate reprint chain.

A reprint magazine featuring science ficton from before the mid-1930's. The issues were quite neat, and even reprinted the original illustrations by such artists as F. R. Paul and L. Morey (often using the inside front and back covers and the back cover for this purpose). From issue No. 7 (Win 1969) there appear to have been many changes in name, the first being *Science Fiction Adventure Classics*.

Notable Fiction:
1967 No. 1 "Politics" (n'te, *AS*, June 1932), M. Leinster [W. F. Jenkins]; illustrations from *The Skylark of Space*
Fall "When the Atoms Failed" (n'te, *AS*, Jan 1930), J. W. Campbell; "The Gostak and the Doshes" (short, *AS*, Mar 1930), M. J. Breuer; illus. of "The Universe Wreckers"
1968 Spr "The Miracle of the Lily" (short, *AS*, Apr 1928), Clare Harris
Sum "The Second Swarm" (short novel, *ASQ*, Spr 1928), J. Schlossel
Fall "Space-Rocket Murders" (n'te, *AS*, Oct 1932), E. Hamilton

Issues:

	Spring	Summer	Fall	Winter	W
1967		1 (nd)	2	3	3
1968	4	5	6		6

SCIENCE FICTION DIGEST   U.S.   Science fiction
2 issues, not dated (*ca.* Feb, May 1954).
Digest size; 160 pp.; 35¢.

Editor: C. Whitehorne.

Publisher: Specific Fiction Corp., New York.

The only attempt in the science fiction field to produce a magazine that was digest in content as well as in size. It reprinted articles and fiction from all sources, even "slick" magazines. Although generally considered to be quite good, there was not enough sf literature, etc., to sustain it, and it ceased even as the third issue was ready for the printers. A companion was the short-lived *Vortex Science Fiction*.

SCIENCE FICTION FORTNIGHTLY See *AUTHENTIC SCIENCE FICTION*

SCIENCE FICTION HORIZONS   British   Criticism
2 issues (Spr 1964 No. 1, Win 1965 No. 2).
Size 5½ x 8¼ in.; 64 pp.; 3/6.

Editors: H. Harrison and B. Aldiss.

Publisher: SF Horizons Ltd. [Business Manager, T. Boardman], Sunningdale, Berks., England.

Art Editor: Roy G. Krenkel.

Science fiction criticism and discussion; it deserved to continue. The main material presented was:

No. 1: C. S. Lewis discusses sf with Kingsley Amis; "Judgment at Jonbar," B. Aldiss (discussion of J. Williamson's *Legion of Time*); "The Use of Language in SF," G. D. Doherty; "Is This Thinking?" J. Blish.

No. 2: William Burroughs discusses science fiction; "British SF Now," B. Aldiss (studies of L. Wright, D. Malcolm, J. G. Ballard); "SF: The Critical Literature," J. Blish.

SCIENCE FICTION MAGAZINE   French   Science fiction
4 issues (Nov 1953—Feb 1954).
Size 22 cm x 30 cm (approx. 8⅝ x 11¾ in.); 18 pp.; monthly; 60 francs.
Published in Paris. Besides French writers, the contributors included B. Berry, S. Mullen, A. Connell, and R. Cummings.

SCIENCE FICTION MONTHLY See *AUTHENTIC SCIENCE FICTION*

SCIENCE FICTION MONTHLY   Australian   Science fiction
18 issues, not dated (Aug 1955—Jan 1957).

Publisher: Atlas Pubs., Melbourne.
Size 5¼ x 7½ in.; 98 pp.; monthly; 2/-; from No. 12, 112 pp. and 2/6; saddle-stapled.

An Australian venture of reasonable quality. Most of its contents were reprinted from the U.S. magazines *Science Fiction Plus*, *Cosmos Science Fiction*, *The Magazine of Fantasy and Science Fiction*, *Planet Stories*, and *Imagination*, and the British *Worlds of Fantasy*. The first five covers were copied from *Science Fiction Plus*, and a number of later ones were from *Planet* and *Imagination*.

Following the page increase, G. Stone's "Science Fiction Scene" department appeared, in which he presented book reviews, topical articles, and outlined '20 Years Ago in SF.' This magazine had a companion paperback series *Science Fiction Library*.

Issues:

	Jan	Feb	Mar	Apr	May	Jun	Jul	Aug	Sep	Oct	Nov	Dec	W
1955								1	2	3	4	5	5
1956	6	7	8	9	10	11	12	13	14	15	16	17	17
1957	18												18

SCIENCE FICTION PLUS   U.S.   Science fiction
7 issues (Mar 1953—Dec 1953).
Large size; 68 pp.; monthly, then bimonthly; 35¢.

Editor: H. Gernsback (with S. Moskowitz, Managing Editor).

Art Editor: F. R. Paul.

Publisher: Gernsback Pubs., New York.

This was probably the best looking sf magazine ever produced [at least until *Omni* in 1978], using slick paper for the first 5 issues. However, the story content did not meet this standard and was somewhat prewar in style. The covers were by Schomburg and Paul, with the latter on the back covers (sometimes with "Tina"—presumably Dorothy Les Tina). Nonfiction was provided by D. Menzel, H. Gernsback, and others.

Notable Fiction:
1953 Apr "Retrograde Evolution," C. D. Simak
May "Worlds in Balance," F. L. Wallace
Jun "Nightmare Planet" (n'te), M. Leinster [W. F. Jenkins] [see *Forgotten Planet*]
Aug "Spacebred Generations" (n'te), C. D. Simak; "Hands Across Space" (short), C. Oliver
Oct "Strange Compulsion" (n'te), P. J. Farmer

Issues:

	Jan	Feb	Mar	Apr	May	Jun	Jul	Aug	Sep	Oct	Nov	Dec	W
1953			1/1	1/2	1/3	1/4		1/5		1/6		1/7	7

SCIENCE FICTION QUARTERLY   U.S.   Science fiction
38 issues in 2 series: 10 issues, Sum 1940—Spr 1943; 28 issues, May 1951—Feb 1958).

Format: First series, pulp size; 144 pp.; quarterly; 25¢. Second series, pulp size; 132 pp. to Aug 1953, then 98 pp., to May 1957, all at 25¢; finally 132 pp. at 35¢.

Editors: C. D. Hornig, Sum 1940—Sum 1941; R. W. Lowndes, Spr 1941 on (including the second series).

Publisher: Double Action, later Columbia Pubs., New York.

Cover Artists: F. R. Paul and H. Bok painted most of the first series covers. Early in the second series M. Luros was the main artist; K. Freas had some covers from Aug 1954; E. Emsh(willer) appeared first in May 1955 and frequently from May 1956.

When Hornig began this magazine he published mainly reprint novels and the magazine was reasonably successful. The second series printed new stories, usually including a short novel, and was of average to good quality. The second series also published J. Blish's articles on science in science fiction, R. H. Macklin's on the same subject, and good editorials, and often ran R. Madle's "Inside Science Fiction" column. *Science Fiction Quarterly*, which had trimmed edges from Aug 1953, was the last of the pulp-sized sf magazines.

Notable Fiction:
1940 Sum *The Moon Conquerors*, R. H. Romans
1941 Win *The Shot Into Infinity*, O. W. Gail
Spr "Rescue From Jupiter" (new), E. E. Repp
Sum *Tarrano the Conqueror*, R. Cummings
1942 Win *Into the Fourth Dimension*, R. Cummings
Spr *The Shadow Girl*, R. Cummings
Sum *The Great Mirror* (new), A. J. Burks
Fall *Brigands of the Moon*, R. Cummings

1943 Win   "The Far Detour," A. J. Burks; "The Growing Wall," D. H. Keller; "Wings Across Time," F. E. Arnold

    Spr   *Wandl the Invader*, R. Cummings

1951 May   "Stopwatch on the World," D. R. Gilgannon; J. Blish articles on sf began.

    Aug   "Second Dawn" (n'te), A. C. Clarke [in *Expedition to Earth*]

1952 Aug   "All the Answers" (n'te), R. Phillips [R. P. Graham]

    Nov   "The Timeless Ones" (short novel), E. F. Russell

1953 Aug   "Common Time" (n'te), J. Blish

1954 May   "The Guthrie Method" (n'te), R. Z. Gallun

    Nov   "Moon Dance" (n'te), W. West

1955 Feb   "The Adventurers" (short), C. M. Kornbluth

    May   "The Eye in the Window" (n'te), S. Merwin

    Aug   "The Time Lockers" (n'te), W. West [enlarged as book]

1956 Nov   "The Last Question" (short), I. Asimov

1957 Feb   "Children of Fortune" (n'te), D. A. Jourdan

1958 Feb   "We, the Marauders," R. Silverberg [*Invaders of Earth*]

Issues:

	Jan	Feb	Mar	Apr	May	Jun	Jul	Aug	Sep	Oct	Nov	Dec	W
1940							1 (Sum)						1
1941		2 (Win)		3 (Spr)			4 (Sum)						4
1942		5 (Win)		6 (Spr)			7 (Sum)		8 (Fall)				8
1943		9 (Win)		10 (Spr)									10
1951				1/1			1/2			1/3			3
1952	1/4			1/5			1/6			2/1			7
1953	1/6*			2/3			2/4			2/5			11
1954	2/6			3/1			3/2			3/3			15
1955	3/4			3/5			3/6			4/1			19
1956	4/2			4/3			4/4			4/5			23
1957	4/6			5/1			5/2			5/3			27
1958	5/4												28

* Sic (misnumbered).

British Edition:

Two series:

(1) 2 issues, not dated, not numbered, in 1943.

    Publisher: C. G. Swan, London.

    These were titled *The Moon Conquerors* and *Into the Fourth Dimension* [the first is listed as an Anonymous Anthology in Vol. 1]. They were a small pulp size, used a greyish paper, had no titles on the spine and no title page, but were practically complete copies of the U.S. Sum 1940 and Win 1942 issues respectively.

(2) 10 issues, numbered but not dated (1952–1955).

    Pulp size; 1/-.

    Publisher: Thorpe & Porter, Leicester.

Issues:

	Jan	Feb	Mar	Apr	May	Jun	Jul	Aug	Sep	Oct	Nov	Dec	W
1943			(#1)			(#2)							2
1952	1			2					3				3
1953			4								5		5
1954			6							7			7
1955	8				9			10					10

SCIENCE FICTION STORIES   U.S.   Science fiction

The blurb "Original" was placed before the title from Sep 1955.

38 issues (No. 1, not numbered, not dated, 1953–May 1960).

Digest size; 130-144 pp.; bimonthly; 35¢.

Editor: R.A.W. Lowndes.

Publisher: Columbia Pubs., New York.

This magazine began as a digest-size one-shot companion to the pulp-size *Future (Science) Fiction*, *Science Fiction Quarterly*, etc. The issue sold well, as did a further "one-shot" issue, so it became a regular magazine, taking over the role of *Future SF* from Jan 1955 and assuming its volume numbering.

Within the limitations of Lowndes' budget (the Columbia magazines were amongst the lowest paying in the science fiction field), this magazine published some quite good material. For a period it ran D. Knight's book review column, and Lowndes also presented much review-type material on science fiction itself in his editorials. Madle's "Inside Science Fiction" department also appeared in many issues. The magazine began publishing reprints from Nov 1959.

The last two issues of *Future Fiction* in 1943 had the title *Science Fiction Stories*, but these are usually indexed under *Future Fiction*. The noted amateur magazine *Science Fiction Times* purchased the rights for the title *Original Science Fiction Stories* in 1961, and one amateur magazine of this title appeared.

Notable Fiction:

1953 No. 1 (nn)   "Sentiment, Inc." (n'te) P. Anderson; "The Way of Decision" (n'te), M. C. Pease

1954 No. 2   "In Human Hands" (n'te), A. Budrys

1955 Jan   "The Gift of the Gods" (n'te), R. F. Jones; "Ripeness" (n'te), M. C. Pease

    Sep   "No More Barriers," G. R. Dickson

    Nov   "Full Cycle," C. D. Simak

1956 Jan   "Giants in the Earth," J. Blish [see *Titans' Daughter*]

    Mar   "The Spaceman's Van Gogh" (short), C. D. Simak

    Sep   "The Songs of Summer" (short), R. Silverberg

    Nov   "Homecalling," J. Merril

1957 Sep   "The Return From Troy" (short), R. R. Winterbotham

    Nov   "Early Bird" (n'te), E. F. Russell

1958 May   *The Tower of Zanid* (sr4), L. S. de Camp

1959 Jan   "Caduceus Wild" (sr4), W. Moore & R. Bradford

    Mar   "Project Starlight" (n'te), K. Wilhelm

    Nov   "Luck, Inc." (short), J. Harmon

Issues:

	Jan	Feb	Mar	Apr	May	Jun	Jul	Aug	Sep	Oct	Nov	Dec	W
1953						1 (nn, nd)							1
1954						2 (nd)							2
1955	5/4		5/5		5/6		6/1		6/2		6/3		8
1956	6/4		6/5		6/6		7/1		7/2		7/3		14
1957	7/4		7/5		7/6		8/1		8/2		8/3		20
1958	8/4		8/5		8/6	8/7	9/1	9/2	9/3		9/4		28
1959	9/5	9/6	10/1		10/2		10/3		10/4		10/5		35
1960	10/6		11/1		11/2								38

British Edition:

11 issues (Nos. 1 to 11, 1957–1960).

Digest size; 2/-.

Publisher: Strato Pubs., London.

Practically complete copies of the corresponding U.S. editions: No. 1 (U.S. Sep 1957); 2 (Nov 1957); 3 (May 1958); 4 (June 1958); 5 (July 1958); 6 (Aug 1958); 7 (Nov 1958); 8 (Jan 1959); 9, 10, 11, not known. A 12th issues appeared, but this was an overstamp at 2/- of the May 1960 U.S. original.

Issues (not dated):

	Jan	Feb	Mar	Apr	May	Jun	Jul	Aug	Sep	Oct	Nov	Dec	W
1957									1				1
1958			2			3			4		5		5
1959	6		7			8			9		10		10
1960	11		12*										12

* Overprinted U.S. edition.

SCIENCE FICTION YEARBOOK   U.S.   Science fiction

Current (1967–) [ceased in 1970, after 4 issues].

Pulp size; annual; 98 pp.; 50¢.

Editor: Helen Tono.

Publisher: Popular Library, Inc., New York.

A continuation of *Treasury of Great Science Fiction Stories*, an annual which began in 1964 with J. Hendryx Jr. as editor. No. 1 was noted as *S-F Yearbook*. This magazine reprinted fiction from old *Thrilling Wonder Stories* and *Startling Stories*, and was generally well received. Fiction of interest includes:

1967 No. 1   "Ring Around the Redhead" (short, *SS*, Nov 1948), J. D. MacDonald; "Fruits of the Agathon" (n'te, *TWS*, Dec 1948), C. L. Harness.

1968 No. 2   "The Dark Angel" (n'te, *SS*, Mar 1946), H. Kuttner; "The Invaders" (n'te, *Space Stories*, Oct 1942), G. R. Dickson.

SCIENCE STORIES   U.S.   Science fiction

4 issues (Oct 1953–Apr 1954).

Digest size; 130 pp.; bimonthly; 35¢.

Editor: R. Palmer with B. Mahaffey.

Publisher: Bell Publications, Chicago, for first issue, then Palmer Publications, Evanston, Illinois.

This magazine was actually a continuation of *Other Worlds Science Stories. Universe Science Fiction* was bought as its companion. During the recession the latter magazine was the only one to remain under Palmer's editorship.

Issues and Notable Fiction:
1953 Oct (No. 1) "Flight to Utopia" (n'te), J. Tourneau
      Dec (No. 2) "Potential Zero," J. Bloodstone
1954 Feb (No. 3) —
      Apr (No. 4) "The Oceans Are Wide," F. Robinson; "School Days" (short), J. Causey.

SCIENCE WONDER QUARTERLY See *WONDER STORY QUARTERLY*

SCIENCE WONDER STORIES   U.S.   Science fiction
12 issues (June 1929 – May 1930).
Large size; 96 pp.; monthly; 25¢.
Editor: H. Gernsback.
Publisher: Stellar Pub. Corp., New York.
Cover Artist: F. R. Paul.

Gernsback started this science fiction magazine after his financial setback caused him to leave *Amazing Stories*. The magazine combined with its companion *Air Wonder Stories* to form *Wonder Stories* from June 1930.

Notable Fiction [many short stories, not listed here, appeared as reprints in *Startling*'s "Hall of Fame."]:
1929 Jul   "The Alien Intelligence" (sr2), J. Williamson
    Aug   *The Radium Pool* (sr2), E. E. Repp; "The Eternal Man" (short), D. D. Sharp
    Sep   "The Human Termites" (sr3), D. H. Keller
    Dec   "The Conquerors" (sr2), D. H. Keller [had sequel]
1930 Jan   "The Fitzgerald Contraction" (n'te), M. J. Breuer [had sequel]
    Feb   "A Rescue From Jupiter" (sr2), G. Edwards [had sequel]
    Mar   "Before the Asteroids" (n'te), H. Vincent
    May   "The City of the Living Dead" (n'te), L. Manning & F. Pratt

Issues:

	Jan	Feb	Mar	Apr	May	Jun	Jul	Aug	Sep	Oct	Nov	Dec	W
1929						1/1	1/2	1/3	1/4	1/5	1/6	1/7	7
1930	1/8	1/9	1/10	1/11	1/12	[merging into *Wonder Stories*]							12

SCIENTIFIC DETECTIVE MONTHLY See *AMAZING DETECTIVE TALES*

SCIENZA FANTASTICA: Avventure dello Spazio Tempo e Dimensione
     Italian   Science fiction
7 issues (Apr 1952 – Mar 1953).
Format: Nos. 1 to 4, 5⅝ x 7¾ in., 96 pp.; Nos. 5 to 7, 4¾ x 7¾ in., 128 pp.
Editor: L. Torossi.
Publisher: Editrice Krator S.R.L., Rome.

Of quite good quality, this was the first Italian sf magazine. It reprinted stories from the U.S. magazines *Galaxy* and *ASF*, but used original illustrations.

The first issue had five stories, including four of U.S. origin by A. C. Clarke, H. B. Fyfe, N. L. Knight, and L. del Rey. The second issue had four stories—three U.S. by C. M. Kornbluth, W. West, and L. del Rey—and a serial by Massimo Zeno.

SCOOPS   British   Science fiction
20 issues (10 Feb 1934 – 23 June 1934).
Large size; 32 pp.; weekly; 2d.
Editor: Hadyn Dimmock.
Publisher: Pearsons, London.

The only English-language weekly science fiction magazine so far produced. It was designed as a juvenile and sold in the comic field but was more appreciated by adults. Of average quality with a tendency to sensationalism, it is now a collector's item. Many stories were not credited, but among those that were, Low's "Space" was serialised from 17 Feb 1934 (10 parts), Doyle's "The Poison Belt" from 5 May 1934 (sr6), and G. E. Rochester's "The Black Vultures" from 18 Apr (sr9)—a novel which had appeared in *Boy's Own Annual*.

A number of stories from various issues later appeared in the anonymously edited volume *The Boys' World of Adventure*.

SCORPION, THE   U.S.   Weird
1 issue (Apr 1939).

The first issue of *The Octopus* not being a success, Norvell Page rewrote the second Octopus novel to feature the Scorpion as the new leader of the Purple Eyes. He attempts to use hypnotic drugs to brainwash New Yorkers into mindless zombies. The story was "Satan's Incubator," by-lined Randolph Craig.

SCRAP BOOK, THE   U.S.   General fiction
Publisher: Frank A. Munsey, New York.

This began March 1906 as a reprint magazine, and later began to print original fiction. The July 1907 issue was divided into two sections—the second, primarily for fiction, became *The Cavalier* after the Sep 1908 issue. The first section remained independent until Jan 1912, when it was absorbed into *The Cavalier*.

In 1906 *The Scrap Book* published many fantasy short stories by such writers as E. A. Poe, A. Bierce, and Sir W. Scott. Two novels of interest were: "The Sky Pirate" (sr6, Apr 1909), G. P. Serviss; *The Radium Terrors* (sr8, Jan 1911; book 1912), A. Dorrington.

SCREEN CHILLS AND MACABRE STORIES   British   Weird
1 issue, not dated (No. 1, Jan 1958).
Size 7¼ x 10 in.; 42 pp.; 2/-.
Publisher: Pep Publishers & Printers, Croydon.

Announced as a monthly, this apparently only had the one issue. It gave story reviews of sf(?)-horror films and illustrations therefrom. The issue that appeared covered the films *The Dead That Walk* and *I Was a Teenage Werewolf*.

SCREEN THRILLS ILLUSTRATED   U.S.   Film articles
One of F. J Ackerman's film review magazines, this began June 1962. It only had a few articles of direct interest to science fiction. There were at least 10 issues, with one sighted for Feb 1965.

SEARCH   U.S.   Occult, etc.
Originally titled *Mystic*, Nov 1953 – July 1956.
Current (?) (Nov 1953 –).
Digest size; 35¢; then pulp size from Oct 1959.
Editor: R. A. Palmer.
Publisher: Palmer Pubs., Evanston, Illinois.

Under the title *Mystic* this published some fiction, but gradually the articles predominated until with the name change in Oct 1959 it became entirely nonfiction. Material in the occult, supernatural and weird fields was presented as fact.

Issues:

	Jan	Feb	Mar	Apr	May	Jun	Jul	Aug	Sep	Oct	Nov	Dec	W
1953											1		1
1954	2		3		4			5		6		7	7
1955		8		9		10		11		12			12
1956	13		14		15		16			17		18	18
1957		19			20	21	22	23				24	24
1958		25		26		27			28		29		29
1959	30			31		32		33		34		35	35
1960		36				37		38				39	39
1961		40			41		42		43		44	44
1962	45		46		47		48		49		50	50
1963		51		52		53		54		55	55
1964		56		57		58		59		60		60
1965	61		62		63		64		65		66		66
1966		67		68		69			70		71		71
1967	72		73		74			75		76		76
1968	77		78		79		80	(later not known)				80+

SECRET AGENT X   U.S.   Spy adventure
41 issues (Feb 1934 – Mar 1939).
Pulp size; 10¢.

A one-character magazine of some interest. Working for the unknown Section K-9 in the U.S. Government, "X" was a master of disguise—usually he masquerades as someone else involved in the case. The stories were written by Paul Chadwick under the pseudonym of Brant House.

Corinth Publications reprinted the foliowing titles in paperback in 1966 (with original appearances noted): *The Torture Trust* (Feb 1934); *Servants of the Skull* (Nov 1934); *Curse of the Mandarin's Fan* (Feb 1938); *City of Living Dead* (June 1934); *The Death-Torch Terror* (Apr 1934); *Octopus of Crime* (Sep 1934); *The Sinister Scourge* (Jan 1935).

Issues:

	Jan	Feb	Mar	Apr	May	Jun	Jul	Aug	Sep	Oct	Nov	Dec	W
1934		1/1	1/2	1/3	2/1	2/2		2/3	3/1	3/2	3/3	4/1	10
1935	4/2	4/3	5/1	5/2	5/3		6/1	6/2	6/3	7/1	7/2	7/3	21
1936	7/4	8/1	8/2	8/3		8/4		9/1		9/2		9/3	29
1937		9/4		11/1*		11/2		11/3		11/3		12/1	35
1938		12/2		12/3		12/4			13/1		13/2		40
1939			13/3										41

* Apparently no Vol. 10 (as per *The Hero-Pulp Index*).

SELECTED SCIENCE-FICTION MAGAZINE
Australian — Science fiction
5 issues (May 1955—Sep 1955), not dated, Nos. 1 to 5.
Size: 5¼ x 7¾ in.; 34 pp.; monthly; 9d.
Publisher: Malian Press, Sydney.
Cover Artist: Stanley Pitt.

The companion to *American Science Fiction Magazine*, reprinting U.S. material, this was of good quality. Each issue presented a short novel plus short stories.

Issues and feature stories were: 1. "Second Variety," P. K. Dick; 2. "Flight to Forever," P. Anderson; 3. "The Enormous Room," H. L. Gold & R. W. Krepps; 4. "Surface Tension," J. Blish; 5. "Category Phoenix," B. Ellanby.

SHADOW, THE
U.S. — Weird mystery
325 issues (Apr/June 1931—Sum 1949).

One of the most noted of the one-character magazines, this is only of associational interest. It was not as fantastic as *Doc Savage*. It appeared twice a month from Oct 1932 to Feb 1943.

Wealthy playboy Lamont Cranston was secretly the Shadow, scourge of the underworld, garbed in black cloak, slouch hat, and a pair of automatics. His skill at disguise and ability to blend into the background enabled him to go undetected by his criminal prey. (The weekly radio-play version was more fantastic than the magazine stories, giving the Shadow the occult power, learned in the Orient, to "cloud men's minds" and thus make himself literally invisible to human eyes.)

The stories appeared under the pseudonym "Maxwell Grant," and were mostly by Walter B. Gibson, but with some by Theodore Tinsley, Lester Dent, and Bruce Elliot.

This character was continued in a new series of paperback books by W. B. Gibson (and others under the "Maxwell Grant" pseudonym), issued by Belmont Books from Sep 1963. Some have been reprinted by Grosset & Dunlap. A more recent paperback series was started by Bantam Books.

SHEENA, QUEEN OF THE JUNGLE
U.S. — Fantasy adventure
1 issue (Spr 1951); no further information.

A one-character magazine, with the orphaned daughter of a white explorer growing up in the jungle.

SHOCK
U.S. — Mystery weird
Two series:
(1) 3 or 4 issues (Mar 1948 [1/1]— ?).
   Pulp size; 98 pp.; 15¢.
   Publisher: New Publications Inc., Chicago.
   B. M. Day lists only two issues.
(2) 3 issues (May 1960—Sep 1960).
   Digest size; 130 pp.; bimonthly; 35¢.
   Editor: Anonymous. **Publisher:** Winston Publications, New York.
General:
The first issue of the first series has been sighted. It presented some recommended off-trail fiction: the novel in Mar 1948 was "Death Is a Dame," Frederick C. Davis; there were two novelettes; the short stories included "Her Black Wings," J. D. MacDonald.

The second series was quite well received by lovers of the macabre, blending good reprints with original material. It was apparently continued as *Shock Mystery Tales* (see below).

Issues and Notable Fiction [second series]:
1960 May (1/1) "Bianca's Hands" (n'te), T. Sturgeon; "Graveyard Rats" (short), H. Kuttner; "The Crowd" (short), R. Bradbury
    Jul (1/2) "9-Finger Jack" (short), A. Boucher; "Yours Truly, Jack the Ripper" (short), R. Bloch
    Sep (1/3) "Final Performance" (short), R. Bloch; "Skin" (short), R. Dahl; "Moon-Face" (short), J. London.

SHOCK MYSTERY TALES
U.S. — Mystery horror
7 issues (Dec 1961 [2/1]—Feb 1963 [3/1]).
Digest size; quarterly; 128 pp.; 35¢.
Publisher: Pontiac Publishing Corp., New York.

This was evidently intended as a continuation of *Shock*, as the issues started as Vol. 2. Each had three novelettes and four short stories. The magazine was very similar in content, layout, and type of illustration to the old *Horror Stories*; apart from size they could be taken as twin publications. The lead novelette for the first issue was "Curse of the Serpent Goddess," Bill Ryder; the second issue (Mar 1962) featured a novelette by Anthony Stuart.

SHRIEK
U.S. — Horror films
4 issues (May 1965, Oct 1965; 1966 issues not known).
First two, large size; 50¢.
Publisher: Acme News Co. Inc., New York (which had some connection with Health Knowledge Inc.).

Subtitled "The Monster Horror Magazine." One issue sighted—Oct 1965—had interviews with Vincent Price, Boris Karloff, and other horror movie stars. It also had illustrated articles on horror movies.

SINISTER STORIES
U.S. — Weird mystery
3 issues (Feb 1940, Mar 1940, May 1940).
Pulp size; 112 pp.; bimonthly; 15¢.
Editor: Costa Carousso.
Publisher: Fictioneers, Inc., Chicago.

A weird-menace (sex/torture) type, this was a companion to *Astonishing Stories* and *Super Science Stories*. The issues are indexed in *The Weird Menace* (B. Jones, 1971), but inadvertently dated there as 1941. Notable stories include "Song of Evil Love," Russell Gray (short, Feb); "School Mistress for the Mad," Hugh Cave (short, Apr).

S.I.P.
Spanish — Science fiction
Over 200 issues, ceasing 1962.

A space-opera magazine series with material by Spanish pulp writers (with English-sounding names). Issues were generally 128 pp.

SKIPPER, THE
U.S. — Adventure fantasy
12 issues (Dec 1936—Dec 1937).
Pulp size; monthly (omitting Aug 1937); 128 pp.; 10¢.
Editor: John Nanovic.
Publisher: Street & Smith, New York.

A one-character magazine presenting novels about the commander of a Q-ship called the *Whirlwind*. Captain John Fury, "The Skipper," sailed around the world investigating piracy. There were also short stories by such writers as Norman A. Daniels, H. B. Cave, C. Jacobi, and Steve Fisher.

After the magazine ceased the series was continued for a further 40 stories in *Doc Savage* magazine (Nov 1937—Dec 1943). The series is listed in *The Hero-Pulp Index*, McKinstry & Weinberg (1970). Volume numbering was Dec 1936—May 1937, 1/1—1/6; June 1937—Dec 1937, 2/1—2/6.

SOLDIERS OF FORTUNE
U.S. — Adventure
5 issues (Sep 1931—May 1932).
Pulp size; bimonthly; 160 pp.; 25¢.
Editor: Harry Bates.
Publisher: Clayton Magazines, New York.

This companion to *Astounding* had some stories of fantastic adventure.

SPACE (Incorporating Speed Age)   U.S.   Nonfiction
2 issues (Jan, Apr 1960).
Publisher: Great American Pubs.

Formerly the hot-rod magazine *Speed Age*, this gave general material on space travel, etc.

SPACE AGE   U.S.   Nonfiction
Quarterly; 50¢.
Publisher: James L. Quinn, Kingston, N.Y.

This magazine began Nov 1958, with issues at least to Nov 1959. It was subtitled "The Fact Reporter for the World of Science and Space."

SPACE FACT AND FICTION   British   Science fiction/nonfiction
8 issues (Mar 1954—Oct 1954); numbered 1—8, last 4 not dated. Size 7¼ x 9½ in.; variable pages; monthly; 6d.
Publisher: Gerald G. Swan, London.

This was slanted to the juvenile audience. It was set in large type, and the fiction presented was reprints from the prewar Columbia sf magazines.

SPACE FICTION   Dutch   Science fiction

A little known magazine published at Amsterdam. It had at least one issue—size 13 cm. x 19 cm. (approx. 5⅛ x 7½ in.); 16 pp.; Dutch equivalent of 25¢ U.S. It was not numbered.

SPACE JOURNAL   U.S.   Science nonfiction
First issue Fall 1958, continuing at least to Dec. 1959.
Editor: B. Spencer Isbell.
Publisher: Space Journal Inc., Huntsville, Alabama.
Quarterly; 46 pp.; 50¢.

Mainly devoted to the astro-sciences, it also presented one short science fiction story per issue.

SPACE SCIENCE FICTION   U.S.   Science fiction
Two unrelated series:
(1) 8 issues (May 1952—Sep 1953).
   Digest size; 160 pp.; bimonthly; 35¢.
   Editor: L. del Rey
   Publisher: Space Pubs., New York [J. Raymond].
(2) 2 issues (Spring, Aug 1957).
   Digest size; 128 pp.; bimonthly?; 35¢.
   Editor: Lyle Kenyon Engel.
   Publisher: Republic Features Syndicate Inc., New York.

The first series was the first magazine edited by Lester del Rey, and was very highly considered. It had a number of companions.

The second series was only of reasonable quality, and had as a companion *Tales of the Frightened*.
Notable Fiction:
1952 Sep "Moon-Blind" (n'te), E. van Lhin [L. del Rey]; "The God
       in the Bowl" (short), R. E. Howard & L. S. de Camp
   Nov "Moonwalk" (n'te), H. B. Fyfe
1953 Feb "Ullr Uprising" (sr2), H. B. Piper [expanded as "Uller Uprising" in *The Petrified Planet* (J. D. Clark), 1952]
   May "Cue for Quiet" (sr2), T. L. Sherred; "Second Variety"
       (n'te), P. K. Dick
   Sep "The Variable Man" (n'te), P. K. Dick [title story of collection]
1957 Aug "The Star Dream" (n'te), R. F. Jones
Issues:

	Jan	Feb	Mar	Apr	May	Jun	Jul	Aug	Sep	Oct	Nov	Dec	W
1952					1/1				1/2		1/3		3
1953		1/4	1/5		1/6		2/1		2/2				8
1957		1/1 (Spr)				1/2							2

British Edition:
8 issues (1952—1953).
Digest size; not dated; 1/6.
Publisher: Archer Press, London.

These were practically full copies of the original U.S. (first series). The first British issue corresponded with the second U.S. (Sep 1952), and so on, with the eighth British reprinting from the first U.S.

Issues:

	Jan	Feb	Mar	Apr	May	Jun	Jul	Aug	Sep	Oct	Nov	Dec	W
1952											1/1		1
1953		1/2	1/3	1/4	1/5	2/1	2/2	2/3					8

SPACE STORIES   U.S.   Science fiction
5 issues (Oct 1952—June 1953).
Pulp size; 130 pp.; bimonthly; 25¢.
Editor: S. Mines.
Publisher: Standard Magazines, New York.

This was to have been titled *Space Adventures*, but the appearance of a comic of that title caused the name to be changed. Of quite good quality, this magazine featured a novel in each issue.
Issues and Notable Fiction:
1952 Oct (1/1) "Man of Two Worlds," B. Walton
   Dec (1/2) "Planet of the Damned," J. Vance [*Slaves of the Klau*];
       "Get Along Little Unicorn" (n'te), K. F. Crossen
1953 Feb (1/3) *The Big Jump*, L. Brackett
   Apr (2/1) "The Gears of Time," W. Morrison
   Jun (2/2) "The Dark Side of the Moon," S. Merwin; "The
       Enemy, Time" (short), R. Dee

SPACE TRAVEL   See *IMAGINATIVE TALES*

SPACE WORLD   U.S.   Science nonfiction
Editor: Otto Binder.
Publisher: Winston Pub.

This magazine, edited by the one-time noted science fiction writer Otto Binder, began successfully March 1960 as large-size at 50¢, then changed to newspaper format in 1962. After the Sep 1963 issue it was purchased by Ray Palmer.

SPACEFLIGHT   British   Astronautics
Current (Oct 1956—).
Quarterly.
Editor: P. A. Moore.
Publisher: British Interplanetary Society.

The popular magazine founded to cater to the general public for whom the B.I.S. *Journal* was too technical. It has presented research work as well as related historical and astronomical material.

SPACEMEN   U.S.   Science fiction film reviews
9 issues (July 1961—1965 Yearbook).
Large size; 66 p.; quarterly?; 35¢.
Editor: F. J Ackerman.
Publisher: Spacemen Inc., Philadelphia [J. Warren].

Written in Ackerman's flamboyant style, this magazine followed on the success of *Famous Monsters of Filmland*, and was specially biased to the science fiction field. The stills presented were of considerable interest, and included the text and photos of the German *Girl in the Moon* (F. Lang). It did not generate the cult following of the monster magazine.
Issues:

	Jan	Feb	Mar	Apr	May	Jun	Jul	Aug	Sep	Oct	Nov	Dec	W
1961							1 (1/1)		2 (1/2)				2
1962			3 (1/3)			4 (1/4)			5 (2/1)				5
1963	6 (2/2)						7 (2/3)						7
1964					8								8
1965	Yearbook												9

SPACEWAY   See *SPACEWAY SCIENCE FICTION*

SPACEWAY SCIENCE FICTION   U.S.   Science fiction
Titled *Spaceway* Dec 1953—June 1954.
8 issues (Dec 1953—June 1955). [Since reissued from June 1969.]
Digest size; 160 pp., first 3, then 128 pp.; bimonthly; 35¢.
Editor: W. L. Crawford, with G. Ford [pseudonym] as Associate Editor.
Publisher: Fantasy Publishing Co. Inc., Los Angeles.

This magazine published fiction of quite reasonable quality at times, though the "Criswell Predicts" column (from Feb 1955) was not highly favoured. Beginning with the second issue, F. J Ackerman's "Scienti-film Parade" column was of interest.

Notable Fiction:
1953 Dec "The Osilans" (sr3), A. J. Burks; "The Glad Season"
(n'te), Gene Hunter
1954 Feb "A Look at the Stars" (short), G. Hunter; "The Midgets of Monoton," S. A. Coblentz
Dec *The Cosmic Geoids* (sr3), J. Taine [E. T. Bell]; "The Festival of Earth" (n'te), C. E. Maine [D. McIlwain]
1955 Jun "Igor" (short), Dan Kelly; also began serials "Stairway to Mars," E. E. Evans, and "The Radio Minds of Mars," R. M. Farley, neither of which was completed.

Issues:

	Jan	Feb	Mar	Apr	May	Jun	Jul	Aug	Sep	Oct	Nov	Dec	W
1953												1/1	1
1954		1/2		1/3		2/1						2/2	5
1955		2/3		3/1		3/2							8

British Edition:
4 issues (1954—1955); not dated; titled *Spaceway.*
Publisher: Regular Publications Ltd., London.
These were nearly complete reprints of the first four U.S. issues. No. 1 omitted two stories; No. 2 omitted two stories and an article; No. 3 was slightly changed; and No. 4 was identical.

Issues:

	Jan	Feb	Mar	Apr	May	Jun	Jul	Aug	Sep	Oct	Nov	Dec	W
1954			1/1			1/2					1/3		3
1955													
1956	1/4												4

SPEED MAGAZINES

These were: *Speed Mystery Stories*; *Speed Detective Stories*; *Speed Adventure Stories*; *Speed Western Stories*; *Super-Detective Stories*; *Private Detective Stories*; *Dan Turner—Hollywood Detective*. These were being published in 1943 by Trojan Pub. Corp., Chicago. Only *Speed Mystery* and *Super-Detective* are of fantasy interest.

SPEED MYSTERY STORIES — U.S. — Borderline weird/fantasy
At least 5 issues (Jan 1943—July 1943).
Pulp size; 112 pp.; 15¢.
Publisher: Trojan Pub. Corp., Chicago.
Of issues sighted, the following stories are of possible interest:
1943 May (1/4) "The Samurai Sword," Clive Trent [V. R. Emanuel]
Jul (1/5) "Shadow Captain," E. H. Price; "Titanium Ship," C. Trent

SPENCER MAGAZINES

Four science fiction magazines and two weird magazines published by John Spencer & Co., London. The sf group were not dated and their first issues were not numbered. The weird magazines were more adult in outlook than the juvenile sf ones; they began with dated issues, though this later ceased.
Science Fiction: *Worlds of Fantasy*, 14 issues (June 1960—late 1954); *Futuristic Science Stories*, 16 issues (Aug 1950—June 1954); *Tales of Tomorrow*, 11 issues (Sep 1950—1954); *Wonders of the Spaceways*, 10 issues (Nov 1950—1954).
Weird: *Supernatural Stories*, 106 issues (May 1954—Sum 1967 [nd]); *Out of This World*, 2 issues (Nov 1954, Jan 1955).
From late 1957 Spencer published science fiction as the Badger SF Series; these and the novels in *Supernatural Stories* are covered in the *PAPERBACKS* section.

SPICY MYSTERY STORIES — U.S. — Mystery weird
72 issues? (July 1934—Dec 1942).
Editor: Lawrence Cadman.
Publisher: probably Culture Publications.
A pulp in the weird menace field that placed emphasis on sex with gruesome consequences. Not highly considered. The Austin *Macabre Index* (1952) lists two issues (Sep 1935 and Feb 1937). Although these had no stories of note, such authors as E. H. Price, W. Blassingame, H. B. Cave, R. E. Howard, H. Wandrei, and R. L. Bellem appeared at times.

SPIDER, THE — U.S. — Borderline fantasy
118 issues (Oct 1933—Dec 1943)
Publisher: Popular Pubs.
Pulp size; monthly to Feb 1943, then bimonthly; mainly 112 pp.; 15¢.
A one-character magazine with The Spider, Master of Men, and his aides fighting fantastic villains and menaces. The stories were by-lined "Grant Stockbridge" (pseudonym for Norvell Page), and are covered in *The Hero-Pulp Index*, McKinstry & Weinberg (1970). Berkley Books began a reprint series late in 1969.

STANDARD MAGAZINES

The science fiction and weird magazines published by Standard Magazines Inc. (or this firm's associate, Better Publications, or predecessor, Beacon Magazines), namely:
Thrilling Wonder Stories (1936—1955); *Startling Stories* (1939—1955); *Strange Stories* (1939—1941); *Captain Future* (1940-1944); *Space Stories* (1952—1953); *Fantastic Story Quarterly* (changing to *Fantastic Story Magazine*) (1950-1955); *Wonder Story Annual* (1950—1954).
In the 1960's Popular Library Inc., New York, took over the assets of Better Publications and issued reprint magazines: *Wonder Stories* (1957, 1963); *(Treasury of) Great Science Fiction Stories* (1964, 1965, 1966); *Science Fiction Yearbook* (1967, 1968, and continuing).

STAR SCIENCE FICTION — U.S. — Science fiction
1 issue (Jan 1958).
Digest size; 128 pp.; 35¢.
Editor: F. Pohl.
Publisher: Ballantine Magazines, Derby, Connecticut.
This magazine was started after the success of the original *Star Science Fiction* anthologies [see POHL, F.]. Poor circulation and bad sales caused it to fold after one much-delayed issue. The name was again continued in the paperback anthology series. The artwork was considered quite poor, and the fiction was not in the class presented in the paperback book series.
The same title had been scheduled twice before for projected science fiction magazines—around 1950 by Gnome Press for a magazine to be edited by Philip Klass, and again later for what eventually appeared under the title *Cosmos Science Fiction and Fantasy Magazine.*

STAR-UTOPIA — Austrian (in German) — Science fiction
10 issues (1957—1958).
Publisher: Josef & Maria Steffek, Vienna.
A magazine series using only Germanic authors, including a few reprints of German books. It ceased in mid-1958 because of German competition on the Austrian market.

STARTLING MYSTERY MAGAZINE — U.S. — Weird mystery
2 issues (Feb, Apr 1940).
Editor: Costa Carousso.
Publisher: Popular Publications.
A weird-menace magazine listed in *The Macabre Index* (Austin) and in *The Weird Menace* (B. Jones, 1972). Stories included such titles as "Flesh for the Flame Worshipper" (n'te) Francis James (Feb), and "Flesh for the Devil's Piper" (novel), Wayne Rogers (Apr).

STARTLING MYSTERY STORIES — U.S. — Weird mystery
18 issues (Sum 1966—Mar 1971).
Digest size; 130 pp., saddle-stapled; 50¢.
Editor: R. A. W. Lowndes.
Publisher: Health Knowledge Inc., New York.
This magazine was begun by Lowndes to cater to weird mystery enthusiasts as a companion to *The Magazine of Horror*. It reprinted from many sources, but especially from *Weird Tales*. Among these were many of Seabury Quinn's "Jules de Grandin" series; a chronological coverage noting those reprinted was published in Sum 1969 (#13). The magazine ceased in 1971.
Notable Fiction:
1966 Sum "House of the Hatchet" (short), R. Bloch; "The Lurking Fear" (short), H. P. Lovecraft; a "Jules de Grandin" story
Fall "Doctor Satan" (n'te), Paul Ernst

1966/67 Win "The Inn of Terror" (n'te), G. Leroux
Spr "The Secret of Lost Valley" (n'te), R. E. Howard; "Si Urag of the Tail," Oscar Cook
Sum "The Darkness on Fifth Avenue" (n'te), M. Leinster [W. F. Jenkins]
Fall "My Lady of the Tunnel" (short), A. J. Burks
1967/68 Win "The Bride of the Peacock" (n'te), E. H. Price
Spr "The Return of the Sorcerer" (short), C. A. Smith; "The Three From the Tomb" (n'te), E. Hamilton
Sum "The Black Mass," Col. S. P. Meek
Fall "The House of the Living Dead" (n'te), Harold Ward
1968/69 Win "Wolf Hollow Bubbles" (short), D. H. Keller; "The Haunter of the Ring" (short), R. E. Howard

Issues:

	Spring	Summer	Fall	Winter*	W
1966		1 (1/1)	2 (1/2)	3 (1/3)	3
1967	4 (1/4)	5 (1/5)	6 (1/6)	7 (2/1)	7
1968	8 (2/2)	9 (2/3)	10 (2/4)	11 (2/5)	11

* "Winter" issues bridged two years, e.g., "Winter 1966-1967."

STARTLING STORIES U.S. Science fiction
99 issues (Jan 1939—Fall 1955).
Editors: M. Weisinger, Jan 1939—May 1941; O. J. Friend, July 1941—Fall 1944; S. Merwin, Win 1945—Sep 1951; S. Mines, Nov 1951—Fall 1954; A. Samalman, Win 1955—Fall 1955.
Publisher: Better Publications, later Standard Magazines, New York.
Format: always pulp size, with trimmed edges from Feb 1953; 114 to 180 pp., varying with price; 15¢ to start, 20¢ from Mar 1948, then 25¢ from Nov 1948; mostly bimonthly but with some periods as quarterly or monthly.

This magazine was the first companion to *Thrilling Wonder Stories*; its policy was to publish long novels (as listed later), plus an exceptional older short story in the "Hall of Fame" section. The reprints were quite successful, but many were abridged, even appearing in the abridged form when used in the anthology *From Off This World* (Margulies & Friend, 1949). This success with reprints caused companions *Fantastic Story Quarterly* (later *Fantastic Story Magazine*) and *Wonder Story Annual* to appear, essentially as reprint magazines. The reprints were then dropped from *Startling* from Nov. 1950.

The cover artists were H. V. Brown to May 1940, then E. K. Bergey for most to 1952; Emsh(willer) and Popp also painted many covers.

After a good beginning, the magazine became somewhat juvenile in the early 1940's. Then S. Merwin built up *Startling* and *Thrilling Wonder* to be the best general-type science fiction magazines in the field. From its first issue until Mar 1953 it ran a fan magazine review department, and was the first professional magazine ever to do so.

Startling finished as the last magazine in the Standard chain. The anthology *The Best From Startling Stories* (S. Mines, 1953) was selected from both this magazine and *Thrilling Wonder*.

Notable Fiction [essentially a listing of all novels; reprints are not covered here, but some are noted in *From Off This World* (Margulies, 1949)]:
1939 Jan *The Black Flame*, S. G. Weinbaum
Mar "The Impossible World," E. Binder
May "The Prisoner of Mars," E. Hamilton [*Tharkol, Lord of the Unknown*]
Jul *Giants From Eternity*, M. W. Wellman
Sep "The Bridge to Earth," R. M. Williams
Nov "The Fortress of Utopia," J. Williamson
1940 Jan "The Three Planeteers," E. Hamilton
Mar "When New York Vanished," H. Kuttner
May *Twice in Time*, M. W. Wellman
Jul "Five Steps to Tomorrow," E. Binder
Sep *The Kid From Mars*, O. J. Friend
Nov "A Million Years to Conquer," H. Kuttner [*The Creature From Beyond Infinity*]
1941 Jan "A Yank at Valhalla," E. Hamilton [*The Monsters of Juntonheim*]
Mar *Sojarr of Titan*, M. W. Wellman
May "The Water World," O. J. Friend
Jul "Gateway to Paradise," J. Williamson [*Dome Around America*]

Sep "The Bottom of the World," J. C. & H. Burroughs
Nov *The Gods Hate Kansas*, J. J. Millard
1942 Jan *Devil's Planet*, M. W. Wellman
Mar *Tarnished Utopia*, M. Jameson
May "Blood on the Sun," H. K. Wells
Jul *The City of Glass*, N. Loomis
Sep "Two Worlds to Save," W. Morrison
Nov "The Day of the Cloud," R. Rocklynne
1943 Jan "World Beyond the Sky," R. M. Williams
Mar "Speak of the Devil," N. A. Daniels
Jun "Wings of Icarus," R. Cummings
Fall "Pirates of the Time Trail," R. Rocklynne
1944 Win "The Giant Atom," M. Jameson [*Atomic Bomb*]
Spr "The Great Ego," N. A. Daniels
Sum "Strangers on the Heights," M. W. Wellman [*The Beasts From Beyond*]
Fall *Shadow Over Mars*, L. Brackett [also as *The Nemesis From Terra*]
1945 Win "Iron Men," N. Loomis [sequel to *The City of Glass*]
Spr "Red Sun of Danger," Brett Sterling [a "Captain Future" novel]
Sum "The Hollow World," F. B. Long
Fall "Aftermath," J. R. Fearn
1946 Win "Outlaw World," E. Hamilton [a "Captain Future" novel]
Mar *Valley of the Flame*, K. Hammond [H. Kuttner]
Spr *Other Eyes Watching*, P. Cross [J. R. Fearn]
Sum *The Dark World*, H. Kuttner
Fall *The Solar Invasion*, M. W. Wellman [a "Captain Future" novel]
1947 Jan *The Star of Life*, E. Hamilton
Mar "The Laws of Chance," M. Leinster [W. F. Jenkins] [*Fight for Life*]
May "Lands of the Earthquake," H. Kuttner
Jul "The Kingdom of the Blind," G. O. Smith [*Path of Unreason*]
Sep "Lord of the Storm," K. Hammond [H. Kuttner]
Nov "The Man in the Iron Cap," M. Leinster [W. F. Jenkins] [*The Brain Stealers*]
1948 Jan "The Blue Flamingo," H. Bok
Mar "One of Three," W. Long [G. O. Smith]
May "The Mask of Circe," H. Kuttner
Jul *The Valley of Creation*, E. Hamilton; first of "Magnus Ridolph" series, J. Vance [see *The Many Worlds of Magnus Ridolph*]
Sep *What Mad Universe*, F. Brown
Nov *Against the Fall of Night*, A. C. Clarke
1949 Jan *The Time Axis*, H. Kuttner
Mar *The Black Galaxy*, M. Leinster [W. F. Jenkins]
May "Flight Into Yesterday," C. L. Harness [*The Paradox Men*]
Jul *Fire in the Heavens*, G. O. Smith
Sep "The Portal in the Picture," H. Kuttner [*Beyond Earth's Gates*]
Nov "The Other World," M. Leinster [W. F. Jenkins]
1950 Jan "The Shadow Men," A. E. van Vogt [*The Universe Maker*]
Mar "The Lady Is a Witch," N. A. Daniels
May "Wine of the Dreamers," J. D. MacDonald [*Planet of the Dreamers*]
Jul *The City at World's End*, E. Hamilton
Sep *The Cybernetic Brains*, R. F. Jones
Nov *The Five Gold Bands*, J. Vance [also *The Space Pirate*]
1951 Jan "Passport to Jupiter," R. Z. Gallun
Mar "The Starmen of Llyrdis," L. Brackett [*The Starmen* and also as *The Galactic Breed*]
May "The Seed From Space," F. Pratt
Jul "The Dark Tower," W. West [*The Memory Bank*]
Sep *House of Many Worlds*, S. Merwin
Nov "The Star Watchers," E. F. Russell [*Sentinels of Space*]
1952 Jan "Journey to Barkut," M. Leinster [W. F. Jenkins] [*Gateway to Elsewhere*]
Feb "Vulcan's Dolls," M. St. Clair [*Agent of the Unknown*]
Mar *The Well of the Worlds*, H. Kuttner
Apr *The Glory That Was*, L. S. de Camp

May	*The Hellflower*, G. O. Smith	
Jun	*Dragon's Island*, J. Williamson [abridged]	
Jul	"Passport to Pax," K. F. Crossen	
Aug	*The Lovers*, P. J. Farmer	
Sep	*Big Planet*, J. Vance	
Oct	*Asylum Earth*, B. Elliott	
Nov	"The Star Dice," R. Dee [R. D. Aycock] [*An Earth Gone Mad*]	
Dec	"The Long View," F. Pratt [in *The Petrified Planet*, Pratt (1952)]	
1953 Jan	"Double Meaning," D. Knight [*The Rithian Terror*]	
Feb	*Troubled Star*, G. O. Smith	
Mar	"Centaurus," S. Merwin	
Apr	"Halos, Inc.," K. F. Crossen	
May	"The Conditioned Captain," F. Pratt [*The Undying Fire*]	
Jun	"Moth and Rust," P. J. Farmer [*A Woman a Day* and also as *Day of Timestop*] [sequel to *The Lovers*]	
Aug	"Journey to Misenum," S. Merwin [*Three Faces of Time*]; "The Wages of Synergy" (n'te), T. Sturgeon	
Oct	*The White Widows*, S. Merwin [also as *The Sex War*]	
1954 Jan	*The Time Masters*, W. Tucker	
Apr	*The Houses of Iszm*, J. Vance	
Sum	"The Spiral of the Ages," F. Pratt	
Fall	"Spacemen Lost," G. O. Smith [*Lost in Space*]	
1955 Win	*The Snows of Ganymede*, P. Anderson	
Spr	"Too Late for Eternity," B. Walton	
Sum	No novel	
Fall	"The Naked Sky," J. E. Gunn [see *The Joy Makers*]; "Jungle Doctor" (n'te), R. F. Young	

Issues:

	Jan	Feb	Mar	Apr	May	Jun	Jul	Aug	Sep	Oct	Nov	Dec	W
1939	1/1		1/2		1/3		2/1		2/2		2/3		6
1940	3/1		3/2		3/3		4/1		4/2		4/3		12
1941	5/1		5/2		5/3		6/1		6/2		6/3		18
1942	7/1		7/2		7/3		8/1		8/2		8/3		24
1943	9/1		9/2			9/3			10/1 (Fall)				28
1944	10/2 (Win)		10/3 (Spr)			11/1 (Sum)			11/2 (Fall)				32
1945	11/3 (Win)		12/1 (Spr)			12/2 (Sum)			12/3 (Fall)				36
1946	13/1 (Win)		13/2	13/3 (Spr)		14/1 (Sum)			14/2 (Fall)				41
1947	14/3		15/1		15/2		15/3		16/1		16/2		47
1948	16/3		17/1		17/2		17/3		18/1		18/2		53
1949	18/3		19/1		19/2		19/3		20/1		20/2		59
1950	20/3		21/1		21/2		21/3		22/1		22/2		65
1951	22/3		23/1		23/2		23/3		24/1		24/2		71
1952	24/3	25/1	25/2	25/3	26/1	26/2	26/3	27/1	27/2	27/3	28/1	28/2	83
1953	28/3	29/1	29/2	29/3	30/1	30/2		30/3		31/1			91
1954	31/2 (Win)		31/3 (Spr)			32/1 (Sum)			32/2 (Fall)				95
1955	32/3 (Win)		33/1 (Spr)			33/2 (Sum)			33/3 (Fall)				99

British Edition:
18 issues (1949—1954), not dated.
Pulp size (6½ x 9½ in.); 64 pp.; 1/-.
Publisher: Pembertons, Manchester.

These were incomplete versions of the American edition. No. 1 was based on Win 1946; 2—Mar 1946; 3—Sum 1946; 4—Sep 1950; 5—May 1951; 6—July 1951; 7—Sep 1951; 8—May 1951 & Apr 1952; 9—May 1952; 10—Oct 1952; 11—Nov 1952; 12—Dec 1952; 13 & 14—Jan 1953; 15—June 1953; 16—Dec 1952; 17—Jan 1954; 18—Spr 1954. The issues were quite slim, varying between 64 and 80 pages. They omitted the extensive letter column and other departments that gave *SS* its special quality. The first issue had "Outlaw World," E. Hamilton.

Issues:

	Jan	Feb	Mar	Apr	May	Jun	Jul	Aug	Sep	Oct	Nov	Dec	W
1949						1						2	2
1950						3						4	4
1951					5						6		6
1952							7	8	9		10		10
1953		11		12			13		14		15		15
1954	16		17		18								18

Canadian Edition:
22 issues (Sum 1945—Fall 1946; May, July, Sep 1948; Mar 1949—Jan 1951).
Publishers: Publication Enterprises Ltd., Toronto, 1945-1946; Pines Publications Ltd., Toronto, 1948; Better Publications of Canada Ltd., Toronto, 1949—1951.
Pulp size, untrimmed; varying 96 to 162 pp.; prices 15¢, 20¢, 25¢; quarterly 1945—1946, then bimonthly.
This magazine was identical to the U.S. edition except for the page size being a half inch longer.

STELLAR: Stories of Imagination U.S. Science fiction
The magazine which Ted White intended to publish co-operatively and sell in bookstores (not newsstands). To appear in 1968, the first issue was dummied and was to have had a wrap-around cover by Jack Gaughan and stories by R. Zelazny, Ted White, Lee Hoffman, and Alexei Panshin. (All the stories have since been published elsewhere.) The magazine was to have been priced at $1.00 and to have more wordage than the sf magazines then current. It never appeared because, like so many fannish dreams, it lacked sufficient capital.

STIRRING SCIENCE STORIES U.S. Science fiction and fantasy
4 issues (Feb 1941—Mar 1942)
Format: first three, pulp size, 130 pp., bimonthly, 15¢; last issue, large size, saddle-stapled, 66 pp., 15¢.
Editor: D. A. Wollheim.
Publisher: Albing Pubs., Holyoke, Mass.
This was the first magazine D. A. Wollheim edited. It printed science fiction and fantasy in separate sections, the title of the magazine changing inside from "Stirring Science Stories" to "Stirring Fantasy Fiction." It had *Cosmic Stories* as companion. C. M. Kornbluth wrote many stories under pseudonym, including all of those below.
Notable Fiction:
1941 Feb "Dead Center" (n'te), S. D. Gottesman; "Thirteen O'Clock," C. Corwin
    Jun "Kazan Collects" (short), C. Corwin
Issues:

	Jan	Feb	Mar	Apr	May	Jun	Jul	Aug	Sep	Oct	Nov	Dec	W
1941		1/1		1/2		1/3							3
1942			2/1										4

STRAND, THE British General fiction, etc.
This magazine presented fiction of quite reasonable standard and had some science fiction and fantasy of interest. This included:
1900 Dec *The First Men in the Moon* (sr9), H. G. Wells
1901 Dec "The New Accelerator," (short), H. G. Wells; "The House Under the Sea" (sr8), Max Pemberton
1902 Oct "The Sorceress of the Strand," L. T. Meade & R. Eustace [a series to Mar 1903]
1903 Dec "The Land Ironclads" (short), H. G. Wells
1912 Apr *The Lost World* (sr8), A. C. Doyle
    Dec *Smith and the Pharaohs* (sr3), H. R. Haggard

STRANGE—The Magazine of True Mystery U.S. Nonfiction
3 issues (Mar, May, July 1952).
Digest size; bimonthly; 35¢.
Publisher: Quinn Pub. Co., New York.
This magazine was actually a companion to the early *If*. It presented articles on weird cults and mysteries, etc.

STRANGE ADVENTURES British Science fiction
2 issues (Sep 1946, Feb 1947), not dated.
Large size; first issue 48 pp., 2/-; second, 32 pp., 1/-.
Publisher: Hamilton & Co., London.
A low-rated sf juvenile and companion to *Futuristic Stories*. The issues featured "Fugitive on Venus," L. Halward, and "The Green Dimension," N. Wesley Firth.

STRANGE DETECTIVE MYSTERIES U.S. Weird mystery
At least 23 issues (Oct 1937—Sep/Oct 1942), including 5 issues (Mar 1938—July 1938) titled *Captain Satan*.
Pulp size; 112 pp.; mainly bimonthly; 10¢.
Publisher: Popular Pubs.
Some issues are listed in W. Austin's *Macabre Index*, but this does not make clear the change in title. The situation is covered in *The Hero-Pulp Index* (Weinberg & McKinstry, 1971). The retitling of a mystery

magazine (at Vol. 1 No. 3) has caused many collectors to seek non-existent No. 1 and No. 2 *Captain Satan* issues. *Captain Satan* was an interesting variant in the genre of *The Spider*. The stories, by William O'Sullivan, concerned Cary Adair, a reformed criminal who led a group of gangsters against the gang lords—a typical Robin Hood of crime who justified the title by pretending to be more than human.

Authors in the non-Captain Satan issues included W. Blassingame, P. Ernst, Russell Gray, C. Woolrich, A. L. Zagat, N. W. Page, and W. Rogers.

STRANGE DETECTIVE STORIES   U.S.   Detective mystery
19 issues? (Aug 1932?—Feb 1934).
Pulp size; 160 pp.; 15¢.
Editor: Ralph Daigh; Associate Editor: H. W. Schuettauff.
Publisher: Nickel Publications, Chicago.

An early example of bizarre detective stories such as E. H. Price's "Pierre d'Artois" series. The issue sighted (the last) had a number of stories of fantasy interest, including "Death's Portrait" (n'te), W. E. Barrett, and "Fangs of Gold" (n'te), R. E. Howard. Howard further appeared under his Patrick Ervin pseudonym with "The Tomb's Secret" (short); A. J. Burks and E. H. Price also had short stories.

STRANGE LOVE STORIES   A Utopian Publication (British), covered as a Paperback.

STRANGE STORIES   U.S.   Weird fantasy
13 issues (Feb 1939—Feb 1941).
Pulp size; bimonthly; 128 pp. & 15¢ to Jun 1940, then 96 pp. & 10¢.
Editor: Probably M. Weisinger for all issues.
Publisher: Better Publications, New York.

One of the lesser-known weird magazines, a companion to *Thrilling Wonder Stories* and *Startling Stories*. It featured the popular authors of the day, including R. Bloch, A. Derleth, H. Kuttner, and M. W. Wellman. Most covers were painted by E. K. Bergey, with at least one by R. Belarski. The magazine is covered in T.G.L. Cockcroft's *Index to the Weird Fiction Magazines* (1962).

Issues:

	Jan	Feb	Mar	Apr	May	Jun	Jul	Aug	Sep	Oct	Nov	Dec	W
1939		1/1		1/2		1/3		2/1		2/2		2/3	6
1940	3/1		3/2		3/3		4/1		4/2		4/3		12
1941	5/1												13

STRANGE TALES of Mystery and Terror   U.S.   Weird
7 issues (Sep 1931—Jan 1933).
Pulp size; 144 pp.; irregular; 25¢.
Editor: H. Bates.
Publisher: Clayton Magazines Inc.

The companion to the Clayton *Astounding Stories*, and now a collector's item. It is covered in T.G.L. Cockcroft's *Index to the Weird Fiction Magazines* (1962). All covers were painted by H. Wesso.
Notable Fiction:
1931 Sep "The Dead Who Walk" (n'te), R. Cummings; "The Dog That Laughed" (short), C. W. Diffin; "The Return of the Sorcerer" (short), C. A. Smith
    Nov "Cassius" (n'te), H. S. Whitehead
1932 Jan "Wolves of Darkness" (n'te), J. Williamson
    Mar "The Duel of the Sorcerers" (n'te), P. Ernst; "The Trap" (short), H. S. Whitehead
    Jun "The Nameless Offspring" (short), C. A. Smith
    Oct "The Curse of Amen Ra" (n'te), V. Rousseau [V. R. Emanuel]; "The Hunters From Beyond" (short), C. A. Smith
1933 Jan "The Thing That Walked on the Wind" (short), A. Derleth; "The Cairn on the Headland" (short), R. E. Howard

The 8th issue, never published, was scheduled to include "The Valley of the Lost," R. E. Howard; "The Seed From the Sepulchre," C. A. Smith; "The Case of the Crusader's Hand," Gordon MacCreagh.
Issues:

	Jan	Feb	Mar	Apr	May	Jun	Jul	Aug	Sep	Oct	Nov	Dec	W
1931									1/1		1/2		2
1932	1/3		2/1			2/2				2/3			6
1933	3/1												7

STRANGE TALES OF THE MYSTERIOUS AND SUPERNATURAL   British   Weird
2 issues, not dated (Feb 1946, Mar 1946).
Digest size; 68 pp.; 9d.
Editor: B. Herbert (actually done by W. Gillings).
Publisher: Utopian Publications, London.

The issues were designated "First Selection" and "Second Selection," with both covers by Alva Rogers. The stories presented were reprints from *Weird Tales*, with C. A. Smith appearing in both issues, and R. Bloch not only in the first issue but twice in the second (once under the pseudonym Tarleton Fiske). No. 2 included "The Moon Devils," J. B. Harris, and "Cool Air," H. P. Lovecraft.

A third selection was ready for the press, but the appearance of too many other similar publications killed it.

STREET AND SMITH
A U.S. publisher which played an active part in science fiction and fantasy publishing.

In 1919 the company published *The Thrill Book*. Then in 1933 it purchased *Astounding Stories* from Clayton and published it (with title changes to *Astounding Science Fiction* and *Analog Science Fiction / Science Fact*) monthly through to Jan. 1961, when it was sold to Condé Nast. *Unknown (Worlds)* was also published by this firm, as well as the noted one-character magazines of interest, *Doc Savage* and *The Shadow*.

To celebrate Street & Smith's 100th anniversary, the book *Fiction Factory: From Pulp Road to Quality Street* was commissioned from Quentin Reynolds (Random House, 1956, $5.00). This gives a great deal of information about the early dime novels published, as well as chapters on the magazines. However, Reynolds was not directly associated with Street & Smith and many points in the book are erroneous. The magazine *Unknown* is not even mentioned.

SUMMER SCIENCE FICTION   U.S.   Science fiction (projected)
The tentative title for a one-shot magazine that Great American Publications planned but did not publish. Edited by H. Santesson, it was to have published material purchased for the defunct *Fantastic Universe*. Planned to be pulp size, 160 pp., 50¢, it was dropped before going to the printers.

SUPER-DETECTIVE   U.S.   Fantasy detective
A one-character pulp about super-hero Jim Anthony, of Irish and American Indian descent. At least one issue has been sighted: Oct 1940; 128 pp.; 15¢; published by Trojan Publishing Corp., New York. The novel "Dealer in Death" was by John Grange. The two short stories in this issue both appear to be of fantasy flavour.

SUPER SCIENCE AND FANTASTIC STORIES   See *SUPER SCIENCE STORIES*

SUPER-SCIENCE FICTION   U.S.   Science fiction
18 issues (Dec 1956—Oct 1959).
Digest size; 128 pp.; bimonthly; 35¢.
Editor: W. W. Scott.
Publisher: Headline Pubs. Inc., New York.

Generally considered a quite readable magazine of the adventure type, this also presented science articles. However, from the Apr 1959 issue it concentrated on "monster" stories, attempting to capitalize on the short-lived success of that genre at the time.
Notable Fiction:
1957 Dec "The Gentle Vultures" (short), I. Asimov
1958 Apr "All the Troubles of the World" (short), I. Asimov
    Jun "Slaves of the Tree" (n'te), E. Rodman [R. Silverberg]
Issues:

	Jan	Feb	Mar	Apr	May	Jun	Jul	Aug	Sep	Oct	Nov	Dec	W
1956											1/1		1
1957		1/2		1/3		1/4		1/5		1/6		2/1	7
1958		2/2		2/3		2/4		2/5		2/6		3/1	13
1959		3/2		3/3		3/4		3/5		3/6			18

SUPER SCIENCE NOVELS   See *SUPER SCIENCE STORIES*

SUPER SCIENCE STORIES   U.S.   Science fiction

31 issues in two series:

(1) 16 issues (Mar 1940–May 1943).

Pulp size; 128 pp.; bimonthly; 15¢ to start, 20¢ from Mar 1941, May 1943 at 25¢.

Titled *Super Science Novels*, Mar 1941–Aug 1941.

Editors: F. Pohl, Mar 1940–Aug 1941; A. H. Norton, Nov 1941–May 1943.

Publisher: Fictioneers, Chicago.

(2) 15 issues (Jan 1949–Aug 1951).

Pulp size; 130 pp.; bimonthly?; 25¢.

Editor: E. Jakobsson.

Publisher: Popular Pubs., New York.

This was originally a companion to *Astonishing Stories*. It ran the fan section "The Science Fictioneers"—with an attempt at organising groups under this name (in a manner similar to the old Science Fiction League). The magazine also presented book and film reviews. When it changed to the *Novels* title it published a number of these of interest.

The second series was a companion to *Famous Fantastic Mysteries* and *Fantastic Novels*. While these were essentially reprint magazines, *Super Science* was designed for original material. Although its first few issues were only fair, it developed into a magazine of quite good quality and its demise was regrettable. It had some departments, including J. Taurasi's "Fandom Corner."

Notable Fiction [From Sep 1950 a reprint was published in each issue; the second series also published the last novels in the "Professor Jameson" series by N. R. Jones]:

1940 May "Let There Be Light" (short), L. Monroe [R. A. Heinlein]

Jul "Before the Universe" (n'te), S. D. Gottesman [C. M. Kornbluth & F. Pohl] [had sequel]

Sep "Invisible One" (n'te), N. R. Jones [in "Durna Rangue" series]

1941 Mar *Genus Homo*, L. S. de Camp & P. S. Miller

Nov "Lost Legion" (short novel), L. Monroe [R. A. Heinlein] [as "Lost Legacy" in *Assignment in Eternity*]; a "Tumithak" series story, C. Tanner

1942 Nov "We Guard the Black Planet," H. Kuttner

1949 Sep "Minion of Chaos" (short novel), J. D. MacDonald

Nov "Gateway to Darkness" (short novel), F. Brown [see *Rogue in Space*]

1950 Mar "Rogue Ship" (short novel), A. E. van Vogt

Nov "Flight to Forever" (short novel), P. Anderson

Issues:

	Jan	Feb	Mar	Apr	May	Jun	Jul	Aug	Sep	Oct	Nov	Dec	W
1940			1/1		1/2		1/3		1/4		2/1		5
1941	2/2		2/3		2/4			3/1			3/2		10
1942		3/3			3/4			4/1			4/2		14
1943		4/3			4/4								16
....													
1949	5/1		5/2		5/3		5/4		6/1				5
1950	6/2		6/3		6/4		7/1		7/2		7/3		11
1951	7/4		8/1		8/2		8/3						15

British Edition:

17 issues in two series.

(1) 3 issues, not dated (1949–1950).

Pulp size; 96 pp.; 1/-.

Publisher: Thorpe & Porter, Leicester.

(2) 14 issues, not dated (1950–1953).

Pulp size; 64 pp.; 1/-.

Publisher: Pembertons, Manchester.

Both series reprinted from the U.S. second series, but later Pemberton issues (from No. 7 or so) reprinted most of their material from the U.S. first series.

Issues:

	Jan	Feb	Mar	Apr	May	Jun	Jul	Aug	Sep	Oct	Nov	Dec	W
1949											1		1
1950		2			3				1				4
1951	2		3	4	5				6				9
1952		7		8	9		10			11			14
1953		12	13	14									17

Canadian Edition:

36 issues in two series.

(1) 21 issues (Aug 1942–Dec 1945).

Pulp size; Nos. 1-10, 96 pp.; 11-21, 80 pp.; 15¢.

Publisher: Popular Pub. Inc., Toronto.

From No. 15 (Dec 1944) the title was changed to *Super Science and Fantastic Stories*.

This magazine reprinted fiction from the U.S. *Super Science*, *Astonishing*, *FFM*, and *Argosy*, but in no set order. Some new stories appeared, such as "And Then the Silence" (short), R. Bradbury, and "The Bounding Crown" (short), J. Blish. The magazines were entirely redrafted; they had their own plates and printing. Some covers were reprinted and others repainted. All the interior illustrations were by Canadian artists; they were generally excellent, and some were 2-page spreads. This magazine is now amongst the rarest of the Canadian magazines.

(2) 15 issues (Jan 1949–Aug 1951).

Pulp size; 130 pp., except 114 pp. for last 3; 25¢.

Publisher: Fictioneers, Inc., a subsidiary of Popular Pub. Co., Inc., Toronto.

This magazine was identical to the U.S. edition second series, except that page size was a half inch longer. The same advertisements appeared on the outside back cover as were used on the Canadian editions of *A. Merritt's Fantasy*, etc.

Issues:

	Jan	Feb	Mar	Apr	May	Jun	Jul	Aug	Sep	Oct	Nov	Dec	W
1942								1/1		1/2		1/3	3
1943		1/4		1/5		1/6		1/7		1/8		1/9	9
1944		1/10		1/11		1/12		1/13		1/14		1/15	15
1945		1/16		1/17		1/18		1/19		1/20		1/21	21

1949–1951 Same issues as the U.S. edition.

SUPER SPAZIO   Italian   Science fiction

10 issues (Nov 1961–Nov 1962), 128 pp.

Editor: G. Jori. **Publisher:** Minerva Editrice, Milan.

SUPERNATURAL STORIES   British   Weird

106 issues (No. 1, May 1954–No. 107, 1966/67; No. 106 not issued).

Pocket book size; around 128 pp. (varied); irregular; began at 1/6, then became 2/-, and from No. 39 was 2/6.

Editor: John S. Manning (pseudonym for Michael Nahum and Sol de Salle).

Publisher: John Spencer, London.

This was one of the Spencer magazines, and the only one to last any reasonable length of time. After appearing for several years as a typical magazine with short stories, from No. 40 (1961) it began to have regular issues devoted exclusively to a novel on each even number. (Earlier novel issues were Nos. 29, 32, and 35.) These are listed as novels in the *PAPERBACKS* section (check Spencer "Badger" SN), as they can be considered an associate series to the Spencer "Badger" SF novels which ran at the same time. The title of the short-lived companion *Out of This World* was used (as *Out of This World and Supernatural Stories*) on certain issues (Nos. 13, 15, 17, 19).

Most issues from No. 39 to 95 were issued in pairs monthly. The fiction was only fair, with most being written by Robert L. Fanthorpe under his own name and various pseudonyms.

Few complete collections of this magazine are known.

SUSPENSE   U.S.   Weird/mystery

4 issues (Spr 1951–Win 1952).

Digest size; 128 pp.; quarterly; 35¢.

Editor: Theodore Irwin.

Publisher: Farrell Pub. Co., Chicago.

This was an attempt at a magazine mixing science fiction, weird, mystery, etc.—"High Tension" stories. It did not succeed.

A number of reprints were used and also new stories by some regular sf writers, including T. Sturgeon, R. Bradbury, and A. E. van Vogt. On the weird side, F. Leiber appeared with one of his "Gray Mouser" series; reprints included "A Voice in the Night," W. H. Hodgson, and "A Horseman in the Sky," Ambrose Bierce.

[The title *Suspense* was also used on a mystery magazine issued in 1946 with Leslie Charteris as editor, only No. 1 of which appeared.]

Issues:

	Winter	Spring	Summer	Fall	W
1951		1/1	1/2	1/3	3
1952	1/4				4

SUSPENSE STORIES   British   Mystery, etc.
At least 3 issues in early 1950's, not numbered and not dated.
Publisher: Curtis Warren Ltd., London.

The fantasy and science fiction that appeared was:

(One issue) "Gordon's Town," Derry Falcon; "What Happened to Clambake," R. S. Evans [both fantasy] (plus 2 stories).

(Another issue) "When Johnny Came Home," G. G. Carson; "Dark Nebula," Harold Slater [both sf] (plus 2 stories).

The other issue known had four stories but none was sf or fantasy.

SWAN AMERICAN MAGAZINE   British   Magazine series
Publisher: G. G. Swan, London.

This series included two science fiction issues:

No. 11, *Future* (1948): Reprint of cover and all but two stories (those by Ackerman and Gordon) of the Dec 1942 U.S. *Future*, but with new illustrations; pulp size, trimmed edges, saddle-stapled; 36 pp.; 9d.

No. 15, *Science Fiction Quarterly* (1950): Reprint of cover, three short novels, and short story by Lambert from the Win 1943 (No. 9) U.S. *SFQ*; same format and price as above, except 49 pp.

SWAN YANKEE MAGAZINE   British   Magazine series
Publisher: G. G. Swan, London.

The only issues of direct interest were:

Science fiction: No. 3 (June 1941); No. 11 (early 1942); No. 21 (July 1942).

Weird: No. 6 (early 1942); No. 19 (May 1942).

T

TALES OF GHOSTS AND HAUNTED HOUSES   British   Weird
1 issue (Dec 1938).
Size 6¾ x 9¼ in., trimmed; 96 pp.; probably 1/-.
Publisher: World's Work, Tadsworth, England.

This was No. 32 in the *Master Thriller* series, and was a special Christmas one-shot magazine featuring ten stories by little-known authors.

TALES OF MAGIC AND MYSTERY   U.S.   Weird/fantasy
5 issues (Dec 1927—Apr 1928).
Pulp size; saddle-stapled; 64 pp.; monthly; 25¢.
Publisher: Personal Arts Co., Camden, New Jersey.

An unusual magazine of interest, now a collector's item. Besides fiction, it published many articles on stage magic, conjuring, Houdini, Indian fakirs, etc.. It was illustrated with photos and some drawings.
Notable Fiction:
1927 Dec "The Black Wall of Wadi" (short), F. Owen; "The Black Pagoda" (sr3), P. Chance
1928 Jan "Ghostly Hands" (short), Miriam A. deFord
     Mar "Cool Air" (short), H. P. Lovecraft
     Apr "The Lure of the Shriveled Hand" (short), F. Owen
Issues:

	Jan	Feb	Mar	Apr	May	Jun	Jul	Aug	Sep	Oct	Nov	Dec	W
1927												1/1	1
1928	1/2	1/3	1/4	1/5									5

TALES OF TERROR   British   Weird
1 issue (possibly 2), not dated (about 1937).
Pulp size; 128 pp.; 1/-.
Publisher: World's Work, Tadsworth, England.

One of the magazines in the *Master Thriller* series, the issue known being No. 17. The stories presented, new and reprint, were "Cracky

Miss Judith," Hector Bolitho; "Young Jackson's Discovery," John Creasey; and 4 others.

TALES OF TERROR FROM BEYOND   U.S.   Weird/fantasy
1 issue (Sum 1964).
Size 8¼ x 11 in.; 82 pp.; announced as quarterly; 50¢.
Editor: Patrick Masulli.
Publisher: Charlton Publications Inc., Derby, Connecticut.

The Summer 1964 issue had 8 items, including a story by Stanton A. Coblentz and another by Stanley Ellin.

TALES OF THE FRIGHTENED   U.S.   Weird
2 issues (Spr 1957; Aug 1957).
Digest size; 128 pp.; 35¢.
Editor: Lyle Kenyon Engel.
Publisher: Republic Features Inc., New York.

Companion to *Space Science Fiction*, this published weird material and was of reasonable standard. A short story of interest in the second issue was "Mr. Tiglath," P. Anderson.

TALES OF THE UNCANNY   British   Weird
3 issues, about 1937/1938.
Publisher: World's Work, Tadsworth, England.

These included Nos. 6 and 19 of this publisher's *Master Thriller* series; no information is available on a reported third issue. These were 128 pp., 1/-.

No. 6 included stories by F. Graves, S. Horler, H. Bolitho, and O. Onions; while No. 19 had R. Thurston Hopkins and Francis H. Gibson.

TALES OF TOMORROW   British   Science fiction
11 issues (Sep 1950—late 1954), not dated.
Publisher: John Spencer, London.
Digest size; irregular; 1/6.

One of the four juvenile Spencer sf magazines; it presented original material. It is listed in G. Stone's *Index to British Science Fiction Magazines 1934-53*, Part 6, 1974.
Issues:

	Jan	Feb	Mar	Apr	May	Jun	Jul	Aug	Sep	Oct	Nov	Dec	W
1950									1	2	3		3
1951													
1952							4			5			5
1953	6				7			8	9				9
1954			10		11								11

TALES OF WONDER   British   Science fiction
16 issues (No. 1, 1937, not dated—No. 16, Spr 1942).
Pulp size; 128 pp., dropping to 72 pp.; 1/-.
Editor: W. Gillings.
Publisher: World's Work, Tadsworth, England.

The first British science fiction magazine (not counting *Scoops*, which was published in the two-penny children's magazine field). It appeared irregularly until forced to cease in World War II. Its policy was middle course, giving new work by British writers and also reprinting much material from the older U.S. sf magazines, with such authors as S. A. Coblentz, D. H. Keller, C. A. Smith, and J. Williamson.
Notable Fiction:
1937 No. 1 "The Prr-r-eet" (short), E. F. Russell
1938 No. 2 "Sleepers of Mars" (n'te), J. Beynon [J. B. Harris] [sequel to *Stowaway to Mars*]
    No. 4 "The Smile of the Sphinx" (short), W. F. Temple
    No. 6 "The Mad Planet" (n'te), M. Leinster [W. F. Jenkins] [see *Forgotten Planet*]
1940 No. 10 "City of the Singing Flame" (n'te), C. A. Smith
1941 No. 15 "The Moon Era" (n'te), J. Williamson
Issues:

	Spring	Summer	Autumn	Winter	W
1937				1	1
1938	2	3	4	5	5
1939	6	7	8	9	9
1940	10	11	12	13*	13
1941	14		15		15
1942	16				16

* Dated "Winter 1941."

TASCHENBUCH, DAS   German   Science fiction
4 issues (1958).
Publisher: Zimmerman, Balve.

A short-lived magazine series giving reprints of German material. The title translates as "Pocket Book."

10 STORY FANTASY   U.S.   Fantasy/science fiction
1 issue (Spr 1951).
Pulp size; 130 pp.; 25¢.
Editor: D. A. Wollheim.
Publisher: Avon Periodicals, Inc., New York.

This magazine published original material of only average quality, even though some noted authors appeared. It was not even true to the title, presenting 11 stories, including "Friend to Man" (short), C. M. Kornbluth, and "Sentinel of Eternity" (short), A. C. Clarke.

TERRA   German   Science fiction
555 issues (*ca.* Aug 1957—1968).
Size 6 x 9 in.; 64 pp.; fortnightly; price began at 0.60 DM, 0.70 DM in 1960, then 0.80 DM.
Editor: W. Ernsting for the early period.
Publisher: Moewig, München.

A science fiction magazine series reprinting novels that had seen prior publication in German, and also many translations of British and U.S. novels. These are covered in the appropriate *WHO'S WHO* author entries

TERRA EXTRA   German   Science fiction
182 issues (mid-1962—early 1968).
Size 6 x 9 in.; 64 pp.; 0.80 DM.
Publisher: Moewig, München.

This magazine series reprinted fiction that had previously appeared in a German sf magazine, e.g., from *Terra*.

TERRA NOVA   German   Science fiction
Current (early 1968—).
Publisher: Moewig, München.

A series begun to replace *Terra* and *Terra Extra*. This published novels by both German and English authors. It had reached about 20 issues at the end of 1968.

TERRA SONDERBAND   German   Science fiction
98 issues (May 1958—1965).
Digest size; 96 pp.; monthly; 1.00 DM.
Editor: W. Ernsting for a period.
Publisher: Moewig, München.

A companion to *Terra* but of better quality, printing original translations, mostly of U.S. writers. See coverage under individual authors. In 1965 it became *Terra Sonderreihe*, a paperback series which reached about No. 159 at the end of 1968.

TERROR TALES   U.S.   Weird horror mystery
50 issues (Sep 1934—Jan/Feb 1941).
Pulp size; began as monthly, then bimonthly.

One of the major weird menace magazines outlined in *The Shudder Pulps* (R. K. Jones, 1975) and indexed in *The Weird Menace* (B. Jones, 1972). It also has many issues listed in W. N. Austin's *Macabre Index* (1952). The first issue featured the novel "House of the Living Death," A. L. Zagat, with such other prominent authors as W. Blassingame, H. B. Cave, and G. T. Fleming-Roberts. Authors besides these writing for the magazine later included A. J. Burks, P. Ernst, N. Schachner, N. W. Page, Russell Gray, and R. Cummings.

Corinth Publishers in 1966 issued two selections in paperback, edited by Jon Hanlon [Earl Kemp]: *Death's Loving Arms*; *The House of Living Death*.
British Edition:
3 issues, not numbered, not dated (1948—1950).

THIS WEEK MAGAZINE   U.S.   General
A weekly newspaper supplement which has published *The Eyes of Fu Manchu* (sr2, 6 Oct 1957), S. Rohmer [reprinted as about 10 pp. in *The*

Secret of Holm Peel], and *Life on Mars* (sr3, 24 Apr 1960), W. Von Braun.

THRILL BOOK, THE   U.S.   General/weird
16 issues (1 Mar 1919—15 Oct 1919).
Semimonthly, on 1st and 15th.
Editors: Eugene A. Clancy and H. Hersey, jointly.
Publisher: Street and Smith, New York.

A publication considered by some authorities to be the first actual weird magazine. Now a collector's item, the exact proportion of fantasy material is not known.

It published a number of stories by Greye La Spina, P. P. Sheehan, M. Leinster, and Tod Robbins. The only one of note to be reprinted was *The Heads of Cerberus* (sr5, 15 Aug 1919), Francis Stevens [G. Bennett].

THRILLER   U.S.   Weird horror
3 issues (Feb, May, July 1962).
Large size; 35¢.
Editor: Harry Schreiner.
Publisher: Tempest Pubs., U.S.A.
Considered to be merely readable.

THRILLING MYSTERY   U.S.   Mystery weird
61 issues (Oct 1935—Fall 1944).
Editor-in-charge: Leo Margulies.

There were apparently two series. Most information is on the first: pulp size, 130 to 114 pp., 10¢, published by Popular Publications. The second series was probably pulp size, published by The Thrilling Group of Publishers.

This was one of the lesser-known terror magazines, of interest principally to the weird enthusiast, as it published many stories by *Weird Tales* contributors. It placed great emphasis on characterization of evil. Authors included R. Cummings, J. Williamson, E. Hamilton, F. B. Long, R. Tooker, H. Kuttner, H. B. Cave, H. K. Wells, A. K. Barnes, C. Jacob, J. R. Fearn, P. Ernst, A. J. Burks, and S. Quinn. Most of the fiction is reputed to be only fair.

Many issues are covered in W. Austin's *Macabre Index*, listing up to Jan 1942; a separate coverage from another enthusiast has a Sep 1942 issue. B. Day only lists to Nov 1939.
Issues:

	Jan	Feb	Mar	Apr	May	Jun	Jul	Aug	Sep	Oct	Nov	Dec	W
1935									1/1		1/2		2
1936	1/3	2/1	2/2	2/3	3/1	3/2	3/3	4/1	4/2	4/3	5/1	5/2	14
1937	5/3	6/1	6/2	6/3	7/1	7/2	7/3	8/1	8/2		8/3		23
1938	9/1		9/2		9/3		10/1		10/2		10/3		29
1939	11/1		11/2		11/3		12/1		12/2		12/3		36
1940	*									15/3			
1941					16/3								
1942	18/1								19/2				
1943													
1944										(Fall)			61

* Information from 1940 onward is incomplete.

THRILLING STORIES A Utopian Publications item (British) covered as a paperback.

THRILLING WONDER STORIES   U.S.   Science fiction
Continuation of *Wonder Stories*.
112 issues (Aug 1936—Win 1955); 189 issues including predecessors *Wonder Stories* and *Science Wonder*.
Format: always pulp size; 114 to 180 pp.; 15¢ to start, 20¢ from Apr 1948, 25¢ from Oct 1948.
Editors: M. Weisinger, Aug 1936—June 1941; O. J. Friend, Aug 1941—Fall 1944; S. Merwin, Win 1945—Oct 1951; S. Mines, Dec 1951—Sum 1954; A. Samalman, Fall 1954, Win 1955.
Publisher: Beacon Magazines; (Aug 1937) Better Publications; (Fall 1943) Standard Magazines [all the same publisher].
Review:

When *Wonder Stories* was purchased from H. Gernsback, a complete policy change was made and the magazine was slanted to the juvenile field, even featuring the comic strip "Zarnak" for a number of issues. After its Tenth Anniversary issue (June 1939), in which S. G. Weinbaum's "Dawn of Flame" was featured, some reasonably good short novels were published in each issue. Then in the early war years the standard dropped, and the presence of "Sergeant Saturn" in control of the letter column from Jan 1941 through Feb 1947 made the general tone quite juvenile.

S. Merwin built up the magazine, along with *Startling Stories* (a companion which began in Jan 1939), as the best general magazines in the sf field. Other early companions were *Captain Future* and *Strange Stories*; more companions appeared in the early 1950's. Toward the end of *Thrilling Wonder*'s career it showed a slight sexy trend in line with modern fiction.

Cover artists were H. V. Brown to Aug 1940 and then E. K. Bergey for most to Oct 1952. Emsh(willer), Popp, and J. Coggins also painted a number of covers.

Notable Fiction:

1936 Aug "The Circle of Zero" (short), S. G. Weinbaum; "The Drone Man" (short), A. Merritt

Oct "Rhythm of the Spheres" (short), A. Merritt; "The Microscopic Giants" (short), P. Ernst

Dec First of "Penton and Blake" series, J. W. Campbell [see *The Planeteers*]; "The Brink of Infinity" (short), S. G. Weinbaum

1937 Aug First of "Anton York" series, E. Binder [see *Anton York, Immortal*]

Oct First of "Gerry Carlyle" series, A. K. Barnes [see *Interplanetary Hunter*]; first of "Via" series, G. A. Giles [E. Binder]

1938 Apr First of "Hollywood on the Moon" series, H. Kuttner

Oct "Of Jovian Build" (short), O. J. Friend

1939 Jun 10th Anniversary Issue, including "The Ultimate Catalyst" (n'te), J. Taine [E. T. Bell]; "Robot Nemesis" (short), Edw. E. Smith; "Stolen Centuries" (short), O. A. Kline.

Aug "Race Around the Moon" (short novel), O. A. Kline; first of "Pete Manx" series, K. Kent [see H. Kuttner]

1940 Jan "The Eternal Light" (short), R. M. Williams

Feb "Doom Over Venus" (short novel), E. Hamilton

Jun "The Sun Maker" (short novel), J. Williamson

1941 Jan "Remember Tomorrow" (short novel), H. Kuttner

Feb "The Teacher From Mars" (short), E. Binder

Aug "Son of Two Worlds" (short novel), E. Hamilton

Oct "John Carstairs" series, F. B. Long, began [*John Carstairs: Space Detective*].

1944 Fall "The Eternal Now" (short novel), M. Leinster [W. F. Jenkins]

1945 Fall "Sword of Tomorrow" (short novel), H. Kuttner

1946 Win "Forgotten World" (short novel), E. Hamilton; "The Disciplinary Circuit" (n'te), M. Leinster [W. F. Jenkins] [with sequels as *The Last Space Ship*]

Fall "Call Him Demon" (n'te), K. Hammond [H. Kuttner]

1947 Apr "Bud Gregory" series, W. Fitzgerald [W. F. Jenkins] began [see *Out of This World*]

Oct "Jerry Is a Man" (n'te), R. A. Heinlein; "The Darker Drink" (n'te), L. Charteris; "Hogben" series, H. Kuttner, began.

1948 Apr "The World of Wulkins" (n'te), F. B. Long

Jun "And the Moon Be Still as Bright" (n'te), R. Bradbury

Aug "Memory" (n'te), T. Sturgeon; "The Earth Men" (short), R. Bradbury

1949 Feb *The Weapon Shops of Isher*, A. E. van Vogt; "The Weakness of RVOG," J. Blish & D. Knight [see *VOR*, Blish]

Jun "Sea Kings of Mars," L. Brackett [*Sword of Rhiannon*]; "The Life-Work of Professor Muntz" (short), M. Leinster [W. F. Jenkins]

Aug *The Lion of Comarre*, A. C. Clarke

Dec "Let the Finder Beware!" J. Blish [*Jack of Eagles*]

1950 Apr "There Shall Be No Darkness," J. Blish [in *Witches Three* (F. Pratt)]

1951 Apr "The Continent Makers," L. S. de Camp [title story of collection]

Jun *Son of the Tree*, J. Vance

Aug *Earthlight*, A. C. Clarke [enlarged as book]

Oct "Asylum Satellite" (short novel), F. Pratt [see *Double in Space*]; "Manning Draco" series, K. F. Crossen, began.

1952 Feb "Abercrombie Station," J. Vance [with sequel as *Monsters in Orbit*]

Apr *Double Jeopardy*, F. Pratt; "Moment Without Time" (short), J. T. Rogers

Dec "What's It Like Out There?" (n'te), E. Hamilton

1953 Feb "The Virgin of Zesh" (short novel), L. S. de Camp

Apr "Turncoat" (short novel), D. Knight [see *Hell's Pavement*]; "The Diploids" (short), K. MacLean [title story of collection]

Nov *The Transposed Man*, D. V. Swain

1954 Win "Second Landing," M. Leinster [W. F. Jenkins]

Fall "Time Pawn," P. K. Dick [enlarged as *Dr. Futurity*]; "Trade In" (short), W. Marks

Sum "The Golden Helix" (short novel), T. Sturgeon

1955 Win "Name Your Pleasure," J. E. Gunn [see *The Joy Makers*]; "Crescendo" (n'te), M. St. Clair

Issues:

	Jan	Feb	Mar	Apr	May	Jun	Jul	Aug	Sep	Oct	Nov	Dec	W
1936	[continuation of *Wonder Stories*]							8/1		8/2		8/3	3
1937		9/1		9/2		9/3		10/1		10/2		10/3	9
1938		11/1		11/2		11/3		12/1		12/2		12/3	15
1939		13/1		13/2		13/3		14/1		14/2		14/3	21
1940	15/1	15/2	15/3	16/1	16/2	16/3	17/1	17/2	17/3	18/1	18/2	18/3	33
1941	19/1	19/2	19/3	20/1		20/2		20/3		21/1		21/2	41
1942	21/3			22/1		22/2		22/3		23/1		23/2	47
1943	23/3			24/1		24/2		24/3		25/1 (Fall)			52
1944	25/2 (Win)			25/3 (Spr)			26/1 (Sum)			26/2 (Fall)			56
1945	26/3 (Win)			27/1 (Spr)			27/2 (Sum)			27/3 (Fall)			60
1946	28/1 (Win)			28/2 (Spr)			28/3 (Sum)			29/1 (Fall)	29/2		65
1947		29/3		30/1		30/2		30/3		31/1		31/2	71
1948		31/3		32/1		32/2		32/3		33/1		33/2	77
1949		33/3		34/1		34/2		34/3		35/1		35/2	83
1950		35/3		36/1		36/2		36/3		37/1		37/2	89
1951		37/3		38/1		38/2		38/3		39/1		39/2	95
1952		39/3		40/1		40/2		40/3		41/1		41/2	101
1953		41/3		42/1		42/2		42/3			43/1		106
1954		43/2 (Win)		43/3 (Spr)			44/1 (Sum)			44/2 (Fall)			110
1955		44/3 (Win)											111

British Edition:

14 issues in two series:

(1) 10 issues, not dated (1949—1950, 1952—1953).

   Publisher: Atlas, London.

   Pulp size; originally 1/-, changing to 9d in 1953.

   Issues were taken from the following U.S. originals (but with fewer stories, etc.): No. 1—Aug 1949; 2—Dec 1949; 3—Oct 1949; 4—Feb 1950; 5—Apr 1952; 6—Oct 1951; 7—June 1952; 8—Dec 1951; 9—Aug 1952; 10—Dec 1952.

(2) 4 issues (No. 101—No. 104).

   Publisher: Pembertons, Manchester.

   Pulp size (6½ x 9½ in.), 64 pp.; 1/-.

   Issues (with fewer stories) based on U.S. originals: 101—Aug 1953; 102—Nov 1953; 103—Win 1954; 104—Spr 1954.

Issues:

	Jan	Feb	Mar	Apr	May	Jun	Jul	Aug	Sep	Oct	Nov	Dec	W
1949												1	1
1950			2	3									3
1951													
1952				4		5		6		7			7
1953		8		9		10 (Sum)				101			11
1954	102			103		104							14

Canadian Edition:

23 issues in three series from three publishers:

(1) Sum 1945—Win 1946, by Publication Enterprises, Toronto.

(2) Spr 1946—Dec 1946, by Pines Publications Ltd., Toronto.

(3) Apr 1948—Feb 1951, by Better Publications of Canada Ltd., Toronto.

Format: Pulp size, untrimmed; varying 98 to 162 pp.; prices 15¢, 20¢, and 25¢; quarterly for first 7 issues, bimonthly next 16 issues.

This magazine was identical to the U.S. edition except that the pages were a half inch longer.

THRILLS   British   Mystery/weird
1 issue, not dated, *ca.* 1938, 9d.

This magazine included one real fantasy: "The Duel of the Sorcerers," P. Ernst [*Strange Tales*, Mar 1932]. A projected second issue was to have included "Wolves of Darkness," J. Williamson [*Strange Tales*, Jan 1932].

THRILLS INCORPORATED   Australian   Science fiction
23 issues, not dated (Mar 1950—June 1952).
Publisher: Associated General Pubs., Sydney [later Transport Pubs. (same firm)].
Format: Nos. 1 to 5, 7½ x 9½ in., 50 pp., 9d; Nos. 6 to 12, 7¾ x 10½ in., 50 pp., 1/-; Nos. 13 to 23, varied around 5½ x 7½ in., 34 pp., 8d, but these had 8-point type compared to 10-point previously.

This Australian attempt at a regular science fiction magazine was quite juvenile in outlook. Although it did not reprint U.S. materials, in the early issues some authors (pseudonymous) copied freely from U.S. stories, unbeknownst to the management, who did not know anything about sf. This practice ceased when attention was drawn to the matter.

The only writer of real interest was the late Norma Hemming, who had a story in each of the last seven issues. Some stories of other writers were reprinted in the British *Amazing Science Stories*.
Issues:

	Jan	Feb	Mar	Apr	May	Jun	Jul	Aug	Sep	Oct	Nov	Dec	W
1950			1	2	3	4	5	6	7	8	9	10	10
1951	11			12, 13		14		15	16	17	18		18
1952	19	20	21	22		23							23

TOMORROW   Occult nonfiction
At least 10 issues, Autumn 1952—.

TOP NOTCH   U.S.   Adventure
An adventure magazine running from the mid-1920's to at least Sep 1935, with two issues per month for a period 1930-32. It was companion to *Astounding Stories*, and was edited by F. Orlin Tremaine from late 1933. It published some material of interest, including the following (not necessarily novels):
1930 1 Apr "Death Zone," Lester Dent
1932 1 Sep "Ghost Town," S. P. Wright
1933 Dec "Pit of the God-Beasts," R. F. Starzl
1934 Feb "Time Turns Back," H. Leslie
     Apr "The Dragon of Iskander," N. Schachner [reprinted in *Fantastic*, July 1962]
     Jul "Forest of Fear," C. W. Diffin
     Oct "Man of Dawn," C. W. Diffin
1935 Jan "Heritage," E. J. Derringer [reprinted in *Fantastic*, Dec 1962]
     Feb "The Walking Cadaver," M. Renard; "Blute, Man of Thor," C. B. Kruse
     May "The Feat of Rah," C. W. Diffin
     Sep "The Ultimate Adventure," C. W. Diffin; "The Curse of Atlantis," H. Leslie

TOPS IN SCIENCE FICTION   U.S.   Science fiction
2 issues (Spr, Fall 1953).
Editors: J. O'Sullivan and M. Reiss, respectively.
Publisher: Love Romances, New York.
Format: first issue (1/1), pulp size, 138 pp., 25¢; second issue, digest size, 128 pp., 35¢.
Issues and Notable Fiction (all reprints from *Planet Stories*:
1953 Spr (1/1) "Citadel of Lost Ships" (n'te, Mar 1943), L. Brackett; "The Million Year Picnic" (short, Sum 1946), R. Bradbury; "The Rocketeers Have Shaggy Ears" (n'te, Spr 1950), K. Bennett
     Fall (1/2) "Lorelei of the Red Mist" (Sum 1946), R. Bradbury & L. Brackett
British Edition:
3 issues, not dated (Nos. 1 to 3), *ca.* Sep 1954, Jan 1955, Aug 1956.
Publisher: Top Fiction Ltd., London.
The first two issues reprinted stories from the first U.S., while the third had selections from the second U.S., including "Lorelei of the Red Mist."

TREASURY OF GREAT SCIENCE FICTION STORIES
                        U.S.   Science fiction
3 issues (1964, 1965, 1966), Nos. 1 to 3, with last titled *Great Science Fiction Stories.*
Pulp size; 98 pp.; annual; 50¢.
Editor: Jim Hendryx Jr.
Publisher: Popular Library Inc., New York.
A continuation of *Wonder Stories* (45/2) 1963, which was edited by J. Hendryx; it has since been replaced by H. Tono's *Science Fiction Yearbook*. Each issue lacks a table of contents, though the stories (or authors only, for No. 3) are listed on the outside back cover—not always in correct order. The stories are reprints from *Thrilling Wonder Stories* and *Startling Stories* for the period 1939 to 1954.
Notable Fiction:
1964 No. 1 "The Rotohouse," M. St. Clair; "Keyhole," M. Leinster [W. F. Jenkins]
1965 No. 2 "Columbus Was a Dope," R. A. Heinlein; "What's It Like Out There?" E. Hamilton
1966 No. 3 "The Naming of Names," R. Bradbury; "A Walk in the Dark," A. C. Clarke

TRUE MYSTIC CRIMES See *MYSTIC MAGAZINE*

TRUE MYSTIC SCIENCE   U.S.   Occult nonfiction
At least 3 issues (1938—1939); issues sighted are Dec 1938 (1/2), Apr 1939 (2/1).
Large size; 66 pp.; noted as monthly.
Editor: R. T. Maitland Scott Jr.
Publisher: Continental News, Minneapolis.
A magazine similar to the present-day *Fate*. It printed material by Talbot Mundy, including "Mystic India Speaks," and other articles such as "Lawrence of Arabia."

TRUE STRANGE   U.S.   Weird nonfiction
7 issues (Oct 1956—Feb 1958).
Large size; irregular, but monthly at times; 35¢.
Publisher: Weider Periodicals, New York.
A continuation of *True Weird Stories*. Subtitled "Incredible, Weird and Factual," it gave sensational "true" weird articles.

TRUE TWILIGHT TALES   U.S.   Ghost stories
2 issues (Fall 1963, Spr 1964).
Large size; 96 pp.; 50¢.
Editor: Helene Gardiner.
Publisher: League Publications Inc., division of MacFadden Pubs., New York.
A magazine that reprinted from *Ghost Stories* of July 1930—June 1931. Each issue had 15 stories. One reprint was the oldie "What Was in the Upper Berth?" (short), F. Marion Crawford.

TRUE WEIRD STORIES   U.S.   Weird nonfiction
3 issues (Nov 1955, Feb 1956, May 1956).
Large size; 82 pp.; quarterly; 25¢.
Publisher: Weider Periodicals, New York.
Subtitled "Strange Fantastic True." A weird-supernatural type of magazine similar to *Fate*, with sensationalised articles. Continued as *True Strange*.

TWO COMPLETE SCIENCE-ADVENTURE BOOKS
                        U.S.   Science fiction
11 issues (Win 1950—Spr 1954).
Pulp size; 112 pp.; 3 per year; 25¢.
Editors: J. Bixby, Win 1950—Sum 1951; M. Reiss, Win 1951—Sum 1953; Katherine Daffron, Win 1953—Spr 1954.
Publisher: Wings Pub. Co., New York.
Companion to *Planet Stories*, this magazine featured two books (usually abridged) or short novels in each issue.
Issues and Contents:
1950 Win (1/1) *Pebble in the Sky*, I. Asimov; *The Kingslayer*, L. R. Hubbard
1951 Spr (1/2) *The Star Kings*, E. Hamilton; "The Seeker of the Sphinx," A. C. Clarke

Sum (1/3) "Sword of Xota," J. Blish [*The Warriors of Day*]; "The Citadel in Space," N. R. Jones
Win (1/4) *The Time Machine*, H. G. Wells; *The Tritonian Ring*, L. S. de Camp
1952 Spr (1/5) *The Humanoids*, J. Williamson; "The Outcasts of Venus," A. Powell
Sum (1/6) "The Cructars Are Coming!" P. L. Payne; *Minions of the Moon*, W. G. Beyer
Win (1/7) *Beyond This Horizon*, R. A. Heinlein; "The Magellanics," A. Coppel
1953 Spr (1/8) "Sargasso of Lost Cities," J. Blish [in "Okie" series]; "Survivor of Mars," J. R. Fearn
Sum (1/9) "The Wanton of Argus," K. H. Brunner [John Brunner]; "Mission to Marakee," B. Berry
Win (1/10) "Silent Victory," P. Anderson [*The War of Two Worlds*]; *Ballroom of the Skies*, J. D. MacDonald
1954 Spr (1/11) "Tombot!" D. Wilcox; "World Held Captive," B. Berry

U

UNCANNY STORIES   U.S.   Weird
1 issue (Apr 1941).
Pulp size; 112 pp.; 15¢.
Editor: Robert O. Erisman.
Publisher: Western Fiction.

A scarce one-shot of minor importance. It featured two short novels: "Coming of the Giant Germs," R. Cummings, and "Beyond Hell," R. D. Miller.

UNCANNY TALES   U.S.   Weird
7 issues (Oct 1938—May 1940).
Pulp size.
Editor: R. O. Erisman.
Publisher: Western Fiction.

One of the lesser-known magazines with sex-emphasizing terror material. A companion to *Marvel Science Stories*, most of its issues are listed in W. N. Austin's Macabre Index (1952). Authors included A. J. Burks, Russell Gray, R. Cummings, Mindret Lord, A. K. Echols, and R. L. Bellem.

UNCANNY TALES   Canadian   Weird/science fiction
21 issues (Nov 1940—Sep 1943).
Publishers: Asam Publishing Co., Toronto, Nov 1940—May 1942; then Norman Book Co., Toronto.
Format: first 4 issues 5¼ x 8⅛ in., 64 pp.; then large size (7 x 10½ in.), 96 pp., with last 2 issues 128 pp.; generally a monthly; price 15¢ except the last at 25¢.

This magazine reprinted fiction from *Stirring Science Stories*, *Cosmic Stories*, *Weird Tales*, and *Amazing Stories Quarterly*. From the last-named appeared "After 12,000 Years," S. A. Coblentz (sr4, with illustrations redrawn from the F. R. Paul originals). However, early issues reprinted most prominently from *Weird Tales*, especially T. P. Kelly's "The Talking Heads," "Terrible Crimes of the Past," "Isle of Madness," "I Found Cleopatra," and "A Million Years in the Future." In the later issues most stories were from *Stirring* and *Cosmic*.
Issues:

	Jan	Feb	Mar	Apr	May	Jun	Jul	Aug	Sep	Oct	Nov	Dec	W
1940											1	2	2
1941	3		4		5	6	7	8	9	10	11	12	12
1942	13	14	15	16	17		18		19			20	20
1943							21						21

UNIVERSE SCIENCE FICTION   U.S.   Science fiction
10 issues (June 1953—Mar 1955).
Digest size; 130 pp.; bimonthly; 35¢.
Editors: G. Bell (pseud?), June & Sep 1953; then R. Palmer & B. Mahaffey.
Publishers: Bell Pubs., Chicago; then Palmer Pubs., Evanston, Illinois.

This magazine began in one of the science fiction booms. It was then bought by R. A. Palmer as companion for his *Science Stories* (the continuation of *Other Worlds Science Stories*). *Universe* remained in the field when *Science Stories* ceased during the sf recession, but after March 1955 reverted to its old name and became the second series of *Other Worlds*, retaining the *Universe* numbering.

This was a typical R. A. Palmer magazine, endeavouring to be sensational and publishing few notable stories. It did, however, bring back "The Club House" from July 1954 (the fan service column previously running in *Amazing Stories*).
Notable Fiction:
1953 Jun "The World Well Lost" (short), T. Sturgeon
Dec "The Adventure of the Misplaced Hound" (short), P. Anderson & G. Dickson [a "Hoka" story]; "The Hungry Hercynian" (short), L. S. de Camp
1954 Mar "Lord Tedric" (n'te), E. E. Smith; "The Door" (short), E. F. Russell
May "The Surgeon's Knife," R. Garrett; "Homecoming" (short), E. C. Tubb
Jul "The Dead End Kids of Space," F. M. Robinson
Sep "Star Man Come Home," E. Hamilton [*The Sun Maker*]
1955 Jan "The Santa Claus Planet" (short), F. M. Robinson
Mar "Mistress of Viridis," M. St. Clair [*The Green Queen*]
Issues:

	Jan	Feb	Mar	Apr	May	Jun	Jul	Aug	Sep	Oct	Nov	Dec	W
1953						1/1			1/2			3	3
1954			4		5		6		7		8		8
1955	9		10										10

UNKNOWN See *UNKNOWN WORLDS*

UNKNOWN WORLDS   U.S.   Fantasy
Title changes: *Unknown*, Mar 1939—Aug 1941; then *Unknown Worlds*.
39 issues (Mar 1939—Oct 1943).
Editor: J. W. Campbell Jr.
Publisher: Street & Smith, New York.
Format: Pulp size, 162 pp., 20¢, to Aug 1941; large size, 130 pp., 25¢, Oct 1941—Apr 1943; pulp size, June 1943—Oct 1943, 162 pp., 25¢; monthly to Dec 1940, then bimonthly.

This unique magazine was germinated when E. F. Russell submitted *Sinister Barrier* to *Astounding Science Fiction*. It gave J. W. Campbell the idea of starting a companion magazine to print fantasy which was logical in its own framework and not just frightening. Russell's novel led off the first issue. *Unknown* published much notable adult fantasy during its career. Such authors as L. del Rey, L. R. Hubbard, and J. Williamson helped Campbell give it a flavour all its own. It became especially known for the whacky type of material at which L. S. de Camp excelled.

Up to June 1940 the covers were conventional paintings by comparatively unknown artists, but did include several by E. Cartier. From July 1940 the cover art consisted of a list of the story content decorated with vignette drawings.

In 1948 Street & Smith published *From Unknown Worlds* (large size, 130 pp., 25¢), a selection of reprints with a notable cover by E. Cartier. It included "The Enchanted Weekend," J. MacCormac; "Nothing in the Rules" (n'te), L. S. de Camp; "The Compleat Werewolf," A. Boucher; plus 11 short stories and 4 poems. This was reportedly intended to test the market for a possible revival of *Unknown*.

An Index to Unknown and Unknown Worlds was published by S. Hoffman, Black Earth, Wisconsin (1955, spiral bound, 34 pp., $1.00).
Notable Fiction:
1939 Mar *Sinister Barrier*, E. F. Russell
Apr "The Ultimate Adventure," L. R. Hubbard; *Divide and Rule* (sr2), L. S. de Camp
May "Returned From Hell," S. Fisher
Jun "Flame Winds," N. W. Page; "The Gnarly Man" (n'te), L. S. de Camp

Jul *Slaves of Sleep*, L. R. Hubbard; "Nothing in the Rules" (n'te), L. S. de Camp

Aug "The Ghoul," L. R. Hubbard; first of "Gray Mouser" series, F. Leiber

Sep "None But Lucifer," H. L. Gold & L. S. de Camp; "The Coppersmith" (short), L. del Rey

Oct "The Elder Gods," D. Stuart [J. W. Campbell]; "Enchanted Weekend," J. MacCormac

Nov "Sons of the Bear-God," N. W. Page

Dec *Lest Darkness Fall*, L. S. de Camp

1940 Jan "Soldiers of the Black Goat," M. O'Hearn; "On the Knees of the Gods" (sr3), J. A. Dunn; "The Sea Thing" (n'te), A. E. van Vogt

Feb *Death's Deputy*, L. R. Hubbard

Mar *The Reign of Wizardry* (sr3), J. Williamson

Apr "The Indigestible Triton," L. R. Hubbard [*Triton*]; "He Shuttles" (n'te), T. Sturgeon

May "The Roaring Trumpet," L. S. de Camp & F. Pratt [see *The Incomplete Enchanter*]; "The Pipes of Pan" (short), L. del Rey

Jun "But Without Horns," N. W. Page; "The Kraken" (short), F. Engelhardt

Jul *Fear*, L. R. Hubbard; "The Spark of Allah" (sr3), M. O'Hearn

Aug "The Devil Makes the Law," R. A. Heinlein [see *Waldo and Magic Inc.*]; "It" (n'te), T. Sturgeon

Sep "The Mathematics of Magic," L. S. de Camp & F. Pratt [see *The Incomplete Enchanter*]

Oct "The Wheels of If," L. S. de Camp [title story of collection]; "The Tommyknocker" (sr2), T. C. McClary

Nov *Typewriter in the Sky*, L. R. Hubbard; "Cartwright's Camera" (short), N. S. Bond

Dec *Darker Than You Think*, J. Williamson

1941 Feb *The Mislaid Charm*, A. M. Phillips; "Shottle Bop" (n'te), T. Sturgeon

Apr *The Castle of Iron*, L. S. de Camp & F. Pratt; "They" (short), R. A. Heinlein

Jun "The Fountain" (short), N. S. Bond

Aug "The Case of the Friendly Corpse," L. R. Hubbard; "Take My Drum to England" (short), N. S. Bond

Oct *The Land of Unreason*, L. S. de Camp; "A Gnome There Was" (n'te), H. Kuttner

Dec "Bit of Tapestry," C. Cartmill; "Mr. Arson" (n'te), L. S. de Camp; "Snulbug" (short), A. Boucher

1942 Feb *The Undesired Princess*, L. S. de Camp; "Etaoin Shrdlu" (short), F. Brown

Apr "Prelude to Armageddon," C. Cartmill; "The Compleat Werewolf" (n'te), A. Boucher

Jun *Solomon's Stone*, L. S. de Camp; "Grab Bags Are Dangerous" (short), F. B. Long

Aug "Hell Is Forever," A. Bester; "The Ghost" (n'te), A. E. van Vogt

Oct "The Unpleasant Profession of Jonathan Hoag," J. Riverside [R. A. Heinlein] [title story of collection]; "Compliments of the Author" (n'te), H. Kuttner

Dec "The Sorcerer's Ship," H. Bok; "It Will Come to You" (short), F. B. Long

1943 Feb "Wet Magic," H. Kuttner; "The Angelic Angleworm" (n'te), F. Brown; "The Ultimate Wish" (short), E. M. Hull

Apr *Conjure Wife*, F. Leiber

Jun "Blind Alley" (n'te), M. Jameson; "Sriberdegibit" (n'te), A. Boucher

Aug "Hell Hath Fury," C. Cartmill; "They Bite" (short), A. Boucher

Oct *The Book of Ptath*, A. E. van Vogt; "The Refugee" (short), J. Rice

Issues:

	Jan	Feb	Mar	Apr	May	Jun	Jul	Aug	Sep	Oct	Nov	Dec	W
1939		1/1	1/2	1/3	1/4	1/5	1/6	2/1	2/2	2/3	2/4		10
1940	2/5	2/6	3/1	3/2	3/3	3/4	3/5	3/6	4/1	4/2	4/3	4/4	22
1941		4/5		4/6		5/1		5/2		5/3		5/4	28
1942		5/5		5/6		6/1		6/2		6/3		6/4	34
1943		6/5		6/6		7/1		7/2		7/3			39

British Edition:

41 issues (Sep 1939—Win 1949)

Pulp size (6½ x 9½ in.), 9d.

Publisher: Atlas Pub. Co., London.

Like the British *Astounding*, this edition of *Unknown* was begun as a wartime measure; it ran chronologically later than the U.S. original.

The issues were abridged from the originals, and naturally not much was reprinted from the first six U.S. issues, as these were available in England through normal channels. The principal novels of later issues that were *omitted* were *The Reign of Wizardry*; "The Spark of Allah"; "The Tommyknocker"; *Typewriter in the Sky*; *The Undesired Princess*; "Prelude to Armageddon"; "Hell Is Forever"; "The Sorcerer's Ship"; *Conjure Wife*; *The Book of Ptath*.

The magazine was titled *Unknown* to Mar 1942, then *Unknown Worlds*. Issues were first numbered corresponding to the U.S. edition, then not numbered, and finally denoted as if the first British issue was Vol. 1 No. 1.

From Unknown Worlds was reprinted in 1952. It was smaller than the original (7 x 9½ in., 124 pp., 2/6), but had all the material except the short story "One Man's Harp," Babette Rosmond. A number of copies were better bound at a higher price.

Issues:

	Jan	Feb	Mar	Apr	May	Jun	Jul	Aug	Sep	Oct	Nov	Dec	W
1939							2/1	2/2	2/3	2/4			4
1940	2/5	2/6	3/1	3/2	3/3	3/4	3/5	3/6	4/1	4/2	4/3	4/4	16
1941		4/5					4/6						18
1942			5/5*			6/1				6/3*			21
1943	6/4				6/5					(nn)			24
1944	(nn)				(nn)			(nn)	(Aut)				27
1945		3/4 (Spr)						3/5 (Aut)			3/6 (Win)		30
1946				3/7 (Sum)							3/8 (Win)		32
1947		3/9 (Spr)			3/10 (Sum)						3/11 (Win)		35
1948		3/12 (Spr)			4/1 (Sum)						4/2 (Win)		38
1949		4/3 (Spr)			4/4 (Sum)						4/5 (Win)		41

* Numbers 5/1 through 5/4, and 6/2, were omitted by the publisher.

UNUSUAL STORIES   U.S.   Science fiction

2 issues (May/June 1935, Win 1935), with an advance issue in Mar 1934 (giving incomplete samples of stories).

Editor and Publisher: W. L. Crawford, Los Angeles.

This was a companion to *Marvel Tales*, but its fiction was not so noted. The advance issue had a brief biography of Richard Tooker and a few pages of "When the Waker Sleeps," Cyril G. Wates. "Waning Moon," Robert A. Wait, was the novelette in the official first issue, and the serial "A Diamond Asteroid," Lowell H. Morrow began in the second issue (and was not finished).

URANIA   Italian   Science fiction

14 issues (Nov 1952—Dec 1953), numbered 1 to 14.

Digest size; 160 pp.; monthly; 150 lire.

Editor: G. Monicelli.

Publisher: Arnoldo Mondadori, Milan.

This was a regular magazine subtitled "Avventure nell'universo e nel tempo." Its features included a letter section and a number of articles selected from *Galaxy Science Fiction*. Fiction selections were from the better U.S. material, with translations of stories by A. E. van Vogt, R. Matheson, M. Leinster, I. Asimov, etc., and even some older material such as "Who Goes There?" by J. W. Campbell and "The Black Pits of Luna" by R. A. Heinlein.

Note: The original companion for this magazine was *I Romanzi di Urania*. Its title was shortened to *Urania* at No. 153 in 1957.

URANUS   Austrian (in German)   Science fiction

18 issues (1957—mid-1958).

Publisher: Josef & Maria Steffek, Vienna.

A juvenile paperback series presenting original space-operas (not translations). It ceased because of German competition in the Austrian market.

UTOPIA   Belgian (in French)   General adventure

24 issues (1961—May 1963).

Approx. monthly; 48 pp.; 8 Belgian francs.

Editor: A. Van Hageland.
Publisher: De Schorpioen, Belgium.

The only pulp magazine Belgium has ever had, presenting for a time a science fiction novelette combined with short articles, and with some short stories by the editor or his wife, A. M. Lamend, also a writer of sf. This attempt to make sf popular in Belgium failed; however, *Utopia* did present interesting German, Belgian, and U.S. writers.

UTOPIA-GROSSBAND   German   Science fiction
204 issues (1954–1963).
Size 6 x 8¾ in.; 94 pp.; monthly; 1 DM.
Editor: W. Ernsting, 1954–1957.
Publisher: Erich Pabel, Rastatt.

An important magazine series which printed many translations of the better British and U.S. novels. These are covered by author in the *WHO'S WHO* section. It is understood that most stories were abridged.

UTOPIA-KLEINBAND See *UTOPIA-ZUKUNFTSROMANE*

UTOPIA-KRIMINAL   German   Science fiction
27 issues (Feb 1956–Feb 1958).
Size 5½ x 8 in.; 94 pp.; monthly; 1 DM.
Editor: W. Ernsting.
Publisher: Erich Pabel.

This magazine often had the title *Utopia-Krimi* on the cover and *Utopia-Kriminalromane* inside. It began as a companion to *Utopia-Grossband* and was devoted to future detective fiction. In 1957 it widened its scope from detective stories to include high-class sf. It published a number of outstanding British and U.S. novels, including some by E. F. Russell, M. Leinster, and H. Clement. These were abridged.

UTOPIA-MAGAZIN   German   Science fiction
Title change: *Utopia-Sonderband* for about the first four issues.
16 issues, not dated (*ca.* Dec 1955–May 1959).
Size 5½ x 8 in. (for No. 8); 112 pp.; 1.50 DM.
Editors: W. Ernsting, 1955 to end of 1957; W. Spiegl, 1958–1959.
Publisher: Erich Pabel.

An experimental first issue appeared late in 1955; this was followed by one in June 1956, then Sep/Oct 1956. It then became bimonthly, and turned monthly around May 1958.

This was the first German science fiction magazine in the strict sense, and was also the last of the magazine field to survive. It presented a selection of short stories, mostly translated from U.S. and British material, but with some original German works. It featured covers by Neutzell and Emsh, and early issues also had a movie column conducted by F. J Ackerman.

UTOPIA-SONDERBAND See *UTOPIA-MAGAZIN*

UTOPIA-TASCHENROMAN   German   Science fiction
13 issues (mid-1957–mid-1959); 96 pp.; 1 DM.
Publisher: Walter Lehning Verlag, Hanover.

A companion to *Luna-Weltall*, this series presented only novels. It reprinted German materials by such writers as K. Merten, A. Jeffers, and J. E. Wells. There were three translations: *Alien From Arcturus*, G. R. Dickson (No. 3); *Atom Curtain*, N. B. Williams (No. 4); *Empire of Chaos*, H. K. Bulmer (No. 11).

UTOPIA-ZUKUNFTSROMANE   German   Science fiction
Title change: Began as *Utopia-Kleinband*, with subtitle "Jim Parkers Abenteuer im Weltraum," and changed to *Utopia-Zukunftsromane* around 1954 (before No. 45).
596 issues (1953–1968), then ceased.
Size 6 x 8¾ in. at start; 46 pp.; monthly, later weekly; 50 pfennigs, then 60 pf in 1960, and later 80 pf.
Editor: W. Ernsting to end of 1957.
Publisher: Erich Pabel.

Essentially a juvenile science fiction series, this at times has published some good British and U.S. translations (though very abridged). For the first 43 issues it was a single-character magazine, covering "Jim Parker's Adventures in the Universe," with a few stories in this series following later, all written by A. Tjörnsen.

The City of Glass, N. Loomis (No. 53), was the first translation, and gradually translations became more frequent. Original German works appeared from such writers as J. Norton, C. Darlton, K. H. Scheer, and W. D. Rohr. As with other German magazines, translations pertinent to works in English are covered by author in the *WHO'S WHO*.

UTOPIAN PUBLICATIONS LTD.
A London firm begun by Benson Herbert in the early years of World War II. It produced a number of magazines and paper-covered items, most of which are now quite scarce. The most interesting publications were *American Fiction*, *Strange Tales of the Mysterious and Weird*, and *New Frontiers*. A number of others were more one-shot in nature, e.g. *Thrilling Stories* and *Strange Love Stories*, and are covered in the *PAPERBACK* section.

V

VANGUARD SCIENCE FICTION   U.S.   Science fiction
1 issue (June 1958).
Digest size; 128 pp.; planned as bimonthly; 35¢.
Editor: J. Blish.
Publisher: Vanguard Science Fiction Inc., New York.

The only issue was generally considered quite high class, with the best story being "Reap the Dark Tide" (n'te), C. M. Kornbluth. The other novelette was "SOS, Planet Unknown," A. B. Chandler. There were three short stories, plus book reviews by L. del Rey. It is understood that sales just broke even.

VARGO STATTEN SCIENCE FICTION MAGAZINE See *BRITISH SPACE FICTION MAGAZINE*

VECKANS AVENTYR See *JULES VERNE MAGASINET*

VENTURE SCIENCE FICTION   U.S.   Science fiction
10 issues (Jan 1957–Jul 1958).
Digest size; 128 pp.; monthly; 35¢.
Editor: R. P. Mills, with A. Boucher as Senior Advisory Editor.
Publisher: Fantasy House, New York.

The companion to *The Magazine of Fantasy and Science Fiction*. Designed to give well-told science fiction adventure, it also gave shock-type fiction with some sexual sadism, in the style of Mickey Spillane, to the detriment of the field.

The best story is considered to be "Two Dooms," C. M. Kornbluth (July 1958). "Virgin Planet," P. Anderson, in the first issue was enlarged as a book, and so was "Too Soon to Die," T. Godwin (Mar 1957) [*The Survivors*]. The magazine was briefly revived in 1969-1970.
Issues:

	Jan	Feb	Mar	Apr	May	Jun	Jul	Aug	Sep	Oct	Nov	Dec	W
1957	1/1		1/2		1/3		1/4		1/5		1/6		6
1958	2/1	2/2	2/3	2/4									10

British Edition:
28 issues (Nov 1963–Feb 1966).
Digest size; 128 pp.; monthly; 2/6, then 3/- from June 1964.
Publisher: Atlas Publications, London.

This reprint magazine was founded to replace the British Edition of *Analog Science Fiction* which had ceased (replaced by the U.S. original). It published material from the U.S. original *Venture* and also material, previously unpublished in Britain, from *The Magazine of Fantasy and Science Fiction*. It was the last of the British reprint magazines.
Issues:

	Jan	Feb	Mar	Apr	May	Jun	Jul	Aug	Sep	Oct	Nov	Dec	W
1963											1	2	2
1964	3	4	5	6	7	8	9	10	11	12	13	14	14
1965	15	16	17	18	19	20	21	22	23	24	25	26	26
1966	27	28											28

VORTEX SCIENCE FICTION   U.S.   Science fiction
2 issues, not dated (1/1 & 1/2, 1953).
Digest size; 160 pp.; 35¢.
Editor: C. Whitehorne.
Publisher: Specific Fiction Corp., New York.

The companion to *Science Fiction Digest*, this magazine concentrated on short stories, presenting 20 and 25 shorts in the two issues that appeared. Although not generally recommended, the material was not as poor as some enthusiasts judged.

WEB TERROR STORIES   U.S.   Weird terror
? issues (Oct 1958—June 1965?).
Editor: Robert C. Sproul.

A terror magazine which was originally *Saturn Science Fiction and Fantasy*. It had a period as *Web Detective Stories* prior to 1962. Most stories were not highly considered, by writers such as Bill Ryder and Al James, with occasional appearances by John Jakes and M. Z. Bradley.

WEIRD AND OCCULT—1/- Library   British   Weird
3 issues, not dated (No. 1 *ca.* May 1960; No. 2 *ca.* Aug 1960; No. 3, ? 1961).
Publisher: G. G. Swan, London.
Size 4¾ x 7 in.; 64 pp.; 1/-.

A companion to *Science Fiction—1/- Library*, this magazine had no title/table of contents page. It reprinted some material and was only fair in quality, using small type on poor paper.

WEIRD STORY MAGAZINE   British   Weird
Two series: (1) No. 1 (Aug 1940); (2) No. 1, not numbered (1947) and No. 2 (June 1948).
Pulp size; 96 pp.; 7d.
Publisher: G. G. Swan, London.

This magazine presented original ghost stories by British writers. The one issue in the first series had a comic strip, and also noted that the second issue would start a serial "The Last Men in the World," E. Bruce; this was never published.

In the second series, the second issue had 8 stories, including "The Horror Undying," W. P. Cockcroft, and "Obscene Parade," N. Wesley Firth.

WEIRD TALES   U.S.   Weird
279 issues (Mar 1923—Sep 1954).
Editors: Edwin Baird, Mar 1923—May 1924; Farnsworth Wright, Nov 1924—Mar 1940; Dorothy McIlwraith, May 1940—Sep 1954.
Format: Pulp size, Mar & Apr 1923; large size, May 1923—May 1924; probably pulp size thereafter, but definitely by Oct 1925, to July 1953 (with slight alteration from Sep 1930); digest size, Sep 1953—Sep 1954. Essentially monthly 1923—Dec 1939, then bimonthly. Price 25¢ to Aug 1939 (except 50¢ for May 1924 compound issue); 15¢, Sep 1939—July 1947; 20¢, Sep 1947—Mar 1949; 25¢, May 1949—July 1953; 35¢, Sep 1953—Sep 1954.
Review:

This was the magazine which developed and popularised the supernatural story as a specialised form of popular fiction in the 1920's and 1930's. It also featured much science fiction—most frequently by Edmond Hamilton. It cradled dozens of fantasy fiction's most popular authors whose names constitute a *Who's Who* of modern weird fiction. These included H. P. Lovecraft, C. A. Smith, C. L. Moore, R. Bloch, R. Bradbury, and R. E. Howard. There were also notable authors whose names were not familiar in other magazines, such as A. W. Bernal,

Greye La Spina, Robert Leitfred, A. Eadie, N. Dyalhis, B. Morgan, Mary E. Counselman, and E. Worrell.

Cover artists included Brosnatch, Senf, Rankin, St. John, Brundage (particularly noted for her beautiful nudes), Finlay, Bok, and Coye.

There is a big band of authors whose book collections are predominantly stories that originally appeared in *Weird Tales*, including H. P. Lovecraft, H. S. Whitehead, R. Bloch, A. Derleth, and F. B. Long. Most modern anthologies in the field use some (if not all) material from its pages, but few notable stories now remain unreprinted; a scanning of the "Notable Fiction" list will indicate why.

The first anthology based on this magazine was the low-price British *Not at Night* series, edited by C. C. Thomson, which appeared approximately annually from the late 1920's. Postwar, A. Derleth presented much material derived from *Weird Tales* in his anthologies. Many stories in *Avon Fantasy Reader* and the more recent *Magazine of Horror* and its companions have also been *WT* reprints. After *Weird Tales* folded, L. Margulies bought its rights and compiled a number of paperback anthologies from its pages. At one stage in the late 1950's Margulies was planning to reissue the magazine.

Enthusiasts generally consider that Wright's editorship was the "golden age" of *Weird Tales*, but even so it tapered off in the 1940's so much that often the reprints from earlier issues are thought to be the best fiction of the issue.

T.G.L. Cockcroft's *Index to the Weird Fiction Magazines* (Title and Author) covers *WT* in its entirety (as well as some other magazines).
Notable Fiction:
1923 Mar "Ooze" (n'te), A. Rud; "The Thing of a Thousand Shapes" (sr2), O. A. Kline
    May *The Moon Terror* (sr2), A. G. Birch [title story of anthology]
    Jul "Sunfire" (sr2), Francis Stevens [G. Bennett]
    Sep *People of the Comet* (sr2), A. Hall
    Oct "The Phantom Farmhouse" (short), S. Quinn; "Dagon" (short), H. P. Lovecraft; "The Man Who Owned the World" (short), F. Owen
    Nov "Dracondra" (sr6), J. M. Leahy
1924 Jan "The Abysmal Horror" (sr2), B. Wallis; "The Picture in the House" (short), H. P. Lovecraft
    Mar "The Spirit Fakers of Hermannstadt" (sr2), H. Houdini; "The Rats in the Walls" (short), H. P. Lovecraft
    Apr "The White Ape" (short), H. P. Lovecraft ["Arthur Jermyn"]
    May "Imprisoned With the Pharaohs" (n'te), H. Houdini & H. P. Lovecraft; "The Loved Dead" (short), C. M. Eddy Jr.; "Tea Leaves" (short), H. S. Whitehead
    Nov "The Tortoise Shell Cat" (short), Greye La Spina
    Dec "Death Waters" (short), F. B. Long; "The Valley of Teeheemen" (sr2), A. Thatcher [had sequel]
1925 Jan "The Fireplace" (short), H. S. Whitehead; "The Ocean Leech" (short), F. B. Long
    Feb "The Statement of Randolph Carter" (short), H. P. Lovecraft; "Sea Change" (short), H. S. Whitehead
    Apr "When the Green Star Waned" (short), N. Dyalhis; *Invaders From the Dark* (sr3), G. La Spina; "The Wind That Tramps the World," F. Owen [Roswell Williams] [title story of collection]
    May "The Music of Erich Zann" (short), H. P. Lovecraft
    Jul *The Werewolf of Ponkert*, H. W. Munn [book has later stories]
    Oct "The Horror on the Links" (short), S. Quinn [first of "Jules de Grandin" series]
    Dec "The Sea Thing" (short), F. B. Long
1926 Feb "The Word of Santiago" (short), E. Hoffmann Price [first of "Pierre D'Artois" series]
    Apr "Wolfshead" (short), R. E. Howard; "The Outsider" (short), H. P. Lovecraft
    May "The Ghosts of Steamboat Coulee" (n'te), A. J. Burks; "Bat's Belfry" (short), A. W. Derleth
    Jun "The Moon-Bog" (short), H. P. Lovecraft
    Jul "Laocoon" (short), B. Morgan; "A Runaway World" (short), Clare W. Harris
    Aug "The Woman of the Wood" (n'te), A. Merritt; "The Monster God of Mamurth" (short), E. Hamilton

Sep "Across Space" (sr2), E. Hamilton; "Case of the Jailor's Daughter" (short), V. Rousseau [V. R. Emanuel] [first of "Surgeon of Souls" series]; "Jumbee" (short), H. S. Whitehead [title story of collection]

Nov "The Star Shell" (sr4), G. C. & B. Wallis

1927 Jan *Drome* (sr5), J. M. Leahy; "The Horror at Red Hook" (n'te), H. P. Lovecraft

Mar "Evolution Island" (n'te), E. Hamilton

Apr *Explorers Into Infinity* (sr3), R. Cummings [book includes sequel]

Aug "The Bride of Osiris" (sr3), O. A. Kline; "The Man With a Thousand Legs" (short), F. B. Long

Oct "The Time Raider" (sr4), E. Hamilton; "Pickman's Model" (short), H. P. Lovecraft; "The Red Brain" (short), D. Wandrei

Dec "The Devils of Po Sung" (n'te), B. Morgan; "The Canal" (n'te), E. Worrell; "The Bells of Oceana" (short), A. J. Burks

1928 Jan "The Giant World" (sr3), R. Cummings; "In Amundsen's Tent" (short), J. M. Leahy

Feb "The Call of Cthulhu" (n'te), H. P. Lovecraft; "The Purple Sea" (short), F. Owen

Mar "The Strange People" (sr3), M. Leinster [W. F. Jenkins]; "The Eighth Green Man" (short), G. G. Pendarves

Jun "The Lurking Fear" (short), H. P. Lovecraft [title story of collection]

Jul "The Space Eaters" (short), F. B. Long

Aug "Red Shadows" (n'te), R. E. Howard [first of "Solomon Kane" series]; *Crashing Suns* (sr2), E. Hamilton [first of "Interstellar Patrol" series]

Nov "The Last Test" (short), A. de Castro

1929 Jan "Bimini" (short), B. Morgan; "The Silver Key" (short), H. P. Lovecraft [had sequel]; "The Chemical Brain" (short), F. Flagg

Mar "The Immortal Hand" (short), A. Eadie; "The Hounds of Tindalos" (short), F. B. Long

Apr "A Dinner at Imola" (short), A. Derleth; "The Dunwich Horror" (n'te), H. P. Lovecraft

Jun "Black Tancrede" (short), H. S. Whitehead

Aug "The Shadow Kingdom" (n'te), R. E. Howard [first of "King Kull" series]

Sep "Automata" (short), S. F. Wright

Oct "Skull-Face" (sr3), R. E. Howard [title story of collection]; "The Battle of the Toads" (short), D. H. Keller [first of "Overlord of Cornwall" series]

Nov "The Curse of Yig" (short), Z. B. Reed [Z. B. Bishop] [title story of collection]

Dec "Beyond the Moon" (sr3), W. E. Backus; "Dancer in the Crystal" (short), F. Flagg

1930 Jan "The Life Masters" (n'te), E. Hamilton

Feb "Thirsty Blades" (n'te), O. A. Kline & E. H. Price; "The Comet-Drivers" (n'te), E. Hamilton

Mar "The Pacer" (short), A. Derleth & M. Schorer

Jun "The Moon of Skulls" (sr2), R. E. Howard; "The Rats in the Walls" (short), H. P. Lovecraft

Aug "Pigmy Island" (n'te), E. Hamilton; "The Electric Executioner" (short), A. de Castro

Sep "A Visitor From Egypt" (short), F. B. Long; "The Phantom Bus" (short), W. E. Backus

Oct "Mrs. Bentley's Daughter" (short), A. W. Derleth; "The Portal to Power" (sr4), Greye La Spina

Nov "Kings of the Night" (n'te), R. E. Howard [first of "Bran Mak Morn" series]

1931 Jan *The Horror From the Hills* (sr2), F. B. Long; "Passing of a God" (short), H. S. Whitehead

Jun *Tam, Son of the Tiger* (sr6), O. A. Kline

Aug "The Whisperer in Darkness" (n'te), H. P. Lovecraft; "Prince Borgia's Mass" (short), A. W. Derleth; *The Wolf-Leader* (sr8), A. Dumas

Oct "The Gods of Bal-Sagoth" (n'te), R. E. Howard [first of "Turlogh O'Brien" series]

Nov "Placide's Wife" (n'te), K. Mashburn [had sequel]

1932 Feb "The Laughing Duke" (short), W. West

Mar "Island of Doom" (short), B. Morgan; "The Thing in the Cellar" (short), D. H. Keller

Apr "The Red Witch" (n'te), N. Dyalhis; "In the Vault" (short), H. P. Lovecraft

May "The Vaults of Yoh-Vombis" (short), C. A. Smith; *Frankenstein* (sr8), M. W. Shelley

Sep "The Sheraton Mirror" (short), A. W. Derleth; "The Empire of Necromancers" (short), C. A. Smith

Nov "Buccaneers of Venus" (sr6), O. A. Kline [*The Port of Peril*]; "Worms of the Earth" (n'te), R. E. Howard

Dec "The Phoenix on the Sword" (n'te), R. E. Howard [first published story of "Conan" series]

1933 Feb "The Chadbourne Episode" (short), H. S. Whitehead; "The Cats of Ulthar" (short), H. P. Lovecraft

Apr *Golden Blood* (sr6), J. Williamson; "Tiger Dust" (short), B. Morgan; "Revelations in Black" (short), C. Jacobi [title story of collection]

Jun "Genius Loci" (short), C. A. Smith [title story of collection]

Jul "The Horror in the Museum" (n'te), Hazel Heald; "The Dreams in the Witch-House" (short), H. P. Lovecraft

Sep "Horror on the Asteroid" (short), E. Hamilton [title story of collection]; "The Return of Andrew Bentley," A. Derleth & M. Schorer; "Death Waters" (short), F. B. Long

Oct "Seed of the Sepulchre" (short), C. A. Smith; "The Cat Woman" (short), M. E. Counselman

Nov "Shambleau" (n'te), C. L. Moore [first of "Northwest Smith" series]

1934 Jan *The Solitary Hunters* (sr3), D. H. Keller

Feb "The Sapphire Goddess" (n'te), N. Dyalhis

Mar "Thundering Worlds" (n'te), E. Hamilton

Apr "Satan's Garden" (sr2), E. Hoffmann Price

Jun "The Colossus of Ylourgne" (short), C. A. Smith; "Colonel Markesan" (short), A. Derleth & M. Schorer

Aug "The Three Marked Pennies" (short), M. E. Counselman

Sep "Naked Lady" (short), Mindret Lord

Oct "The Black God's Kiss" (n'te), C. L. Moore [first of "Jirel of Joiry" series]

Dec "Pale Pink Porcelain" (short), F. Owen

1935 Jan "Rulers of the Future" (sr3), P. Ernst; "The Feast in the Abbey" (short), R. Bloch

Feb "The Metronome" (short), A. Derleth

Mar "Lord of the Lamia" (sr3), O. A. Kline

Apr "Out of the Eons" (short), Hazel Heald

Aug "Doctor Satan" (n'te), P. Ernst [first of "Doctor Satan" series]

Sep "The Shambler From the Stars" (short), R. Bloch

Oct "Mystery of the Last Quest" (short), J. Flanders

Dec "Hour of the Dragon" (sr5), R. E. Howard [*Conan the Conqueror*]; "The Great Brain of Kaldar" (n'te), E. Hamilton

1936 Mar "The Graveyard Rats" (short), H. Kuttner

Apr "The Ruler of Fate" (sr3), J. Williamson

Jun "The Telephone in the Library" (short), A. W. Derleth

Oct "The Opener of the Way" (short), R. Bloch [title story of collection]

Nov "The Crawling Horror" (short), T. McClusky

Dec "The Haunter of the Dark" (n'te), H. P. Lovecraft [title story of collection]

1937 Jan "The Eighth Green Man" (short), G. G. Pendarves

Mar "The Dark Star" (short), G. G. Pendarves

Apr "Fessenden's World" (short), E. Hamilton; "The Shuttered House" (short), A. Derleth

May "The Last Pharaoh" (sr4), T. P. Kelley

Jun "Black Kiss" (short), R. Bloch & H. Kuttner

Jul "The Creeper in the Crypt" (short), R. Bloch

Aug "The Thing of Darkness" (n'te), G. G. Pendarves

Sep "School for the Unspeakable" (short), M. W. Wellman

Nov "Quest of the Starstone" (n'te), C. L. Moore & H. Kuttner

Dec "The Sea-Witch" (n'te), N. Dyalhis; "Fane of the Black Pharaoh" (short), R. Bloch

1938 Jan *Roads*, S. Quinn; "The Hairy Ones Shall Dance" (sr3), Gans T. Field [M. W. Wellman] [first of "Judge Pursuivant" series]

Feb "Jumbee" (short), H. S. Whitehead [title story of collection]

Mar "Dreadful Sleep" (sr3), J. Williamson; "Beyond the Wall of Sleep" (short), H. P. Lovecraft

Apr "The House of Ecstasy" (short), R. M. Farley

May "Thunder in the Dawn" (sr2), H. Kuttner

Jun "The Doom That Came to Sarnath" (short), H. P. Lovecraft

Aug "The Fire Princess" (sr3), E. Hamilton

Nov "I Found Cleopatra" (sr3), T. P. Kelley

Dec "The Sin-Eater" (n'te), G. G. Pendarves

1939 Jan "Medusa's Coil" (n'te), Z. B. Bishop

Feb "The Double Shadow" (short), C. A. Smith [title story of collection]

May *Almuric* (sr3), R. E. Howard

Sep *King of the World's Edge* (sr4), H. W. Munn; "Cool Air" (short), H. P. Lovecraft

Oct "In the Walls of Eryx" (n'te), K. Sterling & H. P. Lovecraft

1940 Jan "A Million Years in the Future" (sr4), T. P. Kelley

May "The Automatic Pistol" (short), F. Leiber

Jul "The Adventure of a Professional Corpse" (short), H. Bedford-Jones [first of series]

Nov "The Sandwin Compact" (short), A. Derleth

1941 Jan "House of the Hatchet" (short), R. Bloch

May *The Case of Charles Dexter Ward* (sr2), H. P. Lovecraft; "There Are Such Things" (n'te), S. Quinn [first of "Carmichael" series]

Nov "Compliments of Spectre" (short), A. Derleth

1942 Jan "The Shadow Over Innsmouth" (n'te), H. P. Lovecraft [title story of collection]

Mar "Child's Play" (short), Alice-Mary Schnirring; "Herbert West: Reanimator" (sr4), H. P. Lovecraft

Nov "Nursemaid to Nightmares" (n'te), R. Bloch; "The Golden Bough" (short), D. H. Keller; "The Candle" (short), R. Bradbury

1943 Mar "Seventh Sister" (short), M. E. Counselman

May "A Wig for Miss Devore" (short), A. W. Derleth

Jul "The Scythe" (short), R. Bradbury; "Yours Truly—Jack the Ripper" (short), R. Bloch [title story of collection]

Nov "The Third Cry to Legba" (short), M. W. Wellman [first of "John Thunstone" series]

1944 Jan "The Master of Cotswold" (n'te), N. S. Bond

Mar "The Trail of Cthulhu" (n'te), A. W. Derleth [first of "Trail of Cthulhu" series]

May "The Lake" (short), R. Bradbury; "The Gothic Window" (short), Dorothy Quick

Nov "A Gentleman From Prague" (short), S. Grendon [A. Derleth]; "The Jar" (short), R. Bradbury

1945 Jan "Ship-in-a-Bottle" (short), P. S. Miller

Jul "The Inn Outside the World" (short), E. Hamilton; "Carnaby's Fish" (short), C. Jacobi

Sep "The Skull of the Marquis de Sade" (n'te), R. Bloch; "Mr. Lupescu" (short), A. Boucher

Nov "Lost Elysium" (n'te), E. Hamilton; "Mrs. Lannisfree" (short), A. W. Derleth

1946 Jan "Mr. Bauer and the Atom" (short), F. Leiber; "Pikeman" (short), A. Derleth

May "The Smiling People" (short), R. Bradbury

Jul "The Night" (short), R. Bradbury; "The Wings" (short), A. V. Harding

Nov "Let's Play 'Poison'" (short), R. Bradbury

1947 Jan "The Hog" (n'te), W. H. Hodgson; "The Extra Passenger" (short), S. Grendon [A. Derleth]; "Cellmate" (short), T. Sturgeon

Mar "Mr. George" (n'te) S. Grendon [A. Derleth] [title story of collection]

Jul "The Churchyard Yew" (short), J. S. Le Fanu [actually A. W. Derleth]; "The Damp Man" (n'te), A. V. Harding [had sequel]

1948 Mar 25th Anniversary issue—material by "name" authors, including: "The October Game" (short), R. Bradbury; "The Professor's Teddy Bear" (short), T. Sturgeon

May "One Foot in the Grave" (short), D. Grubb

Jul "Twilight of the Gods" (n'te), E. Hamilton

Nov "The Perfect Host" (n'te), T. Sturgeon

1949 Jan "Our Fair City" (n'te), R. A. Heinlein; "The 13th Floor" (short), F. Gruber

Mar "The Martian and the Moron" (n'te), T. Sturgeon

Jul "Come and Go Mad" (n'te), F. Brown

Sep "One Foot and the Grave" (n'te), T. Sturgeon

1950 Sep "Legal Rites" (n'te), I. Asimov & J. MacCreigh [F. Pohl]

Nov "The Third Shadow" (short), H. R. Wakefield

1951 Sep "The Metamorphosis of Earth" (n'te), C. A. Smith

Nov "When the Night Wind Howls" (short), L. S. de Camp & F. Pratt [in "Gavagan's Bar" series; others followed]

1953 Jan "Once There Was a Little Girl" (n'te), E. Worrell

Mar "Night Court" (short), Mary E. Counselman

1954 May "Song in the Thicket" (short), M. Banister

Jul "The Survivor" (short), H. P. Lovecraft & A. Derleth [title story of collection]

Issues:

	Jan	Feb	Mar	Apr	May	Jun	Jul	Aug	Sep	Oct	Nov	Dec	W
1923		1/1	1/2	1/3	1/4		2/1		2/2	2/3	2/4		8
1924	3/1	3/2	3/3	3/4		4/2*				4/3	4/4		15
1925	5/1	5/2	5/3	5/4	5/5	5/6	6/1	6/2	6/3	6/4	6/5	6/6	27
1926	7/1	7/2	7/3	7/4	7/5	7/6	8/1	8/2	8/3	8/4	8/5	8/6	39
1927	9/1	9/2	9/3	9/4	9/5	9/6	10/1	10/2	10/3	10/4	10/5	10/6	51
1928	11/1	11/2	11/3	11/4	11/5	11/6	12/1	12/2	12/3	12/4	12/5	12/6	63
1929	13/1	13/2	13/3	13/4	13/5	13/6	14/1	14/2	14/3	14/4	14/5	14/6	75
1930	15/1	15/2	15/3	15/4	15/5	15/6	16/1	16/2	16/3	16/4	16/5	16/6	87
1931	17/1		17/2		17/3		17/4		18/1	18/2	18/3	18/4	18/5	96
1932	19/1	19/2	19/3	19/4	19/5	19/6	20/1	20/2	20/3	20/4	20/5	20/6	108
1933	21/1	21/2	21/3	21/4	21/5	21/6	22/1	22/2	22/3	22/4	22/5	22/6	120
1934	23/1	23/2	23/3	23/4	23/5	23/6	24/1	24/2	24/3	24/4	24/5	24/6	132
1935	25/1	25/2	25/3	25/4	25/5	25/6	26/1	26/2	26/3	26/4	26/5	26/6	144
1936	27/1	27/2	27/3	27/4	27/5	27/6	28/1		28/2	28/3	28/4	28/5	155
1937	29/1	29/2	29/3	29/4	29/5	29/6	30/1	30/2	30/3	30/4	30/5	30/6	167
1938	31/1	31/2	31/3	31/4	31/5	31/6	32/1	32/2	32/3	32/4	32/5	32/6	179
1939	33/1	33/2	33/3	33/4	33/5		34/1		34/2	34/3	34/4	34/5	34/6	190
1940	35/1		35/2		35/3		35/4		35/5		35/6		196
1941	35/7		35/8		35/9		35/10		36/1		36/2		202
1942	36/3		36/4		36/5		36/6		36/7		36/8		208
1943	36/9		36/10		36/11		36/12		37/1		37/2		214
1944	37/3		37/4		37/5		37/6		38/1		38/2		220
1945	38/3		38/4		38/5		38/6		39/1		39/2		226
1946	39/3		39/4		39/5		39/6		39/7		39/8		232
1947	39/9		39/10		39/11		39/11†		39/12		40/1		238
1948	40/2		40/3		40/4		40/5		40/6		41/1		244
1949	41/2		41/3		41/4		41/5		41/6		42/1		250
1950	42/2		42/3		42/4		42/5		42/6		43/1		256
1951	43/2		43/3		43/4		43/5		43/6		44/1		262
1952	44/2		44/3		44/4		44/5		44/6		44/7		268
1953	44/8		45/1		45/2		45/3		45/4		45/5		274
1954	45/6		46/1		46/2		46/3		46/4				279

* There was no Vol. 4 No. 1.

† Correct, number 11 used twice.

British Edition:

Three series, from three publishers:

(1) 3 issues, not dated, from G. G. Swan, London.

No. 1 (Feb 1942) All stories from U.S. *Weird Tales* Sep 1940, with cover story "Seven Seconds to Eternity."

No. 2 (Mar 1942) Stories from U.S. *WT* Nov 1940, cover story "The Last Waltz."

No. 3 (Jun 1942) Stories from U.S. *WT* Jan 1941, cover story "Dragon Moon."

The cover illustrations were the same as the corresponding U.S. editions, but in blue instead of full colour. The paper used was the bluish-grey common to wartime Swan publications.

(2) 1 issue, not numbered, not dated, *ca.* 1946, 36 pp., 1/6, from William C. Merrett, London.

Fiction: "Tiger Cat," D. H. Keller; "Pledged to the Dead," S.

Quinn; "The Shunned House," H. P. Lovecraft [selected from *WT*, Oct 1937].

(3) 28 issues (No. 1, not numbered, not dated, to No. 23, 1953) and (1/1, 1953–1/5, 1954), from Thorpe & Porter, Leicester.

The first 23 were pulp size, with a few of the early ones being dated on the spine, and all numbered after the first. Prices were 1/- to No. 10, 1/6 to around No. 15, and then 1/- again. The last five issues were digest size at 1/6.

The issues were generally fairly complete copies of the U.S. originals except for changed advertisements and occasional omissions of departments. They corresponded as follows: No. 1 (nn) was U.S. July 1949; from No. 2 on they followed quite regularly from U.S. Nov 1949; No. 19 was U.S. Sep 1952 and No. 23 was Mar 1953—issues 20 to 22 have not been sighted, and one may have been U.S. May 1953. The digest-size issues were identical to the U.S. from Sep 1953 to May 1954, but ceased before covering the final two U.S. originals.

An interesting point is that although the original U.S. edition was banned in Australia from 1938 or so, some issues of this British series were available. (The ban is understood to have been lifted in more recent years.)

Issues:

	Jan	Feb	Mar	Apr	May	Jun	Jul	Aug	Sep	Oct	Nov	Dec	W
1942		1	2			3							3
1946											(nn)		4
1949											1 (nn)		5
1950	2			3		4					5		9
1951		6		7		8	9	10			11	12	16
1952	13		14	15				16		17			21
1953	18	19		20		21			22	1/1*	23		28
1954	1/2		1/3	1/4	1/5								32

* Change to digest size, different numbering.

Canadian Edition: Two series.

(1) 14 issues (June 1935–July 1936).

Pulp size; 128 pp.; monthly; 25¢.

Publisher: The American News Co. Ltd., Toronto.

Identical with U.S. edition except with "Printed in Canada" overprinted on the cover. An unusual cover was that of Nov 1935, where a nude on the U.S. edition was covered by a white patch bearing the words "Magazine of the Bizarre and Unusual" and "November 25¢."

(2) 58 issues? (May 1942–Nov 1951).

Pulp size; 128 pp., later 96 pp.; bimonthly; 20¢ until Mar 1949, then 25¢.

Publisher: The American News Co. Ltd., Toronto.

Identical to the U.S. edition except that it ran one issue behind—i.e, Canadian May 1942 reprinted U.S. Mar 1942—and had different advertisements. It is understood that it ceased with the Nov 1951 issue; the Sep 1951 issue has been sighted.

At first Canadian illustrations appeared instead of the U.S. originals, then some of both were used, and finally for the last 18 or so issues all the U.S. illustrations were presented.

WEIRD WORLD   British   Weird fiction

2 issues, not dated (Aut 1955, Spr 1956); noted as 1/1, 1/2.

Publisher: Gannet Press (Sales) Ltd., Birkenhead.

Format (2nd issue, sighted): size 7 x 9¼ in.; 48 pp.; 1/-.

This presented short horror stories of fair quality, with the best being "The Man Who Loved Cats," Konstantin Faber. The oft-reprinted "The Fall of the House of Usher," E. A. Poe, was reprinted in the second issue. A companion, *Fantastic World*, was advertised on the back cover of the first issue, but never appeared.

WELTRAUMFAHRER, DER   German   Science fiction

8 issues (1958), not dated.

Probably monthly; 1 DM.

Publisher: A. Semrau, Hamburg.

A German series which reprinted some high-class U.S. translations, including *The Skylark of Space*, E. E. Smith (No. 1); *Who*, A. Budrys (No. 3); *The Secret People*, R. F. Jones (No. 6).

WEREWOLVES AND VAMPIRES   U.S.   Horror nonfiction

1 issue (1962, 1/1); 64 pp.; 35¢.

Publisher: Charlton Publications, Inc., Derby, Connecticut.

Articles on werewolves and vampires.

British Edition: 1 issue, 1964, not dated; could be a reprint.

WHISPERER, THE   U.S.   Weird mystery

24 issues (14 issues, Oct 1936–Dec 1937; 10 issues, Oct 1940–Apr 1942).

Publisher: Street & Smith, New York.

A one-character magazine which ran for two series. The novels by Clifford Goodrich (pseud. of Alan Hathway) covered the macabre exploits of "Wildcat" Gordon, a New York Police Commissioner who stalked criminals in a disguise including special false teeth (hence his nickname). After failing in the first series, the stories were carried in alternate issues of *The Shadow* (22 appearances from 1 Dec 1937 to 1 Dec 1939). They were then so successful that the character was given a second chance in a new series. The story series is listed in *The Hero-Pulp Index*, McKinstry & Weinberg (1970).

WITCH'S TALES   U.S.   Weird

2 issues (Nov, Dec 1936). Large size.

Editor: Tom Chadburn.

This was inspired by the radio programme of the same name, and included lead novels by Alonzo D. Cole, the programme's mainstay. Other fiction was reprinted from turn-of-the-century U.K. magazines; there were also some "true" experience articles.

WONDER STORIES   U.S.   Science fiction

66 issues (June 1930–Apr 1936).

Combined from *Air Wonder Stories* and *Science Wonder Stories*; continued as *Thrilling Wonder Stories*.

Editor: H. Gernsback. Associate Editors: D. Lasser, June 1930–Oct 1933; C. D. Hornig, Nov 1933–Apr 1936.

Publisher: Stellar Pub. Corp., New York.

Format: Large size, 96 pp., June 1930–Oct 1930; pulp size, 144 pp., Nov 1930–Oct 1931; large size, 96 pp., Nov 1931–Nov 1932; large size, 64 pp., Dec 1932–Mar 1933; pulp size, 128 pp., Nov 1933–Apr 1936. Price 25¢ June 1930–Oct 1932; 15¢ Nov 1932–Mar 1933; 25¢ Apr 1933–May 1935; 15¢ June 1935–Apr 1936.

Review:

After Hugo Gernsback was forced to leave Teck Publications, where he had published *Amazing Stories* and associated magazines, he began the "Wonder" magazines. He combined *Air Wonder Stories* and *Science Wonder Stories* to form *Wonder Stories*, and operated this title for about six years. A quite colourful magazine, it presented many notable novels and series (as can be seen by scanning the fiction listing below). It featured the late F. R. Paul on every cover, and also presented a considerable quantity of translated foreign science fiction. Before the magazine was sold, the June 1936 issue had been partially prepared.

In 1934 *Wonder Stories* sponsored the formation of The Science Fiction League, giving it a special section in the magazine. The League's activities included "Science Fiction Tests" (Jan 1935, July 1935, Feb 1936), which were graded and "degrees" in science fiction granted.

It is of interest that a *Wonder Stories Reprint Annual* was planned to appear in 1934, but never eventuated. It was to have contained "The Human Termites," D. H. Keller; "The Hidden World," E. Hamilton; "The City of the Living Dead," L. Manning & F. Pratt; "The City of the Singing Flame," C. A. Smith.

A follow-on to the Standard publications of the 1950's was entitled *Wonder Stories: An Anthology of the Best in Science Fiction.* A digest-sized issue appeared in 1957 as Vol. 45 No. 1 (128 pp., 35¢); then in 1963 a pulp-sized issue appeared as Vol. 45 No. 2 (96 pp., 50¢), with practically identical contents—John D. MacDonald's 1950 short novel "Shadow on the Sand" was the main item repeated. An *Index to the Wonder Group* was compiled by Fred Cook in 1966.

Notable Fiction [Many short stories were later republished in the *Startling Stories* "Hall of Fame" department (often abridged) and in *Fantastic Story Magazine*.]:

1930 Jul   "The Red Plague" (short), P. S. Miller

      Sep   "In 20,000 A.D." (short), N. Schachner & A. L. Zagat [had sequel]

Oct "Marooned in Andromeda" (short), C. A. Smith

Nov "Hornets in Space" (short), R. F. Starzl

1931 Jan "The Satellite of Doom" (n'te), D. D. Sharp

Feb "The World Without" (short), B. Herbert [had sequel]

Mar "The Return From Jupiter" (sr2), G. Edwards [sequel to serial in *Science Wonder*]

Apr "The Man Who Evolved" (short), E. Hamilton

May "Utopia Island" (sr2), O. Von Hanstein; "The Cosmic Gun" (short), M. Colladay [had sequel]

Jul "The Time Projector" (sr2), D. Lasser & D. H. Keller; "The City of Singing Flame" (short), C. A. Smith [had sequel]

Sep "Exiles of the Moon" (sr3), N. Schachner & A. L. Zagat; "A Mutiny in Space" (n'te), G. Edwards

Nov "Tetrahedra of Space" (n'te), P. S. Miller; "The Superman of Dr. Jukes" (short), F. Flagg

Dec *The Time Stream* (sr4), J. Taine [E. T. Bell]

1932 Feb "The Moon Era" (n'te), J. Williamson; "A Conquest of Two Worlds" (short), E. Hamilton

Mar "The Final War" (sr2), C. Spohr; "The Eternal World" (short), C. A. Smith

May *Brood of Helios* (sr3), J. Bertin; "The Venus Adventure" (short), J. B. Harris

Jun "The Invisible City" (short), C. A. Smith; "Power Satellite" (short), R. F. Starzl

Jul "In the Year 8000" (sr3), O. Von Hanstein

Sep "The Death of Iron" (sr4), S. S. Held

Oct *The Planet of Youth* (n'te), S. A. Coblentz; "Master of the Asteroid" (short), C. A. Smith

Dec "The Wreck of the Asteroid" (sr3), L. Manning [had sequel]

1933 Feb "The Moon Doom" [first of series with different authors for each part]

Mar "The Man Who Awoke" (n'te), L. Manning [first of series of same title]; "Wanderers of Time" (n'te), J. B. Harris

Apr "Revolt of the Scientists" (n'te), N. Schachner [first of series of same title]; "The Light From Beyond" (short), C. A. Smith

May "The Visitors of Mlok" (short), C. A. Smith; "The Island of Unreason" (short), E. Hamilton

Jun "The Radio Terror" (sr3), E. Thebault

Jul/Aug "The Isotope Man" (n'te), F. Pragnell

Nov "The End of Tyme" (short), A. Fedor & H. Hasse [had sequel]; first of "Stranger Club" series, L. Manning; "The Man With X-Ray Eyes" (short), E. Hamilton

Dec "Evolution Satellite" (sr2), J. H. Haggard

1934 Jan "The Exile of the Skies" (sr3), R. Vaughan; "The Man From Ariel" (short), D. A. Wollheim

Feb "The Sublime Vigil" (short), C. D. Cuthbert

Mar "Xandulu" (sr3), J. Williamson; "The Literary Corkscrew" (short), D. H. Keller

May "Druso" (sr3), F. Freksa

Jul *Enslaved Brains* (sr3), E. Binder; "A Martian Odyssey" (short), S. G. Weinbaum [had sequel; also title story of collection]

Sep "The Fall of the Eiffel Tower" (sr3), C. de Richter; "The Man From Beyond" (short), J. B. Harris

Nov "Dawn to Dusk" (sr3), E. Binder

1935 Jan "The Hidden Colony" (sr3), O. Von Hanstein; "One Way Tunnel" (short), D. H. Keller

Feb "The Truth Gas" (short), E. Hamilton

Mar "In Caverns Below" (sr3), S. A. Coblentz [*Hidden World*]; "The Eternal Cycle" (short), E. Hamilton

May *The Waltz of Death* (sr3), P. B. Maxon; "The Living Machine" (short), D. H. Keller

Jun "Pygmalion's Spectacles" (short), S. G. Weinbaum

Jul *The Green Man of Graypec* (sr3), F. Pragnell

Aug "The Reign of the Reptiles" (n'te), A. Connell; first of "Professor Manderpootz" series, S. G. Weinbaum; "The Branches of Time" (short), D. R. Daniels

Sep "World of the Mist" (sr2), L. Manning

Oct "The Perfect World" (sr3), B. Herbert [*Crisis—1992*]; "The Cosmic Pantograph" (short), E. Hamilton; "Martian Gesture" (short), A. M. Phillips

Dec "Dream's End" (short), A. Connell

1936 Feb "A World Unseen" (sr2), J. W. Skidmore

Apr "The Cosmic Cocktail" (short), S. Wagener

Issues:

	Jan	Feb	Mar	Apr	May	Jun	Jul	Aug	Sep	Oct	Nov	Dec	W
1930	[*Science Wonder Stories*]				2/1	2/2	2/3	2/4	2/5	2/6	2/7		7
1931	2/8	2/9	2/10	2/11	2/12	3/1	3/2	3/3	3/4	3/5	3/6	3/7	19
1932	3/8	3/9	3/10	3/11	3/12	4/1	4/2	4/3	4/4	4/5	4/6	4/7	31
1933	4/8	4/9	4/10	4/11	4/12	5/1		5/2		5/3	5/4	5/5	41
1934	5/6	5/7	5/8	5/9	5/10	6/1	6/2	6/3	6/4	6/5	6/6	6/7	53
1935	6/8	6/9	6/10	6/11	6/12	7/1	7/2	7/3	7/4	7/5		7/6	64
1936	7/7		7/8	[sold to become *Thrilling Wonder Stories*]									66

WONDER STORIES QUARTERLY   U.S.   Science fiction

14 issues (Fall 1929—Win 1933).

Titled *Science Wonder Quarterly* for first 3 issues (Fall 1929—Spr 1930). Large size; 144 pp.; quarterly; 50¢ (last 2 issues, 96 pp., 25¢).

Editor: H. Gernsback.

Publisher: Stellar Pub. Corp., New York.

This magazine concentrated on publishing novels and gave many classics. A number of translated foreign novels also appeared. All covers were by F. R. Paul. Of interest were a number of stories written by noted authors from readers' pet ideas, beginning Fall 1931.

Notable Fiction:

1929 Fall "The Shot Into Infinity" O. W. Gail; "The Hidden World," E. Hamilton

1930 Win "The Moon Conquerors," R. H. Romans

Spr "The Stone From the Moon," O. W. Gail

Sum "The War of the Planets," R. H. Romans; "Electropolis," O. Von Hanstein

Fall "Between the Earth and the Moon," O. Von Hanstein

1931 Win "The Scarlet Planet," D. M. Lemon

Spr *Into Plutonian Depths*, R. Cummings; "When the Planets Clashed" (short), M. W. Wellman

Sum *Vandals of the Void*, J. M. Walsh; "The Man From Mars" (short), P. S. Miller

Fall "The Cosmic Cloud," B. H. Burgel

1932 Win "The Onslaught From Rigel," F. Pratt [*Invaders From Rigel*]

Spr *The Vanguard to Neptune*, J. M. Walsh

Sum "Beyond Pluto," J. S. Campbell; "The Voyage of the Asteroid" (n'te), L. Manning

Fall "Emissaries of Space," N. Schachner

1933 Win "Interplanetary Bridges," L. Anton; "Exiles of Asperus" (n'te), J. B. Harris

Issues:

	Winter	Spring	Summer	Fall	W
1929				1/1	1
1930	1/2	1/3	1/4	2/1	5
1931	2/2	2/3	2/4	3/1	9
1932	3/2	3/3	3/4	4/1	13
1933	4/2				14

WONDER STORY ANNUAL   U.S.   Science fiction

4 issues (1950—1953).

Editors: S. Merwin, 1950, 1951; S. Mines, 1952, 1953.

Publishers: First issue, Better Publications; then from second issue, Best Books, New York.

Format: First issue, 6½ x 9⅜ in., 196 pp.; from 2nd issue, 6½ x 8¾ in., 162 pp.; 25¢.

This was the first annual in the science fiction field to exceed one issue. The stories used were all reprints from *Wonder Stories* and related magazines. It may therefore be considered an offshoot of *Fantastic Story Magazine*.

Issues and Notable Fiction:

1950   "The Onslaught From Rigel" F. Pratt [*Invaders From Rigel*]

1951 (1/2) *Twice in Time*, M. W. Wellman

1952 (1/3) "The Death of Iron," S. S. Held

1953 (2/1) "Gateway to Paradise," J. Williamson [*Dome Around America*]

Canadian Edition:
Publisher: Better Publications of Canada Ltd., Toronto.
Pulp size, trimmed; 194 pp.; 25¢.
Identical to the U.S. edition.

WONDERS OF THE SPACEWAYS   British   Science fiction
10 issues, not dated (Nov 1950—No. 10, 1954).
Pocket book size; irregular; 1/6.
Publisher: John Spencer, London.
A publication of only minor interest; one of the four juvenile science fiction Spencer magazines. It is listed in G. Stone's *Index to British Science Fiction Magazines 1934-53*, Part 6 (1974).
Issues:

	Jan	Feb	Mar	Apr	May	Jun	Jul	Aug	Sep	Oct	Nov	Dec	W
1950											1(nn)		1
1951													
1952			2	3							4	5	5
1953			6				7			8			8
1954	9			10									10

WORLD FAMOUS CREATURES   U.S.   Horror
4 issues (Oct 1958, Dec 1958, Feb 1959, June 1959).
Editor: M. Leon Howard.
Publisher: Magsyn Pubs., New York [J. B. Musachia].
One of the "monster" magazines.
British Edition:
1 issue—Collector's Edition No. 1 (1959).
Issued by Brook St. Publications, London.

WORLDS BEYOND   U.S.   Science fiction
3 issues (Dec 1950—Feb 1951).
Editor: D. Knight.
Publisher: Hillman Periodicals, Chicago.
Digest size; 128 pp.; monthly; 25¢.
This was the first magazine Damon Knight edited, and is generally considered to be of quite good quality. It did not sell as well as the publisher anticipated and hence was terminated. Some stories were reprints. Van Dongen painted the last two covers.
Issues and Notable Fiction:
1950 Dec (1/1) "The Mindworm" (short), C. M. Kornbluth [title story of collection]; "The Smile of the Sphinx" (n'te), W. F. Temple.
1951 Jan (1/2) "The Tourist Trade" (short), Bob Tucker; "The Green Cat" (short), C. Cartmill.
Feb (1/3) "The Acolytes" (short), P. Anderson; "The Rocket of 1955" (short), C. M. Kornbluth

WORLDS OF FANTASY   British   Science fiction
14 issues (June 1950—mid-1954), not dated.
Pocket book size; irregular; 1/6.
Publisher: John Spencer, London.
One of the four juvenile science fiction Spencer magazines, this is a publication of only minor interest. It is listed in G. Stone's *Index to British Science Fiction Magazines 1934-53*, Part 6 (1974).
Issues:

	Jan	Feb	Mar	Apr	May	Jun	Jul	Aug	Sep	Oct	Nov	Dec	W
1950						1		2		3			3
1951	4												4
1952					5			6			7		7
1953	8					9	10		11				11
1954		12	13			14							14

WORLDS OF FANTASY   U.S.   Fantasy
Current (Sep 1968—), not dated. [Ceased with 4th issue, Spr 1971.]
Digest size; 130 pp.; 60¢.
Editor: L. del Rey.
Publisher: Galaxy Pub. Corp., New York [R. M. Guinn].
A magazine started as a one-shot, and then continued. The first issue had a report about J.R.R. Tolkien and 10 stories, including "The Mirror of Wizardry" (short novel), J. Jakes; "However" (short novel), R. Lory; and a Conan novelette by L. Carter & L. S. de Camp.

WORLDS OF THE UNIVERSE   British   Science fiction
1 issue (1/1), not dated, late 1953.
Pocket book size; 102 pp.; 1/6.
Publisher: Gould Light Co., London.
The one issue was quite well received. The cover and illustrations were by "Marcus." The stories were "Waters of Eternity" (n'te), M. Denholm; "Lilliput Minor" (short), M. Stern; "Spawn of the Void!" (short), J. Sylvassey.

WORLDS OF TOMORROW   U.S.   Science fiction
23 issues (Apr 1963—May 1967). [Second series, 3 issues, 1970—Spr 1971.]
Digest size; 162 pp.; mainly bimonthly; 50¢.
Editor: F. Pohl.
Publisher: Galaxy Pub. Corp., New York.
An interesting magazine of good standard. From Nov 1965 it ran an article series by S. Moskowitz, covering such topics as the sleuth in sf, Tom Swift, and the Jew in sf.
Notable Fiction:
1963 Apr "People of the Sea" (sr2), A. C. Clarke [*Dolphin Island*]
Aug "All We Marsmen" (sr3), P. K. Dick [*Martian Timeslip*]
1964 Feb "Lord of the Uffts," M. Leinster [W. F. Jenkins] [*The Duplicators*]
Apr *The Dark Light-Years*, B. W. Aldiss; "Under the Gaddyl," C. C. MacApp
Aug "Valentine's Planet," A. Davidson
1965 Jan "Day of the Great Shout," P. J. Farmer [first of "Riverworld" series]
Mar *World of Ptavvs*, L. Niven
Jul *Of Godlike Power* (sr2), M. Reynolds; "World of the Spectrum," E. Petaja [*The Prism*]
Nov "Project Ploughshare" (sr2), P. K. Dick [*The Zap Gun*]
1966 May "The Ultra Man" (n'te), A. E. van Vogt
Nov "Report on the Slow Freeze" (article), R.C.W. Ettinger
1967 Feb "The Star-Pit" (n'te), S. R. Delany
May "Stone Man" (n'te), F. Saberhagen
Issues:

	Jan	Feb	Mar	Apr	May	Jun	Jul	Aug	Sep	Oct	Nov	Dec	W
1963				1/1		1/2		1/3		1/4		1/5	5
1964		1/6		2/1		2/2		2/3		2/4			10
1965	2/5		2/6		3/1		3/2		3/3		3/4		16
1966	3/5		3/6		3/7			4/1			4/2		21
1967		4/3			4/4								23

X,Z

X SCIENCE FICTION   U.S. (projected)   Science fiction
This was planned to appear in Fall 1954, with Jim Harmon as editor, but never eventuated.

ZAUBERKREIS SF   German   Science fiction
Current.
Fortnightly, 64 pp.
Publisher: Zauberkreis Verlag, Rastatt.
A German series which reached No. 182 around the end of 1968. Only German authors are published; these include Marcus T. Orban, Jurgen Grasse, Peter Childs, C. R. Munro, and "Spencer."

ZIFF-DAVIS PUBLISHING CO.
Ziff-Davis Pub. Co., Chicago, bought *Amazing Stories* in 1938, and in 1939 added a "twin" companion magazine, *Fantastic Adventures*, which ran to 1953. When the latter was dropped, *Fantastic* (which had begun slightly earlier) became the twin to *Amazing* and has continued through several title variations. In the early 1950's Ziff-Davis moved its editorial offices to New York.

PAPERBACKS

System and Abbreviations

Paperback books and similar paper-covered items are listed in three sections:

AUTHORS (including Editors, Anthologists, Compilers, etc.): complete data on each title, including multiple editions. Works of unknown authorship are listed under Anonymous.

PUBLISHERS: In most cases the listings are sequential by book series (publisher's serial number) within each year; some are alphabetical by author within each year. There is also a supplementary section on *Ephemerals* (see below).

TITLES: Entries are similar to the *WHO'S WHO Titles* section (in Volume 2), except that juveniles are not so noted.

This coverage is as complete as possible for titles to the end of 1968. The listing includes *Authentic Science Fiction* in its various forms through to No. 28, and all the *Galaxy Science Fiction Novels* (including the later continuation by Beacon). It also includes many English titles *circa* World War II as well as Australian ones from 1940-1950, now virtually unobtainable.

A supplementary coverage of *Ephemerals* is given at the end of the *PUBLISHERS* section, listing certain series of nominal interest, such as the *Boy's Friend Library* and similar titles, the Haldeman-Julius *Little Blue Books*, titles by some specialist publishers such as Ed Aprill, and newspaper supplements such as the Toronto *Star Weekly*. These "Ephemeral" titles are listed in the *TITLES* section with the notation *Eph.*, but are not listed in the *AUTHORS* section. Instead, there are "see also" notes under each author, referring to the publisher and page number in the *Ephemerals* section.

The listing does not cover paper-covered editions of most works to the mid-1930's (except a few directly brought to my attention), when the present paperback era can be considered to have begun. Titles by specialist fan presses are generally not included, nor are any foreign series (though the more important of these are mentioned in the *GENERAL* section).

Nonfiction is not completely covered, but an attempt has been made to provide reasonable leads to titles concerning "unidentified flying objects" and related material, supernatural "fact" and "true" ghost stories, witchcraft, and of course nonfiction concerning science fiction and fantasy. Astronomy is not gen-

erally covered, nor early nonfiction on space travel and rocketry, except some titles from contemporary science fiction writers or learned essayists such as A. C. Clarke and W. Ley.

The listing contains few sex science fiction and fantasy titles, as most have been issued by obscure publishers and have not been available through normal sales channels.

The coverage has been rechecked since the appearance of Volumes 1 and 2 of the *Encyclopedia*, and some changes have been made in the light of new information. Entries herewith should be taken as more accurate than the *Who's Who* coverage in Volumes 1 and 2 – in particular the redating of many of the British paperbacks of the early 1950's. Some changes in author alphabetising have been made because of their pseudonyms; two examples are John Newton Chance (for pseudonym John Lymington) and Charles Beaumont (the present legal name for the former Charles Nutt).

I acknowledge in particular the help of Gerald Bishop, Bob Gaines, and the late Ron Graham in updating the original manuscript for this section.

Abbreviations: Each column in the *AUTHORS* section is headed by the line:

Author and Title   Publisher   Serial   Date   Pp.   Price   Type

Publisher abbreviations are spelled out in the *PUBLISHER* section, with cross-references where the abbreviation is alphabetized differently from the publisher's full name. *Serial* is the publisher's serial number or order code; an asterisk (*) indicates that the book is a "double" containing another title, see the *PUBLISHERS* listing. *Pp.* is the number of pages. *Type* is the book category, as follows:

A   anthology
C   collection
J   juvenile
M   reprinted directly from a magazine
N   nonfiction
R   reprinted from a book

Paperback Authors

Author and Title	Publisher	Serial	Date	Pp.	Price	Type

A

ABBOTT, EDWIN A(BBOTT) (1838—1926)

Flatland	Dover		1952	103	$2.25	R
			1955	103	$1.00	R

ABEL, R. COX

Trivana 1 [with C. Barren]	Panther	2077	1966	171	3/6	R

ACKERMAN, FORREST J (1916—)
The Best From Famous Monsters of Filmland

	Paperback	52-290	1964	162	50¢	N,M

Famous Monsters of Filmland Strike Back

	Paperback	52-813	1965	161	50¢	N,M

Son of Famous Monsters of Filmland

	Paperback	52-504	1964	162	50¢	N,M

ADAM, ROBERT J. See MacTYRE, PAUL (pseud)

ADAMS, JOHN (pseud) See GLASBY, J. S.

ADAMSKI, GEORGE (1891—)
Behind the Flying Saucer Mystery

	Paperback	53-439	1967	159	60¢	N,R

The Flying Saucers Have Landed [with D. Leslie]

	Panther	663	1957	237	2/6	N

Inside the Flying Saucers	Paperback	53-428	1967	192	60¢	N,R

ADDAMS, CHARLES (SAMUEL) (1912—)

Dear Dead Days	Berkley	F1175	1966	124	50¢	R
Drawn and Quartered	Bantam	37	1946	128	35¢	R

ADLER, ALLEN (1916—)
Terror on Planet Ionus (originally *Mach 1*)

	Paperback	52-941	1966	160	50¢	R

ADLER, BILL
Letters to the Air Force on UFO's

	Dell	4748	1967	157	50¢	N

AHMED, R(OLLO) (Deceased)

The Black Art	Arrow	924	1966	320	5/-	N,R
	Paperback	54-617	1968	318	75¢	N,R

AICKMAN, ROBERT (1914—1981)

Dark Entries	Fontana	981	1964	173	3/6	C

The Fontana Book of Great Ghost Stories

	Fontana	1055	1964	256	3/6	A

The Fourth Fontana Book of Great Ghost Stories

	Fontana	1635	1967	192	3/6	A

Powers of Darkness	Fontana	1827	1968	190	5/-	C,R

The Second Fontana Book of Great Ghost Stories

	Fontana	1227	1966	252	3/6	A

The Third Fontana Book of Great Ghost Stories

	Fontana	1465	1966	224	3/6	A

We Are for the Dark [with E. J. Howard]

	Mayflower	9438	1965	174	3/6	C

AINSBURY, RAY (pseud) See VERRILL, A. H.

AINSWORTH, WILLIAM H. (1805—1882)

The Elixir of Life	FSB	1576	1966	122	3/6	R

ALBERT, MARVIN H.

Goodbye Charlie	Dell	2923	1964	157	40¢	

ALBERTSON, GARRETT V.

A Visit to Mars	Moody 'Colportage'					
		200	nd	124	35¢	

ALDISS, BRIAN W(ILSON) (1925—)

The Airs of Earth	FSB	1325	1965	190	3/6	C,R

All About Venus

[with H. Harrison]	Dell	0085	1968	219	60¢	A

Best SF: 1967 (also titled *Year's Best Science Fiction*)

[with H. Harrison]	Berkley	S1529	1968	256	75¢	A

Bow Down to Nul (also titled *The Interpreter*)

	Ace	D-443*	1960	145	35¢	M
	Ace	F-382	1966	145	40¢	R

The Canopy of Time	FSB	821	1963	191	2/6	C,R
	FSB	1078	1964	191	3/6	C,R

The Dark Light-Years	Signet D2497 (2 ed)		1964	128	50¢	M,R
	FSB	1437	1966	159	3/6	M,R

Earthworks	FSB	1741 (2 ed)	1966	126	3/6	M,R
	Signet	P3116	1967	128	60¢	M,R

Equator (originally *Vanguard From Alpha*)

	Digit	R533	1961	160	2/6	C
	Digit	R695	1963	157	2/6	C

Galaxies Like Grains of Sand

	Signet	S1815	1960	144	35¢	C

Greybeard	Signet	P2689	1965	207	60¢	R
	Panther	024603	1968	219	5/-	R

Hothouse (originally *The Long Afternoon of Earth*)

	FSB	1147	1964	206	3/6	C

The Interpreter (originally *Bow Down to Nul*)

	Digit	R506	1961	156	2/6	R
	Digit	R766	1963	158	2/6	R
	FSB	1970	1967	126	3/6	R

Introducing Science Fiction

	Faber		1967	224	6/-	A,R

The Long Afternoon of Earth (also titled *Hothouse*)

	Signet	D2018	1962	192	50¢	

The Male Response	Beac (Gal)	305	1961	188	35¢	
	FSB	1623	1966	174	3/6	R

More Penguin Science Fiction

	Penguin	1963	1963	236	3/6	A

Nebula Award Stories 2 [with H. Harrison]

	Pocket Bks	75114	1968	244	75¢	A,R

No Time Like Tomorrow	Signet	S1683	1959	160	35¢	C

Non-Stop (also titled *Starship*)

	Digit	R396	1960	160	2/6	M,R
	Faber		1965	252	7/6	M,R

Penguin Science Fiction	Penguin	1638	1961	236	3/6	A
	Penguin	1638	1966	236	3/6	A

The Primal Urge	Ballantine	F555	1961	191	50¢	
	Sphere	10820	1967	191	5/-	

The Saliva Tree and Other Strange Growths

	Sphere	10839	1968	253	5/-	C

Space, Time and Nathaniel

	FSB	1496	1966	159	3/6	C,R

Starship (originally *Non-Stop*)

	Signet	S1779	1960	160	35¢	R
	Signet	D2271	1963	160	50¢	R

Starswarm	Signet	D2411	1964	159	50¢	C

Vanguard From Alpha (also titled *Equator*)

	Ace	D-369*	1959	109	35¢	M

Who Can Replace a Man? (originally *Best Science Fiction Stories of Brian Aldiss*)

	Signet	P3311	1967	215	60¢	C,R

Year's Best Science Fiction (originally *Best SF:1967*)

[with H. Harrison]	Sphere	43311	1968	207	5/-	A

Yet More Penguin Science Fiction

	Penguin	2189	1964	205	3/6	A
	Penguin	2189	1966	205	3/6	A

Author and Title	Publisher	Serial	Date	Pp.	Price	Type
ALEXANDER, DAVID (1907—)						
Tales for a Rainy Night	Crest	d557	1962	192	50¢	A,R
ALEXANDER, LLOYD (1924—)						
Time Cat	Avon	ZS139	1968	191	60¢	J
ALGREN, NELSON						
Book of Lonesome Monsters						
	Panther	1627	1964	206	3/6	A
ALLEN, MARION C. (1914—)						
Shock!	Popular	SP375	1965	144	50¢	A
ALLEN, VIRGINIA FRENCH						
Times 4	Noble	F227	1968	160	75¢	A
ALLINGHAM, H. J. See BOY'S FRIEND LIBRARY, page 789.						
ALLINGHAM, MARGERY (1904—1966)						
The Mind Readers	Macfadden	75-175	1967	224	75¢	R
	Penguin	C2779	1968	250	4/6	R
ALLISON, CLYDE (pseud of William Knoles)						
The Desdamona Affair	Ember Lib		1966	159	75¢	
The Desert Damsels	Candid Reader					
		CA930	1968	159		
For Your Sighs Only	Ember Lib	EL329	1966	159	75¢	
From Rapture to Love	Leisure		1966	159		
Gamefinger	Ember Lib	EL321	1966	159	75¢	
Go-Go Sadisto	Ember Lib	EL313	1966	160	75¢	
The Ice Maiden	Ember Lib	EL365	1967	159	75¢	
The Lost Bomb	Ember Lib	EL333	1966	159	75¢	
The Merciless Mermaids	Leisure	LB1159	1966	159		
Mondo Sadisto	Leisure	LB1160	1966	159		
Nautipuss	Ember Lib	EL309	1965	160	75¢	
Our Girl From Mephisto	Ember Lib	EL305	1965	160		
Our Man From Sadisto	Ember Lib	EL301	1965	160		
Platypussy	Nightstand	NB1877	1968			
Roburta the Conqueress	Leisure	LB1176	1966	159	75¢	
Sadisto Royale	Ember Lib	EL325	1966	160	75¢	
The Sex Ray	Leisure	LB1174	1966	159	75¢	
The Sin Funnel	Candid Reader					
		CA901	1967	159		
0008 Meets Gnatman	Leisure	LB1140	1968	159	75¢	
0008 Meets Modesta Blaze	Leisure	LB1169	1966	159		
AMIS, KINGSLEY (1922—)						
The Anti-Death League	Ballantine	U6114	1967	317	75¢	R
	Penguin	2803	1968	304	5/-	R
New Maps of Hell	Ballantine	479K	1961	141	35¢	N,R
	FSB	863	1963	141	2/6	N,R
Spectrum [with R. Conquest]						
	Berkley	F733	1963	190	50¢	A,R
	Pan	M61	1964	317	5/-	A,R
	Berkley	A1595	1968		75¢	A,R
Spectrum II [with R. Conquest]						
	Berkley	F950	1964	256	50¢	A,R
	Pan	M75	1965	286	5/-	A,R
Spectrum 3 [with R. Conquest]						
	Berkley	X1108	1965	254	60¢	A,R
	Pan	M113	1966	287	5/-	A,R
Spectrum 4 [with R. Conquest]						
	Berkley	S1272	1966	287	75¢	A,R
	Pan	M193	1967	335	5/-	A,R
Spectrum 5 [with R. Conquest]						
	Berkley	A1595	1968	303	50¢	A,R
AMPER, DRAX						
Far Beyond the Blue	Gannet	7	1954	128	1/6	
ANDERSON, CHESTER (1932—)						
The Butterfly Kid	Pyramid	X1730	1967	190	60¢	
Ten Years to Doomsday [with M. Kurland]						
	Pyramid	F1015	1964	158	40¢	
	Pyramid	R1015	1964	158	50¢	R
ANDERSON, GERALD and SYLVIA						
Thunderbirds Are Go	Armada	C162	1966	127	2/6	J
ANDERSON, POUL (1926—)						
After Doomsday	Ballantine	579	1962	128	35¢	M
	Panther	1798	1965	185	3/6	R
Brain Wave	Ballantine	80	1954	164	35¢	
	Ballantine	393K	1960	164	35¢	R
	Ballantine	U2342	1966	164	50¢	R
	Mayflower	0765	1965	159	3/6	R
The Corridors of Time	Lancer	73505	1966	222	60¢	M,R
	Panther	025693	1968	223	5/-	R
Earthman, Go Home!	Ace	D-479*	1960	110	35¢	
The Enemy Stars	Berkley	G289	1959	142	35¢	M,R
	Berkley	F1112	1965	142	50¢	R
Ensign Flandry	Lancer	73-677	1967	224	60¢	M,R
Guardians of Time	Ballantine	422K	1960	140	35¢	M,C
	Pan	G660	1964	160	2/6	C,R
The High Crusade	Dolphin	C351	1962	191	95¢	M,R
	Macfadden	50-211	1964	160	50¢	M,R
	Macfadden	60-349	1968	160	60¢	R
The Horn of Time	Signet	P3349	1968	144	60¢	C
Is There Life on Other Worlds?						
	Collier	01625	1968	223	95¢	N,R
Let the Spacemen Beware!	Ace	F-209*	1963	98	40¢	M
The Makeshift Rocket	Ace	F-139*	1962	97	40¢	M
Mayday Orbit	Ace	F-104*	1961	126	40¢	M
No World of Their Own	Ace	D-110*	1955	158	35¢	M
	Ace	D-550	1962	158	35¢	R
Orbit Unlimited	Pyramid	G615	1961	158	35¢	C
	Pyramid	F818	1963	158	40¢	C,R
Planet of No Return	Ace	D-199*	1956	105	35¢	M
Shield	Berkley	F743	1963	158	50¢	M
The Snows of Ganymede	Ace	D-303*	1958	96	35¢	M
The Star Fox	Signet	P2920	1966	207	60¢	M,R
	Panther	026312	1968	204	5/-	R
Star Ways	Ace	D-255*	1957	143	35¢	R
	Ace	D-568	1963	143	35¢	R
Strangers From Earth	Ballantine	483K	1961	144	35¢	C
	Mayflower	8345	1964	190	3/6	C
Three Hearts and Three Lions						
	Avon	G1127	1962	160	50¢	M,R
Three Worlds to Conquer	Pyramid	R994	1964	143	50¢	M
	Pyramid	X1875	1968	143	60¢	R
	Mayflower	8873	1966	142	3/6	R
Time and Stars	Macfadden	60-206	1965	190	60¢	C,R
	Panther	2109	1966	169	3/6	C,R
Trader to the Stars	Berkley	F1284	1966	159	50¢	C,R
	Panther	2214	1967	144	3/6	C,R
The Trouble Twisters	Berkley	X1417	1967	190	60¢	C,R
Twilight World	Panther	1676	1964	127	2/6	R
Un-Man and Other Novellas						
	Ace	F-139*	1962	158	40¢	C
Virgin Planet	Beac (Gal)	270	1960	160	35¢	R
	Mayflower	9336	1966	156	3/6	R
War of the Wing-Men	Ace	D-303*	1958	160	35¢	M
	Ace	G-634	1967	160	50¢	R
The War of Two Worlds	Ace	D-335*	1959	108	35¢	M
We Claim These Stars!	Ace	D-407*	1959	125	35¢	M
	Ace	G-697	1968	125	50¢	R
World Without Stars	Ace	F-425	1967	125	40¢	M

Author and Title	Publisher	Serial	Date	Pp.	Price	Type
ANDERSON, WILLIAM C. (1920—)						
Five, Four, Three, Two, One—Pffff						
	Ace	D-467	1960	157	35¢	
Penelope	Pocket Bks	50126	1965	197	50¢	R
ANDREZEL, PIERRE (pseud) See BLIXEN, K.						
ANDRZEYEVSKI, G.						
The Gates of Paradise	Panther	2242	1967	125	3/6	
ANONYMOUS						
Bedside Tales of Mystery and Suspense						
	Panther	1475	1963	126	2/6	A
Benn's Bedside Book	Benn		1958	319	3/6	A
Beyond	Berkley	F712	1963	160	50¢	A
Beyond the Stars and Other Stories						
	Satellite	211	1958	113	2/-	A
Black Tales	Corgi	GN7272	1965	158	3/6	A
Dr. Jekyll and Mr. Hyde and Other Macabre Stories						
	Corgi	SN7049	1964	141	2/6	A
(see also STEVENSON, R. L.)						
The Dome of Survival	Pearson	T-B	1954	21	9d	
Four in One Weird and Occult Shorts						
	Swan		1948	144	9d	A
The Frozen Planet and Four Other Science-Fiction Novellas						
	Macfadden	60-229	1966	160	60¢	A
Great Ghost Stories	New Era	22	nd	48	25¢	A
Grimm's Fairy Tales	Airmont	CL168	1968	191	60¢	C,R
The Haunted Hotel and 25 Other Ghost Stories						
	Avon	6	nd	240	25¢	A,R
	Avon	6	nd	256	25¢	A,R
The Haunters and the Haunted and Other Ghost Stories						
	Corgi	SN1404	1963	158	2/6	A
The Heart of the Serpent	FLPH		nd	267	np	A
Horror Stories	Elek	Bestseller	1961	256	3/6	A
Imperial Overture and Other Stories						
	Pictorial		nd (1941-46)	32	6d	A
Masters of Science Fiction	Belmont	92-606	1964	157	50¢	A
The Mindworm	Tandem	T118	1967	191	3/6	A
The Molecule Monsters	Whitman		1951	32	8d	A
The Moon Conquerors	Swan		1943	176	7d	A,R
More Soviet Science Fiction						
	Collier	AS295V	1962	190	95¢	A,R
	Collier	01647	1967	190	95¢	A,R
More Tales of Terror and Surprise						
	Everybody's		nd	127	1/6	A
Now and Beyond	Belmont	B50-646	1965	157	50¢	A
Occult: A Collection of the Supernatural						
	Swan		1945	36	7d	A
Occult Shorts: Second Collection						
	Swan		nd	36	7d	A
A Pair From Space	Belmont	92-612	1965	155	50¢	A
	Belmont	B50-813	1968	155	50¢	A,R
Path Into the Unknown	Dell	6862	1968	189	60¢	A
Peter Rugg, the Missing Man						
	Todd	Polybook	1943	16	4d	
Planet of Doom and Other Stories						
	Satellite	214	1958	114	2/-	A
The Premature Burial and Other Tales of Horror						
	Corgi	GN7509	1966	157	3/6	A
The Sands of Mars and Other Stories						
	Satellite	213	1958	113	2/-	A
Science Fiction	International	3	1964	174	5/-	A
Second Arrow Book of Horror Stories						
	Arrow	800	1965	222	3/6	A,R
The 6 Fingers of Time and Other Stories						
	Macfadden	50-244	1965	128	50¢	A
Sometime, Never	Ballantine	215	1957	185	35¢	A
	Ballantine	F657	1962	185	50¢	A,R
	Ballantine	U2853	1967	185	50¢	A,R
Soviet Science Fiction	Collier	AS279V	1962	189	95¢	A
	Collier	AS279V	1965	189	95¢	A,R
	Collier	01655	1966	189	95¢	A,R
Space Station 42 and Other Stories						
	Satellite	212	1958	113	2/-	A
Stories About Giants, Witches and Dragons To Read Aloud						
	Wonder	2046	1964	127	39¢	J,C
Stories of Suspense	Scholastic	T487	1963	220	45¢	A
Strange Love Stories	Utopian	nd		72	1/-	A
Suspense Stories	Curtis War.		1951	95	1/-	A
Tales From the Crypt	Ballantine	U2106	1965	191	50¢	A
[comic-book format]						
Tales of Murder and Mystery						
	Everybody's		nd	50	1/-	A
Tales of Mystery and Surprise						
	Everybody's		nd	32	6d	A
Tales of Terror and the Unknown						
	Everybody's		1944	96	2/-	A
Tales of the Incredible	Ballantine	U2140	1965	190	50¢	A
[comic-book format]						
Tales of the Supernatural	Pan	22	1947	183	2/-	A
	Pan	22	1951	186	2/-	A,R
Tales of the Supernatural	Panther	1397	1962	124	2/6	A
Tales of the Uncanny	Panther	1454	1962	128	2/6	A
Third Finger—Left Hand and Other Thrilling Stories						
	Everybody's		nd	34	1/-	A
	Strothers		nd	34	1/-	A
Thrilling Stories—Romance, Adventure						
	Utopian		nd	36	9d	A
Thrilling Tales of Unusual Interest						
	Gulliver		nd	47	7d	A
Time Untamed	Belmont	B50-781	1967	175	50¢	A
Twenty-Five Great Ghost Stories						
	Avon	6	1943	190	25¢	A
20 Great Ghost Stories	Avon	630	1955	127	25¢	A
The Vault of Horror	Ballantine	V2107	1965	189	50¢	A
[comic-book style]						
A Visitor From Outer Space						
	FLPH		nd	202	np	A
Weird and Occult Miscellany						
	Swan		1960	105	2/6	A
Weird Shorts: First Selection						
	Swan		nd	34	7d	A
ANSTEY, F. (pseud) See GUTHRIE, T. A.						
ANTHONY, PIERS (pseud) See JACOB, P.A.D.						
ANVIL, CHRISTOPHER (pseud) See CROSBY, H. C.						
APPEL, BENJAMIN (1907—)						
The Funhouse	Ballantine	345K	1959	157	35¢	
APRILL, EDWARD M. Jr. See page 789.						
ARCHER, RON (pseud) See WHITE, TED						
ARNOLD, EDWIN L. (1887—1935)						
Gulliver of Mars (originally *Lieut. Gulliver of Mars*)						
	Ace	F-296	1964	224	40¢	R
ARNOLD, FRANK E. (1914—)						
Wings Across Time	Pendulum	ST1	1946	118	2/-	C
ARTHUR, ROBERT (1909—1971)						
Monster Mix	Dell	5797	1968	284	60¢	A
ASCHER, EUGENE						
The Grim Caretaker	Everybody's		1944	49	9d	

Author and Title	Publisher	Serial	Date	Pp.	Price	Type
There Were No Asper Ladies (also titled *To Kill a Corpse*)						
	Mitre		1944	126	1/6	
To Kill a Corpse	WDL	M839	1959	160	2/-	R
	Consul	1433	1965	160	3/6	R
Uncanny Adventures	Everybody's		1944	38	9d	C
ASH, ALAN						
Conditioned for Space	Ward Lock	38	1956	192	2/6	R
	Digit	D478	1961	160	2/6	R
	Digit	R754	1963	157	2/6	R
ASH, FENTON (pseud) See ATKINS, F.						
ASHTON, FRANCIS (1904—) **and STEPHEN**						
The Wrong Side of the Moon						
	Boardman	159	1954	190	2/-	R
ASHTON, MARVIN						
People of Asa	Curtis War.		1953	159	1/6	
(also hardcover edition, 6/-)						
ASIMOV, ISAAC (1920—)						
The Caves of Steel	Signet	S1240	1955	189	35¢	M,R
	Panther	835	1958	189	2/6	R
	Panther	835	1964	189	3/6	R
	Panther	835	1967	206	5/-	R
	Pyramid	F784	1962	189	40¢	R
	Pyramid	X1824	1968	189	60¢	R
The Currents of Space	Signet	1082	1953	176	25¢	M,R
	Panther	824	1958	192	2/6	R
	Panther	824	1964	192	3/6	R
	Panther	824	1967	205	5/-	R
	Lancer	74-816	1963	191	75¢	R
	Lancer	72-104	1966	191	50¢	R
	Lancer	73-703	1968	191	60¢	R
Earth Is Room Enough	Bantam	A1978	1959	166	35¢	C,R
	Panther	1042	1960	176	2/6	C,R
	Panther	1042	1967	176	3/6	C,R
The End of Eternity	Signet	S1493	1958	192	35¢	R
	Panther	881	1959	191	2/6	R
	Panther	881	1964	207	3/6	R
	Panther	881	1965	189	3/6	R
	Panther	024409	1968	189	5/-	R
	Lancer	74-818	1963	176	75¢	R
	Lancer	72-107	1966	176	50¢	R
	Lancer	73-701	1968	176	60¢	R
Environments Out There	Scholastic	TX757	1967	96	50¢	N
Fantastic Voyage	Bantam	H3177	1966	186	60¢	R
	Corgi	GS7366	1966	186	3/6	R
Fifty Short Science Fiction Tales [with G. Conklin]						
	Collier	AS516	1963	287	95¢	A
	Collier	01639	1966	287	95¢	A
Foundation	Panther	1080	1960	189	2/6	R
	Panther	1080	1964	189	3/6	R
	Panther	1080	1965	189	3/6	R
	Panther	1080	1966	189	3/6	R
	Avon	S224	1966	200	60¢	R
	Avon	V2248	1968	200	75¢	R
Foundation and Empire	Panther	1355	1962	172	2/6	R
	Panther	1355	1964	172	3/6	R
	Panther	1355	1965	172	3/6	R
	Avon	S234	1966	224	60¢	R
	Avon	V2236	1968	224	75¢	R
The Hugo Winners	Avon	S127	1963	320	60¢	A,R
	Penguin	1905	1964	342	4/6	A,R
I, Robot	Gnome		1950	253	35¢	C
(also hardcover edition, $2.50)						
	Signet	S1282	1956	192	35¢	C,R
	Signet	S1885	1961	192	35¢	C,R
	Signet	D2458	1964	192	50¢	C,R

Author and Title	Publisher	Serial	Date	Pp.	Price	Type
	Signet	P3540	1968	192	60¢	C,R
	Digit	D164	1958	158	2/-	C,R
	Panther	025324	1968	206	5/-	C,R
Is Anyone There?	Ace	N-4	1968	319	95¢	N
The Man Who Upset the Universe (originally *Foundation and Empire*)						
	Ace	D-125	1955	254	35¢	R
	Ace	F-216	1963	254	40¢	R
The Martian Way	Signet	S1433	1957	159	35¢	C,R
	Panther	1799	1965	192	3/6	C,R
	Panther	1799	1967	192	3/6	C,R
The Naked Sun	Bantam	A1731	1958	178	35¢	M,R
	Panther	1016	1960	189	2/6	R
	Panther	1016(2 ed)	1964	202	3/6	R
	Panther	1016	1965	202	3/6	R
	Panther	1016	1967	202	5/-	R
	Lancer	72-753	1964	189	50¢	R
	Lancer	72-108	1966	191	50¢	R
	Lancer	73-702	1968	191	60¢	R
Nine Tomorrows	Bantam	A2121	1960	198	35¢	C,R
	Pan	M171	1966	251	5/-	C,R
The 1,000 Year Plan (originally *Foundation*)						
	Ace	D-110*	1955	169	35¢	R
	Ace	D-538	1962	160	35¢	R
	Ace (spec.)	D-110	1965	160		R
Pebble in the Sky	Galaxy Nov	14	1953	153	35¢	R
	Bantam	A1646	1957	200	35¢	R
	Bantam	EP47	1964	200	45¢	R
	Bantam	FP47	1968	200	50¢	R
	Corgi	S583	1958	220	2/6	R
The Rebellious Stars (originally *The Stars, Like Dust*)						
	Ace	D-84*	1954	176	35¢	R
The Rest of the Robots	Pyramid	R1283	1966	159	50¢	C,R
	Pyramid	R1783	1968	159	50¢	C,R
	Panther	025944	1968	223	5/-	C,R
Second Foundation: Galactic Empire (originally *Second Foundation*)						
	Avon	T232	1958	192	35¢	R
	Avon	G1248	1964	191	50¢	R
	Avon	S237	1966	191	60¢	R
	Avon	S237	1968	191	60¢	R
	Digit	D192	1958	160	2/-	R
	Panther	1713	1964	187	3/6	R
	Panther	1713	1965	187	3/6	R
	Panther	17135	1967	187	5/-	R
The Stars, Like Dust (also titled *The Rebellious Stars*)						
	Panther	863	1958	191	2/6	M,R
	Panther	863	1964	204	3/6	R
	Panther	863	1965	189	3/6	R
	Panther	024417	1968	189	5/-	R
	Lancer	74-815	1963	192	75¢	R
	Lancer	72-103	1966	192	50¢	R
	Lancer	73-704	1968	192	60¢	R
Through a Glass, Clearly	FSB	1866	1967	124	3/6	C
ASQUITH, (LADY) CYNTHIA (1887—1960)						
The Black Cap	Hutchinson		nd	352		A,R
The Ghost Book	Hutchinson	123	1945?	287	1/6	A,R
The Second Ghost Book	Pan	393	1956	222	2/-	A,R
	Pan	G315	1959	223	2/6	A,R
	Pan	G315	1961	223	2/6	A,R
	Pan	G315	1963	223	2/6	A,R
The Third Ghost Book	Pan	GP86	1957	253	2/6	A,R
	Pan	GP86	1960	253	2/6	A,R
	Pan	GP86	1963	253	3/6	A,R
	Pan	02061	1968	253	5/-	A,R
What Dreams May Come	FSB	1283	1965	158	3/6	C,R
When Churchyards Yawn	Arrow	679	1963	192	2/6	A,R
ASTURIAS, MIGUEL ANGEL (1899—1974)						
Mulata	Dell	5915	1968	348	95¢	R

Author and Title	Publisher	Serial	Date	Pp.	Price	Type
ATHELING, WILLIAM Jr. (pseud) See BLISH, J.						
ATHOLL, JUSTIN						
Death in the Green Fields	Mitre		1945?	36	np	
The Grey Beast	Everybody's		1944	48	9d	
Land of Hidden Death	Everybody's		1944	50	9d	
The Man Who Tilted the Earth						
	Mitre		1944	63	1/6	
The Oasis of Sleep	Mitre		1944	62	1/6	
ATKINS, FRANK						
As Fenton Ash, see BOY'S FRIEND LIBRARY, page 789.						
As Frank Aubrey, see BOY'S FRIEND LIBRARY, page 789.						
AUBREY, FRANK (pseud) See ATKINS, F.						
AVALLONE, MICHAEL (1924—)						
The Birds-of-a-Feather Affair						
	Signet		1966	128		
The Blazing Affair	Signet		1966	127		
The Coffin Things	Lancer	74-942	1968	221	75¢	
Edwina Noone's Gothic Sampler [as Edwina Noone (pseud)]						
	Award	A199X	1967	159	60¢	A
The Night Walker [as Sidney Stuart (pseud)]						
	Award	A124F	1964	139	50¢	
	Brown-Wat.	R913	1965	156	3/6	R
Tales of the Frightened	Belmont	90-297	1963	128	40¢	C
	Belmont	B50-736	1967	128	50¢	C,R
	Mayflower	8474	1964	126	2/6	C,R
The Thousand Coffins Affair						
	Ace	G-553	1965	160	50¢	
AYCOCK, ROGER DEE (1924—) [as Roger Dee (pseud)]						
An Earth Gone Mad	Ace	D-84*	1954	144	35¢	M
AYLESWORTH, JOHN (1938—)						
Fee, Fei, Fo, Fum!	Avon	G1166	1963	158	50¢	
AYMÉ, MARCEL (1902—)						
Across Paris and Other Stories (also titled *The Walker-Through-Walls*)						
	Ace (Brit.)	H380	1960	187	2/6	C,R
The Fable and the Flesh	Mayflower	2450	1965	190	3/6	R
The Grand Seduction (originally *The Second Face*)						
	Ace (Brit.)	H278	1959	192	4/-	R
The Green Mare	Penguin	1516	1961	237	3/6	R
The Walker-Through-Walls (originally *Across Paris and Other Stories*)						
	Berkley	F634	1962	191	50¢	C,R

B

Author and Title	Publisher	Serial	Date	Pp.	Price	Type
B.B. (pseud) See WATKINS-PITCHFORD, D. J.						
BACH, M.						
Strange Altars	Signet	T3484	1968	176	75¢	
BACHELOR, GEORGE C.						
True Ghost Stories	Gulliver		nd	49	6d	C
Uncanny	Mitre		1945	32	1/-	C
BAHNSON, AGNEW H. (? —1964)						
The Stars Are Too High	Bantam	A2048	1960	183	35¢	R

Author and Title	Publisher	Serial	Date	Pp.	Price	Type
BAILEY, CHARLES W. (1929—) See KNEBEL, F. (co-author)						
BAKER, FRANK (1908—)						
The Birds	Panther	1635	1964	224	3/6	R
Miss Hargreaves	Penguin	783	1950	315	1/6	R
	Panther	1959	1965	234	3/6	R
BAKER, RUSSELL						
Our Next President	Dell	6762	1968	108	75¢	
BALDERSTON, JOHN L. See DEANE, H. (co-author)						
BALL, BRIAN N. (1932—)						
Sundog	Corgi	GS7451	1966	190	3/6	R
Tales of Science Fiction	Peacock	PK63	1968	173	4/-	A,R
BALLARD, J(AMES) G(RAHAM) (1930—)						
Billenium	Berkley	F667	1962	159	50¢	C
The Burning World (also titled *The Drought*)						
	Berkley	F961	1964	160	50¢	
The Crystal World	Berkley	X1380	1967	160	60¢	R
	Panther	024190	1968	175	5/-	R
The Day of Forever	Panther	2307	1967	141	3/6	C
The Drought (originally *The Burning World*)						
	Penguin	2753	1968	176	3/6	R
The Drowned World	Berkley	F655	1962	158	50¢	M
	Berkley	F1266	1966	158	50¢	R
	Penguin	2229	1965	171	3/6	R
The Four-Dimensional Nightmare						
	Penguin	2345	1965	223	3/6	C,R
The Impossible Man	Berkley	F1204	1966	160	50¢	C
The Overloaded Man	Panther	2336	1967	158	3/6	C
Passport to Eternity	Berkley	F823	1963	160	50¢	C
Terminal Beach	Berkley	F928	1964	160	50¢	C,R
	Penguin	2499	1966	224	4/6	C,R
The Voices of Time and Other Stories						
	Berkley	F607	1962	158	50¢	C
	Berkley	F1243	1966	158	50¢	C
The Wind From Nowhere	Berkley	F600	1962	160	50¢	M
	Berkley	F1198	1966	160	50¢	M,R
	Penguin	2591	1967	186	4/-	M,R
BALLINGER, W. A. (pseud) See McNEILLY, W. G.						
BALMER, EDWIN (1883—1959) See WYLIE, P. (co-author)						
BANISTER, MANLY (1914—)						
Conquest of Earth	Airmont	SF7	1964	128	40¢	R
BARDENS, D(ENNIS)						
Ghosts and Hauntings	Fontana	1610	1967	256	5/-	N,R
BARKER, GRAY						
They Knew Too Much About Flying Saucers (also titled *The Unidentified*)						
	Tower	43817	1967	190	60¢	N,R
The Unidentified (originally *They Knew Too Much About Flying Saucers*)						
	Badger	SS3	1960	156	2/6	N,R
BARKIN, G.						
The Sardonic Humour of Ambrose Bierce						
	Dover	T768	1963	232	$1.00	C
BARNARD, ALLAN						
The Harlot Killer	Dell	797	1954	224	25¢	A,R
BARR, DENSIL N. (pseud of Douglas C. Buttrey)						
The Man With Only One Head						
	Digit	R558	1962	156	2/6	R

Author and Title	Publisher	Serial	Date	Pp.	Price	Type
BARR, TYRONE C.						
The Last Fourteen (originally *Split Worlds*)						
	Chariot	CB150	1960	156	50¢	R
Split Worlds (also titled *The Last Fourteen*)						
	Digit	D248	1959	156	2/-	
	Digit	R563	1962	160	2/6	R
BARREN, CHARLES See ABEL, R. C. (co-author)						
BARRETT, WILLIAM E. (1900—)						
The Fools of Time	Pocket Bks	50003	1964	309	50¢	R
BARRON, D(ONALD) G. (1922—)						
The Zilov Bombs	Pan	G698	1965	125	2/6	R
BARRY, RAY (pseud) See HUGHES, DEN						
BARTER, ALAN F. (1933—)						
Untravelled Worlds [with R. Wilson]						
	Papermac		1966	168	np	A
BARTH, JOHN (1930—)						
Giles Goat-Boy	Crest	P1052	1967	766	$1.25	R
	Penguin	2728	1967	813	8/6	R
BARTHELME, DONALD (1933—)						
Come Back, Dr. Caligari	Anchor	470	1965	138	95¢	C,R
BARTON, ERLE (pseud) See FANTHORPE, R. L.						
BARTON, LEE (pseud) See FANTHORPE, R. L.						
BARZMAN, BEN						
Echo X (originally *Twinkle, Twinkle, Little Star*; also titled *Out of This World*)						
	Paperback	52-130	1962	252	50¢	R
	Paperback	52-329	1964	252	50¢	R
	Paperback	54-684	1968	252	75¢	R
Out of This World (originally *Twinkle, Twinkle, Little Star*)						
	Fontana	681	1963	255	3/6	R
BATEMAN, ROBERT (1922—)						
The Hands of Orlac (revision of novel of same title by Maurice Renard)						
	FSB	289	1960	128	2/6	
	Horwitz	FH24	1962	130	4/-	R
When the Whites Went	Digit	R854	1964	158	2/6	R
BATT, LEON						
Formula for Power	Pinnacle (Sydney)		1941	64	6d	
BAUM, L(YMAN) FRANK (1856—1919)						
The Land of Oz	Airmont	CL181	1968		50¢	J,R
	Avon	ZV147	1968	287	75¢	J,R
The Marvelous Land of Oz	Dover	T692	1961	287	$1.50	J,R
The Surprising Adventures of the Magical Monarch of Mo						
	Dover	T-1892	1968	237	$2.00	J,R
The Wizard of Oz	Crest	s395	1960	192	35¢	J,R
	Crest	K674	1963	192	40¢	J,R
	Avon	ZS122	1967	199	60¢	J,R
	Gold Medal	d1883	1968	162	50¢	J,R
	Scholastic	TX163	1968	156	60¢	J,R
The Wonderful Wizard of Oz						
	Dover	T-691	1960	268	$1.45	J,R
	Airmont	CL69	1965	160	50¢	J,R
BAWDEN, NINA See MONTREAL STAR, page 790.						
BAXTER, JOHN (1939—)						
The God Killers (the original title, but preceded by *The Off-Worlders*)						
	Horwitz	PB345	1968	127	55¢	R
The Off-Worlders	Ace	G-588*	1966	127	50¢	M
Pacific Book of Australian Science Fiction						
	Pacific	92	1968	180	$1.00	A
BEAGLE, PETER S. (1939—)						
A Fine and Private Place	Dell	Delta 2530	1960	272	$1.85	R
	Corgi	GN1273	1963	222	3/6	R
BEARNE, A. W.						
Flying Saucers Over the West						
	Bearne		1968	24	3/6	N
BEAUMONT, CHARLES (1929—1967) [Legal name of the former Charles Nutt]						
The Edge	Panther	2151	1966	143	3/6	C
The Fiend in You	Ballantine	F641	1962	158	50¢	A
The Hunger and Other Stories (also titled *Shadow Play*)						
	Bantam	A1917	1959	183	35¢	C,R
The Magic Man	Gold Medal	d1586	1965	256	50¢	C
	Coronet	F109	1966	258	3/6	C,R
Night Ride and Other Journeys						
	Bantam	A2087	1960	184	35¢	C
Shadow Play (originally *The Hunger and Other Stories*)						
	Panther	1767	1964	190	3/6	C,R
Yonder	Bantam	A1759	1958	184	35¢	C,R
BECHER, DON						
A Ticket to Nowhere	Vega	VSF13	1966	160	50¢	
BECK, CALVIN T. (1930—)						
The Frankenstein Reader	Ballantine	F680	1962	159	50¢	A
BECKFORD, WILLIAM (1760—1844)						
Vathek	FSB	1575	1966	123	3/6	R
See also *Three Gothic Novels* [E. F. Bleiler]						
BEEMISH, CRAGG						
Worlds Away	Gannet	9	1953	127	1/6	
BEERBOHM, MAX (1872—1956)						
Seven Men	Armed	c-67	nd		np	C,R
Seven Men and Two Others						
	Penguin	1010	1954	185	2/-	C,R
BELFIELD, H. WEDGWOOD See CHAMPION LIBRARY, page 789.						
BELL, ERIC T. (1883—1960) [as John Taine (pseud)]						
G.O.G. 666	Arrow	705	1963	192	2/6	R
The Greatest Adventure	Ace	D-473	1960	256	35¢	R
See also *Three Science Fiction Novels*						
The Purple Sapphire See *Three Science Fiction Novels*						
Seeds of Life	Galaxy Nov	13	1953	174	35¢	M,R
	Panther	784	1958	157	2/6	R
Seeds of Life & The White Lily						
	Dover	T-1626	1966	367	$2.00	C,R
Three Science Fiction Novels [*The Time Stream*; *The Greatest Adventure*; *The Purple Sapphire*] Dover		T-1180	1964	532	$2.00	C,R
The Time Stream See *Three Science Fiction Novels*						
The White Lily See *The Seeds of Life*						
BELL, NEIL (pseud) See SOUTHWOLD, S.						
BELL, THORNTON (pseud) See FANTHORPE, R. L.						
BELLAMY, EDWARD (1850—1898)						
Looking Backward	Routledge		1904	156	np	R
	Judd		1932	220	2/-	R
	Dolphin	C55	nd	234	95¢	R
	Signet	CD26	1960	222	50¢	R
	Lancer	13-440	1968	349	60¢	R
BELLAMY, FRANCIS R. (1886—)						
Atta	Ace	D-79*	1954	179	35¢	R

Author and Title	Publisher	Serial	Date	Pp.	Price	Type
BELLMORE, DON						
By Lust Possessed	Pleasure Reader PR180		1968			
Leopard Lust	Nightstand NB1864		1967			
Sin Seance	Candid Reader CA940		1968			
BENEDICT, STEWART H. (1924—)						
Tales of Terror and Suspense	Dell	8466	1963	288	45¢	A
BENEFIELD, (JOHN) B(ARRY) (1883—)						
Eddie and the Archangel Mike	Armed	710	nd	320	np	
BENÉT, STEPHEN V. (1898—1943)						
The Devil and Daniel Webster and Other Stories	Washington	29013	1968	120	50¢	C,R
O'Halloran's Luck and Other Short Stories	Penguin-US		1944?		25¢	C
Short Stories of Stephen Vincent Benét	Armed	c77	nd	320	np	C
The Stephen Vincent Benét Pocket Book	Pocket Bks	360	1946	414	25¢	C
BENNETT, ALFRED GORDON (1901—1962)						
Whom the Gods Destroy	Pharos		1946	100	2/-	
BENNETT, GEOFFREY						
This Creeping Evil	Arrow	693	1963	190	2/6	R
BENNETT, GEORGE						
Great Tales of Action and Adventure	Dell	LB126	1959	256	35¢	A
BENNETT, JAY						
Catacombs	Panther	1287	1962	156	2/6	
BENNETT, W. See BURNLEY, COUNTY BOROUGH OF, page 789.						
BENOIT, PIERRE (1886—1962)						
Atlantida (also titled *The Queen of Atlantis*)	Ace	F-281	1964	192	40¢	R
The Queen of Atlantis	Hutchinson	359	nd	128	6d	R
BENSEN, D(ONALD) R. (1927—)						
The Unknown	Pyramid	R851	1963	192	50¢	A
The Unknown Five	Pyramid	R962	1964	190	50¢	A
BENSON E(DWARD) F(REDERICK) (1867—1940) See HALDE-MAN-JULIUS CO., page 790.						
BENTLIF, SYD						
Horror Anthology	Mayflower	3720	1965	126	3/6	A
BERESFORD, J(OHN) D(AVYS) (1873—1947)						
The Hampdenshire Wonder	Penguin	92	1937	256	6d	R
BERESFORD, L. See BOY'S FRIEND LIBRARY, page 789.						
BERGIER, JACQUES See PAUWELS, L. (co-author)						
BERKLEY, T.						
Legend of the Holocaust	Scripts	PB376	1968	129	55¢	
BERNARD, CHRISTINE (1926—)						
The Armada Ghost Book	Armada	C197	1967	158	2/6	A,J
The Fontana Book of Great Horror Stories	Fontana	1232	1966	221	3/6	A
	Fontana	1748	1968	221	3/6	A,R
The Second Armada Ghost Book	Armada	C253	1968	126	2/6	A,J
The Third Fontana Book of Great Horror Stories	Fontana	1702	1968	188	3/6	A
BERNARD, JOEL						
The Thinking Machine Affair	FSB		1967	128		
BERNARD, RAFE						
Army of the Undead (originally *The Halo Highway*)	Pyramid	R1711	1967	142	50¢	
The Halo Highway (also titled *Army of the Undead*)	Corgi	GS7742	1967	158	3/6	
Wheel in the Sky	Ward Lock	26	1955	193	2/6	R
BERNSTEIN, MOREY (1930?—)						
The Search for Bridey Murphy	Pocket Bks	GC37	1956	324	50¢	N,R
BERRY, BRYAN (1930—1955)						
Aftermath	Authentic	24	1952	109	1/6	
And the Stars Remain	Panther	nn	1952	112	1/6	
	Atlas	SFL7	1956	114	2/-	R
Born in Captivity	Hamilton		1952	191	2/-	
(identical hardcover edition 8/6)						
Dread Visitor	Panther	28	1952	127	1/6	
From What Far Star?	Panther	40	1953	143	1/6	
(identical hardcover edition 6/-)						
	Atlas	SFL3	1955	114	2/-	R
The Immortals [as Rolf Garner]	Panther	78	1953	159	1/6	
(identical hardcover edition 6/-)						
The Indestructible [as Rolf Garner]	Panther	104	1954	159	1/6	
(identical hardcover edition 6/-)						
Resurgent Dust [as Rolf Garner]	Panther	68	1953	160	1/6	
(identical hardcover edition 6/-)						
Return to Earth	Hamilton		1952	110	1/6	
The Venom-Seekers	Panther	57	1953	160	1/6	
(identical hardcover edition 6/-)						
BESTER, ALFRED (1913—)						
The Dark Side of Earth	Signet	D2474	1964	160	50¢	C
The Demolished Man	Signet	1105	1954	175	25¢	M,R
	Signet	S1593	1958	175	35¢	R
	Signet	D2679	1965	174	50¢	R
	Panther	933	1959	189	2/6	R
	Penguin	2536	1967	191	3/6	R
Starburst	Signet	S1524	1958	160	35¢	C
	Signet	D2672	1965	160	50¢	C,R
	Sphere	16071	1968	158	5/-	C,R
The Stars My Destination (also titled *Tiger! Tiger!*)	Signet	S1389	1957	197	35¢	M,R
	Signet	S1931	1961	197	35¢	R
	Panther	973	1959	192	2/6	R
Tiger! Tiger! (originally *The Stars My Destination*)	Penguin	2620	1967	249	4/6	R
BEYMER, WILLIAM GILMORE (1881—)						
The Middle of Midnight	Armed	1258	nd		np	R
BEYNON, JOHN (pseud) See HARRIS, J. B.						
BIDSTON, LESTER See BOY'S FRIEND LIBRARY, page 789.						

Author and Title	Publisher	Serial	Date	Pp.	Price	Type
BIERCE, AMBROSE (1842—1914)						
See also HALDEMAN-JULIUS CO., page 790.						
Collected Writings of Ambrose Bierce						
	Citadel		1963	810	$2.75	C,R
Ghost and Horror Stories of Ambrose Bierce						
	Dover	T-767	1964	199	$1.00	C
	Dover	T-767	1967	199	$1.25	C,R
In the Midst of Life	Penguin	199	1939	215	1/-	C,R
	Signet	CD60	1961	256	60¢	C,R
The Monk and the Hangman's Daughter						
	Avon	628	1955	127	25¢	C
The Sardonic Humour of Ambrose Bierce [editor, G. Barkin]						
	Dover	T-768	1963	232	$1.00	C
BIGGERS, W. WATTS						
The Man Inside	Ballantine	72008	1968	192	75¢	
BIGGLE, LLOYD Jr. (1923—)						
All the Colors of Darkness	Paperback	52-514	1965	176	50¢	R
	Paperback	53-746	1968	176	60¢	R
	Penguin	2387	1966	204	4/-	R
The Angry Espers	Ace	D-485*	1961	136	35¢	M
The Fury Out of Time	Berkley	X1393	1967	223	60¢	R
	Sphere	16519	1968	192	5/-	R
BINDER, EARL (1904—) and **OTTO** (1911—1974)) [as Eando Binder]						
See also BIZARRE SERIES, page 789.						
Adam Link in the Past	Whitman		1950	48	8d	M
Adam Link, Robot	Paperback	52-847	1965	174	50¢	M
	Paperback	53-763	1968	174	60¢	R
Anton York, Immortal	Belmont	B50-627	1965	158	50¢	M
Martian Martyrs [as John Coleridge]						
	Columbia	SFC1	nd	23	10¢	M
The New Life [as John Coleridge]						
	Columbia	SFC4	nd	23	10¢	M
The Three Eternals	Whitman		1949	48	6d	M
Where Eternity Ends	Whitman		1950	32	6d	M
BINDER, OTTO (1911—1974)						
The Avengers Battle the Earth-Wrecker						
	Bantam	F3569	1967	122	50¢	
Flying Saucers Are Watching Us						
	Belmont	B75-218	1968	189	75¢	N
What We Really Know About Flying Saucers						
	Gold Medal		1967		75¢	N
BINGHAM, CARSON (pseud) See CASSIDAY, B.						
BIRD, WILLIAM HENRY FLEMING (1896—1971)						
Blast-Off Into Space [as Harry Fleming]						
	Cape		1966	128		
Cosmic Conquest [as Adrian Blair]						
	Curtis War.		1953	159	1/6	
(identical hardcover edition 6/-)						
Operation Orbit [as Kris Luna]						
	Curtis War.		1954	159	1/6	
(identical hardcover edition 6/-)						
The Third Mutant [as Lee Elliot]						
	Curtis War.		1953	160	1/6	
(identical hardcover edition 6/-)						
Two Worlds [as Paul Lorraine]						
	Curtis War.		1952	128	1/6	
(identical hard cover edition 5/- [?])						
War of Argos [as Rand Le Page]						
	Curtis War.		1952	127	1/6	
BIRKIN, CHARLES (1907—)						
Dark Menace	Tandem	T199	1968	188	3/6	C
The Haunted Dancers (originally *The Tandem Book of Ghost Stories*)						
	Paperback	52-472	1967	159	50¢	A,R

Author and Title	Publisher	Serial	Date	Pp.	Price	Type
The Kiss of Death and Other Horror Stories						
	Tandem	T2	1964	235	3/6	C
	Tandem	T2	1967	192	3/6	C,R
My Name Is Death and Other New Tales of Horror						
	Panther	2150	1966	139	3/6	C
The Smell of Evil	Tandem	T28	1965	189	3/6	C
The Tandem Book of Ghost Stories (also titled *The Haunted Dancers*)						
	Tandem	T52	1965	192	3/6	A
The Tandem Book of Horror Stories (also titled *The Witch Baiter*)						
	Tandem	T49	1965	192	3/6	A
Where Terror Stalked	Tandem	T80	1967	192	3/6	C
The Witch Baiter (originally *The Tandem Book of Horror Stories*)						
	Paperback	52-468	1967	159	50¢	A,R
BIXBY, JEROME (1923—)						
Devil's Scrapbook	Brandon	625	1964	158	60¢	C
Space by the Tale	Ballantine	U2203	1964	159	50¢	C
BLACK, PANSY E.						
The Men From the Meteor	Stellar	SFS13	1932	24	10¢	
The Valley of the Great Ray						
	Stellar	SFS11	1930	28	10¢	
BLACKBURN, JOHN (1923—)						
Children of the Night	Panther	024689	1968	158	5/-	R
A Scent of New-Mown Hay (also titled *The Reluctant Spy*)						
	Penguin	1615	1961	191	2/6	R
	Digit	R846	1964	158	2/6	R
	NEL	2056	1968	160	6/-	R
The Reluctant Spy (originally *The Scent of New-Mown Hay*)						
	Lancer	73509	1966	152	60¢	R
BLACKSTOCK, CHARITY (pseud of Ursula Torday)						
Witches' Sabbath	Paperback	52527	1967	174	50¢	
BLACKWOOD, ALGERNON (1869—1951)						
Ancient Sorceries and Other Stories						
	Penguin	2904	1968	203	5/-	C,R
The Centaur	Penguin	166	1938	280	np	R
The Dance of Death	Pan	G645	1963	126	2/6	C,R
The Insanity of Jones and Other Tales (originally *Tales of Terror and the Unknown*)	Penguin	2527	1966	365	6/-	C,R
Selected Short Stories of Algernon Blackwood						
	Armed	s-26	nd	287	np	C
Selected Tales of Algernon Blackwood						
	Penguin	393	1948	173	1/6	C
Tales of Terror and the Unknown (also titled *The Insanity of Jones and Other Tales*)	Everyman Dutt.					
		D166	1965	381	$1.75	C
BLAIR, ADRIAN (pseud) See BIRD, W. H. F.						
BLAIR, CLAY						
The Atomic Submarine	Beac (Odh)	B17	1957	256	2/6	N
BLAIR, ERIC (1903—1950) [as George Orwell]						
Animal Farm	Penguin	838	1951	120	1/6	R
	Penguin	838	1954	120	2/-	R
	Penguin	838	1959	120	2/6	R
	Penguin	838	1962	120	2/6	R
	Penguin	838	1968	120	3/-	R
	Signet	1289	1956	128	25¢	R
	Signet	D1615	1958	128	50¢	R
	Signet	CD3	1959	128	50¢	R
	Signet	CP121	1962	128	60¢	R
	Signet	CT304	1966	128	75¢	R
1984	Signet	798	1950	237	25¢	R
	Signet	S798	1956	237	35¢	R
	Signet	D1640	1959	256	50¢	R
	Signet	CP100	1961	267	60¢	R

Author and Title	Publisher	Serial	Date	Pp.	Price	Type
	Signet	CT311	1966	267	75¢	R
	Penguin	972	1954	251	2/-	R
	Penguin	972	1959	251	2/6	R
	Penguin	972	1962	251	3/6	R
	Penguin	972	1967	251	4/-	R
BLAISDELL, ANNE						
Nightmare	Crest	s518	1962	176	35¢	
	Corgi	GN7020	1964	190	3/6	R
	Lancer	73-653	1967	222	60¢	R

BLAKE, S. See BOY'S FRIEND LIBRARY, page 789.

BLAUSTEIN, A. P. See DeGRAEFF, A. P. (joint pseud. with G. Conklin)

BLAVATSKY, HELEN P. (1831—1891) See THEOSOPHICAL SOCIETY, page 791.

BLEILER, EVERETT F. (1920—)
Frontiers in Space [with T. E. Dikty]

Author and Title	Publisher	Serial	Date	Pp.	Price	Type
	Bantam	1328	1955	166	25¢	A,R

Imagination Unlimited [with T. E. Dikty]

	Berkley	G233	1959	172	35¢	A,R
	Mayflower	3985	1964	190	3/6	A,R

Three Gothic Novels [*The Castle of Otranto*; *Vathek*; *The Vampyre*]

	Dover	T1232	1966	291	$2.00	A

BLISH, JAMES (1921—1975)

Author and Title	Publisher	Serial	Date	Pp.	Price	Type
A Case of Conscience	Ballantine	256	1958	188	35¢	
	Ballantine	U2251	1966	188	50¢	R
	Penguin	1809	1963	192	3/-	R

The Duplicated Man [with R. A. W. Lowndes]

	Airmont	SF8	1964	128	40¢	R
Earthman, Come Home	Avon	T225	1958	191	35¢	R
	Avon	S218	1966	254	60¢	R
	Avon	S218	1968	254	60¢	R
	Mayflower	2205	1963	222	3/6	R

ESP-er (originally *Jack of Eagles*)

	Avon	T268	1958	190	35¢	R

Fallen Star (originally *The Frozen Year*)

	FSB	340	1961	156	2/6	R

The Frozen Year (also titled *Fallen Star*)

	Ballantine	197	1957	155	35¢	

(identical hardcover edition $2.75)

Author and Title	Publisher	Serial	Date	Pp.	Price	Type
Galactic Cluster	Signet	S1719	1959	176	35¢	C
	Signet	D2790	1965	176	50¢	C,R
	FSB	889	1963	128	2/6	C,R
	FSB	2229	1968	128	3/6	C,R

The Issue at Hand [as W. Atheling Jr.]

	Advent		1967	136	$1.95	N,R

Jack of Eagles (also titled *ESP-er*)

	Galaxy Nov	19	1954	128	35¢	M
	Nova	NS4	1955	159	2/-	R
	Avon	S337	1968	176	60¢	R
A Life for the Stars	Avon	H107	1963	143	45¢	M,R
	Avon	G1280	1966	144	50¢	R
	Avon	G1280	1968	144	50¢	R

New Dreams This Morning

	Ballantine	U2331	1966	190	50¢	A
The Night Shapes	Ballantine	F647	1962	125	50¢	
	FSB	942	1963	125	2/6	R
	FSB	1305	1965	127	3/6	R
The Seedling Stars	Signet	S1622	1959	158	35¢	R
	Signet	D2549	1964	158	50¢	R
So Close to Home	Ballantine	465K	1961	142	35¢	C
	Ballantine	632	1962	142	35¢	C,R
The Star Dwellers	Avon	F122	1962	128	40¢	R
	Avon	G1268	1965	128	50¢	R
Star Trek	Bantam	F3459	1967	136	50¢	C

Author and Title	Publisher	Serial	Date	Pp.	Price	Type
Star Trek 2	Bantam	F3439	1968	122	50¢	C

They Shall Have Stars (first paperback version was *Year 2018!*)

	Avon	S210	1966	159	60¢	R
	Avon	V2216	1967	159	60¢	R
	NEL	2303	1968	159	5/-	R
Titans' Daughter	Berkley	G507	1961	142	35¢	
	Berkley	F1163	1966	142	50¢	R
	FSB	912	1963	142	2/6	R
	FSB	1307	1965	142	3/6	R

A Torrent of Faces [with Norman L. Knight]

	Ace	A-29	1968	286	75¢	R
The Triumph of Time	Avon	T279	1958	158	35¢	
	Avon	S221	1966	158	60¢	R
	Avon	S221	1968	158	60¢	R
VOR	Avon	T238	1958	159	35¢	
	Avon	S313	1967	158	60¢	R
	Corgi	S681	1959	156	2/6	R
The Warriors of Day	Galaxy Nov	16	1953	125	35¢	M
	Lancer	73-580	1967	159	60¢	R

Year 2018! (see also *They Shall Have Stars*)

	Avon	T193	1957	159	35¢	R
	FSB	954	1964	158	2/6	R
	FSB	1306	1965	159	3/6	R

BLIXEN, KAREN (1885—1962)
The Angelic Avengers [as Pierre Andrezel]

	Ace	K-167	1963	252	50¢	R

Last Tales [as Isak Dinesen]

	FSB	1797	1967	223	7/6	C,R

Seven Gothic Tales [as Isak Dinesen]

	Armed	687	nd	448	np	C,R
	Penguin	1952	1963	364	5/-	C,R

Winter's Tales [as Isak Dinesen]

	Armed	802	nd	384	np	C,R
	Dell	D191	1957	287	35¢	C,R

BLOCH, ROBERT (1917—)

Author and Title	Publisher	Serial	Date	Pp.	Price	Type
Atoms and Evil	Gold Medal	s1231	1962	160	35¢	C
	Muller	GM638	1963	160	2/6	C,R
Blood Runs Cold	Popular	K18	1963	206	40¢	C,R
	Corgi	SC7021	1964	127	3/6	C,R
Bogey Men	Pyramid	F839	1963	159	40¢	C
Chamber of Horrors	Award	A187X	1966	139	60¢	C
The Eighth Stage of Fandom						
	Advent		1962	176	$1.95	N,R
Firebug	Regency	RB101	1961	160	50¢	
	Lancer	73-615	1967	160	60¢	R
Horror-7	Belmont	90-275	1963	125	40¢	C
	Horwitz	PB160	1963	130	4/-	C,R
	FSB	1196	1964	125	2/6	C,R
	FSB	1196	1965	125	3/6	C,R

The House of the Hatchet (originally *Yours Truly, Jack the Ripper*)

	Tandem	T19	1965	190	3/6	C,R
The Living Demons	Belmont	B50-787	1967	156	50¢	C
More Nightmares	Belmont	L92-530	1962	173	50¢	C

Nightmares (reprinted from *Pleasant Dreams*)

	Belmont	233	1961	140	35¢	C,R

The Scarf (original title; see also *The Scarf of Passion*)

	Gold Medal	d1727	1967	160	50¢	R

The Scarf of Passion (originally titled *The Scarf*)

	Avon Monthly Novel					
		9	1948	125	35¢	R
	Avon	211	1949	154	25¢	R
	Avon	494	1952	154	25¢	R
Sea-Kissed	Utopian	AF nn	nd	39	1/-	C
The Shooting Star	Ace	D-265*	1958	159	35¢	

The Skull of the Marquis de Sade

	Pyramid	R1247	1965	157	50¢	C
Tales in a Jugular Vein	Pyramid	R1139	1965	144	50¢	C
Terror in the Night	Ace	D-265*	1958	129	35¢	

Author and Title	Publisher	Serial	Date	Pp.	Price	Type

This Crowded Earth & Ladies' Day
Belmont · B60-080 · 1968 · 172 · 60¢ · C,M
Yours Truly, Jack the Ripper (also titled *The House of the Hatchet*)
Belmont · L92-527 · 1962 · 189 · 50¢ · C

BLOW, ERNEST J.
Appointment in Space · Consul · · 1270 · 1963 · 221 · 2/6

BOARDMAN, TOM (1930—)
An ABC of Science Fiction FSB · 1652 · 1966 · 207 · 3/6 · A
. Avon · V2249 · 1968 · 223 · 75¢ · A,R
Connoisseur's Science Fiction
Penguin · 2223 · 1964 · 234 · 3/6 · A
Penguin · 2223 · 1965 · 234 · 3/6 · A,R
Penguin · 2223 · 1966 · 234 · 3/6 · A,R
The Unfriendly Future FSB · 1347 · 1965 · 173 · 3/6 · A

BOGGON, MARTYN
The Inevitable Hour · Tandem · T169 · 1968 · 188 · 3/6
Award · A3985 · 1968 · 188 · · R

BOHLE, E.
The Man Who Disappeared
Dell · 1013 · 1960 · 159 · 25¢

BOILEAU, PIERRE (1906—) [with T. Narcejac]
Choice Cuts · Bantam · S3578 · 1968 · 198 · 75¢ · R
Panther · 024700 · 1968 · 191 · 5/- · R
The Evil Eye · FSB · 349 · 1961 · 128 · 2/6 · R
The Living and the Dead · Arrow · 505 · 1958 · 190 · 2/- · R
Arrow · 505 · 1965 · 192 · 3/6 · R

BOLAND, JOHN (1913—)
No Refuge · Mayflower · 6458 · 1963 · 191 · 3/6 · R
White August · Brown-Wat. · · 1957 · 189 · 2/6 · R
Mayflower · 9514 · 1963 · 192 · 3/6 · R

BOND, J. HARVEY (pseud) See WINTERBOTHAM, R. R.

BOND, NELSON S. (1908—)
See also SUNDAY TELEGRAPH, page 791.
Exiles of Time · Paperback · 52-804 · 1965 · 159 · 50¢ · R
Mr. Mergenthwirker's Lobblies
French · · nd · 85 · $1.00 · R
No Time Like the Future Avon · T80 · 1954 · 221 · 35¢ · C
The 31st of February · Gnome · · 1949 · 272 · 35¢ · C
(identical hardcover edition $3.00)

BONE, J(ESSE) F. (1916—)
The Lani People · Bantam · J2363 · 1962 · 152 · 40¢
Corgi · SS1181 · 1963 · 152 · 2/6 · R

BONFIGLIOLI, KYRIL
SF Reprise 3 · Compact · H325 · 1966 · 384 · 5/- · A,M
(bound copies of *Science-Fantasy* Nos. 67-69, 1964-65)
SF Reprise 4 · Compact · H326 · 1967 · 256 · 5/- · A,M
(bound copies of *Science-Fantasy* Nos. 70-71, 1965)
SF Reprise 6 · Compact · H331 · 1967 · 251 · 5/- · A,M
(bound copies of *Science-Fantasy* Nos. 72-73, 1965)

BOOTHBY, GUY (1867—1905)
Dr. Nikola · Ward Lock · 33 · 1955 · 192 · 1/6 · R

BORGES, JORGE LUIS (1899—)
Ficciones · Grove · E368 · 1962 · 174 · $2.45 · C,R
Fictions · Jupiter · J7 · 1965 · 159 · 6/6 · C,R
Labyrinths · New Direc. NDP186 · 1964 · 260 · $1.90 · C,R

BORGIA, ANTHONY
Beyond This Life · Feature · · 1942 · 125 · np

BORN, FRANZ
Jules Verne: The Man Who Invented the Future
Scholastic · T838 · 1968 · 143 · 50¢ · N

BORODIN, GEORGE (pseud) See SAVA, G.

BOUCHER, ANTHONY (pseud. of W. A. P. White) (1911—1968)
The Best From Fantasy and Science Fiction, Third Series [with J. F.
McComas, co-anthologist] Ace · D-422 · 1960 · 256 · 35¢ · A,R
Ace · G-712 · 1968 · 256 · 50¢ · A,R
The Best From Fantasy and Science Fiction, Fourth Series
Ace · D-455 · 1960 · 255 · 35¢ · A,R
Ace · G-713 · 1968 · 255 · 50¢ · A,R
The Best From Fantasy and Science Fiction, Fifth Series
Ace · F-105 · 1961 · 254 · 40¢ · A,R
Ace · G-714 · 1968 · 254 · 50¢ · A,R
The Best From Fantasy and Science Fiction, Sixth Series
Ace · F-131 · 1962 · 254 · 40¢ · A,R
Ace · G-715 · 1968 · 254 · 50¢ · A,R
The Best From Fantasy and Science Fiction, Seventh Series
Ace · F-162 · 1962 · 252 · 40¢ · A,R
The Best From Fantasy and Science Fiction, Eighth Series
Ace · F-217 · 1963 · 224 · 40¢ · A,R
[Series later compiled by R. P. Mills, A. Davidson]
Far and Away · Ballantine · 109 · 1955 · 166 · 35¢ · C
(identical hardcover edition $2.00)
Rocket to the Morgue [as H. H. Holmes]
Dell · · 1943 · · 25¢ · R
Dell · 591 · 1952 · 223 · 25¢ · R
Pyramid · X1681 · 1967 · · 60¢ · R

BOULLE, PIERRE (1912—)
Garden on the Moon · Signet · P3031 · 1966 · 255 · 60¢ · R
Monkey Planet (originally *Planet of the Apes*)
Penguin · 2401 · 1966 · 174 · 3/6 · R
Planet of the Apes (also titled *Monkey Planet*)
Signet · D2547 · 1964 · 128 · 50¢ · R
Signet · P3399 · 1968 · 128 · 60¢ · R
Signet · T3423 · 1968 · 128 · 75¢ · R

BOUMPHREY, GEOFFREY See K. WALKER (co-author)

BOUNDS, SYDNEY J. (1920—)
Dimension of Horror · Panther · 70 · 1953 · 160 · 1/6
(identical hardcover edition 6/-)
The Moon Raiders · Digit · nn · 1958 · 158 · 2/- · R
The Robot Brains · Digit · nn · 1957 · 160 · 2/-
Digit · R521 · 1961 · 160 · 2/6 · R
Digit · R819 · 1964 · 158 · 2/6 · R
The World Wrecker · Digit · R885 · 1964 · 158 · 2/6 · R

BOURNE, FRANK
The Thought Stealer · Stellar · SFS7 · 1930 · 12 · 10¢
(part of booklet also containing *The Mechanical Man*, A. R. Long)

BOWEN, ELIZABETH (1899—)
Encounters · Ace (Brit.) · H457 · 1961 · 125 · 2/6 · C,R
Stories · Vintage · K79 · 1959 · 306 · $1.25 · C

BOWEN, JOHN (1925—)
After the Rain · Ballantine · 284K · 1959 · 158 · 35¢ · R
Ballantine · U2248 · 1965 · 158 · 50¢ · R
Penguin · 1634 · 1961 · 144 · 2/6 · R
Panther · 2241 · 1967 · 140 · 3/6 · R

BOWEN, ROBERT SIDNEY (1900—1977)
Black Invaders vs. the Battle Birds
Corinth · CR148 · 1966 · 159 · 60¢ · C,M

Author and Title	Publisher	Serial	Date	Pp.	Price	Type
Black Lightning	Corinth	CR133	1966	160	60¢	M
Crimson Doom	Corinth	CR137	1966	160	60¢	M
Purple Tornado	Corinth	CR141	1966	159	60¢	M
The Telsa Raiders	Corinth	CR145	1966	160	60¢	M

BOWERS, R. L. (pseud) See GLASBY, J. S.

BOWLES, PAUL (1910—)
The Delicate Prey and Other Stories

	Publisher	Serial	Date	Pp.	Price	Type
	Signet	1296	1956	192	25¢	C,R

BOYS OF YING WA COLLEGE See OPIUM BOOKS, page 790.

BRACK, VEKTIS

Author and Title	Publisher	Serial	Date	Pp.	Price	Type
Castaway From Space	Gannet	5	1953	128	1/6	C
(includes short story "The Terror of Marinda," 19 pp.)						
Odyssey in Space	Gannet	3	1954	127	1/6	
The X People	Gannet	8	1953	128	1/6	

BRACKETT, LEIGH (1915—1978)

Author and Title	Publisher	Serial	Date	Pp.	Price	Type
Alpha Centauri—or Die!	Ace	F-187*	1963	121	40¢	M
The Big Jump	Ace	D-103*	1955	131	35¢	M
	Ace	G-683	1967	128	50¢	R
The Coming of the Terrans	Ace	G-669	1967	157	50¢	M,C
The Galactic Breed (originally The Starmen)						
	Ace	D-99*	1955	168	35¢	R
The Long Tomorrow	Ace	F-135	1962	223	40¢	R
	Mayflower	B57	1962	223	3/6	R
The Nemesis From Terra (originally Shadow Over Mars)						
	Ace	F-123*	1961	120	40¢	R
People of the Talisman	Ace	M-101*	1964	128	45¢	M
The Secret of Sinharat	Ace	M-101*	1964	95	45¢	M
Shadow Over Mars (also titled The Nemesis From Terra)						
	WDL	WFC	1951	128	1/6	M
The Sword of Rhiannon	Ace	D-36*	1953	187	35¢	M
	Ace	F-422	1967	128	40¢	R

BRADBURY, EDWARD P. (pseud) See MOORCOCK, M.

BRADBURY, RAY (1920—)

Author and Title	Publisher	Serial	Date	Pp.	Price	Type
The Anthem Sprinters	Apollo	A75	1963	159	$1.95	C,R
The Autumn People	Ballantine	U2141	1965	122	50¢	C
(comic-book versions of some stories)						
The Circus of Dr. Lao and Other Improbable Stories						
	Bantam	A1519	1956	210	35¢	A
Dandelion Wine	Bantam	A1922	1959	184	35¢	C,R
	Bantam	FP55	1964	184	50¢	C,R
	Bantam	HP55	1967	184	60¢	C,R
	Bantam	HP4197	1968	184	60¢	C,R
	Corgi	GN7240	1965	184	3/6	C,R
The Day It Rained Forever (originally A Medicine for Melancholy)						
	Penguin	1878	1963	233	3/6	C,R
Fahrenheit 451	Ballantine	41	1953	199	35¢	C
(identical hardcover edition $2.50)						
	Ballantine	382K	1960	147	35¢	R
	Ballantine	F676	1962	147	50¢	R
	Ballantine	U2138	1963	147	50¢	R
	Ballantine	U2843	1967	147	50¢	R
	Ballantine	U5060	1967	147	60¢	R
	Ballantine	70002	1968	147	50¢	R
	Corgi	T389	1957	157	2/-	R
	Corgi	SS821	1960	159	2/6	R
	Corgi	YS1367	1963	126	3/-	R
	Corgi	GS7186	1965	158	3/6	R
	Corgi	GS7654	1967	158	3/6	R
The Golden Apples of the Sun						
	Bantam	A1241	1954	200	35¢	C,R
	Bantam	J2306	1961	169	40¢	C,R
	Bantam	H3357	1967	169	60¢	C,R
	Corgi	1241	1956	189	2/-	C,R

Author and Title	Publisher	Serial	Date	Pp.	Price	Type
	Corgi	SS820	1960	189	2/6	C,R
	Corgi	GS7130	1964	169	3/6	C,R
	Corgi	GS7130	1966	169	3/6	C,R
The Illustrated Man	Bantam	991	1952	246	25¢	C,R
	Bantam	1282	1954	186	25¢	C,R
	Bantam	F2588	1963	186	50¢	C,R
	Bantam	FP127	1965	186	50¢	C,R
	Bantam	H3484	1967	186	60¢	C,R
	Corgi	1282	1955	246	2/-	C,R
	Corgi	SS818	1960	246	2/6	C,R
	Corgi	YS1349	1963	186	3/-	C,R
	Corgi	GS7184	1965	186	3/6	C,R
The Machineries of Joy	Bantam	H2988	1965	213	60¢	C,R
	Corgi	GN7489	1966	213	3/6	C,R
The Martian Chronicles (also titled The Silver Locusts)						
	Bantam	886	1951	181	25¢	C,R
	Bantam	1261	1954	181	25¢	C,R
	Bantam	A1885	1959	181	35¢	C,R
	Bantam	F2438	1962	181	50¢	C,R
	Bantam	H3243	1967	181	60¢	C,R
	Time Inc.		1963	267		C,R
A Medicine for Melancholy (also titled The Day It Rained Forever)						
	Bantam	A2069	1960	183	35¢	C,R
	Bantam	F2637	1963	183	50¢	C,R
	Bantam	H3398	1967	183	60¢	C,R
The October Country	Ballantine	F139	1956	276	50¢	C
(identical hardcover edition $3.50)						
	Ballantine	F580	1962	276	50¢	C,R
	Ballantine	U2139	1965	276	50¢	C,R
	Ballantine	72138	1968	277	75¢	C,R
	Ace (Brit.)	H422	1961	142	2/6	C,R
	FSB	H422	1963	158	2/6	C,R
	FSB	1233	1965	158	3/6	C,R
R Is for Rocket	Bantam	F2915	1965	184	50¢	C,R
	Bantam	FP164	1967	184	50¢	C,R
	Bantam	FP4078	1968	184	50¢	C,R
The Silver Locusts (also titled The Martian Chronicles)						
	Corgi	886	1956	256	2/-	C,R
	Corgi	SS819	1960	221	2/6	C,R
	Corgi	YS1350	1963	181	3/-	C,R
	Corgi	GS7185	1965	181	3/6	C,R
The Small Assassin	Ace (Brit.)	H521	1962	144	2/6	C
	FSB	1234	1965	144	3/6	C,R
Something Wicked This Way Comes						
	Bantam	H2630	1963	215	60¢	R
	Bantam	S3408	1967	215	75¢	R
	Corgi	GN7114	1965	215	3/6	R
Timeless Stories for Today and Tomorrow						
	Bantam	A944	1952	306	35¢	A
	Bantam	A2343	1961	258	60¢	A,R
	Bantam	H3358	1967	258	60¢	A,R
Tomorrow Midnight	Ballantine	U2142	1966	188	50¢	C
(comic-book versions of some stories)						
The Vintage Bradbury	Vintage	V294	1965	329	$1.45	C

BRADDON, RUSSELL (1921—)
The Year of the Angry Rabbit

	Publisher	Serial	Date	Pp.	Price	Type
	Pan	X625	1967	159	3/6	R

BRADFORD, M.
Invasion From Space

	Publisher	Serial	Date	Pp.	Price	Type
	Atlantic		1954	128	1/6	

BRADFORD, ROARK (1896—1948)
Ol' Man Adam an' His Chillun

	Publisher	Serial	Date	Pp.	Price	Type
	Armed	i-244	nd		np	C,R
	Military	M638	1944	187	25¢	C,R

BRADLEY, JACK
The Torch of Ra

	Publisher	Serial	Date	Pp.	Price	Type
	Stellar	SFS8	1930	24	10¢	

Author and Title	Publisher	Serial	Date	Pp.	Price	Type
BRADLEY, MARION ZIMMER (1930—)						
The Bloody Sun	Ace	F-303	1964	191	40¢	
The Colors of Space	Monarch	368	1963	124	35¢	
The Dark Intruder and Other Stories						
	Ace	F-273*	1964	124	40¢	C
The Door Through Space	Ace	F-117*	1961	132	40¢	M
Falcons of Narabedla	Ace	F-273*	1964	127	40¢	
The Planet Savers	Ace	F-153*	1962	91	40¢	M
Seven From the Stars	Ace	F-127*	1962	120	40¢	M
Star of Danger	Ace	F-350	1965	160	40¢	
The Sword of Aldones	Ace	F-153*	1962	164	40¢	
BRAMAH, ERNEST (pseud) See SMITH, ERNEST BRAMAH						
BRAUTIGAN, RICHARD (1935—)						
In Watermelon Sugar	Dell		1968	138		R
BREDE, ARNOLD						
Sister Earth	Scion		1951	112	1/6	
BREDESON, LENORE						
More From One Step Beyond						
	Citadel		1961	123	$1.00	C
	Digit	R552	1961	156	2/6	C,R
	Digit	R676	1963	158	2/6	C,R
One Step Beyond	Citadel		1960	122	$1.00	C
	Digit	R468	1961	156	2/6	C,R
	Digit	R468	1962	156	2/6	C,R
BREDON, J. See BOY'S FRIEND LIBRARY, page 789.						
BRENNAN, FREDERICK HAZLITT						
One of Our H-Bombs Is Missing						
	Gold Medal	498	1955	159	25¢	
BRENNAN, JOSEPH P. (1918—)						
Nine Horrors and a Dream	Ballantine	587	1962	121	35¢	C,R
BRENT, LYNTON WRIGHT						
The Sex Demon of Vangal	Brentwood	FB1007	1964			
BRENT, PETER See PETERS, L. (pseud)						
BRETNOR, REGINALD (1911—)						
Through Time and Space With Ferdinand Feghoot [as Grendel Briarton]						
	Paradox		1962	74	$1.25	C,M
BRETT, LEO (pseud) See FANTHORPE, R. L.						
BREUER, MILES J. (1889—1947)						
The Girl From Mars [with J. Williamson]						
	Stellar	SFS1	1929	24	10¢	
BREWSTER, DENNIS						
I Dream of Jeannie	Pocket Bks	10130	1966	124	60¢	
BRIARTON, GRENDEL (pseud) See BRETNOR, R.						
BRIDGMAN, BILL						
The Lonely Sky	Panther	755	1958	208	2/6	
BRINEY, ROBERT E. (1933—)						
Shanadu	SSSR Pubs		1953	101	$1.50	A
BRINK, CAROL RYRIE						
Andy Buckram's Tin Men	Tempo	4851	1967	157	50¢	J
	Tempo	T151	1967	157	50¢	J
BRINTON, HENRY (1901—)						
Purple-6	Arrow	701	1963	191	2/6	R
	Avon	S135	1963	192	60¢	R
BRITTON, L.						
Brain (A Play of the Whole Earth)						
	G. Putnam's		1930	129	3/6	R
BRODERICK, DAMIEN						
A Man Returned	Horwitz	PB216	1965	130	4/6	C
BROMFIELD, LOUIS (1896—1956)						
The Strange Case of Miss Annie Spragg						
	Penguin	19	1935	255	6d	R
	Penguin	19	1959	240	2/6	R
	Berkley	G36	1956	219	35¢	R
BRONDFIELD, JEROME						
Night in Funland	Scholastic	TK1056	1968	238	75¢	A
BROOKS, WALTER ROLLIN (1886—1958)						
The Original Mr. Ed	Bantam	J2530	1963	118	40¢	
BROPHY, BRIGID (1929—)						
Hackenfeller's Ape	Penguin	2560	1968	121	3/6	R
BROWN, CHARLES BROCKDEN (1771—1810)						
Arthur Mervyn	Holt	N112	1962	430	$1.75	R
Ormond	Hafner	24	1963	242	$2.75	R
Wieland, or the Transformation						
	Dolphin	C320	1962	276	95¢	R
	Hafner	17	1958	351	$1.95	R
BROWN, DOUGLAS [with S. Serpell]						
If Hitler Comes	Guild	13	1941	142	6d	
BROWN, FREDRIC (1906—1972)						
Angels and Spaceships (also titled Star Shine)						
	FSB	709	1962	160	2/6	C,R
Daymares	Lancer	73-727	1968	317	60¢	C
Honeymoon in Hell	Bantam	A1812	1958	170	35¢	C
	Bantam	J2650	1963	150	40¢	C,R
The Lights in the Sky Are Stars (also titled Project Jupiter)						
	Bantam	1285	1955	149	25¢	R
	Bantam	J2578	1963	149	40¢	R
Martians, Go Home	Bantam	A1546	1956	159	35¢	R
The Mind Thing	Bantam	A2187	1961	149	35¢	
Nightmares and Geezenstacks						
	Bantam	J2296	1961	137	40¢	C
	Corgi	SS1167	1962	137	2/6	C,R
Project Jupiter (originally The Lights in the Sky Are Stars)						
	Digit	D173	1958	156	2/-	R
	Digit	R828	1964	160	2/6	R
Rogue in Space	Bantam	A1701	1957	163	35¢	R
Science Fiction Carnival [with M. Reynolds]						
	Bantam	A1615	1957	167	35¢	A,R
Space on My Hands	Bantam	1077	1953	239	25¢	C,R
	Corgi	1077	1953	239	2/-	C,R
Star Shine (originally Angels and Spaceships)						
	Bantam	1423	1956	138	25¢	C,R
What Mad Universe	Bantam	835	1950	199	25¢	R
	Bantam	1253	1954	184	25¢	R
	Boardman	154	1954	192	2/-	R
BROWN, PETER C.						
Smallcreeps Day	Panther	023879	1968	285	5/-	
BROWN, ROSEL GEORGE (1926—1967)						
Earthblood [with K. Laumer]						
	Berkley	S1544	1968	287	75¢	R
Galactic Sibyl Sue Blue (originally Sybil Sue Blue)						
	Berkley	X1503	1968	158	60¢	R
A Handful of Time	Ballantine	F703	1963	160	50¢	C

Author and Title	Publisher	Serial	Date	Pp.	Price	Type
BROWNE, GEORGE SHELDON						
Destination Mars	Edw. Self		1952	128	1/6	
The Planetoid Peril	Edw. Self		1952	128	1/6	
The Yellow Planet	Edw. Self		1954	100	1/-	
BRULLER, JEAN (1902—) [as Vercors]						
The Murder of the Missing Link (originally *You Shall Know Them*)						
	Pocket Bks	1206	1958	196	25¢	R
Sylva	Crest	d586	1963	175	50¢	R
You Shall Know Them (also titled *The Murder of the Missing Link*)						
	Pocket Bks	1038	1955	196	25¢	R
	Popular	60-2202	1967	191	60¢	R
BRUNNER, JOHN (1934—)						
The Altar on Asconel	Ace	M-123*	1965	143	45¢	M
The Astronauts Must Not Land						
	Ace	F-227*	1963	138	40¢	
The Atlantic Abomination	Ace	D-465*	1960	128	35¢	
Bedlam Planet	Ace	G-709	1968	159	50¢	
Born Under Mars	Ace	G-664	1967	127	50¢	M
Castaways' World	Ace	F-242*	1963	127	40¢	
Catch a Falling Star	Ace	G-761	1968	158	50¢	
The Day of the Star Cities	Ace	F-361	1965	158	40¢	
The Dreaming Earth	Pyramid	F829	1963	159	40¢	M
Echo in the Skull	Ace	D-385*	1959	94	35¢	M
Endless Shadow	Ace	F-299*	1964	97	40¢	M
Enigma From Tantalus	Ace	M-115*	1965	102	45¢	M
Father of Lies	Belmont	B60-081*	1968	85	60¢	
Galactic Storm [as Gill Hunt]						
	Curtis War.		1951	110	1/6	
I Speak for Earth [as Keith Woodcott]						
	Ace	D-497*	1961	120	35¢	
Into the Slave Nebula (revised from *Slavers of Space*)						
	Lancer	73-797	1968	176	60¢	
The Ladder in the Sky [as Keith Woodcott]						
	Ace	F-141*	1962	137	40¢	
Listen! The Stars!	Ace	F-215*	1963	96	40¢	M
The Long Result	Ballantine	U2329	1966	190	50¢	R
	Penguin	2804	1968	186	4/-	R
The Martian Sphinx [as Keith Woodcott]						
	Ace	F-320	1965	149	40¢	
Meeting at Infinity	Ace	D-507*	1961	155	35¢	
No Future in It	Panther	1840	1965	192	3/6	C,R
No Other Gods But Me	Compact	F317	1966	159	3/6	C,M
Not Before Time	FSB	2138	1968	128	3/6	C
Now Then!	Mayflower	6500	1965	143	3/6	C
	Avon	S323	1968	160	60¢	C,R
The 100th Millennium	Ace	D-362*	1959	110	35¢	M
Out of My Mind	Ballantine	U5064	1967	220	60¢	C
	FSB	2102	1968	128	3/6	C
(contents of two editions substantially different)						
A Planet of Your Own	Ace	G-592*	1966	99	50¢	M
The Productions of Time	Signet	P3113	1967	139	60¢	M
The Psionic Menace [as Keith Woodcott]						
	Ace	F-199*	1963	108	40¢	M
The Repairmen of Cyclops	Ace	M-115*	1965	150	45¢	M
The Rites of Ohe	Ace	F-242*	1963	129	40¢	
Sanctuary in the Sky	Ace	D-471*	1960	122	35¢	
Secret Agent of Terra	Ace	F-133*	1962	127	40¢	
The Skynappers	Ace	D-457*	1960	117	35¢	
Slavers of Space (revised as *Into the Slave Nebula*)						
	Ace	D-421*	1960	118	35¢	
The Space-Time Juggler	Ace	F-227*	1963	84	40¢	M
The Squares of the City	Ballantine	U6035	1965	319	75¢	
The Super Barbarians	Ace	D-547	1962	160	35¢	
Telepathist (originally *The Whole Man*)						
	Penguin	2715	1968	190	4/-	R
Threshold of Eternity	Ace	D-335*	1959	148	35¢	M
Times Without Number	Ace	F-161*	1962	139	40¢	C,M
To Conquer Chaos	Ace	F-277	1964	192	40¢	M

Author and Title	Publisher	Serial	Date	Pp.	Price	Type
The Whole Man (also titled *Telepathist*)						
	Ballantine	U2219	1964	188	50¢	R
The World Swappers	Ace	D-391*	1959	153	35¢	
	Ace	G-649	1967	153	50¢	R
BRYAN, L. S.						
Mystery Ship	Armed	D-103	nd	318	np	
BRYANT, PETER (pseud) See GEORGE, P.						
BUCHAN, JOHN (1875—1940)						
The Watcher by the Threshold						
	Digit	R613	1962	157	2/6	R
BUCK, PEARL S. (1892—1973)						
Command the Morning	Pan	G561	1963	238	2/6	R
	Pan	G561	1964	238	2/6	R
	Pan	M224	1967	238	5/-	R
BUCKNER, ROBERT (1906—)						
Moon Pilot (also titled *Starfire*)						
	Permabks	M4241	1962	138	35¢	R
Starfire (also titled *Moon Pilot*)						
	Permabks	M4185	1960	139	35¢	M
BUDRYS, ALGIS (1931—)						
The Amsirs and the Iron Thorn						
	Gold Medal	d1852	1967	159	50¢	M
Budrys' Inferno (also titled *The Furious Future*)						
	Berkley	F799	1963	160	50¢	C
The Falling Torch	Pyramid	G416	1959	158	35¢	
	Pyramid	F693	1962	158	40¢	R
	Pyramid	F1028	1965	158	40¢	R
	Pyramid	R1028	1965	158	50¢	R
	Pyramid	X1837	1968	158	60¢	R
False Night (later version, *Some Will Not Die*)						
	Lion	230	1954	127	25¢	
The Furious Future (originally *Budrys' Inferno*)						
	Panther	2019	1966	174	3/6	C,R
Man of Earth	Ballantine	243	1958	144	35¢	M
Rogue Moon	Gold Medal	s1057	1960	176	35¢	M
	Gold Medal	L1474	1964	176	45¢	R
	Muller	GM540	1962	173	2/6	R
	Hodder	04455	1968	159	3/6	R
Some Will Not Die (derived from *False Night*)						
	Regency	RB110	1961	159	50¢	
	Mayflower	8103	1964	159	3/6	R
The Unexpected Dimension						
	Ballantine	388K	1960	159	35¢	C
	Panther	1649	1964	125	2/6	C,R
	Panther	1649	1966	125	3/6	C,R
Who?	Pyramid	G339	1958	157	35¢	
	Badger	SF28	1960	142	2/-	R
	Penguin	2217	1964	159	3/6	R
	Lancer	73-810	1968	191	60¢	R
BULGAKOV, MIKHAIL (1891—1940)						
The Heart of a Dog	Harvest	HB 142	1968	146	$1.45	R
The Master and Margarita	Signet	Q3397	1967	384	95¢	R
BULL, RANDOLPH C.						
Great Tales of Terror (originally *Great Tales of Mystery*)						
	Panther	1489	1963	224	3/6	A,R
Perturbed Spirits	Barker	D20	1958	191	2/6	A,R
BULMER, (HENRY) KEN(NETH) (1921—)						
Behold the Stars	Ace	M-131*	1965	120	45¢	
	Mayflower	0529	1966	126	3/6	R
Beyond the Silver Sky	Ace	D-507*	1961	100	35¢	M
Challenge	Curtis War.		1954	160	1/6	

Author and Title	Publisher	Serial	Date	Pp.	Price	Type
The Changeling Worlds	Ace	D-369*	1959	145	35¢	
	Digit	D466	1961	156	2/6	R
	Digit	R758	1963	159	2/6	R
City Under the Sea	Ace	D-255*	1957	175	35¢	M
	Digit	R505	1961	158	2/6	R
	Digit	R672	1963	158	2/6	R
Cybernetic Controller [with A. V. Clarke]						
	Panther	nn	1952	112	1/6	
Cycle of Nemesis	Ace	G-680	1967	190	50¢	
Defiance	Digit	R666	1963	160	2/6	
The Demons (originally *Demons' World*)						
	Compact	F277	1965	190	3/6	R
Demons' World (also titled *The Demons*)						
	Ace	F-289*	1964	139	40¢	
The Earth Gods Are Coming (also titled *Of Earth Foretold*)						
	Ace	D-453*	1960	107	35¢	M
Earth's Long Shadow (also titled *No Man's World*)						
	Digit	R572	1962	159	2/6	M,R
Empire of Chaos	Panther	69	1953	158	1/6	
(identical hardcover edition 6/-)						
Encounter in Space	Panther	29	1952	126	1/6	
The Fatal Fire	Digit	D597	1962	160	2/6	M
Galactic Intrigue	Panther	60	1953	159	1/6	
(identical hardcover edition 6/)						
Home Is the Martian [as Philip Kent]						
	Pearson	T-B	1954	64	9d	
The Key to Irunium	Ace	H-20*	1967	138	60¢	
The Key to Venudine	Ace	H-65*	1968	122	60¢	
Land Beyond the Map	Ace	M-111*	1965	136	45¢	M
The Million Year Hunt	Ace	F-285*	1964	133	40¢	
Mission to the Stars [as Philip Kent]						
	Pearson	T-B	1954	64	9d	
No Man's World (also titled *Earth's Long Shadow*)						
	Ace	F-104*	1961	128	40¢	M
Of Earth Foretold (also titled *The Earth Gods Are Coming*)						
	Digit	R539	1961	160	2/6	
	Digit	R681	1963	159	2/6	R
Peril From Space [as Karl Maras]						
	Comyns		1955	128	1/6	
The Secret of ZI	Ace	D-331*	1958	161	35¢	
	Digit	R515	1961	156	2/6	R
Slaves of the Spectrum [as Philip Kent]						
	Pearson	T-B	1954	64	9d	
Space Salvage	Panther	37	1953	143	1/6	
Space Treason [with A. V. Clarke]						
	Panther	nn	1952	112	1/6	
The Stars Are Ours	Panther	48	1953	158	1/6	
(identical hardcover edition 6/-)						
	Atlas	SFL6	1956	114	2/-	R
To Outrun Doomsday	Ace	G-625	1967	159	50¢	
Vassals of Venus [as Philip Kent]						
	Pearson	T-B	1955	64	9d	
The Wind of Liberty	Digit	R607	1962	159	2/6	C,M
The Wizard of Starship Poseidon						
	Ace	F-209*	1963	124	40¢	
World Aflame	Panther	159	1954	144	1/6	
(identical hardcover edition 6/-)						
Worlds for the Taking	Ace	F-396	1966	159	40¢	
Zhorani [as Karl Maras]	Comyns		1953	128	1/6	

BULWER-LYTTON, EDWARD See HALDEMAN-JULIUS CO., page 790.

BUNYAN, JOHN

Author and Title	Publisher	Serial	Date	Pp.	Price	Type
The Pilgrim's Progress	Washington	W253	1964	308	45¢	R

BURDICK, EUGENE (1918—1965)
Fail-Safe [with J. H. Wheeler]

Author and Title	Publisher	Serial	Date	Pp.	Price	Type
	Dell	2459	1963	285	75¢	R
	Pan	X388	1965	205	3/6	R

BURGER, DIONYS

Author and Title	Publisher	Serial	Date	Pp.	Price	Type
Sphereland: A Fantasy	Crowell	Apollo A184	1968	208	$1.95	R

BURGESS, ANTHONY See WILSON, J. B.

BURKE, JOHN F. (1922—) [His early works to and including 1965 were bylined Jonathan Burke]

Author and Title	Publisher	Serial	Date	Pp.	Price	Type
The Dark Gateway	Panther	94	1954	223	2/-	
(identical hardcover edition 8/6)						
Deep Freeze	Panther	182	1955	143	1/6	
(identical hardcover edition 6/-)						
Dr. Terror's House of Horrors						
	Pan	G692	1965	159	2/6	
The Echoing Worlds	Panther	103	1954	159	1/6	
(identical hardcover edition 6/-)						
	Atlas	SFL1	1955	114	2/-	R
Exodus From Elysium	Horwitz	PB238	1965	159	4/9	C
The Hammer Horror Omnibus						
	Pan	X520	1966	331	5/-	A
Hotel Cosmos	Panther	135	1954	142	1/6	
(identical hardcover edition 6/-)						
Pattern of Shadows	Horwitz	PB233	1965	128	4/-	R
Privilege	Avon	S304	1967	160	60¢	R
Pursuit Through Time	Digit	R612	1962	159	2/6	R
Revolt of the Humans	Panther	192	1955	141	1/6	
(identical hardcover edition 6/-)						
The Second Hammer Horror Film Omnibus						
	Pan	M223	1967	349	5/-	A
Tales of Unease	Pan	X482	1966	271	3/6	A
Twilight of Reason	Panther	118	1954	159	1/6	
(identical hardcover edition 6/-)						

BURKE, THOMAS (1886—1945)

Author and Title	Publisher	Serial	Date	Pp.	Price	Type
Limehouse Nights	Digit	R486	1961	156	2/6	C,R

BURKETT, WILLIAM R. (1943—)

Author and Title	Publisher	Serial	Date	Pp.	Price	Type
Sleeping Planet	Paperback	54-445	1967	285	75¢	R
	Panther	023704	1968	285	5/-	R

BURKS, ARTHUR J. (1898—)

Author and Title	Publisher	Serial	Date	Pp.	Price	Type
The Great Mirror	Swan		1952	128	1/-	M
Look Behind You	Shroud		1954	73	$1.00	C

BURNETT, WHIT (1899—) [with Hallie Burnett]

Author and Title	Publisher	Serial	Date	Pp.	Price	Type
19 Tales of Terror	Bantam	A1550	1957	229	35¢	A
Things With Claws	Ballantine	466K	1961	159	35¢	A
	Ballantine	U2816	1965	159	50¢	A,R

BURROUGHS, EDGAR RICE (1875—1950)

Author and Title	Publisher	Serial	Date	Pp.	Price	Type
At the Earth's Core (see also *Three Science Fiction Novels*)						
	Ace	F-156	1962	142	40¢	R
	Ace	G-733	1968	142	50¢	R
Back to the Stone Age	Ace	F-245	1963	221	40¢	R
	Ace	G-737	1968	221	50¢	R
The Beasts of Tarzan	Goulden	18 (2 ed)	1951	136	2/-	R
	FSB	240	1960	157	2/6	R
	FSB	240	1964	157	2/6	R
	Ballantine	F747	1963	159	50¢	R
	Ballantine	U2003	1963	159	50¢	R
	Ace	F-203	1963	191	40¢	R
(abridged)	Dragon	D44	1967	140	2/6	R
Beyond the Farthest Star	Ace	F-282	1964	125	40¢	M
(included in *Tales of Three Planets*)						
Carson of Venus	Goulden	9	1950	136	1/6	R
	Goulden	9	1952	136	2/-	R
	Ace	F-247	1963	192	40¢	R
	FSB	1726	1967	155	3/6	R
The Cave Girl	Dell	320	1949	240	25¢	R
	Pinnacle	35	1954	153	2/-	R
	Ace	F-258	1964	224	40¢	R

Author and Title	Publisher	Serial	Date	Pp.	Price	Type
The Chessmen of Mars	Pinnacle	36	1954	151	2/-	R
	Ace	F-170	1962	256	40¢	R
	FSB	661	1962	205	2/6	R
	FSB	661	1964	205	2/6	R
	FSB	1403	1965	205	3/6	R
	Ballantine	F776	1963	220	50¢	R
(see also *Three Martian Novels*)						
Escape on Venus	Ace	F-268	1964	254	40¢	R
	FSB	1660	1966	222	3/6	R
The Eternal Lover (also titled *The Eternal Savage*)						
	Pinnacle	28	1953	152	2/-	R
The Eternal Savage (originally *The Eternal Lover*)						
	Ace	F-234	1963	192	40¢	R
A Fighting Man of Mars	Pinnacle	33	1954	154	2/-	R
	Pinnacle	33	1955	154	2/-	R
	Ace	F-190	1963	253	40¢	R
	Ballantine	U2037	1963	192	50¢	R
	FSB	1638	1966	192	3/6	R
A Fighting Man of Mars & A Princess of Mars						
	Dover	T-1140	1964	356	$1.75	C
The Gods of Mars	Pinnacle	30	1953	160	2/-	R
	FSB	353	1961	192	2/6	R
	FSB	353	1962	192	2/6	R
	FSB	1199	1964	192	3/6	R
	FSB	1199	1965	192	3/6	R
	Ballantine	F702	1963	190	50¢	R
	Ballantine	U2032	1963	190	50¢	R
(abridged)	Dragon	D77	1968	158	2/6	R
John Carter of Mars	Ballantine	U2041	1965	157	50¢	C,R
	FSB	1758	1968	126	3/6	C,R
Jungle Tales of Tarzan (also titled *Tarzan's Jungle Tales*)						
	Pinnacle	32	1954	190	2/-	R
	Ace	F-206	1963	220	40¢	R
	Ballantine	F750	1963	191	50¢	R
	Ballantine	U2006	1963	191	50¢	R
The Lad and the Lion	Ballantine	U2048	1964	192	50¢	R
The Land of Hidden Men (originally *Jungle Girl*)						
	Ace	F-232	1963	191	40¢	R
Land of Terror	Ace	F-256	1963	175	40¢	R
	Ace	G-738	1968	175	50¢	R
The Land That Time Forgot						
	Ace	F-213	1963	126	40¢	R
The Land That Time Forgot & The Moon Maid						
	Dover	T-358	1963	552	$2.00	C,R
Llana of Gathol	Ballantine	F762	1963	191	50¢	R
	Ballantine	U2040	1965	191	50¢	R
	FSB	1746	1967	191	3/6	R
The Lost Continent (originally *Beyond Thirty*)						
	Ace	F-235	1963	123	40¢	R
Lost on Venus	Pinnacle	23	1953	136	2/-	R
	Ace	F-221	1963	192	40¢	R
	FSB	1215	1965	190	3/6	R
Lost on Venus & Pirates of Venus						
	Dover	T-1053	1963	350	$1.75	C,R
The Mad King	Ace	F-270	1964	255	40¢	R
The Master Mind of Mars	Pinnacle	38	1955	158	1/6	R
	FSB	751	1962	144	2/6	R
	FSB	1216	1964	144	3/6	R
	FSB	1216	1965	144	3/6	R
	Ace	F-181	1963	159	40¢	R
	Ballantine	U2036	1963	160	50¢	R
(see also *Three Martian Novels*)						
The Monster Men	Ace	F-182	1963	159	40¢	R
The Moon Maid	Ace	F-157	1962	176	40¢	R
	Ace	G-745	1968	176	50¢	R
The Moon Maid & The Land That Time Forgot						
	Dover	T-358	1963	552	$2.00	C,R
The Moon Men	Ace	F-159	1962	222	40¢	R
	Ace	G-748	1968	222	50¢	R
The Mucker	Ballantine	U6039	1966	320	75¢	R
Out of Time's Abyss (part of full version of *The Land That Time Forgot*)						
	Ace	F-233	1963	125	40¢	R
Pellucidar	Pinnacle	39	1955	159	2/-	R
	Ace	F-158	1962	160	40¢	R
	Ace	G-734	1968	160	50¢	R
(see also *Three Science Fiction Novels*)						
The People That Time Forgot (part of full version of *The Land That Time Forgot*)						
	Ace	F-220	1963	124	40¢	R
Pirates of Venus	Pinnacle	34	1954	153	2/-	R
	Ace	F-179	1962	173	40¢	R
	FSB	820	1963	159	2/6	R
	FSB	1217	1964	159	3/6	R
	FSB	1217	1965	159	3/6	R
Pirates of Venus & Lost on Venus						
	Dover	T-1053	1963	340	$1.75	C,R
A Princess of Mars	Goulden	nn (2 ed)	1948	127	1/6	R
	FSB	306	1961	160	2/6	R
	FSB	306	1962	160	2/6	R
	FSB	1401	1965	160	3/6	R
	Ballantine	F701	1963	159	50¢	R
	Ballantine	U2031	1963	159	50¢	R
(abridged)	Dragon	D76	1968	156	2/6	R
A Princess of Mars & A Fighting Man of Mars						
	Dover	T-1140	1964	356	$1.75	C,R
The Return of Tarzan	Armed	o-22	nd		np	R
	Goulden	19 (2 ed)	1951	136	2/-	R
	FSB	93 (2 ed)	1959	253	2/6	R
	FSB	93	1960	253	2/6	R
	FSB	93	1961	253	2/6	R
	FSB	93	1964	253	2/6	R
	Ballantine	F746	1963	221	50¢	R
	Ballantine	U2002	1963	221	50¢	R
	Ballantine	U2002	1967	221	50¢	R
(abridged)	Dragon	D43	1967	156	2/6	R
Savage Pellucidar	Ace	F-280	1964	221	40¢	R
	Ace	G-739	1968	221	50¢	R
The Son of Tarzan	Ransom		1929	128	6d	R
	Pinnacle	21	1953	136	2/-	R
	FSB	183	1959	224	2/6	R
	FSB	183	1962	224	2/6	R
	FSB	1062	1964	224	3/6	R
	Ace	F-193	1963	255	40¢	R
	Ballantine	F748	1963	222	50¢	R
	Ballantine	U2004	1963	222	50¢	R
(abridged)	Dragon	D45	1967	157	2/6	R
Swords of Mars	Ballantine	F728	1963	191	50¢	R
	Ballantine	U2038	1965	191	50¢	R
	FSB	1676	1966	191	3/6	R
Synthetic Men of Mars	Ballantine	F739	1963	160	50¢	R
	Ballantine	U2039	1965	160	50¢	R
	FSB	1153	1964	160	3/6	R
Tanar of Pellucidar	Pinnacle	29	1953	154	2/-	R
	Ace	F-171	1962	224	40¢	R
	Ace	G-735	1968	224	50¢	R
(see also *Three Science Fiction Novels*)						
Tarzan and the Ant Men	Pinnacle	24	1953	136	2/-	R
	FSB	186	1959	192	2/6	R
	FSB	1059	1964	192	3/6	R
	FSB	1059	1967	192	3/6	R
	Ballantine	F754	1963	188	50¢	R
	Ballantine	U2010	1963	188	50¢	R
(abridged)	Dragon	D64	1967	140	2/6	R
Tarzan and the Castaways	Ballantine	U2024	1965	191	50¢	C,R
	FSB	1552	1966	191	3/6	C,R
	FSB	1552	1967	191	3/6	C,R

Author and Title	Publisher	Serial	Date	Pp.	Price	Type
Tarzan and the City of Gold						
	Goulden	11	1950	136	1/6	R
	Goulden	11	1951	136	1/6	R
	Goulden	11	1952	136	2/-	R
	FSB	358	1961	160	2/6	R
	FSB	1060	1964	160	3/6	R
	FSB	1060	1967	160	3/6	R
	Ace	F-205	1963	191	40¢	R
	Ballantine	U2016	1964	190	40¢	R
Tarzan and the Forbidden City (also abridged as *Tarzan in the Forbidden City*)						
	Goulden	8	1950	136	1/6	R
	Goulden	8	1952	126	2/-	R
	Ballantine	U2020	1964	191	50¢	R
	FSB	1181	1965	191	3/6	R
	FSB	1181	1968	191	3/6	R
Tarzan and the "Foreign Legion"						
	Goulden	13	1950	128	1/6	R
	Goulden	13	1952	124	2/-	R
	Pinnacle	nn	1958	192	2/6	R
	FSB	996	1964	175	3/6	R
	Ballantine	U2022	1964	192	50¢	R
Tarzan and the Golden Lion						
	Pinnacle	20	1953	136	2/-	R
	FSB	261	1960	221	2/6	R
	FSB	261	1961	221	2/6	R
	FSB	1095	1964	222	3/6	R
	Ballantine	F753	1963	191	50¢	R
	Ballantine	U2009	1963	191	50¢	R
Tarzan and the Jewels of Opar						
	Goulden	17 (2 ed)	1951	136	1/6	R
	FSB	184	1959	160	2/6	R
	FSB	184	1960	160	2/6	R
	FSB	184	1962	160	2/6	R
	FSB	1111	1964	160	3/6	R
	FSB	1111	1968	160	3/6	R
	Ace	F-204	1963	192	40¢	R
	Ballantine	F749	1963	158	50¢	R
	Ballantine	U2005	1963	158	50¢	R
	House of Greystoke		1964	124	np	R
(Part 1)	Dragon	D62	1967	123	2/6	R
(Part 2)	Dragon	D63	1967	123	2/6	R
Tarzan and the Leopard Men						
	Goulden	10	1950	136	1/6	R
	Goulden	10	1952	128	2/-	R
	FSB	380	1961	160	2/6	R
	FSB	1132	1964	160	3/6	R
	FSB	1132	1967	160	3/6	R
	Ballantine	U2018	1964	192	50¢	R
Tarzan and the Lion Man	Goulden	7	1950	136	1/6	R
	Ace	F-212	1963	223	40¢	R
	Ballantine	U2017	1964	192	50¢	R
	FSB	1253	1965	191	3/6	R
Tarzan and the Lost Empire						
	Goulden	nn	1949	128	1/6	R
	Goulden	1	1950	128	1/6	R
	Goulden	1	1951	128	2/-	R
	Goulden	1	1952	128	2/-	R
	Pinnacle	nn	1958	192	2/6	R
	Dell	536	1951	192	25¢	R
	Ace	F-169	1962	192	40¢	R
	Ballantine	F777	1963	159	50¢	R
	Ballantine	U2012	1963	159	50¢	R
	FSB	971	1964	175	2/6	R
	FSB	1405	1965	175	3/6	R
Tarzan and the Madman	Ballantine	U2023	1965	160	50¢	R
	FSB	1422	1966	156	3/6	R
	FSB	1422	1968	156	3/6	R
Tarzan at the Earth's Core	Wren	22	1941	141	6d	R
	Goulden	nn	1949	128	1/6	R
	Goulden	4	1951	128	1/6	R
	Goulden	4	1952	128	1/6	R
	FSB	168	1959	188	2/6	R
	FSB	168	1962	188	2/6	R
	FSB	1061	1964	188	3/6	R
	FSB	1061	1967	188	3/6	R
	Ace	F-180	1963	223	40¢	R
	Ace	G-736	1968	223	50¢	R
	Ballantine	U2013	1964	191	50¢	R
Tarzan in the Forbidden City (abridgement of *Tarzan and the Forbidden City*)						
	Bant.		1940	100	10¢	R
Tarzan, Lord of the Jungle	Goulden	nn (2 ed)	1949	136	1/6	R
	Pinnacle	2	1953	128	2/-	R
	Pinnacle	nn	1958	192	2/6	R
	Ballantine	F772	1963	191	50¢	R
	Ballantine	U2011	1963	191	50¢	R
	FSB	933	1963	192	2/6	R
	FSB	1404	1965	192	3/6	R
Tarzan of the Apes	Armed	m-16	nd	352	np	R
	Goulden	15 (2 ed)	1951	136	1/6	R
	Goulden	15	1952	136	2/-	R
	FSB	87	1959	222	2/6	R
	FSB	87	1961	222	2/6	R
	FSB	997	1964	223	3/6	R
	FSB	1995	1967	223	5/-	R
	Ballantine	F745	1963	219	50¢	R
	Ballantine	U2001	1963	219	50¢	R
	Ballantine	U2001	1966	220	50¢	R
(abridged)	Dragon	D42	1967	155	2/6	R
Tarzan the Invincible	Goulden	nn	1949	127	1/6	R
	Goulden	3	1952	127	1/6	R
	Pinnacle	nn	1958	192	2/6	R
	FSB	319	1961	190	2/6	R
	FSB	1043	1964	190	3/6	R
	FSB	1043	1967	190	3/6	R
	Ace	F-189	1963	220	40¢	R
	Ballantine	U2014	1964	192	50¢	R
Tarzan the Magnificent	Goulden	14	1950	128	1/6	R
	Goulden	14	1952	127	2/-	R
	FSB	152 (2 ed)	1959	191	2/6	R
	FSB	152	1960	191	2/6	R
	FSB	152	1964	191	2/6	R
	FSB	1399	1965	192	3/6	R
	FSB	1399	1967	192	3/6	R
	Horwitz	FH116	1961	193	4/6	R
	Ballantine	U2021	1964	192	50¢	R
Tarzan the Terrible	Pinnacle	22	1953	136	2/-	R
	FSB	254	1960	224	2/6	R
	FSB	254	1961	224	2/6	R
	FSB	984	1964	224	3/6	R
	Ballantine	F752	1963	220	50¢	R
	Ballantine	U2008	1963	220	50¢	R
Tarzan the Untamed	Goulden	16	1950	128	1/6	R
	Goulden	16	1952	136	2/-	R
	FSB	185	1959	256	2/6	R
	FSB	1094	1964	256	3/6	R
	Ballantine	F751	1963	254	50¢	R
	Ballantine	U2007	1963	254	50¢	R
Tarzan Triumphant	Goulden	12 (2 ed)	1950	128	1/6	R
	Goulden	12	1952	128	2/-	R
	FSB	339	1961	191	2/6	R
	FSB	1077	1964	256	3/6	R
	Ace	F-194	1963	222	40¢	R
	Ballantine	U2015	1964	192	50¢	R
Tarzan's Jungle Tales (originally *Jungle Tales of Tarzan*)						
	FSB	284	1961	192	2/6	R

Author and Title	Publisher	Serial	Date	Pp.	Price	Type
	FSB	1133	1964	192	3/6	R
	FSB	1133	1967	192	3/6	R
Tarzan's Quest	Goulden	nn (2 ed)	1949	127	1/6	R
	Goulden	5	1952	127	2/-	R
	FSB	266	1960	192	2/6	R
	FSB	266	1962	192	2/6	R
	FSB	1044	1964	192	3/6	R
	FSB	1044	1967	192	3/6	R
	Ballantine	U2019	1964	191	50¢	R
(abridged)	Dragon	D65	1967	159	2/6	R

Three Martian Novels [*Thuvia, Maid of Mars*; *The Chessmen of Mars*;
The Master Mind of Mars] Dover		T-39	1962	499	$1.75	C,R

Three Science Fiction Novels [*At the Earth's Core*; *Pellucidar*; *Tanar of
Pellucidar*]	Dover		T-1051	1963	433	$2.00	C,R

Thuvia, Maid of Mars	Pinnacle	25	1953	136	2/-	R
	FSB	613	1962	127	2/6	R
	FSB	613	1964	127	2/6	R
	FSB	1402	1965	127	3/6	R
	Ace	F-168	1962	143	40¢	R
	Ballantine	F770	1963	158	50¢	R
	Ballantine	U2034	1965	158	50¢	R
(abridged)	Dragon	D106	1968	124	2/6	R

Two Martian Novels [*A Princess of Mars*; *A Fighting Man of Mars*]
		Dover		T-1140	1964	356	$1.75	C,R

The Warlord of Mars	Pinnacle	26	1953	152	2/-	R
	FSB	367	1961	128	2/6	R
	FSB	1232	1965	160	3/6	R
	Ballantine	F711	1963	158	50¢	R
	Ballantine	U2033	1965	185	50¢	R
(abridged)	Dragon	D105	1968	138	2/6	R

BURROUGHS, JOHN COLEMAN (1913—1979)
Treasure of the Black Falcon

	Ballantine	U6085	1967	253	75¢	

BURROUGHS, WILLIAM S(EWARD) (1914—)

Dead Fingers Talk	Tandem	T55	1966	224	3/6	
The Nova Express	Evergreen	BC-102	1965	155	95¢	R
	Panther	023771	1968	157	5/-	R
The Soft Machine	Grove	BC131	1967	182	95¢	R
The Ticket That Exploded	Evergreen	B164	1968	217	$1.25	R

BURTON, EDMUND
See also BOY'S FRIEND LIBRARY, page 789.
In Quest of the Golden Orchid

	Cole		1942	80	4/-	J
Peril of Creation	UTB	nd, 1941-1945		33	np	
The Radium King	Cole		1942	66	3/6	J

BUTLER, I. (pseud)

The Horror Film	Zwemmer		1967	176	$2.25	N,R

BUTLER, SAMUEL (1835—1902)

Erewhon	Penguin	20	1936	256	6d	R
	Penguin	20	1954	217	2/-	R
	Signet	CD41	1961	240	50¢	R
	Collier	HS16	1961		65¢	R
	Airmont	CL130	1967	192	50¢	R
	Lancer	13-445	1968	348	60¢	R

BUTLER, WILLIAM (1929—)

The Butterfly Revolution	Ballantine	U6099	1967	221	75¢	R
	Panther	2286	1967	158	3/6	R

BUTTERWORTH, OLIVER (1915—)

The Enormous Egg	Scholastic	TX306	1961	188	50¢	J,R

BUTTREY, DOUGLAS C. See BARR, D. N. (pseud)

C

CABELL, JAMES BRANCH (1879—1958)

Jurgen	Penguin	268 (2 ed)	1940	247	6d	R
	Penguin-US	601	1946	275	25¢	R
	Xanadu		1962	368	$1.45	R
	Avon	VS7	1964	287	75¢	R

CAIDIN, MARTIN (1927—)

Marooned	Bantam	S2965	1965	314	75¢	R
	Corgi	FN7217	1965	314	5/-	R

CALDER-MARSHALL, ARTHUR (1908—)

The Scarlet Boy	Corgi	SN1161	1962	190	2/6	R

CALDWELL, TAYLOR (1900—)

The Devil's Advocate	Macfadden	75-126	1964	349	75¢	R
	Macfadden	75-184	1967	349	75¢	R
Your Sins and Mine	Gold Medal	156	1956	140	25¢	
	Muller	GM156	1956	140	2/-	R
	Muller	GM nn	nd	140	3/-	R
	Popular	G556	1961	126	35¢	R

CALLAHAN, WILLIAM (pseud) See GALLUN, R. Z.

CAMERON, BERL (house pseud)
Black Infinity See O'BRIEN, D.
Cosmic Echelon See GLASBY, J. S.
Destination Alpha See HOLLOWAY, B.
Lost Aeons See HUGHES, DEN
Photomesis See O'BRIEN, D.

Solar Gravita	Curtis War.		1953	159	1/6	
(identical hardcover edition 6/-)						

Sphero Nova See GLASBY, J. S.

CAMERON, ELEANOR (1912—)
The Wonderful Flight to the Mushroom Planet

	Scholastic	TX 913	1966	172	50¢	J,R

CAMP, LON

The Experiment	Softcover	B924X	1966			

CAMPBELL, HERBERT J. (1925—)
Another Space—Another Time

	Panther	67	1953	158	1/6	
(identical hardcover edition 6/-)						

Atoms in Action [as Roy Sheldon]

	Panther	47	1953	159	1/6	
(identical hardcover edition 1/6)						
Beyond the Visible	Hamilton		1953	189	2/-	
(identical hardcover edition 8/6)						
Brain Ultimate	Panther	86	1953	157	1/6	
(identical hardcover edition 6/-)						
Chaos in Miniature	Authentic	18	1952	109	1/6	

House of Entropy [as Roy Sheldon]

	Panther	59	1953	160	1/6	
(identical hardcover edition 6/-)						
The Last Mutation	Authentic	11	1951	105	1/6	

Mammoth Man [as Roy Sheldon]

	Hamilton		1952	110	1/6	

The Menacing Sleep [as Roy Sheldon]

	Panther	16	1952	126	1/6	
Mice or Machines	Authentic	22	1952	109	1/6	

Author and Title	Publisher	Serial	Date	Pp.	Price	Type
The Moon Is Heaven	Authentic	16	1951	110	1/6	
Once Upon a Space	Panther	160	1954	142	1/6	
(identical hardcover edition 6/-)						
The Red Planet	Panther	77	1953	159	1/6	
(identical hardcover edition 6/-)						
Sprague de Camp's New Anthology [editor]						
	Panther	92	1953	159	1/6	C
(identical hardcover edition 7/6)						
Tomorrow's Universe	Panther	101	1954	224	2/-	A
(identical hardcover edition 8/6)						
Two Days of Terror [as Roy Sheldon]						
	Panther	nn	1951	112	1/6	
World in a Test Tube	Authentic	8	1951	106	1/6	

CAMPBELL, JOHN W(OOD) Jr. (1910-1971)

Author and Title	Publisher	Serial	Date	Pp.	Price	Type
Analog 1	Paperback	52-293	1964	160	50¢	A,R
	Panther	2256	1967	169	3/6	A,R
Analog 2	Paperback	52-509	1965	207	50¢	A,R
	Panther	2254	1967	218	5/-	A,R
Analog 3	Panther	025952	1968	300	5/-	A,R
The Astounding Science Fiction Anthology						
	Berkley	G41	1956	188	35¢	A,R
	Berkley	F875	1963	192	50¢	A,R
	Berkley	X1490	1967	192	60¢	A,R
Astounding Tales of Space and Time						
	Berkley	G47	1957	189	35¢	A
	Berkley	F951	1964	190	50¢	A,R
The Black Star Passes	Ace	F-346	1965	223	40¢	C,R
Brigands of the Moon	Duchess					
(wrongly credited to Campbell; see listing under R. Cummings)						
The First Astounding Science Fiction Anthology						
	FSB	1166	1964	320	5/-	A
Invaders From the Infinite	Ace	M-154	1966	192	45¢	R
Islands of Space	Ace	M-143	1966	191	45¢	R
The Mightiest Machine	Ace	F-364	1965	220	40¢	R
The Moon Is Hell	Fantasy	2	1956	256	$1.00	C,R
The Planeteers	Ace	G-585*	1966	150	50¢	C,M
Prologue to Analog	Panther	2255	1967	236	5/-	A,R
The Second Astounding Science Fiction Anthology						
	FSB	1211	1965	320	5/-	A
The Thing and Other Stories	Kemsley	CT408	1952	190	1/6	C,R
The Thing From Outer Space						
	Tandem	T75	1966	220	3/6	C,R
The Ultimate Weapon	Ace	G-585*	1966	106	50¢	M
Who Goes There? and Other Stories						
	Dell	D150	1955	254	35¢	C,R

CAMRA, ROY (pseud)

Author and Title	Publisher	Serial	Date	Pp.	Price	Type
Assault (also titled *Sex Machine* and *Space Sex*)						
	Epic	144	1962			
Sex Machine (retitling of *Assault*, but published anonymously)						
	Ram	RB104	1963	159	75¢	R
Space Sex (retitling of *Assault*, as by Roy Warren)						
	Heart	105	nd			

CANTOR, HAL

Author and Title	Publisher	Serial	Date	Pp.	Price	Type
Ghosts and Things	Berkley	F666	1962	160	50¢	A

CANTRIL, HADLEY

Author and Title	Publisher	Serial	Date	Pp.	Price	Type
The Invasion From Mars	Harper	TB1282	1966	220	$1.95	N,R

CAPEK, KAREL (1890−1938)

Author and Title	Publisher	Serial	Date	Pp.	Price	Type
R.U.R. & The Insects [latter with J. Capek]						
	Oxford	PB34	1961	177	7/6	C,R
	Oxford	34	1961	177	$1.85	C,R
War With the Newts	Bantam	A1292	1955	236	35¢	R
	Bantam	FC46	1959	241	50¢	R
	Bantam	FC46	1963	241	50¢	R
	Bantam	QC250	1965	241	$1.25	R
	Berkley	S1404	1967	241	75¢	R

CAPON, PAUL (1912−)

Author and Title	Publisher	Serial	Date	Pp.	Price	Type
Down to Earth	Digit	R842	1964	158	2/6	R
Into the Tenth Millennium						
	Brown-Wat.	R895	1965	224	3/6	R
Phobos the Robot Planet	Digit	R887	1964	160	2/6	J,R
The World at Bay	Digit	R863	1954	158	2/6	R

CAPOTE, TRUMAN (1924−)

Author and Title	Publisher	Serial	Date	Pp.	Price	Type
Other Voices, Other Rooms	Penguin	2135	1964	173	3/6	R

CAPPS, CARROLL M. (1917?−1971) [as C. C. MacApp]

Author and Title	Publisher	Serial	Date	Pp.	Price	Type
Omha Abides	Paperback	52-649	1968	160	50¢	M

CARAS, R. A. (1928−) [as Roger Sarac]

Author and Title	Publisher	Serial	Date	Pp.	Price	Type
The Throwbacks	Belmont	B50-642	1965	140	50¢	

CAREY, Dr. GEORGE W.

Author and Title	Publisher	Serial	Date	Pp.	Price	Type
Road to the Moon	Yates & Mann		1924	48	np	

CARNELL, EDWARD JOHN (1912−1972)

Author and Title	Publisher	Serial	Date	Pp.	Price	Type
The Best From New Worlds Science Fiction						
	Boardman	163	1955	190	2/-	A
Gateway to Tomorrow	Panther	1460	1963	160	2/6	A,R
Jinn and Jitters	Pendulum		1946	116	2/-	A
Lambda 1 and Other Stories	Berkley	F883	1964	175	50¢	A
	Penguin	2275	1965	206	3/6	A,R
[contents of two editions differ substantially]						
New Writings in SF 1	Corgi	GS7083	1964	190	3/6	A,R
(Corgi editions in this series usually followed D. Dobson edition, but occasionally were first)						
	Bantam	F3245	1966	147	50¢	A,R
New Writings in SF 2	Corgi	GS7125	1965	191	3/6	A,R
	Bantam	F3379	1966	150	50¢	A,R
New Writings in SF 3	Corgi	GS7199	1965	189	3/6	A,R
	Bantam	F3380	1967	168	50¢	A,R
New Writings in SF 4	Corgi	GS7262	1965	186	3/6	A,R
	Bantam	F3763	1968	154	50¢	A,R
New Writings in SF 5	Corgi	GS7329	1966	190	3/6	A,R
New Writings in SF 6	Corgi	GS7383	1966	190	3/6	A,R
New Writings in SF 7	Corgi	GS7469	1966	190	3/6	A,R
New Writings in SF 8	Corgi	GS7564	1966	188	3/6	A,R
New Writings in SF 9	Corgi	GS7650	1967	187	3/6	A,R
New Writings in SF 10	Corgi	GS7722	1967	189	3/6	A,R
New Writings in SF 11	Corgi	GS7803	1967	190	3/6	A,R
New Writings in SF 12	Corgi	07878	1968	188	3/6	A,R
New Writings in SF 13	Corgi	08037	1968	190	3/6	A,R
No Place Like Earth	Boardman	140	1954	192	2/-	A,R
	Panther	1252	1961	190	2/6	A,R
Weird Shadows From Beyond						
	Corgi	GS7208	1965	157	3/6	A

CARNELLE, INGE

Author and Title	Publisher	Serial	Date	Pp.	Price	Type
The Girl From B.U.S.T.	Bee-Line	145	1966			
Joy Ride	Bee-Line	194	1967			

CARPENTER, ELMER J.

Author and Title	Publisher	Serial	Date	Pp.	Price	Type
Moonspin	Flagship	00715	1967	159	60¢	

CARR, CHARLES

Author and Title	Publisher	Serial	Date	Pp.	Price	Type
Colonists of Space	Ward Lock	25	1955	193	1/6	R
	Digit	R617	1962	158	2/6	R
Salamander War	Digit	R616	1962	160	2/6	R

CARR, JOHN DICKSON (1906−1977)
See also MONTREAL STAR, page 790.

Author and Title	Publisher	Serial	Date	Pp.	Price	Type
The Burning Court	Popular		1944	221	25¢	R
	Guild		1952	192	2/-	R
	Bantam	1207	1954	215	25¢	R
	Bantam	J2706	1963	215	40¢	R

Author and Title	Publisher	Serial	Date	Pp.	Price	Type
The Department of Queer Complaints [as Carter Dickson]						
	Pan	X208	1963	223	3/6	C,R
The Devil in Velvet	Bantam	A1009	1952	378	35¢	R
	Bantam	A2052	1960	312	50¢	R
	Bantam	S3637	1968	312	75¢	R
	Penguin	1242	1957	352	3/6	R
Fear Is the Same [as Carter Dickson]						
	Bantam	A2000	1959	199	35¢	R
	WDL	HN847	1959	257	2/6	R
Fire, Burn!	Bantam	A1847	1958	214	35¢	R
	Bantam	S3638	1968	214	75¢	R
	Penguin	1622	1961	269	3/6	R
	Penguin	C1622	1965	269	3/6	R
CARR, ROBERT S. (1909—)						
Beyond Infinity	Dell	781	1954	223	25¢	C,R
CARR, TERRY (1937—)						
Invasion From 2500 [as Norman Edwards, joint pseudonym with Ted White]	Monarch	453	1964	126	40¢	
New Worlds of Fantasy	Ace	A-12	1967	253	75¢	A
Science Fiction for People Who Hate Science Fiction						
	Funk & Wag.	F47	1968	190	95¢	A,R
Warlord of Kor	Ace	F-177*	1963	97	40¢	
World's Best Science Fiction See WOLLHEIM, D. A. (co-anthologist)						
CARRINGTON, RICHARD (1921—)						
Mermaids and Mastodons	Grey Arrow	G40	1960	256	5/-	N,R
CARROLL, LESLIE						
You Can't Hang the Dead	Mitre		1941	31	1/-	
CARTER, DEE (pseud) See HUGHES, DEN						
CARTER, JOHN FRANKLIN (1897—) [as Jay Franklin]						
Rat Race	Galaxy Nov 10		1952	160	35¢	R
CARTER, LIN(WOOD VROOMAN) (1930—) See also R. E. HOWARD						
Conan of the Isles [with L. S. de Camp]						
	Lancer	73-800	1968	189	60¢	
Destination: Saturn [with D. Grinnell (pseud. of D. A. Wollheim)]						
	Ace	H-85*	1968	107	60¢	
The Flame of Iridar	Belmont	B50-759*	1967	99	50¢	
The Man Without a Planet	Ace	G-606*	1966	113	50¢	
The Star Magicians	Ace	G-588*	1966	124	50¢	
The Thief of Thoth	Belmont	00809*	1968	85	50¢	
Thongor Against the Gods	Paperback	52-586	1967	157	50¢	
Thongor at the End of Time						
	Paperback	53-780	1968	158	60¢	
Thongor in the City of Magicians						
	Paperback	53-665	1968	160	60¢	
Thongor of Lemuria	Ace	F-383	1966	127	40¢	
Tower at the Edge of Time	Belmont	00804	1968	141	50¢	
The Wizard of Lemuria	Ace	F-326	1965	127	40¢	
CARTER, NICK (pseud)						
Operation Moon Rocket	Award	A295X	1968	160	60¢	
CARTMELL, V. H. (1896—) [with C. Grayson]						
The Golden Argosy	Bantam	F1441	1956	403	50¢	A,R
CASEWIT, CURTIS W. (1922—)						
The Peacemakers	Digit	R704	1963	191	2/6	R
	Macfadden	60-321	1968	143	60¢	R
CASSIDAY, BRUCE (1920—) [as Carson Bingham]						
Gorgo	Monarch	MM603	1960	141	35¢	
CASSON, MILES						
Time Drug	Curtis War.		1954	159	1/6	
(identical hardcover edition 6/-)						

Author and Title	Publisher	Serial	Date	Pp.	Price	Type
CASTLE, JEFFREY L. (1898—)						
Satellite E One	Bantam	A1766	1958	164	35¢	R
	Consul	1140	1962	157	2/6	R
CASTLE, JOHN						
The 7th Fury	Horwitz	PB265	1966	255	65¢	
CAUSETT, WILLIAM						
Pirates in Space	Baker	FST2	1953	63	9d	
CAYROL, JEAN						
All in a Night	FSB	687	1962	144	2/6	
CERF, BENNETT (1889—1971)						
Famous Ghost Stories	Vintage	V140	1960	361	$1.25	A,R
	Modern Lib	P21	1963	361	95¢	A,R
Stories Selected From The Unexpected						
	Bantam	FP30	1963	184	50¢	A
The Unexpected	Bantam	502	1948	273	25¢	A
CERF, CHRISTOPHER						
The Vintage Anthology of Science Fantasy						
	Vintage	V326	1966	310	$1.65	A
CHADWICK, PAUL [as Brant House]						
City of Living Dead	Corinth	CR134	1966	160	60¢	M
Curse of the Mandarin's Fan						
	Corinth	CR130	1966	158	60¢	M
The Death-Torch Terror	Corinth	CR138	1966	160	60¢	M
Octopus of Crime	Corinth	CR142	1966		60¢	M
Servants of the Skull	Corinth	CR126	1966	160	60¢	M
The Sinister Scourge	Corinth	CR146	1966	160	60¢	M
The Torture Trust	Corinth	CR122	1966	160	60¢	M
CHAMBERLAIN, WILLIAM (1903—)						
China Strike	Gold Medal	d1783	1967	191	50¢	
Red January	Paperback	52-501	1964	158	50¢	
CHAMBERS, DANA						
The Last Secret	Quinn	H34	1945		25¢?	
CHAMBERS, ROBERT W. (1865—1933)						
The King in Yellow	Ace	M-132	1965	253	45¢	C,R
The Maker of Moons	Shroud		1954	78	$1.00	R
The Tracer of Lost Persons	Newnes		nd	252	np	R
CHAMBERS, WHITMAN						
Invasion	Hillman	TNC13	1950?			
CHANDLER, A. BERTRAM (1912—)						
See also STAR WEEKLY, page 791.						
The Alternate Martians	Ace	M-129*	1965	129	45¢	
Beyond the Galactic Rim	Ace	F-237*	1963	114	40¢	C,M
Bring Back Yesterday	Ace	D-517*	1961	173	35¢	
The Coils of Time	Ace	M-107*	1964	128	45¢	M
Contraband From Otherspace						
	Ace	G-609*	1967	104	50¢	M
The Deep Reaches of Space	Mayflower	1885	1967	128	3/6	R
Empress of Outer Space	Ace	M-129*	1965	127	45¢	
False Fatherland	Horwitz	PB374	1968	161	65¢	M
The Hamelin Plague	Monarch	390	1963	126	35¢	
Into the Alternate Universe	Ace	M-107*	1964	128	45¢	
Nebula Alert	Ace	G-632*	1967	121	50¢	
Rendezvous on a Lost World						
	Ace	F-117*	1961	124	40¢	M
The Rim of Space	Ace	F-133*	1962	128	40¢	R
The Road to the Rim	Ace	H-29*	1967	117	60¢	
The Ship From Outside	Ace	F-237*	1963	108	40¢	M
Space Mercenaries	Ace	M-133*	1965	131	45¢	

Author and Title	Publisher	Serial	Date	Pp.	Price	Type
CHAPELA, E. SALAZAR						
Naked in Piccadilly	FSB	1559	1966	253	5/-	R
CHAPPELL, GEORGE S(HEPARD) (1877—1946)						
Through the Alimentary Canal With Gun and Camera						
	Dover	T-376	1963	114	$1.00	R
CHARBONNEAU, LOUIS (1925—)						
Corpus Earthling	Zenith	ZB40	1960	160	35¢	
	Digit	R753	1963	159	2/6	R
Down to Earth	Bantam	F3442	1967	187	50¢	
No Place on Earth	Crest	s342	1959	160	35¢	R
Psychedelic-40	Bantam	F2929	1965	184	50¢	
The Sensitives	Bantam	H3759	1968	203	60¢	
The Sentinel Stars	Bantam	J2686	1963	156	40¢	
	Corgi	GS1480	1964	156	3/-	R
CHARKIN, PAUL (SAMUEL) (1907—)						
Light of Mars	Badger	SF12	1959	155	2/-	
The Living Gem	Digit	R782	1963	159	2/6	
The Other Side of Night	Badger	SF24	1960	158	2/-	
CHARLES, NEIL (house pseud)						
Beyond Zoaster	Curtis War.		1953	159	1/6	
(identical hardcover edition 6/-)						
The Land of Esa See HUGHES, DEN						
Para-Robot See JENNISON, J. W.						
Planet Tha	Curtis War.		1953	159	1/6	
(identical hardcover edition 6/-)						
Pre-Gargantua	Curtis War.		1953	159	1/6	
(identical hardcover edition 6/-)						
Research Opta	Curtis War.		1953	160	1/6	
(identical hardcover edition 6/-)						
Titan's Moon See HOLLOWAY, B.						
Twenty-Four Hours See HUGHES, DEN						
World of Gol	Curtis War.		1953	159	1/6	
(identical hardcover edition 6/-)						
CHARLES, T.						
Lady in the Mist	Ace	G-566	1964	189	50¢	
CHARTERIS, LESLIE (1907—)						
The Saint's Choice of Impossible Crime						
	Bond-Charteris		1945	125	25¢	A
CHASE, JAMES H. (pseud) See RAYMOND, R.						
CHEEVER, JOHN (1912—)						
The Enormous Radio	Berkley	G119	1958	190	35¢	C,R
CHESTER, WILLIAM L. (1907—)						
Hawk of the Wilderness	Ace	G-586	1966	287	50¢	R
CHESTERTON, G(ILBERT) K(EITH) (1874—1936)						
The Flying Inn	Penguin	1338	1958	288	2/6	R
The Man Who Was Thursday						
	Penguin	95	1937	184	6d	R
	Penguin	95	1940	184	6d	R
	Penguin	95	1958	188	2/6	R
	Penguin	95	1962	188	3/6	R
	Penguin	95	1967	186	3/6	R
	Armed	984	nd		np	R
	Capricorn	CAP27	1960	192	$1.35	R
The Napoleon of Notting Hill						
	Penguin	550	1946		1/6	R
	WDL	H947	1960	192	2/6	R
CHETWYND-HAYES, R(ONALD) (1919—)						
The Man From the Bomb	Badger	SF21	1959	157	2/-	

Author and Title	Publisher	Serial	Date	Pp.	Price	Type
CHILTON, CHARLES (1927—)						
Journey Into Space	Pan	437	1958	189	2/-	R
	Digit	R811	1963	160	2/6	R
The Red Planet	Pan	G274	1960	185	2/6	R
	Digit	R770	1963	158	2/6	R
The World in Peril	Pan	G579	1962	191	2/6	R
CHILTON, IRMA (1930—)						
String of Time	Topliner	02047	1968	111	3/6	
CHOPPING, R.						
The Fly	Signet	T2835	1966	223	75¢	
	Pan	M228	1967	256	5/-	R
CHRISTIE, AGATHA (1890—1976)						
The Hound of Death and Other Stories						
	Pan	G377	1960	219	2/6	C,R
	Fontana	970	1966	190	3/6	C,R
CHRISTOPHER, JOHN (pseud) See YOUD, C. S.						
CHURCHILL, ALLEN						
They Never Came Back	Ace	F-218	1963	159	40¢	
CHURCHWARD, JAMES (1854—1936)						
Children of Mu	Paperback	54-639	1968	223	75¢	N,R
The Cosmic Forces of Mu	Paperback	54-678	1968	191	75¢	N,R
The Lost Continent of Mu	Xanadu		1962	335	$1.95	N,R
	Paperback	54-616	1968	286	75¢	N,R
The Sacred Symbols of Mu	Paperback	54-663	1968	222	75¢	N,R
The Second Book of the Cosmic Forces of Mu						
	Paperback	54-754	1968	224	75¢	N,R
CICELLIS, KAY (1926—)						
The Day the Fish Came Out						
	Bantam	K3656	1967	138	60¢	
CLARENS, CARLOS (1936—)						
An Illustrated History of the Horror Film						
	Capricorn Giant	295	1967	256	$2.75	N,R
CLARK, CURT (pseud) See WESTLAKE, D. E.						
CLARKE, A. V(INCENT) [with (H.) K. Bulmer]						
Cybernetic Controller	Panther	nn	1952	112	1/6	
Space Treason	Panther	nn	1952	112	1/6	
CLARKE, ALFRED C(HARLES) G(EORGE)						
Into the Darkness	Digit	R550	1961	160	2/6	
The Mind Master	Digit	R654	1962	160	2/6	
CLARKE, ARTHUR C. (1917—)						
See also STAR WEEKLY, page 791.						
Against the Fall of Night (revised into *The City and the Stars*)						
	Permabks	310	1954	160	25¢	M
	Pyramid	G554	1960	159	35¢	R
	Pyramid	F754	1962	159	40¢	R
	Pyramid	X1703	1967	159	60¢	R
The Challenge of the Space Ship						
	Ballantine	F528	1961	189	50¢	N,R
Childhood's End	Ballantine	33	1953	214	35¢	
(identical hardcover edition $2.00)						
	Ballantine	398K	1960	214	35¢	R
	Ballantine	U2111	1963	214	50¢	R
	Ballantine	U5066	1967	222	60¢	R
	Pan	369	1956	189	2/-	R
	Pan	G463	1961	189	2/6	R
	Pan	G463	1963	189	2/6	R
	Pan	X573	1966	189	3/6	R

Author and Title	Publisher	Serial	Date	Pp.	Price	Type
The City and the Stars (revision of *Against the Fall of Night*)						
	Corgi	G443	1957	319	3/6	R
	Corgi	GS933	1960	283	3/6	R
	Corgi	FS7295	1965	254	5/-	R
	Signet	S1464	1957	191	35¢	R
	Signet	D1858	1960	191	50¢	R
	Signet	P3429	1968	191	60¢	R
	Harbrace	HPL1	1966	227	75¢	R
The Deep Range	Signet	S1583	1958	144	35¢	R
	Signet	D2528	1964	175	50¢	R
Dolphin Island	Berkley	F1495	1968	140	50¢	R
	Dragon	D88	1968	126	2/6	R
Earthlight	Ballantine	97	1955	155	35¢	
(identical hardcover edition $2.75)						
	Ballantine	249	1957	155	35¢	R
	Ballantine	F698	1963	155	50¢	R
	Ballantine	U2824	1965	155	50¢	R
	Pan	420	1957	158	2/-	R
	Pan	G641	1963	158	2/6	R
	Pan	X574	1966	158	3/6	R
Expedition to Earth	Ballantine	52	1953	165	35¢	C
(identical hardcover edition $2.00)						
	Ballantine	472K	1961	167	35¢	C,R
	Ballantine	U2112	1965	167	50¢	C,R
	Corgi	S650	1959	192	2/6	C,R
	Pan	X462	1966	174	3/6	C,R
	Sphere	23973	1968	174	5/-	C,R
The Exploration of Space	Cardinal	C135	1954	210	35¢	N,R
	Pelican	A434	1958	192	3/6	N,R
(revised)	Premier	d102	1961	192	50¢	N
	Premier	R228	1964	183	60¢	N,R
A Fall of Moondust	Dell	2463	1963	240	50¢	R
	Pan	X280 (2 eds.)	1964	206	3/6	R
Islands in the Sky	Signet	S1769	1960	127	35¢	J,R
	Signet	KD510	1965	157	50¢	J,R
	Digit	R802	1964	158	2/6	J,R
Master of Space (originally *Prelude to Space*)						
	Lancer	72-610	1961	158	50¢	R
The Other Side of the Sky	Signet	S1729	1959	158	35¢	C,R
	Signet	D2433	1964	160	50¢	C,R
	Corgi	YS1289	1963	158	3/-	C,R
	Corgi	GS7531	1966	158	3/6	C,R
	Harbrace	HPL25	1968	248	75¢	C,R
Prelude to Space (also titled *Master of Space*)						
	Galaxy Nov	3	1951	160	25¢	
	Pan	301	1954	156	2/-	R
	Ballantine	68	1954	166	35¢	R
	FSB	755	1962	159	2/6	R
	FSB	1097	1964	159	2/6	R
	FSB	2147	1968	159	3/6	R
Profiles of the Future	Bantam	H2734	1964	235	60¢	N,R
	Pan	XP54	1964	223	3/6	N,R
Reach for Tomorrow	Ballantine	135	1956	166	35¢	C
(identical hardcover edition $2.00)						
	Ballantine	U2110	1963	166	50¢	C,R
Sands of Mars	Corgi	T43	1954	251	2/-	R
	Corgi	S564	1958	251	2/6	R
	Pocket Bks	989	1954	217	25¢	R
	Permabks	M4149	1959	217	35¢	R
	Pan	X281 (2 eds.)	1964	207	3/6	R
Tales From the White Hart	Ballantine	186	1957	148	35¢	C
	Ballantine	539	1961	151	35¢	C,R
	Ballantine	U2113	1966	151	50¢	C,R
Tales of Ten Worlds	Dell	8467	1964	224	50¢	C,R
	Pan	X424	1965	204	3/6	C,R
Time Probe	Dell	8925	1967	238	75¢	A,R
2001: A Space Odyssey	Signet	Q3580	1968	221	95¢	R
	Arrow	153	1968	256	5/-	R

Author and Title	Publisher	Serial	Date	Pp.	Price	Type
CLAYTON, RICHARD (1907—) [as William Haggard]						
Slow Burner	Corgi	S669	1959	223	2/6	R
	Penguin	2233	1965	159	3/6	R
	Signet	D2773	1965	143	50¢	R
CLEARY, JOHN (1917—)						
A Flight of Chariots	Paperback	54-830	1965	320	75¢	R
CLEMENS, SAMUEL L. (1835—1911) [as Mark Twain]						
A Connecticut Yankee in King Arthur's Court						
	Armed	e-139	nd	319	np	R
	Pocket Bks	497	1948	360	25¢	R
	Cardinal	C107	1954	360	35¢	R
	Washington	W150	1960	360	35¢	R
	Washington	RE301	1964	360	75¢	R
	Royal Giant (½)		nd	218	50¢	R
	Signet	CD158	1963	334	50¢	R
The Mysterious Stranger	Armed	n-1	nd	128	np	R
Selected Short Stories of Mark Twain						
	Armed	m-3	nd		np	C
CLEMENT, HAL (pseud) See STUBBS, H. C.						
CLIFTON, MARK (1906—1963)						
Eight Keys to Eden	Ballantine	F639	1962	160	50¢	R
	Pan	X353	1965	173	3/6	R
The Forever Machine [with F. Riley] (originally *They'd Rather Be Right*)						
	Galaxy Nov	35	1959	159	35¢	R
When They Come From Space						
	Macfadden	40-105	1963	144	40¢	R
	Macfadden	50-341	1967	144	50¢	R
	FSB	1128	1964	192	3/6	R
CLINGERMAN, MILDRED (1918—)						
A Cupful of Space	Ballantine	519K	1961	142	35¢	C
CLIVE, DENNIS (pseud) See FEARN, J. R.						
COATES, ROBERT M. (1897—)						
The Eater of Darkness	Capricorn	CAP-18	1959	238	$1.15	R
COBLENTZ, STANTON A. (1896—)						
Hidden World	Airmont	SF6	1964	127	40¢	R
Into Plutonian Depths	Avon	281	1950	159	25¢	M
The Sunken World	Kemsley	CT402	1951	190	1/6	R
Youth Madness	Utopian	AF8	nd	38	1/-	M
COCKCROFT, W. P.						
They Came From Mars	Swan		1945	16	2d	
COCKRELL, MARIAN						
Shadow Castle	Scholastic	TX 519	1963	143	45¢	
CODY, C. S. (pseud) See WALLER, L.						
COGSWELL, THEODORE R. (1918—)						
The Third Eye	Belmont	B50-840	1968	175	50¢	C
The Wall Around the World						
	Pyramid	F703	1962	160	40¢	C
COLBY, C(ARROLL) B. (1904—)						
The Weirdest People in the World						
	Popular	SP385	1965	143	50¢	N
COLEMAN, JAMES NELSON						
Seeker From the Stars	Berkley	X1438	1967	159	60¢	
COLERIDGE, JOHN (pseud) See BINDER, E.						

Author and Title	Publisher	Serial	Date	Pp.	Price	Type
COLLADAY, MORRISON						
When the Moon Fell	Stellar	SFS6	1929	24	10¢	
COLLIER, JOHN (1901−1980)						
Fancies and Goodnights	Bantam	A1106	1953	506	35¢	C,R
	Bantam	F1703	1957	375	50¢	C,R
	Bantam	SC91	1964	418	75¢	C,R
Green Thoughts and Other Strange Tales						
	Armed	871	nd	287	np	C,R
Of Demons and Darkness	Corgi	FS7126	1965	303	5/-	C,R
COLLINS, CHARLES M.						
A Feast of Blood	Avon	S277	1967	190	60¢	A
Fright	Avon	G1178	1963	141	50¢	A
COLLINS, E(RROLL)						
Conquerors of Space	Baker	FST5	1953	60	1/-	

COLLINS, HUNT (pseud) See HUNTER, E.

COLLINS, WILLIAM WILKIE (1825−1889)

See also HALDEMAN-JULIUS CO., page 790, and LIPPSIUS & TISCHER, page 790.

Author and Title	Publisher	Serial	Date	Pp.	Price	Type
The Moonstone	Penguin	1072	1955		2/6	R
	Penguin	EL14	1966	528	5/-	R
	Pyramid	19	1950	320	25¢	R
	Pyramid	G88	1953	320	25¢	R
	Pyramid	PR11	1958		35¢	R
	Pyramid	X1402	1966	416	60¢	R
	Airmont	CL76	1965	415	60¢	R
	Perennial	P3029	1967	462	75¢	R
	Paperback	54-960	1966	414	75¢	R

COLLODI, CARLO (pseud of Carlo Lorenzini)

Author and Title	Publisher	Serial	Date	Pp.	Price	Type
The Adventures of Pinocchio						
	Lancer	13-448	1968	222	60¢	R

COLVIN, JAMES (pseud) See MOORCOCK, M.

Author and Title	Publisher	Serial	Date	Pp.	Price	Type
COMER, RALPH (pseud of John Sanders)						
The Witchfinders	Award	A352X	1968	189	60¢	
COMPTON, D(AVID) G(UY) (1930−)						
Synthajoy	Ace	H-86	1968	189	60¢	R
CONDON, RICHARD (1915−)						
The Manchurian Candidate						
	Signet	T1826	1960	351	75¢	R
	Pan	X156	1962	272	3/6	R
	Pan	X156	1963	272	3/6	R
	Pan	X156	1966	272	3/6	R
	Pan	X156	1967	272	3/6	R
CONDRAY, BRUNO G.						
The Dissentizens	Pearson	T-B	1954	64	9d	
Exile From Jupiter	Pearson	T-B	1955	64	9d	
CONGDON, DON						
Alone by Night [with Michael Congdon]						
	Ballantine	563	1961	144	35¢	A
	Ballantine	U2852	1967	144	50¢	A,R
Stories for the Dead of Night						
	Dell	B107	1957	288	35¢	A
	Dell	8295	1967	240	50¢	A,R
Tales of Love and Horror	Ballantine	522K	1961	144	35¢	A

CONGDON, MICHAEL See CONGDON, D. (coanthologist)

Author and Title	Publisher	Serial	Date	Pp.	Price	Type
CONKLIN, GROFF (1904−1968)						
Another Part of the Galaxy	Gold Medal	d1628	1966	224	50¢	A

Author and Title	Publisher	Serial	Date	Pp.	Price	Type
The Best of Science Fiction	Bonanza		1963	440	$1.95	A,R
Big Book of Science Fiction	Berkley	G53	1957	187	35¢	A,R
	Berkley	F975	1964	176	50¢	A,R
Br-r-r!	Avon	T289	1959	192	35¢	A
Crossroads in Time	Permabks	P254	1953	312	35¢	A
Dimension 4	Pyramid	F973	1964	159	40¢	A
Elsewhere and Elsewhen	Berkley	S1561	1968	253	75¢	A
Enemies in Space (abridgement of *Invaders of Earth*)						
	Digit	R577	1962	159	2/6	A,R
	Digit	R883	1964	158	2/6	A,R
Fifty Short Science Fiction Tales [with Isaac Asimov]						
	Collier	AS516	1963	287	95¢	A
	Collier	01639	1966	287	95¢	A,R
Five−Odd	Pyramid	R1056	1964	188	50¢	A
5 Unearthly Visions	Gold Medal	d1549	1965	175	50¢	A
	Gold Medal	D1868	1967	175	50¢	A,R
Four for the Future	Pyramid	G434	1959	160	35¢	A
	Pyramid	F743	1962	160	40¢	A,R
	Consul	N1018	1961	174	2/6	A,R
Giants Unleashed	Tempo	T111	1966	248	50¢	A,R
The Graveyard Reader	Ballantine	257	1958	156	35¢	A
	Ballantine	U2822	1965	156	50¢	A,R
Great Science Fiction About Doctors [with Noah D. Fabricant]						
	Collier	AS518	1963	412	95¢	A
	Collier	01895	1965	412	95¢	A,R
	Collier	01895	1966	412	95¢	A,R
Great Science Fiction by Scientists						
	Collier	AS218	1962	313	95¢	A
	Collier	01903	1966	313	95¢	A,R
Great Stories of Space Travel						
	Tempo	T39	1963	256	50¢	A
Human and Other Beings [as Allen DeGraeff (joint pseud. with A. P. Blaustein)]	Collier	AS567	1963	319	95¢	A
In the Grip of Terror	Permabks	P117	1951	364	35¢	A
Invaders of Earth	Pocket Bks	1074	1955	257	25¢	A,R
	Digit	R562	1962	160	2/6	A,R
(companion to Digit edition is *Enemies in Space*)						
	Tempo	T6	1962	382	50¢	A,R
Operation Future	Permabks	M4022	1955	356	35¢	A
Possible Worlds of Science Fiction						
	Berkley	G-3	1955	189	35¢	A,R
	Berkley	G471	1960	188	35¢	A,R
	Berkley	X1633	1968	188	60¢	A,R
Science Fiction Adventures in Dimension						
	Berkley	F1053	1965	174	50¢	A,R
Science Fiction Adventures in Mutation						
	Berkley	F1096	1965	174	50¢	A,R
Science Fiction Galaxy	Permabks	P67	1950	242	35¢	A
Science Fiction Oddities	Berkley	S1311	1966	256	75¢	A
Science Fiction Omnibus (selections from *The Omnibus of Science Fiction*)	Berkley	G31	1956	187	35¢	A,R
	Berkley	F851	1963	190	50¢	A,R
Science Fiction Terror Tales						
	Pocket Bks	1045	1955	262	25¢	A,R
Science Fiction Thinking Machines (also titled *Selections From Science Fiction Thinking Machines*)	Bantam	1352	1955	183	25¢	A,R
	Bantam	EP63	1964	201	45¢	A,R
Seven Come Infinity	Gold Medal	d1752	1966	288	50¢	A
	Coronet	02880	1967	288	3/6	A,R
Seven Trips Through Time and Space						
	Gold Medal	R1924	1968	256	60¢	A
17 X Infinity	Dell	7746	1963	272	50¢	A
	Mayflower	7746	1964	272	3/6	A,R
6 Great Short Novels of Science Fiction						
	Dell	D9	1954	384	35¢	A
Six Great Short Science Fiction Novels						
	Dell	C111	1960	350	50¢	A
The Supernatural Reader [with Lucy Conklin]						
	WDL	M706	1958	252	2/6	A,R
	Collier	AS392X	1962	352	95¢	A,R

Author and Title	Publisher	Serial	Date	Pp.	Price	Type
	Collier	01911	1966	352	95¢	A,R
	Collier	01911	1968	352	95¢	A,R
13 Above the Night	Dell	8741	1965	286	60¢	A
13 Great Stories of Science Fiction						
	Gold Medal	s997	1960	192	35¢	A
	Gold Medal	k1243	1962	192	40¢	A,R
	Gold Medal	d1444	1964	192	50¢	A,R
	Coronet	2482	1967	192	3/6	A,R
A Treasury of Science Fiction						
	Berkley	G63	1957	186	35¢	A,R
	Berkley	F1047	1965	186	50¢	A,R
12 Great Classics of Science Fiction						
	Gold Medal	d1366	1963	192	50¢	A
	Gold Medal	d1669	1966	192	50¢	A,R
Twisted	Belmont	L92-535	1962	189	50¢	A
	Belmont	B50-771	1967	189	50¢	A,R
	Horwitz	PB153	1963	130	4/-	A,R
	FSB	1379	1965	189	3/6	A,R
A Way Home [collection of T. Sturgeon, *q.v.*]						
Worlds of When	Pyramid	F733	1962	159	40¢	A

CONNELL, ALAN

Author and Title	Publisher	Serial	Date	Pp.	Price	Type
Lords of Serpent Land	Currawong		1945	62	9d	
Prisoners of Serpent Land	Currawong		1945	62	9d	
Warriors of Serpent Land	Currawong		1945	62	9d	

CONNINGTON, J. J. (pseud) See STEWART, A. W.

CONQUEST, ROBERT (1917—)
Spectrum . . . [with K. Amis] See AMIS, K. (co-anthologist)

Author and Title	Publisher	Serial	Date	Pp.	Price	Type
A World of Difference	Ballantine	U2213	1964	192	50¢	R

CONRAD, EARL (1912—)

Author and Title	Publisher	Serial	Date	Pp.	Price	Type
The Premier	Pyramid	X-1005	1964	254	60¢	R

CONRAD, JOSEPH (1857—1924)

Author and Title	Publisher	Serial	Date	Pp.	Price	Type
The Shadow Line	Armed	J-273	nd		np	R

CONROY, RICK
Martians in a Frozen World

Author and Title	Publisher	Serial	Date	Pp.	Price	Type
	Authentic	26	1952	108	1/6	
Mission From Mars	Panther	nn	1952	112	1/6	

COOK, W(ILLIAM) W(ALLACE) (1867—1933) See ADVENTURE LIBRARY, page 789.

COOLIDGE, OLIVIA E.
Hercules and Other Tales From Greek Myths

Author and Title	Publisher	Serial	Date	Pp.	Price	Type
	Scholastic	TX219	1967	113	35¢	

COOMBS, CHARLES I. (1914—)

Author and Title	Publisher	Serial	Date	Pp.	Price	Type
Mystery of Satellite 7	Tempo	T9	1962	192	50¢	R
Survival in the Sky	Badger	SS2	1959		2/6	N,R

COON, HORACE (1897—1961)

Author and Title	Publisher	Serial	Date	Pp.	Price	Type
43,000 Years Later	Signet	S1534	1958	143	35¢	
	Panther	975	1959	157	2/6	R

COONEY, MICHAEL (1921—)

Author and Title	Publisher	Serial	Date	Pp.	Price	Type
Doomsday England	Corgi	08032	1968	221	5/-	R

COOPER, EDMUND (1926—1982)

Author and Title	Publisher	Serial	Date	Pp.	Price	Type
All Fools' Day	Berkley	X1469	1967	176	60¢	R
	Hodder	02860	1967	192	3/6	R
Deadly Image (also titled *The Uncertain Midnight*)						
	Ballantine	260	1958	190	35¢	
	Panther	988	1959	192	2/6	R
A Far Sunset	Berkley	X1607	1968	160	60¢	R
	Hodder	04364	1967	189	3/6	R
News From Elsewhere	Mayflower	6304	1968	128	3/6	C

Author and Title	Publisher	Serial	Date	Pp.	Price	Type
Seed of Light	Ballantine	327	1959	159	35¢	R
	Panther	1094	1960	189	2/6	R
Tomorrow Came	Panther	1511	1963	123	2/6	C
Tomorrow's Gift	Ballantine	279K	1958	164	35¢	C
	Digit	D280	1959	160	2/-	C,R
Transit	Lancer	72-758	1964	159	50¢	R
	Lancer	73-690	1967	287	60¢	R
	FSB	1391	1965	190	3/6	R
Voices in the Dark	Digit	D349	1960	157	2/-	C
	Digit	R663	1963	157	2/6	C,R

COOPER, GILES (1918—1966)

Author and Title	Publisher	Serial	Date	Pp.	Price	Type
The Other Man	Panther	1757	1964	207	3/6	

COOPER, JOHN C.

Author and Title	Publisher	Serial	Date	Pp.	Price	Type
The Grip of the Strangler	Digit	R214	1958	189	2/6	
The Haunted Strangler	Ace	D-359	1958	190	35¢	

COOPER, MERIAM C.
King Kong See WALLACE, E. (co-author)

COOPER, MORTON

Author and Title	Publisher	Serial	Date	Pp.	Price	Type
The Munsters	Avon	G1237	1964	143	50¢	

COOPER, SUSAN (1935—)

Author and Title	Publisher	Serial	Date	Pp.	Price	Type
Mandrake	Penguin	2491	1966	238	4/-	R
Over Sea, Under Stone	Puffin	PS362	1968	221	5/-	J

COPPARD, A(LFRED) E. (1878—1957)
Adam and Eve and Pinch Me

Author and Title	Publisher	Serial	Date	Pp.	Price	Type
	Penguin	595	1946	168	1/-	C,R

COPPEL, ALFRED (1921—)

Author and Title	Publisher	Serial	Date	Pp.	Price	Type
Dark December	Gold Medal	s989	1960	208	35¢	

COPPER, BASIL (1924—)

Author and Title	Publisher	Serial	Date	Pp.	Price	Type
Not After Nightfall	FSB	1845	1967	190	5/-	C

CORREY, LEE (pseud) See STINE, G. H.

CORWIN, NORMAN (LEWIS) (1910—)

Author and Title	Publisher	Serial	Date	Pp.	Price	Type
Selected Radio Plays	Armed	T-7	nd		np	C

CORY, HOWARD L. (pseud) See JARDINE, J. O.

COULSON, JUANITA (RUTH) (1933—)

Author and Title	Publisher	Serial	Date	Pp.	Price	Type
Crisis on Cheiron	Ace	H-27*	1967	129	60¢	
The Singing Stones	Ace	H-77*	1968	132	60¢	

COULSON, ROBERT (1928—)
The Invisibility Affair [with Gene DeWeese, as Thomas Stratton]

Author and Title	Publisher	Serial	Date	Pp.	Price	Type
	Ace	G-645	1967	158	50¢	

The Mind Twisters Affair [with Gene DeWeese, as Thomas Stratton]

Author and Title	Publisher	Serial	Date	Pp.	Price	Type
	Ace	G-663	1967	158	50¢	

COUNSELMAN, MARY E. (1911—)

Author and Title	Publisher	Serial	Date	Pp.	Price	Type
Half in Shadow	Consul	788	1964	189	3/6	C

COVE, JOSEPH W. (1891—) [as Lewis Gibbs]

Author and Title	Publisher	Serial	Date	Pp.	Price	Type
Late Final	Digit	R487	1961	156	2/6	R

COX, ERLE (1873—1950)

Author and Title	Publisher	Serial	Date	Pp.	Price	Type
Fool's Harvest	Robertson & Mullen		1939	194	2/-	

COZZENS, JAMES G. (1903—)

Author and Title	Publisher	Serial	Date	Pp.	Price	Type
Castaway	Armed	s-4	nd		np	R
	Bantam	1007	1952	121	25¢	R
	Corgi	1007	1952	121	2/-	R
	Modern Lib	P7	1957	182	95¢	C,R

Author and Title	Publisher	Serial	Date	Pp.	Price	Type
CRANE, ROBERT (pseud) See GLEMSER, B.						
CRANE, STEPHEN (1871—1900) See HALDEMAN-JULIUS CO., page 790.						
CRAWFORD, WILLIAM (1911—)						
The Garden of Fear	Crawford		1945	79	25¢	A
CREASEY, JOHN (1908—1973)						
The Black Spiders	Corgi	SC1238	1962	158	2/6	R
The Children of Despair	Jay Books	31	1958	188	2/6	R
Dark Peril	Arrow	779	1964	192	2/6	R
The Depths	Hodder	2485	1967	190	3/6	R
	Berkley	X1613	1968	175	60¢	R
The Flood	Hodder	C350	1958	191	2/6	R
The Inferno	Berkley	X1627	1968	192	60¢	R
	Hodder	2790	1967	190	3/6	R
The League of Light	Arrow	717	1963	192	2/6	R
The Man Who Shook the World						
	Suspense	J32	1958	191	3/3	R
	Arrow	718	1963	192	2/6	R
The Mists of Fear	FSB	868	1963	223	2/6	R
The Peril Ahead	Arrow	780	1964	192	2/6	R
The Perilous Country	Arrow	862	1966	192	3/6	R
The Plague of Silence	Hodder	542	1962	188	2/6	R
The Sons of Satan	Arrow	699	1963	190	2/6	R
The Terror	Hodder	772	1966	191	3/6	R
	Berkley	X1639	1968	159	60¢	R
CRISP, FRANK (1915—)						
The Night Callers	Panther	1276	1961	156	2/6	R
CRISPIN, EDMUND (pseud) See MONTGOMERY, R. B.						
CROMPTON, RICHMAL (1890—1969)						
Richard and the Moon Rocket						
	Merlin	M-37	1968		2/6	J
Richard and the Space Animal						
	Merlin	M-18	1967		2/6	J
CRONIN, BERNARD C. (1884—late 1960's) [as Eric North]						
The Ant Men	Macfadden	60-277	1967	175	60¢	R
CROSBY, HARRY C. [as Christopher Anvil]						
The Day the Machines Stopped						
	Monarch	478	1964	124	40¢	
CROSS, GENE						
Nude in Orbit	Nightstand	NB1883	1968	160	95¢	
CROSS, JOHN KEIR (1914—1967)						
Best Black Magic Stories	Faber		1963	269	6/-	A,R
Best Horror Stories	Faber		1962	300	6/-	A,R
The Other Passenger	Ballantine	480K	1961	159	35¢	C,R
CROSSEN, KENDELL FOSTER (1910—1981)						
Adventures in Tomorrow	Belmont	B75-215	1968	236	75¢	A,R
The Rest Must Die [As Richard Foster]						
	Gold Medal	s853	1959	176	35¢	
	Muller	GM462	1960	160	2/-	R
Year of Consent	Dell	32	1954	224	25¢	
CROWN, PETER J. See LEWIS, PETE (pseud)						
CRUMLEY, THOMAS W.						
Star Trail	Vega	VSF14	1966	158	50¢	
CUMMINGS, M(ONETTE) A.						
Exile and Other Tales of Fantasy						
	Flagship	00864	1968	160	60¢	C

Author and Title	Publisher	Serial	Date	Pp.	Price	Type
CUMMMINGS, RAY (1887—1957)						
Beyond the Stars	Ace	F-248	1963	160	40¢	M
Beyond the Vanishing Point						
	Ace	D-331*	1958	95	35¢	M
A Brand New World	Ace	F-313	1964	158	40¢	M
Brigands of the Moon	Duchess		nd	191	25¢	R
(Duchess edition wrongly credited to J. W. Campbell, Jr.)						
	Ace	D-324	1958	224	35¢	R
	Consul	1481	1966	191	3/6	R
The Exile of Time	Ace	F-343	1965	157	40¢	M
The Man on the Meteor	Swan		nd	125	1/-	M
The Man Who Mastered Time						
	Ace	D-173*	1956	172	35¢	M
The Princess of the Atom	Avon	FN1	1950	158	25¢	R
The Shadow Girl	Ace	D-535	1962	159	35¢	R
Tama of the Light Country	Ace	F-363	1965	124	40	M
Tama, Princess of Mercury	Ace	F-406	1966	128	40¢	M
Wandl the Invader	Ace	D-497*	1961	135	35¢	M
CUNNINGHAM, E. V. (pseud) See FAST, H.						
CURTIS, PETER (pseud) See LOFTS, N.						
CURTIS, RICHARD (ALAN) (1937—)						
Future Tense	Dell	2769	1968	220	60¢	A
CUSACK, FRANK						
True Australian Ghost Stories						
	Pacific	101	1968	177	80¢	N,C,R

D

Author and Title	Publisher	Serial	Date	Pp.	Price	Type
DAGMAR, PETER						
Alien Skies	Digit	R605	1962	160	2/6	
Once in Time	Digit	R746	1963	160	2/6	
The Sands of Time	Digit	R696	1963	155	2/6	
Spykos 4	Digit	R609	1962	154	2/6	
DAHL, ROALD (1916—)						
Kiss, Kiss	Dell	F128	1961	288	50¢	C,R
	Dell	4752	1965	223	60¢	C,R
	Penguin	1832	1962	233	3/6	C,R
	Penguin	1832	1966	233	4/6	C,R
Someone Like You	Dell	F139	1961	320	50¢	C,R
	Dell	8116	1965	253	60¢	C,R
	FSB	1229	1965	252	3/6	C,R
DALE, CORLEY						
Chief Sexecutive	Greenleaf 'Adult'					
		AB417	1968			
DALY, C. J.						
The Legion of the Living Dead						
	Popular Pub		1947	96	1/-	
DANE, D. See CHAMPION LIBRARY, page 789.						
DANFORTH, MILDRED						
From Outer Space	Digit	R760	1963	160	2/6	

Author and Title	Publisher	Serial	Date	Pp.	Price	Type
DANIELS, NORMAN A.						
Cold Death See DENT, L.						
Murder Melody See DENT, L.						
Spy Ghost	Pyramid	R1190	1965	126	50¢	
DARAUL, ARKON						
Witches and Sorcerers	Tandem	T35	1965	224	5/-	N
DARK, JAMES (pseud) See WORKMAN, J.						
DARLINGTON, W(ILLIAM) A. (1890—)						
Alf's Button	Collins	Thriller 15	nd	128	np	R
DAVENPORT, BASIL (1905—1966)						
Deals With the Devil	Ballantine	326K	1959	160	35¢	A
	Ballantine	U2828	1966	160	50¢	A,R
Ghostly Tales To Be Told	Faber		1963	320	7/6	A,R
Horror Stories From Tales To Be Told in the Dark						
	Ballantine	380K	1960	159	35¢	A,R
	Ballantine	U2807	1965	159	50¢	A,R
Invisible Men	Ballantine	401K	1960	158	35¢	A
	Ballantine	U2842	1966	158	50¢	A,R
Tales To Be Told in the Dark						
	Faber		1967	288	7/6	A
DAVENTRY, LEONARD (1915—)						
A Man of Double Deed	Pan	X650	1967	174	3/6	R
	Berkley	X1491	1967	159	60¢	R
DAVID, JAY						
The Flying Saucer Reader	Signet	T3278	1967	252	75¢	N
DAVIDSON, AVRAM (1923—)						
The Best From Fantasy and Science Fiction, Twelfth Series						
	Ace	G-611	1967	254	50¢	A,R
	Panther	2275	1967	176	3/6	A,R
The Best From Fantasy and Science Fiction, 13th Series						
	Ace	H-26	1967	256	60¢	A,R
	Panther	026185	1968	219	5/-	A,R
The Best From Fantasy and Science Fiction, 14th Series						
	Ace	A-17	1968	255	75¢	A,R
Clash of Star-Kings	Ace	G-576*	1966	105	50¢	
The Enemy of My Enemy	Berkley	X1341	1966	160	60¢	
Joyleg [with W. Moore]	Pyramid	F805	1962	160	40¢	M
The Kar-Chee Reign	Ace	G-574*	1966	138	50¢	
Masters of the Maze	Pyramid	R1208	1965	156	50¢	
Mutiny in Space	Pyramid	R1069	1964	159	50¢	M
Or All the Seas With Oysters						
	Berkley	F639	1962	176	50¢	C
Rogue Dragon	Ace	F-353	1965	142	40¢	M
Rork!	Berkley	F1146	1965	144	50¢	
What Strange Stars and Skies						
	Ace	F-330	1965	188	40¢	C
DAVIES, FREDERICK (pseud) See ELLIK, R.						
DAVIES, L(ESLIE) P(URNELL) (1914—)						
The Artificial Man	Mayflower	113087	1968	170	3/6	R
	Scholastic	TK 1248	1968	253	60¢	R
Man Out of Nowhere	Mayflower	112625	1968	175	3/6	R
The Paper Dolls	Signet	P3027	1966	176	60¢	R
	Mayflower	6840	1967	157	3/6	R
Psychogeist	Mayflower	7175	1967	188	5/-	R
	Tower	44115	1968	218	75¢	R
DAVIES, VALENTINE (1905—1961)						
It Happens Every Spring	Avon	249	1950	126	25¢	R
Miracle on 34th Street	Pocket Bks	903	1952	117	25¢	R

Author and Title	Publisher	Serial	Date	Pp.	Price	Type
DAVIS, RICHARD						
Tandem Horror 2	Tandem	T198	1968	192	3/6	A
DAY, L. See BOY'S FRIEND LIBRARY, page 789.						
DE BIBIENA, JEAN GALLI						
Amorous Philandre	Avon	171	1948	124	25¢	
DE CAMP, L(YON) SPRAGUE (1907—) See also HOWARD, R. E.						
The Carnelian Cube [with F. Pratt]						
	Lancer	73-62	1967	222	60¢	R
The Castle of Iron [with F. Pratt]						
	Pyramid	F722	1962	159	40¢	R
Conan of the Isles [with L. Carter]						
	Lancer	73-800	1968	189	60¢	
Conan series [subedited, check HOWARD, R. E.]						
Cosmic Manhunt (also titled *A Planet Named Krishna*)						
	Ace	D-61*	1954	128	35¢	M
Divide and Rule	Lancer	72-768	1964	160	50¢	C,R
The Fantastic Swordsmen	Pyramid	R1621	1967	204	50¢	A
The Floating Continent (originally *The Search for Zei*)						
	Compact	F321	1966	158	3/6	R
Genus Homo [with P. S. Miller]						
	Berkley	G536	1961	157	35¢	R
The Goblin Tower	Pyramid	T1927	1968	253	75¢	
The Hand of Zei	Ace	F-249*	1963	113	40¢	R
The Incomplete Enchanter [with F. Pratt]						
	Pyramid	G530	1960	192	35¢	R
	Pyramid	F723	1962	192	40¢	R
	Pyramid	X1928	1968	192	60¢	R
Lest Darkness Fall	Galaxy Nov	24	1955	125	35¢	R
	Pyramid	F817	1963	174	40¢	R
A Planet Named Krishna (originally *Cosmic Manhunt*)						
	Compact	F311	1966	158	3/6	R
Rogue Queen	Dell	600	1952	192	25¢	R
	Pinnacle	nn	1954	160	2/-	R
	Ace	F-333	1965	189	40¢	R
The Search for Zei (also titled *The Floating Continent*)						
	Ace	F-249*	1963	143	40¢	R
The Spell of Seven	Pyramid	R1192	1965	192	50¢	A
Sprague de Camp's New Anthology of Science Fiction						
	Panther	92	1953	159	1/6	C
(identical hardcover edition 7/6 [editor—H. J. Campbell])						
Swords and Sorcery	Pyramid	F950	1963	186	40¢	A
	Pyramid	R950	1963	186	50¢	A,R
The Tower of Zanid	Airmont	SF2	1963	128	35¢	R
The Tritonian Ring	Paperback	53-618	1968	224	60¢	R
DE LA MARE, WALTER (1873—1956)						
The Return	Penguin	38	1936	254	6d	R
	Pan	270	1954	221	2/-	R
Some Stories	Faber		1962	192	6/-	C,R
DE ROUEN, REED						
Split Image	Panther	763	1958	160	2/-	R
	Digit	R728	1963	160	2/6	R
DE TIMMS, GRAEME						
Split	Digit	R807	1963	160	2/6	
Three Quarters	Digit	R740	1963	158	2/6	
DE VET, CHARLES V. (1911—)						
Cosmic Checkmate [with K. MacLean]						
	Ace	F-149*	1962	96	40¢	M
DEAKIN, BASIL						
The Menace of Mask	Spitfire		1967	128	np	J
DEANE, HAMILTON [with John L. Balderston]						
Dracula	French		late 1940's	109		

Author and Title	Publisher	Serial	Date	Pp.	Price	Type
DEE, ROGER (pseud) See AYCOCK, R. D.						
DEEGAN, JON J. (pseud) See SHARP, R. (G.)						
DEER, M. J. (pseud) See SMITH, GEORGE H.						
DEFOE, DANIEL (1659—1731)						
Tales of Piracy, Crimes and Ghosts	Penguin—US	554	1945	247	25¢	C
deFORD, MIRIAM ALLEN (1888—1975)						
Space, Time and Crime	Paperback	52502	1964	174	50¢	A
	Paperback	52622	1968	174	50¢	A,R
DeGRAEFF, ALLEN (pseud) See CONKLIN, G.						
DEIGHTON, LEN						
Billion-Dollar Brain	Penguin	2662	1967	255	5/-	R
DEL MARTIA, ASTRON (pseud) See FEARN, J. R.						
DEL REY, LESTER (1915—)						
. . . And Some Were Human						
	Ballantine	552	1961	160	35¢	C,R
Badge of Infamy (combined with *The Sky Is Falling*)						
	Magabook	1*	1963	76	50¢	M
Day of the Giants	Airmont	SF5	1964	128	40¢	R
The Eleventh Commandment						
	Regency	RB113	1962	159	50¢	
Marooned on Mars	Paperback	52-415	1967	158	50¢	J,R
Mortals and Monsters	Ballantine	U2236	1965	188	50¢	C
	Tandem	T88	1967	192	3/6	C,R
Nerves	Ballantine	151	1956	153	35¢	M
(identical hardcover edition $2.00)						
	Ballantine	U2344	1966	153	50¢	R
Robots and Changelings	Ballantine	246	1958	175	35¢	C
Rockets Through Space	Premier	d93	1960	192	50¢	N,R
The Runaway Robot	Scholastic	TX863	1966	188	50¢	R
The Scheme of Things	Belmont	B50-682	1966	157	50¢	
Siege Perilous	Lancer	73-468	1966	157	60¢	
The Sky Is Falling (combined with *Badge of Infamy*)						
	Magabook	1*	1963	182	50¢	C,R
Step to the Stars	Paperback	52-955	1966	160	50¢	J,R
Tunnel Through Time	Scholastic	TX1065	1967	160	50¢	J,R
DELANY, SAMUEL R. (1942—)						
Babel-17	Ace	F-388	1966	173	40¢	
The Ballad of Beta2	Ace	M-121*	1965	96	45¢	
Captives of the Flame (revised as *Out of the Dead City*)						
	Ace	F-199*	1963	147	40¢	
City of a Thousand Suns	Ace	F-322	1965	156	40¢	
The Einstein Intersection	Ace	F-427	1967	142	40¢	
Empire Star	Ace	M-139*	1966	102	45¢	
The Jewels of Aptor	Ace	F-173*	1962	156	40¢	
	Ace	G-706	1968	159	50¢	
Out of the Dead City (revision of *Captives of the Flame*)						
	Sphere	28835	1968	143	5/-	
The Towers of Toron	Ace	F-261*	1964	140	40¢	
	Sphere	28843	1968	140	5/-	R
DELL, JEFFREY						
News for Heaven	Consul	1290	1964	190	3/6	R
DELRAY, CHESTER						
Realm of the Alien	Grafton		ca.1945		64	7d
DEMPSTER, D. D. See GATLAND, K. W. (co-author)						
DENHAM, ALICE						
The Ghost and Mrs. Muir	Popular	602348	1968	127	60¢	R

Author and Title	Publisher	Serial	Date	Pp.	Price	Type
DENIS, ARMAND						
Taboo	Berkley	S1464	1967	172	75¢	
DENNIS, NIGEL (1912—)						
Cards of Identity	Penguin	1468	1960	302	3/6	R
	Signet	P2431	1964	272	60¢	R
DENT, LESTER (1905—1959) [as Kenneth Robeson, for Doc Savage series only; several of these were by other authors, as noted, but are included here for completeness]						
The Annihilist	Bantam	F3885	1968	138	50¢	M
Brand of the Werewolf	Bantam	E3016	1965	138	45¢	M
	Bantam	F3573	1967	138	50¢	R
Cold Death [actually by Norman A. Daniels]						
	Bantam	F3584	1968	121	50¢	M
The Czar of Fear	Bantam	F3667	1968	140	50¢	M
The Deadly Dwarf (magazine title was "Repel")						
	Bantam	F3839	1968	115	50¢	M
Death in Silver	Bantam	F3805	1968	134	50¢	M
The Devil's Playground (actually by Alan Hathway)						
	Bantam	F3841	1968	119	50¢	M
The Fantastic Island	Bantam	F3269	1966	135	50¢	M
Fear Cay	Bantam	E3146	1966	138	45¢	M
	Bantam	F3455	1967	138	50¢	R
The Flaming Falcons	Bantam	F3897	1968	118	50¢	M
Fortress of Solitude	Bantam	F3716	1968	116	50¢	M
The Green Eagle	Bantam	F3782	1968	114	50¢	M
Land of Always-Night	Bantam	E3202	1966	138	45¢	M
	Bantam	F3520	1967	138	50¢	R
The Land of Terror	Bantam	E3042	1965	155	45¢	M
The Lost Oasis	Bantam	E3017	1965	123	45¢	M
	Bantam	F3498	1967	123	50¢	R
The Man of Bronze	Bantam	E2853	1964	135	45¢	M
	Bantam	F3496	1967	135	50¢	R
Meteor Menace	Bantam	E2855	1964	140	45¢	M
The Monsters	Bantam	E3033	1965	138	45¢	M
	Bantam	F3499	1967	138	50¢	R
Murder Melody [actually by Norman A. Daniels]						
	Bantam	F3755	1968	120	50¢	M
The Mystic Mullah	Bantam	E3115	1965	137	45¢	M
	Bantam	F3464	1967	137	50¢	R
The Other World	Bantam	F3877	1968	119	50¢	M
The Phantom City	Bantam	E3047	1966	137	45¢	M
	Bantam	F3047	1967	137	50¢	R
Pirate of the Pacific	Bantam	F3486	1967	136	50¢	M
The Polar Treasure	Bantam	E3015	1965	122	45¢	M
Quest of Qui	Bantam	E3110	1966	119	45¢	M
	Bantam	F3456	1967	119	50¢	R
The Red Skull	Bantam	F3387	1967	124	50¢	M
The Sargasso Ogre	Bantam	F3441	1967	140	50¢	M
The Secret in the Sky	Bantam	F3533	1967	119	50¢	M
The Spook Legion	Bantam	F3340	1967	122	50¢	M
The Thousand-Headed Man						
	Bantam	E2854	1964	150	45¢	M
DERLETH, AUGUST W. (1909—1971)						
Beachheads in Space (see also *From Other Worlds*)						
	Berkley	G77	1957	190	35¢	A,R
	FSB	1073	1964	219	3/6	A,R
Beyond Time and Space	Berkley	G104	1958	174	35¢	A,R
Dark Mind, Dark Heart	Mayflower	1655	1963	222	3/6	A,R
	Mayflower	1655	1966	222	5/-	A,R
Far Boundaries	Consul	1443	1965	233	3/6	A,R
	Sphere	28924	1967	219	3/6	A,R
From Other Worlds (derived from U.S. hardcover edition of *Beachheads in Space*)						
	FSB	1107	1964	186	3/6	A,R
The Mask of Cthulhu	Consul	HS1036	1961	175	2/6	C,R
Mr. George and Other Odd Persons (also titled *When Graveyards Yawn*)						
	Belmont	L92-594	1964	176	50¢	C,R

Author and Title	Publisher	Serial	Date	Pp.	Price	Type
New Worlds for Old (derived from U.S. hardcover edition of *Worlds of*						
Tomorrow)	FSB	842	1963	126	1/6	A,R
The Night Side	FSB	1657	1966	270	5/-	A,R
Night's Yawning Peal	Consul	1368	1965	160	3/6	A,R
Not Long for This World	Ballantine	542	1961	159	35¢	C,R
The Other Side of the Moon	Berkley	G249	1959	172	35¢	A,R
	Panther	1541	1963	144	2/6	A,R
	Mayflower	6740	1966	159	3/6	A,R
The Outer Reaches (see also *The Time of Infinity*)						
	Berkley	G116	1958	174	35¢	A,R
	Consul	1267	1963	173	2/6	A,R
Sleep No More	Armed	R-33	1944	384	np	A,R
	Panther	1770	1964	188	3/6	A,R
	Panther	1770	1965	188	3/6	A,R
	Bantam	H3425	1967	148	60¢	A,R
The Sleeping and the Dead (see also *The Unquiet Grave*)						
	FSB	943	1963	253	3/6	A,R
Some Notes on H. P. Lovecraft						
	Arkham		1959	42	$1.25	N
Strange Ports of Call	Berkley	G131	1958	173	35¢	A,R
The Time of Infinity (derived from U.S. hardcover edition of *The*						
Outer Reaches)	Consul	1268	1963	205	2/6	A,R
Time to Come	Berkley	G189	1958	172	35¢	A,R
	Consul	1239	1963	190	3/6	A,R
	Tower	43-461	1965	221	60¢	A,R
The Unquiet Grave (derived from U.S. hardcover edition of *The Sleep-*						
ing and the Dead)	FSB	982	1964	254	3/6	A,R
When Evil Wakes	Corgi	GN7107	1965	223	3/6	A,R
When Graveyards Yawn (originally *Mr. George and Other Odd Persons*)						
	Tandem	T30	1965	176	3/6	C,R
Who Knocks?	Panther	1769	1964	191	3/6	A,R
Worlds of Tomorrow (see also *New Worlds for Old*)						
	Berkley	G163	1958	172	35¢	A,R
	FSB	794	1963	160	2/6	A,R

DESMOND, HUGH

Author and Title	Publisher	Serial	Date	Pp.	Price	Type
A Pact With the Devil	Streamline	1	*ca.*1950	96	6d	

DETZER, DIANE (1930—) [as Adam Lukens]

Author and Title	Publisher	Serial	Date	Pp.	Price	Type
Sons of the Wolf	Consul	1207	1963	158	3/6	R

DeWEESE, GENE See COULSON, R. (co-author)

DEXTER, J. B. (pseud) See GLASBY., J. S.

DEXTER, JOHN (house pseud)

Author and Title	Publisher	Serial	Date	Pp.	Price	Type
Carnaby Consort	Leisure	LB1175	1966			
Garden of Shame	Ember Lib	EL323	1966	159		
The Sin Veldt	Leisure	LB1152	1966	160		
The Sinners of Hwang	Leisure	LB1106	1965	160		

DICK, PHILIP K. (1928—1982)

Author and Title	Publisher	Serial	Date	Pp.	Price	Type
Clans of the Alphane Moon	Ace	F-309	1964	192	40¢	
The Cosmic Puppets	Ace	D-249*	1957	127	35¢	M
Counter-Clock World	Berkley	X1372	1967	160	60¢	
	Sphere	19564	1968	160	5/-	R
The Crack in Space	Ace	F-377	1966	190	40¢	M
Dr. Bloodmoney, Or How We Got Along After the Bomb						
	Ace	F-337	1965	222	40¢	
Dr. Futurity	Ace	D-421*	1960	138	35¢	M
Eye in the Sky	Ace	D-211	1957	255	35¢	
	Ace	H-39	1968	255	60¢	R
The Game-Players of Titan	Ace	F-251	1963	191	40¢	
The Ganymede Takeover [with Ray Nelson]						
	Ace	G-637	1967	157	50¢	
A Handful of Darkness	Panther	2108	1966	186	3/6	C,R
The Man in the High Castle						
	Popular	SP250	1964	191	50¢	R
	Popular	60-2289	1968	191	60¢	R
	Penguin	2376	1965	236	5/-	R

Author and Title	Publisher	Serial	Date	Pp.	Price	Type
The Man Who Japed	Ace	D-193*	1956	160	35¢	
Martian Time-Slip	Ballantine	U2191	1964	220	50¢	M
Now Wait for Last Year	Macfadden	60352	1968	224	60¢	R
The Penultimate Truth	Belmont	92-603	1964	174	50¢	
The Simulacra	Ace	F-301	1964	192	40¢	
Solar Lottery (also titled *World of Chance*)						
	Ace	D-103*	1955	188	35¢	
	Ace	D-340	1959	188	35¢	R
	Ace	G-718	1968	188	50¢	R
The Three Stigmata of Palmer Eldritch						
	Macfadden	60-240	1966	191	60¢	R
Time out of Joint	Belmont	92-618	1965	175	50¢	R
The Unteleported Man	Ace	G-602*	1966	100	50¢	M
The Variable Man and Other Stories						
	Ace	D-261	1957	255	35¢	C
Vulcan's Hammer	Ace	D-457*	1960	139	35¢	M
The World Jones Made	Ace	D-150*	1956	192	35¢	
	Ace	F-429	1967	192	40¢	R
World of Chance (originally *Solar Lottery*)						
	Panther	785	1958	156	2/6	R
The Zap Gun	Pyramid	R1569	1967	176	50¢	M

DICKENS, CHARLES (1812—1870) See HALDEMAN-JULIUS
  CO., page 790.

DICKINSON, H. O.

Author and Title	Publisher	Serial	Date	Pp.	Price	Type
The Sex Serum	Utopian	AF9	nd	36	1/-	C

DICKSON, CARTER (pseud) See CARR, J. D.

DICKSON, GORDON R. (1923—)

Author and Title	Publisher	Serial	Date	Pp.	Price	Type
Alien From Arcturus	Ace	D-139*	1956	150	35¢	
The Alien Way	Bantam	F2941	1965	184	50¢	M
Delusion World	Ace	F-119*	1961	100	40¢	
The Genetic General	Ace	D-449*	1960	149	35¢	M
	Ace	F-426	1967	159	40¢	R
	Digit	R437	1961	156	2/-	R
Mankind on the Run	Ace	D-164*	1956	151	35¢	
Mission to Universe	Berkley	F1147	1965	175	50¢	
Naked to the Stars	Pyramid	F682	1961	159	40¢	M
Necromancer (also titled *No Room for Man*)						
	Mayflower	0799	1963	190	3/6	R
No Room for Man (originally *Necromancer*)						
	Macfadden	50-179	1963	158	50¢	R
	Macfadden	50-329	1966	158	50¢	R
Planet Run [with K. Laumer]						
	Berkley	X1588	1968	143	60¢	R
Secret Under the Sea	Scholastic	TX959	1966	128	45¢	R
Soldier, Ask Not	Dell	8090	1967	222	60¢	M
The Space Swimmers	Berkley	X1371	1967	160	60¢	
Spacial Delivery	Ace	F-119*	1961	123	40¢	M
Time to Teleport	Ace	D-449*	1960	60	35¢	M

DIKTY, T(HADDEUS) E. (1920—)

Author and Title	Publisher	Serial	Date	Pp.	Price	Type
Five Tales From Tomorrow (abridgment of *Best Science Fiction Stories*						
and Novels 1955)	Crest	s197	1957	176	35¢	A,R
	Crest	d597	1963	176	50¢	A,R
	Crest	D996	1967	176	50¢	A,R
Frontiers in Space [with E. F. Bleiler]						
	Bantam	1328	1955	166	25¢	A,R
Imagination Unlimited [with E. F. Bleiler]						
	Berkley	G233	1959	172	35¢	A,R
	Mayflower	3985	1964	190	3/6	A,R
6 From Worlds Beyond (abridgment of *Best Science Fiction Stories and*						
Novels 1956)	Crest	s258	1958	160	35¢	A,R

DINESEN, ISAK (pseud) See BLIXEN, K.

DINGWALL, ERIC J.

Author and Title	Publisher	Serial	Date	Pp.	Price	Type
The Unknown—Is It Nearer? [with J. Langdon-Davies]						
	Signet	Ks336	1956	160	35¢	N

Author and Title	Publisher	Serial	Date	Pp.	Price	Type
DISCH, THOMAS M. (1940—)						
Echo Round His Bones	Berkley	X1349	1967	144	60¢	M
The Genocides	Berkley	F1170	1965	143	50¢	
	Panther	024204	1968	188	5/-	R
Mankind Under the Leash	Ace	G-597*	1966	140	50¢	M
One Hundred and Two H-Bombs						
	Compact	F327	1967	192	3/6	C
DIVINE, ARTHUR D. (1904—)						
Atom at Spithead [as David Divine]						
	Hale		1955	160	2/-	R
Tunnel From Calais [as David Rame]						
	Armed	t-22	nd	np		R
DIVINE, DAVID (pseud) See DIVINE, ARTHUR D.						
DIXON, RICHARD						
Destination: Amaltheia	FLPH		1963	420	np	A
DONNELLY, IGNATIUS (1831—1901)						
Atlantis: The Antediluvian World						
	Xanadu		1963	355	$1.65	N,R
DORNBERGER, WALTER (1895—1980)						
V-2	Panther	747	1958	192	2/6	N,R
	Ballantine	273K	1958	237	50¢	N,R
DOUGLAS, BRYAN						
Great Stories of Mystery and Imagination						
	Fontana	1324	1966	224	3/6	A
DOYLE, A. CONAN (1859—1930)						
The Land of Mist	Consul	1212	1963	223	3/6	R
The Lost World	Pan	100	1949	224	2/-	R
	Pan	100(2 ed)	1950	224	2/-	R
	Pan	100	1952	224	2/-	R
	Pan	100	1953	224	2/-	R
	Pan	100	1955	224	2/-	R
	Harlequin	238	1953			R
	Permabks	279	1954	200	25¢	R
	Pyramid	PR15	1959	192	35¢	R
	Pyramid	G514	1960	192	35¢	R
	Pyramid	F713	1962	192	40¢	R
	Murray		1960	215	3/6	R
	Berkley	F1162	1965	176	50¢	R
The Maracot Deep	Murray		1961	153	3/-	R
	Murray		1968	153	3/6	R
The Poison Belt	Berkley	F1203	1966	158	50¢	R
Tales of Terror and Mystery						
	Murray		1968	190		C
When the World Screamed	Murray		1968	173	5/-	R
DRACHMAN, T. S.						
Cry Plague!	Ace	D-13*	1953	153	35¢	
DRING, NAT						
The Earth Is Your Spaceship						
	Space Age		1967	118	$1.89	
(identical hardcover edition $2.95)						
DRUCKER, PETER F.						
The Future of Industrial Man						
	Mentor	MT625	1965	208	75¢	N
DRURY, ALLEN (1918—)						
Advise and Consent	Pocket Bks	GC952	1961	760	95¢	R
	Corgi	EN1239	1962	624	7/-	R
Capable of Honor	Dell	1031	1968	603	$1.25	R
A Shade of Difference	Pocket Bks	GC961	1963	773	95¢	R

Author and Title	Publisher	Serial	Date	Pp.	Price	Type
DU BOIS, THEODORA (1890—)						
Solution t-25	Kemsley	CT411	1952	190	1/6	R
DU MAURIER, DAPHNE (1907—)						
Kiss Me Again, Stranger	?		1956		35¢	C,R
DUKE, MADELAINE (1925—)						
Claret, Sandwiches and Sin	FSB	1564	1966	143	3/6	R
DUNCAN, BRUCE (pseud) See GREENFIELD, I. A.						
DUNCAN, DAVID (1913—)						
Beyond Eden	Ballantine	102	1955	169	35¢	
(identical hardcover edition $2.00)						
Dark Dominion	Ballantine	56	1954	206	35¢	
(identical hardcover edition $2.50)						
	Consul	SF1021	1961	221	2/6	R
Occam's Razor	Ballantine	230	1957	165	35¢	
	FSB	646	1962	160	2/6	R
DUNKEE, D. See CHAMPION LIBRARY, page 789.						
DUNN, J. A. See BOY'S FRIEND LIBRARY, page 789.						
DUNSANY, LORD (1878—1957)						
Carcassonne	Luce		nd	32	np	R
[special edition, very scarce]						
The Fourth Book of Jorkens						
	Jarrolds	'Cresta'	nd	176	np	C,R
DUTHIE, ERIC						
Tall Short Stories	Ace	K-113	1960	352	50¢	A,R
DUTOURD, JEAN (1920—)						
A Dog's Head	Lion	196	1954	128	25¢	R
	Avon	H102	1963	127	45¢	R
DYE, CHARLES (1927—1960?)						
Prisoner in the Skull	Corgi	S486	1957	219	2/6	R

E

Author and Title	Publisher	Serial	Date	Pp.	Price	Type
EARLE, RICHARD						
Forever Ember	Bee-Line	133	1966	157		
EBERLE, MERAB						
The Thought Translator	Stellar	SFS9	1930	17	10¢	
(part of booklet also containing "The Creation," M. Mitchell)						
EDDISON, E(RIC) R. (1882—1945)						
A Fish Dinner in Memison	Ballantine	U7064	1968	319	95¢	R
Mistress of Mistresses	Ballantine	U7063	1967	405	95¢	R
The Worm Ouroboros	Xanadu	X5	1962	446	$1.95	R
	Ballantine	U7061	1967	520	95¢	R
EDEL, LEON						
Ghostly Tales of Henry James						
	Univ. Lib.	UL-161	1963	433	$2.25	C,R
EDEN, DOROTHY						
Cat's Prey	Hodder	779	1966	191	3/6	
The Voice of the Dolls	Hodder	780	1966	191	3/6	

Author and Title	Publisher	Serial	Date	Pp.	Price	Type
EDGAR, ALFRED See BOY'S FRIEND LIBRARY, page 789.						
EDGAR, PETER (pseud) See KING-SCOTT, PETER						
EDGLEY, LESLIE						
The Judas Goat	Ace	D-13*	1953	166	35¢	
EDMONDSON, G. C. (1917—)						
The Ship That Sailed the Time Stream						
	Ace	M-109*	1965	167	45¢	
Stranger Than You Think	Ace	M-109*	1965	87	45¢	C
"EDWARD"						
The Laboratory Medium	Biddle		nd	12	np	
EDWARDS, FRANK (1908—1968?)						
Flying Saucers—Here and Now						
	Bantam	S3631	1968	162	75¢	N
Flying Saucers—Serious Business						
	Bantam	S3378	1966	185	75¢	N
	Mayflower	2627	1967	192	5/-	N
Strange People	Popular	PC1046	1965	191	50¢	N,R
	Pan	X484	1966	236	3/6	N,R
Strange World	Ace	K-206	1965	251	50¢	N,R
Stranger Than Science	Ace	K-117	1959	224	50¢	N
	Bantam	H3469	1967	181	60¢	N,R
	Bantam	S4323	1968	180	75¢	N,R
	Pan	X252	1963	207	3/6	N,R
Strangest of All	Ace	K-144	1962	189	50¢	N
EDWARDS, NORMAN (pseud) See CARR, T., and WHITE, TED						
EENHOORN, MICHAEL						
An Omnibus of American Mysteries						
	Juniper		1959	383	$1.45	A
EHRLICH, MAX (1909—)						
The Big Eye	Popular	273	1950	223	25¢	R
	Boardman	149	1954	192	2/-	R
	Bantam	A1860	1958	181	35¢	R
	Corgi	SS844	1960	252	2/6	R
EINSTEIN, CHARLES (1926—)						
The Day New York Went Dry						
	Gold Medal	k1446	1964	160	40¢	
ELAM, RICHARD M. Jr. (1920—)						
Science Fiction Stories (originally *Young Readers Science Fiction Stories*)	Lantern	50096	1964	212	50¢	C,R
Super Science Stories (originally *Teen-Age Super Science Stories*)	Lantern	50526	1967	231	50¢	C,R
ELDRIDGE, PAUL (1888—) See VIERECK, G. S. (co-author)						
ELG, STEFAN						
Beyond Belief	Tower	43-762	1967	155	60¢	N,R
ELIOT, T(HOMAS) S(TEARNS) (1888—1965)						
The Family Reunion	Faber	34	1968	126	30p	R
ELIOTT, E. C. (pseud) See MARTIN, R. A.						
ELLIK, RON (1938—1968)						
The Cross of Gold Affair [with Fredric Langley, as Frederick Davies]	Ace	G-689	1968	156	50¢	
The Universes of E. E. Smith [with B. Evans]	Advent		1968	272	$2.45	N,R
ELLIN, STANLEY						
The Blessington Method	Signet	D2805	1966	127	50¢	C,R
Quiet Horror	Signet	D2806	1965	175	50¢	C
ELLIOT, JOHN See HOYLE, F. (coauthor)						
ELLIOT, LEE (house pseud)						
Bio-Muton See HUGHES, DEN						
Overlord New York	Curtis War.		1953	159	1/6	
(identical hardcover edition)						
The Third Mutant See BIRD, W. H. F.						
ELLIOTT, BRUCE (pseud of Walter Stacy) (1914?—1973)						
Asylum Earth	Belmont	B50-819	1968	157	50¢	M
ELLIOTT, GEORGE						
The Case of the Missing Airman						
	Swan		1944	36	4d	
ELLIOTT, R. C.						
Sabotage	Barrington		1955	128	1/6	
ELLIS, D. E.						
A Thousand Ages	Digit	R549	1961	156	2/6	
	Digit	R757	1963	159	2/6	R
ELLISON, HARLAN (1934—)						
Doomsman	Belmont	B50-779*	1967	74	50¢	
Earthman, Go Home (originally *Ellison Wonderland*)						
	Paperback	52-508	1964	191	50¢	C,R
	Paperback	53-727	1968	191	60¢	C,R
Ellison Wonderland (also titled *Earthman, Go Home*)						
	Paperback	52-149	1962	191	50¢	C
From the Land of Fear	Belmont	B60-069	1967	176	60¢	C
I Have No Mouth and I Must Scream						
	Pyramid	X1611	1967	175	60¢	C
The Man With Nine Lives	Ace	D-413*	1960	133	35¢	M
Paingod and Other Delusions						
	Pyramid	R1270	1965	157	50¢	C
A Touch of Infinity	Ace	D-413*	1959	123	35¢	C
ELTON, JAMES						
The Quest of the Seeker	Badger	SF10	1958	158	2/-	
ELTON, JOHN (pseud) See MARSH, J.						
ELWOOD, ROGER (1943—)						
Alien Worlds	Paperback	52-320	1964	176	50¢	A
	Paperback	53-667	1968	176	60¢	A,R
The Human Zero [with S. Moskowitz]						
	Tower	43-906	1967	224	60¢	A
Invasion of the Robots	Paperback	52-519	1965	157	50¢	A
The Time Curve [with S. Moskowitz]						
	Tower	43-986	1968	189	60¢	A
ELY, DAVID (1927—)						
Seconds	Signet	P2507	1964	159	60¢	R
	FSB	1290	1965	159	3/-	R
EMERSON, CAROLINE D.						
The Magic Tunnel	Scholastic	TX 533	1966	127	45¢	J,R
EMERSON, WILLIS GEORGE (1856—1918)						
The Smoky God	Health Research		1965	186	$4.00	R
	Inspired Nov	D3	1965	176	$2.50	R
ENDORE, GUY (1900—1970)						
The Furies in Her Body (originally *Methinks the Lady*)						
	Avon	323	1951	220	25¢	R
Nightmare (originally *Methinks the Lady*)						
	Dell	D183	1956	256	35¢	R
The Werewolf of Paris	Pocket Bks	97	1941			R
	Avon	354	1951	189	25¢	R
	Ace	K-160	1962	223	50¢	R
	Panther	1555	1963	222	3/6	R

Author and Title	Publisher	Serial	Date	Pp.	Price	Type

ENEY, RICHARD (1932–)
Proceedings of the 21st World Science Fiction Convention: Discon

| | Advent | | 1965 | 191 | $3.50 | N |
| | Advent | | 1966 | 191 | $1.95 | N |

ENGLE, E(LOISE) (1923–)
Countdown for Cindy Bantam J2753 1964 122 40¢ R

ENGLISH, CHARLES (pseud) See NUETZEL, C.

ERSKINE, JOHN (1879–1951)
The Private Life of Helen of Troy

| | Popular | 147 | 1948 | 222 | 25¢ | R |
| | Graphic | G-216 | 1956 | 285 | 35¢ | R |

ESHBACH, LLOYD ARTHUR (1910–)
Of Worlds Beyond Advent 1964 104 $1.95 N,R
(identical hardcover edition $3.50)

ETTINGER, ROBERT C. W. (1918–)
The Prospect of Immortality

| | Macfadden | 75-166 | 1966 | 160 | 75¢ | N,R |

EVANS, BILL See ELLIK, R. (co-author)

EVANS, E. EVERETT (1893–1958)
Man of Many Minds Pyramid G458 1959 192 35¢ R
| | Pyramid | X1891 | 1968 | 192 | 60¢ | R |

EVANS, I(DRISYN) O(LIVER) (1894–) [Also translator of many novels by J. VERNE, *q.v.*]
Science Fiction Through the Ages 1
| | Panther | 2152 | 1966 | 156 | 3/6 | A |
Science Fiction Through the Ages 2
| | Panther | 2159 | 1966 | 173 | 3/6 | A |

EYRE, KATHERINE W(IGMORE) (1901–1970)
The Lute and the Glove Ace K-165 1963 223 50¢ R

F

FABRICANT, DON See CONKLIN, G. (co-anthologist)

FADIMAN, CLIFTON (1904–)
Fantasia Mathematica Simon & Schuster 1962 298 $1.45 A,R
The Mathematical Magpie Simon & Schuster 1963 300 $1.75 A,R

FAGAN, J.
Jules Verne's Rocket to the Moon
| | Horwitz | PB364 | 1967 | 129 | 55¢ | |

FAIRCLOUGH, PETER
Three Gothic Novels Penguin EL36 1968 505 8/- A

FAIRMAN, PAUL W. (1916–1977)
City Under the Sea Pyramid R1162 1965 141 50¢ R
I, the Machine Lancer 73-735 1968 205 60¢
Rest in Agony [as Ivar Jorgensen (pseud)]
| | Monarch | 362 | 1963 | 125 | 35¢ | |
| [as P. Fairman] | Lancer | 74-905 | 1967 | 223 | 75¢ | R |
The World Grabbers Monarch 471 1964 126 40¢

FALKNER, J(OHN) MEADE (1858–1932)
The Lost Stradivarius Penguin 487 1945 157 1/- R

FALKNER, JOHN (pseud of E. F. Gale)
Overlords of Andromeda Panther 193 1955 144 1/6
(identical hardcover edition 6/-)
Untrodden Streets of Time Panther 136 1954 143 1/6
(identical hardcover edition)

FANE, BRON (pseud) See FANTHORPE, R. L.

FANTHORPE, ROBERT L. (1935–)
Alien From the Stars Badger SF15 1959 156 2/-
The Alien Ones [as Leo Brett]
| | Badger | SF94 | 1963 | 158 | 2/6 |
Android [as Karl Zeigfreid (h)]
| | Badger | SF79 | 1962 | 158 | 2/6 |
Asteroid Man Badger SF35 1960 142 2/-
Atomic Nemesis [as Karl Zeigfreid (h)]
| | Badger | SF80 | 1962 | 158 | 2/6 |
Barrier 346 [as Karl Zeigfreid (h)]
| | Badger | SF113 | 1965 | 158 | 2/6 |
Beyond the Veil [as Neil Thanet]
| | Badger | SN86 | 1964 | 160 | 2/6 |
Beyond the Void [as John E. Muller (h)]
| | Badger | SF112 | 1965 | 158 | 2/6 |
Beyond Time [as John E. Muller (h)]
| | Badger | SF71 | 1962 | 158 | 2/6 |
Black Infinity [as Leo Brett]
| | Badger | SN44 | 1961 | 158 | 2/6 |
Chaos [as Thornton Bell] Badger SN92 1964 158 2/6
Crimson Planet [as John E. Muller (h)]
| | Badger | SF60 | 1961 | 158 | 2/6 |
Cyclops in the Sky [as Lionel Roberts]
| | Badger | SF26 | 1960 | 156 | 2/- |
Dark Continuum [as John E. Muller (h)]
| | Badger | SF104 | 1964 | 160 | 2/6 |
Dawn of the Mutants [as Lionel Roberts]
| | Badger | SF18 | 1959 | 156 | 2/- |
The Day the World Died [as John E. Muller (h)]
| | Badger | SF73 | 1962 | 159 | 2/6 |
| | Vega | VSF3 | 1963 | 137 | 50¢ | R |
Destination Moon [as L. P. Kenton (h)]
| | Badger | SF14 | 1959 | 157 | 2/- |
Doomed World Badger SF25 1960 157 2/-
Escape to Infinity [as Karl Zeigfreid (h)]
| | Badger | SF82 | 1963 | 158 | 2/6 |
Exit Humanity [as Leo Brett]
| | Badger | SF40 | 1960 | 142 | 2/- |
The Exorcists [as John E. Muller (h)]
| | Badger | SN94 | 1965 | 158 | 2/6 |
The Eye of Karnak [as John E. Muller (h)]
| | Badger | SN56 | 1962 | 158 | 2/6 |
Face in the Night [as Leo Brett]
| | Badger | SN58 | 1962 | 158 | 2/6 |
The Face of Fear [as Pel Torro]
| | Badger | SN82 | 1963 | 158 | 2/6 |
The Face of X [as Lionel Roberts]
| | Badger | SF39 | 1960 | 141 | 2/- |
Faceless Planet [as Leo Brett]
| | Badger | SF47 | 1960 | 158 | 2/6 |
Fiends Badger SF22 1959 157 2/-
Five Faces of Fear [as Trebor Thorpe]
| | Badger | SN32 | 1960 | 156 | 2/- |
Flame Goddess [as Lionel Roberts]
| | Badger | SN46 | 1961 | 158 | 2/6 |
Flame Mass Badger SF49 1960 158 2/6
The Forbidden [as Leo Brett]
| | Badger | SN72 | 1963 | 158 | 2/6 |

Author and Title	Publisher	Serial	Date	Pp.	Price	Type
Forbidden Planet [as John E. Muller (h)]						
	Badger	SF63	1961	158	2/6	
Force 97X [as Pel Torro]	Badger	SF110	1965	158	2/6	
Formula 29X [as Pel Torro]	Badger	SF87	1963	158	2/6	
From Realms Beyond [as Leo Brett]						
	Badger	SN74	1963	158	2/6	
Frozen Planet [as Pel Torro]						
	Badger	SF42	1960	142	2/-	
Galaxy 666 [as Pel Torro]	Badger	SF86	1963	158	2/6	
The Girl From Tomorrow [as Karl Zeigfreid (h)]						
	Badger	SF114	1966	158	2/6	
Gods of Darkness [as Karl Zeigfreid (h)]						
	Badger	SN64	1962	158	2/6	
The Golden Chalice	Badger	SN50	1961	158	2/6	
Hand of Doom	Badger	SF44	1960	158	2/6	
Hyper Space	Badger	SF17	1959	157	2/-	
The Immortals [as Leo Brett]						
	Badger	SN62	1962	158	2/6	
The In-World [as Lionel Roberts]						
	Badger	SF37	1960	142	2/-	
Infinity Machine [as John E. Muller (h)]						
	Badger	SF72	1962	158	2/6	
The Intruders [as Bron Fane]						
	Badger	SF89	1963	158	2/6	
Juggernaut [as Bron Fane]	Badger	SF41	1960	142	2/-	
The Last Astronaut [as Pel Torro]						
	Badger	SF93	1963	158	2/6	
The Last Man on Earth [as Bron Fane]						
	Badger	SF46	1960	158	2/6	
The Last Valkyrie [as Lionel Roberts]						
	Badger	SN40	1961	158	2/6	
Legion of the Lost [as Pel Torro]						
	Badger	SN66	1962	158	2/6	
Lightning World [as Trebor Thorpe]						
	Badger	SF38	1960	142	2/-	
The Macabre Ones [as Bron Fane]						
	Badger	SN90	1964	160	2/6	
The Man From Beyond [as John E. Muller (h)]						
	Badger	SF111	1965	158	2/6	
The Man Who Came Back [as Neil Thanet]						
	Badger	SN88	1964	158	2/6	
The Man Who Conquered Time [as John E. Muller (h)]						
	Badger	SF68	1962	156	2/6	
March of the Robots [as Leo Brett]						
	Badger	SF53	1961	159	2/6	
Mark of the Beast [as John E. Muller (h)]						
	Badger	SF105	1964	158	2/6	
Menace From Mercury [as Victor La Salle (h)]						
	Spencer	nn	1954	128	1/6	
Micro Infinity [as John E. Muller (h)]						
	Badger	SF70	1962	158	2/6	
The Microscopic Ones [as Leo Brett]						
	Badger	SF43	1960	158	2/6	
Mind Force [as Leo Brett]	Badger	SF54	1961	157	2/6	
The Mind Makers [as John E. Muller (h)]						
	Badger	SF58	1961	158	2/6	
Negative Minus	Badger	SF88	1963	158	2/6	
The Negative Ones [as John E. Muller (h)]						
	Badger	SF109	1965	158	2/6	
Nemesis [as Bron Fane]	Badger	SF100	1964	158	2/6	
Neuron World	Badger	SF108	1965	159	2/6	
Nightmare [as Leo Brett]	Badger	SN54	1962	158	2/6	
No Way Back [as Karl Zeigfreid (h)]						
	Badger	SF107	1964	160	2/6	
Orbit One [as John E. Muller (h)]						
	Badger	SF69	1962	158	2/6	
	Pitt Bond	PB512	1963	130	3/6	R
Out of the Darkness	Badger	SN35	1960	142	2/6	
Out of the Night [as John E. Muller (h)]						
	Badger	SN100	1966	159	3/6	

Author and Title	Publisher	Serial	Date	Pp.	Price	Type
Perilous Galaxy [as John E. Muller (h)]						
	Badger	SF66	1962	160	2/6	
The Phantom Ones [as Pel Torro]						
	Badger	SN48	1961	158	2/6	
Phenomena X [as John E. Muller (h)]						
	Badger	SF116	1966	143	2/6	
The Planet Seekers [as Erle Barton]						
	Badger	SF99	1963	158	2/6	
	Vega	VSF7	1964	158	50¢	R
Power Sphere [as Leo Brett]	Badger	SF95	1963	158	2/6	
Projection Infinity [as Karl Zeigfreid (h)]						
	Badger	SF103	1964	158	2/6	
	Vega	VSF-12	1965	155	60¢	R
Radar Alert [as Karl Zeigfreid (h)]						
	Badger	SF83	1963	157	2/6	
	Vega	VSF4	1963	134	50¢	R
Reactor XK9 [as John E. Muller (h)]						
	Badger	SF96	1963	158	2/6	
The Return [as Pel Torro]	Badger	SF101	1964	158	2/6	
	Vega	VSF10	1964	155	50¢	R
The Return of Zeus [as John E. Muller (h)]						
	Badger	SN52	1962	160	2/6	
Rodent Mutation [as Bron Fane]						
	Badger	SF55	1961	157	2/6	
Satellite	Badger	SF27	1960	157	2/-	
Shadow Man [as Lee Barton]						
	Badger	SN104	1966	158	2/6	
Softly by Moonlight [as Bron Fane]						
	Badger	SN80	1963	158	2/6	
Somewhere Out There [as Bron Fane]						
	Badger	SF92	1963	158	2/6	
Space-Borne	Badger	SF20	1959	156	2/-	
Space Fury	Badger	SF77	1962	159	2/6	
	Vega	VSF2	1963	146	50¢	R
Space No Barrier [as Pel Torro]						
	Badger	SF106	1964	160	2/6	
Space Trap [as Thornton Bell]						
	Badger	SF98	1964	158	2/6	
Special Mission [as John E. Muller (h)]						
	Badger	SF97	1963	158	2/6	
	Vega	VSF8	1964	155	50¢	R
Spectre of Darkness [as John E. Muller (h)]						
	Badger	SN98	1965	158	2/6	
The Strange Ones [as Pel Torro]						
	Badger	SN70	1963	159	2/6	
Survival Project [as John E. Muller (h)]						
	Badger	SF117	1966	143	2/6	
Suspension [as Bron Fane]	Badger	SF102	1964	160	2/6	
	Vega	VSF9	1964	157	60¢	R
The Synthetic Ones [as Lionel Roberts]						
	Badger	SF52	1961	158	2/6	
They Never Come Back [as Leo Brett]						
	Badger	SN68	1963	158	2/6	
A 1,000 Years On [as John E. Muller (h)]						
	Badger	SF50	1961	160	2/6	
Through the Barrier [as Pel Torro]						
	Badger	SF91	1963	158	2/6	
Time Echo [as Lionel Roberts]						
	Badger	SF23	1959	157	2/-	
The Timeless Ones [as Pel Torro]						
	Badger	SN76	1963	158	2/6	
The Triple Man	Badger	SN96	1965	158	2/6	
U.F.O. 517 [as Bron Fane]	Badger	SF115	1966	158	2/6	
The Ultimate Man [as John E. Muller (h)]						
	Badger	SF56	1961	158	2/6	
The Unconfined	Badger	SN102	1966	158	2/6	
The Uninvited [as John E. Muller (h)]						
	Badger	SF57	1961	158	2/6	
The Unknown Destiny [as Bron Fane]						
	Badger	SN84	1963	158	2/6	

Author and Title	Publisher	Serial	Date	Pp.	Price	Type
The Unseen [as Lee Barton] Badger		SN78	1963	158	2/6	
Uranium 235 [as John E. Muller (h)]						
	Badger	SF67	1962	158	2/6	
The Vengeance of Siva [as John E. Muller (h)]						
	Badger	SN60	1962	160	2/6	
The Venus Venture [as John E. Muller (h)]						
	Badger	SF62	1961	158	2/6	
	Vega	VSF11	1965	155	60¢	R
The Waiting World	Badger	SF1	1957	158	2/-	
Walk Through To-morrow [as Karl Zeigfreid (h)]						
	Badger	SF78	1962	158	2/6	
	Vega	VSF-1	1963	144	50¢	R
Watching World	Badger	SF118	1966	142	2/6	
World of the Gods [as Pel Torro]						
	Badger	SF45	1960	158	2/6	
World of Tomorrow [as Karl Zeigfreid (h)]						
	Badger	SF84	1963	158	2/6	
The World That Never Was [as Karl Zeigfreid (h)]						
	Badger	SF85	1963	158	2/6	
The X-Machine [as John E. Muller (h)]						
	Badger	SF74	1962	157	2/6	
Zero Minus X [as Karl Zeigfreid (h)]						
	Badger	SF81	1962	160	2/6	

FARADAY, ROBERT

Author and Title	Publisher	Serial	Date	Pp.	Price	Type
The Anytime Rings	Dell	0241	1963	119	35¢	J

FARJEON, J(OSEPH) JEFFERSON (1883—1955)

Author and Title	Publisher	Serial	Date	Pp.	Price	Type
Death of a World	Collins	205c	1952	192	1/6	R
The Invisible Companion and Other Stories						
	Todd	Polybook	1946	62	6d	C

FARLEY, RALPH MILNE (pseud) See HOAR, R. S.

FARMER, ARTHUR (pseud) See JARDINE, J. O.

FARMER, PHILIP JOSÉ (1918—)

Author and Title	Publisher	Serial	Date	Pp.	Price	Type
The Alley God	Ballantine	F588	1962	176	50¢	C
Cache From Outer Space	Ace	F-165*	1962	139	40¢	
The Celestial Blueprint	Ace	F-165*	1962	114	40¢	C
Dare	Ballantine	U2193	1965	159	50¢	
The Day of Timestop (originally *A Woman a Day*)						
	Lancer	73-715	1968	192	60¢	R
Flesh	Beac (Gal)	277	1960	160	35¢	
The Gate of Time	Belmont	B50-717	1966	176	50¢	
The Gates of Creation	Ace	F-412	1966	159	40¢	
The Green Odyssey	Ballantine	210	1957	152	35¢	
(identical hardcover edition $2.75)						
	Ballantine	U2345	1966	152	50¢	R
The Image of the Beast	Essex House	0108	1968	255	$1.95	
Inside Outside	Ballantine	U2192	1964	156	50¢	
The Lovers	Ballantine	507K	1961	160	35¢	
The Maker of Universes	Ace	F-367	1965	191	40¢	
Night of Light	Berkley	F1248	1966	160	50¢	M
A Private Cosmos	Ace	G-724	1968	192	50¢	
Strange Relations	Ballantine	391K	1960	190	35¢	C
	Panther	2092	1966	187	3/6	C,R
Tongues of the Moon	Pyramid	R1055	1964	143	50¢	M
A Woman a Day (also titled *The Day of Timestop*)						
	Beac (Gal)	291	1960	160	35¢	

FARR, CAROLINE

Author and Title	Publisher	Serial	Date	Pp.	Price	Type
House of Tombs	Signet	D3062	1966	128	50¢	

FARRAR, CLYDE

Author and Title	Publisher	Serial	Date	Pp.	Price	Type
The Life Vapor	Stellar	SFS12	1930	11	10¢	
(part of booklet also containing "30 Miles Down," D. D. Sharp)						

FAST, HOWARD (1914—)

Author and Title	Publisher	Serial	Date	Pp.	Price	Type
The Edge of Tomorrow	Bantam	A2254	1961	120	35¢	C

Author and Title	Publisher	Serial	Date	Pp.	Price	Type
	Bantam	F3309	1966	121	50¢	C,R
	Corgi	SS1107	1962	125	2/6	C,R
Phyllis [as E. V. Cunningham]						
	Crest	s595	1963	143	35¢	R
	Pan		1964	160	2/6	R

FAST, JULIUS (1918—)

Author and Title	Publisher	Serial	Date	Pp.	Price	Type
Out of This World	Penguin-US	537	1944	232	25¢	A

FAUCETTE, JOHN M. (1943—)

Author and Title	Publisher	Serial	Date	Pp.	Price	Type
The Age of Ruin	Ace	H-103*	1968	114	60¢	
Crown of Infinity	Ace	H-51*	1968	129	60¢	

FEAR, W. H.

Author and Title	Publisher	Serial	Date	Pp.	Price	Type
Lunar Flight	Badger	SF7	1958	158	2/-	
Operation Satellite	Badger	SF5	1958	158	2/-	
Return to Space	Badger	SF9	1958	158	2/-	
The Ultimate	Badger	SF3	1958	158	2/-	

FEARN, JOHN RUSSELL (1908—1960) [The following excludes novel supplements—check in the *Ephemerals* section under *Long Island Sunday Press* (page 790); *Star Weekly*, Toronto (pages 790, 791); and *Sunday Star Ledger* (page 791). The *Star* novels include the *Golden Amazon* series also listed in the *Who's Who* entry. Works shown below as by Astron Del Martia are listed here only for convenience, as only *The Trembling World* is known to be by Fearn; the others may or may not be. Volsted Gridban is a house pseudonym also used by E. C. Tubb, *q.v.*]

Author and Title	Publisher	Serial	Date	Pp.	Price	Type
Across the Ages [as Vargo Statten]						
	Scion		1952	96	1/6	M
Anjani the Mighty [as Earl Titan]						
	Scion		1951	128	1/6	
Annihilation [as Vargo Statten]						
	Scion		1950	128	1/6	
The Avenging Martian [as Vargo Statten]						
	Scion		1951	128	1/6	M
The Black Avengers [as Vargo Statten]						
	Scion		1953	128	1/6	
Black Bargain [as Vargo Statten]						
	Scion		1953	128	1/6	
Black Wing of Mars [as Vargo Statten]						
	Scion		1953	128	1/6	M
Born of Luna [as Vargo Statten]						
	Scion		1951	128	1/6	
Cataclysm [as Vargo Statten]						
	Scion		1951	128	1/6	M
The Catalyst [as Vargo Statten]						
	Scion		1951	112	1/6	
Cosmic Exodus [as Conrad G. Holt]						
	Pearson	T-B	1953	64	9d	
The Cosmic Flame [as Vargo Statten]						
	Scion		1950	128	1/6	
The Creature From the Black Lagoon [as Vargo Statten]						
	Dragon Pub.	3	1954	176	2/-	
Dark Boundaries [as Paul Lorraine]						
	Curtis War.		1953	159	1/6	
(identical hardcover edition 6/-)						
Dawn of Darkness [as Astron Del Martia]						
	Gaywood		1951	98	1/6	
Deadline to Pluto [as Vargo Statten]						
	Scion		1951	128	1/6	
The Deathless Amazon	Harlequin	320	1954	160	35¢	
Decreation [as Vargo Statten]						
	Scion		1952	96	1/6	
The Devouring Fire [as Vargo Statten]						
	Scion		1951	112	1/6	
The Dust Destroyer [as Vargo Statten]						
	Scion		1953	127	1/6	
The Dyno-Depressant [as Volsted Gridban]						
	Scion		1953	128	1/6	

Author and Title	Publisher	Serial	Date	Pp.	Price	Type
Earth-2 [as Vargo Statten] Dragon Pub.			1955	128	1/6	
The Eclipse Express [as Vargo Statten]						
	Scion		1952	112	1/6	
Emperor of Mars	Hamilton		1950	127	1/6	
Exit Life [as Volsted Gridban]						
	Scion		1953	128	1/6	
The Frozen Limit [as Volsted Gridban]						
	Scion		1954	128	1/6	
The G-Bomb [as Vargo Statten]						
	Scion		1952	112	1/6	
The Genial Dinosaur [as Volsted Gridban]						
	Scion		1954	128	1/6	
Goddess of Mars	Hamilton		1950	126	1/6	
The Gold of Akada [as Earl Titan]						
	Scion		1951	128	1/6	
The Golden Amazon	Harlequin	218	1953	192	35¢	
The Golden Amazon's Triumph						
	Harlequin	421	1958	160	35¢	
The Grand Illusion [as Vargo Statten—spine credits V. Gridban						
as author]	Scion		1953	128	1/6	
The Hell Fruit [as Lawrence F. Rose]						
	Pearson	T-B	1953	64	9d	
I Came—I Saw—I Wondered [as Volsted Gridban]						
	Scion		1954	128	1/6	
I Spy [as Vargo Statten]	Scion		1954	128	1/6	
Inferno! [as Vargo Statten]	Scion		1950	128	1/6	
The Inner Cosmos [as Vargo Statten]						
	Scion		1952	112	1/6	
The Interloper [as Vargo Statten]						
	Scion		1953	128	1/6	
Interstellar Espionage [as Astron Del Martia]						
	Gaywood		1952	100	1/6	
The Last Martian [as Vargo Statten]						
	Scion		1952	96	1/6	
Laughter in Space [as Vargo Statten]						
	Scion		1952	96	1/6	M
The Lie Destroyer [as Vargo Statten]						
	Scion		1953	127	1/6	
The Lonely Astronomer [as Volsted Gridban]						
	Scion		1954	128	1/6	
Magnetic Brain [as Volsted Gridban]						
	Scion		1953	128	1/6	
Man From Tomorrow [as Vargo Statten]						
	Scion		1952	112	1/6	M
Man in Duplicate [as Vargo Statten]						
	Scion		1953	128	1/6	
Man of Two Worlds [as Vargo Statten]						
	Scion		1953	128	1/6	
The Master Must Die [as Volsted Gridban]						
	Scion		1953	128	1/6	
The Micro Men [as Vargo Statten]						
	Scion		1950	128	1/6	
Moons for Sale [as Volsted Gridban]						
	Scion		1953	128	1/6	
The Multi-Man [as Vargo Statten]						
	Scion		1954	128	1/6	
Nebula X [as Vargo Statten]	Scion		1950	128	1/6	
The New Satellite [as Vargo Statten]						
	Scion		1951	112	1/6	
Odyssey of Nine [as Vargo Statten]						
	Scion		1953	128	1/6	
1,000-Year Voyage [as Vargo Statten]						
	Dragon Pub	1	1954	128	1/6	
Operation Venus	Scion		1949	128	1/6	
Other Eyes Watching [as Polton Cross]						
	Pendulum		1946	120	2/-	M
The Petrified Planet [as Vargo Statten]						
	Scion		1951	112	1/6	
Pioneer 1990 [as Vargo Statten]						
	Scion		1953	128	1/6	M

Author and Title	Publisher	Serial	Date	Pp.	Price	Type
The Purple Wizard [as Volsted Gridban]						
	Scion		1953	128	1/6	
The Red Insects [as Vargo Statten]						
	Scion		1951	128	1/6	
Red Men of Mars	Hamilton		1950	127	1/6	
The Renegade Star [as Vargo Statten]						
	Scion		1952	112	1/6	M
Science Metropolis [as Vargo Statten]						
	Scion		1952	128	1/6	M
Scourge of the Atom [as Volsted Gridban]						
	Scion		1953	128	1/6	
Slaves of Ijax	Kaner		1948	80	1/-	
Space Pirates [as Astron Del Martia]						
	Gaywood		1951	112	1/6	
The Space Warp [as Vargo Statten]						
	Scion		1952	112	1/6	
The Sun Makers [as Vargo Statten]						
	Scion		1950	128	1/6	
A Thing of the Past [as Volsted Gridban]						
	Scion		1953	128	1/6	
A Time Appointed [as Vargo Statten]						
	Scion		1954	128	1/6	
The Time Bridge [as Vargo Statten]						
	Scion		1952	112	1/6	
The Time Trap [as Vargo Statten]						
	Scion		1952	96	1/6	
To the Ultimate [as Vargo Statten]						
	Scion		1952	128	1/6	
The Trembling World [as Astron Del Martia]						
	Gaywood		1950	128	1/6	
2,000 Years On [as Vargo Statten]						
	Scion		1950	128	1/6	
Ultra Spectrum [as Vargo Statten]						
	Scion		1953	128	1/6	
Valley of Pretenders [as Dennis Clive]						
	Columbia	SFC2	nd	24	10¢	R
The Voice Commands [as Dennis Clive]						
	Columbia	SFC5	nd	24	10¢	R
Wanderer of Space [as Vargo Statten]						
	Scion		1950	128	1/6	
Warrior of Mars	Hamilton		1950	127	1/6	
Wealth of the Void [as Vargo Statten]						
	Scion		1954	128	1/6	
Worlds to Conquer [as Vargo Statten]						
	Scion		1952	96	1/6	
Z Formations [as Bryan Shaw]						
	Curtis War.		1953	159	1/6	
Zero Hour [as Vargo Statten]						
	Scion		1953	128	1/6	M
FENTON, CRAWLEY						
The Seeing Knife	Curtis War.		1954		1/6	
FERMAN, JOSEPH W. (1906—)						
No Limits	Ballantine	U2220	1964	192	50¢	A
	Ballantine	U2220	1968	192	50¢	A,R
FESSIER, MICHAEL (1907—)						
Fully Dressed and in His Right Mind						
	Lion	214	1954	126	25¢	R
FIELD, GANS T. (pseud) See WELLMAN, M. W.						
FINE, PETER [as Peter Heath]						
Assassins From Tomorrow	Lancer	73-631	1967	160	60¢	
Men Who Die Twice	Lancer	73-783	1968	160	60¢	
[part of series, and published as SF, but is not]						
The Mind Brothers	Lancer	73-600	1967	159	60¢	

Author and Title	Publisher	Serial	Date	Pp.	Price	Type
FINN, RALPH L. (1912—)						
Captive on the Flying Saucer						
	Gaywood		1952	123	1/6	
Freaks Against Supermen	Gaywood		1951	123	1/6	
FINNEY, CHARLES G. (1905—)						
The Circus of Dr. Lao	Compass	C82	1961	160	$1.25	R
	Bantam	F2755	1964	119	50¢	R
	Penguin	2537	1966	126	3/6	R
The Ghosts of Manacle	Pyramid	R1042	1964	159	50¢	C
The Unholy City & Magician out of Manchuria						
	Pyramid	X-1818	1968	221	60¢	C
FINNEY, JACK (1911—)						
The Body Snatchers	Dell	42	1955	191	25¢	M
	Dell	B204	1961	191	35¢	R
	Dell	0674	1967	191	60¢	R
	Beac (Odh)		1957	191	2/-	R
The Clock of Time (originally *The Third Level*)						
	Panther	1193	1961	156	2/6	C,R
I Love Galesburg in the Springtime						
	Pan	02021	1968	172	3/6	C,R
The Third Level (also titled *The Clock of Time*)						
	Dell	D274	1959	192	35¢	C,R
FIRTH, N. WESLEY						
Spawn of the Vampire	Bear Hudson		nd	80	1/6	
	Bear Hudson	538	1957	80	1/6	R
[both editions include non-sf "All Set for Murder," Frank Griffin]						
The Terror Strikes	Hamilton		nd	80	1/6	
FISCHER, LEONARD						
Let Out the Beast	Export	KN18A	1950	159	25¢	
FISHER, VARDIS (1895—1968) [Titles of sf interest in the *Testament of Man* series]						
Adam and the Serpent	Pyramid	R677	1961	254	50¢	R
Darkness and the Deep	Pyramid	R527	1960	256	50¢	R
	Pyramid	R738	1962	256	50¢	R
	Pyramid	R738	1965	256	50¢	R
The Divine Passion	Pyramid	R419	1959	318	50¢	R
	Pyramid	R628	1961	318	50¢	R
	Pyramid	X845	1963	318	60¢	R
The Golden Rooms	Armed	713	nd		np	R
	Pyramid	R472	1960	256	50¢	R
	Pyramid	X696	1962	256	60¢	R
Intimations of Eve	Pyramid	R657	1961	254	50¢	R
	Pyramid	R883	1965	254	50¢	R
FITZGERALD, F. SCOTT (1896—1940)						
This Side of Paradise	Dell		1954		25¢	R
	Penguin	1867	1963	256	3/6	R
FITZGIBBON, CONSTANTINE (1919—)						
When the Kissing Had to Stop						
	Bantam	F2255	1961	230	50¢	R
	Pan	G543	1962	252	2/6	R
	Pan	X186	1963	252	3/6	R
FLACKES, B.						
Duel in Nightmare Worlds	Hamilton		1952	112	1/6	
FLAGG, FRANCIS (pseud) See WEISS, G. H.						
FLAIR, TIFFANY						
Psychic Passion	PEC Giant	G-1130	1968			
FLANNIGAN, ROY						
County Court	Mercury		nd	126	25¢	

Author and Title	Publisher	Serial	Date	Pp.	Price	Type
FLEISCHMAN, THEO						
Double Exposure	Popular	SP214	1963	172	50¢	R
FLEMING, HARRY (pseud) See BIRD, W. H. F.						
FLEMING, IAN (1908—1964)						
Chitty-Chitty-Bang-Bang	Signet	T3705	1968	153	75¢	J,R
Moonraker (also titled *Too Hot to Handle*)						
	Pan	392	1956	185	2/-	R
	Pan	G216	1959	190	2/6	R
	Pan	X234	1963	190	3/6	R
	Signet	S1850	1960	175	35¢	R
	Signet	D2053	1963	175	50¢	R
Too Hot to Handle (originally *Moonraker*)						
	Permabks	M3070	1957	185	25¢	R
FLEMING, JOAN						
The Chill and the Kill	Fontana	1599	1967	256	3/6	
FLES, BARTHOLD (1902—)						
The Saturday Evening Post Fantasy Stories						
	Avon	389	1951	126	25¢	A
FLETCHER, GEORGE U. (pseud) See PRATT, F.						
FLINT, HOMER EON (189?—1924)						
The Blind Spot [with A. Hall]						
	Ace	G-547	1964	318	50¢	R
The Devolutionist and The Emancipatrix						
	Ace	F-355	1965	191	40¢	M
The Lord of Death and The Queen of Life						
	Ace	F-345	1965	143	40¢	M
FOLEY, DAVE See HATCH, G. (pseud)						
FOLEY, JOHN						
Man in the Moon	FSB	271	1960	160	2/6	
	Horwitz	FH15	1961	129	4/6	R
FOLLETT, BARBARA NEWHALL (1914—?)						
The House Without Windows						
	Avon	ZS127	1968	142	60¢	R
FONTENAY, CHARLES L(OUIS) (1917—)						
The Day the Oceans Overflowed						
	Monarch	443	1964	128	40¢	
Rebels of the Red Planet	Ace	F-113*	1961	143	40¢	
Twice Upon a Time	Ace	D-266*	1958	152	35¢	
FORBES, ESTHER (1891—1967)						
A Mirror for Witches	Sentry	29	1963	215	$1.75	N,R
FORD, A.						
Nothing So Strange	Paperback	54-629	1968	217	75¢	
FORD, KEN						
Prototype P.Z.642	Curtis War.		1953	111	1/6	
Sky Fighters	Curtis War.		1953		1/6	
FOREST, JEAN-CLAUDE						
Barbarella [comic-book version]						
	Grove	GS2	1968	68	$1.50	R
	Corgi	07924.3	1968	68	12/6	R
FORSTER, E(DWARD) M. (1879—1970)						
Collected Short Stories	Penguin	1031	1954	222	2/-	C,R
	Penguin	1031	1956	222	2/6	C,R
	Penguin	1031	1961	222	3/6	C,R
The Eternal Moment and Other Stories						
	Univ. Lib.	UL172	1964	245	$1.65	C

Author and Title	Publisher	Serial	Date	Pp.	Price	Type
FORT, CHARLES (1874—1932)						
The Book of the Damned	Ace	K-156	1962	287	50¢	N,R
	Ace	H-24	1967	287	60¢	N,R
Lo!	Ace	K-217	1965	284	50¢	N,R
New Lands	Ace	H-74	1968	222	60¢	N,R
Wild Talents	Ace	H-88	1968	222	60¢	N,R
FOSTER, GEORGE C(ECIL) (1893—)						
The Change	Digit	R721	1963	160	2/6	
FOSTER, LIONEL B.						
The Hocus Root	Hogbin, Poole		1944	155	2/6	
FOSTER, RICHARD (pseud) See CROSSEN, K. F.						
FOWEY, ROGER See BOY'S FRIEND LIBRARY, page 789.						
FOX, GARDNER F. (1911—)						
Abandon Galaxy [as Bart Somers]						
	Paperback	52-430	1967	160	50¢	
The Arsenal of Miracles	Ace	F-299*	1964	156	40¢	
Beyond the Black Enigma	Paperback	52-848	1965	156	50¢	
	Paperback	53-785	1968	156	60¢	R
The Druid Stone [as Simon Majors]						
	Paperback	52-488	1967	157	50¢	
Escape Across the Cosmos	Paperback	52-273	1964	160	50¢	
	Paperback	52-635	1968	160	50¢	R
The Hunter out of Time	Ace	F-354	1965	126	40¢	
Thief of Llarn	Ace	F-399	1966	158	40¢	
Warrior of Llarn	Ace	F-307	1964	160	40¢	
FOX, LESLIE H. (deceased)						
The Vampire and Sixteen Other Stories						
	Alliance		1945	32	1/6	C
FRANCE, ANATOLE (1844—1924)						
Penguin Island	Penguin	617	1948	293	2/6	R
	Bantam	FC13	1958	239	50¢	R
	Bantam	SC247	1965	239	75¢	R
Revolt of the Angels	Xanadu		1962	348	$1.45	R
FRANK, PAT (1907—)						
Alas, Babylon	Bantam	F2054	1960	279	50¢	R
	Bantam	HP70	1964	279	60¢	R
	Pan	X105	1961	283	3/6	R
Forbidden Area (also titled *Seven Days to Never*)						
	Bantam	A1553	1957	214	35¢	R
Mr. Adam	Armed	1217	nd		np	R
	Pocket Bks	498	1948	231	25¢	R
	Pocket Bks	2498	1955	204	25¢	R
	Panther	688	1957	192	2/-	R
Seven Days to Never (originally *Forbidden Area*)						
	Pan	G255	1959	219	2/6	R
FRANKAU, PAMELA (1908—)						
The Bridge	FSB	137	1959	288	3/6	R
FRANKLIN, H. BRUCE (1934—)						
Future Perfect	Oxford	GB241	1968	402	$2.25	A,R
FRANKLIN, JAY (pseud) See CARTER, J. F.						
FRASER, PHYLLIS See WISE, HERBERT A.						
FRATER OM						
The Mongolian Master and His Disciple						
	H. J. Service		1943	8	np	play
FRAYN, MICHAEL (1933—)						
The Tin Men	Fontana	1419	1966	158	3/6	

Author and Title	Publisher	Serial	Date	Pp.	Price	Type
FRAZEE, STEVE (1909—)						
The Sky Block	Lion	LL3	1954	192	35¢	R
	Pyramid	PG13	1958	192	35¢	R
	Mayflower	8014	1964	143	2/6	R
FRIEDBERG, GERTRUDE (1908—)						
The Revolving Boy	Ace	H-58	1968	192	60¢	R
FRIEDMAN, BRUCE J.						
Black Humour	Corgi	GN7268	1965	174	5/-	C
FRIEND, ED						
The Green Hornet in the Infernal Light						
	Dell	3231	1966	127	50¢	
FRIEND, OSCAR J. (1897—1963)						
The Kid From Mars	Kemsley	CT401	1951	190	1/6	R
My Best Science Fiction Story [with Leo Margulies]						
	Pocket Bks	1007	1954	263	25¢	A,R
Roar of the Rocket	Whitman		1950	32	8d	M
FULLER, JOHN G.						
Incident at Exeter	Berkley	S1354	1967	221	75¢	N,R
The Interrupted Journey	Dell	4068	1967	350	95¢	N,R
FULLER, ROGER						
Son of Flubber	Permabks	M4279	1963	135	35¢	
FURMAN, ABRAHAM L. (1902—)						
Ghost Stories (originally *Teen-Age Ghost Stories*)						
	Lantern	50092	1964	163	50¢	A,R
More Ghost Stories (originally *More Teen-Age Ghost Stories*)						
	Lantern	50593	1968	152	50¢	A,R
The Mystery Companion	Popular	130	1943	192	25¢	A,R
Outer Space Stories (originally *Teen-Age Outer Space Stories*)						
	Lantern	50260	1965	173	50¢	A,R
FURNEAUX, RUPERT						
The World's Strangest Mysteries						
	Ace	K-163	1963	256	50¢	N,R
FUTURE, STEVE (pseud)						
Doomed Nation of the Skies	Pearson	T-B	1953	64	9d	
Slave Traders of the Sky	Pearson	T-B	1954	64	9d	
FYFE, HORACE B. (1918—)						
D-99	Pyramid	F794	1962	144	40¢	
FYSH, G.						
Planetary War	Archer		1952	96	1/6	

G

Author and Title	Publisher	Serial	Date	Pp.	Price	Type
GABOR, DENNIS						
Inventing the Future	Pelican	A663	1964	199	6/6	N,R
GADDIS, VINCENT H. (1913—)						
Invisible Horizons	Ace	H-14	1965	256	60¢	N
Mysterious Fires and Lights						
	Dell	6244	1968	236	75¢	N,R

Author and Title	Publisher	Serial	Date	Pp.	Price	Type
GALBRAITH, JOHN KENNETH (1908—)						
The McLandress Dimension						
	Signet	T3617	1968	126	75¢	R
GALE, E. F. See FALKNER, JOHN (pseud)						
GALLANT, JOSEPH (1907—1957)						
Stories of Scientific Imagination						
	Oxford		1954	152	70¢	A
GALLICO, PAUL (1897—1976)						
Adventures of Hiram Holliday						
	Penguin	2755	1967	221	4/6	
The Man Who Was Magic	Pan	02194	1968	191	5/-	J,R
Too Many Ghosts	Cardinal	C426	1961	278	35¢	R
	Pan	M144	1966	267	5/-	R
GALLUN, RAYMOND Z. (1911—)						
The Machine That Thought [as William Callahan]						
	Columbia	SFC3	nd	24	10¢	M
The Moon Mirage	Stellar	SFS18	1932	24	10¢	
[in booklet also containing "The Ship From Nowhere," S. Patzer]						
People Minus X	Ace	D-291*	1958	160	35¢	R
The Planet Strappers	Pyramid	G658	1961	157	35¢	
GALOUYE, DANIEL F(RANCIS) (1920—1976)						
Dark Universe	Bantam	J2266	1961	154	40¢	
	Sphere	37435	1967	175	5/-	R
The Last Leap and Other Stories						
	Corgi	GS7043	1964	172	3/6	C
Lords of the Psychon	Bantam	J2555	1963	153	40¢	
The Lost Perception (also titled *A Scourge of Screamers*)						
	Corgi	GS7819	1968	173	3/6	R
A Scourge of Screamers (originally *The Lost Perception*)						
	Bantam	F3585	1968	172	50¢	R
Simulacron-3	Bantam	J2797	1964	152	40¢	
GANTZ, KENNETH F(RANKLIN) (1905—)						
Not in Solitude	Berkley	Y582	1961	192	40¢	R
GARDNER, ALAN						
The Escalator	Consul	1411	1965	218	3/6	
Six Day Week	Berkley	X1401	1967	190	60¢	
GARDNER, DICK						
The Impossible	Ballantine	F636	1962	159	50¢	N
GARDNER, GERALD B. (1884—)						
Witchcraft Today	Pedigree		1960	191	3/6	N,R
	Arrow	926	1966	192	3/6	N,R
GARDNER, MARTIN (1914—)						
Fads and Fallacies in the Name of Science						
	Ballantine	F446K	1960		50¢	N,R
GARNER, ALAN (1934—)						
Elidor	Puffin	PS317	1967	171	3/6	J,R
Moon of Gomrath	Puffin	PS242	1965	171	3/-	J,R
	Ace	G-753	1968	157	50¢	J,R
The Weirdstone of Brisingamen						
	Puffin	PS193	1963	236	4/-	J,R
	Ace	G-570	1966	192	50¢	J,R
GARNER, ROLF (pseud) See BERRY, B.						
GARNETT, DAVID (1892—)						
Lady Into Fox	Armed	p-1	nd	96	np	R
Lady Into Fox and A Man in the Zoo						
	Penguin-US	615	1946	135	35¢	R

Author and Title	Publisher	Serial	Date	Pp.	Price	Type
GARNETT, RICHARD (1835—1906)						
Twilight of the Gods	Penguin	586	1947	183	1/6	R
GARRETT, RANDALL (1927—)						
Anything You Can Do [as Darrel T. Langart]						
	Mayflower	0238	1963	190	3/6	R
Brain Twister [as Mark Phillips (pseud with L. M. Janifer)]						
	Pyramid	F783	1962	144	40¢	M
The Dawning Light [as Robert Randall (pseud with R. Silverberg)]						
	Mayflower	1678	1964	189	3/6	R
	Mayflower	1678	1966	189	3/6	R
The Impossibles [as Mark Phillips (pseud with L. M. Janifer)]						
	Pyramid	F875	1963	157	40¢	M
	Pyramid	R1299	1966	157	50¢	R
Pagan Passions [with L. M. Harris (pseud)]						
	Beac (Gal)	263	1959	158	35¢	
The Shrouded Planet [as Robert Randall (pseud with R. Silverberg)]						
	Mayflower	7881	1963	192	3/6	R
Supermind [as Mark Phillips (pseud with L. M. Janifer)]						
	Pyramid	F909	1963	192	40¢	M
Unwise Child	Mayflower	9220	1963	192	3/6	R
GARRON, MARCO						
Black Fury	Curtis War.		nd	111	1/6	
Black Sport	Curtis War.		1952	128	1/6	
Bush Claws	Curtis War.		nd	111	1/6	
Jungle Allies	Curtis War.		1952	111	1/6	
Jungle Fever*	Curtis War.	109	*ca.*1952	128	1/6	
King Hunters*	Curtis War.	95	1952	128	1/6	
Leopard God	Curtis War.		1952	111	1/6	
The Lost City*	Curtis War.	111	1952	128	1/6	
The Missing Safari*	Curtis War.	96	1952	128	1/6	
Silent River	Curtis War.		1952	111	1/6	
Snake Valley	Curtis War.		1952	111	1/6	
Tribal War*	Curtis War.	94	1952	112	1/6	
Veldt Warriors	Curtis War.		1952	111	1/6	
White Fangs*	Curtis War.	110	1952	112	1/6	
* (These 6 form the *Azan the Ape Man* series; it is understood they were withdrawn from circulation after being issued.)						
GARY, ROMAIN (1914—1980)						
Hissing Tales	FSB	1516	1966	160	5/-	C,R
GASKELL, JANE (1941—)						
Atlan	Sphere	37818	1967	286	5/-	R
	Sphere	37818	1968	286	5/-	R
	Paperback	55-738	1968	287	95¢	R
The City	Sphere	37826	1967	191	5/-	R
	Sphere	37826	1968	191	5/-	R
	Paperback	64-019	1968	176	75¢	R
The Serpent	Sphere	37834	1967	479	5/-	R
	Paperback	55-693	1968	477	95¢	R
GATES, T.						
I Was Walking Down Below						
	Corgi	GN7732	1967	158	3/6	
GATLAND, KENNETH W. (1924—)						
The Inhabited Universe [with D. D. Dempster]						
	Premier	d83	1959	206	50¢	N,R
GEIS, RICHARD E(RWIN) (1927—)						
The Endless Orgy	Brandon	2061	1968	190	$1.25	
The Sex Machine	Brandon	1070	1967	190	95¢	
GEORGE, BRIAN						
Atom of Doubt	FSB	196	1961	160	2/6	
	Horwitz	FH28	1962	162	4/6	R

Author and Title	Publisher	Serial	Date	Pp.	Price	Type
GEORGE, PETER (1924—1966)						
Commander-1	Dell	1430	1966	251	75¢	R
	Pan	X524	1966	222	3/6	R
Dr. Strangelove	Bantam	F2679	1964	145	50¢	
	Bantam	S3856	1968	145	75¢	R
	Corgi	SN1453	1964	145	2/6	R
Red Alert [as Peter Bryant] (originally *Two Hours to Doom*)						
	Ace	D-350	1959	191	35¢	R
	Ace	F-210	1963	191	40¢	R
Two Hours to Doom [as Peter Bryant] (also titled *Red Alert*)						
	Corgi	SN1091	1961	189	2/6	R
GEORGE, S(IDNEY) C(HARLES) (1898—)						
The Blue Ray	3-Star		1953	190	np	
GERARD, FRANCIS (1905—)						
The Mark of the Moon	Popular	544	1953	191	25¢	R
GERNSBACK, HUGO (1884—1967)						
Ralph 124C 41 +	Kemsley	CT406	1952	190	1/6	R
	Crest	s226	1958	142	35¢	R
GESTON, MARK S. (1946—)						
Lords of the Starship	Ace	G-673	1967	156	50¢	
GIBBONS, GAVIN (1922—)						
On Board the Flying Saucers						
	Paperback	53-585	1967	192	60¢	N,R
GIBBONS, STELLA						
Cold Comfort Farm	Penguin	140	1938	246	6d	R
	Penguin	140	1951	248	1/6	R
	Penguin	140	1956	248	2/6	R
	Mayflower	113036	1968	190	5/-	R
GIBBS, LEWIS (pseud) See COVE, J. W.						
GIBSON, TONY						
Breaking in the Future	Zenith (UK)	1	1965	128	5/-	N
GIBSON, WALTER B(ROWN) (1897—)						
Cry Shadow! [as Maxwell Grant]						
	Belmont	92-624	1965	157	50¢	
Destination: Moon [as Maxwell Grant]						
	Belmont	B50-737	1967	156	50¢	
Mark of the Shadow [as Maxwell Grant]						
	Belmont	B50-683	1966	157	50¢	
The Night of the Shadow [as Maxwell Grant]						
	Belmont	B50-725	1966	156	50¢	
Return of the Shadow	Belmont	90-298	1963	141	40¢	
Shadow Beware [as Maxwell Grant]						
	Belmont	92-615	1965	157	50¢	
Shadow—Go Mad! [as Maxwell Grant]						
	Belmont	B50-709	1966	160	50¢	
The Shadow Strikes Back [as Maxwell Grant]						
	Belmont	92-602	1964	157	50¢	
The Shadow's Revenge [as Maxwell Grant]						
	Belmont	B50-647	1965	156	50¢	
GILES, RAYMOND (pseud) See HOLT, J. R.						
GILLIATT, PENELOPE (1932—)						
One by One	Panther	2234	1967	157	3/6	
GILLON, DIANA (1915—)						
The Unsleep [with Meir Gillon]						
	Ballantine	F571	1962	207	50¢	
	FSB	811	1963	223	3/6	R

Author and Title	Publisher	Serial	Date	Pp.	Price	Type
GILLON, MEIR (1907—) See GILLON, D. (co-author)						
GILSON, Major CHARLES (1878—1943)						
The Lost City	Wren		1941	190	6d	
GLASBY, JOHN S(TEPHEN) (1928—)						
Alien [as John E. Muller (h)]						
	Badger	SF61	1961	158	2/6	
Barrier Unknown [as A. J. Merak]						
	Badger	SF30	1960	142	2/-	
Black Abyss [as J. L. Powers]						
	Badger	SF32	1960	142	2/-	
Cosmic Echelon [with Arthur Roberts, as Berl Cameron]						
	Curtis War.		1952	128	1/6	
(identical hardcover edition 5/-)						
Dark Andromeda [as A. J. Merak]						
	Panther	95	1954	159	1/6	
(identical hardcover edition 6/-)						
Dark Centauri [as Karl Zeigfreid]						
	Spencer		1954	130	1/6	
Dark Conflict [as A. J. Merak]						
	Badger	SN29	1959	157	2/-	
The Dark Millennium [as A. J. Merak]						
	Badger	SF19	1959	157	2/-	
Dawn of the Half-Gods [as Victor La Salle]						
	Spencer		1953	128	1/6	
Day of the Beasts [as John E. Muller (h)]						
	Badger	SF51	1961	158	2/6	
Hydrosphere [as A. J. Merak]						
	Badger	SF36	1960	142	2/-	
No Dawn and No Horizon [as A. J. Merak]						
	Badger	SF16	1959	158	2/-	
Satellite B.C. [with Arthur Roberts, as Rand Le Page]						
	Curtis War.		1952	127	1/6	
Sphero Nova [with Arthur Roberts, as Berl Cameron]						
	Curtis War.		1952	159	1/6	
(identical hardcover edition 6/-)						
This Second Earth [as R. L. Bowers]						
	Cobra	SS1	1957	158	2/-	
Time and Space [with Arthur Roberts, as Rand Le Page]						
	Curtis War.		1952	128	1/6	
(identical hardcover edition 5/-)						
The Time Kings [as J. B. Dexter]						
	Badger	SF6	1958	158	2/-	
Twilight Zone [as Victor La Salle]						
	Spencer		1954	130	1/6	
	Badger	SF13	1959	158	2/-	R
The Unpossessed [as John E. Muller (h)]						
	Badger	SN42	1961	158	2/6	
The Uranium Seekers [as Karl Zeigfreid]						
	Spencer		1953	128	1/6	
When the Gods Came [as John Adams]						
	Badger	SF31	1960	142	2/6	
The World Makers [as John C. Maxwell]						
	Badger	SF2	1938	160	2/-	
Zenith-D [with Arthur Roberts, as Paul Lorraine]						
	Curtis War.		1952	159	1/6	
Zero Point [with Arthur Roberts, as Rand Le Page]						
	Curtis War.		1952	128	1/6	
(identical hardcover edition 5/-)						
GLASKIN, GERALD M. (1923—)						
A Change of Mind	Ace (Brit.)	H489	1961	188	2/6	R
GLEMSER, BERNARD (1908—)						
Hero's Walk [as Robert Crane]						
	Ballantine	71	1954	196	35¢	
(identical hardcover edition $2.50)						

Author and Title	Publisher	Serial	Date	Pp.	Price	Type
GLENNING, RAYMOND						
The Corpse Sat Up	Transport	ST	1951	30	8d	
[cover credits Paul Valdez as author]						
Seven for Murder	Transport	ST	1951	30	8d	
GLYNN, A(NTHONY) A(RTHUR) (1929—)						
Plan for Conquest	Badger	SF90	1963	157	2/6	
	Vega	VSF5	1964	141	50¢	R
Search the Dark Stars [as J. E. Muller]						
	Badger	SF48	1961	158	2/6	
GODWIN, FRANCIS (1562—1633)						
The Man in the Moone	Negram		1959	48	5/-	R
GODWIN, TOM (1915—)						
The Space Barbarians	Pyramid	R993	1964	169	50¢	
Space Prison (originally *The Survivors*)						
	Pyramid	G480	1960	158	35¢	R
	Pyramid	F774	1962	158	40¢	R
GODWIN, WILLIAM (1756—1836)						
Caleb Williams	FSB	1578	1966	317	6/-	
GOFF, J. M.						
Fantastic Seducer	Merit	GM417	1964	128	60¢	
GOLD, H(ORACE) L. (1914—)						
Bodyguard and Four Other Short Science Fiction Novels From Galaxy						
	Permabks	M4252	1962	273	35¢	A,R
The Fifth Galaxy Reader	Pocket Bks	6163	1963	241	35¢	A,R
Five Galaxy Short Novels	Permabks	M4158	1960	292	35¢	A,R
The Fourth Galaxy Reader	Permabks	M4184	1960	239	35¢	A,R
Mind Partner and 8 Other Novelets From Galaxy						
	Permabks	M4287	1963	241	35¢	A,R
The Third Galaxy Reader	Permabks	M4172	1960	235	35¢	A,R
The Weird Ones	Belmont	L92-541	1962	173	50¢	A
	Corgi	GS7592	1967	190	3/6	A,R
The World That Couldn't Be and 8 Other Novelets From Galaxy						
	Permabks	M4197	1961	260	35¢	A,R
GOLDING, LOUIS (1895—1958)						
The Call of the Hand and Other Stories						
	Poynings		1944	32	1/-	C
The Miracle Boy	Penguin	475	1944	240	9d	R
GOLDING, WILLIAM (1911—)						
The Inheritors	Harcourt		1963	233	$1.65	R
	Faber		1964	282	6/6	R
	Cardinal	GC787	1964	273	75¢	R
	Cardinal	75169	1966	213	75¢	R
Lord of the Flies	Faber		1958	248	5/-	R
	Faber		1963	248	6/-	R
	Faber		1967	223	3/6	R
	Capricorn	CAP14	1959	256	$1.25	R
	Capricorn	CAP14 (13th imp.)				
			ca.1963	192	$1.25	R
	Capricorn	CAP14 (27th imp.)				
			ca.1967	192	$1.25	R
	Penguin	1471	1960	192	2/6	R
Pincher Martin	Faber		1960	208	5/-	R
	Penguin	1686	1962	190	2/6	R
	Capricorn	66	nd	216	$1.25	R
The Spire	Harcourt		1965	214	$1.35	R
GOLDSTON, ROBERT C. (1927—)						
The Catafalque	Popular	75-1260	1968	272	75¢	R
The Last of Lazarus	Avon	V2166	1967	224	75¢	
Satan's Disciples	Ballantine	F581	1962	189	50¢	N

Author and Title	Publisher	Serial	Date	Pp.	Price	Type
GOODWIN, HAROLD L. (1914—)						
The Science Book of Space Travel						
	Cardinal	C207	1956	213	35¢	N
Space Frontier Unlimited	Van Nostrand		1967	144	$1.45	N
GORDON, DONALD (pseud) See PAYNE, D. G.						
GORDON, FRITZ						
Flight of the Bamboo Saucer						
	Tandem	T131	1967	176	3/6	
	Award	A244XK	1967	176	60¢	R
GORDON, MILDRED and GORDON						
Power Play [as The Gordons]						
	Bantam	S3267	1966	281	75¢	R
	Corgi	FN7792	1967	282	5/-	R
GORDON, REX (pseud) See HOUGH, S. B.						
GORDON, RICHARD See BOY'S FRIEND LIBRARY, page 789.						
GOTLIEB, PHYLLIS (1926—)						
Sunburst	Gold Medal	k1488	1964	160	40¢	M
	Coronet	F117	1966	160	3/6	R
GOUSCHEV, S. See VASSILIEV, M. (co-author)						
GRAHAM, ROGER P. (1909—1965) [as Rog Phillips]						
Time Trap	Century	116	1949	158	25¢	
	Atlas	SFL8	1956	114	2/6	R
World of If	Century	B13	1951	126	35¢	
Worlds Within	Century	124	1950	159	25¢	
	Export	MDS142	1950	160	25¢	R
GRAHAME, KENNETH						
The Wind in the Willows	Methuen		1961	256	3/6	J,R
	Avon	SS4	1965	224	60¢	J,R
	Lancer	12-404	1967	253	60¢	J,R
GRANT, JOAN (1907—)						
Winged Pharaoh	FSB	11	1958	255	2/6	R
GRANT, MATTHEW						
Hyper-Drive	Digit	R673	1963	160	2/6	
GRANT, MAXWELL (pseud) See GIBSON, W. B.						
GRAVES, ROBERT (1895—)						
Hercules, My Shipmate (originally *The Golden Fleece*)						
	Univ. Lib.	UL19	1957	467	$1.25	R
	Pyramid	S1346	1966	463	85¢	R
Watch the North Wind Rise (originally *Seven Days in New Crete*)						
	Avon	V2075	1964	254	75¢	R
The White Goddess	Vintage	K56	1958	541	$1.25	R
GRAY, ANTHONY (pseud)						
The Penetrators	Dell	6873	1966	255	75¢	R
GRAYSON, CHARLES (1905—) See CARTMELL, V. H. (co-anthologist)						
GREEN, GABRIEL						
Let's Face the Facts About Flying Saucers						
	Popular	60-2223	1967	127	60¢	N
GREEN, JOSEPH L. (1931—)						
The Loafers of Refuge	Ballantine	U2233	1965	160	50¢	C,M
	Pan	X651	1967	175	3/6	C,R

Author and Title	Publisher	Serial	Date	Pp.	Price	Type
GREEN, ROGER L. (1918—)						
Two Satyr Plays [translated]						
	Penguin	L76	1957		2/6	C
GREENBERG, MARTIN L. (1918—)						
Men Against the Stars	Pyramid	G234	1957	191	35¢	A,R
	Pyramid	F852	1963	191	40¢	A,R
GREENE, GRAHAM (1904—)						
Nineteen Stories	Lion	LL31	1955	192	35¢	C,R
GREENER, LESLIE (1900—1974)						
Moon Ahead!	Puffin	PS107	1957	160	2/6	J,R
GREENFIELD, IRVING A. (1928—)						
Mirror Image [as Bruce Duncan]						
	Belmont	B60-081*	1968	90	60¢	
UFO Report	Lancer	73-624	1967	141	60¢	N
Waters of Death	Lancer	73-672	1967	157	60¢	

GREGORY, D. See BOY'S FRIEND LIBRARY, page 789.

GREGORY, FRANKLIN (1905—)						
The White Wolf	Hillman	TNC10	ca.1950			R

GREY, CHARLES (pseud) See TUBB, E. C.

GRIBBLE, LEONARD						
Atomic Murder	Digit	nn	1956	160	2/-	

GRIBBON, WILLIAM LANCASTER See MUNDY, T. (pseud)

GRIDBAN, VOLSTED (pseud) See FEARN, J. R., and TUBB, E. C.

GRIFFEN, ELIZABETH L.						
The Shaggy Dog	Scholastic	TX1111	1967	96	50¢	J
GRIFFITH, MAXWELL						
The Gadget Maker	Cardinal	C215	1956	353	35¢	
GRIFFITHS, DAVID ARTHUR						
Astro Race [as King Lang]	Curtis War.		1951	112	1/6	
Fission [as Gill Hunt]	Curtis War.		1952	111	1/6	
Gyrator Control [as King Lang]						
	Curtis War.		1951	112	1/6	
Laboratory "X" [as David Shaw]						
	Curtis War.		1950	128	1/6	
Planet Federation [as David Shaw]						
	Curtis War.		1950	128	1/6	
Rocket Invasion [as King Lang]						
	Curtis War.		1951	111	1/6	
Space Men [as David Shaw]	Curtis War.		1951	128	1/6	
Task Flight [as King Lang]	Curtis War.		1951	112	1/6	
Vega [as Gill Hunt]	Curtis War.		1951	111	1/6	
GRIMM, BENJAMIN						
Conception of the Beast	Ophelia	OPS-132	1968	218	$1.75	

GRINNELL, DAVID (pseud) See WOLLHEIM, D. A.

GRUBB, DAVIS (1919—)						
One Foot in the Grave	Arrow	925	1967	186	3/6	C
Twelve Tales of Suspense and the Supernatural						
	Crest	d814	1965	144	50¢	C,R
GRUEN, VON						
The Mortals of Reni	Curtis War.		1953	159	1/6	
(identical hardcover edition 6/-)						

Author and Title	Publisher	Serial	Date	Pp.	Price	Type
GUIN, WYMAN (1915—)						
Living Way Out	Avon	S298	1967	208	60¢	C
GUNN, JAMES E. (1923—)						
Future Imperfect	Bantam	J2717	1964	137	40¢	C
The Immortals	Bantam	J2484	1962	154	40¢	C
	Bantam	H3915	1968	154	60¢	C,R
The Joy Makers	Bantam	A2219	1961	160	35¢	M
Star Bridge [with J. Williamson]						
	Ace	D-169	1956	255	35¢	
	Ace	F-241	1963	255	40¢	R
Station in Space	Bantam	A1825	1958	156	35¢	C
This Fortress World	Ace	D-223*	1957	190	35¢	R
GUNTHER, JOHN						
Jason and the Golden Fleece						
	Scholastic	TX 517	1964	64	35¢	
GUTHRIE, THOMAS A. (1856—1934) [as F. Anstey]						
See also DAILY MAIL 6d NOVELS, page 789.						
The Brass Bottle	Penguin	542	1946	227	1/6	R
	Penguin-US		1953	187	35¢	R
Vice Versa	?		1947	78	2/-	R

H

Author and Title	Publisher	Serial	Date	Pp.	Price	Type
HABER, HEINZ (1913—)						
Stars, Men and Atoms	Washington	W924	1966	159	75¢	N
HADFIELD, JOHN (1907—)						
A Chamber of Horrors	Fontana	1484	1967	286	5/-	A,R
HADLEY, ARTHUR T. (1924—)						
The Joy Wagon	Berkley	G466	1960	158	35¢	R

HADLEY, FRANKLIN (pseud) See WINTERBOTHAM, R. R.

HAGGARD, H. RIDER (1856—1925)						
See also MASTERPIECE LIBRARY, page 790.						
Allan Quatermain	Hodder	C118	1951	256	2/-	R
	Hodder	C118	1958	256	2/6	R
	Hodder	118	1966	255	3/6	R
	Royal Giant	18*	195?	170	50¢	R
	Ballantine	X743	1963	222	60¢	R
Ayesha: Return of She	Icon	F14	1964	288	5/-	R
Benita	Chariot (Brit.)	6	1952	182	2/-	R
Cleopatra	Hodder	620	1963	256	3/6	R
	Pocket Bks	7025	1963	290	50¢	R
King Solomon's Mines	Armed	795	nd	319	np	R
	Dell	433	1950	192	25¢	R
	Dell	LC172	1961	288	50¢	R
	Pan	163	1951	191	1/6	R
	Royal Giant	18*	195?	149	50¢	R
	Puffin	PS111	1957	256	3/6	R
	Puffin	PS111	1966	256	3/6	R
	Puffin	PS111	1968	256	4/-	R
	Collier	HS51V	1962	319	65¢	R
	Ballantine	X733	1963	190	60¢	R
The Return of She: Ayesha (also titled *Ayesha*)						
	Lancer	74-899	1967	350	75¢	R

Author and Title	Publisher	Serial	Date	Pp.	Price	Type
She	Masterpiece Lib.		1896	68	1d	R
	Newnes		1899	190	6d	R
	Armed	881	nd		np	R
[rewritten by Don Ward]	Dell	339	1949	192	25¢	R
	Dell	1339	nd	192	25¢	R
	Hodder	119	1949	255	2/-	R
	Hodder	C119	1953	256	2/-	R
	Hodder	119	1961	255	3/6	R
	Hodder	119	1965	255	3/6	R
	Hodder	1808	1968	255	5/-	R
	Lancer	72-614	1961	256	50¢	R
	Lancer	72-925	1965	256	50¢	R
	Lancer	72-140	1966	256	50¢	R
	Pyramid	X1403	1966	238	60¢	R
	Airmont	CL146	1967		60¢	R
She and Allan	Arrow	587	1960	288	2/6	R
Wisdom's Daughter	Hutchinson	303	*ca.*1925	128	6d	R

HAGGARD, WILLIAM (pseud) See CLAYTON, R.

HAILE, TERENCE

Author and Title	Publisher	Serial	Date	Pp.	Price	Type
Galaxies Ahead	Digit	R652	1962	160	2/6	
Space Train	Digit	R584	1962	160	2/6	

HAILEY, ARTHUR (1920—)

Author and Title	Publisher	Serial	Date	Pp.	Price	Type
In High Places	Bantam	S2526	1962	376	75¢	R
	Corgi	FN1339	1963	376	5/-	R

HAINING, PETER (1940—)

Author and Title	Publisher	Serial	Date	Pp.	Price	Type
Beyond the Curtain of Dark	FSB	1634	1966	320	5/-	A
The Craft of Terror	FSB	1678	1966	188	3/6	A
Devil Worship in Britain [with A. V. Sellwood]						
	Corgi	GS7084	1964	124	3/6	N
The Hell of Mirrors	FSB	1423	1965	189	3/6	A
Legends for the Dark	FSB	2094	1968	127	3/6	A
Summoned From the Tomb	Brown-Wat.	R968	1966	160	3/6	A
Where Nightmares Are	Mayflower	9504	1966	174	3/6	A

HALDANE, J(OHN) B(URDON) S(ANDERSON) (1892—1964)

Author and Title	Publisher	Serial	Date	Pp.	Price	Type
My Friend Mr. Leaky	Puffin	PS16	1948	124	1/6	J

HALDEMAN-JULIUS, E. See HALDEMAN-JULIUS CO., page 790.

HALEY, CLAUD

Author and Title	Publisher	Serial	Date	Pp.	Price	Type
Beyond the Solar System	Arc	1	1954	141	1/6	

HALIFAX, LORD (1839—1934)

Author and Title	Publisher	Serial	Date	Pp.	Price	Type
Lord Halifax's Ghost Book	Fontana	603	1961	287	3/6	N,R
	Fontana	603	1964	287	3/6	N,R
	Fontana	1856	1968	287	5/-	N,R

HALL, AUSTIN (*ca.*1882—1933)

Author and Title	Publisher	Serial	Date	Pp.	Price	Type
The Blind Spot [with H. E. Flint]						
	Ace	G-547	1964	318	50¢	R
The Spot of Life	Ace	F-318	1964	187	40¢	M

HALL, J. N.

Author and Title	Publisher	Serial	Date	Pp.	Price	Type
Dr. Dogbody's Leg	Armed	t-179	nd		np	

HALLUMS, JAMES R.

Author and Title	Publisher	Serial	Date	Pp.	Price	Type
They Came, They Saw	Digit	R920	1965	159	2/6	

HAMILTON, ALEXANDER (1930—)

Author and Title	Publisher	Serial	Date	Pp.	Price	Type
Beam of Malice	Corgi	GN7812	1968	190	3/6	C
The Cold Embrace	Corgi	GN7508	1966	188	3/6	A
My Blood Ran Cold [as Donald Speed]						
	Corgi	GN7507	1966	188	3/6	A

HAMILTON, EDMOND (1904—1977)
See also STAR WEEKLY, page 791.

Author and Title	Publisher	Serial	Date	Pp.	Price	Type
Battle for the Stars	Mayflower	0480	1963	190	3/6	R
	Paperback	52-311	1964	159	50¢	R
	Paperback	52-609	1967	159	50¢	R
Beyond the Moon (originally *The Star Kings*)						
	Signet	812	1950	167	25¢	R
City at World's End	Galaxy Nov	18	1953	128	35¢	R
	Corgi	T58	1954	221	2/-	R
	Crest	s184	1957	160	35¢	R
	Crest	s494	1961	160	35¢	R
	Crest	L758	1964	160	45¢	R
The Closed Worlds	Ace	G-701	1968	157	50¢	
Crashing Suns	Ace	F-319	1965	192	40¢	C,M
Danger Planet [as Brett Sterling]						
	Popular	60-2335	1968	128	60¢	M
Doomstar	Belmont	B50-657	1966	158	50¢	
Fugitive of the Stars	Ace	M-111*	1965	116	45¢	M
The Haunted Stars	Pyramid	F698	1962	159	40¢	R
The Monsters of Juntonheim (originally *A Yank at Valhalla*)						
	WDL	WFC	1950	160	1/6	M
Murder in the Clinic	Utopian	AF7	nd	36	1/-	C
Outlaw World	Popular	60-2376	1968	126	60¢	M
Outside the Universe	Ace	F-271	1964	173	40¢	M
The Star Kings (also titled *Beyond the Moon*)						
	Paperback	53-538	1967	190	60¢	R
The Star of Life	Crest	s329	1959	187	35¢	R
The Sun Smasher	Ace	D-351*	1959	110	35¢	M
Tharkol, Lord of the Unknown (originally *The Prisoner of Mars*)						
	WDL	WFC	1950	160	1/6	M
Tiger Girl	Utopian	AFnn	nd	36	1/-	A
The Valley of Creation	Lancer	72-721	1964	159	50¢	M
	Lancer	73-577	1967	159	60¢	R
The Weapon From Beyond	Ace	G-639	1967	158	50¢	
World of the Starwolves	Ace	G-766	1968	158	50¢	

HAMMETT, DASHIELL (1894—1961)

Author and Title	Publisher	Serial	Date	Pp.	Price	Type
Breakdown	FSB	1784	1968	128	3/6	A
Creeps by Night (half of stories in hardcover edition; see also *The Red Brain*)						
	Belmont	230	1961	141	35¢	A,R
	FSB	1438	1966	141	3/6	A,R
The Red Brain (other half of stories in hardcover *Creeps by Night*)						
	Belmont	239	1961	141	35¢	A,R
	FSB	1328	1965	159	3/6	A,R

HAMMOND, KAY

Author and Title	Publisher	Serial	Date	Pp.	Price	Type
The Dark City	Swan		nd	48	4d	

HAMPDEN, JOHN (1898—)

Author and Title	Publisher	Serial	Date	Pp.	Price	Type
Ghost Stories	Everyman	952	1961	384	5/-	A,R

HANLON, JON (pseud) See KEMP, E.

HANSEN, VERN

Author and Title	Publisher	Serial	Date	Pp.	Price	Type
Claws of the Night	Digit	R803	1964	158	2/6	
Creatures of the Mist	Digit	R780	1963	160	2/6	
The Grip of Fear	Digit	R840	1964	158	2/6	C
The Twisters	Digit	R727	1963	157	2/6	

HARDIE, JOHN L.

Author and Title	Publisher	Serial	Date	Pp.	Price	Type
Another Seven Strange Stories						
	Art & Educ.		*ca.*1945	80	1/3	A,R
Seven More Strange Stories	Art & Educ.		*ca.*1945	80	1/3	A,R
Seven Strange Stories	Art & Educ.		*ca.*1945	80	1/3	A,R
Strange Stories—The Last Seven						
	Art & Educ.		*ca.*1945	80	1/3	A,R

HARDY, A. S. See BOY'S FRIEND LIBRARY, page 789.

Author and Title	Publisher	Serial	Date	Pp.	Price	Type
HARDY, PHILIP						
The Buried Country	Swan		nd (1945)	32	np	
Smith Minor on the Moon	Swan		nd (1945)	32	np	
[The above pair are Nos. 26 & 19 in Swan's "Schoolboys' Pocket Library," but as listed are in chronological order.]						
HARKER, KENNETH (1927—)						
The Symmetrians	Compact	F308	1966	160	3/6	
HARKON, FRANZ						
Spawn of Space	Scion		1952	112	1/6	
HARMON, JIM (1933—)						
The Great Radio Heroes	Ace	A-27	1968	253	75¢	N,R
HARNESS, CHARLES L. (1915—)						
The Paradox Men	Ace	D-118*	1955	187	35¢	M
	FSB	1769	1967	158	3/6	R
The Ring of Ritornel	Berkley	X1630	1968	191	60¢	R
The Rose	Compact	F295	1966	189	3/6	C
HARRIS, JOHN B. (1903—1969) [as John Wyndham except as noted]						
Chocky	Ballantine	U6199	1968	221	75¢	M
The Chrysalids [originally *Re-Birth*]						
	Penguin	1308	1958	200	2/6	R
	Penguin	1308	1961	200	2/6	R
	Penguin	1308	1967	200	3/6	R
	Penguin	1308	1968	200	4/-	R
	Horwitz	H1308	1961	198	5/-	R
Consider Her Ways and Others (also titled *The Infinite Moment*)						
	Penguin	2231	1965	190	3/6	C,R
The Day of the Triffids (also titled *Revolt of the Triffids*)						
	Penguin	993	1954	272	2/-	R
	Penguin	993	1958	272	2/6	R
	Penguin	993	1968	272	4/-	R
	Horwitz	H993	1961	272	5/6	R
	Crest	D531	1962	191	50¢	R
	Crest	d741	1964	191	50¢	R
	Crest	R1049	1967	191	60¢	R
	Dolphin	C130	nd	233	95¢	R
The Infinite Moment (also titled *Consider Her Ways*)						
	Ballantine	546	1961	159	35¢	C
Jizzle	FSB	730	1962	191	2/6	C,R
	FSB	730	1963	191	2/6	C,R
	FSB	1308	1965	191	3/6	C,R
The Kraken Wakes (also titled *Out of the Deeps*)						
	Penguin	1075	1955	240	2/6	R
	Penguin	1075	1956	240	2/6	R
	Penguin	1075	1961	240	3/6	R
	Penguin	1075	1964	240	3/6	R
	Penguin	1075	1966	240	3/6	R
Love in Time [as Johnson Harris]						
	Utopian	AF nn	nd	36	1/-	M
The Midwich Cuckoos (also titled *Village of the Damned*)						
	Ballantine	299K	1959	189	35¢	R
	Ballantine	U2840	1966	189	50¢	R
	Penguin	1440	1960	220	2/6	R
	Penguin	1440	1967	220	3/6	R
Out of the Deeps (also titled *The Kraken Wakes*)						
	Ballantine	50	1953	182	35¢	R
(identical hardcover edition $2.00)						
	Ballantine	545	1961	182	35¢	R
	Ballantine	U2814	1965	182	50¢	R
The Outward Urge [as John Wyndham with Lucas Parkes, both pseud. for Harris]						
	Ballantine	341K	1959	143	35¢	R
	Ballantine	U2809	1965	143	50¢	R
	Penguin	1544	1962	187	3/-	R
Re-Birth (also titled *The Chrysalids*)						
	Ballantine	104	1955	185	35¢	R
(identical hardcover edition $2.00)						

Author and Title	Publisher	Serial	Date	Pp.	Price	Type
	Ballantine	423K	1960	185	35¢	R
	Ballantine	U2820	1965	185	50¢	R
Revolt of the Triffids (originally *The Day of the Triffids*)						
	Popular	411	1952	224	25¢	R
The Secret People [as John B. Harris]						
	Lancer	72-701	1964	175	50¢	R
	Lancer	72-155	1967	175	50¢	R
The Seeds of Time	Penguin	1385	1959	222	2/6	C,R
	Penguin	1385	1961	222	2/6	C,R
	Horwitz	H1385	1961	220	5/-	C,R
Stowaway to Mars [as John Beynon]						
	Nova	1	1953	128	1/6	R
Tales of Gooseflesh and Laughter						
	Ballantine	182	1956	150	35¢	C
	Ballantine	U2832	1966	151	50¢	C,R
Trouble With Lichen	Ballantine	449K	1960	160	35¢	R
	Penguin	1986	1963	204	3/6	R
	Penguin	1986	1965	204	3/6	R
Village of the Damned (originally *The Midwich Cuckoos*)						
	Ballantine	453K	1960	189	35¢	R
HARRIS, JOHNSON (pseud) See HARRIS, JOHN B.						
HARRIS, KATHLEEN						
Jane Arden: Space Nurse	Popular	K38	1963	126	40¢	R
HARRIS, LARRY M. (pseud) See JANIFER, L. M.						
HARRISON, HARRY (1925—)						
Best SF: 1967 [with B. W. Aldiss] (also titled *Year's Best Science Fiction*)						
	Berkley	S1529	1968	256	75¢	A
Bill, the Galactic Hero	Berkley	F1186	1966	143	50¢	R
Deathworld	Bantam	A2160	1960	154	35¢	R
	Penguin	2095	1964	158	3/-	R
	Penguin	2095	1966	158	3/6	R
Deathworld 2	Bantam	F2838	1964	151	50¢	M
Deathworld 3	Dell	1849	1968	188	60¢	M
Make Room! Make Room!	Berkley	X1416	1967	208	60¢	R
	Penguin	2664	1967	224	4/6	R
The Man From P.I.G.	Avon	ZS136	1968	120	60¢	M
Nebula Award Stories 2 [with B. W. Aldiss]						
	Pocket Bks	75114	1968	244	75¢	A,R
Plague From Space	Bantam	F3640	1968	154	50¢	R
Planet of the Damned	Bantam	J2316	1962	135	40¢	M
SF: Author's Choice	Berkley	S1567	1968	224	75¢	A
The Stainless Steel Rat	Pyramid	F672	1961	158	40¢	M
	FSB	1605	1966	158	3/6	R
The Technicolor Time Machine						
	Berkley	X1640	1968	174	60¢	R
Two Tales and Eight Tomorrows						
	Bantam	F3722	1968	147	50¢	C,R
War With the Robots	Pyramid	F771	1962	158	40¢	C
	Pyramid	X1898	1968	158	60¢	C,R
Year's Best Science Fiction [with B. W. Aldiss] (originally *Best SF: 1967*)						
	Sphere	43311	1968	207	5/-	A,R
HARTE, BRET (1836—1902)						
Selected Short Stories of Bret Harte						
	Armed	t62	nd		np	C
HARTLEY, LESLIE P. (1895—1972)						
Facial Justice	Penguin	2455	1966	220	4/6	R
The Travelling Grave	Barker	D40	1959	192	2/6	C,R
HARVEY, FRANK (1913—)						
Air Force!	Ballantine	329K	1959	142	35¢	C
HARVEY, WILLIAM F. (1885—1937)						
The Beast With Five Fingers						
	Guild	4	1941	158	3/6	C
	Aldine	10	1962	200	5/-	C,R

Author and Title	Publisher	Serial	Date	Pp.	Price	Type

HATCH, GERALD (pseud of Dave Foley)
The Day the Earth Froze — Monarch — 354 — 1963 — 125 — 35¢

HATHWAY, ALAN See DENT, L. (some "Doc Savage" stories under Kenneth Robeson pseudonym)

HAWKE, CAPT. ROBERT See BOY'S FRIEND LIBRARY, page 789.

HAWKES, JACQUETTA (1910—)
Providence Island — Grey Arrow — G89 — 1961 — 199 — 3/6 — R

HAWKINS, PETER [as Karl Maras (a pseud. also used by K. Bulmer)]
The Plant From Infinity — Paladin — — 1954 — 128 — 1/6

HAWTHORNE, JULIAN (1846—1934)
The Gray Champion and Other Tales
— Armed — 863 — nd — — np — C

HAWTHORNE, NATHANIEL (1804—1864)
See also HALDEMAN-JULIUS CO., page 790.
The Birthmark and Other Stories
— Scholastic — TK700 — 1968 — 240 — 75¢ — C
The Celestial Railroad and Other Stories
— Signet — CP153 — 1963 — 301 — 60¢ — C
Tanglewood Tales — Airmont — CL175 — 1968 — 190 — 60¢ — C,R
Twice-Told Tales and Other Short Stories
— Washington — W580 — 1961 — 430 — 50¢ — C,R
— Airmont — CL66 — 1965 — 288 — 60¢ — C,R
A Wonder Book — Lancer — 13-452 — 1968 — 221 — 60¢ — C,R

HAY, GEORGE (1922—)
Flight of the "Hesper" — Hamilton — — 1952 — 112 — 1/6
Man, Woman and Android — Authentic — 10 — 1951 — 106 — 1/6
Moment out of Time [as Roy Sheldon]
— Hamilton — — 1952 — 110 — 1/6
Terra! [as King Lang] — Curtis War. — — 1952 — 112 — 1/6
This Planet for Sale — Hamilton — — 1952 — 110 — 1/6

HAYMAN, ART
Murder Gives Notice — Transport — ST — 1951 — 32 — 8d
[cover credits Paul Valdez as author; inside credits Hayman]

HAYNES, JOHN R. (pseud) See WILDING, P.

HAYWARD, DAGNEY See BOY'S FRIEND LIBRARY, page 789.

HEALY, DOMINIC
A Voyage to Venus — Currawong — — 1943 — 165 — 2/9

HEALY, RAYMOND J. (1907—)
Adventures in Time and Space [with J. F. McComas] (selections from hardcover edition) — Bantam — P44 — 1954 — 200 — 25¢ — A,R
— Bantam — F3102 — 1966 — 181 — 50¢ — A,R
More Adventures in Time and Space [with J. F. McComas] (more selections from hardcover edition of Adventures in Time and Space)
— Bantam — 1310 — 1955 — 142 — 25¢ — A,R
— Bantam — F3261 — 1966 — 142 — 50¢ — A,R
New Tales of Space and Time
— Pocket Bks — 908 — 1952 — 273 — 25¢ — A,R
— Cardinal — C319 — 1958 — 273 — 35¢ — A,R

HEARD, HENRY F. (or GERALD) (1889—1971)
Doppelgangers — Ace — M-142 — 1966 — 253 — 45¢ — R
Is Another World Watching?
— Bantam — 1079 — 1953 — 182 — 35¢ — N,R
Reply Paid — Lancer — 72-754 — 1964 — 158 — 50¢ — R
A Taste for Honey (also titled A Taste for Murder)
— Avon — 108 — 1946 — 186 — 25¢ — R
— Penguin — 1624 — 1961 — 256 — 2/6 — R
— Lancer — 72-752 — 1964 — 142 — 50¢ — R
— Lancer — 73-647 — 1967 — 142 — 60¢ — R
A Taste for Murder (originally titled A Taste for Honey)
— Avon — 808 — 1958 — 127 — 25¢ — R

HEARN, LAFCADIO (1850—1904)
Kwaidan: Stories and Studies of Strange Things
— Dover — 21901-1 — 1968 — 113 — $1.25 — C
Selected Writings of Lafcadio Hearn
— Citadel — — 1959 — 566 — $1.75 — C

HEATH, PETER (pseud) See FINE, P.

HECHT, BEN (1893—1964)
Concerning a Woman in Sin and Other Stories
— Armed — 921 — nd — — np — C

HEINE, IRVING
Dimension of Illion — Pearson — T-B — 1954 — 64 — 9d

HEINKEL, STANFORD
King Rat — Transport — ST — 1950 — 48 — 6d

HEINLEIN, ROBERT A. (1907—)
Assignment in Eternity (see also Lost Legacy)
— Signet — 1161 — 1954 — 192 — 25¢ — C,R
— Signet — D2587 — 1965 — 192 — 50¢ — C,R
— Signet — P3163 — 1967 — 192 — 60¢ — C,R
— Digit — D368 — 1960 — 156 — 2/- — C,R
— Digit — R636 — 1962 — 156 — 2/6 — C,R
[Digit edition and Lost Legacy together give full contents of U.S. editions.]
Between Planets — Scribner's — SL67 — 1962 — 222 — $1.45 — J,R
Beyond This Horizon — Signet — S1891 — 1960 — 158 — 35¢ — R
— Signet — D2539 — 1964 — 158 — 50¢ — R
— Panther — 23488 — 1967 — 206 — 5/- — R
The Day After Tomorrow (originally Sixth Column)
— Signet — 882 — 1951 — 160 — 25¢ — R
— Signet — S1577 — 1958 — 144 — 35¢ — R
— Signet — D2649 — 1965 — 144 — 50¢ — R
— Mayflower — A36 — 1962 — 159 — 2/6 — R
The Door Into Summer — Signet — S1639 — 1959 — 159 — 35¢ — R
— Signet — D2443 — 1964 — 159 — 50¢ — R
— Panther — 1021 — 1960 — 160 — 2/6 — R
Double Star — Signet — S1444 — 1957 — 159 — 35¢ — R
— Signet — D2419 — 1964 — 128 — 50¢ — R
— Panther — 1120 — 1960 — 158 — 2/6 — R
— Panther — 1120 — 1963 — 127 — 2/6 — R
— Panther — 025022 — 1968 — 143 — 3/6 — R
Farmer in the Sky — Pan — X713 — 1967 — 174 — 3/6 — J,R
— Dell — 2518 — 1968 — 221 — 50¢ — J,R
Farnham's Freehold — Signet — T2704 — 1965 — 256 — 75¢ — R
— Signet — T2704 — 1968 — 256 — 75¢ — R
— Corgi — FS7577 — 1967 — 254 — 5/- — R
Glory Road — Avon — V2102 — 1964 — 288 — 75¢ — R
— Avon — V2102 — 1966 — 288 — 75¢ — R
— Avon — V2202 — 1967 — 288 — 75¢ — R
— FSB — 1300 — 1965 — 256 — 3/6 — R
— FSB — 2250 — 1968 — 256 — 5/- — R
The Green Hills of Earth — Signet — 943 — 1952 — 176 — 25¢ — C,R
— Signet — S1537 — 1958 — 176 — 35¢ — C,R
— Signet — D2348 — 1963 — 176 — 50¢ — C,R
— Signet — T3193 — 1967 — 176 — 75¢ — C,R
— Pan — 377 — 1956 — 189 — 2/- — C,R
— Pan — X679 — 1967 — 189 — 3/6 — C,R
— Digit — R583 — 1962 — 160 — 2/6 — C,R
Lost Legacy (see also Assignment in Eternity)
— Digit — D386 — 1960 — 156 — 2/- — C,R
The Man Who Sold the Moon
— Signet — 847 — 1951 — 167 — 25¢ — C,R
— Signet — S1644 — 1959 — 159 — 35¢ — C,R

Author and Title	Publisher	Serial	Date	Pp.	Price	Type
	Signet	D2358	1963	159	50¢	C,R
	Pan	327	1955	251	2/-	C,R
	Pan	X227	1963	238	3/6	C,R
The Menace From Earth	Signet	D2105	1962	189	50¢	C,R
	Signet	D2105	1964	189	50¢	C,R
	Corgi	07860	1968	189	3/6	C,R
Methuselah's Children	Signet	S1752	1960	160	35¢	R
	Signet	D2191	1962	160	50¢	R
	Signet	D2621	1965	160	50¢	R
	Pan	X526	1966	191	3/6	R
The Moon Is a Harsh Mistress						
	Berkley	N1601	1968	302	95¢	R
Orphans of the Sky	Signet	D2618	1965	128	50¢	C,R
	Signet	P3344	1968	128	60¢	C,R
	Mayflower	6705	1965	111	2/6	C,R
Podkayne of Mars	Avon	G1211	1964	159	50¢	J,R
	Avon	S335	1968	159	60¢	J,R
The Puppet Masters	Signet	980	1952	175	25¢	R
	Signet	S1544	1958	175	35¢	R
	Signet	D2366	1963	175	50¢	R
	Signet	P2863	1966	175	60¢	R
	Panther	1001	1960	190	2/6	R
Red Planet	Scribner's	SL100	1964	211	$1.25	J,R
	Pan	X712	1967	173	3/6	J,R
Revolt in 2100	Signet	1194	1955	192	25¢	C,R
	Signet	S1699	1959	192	35¢	C,R
	Signet	D2638	1965	192	50¢	C,R
	Signet	P3563	1968	192	60¢	C,R
	Digit	D235	1959	159	2/-	C,R
	Pan	M172	1966	253	5/-	C,R
6 X H (originally The Unpleasant Profession of Jonathan Hoag)						
	Pyramid	G642	1961	191	35¢	C,R
	Pyramid	F910	1963	191	40¢	C,R
Starman Jones	Puffin	PS267	1966	250	4/6	J,R
	Dell	8246	1967	252	60¢	J,R
Starship Troopers	FSB	299	1961	224	2/6	J,R
	FSB	1803	1967	222	5/-	J,R
	Signet	D1987	1961	208	50¢	J,R
	Signet	D2381	1963	208	50¢	J,R
	Berkley	S1560	1968	208	75¢	J,R
Stranger in a Strange Land	Avon	V2056	1962	414	75¢	R
	Avon	V2191	1967	414	75¢	R
	FSB	1282	1965	400	5/-	R
	FSB	2124	1968	400	7/6	R
	Berkley	N1571	1968	414	95¢	R
Time for the Stars	Pan	02028	1968	190	3/6	J,R
Tomorrow, the Stars	Signet	1044	1953	207	25¢	A,R
	Berkley	S1426	1967	224	75¢	A,R
Tunnel in the Sky	Pan	02029	1968	221	5/-	J,R
Universe	Dell	36	1951	64	10¢	M
The Unpleasant Profession of Jonathan Hoag (also titled 6 X H)						
	Penguin	2510	1966	221	4/-	C,R
Waldo & Magic Inc. (also titled Waldo: Genius in Orbit)						
	Pyramid	F859	1963	191	40¢	C,R
	Pyramid	X1286	1966	191	60¢	C,R
	Pyramid	X1758	1968	191	60¢	C,R
	Signet	T3690	1968		75¢	C,R
Waldo: Genius in Orbit (originally Waldo & Magic Inc.)						
	Avon	T-261	1958	191	35¢	C,R
The Worlds of Robert A. Heinlein						
	Ace	F-375	1966	189	40¢	C

HEMING, JOHN W. (1900—1953)

Author and Title	Publisher	Serial	Date	Pp.	Price	Type
From Earth to Mars	Currawong		1941	64	9d	
In Aztec Hands	Currawong		1942	64	9d	
King of the Underseas	Currawong		1941	64	6d	
The Living Dead	Currawong		1940	80	6d	
The Lost World of the Colorado						
	3-Star		nd	189	np	
Other Worlds	Currawong		1941	60	6d	

Author and Title	Publisher	Serial	Date	Pp.	Price	Type
Subterranean City	Currawong		1940	80	6d	
Time Marches Off [as Paul de Wreder]						
	Currawong		1942	80	6d	

HENDERSON, PHILIP (1906—)
Shorter Novels of the 18th Century

	Dutton		1954	278	$1.64	A,R

HENDERSON, ZENNA (1917—)
The People: No Different Flesh

	Avon	S328	1968	221	60¢	C,R

Pilgrimage: The Book of the People

	Avon	G1185	1963	255	50¢	C,R
	Avon	S243	1966	255	60¢	C,R
	Panther	1971	1965	208	3/6	C,R

HEPPER, ELIZABETH P.

Palace Under the Sea	Acorn	AB18	1963	178	79¢	J

HERBERT, A(LAN) P(ATRICK) (1890—1971)

Watch This Space	Methuen		1964	196	np	

HERBERT, BENSON (1912—)

Hand of Glory	Cole		nd (1941-45)	31	8d	
The Red-Haired Girl	Cole		nd (1941-45)	36	8d	
Strange Romance	Cole		nd (1941-45)	95	1/6	
Thieves of the Air [with F. Pragnell]						
	Cole		nd (1941-45)	27	9d	

HERBERT, FRANK (1920—)

Destination: Void	Berkley	F1249	1966	190	50¢	M
	Penguin	2689	1967	219	4/6	R
The Dragon in the Sea (also titled 21st Century Sub)						
	Penguin	1886	1963	219	3/6	R
	Avon	S290	1967	189	60¢	R
Dune	Ace	N-3	1967	544	95¢	R
	FSB	2176	1968	510	10/6	R
The Eyes of Heisenberg	Berkley	F1283	1966	158	50¢	M
	Sphere	45179	1968	157	5/-	R
The Green Brain	Ace	F-379	1966	160	40¢	M
The Heaven Makers	Avon	S319	1968	159	60¢	M
The Santaroga Barrier	Berkley	S1615	1968	255	75¢	M
21st Century Sub (originally titled The Dragon in the Sea)						
	Avon	T146	1956	190	35¢	R
	Avon	G1092	1961	190	50¢	R

HERSCHOLT, WOLFE

The Curse of Blood	Transport	ST	1949	48	6d	
Magnetic Peril	Transport	ST	1949	48	6d	
X-Ray Menace	Transport	ST	1949	48	6d	

HERSEY, JOHN (1914—)

The Child Buyer	Bantam	H2290	1961	229	60¢	R
	Penguin	2152	1965	262	4/6	R
Too Far To Walk	Bantam	N3400	1967	218	95¢	R
White Lotus	Bantam	Q3095	1966	691	$1.25	R
	Corgi	EN7568	1967	704	7/6	R

HERVEY, MICHAEL (1920—)

Creeps Medley	Hampton		nd (1941-45)	64	np	C
Death at My Heels	Mitre		ca.1946	32	9d	C
Horror Medley	Hampton		nd (1941-45)	32	1/-	C
Queer-Looking Box: Seven Gripping Mystery Stories						
	Everybody's		1944	32	6d	C
Strange Happenings	Ace	K-259	1967	189	50¢	N
Strange Hunger	Hamilton		ca.1946	128	np	
Thrilling Tales	Gulliver		nd	48	6d	C

HESKY, OLGA (? —1974)

The Purple Armchair	Mayflower	7166	1963	221	3/6	R

Author and Title	Publisher	Serial	Date	Pp.	Price	Type
HEYWOOD, ROSALIND						
The Infinite Hive	Pan	23102	1966	252	3/6	N,R
HIGGINSON, H. W.						
The Elixir	Stellar	SFS10	1930	24	10¢	
HIGH, PHILIP E. (1914—)						
Invader on My Back	Ace	H-85*	1968	146	60¢	
The Mad Metropolis	Ace	M-135*	1966	142	45¢	
No Truce With Terra	Ace	F-275*	1964	110	40¢	
The Prodigal Sun	Ace	F-255	1963	192	40¢	
	Compact	F273	1965	190	3/6	R
Reality Forbidden	Ace	G-609*	1967	151	50¢	
These Savage Futurians	Ace	G-623*	1967	134	50¢	
The Time Mercenaries	Ace	H-59*	1968	118	60¢	
Twin Planets	Paperback	52-392	1967	159	50¢	
HIGHAM, CHARLES (1931—)						
The Curse of Dracula and Other Terrifying Tales						
	Horwitz	PB111	1962	130	3/9	A
Nightmare Stories	Horwitz	PB117	1962	130	3/9	A
Spine-Tingling Tales	Horwitz	PB98	1962	162	3/9	A
Tales of Horror	Horwitz	PB104	1962	160	3/9	A
Tales of Terror	Horwitz	PB93	1961	194	4/6	A
Weird Stories	Horwitz	PB82	1961	127	3/9	A
HILL, DOUGLAS (1935—)						
The Supernatural [with Pat Williams]						
	Signet	Q3256	1967	240	95¢	N,R
Way of the Werewolf	Panther	2149	1966	143	3/6	A
HILL, ERNEST (1914—)						
Pity About Earth	Ace	H-56*	1968	132	60¢	
HILL, ROBERT See ZUGSMITH, A. (co-author)						
HILTON, JAMES (1900—1954)						
Lost Horizon	Pocket Bks	1	1939	181	25¢	R
	Pocket Bks	1	1945	239	25¢	R
	Pocket Bks	1	1952	169	25¢	R
	Pocket Bks		1956	169	25¢	R
	Pocket Bks		1959	169	25¢	R
	Armed		nd	182	np	R
	Pan	2	1947	192	1/6	R
	Pan	2	1949	189	2/-	R
	Pan	2	1950	189	1/6	R
	Pan	2	1953	189	2/-	R
	Pan	2	1954	184	2/-	R
	Pan	2	1957	184	2/-	R
	Pan	G330	1960	186	2/6	R
	Pan	G330	1962	186	2/6	R
	Pan	X588	1966	186	3/6	R
	Washington	RE108	1964	236	60¢	R
HINE, AL						
Bewitched	Dell	0551	1965	157	45¢	
	Mayflower	0551	1965	157	3/6	R
HIRSCH, PHIL						
Ghoul Days [cartoons]	Pyramid	F1101	1964	128	40¢	
HITCHCOCK, ALFRED (1899—1980)						

[The prefix *Alfred Hitchcock Presents:* is omitted from many of the titles below; see Volume 1. It is understood that most Hitchcock anthologies are "ghost" edited.]

Author and Title	Publisher	Serial	Date	Pp.	Price	Type
Alfred Hitchcock's Ghostly Gallery						
	Puffin	PS319	1967	223	5/-	A,R
Alfred Hitchcock's Haunted Household						
	FSB	1471	1966	189	5/-	A,R
Alfred Hitchcock's Witches' Brew						
	Dell	9613	1965	192	50¢	A
A Baker's Dozen of Suspense Stories						
	Dell	3626	1963	192	50¢	A
Bar the Doors	Dell	143	1946	192	25¢	A
	Dell	F166	1962	192	50¢	A,R
	Dell	0436	1965	192	50¢	A,R
	Mayflower	0436	1963	192	50¢	A,R
Behind the Locked Door and Other Strange Tales						
	FSB	1773	1967	160	5/-	A
Fear and Trembling	Dell	264	1948	192	25¢	A
	Dell	2495	1963	192	50¢	A,R
14 of My Favourites in Suspense (selections from *My Favourites in Suspense*)	Dell	F125	1960	286	50¢	A,R
14 Suspense Stories to Play Russian Roulette By (originally *Suspense*)						
	Dell	3632	1964	208	50¢	A,R
	Mayflower	3632	1964	208	3/6	A,R
The Graveyard Man	NEL	2281	1968	95	3/6	A
Guaranteed Rest in Peace	FSB	1656	1966	223	5/-	A
A Hangman's Dozen	Dell	3428	1962	222	50¢	A
	Mayflower	3428	1964	222	2/6	A,R
Hold Your Breath	Dell	206	1947	192	25¢	A
	Dell	3658	1963	192	50¢	A,R
	Mayflower	3658	1964	192	2/6	A,R
The Late Unlamented	FSB	1979	1967	128	3/6	A
Meet Death at Night	FSB	1869	1967	160	5/-	A
More of My Favourites in Suspense (selections from *My Favourites in Suspense*)	Dell	F130	1961	287	50¢	A,R
	Dell	3620	1964	287	50¢	A,R
More Stories for Late at Night (selections from *Stories for Late at Night*)	Dell	5815	1962	207	50¢	A,R
	Dell	5815	1967	207	50¢	A,R
More Stories My Mother Never Told Me (selections from *Stories My Mother Never Told Me*)	Dell	5816	1965	190	50¢	A,R
My Favourites in Suspense (part of U.S. hardcover original)						
	Pan	X177	1963	269	3/6	A,R
	Pan	10271	1968	269	5/-	A,R
My Favourites in Suspense II (rest of U.S. hardcover original)						
	Pan	X271	1963	269	3/6	A,R
	Pan	10271	1968	269	5/-	A,R
Once Upon a Dreadful Time						
	Dell	6622	1964	192	50¢	A
16 Skeletons From My Closet						
	Dell	8011	1963	221	50¢	A
	Mayflower	8011	1964	221	3/6	A,R
Stories for Late at Night I (selections from U.S. hardcover original)						
	Pan	X344	1964	285	3/6	A,R
Stories for Late at Night II (selections from U.S. hardcover original)						
	Pan	X457	1965	237	3/6	A,R
Stories My Mother Never Told Me						
	Dell	8290	1965	223	50¢	A,R
Stories My Mother Never Told Me I (selections from U.S. hardcover original)	Pan	X581	1966	255	3/6	A,R
Stories My Mother Never Told Me II (selections from U.S. hardcover original)	Pan	M250	1967	235	5/-	A,R
Stories Not for the Nervous	Dell	8288	1966	188	50¢	A,R
Stories Not for the Nervous I						
	Pan	02195	1968	187	5/-	A,R
Stories They Wouldn't Let Me Do on TV						
	Pan	X71	1960	378	3/6	A,R
	Pan	M251	1967	378	5/-	A,R
Suspense (see also *14 Suspense Stories to Play Russian Roulette By*)						
	Dell	92	1945	192	25¢	A
Suspense Stories	Dell	367	1949	192	25¢	A
13 More Stories They Wouldn't Let Me Do on TV (selections from *Stories They Wouldn't Let Me Do on TV*)						
	Dell	D281	1959	224	35¢	A,R
This Day's Evil	FSB	1723	1967	204	5/-	A
12 Stories for Late at Night (selections from *Stories for Late at Night*)						
	Dell	9178	1962	223	50¢	A,R

Author and Title	Publisher	Serial	Date	Pp.	Price	Type
12 Stories They Wouldn't Let Me Do on TV (selections from *Stories They Wouldn't Let Me Do on TV*)						
	Dell	D231	1958	224	35¢	A,R
	Dell	F206	1961	224	50¢	A,R
	Dell	3645	1962	224	50¢	A,R
HOAR, ROGER S. (1887—1963) [as Ralph Milne Farley]						
Dangerous Love	Utopian		nd	63	9d	C
An Earthman on Venus (originally *The Radio Man*)						
	Avon	285	1950	125	25¢	M
The Immortals	Popular Pub.		1947	46	1/-	M
The Radio Beasts	Ace	F-304	1964	191	40¢	M
The Radio Planet	Ace	F-312	1964	224	40¢	M
HODDER-WILLIAMS, CHRISTOPHER (1926—)						
Chain Reaction	Hodder	485	1961	258	3/6	R
	Corgi	GS7484	1966	190	3/6	R
Final Approach	Hodder		1961	252	3/6	R
The Main Experiment	Ballantine	U6049	1966	238	75¢	R
	Corgi	GN7390	1966	190	3/6	R
HODGSON, WILLIAM H. (1877—1918)						
The House on the Borderland						
	Ace	D-553	1962	159	35¢	R
HOFFE, ARTHUR						
Something Evil	Avon	S368	1968	175	60¢	
HOFFMAN, KURT						
Blackmarket Brains	Transport	ST	1949	48	6d	
HOFFMAN, LEE (1932—)						
Telepower	Belmont	B50-779*	1967	85	50¢	
HOFFMANN, E. T. A. (1776—1822)						
The Best Tales of Hoffmann [Editor—E. F. Bleiler]						
	Dover	21793	1967	419	$2.50	C
Tales of Hoffmann [Editor—C. Lazare]						
	Grove	E147	1959	509	$2.45	C
HOLBERG, LUDWIG (1684—1754)						
Journey of Niels Klim to the World Underground						
	Bison	BB102	1960	336	$1.40	R
HOLDEN, RICHARD C.						
Snow Fury	Permabks	M3034	1956	194	25¢	R
HOLE, CHRISTINA (1896—)						
A Mirror of Witchcraft	Pedigree		1960	245	3/6	N
Witchcraft in England	Collier	02886	1968	222	$1.50	N
HOLLAND, BOB						
The Permabook of Ghost Stories						
	Permabks	P94	1950	188	35¢	A,R
HOLLEDGE, JAMES						
Black Magic	Scripts	40	1967	160	60¢	N
Flying Saucers Over Australia						
	Horwitz	36	1965	130	5/-	N
HOLLIDAY, DON						
Three on a Broomstick	Adult	AB40	1967			
HOLLOWAY, BRIAN						
"A" Men [as Rand Le Page]	Curtis War.		1952	127	1/6	
Destination Alpha [as Berl Cameron]						
	Curtis War.		1952	127	1/6	
Red Storm [as Brian Storm]	Curtis War.		1952	112	1/6	
Titan's Moon [as Neil Charles]						
	Curtis War.		1952	112	1/6	
Trans-Mercurian [as King Lang]						
	Curtis War.		1952	112	1/6	

Author and Title	Publisher	Serial	Date	Pp.	Price	Type
HOLLY, J. HUNTER (pseud) See HOLLY, JOAN						
HOLLY, JOAN C. (1932—) [as J. Hunter Holly]						
The Assassination Affair	Ace	G-636	1967	158	50¢	
Encounter	Monarch	240	1962	142	35¢	R
The Flying Eyes	Monarch	260	1962	140	35¢	R
The Green Planet	Monarch	213	1961	143	35¢	R
The Grey Aliens	Mayflower	3255	1964	125	2/6	R
The Mind Traders	Macfadden	60-291	1967	143	60¢	R
The Running Man	Monarch	342	1963	142	35¢	
The Time Twisters	Avon	G1231	1964	160	50¢	
HOLMES, D. C.						
The Search for Life on Other Worlds						
	Bantam	SA2	1967	184	75¢	N
HOLT, CONRAD G. (pseud) See FEARN, J. R.						
HOLT, JOHN R. [as Raymond Giles]						
Night of the Warlock	Paperback	53-677	1968	160	60¢	
HOLTON, LEONARD						
A Pact With Satan	Dell	6809	1963	142	40¢	
HOLZER, HANS W. (1920—)						
ESP and You	Ace	H-100	1968	220	60¢	N
Ghost Hunter	Ace	K-210	1965	160	50¢	N
Ghosts I've Met	Ace	H-16	1966	253	60¢	N
Lively Ghosts of Ireland	Ace	H-47	1968		60¢	N
Yankee Ghosts	Ace	K-272	1967	191	50¢	N
HOME-GALL, EDWARD R(EGINALD)						
The Human Bat	Goulden		*ca.*1949	127	1/6	
The Human Bat v. the Robot Gangster						
	Goulden		*ca.*1949	128	1/6	
HOMER						
A Bedside Odyssey (understood to be a sexed-up version)						
	Olympia	TC206	1967	192	$1.25	R
Odyssey	Armed	925	nd		np	R
HOOPES, NED E(DWARD) (1932—)						
Speak of the Devil	Dell	8184	1967	205	60¢	A
HOPKINS, R. THURSTON (1884—1958)						
Cavalcade of Ghosts	Panther	1502	1963	219	3/6	N,R
Horror Parade	Mitre		1945	63	1/-	C
Uncanny Tales	Mitre		1944	32	9d	C
Weird and Uncanny Stories	Mitre		1945	32	1/-	C
The World's Strangest Ghost Stories						
	Cedar	57	1958	317	5/-	C,R
HOPLEY, GEORGE (pseud) See WOOLRICH, C.						
HORAN, KEITH						
The Squid	Bernardo		1946	64	1/6	
HORLER, SYDNEY (1888—1954)						
The Curse of Doone	Hodder	C215	1955	192	2/-	
	Paperback	53-931	1966	224	60¢	R
Lord of Terror	Hillman	TNC 5	*ca.*1950		25¢	R
HOUGH, STANLEY B. (1917—) [as Rex Gordon except as noted]						
Extinction Bomber [as S. B. Hough]						
	WDL	W419	1958	190	2/6	R
First on Mars (originally *No Man Friday*)						
	Ace	D-233	1957	192	35¢	
First Through Time (also titled *The Time Factor*)						
	Ace	F-174	1962	160	40¢	
First to the Stars (also titled *The Worlds of Eclos*)						
	Ace	D-405	1959	190	35¢	

Author and Title	Publisher	Serial	Date	Pp.	Price	Type
No Man Friday (also titled *First on Mars*)						
	Corgi	S569	1958	222	2/6	R
The Paw of God (originally *Utopia Minus X*)						
	Tandem	T107	1967	189	3/6	R
The Time Factor (originally *First Through Time*)						
	Panther	1921	1965	121	3/6	R
Utopia Minus X (also titled *The Paw of God*)						
	Ace	F-416	1966	190	40¢	
Utopia 239	Consul	SF1053	1961	222	2/6	R
The Worlds of Eclos (originally *First to the Stars*)						
	Consul	SF1050	1961	160	2/6	R

HOUGHTON, CLAUDE (pseud of Claude Houghton Oldfield [1889–1961])

The Man Who Could Still Laugh						
	Todd	'Bantam'	1943	16	6d	
The Passing of the Third Floor Back						
	Readers' Library	nd		128	1/6	
Three Fantastic Tales	Todd	'Polybook'	1943	16	4d	C

HOUSE, BRANT (pseud) See CHADWICK, P.

HOUSEHOLD, GEOFFREY (1900–)

The Spanish Cave (originally *The Terror of the Villadonga*)						
	Comet	12	1948	178	np	C
	Berkley	F1315	1966	143	50¢	R

HOWARD, DANA

My Flight to Venus	Regency (Brit)		nd	64	5/-	

HOWARD, ELIZABETH J. See AICKMAN, R. (co-author)

HOWARD, HAYDEN

The Eskimo Invasion	Ballantine	U6112	1967	380	75¢	M

HOWARD, IVAN

Escape to Earth	Belmont	L92-571	1963	173	50¢	A
Novelets of Science Fiction	Belmont	L92-567	1963	173	50¢	A
	Belmont	B50-770	1967	173	50¢	A,R
Rare Science Fiction	Belmont	L92-557	1963	173	50¢	A
6 and the Silent Scream	Belmont	L92-564	1963	173	50¢	A
	Consul	1298	1964	206	2/6	A,R
Things	Belmont	L92-582	1964	157	50¢	A
	Mayflower	7815	1965	173	3/6	A,R
Way Out	Belmont	L92-575	1963	173	50¢	A

HOWARD, ROBERT E. (1906–1936)
[For completeness, all *Conan* series paperbacks are listed here, though some are revised—or written entirely—by other authors, as noted: L. Sprague de Camp (L.S. de C.), Lin Carter (L.C.), and Björn Nyberg (B.N.). The series was not yet complete during the period of this coverage; see Volume 1.]

Almuric	Ace	F-305	1964	157	40¢	M
Conan [with L.S. de C. & L.C.]						
	Lancer	73-685	1967	221	60¢	C
	Lancer	74-958	1968	221	75¢	C,R
Conan of the Isles [by L.S. de C. & L.C.]						
	Lancer	73-800	1968	189	60¢	
Conan the Adventurer [with L.S. de C.]						
	Lancer	73-526	1966	224	60¢	C
Conan the Avenger [by L.S. de C. & B.N.]						
	Lancer	73-680	1968	192	60¢	
Conan the Conqueror	Ace	D-36*	1954	131	35¢	R
	Lancer	73-572	1967	224	60¢	R
Conan the Freebooter [with L.S. de C.]						
	Lancer	74-963	1968	223	75¢	C
Conan the Usurper [with L.S. de C.]						
	Lancer	73-599	1967	256	60¢	C
Conan the Wanderer [with L.S. de C. & L.C.]						
	Lancer	74-976	1968	222	95¢	C

Author and Title	Publisher	Serial	Date	Pp.	Price	Type
Conan the Warrior [with L.S. de C.]						
	Lancer	73-549	1967	222	60¢	C
King Kull [with L.C., edited by Glenn Lord]						
	Lancer	73-650	1967	223	60¢	C
Wolfshead	Lancer	73-721	1968	190	60¢	C

HOWELLS, WILLIAM D. (1837–1920)

A Traveler From Altruria	Sagamore	S16	1957	211	$1.35	R

HOYLE, FRED (1915–)

A for Andromeda [with J. Elliot]						
	Corgi	YS1300	1963	172	3/-	R
	Corgi	GS7348	1966	174	3/6	R
	Crest	d773	1964	205	50¢	R
	Crest	R1205	1968	205	60¢	R
Andromeda Breakthrough [with J. Elliot]						
	Corgi	GS7347	1966	190	3/6	R
	Crest	R1080	1967	192	60¢	R
The Black Cloud	Signet	S1673	1959	191	35¢	R
	Signet	D2202	1962	191	50¢	R
	Signet	P3384	1968	191	60¢	R
	Penguin	1466	1960	219	2/6	R
	Penguin	1466	1963	219	3/-	R
	Penguin	1466	1968	219	4/-	R
	Perennial	P37	1965	214	50¢	R
Element 79	Signet	P3463	1968	143	60¢	C,R
Encounter With the Future	Simon & Schuster		1968	108	$1.95	N
Fifth Planet [with Geoffrey Hoyle]						
	Crest	d812	1965	192	50¢	R
	Penguin	2244	1965	220	3/6	R
Frontiers of Astronomy	Mentor	MD200	1957	317	50¢	N,R
	Signet	T2309	1963		75¢	N,R
The Nature of the Universe	Signet		1954	128	35¢	N,R
	Signet	P2331	1963	125	60¢	N,R
October the First Is Too Late						
	Crest	R1155	1968	160	60¢	R
	Penguin	2886	1968	175	4/-	R
Ossian's Ride	Berkley	G495	1961	153	35¢	R
	Berkley	X1506	1968	153	60¢	R
	FSB	317	1961	189	2/6	R
	FSB	2051	1967	189	3/6	R
	Harper	P60A	1965	181	50¢	R

HUBBARD, L. RON (1911–)

Fear	Galaxy Nov	29	1957	125	35¢	R
Return to Tomorrow	Ace	S-66	1954	157	25¢	M
	Panther	692	1957	144	2/-	R
Slaves of Sleep	Lancer	73-573	1967	176	60¢	R
Typewriter in the Sky & Fear						
	Kemsley	CT409	1952	190	1/6	R

HUDSON, DEAN

Dreamlover	Idle Hour	IH576	1966			
Nightmare Clinic	Ember Lib	EL303	1965			
The N.U.D.E. Caper	Candid Reader					
		CA909	1967			

HUDSON, JAN (pseud) See SMITH, GEORGE H.

HUDSON, W(ILLIAM) H. (1841–1922)

A Crystal Age	Armed	G-196	nd	256	np	R
Green Mansions	Pocket Bks	16	1939	271	25¢	R
	Armed	c-71	nd	285	np	R
	Guild	420	1950	216	1/6	R
	Bantam	63	1946	275	np	R
	Bantam	F1878	1959	298	50¢	R
	Bantam	HP103	1965	298	60¢	R
	Airmont	CL87	1965	224	50¢	R
	Paperduck	9	1966	283	10/6	R

Author and Title	Publisher	Serial	Date	Pp.	Price	Type
HUGHES, CLEDWYN						
He Dared Not Look Behind!						
	Export	60	1949	160	25¢	
HUGHES, DEN(NIS)						
Bio-Muton [as Lee Elliot]						
	Curtis War.		1952	128	1/6	
(identical hardcover edition 5/-)						
Biology "A" [as Brad Kent]	Curtis War.		1952	128	1/6	
Blue Cordon [as Dee Carter]	Curtis War.		1952	128	1/6	
(identical hardcover edition 5/-)						
Blue Peril [as Ray Barry]	Curtis War.		1952	128	1/6	
Catalyst [as Brad Kent]	Curtis War.		1952	112	1/6	
Chloroplasm [as Dee Carter]						
	Curtis War.		1953	159	1/6	
(identical hardcover edition 5/-)						
Death Dimension [as Ray Barry]						
	Curtis War.		1952	112	1/6	
The Earth Invasion Battalion						
	Curtis War.		1950	128	1/6	
Elektron Union [as Gill Hunt]						
	Curtis War.		1951	112	1/6	
The Fatal Law [as Brad Kent]						
	Curtis War.		1952	112	1/6	
Formula 695	Curtis War.		*ca.*1950	128	1/6	
Gamma Product [as Ray Barry]						
	Curtis War.		1952	127	1/6	
Hostile Worlds [as Gill Hunt]						
	Curtis War.		1951	112	1/6	
House of Many Changes [as Van Reed]						
	Curtis War.		1952	128	1/6	
(identical hardcover edition 5/-)						
Humanoid Puppets [as Ray Barry]						
	Curtis War.		1952	127	1/6	
The Land of Esa [as Neil Charles]						
	Curtis War.		1952	128	1/6	
Lost Aeons [as Berl Cameron]						
	Curtis War.		1953	159	1/6	
(identical hardcover edition 6/-)						
Maid of Thuro [as John Lane]						
	Curtis War.		1952	128	1/6	
(identical hardcover edition 5/-)						
Moon War	Curtis War.		1951	128	1/6	
Murder by Telecopter	Curtis War.		1950	127	1/6	
Ominous Folly [as Ray Barry]						
	Curtis War.		1952	112	1/6	
Planet X [as Gill Hunt]	Curtis War.		1951	112	1/6	
Purple Islands [as Dee Carter]						
	Curtis War.		1953	159	1/6	
(identical hardcover edition 6/-)						
The Queen People [as Russell Rey]						
	Curtis War.		1952	127	1/6	
(identical hardcover edition 5/-)						
Space Flight [as Gill Hunt]	Curtis War.		1951	111	1/6	
Spatial Ray [as Gill Hunt]	Curtis War.		1951	111	1/6	
Twenty-Four Hours [as Neil Charles]						
	Curtis War.		1952	128	1/6	
(identical hardcover edition 5/-)						
War Lords of Space	Curtis War.		1950	128	1/6	
HUGHES DOROTHY B(ELLE) (1904—)						
The Delicate Ape	Armed	828	nd		np	R
HUGHES, JEAN						
Ditta's Tree	Puffin	PS57	1952	109	np	J
	Puffin	PS57	1968	109	3/6	J,R
HUGHES, PENNETHORNE						
Witchcraft	Pelican	A745	1965	236	5/-	N

Author and Title	Publisher	Serial	Date	Pp.	Price	Type
HUGHES, RILEY (? —1981)						
The Hills Were Liars	All-Saints	AS230	1962	216	50¢	R
HUGHES, WALTER L. (1910—) [as Hugh Walters]						
Blast Off at Woomera	Faber		1965	202	6/6	J,R
First on the Moon	Tempo	T13	1962	192	50¢	J,R
HULL, E. MAYNE See VAN VOGT, A. E. (co-author)						
HUME, FERGUS See A. M. GARDNER, page 790.						
HUNGER, ANNA See MILLER, R. D. (co-author)						
HUNT, GILL (house pseudonym)						
Elektron Union See HUGHES, DEN						
Fission See GRIFFITHS, D. A.						
Galactic Storm See BRUNNER, J.						
Hostile Worlds See HUGHES, DEN						
Planet Fall See TUBB, E. C.						
Planet X See HUGHES, DEN						
Space Flight See HUGHES, DEN						
Spatial Ray See HUGHES, DEN						
Station 7 See JENNISON, J. W.						
Vega See GRIFFITHS, D. A.						
Zero Field See JENNISON, J. W.						
HUNTER, EVAN [former pseudonym, now legal name of S. A. Lombino] (1926—)						
The Last Spin	Corgi	GN1021	1961	220	3/6	C,R
Tomorrow and Tomorrow [as Hunt Collins]						
	Pyramid	G214	1956	190	35¢	R
	Pyramid	G654	1961	190	35¢	R
	Pyramid	R1170	1965	190	50¢	R
HUNTER, MOLLIE (pseud of Maureen Mollie McIlwraith [1922—])						
The Kelpie's Pearls	Avon	ZS146	1968	112	60¢	R
HUNTER, NORMAN						
The Incredible Adventures of Professor Branestawm						
	Puffin	PS33	1946	208	1/6	J,R
	Puffin	PS33	1950	208	1/6	J,R
	Puffin	PS33	1959	208	2/6	J,R
Professor Branestawm's Treasure Hunt						
	Puffin	PS275	1966	197	3/6	C,J
HURKOS, PETER						
Psychic	Tandem	T114	1967	160	3/6	N?
HURLEY, RICHARD J(AMES) (1906—)						
Beyond Belief	Scholastic	T573	1966	188	45¢	A
HURWOOD, BERNHARDT J(ACKSON) (1926—)						
The Dirty Rotten Depriving Ray [as Mallory T. Knight]						
	Award	287X	1967	191	60¢	
The Dozen Deadly Dragons of Joy [as Mallory T. Knight]						
	Award		1967	175		
The First Occult Review Reader						
	Award	A346SK	1968	188	75¢	N
The Malignant Metaphysical Menace [as Mallory T. Knight]						
	Award		1968	156		
The Million Missing Maidens [as Mallory T. Knight]						
	Award		1967	192		
Monsters and Nightmares	Belmont	B50-735	1967	156	50¢	C,N
Monsters Galore	Gold Medal	d1544	1965	224	50¢	A
Strange Talents	Ace	K-276	1967	189	50¢	N
The Terrible Ten [as Mallory T. Knight]						
	Award		1967	190		
Terror by Night	Lancer	72-656	1963	127	50¢	N
Tsimmis in Tangier [as Mallory T. Knight]						
	Award		1968	156		
Vampires, Werewolves and Ghouls						
	Ace	H-83	1968	158	60¢	N

Author and Title	Publisher	Serial	Date	Pp.	Price	Type
HUXLEY, ALDOUS (1894—1963)						
After Many a Summer Dies the Swan						
	Avon	388	1951	250	25¢	R
	Avon	AT435	1952	250	35¢	R
	Avon	T75	1954	254	35¢	R
	Avon	G2001	ca.1960	254	50¢	R
	Avon	VS1	1964	254	75¢	R
	Penguin	1049	1955	251	4/-	R
	Penguin	1049	1959	251	4/-	R
	Penguin	1049	1961	251	4/-	R
	Penguin	1049	1965	251	5/6	R
Ape and Essence	Bantam	A1793	1958	152	35¢	R
	Bantam	HC262	1964	152	60¢	R
Brave New World	Bantam	A1071	1953	266	35¢	R
	Bantam	A1369	1955	177	35¢	R
	Bantam	AC1	1959	177	35¢	R
	Bantam	FC85	1962	177	50¢	R
	Bantam	FC189	1962	177	50¢	R
	Bantam	HC206	1964	177	60¢	R
	Bantam	SY4172	1968	177	75¢	R
	Penguin	1052	1955	201	4/-	R
	Penguin	1052	1958	201	4/-	R
	Penguin	1052	1966	201	5/6	R
Brave New World Revisited	Bantam	F2124	1960	116	50¢	N,R
	Perennial	P23	1965	118	50¢	N,R
The Gioconda Smile and Other Weird Stories						
	Armed	926	nd		np	C
Island	Bantam	S2695	1963	295	75¢	R
	Bantam	N3481	1968	295	95¢	R
	Penguin	2193	1964	297	4/6	R
	Penguin	2193	1966	297	5/-	R
	Penguin	2193	1968	297	5/-	R
Time Must Have a Stop	Berkley	X834	1963	239	60¢	R
Tomorrow and Tomorrow and Tomorrow						
	Signet	P2450	1964	222	60¢	N

I,J

Author and Title	Publisher	Serial	Date	Pp.	Price	Type
IBSEN, HENRIK (1828—1906)						
Peer Gynt	Signet	CP215	1964	253	60¢	R
IGGULDEN, JOHN M. (1917—)						
Breakthrough	FSB	873	1963	221	3/6	R
INNES, HAMMOND						
The Survivors	Collier	AS144	1962	256	95¢	
IRISH, WILLIAM (pseud) See WOOLRICH, C.						
IRVING, CLIFFORD						
The Thirty-Eighth Floor	Pan	30044	1968	304	6/-	
IRVING, WASHINGTON (1783—1859)						
See also HALDEMAN-JULIUS CO., page 790.						
The Legend of Sleepy Hollow and Other Stories						
	Washington	W581	1962	265	60¢	C
	Airmont	CL50	1964	190	50¢	C
	Lancer	13-453	1968	318	60¢	C
The World of Washington Irving						
	Dell	9700	1965	320	50¢	C

Author and Title	Publisher	Serial	Date	Pp.	Price	Type
JACKSON, NORMAN						
The Daring Adventures of Captain Sex						
	Lancer	73-809	1968	190	60¢	
JACKSON, SHIRLEY (1919—1965)						
The Bird's Nest (also titled *Lizzie*)						
	Tower		1965			R
	Tower	44-775	1967	254	75¢	R
Hangsaman	Ace	K-185	1964	191	50¢	
The Haunting of Hill House						
	Popular	K6	1962	174	40¢	R
	Popular	60-2121	1968	174	60¢	R
	FSB	848	1963	190	2/6	R
Lizzie (retitling of *The Bird's Nest*)						
	Signet		1957			
The Lottery	Lion	14	1950	238	25¢	C,R
	Avon	T449	1960	222	35¢	C,R
	Avon	S197	1965	219	60¢	C,R
The Sundial	Ace	K-166	1963	192	50¢	R
	Ace	H-96	1968	192	60¢	R
JACOB, PIERS ANTHONY DILLINGHAM (1934—) [as Piers Anthony]						
Chthon	Ballantine	U6107	1967	254	75¢	
Omnivore	Ballantine	72014	1968	221	75¢	
The Ring [as Piers Anthony, with R. Margroff]						
	Ace	A-19	1968	254	75¢	
Sos, the Rope	Pyramid	X-1890	1968	157	60¢	M
JAKES, JOHN (1932—)						
Brak the Barbarian	Avon	S363	1968	173	60¢	
When the Star Kings Die	Ace	G-656	1967	160	50¢	
JAMES, HENRY (1843—1916)						
See also HALDEMAN-JULIUS CO., page 790.						
The Aspern Papers & The Turn of the Screw						
	Everyman	1912	1964	299	6/-	C
[*The Aspern Papers* is not weird or sf.]						
Ghostly Tales of Henry James [Editor—L. Edel]						
	Univ. Lib.	UL-161	1963	433	$2.25	C
The Turn of the Screw (see also *The Aspern Papers*)						
	Zephyr	159	1947			C
	Penguin		1946			
	Dell	D181	1956		25¢	C
	WDL	W937	1960	143	2/6	
	Airmont	CL155	1967	127	50¢	
The Turn of the Screw & Daisy Miller						
	Dell	800	1954	121	25¢	C
	Lancer	13-433	1968	284	60¢	C
The Turn of the Screw and Other Stories						
	Scholastic	TK650	1966	316	60¢	C
JAMES, M(ONTAGUE) R. (1862—1936)						
Ghost Stories of an Antiquary						
	Penguin	91	1937	256	np	C,R
	Penguin	91	1959	153	2/6	C,R
	Penguin	91	1960	153	2/6	C,R
	Pan	266	1953	159	2/-	C,R
More Ghost Stories of an Antiquary						
	Pan	359	1955	160	2/-	C,R
	Penguin	1347	1959	152	2/6	C,R
	Penguin	1347	1962	154	2/6	C,R
Selected Ghost Stories of M. R. James						
	Armed	o-28	1944	352	np	C
JAMESON, MALCOLM (1891—1945)						
Atomic Bomb	Bond-Charteris		1945	128	25¢	M
Tarnished Utopia	Galaxy Nov	27	1956	126	35¢	M
JANES, GENE						
Come and Go Mad	Calvert		1964	126	4/-	

Author and Title	Publisher	Serial	Date	Pp.	Price	Type
JANIFER, LAURENCE M. (1933—)						
Bloodworld (originally *You Sane Men*)						
	Lancer	73-752	1968	159	60¢	R
Brain Twister [as Mark Phillips, pseud. with R. Garrett]						
	Pyramid	F783	1962	144	40¢	M
Impossible?	Belmont	B50-810	1968	159	50¢	C
The Impossibles [as Mark Phillips, pseud. with R. Garrett]						
	Pyramid	F875	1963	157	40¢	M
	Pyramid	R1299	1966	157	50¢	R
Master's Choice 1 (part of hardcover edition)						
	Tandem	PB380	1968	175	3/6	A,R
Master's Choice 2 (rest of hardcover edition)						
	Tandem	PB381	1968	160	3/6	A,R
Pagan Passions [as Larry M. Harris, with R. Garrett]						
	Beacon	263	1959	158	35¢	
A Piece of Martin Cann	Belmont	B50-811	1968	141	50¢	
Slave Planet	Pyramid	F840	1963	142	40¢	
Supermind [as Mark Phillips, pseud. with R. Garrett]						
	Pyramid	F909	1963	192	40¢	M
Target: Terra [with J. Treibich]						
	Ace	H-91*	1968	104	60¢	
The Wonder War	Pyramid	F963	1964	128	40¢	
	Pyramid	R963	1964	128	50¢	R
You Sane Men (also titled *Bloodworld*)						
	Lancer	72-789	1965	159	50¢	
JANSON, HANK (house pseud)						
Tomorrow and a Day	Alex Moring		1955	160		
The Unseen Assassin	Alex Moring		1950	159	2/6	
	Top Fiction		1953	142	2/-	R
JARDINE, JACK OWEN (1931—)						
The Emerald Elephant Gambit [as Larry Maddock]						
	Ace	G-644	1967	158	50¢	
The Flying Saucer Gambit [as Larry Maddock]						
	Ace	G-605	1966	159	50¢	
The Golden Goddess Gambit [as Larry Maddock]						
	Ace	G-620	1967	158	50¢	
The Mind Monsters [as Howard L. Cory (pseud. with Julie A. Jardine)]						
	Ace	G-602*	1966	156	50¢	
The Nymph and the Satyr [as Arthur Farmer]						
	All Star	518	1962	154		
The Sword of Lankor [as Howard L. Cory (pseud. with Julie A. Jardine)]						
	Ace	F-373	1966	158	40¢	
JARDINE, JULIE A. See JARDINE, JACK O. (co-author)						
JASON, JERRY						
Sexodus	Boudoir	1027	1963	160	60¢	
JAVOR, FRANK A.						
The Rim-World Legacy	Signet	P3183	1967	144	60¢	
JENKINS, WILL(IAM) F(ITZGERALD) (1896—1975) [as Murray Leinster unless otherwise noted]						
The Aliens	Berkley	G410	1960	144	35¢	C
	Berkley	F1139	1965	144	50¢	C,R
The Black Galaxy	Galaxy Nov	20	1954	127	35¢	M
The Brain Stealers	Ace	D-79*	1954	139	35¢	M
	Badger	SF33	1960	141	2/-	R
Checkpoint Lambda	Berkley	F1263	1966	143	50¢	M
City on the Moon	Ace	D-277*	1958	151	35¢	R
Creatures of the Abyss	Berkley	G549	1961	143	35¢	
Destroy the U.S.A. [as Will F. Jenkins] (originally *The Murder of the U.S.A.*)						
	Export Newsstand					
		141	1950	157	25¢	R
Doctor to the Stars	Pyramid	F987	1964	176	40¢	M
The Duplicators	Ace	F-275*	1964	143	40¢	M
Fight for Life	Crestwood	Prize 10	1949	118	25¢	M
The Forgotten Planet	Ace	D-146*	1956	175	35¢	R
	Ace	D-528	1961	175	35¢	R
Four From Planet Five	Gold Medal	s937	1959	160	35¢	M
	Gold Medal	K1397	1964	160	40¢	R
Gateway to Elsewhere	Ace	D-53*	1954	139	35¢	M
Get Off My World!	Belmont	B50-676	1966	157	50¢	C,M
The Greks Bring Gifts	Macfadden	50-224	1964	143	50¢	
	Macfadden	50-418	1968	143	50¢	R
Invaders of Space	Berkley	F1022	1964	144	50¢	
	Tandem	T201	1968	141	3/6	R
Land of the Giants	Pyramid	X1846	1968	156	60¢	
The Last Space Ship	Kemsley	CT404	1952	190	1/6	R
	Galaxy Nov	25	1955	126	35¢	R
Men Into Space	Berkley	G461	1960	142	35¢	
Miners in the Sky	Avon	G1310	1967	127	50¢	
	Sphere	54828	1968	125	5/-	R
The Monster From Earth's End						
	Gold Medal	s832	1959	176	35¢	
	Muller	GM433	1960	159	2/-	R
Monsters and Such	Avon	T345	1959	174	35¢	C
The Murder of the U.S.A. [as Will F. Jenkins] (also titled *Destroy the U.S.A.*)						
	Quinn	H62	1947	127	20¢	R
The Mutant Weapon	Ace	D-403*	1959	93	35¢	M
Operation: Outer Space	Fantasy	3	1956	208	$1.00	R
	Signet	S1346	1957	160	35¢	R
Operation Terror	Berkley	F694	1962	160	50¢	
	Tandem	T200	1968	160	3/6	R
The Other Side of Here	Ace	D-94*	1955	134	35¢	M
The Other Side of Nowhere	Berkley	F918	1964	142	50¢	M
The Pirates of Zan	Ace	D-403*	1959	163	35¢	M
The Planet Explorer (originally *Colonial Survey*)						
	Avon	T202	1957	171	35¢	R
S.O.S. From Three Worlds	Ace	G-647	1967	140	50¢	C,M
Space Captain	Ace	M-135*	1966	112	45¢	M
Space Gypsies	Avon	G1318	1967	128	50¢	
	Sphere	54798	1968	127	5/-	R
Space Platform	Pocket Bks	920	1953	167	25¢	J,R
	Belmont	92625	1965	157	50¢	J,R
Space Tug	Pocket Bks	1037	1955	154	25¢	J,R
	Belmont	B50-632	1965	157	50¢	J,R
	Belmont	B50-846	1968	157	50¢	J,R
Talents, Incorporated	Avon	G1120	1962	159	50¢	
This World Is Taboo	Ace	D-525	1961	127	35¢	M
Time Tunnel	Pyramid	R1043	1964	140	50¢	
The Time Tunnel	Pyramid	R1522	1967	143	50¢	
[Above two novels are different stories, the latter adapted from the TV series.]						
Timeslip!	Pyramid	R1680	1967	140	50¢	
Twists in Time	Avon	T389	1960	160	35¢	C
The Wailing Asteroid	Avon	T483	1961	143	35¢	
	Avon	G1306	1966	143	50¢	R
	Sphere	34801	1968	142	5/-	R
War With the Gizmos	Gold Medal	s751	1958	156	35¢	M
	Muller	GM368	1960	159	2/-	R
	Muller	nn	nd	159	3/-	R
JENNISON, JOHN W(ILLIAM)						
Para-Robot [as Neil Charles]						
	Curtis War.		1952	112	1/6	
Space Line [as King Lang]	Curtis War.		1952	112	1/6	
Station 7 [as Gill Hunt]	Curtis War.		1952	112	1/6	
Zero Field [as Gill Hunt]	Curtis War.		1952	112	1/6	
JESSUP, MORRIS K.						
The Case for the UFO	Bantam	A1374	1955	208	35¢	N,R
JOHNSON, EDWIN						
Strangers in Space	Spitfire		1967	128	1/-	J

Author and Title	Publisher	Serial	Date	Pp.	Price	Type
JOHNSON, J. W.						
Utopian Literature: A Selection						
	Random College	T96	1968		$1.95	N
JOHNSTON, WILLIAM (1924—)						
And Loving It	Tempo		1967	153		
Captain Nice	Tempo	T-158	1967	188	60¢	
Get Smart!	Tempo		1965	159		
Get Smart Once Again!	Tempo		1966	154		
The Littlest Rebels	Ace		1968	175		
Max Smart and the Perilous Pellets						
	Tempo		1966	154		
Max Smart Loses Control	Tempo		1968	148		
Max Smart—The Spy Who Went Out to the Cold						
	Tempo		1968	152		
Miracle at San Tanco	Ace	G-702	1968	175	50¢	
Missed It By That Much!	Tempo		1967	151		
Sorry, Chief	Tempo		1966	154		
JONES, CONSTANCE B. See JONES, GUY P. (co-author)						
JONES, D(ENNIS) F(ELTHAM) (*ca.*1915—1981)						
Colossus	Berkley	X1455	1967	223	60¢	R
	Pan	02110	1968	221	5/-	R
JONES, FRANK EARL						
The Big-Ball	Jones		1958	156	$1.00	
JONES, GUY PEARCE						
Peabody's Mermaid [with Constance B. Jones]						
	Pocket Bks	503	1948	184	25¢	R
JONES, H. SPENCER (1890—1960)						
Life on Other Worlds	Mentor	M39	1949	160	35¢	N,R
	Mentor	MD144	1956	160	50¢	N,R
	Mentor	MP440	1962	160	60¢	N,R
	Hodder	360	1959	251	3/6	N,R
JONES, NEIL R. (1909—)						
Doomsday on Ajiat	Ace	G-719	1968	159	50¢	C,M
The Planet of the Double Sun						
	Ace	F-420	1967	123	40¢	C,M
Space War	Ace	G-650	1967	158	50¢	C,M
The Sunless World	Ace	G-631	1967	189	50¢	C,M
Twin Worlds	Ace	G-681	1967	157	50¢	C,M
JONES, RAYMOND F. (1915—)						
The Alien	Galaxy Nov	6	1951	160	35¢	
	Belmont	B50-708	1966	157	50¢	R
The Deviates (originally *The Secret People*)						
	Beac (Gal)	242	1959	160	35¢	R
Man of Two Worlds (originally *Renaissance*)						
	Pyramid	F941	1963	268	40¢	R
The Non-Statistical Man	Belmont	L92-588	1964	158	50¢	C
	Belmont	B50-820	1968	158	50¢	C,R
	Brown-Wat.	R904	1965	192	3/6	C,R
JORGENSON, IVAR (pseud) [also spelled JORGENSEN]						
Rest in Agony See FAIRMAN, P. W.						
Starhaven See SILVERBERG, R.						
Ten From Infinity	Monarch	297	1963	139	35¢	
Whom the Gods Would Slay						
	Belmont	B50-849	1968	140	50¢	
JUDD, CYRIL (pseud) See KORNBLUTH, C. M., and MERRIL, J.						
JUENGER, ERNST (1895—)						
The Glass Bees	Noonday	204	1961	149	$1.65	R
JUSTER, NORTON (1929—)						
The Phantom Tollbooth	Puffin	PS236	1965	214	4/-	J

K

Author and Title	Publisher	Serial	Date	Pp.	Price	Type
KAFKA, FRANZ (1883—1924)						
The Castle	Penguin	1235	1957	298	3/6	R
	Penguin	1235	1962	298	6/-	R
The Metamorphosis	Schocken	SB172	1968	127	$1.95	R
The Metamorphosis and Other Stories						
	Penguin	1572	1968	218	4/-	C,R
The Trial	Penguin	907	1953	256	2/-	R
	Penguin	907	1966	256	3/6	R
KAHLER, JACK						
Rubber Dolly	PEC Giant	G-1117	1966			
KAINEN, RAY						
The Day the Universe Came [as Ray Kalnen]						
	Nightstand	NB 1889	1968	160	95¢	
The Love Box [as Ray Kalnen]						
	Greenleaf	GC218	1967	160		
A Sea of Thighs	Traveller's Comp.					
		TC-432	1968	181		
KALNEN, RAY (pseud) See KAINEN, R.						
KANER, H.						
Ape-Man's Offering	Kaner		nd	64	1/6	C
Cynic's Desperate Mission	Kaner		nd	64	1/-	
Fire Watcher's Night	Kaner		1944	56	1/6	C
Hot Swag	Kaner		*ca.*1945	64	1/6	C
Squaring the Triangle and Other Short Stories						
	Kaner		1944	64	2/-	C
KANTOR, MacKINLAY (1904—)						
If the South Had Won the Civil War						
	Bantam	A2241	1961	113	35¢	
KAPP, COLIN (1929?—)						
The Dark Mind (original title, but first paperback edition was *Transfinite Man*)						
	Corgi	GS7160	1965	158	3/6	R
Transfinite Man (see also *The Dark Mind*)						
	Berkley	F974	1964	160	50¢	M
KARLOFF, BORIS (pseud) See PRATT, W.						
KARLOVA, IRINA						
Dreadful Hollow	Dell	125	1946	240	25¢	R
	Paperback	53-860	1965	221	60¢	R
KARLSON, H.						
Atomic Death	Assoc. G.P.		1948	48	6d	
KARP, DAVID (1922—)						
The Brotherhood of Velvet	Banner	B50-113	1967	159	50¢	
Escape to Nowhere (originally *One*)						
	Lion	LL10	1955	222	35¢	R
One (also titled *Escape to Nowhere*)						
	Penguin	1459	1960	220	2/6	R
	Univ. Lib.	UL126	1962	311	$1.65	R
KARP, MARVIN ALLEN						
Suddenly [with Irving Settel]						
	Popular	SP351	1965	144	50¢	A
The Unhumans	Popular	SP405	1965	141	50¢	A

Author and Title	Publisher	Serial	Date	Pp.	Price	Type
KASSIRER, NORMA						
Magic Elizabeth	Scholastic	TX 1119	1967	192	50¢	J,R
KASTLE, HERBERT (1924—)						
The Reassembled Man	Gold Medal	L1494	1964	192	45¢	
KEDABRA, ABBY (pseud)						
Nine Witch Tales	Scholastic	TX1308	1968	112	50¢	A
KEEL, JOHN A.						
The Fickle Finger of Fate	Gold Medal	d1719	1966	160	50¢	
Jadoo	Tower	43-620	1966	188	60¢	R
KEENE, DAY						
World Without Women [with Leonard Pruyn]						
	Gold Medal	s975	1960	176	35¢	
	Gold Medal	L1504	1965	176	45¢	R
	Muller	GM531	1961	158	2/6	R
	Muller	GM nn	nd	158	3/-	R
KEIGHTLEY, DAVID N. (1932—) [as Noel Keyes]						
Contact!	Paperback	52-211	1963	176	50¢	A
	Paperback	52-837	1965	176	50¢	A,R
KELLAR, VON (house pseud)						
Ionic Barrier	Curtis War.		1953	159	1/6	
(identical hardcover edition 6/-)						
Tri-Planet	Curtis War.		1953	159	1/6	
(identical hardcover edition 6/-)						
KELLEAM, JOSEPH E. (1913—)						
Overlords From Space	Ace	D-173*	1956	146	35¢	
KELLER, DAVID H. (1880—1966)						
See also BIZARRE SERIES, page 789.						
The Thought Projector	Stellar	SFS2	1929	24	10¢	
KELLEY, LEO P. (1928—)						
The Counterfeits	Belmont	B50-797	1967	157	50¢	
Odyssey to Earthdeath	Belmont	B50-845	1968	174	50¢	
	Belmont	B60-085	1968	174	60¢	R
KELLEY, THOMAS P.						
The Gorilla's Daughter	Export	122	1950	160	25¢	
I Found Cleopatra	Export		1946	126	9d	M
KEMP, EARL (1929—)						
Death's Loving Arms and Other Terror Tales [as Jon Hanlon]						
	Corinth	CR147	1966	159	60¢	A,M
House of Living Death and Other Terror Tales [as Jon Hanlon]						
	Corinth	CR143	1966	160	60¢	A,M
Proceedings of the 20th World Science Fiction Convention—Chicon III						
	Advent		1963	208	$3.50	N
	Advent		1966	208	$1.95	N
Stories From Doctor Death and Other Terror Tales [as Jon Hanlon]						
	Corinth	CR129	1966	160	60¢	A,M
KEMPER, WILLIAM E. Jr.						
Another Man's Hell	Chicago	A108	1962	190	50¢	
KENDALL, CAROL (1917—)						
The Gammage Cup	Voyager	AVB-43	1966	221	65¢	R
KENNAWAY, JAMES (pseud) See PEEBLES, J. E.						
KENNEDY, EDGAR REE						
Conquerors of Venus	Edw. Self	7	1953	128	1/6	
The Mystery Planet	Edw. Self		1952	128	1/6	

Author and Title	Publisher	Serial	Date	Pp.	Price	Type
KENNERLEY, JUBA						
The Terror of the Leopard Men						
	Avon	339	1951	192	25¢	
KENSCH, OTTO						
Death Is a Habit	Transport	ST	1949	48	6d	
Image of Death	Transport	ST	1950	48	6d	
Murder Has Wings	Transport	ST	1949	48	6d	
Sleep Is Death	Transport	ST	1950	48	6d	
Time Has a Door	Transport	ST	1949	48	6d	
KENT, BRAD (house pseud)						
Biology "A" See HUGHES, DEN						
Catalyst See HUGHES, DEN						
The Fatal Law See HUGHES, DEN						
Out of the Silent Places	Curtis War.		1952	127	1/6	
KENT, PHILIP (pseud) See BULMER, K.						
KENTON, L. P. See FANTHORPE, R. L.						
KEROUAC, JACK						
Doctor Sax	Grove	E160	1959	245	$1.75	
KERR, GEOFFREY (1895—)						
Under the Influence	Pan	G138	1958	190	2/6	R
	Berkley	G518	1961	189	35¢	R
KERRUISH, JESSIE D(OUGLAS) (? —1949)						
The Undying Monster	Award	A351S	1968	218	75¢	R
KERSH, GERALD (1911—1968)						
The Battle of the Singing Men						
	Staples		1944	61	1/6	C
Men Without Bones	WDL	SF975	1960	156	2/6	C,R
	Paperback	52-127	1962	223	50¢	C,R
[contents of two editions are substantially different]						
Nightshade and Damnation						
	Gold Medal	R1887	1968	192	60¢	C
On an Odd Note	Ballantine	268	1958	154	35¢	C
The Secret Masters	Ballantine	28	1953	225	35¢	
(identical hardcover edition $2.00)						
KEY, ALEXANDER (1904—)						
The Forgotten Door	Scholastic	TX791	1968	140	45¢	J,R
KEY, DAVID						
The Sex Machine	Bee-Line	307N	1968	155		
KEYES, DANIEL (1927—)						
Flowers for Algernon	Bantam	S3339	1967	216	75¢	R
	Bantam	S3339	1968	217	75¢	R
	Pan	02094	1968	238	5/-	R
KEYES, NOEL (pseud) See KEIGHTLEY, D. N.						
KEYHOE, DONALD E. (1897—)						
The Flying Saucers Are Real						
	Fawcett		1948	38	np	N
	Gold Medal	107	1950	175	25¢	N,R
	Arrow		1950	192	2/-	N,R
Flying Saucers From Outer Space						
	Permabks	297	1954	241	25¢	N
	Arrow	402H	1955	256	2/-	N,R
KING, JOHN (pseud of Ernest Lionel McKeag [1896—])						
Shuna and the Lost Tribe	Harborough		1951	128	1/6	
Shuna, White Queen of the Jungle						
	Harborough		1951	128	1/6	

Author and Title	Publisher	Serial	Date	Pp.	Price	Type
KING-HALL, (WILLIAM) STEPHEN (RICHARD) (1893—1966)						
Moment of No Return	Ballantine	F543	1961	192	50¢	R
KING-SCOTT, PETER [as Peter Edgar]						
Cities of the Dead	Digit	R796	1963	160	2/6	
KINLEY, GEORGE						
Ferry Rocket	Curtis War.		1954	159	1/6	
(identical hardcover edition 6/-)						
KINROSS, ALBERT (1870—1929)						
The Fearsome Island	Shroud		1965	68	np	R
KIPLING, RUDYARD (1865—1936)						
See also HALDEMAN-JULIUS CO., page 790.						
Puck of Pook's Hill	Papermac	P76	1967	222	5/-	C,R
KIRK, RUSSELL (1918—)						
Lost Lake (originally *The Surly Sullen Bell*)						
	Paperback	52-365	1966	159	50¢	C,R
Old House of Fear	Avon	G1134	1961	192	50¢	R
	Avon	G1262	1965	192	50¢	R
The Surly Sullen Bell (also titled *Lost Lake*)						
	Paperback	52-316	1964	159	50¢	C,R
	Paperback	52-365	1966	159	50¢	C,R
KIRST, HANS HELLMUT (1914—)						
No One Will Escape (originally *The Seventh Day*)						
	WDL	N961	1960	446	5/6	R
The Seventh Day (also titled *No One Will Escape*)						
	Ace	K-110	1960	384	50¢	R
	Pyramid	T1215	1965	382	75¢	R
KJELGAARD, JIM						
Fire-Hunter	Scholastic	T388	1966	218	50¢	R
KLASS, PHILIP (1920—) [as William Tenn]						
The Human Angle	Ballantine	159	1956	152	35¢	C
	Ballantine	U2190	1964	152	50¢	C,R
	Ballantine	U6135	1968	153	75¢	C,R
A Lamp for Medusa	Belmont	B60-077*	1968	78	60¢	M
Of All Possible Worlds	Ballantine	99	1955	159	35¢	C
(identical hardcover edition $2.00)						
	Ballantine	407K	1960	160	35¢	C,R
	Ballantine	U6136	1968	161	75¢	C,R
	Mayflower	6532	1963	190	3/6	C,R
	Mayflower	6532	1966	190	3/6	C,R
Of Men and Monsters	Ballantine	U6131	1968	251	75¢	
Outsiders: Children of Wonder (originally *Children of Wonder*)						
	Permabks	P291	1954	355	35¢	A,R
The Seven Sexes	Ballantine	U6134	1968	236	75¢	C
The Square Root of Man	Ballantine	U6132	1968	220	75¢	C
Time in Advance	Bantam	A1786	1958	153	35¢	C
	Panther	2037	1966	173	3/6	C,R
The Wooden Star	Ballantine	U6133	1968	251	75¢	C
KLINE, OTIS ADELBERT (1891—1946)						
Jan of the Jungle (also titled *The Call of the Jungle*)						
	Ace	F-400	1966	172	40¢	R
The Man Who Limped and Other Stories						
	Saint Enter.	22	1946	128	25¢	C,M
Maza of the Moon	Ace	F-321	1965	144	40¢	M
The Outlaws of Mars	Ace	D-531	1961	158	35¢	R
	Ace	G-693	1967	158	50¢	R
Planet of Peril	Ace	F-211	1963	160	40¢	M
The Port of Peril	Ace	F-294	1964	192	40¢	R
Prince of Peril	Ace	F-259	1964	174	40¢	R
The Swordsman of Mars	Ace	D-516	1961	174	35¢	R
	Ace	G-692	1967	174	50¢	R

Author and Title	Publisher	Serial	Date	Pp.	Price	Type
KNEALE, NIGEL (1922—)						
Quatermass and the Pit	Penguin	1449	1960	188	2/6	
The Quatermass Experiment						
	Penguin	1421	1959	192	2/6	
Quatermass II	Penguin	1448	1960	174	2/6	
Tomato Cain	Fontana	561	1961	190	2/6	C,R
KNEBEL, FLETCHER (1911—)						
Night of Camp David [with C. W. Bailey]						
	Bantam	H3152	1966	312	95¢	R
Seven Days in May [with C. W. Bailey]						
	Bantam	N2640	1963	372	95¢	R
	Corgi	FN1455	1964	372	5/-	R
KNERR, MICHAEL						
The Sex Life of the Gods	Uptown	703	1962	160	50¢	
KNIGHT, DAMON (1922—)						
A for Anything (another version is *The People Maker*)						
	FSB	382	1961	160	2/6	R
	Berkley	F1136	1965	160	50¢	R
Analogue Men (originally *Hell's Pavement*)						
	Berkley	F647	1962	160	50¢	R
	Sphere	53031	1967	191	3/6	R
Beyond the Barrier	Macfadden	50-234	1965	142	50¢	R
	Corgi	GS7502	1966	123	3/6	R
A Century of Great Short Science Fiction Novels						
	Dell	1158	1965	447	75¢	A,R
	Mayflower	1168	1968	np	5/-	A,R
A Century of Science Fiction						
	Dell	1157	1963	384	75¢	A,R
	Pan	T19	1966	446	6/-	A,R
Cities of Wonder	Macfadden	75-183	1967	251	75¢	A,R
The Dark Side	Corgi	GS7788	1967	172	3/6	A,R
Far Out	Berkley	F616	1962	192	50¢	C,R
	Corgi	GS1439	1963	221	3/6	C,R
First Flight	Lancer	72-672	1963	160	50¢	A
	Lancer	72-145	1966	160	50¢	A,R
Hell's Pavement (also titled *Analogue Men*)						
	Lion	LL13	1955	192	35¢	
	Miller	Banner 59	1958	160	2/-	R
In Deep	Berkley	F760	1963	158	50¢	C
	Corgi	GS7399	1966	174	3/6	C,R
In Search of Wonder	Advent		1960	180	$1.65	N,R
	Advent	(2 ed)	1968	306	$2.45	N,R
Masters of Evolution	Ace	D-375*	1959	96	35¢	M
The Metal Smile	Belmont	B60-082	1968	158	60¢	A
Mind Switch (also titled *The Other Foot*)						
	Berkley	F1160	1965	144	50¢	M
Nebula Award Stories (1)	Pocket Bks	75275	1967	244	75¢	A,R
Off Center	Ace	M-113*	1965	141	45¢	C
Orbit 1	Berkley	F1291	1966	192	50¢	A,R
	Panther	2325	1967	156	3/6	A,R
Orbit 2	Berkley	S1448	1967	255	75¢	A,R
Orbit 3	Berkley	S1608	1968	224	75¢	A,R
The Other Foot (originally *Mind Switch*)						
	Corgi	07994	1968	125	3/6	R
The People Maker (also titled *A for Anything*)						
	Zenith	ZB-14	1959	159	35¢	
The Rithian Terror	Ace	M-113*	1965	111	45¢	M
Science Fiction Inventions	Lancer	73-691	1967	256	60¢	A
The Shape of Things	Popular	SP352	1965	206	50¢	A
The Sun Saboteurs	Ace	F-108*	1961	101	40¢	M
13 French Science-Fiction Stories						
	Bantam	F2817	1965	167	50¢	A
	Corgi	GS7312	1965		3/6	A,R
Tomorrow X 4	Gold Medal	d1428	1964	176	50¢	A
	Coronet	F124	1967	176	3/6	A,R
Turning On	Ace	G-677	1967	160	50¢	C,R
Worlds to Come	Gold Medal	R1942	1968	254	60¢	A,R

Author and Title	Publisher	Serial	Date	Pp.	Price	Type
KNIGHT, ERIC (1897–1943)						
The Flying Yorkshireman (also titled *Sam Small Flies Again*)						
	Armed	g-187	nd	318	np	C,R
	Pocket Bks	493	1948	273	25¢	C,R
Sam Small Flies Again (also titled *The Flying Yorkshireman*)						
	Guild		1945			C,R
KNIGHT, MALLORY T. (pseud) See HURWOOD, B. J.						
KNIGHT, NORMAN L. (1895–)						
A Torrent of Faces [with James Blish]						
	Ace	A-29	1968	286	75¢	R
KNOLES, WILLIAM See ALLISON, C. (pseud)						
KNOWLER, JOHN						
The Trap	Avon	S208	1966	192	60¢	
KNOX, CALVIN M. (pseud) See SILVERBERG, R.						
KOESTLER, ARTHUR (1905–)						
The Age of Longing	Mayflower	B12	1961	320	3/6	R
KOMROFF, M. See HALDEMAN-JULIUS CO., page 790.						
KOONTZ, DEAN R. (1945–)						
Star Quest	Ace	H-70*	1968	127	60¢	
KOPF, SEYMOUR See EDITORIAL TECNICA, page 789.						
KORNBLUTH, CYRIL (1923–1958) [as C. M. Kornbluth unless otherwise noted]						
Christmas Eve (originally *Not This August*)						
	Digit	nn	1957	160	2/-	R
The Explorers	Ballantine	86	1954	145	35¢	C
	Ballantine	F708	1963	145	50¢	C,R
Gladiator-at-Law [with F. Pohl]						
	Ballantine	107	1955	171	35¢	
(identical hardcover edition $2.00)						
	Ballantine	F570	1962	171	50¢	R
	Ballantine	U2343	1967	171	50¢	R
	Digit	D157	1958	160	2/-	R
	Pan	X571	1966	187	3/6	R
Gunner Cade [as Cyril Judd (pseud. with J. Merril)]						
	Ace	D-227*	1957	198	35¢	R
	Penguin	2460	1966	199	3/6	R
The Marching Morons	Ballantine	303K	1959	158	35¢	C
	Ballantine	F760	1963	158	50¢	C,R
A Mile Beyond the Moon	Macfadden	40-100	1962	175	40¢	C,R
	Macfadden	50-288	1966	175	50¢	C,R
Not This August (also titled *Christmas Eve*)						
	Bantam	A1492	1956	165	35¢	R
Outpost Mars [as Cyril Judd (pseud. with J. Merril)] (see also *Sin in Space*)						
	Dell	760	1954	223	25¢	R
	FSB	1585	1966	187	3/6	R
Search the Sky [with F. Pohl]						
	Ballantine	61	1954	165	35¢	
(identical hardcover edition $2.00)						
	Ballantine	F738	1963	165	50¢	R
	Digit	D352	1960	159	2/-	R
	Digit	R662	1963	158	2/6	R
Sin in Space [as Cyril Judd (pseud. with J. Merril)] (sexed-up version of *Outpost Mars*)						
	Beac (Gal)	312	1961	190	35¢	R
The Space Merchants [with F. Pohl]						
	Ballantine	21	1953	179	35¢	M
(identical hardcover edition $2.00)						
	Ballantine	381K	1960	158	35¢	R
	Ballantine	U2173	1964	158	50¢	R
	Digit	D327	1960	158	2/-	R
	Digit	R499	1961	156	2/6	R
	Penguin	2224	1965	170	3/6	R

Author and Title	Publisher	Serial	Date	Pp.	Price	Type
The Syndic	Bantam	1317	1955	142	25¢	R
	Berkley	F1032	1965	144	50¢	R
	Sphere	53171	1968	160	5/-	R
Takeoff	Bantam	P15	1953	149	25¢	R
Wolfbane [with F. Pohl]	Ballantine	335K	1959	140	35¢	M
	Penguin	2561	1967	160	3/6	R
The Wonder Effect [with F. Pohl]						
	Ballantine	F638	1962	159	50¢	C
KORNBLUTH, MARY (1920–)						
Science Fiction Showcase	Mayflower	112250	1968	204	5/-	A,R
KRAMER, NORA						
Arrow Book of Ghost Stories						
	Scholastic	TX232	1960	116	25¢	J,A
KREMER, RAYMOND DE (1887–1964) [as Jean Ray]						
Ghouls in My Grave	Berkley	F1071	1965	143	50¢	C
KRESSING, HARRY						
The Cook	Panther	2311	1967	223	5/-	R
	Panther	026037	1968	223	5/-	R
KUMMER, FREDERIC ARNOLD						
Ladies in Hades	Dell	415	1950	158	25¢	
KURLAND, MICHAEL (1938–) See also ANDERSON, C. (co-author)						
Mission: Tank War	Pyramid	X1976	1968	188	60¢	
KUTTNER, HENRY (1914–1958)						
Ahead of Time	Ballantine	30	1953	177	35¢	C
(identical hardcover edition $2.00)						
	Ballantine	U2341	1966	177	50¢	C,R
	FSB	371	1961	160	2/6	C,R
	FSB	371	1964	160	2/6	C,R
	FSB	1990	1967	160	3/6	C,R
The Best of Kuttner 1	Mayflower	0547	1965	286	5/-	C
The Best of Kuttner 2	Mayflower	0547	1966	288	5/-	C
Beyond Earth's Gates [as L. Padgett, with C. L. Moore]						
	Ace	D-69*	1954	138	35¢	M
Bypass to Otherness	Ballantine	497K	1961	144	35¢	C
	Consul	1269	1963	155	2/6	C,R
Chessboard Planet [as Lewis Padgett] (originally *The Fairy Chessmen*)						
	Galaxy Nov	26	1956	124	35¢	R
The Creature From Beyond Infinity						
	Popular	602355	1968	125	60¢	M
The Dark World	Ace	F-327	1965	126	40¢	M
	Mayflower	1657	1966	127	3/6	R
Destination Infinity (originally *Fury*)						
	Avon	T275	1958	192	35¢	R
Earth's Last Citadel [with C. L. Moore]						
	Ace	F-306	1964	128	60¢	
The Far Reality [as Lewis Padgett] (originally *The Fairy Chessmen*)						
	Consul	1266	1963	155	2/6	R
Fury (also titled *Destination Infinity*)						
	Digit	R413	1960	156	2/6	R
	Mayflower	2779	1963	190	3/6	R
Line to Tomorrow [as Lewis Padgett]						
	Bantam	1251	1954	184	25¢	C
Mutant	Mayflower	B27	1962	192	2/6	R
	Ballantine	F724	1963	191	50¢	R
	Ballantine	U2859	1968	191	50¢	R
No Boundaries [with C. L. Moore]						
	Ballantine	122	1955	149	35¢	C
(identical hardcover edition $2.00)						
	Consul	SF1025	1961	159	2/6	C,R
Return to Otherness	Ballantine	F619	1962	240	50¢	C
	Mayflower	7401	1965	288	5/-	C,R
The Time Axis	Ace	F-356	1965	142	40¢	M
Tomorrow and Tomorrow [as Lewis Padgett]						
	Consul	1265	1963	106	2/6	R

Author and Title	Publisher	Serial	Date	Pp.	Price	Type
Valley of the Flame	Ace	F-297	1964	156	40¢	M
Well of the Worlds [as Lewis Padgett]						
	Galaxy Nov	17	1953	127	35¢	M
[as H. Kuttner]	Ace	F-344	1965	142	40¢	R

L

Author and Title	Publisher	Serial	Date	Pp.	Price	Type
LA SALLE, VICTOR (house pseud)						
After the Atom	Spencer		1953	108	1/6	
Assault From Infinity	Spencer		1953	108	1/6	
The Black Sphere	Spencer		1952	108	1/6	
Dawn of the Half-Gods See GLASBY, J. S.						
Menace From Mercury See FANTHORPE, R. L.						
The Seventh Dimension	Spencer		1953	124	1/6	
Suns in Duo	Spencer		1953	108	1/6	
Twilight Zone See GLASBY, J. S.						
LA SPINA, GREYE (1880—1969)						
Shadow of Evil (originally *Invaders From the Dark*)						
	Paperback	52334	1966	160	50¢	R
LAFFERTY, R(APHAEL) A. (1914—)						
Past Master	Ace	H-54	1968	191	60¢	
The Reefs of Earth	Berkley	X1528	1968	144	60¢	
Space Chantey	Ace	H-56*	1968	123	60¢	
LAFOND (pseud)						
Diane	Utopian		1940's	32	np	
LAING, ALEXANDER (1903—)						
The Cadaver of Gideon Wyck						
	Armed	685	nd	381	np	R
	Collier	AS257X	1962	250	95¢	R
LAMPMAN, EVELYN SIBLEY						
The Shy Stegosaurus of Cricket Creek						
	Scholastic	TX 409	1962	189	50¢	R
LANE, JOHN (house pseud)						
Maid of Thuro See HUGHES, DEN						
Mammalia	Curtis War.		1953	159	1/6	
(identical hardcover edition 6/-)						
LANG, ANDREW (1844—1912)						
Tales From the Red Fairy Book						
	Scholastic	TX235	1962	116	35¢	C,R
LANG, KING (house pseud)						
Astro Race See GRIFFITHS, D. A.						
Gyrator Control See GRIFFITHS, D. A.						
Projectile War	Curtis War.		1951	111	1/6	
Rocket Invasion See GRIFFITHS, D. A.						
Saturn Patrol See TUBB, E. C.						
Space Line See JENNISON, J. W.						
Task Flight See GRIFFITHS, D. A.						
Terra! See HAY, G.						
Trans-Mercurian See HOLLOWAY, B.						
LANGART, DARREL T. (pseud) See GARRETT, R.						
LANGDON-DAVIES, JOHN See DINGWALL, E. J. (co-author)						
LANGE, JOHN F. (1931—) [as John Norman]						
Outlaw of Gor	Ballantine	U6072	1967	255	75¢	
Priest-Kings of Gor	Ballantine	72015	1968	317	75¢	
Tarnsman of Gor	Ballantine	U6071	1966	219	75¢	
LANGELAAN, GEORGE (1908—)						
Out of Time	FSB	1129	1964	190	3/6	C
LANGLEY, FREDRIC See ELLIK, R. (co-author)						
LANNING, GEORGE (1925—)						
The Pedestal	Avon	S376	1968	158	60¢	R
LARNACH, S. L.						
A Checklist of Australian Fantasy						
	Futurian		1950	22	6/-	N
LASKI, MARGHANITA (1915—)						
The Offshore Island	Mayfair	1	1961	96	2/6	
The Victorian Chaise-Longue						
	Guild	07	1953	159	2/-	R
	Ballantine	441K	1960	125	35¢	R
	Ballantine	70005	1968	125	50¢	R
	Penguin	1835	1962	160	4/-	R
LATTER, SIMON						
The Global Globule Affair	FSB		1967	126		
The Golden Boats of Taradata Affair						
	FSB		1967	128		
LAUMER, KEITH (1925—)						
Assignment in Nowhere	Berkley	X1596	1968	143	60¢	
Catastrophe Planet	Berkley	F1273	1966	158	50¢	
Earthblood [with Rosel G. Brown]						
	Berkley	S1544	1968	287	75¢	R
Enemies From Beyond	Pyramid	X1689	1967	159	60¢	
Envoy to New Worlds	Ace	F-223*	19683	134	40¢	C
Galactic Diplomat	Berkley	X1240	1966	223	60¢	C,R
Galactic Odyssey	Berkley	X1447	1967	160	60¢	M
The Great Time Machine Hoax						
	Pocket Bks	50156	1965	176	50¢	R
Greylorn	Berkley	X1514	1968	192	60¢	C
The Invaders (also titled *The Meteor Men*)						
	Pyramid	R1664	1967	142	50¢	
It's a Mad, Mad, Mad Galaxy						
	Berkley	X1641	1968	160	60¢	C
The Meteor Men [as A. Lebaron—pseudonym used without author's knowledge] (originally *The Invaders*)						
	Corgi	GS7836	1968	127	3/6	R
The Monitors	Berkley	X1340	1966	160	60¢	
The Other Side of Time	Berkley	F1129	1965	160	50¢	M
A Plague of Demons	Berkley	F1086	1965	159	50¢	M
	Penguin	2698	1967	170	3/6	R
Planet Run [with G. R. Dickson]						
	Berkley	X1588	1968	143	60¢	R
Retief's War	Berkley	X1427	1967	175	60¢	R
The Time Bender	Berkley	F1185	1966	160	50¢	
A Trace of Memory	Berkley	F780	1963	174	50¢	M
	Mayflower	11329X	1968	188	5/-	R
Worlds of the Imperium	Ace	F-127*	1962	133	40¢	M
	Ace	M-165	1967	133	45¢	R
LAWRENCE, H(ENRY) L(IONEL) (1908—)						
Children of Light	Consul	1167	1962	191	2/6	
LAWSON, ROBERT (1892—1957)						
Mr. Wilmer	Armed	899	nd		np	R
LE FANU, J. SHERIDAN (1814—1873)						
Best Ghost Stories	Dover	T415	1964	467	$2.00	C
The Diabolical Genius	Juniper	3	1959	384	$1.45	C

Author and Title	Publisher	Serial	Date	Pp.	Price	Type
Green Tea	Todd	Polybook	1943	16	4d	
Uncle Silas	Penguin		1947	191	1/3	R
	Corgi	FN7506	1966	382	5/-	R
	Dover	T1715	1966	436	$2.00	R
	Paperback	54-390	1967	351	75¢	R

LE GUIN, URSULA (1929—)
City of Illusions	Ace	G-626	1967	160	50¢	
Planet of Exile	Ace	G-597*	1966	113	50¢	
Rocannon's World	Ace	G-574*	1966	117	50¢	

LE PAGE, RAND (house pseud)
"A" Men See HOLLOWAY, B.
Asteroid Forma	Curtis War.		1953	159	1/6	

(identical hardcover edition 6/-)
Beyond These Suns See PROTHEROE, C.
Blue Asp See O'BRIEN, D.
Satellite B.C. See GLASBY, J. S.
Time and Space See GLASBY, J. S.
War of Argos See BIRD, W. H. F.
Zero Point See GLASBY, J. S.

LEACOCK, STEPHEN (1869—1944)
Laugh With Leacock	Corgi	GH736	1959	288	3/6	C

LEBARON, A. (pseud) See LAUMER, K.

LEDERMAN, FRANK
Tremor	Kaye		nd	112	1/6	

LEE, CHRISTOPHER (1923—)
Christopher Lee's Treasury of Terror [comic-book versions]
	Pyramid	R1498	1966	144	50¢	A

LEE, ELIZABETH
More Horror Stories	Elek	Bestseller	1962	222	3/6	A

LEE, ELSIE
Comedy of Terrors	Lancer	70-067	1964	126	40¢	

LEE, VERNON (pseud) See PAGET, V.

LEIBER, FRITZ (1910—)
The Big Time	Ace	D-491*	1961	129	35¢	M
	Ace	G-627	1967	129	50¢	R
	FSB	1267	1965	127	3/6	R
Conjure Wife	Lion	179	1954	192	25¢	R
	Berkley	F621	1962	176	50¢	R
	Award	A341	1968	188	60¢	R
Destiny Times Three	Galaxy Nov	28	1957	126	35¢	M
Gather, Darkness!	Berkley	F679	1962	174	50¢	R
	FSB	1548	1966	192	3/6	R
The Green Millennium	Lion	LL7	1954	192	35¢	R
	Icon	SF3	1964	160	3/6	R
The Mind Spider and Other Stories						
	Ace	D-491*	1961	127	35¢	C
The Night of the Wolf	Ballantine	U2254	1966	221	50¢	C
Night's Black Agents	Ballantine	508K	1961	143	35¢	C,R
A Pail of Air	Ballantine	U2216	1964	191	50¢	C
Shadows With Eyes	Ballantine	577	1962	128	35¢	C
Ships to the Stars	Ace	F-285*	1964	122	40¢	C
The Silver Eggheads	Ballantine	F561	1961	192	50¢	M
	FSB	1629	1966	192	5/-	R
The Sinful Ones	Universal	G-5	1953	318	50¢	M
Swords Against Wizardry	Ace	H-73	1968	188	60¢	C,M
Swords in the Mist	Ace	H-90	1968	190	60¢	C,M
The Swords of Lankhmar	Ace	H-38	1968	224	60¢	M
Tarzan and the Valley of Gold						
	Ballantine	U6125	1966	317	75¢	
The Wanderer	Ballantine	U6010	1964	318	75¢	

LEINSTER, MURRAY (pseud) See JENKINS, W. F.

L'ENGLE, MADELEINE (1918—)
A Wrinkle in Time	Puffin	PS288	1967	185	3/6	J,R

LEONARDO DA VINCI (1452—1519)
The Deluge [with R. Payne]	Lion	233	1955	124	25¢	R

LESLIE, DESMOND (1921—)
The Amazing Mr. Lutterworth
	Digit	D315	1960	159	2/-	R
The Flying Saucers Have Landed [with George Adamski]						
	Panther	663	1957	237	2/6	N,R

LESLIE, PETER (1912—)
The Cornish Pixie Affair	FSB		1967	117		
The Diving Dames Affair	Ace	G-617	1967		50¢	
	FSB		1967	140		R
The Finger in the Sky Affair						
	FSB		1966	117		
Night of the Trilobites	Corgi	07879	1968	128	3/6	
The Radioactive Camel Affair						
	Ace	G-600	1966		50¢	
	FSB		1966	141		
The Splintered Sunglasses Affair						
	Ace	G-752	1968		50¢	
	FSB		1968	124		
The Unfair Fare Affair	FSB		1968	127		

LESLIE, SHANE (1885—1971)
Shane Leslie's Ghost Book	FSB	1150	1964	191	3/6	C,N

LESSER, MILTON (1928—)
Recruit for Andromeda	Ace	D-358*	1959	117	35¢	M
Secret of the Black Planet	Belmont	92-621	1965	157	50¢	M

LEVENE, PHILIP
The City of Hidden Eyes [with J. L. Morrissey]
	WDL	SF973	1960	160	2/6	

LEVIE, REX DEAN
The Insect Warriors	Ace	F-334	1965	143	40¢	

LEVIN, IRA (1929—)
Rosemary's Baby	Dell	7509	1968	218	95¢	R
	Pan	02115X	1968	205	5/-	R

LEWIS, C(LIVE) S(TAPLES) (1898—1963)
The Great Divorce	Macmillan	08678	1968	128	95¢	R
The Horse and His Boy	Puffin	PS244	1965	188	3/6	J,R
The Last Battle	Puffin	PS205	1964	165	3/6	J,R
The Lion, the Witch, and the Wardrobe						
	Puffin	PS132	1959	171	3/-	J,R
The Magician's Nephew	Puffin	PS192	1963	171	3/-	J,R
Out of the Silent Planet	Avon	195	1949	159	25¢	R
	Avon	T127	1956	159	35¢	R
	Avon	T410	1960	159	35¢	R
	Pan	213	1952	190	2/-	R
	Pan	213	1955	190	2/-	R
	Pan	213	1956	190	2/-	R
	Pan	G403	1960	190	2/6	R
	Pan	G403	1961	190	2/6	R
	Pan	G403	1962	190	2/6	R
	Pan	X270	1963	190	3/6	R
	Pan	X270	1965	190	3/6	R
	Pan	02172	1968	190	5/-	R
	Collier	AS207V	1962	160	95¢	R
	Macmillan	08688	1965	160	95¢	R

Author and Title	Publisher	Serial	Date	Pp.	Price	Type
Perelandra (also titled *Voyage to Venus: Perelandra*)						
	Avon	277	1950	191	25¢	R
	Avon	T157	1957	191	35¢	R
	Collier	AS183	1962	222	95¢	R
	Collier	AS183V	1968	222	95¢	R
	Macmillan		1965	222	95¢	R
Prince Caspian	Puffin	PS173	1962	190	3/-	J,R
The Screwtape Letters	Fontana	49B	1955	160	2/-	R
	Macmillan		1960	160	75¢	R
	Macmillan	08686	1966	172	95¢	R
The Silver Chair	Puffin	PS240	1965	206	3/6	J,R
That Hideous Strength (also titled *The Tortured Planet*)						
	Pan	321	1955	252	2/-	R
	Pan	321	1956	252	2/6	R
	Pan	G421	1960	252	2/6	R
	Pan	G421	1962	252	2/6	R
	Pan	X266	1963	252	3/6	R
	Pan	X266	1965	252	3/6	R
	Pan	02170	1968	252	5/-	R
	Collier	BS58V	1961	382	$1.50	R
	Macmillan	08692	1965	382	$1.50	R
Till We Have Faces	Eerdsmans		1964	313	$1.95	R
The Tortured Planet (originally *That Hideous Strength*)						
	Avon	T211	1958	254	35¢	R
The Voyage of the "Dawn Treader"						
	Puffin	PS229	1965	212	3/6	J,R
Voyage to Venus (Perelandra) (originally *Perelandra*)						
	Pan	253	1953	188	2/-	R
	Pan	253	1955	188	2/-	R
	Pan	253	1956	188	2/-	R
	Pan	G404	1960	188	2/6	R
	Pan	G404	1961	188	2/6	R
	Pan	G404	1962	188	2/6	R
	Pan	X268	1963	206	3/6	R
	Pan	X268	1965	206	3/6	R
	Pan	02171	1968	188	5/-	R
LEWIS, IRWIN						
The Day New York Trembled						
	Avon	G1315	1967	144	50¢	
The Day They Invaded New York						
	Avon	G1227	1964	160	50¢	
LEWIS, MATTHEW G. (1775—1818)						
The Monk	Grove	E163	1959	445	$2.45	R
	Elek	Bestseller	1960	256	3/6	R
LEWIS, PETE (pseud of Peter J. Crown)						
Father of the Amazons	Kozy	K136	1961	158	50¢	
LEWIS, ROY (1913—)						
The Evolution Man (originally *What We Did to Father*)						
	Penguin	2004	1964	123	2/6	R
LEWIS, SINCLAIR (1885—1951)						
It Can't Happen Here	Mayflower	4128	1965	382	5/-	R
LEWIS, (PERCY) WYNDHAM (1884—1957)						
The Childermass	Jupiter	J8	1966	320	10/6	R
Malign Fiesta	Jupiter	J16	1966	240	6/6	R
Monstre Gai	Jupiter	J12	1966	254	6/6	R
LEY, ROBERT A. (1921—1968) [as Arthur Sellings except as noted]						
Intermind [as Ray Luther]	Banner	B50-117	1967	144	50¢	
The Quy Effect	Berkley	X1350	1967	144	60¢	R
The Silent Speakers (originally *Telepath*)						
	Panther	1787	1965	127	2/6	R
Telepath (also titled *The Silent Speakers*)						
	Ballantine	F609	1962	160	50¢	R
Time Transfer	Compact	F302	1966	189	3/6	C,R
The Uncensored Man	Berkley	X1379	1967	160	60¢	R

Author and Title	Publisher	Serial	Date	Pp.	Price	Type
LEY, WILLY (1906—1969) [nonfiction on contemporary space-flight is not covered]						
Exotic Zoology	Capricorn	273	1966	468	$2.65	N,R
Missiles, Moonprobes and Megaparsecs						
	Signet	P2445	1964	189	60¢	N,R
On Earth and in the Sky	Ace	H-55	1968	192	60¢	N,R
Project Mars [with W. Von Braun] (originally *The Exploration of Mars*)						
	Badger	SS4	1962	184	2/6	N,R
Satellites, Rockets and Outer Space						
	Signet	KS360	1958	128	35¢	N,R
LICATA, TONY						
Great Science Fiction	Three Star	102	1965	128	60¢	A
LIEBER, MAXIM						
Ghosts, Ghouls and Other Nuisances						
	Seven Seas		1959	272	2/6	A
LINCOLN, M. See BOY'S FRIEND LIBRARY, page 789.						
LIND, JAKOV						
Soul of Wood and Other Stories						
	Crest	R897	1966	158	60¢	C
LINDNER, ROBERT (1914—1956)						
The Fifty-Minute Hour	Bantam		1956	207	35¢	N,R
	Corgi	GG1137	1962	207	3/6	N,R
LINDSAY, DAVID (1876—1945)						
A Voyage to Arcturus	Ballantine	73010	1968	287	95¢	R
LINEBARGER, PAUL M. A. (1913—1966) [as Cordwainer Smith]						
The Planet Buyer	Pyramid	R1084	1964	156	50¢	M
Quest of the Three Worlds	Ace	F-402	1966	174	40¢	C,M
Space Lords	Pyramid	R1183	1965	206	50¢	C
	Pyramid	X1911	1968	206	60¢	C,R
The Underpeople	Pyramid	X1910	1968	159	60¢	
You Will Never Be the Same						
	Regency	RB309	1963	156	50¢	C
LIPSKY, ELEAZAR						
The Scientists	Panther	1570	1963	315	5/-	
LITTLE, JANE						
Spook	Scholastic	TX 1001	1967	80	45¢	J
LITTLEDALE, FREYA						
13 Ghostly Tales	Scholastic	TX875	1966	92	45¢	A
LIVESEY, ERIC M.						
The Desolate Land	Digit	R877	1964	158	2/6	
LIVINGSTON, ARMSTRONG						
Magic for Murder	Cavalcade	2	nd	127	25¢	
LIVINGSTON, HAROLD (1924—)						
The Climacticon	Ballantine	406K	1960	191	35¢	
LLOYD, J.						
Tales From the Beyond	Tandem	T56	1966	200	3/6	C
LLOYD, JOHN URI (1849—1936)						
Etidorhpa	Inspired Nov	A3	1962	234	$2.00	R
LLOYD, STEPHANIE						
Graveswood	Paperback	52-364	1966	158	50¢	
LOFTS, NORAH (1904—)						
The Witches [as Peter Curtis] (originally *The Devil's Own*)						
	Pan	X591	1966	254	3/6	R

Author and Title	Publisher	Serial	Date	Pp.	Price	Type

LOMBINO, S. A. Name changed to HUNTER, EVAN, *q.v.*

LONDON, JACK (1876—1916)
Children of the Frost	Panther	1954	1965	155	3/6	C,R
The Iron Heel	Penguin	461	1945	219	9d	R

LONG, AMELIA R. (1904—)
The Mechanical Man	Stellar	SFS7	1930	14	10¢	

[part of booklet also containing "The Thought Stealer," F. Bourne]

LONG, FRANK B. (1903—)
See also SUNDAY TELEGRAPH, page 791.

. . . And Others Shall Be Born	Belmont	B50-809	1968	87	50¢	
The Dark Beasts	Belmont	L92-579	1964	141	50¢	C,R

[some stories from hardcover *The Hounds of Tindalos*]

The Goblin Tower [verse]	New Collectors		1949	30	50¢	C
The Horror From the Hills (also titled *Odd Science Fiction*)						
	Brown-Wat.	R907	1965	159	3/6	C,R
The Hounds of Tindalos	Belmont	L92-569	1963	173	50¢	C,R

[some stories from hardcover ed.; see also *The Dark Beasts*]

It Was the Day of the Robot	Belmont	90-277	1963	141	40¢	
John Carstairs: Space Detective						
	Kemsley	CT400	1951	192	1/6	C,R
Journey Into Darkness	Belmont	B50-757	1967	156	50¢	
Lest Earth Be Conquered	Belmont	B50-726	1966	144	50¢	
Mars Is My Destination	Pyramid	F742	1962	158	40¢	
Mating Center	Chariot	CB162	1961	160	50¢	
Odd Science Fiction (originally *The Horror From the Hills*)						
	Belmont	L92-600	1964	141	50¢	C,R
So Dark a Heritage	Lancer	72-106	1966	175	50¢	
Space Station No. 1	Ace	D-242*	1957	157	35¢	
	Ace	D-544	1962	157	35¢	R
This Strange Tomorrow	Belmont	B50-663	1966	158	50¢	
	Brown-Wat.	R965	1966	158	3/6	R
Woman From Another Planet						
	Chariot	CB123	1960	190	50¢	

LOOMIS, NOEL (1905—1969)
City of Glass	Columbia	DAB	1955	128	35¢	M
The Man With Absolute Motion [as Silas Water]						
	Arrow	795	1964	192	3/6	R
	Arrow	795	1966	192	3/6	R

LORAINE, PHILIP
13 (originally *Day of the Arrow*)
	Lancer	73-540	1966	158	60¢	R

LORENZEN, CORAL E. (1925—)
Flying Saucer Occupants	Signet	T3205	1967	215	75¢	N
Flying Saucers: The Startling Evidence of the Invasion From Outer Space	Signet	T3058	1966	278	75¢	N
UFO's Over the Americas	See LORENZEN, J. (co-author)					

LORENZEN, JIM
UFO's Over the Americas [with Coral E. Lorenzen]
	Signet	T3513	1968	254	75¢	N

LORENZINI, CARLO See COLLODI, C. (pseud)

LORRAINE, LILITH (1894—)
The Brain of the Planet	Stellar	SFS5	1929	23	10¢	

LORRAINE, PAUL (house pseud)
Dark Boundaries See FEARN, J. R.
Two Worlds See BIRD, W. H. F.
Zenith-D See GLASBY, J. S.

LOUYS, PIERRE (1870—1925)
Aphrodite	Avon	113	1946	186	25¢	
The Collected Works of Pierre Louys						
	Avon	G1003	1961	628	50¢	C

LOVECRAFT, H(OWARD) P(HILLIPS) (1890—1937)
At the Mountains of Madness						
	Panther	025960	1968	300	5/-	C,R
The Case of Charles Dexter Ward						
	Panther	1513	1963	127	2/6	R
	Belmont	92-617	1965	141	50¢	R
The Colour Out of Space and Others						
	Lancer	73-425	1964	222	60¢	C
	Lancer	73-608	1967	222	60¢	C,R
Cry Horror! (originally *The Lurking Fear*)						
	Avon	T284	1958	191	35¢	C,R
	WDL	HS853	1960	160	2/6	C,R
The Dream-Quest of Unknown Kadath						
	Shroud		1955	107	$1.25	M
The Dunwich Horror	Bart House	12	1945	186	25¢	C
The Dunwich Horror and Other Weird Tales						
	Armed	730	1943	384	np	C
The Dunwich Horror and Others						
	Lancer	72-702	1963	158	50¢	C,R
The Haunter of the Dark	Panther	1474	1963	256	3/6	C,R
	Panther	1474	1964	256	3/6	C,R
	Panther	1474	1965	256	3/6	C,R
The Lurking Fear (also titled *Cry Horror!*)						
	Avon	136	1947	223	25¢	C
The Lurking Fear and Other Stories						
	Panther	1759	1964	208	3/6	C
The Survivor and Others [stories completed by A. Derleth]						
	Ballantine	629	1962	143	35¢	C,R
The Weird Shadow Over Innsmouth						
	Bart House	4	1944	190	25¢	C

LOW, A(RCHIBALD) M. (1888—1956)
Satellite in Space	Digit	R734	1963	160	2/6	J,R

LOWE, ARTHUR
Death of the Last Taxpayer	Forward		1944	23		np

LOWNDES, ROBERT A. W. (1916—)
The Duplicated Man [with J. Blish]						
	Airmont	SF8	1964	128	40¢	R
The Puzzle Planet	Ace	D-485*	1961	119	35¢	

LOWTHER, GEORGE (FRANCIS) (1913—1975)
Adventures of Superman	Armed	656	nd		np	R

LUDLAM, HARRY
The Coming of Jonathan Smith
	Arrow	838	1965	184	3/6	

LUDWIG, BORIS
Jaws of Doom	Assoc. G.P.		1948	48	6d	
The Whistle of Doom	Transport	ST	1949	48	6d	

LUIGI, BELLI
Cosmic Calamity	Transport	ST	1949	48	6d	
Crime Flies	Transport	ST	1950	48	6d	
The Curse of the Mummy	Transport	ST	1950	48	6d	
Death Has No Weight	Transport	ST	1949	48	6d	
Depths of Death	Transport	ST	1950	48	6d	
The Freezing Peril Strikes	Transport	ST	1951	32	8d	
The Glowing Globe	Transport	ST	1950	48	6d	
Lightning Crime	Transport	ST	1949	48	6d	
The Lost Underworld	Transport	ST	1950	48	6d	
The Master-Mind Menace	Transport	ST	1950	48	6d	
	WDL	WFC	1950	128	1/6	R
The Metal Monster	WDL	WFC	1950	128	1/6	
The Mummy Walks	Transport	ST	1950	48	6d	
Toppling Terror	Transport	ST	1950	48	6d	

LUKENS, ADAM (pseud) See DETZER, D.

Author and Title	Publisher	Serial	Date	Pp.	Price	Type

LUNA, KRIS (house pseud)
Operation Orbit See BIRD, W. H. F.
Stellar Radium Discharge See O'BRIEN, D.

LUPOFF, RICHARD A. (1935—)
Edgar Rice Burroughs: Master of Adventure

	Ace	N-6	1968	315	95¢	N,R
One Million Centuries	Lancer	74-892	1967	352	75¢	

LURIE, ALLISON
Imaginary Friends Avon N191 1968 288 95¢ R

LUTHER, RAY (pseud) See LEY, R. A.

LYMINGTON, JOHN (pseud) [most by John Chance]
The Coming of the Strangers

	Corgi	YS1267	1963	142	3/-	R
Froomb!	Hodder	818	1967	191	3/6	R
	Macfadden	60-287	1967	224	60¢	R
The Giant Stumbles	Corgi	SS1063	1961	157	2/6	R
	Hodder	753	1965	157	2/6	R
The Grey Ones	Corgi	SS1227	1962	126	2/6	R
The Night of the Big Heat	Corgi	SS982	1961	157	2/6	R
	Hodder	738	1965	126	2/6	R
The Night Spiders	Corgi	GS1540	1964	159	3/6	C
The Screaming Face	Corgi	GS7142	1965	159	3/6	R
The Sleep Eaters	Corgi	GS7066	1964	174	3/6	R
The Star Witches	Hodder	737	1965	128	2/6	R
A Sword Above the Night	Corgi	SS1334	1963	126	2/6	R

LYNDON, BARRE
The Man Who Could Cheat Death [with J. Sangster]

	Avon	T362	1960	160	35¢	

The Man Who Could Cheat Death [as John Sansom (pseud)]

	Ace (Brit.)	H280	1959	188	2/6	R

LYNN, DAVID
Cybro Sex Nightstand NB 1910 1968 160
Zardoc, Warrior Stud Leisure LB 1207 1967

LYNN, G.
The Return of Karl Marx Chancery 1951 117 1/6

LYON, WINSTON
Batman vs. the Fearsome Foursome

	Signet	D2995	1966	128	50¢	

Batman vs. Three Villains of Doom

	Signet	D2940	1966	128	50¢	

M

MacAPP, C. C. (pseud) See CAPPS, C. M.

MACARDLE, DOROTHY (1889—)

Dark Enchantment	Bantam	H3329	1967	259	60¢	R
The Unforeseen	Armed	1185	nd		np	R
	Bantam	915	1951	279	25¢	R
	Bantam	H3211	1966	218	60¢	R
	Corgi	915	1953	279	2/-	R
	Corgi	ZR7435	1966	218	4/-	R

The Uninvited	Armed	b-51	nd		np	R
	Bantam	90	1947	341	25¢	R
	Bantam	H3148	1966	278	60¢	R
	Corgi	ZR7453	1966	278	4/-	R

MacARTHUR, ARTHUR (1896—)
Aphrodite's Lover (originally *After the Afternoon*)

	Universal	Giant 9	1953	287	50¢	R

MACAULAY, KEN
The Nuclear Nazis Scripts PB366 1968 129 55¢

McCABE, J. See HALDEMAN-JULIUS CO., page 790.

McCALL, ANTHONY
Holocaust Pocket Bks 55052 1968 185 60¢ R

McCAFFREY, ANNE (1926—)

Dragonflight	Ballantine	U6124	1968	309	75¢	M
Restoree	Ballantine	U6108	1967	252	75¢	

McCANN, EDSON (pseud) See POHL, F.

MacCARTNEY, CLEM

Dark Side of Venus	Hamilton	nn	nd	111	1/6	
Ten Years to Oblivion	Authentic	12	1951	109	1/6	

McCLARY, THOMAS C.

Rebirth	Bart House	6	1944	187	25¢	M
Three Thousand Years	Ace	D-176*	1956	190	35¢	R

McCOMAS, J. FRANCIS (1910—) See HEALY, R. J. (co-anthologist)

McCULLAGH, SHEILA K.
The Kingdom Under the Sea

	Hulton		1967	32	50¢	J

McCUTCHAN, PHILIP (1920—)
Skyprobe Berkley X1526 1968 175 60¢ R

McDANIEL, DAVID (1939—1977)

The Arsenal out of Time	Ace	G-667	1967	156	50¢	
The Dagger Affair	Ace	G-571	1965	159	50¢	
The Monster Wheel Affair	Ace	G-613	1967	159	50¢	
The Rainbow Affair	Ace	G-670	1967	157	50¢	
The Utopia Affair	Ace	G-729	1968	157	50¢	
The Vampire Affair	Ace	G-590	1966	159	50¢	

MacDONALD, GEORGE (1824—1905)
At the Back of the North Wind

	Airmont	CL100	1966	288	60	R
Phantastes and Lilith	Eerdmans		1964	420	$2.45	C,R
The Princess and Curdie	Puffin	PS260	1966	221	3/6	J,R
The Princess and the Goblin						
	Puffin	PS220	1964	207	3/6	J,R
	Puffin	PS220	1966	207	3/6	J,R

MacDONALD, JOHN D. (1916—)

Ballroom of the Skies	Gold Medal	R1993	1968	176	60¢	R
The Girl, the Gold Watch and Everything						
	Gold Medal	s1259	1962	207	35¢	
	Gold Medal	K1513	1965	207	40¢	R
	Gold Medal	d1792	1967	207	50¢	R
	Muller	GM694	1964	172	2/6	R
	Coronet	02679	1968	205	3/6	R

Planet of the Dreamers (originally *Wine of the Dreamers*)

	Pocket Bks	943	1953	164	25¢	R
	Viking	SF228	1957	189	2/-	R
	Corgi	SS1143	1962	158	2/6	R

Wine of the Dreamers (also titled *Planet of the Dreamers*)

	Gold Medal	R1994	1968	175	60¢	R

Author and Title	Publisher	Serial	Date	Pp.	Price	Type
McDOUGLE, WILLIAM						
The Female Demon [verse] Shroud			1955	76	$1.25	C
McGAUGHY, DUDLEY DEAN [as Dean Owen]						
The Brides of Dracula	Monarch	MM602	1960	141	35¢	
End of the World	Ace	D-548	1962	127	35¢	
Konga	Monarch	MM604	1960	144	35¢	
Reptilicus	Monarch	MM605	1961	143	35¢	
MacGREGOR, ELLEN (1906—1954)						
Miss Pickerell Goes to Mars						
	Scholastic	TX101	1961	94		J
Miss Pickerell Goes Undersea						
	Scholastic	TX302	1964	123	35¢	J
MacGREGOR, JAMES M. (1925—) [as J. T. McIntosh]						
Born Leader (also titled *Worlds Apart*)						
	Corgi	SS1083	1961	190	2/6	R
The Fittest (also titled *The Rule of the Pagbeast*)						
	Corgi	SS1051	1961	220	2/6	R
The Million Cities	Pyramid	F898	1963	141	40¢	M
The Noman Way	Digit	R882	1964	158	2/6	
One in 300	Ace	D-113*	1955	222	35¢	R
	Corgi	SS960	1961	190	2/6	R
Out of Chaos	Brown-Wat.	R888	1965	159	2/6	
The Rule of the Pagbeasts (originally *The Fittest*)						
	Crest	150	1956	192	25¢	R
Snow White and the Giants (also titled *Time for a Change*)						
	Avon	S347	1968	159	60¢	R
200 Years to Christmas	Ace	F-113*	1961	81	40¢	M
World out of Mind	Permabks	M3027	1956	166	25¢	R
	Corgi	SS995	1961	188	2/6	R
Worlds Apart (originally *Born Leader*)						
	Avon	T249	1958	189	35¢	R
MacGREGOR, RICHARD						
The Creeping Plague	Digit	R768	1963	160	2/6	
The Day a Village Died	Digit	R628	1962	158	2/6	
The Deadly Sun	Digit	R856	1964	158	2/6	
Horror in the Night	Digit	R715	1963	158	2/6	
McGUIRE, JOHN J. (1917—) See PIPER, H. B. (co-author)						
MACHEN, ARTHUR (1863—1947)						
See also HALDEMAN-JULIUS CO., page 790.						
Black Crusade (originally *The Three Impostors*)						
	Corgi	GN7392	1966	158	3/6	R
The Great God Pan	Armed	940	nd		np	R
The Hill of Dreams	Corgi	GN7712	1967	156	3/6	R
Holy Terrors	Penguin	526	1946	140	1/-	C
The Novel of the Black Seal						
	Corgi	GN7269	1965	158	3/6	C
The Novel of the White Powder						
	Corgi	GN7270	1965	158	3/6	C
The Strange World of Arthur Machen						
	Juniper	VI	nd	381	$1.65	C
Tales of Horror and the Supernatural						
	Panther	1537	1963	224	3/6	C
McHUGH, VINCENT (1904—)						
I Am Thinking of My Darling						
	Signet	778	1950	224	25¢	
McILWAIN, DAVID (1921—) [as Charles Eric Maine]						
B.E.A.S.T.	Ballantine	U6092	1967	191	75¢	R
	Coronet	02863	1967	190	3/6	R
Calculated Risk	Corgi	SS1118	1962	126	2/6	R
Countdown (also titled *Fire Past the Future*)						
	Corgi	GS7027	1964	158	3/6	R
Crisis 2000	Corgi	S520	1958	224	2/6	R

Author and Title	Publisher	Serial	Date	Pp.	Price	Type
The Darkest of Nights (also titled *Survival Margin*)						
	Panther	1779	1965	205	3/6	R
Fire Past the Future (originally *Countdown*)						
	Ballantine	360K	1960	160	35¢	R
He Owned the World (also titled *The Man Who Owned the World*)						
	Avon	T-524	1961	144	35¢	R
High Vacuum	Ballantine	218	1957	185	35¢	R
	Corgi	SS714	1959	220	2/6	R
The Isotope Man	Corgi	S631	1959	189	2/6	R
The Man Who Owned the World (originally *He Owned the World*)						
	Panther	1610	1964	123	2/6	R
The Mind of Mr. Soames	Panther	1700	1964	192	3/6	R
Spaceways	Pan	297	1954	190	2/-	R
Subterfuge	Hodder	511	1962	192	2/6	R
Survival Margin (originally *The Darkest of Nights*)						
	Gold Medal	R1918	1968	192	60¢	R
The Tide Went Out	Ballantine	290K	1959	156	35¢	R
	Corgi	SS873	1960	220	2/6	R
Timeliner	Bantam	A1470	1956	182	35¢	R
	Corgi	S554	1958	222	2/6	R
	Corgi	GS1512	1964	190	3/6	R
World Without Men	Ace	D-274	1958	190	35¢	
	Digit	R808	1963	158	2/6	R
McILWRAITH, MAUREEN MOLLIE See HUNTER, M. (pseud)						
McINNES, GRAHAM (1912—)						
Lost Island	Signet	S1215	1955	191	35¢	R
McINTOSH, J. T. (pseud) See McGREGOR, J. M.						
MACK, THOMAS						
The Spectre Bullet	Stellar	SFS17*	1932	13	10¢	
(part of booklet also containing "The Avenging Note," A. Sprissler)						
McKEAG, ERNEST LIONEL See KING, J. (pseud)						
McKENZIE, NIGEL						
Day of Judgment	Brown-Wat.		1960	160	2/-	R
McLAUGHLIN, DEAN (1931—)						
Dome World	Pyramid	F763	1962	159	40¢	
The Fury From Earth	Pyramid	F923	1963	192	40¢	
The Man Who Wanted Stars						
	Lancer	73-441	1965	222	60¢	
	Lancer	74-949	1968	222	75¢	R
MacLEAN, ALISTAIR (1922—)						
The Satan Bug [as Ian Stuart]						
	Popular	SP231	1963	224	50¢	R
[as Ian Stuart]	Fontana	917	1963	223	2/6	R
[as Alistair MacLean]	Fontana	1173	1965	223	3/6	R
MacLEAN, KATHERINE (1925—)						
Cosmic Checkmate [with Charles V. DeVet]						
	Ace	F-149*	1962	96	40¢	
The Diploids	Avon	G1143	1962	192	50¢	C
McNEILLY, WILFRED G. (1921—)						
Drums of the Dark Gods [as W. A. Ballinger]						
	Mayflower	2153	1966	126	3/6	
	Paperback	52-584	1967	159	50¢	R
McSHANE, MARK (1930—)						
Seance on a Wet Afternoon Crest		k781	1965	128	50¢	R
	Pan	G608	1963	156	3/6	R
MacTYRE, PAUL (pseud of Robert J. Adam [1925—])						
Doomsday, 1999 (originally *Midge*)						
	Ace	F-201	1963	158	40¢	R

Author and Title	Publisher	Serial	Date	Pp.	Price	Type
MacVICAR, ANGUS (1908—)						
Red Fire on Lost Planet	Burke	JP	1964	158	2/6	
MADDOCK, LARRY (pseud) See JARDINE, J. O.						
MADDOX, CARL (pseud) See TUBB, E. C.						
MAGEE, BRYAN						
Towards 2000	MacDonald		1965	156	np	N
MAGROON, VICTOR						
The Burning Void	Scion		1953	128	1/6	
MAINE, CHARLES ERIC (pseud) See McILWAIN, D.						
MAIR, GEORGE B. (1917—)						
The Day Khrushchev Panicked	Digit	R649	1962	188	2/6	
	Macfadden	50-183	1963	159	50¢	R
MAJORS, SIMON (pseud) See FOX, G. F.						
MAKEPEACE-LOTT, S.						
Escape to Venus	Panther	786	1958	192	2/6	R
MALAMUD, BERNARD (1914—)						
Idiots First	Dell	3946	1966	192	75¢	C,R
The Magic Barrel	Dell	5613	1966	188	75¢	R
MALCOLM-SMITH, GEORGE (1901—)						
The Grass Is Always Greener	Bantam	410	1948	184	25¢	R
MANNHEIM, KARL						
Vampires of Venus	WDL	WFC	1950	128	1/6	
When the Earth Died	WDL	WFC	1950	128	1/6	
MANNING, P. L.						
The Destroyers	Badger	SF11	1958	158	2/-	
MANNING, ROSEMARY (1911—)						
Green Smoke	Puffin	PS297	1967	143	75¢	J,R
MANSFIELD, ROGER (1939—)						
The Starlit Corridor	Pergamon	103370	1967	145	9/6	A
(identical hardcover edition 21/-)						
[Teacher's edition]	Pergamon	103349	1967	160	np	A
MANTLEY, JOHN (1920—)						
The 27th Day	Crest	s209	1958	176	35¢	R
	Odhams	B26	1958	156	2/6	R
	FSB	363	1961	192	2/6	R
	FSB	1162	1964	192	3/6	R
MANUEL, F. E.						
Utopias and Utopian Thought	Beac (Prs)	BP251	1967	321	$2.45	N
MANVELL, ROGER (1909—)						
The Dreamers	Bantam	F2697	1963	165	50¢	R
	Bantam	H3494	1967	165	60¢	R
	Corgi	GN7012	1964	165	3/6	R
MAPLE, ERIC						
The Dark World of Witches	Pan	X373	1965	205	3/6	N,R
The Domain of Devils	Pan	02231	1968	223	5/-	N
The Realm of Ghosts	Pan	M219	1967	220	5/-	N,R
MARAS, KARL (pseud) See BULMER, K. (2 novels), and HAWKINS, P. (1 novel)						

Author and Title	Publisher	Serial	Date	Pp.	Price	Type
MARCELIN, PHILIPPE THOBY (1908—) See MARCELIN, PIERRE (co-author)						
MARCELIN, PIERRE (1904—)						
The Beast of the Haitian Hills (with Philippe Thoby Marcelin)						
	Time Inc.		1964	172	np	R
MARFAX, CLYDE						
Planets of Peril	Baker	FST4	1953	62	9d	
MARGOLIES, JOSEPH A. (1889—)						
Strange and Fantastic Stories [abridged]						
	Armed	1223	nd		np	A,R
MARGROFF, ROBERT See JACOB, P.A.D. (co-author)						
MARGULIES, LEO (1900—1975)						
Get Out of My Sky	Crest	s362	1960	176	35¢	A
	Crest	L728	1964	176	45¢	A,R
The Ghoul Keepers	Pyramid	G665	1961	157	35¢	A
	Pyramid	R1210	1965	157	50¢	A,R
My Best Science Fiction Story [with Oscar J. Friend]						
	Pocket Bks	1007	1954	263	25¢	A,R
Race to the Stars [with Oscar J. Friend] (selections from *Giant Anthology of Science Fiction*)	Crest	s245	1958	224	35¢	A,R
3 From Out There	Crest	s282	1959	192	35¢	A
	Panther	1057	1960	190	2/6	A,R
	Panther	1057	1964	207	3/6	A,R
Three in One	Pyramid	F899	1963	144	40¢	A
Three Times Infinity	Gold Medal	s726	1958	176	35¢	A
	Gold Medal	d1324	1963	176	50¢	A,R
	Gold Medal	d1680	1966	176	50¢	A,R
The Unexpected	Pyramid	G590	1961	160	35¢	A
	Pyramid	F795	1962	160	40¢	A,R
Weird Tales	Pyramid	R1029	1964	155	50¢	A
Worlds of Weird	Pyramid	R1125	1965	158	50¢	A
MARLOWE, GABRIEL						
Chez Robert and Other Romances						
	Utopian		nd	44	1/-	C
MARQUIS, DON (1878—1937)						
Archy and Mehitabel	Dolphin	C26	1960	193	95¢	R
MARQUIS, ROY						
The Moon Monsters	Barrington	1	ca.1954	128	1/6	
MARRYAT, FREDERICK (1792—1848)						
The Phantom Ship	FSB	1577	1966	318	5/-	R
MARS, ALASTAIR (CAMPBELL GILLESPIE) (1915—)						
Arctic Submarine	Horwitz	NA13	1959	224	4/6	
Atomic Submarine	Horwitz	NS14	1959	223	4/6	
MARSH, JOHN (1907—) [as John Elton]						
The Green Plantations	Ward Lock	37	1956	194	2/6	R
MARSH, RICHARD (1867—1915)						
The Beetle	Hutchinson 9d Lib	nd	152	9d	R
	WDL	GC833	1959	263	3/6	R
	Consul	1378	1965	253	3/6	R
MARSHALL, BRUCE (1899—)						
Father Malachy's Miracle	Pocket Bks	435	1947	201	25¢	R
	Pan	207	1952	191	1/6	R
	Fontana	742R	1962	159	2/6	R
MARSHALL, EDISON (TESLA) (1894—1967)						
Earth Giant	Popular	W1110	1961	380	75¢	R

Author and Title	Publisher	Serial	Date	Pp.	Price	Type
MARTIN, A. E.						
The Shudder Show	N.S.W. Bookstall		nd	48	1/-	C
MARTIN, ED(GAR A.)						
Busy Bodies	Traveller's Comp.					
		TC-2227	1968	246		
MARTIN, REGINALD ALEC [as E. C. Eliott]						
Kemlo and the Martian Ghosts						
	Nelson	Junior	1959	202	2/6	J,R
Kemlo and the Space Lanes						
	Nelson	Junior	1959	200	2/6	J,R
	Merlin	M39	1968	125	2/6	J,R
Kemlo and the Star Men	Merlin	M40	1968	126	2/6	J,R
Kemlo and the Zones of Silence						
	Nelson	Junior	1959	200	2/6	J,R
Tas and the Postal Rocket	Nelson	Panther	ca.1960	127	np	J,R
Tas and the Space Machine	Nelson	Panther	ca.1960	127	np	J,R
MARTIN, S. See BOY'S FRIEND LIBRARY, page 789.						
MARTIN, THOMAS (1913—)						
Beyond the Spectrum [as Martin Thomas]						
	Digit	R864	1964	158	2/6	
	Paperback	52-554	1967	160	50¢	R
The Curse of Rathlaw [as Peter Saxon (house pseud.)]						
	Lancer	73-750	1968	190	60¢	R
Hand of Cain [as Martin Thomas] (originally *The Hands of Cain*)						
	Lancer	73-660	1967	159	60¢	R
The Hands of Cain [as Martin Thomas] (also titled *Hand of Cain*)						
	Mayflower	3425	1966	158	3/6	
Laird of Evil [as Martin Thomas]						
	Mayflower	4622	1965	111	2/6	
Sorcerers of Set	Mayflower	8156	1966	141	3/6	
MASEFIELD, JOHN E. (1878—)						
The Box of Delights	Puffin	PS234	1965	269	4/6	J,R
The Midnight Folk	Puffin	PS187	1963	232	3/6	J,R
MASON, A(LFRED) E(DWARD) W(OODLEY) (1865—1948)						
The Prisoner in the Opal	Hodder		1953	191	2/-	
MASON, DOUGLAS R. (1918—)						
Eight Against Utopia (originally *From Carthage Then I Came*)						
	Paperback	52-599	1967	158	50¢	R
Interstellar Two-Five [as John Rankine]						
	Corgi	07979	1968	123	3/6	R
MASSON, LOUYS						
The Barbed Wire Fence	Panther	1634	1964	203	3/6	
MASTERS, DEXTER (1908—)						
The Accident	Panther	1024	1960	316	3/6	R
MASTERS, R. & L.						
The Mystery of the Ming Tree						
	French		nd	59	$1.00	
MASTERSON, WHIT (pseud of R. Wade and B. Miller)						
The Dark Fantastic	Avon	S212	1966	207	60¢	
MATHESON, HUGH						
Balance of Fear	Panther	1983	1966	189	3/6	
MATHESON, RICHARD (1926—)						
I Am Legend	Gold Medal	417	1954	160	25¢	
	Corgi	T197	1956	192	2/-	R
	Corgi	SS854	1960	188	2/6	R
	Corgi	SS1213	1962	141	2/6	R
	Bantam	J2744	1964	122	40¢	R

Author and Title	Publisher	Serial	Date	Pp.	Price	Type
Shock	Dell	B195	1961	191	35¢	C
	Dell	7828	1966	191	50¢	C,R
	Corgi	SN1180	1962	160	2/6	C,R
Shock II	Dell	7829	1964	192	50¢	C
	Corgi	GN7289	1965	158	3/6	C,R
Shock III	Dell	7830	1966	192	50¢	C
	Corgi	GN7694	1967	190	3/6	C,R
The Shores of Space	Bantam	A1571	1957	184	35¢	C
	Corgi	S614	1958	221	2/6	C,R
	Corgi	GS7230	1965	176	3/6	C,R
The Shrinking Man	Gold Medal	s577	1956	192	35¢	
	Gold Medal	d1203	1962	192	50¢	R
	Muller	GM259	1958	190	2/-	R
	Muller	nn	nd	130	3/-	R
A Stir of Echoes	Crest	s308	1959	175	35¢	R
	Corgi	SS886	1960	190	2/6	R
	Corgi	GS7097	1965	158	3/6	R
Third From the Sun (selections from *Born of Man and Woman*)						
	Bantam	1294	1955	180	25¢	C,R
	Bantam	J2467	1962	180	40	C,R
	Corgi	SS1027	1961	190	2/6	C,R
MATHEWS, BRANDER See HALDEMAN-JULIUS CO., page 790.						
MATSON, NORMAN (1893—)						
Bats in the Belfry	Popular	200	1948	192	25¢	R
The Passionate Witch [completed by Matson] See SMITH, THORNE						
MATURIN, CHARLES (1780—1824)						
Melmoth the Wanderer	Bison		1963	413	$1.70	R
	FSB	1561	1966	542	7/6	R
MAUGHAM, ROBIN						
The Man With Two Shadows						
	FSB	1894	1967	124	5/-	
The 1946 Ms	War Facts		1943	44	1/-	
MAUGHAM, W(ILLIAM) SOMERSET (1874—1965)						
The Magician	Pocket Bks		1958		35¢	
MAXON, P. B. (? —1934?)						
The Waltz of Death	Bart House	9	1944	188	25¢	R
MAXWELL, J. See CHAMPION LIBRARY, page 789.						
MAXWELL, JOHN C. (pseud) See GLASBY, J. S.						
MEAD, (EDWARD) SHEPHERD (1914—)						
The Big Ball of Wax	Ballantine	174	1956	181	35¢	R
	Avon	G1129	1962	181	50¢	R
	Mayflower	B35	1962	160	3/6	R
The Sex Machine (originally *The Magnificent McInnes*)						
	Popular	228	1949	160	25¢	R
MEAD, HAROLD (1910—)						
The Bright Phoenix	Ballantine	147	1956	184	35¢	
(identical hardcover edition $2.00)						
	Corgi	GS784	1960	287	3/6	R
MEADE, RICHARD						
The Sword of Morning Star	Signet	P3774	1968	144	60¢	
MEEK, S(TERNER) (ST.) P(AUL) (1894—)						
Arctic Bride	Utopian	AF nn	nd	36	9d	C
MEITER, WALTER						
The Deadly Organ	Olympic	F-111	1968			

Author and Title	Publisher	Serial	Date	Pp.	Price	Type

MELDE, G. R.
| Pacific Advance | Curtis War. | | 1954 | 159 | 1/6 | |

(identical hardcover edition 6/-)

MELTZER, DAVID (1937—)
The Agency	Essex House	0102	1968	160	$1.95	
The Agent	Essex House	0104	1968	160	$1.95	
How Many Blocks in the Pile?						
	Essex House	0107	1968	160	$1.95	

MENDELSOHN, FELIX Jr. (1906—)
| Club Tycoon Sends Man to Moon | | | | | | |
| | Book Amer. | 13 | 1964 | 122 | 75¢ | |

MENEN, AUBREY (1912—)
| The Fig Tree | Penguin | 1928 | 1963 | | 3/6 | R |
| The Prevalence of Witches | Penguin | 1215 | 1957 | 216 | 2/6 | R |

MENGER, H.
| From Outer Space | Pyramid | T1630 | 1967 | 254 | 75¢ | |

MERAK, A. J. (pseud) See GLASBY, J. S.

MERRIL, JUDITH (1923—)
The Best of Sci-Fi (originally *The Year's Best S-F: 6th Annual Edition*)						
	Mayflower	0543	1963	384	5/-	A,R
The Best of Sci-Fi 2 (originally *The Year's Best S-F: 7th Annual Edition*)						
	Mayflower	9773	1964	399	5/-	A,R
The Best of Sci-Fi 3 See SMITH, CORDELIA TITCOMB						
The Best of Sci-Fi 4 (originally *The Year's Best S-F: 8th Annual Edition*)						
	Mayflower	0544	1965	382	5/-	A,R
The Best of Sci-Fi 5 (originally *The Year's Best S-F: 5th Annual Edition*)						
	Mayflower	0531	1966	317	5/-	A,R
Beyond Human Ken See *Selections From Beyond Human Ken*						
Galaxy of Ghouls (also titled *Off the Beaten Orbit*)						
	Lion	LL25	1955	192	35¢	A
Gunner Cade [as Cyril Judd (pseud. with Cyril Kornbluth)]						
	Ace	D-227*	1957	198	35¢	R
	Penguin	2460	1966	199	3/6	R
Human?	Lion	205	1954	190	35¢	A
Off the Beaten Orbit (originally *Galaxy of Ghouls*)						
	Pyramid	G397	1959	192	35¢	A,R
	Pyramid	F683	1961	192	40¢	A,R
Out of Bounds	Pyramid	G499	1960	160	35¢	C
	Pyramid	F830	1963	160	40¢	C,R
Outpost Mars [as Cyril Judd (pseud. with Cyril Kornbluth)] (see also						
Sin in Space)	Dell	760	1954	223	25¢	R
	FSB	1585	1966	187	3/6	R
S-F: The Best of the Best	Dell	0508	1967	408	95¢	A,R
S-F: The Year's Greatest Science-Fiction and Fantasy						
	Dell	B103	1956	352	35¢	A
(identical hardcover edition from Gnome Press, $3.50)						
S-F: The Year's Greatest Science-Fiction and Fantasy: Second Annual Volume	Dell	B110	1957	320	35¢	A
(identical hardcover edition from Gnome Press, $3.95)						
S-F: The Year's Greatest Science-Fiction and Fantasy: Third Annual Volume	Dell	B119	1958	255	35¢	A
(identical hardcover edition from Gnome Press, $3.50)						
S-F: The Year's Greatest Science-Fiction and Fantasy: Fourth Annual Volume	Dell	B129	1959	256	35¢	A
(identical hardcover edition from Gnome Press, $3.50)						
[Series continued as *Year's Best S-F: . . .*]						
Selections From Beyond Human Ken						
	Bantam	P56	1954	248	25¢	A,R
Shadow on the Hearth	Compact	F325	1966	192	3/6	R
Shot in the Dark	Bantam	751	1950	310	25¢	A
Sin in Space [as Cyril Judd (pseud. with Cyril Kornbluth)] (sexed-up						
version of *Outpost Mars*)	Beacon	312	1961	190	35¢	R
The Tomorrow People	Pyramid	G502	1960	192	35¢	
	Pyramid	F806	1962	192	40¢	R
	Pyramid	X1802	1968	192	60¢	R

The Year's Best S-F: 5th Annual Edition (also titled *The Best of Science Fiction 5*)
| | Dell | F118 | 1961 | 320 | 50¢ | A,R |

[From here on until the *9th Annual*, Simon & Schuster published a hardcover edition first; beginning with the *10th Annual*, Delacorte published the hardcover edition.]

The Year's Best S-F: 6th Annual Edition (also titled *The Best of Sci-Fi*)
| | Dell | 9772 | 1962 | 384 | 50¢ | A,R |

The Year's Best S-F: 7th Annual Edition (also titled *The Best of Sci-Fi 2*)
| | Dell | 9773 | 1963 | 399 | 75¢ | A,R |

The Year's Best S-F: 8th Annual Edition (also titled *The Best of Sci-Fi 4*)
| | Dell | 9774 | 1964 | 382 | 75¢ | A,R |

The Year's Best S-F: 9th Annual Edition
| | Dell | 9775 | 1965 | 384 | 75¢ | A,R |
| | Mayflower | 9775 | 1967 | 381 | 5/- | A,R |

The Year's Best S-F: 10th Annual Edition
| | Dell | 8611 | 1966 | 382 | 75¢ | A,R |
| | Mayflower | 8611 | 1967 | 382 | 5/- | A,R |

The Year's Best S-F: 11th Annual Edition
| | Dell | 2241 | 1967 | 384 | 75¢ | A,R |

MERRITT, A(BRAHAM) (1884—1943)
See also BIZARRE SERIES, page 789.

Burn, Witch, Burn!	Avon	MM5	1942	223	25¢	R
	Avon	43	1943		25¢	R
	Avon	MM43	1946	161	25¢	R
	Avon	392	1951	161	25¢	R
	Pedigree		1957	192	2/6	R
	Corgi	SN1343	1963	126	2/6	R
Creep, Shadow, Creep!	Avon	MM11	1943	188	25¢	R
	Avon	MM47	1946		25¢	R
	Avon	117	1947	255	25¢	R
Dwellers in the Mirage	Avon	MM24	1944	158	25¢	R
	Avon	413	1952	220	25¢	R
	Avon	S271	1967	222	60¢	R
	Paperback	52-142	1962	192	50¢	R
	Paperback	52-516	1965	192	50¢	R
The Face in the Abyss	Avon	MM29	1945	205	25¢	R
	Avon	T161	1957	253	35¢	R
	Collier	AS34X	1961	255	95¢	R
	Collier	02279	1967	255	95¢	R
The Fox Woman	Avon	214	1949	157	25¢	C
The Metal Monster	Avon	MM41	1946	203	25¢	R
	Avon	315	1951	252	25¢	R
	Avon	T172	1957	222	35¢	R
	Avon	S231	1966	238	60¢	R
The Moon Pool	Avon	MM18	1944	201	25¢	R
	Avon	370	1951	254	25¢	R
	Avon	T135	1956	254	35¢	R
	Collier	AS103X	1962	254	95¢	R
	Collier	02287	1966	254	95¢	R
Seven Footprints to Satan	Avon	MM1	1942	310	25¢	R
	Avon	26	1942	320	25¢	R
	Avon	235	1949	187	25¢	R
	Avon	T115	1955	187	35¢	R
	Avon	T208	1957	187	35¢	R
	Avon	G1192	1964	192	50¢	R
	Avon	S280	1968	192	60¢	R
The Ship of Ishtar	Avon	MM34	1945	168	25¢	R
	Avon	324	1951	220	25¢	R
	Avon	T152	1956	220	35¢	R
	Avon	S229	1966	207	60¢	R

MERWIN, SAM Jr. (1910—)
The House of Many Worlds
	Galaxy Nov	12	1952	154	35¢	R
Killer to Come	Galaxy Nov	22	1954	125	35¢	R
	Digit	R651	1962	160	2/6	R
The Sex War (originally *The White Widows*)						
	Beac (Gal)	284	1960	160	35¢	R
Three Faces of Time	Ace	D-121*	1955	135	35¢	M
	Badger	SF29	1960	142	2/-	R

Author and Title	Publisher	Serial	Date	Pp.	Price	Type
MEYER, BILL						
Ultimatum	Signet	P2923	1966	189	60¢	
MEYER, J. A. See NOURSE, A. E. (co-author)						
MEYERS, ROY (1910—)						
Daughters of the Dolphin	Ballantine	72001	1968	224	75¢	
Dolphin Boy	Ballantine	U6100	1967	224	75¢	
MEYRINK, GUSTAV (1868—1932)						
The Golem	Unger	2139	1964	288	$1.75	R
MICHAEL, SCOTT						
Journey Into Limbo	Macfadden	60-140	1963	192	60¢	
MICHEL, AIME (1919—)						
The Truth About Flying Saucers						
	Corgi	S576	1958	253	2/6	N,R
	Pyramid	T1647	1967	270	75¢	N,R
MICHELET, JULES (1798—1874)						
Satanism and Witchcraft	Pedigree		1958	288	3/6	N
	Citadel	C89	1967	332	$1.75	N,R
MICHELMORE, REG						
An Adventure in Venus	Stellar	SFS3	1929	24	10¢	
MILLARD, JOSEPH J. (1908?—)						
The Gods Hate Kansas	Monarch	414	1964	126	40¢	M
MILLER, BILL See MASTERTON, W. (pseud, with R. Wade)						
MILLER, P. SCHUYLER (1912—1974)						
Genus Homo [with L. S. de Camp]						
	Berkley	G536	1961	157	35¢	R
MILLER, R(ICHARD) DeWITT (1910—1958)						
Impossible—Yet It Happened						
	Ace	F-137	1962	128	40¢	N
	Ace	K-229	1966	128	50¢	N,R
The Man Who Lived Forever [with Anna Hunger] (also titled *Year 3097*)						
	Ace	D-162*	1956	137	35¢	
Reincarnation—The Whole Startling Story						
	Bantam	1507	1956	118	25¢	N
Stranger Than Life	Ace	K-168	1964	190	50¢	N
Year 3097 [with Anna Hunger] (originally *The Man Who Lived Forever*)						
	Satellite	215	1958	129	3/-	R
MILLER, SUTRO						
H for Horrific	Sentinel		1947	80	1/6	C
MILLER, WALTER M. Jr. (1922—)						
A Canticle for Leibowitz	Bantam	F2212	1961	278	50¢	R
	Bantam	H2618	1963	278	60¢	R
	Bantam	S2973	1965	278	75¢	R
	Corgi	GS1401	1963	278	3/6	R
Conditionally Human	Ballantine	F626	1962	191	50¢	C
	Panther	1989	1966	174	3/6	C,R
The View From the Stars	Ballantine	U2212	1965	192	50¢	C
	Panther	23852	1968	223	5/-	C,R
MILLER, WARREN						
Looking for the General	Crest	R793	1965	176	60¢	R
The Siege of Harlem	Crest	R833	1965	128	60¢	R
MILLS, ROBERT P. (1920—)						
The Best From Fantasy and Science Fiction, Ninth Series						
	Ace	F-267	1964	256	40¢	A,R
	Panther	1738	1964	207	3/6	A,R

Author and Title	Publisher	Serial	Date	Pp.	Price	Type
The Best From Fantasy and Science Fiction, Tenth Series						
	Ace	M-116	1965	252	45¢	A,R
The Best From Fantasy and Science Fiction, Eleventh Series						
	Ace	M-137	1966	254	45¢	A,R
[noted as No. 11]	Panther	2052	1966	189	3/6	A,R
A Decade of Fantasy and Science Fiction						
	Dell	X12	1962	416	75¢	A,R
	Corgi	FS7028	1964	319	5/-	A,R
The Worlds of Science Fiction						
	Paperback	54-819	1965	287	75¢	A,R
	Paperback	54-577	1967	287	75¢	A,R
	Panther	2124	1966	288	5/-	A,R
MILNE, A(LAN) A(LEXANDER) (1882—1956)						
Once on a Time	Camelot	ZS103	1966	242	60¢	J,R
	Puffin	PS377	1968	203	5/-	J,R
MILTON, HENRY A.						
The President Is Missing!	Banner	B60-105	1967	175	60¢	
MIRBEAU, OCTAVE (1850—1917)						
Torture Garden	Berkley	111	1955	187	25¢	R
	Berkley	G39	1956	157	35¢	R
	Lancer	74-840	1965	191	75¢	R
MISTRAL, BERGO						
The Brains of Helle	Gannet	4	1953	127	1/6	
Pirates of Cerelius	Gannet	1	1953	128	1/6	
Space Flight 139	Gannet	2	1953	128	1/6	
MITCHELL, J. LESLIE (1901—1935)						
Three Go Back	Galaxy	Nov 15	1953	124	35¢	R
MITCHELL, MILTON						
The Creation	Stellar	SFS9*	1930	10	10¢	
[part of booklet also containing "The Thought Translator," M. Eberle]						
MITCHISON, NAOMI (1897—)						
Memoirs of a Spacewoman	FSB	1090	1964	190	3/6	R
MITTELHÖLZER, EDGAR (1909—1965)						
My Bones and My Flute	Corgi	S606	1958	224	2/6	R
	Corgi	GN7373	1966	174	3/6	R
MOIS, JOSEPH						
A Spot on the Sun	Baker	FST3	1953	52	9d	
MOLESWORTH, VOL (1924—1964)						
Ape of God	Currawong		1943	64	6d	
Blinded They Fly	Futurian		1951	31	6/-	
Let There Be Monsters	Futurian		1952	23	6/-	
Monster at Large	Currawong		1943	63	9d	
An Outline History of Australian Fandom (Part 1)						
	Futurian		1953	26	6/-	N
Prelude for Death	Currawong		1944	64	9d	
Satan's Understudy	Currawong		1944	64	9d	
Spaceward Ho!	Transport	RR6/18	1943	48	6d	
Stratosphere Patrol	Transport	RR5/64	1943	48	6d	
The Three Rocketeers	Transport	RR6/37	1944	50	6d	
Wolfblood	Dennett	*ca.*1944		64	9d	
MONAHAN, JAMES L.						
Masterpieces of Surprise	Hart		1966	256	75¢	A
MONSARRAT, NICHOLAS (1910—1978?)						
The Time Before This	Pan	G694	1965	127	2/6	R
	Pocket Bks	50499	1966	128	50¢	R

Author and Title	Publisher	Serial	Date	Pp.	Price	Type
MONTELHEIT, HUBERT						
Return From the Ashes	Signet	D2414	1964	124	50¢	
	Signet	D2414	1965	124	50¢	R
MONTGOMERY, ROBERT B. (1921–1978) [as Edmund Crispin]						
Best SF	Faber		1958	368	6/-	A,R
Best SF Two	Faber		1960	296	6/-	A,R
Best SF Three	Faber		1962	224	6/-	A,R
Best SF Four	Faber		1965	224	6/6	A,R
Best Tales of Terror	Faber		1966	255	6/6	A,R
Buried for Pleasure	Pyramid	X1937	1968	174	60¢	R
The Stars and Under	Faber		1968	174	5/6	A,R
MOORCOCK, MICHAEL (1939–)						
Barbarians of Mars [as Edward P. Bradbury]						
	Compact	F291	1965	158	3/6	
	Lancer	72-127	1966	158	50¢	R
The Best of New Worlds	Compact	H287	1965	318	5/-	A
Best SF Stories From New Worlds						
	Panther	2243	1967	141	3/6	A
	Berkley	X1513	1968	158	60¢	A,R
Best SF Stories From New Worlds 3						
	Panther	024956	1968	157	3/6	A
Best Stories From New Worlds 2						
	Panther	023690	1968	157	3/6	A
Blades of Mars [as Edward P. Bradbury]						
	Compact	F279	1965	158	3/6	
	Lancer	72-122	1966	159	50¢	R
The Deep Fix [as James Colvin]						
	Compact	F305	1966	159	3/6	C
The Final Programme	Avon	S351	1968	191	60¢	
The Fireclown	Compact	F281	1965	189	3/6	
	Paperback	52-475	1967	158	50¢	R
The Jewel in the Skull	Lancer	73-688	1967	175	60¢	
SF Reprise 2	Compact	H324	1966	216	5/-	A
[double binding of *New Worlds* Nos. 146 and 147]						
SF Reprise 5	Compact	H329	1967	358	5/-	A
[double binding of *New Worlds* Nos. 149, 150, and 151]						
Sorcerer's Amulet	Lancer	73-707	1968	190	60¢	
The Stealer of Souls	Lancer	73-545	1967	190	60¢	C,R
	Mayflower	113443	1968	173	5/-	C,R
Stormbringer	Lancer	73-579	1967	191	60¢	C,R
	Mayflower	113435	1968	189	5/-	C,R
The Sundered Worlds	Compact	F266	1965	190	3/6	M
	Paperback	52-368	1966	159	50¢	R
Sword of the Dawn	Lancer	73-761	1968	191	60¢	
The Twilight Man	Compact	F313	1966	190	3/6	M
Warriors of Mars [as Edward P. Bradbury]						
	Compact	F275	1965	157	3/6	
	Lancer	72-118	1966	159	50¢	R
Wrecks of Time	Ace	H-36*	1967	135	60¢	M
MOORE, CATHERINE L. (1911–)						
Beyond Earth's Gates [with Lewis Padgett (pseud. of Henry Kuttner)]						
	Ace	D-69*	1954	138	35¢	M
Doomsday Morning	Avon	T297	1959	221	35¢	R
	Avon	S378	1968	208	60¢	R
	WDL	SF963	1960	192	2/6	R
Earth's Last Citadel [with H. Kuttner]						
	Ace	F-306	1964	128	40¢	M
Judgment Night	Paperback	52-863	1965	156	50¢	R
No Boundaries [with H. Kuttner]						
	Ballantine	122	1955	149	35¢	C
(identical hardcover edition $2.00)						
	Consul	SF1025	1961	159	2/6	C,R
Shambleau	Galaxy Nov	31	1958	127	35¢	C,R
	Consul	SF1009	1961	222	2/6	C,R

Author and Title	Publisher	Serial	Date	Pp.	Price	Type
MOORE, ISABEL						
The Day the Communists Took Over America						
	Wisdom House G-1		1961	158	50¢	
MOORE, PATRICK (1923–)						
Once Upon a Friday	Tower	43-528	1965	190	60¢	
Raiders of Mars	Burke	JP	1964	159	2/6	J
MOORE, WARD (1903–1978)						
Bring the Jubilee	Ballantine	38	1953	194	35¢	M
(identical hardcover edition $2.00)						
	FSB	1378	1965	189	3/6	
Greener Than You Think	Ballantine	527	1961	185	35¢	R
Joyleg [with A. Davidson]	Pyramid	F805	1962	160	40¢	M
MORGAN, DAN (1925–)						
Cee-Tee Man	Panther	181	1955	144	1/6	
(identical hardcover edition 6/-)						
The New Minds	Corgi	GS7630	1967	158	3/6	
The Richest Corpse in Show Business						
	Compact	F299	1966	190	3/6	
The Uninhibited	Digit	R532	1961	159	2/6	M
	Digit	R771	1963	160	2/6	R
MORLEY, CHRISTOPHER (1890–1957)						
Thunder on the Left	Penguin-US	S37	1944	245	25¢	R
	Penguin-US	582	1946	184	25¢	R
MORRIS, ROSAMUND						
Masterpieces of Horror	Hart		1966	255	75¢	A
Masterpieces of Mystery and Detection						
	Hart		1965	256	75¢	A
Masterpieces of Suspense	Hart		1966	254	75¢	A
MORRISON, ROBERTA						
Tree of Evil	Paperback	52376	1966	158	50¢	
MORRISSEY, J. L. See LEVENE, P. (co-author), and SAXON, R.						
(pseud)						
MORTON, HENRY C. V(OLLAM) (1892–)						
I, James Blunt	Methuen		1942	56	6d	
MOSKOWITZ, SAM (1920–)						
The Coming of the Robots	Collier	AS548	1963	254	95¢	A
Doorway Into Time†	Macfadden	50311	1966	144	50¢	A
Explorers of the Infinite	Meridian	M202	1966	354	$1.95	N,R
Exploring Other Worlds	Collier	AS551	1963	256	95¢	A
	Collier	02311	1967	256	95¢	A,R
The Human Zero and Other Science Fiction Masterpieces						
[with R. Elwood]	Tower	43-906	1967	224	60¢	A
Microcosmic God and Other Stories†						
	Macfadden	60-335	1968	142	60¢	A
Seekers of Tomorrow	Ballantine	U7083	1967	450	95¢	N,R
The Time Curve [with R. Elwood]						
	Tower	43-986	1968	189	60¢	A
The Vortex Blasters†	Macfadden	60-325	1968	144	60¢	A
† These three together reprint most of the stories in the hardcover *Modern Masterpieces of Science Fiction*.						
MOUDY, WALTER F. (1929–1973)						
No Man on Earth	Berkley	F987	1964	176	50¢	
	Corgi	GS7598	1967	172	3/6	R
MOXLEY, F(RANK) WRIGHT (1889–1937)						
Red Snow	Simon Schuster		1930	411	$1.00	R

Author and Title	Publisher	Serial	Date	Pp.	Price	Type
MULLEN, STANLEY (1911—1973?)						
The Sphinx Child	New Collectors		1948	23	35¢	
MULLER, JOHN E. (house pseud)						
Alien See GLASBY, J. S.						
Day of the Beasts See GLASBY, J. S.						
Edge of Eternity	Badger	SF65	1962	158	2/6	
	Pitt & Bond	516	1963	130	3/6	R
Forbidden Planet See FANTHORPE, R. L.						
In the Beginning	Badger	SF76	1962	159	2/6	
	Vega	VSF6	1964	146	50¢	R
Infinity Machine See FANTHORPE, R. L.						
The Mind Makers See FANTHORPE, R. L.						
Night of the Big Fire	Badger	SF75	1962	159	2/6	
Search the Dark Stars See GLYNN, A. A.						
Space Void	Badger	SF34	1960	141	2/-	
The Unpossessed See GLASBY, J. S.						
Uranium 235 See FANTHORPE, R. L.						
MUNBY, A(LAN) N(OEL) L(ATIMER) (1913—1974)						
The Alabaster Hand	FSB	932	1963	143	2/6	C,R
MUNDY, TALBOT (pseud of William Lancaster Gribbon [1879—1940])						
The Devil's Guard	Avon	V2230	1968	255	75¢	R
Full Moon	Royal Giant	C20*	1953	225	50¢	R
Helene†	Avon	S318	1967	159	60¢	R
Helma†	Avon	S309	1967	240	60¢	R
Jimgrim (also titled *Jimgrim Sahib*)						
	Avon	V2220	1968	288	75¢	R
Jimgrim Sahib (originally *Jimgrim*)						
	Royal Giant	12	*ca.*1952	319	50¢	R
King—of the Khyber Rifles	Beac (Pub)	105	*ca.*1945	288	35¢	R
Liafail†	Avon	S316	1967	255	60¢	R
The Nine Unknown	Avon	V2242	1968	254	75¢	R
Om: The Secret of Ahbor Valley						
	Xanadu		1962	392	$1.65	R
	Avon	V2212	1967	336	75¢	R
Queen Cleopatra	Ace	K-149	1962	319	50¢	R
Trek East (The Ivory Trail)						
	Royal Giant	19	1953	319	50¢	R
Tros†	Avon	S303	1967	239	60¢	R

† *Tros, Helma, Liafail,* and *Helene* comprise the text of the hardcover *Tros of Samothrace.*

Author and Title	Publisher	Serial	Date	Pp.	Price	Type
MUNN, H. WARNER (1903—1981)						
King of the World's Edge	Ace	M-152	1966	191	45¢	M
The Ship From Atlantis	Ace	G-618*	1967	117	50¢	
MUNRO, H. H. (1870—1916) [as Saki]						
The Best of Saki	Guild	423	1950	179	1/6	C
	Grey Arrow	G65	1961	192	3/6	C,R
	Humorbooks	H47	1968	179	80¢	C,R
Humor, Horror, and the Supernatural						
	Scholastic	T599	1965	156	35¢	C
Incredible Tales	Dell	4031	1966	191	50¢	C,R
A Saki Sampler	Superior	M656	1945	155	25¢	C
Selected Short Stories of Saki						
	Armed	m-3	nd	160	np	C
	Penguin	184	1940	216	?	C
The She-Wolf	Military	143	1945	155	25¢	C
MURDOCH, TEMPLE See BOY'S FRIEND LIBRARY, page 789.						
MURRAY, MARGARET A. (1863—1963)						
The God of the Witches	Anchor	A212	1963	222	$1.45	N,R
The Witch-Cult in Western Europe						
	Oxford	53	1962	303	$1.50	N
MYERS, JOHN MYERS (1906—)						
Silverlock	Ace	A-8	1966	347	75¢	R

N

Author and Title	Publisher	Serial	Date	Pp.	Price	Type
NARCEJAC, THOMAS See BOILEAU, P. (co-author)						
NATHAN, RICK						
The Love Pill	Softcover Lib.	B953X	1966			
NATHAN, ROBERT (1894—)						
The Bishop's Wife	Armed	800	nd		np	
The Enchanted Voyage	Armed	737	nd	128	np	R
Portrait of Jennie	Armed	655	nd		np	R
	Penguin-US	638	1947	138	np	R
So Love Returns	Pyramid	G438	1959	128	35¢	R
	Pyramid	R772	1962	128	50¢	R
NEAL, JAMES H.						
Jungle Magic	FSB	1959	1967	159	5/-	N
NEILL, ROBERT						
Witch Bane	Avon	S377	1968	174	60¢	
NELSON, RAY See DICK, P. K. (co-author)						
NESBIT, EDITH (1858—1924)						
Five Children and It	Puffin	PS128	1959	215	3/6	J,R
	Puffin	PS128	1961	215	3/6	J,R
	Puffin	PS128	1965	215	3/6	J,R
The Phoenix and the Carpet						
	Puffin	PS129	1967	250	4/6	J
The Story of the Amulet	Puffin	PS130	1965	281	5/-	J
NEVILLE, KRIS (1925—1980)						
The Mutants	Belmont	B50-730	1966	158	50¢	
Peril of the Starmen	Belmont	B50-759*	1967	72	50¢	M
Special Delivery	Belmont	B50-788*	1967	84	50¢	M
The Unearth People	Belmont	92-611	1964	157	50¢	
	Belmont	B50-843	1968	157	50¢	R
NEWMAN, BERNARD (1897—1968)						
Armoured Doves: A Peace Book						
	Jackdaw	10	1937	256	1/-	
The Blue Ants	Digit	R730	1963	159	2/6	R
NEWTON, JULIUS P.						
The Forgotten Race	Digit	R747	1963	158	2/6	
NICHOLS, BEVERLEY						
The Powers That Be	Popular	60-2195	1966	192	60¢	
NICOLSON, J(OHN) U(RBAN) (1885—)						
Fingers of Fear	Paperback	53-976	1966	224	60¢	
NICOLSON, MARJORIE HOPE (1894—1981)						
Science and Imagination	Cornell	Great Seal	1956	238	np	N,R
Voyages to the Moon	Macmillan	MP7	1960	297	$1.75	N,R
NILE, DOROTHEA						
The Vampire Cameo	Lancer	73-706	1968	180	60¢	
NIVEN, LARRY (1938—)						
A Gift From Earth	Ballantine	72113	1968	254	75¢	M
Neutron Star	Ballantine	U6120	1968	285	75¢	C
World of Ptavvs	Ballantine	U2328	1966	188	50¢	M

Author and Title	Publisher	Serial	Date	Pp.	Price	Type
NOEL, STERLING (1903—)						
I Killed Stalin	Eton	E119	1952	190	25¢	R
We Who Survived	Avon	T360	1959	160	35¢	
NOLAN, WILLIAM F. (1928—)						
Impact-20	Paperback	52-250	1963	158	50¢	C
	Paperback	52-971	1966	158	50¢	C,R
	Corgi	GN7357	1965	158	3/6	C,R
Man Against Tomorrow	Avon	G1278	1965	191	50¢	A
The Pseudo-People	Berkley	S1437	1967	256	75¢	A,R
	Mayflower	7172	1967	224	5/-	A,R
Ray Bradbury Review	Nolan		1952	64	50¢	N
[a privately printed comprehensive bibliography]						
3 to the Highest Power	Avon	S336	1968	160	60¢	A
NOONE, EDWINA (pseud) See AVALLONE, M.						
NORMAN, JOHN (pseud) See LANGE, J. F.						
NORTH, ANDREW (pseud) See NORTON, ALICE M.						
NORTH, ERIC (pseud) See CRONIN, B. C.						
NORTON, ALDEN H. (1903—)						
Award Science Fiction Reader						
	Award	A181X	1966	188	60¢	A
Horror Times Ten	Berkley	X1414	1967	175	60¢	A
Masters of Horror	Berkley	X1497	1968	192	60¢	A
NORTON, ALICE M. (1912—) [as Andre Norton]						
The Beast Master	Ace	D-509*	1961	159	35¢	R
	Ace	F-315	1964	159	40¢	R
	Ace	G-690	1967	159	50¢	R
	Peacock	PK61	1968	185	4/-	R
Catseye	Ace	F-167	1962	176	40¢	R
	Ace	G-654	1967	176	50¢	R
	Puffin	PS315	1967	206	4/-	R
The Crossroads of Time	Ace	D-164*	1956	169	35¢	
	Ace	D-546	1962	169	35¢	R
	Ace	F-391	1966	169	40¢	R
Daybreak—2250 A.D. (originally *Star Man's Son*)						
	Ace	D-69*	1954	182	35¢	R
	Ace	D-534	1962	182	35¢	R
	Ace	F-323	1965	182	40¢	R
	Ace	G-717	1968	182	50¢	R
The Defiant Agents	Ace	F-183	1963	192	40¢	R
	Ace	M-150	1966	192	45¢	R
Eye of the Monster	Ace	F-147*	1962	80	40¢	R
Galactic Derelict	Ace	D-498	1961	192	35¢	R
	Ace	F-310	1964	192	40¢	R
Gray Magic (originally *Steel Magic*)						
	Scholastic	TX918	1967	155	50¢	R
Huon of the Horn	Ace	F226	1963	128	40¢	R
Judgment on Janus	Ace	F-308	1964	190	40¢	R
Key out of Time	Ace	F-287	1964	189	40¢	R
	Ace	M-156	1967	189	45¢	R
The Last Planet (originally *The Star Rangers*)						
	Ace	D-96*	1955	192	35¢	R
	Ace	D-542	1962	192	35¢	R
	Ace	F-366	1965	192	40¢	R
	Ace	M-151	1967	192	45¢	R
Lord of Thunder	Ace	F-243	1963	174	40¢	R
	Ace	G-691	1967	174	50¢	R
	Peacock	PK62	1968	188	4/-	R
Moon of Three Rings	Ace	H-33	1967	256	60¢	R
Night of Masks	Ace	F-365	1965	191	40¢	R
Ordeal in Otherwhere	Ace	F-325	1965	191	40¢	R
Plague Ship [as Andrew North]						
	Ace	D-345*	1959	178	35¢	R
	Ace	F-291	1964	178	40¢	R

Author and Title	Publisher	Serial	Date	Pp.	Price	Type
Quest Crosstime	Ace	G-595	1966	220	50¢	R
Sargasso of Space [as Andrew North]						
	Ace	D-249*	1957	192	35¢	R
	Ace	F-279	1964	192	40¢	R
Sea Siege	Ace	F-147*	1962	176	40¢	R
Secret of the Lost Race	Ace	D-381*	1959	132	35¢	
The Sioux Spaceman	Ace	D-437*	1960	133	35¢	
	Ace	F-408	1966	133	40¢	R
Sorceress of the Witch World						
	Ace	H-84	1968	221	60¢	
Star Born	Ace	D-299*	1958	186	35¢	R
	Ace	F-192	1963	186	40¢	R
	Ace	M-148	1966	186	45¢	R
Star Gate	Ace	F-231	1963	190	40¢	R
	Ace	M-157	1966	190	45¢	R
Star Guard	Ace	D-199*	1956	214	35¢	R
	Ace	D-527	1961	214	35¢	R
	Ace	G-599	1966	214	50¢	R
Star Hunter	Ace	D-509*	1961	96	35¢	
Star Hunter & Voodoo Planet						
	Ace	G-723	1968	159	50¢	C,R
The Stars Are Ours	Ace	D-121*	1955	183	35¢	R
	Ace	D-121	1955	183	35¢	R
	Ace	F-207	1963	183	40¢	R
	Ace	M-147	1966	183	45¢	R
Storm Over Warlock	Ace	F-109	1961	192	40¢	R
	Ace	F-329	1965	192	40¢	R
Three Against the Witch World						
	Ace	F-332	1965	189	40¢	
The Time Traders	Ace	D-461	1960	191	35¢	R
	Ace	F-236	1963	191	40¢	R
	Ace	F-386	1966	191	40¢	R
Victory on Janus	Ace	G-703	1968	190	50¢	R
Voodoo Planet [as Andrew North]						
	Ace	D-345*	1959	78	35¢	R
(see also *Star Hunter & Voodoo Planet* [as Andre Norton])						
Warlock of the Witch World						
	Ace	G-630	1967	222	50¢	R
Web of the Witch World	Ace	F-263	1964	192	40¢	
	Ace	G-716	1968	192	50¢	R
Witch World	Ace	F-197	1963	222	40¢	
The X Factor	Ace	G-646	1967	158	50¢	R
Year of the Unicorn	Ace	F-357	1965	224	40¢	
NORTON, ANDRE (pseud) See NORTON, ALICE M.						
NORTON, MARY						
The Borrowers Aloft	Aldine	33	1964	154	5/-	R
NORWAY, NEVIL S. (1899—1960) [as Nevil Shute]						
In the Wet	Permabks	M4095	1957	280	35¢	R
	Ballantine	U5004	1964	255	60¢	R
No Highway	Pan	X224	1963	281	3/6	R
	Pan	X224	1964	281	3/6	R
	Pan	X224	1965	281	3/6	R
	Pan	X224	1966	281	3/6	R
	Pan	02072	1968	288	5/-	R
An Old Captivity	Lancer	72-645	1962	224	50¢	R
	Lancer	73-432	1964	224	60¢	R
On the Beach	Signet	D1562	1958	238	50¢	R
	Morrow	Apollo 97	1964	320	$1.75	R
	Pan	X570	1966	272	3/6	R
	Pan	X570	1967	272	3/6	R
	Perennial	P99B	1966	234	60¢	R
	Bantam	S3875	1968	238	95¢	R
	Scholastic	TK1172	1968	234	60¢	R
What Happened to the Corbetts						
	Pan	X380	1965	224	3/6	R
	Pan	X380	1966	224	3/6	R
	Pan	X380	1967	224	3/6	R

Author and Title	Publisher	Serial	Date	Pp.	Price	Type
NORWOOD, VICTOR (1920—)						
The Caves of Death	Scion		1951	112	1/6	
Cry of the Beast	Scion		1953	128		
Drums Along the Amazon	Scion		1953			
The Island of Creeping Death						
	Scion		1952	112		
Night of the Black Horror	Badger	SF64	1962	158	2/6	
The Skull of Kanaima	Scion		1951	112	1/6	
The Temple of the Dead	Scion		1951	112	1/6	
The Untamed	Scion		1951	112	1/6	
NOURSE, ALAN E. (1928—)						
Beyond Infinity (originally *Tiger by the Tail*)						
	Corgi	GS1526	1964	174	3/6	C,R
The Counterfeit Man	Corgi	GS7143	1965	174	3/6	C,R
	Scholastic	T941	1967	224	45¢	C,R
The Invaders Are Coming [with J. A. Meyer]						
	Ace	D-366	1959	223	35¢	M
A Man Obsessed (later expanded as *The Mercy Men*)						
	Ace	D-96*	1955	127	35¢	
Nine Planets	Pyramid	WS3	1965	288	75¢	N,R
Psi High and Others	Ace	G-730	1968	157	50¢	C,R
Raiders From the Rings	Pyramid	R933	1963	160	40¢	R
Rocket to Limbo	Ace	D-385*	1959	162	35¢	R
Scavengers in Space	Ace	D-541	1962	158	35¢	R
Star Surgeon	Scholastic	T625	1964	180	45¢	R
Tiger by the Tail and Other Science Fiction Stories (also titled *Beyond Infinity*)						
	Macfadden	50-199	1964	144	50¢	C,R
	Macfadden	60-309	1968	144	60¢	C,R
Trouble on Titan	Lancer	72-159	1967	174	50¢	R
The Universe Between	Paperback	52-462	1967	160	50¢	R
NOWLAN, PHILIP F. (1888—1940)						
See also APRILL, EDWARD M., page 789.						
Armageddon 2419 A.D.	Ace	F-188	1963	190	40¢	R
NUETZEL, CHARLES (1934—)						
If This Goes On	Book Amer.	015	1965	256	75¢	A
Lovers: 2075 [as Charles English]						
	Scorpion	104	1964	160	75¢	
Queen of Blood	Greenleaf	GC206	1966	160	75¢	
NUNES, CLAUDE (1924—)						
Inherit the Earth	Ace	G-580*	1966	127	50¢	

NUTT, CHARLES Original name of Charles Beaumont, *q.v.*

NYBORG, BJÖRN See HOWARD, R. E.

O

Author and Title	Publisher	Serial	Date	Pp.	Price	Type
O'BRIEN, BARBARA						
Operators and Things	Ace	K-199	1964	157	50¢	N
O'BRIEN, DAVID						
Black Infinity [as Berl Cameron]						
	Curtis War.		1952	127	1/6	
(identical hardcover edition 5/-)						
Blue Asp [as Rand Le Page]						
	Curtis War.		1952	128	1/6	
(identical hardcover edition 5/-)						

Author and Title	Publisher	Serial	Date	Pp.	Price	Type
Photomesis [as Berl Cameron]						
	Curtis War.		1952	127	1/6	
Ships of Vero [as Brian Shaw]						
	Curtis War.		1952	128	1/6	
(identical hardcover edition 5/-)						
Stellar Radium Discharge [as Kris Luna]						
	Curtis War.		1952	128	1/6	
(identical hardcover edition 6/-)						

O'BRIEN, FITZ-JAMES (1828-1862) See HALDEMAN-JULIUS CO., page 790.

O'BRIEN, FLANN (pseud) See O NOLAN, B.

Author and Title	Publisher	Serial	Date	Pp.	Price	Type
O'DONNELL, ELLIOTT (1872—1965)						
Caravan of Crime	Grafton		nd	64	1/-	C
Dangerous Ghosts	Consul	1174	1962	190	2/6	N,R
The Dead Riders	Arrow	784	1964	192	2/6	R
	Paperback	53-567	1967	224	60¢	R
Dread of Night	Pillar		nd	32	1/-	C
Family Ghosts	Consul	1392	1965	187	3/6	N,R
Ghosts	Consul	GS1043	1961	192	2/6	N,R
Ghosts With a Purpose	Digit	R745	1963	222	3/6	N,R
Haunted and Hunted	Grafton		nd	96	1/-	C
Haunted Britain	Consul	1241	1963	222	3/6	N,R
Haunted People	Digit	R781	1963	160	2/6	N,R
Hell Ships of Many Waters	Grafton		nd	64	1/-	C
The Midnight Hearse	FSB	1954	1967	127	3/6	N,R
Phantoms of the Night	Digit	R750	1963	218	3/6	N,R
The Screaming Skull and Other Ghost Stories						
	FSB	1608	1966	160	3/6	N,R
Shadows of Evil	Digit	R792	1963	160	2/6	N,R
O'FARRELL, WILLIAM (1909—)						
Repeat Performance	Bantam	P55	1954	198	25¢	R
OFFUTT, ANDREW J. (1934—)						
The Sex Pill [as J. X. Williams]						
	Pleasure	PR172	1968			
O'GRADY, ROHAN (pseud) See SKINNER, J.						
OLDFIELD, CLAUDE HOUGHTON See HOUGHTON, C. (pseud)						
OLEMY, P. T. (pseud)						
The Clones	Flagship	00840	1968	160	60¢	
OLIN, ROSS						
Lust Planet	France	F14	1962	160	50¢	
OLIVER, CHAD(WICK) (1928—)						
Another Kind	Ballantine	113	1955	170	35¢	C
(identical hardcover edition $2.00)						
Shadows in the Sun	Ballantine	91	1954	152	35¢	
(identical hardcover edition $2.00)						
	Ballantine	U2857	1968	152	50¢	R
	FSB	1177	1965	190	3/6	R
Unearthly Neighbors	Ballantine	365K	1960	144	35¢	
The Winds of Time	Pocket Bks	1222	1959	153	25¢	R
OLSEN, BOB [ALFRED JOHANNES Jr.] (1884—1956)						
Rhythm Rides the Rocket	Columbia	SFC6	nd	23	10¢	R
OLSON, EUGENE [as Brad Steiger]						
Flying Saucers Are Hostile [with Joan Whritenour]						
	Award	A234K	1967	160	75¢	N
	Tandem	T134	1967	160	5/-	N,R
Monsters, Maidens and Mayhem						
	Merit	GM490	1965	127	60¢	N

Author and Title	Publisher	Serial	Date	Pp.	Price	Type
New UFO Breakthrough [with Joan Whritenour]						
	Award	A339S	1968	155	75¢	N
	Tandem	T230	1968	155	3/6	N,R
Real Ghosts, Restless Spirits and Haunted Minds						
	Tandem	T182	1968	184	3/6	N
Strange Guests	Ace	K-241	1966		50¢	N
Strangers From the Skies	Award	A171X	1966	158	60¢	N
We Have Lived Before	Ace	K-291	1967		50¢	N
O'NEILL, SCOTT						
Martian Sexpot	Jade		211	1963	159	75¢
ONIONS, OLIVER (1873—1961)						
Widdershins	Penguin	222	1939	246	1/-	C,R
O NOLAN, BRIAN (1911—1966) [as Flann O'Brien]						
At Swim-Two-Birds	FSB	759	1962	208	3/6	R
	Penguin	2636	1967		6/-	R
	Compass		1967			R
ORAM, JOHN [pseud of John O. Thomas]						
The Copenhagen Affair	Ace	G-564	1965	144	50¢	
The Stone-Cold Dead in the Market Affair						
	FSB	?	1966	126		
ORKOW, BEN (1896—)						
When Time Stood Still	Signet	D2150	1962	174	50¢	
O'ROURKE, FRANK						
Instant Gold	FSB	1478	1966	125	3/6	R
ORWELL, GEORGE (pseud) See BLAIR, E.						
OWEN, BETTY M.						
Stories of the Supernatural	Scholastic	T896	1967	224	45¢	A
OWEN, DEAN (pseud) See McGAUGHY, D. D.						
OWEN, TOM						
Circus of Horrors	Panther	1041	1960	125	2/6	

P

PADGETT, LEWIS (pseud) See KUTTNER, H.

PAGET, VIOLET (1856—1935) [as Vernon Lee]
Ravenna and Her Ghosts (originally *Pope Jacynth and Other Fantastic Tales*)   Corgi   SN1229 1962 126 2/6 C,R
The Snake Lady and Other Stories (also titled *The Virgin of the Seven Daggers*)   Grove   E13 1954 288 $1.25 C
The Virgin of the Seven Daggers (originally *The Snake Lady*)   Corgi   SN1163 1962 158 2/6 C,R

PAINE, LAUREN (1916—)
This Time Tomorrow   Consul   1214 1963 154 3/6

PALMER, BERNARD (1914—)
Jim Dunlap and the Mysterious Orbiting Rocket
   Moody   34-196 1968 128 60¢ J,R
Jim Dunlap and the Secret Rocket Formula
   Moody   34- ? 1968 128 60¢ J,R

Author and Title	Publisher	Serial	Date	Pp.	Price	Type
Jim Dunlap and the Strange Dr. Brockton						
	Moody	34- ?	1967	127		J,R
Jim Dunlap and the Wingless Plane						
	Moody	34- ?	1968	127	60¢	J,R
PALMER, RAYMOND A. (1910—1977)						
Strange Offspring	Utopian	AF10	nd	36	1/-	A
PANGBORN, EDGAR (1909—1976)						
Davy	Ballantine	U6018	1964	265	75¢	R
The Judgment of Eve	Dell	4292	1967	159	50¢	R
A Mirror for Observers	Dell	D246	1958	223	35¢	R
	Penguin	2454	1966	207	3/6	R
West of the Sun	Dell	9442	1966	219	50¢	R
PANKEY, KAY						
Spooks in Your Cupboard	Seven Seas		1966	260	3/6	A
PANSHIN, ALEXEI (1940—)						
Rite of Passage	Ace	A-16	1968	254	75¢	
Star Well	Ace	G-756	1968	157	50¢	
The Thurb Revolution	Ace	G-762	1968	159	50¢	
PAPE, RICHARD (1916—)						
And So Ends the World	Panther	1493	1963	220	3/6	R
PARKER, BERTHA MORRIS						
Beyond the Solar System	Rowe		nd	36	np	
PARKER, E. FRANK						
Girl in Trouble	Utopian	AF	nd	36	9d	
PARKES, LUCAS (pseud) See HARRIS, J. B.						
PARRISH, ANNE						
Floating Island	Tempo	T-190	1968	177	60¢	J,R
PATRICK, Q. (pseud)						
The Grindle Nightmare	Ballantine	F722	1963	157	50¢	
PATZER, SIDNEY						
The Ship From Nowhere	Stellar	SFS18	1932	24	10¢	
PAUL, AUREN						
The Love Machine	Merit	503	1960	160	50¢	
PAUL, F. W.						
The Orgy at Madame Dracula's						
	Lancer	73-754	1968	157	60¢	
Sock It to Me, Zombie!	Lancer	73-759	1968	189	60¢	
PAUL, HUGO						
Master of the Undead	Lancer	73-746	1968	221	60¢	

PAUWELS, LOUIS (1920—)
The Dawn of Magic [with Jacques Bergier] (also titled *The Morning of the Magicians*)   Panther   1743 1964 304 5/- N,R
   Panther   1743 1967 304 5/- N,R
The Morning of the Magicians [with Jacques Bergier] (originally *The Dawn of Magic*)   Avon   N192 1968 416 95¢ N,R

PAYNE, DONALD GORDON (1924—) [as Donald Gordon]
Star Raker   Hodder   1964 224 3/6

PEAKE, MERVYN (1911—1968)						
Gormenghast	Ballantine	73008	1968	568	95¢	R
Titus Alone	Ballantine	73009	1968	284	95¢	R
Titus Groan	Ballantine	73007	1968	543	95¢	R
	Penguin	2762	1968	506	10/6	R

Author and Title	Publisher	Serial	Date	Pp.	Price	Type
PECK, IRA						
A Treasury of Great Ghost Stories	Popular	SP397	1965	256	50¢	A
PEEBLES, JAMES E. (1928–1968) [as James Kennaway]						
The Mind Benders	Pan	G632	1963	157	2/6	
	Signet	P2515	1964	159	60¢	R
PENDLETON, DON						
Revolt!	Bee-Line	313-N	1968	247		
PERKINS, MICHAEL (1942–)						
Evil Companions	Essex	0109	1968	176	$1.95	
PERRY, DICK See WINFIELD, D. (pseud)						
PERUTZ, LEO (1884–)						
The Master of the Day of Judgment	Collier	AS528V	1963	160	95¢	R
PETAJA, EMIL (1915–)						
Alpha Yes, Terra No!	Ace	M-121*	1965	156	45¢	
The Caves of Mars	Ace	M-133*	1965	125	45¢	
Doom of the Green Planet	Ace	H-70*	1968	127	60¢	
Lord of the Green Planet	Ace	H-22*	1967	118	60¢	
The Prism	Ace	H-51*	1968	126	60¢	
Saga of Lost Earths	Ace	F-392	1966	124	40¢	
The Star Mill	Ace	F-414	1966	128	40¢	
The Stolen Sun	Ace	G-618*	1967	136	50¢	
The Time Twister	Dell	8911	1968	158	50¢	
Tramontane	Ace	H-36*	1967	119	60¢	
PETERKIEWICZ, JERZY (pseud) See PIETRKIEWICZ, J.						
PETERS, LUDOVIC (pseud of Peter Brent)						
Riot '71	Hodder	4362	1968	223	5/-	
PETERSON, JOHN						
The Littles	Scholastic	TW 1158	1967	80	50¢	J
PETTY, JOHN (1919–)						
The Last Refuge	Penguin	2734	1968	192	4/6	R
PHELPS, GILBERT (1915–)						
The Winter People	Penguin	2700	1968	208	5/-	R
PHILLIFENT, JOHN T. (1916–1976) [as John Rackham]						
Alien Sea	Ace	H-40*	1968	154	60¢	
Alien Virus	Pearson	T-B	1955	64	9d	
The Beasts of Kohl	Ace	G-592*	1966	154	50¢	
The Corfu Affair	FSB		1967	125		
Danger From Vega	Ace	G-576*	1966	149	50¢	
The Double Invaders	Ace	G-623*	1967	120	50¢	
Jupiter Equilateral	Pearson	T-B	1954	64	9d	
The Mad Scientist Affair	Ace	G-581	1966	159	50¢	
The Master Weed	Pearson	T-B	1954	64	9d	
The Power Cube Affair	FSB		1967	127		
The Proxima Project	Ace	H-91*	1968	149	60¢	
Space Puppet	Pearson	T-B	1954	64	9d	
Time to Live	Ace	G-606*	1966	141	50¢	
The Touch of Evil	Digit	R658	1963	157	2/6	M
We, the Venusians	Ace	M-127*	1965	138	45¢	
PHILLIPS, MARK (joint pseud) See GARRETT, R., and JANIFER, L. M.						
PHILLIPS, ROG (pseud) See GRAHAM, R. P.						
PICKERSGILL, FREDERICK						
And Graves Give Up Their Dead	Corgi	GS1497	1964	174	3/6	A
	Corgi	GS7271	1965	157	3/6	A
Horror-7						
No Such Thing as a Vampire	Corgi	SN7050	1964	126	2/6	A
PIETRKIEWICZ, JERZY [as Jerzy Peterkiewicz]						
Inner Circle	Panther	025650	1968	202	6/-	R
PINCHER, CHAPMAN (1914–)						
Not With a Bang	Signet	P2888	1965	224	60¢	R
	Signet	P2888	1966	224	60¢	R
	NEL	1734	1967	256	5/-	R
PINCKNEY, JOSEPHINE (1895–1957)						
Great Mischief	Popular	SP329	1964	157	50¢	R
PINNER, DAVID						
Ritual	Arrow	127	1968	222	5/-	
PIPER, H. BEAM (1904–1964)						
The Cosmic Computer (originally *Junkyard Planet*)	Ace	F-274	1964	190	50¢	R
Crisis in 2140 [with J. J. McGuire]	Ace	D-227*	1957	120	35¢	M
Little Fuzzy	Avon	F118	1962	160	40¢	
Lord Kalvan of Otherwhen	Ace	F-342	1965	192	40¢	
The Other Human Race	Avon	G1220	1964	190	50¢	
A Planet for Texans [with J. J. McGuire]	Ace	D-299*	1958	101	35¢	M
Space Viking	Ace	F-225	1963	191	40¢	
PIZER, LAURETTE						
Great Psychological Stories	Panther	2334	1967	155	3/6	A
More Stories Strange and Sinister	Panther	2333	1967	127	3/6	A
Stories Strange and Sinister	Panther	1960	1965	173	3/6	A
PLATO (427?–347 B.C.)						
The Republic	Airmont	CL172	1968		75¢	R
PLATT, CHARLES (1944–)						
Garbage World	Berkley	X1470	1967	144	60¢	M
	Panther	026177	1968	144	3/6	R
PLAYBOY (Magazine) See RUSSELL, R.						
POE, EDGAR ALLAN (1809–1849)						
See also HALDEMAN-JULIUS CO., page 790.						
Bizarre and Arabesque	Panther	2306	1967	202	5/-	C
The Black Cat and Other Stories	Todd	Bantam	1943?		6d	C
Descent Into the Maelstrom	Ivor Nich.?		1948	128	1/-	C
	Digit	R512	1961	160	2/6	C
Eight Tales of Terror	Scholastic	T290	1961	197	35¢	C
18 Best Stories by Edgar Allan Poe [ed. by Vincent Price & Chandler Brossard]	Dell	2227	1967	287	50¢	C
The Fall of the House of Usher	Signet	CD29	1960	383	50¢	C
	Digit	R461	1961	156	2/6	C
The Gold Bug	Digit	D350	1960	160	50¢	C
Great Tales and Poems of Edgar Allan Poe	Pocket Bks	39	1940	356	25¢	C,R
	Cardinal	C45	1952	432	35¢	C,R
	Pocket Bks	PL46	1956	432	35¢	C,R
	Washington	W246	1960	432	45¢	C,R
Great Tales of Horror	Bantam	FP58	1964	151	50¢	C
The Masque of the Red Death [adapted by Elsie Lee]	Lancer	72-725	1964	142	50¢	

Author and Title	Publisher	Serial	Date	Pp.	Price	Type
The Murders in the Rue Morgue and Other Tales						
	Condor	1	*ca.*1965	192	np	C
The Mystery of Arthur Gordon Pym [with J. Verne]						
	Panther	1671	1964	207	3/6	R
The Pit and the Pendulum Ivor Nich.			1948	128	1/-	C
[adapted by Lee Sheridan] Lancer		71-303	1961	144	35¢	
	Digit	R565	1962	159	2/6	C
Poe's Tales of Mystery and Terror						
	Lancer	13-404	1967	319	60¢	C
Poe's Tales of Terror [adapted by Eunice Sudak]						
	Lancer	71-325	1962	126	35¢	C
The Portable Edgar Allan Poe						
	Viking Press	P12	1959	665	$1.45	C
Premature Burial [adapted by Max Hallan Danne]						
	Lancer	71-313	1962	128	35¢	R
The Raven [adapted by Eunice Sudak]						
	Lancer	70-034	1963	127	40¢	
Selected Short Stories of Edgar Allan Poe						
	Armed	j-297	nd	352	np	C
	Armed	767	nd	352	np	C
Selected Tales of Edgar Allan Poe						
	Penguin	1109	1956			C
Selected Writings of Edgar Allan Poe						
	Penguin	EL28	1967	540	np	C
Tales of Mystery and Imagination						
	Pocket Bks	39	1940	358	25¢	C
	Pan	G321	1960	223	2/6	C,R
	Pan	X741	1968	223	3/6	C,R
Tales of the Grotesque and Arabesque						
	Dolphin	C50	1950	317	95¢	C,R
Ten Great Mysteries of Edgar Allan Poe [edited by G. Conklin]						
	TAB	T210	1960	210	35¢	C
	TAB	T210	1962	210	50¢	C,R
POHL, FREDERIK (1919–)						
The Abominable Earthman Ballantine		F685	1963	159	50¢	C
Alternating Currents	Ballantine	130	1956	154	35¢	C
(identical hardcover edition $2.00)						
	Penguin	2452	1966	190	3/6	C,R
Beyond the End of Time Permabks		P145	1952	407	35¢	A
The Case Against Tomorrow						
	Ballantine	206	1957	150	35¢	C
	Ballantine	U2175	1965	150	50¢	C,R
Digits and Dastards	Ballantine	U2178	1966	192	50¢	C
Drunkard's Walk	Ballantine	439K	1960	142	35¢	M
	Penguin	2521	1966	166	3/6	R
The Eighth Galaxy Reader Pan		02109	1968	237	5/-	A,R
The Expert Dreamers	Pan	X463	1966	219	3/6	A,R
	Avon	S355	1968	207	60¢	A,R
Gladiator-at-Law [with Cyril Kornbluth]						
	Ballantine	107	1955	171	35¢	M
(identical hardcover edition $2.00)						
	Ballantine	F570	1962	171	50¢	R
	Ballantine	U2343	1967	171	50¢	R
	Digit	D157	1958	160	2/-	R
	Pan	X571	1966	187	3/6	R
The If Reader of Science Fiction						
	Ace	H-19	1967	220	60¢	A,R
The Man Who Ate the World						
	Ballantine	397K	1960	144	35¢	C
	Ballantine	597	1962	144	35¢	C,R
The Ninth Galaxy Reader Pocket Bks		50532	1967	227	50¢	A,R
A Plague of Pythons Ballantine		U2174	1965	158	50¢	M
Preferred Risk [as Edson McCann (pseud. with L. del Rey)]						
	Dell	R114	1962	190	40¢	R
The Reefs of Space [with Jack Williamson]						
	Ballantine	U2172	1964	188	50¢	M
Search the Sky [with Cyril Kornbluth]						
	Ballantine	61	1954	165	35¢	
(identical hardcover edition $2.00)						

Author and Title	Publisher	Serial	Date	Pp.	Price	Type
	Ballantine	F738	1963	165	50¢	R
	Digit	D352	1960	159	2/-	R
	Digit	R662	1963	158	2/6	R
The Seventh Galaxy Reader						
	Pan	M192	1967	237	5/-	A,R
Shadow of Tomorrow	Permabks	P236	1953	379	35¢	A
Slave Ship	Ballantine	192	1957	147	35¢	M
(identical hardcover edition $2.75)						
	Ballantine	U2177	1966	148	50¢	R
	FSB	857	1963	127	2/6	R
	FSB	1986	1967	127	3/6	R
The Space Merchants [with Cyril Kornbluth]						
	Ballantine	21	1953	179	35¢	M
(identical hardcover edition $2.00)						
	Ballantine	381K	1960	158	35¢	R
	Ballantine	U2173	1964	158	50¢	R
	Digit	D327	1960	158	2/-	R
	Digit	R499	1961	156	2/6	R
	Penguin	2224	1965	170	3/6	R
Star Fourteen (originally *Star of Stars*)						
	Pan	02043	1968	236	5/-	A,R
Star of Stars (also titled *Star Fourteen*)						
	Ballantine	U2171	1964	224	50¢	A
Star Science Fiction Stories						
	Ballantine	16	1953	202	35¢	A
(identical hardcover edition $1.50)						
[as *No. 1*]	Ballantine	521K	1961	202	35¢	A,R
Star Science Fiction Stories No. 2						
	Ballantine	55	1953	195	35¢	A
(identical hardcover edition $2.00)						
	Ballantine	612	1962	195	35¢	A,R
Star Science Fiction Stories No. 3						
	Ballantine	96	1954	186	35¢	A
(identical hardcover edition $2.00)						
	Ballantine	F675	1962	186	35¢	A,R
Star Science Fiction Stories No. 4						
	Ballantine	272K	1958	157	35¢	A
Star Science Fiction Stories No. 5						
	Ballantine	308K	1959	159	35¢	A
Star Science Fiction No. 6 Ballantine		353K	1959	156	35¢	A
Star Short Novels	Ballantine	89	1954	165	35¢	A
(identical hardcover edition $2.00)						
	Ballantine	F730	1963	168	50¢	A,R
Starchild [with Jack Williamson]						
	Ballantine	U2176	1965	191	50¢	M
Tomorrow Times Seven	Ballantine	325K	1959	160	35¢	C
Turn Left at Thursday	Ballantine	476K	1961	159	35¢	C
Wolfbane [with Cyril Kornbluth]						
	Ballantine	335K	1959	140	35¢	M
	Penguin	2561	1967	160	3/6	R
The Wonder Effect [with Cyril Kornbluth]						
	Ballantine	F638	1962	159	50¢	C
POTOCKI, JAN (1761–1815)						
The Saragossa Manuscript Avon		G1090	1961	224	50¢	C,R
POWERS, J. L. (pseud) See GLASBY, J. S.						
POWYS, T(HEODORE) F(RANCIS) (1875-1953)						
Mr. Weston's Good Wine Penguin		73	1937	288	2/6	R
PRAGNELL, FESTUS (1905–)						
The Terror of Timorkal	Bear		1946			
Thieves of the Air [with Benson Herbert]						
	Cole		nd	27	9d	
PRATT, FLETCHER (1897–1956)						
Alien Planet	Ace	F-257	1963	188	40¢	R
The Carnelian Cube [with L. Sprague de Camp]						
	Lancer	73-662	1967	222	60¢	R

Author and Title	Publisher	Serial	Date	Pp.	Price	Type
The Castle of Iron [with L. Sprague de Camp]						
	Pyramid	F722	1962	159	40¢	R
Double Jeopardy	Galaxy Nov	30	1957	128	35¢	R
The Incomplete Enchanter [with L. Sprague de Camp]						
	Pyramid	G530	1960	192	35¢	R
	Pyramid	F723	1962	192	40¢	R
	Pyramid	X1928	1968	192	60¢	R
Invaders From Rigel	Airmont	SF4	1964	127	40¢	R
The Undying Fire	Ballantine	25	1953	148	35¢	M
(identical hardcover edition $2.00)						
The Well of the Unicorn	Lancer	74-911	1967	384	75¢	R
[hardcover edition, 1948, under pseud. George U. Fletcher]						

PRATT, THEODORE (1901-1969)

The White God	Pyramid	R856	1963	190	50¢	

PRATT, WILLIAM H. (1887—1969) [as Boris Karloff]

The Boris Karloff Horror Anthology (also titled *Boris Karloff's Favourite Horror Stories*)						
	Corgi	GN7621	1967	158	3/6	A,R
Boris Karloff's Favourite Horror Stories (originally *The Boris Karloff Horror Anthology*)						
	Avon	G1254	1965	176	50¢	A,R

PRESTON, EDNA MITCHELL

Arrow Book of Spooky Stories						
	Scholastic	TX331	1964	90	35¢	J,A

PRIESTLEY, J(OHN) B(OYNTON) (1894—)

The Doomsday Men	Pan	109	1949	256	2/-	R
	Popular	SP195	1962	224	50¢	R
	Corgi	GN1392	1963	222	3/6	R
The Magicians	FSB	1	1957	192	2/-	R
	Corgi	SN1431	1963	156	2/6	R
The Other Place	Corgi	SN1390	1963	142	2/6	C,R
Saturn Over the Water	Pocket Bks	GC165	1963	279	50¢	R
The Shapes of Sleep	Popular	SP232	1963	159	50¢	R
	Corgi	GN1519	1964	188	4/6	R
The 31st of June	Corgi	SN1388	1963	126	2/6	R
Three Time Plays	Pan	7	1947	270	1/6	C
	Pan	7	1949	270	2/-	C,R
	Pan	GP13	1952	270	2/6	C,R

PRINCE, DON

Tom's Temptations	Diversey	4	1949	123	25¢	

PRITCHARD, JOHN WALLACE (1912—) [as Ian Wallace]

Croyd	Berkley	X1616	1968	184	60¢	R

PRITCHARD, WILLIAM T. (1909—) [as William Dexter]

Children of the Void	Consul	1220	1963	188	3/6	R
	Paperback	52-357	1966	159	50¢	R
World in Eclipse	Consul	1192	1962	160	2/6	R
	Paperback	52-338	1966	158	50¢	R

PROTHEROE, CYRIL

Beyond These Suns [as Rand Le Page]						
	Curtis War.		1952	128	1/6	
(identical hardcover edition 6/-)						

PRUYN, LEONARD

World Without Women [with D. Keene]						
	Gold Medal	s975	1960	176	35¢	
	Gold Medal	L1504	1965	176	45¢	R
	Muller	GM531	1961	158	2/6	R
	Muller	GM nn	nd	158	3/-	R

PURDOM, TOM (1936—)

Five Against Arlane	Ace	H-22*	1967	136	60¢	
I Want the Stars	Ace	F-289*	1964	115	40¢	
The Tree Lord of Imeten	Ace	M-139*	1966	152	45¢	

Author and Title	Publisher	Serial	Date	Pp.	Price	Type
PYLE, HOWARD (1853—1911)						
Twilight Land	Dover	T1879	1968	438	$2.00	C,R
PYNCHON, THOMAS (1937—)						
The Crying of Lot 49	Bantam	N5764	1967	138		

Q,R

QUAYNE, J.						
The Jasper Gate	Lancer	75-020	1967	248	95¢	
QUERRY, SIMON						
Adventures on the Planets	Baker	FST1	1953	64	9d	
QUINN, JAMES L.						
The First World of If [with Eve Wulff]						
	Quinn		1957	160	50¢	A
The Second World of If [with Eve Wulff]						
	Quinn		1958	159	50¢	A

RACKHAM, JOHN (pseud) See PHILLIFENT, J. T.

RADCLIFFE, A(NN) (1764—1823)						
The Mysteries of Udolpho	Juniper	7	1963	383	$1.65	R
RAFCAM, NAL (pseud)						
The Troglodytes	Digit	R587	1962	160	2/6	

RAME, DAVID (pseud) See DIVINE, A. D.

RAMPTON, ANTHONY						
The First Panther Book of Horror (also titled *The Panther Book of Horror*)						
	Panther	1956	1965	268	5/-	A
The Panther Book of Horror (originally *The First Panther Book of Horror*)						
	Panther	025855	1968	267	5/-	A,R
RAND, AYN (1905—1982)						
Anthem	Signet	D1985	1961	123	50¢	R
	Signet	D1985	1963	123	50¢	R
	Signet	P2809	1966	123	60¢	R
Atlas Shrugged	Signet	Q1702	1959	1084	95¢	R

RANDALL, ROBERT (joint pseud) See GARRETT, R., and SILVERBERG, R.

RANKINE, JOHN (pseud) See MASON, D. R.

RANZETTA, LUAN						
The Maru Invasion	Digit	R606	1962	159	2/6	
The Night of the Death Rain						
	Digit	R717	1963	157	2/6	
The Uncharted Planet	Digit	R557	1961	156	2/6	
The World in Reverse	Digit	R618	1962	154	2/6	
Yellow Inferno	Digit	R836	1964	158	2/6	
RAPHAEL, RICK (1919—)						
Code Three	Berkley	X1394	1967	176	60¢	R
	Panther	025707	1968	191	5/-	R
The Thirst Quenchers	Panther	024026	1968	142	3/6	C,R
RASCOVICH, MARK (1918—)						
The Bedford Incident	Pocket Bks	GC789	1964	291	75¢	R

Author and Title	Publisher	Serial	Date	Pp.	Price	Type
RATHBONE, BASIL (1892—1967)						
Basil Rathbone Selects Strange Tales						
	Belmont	B50633	1965	157	50¢	A
	Belmont	B50839	1968	157	50¢	A,R
RAVEN, SIMON (1927—)						
Doctors Wear Scarlet	Avon	G1170	1962	222	50¢	
	FSB	758	1962	222	3/6	R
	Panther	1991	1966	191	3/6	R
	Panther	1991	1967	191	3/6	R
	Berkley	S1435	1967	222	75¢	R
RAY, D.						
End of the Fourth Reich	Panther	2142	1966	143	3/6	
RAY, JEAN (pseud) See KREMER, R. DE						
RAY, RENÉ						
The Strange World of Planet X						
	Digit	R735	1963	160	2/6	R
RAY, ROBERT						
No Stars for Us	Digit	R876	1964	158	2/6	
RAYER, FRANCIS G. (1921—)						
Cardinal of the Stars	Digit	R851	1964	158	2/6	
Coming of the Darakua	Authentic	17	1952	109	1/6	
Earth Our New Eden	Authentic	20	1952	109	1/6	
The Iron and the Anger	Digit	R860	1964	158	2/6	
The Star Seekers	Pearson	T-B	1954	64	9d	M
Tomorrow Sometimes Comes						
	Icon	SF1	1962	192	3/6	R
We Cast No Shadow	Authentic	28	1952	108	1/6	
Worlds at War [as anonymous]						
	Tempest		1950	128	1/6	A
RAYMOND, BEN						
The Miracle of the Foomtra						
	E.L. Pub. Co.	L-21	1968	149		
RAYMOND, RENÉ [as James H. Chase]						
Miss Shumway Waves a Wand						
	Panther	1116	1960	224	2/6	
READ, HERBERT (1893—1968)						
The Green Child	New Direc.	NDP208	1966	194	$1.50	R
REED, CLIFFORD C. (1911—)						
Martian Enterprise	Digit	R638	1962	160	2/6	M
REED, DAVID V. (pseud) See VERN, D.						
REED, VAN (house pseud)						
Dwellers in Space	Curtis War.		1953	159	1/6	
(identical hardcover edition 6/-)						
House of Many Changes See HUGHES, DEN						
REEVE, BRYANT and HELEN						
Flying Saucer Pilgrimage	Inspired Nov	D4	1965	304	$2.50	N
REID, DESMOND						
Let My People Be	Mayflower	7764	1965	96	2/6	
The Slave Brain	Mayflower	8022	1967	128	3/6	
The World Shakers	Sexton Blake Lib	457	1960	64	1/-	
REIN, HAROLD						
Few Were Left	WDL	S248	1957	191	2/-	R
REISEN, MARX						
Before the Beginning	Pearson	T-B	1954	64	9d	
RENARD, MAURICE (18751940)						
The Flight of the Aerofix	Stellar	SFS14	1932	23	10¢	
RESNICK, MICHAEL D. (1942—)						
The Goddess of Ganymede	Paperback	52-687	1968	160	50¢	R
Pursuit on Ganymede	Paperback	52-760	1968	144	50¢	
REY, RUSSELL (house pseud)						
The Queen People See HUGHES, DEN						
Valley of Terror	Curtis War.		1953	159	1/6	
(identical hardcover edition 6/-)						
REYNOLDS, JAMES (1891—)						
Ghosts in American Houses						
	Paperback	53-487	1967	223	60¢	N,R
Ghosts in Irish Houses	Paperback	54-691	1968	287	75¢	N,R
More Ghosts in Irish Houses						
	Paperback	64-006	1968	288	75¢	N,R
REYNOLDS, MACK (1917—)						
After Some Tomorrow	Belmont	B50-795	1967	158	50¢	
Code Duello	Ace	H-103*	1968	141	60¢	
Computer War	Ace	H-34*	1967	111	60¢	M
Dawnman Planet	Ace	G-580*	1966	123	50¢	M
Earth Unaware (originally *Of Godlike Power*)						
	Belmont	B50-826	1968	174	50¢	R
The Earth War	Pyramid	F886	1963	141	40¢	M
	FSB	1195	1965	141	3/6	R
Mercenary From Tomorrow	Ace	H-65*	1968	137	60¢	
Of Godlike Power (also titled *Earth Unaware*)						
	Belmont	B50680	1966	174	50¢	
Planetary Agent X	Ace	M-131*	1965	133	45¢	M
The Rival Rigellians	Ace	G-632*	1967	132	50¢	M
Science Fiction Carnival [with F. Brown]						
	Bantam	A1615	1957	167	35¢	A,R
Space Pioneer	FSB	1671	1966	160	3/6	M
Time Gladiator	FSB	1459	1966	157	3/6	M
REYNOLDS, STANLEY						
Better Dead Than Red	Panther	2112	1966	191	3/6	
RHODES, HENRY (1898—)						
The Satanic Mass	Pedigree		1960	224	3/6	N,R
	Arrow	789	1965	256	5/-	N,R
RICE, ELMER (1892—1967)						
A Voyage to Purilia	Penguin	901	1954	185	2/-	R
RICHARDS, FRANK						
Bunter and the Phantom of the Towers						
	Armada	C107	1965	160	2/6	J
RICHMOND, CHARLES						
A Step Into Infinity, or, At the Margin of Destiny [play]						
	Caxton		1946	41	np	
RICHMOND, LEIGH See RICHMOND, WALTER						
RICHMOND, WALTER (1922—1977) [with Leigh Richmond]						
The Lost Millennium	Ace	H-29*	1967	137	60¢	
Shock Wave	Ace	G-614*	1967	127	50¢	
RICHTER, CONRAD (1890—1968)						
The Waters of Kronos	Bantam	F2329	1961	119	50¢	R
RIDLER, ANNE (1912—)						
Best Ghost Stories	Faber		1960	360	6/6	A
RIEFE, ALAN (1925—)						
Tales of Horror	Pocket Bks	10063	1965	64	$1.00	C

Author and Title	Publisher	Serial	Date	Pp.	Price	Type
RIMMER, ROBERT H.						
The Zolotov Affair	Bantam	N3687	1968	250	95¢	R
RINKOFF, BARBARA						
The Dragon's Handbook	Scholastic	TW1145	1967	112	60¢	J,R
Elbert the Mind Reader	Scholastic	TX1276	1968	112	60¢	J
RÍOS, TERE (1917—)						
The Fifteenth Pelican	Avon	G1299	1966	125	50¢	R
RIVA, VALERIA See VOLTA, O. (co-author)						
RIVERE, ALEC						
Lost City of the Damned	Pike	101	1961	160	50¢	
ROBB, JOHN						
Space Beam	Hamilton		nd	111	1/6	
ROBERTS, ARTHUR See GLASBY, J. (co-author)						
ROBERTS, COLIN						
Nuclear Subtraction	Digit	R683	1963	159	2/6	
ROBERTS, JANE (1929—)						
The Rebellers	Ace	F-215*	1963	155	40¢	
ROBERTS, KEITH (1935—)						
The Furies	Berkley	F1177	1966	192	50¢	M
ROBERTS, LIONEL (pseud) See FANTHORPE, R. L.						
ROBERTS, MURRAY See BOY'S FRIEND LIBRARY, page 789.						
ROBESON, KENNETH (pseud) See DENT, L.						
ROBINSON, FRANK M. (1926—)						
The Power	Bantam	A1593	1957	181	35¢	R
	Corgi	S658	1959	223	2/6	R
	Sphere	74160	1968	159	5/-	R
	Popular	60-8059	1968	175	60¢	R
ROCHESTER, GEORGE E. See BOY'S FRIEND LIBRARY, page 789.						
RODDENBERRY, GENE						
The Making of Star Trek [with S. E. Whitfield]						
	Ballantine	73004	1968	414	95¢	N
ROE, IVAN See SAVAGE, R. (pseud)						
ROGERS, ALVA (1923—1982)						
A Requiem for Astounding	Advent		1967	224	$2.45	N,R
ROGERSOHN, WILLIAM						
Amiro	Brown-Wat.	107	1954	107	1/6	
North Dimension	Brown-Wat.		1954	107	1/6	
ROHMER, SAX (1883—1959)						
The Bride of Fu Manchu (also titled *Fu Manchu's Bride*)						
	Consul	1094	1961	252	2/6	R
	Pyramid	F761	1962	190	40¢	R
	Corgi	GC7698	1967	190	3/6	R
Brood of the Witch Queen	Pyramid	R1314	1966	190	50¢	R
Daughter of Fu Manchu	Avon	189	1949	190	25¢	R
	WDL	M913	1960	224	2/6	R
	Pyramid	R-1032	1964	190	50¢	R
	Corgi	GC7624	1967	190	3/6	R
The Day the World Ended	Ace	F-283	1964	223	40¢	R
The Devil Doctor (originally *The Return of Dr. Fu-Manchu*)						
	Consul	M1023	1961	222	2/6	R
	Corgi	GC7588	1967	190	3/6	R
The Dream Detective	Pyramid	R1316	1966	191	50¢	R
The Drums of Fu Manchu	Pyramid	F804	1962	192	40¢	R
	Pyramid	R1307	1966	192	50¢	R
	Consul	1246	1963	240	3/6	R
	Corgi	07945	1968	192	3/6	R
Emperor Fu Manchu	Gold Medal	s929	1959	190	35¢	R
	Panther	1123	1960	189	2/6	R
	Pyramid	R1310	1966	190	50¢	R
The Fire Goddess	Gold Medal	283	1952	192	25¢	
The Golden Scorpion	Hillman	TNC9	nd	128	25¢	R
	Pyramid	R1315	1966	188	50¢	R
The Hand of Fu-Manchu (also titled *The Si-Fan Mysteries*)						
	Pyramid	F688	1962	192	40¢	R
	Pyramid	R1306	1966	192	50¢	R
Hangover House	Graphic	504	1956			R
The Insidious Doctor Fu-Manchu (also titled *The Mystery of Dr. Fu Manchu*)						
	Hillman	TNC4	nd	128	25¢	R
	Pyramid	G579	1961	191	35¢	R
	Pyramid	F908	1963	191	40¢	R
	Pyramid	R1301	1966	191	50¢	R
The Island of Fu Manchu	Consul	1234	1963	296	3/6	R
	Pyramid	F858	1963	208	40¢	R
	Pyramid	R1305	1966	208	50¢	R
	Corgi	07874	1968	223	3/6	R
The Mask of Fu Manchu	WDL	M924	1960	222	2/6	R
	Pyramid	F740	1962	191	40¢	R
	Pyramid	R1303	1966	191	50¢	R
	Corgi	GC7664	1967	221	3/6	R
The Moon Is Red	Digit	R824	1963	160	2/6	R
The Mystery of Dr. Fu Manchu (originally *The Insidious Doctor Fu-Manchu*)						
	Penguin	157	1938	278	np	R
	Guild	?	1953			R
	WDL	M905	1960	222	2/6	R
	Corgi	GC7587	1967	190	3/6	R
Nude in Mink (also titled *Sins of Sumuru*)						
	Gold Medal	105	1950	174	25¢	
President Fu Manchu	Consul	1093	1961	255	2/6	R
	Pyramid	F946	1963	223	40¢	R
	Corgi	GC7738	1967	223	3/6	R
The Quest of the Sacred Slipper						
	Pyramid	R1313	1966	189	50¢	R
Re-Enter Fu Manchu	Gold Medal	s684	1957	144	35¢	
	Gold Medal	K1458	1964	144	40¢	R
	Panther	1084	1960	158	2/6	R
	Pyramid	X1774	1968	159	60¢	R
	Corgi	GC7784	1967	157	3/6	R
The Return of Dr. Fu-Manchu (also titled *The Devil Doctor*)						
	Pyramid	G641	1961	192	35¢	R
	Pyramid	R1302	1965	192	50¢	R
Return of Sumuru (also titled *Sand and Satin*)						
	Gold Medal	408	1954	172	25¢	
	Gold Medal	868	1959	160	25¢	R
Sand and Satin (originally *Return of Sumuru*)						
	Digit	R843	1964	158	2/6	R
Shadow of Fu Manchu	Panther	1060	1960	191	2/6	R
	Pyramid	F837	1963	159	40¢	R
	Pyramid	R1304	1966	159	50¢	R
The Si-Fan Mysteries (originally *The Hand of Fu-Manchu*)						
	Consul	M1024	1961	253	2/6	R
	Corgi	GC7589	1967	190	3/6	R
Sinister Madonna	Gold Medal	555	1956	128	25¢	
	FSB	886	1964	153	2/6	R
Sins of Sumuru (originally *Nude in Mink*)						
	Digit	R835	1964	158	2/6	R
Slaves of Sumuru (originally *Sumuru*)						
	Panther	1074	1960	156	2/6	R
Sumuru (also titled *Slaves of Sumuru*)						
	Gold Medal	199	1951	179	25¢	
	Gold Medal	s757	1958	159	35¢	R
Tales of Chinatown	Popular	217	1950	224	25¢	C,R

Author and Title	Publisher	Serial	Date	Pp.	Price	Type
The Trail of Fu Manchu	Consul	1227	1963	253	3/6	R
	Pyramid	R1003	1964	220	50¢	R
	Pyramid	R1308	1966	220	50¢	R
	Corgi	GC7814	1968	180	3/6	R
The Yellow Claw	Pyramid	R1317	1966	254	50¢	R

ROMILUS, ARN
Beyond Geo	Curtis War.		1953	159	1/6	
(identical hardcover edition 6/-)						
Brain Palaeo	Curtis War.		1953	159	1/6	
(identical hardcover edition 6/-)						
Organic Destiny	Curtis War.		1954	159	1/6	
(identical hardcover edition 6/-)						

RONALD, BRUCE W. (1931—)
Our Man in Space	Ace	M-117*	1965	131	45¢	

ROSCOE, THEODORE
A Grave Must Be Deep	Popular Pub.		1947	95	np	

ROSE, LAWRENCE F. (pseud) See FEARN, J. R.

ROSHWALD, MORDECAI (1921—)
Level 7	Signet	D1956	1961	143	50¢	R
	Signet	D2659	1965	143	50¢	R
	Ace (Brit.)	H497	1961	143	2/6	R
A Small Armageddon	FSB	1418	1966	159	3/6	R

ROSMANITH, OLGA
Unholy Flame	Gold Medal	273	1952	184	25¢	

ROSNY, J. H. AÏNÉ (1856—1940)
Quest of the Dawn Man (originally *The Giant Cat*)
	Ace	F-269	1964	156	40¢	R

ROSS, MARILYN (pseud) See ROSS, W.

ROSS, WILLIAM (1912—) [as Marilyn Ross]
Barnabas Collins	Paperback	62-001	1968	157	60¢	
The Curse of Collinwood	Paperback	63-368	1968	158	60¢	
Dark Shadows	Paperback	52-386	1966	159	50¢	
The Mystery of Collinwood	Paperback	52-610	1968	159	50¢	
The Mystery of Fury Castle	Paperback	52-452	1967	157	50¢	
Strangers at Collins House	Paperback	52-543	1967	159	50¢	
Victoria Winters	Paperback	52421	1967	160	50¢	

ROTH, HOLLY (1916—1964)
The Mask of Glass	Penguin	1237	1957	154	2/6	R
	FSB	1606	1966	128	3/6	R

ROWE, J. G. See NUGGET LIBRARY, page 790.

ROYCE, E. R.
Experiment in Telepathy	Curtis War.		1954	159	1/6	

RUD, ANTHONY (1893—1942)
The Stuffed Men	Duchess		1944	128	25¢	R

RUNYAN, POKE
Commando X	Pyramid	X1693	1967		60¢	

RUPPELT, EDWARD J.
The Report on Unidentified Flying Objects
	Ace	D-200	1956	318	35¢	N,R
	Ace	G-537	1964	318	50¢	N,R

RUSS, JOANNA (1937—)
Picnic on Paradise	Ace	H-72	1968	157	60¢	

RUSSELL, ARTHUR
Crocodile City	Transport	RR	nd	66	6d	

RUSSELL, BERTRAND (1872—1970)
Nightmares of Eminent Persons
	Penguin	1858	1962	174	4/6	C,R
Satan in the Suburbs and Other Stories						
	Penguin	1645	1961	157	2/6	C,R

RUSSELL, ERIC FRANK (1905—1978)
Dark Tides	Panther	1599	1963	128	2/6	C,R
Deep Space	Bantam	1362	1955	165	25¢	C,R
Dreadful Sanctuary	Lancer	74-819	1963	174	75¢	R
	Lancer	72-149	1967	174	50¢	R
	FSB	1719	1967	255	5/-	R
Far Stars	Panther	1691	1964	130	2/6	C,R
The Great Explosion	Pyramid	F862	1963	160	40¢	R
	Panther	1625	1964	144	2/6	R
Great World Mysteries	Mayflower	B32	1962	160	3/6	N,R
	Mayflower	3230	1967	160	3/6	N,R
Men, Martians and Machines						
	Corgi	S424	1957	190	2/6	C,R
	Berkley	G148	1958	174	35¢	C,R
	Berkley	F1088	1965	175	50¢	C,R
	Panther	1890	1965	191	3/6	C,R
	Panther	018905	1968	191	5/-	C,R
The Mindwarpers (originally *With a Strange Device*)						
	Lancer	72-942	1965	158	50¢	R
Next of Kin (also titled *The Space Willies*)						
	Mayflower	A14	1962	160	2/6	R
Sentinels From Space	Ace	D-44*	1954	179	35¢	R
	Ace	D-468	1960	179	35¢	R
Sinister Barrier	Galaxy Nov	1	1950	158	25¢	R
	Kemsley	CT407	1952	190	1/6	R
	Paperback	52-287	1964	176	50¢	R
	Paperback	52-384	1966	176	50¢	R
Six Worlds Yonder	Ace	D-315*	1958	125	35¢	C
Somewhere a Voice	Ace	F-398	1966	174	40¢	C,R
	Penguin	2722	1968	188	4/-	C,R
The Space Willies (also titled *Next of Kin*)						
	Ace	D-315*	1958	131	35¢	M
Three to Conquer	Ace	D-215*	1957	181	35¢	R
	Corgi	S596	1958	224	2/6	R
	Penguin	2005	1963	202	3/6	R
Wasp	Permabks	M4120	1959	170	35¢	R
	Panther	1487	1963	143	2/6	R
	Panther	01487X	1968	143	3/6	R
With a Strange Device (also titled *The Mind Warpers*)						
	Penguin	2358	1965	155	3/6	R

RUSSELL, JOHN (1885—1956)
The Lost God and Other Adventure Stories
	Pocket Bks	408	1946	309	25¢	C
Selected Short Stories of John Russell						
	Armed	0-20	nd		np	C
	Armed	1042	nd		np	C,R
Where the Pavement Ends	Pan	60	1948	250	np	C,R

RUSSELL, RAY (1924—)
The Case Against Satan	Paperback	52-210	1963	160	50¢	R
	Pan	X405	1965	173	3/6	R
The Playboy Book of Horror and the Supernatural [anonymously]						
	Playboy	BA0119	1968	390	95¢	A,R
The Playboy Book of Science Fiction and Fantasy [anonymously]						
	Playboy	BA0115	1968	402	95¢	A,R
Sardonicus and Other Stories						
	Ballantine	540	1961	143	35¢	C
Unholy Trinity	Bantam	H3428	1967	114	60¢	C

Author and Title	Publisher	Serial	Date	Pp.	Price	Type

S

SABERHAGEN, FRED (1930–)

Author and Title	Publisher	Serial	Date	Pp.	Price	Type
Berserker	Ballantine	U5063	1967	190	60¢	C
The Broken Lands	Ace	G-740	1968	191	50¢	
The Golden People	Ace	M-103*	1964	118	45¢	
The Water of Thought	Ace	M-127*	1965	117	45¢	

SAFRONI-MIDDLETON, A(RNOLD)

The Dreaming Skull	World Wide		1948	244	np	

ST. CLAIR, MARGARET (1911–)

Agent of the Unknown	Ace	D-150*	1956	128	35¢	M
The Dolphins of Altair	Dell	2079	1967	188	50¢	
The Games of Neith	Ace	D-453*	1960	149	35¢	
The Green Queen	Ace	D-176*	1956	128	35¢	M
Message From the Eocene	Ace	M-105*	1964	114	45¢	
Sign of the Labrys	Bantam	J2617	1963	139	40¢	
	Corgi	YS1423	1963	139	3/-	R
Three Worlds of Futurity	Ace	M-105*	1964	142	45¢	C

SAINT-EXUPÉRY, ANTOINE DE (1900–1944)

The Little Prince	Puffin	PS160	1963	255	4/-	J

SAKI (pseud) See MUNRO, H. H.

SALE, RICHARD (1911–)

Lazarus Number Seven	Quinn	H13	1943		25¢?	
	Harlequin	79	1950		35¢	R
Not Too Narrow, Not Too Deep						
	Guild	104	1941	190	3/6	R
	Armed	s-7	nd		np	R
	Corgi	GN7103	1965	158	3/6	R

SAMBROT, WILLIAM (1930–)

Island of Fear and Other Science Fiction Stories

	Permabks	M4278	1963	166	35¢	C
	Mayflower	4120	1964	166	2/6	C,R

SANDERS, JOHN See COMER, R. (pseud)

SANDERS, LEONARD M. (1929–) [as Dan Thomas]

The Seed	Ballantine	U6115	1968	252	75¢	

SANDERSON, IVAN T. (1911–1973)

Things	Pyramid	T1692	1967	188	75¢	N

SANGSTER, JIMMY (1927–)

The Man Who Could Cheat Death [with B. Lyndon; see also SAN-
SOM, J.]

	Avon	T362	1959	160	35¢	
The Revenge of Frankenstein						
	Panther	839	1958	158	2/6	
The Terror of the Tongs	Digit	R560	1962	156	2/6	

SANSOM, JOHN (pseud of J. Sangster [*q.v.*] and B. Lyndon)

The Man Who Could Cheat Death

	Ace (Brit.)	H280	1959	188	2/6	R

SANTESSON, HANS STEFAN (1914–1975)

The Fantastic Universe Omnibus

	Panther	1414	1962	223	3/6	A,R
	Paperback	54-633	1968	254	75¢	A,R

Flying Saucers in Fact and Fiction

	Lancer	74-953	1968	224	75¢	A
Gods for Tomorrow	Award	A240X	1967	208	60¢	A
	Tandem	T130	1967	208	3/6	A,R
Rulers of Men	Pyramid	R1227	1965	173	50¢	A

SARAC, ROGER (pseud) See CARAS, R. A.

SARBAN (pseud) See WALL, J. W.

THE SATURDAY EVENING POST, Editors of [see also FLES, B.]

The Post Reader of Fantasy and Science Fiction (also titled *The Saturday Evening Post Reader of Fantasy and Science Fiction*)

	Corgi	GS7450	1966	220	3/6	A,R

The Saturday Evening Post Reader of Fantasy and Science Fiction
(originally *The Post Reader of Fantasy and Science Fiction*)

	Popular	SP331	1964	240	50¢	A,R

SAUL, GEORGE B. (1901–)

Owls' Watch	Crest	R836	1965	238	60¢	A

SAUNDERS, PHILIP I.

Scorched Earth	Currawong		1943	154	2/9	

SAVA, GEORGE (1903–) [as George Borodin]

Threatened People	Regular Pubs.		nd	160	2/-	R

SAVAGE, HARDLEY (pseud)

Jetman Meets the Mad Madam

	Bee-Line	118	1966			

SAVAGE, MARY

The Coach Draws Near	Dell	1307	1967	208	50¢	R
A Likeness to Voices	Dell	4794	1965	159	45¢	

SAVAGE, RICHARD (pseud of I. Roe)

When the Moon Died	Ward Lock	54	1957	191	2/-	R
	Digit	R674	1963	192	2/6	R

SAVILLE, MALCOLM

Saucers Over the Moor	Merlin	M8	1967	188	2/6	J

SAXON, PETER (apparently a house pseud.; see also MARTIN, T.)

Black Honey	Mayflower	112145	1968	157	3/6	
Corruption	Sphere	24562	1968	144	5/-	
The Darkest Night	Mayflower	1659	1966	157	3/6	
	Paperback	52-562	1967	159	50¢	R
The Disorientated Man (also titled *Scream and Scream Again*)						
	Mayflower	1947	1966	126	3/6	
Satan's Child	Lancer	73-784	1968	189	60¢	
Scream and Scream Again (originally *The Disorientated Man*)						
	Paperback	52-598	1967	158	50¢	R
Through the Dark Curtain	Lancer	73-714	1968	190	60¢	
The Torturer	Mayflower	8967	1966	159	3/6	
	Paperback	52-469	1967	158	50¢	R

SAXON, RICHARD (pseud of J. L. Morrissey [1905–])

Cosmic Crusade	Consul	1335	1964	160	2/6	
Future for Sale	Consul	1344	1964	151	3/6	
The Hour of the Phoenix	Consul	1308	1964	140	2/6	
The Stars Came Down	Consul	1292	1964	167	2/6	

SAYERS, DOROTHY L. (1898–1957)

Human and Inhuman Stories†

	Macfadden	50-156	1963	176	50¢	A
	Macfadden	60-298	1967	176	60¢	A,R

Stories of the Supernatural†

	Macfadden	50-170	1963	144	50¢	A
	Macfadden	50-300	1967	144	50¢	A,R

† Both derived from *Great Short Stories of Detection, Mystery and Horror* series.

Author and Title	Publisher	Serial	Date	Pp.	Price	Type
SCAEVOLA, PETER						
'68—A Novel of Presidential Politics						
	Signet	T2503	1964	302	75¢	R
SCHAFER, ROBERT (1915—)						
The Naked and the Damned (originally *The Conquered Place*)						
	Popular	686	1955	207	25¢	R
SCHMITZ, JAMES H. (1911—1981)						
Agent of Vega	Permabks	M-4242	1962	185	35¢	C,R
	Mayflower	0045	1964	192	3/6	C,R
The Demon Breed	Ace	H-105	1968	157	60¢	M
A Tale of Two Clocks	Belmont	B50-643	1965	172	50¢	R
The Universe Against Her	Ace	F-314	1964	160	40¢	M
The Witches of Karres	Ace	A-13	1968	286	75¢	R
SCHNEIDER, JOHN						
The Golden Kazoo	Dell	D178	1956	192	35¢	R
SCHOEPFLIN, HAROLD VINCENT (1893—1968) [as Harl Vincent]						
The Doomsday Planet	Tower	42-621	1966	141	50¢	
	Tower	42-947	1968	141	50¢	R
Master of Dreams	Utopian	AF12	nd	36	1/-	M
SCHOONOVER, LAWRENCE (1906—)						
Central Passage	Dell	1155	1964	192	50¢	R
SCHWARTZ, ALAN						
The Wandering Tellurian	Ace	H-20*	1967	116	60¢	
SCHWARTZ, B.						
Crimson Clay	Panther	nn	1955	144	1/6	
(identical hardcover edition 6/-)						
SCOTT, J.						
The Death Dealer	Horwitz	246	1965	130	48¢	
SCOTT, PETER [as Barton Werper] [All titles below were withdrawn						
from circulation after protest by Burroughs Inc.]						
Tarzan and the Abominable Snowman						
	Gold Star	IL7-60	1965	126	40¢	
Tarzan and the Cave City	Gold Star	IL7-49	1964	126	40¢	
Tarzan and the Silver Globe						
	Gold Star	IL7-42	1964	126	40¢	
Tarzan and the Snake People						
	Gold Star	IL7-54	1964	126	40¢	
Tarzan and the Winged Invaders						
	Gold Star	IL7-65	1965	125	40¢	
SCOTT, WARWICK (pseud) See TREVOR, E.						
SCOTT-MONCRIEFF, D.						
Not for the Squeamish	Background		1948	108	1/6	C
The Vaivaisukko's Bride	Horror Club		195?	63	1/-	C
SCULLY, FRANK (1892—1964)						
Behind the Flying Saucers	Popular	326	1951	192	25¢	N,R
SEABROOK, WILLIAM B. (1886—1945)						
The Magic Island	Lancer	75-038	1968	350	95¢	N,R
Witchcraft	Lancer	74-924	1968	351	75¢	N,R
SEAMARK (pseud) See SMALL, A. J.						
SEARLS, HANK [HENRY] (1922—)						
The Astronaut	Pocket Bks	6093	1962	149	35¢	
The Big X	Dell	F124	1960	288	50¢	R
	FSB	274	1961	224	2/6	R
	Horwitz	FH22	1962	226	5/-	R
The Pilgrim Project	Crest	R798	1965	224	60¢	R
	Mayflower	6917	1966	221	5/-	R

Author and Title	Publisher	Serial	Date	Pp.	Price	Type
SELLERS, CON(NIE)						
F.S.C.	Novel Books	6081	1963	128	60¢	
Red Rape	Headline	105	1960	188	50¢	
SELLINGS, ARTHUR (pseud) See LEY, R. A.						
SELLWOOD, A. V.						
Children of the Damned	FSB	990	1964	128	2/6	
Devil Worship in Britain [with P. Haining]						
	Corgi	GS7084	1964	124	3/6	N
SERLING, ROBERT J.						
The President's Plane Is Missing						
	Dell	7102	1968	287	95¢	
SERLING, ROD(MAN) (1924—1975)						
Chilling Stories From Rod Serling's The Twilight Zone [adapted,						
Walter B. Gibson]	Tempo	T89	1965	190	50¢	C
More Stories From The Twilight Zone						
	Bantam	A2227	1961	149	35¢	C
	Bantam	J2880	1964	149	40¢	C,R
	Bantam	EP169	1966	149	45¢	C,R
	Bantam	E3150	1967	149	45¢	C,R
New Stories From The Twilight Zone						
	Bantam	A2412	1962	122	35¢	C
	Bantam	J2872	1964	122	40¢	C,R
	Bantam	EP121	1965	121	45¢	C,R
Rod Serling's Devils and Demons						
	Bantam	H3324	1967	212	60¢	A
Rod Serling's Triple W: Witches, Warlocks and Werewolves						
	Bantam	J2623	1963	181	40¢	A
	Bantam	F2980	1965	181	50¢	A,R
	Bantam	H3493	1967	181	60¢	A,R
Rod Serling's Twilight Zone Revisited [adapted, Walter B. Gibson]						
	Tempo	T171	1967	189	50¢	C
The Season To Be Wary	Bantam	S3851	1968	182	75¢	C
Stories From The Twilight Zone						
	Bantam	A2046	1960	151	35¢	C
	Bantam	J2693	1963	151	40¢	C,R
	Bantam	EP89	1964	151	45¢	C,R
	Bantam	FP4094	1968	151	50¢	C,R
SETTEL, I. See KARP, N. A. (co-anthologist)						
SEVERANCE, FELIX See OPIUM BOOKS, page 790.						
SEVERN, DAVID (pseud) See UNWIN, D. S.						
SHAPLEY, HARLOW (1885—1972)						
Of Stars and Men	Washington	W601	1959	145	50¢	N,R
The View From a Distant Star						
	Dell	9312	1967	190	75¢	N,R
SHARKEY, JACK (1931—)						
The Addams Family	Pyramid	R1229	1965	175	50¢	
The Secret Martians	Ace	D-471*	1960	132	35¢	
Ultimatum in 2050 A.D.	Ace	M-117*	1965	120	45¢	M
SHARP, D(RURY) D.						
Thirty Miles Down	Stellar	SFS12*	1930	12	10¢	
(part of booklet also containing *The Life Vapor*, C. Farrar)						
SHARP, MARGERY (1905—)						
Miss Bianca	Berkley	F1014	1964	152	50¢	
The Stone of Chastity	Armed	t12	nd		np	R
	Collins	215	1945	192	25¢	R
	Avon	165	1948	186	25¢	R
	Avon	624	1955	173	25¢	R
	Pan	246	1953	191	2/-	R
	Fontana		1956	192	2/6	R
	Fontana	532	1961	192	2/6	R
	Berkley	X1144	1965	160	60¢	R

Author and Title	Publisher	Serial	Date	Pp.	Price	Type
SHARP, ROBERT (GEORGE) [all as Jon J. Deegan, but appearances noted in *Authentic* are not verified]						
Amateurs in Alchemy	Panther	32	1953	128	1/6	
Antro the Life-Giver	Panther	39	1953	144	1/6	
(identical hardcover edition 6/-)						
Beyond the Fourth Door	Panther	96	1954	159	1/6	
(identical hardcover edition 6/-)						
Corridors of Time	Panther	85	1953	159	1/6	
(identical hardcover edition 6/-)						
Exiles in Time	Panther	117	1954	159	1/6	
(identical hardcover edition 6/-)						
The Great Ones	Panther	58	1953	158	1/6	
(identical hardcover edition 6/-)						
Old Growler	Authentic	4	1951	124	1/6	
Old Growler and Orbis	Authentic	9	1951	194	1/6	
Planet of Power	Authentic	14	1952	110	1/6	
Reconnoitre Krellig II	Authentic	2	1951	126	1/6	
The Singing Spheres	Authentic	23	1952	109	1/6	
Underworld of Zello	Panther	17	1952	127	1/6	
SHAW, BOB (1931—)						
Night Walk	Banner	B60110	1967	160	60¢	
The Two-Timers	Ace	H-79	1968	191	60¢	
SHAW, BRIAN (house pseudonym)						
Argentis See TUBB, E. C.						
Lost World	Curtis War.		1953	159	1/6	
(identical hardcover edition 6/-)						
Ships of Vero See O'BRIEN, D.						
Z Formations [as Bryan Shaw] See FEARN, J. R.						
SHAW, DAVID (pseud) See GRIFFITHS, D. A.						
SHAW, FREDERICK L. Jr. (1928—)						
Envoy to the Dog Star	Ace	G-614*	1967	127	50¢	
SHAW, LARRY [LAWRENCE] T. (1924—)						
Great Science Fiction Adventures						
	Lancer	72-697	1963	174	50¢	A
	Lancer	73-740	1968	285	60¢	A,R
	Lancer	74-944	1968	285	75¢	A,R
Terror!	Lancer	72-139	1966	192	50¢	A
SHEARING, DAVID						
The Spectral Bride	Mercury	99	nd	128	25¢	
SHECKLEY, ROBERT (1928—)						
Citizen in Space	Ballantine	126	1955	200	35¢	C
(identical hardcover edition $2.00)						
	Ballantine	F648	1962	200	50¢	C,R
	Ballantine	U2862	1968	200	50¢	C,R
Dimension of Miracles	Dell	1940	1968	190	50¢	C
Immortality, Inc. (originally *Immortality Delivered*)						
	Bantam	A1991	1959	152	35¢	R
Journey Beyond Tomorrow	Signet	D2223	1962	144	50¢	M
	Corgi	GS7365	1966	158	3/6	R
Mindswap	Dell	5643	1967	157	60¢	R
	Mayflower	5644	1968	157	3/6	R
Notions: Unlimited	Bantam	A2003	1960	170	35¢	C
	Bantam	F3850	1968	170	50¢	C,R
The People Trap	Dell	6881	1968	204	60¢	C
Pilgrimage to Earth	Bantam	A1672	1957	167	35¢	C
	Bantam	F2812	1964	167	50¢	C,R
	Corgi	SS746	1959	190	2/6	C,R
Shards of Space	Bantam	J2443	1962	152	40¢	C
	Corgi	YS1252	1962	152	3/-	C,R
	Corgi	GS7503	1966	152	3/6	C,R
The Status Civilization	Signet	S1840	1960	127	35¢	M
	FSB	1873	1967	127	3/6	R
	Dell	8249	1968	156	60¢	R

Author and Title	Publisher	Serial	Date	Pp.	Price	Type
Store of Infinity	Bantam	A2170	1960	151	35¢	C
The 10th Victim	Ballantine	U5050	1965	158	60¢	
	Mayflower	8604	1966	109	3/6	R
Time Limit	Bantam	F3381	1967	137	50¢	
Untouched by Human Hands						
	Ballantine	73	1954	169	35¢	C
(identical hardcover edition $2.00)						
	Ballantine	437K	1960	169	35¢	C,R
	Ballantine	U2855	1967	169	50¢	C,R
	FSB	1804	1967	125	3/6	C,R
SHELDON, ROY (house pseudonym)						
Atoms in Action See CAMPBELL, H. J.						
Beam of Terror	Authentic	13	1951	110	1/6	
Energy Alive	Authentic	7	1951	101	1/6	
Gold Men of Aureus	Authentic	3	1951	126	1/6	
House of Entropy See CAMPBELL, H. J.						
Mammoth Man See CAMPBELL, H. J.						
The Menacing Sleep See CAMPBELL, H. J.						
The Metal Eater See TUBB, E. C.						
Moment out of Time See HAY, G.						
Phantom Moon	Authentic	6	1951	117	1/6	
The Plastic Peril	Authentic	25	1952	109	1/6	
Space Warp	Authentic	19	1952	109	1/6	
Star of Death	Authentic	27	1952	108	1/6	
Two Days of Terror See CAMPBELL, H. J.						
SHELLEY, MARY WOLLSTONECRAFT (1797—1851)						
Frankenstein	Armed	909	nd		np	R
	Lion	146	1953	222	25¢	R
	Pyramid	R290	1957	192	35¢	R
	Pyramid	F1212	1965	192	40¢	R
	WDL	GC294	1958	252	2/6	R
	Everyman	P616	1961	256	3/6	R
	Collier	HS3V	1961	190	65¢	R
	Collier	HS3V	1963	190	65¢	R
	Collier	02527	1966	190	65¢	R
	Airmont	CL19	1963	223	50¢	R
	Corgi	GN7048	1964	158	2/6	R
	Dell	2717	1965	221	45¢	R
	Bantam	FP165	1967	206	50¢	R
The Last Man	Bison	BB323	1965	342	$1.95	R
SHERMAN, HAROLD M(ORROW) (1898—)						
The Green Man	Century	104	1946	128	25¢	M
You Live After Death	Crest	s145	1956	174	35¢	N
SHERRIFF, ROBERT C. (1896—)						
See also SUNDAY TELEGRAPH, page 791.						
The Cataclysm (originally *The Hopkins Manuscript*)						
	Pan	G186	1958	253	2/6	R
SHIEL, M(ATTHEW) P(HIPPS) (1865—1947)						
How the Old Woman Got Home						
	Collier	AS109X	1962	318	95¢	R
Lord of the Sea	Xanadu		1962	299	$1.45	R
The Purple Cloud	Paperback	52-232	1963	191	50¢	R
	Paperback	52-944	1966	191	50¢	R
SHIPLEY, M(AYNARD) See HALDEMAN-JULIUS CO., page 790.						
SHIRAS, WILMAR H. (1908—)						
Children of the Atom	Avon	T221	1958	192	35¢	R
SHIRLEY, R. See NEWSPAPERS PUBLICITY CO., page 790.						
SHULMAN, SANDRA						
The Daughters of Astaroth	Paperback	53-689	1968	159	60¢	
SHUTE, NEVIL (pseud) See NORWAY, N. S.						

Author and Title	Publisher	Serial	Date	Pp.	Price	Type
SIEVEKING, LANCE (1896–)						
A Private Volcano	Ward Lock	59	1957	256	2/6	R
SILLITOE, ALAN (1928–)						
The General	Signet	D2077	1962	142	50¢	R
SILVERBERG, ROBERT (1935–)						
Collision Course	Ace	F-123*	1961	135	40¢	R
Conquerors From the Darkness						
	Dell	1456	1968	156	50¢	J,R
The Dawning Light [as Robert Randall (joint pseud. with R. Garrett)]						
	Mayflower	1678	1964	189	3/6	R
	Mayflower	1678	1966	189	3/6	R
Earthmen and Strangers	Dell	2206	1968	191	50¢	A,R
Godling, Go Home!	Belmont	L92-591	1964	157	50¢	C
Invaders From Earth	Ace	D-286*	1958	169	35¢	M
	Avon	S365	1968	142	60¢	R
[also contained in *A Pair From Space* (Anonymous)]						
Lest We Forget Thee, Earth [as Calvin M. Knox]						
	Ace	D-291*	1958	126	35¢	M
Lost Race of Mars	Scholastic	TX535	1964	123	35¢	J,R
The Masks of Time	Ballantine	U6121	1968	252	75¢	
Master of Life and Death	Ace	D-237*	1957	163	35¢	
	Avon	S329	1968	144	60¢	R
Needle in a Timestack	Ballantine	U2330	1966	190	50¢	C
	Sphere	78417	1967	190	5/-	C,R
Next Stop the Stars	Ace	F-145*	1962	114	40¢	C
One of Our Asteroids Is Missing [as Calvin M. Knox]						
	Ace	F-253*	1964	124	40¢	
The Planet Killers	Ace	D-407*	1959	131	35¢	M
The Plot Against Earth [as Calvin M. Knox]						
	Ace	D-358*	1959	138	35¢	
Recalled to Life	Lancer	74-810	1962	144	75¢	M
	Lancer	72-156	1967	144	50¢	R
Regan's Planet	Pyramid	F986	1964	141	40¢	
Revolt on Alpha C	TAB	TX137	1959	118	25¢	J,R
	TAB	TX137	1963	118	25¢	J,R
The Seed of Earth	Ace	F-145*	1962	139	40¢	M
The Shrouded Planet [as Robert Randall (joint pseud. with R. Garrett)]						
	Mayflower	7881	1963	192	3/6	R
The Silent Invaders	Ace	F-195*	1963	117	40¢	M
Starhaven [as Ivar Jorgenson (house pseud.)]						
	Ace	D-351*	1959	146	35¢	R
Stepsons of Terra	Ace	D-311*	1958	128	35¢	M
The 13th Immortal	Ace	D-223*	1957	129	35¢	
Thorns	Ballantine	U6097	1967	222	75¢	
Those Who Watch	Signet	P3160	1967	143	60¢	
The Time Hoppers	Avon	S372	1968	158	60¢	R
Time of the Great Freeze	Dell	8922	1966	192	50¢	J,R
To Open the Sky	Ballantine	U6093	1967	222	75¢	M
SIMAK, CLIFFORD D. (1904–)						
Aliens for Neighbours (selections from hardcover *The Worlds of Clifford Simak*)	FSB	929	1963	159	2/6	C,R
All Flesh Is Grass	Berkley	X1312	1966	224	60¢	R
	Pan	02042	1968	255	5/-	R
All the Traps of Earth and Other Stories						
	Macfadden	50-165	1963	158	50¢	C,R
	Macfadden	50-388	1967	158	50¢	C,R
	FSB	993	1964	143	2/6	C,R
City	Permabks	264	1954	192	25¢	R
	Ace	D-283	1958	255	35¢	R
	Ace	H-30	1967	255	60¢	R
	FSB	1250	1965	189	3/6	R
Cosmic Engineers	Gnome		1950	224	35¢	M
(identical hardcover edition $2.50)						
	Paperback	52-506	1964	159	50¢	R
	Paperback	52-498	1967	159	50¢	R
The Creator	Crawford		1946	48	np	M
Empire	Galaxy Nov	7	1951	160	35¢	
First He Died (originally *Time and Again*)						
	Dell	680	1953	222	25¢	R
The Night of the Puudly (selections from hardcover *All the Traps of Earth*)	FSB	1040	1964	143	3/6	C,R
	FSB	1040	1965	143	2/6	C,R
	FSB	1040	1968	143	3/6	C,R
Other Worlds of Clifford Simak (selections from hardcover *The Worlds of Clifford Simak*)	Avon	G1124	1962	143	50¢	C,R
Ring Around the Sun	Ace	D-61*	1954	190	35¢	R
	Ace	D-339	1959	190	35¢	R
	WDL	SF881	1960	190	2/6	R
	Avon	S270	1967	200	60¢	R
	FSB	1971	1967	192	4/-	R
So Bright the Vision	Ace	H-95*	1968	141	60¢	C
Strangers in the Universe	Berkley	G71	1957	190	35¢	C,R
	Berkley	G835	1963	191	50¢	C,R
	Berkley	X1589	1968	191	60¢	C,R
	Panther	1332	1962	191	2/6	C,R
They Walked Like Men	Macfadden	50-184	1963	176	50¢	R
	Macfadden	50-381	1967	176	50¢	R
	Pan	X425	1965	220	3/6	R
Time and Again (earlier paperback as *First He Died*)						
	Ace	F-239	1963	256	40¢	R
	Penguin	2596	1967	235	5/-	R
Time Is the Simplest Thing						
	Crest	d547	1962	192	50¢	R
	Crest	d752	1964	192	50¢	R
	Pan	X340	1964	206	3/6	R
The Trouble With Tycho	Ace	D-517*	1961	82	35¢	M
Way Station	Macfadden	60-198	1964	190	60¢	R
	Pan	X572	1966	208	3/6	R
The Werewolf Principle	Berkley	S1463	1968	216	75¢	R
Why Call Them Back From Heaven?						
	Ace	H-42	1968	191	60¢	R
The Worlds of Clifford Simak (selections from hardcover; see also *Other Worlds of Clifford Simak*)	Avon	G1096	1961	191	50¢	C,R
Worlds Without End	Belmont	L92-584	1964	140	50¢	C
	Belmont	B50-791	1967	140	50¢	C,R
SINCLAIR, DAVID						
The Gilead Bomb	Dell	2876	1963	120	35¢	J
The Project	Tower	43-571	1960	188	60¢	R
SINCLAIR, UPTON (1878–1968)						
A Giant's Strength	Laurie		1948	87	2/6	R
The Gnomobile	Tempo	T112	1966	157	50¢	J,R
	FSB	2085	1967	128	3/6	J,R
SINCLAIR-STEVENSON, C.						
A Book of Princes	Puffin	PS378	1968	224	5/-	A,J
SINGER, KURT (1911–)						
The Gothic Reader	Ace	K-244	1966	253	50¢	A
Horror Omnibus	Panther	2158	1966	283	5/-	A,R
I Can't Sleep at Night	Corgi	GN7676	1967	174	3/6	A,R
Kurt Singer's Ghost Omnibus (selections from hardcover ed.)	FSB	1961	1967	126	3/6	A,R
Kurt Singer's Second Ghost Omnibus (more selections from hardcover *Kurt Singer's Ghost Omnibus*)	FSB	1982	1967	125	3/6	A,R
The Unearthly	Belmont	92-622	1965	156	50¢	C
The World's Greatest Stories of the Occult	Panther	1861	1965	192	3/6	C
SINSTADT, GERALD						
Ship of Spies	Lancer	73-566	1967	192	60¢	

Author and Title	Publisher	Serial	Date	Pp.	Price	Type
SIODMAK, CURT (1902—)						
Donovan's Brain	Armed	0-9	nd	256	np	R
	Bantam	819	1950	181	25¢	R
	Corgi	819	1952	181	2/-	R
	Corgi	S853	1960	189	2/6	R
	Popular	G560	1961	160	35¢	R
Riders to the Stars [novelisation by Robert Smith of screenplay by Siodmak]						
	Ballantine	58	1954	166	35¢	
Skyport	Signet	S1939	1961	159	35¢	R
SISSONS, MICHAEL						
Asleep in Armageddon	Panther	1379	1962	189	2/6	A
In the Dead of Night	Panther	1349	1962	155	2/6	A,R
	Panther	025847	1968	155	3/6	A,R
The Masque of the Red Death and Other Tales of Horror						
	Panther	1755	1964	192	3/6	A,R
SKELTON, RED [RICHARD]						
Red Skelton's Favorite Ghost Stories (originally *A Red Skelton in Your Closet*)						
	Tempo	T-182	1968	187	75¢	A,R
SKINNER, B(URRHUS) F(REDERIC) (1904—)						
Walden Two	Macmillan	115	1964	320	$1.75	R
SKINNER, JUNE (1922—) [as Rohan O'Grady]						
Pippin's Journal	Panther	1768	1964	190	3/6	R
SLAUGHTER, FRANK G. (1908—)						
Epidemic!	Arrow	685	1962	255	2/6	R
	Permabks	M5044	1962	277	50¢	R
SLEIGH, BARBARA (1906—)						
Carbonel	Puffin	PS155	1967	188	3/6	J
SLOANE, WILLIAM (1906—1974)						
The Edge of Running Water (also titled *The Unquiet Corpse*)						
	Armed	t-23	nd	352	np	R
	Armed	1169	nd	352	np	R
	Panther	1957	1965	203	3/6	R
	Bantam	H3427	1967	204	60¢	R
To Walk the Night	Armed	b-40	nd	315	np	R
	Penguin-US	550	1944	218	25¢	R
	Dell	856	1955	223	25¢	R
	Panther	1958	1965	189	3/6	R
	Bantam	H3426	1967	181	60¢	R
The Unquiet Corpse (originally *The Edge of Running Water*)						
	Dell	928	1956	223	25¢	R
	Dell	928	1964	254	3/6	R
SMALL, AUSTIN J. (?—1929) [as Seamark]						
The Avenging Ray	Hodder	C10	1952	191	2/-	R
SMITH, CLARK ASHTON (1893—1961)						
The Immortals of Mercury	Stellar	SFS16	1932	24	10¢	
SMITH, CORDELIA TITCOMB (1902—)						
The Best of Sci-Fi 3 (originally *Great Science Fiction Stories*)						
	Mayflower	3160	1964	288	5/-	A,R
Great Science Fiction Stories (also titled *The Best of Sci-Fi 3*)						
	Dell	3160	1963	288	50¢	A
SMITH, CORDWAINER (pseud) See LINEBARGER, P. M. A.						
SMITH, EDWARD E(LMER) (1890—1965)						
Children of the Lens	Pyramid	X1294	1966	254	60¢	R
	Pyramid	X1294	1967	255	60¢	R
First Lensman	Pyramid	R1114	1964	252	50¢	R
	Pyramid	X1456	1966	252	60¢	R
	Pyramid	X1456	1967	252	60¢	R

Author and Title	Publisher	Serial	Date	Pp.	Price	Type
Galactic Patrol	Fantasy	1	1956	273	$1.00	R
	Pyramid	R1103	1964	237	50¢	R
	Pyramid	X1457	1966	237	60¢	R
	Pyramid	X1457	1967	237	60¢	R
The Galaxy Primes	Ace	F-328	1965	192	40¢	M
Gray Lensman	Pyramid	R1245	1965	253	50¢	R
	Pyramid	X1245	1965	253	60¢	R
	Pyramid	X1245	1967	253	60¢	R
Masters of the Vortex (originally *The Vortex Blaster*)						
	Pyramid	X1851	1968	191	60¢	R
Second Stage Lensmen	Pyramid	R1262	1965	271	50¢	R
	Pyramid	X1262	1967	271	60¢	R
	Pyramid	X1262	1968	271	60¢	R
Skylark DuQuesne	Pyramid	X1539	1966	238	60¢	M
The Skylark of Space	Pyramid	G332	1958	159	35¢	R
	Pyramid	F764	1962	159	35¢	R
	Pyramid	X1350	1966	159	60¢	R
	Pyramid	X1350	1968	159	60¢	R
	Digit	D266	1959	159	2/-	R
Skylark of Valeron	Pyramid	F-948	1963	206	40¢	R
	Pyramid	X1458	1966	207	60¢	R
Skylark Three	Pyramid	F924	1963	207	40¢	R
	Pyramid	X1459	1966	207	60¢	R
Spacehounds of IPC	Ace	F-372	1966	252	40¢	R
Subspace Explorers	Ace	H-102	1968	255	60¢	R
Triplanetary	Pyramid	R1222	1965	240	50¢	R
	Pyramid	X1455	1966	240	60¢	R
SMITH, ERNEST BRAMAH (1869?—1942) [as Ernest Bramah]						
Kai Lung Unrolls His Mat	Penguin	108	1937	249	6d	R
	Penguin	108	1939			R
	Penguin	108	1941	222		R
Kai Lung's Golden Hours	Penguin	174	1938	280	6d	R
	Penguin	174	1949	254	1/6	R
	Xanadu	3	1962	312	$1.45	R
The Wallet of Kai Lung	Penguin	39	1936	256	1/-	C,R
SMITH, EVELYN E. (1927—)						
The Perfect Planet	Lancer	72-679	1963	144	50¢	R
SMITH, GARRET						
Between Worlds	Stellar	SFC1	ca.1929	93	np	
SMITH, GEORGE H. (1922—1981)						
The Coming of the Rats	Pike	203	1961	158	50¢	
	Digit	R862	1964	158	2/6	R
Doomsday Wing	Monarch	388	1963	124	35¢	
Flames of Desire [as M. J. Deer]						
	France		1963	160		
The Four Day Weekend	Belmont	B5-0699	1966	157	50¢	
Love Cult [as Jan Hudson]	Pike	205	1961			
1976—The Year of Terror	Epic	103	1961	154	50¢	
A Place Named Hell [as M. J. Deer]						
	France		1963	160		
Scourge of the Blood Cult	Epic	110	1961			
Those Sexy Saucer People [as Jan Hudson]						
	Greenleaf	GC220	1967	176	95¢	
The Unending Night	Monarch	464	1964	128	40¢	
The Year of Love [Anonymous]						
	Moonlight Reader	103	nd			
SMITH, GEORGE O. (1911—1981)						
The Brain Machine (originally *The Fourth "R"*)						
	Lancer	74-936	1968	221	75¢	R
Fire in the Heavens	Ace	D-375*	1959	159	35¢	R
The Fourth "R" (also titled *The Brain Machine*)						
	Ballantine	316K	1959	160	35¢	
Hellflower	Pyramid	G298	1957	160	35¢	R
	Mayflower	3569	1964	192	3/6	R

Author and Title	Publisher	Serial	Date	Pp.	Price	Type
Highways in Hiding (earlier paperback titled *Space Plague*)						
	Lancer	73-636	1967	256	60¢	R
Lost in Space	Ace	D-431*	1960	142	35¢	R
Operation Interstellar	Century	B10	1950	127	25¢	
Pattern for Conquest	Gnome		1949	252	35¢	M
(identical hardcover edition $2.50)						
Space Plague (originally *Highways in Hiding*)						
	Avon	T180	1957	191	35¢	R
	Avon	G1154	1963	191	50¢	R
Troubled Star	Beac (Gal)	256	1959	159	35¢	R
Venus Equilateral	Pyramid	T1724	1967	367	75¢	C,R
SMITH, H. ALLEN (1907–1976)						
The Age of the Tail	Bantam	1541	1956	117	25¢	R
Rhubarb	Pocket Bks	695	1950	270	25¢	R
	Pocket Bks	75287	1968	270	75¢	R
SMITH, KEITH						
Ogf	Humorbooks	H29	1966	259	95¢	R
SMITH, L. E. See HALDEMAN-JULIUS CO., page 790.						
SMITH, ROBERT						
Riders to the Stars [novelisation of screenplay by C. Siodmak]						
	Ballantine	58	1953	166	35¢	
SMITH, THORNE (1892–1934)						
The Bishop's Jaegers	Armed	h-230	nd		np	
The Glorious Pool	Armed	g-181	1944		np	R
	Armed	671	1945		np	R
	Pocket Bks	409	1946	240	25¢	R
[numerous other Pocket Books printings]						
	Pocket Bks	6189	1963	240	35¢	R
	May Fair	43	1962	192	2/6	R
The Jovial Ghosts (originally *Topper*)						
	May Fair	22	1961	192	2/6	R
	Tandem	T47	1965	192	3/6	R
The Night Life of the Gods						
	Armed	s-28	nd	320	np	R
	Pocket Bks	428	1947	310	25¢	R
[2 eds. in 1947 with different covers; numerous printings follow.]						
	Pocket Bks	2428	1955	248	25¢	R
	Penguin	1218	1957	272	2/6	R
	Pyramid	R630	1961	256	50¢	R
The Passionate Witch	Armed	q-13	nd		np	R
	Armed	953	nd		np	R
	Pocket Bks	401	1946	243	25¢	R
[numerous printings follow]						
	Pocket Bks	6207	1963	243	35¢	R
	May Fair	31	1961	192	2/6	R
	Tandem	T93	1966	165	3/6	R
Rain in the Doorway	Armed	922	nd		np	R
	Pocket Bks	546	1949	294	25¢	R
	May Fair	57	1962	254	25¢	R
Skin and Bones	Armed	j-284	nd		np	R
	Pocket Bks	490	1948	274	25¢	R
	May Fair	50	1962	288	3/6	R
The Stray Lamb	Armed	k-15	nd		np	R
	Avon	69	1945	262	25¢	R
	Pocket Bks	518	1948	262	25¢	R
	May Fair	9	1961	192	2/6	R
	Tandem	T97	1966	191	3/6	R
Topper (also titled *The Jovial Ghosts*)						
	Pocket Bks	4	1943	241	25¢	R
Topper Takes a Trip	Pocket Bks	209	1945	312	25¢	R
	Pocket Bks	2209	1955	248	25¢	R
	Penguin	1219	1957	255	2/6	R
	Penguin	1219	1958	255	2/6	R
	Pyramid	F728	1962	248	40¢	R

Author and Title	Publisher	Serial	Date	Pp.	Price	Type
Turnabout	Armed	117	nd		np	R
	Pocket Bks	447	1947	277	25¢	R
	May Fair	66	1962	192	2/6	R
	Paperback	52-201	1963	192	50¢	R
	Paperback	53-603	1965	192	60¢	R
	Tandem	T54	1966	192	3/6	R
SNYDER, ZILPHA KEATLEY						
Black and Blue Magic	Scholastic	T1112	1967	256	50¢	R
SOHL, JERRY (1913–)						
The Altered Ego	Bantam	P75	1954	120	25¢	
Costigan's Needle	Bantam	1278	1954	169	25¢	R
	Avon	S349	1968	174	60¢	R
The Haploids	Lion	118	1953	191	25¢	R
The Mars Monopoly	Ace	D-162*	1956	183	35¢	
	Satellite	216	1958	129	3/-	R
Night Slaves	Gold Medal	d1561	1965	174	50¢	
The Odious Ones	Consul	SF1007	1961	160	2/6	R
	Sphere	80098	1967	127	3/6	R
One Against Herculum	Ace	D-381*	1959	124	35¢	M
Point Ultimate	Bantam	A1952	1959	151	35¢	
The Time Dissolver	Avon	T186	1957	158	35¢	
	Sphere	80101	1967	158	4/-	R
The Transcendent Man	Bantam	A1971	1959	154	35¢	R
SOMERS, BART (pseud) See FOX, G. F.						
SOULE, GARDNER (1913–)						
The Mystery Monsters	Ace	H-13	1965	192	60¢	N,R
SOULE, GEORGE (1887–1970)						
The Shape of Tomorrow	Signet	Ks352	1958	144	35¢	N
SOUTHERN, TERRY						
The Magic Christian	Berkley	BG500	1961	137	50¢	
	Bantam	H2917	1965	134	50¢	R
SOUTHWELL, SAMUEL B. (1922–)						
If All the Rebels Die	Avon	N189	1968	408	95¢	
SOUTHWOLD, STEPHEN (1887–) [as Neil Bell]						
The Gas War of 1940	Collins	505	*ca.*1939	251	1/6	R
Life Comes to Seathorpe	Guild	465	1953	192	2/-	R
Who Walk in Fear	Panther	1288	1962	156	2/6	C,R
SPARK, MURIEL (1918–)						
The Go-Away Bird and Other Stories						
	Penguin	1912	1963	189	3/6	C,R
SPECTOR, ROBERT D. (1922–)						
Seven Masterpieces of Gothic Horror						
	Bantam	NC171	1963	466	95¢	A
SPEED, DONALD (pseud) See HAMILTON, A.						
SPINRAD, NORMAN (1940–)						
Agent of Chaos	Belmont	B50-739	1967	157	50¢	
The Solarians	Paperback	52-985	1966	160	50¢	
SPRISSLER, ALFRED						
The Avenging Note	Stellar	SFS17*	1932	11	10¢	
[part of booklet also containing *The Spectre Bullet*, T. Mack]						
STACY, WALTER See ELLIOTT, B. (pseud)						
STAHL, BEN						
Blackbeard's Ghost	Scholastic	TK1115	1968	144	60¢	R

Author and Title	Publisher	Serial	Date	Pp.	Price	Type
STANTON, L. J.						
Flying Saucers—Hoax or Reality?						
	Belmont	B50-761	1966	157	50¢	N
STANTON, LEE						
Mushroom Men From Mars						
	Authentic	1	1951	127	1/6	
Report From Mandazo	Authentic	15	1951	110	1/6	
Seven to the Moon	Authentic	5	1951	125	1/6	
STANTON, PAUL						
Village of Stars	Permabks	M4230	1962	213	35¢	R
	FSB	697	1962	223	3/-	R
STAPLEDON, OLAF (1886—1950)						
Last and First Men	Pelican	A3	1937	288	6d	R
	Penguin	1875	1963	327	3/6	R
	Penguin	1875	1966	327	5/-	R
Last and First Men & Star Maker						
	Dover	T1962	1968	438	$2.00	C,R
Odd John	Galaxy Nov	8	1952	160	35¢	R
	Beac (Gal)	236	1959	191	35¢	R
	Berkley	F1128	1965	191	50¢	R
Sirius	Penguin	1999	1964	188	3/6	R
Star Maker (see also *Last and First Men & Star Maker*)						
	Berkley	F563	1961	222	50¢	R
STATTEN, VARGO (pseud) See FEARN, J. R.						
STEARN, JESS						
The Door to the Future	Macfadden	75-152	1964	285	75¢	N,R
STEEL, MARK						
Trouble Planet	Gannet	10	1954	127	1/6	
STEELE, C(URTIS) (pseud of EMILE TEPPERMAN)						
The Army of the Dead	Corinth	CR120	1966	160	60¢	M
Blood Reign of the Dictator	Corinth	CR136	1966	160	60¢	M
Hosts of the Flaming Death						
	Corinth	CR132	1966	159	60¢	M
Invasion of the Yellow Warlords						
	Corinth	CR144	1966	160	60¢	M
The Invisible Empire	Corinth	CR124	1966	159	60¢	M
Legions of the Death Master						
	Corinth	CR116	1966	160	60¢	M
March of the Flame Marauders						
	Corinth	CR140	1966	159	60¢	M
Master of Broken Men	Corinth	CR128	1966	158	60¢	M
STEIGER, BRAD (pseud) See OLSON, E.						
STEINBECK, JOHN (1902—1968)						
The Short Reign of Pippin IV						
	Bantam	A1753	1958	151	35¢	R
	Pan	G252	1959	159	2/6	R
STEPHENS, JAMES (1882—1950)						
The Crock of Gold	Armed	N-5	nd	256	np	R
	Armed	1121	nd	256	np	R
	Pan	262	1953	191	2/-	R
	Pan	X361	1965	173	3/6	R
	Collier	02551	1967	228	$1.95	R
Etched in Moonlight	Armed	1-4	nd	124	np	C,R
STERLING, BRETT (house pseudonym) See HAMILTON, E.						
STERN, DAVID (1909—)						
Francis	Armed	1228	nd	192	np	R
	Dell	507	1950	192	25¢	R
STERN, PHILIP VAN DOREN (1900—)						
Great Ghost Stories (selections from hardcover *The Midnight Reader*)						
	Washington	W592	1962	326	50¢	A,R
	Washington		1967	326	60¢	A,R
Great Tales of Fantasy and Imagination (originally *The Moonlight Traveller*)						
	Cardinal	C156	1954	485	35¢	A,R
	Washington	W704	1965	485	60¢	A,R
The Midnight Reader (abridged; see also *The Pocket Book of Ghost Stories* and *Great Ghost Stories*)						
	WDL	HH970	1960	254	2/6	A,R
The Moonlight Traveller (abridged; see also *Great Tales of Fantasy and Imagination*)						
	WDL	HH981	1960	224	2/6	A,R
The Pocket Book of Ghost Stories (selections from hardcover *The Midnight Reader*)						
	Pocket Bks	384	1947	405	25¢	A,R
The Portable Edgar Allan Poe						
	Viking	P12	1959	665	$1.45	C
Strange Beasts and Unnatural Monsters						
	Crest	R1166	1968	224	60¢	A
STERNBERG, JACQUES						
Sexualis '95	Berkley	X1408	1967	160	60¢	R
STEVENSON, ROBERT LOUIS (1850—1894)						
See also HALDEMAN-JULIUS CO., page 790.						
Dr. Jekyll and Mr. Hyde (some editions, such as the Armed and the Dent, are titled *The Strange Case of Dr. Jekyll and Mr. Hyde*)						
	Armed	885	nd	96	np	C
	Kangaroo	1	nd		1/6	R
	Zephyr	129	1950	125	2/6	C
	Pedigree		1959	128	2/-	R
	Digit	R581	1962	156	2/5	R
	Popular	K64	1963	93	40¢	R
	Everyman	1767	1964	244	5/-	C
	Airmont	CL47	1964	126	50¢	R
	Bantam	FP166	1967	106	50¢	R
Dr. Jekyll and Mr. Hyde and Other Macabre Stories						
	Corgi	SN7049	1964	141	2/6	A
Dr. Jekyll and Mr. Hyde and Other Stories						
	Scholastic	T550	1963	216	40¢	C
Great Short Stories of Robert Louis Stevenson						
	Pocket Bks	PL14	1954	370	35¢	C
The Strange Case of Dr. Jekyll and Mr. Hyde and Other Stories						
	Pocket Bks	123	1941	375	25¢	C
STEWART, ALFRED W. (1880—1947) [as J. J. Connington]						
Nordenholt's Million	Penguin	582	1946	286	1/-	R
STEWART, GEORGE R(IPPEY) (1895—1980)						
Earth Abides	Corgi	G184	1956	384	3/6	R
	Corgi	GS1095	1961	316	3/6	R
	Corgi	FS7263	1965	316	5/-	R
	Ace	K-154	1962	318	50¢	R
STEWART, WILL (pseud) See WILLIAMSON, J.						
STINE, G. HARRY (1928—)						
Contraband Rocket [as Lee Correy]						
	Ace	D-146*	1956	143	35¢	
Earth Satellites	Ace	D-239	1957	191	35¢	N
STINE, HANK						
Season of the Witch	Essex	0112	1968	228	$1.95	
STOKER, BRAM (1847—1912)						
Dracula	Armed	1-25	nd	448	np	R
	Armed	851	nd	448	np	R
	Pocket Bks	452	1947	408	25¢	R
	Rider		1954	335	2/-	R
	Permabks	M4088	1957	376	35¢	R
[different cover]	Permabks	M4088	1958	376	35¢	R
	Arrow	370	1957	336	2/6	R

Author and Title	Publisher	Serial	Date	Pp.	Price	Type
	Airmont	CL72	1965	317	50¢	R
	Signet	P2793	1965	382	60¢	R
	Pyramid	R1213	1965	352	50¢	R
	Dell	2148	1965	416	60¢	R
[comic-book version]	Ballantine	U2271	1966	159	50¢	R
Dracula's Curse and The Jewel of Seven Stars (*Dracula's Curse* was originally *Dracula's Guest*)						
	Tower	43970	1968	218	60¢	C,R
Dracula's Guest (also titled *Dracula's Curse*)						
	Arrow	916	1967	192	3/6	C,R
The Garden of Evil (originally *The Lair of the White Worm*)						
	Paperback	53946	1966	220	60¢	R
The Jewel of Seven Stars (see also *Dracula's Curse*)						
	Arrow	630	1962	254	2/6	R
	Arrow	630	1967	254	3/6	R
The Lady of the Shroud	Arrow	644	1962	192	2/6	R
	Arrow	644	1967	192	3/6	R
	Paperback	54-962	1966	287	75¢	R
The Lair of the White Worm (also titled *The Garden of Evil*)						
	Foulsham		1950	188	1/6	R
	Arrow	585	1960	191	1/6	R
	Arrow	585	1963	191	2/6	R
STONE, GRAHAM B. (1926—)						
Australian SF Index 1925-1967						
	Australian SF Assn		1968	158	$3.00	N
Zero Equals Nothing [with R. Williams]						
	Futurian		1951	27	6/-	
STONE, LESLIE F. (1905—)						
When the Sun Went Out	Stellar	SFS4	1929	24	10¢	
STOPECK, PHILIP						
Promiscuous Philbert	Nite-Time	96	1964	159	75¢	
STORM, BRIAN (pseud) See HOLLOWAY, B.						
STOUT, REX (1886—1975)						
The President Vanishes	Pyramid	X1698	1967	203	60¢	
STRATING, J. J.						
European Tales of Terror	Fontana	1852	1968	222	5/-	A
STRATTON, THOMAS (pseud) See COULSON, R.						
STUART, IAN (pseud) See MacLEAN, A.						
STUART, SIDNEY (pseud) See AVALLONE, M.						
STUART, W. J.						
Forbidden Planet	Bantam	A1443	1956	184	35¢	R
	Corgi	1443	1956	192	2/-	R
	Paperback	52-572	1967	159	50¢	R
STUBBS, HARRY CLEMENT (1922—) [as Hal Clement]						
Close to Critical	Ballantine	U2215	1964	190	50¢	M
	Corgi	07915	1968	158	3/6	R
Cycle of Fire	Ballantine	200	1957	185	35¢	
(identical hardcover edition $2.75)						
	Ballantine	70007	1968	185	50¢	R
	Corgi	GS7417	1966	171	3/6	R
From Outer Space (originally *Needle*)						
	Avon	T-175	1957	188	35¢	R
	Avon	G1168	1963	188	50¢	R
Mission of Gravity	Galaxy Nov	33	1958	191	35¢	R
	Pyramid	F786	1962	174	40¢	R
	Penguin	1978	1963	200	3/6	R
Natives of Space	Ballantine	U2235	1965	156	50¢	C
Needle (also titled *From Outer Space*)						
	Corgi	YS1383	1963	158	3/-	R
	Avon	S255	1967	207	60¢	R

Author and Title	Publisher	Serial	Date	Pp.	Price	Type
STURGEON, THEODORE (1918—)						
Aliens 4	Avon	T304	1959	224	35¢	C
... And My Fear Is Great & Baby Is Three (latter is also part of *More Than Human*)						
	Magabook	3*	1965	127	50¢	C
Beyond	Avon	T439	1960	157	35¢	C
Caviar	Ballantine	119	1955	167	35¢	C
(identical hardcover edition $2.00)						
	Ballantine	F562	1962	167	35¢	C,R
	Sphere	82244	1968	158	5/-	C,R
The Cosmic Rape	Dell	B120	1958	160	35¢	
	Dell	1512	1968	160	60¢	R
The Dreaming Jewels (also titled *The Synthetic Man*)						
	Nova	NS3	1955	156	2/-	R
E Pluribus Unicorn	Ballantine	179	1956	211	35¢	C,R
	Ballantine	U2247	1965	212	50¢	C,R
	Panther	1183	1961	192	2/6	C,R
	Panther	011838	1968	192	5/-	C,R
The Joyous Invasions	Penguin	2702	1968	207	5/-	C,R
More Than Human (see also *... And My Fear Is Great & Baby Is Three*)						
	Ballantine	46	1953	233	35¢	
(identical hardcover edition $2.00)						
	Ballantine	462K	1960	188	35¢	R
	Ballantine	U2231	1965	188	50¢	R
	Ballantine	72009	1968	188	75¢	R
	Penguin	2309	1965	234	3/6	R
Not Without Sorcery (originally *Without Sorcery*)						
	Ballantine	506K	1961	160	35¢	C,R
Some of Your Blood	Ballantine	458K	1961	143	35¢	
	Ballantine	U2253	1966	143	50¢	R
	Sphere	82235	1967	141	3/6	R
Starshine	Pyramid	X-1543	1966	174	60¢	C
Sturgeon in Orbit	Pyramid	F974	1964	159	40¢	C
The Synthetic Man (originally *The Dreaming Jewels*)						
	Pyramid	G247	1957	174	35¢	R
	Pyramid	G636	1961	174	35¢	R
	Pyramid	R1126	1965	174	50¢	R
	Pyramid	X1691	1967	174	60¢	R
A Touch of Strange	Berkley	G280	1959	174	35¢	C,R
	Berkley	F1058	1965	174	50¢	C,R
Venus Plus X	Pyramid	G544	1960	160	35¢	
	Pyramid	F732	1962	159	50¢	R
	Pyramid	X1773	1968	160	60¢	R
Voyage to the Bottom of the Sea						
	Pyramid	G622	1961	159	35¢	
	Pyramid	R1068	1964	159	50¢	R
	Pyramid	R1068	1967	159	50¢	R
A Way Home [edited by G. Conklin]						
	Pyramid	G184	1956	192	35¢	C,R
	Pyramid	F673	1961	192	40¢	C,R
	Pyramid	X1739	1968	192	60¢	C,R
SUDAK, EUNICE						
The Raven See POE, E. A.						
X	Lancer	70-052	1963	126	40¢	
SUDDABY, DONALD (1900—)						
The Star Raiders	Scottie	J7	1955	188	2/-	R
SULLIVAN, WALTER (1918—)						
We Are Not Alone	Signet	T2872	1966	319	75¢	N,R
SULLY, KATHLEEN (1910—)						
Skrine	Consul	1198	1963	159	2/6	R
SUMMERS, MONTAGUE (1880—1948)						
The Supernatural Omnibus I (selections from hardcover *Supernatural Omnibus*)	Panther	2199	1967	332	5/-	A,R
The Supernatural Omnibus II (more selections from hardcover)						
	Panther	2228	1967	250	5/-	A,R
Witchcraft and Black Magic						
	Arrow	785	1964	320	5/-	N,R

Author and Title	Publisher	Serial	Date	Pp.	Price	Type
SUTTON, JEFF(ERSON) (1913—)						
Apollo at Go	Popular	SP305	1964	159	50¢	R
	Mayflower	0244	1964	127	2/6	R
The Atom Conspiracy	Ace	F-374	1966	158	40¢	R
Bombs in Orbit	Ace	D-377	1959	192	35¢	
First on the Moon	Ace	D-327	1958	192	35¢	
	Ace	F-222	1963	192	40¢	R
H-Bomb Over America	Ace	H-18	1967	190	60¢	
The Man Who Saw Tomorrow						
	Ace	H-95*	1968	115	60¢	
Spacehive	Ace	D-478	1960	192	35¢	
SWAIN, DWIGHT V. (1915—)						
The Transposed Man	Ace	D-113*	1955	97	35¢	M
	Panther	696	1957	143	2/-	R
SWANN, THOMAS BURNETT (1928—1976)						
Day of the Minotaur	Ace	F-407	1966	159	40¢	M
The Dolphin and the Deep	Ace	G-694	1968	160	50¢	C
Moondust	Ace	G-758	1968	159	50¢	
The Weirwoods	Ace	G-640	1967	125	50¢	M
SWIFT, JONATHAN (1667—1745)						
See also HALDEMAN-JULIUS CO., page 790.						
Gulliver's Travels	Penguin	C10	1938	280	6d	R
	Penguin	EL22	1968	360	5/-	R
	Pocket Bks	34	1939	304	np	R
	Zephyr	70	1947		np	R
	Washington	W251	1960	300	45¢	R
	Dell	LC164	1961	351	50¢	R
	Dell	3308	1966	351	50¢	R
	Signet	CD14	1961	319	50¢	R
	Collier	HS7	1961		65¢	R
	Everyman	1060	1960	384	4/6	R
	Airmont	CL15	1963	285	50¢	R
	Perennial	P3018	1965	232	50¢	R
	Random College					
		T92	1968		95¢	R
	Lancer	74-603	1968		75¢	R
Gulliver's Travels and Other Writings						
	Bantam	SC165	1964	537	75¢	C,R
SYMONDS, JOHN						
In the Astral Light	Panther	1961	1965	207	3/6	
The 31st of February	Fontana		1962	192	2/6	
SYMPOSIUM						
The Science Fiction Novel	Advent		1964	160	$1.95	N,R
SZILARD, LEO (1898—1964)						
The Voice of the Dolphins and Other Stories						
	Simon & Schuster		1961	122	$1.00	C,R
	Sphere	83208	1967	126	3/6	C,R

T

Author and Title	Publisher	Serial	Date	Pp.	Price	Type
T., M.						
Venus Speaks	Regency (Brit)		nd	63	5/-	
TABOR, PAUL (1908—1974) [as Paul Tabori]						
The Doomsday Brain	Tandem	3455	1968	190	3/6	
The Green Rain	Pyramid	G624	1961	192	35¢	
	Pyramid	R1152	1965	192	50¢	R

Author and Title	Publisher	Serial	Date	Pp.	Price	Type
The Invisible Eye	Pyramid	X1728	1967	173	60¢	
The Survivors	Consul	1338	1964	170	3/6	
TABORI, PAUL (pseud) See TABOR, P.						
TAINE, JOHN (pseud) See BELL, E. T.						
TALLANT, ROBERT (1909—1957)						
Voodoo in New Orleans	Collier	AS481	1962	253	95¢	N,R
	Collier	09676	1967	252	95¢	N,R
TAMBLING, R.						
Flying Saucers: Where Do They Come From?						
	Scripts	PB316	1967	158	60¢	N
TAPSELL, R. F.						
The Year of the Horsetails	Berkley	N1610	1968	254	95¢	
TAYLOR, ANN						
Door of Desire	Nite-Time	116	1964	160	75¢	
TAYLOR, FRANK						
House of the Hunter	Chicago	A107	1962	256		
TAYLOR, GEOFF						
Court of Honor	Avon	N161	1967	351	95¢	
TAYLOR, RAY WARD						
Doomsday Square	Paperback	53-640	1968	223	60¢	
TAYLOR, ROBERT LEWIS (1912—)						
Adrift in a Boneyard	Avon	G1132	1963	191	50¢	R
TEMPLE, WILLIAM F. (1914—)						
The Automated Goliath	Ace	F-129*	1962	143	40¢	
Battle on Venus	Ace	F-195*	1963	104	40¢	M
Four-Sided Triangle	Galaxy Nov	9	1952	159	25¢	R
Shoot at the Moon	Macfadden	60-239	1967	176	60¢	R
	Panther	2298	1967	171	3/6	R
The Three Suns of Amara	Ace	F-129*	1962	80	40¢	M
TENN, WILLIAM (pseud) See KLASS, P.						
TEPPERMAN, EMILE See STEELE, C. (pseud)						
TEVIS, WALTER						
The Man Who Fell to Earth						
	Gold Medal	k1276	1963	144	40¢	
THACKERAY, WILLIAM (1811—1863)						
The Rose and the Ring	Puffin	PS223	1964	151	3/-	J,R
THANET, NEIL (pseud) See FANTHORPE, R. L.						
THAYER, TIFFANY (1902—1959)						
One-Man Show	Avon	327	1951	251	25¢	R
THEYDON, JOHN						
The Angels and the Creeping Enemy						
	Armada	C209	1968	125	2/6	J
Calling Thunderbirds	Armada	C144	1966	125	2/6	J
Captain Scarlet and the Mysterons						
	Armada	C201	1967	128	2/6	J
Captain Scarlet and the Silent Saboteur						
	Armada	C202	1967	128	2/6	J
Lady Penelope: The Albanian Affair						
	Armada	C163	1967	128	2/6	J
Stingray	Armada	C131	1965	157	2/6	J
Stingray and the Monster	Armada	C148	1966	125	2/6	J
Thunderbirds	Armada	C141	1966	126	2/6	J
Thunderbirds Ring of Fire	Armada	C161	1966	125	2/6	J

Author and Title	Publisher	Serial	Date	Pp.	Price	Type
THOM, ROBERT						
Wild in the Streets	Pyramid	X-1798	1968	128	60¢	R
	Sphere	84425	1968	140	5/-	R
THOMAS, DAN (pseud) See SANDERS, L. M.						
THOMAS, JACK						
Witches Stay Away From My Door						
	Wolfe	1	1967	96	5/-	N
THOMAS, JOHN ORAM See ORAM, J. (pseud)						
THOMAS, MARTIN (pseud) See MARTIN, THOMAS						
THOMAS, THEODORE L. (1920—)						
The Clone [with Kate Wilhelm]						
	Berkley	F1169	1965	143	50¢	
THOMSON, CHRISTINE CAMPBELL						
More Not at Night†	Arrow	608	1961	192	2/6	A
Not at Night†	Arrow	586	1960	192	2/6	A
Still Not at Night†	Arrow	671	1962	192	2/6	A
† All selected from original *Not at Night* series, 192537.						
THORNDIKE, RUSSELL (1885—1972)						
The Master of the Macabre Cresta		nn	nd	192	np	R
THORPE, TREBOR (pseud) See FANTHORPE, R. L.						
THURBER, JAMES (1894—1961)						
The 13 Clocks & The Wonderful O						
	Puffin	PS180	1962	158	3/6	J,R
TINDALL, GILLIAN (1938—)						
A Handbook on Witches	Panther	2290	1967	158	5/-	N
TITAN, EARL (pseud) See FEARN, J. R.						
TITTERTON, W(ILLIAM) R.						
Death Ray Dictator and Other Stories						
	Organ		nd	127	2/6	C
TODD, RUTHVEN (1914—)						
The Lost Traveller	Dover	T2191	1968	165	$1.50	R
TOLKIEN, J(OHN) R(ONALD) R(EUEL) (1892—1973)						
The Fellowship of the Ring (also part of *The Lord of the Rings*)						
	Ace	A-4	1965	448	75¢	R
	Ballantine	U7040	1965	527	95¢	R
The Hobbit	Puffin	PS161	1961	284	3/6	J,R
	Ballantine	U7039	1965	287	95¢	J,R
	Allen Unwin	65	1968	279	8/6	J,R
The Lord of the Rings (the trilogy: *The Fellowship of the Ring*; *The Two Towers*; *The Return of the King*)						
	Allen Unwin	823087.1	1968	1077	30/-	C
The Return of the King (also part of *The Lord of the Rings*)						
	Ace	A-6	1965	444	75¢	R
	Ballantine	U7042	1965	544	95¢	R
The Tolkien Reader	Ballantine	U7038	1966	179	95¢	C
Tree and Leaf	Allen Unwin	54	1964	92	5/-	C
The Two Towers (also part of *The Lord of the Rings*)						
	Ace	A-5	1965	381	75¢	R
	Ballantine	U7041	1965	447	95¢	R
TOLSTOY, LEO (1882—1945)						
Fables and Fairy Tales	Signet	CP132	1962	141	50¢	C
TOPOR, R.						
The Tenant	FSB	1729	1968	127	3/6	
TORDAY, URSULA See BLACKSTOCK, C. (pseud)						
TORRO, PEL (pseud) See FANTHORPE, R. L.						
TRALINS, ROBERT (1926—)						
The Cosmozoids	Belmont	B50-692	1966	143	50¢	
The Ring-a-Ding UFO's	Belmont	B50-745	1967	156	50¢	
TRAVERS, P(AMELA) L. (1906—)						
Mary Poppins	Puffin	PS182	1965	184	3/6	J,R
TREECE, HENRY (1912—1966)						
The Green Man	Paperback	55-752	1968	222	95¢	R
TREGASKIS, RICHARD (1916—1973)						
China Bomb	Avon	N179	1968		95¢	
TREIBICH, J. See JANIFER, L. M. (co-author)						
TRENCH, BRINSLEY LE POER						
The Flying Saucer Story	Ace	H-64	1968	190	60¢	N,R
TREVOR, ELLESTON (1920—)						
Doomsday [as Warwick Scott]						
	Lion	148	1953	158	25¢	R
Dream of Death	Digit	nn	1957	192	2/6	
The Shoot	NEL	1627	1966	157	5/-	R
	Avon	S301	1967	176	60¢	R
TREW, ANTHONY (1906—)						
Two Hours to Darkness	Bantam	H2728	1964	213	60¢	R
TRIMBLE, LOUIS (1917—)						
Anthropol	Ace	H-59*	1968	136	60¢	
TUBB, E(DWIN) C(HARLES) (1919—)						
Alien Impact	Authentic	21	1952	109	1/6	
Alien Life	Paladin		1956	128	1/6	
Alien Universe [as Volsted Gridban]						
	Scion		1952	94	1/6	
Argentis [as Brian Shaw]	Curtis War.		1952	112	1/6	
Atom-War on Mars	Panther	nn	1952	112	1/6	
City of No Return	Scion		1954	144	2/-	
C.O.D. Mars	Ace	H-40*	1968	99	60¢	
De Bracy's Drug [as Volsted Gridban]						
	Scion		1953	127	1/6	
Death Is a Dream	Ace	H-34*	1967	145	60¢	R
Derai	Ace	H-77*	1968	121	60¢	
Dynasty of Doom [as Charles Grey]						
	Milestone	1062	1953	126	1/6	
Enterprise 2115 [as Charles Grey] (also titled *The Mechanical Monarch*)						
	Milestone		1954	160	2/-	
(identical hardcover edition 6/6)						
The Extra Man [as Charles Grey]						
	Milestone		1954	128	1/6	
Fugitive of Time [as Volsted Gridban]						
	Milestone		1953	112	1/6	
The Hand of Havoc [as Charles Grey]						
	Milestone		1954	128	1/6	
Hell Planet	Scion		1954	140	2/-	
I Fight for Mars [as Charles Grey]						
	Milestone		1953	128	1/6	
Journey to Mars	Scion		1954	144	2/-	
The Living World [as Carl Maddox]						
	Pearson	T-B	1954	64	9d	
The Mechanical Monarch (originally *Enterprise 2115*)						
	Ace	D-266*	1958	167	35¢	R
Menace From the Past [as Carl Maddox]						
	Pearson	T-B	1954	64	9d	

Author and Title	Publisher	Serial	Date	Pp.	Price	Type
The Metal Eater [as Roy Sheldon]						
	Panther	109	1954	159	1/6	
(identical hardcover edition 6/-)						
Moon Base	Ace	F-293	1964	191	40¢	M
	Mayflower	5810	1967	112	3/6	R
The Mutants Rebel	Panther	38	1953	144	1/6	
Planet Fall [as Gill Hunt]	Curtis War.		1952	111	1/6	
Planetoid Disposals Ltds. [as Volsted Gridban]						
	Milestone	1019	1953	112	1/6	
The Resurrected Man	Scion		1954	120	1/6	
Reverse Universe [as Volsted Gridban]						
	Scion		1952	124	1/6	
Saturn Patrol [as King Lang]						
	Curtis War.		1952	111	1/6	
The Space-Born	Ace	D-193*	1956	158	35¢	M
	Digit	R449	1961	156	2/6	R
Space Hunger [as Charles Grey]						
	Milestone		1953	128	1/6	
The Stellar Legion	Scion		1954	144	2/-	
Ten From Tomorrow	Sphere	86061	1968	158	5/-	C,R
Tormented City [as Charles Grey]						
	Milestone	1066	1953	126	1/6	
Venusian Adventure	Comyns		1953	128	1/6	
The Wall [as Charles Grey]	Milestone	1044	1953	128	1/6	
The Winds of Gath	Ace	H-27*	1967	126	60¢	
World at Bay	Panther	110	1954	159	1/6	
(identical hardcover edition 6/-)						
	Atlas	SFL2	1955	114	2/-	R

TUCKER, (ARTHUR) WILSON (1914—)

Author and Title	Publisher	Serial	Date	Pp.	Price	Type
The City in the Sea	Galaxy Nov	11	1952	159	35¢	R
	Nova	NS2	1954	154	2/-	R
The Lincoln Hunters	Ace	H-62	1968	192	60¢	R
The Long Loud Silence	Guild	05	1953	191	2/-	R
	Dell	791	1954	192	25¢	R
The Man From Tomorrow (originally *Wild Talent*)						
	Bantam	1343	1955	148	25¢	R
The Time Masters	Signet	1127	1954	128	25¢	R
Time: X (originally *The Science Fiction Sub-Treasury*)						
	Bantam	1400	1955	140	25¢	C,R
To the Tombaugh Station	Ace	D-479*	1960	145	35¢	M
Tomorrow Plus X (originally *Time Bomb*)						
	Avon	T168	1957	158	35¢	R
Wild Talent (also titled *The Man From Tomorrow*)						
	Avon	G1301	1966	176	50¢	R

TULIP, J.

Author and Title	Publisher	Serial	Date	Pp.	Price	Type
The Moon Goddess	Halle		nd, 1945?	64	np	

TURNER, JAMES (1909—)

Author and Title	Publisher	Serial	Date	Pp.	Price	Type
The Fourth Ghost Book	Pan	02050	1968	286	5/-	A,R

TURNEY, CATHERINE

Author and Title	Publisher	Serial	Date	Pp.	Price	Type
The Other One (also titled *Possessed*)						
	Dell	695	1953	224	25¢	R
Possessed (originally *The Other One*)						
	Paperback	54-662	1968	206	75¢	R

TUTUOLA, AMOS (1920—)

Author and Title	Publisher	Serial	Date	Pp.	Price	Type
The Palm-Wine Drinkard and His Dead Palm-Wine Tapster in the Deads' Town	Grove	E15	1953	130	$1.00	R
	Faber		1962	125	6/-	R

TWAIN, MARK (pseud) See CLEMENS, S. L.

TWEED, THOMAS F(REDERICK) (1890—1940)
Gabriel Over the White House

Author and Title	Publisher	Serial	Date	Pp.	Price	Type
	Kemsley	CT405	1952	190	1/6	R

TWEEDALE, VIOLET

Author and Title	Publisher	Serial	Date	Pp.	Price	Type
Phantoms of the Dawn	Long	2	1938	255	6d	R

TYLER, STEPHEN

Author and Title	Publisher	Serial	Date	Pp.	Price	Type
Are the Invaders Coming?	Tower	43-892	1968	155	60¢	N

U,V

UNWIN, DAVID S. (1918—) [as David Severn]

Author and Title	Publisher	Serial	Date	Pp.	Price	Type
The Future Took Us	Puffin	PS177	1962	159	3/-	J,R
	Puffin	PS177	1968	159	3/6	J,R

UPDIKE, JOHN (1932—)

Author and Title	Publisher	Serial	Date	Pp.	Price	Type
The Centaur	Crest	R682	1964	224	60¢	R
	Crest	R1050	1967	224	60¢	R

USTINOV, PETER

Author and Title	Publisher	Serial	Date	Pp.	Price	Type
And a Dash of Pity	Pan	G503	1964	158	2/6	C,R

VALDEZ, PAUL

Author and Title	Publisher	Serial	Date	Pp.	Price	Type
Celluloid Suicide	Transport	ST	1951	32	8d	
The Corpse Sat Up	Transport	ST	1951	30	8d	
[credited to Valdez on cover, but to R. Glenning inside]						
The Fatal Focus	Transport	ST	1950	48	6d	
Feline Frame-Up	Transport	ST	1952	32	8d	
Flight Into Horror	Transport	ST	1951	32	8d	
Ghosts Don't Kill	Transport	ST	1951	32	8d	
Hypnotic Death	Transport	ST	1949	48	6d	
Kill Him Gently	Transport	ST	1951	32	8d	
Killer by Night	Transport	ST	1951	30	8d	
The Killer Who Wasn't There						
	Transport	ST	1952	32	8d	
The Maniac Murders	Transport	ST	1952	32	8d	
Murder Gives Notice	Transport	ST	1951	32	6d	
[credited to Valdez on cover, but to Art Hayman inside]						
The Murder I Don't Remember						
	Transport	ST	1952	32	8d	
Satan's Sabbath	Transport	ST	1951	32	8d	
There's No Future in Murder						
	Transport	ST	1952	32	8d	
The Time Thief	Transport	ST	1951	32	8d	
You Can't Keep Murder Out						
	Transport	ST	1951	32	8d	

VALE, RENA (1898—)

Author and Title	Publisher	Serial	Date	Pp.	Price	Type
Beyond the Sealed World	Paperback	52-811	1965	192	50¢	
	Paperback	52-651	1968	192	50¢	R

VALENTINE, VICTOR

Author and Title	Publisher	Serial	Date	Pp.	Price	Type
A Cure for Death	FSB	328	1961	160	2/6	R

VALLANCE, KARL

Author and Title	Publisher	Serial	Date	Pp.	Price	Type
Global Blackout	Gannet	6	*ca.*1953	126	1/6	

VALLEE, JACQUES (1939—)

Author and Title	Publisher	Serial	Date	Pp.	Price	Type
Anatomy of a Phenomenon	Ace	H-17	1966	255	60¢	N,R
Challenge to Science—The UFO Enigma [with Janine Vallee]						
	Ace	H-28	1967	256	60¢	N,R

VALLEE, JANINE See VALLEE, JACQUES (co-author)

Author and Title	Publisher	Serial	Date	Pp.	Price	Type

VAN ARNAM, DAVE [DAVID G.]

Author and Title	Publisher	Serial	Date	Pp.	Price	Type
Lost in Space [with Ron Archer (pseud. of Ted White)]						
	Pyramid	X1679	1967	157	60¢	
The Players of Hell	Belmont	B60-077*	1968	95	60¢	
Sideslip [with Ted White]						
	Pyramid	X1787	1968	188	60¢	
Star Gladiator	Belmont	B50-788*	1967	89	50¢	

VAN DER ELST, VIOLET (1882−1966)

The Brain Master	Van Der Elst	6	1946	80	1/6	C
Death of the Vampire Baroness						
	Van Der Elst	1	1945	80	1/6	C
The Mummy Comes to Life and Other Thrilling Stories						
	Van Der Elst	4	1945	79	1/6	C
The Satanic Power	Van Der Elst	5	1946	81	1/6	C
The Secret Power	Van Der Elst	nn	1945	80	1/6	C
The Strange Doctor and Other Mystic Stories						
	Van Der Elst	3	ca.1945	81	1/6	C

VAN DRUTEN, JOHN

Bell, Book and Candle	Bantam	A1842	1958	116	35¢	R

VAN HELLER, MARCUS

The Ring	Ophelia	OPH-112	1968			

VAN LODEN, ERLE

Curse of Planet Kuz	Edw. Self	1	ca.1952	128	1/6	
Voyage Into Space	Edw. Self		1954	100	1/-	

VAN THAL, HERBERT (1904−)

A Book of Strange Stories	Pan	315	1954	188	2/-	A
The Eighth Pan Book of Horror Stories						
	Pan	X699	1967	236	3/6	A
	Pan	X699	1968	236	3/6	A,R
Famous Tales of the Fantastic						
	Panther	2335	1967	140	3/6	A
The Fifth Pan Book of Horror Stories						
	Pan	X331	1964	267	3/6	A
The Fourth Pan Book of Horror Stories						
	Pan	X261	1963	271	3/6	A
Great Ghost Stories	Panther	1426	1962	143	2/6	A
Lie Ten Nights Awake	Coronet	2690	1967	190	3/6	A
	Berkley	X1558	1968	143	60¢	A,R
The Ninth Pan Book of Horror Stories						
	Pan	02144	1968	252	5/-	A
The Pan Book of Horror Stories						
	Pan	X45	1959	317	3/6	A
	Gold Medal	d1693	1966	254	50¢	A,R
The Second Pan Book of Horror Stories						
	Pan	X67	1960	319	3/6	A
The Seventh Pan Book of Horror Stories						
	Pan	X555	1966	239	3/6	A
The Sixth Pan Book of Horror Stories						
	Pan	X447	1965	222	3/6	A
The Third Pan Book of Horror Stories						
	Pan	X161	1962	268	3/6	A
Told in the Dark	Pan	152	1950	256		A
	Pan	152	1952	256		A,R

VAN VOGT, A(LFRED) E(LTON) (1912−)

Away and Beyond	Avon	548	1953	252	25¢	C,R
	Berkley	G215	1959	172	35¢	C,R
	Berkley	F812	1963	190	50¢	C,R
	Panther	1569	1963	219	3/6	C,R
	Panther	024379	1968	219	5/-	C,R
The Beast	Macfadden	60-169	1964	160	60¢	R
	Macfadden	60-343	1968	160	60¢	R
The Changeling	Macfadden	50-335	1967	96	50¢	R
Destination: Universe	Signet	1007	1953	160	25¢	C,R
	Signet	S1558	1958	160	35¢	C,R
	Panther	1063	1960	160	2/6	C,R
	Panther	1063	1963	144	2/6	C,R
	Panther	024840	1968	172	5/-	C,R
	Berkley	F893	1964	160	50¢	C,R
Earth's Last Fortress (originally *Masters of Time*)						
	Ace	D-431*	1960	114	35¢	R
Empire of the Atom	Ace	D-242*	1957	162	35¢	R
	Macfadden	60-267	1966	160	60¢	R
The Far-Out Worlds of A. E. van Vogt						
	Ace	H-92	1968	223	60¢	C
The House That Stood Still (also titled *The Mating Cry*)						
	Harlequin	177	1952	224	35¢	R
	Digit	D361	1960	160	2/-	R
	Digit	R623	1962	160	2/6	R
	Paperback	52-873	1965	159	50¢	R
	Paperback	63-016	1968	159	60¢	R
Masters of Time (see also *Earth's Last Fortress*)						
	Macfadden	50-334	1967	128	50¢	R
The Mating Cry (originally *The House That Stood Still*)						
	Beac (Gal)	298	1960	160	35¢	R
The Mind Cage	Avon	T252	1958	191	35¢	R
	Panther	1112	1960	189	2/6	R
	Panther	1112	1963	189	2/6	R
	Panther	011129	1968	171	5/-	R
	Tower	43-503	1965	251	60¢	R
	Tower	43-776	1967	251	60¢	R
Mission: Interplanetary (originally *The Voyage of the Space Beagle*)						
	Signet	914	1952	175	25¢	R
Mission to the Stars (originally *The Mixed Men*)						
	Berkley	344	1955	126	25¢	R
	Berkley	F704	1962	126	50¢	R
	Digit	D343	1960	160	2/-	R
	Digit	R637	1962	160	2/6	R
Monsters [edited by F. J Ackerman]						
	Paperback	52-515	1965	154	50¢	C
[2nd ed. retitled *Science Fiction Monsters* on cover only]						
	Paperback	52-555	1967	154	50¢	C,R
One Against Eternity (originally *The Weapon Makers*)						
	Ace	D-94*	1955	186	35¢	R
The Pawns of Null-A (originally *The Players of $\overline{A}$*)						
	Ace	D-187	1956	254	35¢	M
	Digit	D377	1960	191	2/6	R
Planets for Sale [with E. M. Hull; hardcover credited to Hull only]						
	Book Amer.	014	1965	171	50¢	C,R
The Players of Null-A (also titled *The Pawns of Null-A*)						
	Berkley	F1195	1966	192	50¢	R
Rogue Ship	Berkley	F1292	1966	157	50¢	R
Science Fiction Monsters See *Monsters*						
Siege of the Unseen (originally *The Chronicler*)						
	Ace	D-391*	1959	103	35¢	R
Slan	Dell	696	1953	223	25¢	R
	Panther	1132	1960	156	2/6	R
	Panther	024387	1968	156	5/-	R
	Ballantine	511K	1961	159	35¢	R
	Berkley	X1543	1968	191	60¢	R
The Twisted Men	Ace	F-253*	1963	130	40¢	
Two Hundred Million A.D. (originally *The Book of Ptath*)						
	Paperback	52-304	1964	159	50¢	R
	Paperback	52-406	1967	159	50¢	R
The Universe Maker	Ace	D-31*	1953	138	35¢	M
	Ace	G-660	1967	127	50¢	R
The Voyage of the Space Beagle (also titled *Mission Interplanetary*)						
	Panther	990	1959	192	2/6	R
	Panther	990	1963	189	3/6	R
	Panther	024395	1968	191	5/-	R
	Macfadden	60-146	1963	176	60¢	R
	Macfadden	60-318	1968	192	60¢	R
The War Against the Rull	Panther	1168	1961	156	2/6	R
	Permabks	M4263	1962	187	35¢	R

Author and Title	Publisher	Serial	Date	Pp.	Price	Type
The Weapon Makers (also titled *One Against Eternity*)						
	Digit	R454	1961	156	2/6	R
	Ace	M-153	1966	186	45¢	R
The Weapon Shops of Isher	Ace	D-53*	1954	179	35¢	R
	Ace	D-482	1960	178	35¢	R
	Nova	NS1	1955	179	2/-	R
The Winged Man [with E. M. Hull]						
	Berkley	X1403	1967	159	60¢	M
The Wizard of Linn	Ace	F-154	1962	190	40¢	M
	Macfadden	60-366	1968	176	60¢	R
The World of Null-A (hardcover titled *World of $\overline{A}$*)						
	Ace	D-31*	1953	182	35¢	R
	Ace	F-295	1964	190	40¢	R

VANCE, JACK (1916—)

Author and Title	Publisher	Serial	Date	Pp.	Price	Type
Big Planet	Ace	D-295*	1958	158	35¢	R
	Ace	G-661	1967	158	50¢	R
The Blue World	Ballantine	U2169	1966	190	50¢	M
The Brains of Earth	Ace	M-141*	1966	108	45¢	
City of the Chasch	Ace	G-688	1968	157	50¢	
The Dragon Masters	Ace	F-185*	1963	102	40¢	M
	Panther	2186	1967	123	3/6	R
The Dying Earth	Hillman	41	1950	175	25¢	C
	Lancer	74-807	1962	160	75¢	C,R
The Eyes of the Overworld	Ace	M-149	1966	189	45¢	C,M
The Five Gold Bands (also titled *The Space Pirate*)						
	Ace	F-185*	1963	122	40¢	R
Future Tense	Ballantine	U2214	1964	160	50¢	C
The Houses of Iszm	Ace	F-265*	1964	112	40¢	M
The Killing Machine	Berkley	F1003	1964	158	50¢	
The Languages of Pao	Ace	F-390	1966	157	40¢	R
The Last Castle	Ace	H-21*	1967	71	60¢	M
The Many Worlds of Magnus Ridolph						
	Ace	M-141*	1966	146	45¢	C,M
Monsters in Orbit	Ace	M-125*	1965	119	45¢	M
The Palace of Love	Berkley	X1454	1967	189	60¢	
Slaves of the Klau	Ace	D-295*	1958	129	35¢	M
Son of the Tree	Ace	F-265*	1964	111	40¢	M
Space Opera	Pyramid	R1140	1965	143	50¢	
The Space Pirate (also titled *The Five Gold Bands*)						
	Toby		1953	128	35¢	M
The Star King	Berkley	F905	1964	158	50¢	M
	Panther	02476X	1968	206	5/-	R
To Live Forever	Ballantine	167	1956	185	35¢	
(identical hardcover edition $2.75)						
	Ballantine	U2346	1966	185	50¢	R
The World Between and Other Stories						
	Ace	M-125*	1965	134	45¢	C

VANDEL, JEAN-GASTON

Author and Title	Publisher	Serial	Date	Pp.	Price	Type
Enemy Beyond Pluto	Hector Kelly		1954	192	2/-	
(Identical hardcover edition)						

VASSILIEV, M(IKHAIL) V.

Author and Title	Publisher	Serial	Date	Pp.	Price	Type
Life in the Twenty-First Century [with S. Gouschev]						
	Penguin	S195	1961	222	3/6	N,R
Sputnik Into Space [with V. V. Dobronravov]						
	Badger	SS1	1959	159	2/6	N,R

VEHEYNE, C.

Author and Title	Publisher	Serial	Date	Pp.	Price	Type
Horror	Digit	R553	1962	160	2/6	

VELIKOVSKY, IMMANUEL (1895—1982)

Author and Title	Publisher	Serial	Date	Pp.	Price	Type
Earth in Upheaval	Dell	Delta 2203	1965	308	$1.85	N,R
	Dell	2203	1968	288	95¢	N,R
Worlds in Collision	Dell	Delta 9702	1965	401	$1.95	N,R
	Dell	9702	1967	400	95¢	N,R

VERCORS (pseud) See BRULLER, J.

VERISSIMO, ERICO

Author and Title	Publisher	Serial	Date	Pp.	Price	Type
Night	Pedigree		1959	160	2/6	

VERN, DAVID (1924—) [as David V. Reed]

Author and Title	Publisher	Serial	Date	Pp.	Price	Type
Murder in Space	Galaxy Nov	23	1954	127	35¢	M
The Thing That Made Love	Universal	15	1952	160	35¢	M
The Whispering Gorilla	WDL	WFC	1950	160	1/6	M

VERNE, JULES (1828—1905)

See also HALDEMAN-JULIUS CO., page 790

Author and Title	Publisher	Serial	Date	Pp.	Price	Type
The Begum's Fortune	Ace	H-49	1968	191	60¢	R
Black Diamonds	Panther	1729	1964	187	3/6	R
Carpathian Castle	Panther	1575	1963	128	2/6	R
	Ace	H-60	1968	190	60¢	R
The City in the Sahara (Part 2 of *The Barsac Mission*)						
	Consul	1425	1965	174	3/6	R
	Ace	H-43	1968	191	60¢	R
The Clipper of the Clouds (originally *Master of the World*)						
	Scottie	J48	1956	222	2/-	R
Five Weeks in a Balloon	Pyramid	F753	1962	158	40¢	R
(Pyramid edition is by Gardner Fox, novelized version of screenplay)						
	Panther	1731	1964	188	3/6	R
	Everyman	1779*	1963	374	6/-	R
From the Earth to the Moon	Crest	s216	1958	222	35¢	R
	Digit	D217	1958	155	2/-	R
	Scholastic	T619	1966	188	45¢	R
	Airmont	CL142	1967	128	50¢	R
	Bantam	FP161	1967	154	50¢	R
From the Earth to the Moon and All Around the Moon						
	Dover	T633	1960	470	$1.75	C,R
The Hunt for the Meteor	Ace	H-78	1968	189	60¢	R
Into the Niger Bend (Part 1 of *The Barsac Mission*)						
	Ace	H-41	1968	192	60¢	R
A Journey to the Center of the Earth						
	Ace	D-155	1956	256	35¢	R
	Ace	D-397	1959	256	35¢	R
	Ace	F-191	1963	256	40¢	R
	Ace	M-119	1965	256	45¢	R
	Ace	G-582	1966	256	50¢	R
	Scottie	J11	1956	187	2/-	R
	Permabks	M4161	1959	263	35¢	R
	Digit	R335	1960	160	2/6	R
	Penguin	2265	1965	254	3/6	R
	Penguin	2265	1968	254	3/6	R
	Airmont	CL60	1965	253	50¢	R
	Consul	1375	1965	223	3/6	R
	Scholastic	T618	1966	318	45¢	R
	Collier	02623	1967	347	95¢	R
	Lancer	13-409	1967		60¢	R
	Blackie	1	1967	224	2/6	R
Master of the World (also titled *The Clipper of the Clouds*)						
	Airmont	CL73	1965	127	50¢	R
	Lancer	13-425	1968	191	60¢	R
Master of the World and Robur the Conqueror						
	Ace	D-504	1961	254	35¢	R
The Mysterious Island	Permabks	M6002	1962	554	60¢	R
	Airmont	CL77	1965		50¢	R
	Scholastic	T250	1961	312	35¢	R
	Scholastic	TX250	1967	312	50¢	R
The Mystery of Arthur Gordon Pym [with Edgar Allan Poe]						
	Panther	1671	1964	207	3/6	R
Off on a Comet (originally *Hector Servadac*; see also *To the Sun*)						
	Ace	D-245	1957	318	35¢	R
Propellor Island	Panther	1783	1965	191	3/6	R
The Purchase of the North Pole						
	Ace	D-434	1960	159	35¢	R
Robur the Conqueror See *Master of the World and Robur the Conqueror*						
Round the Moon (sequel to *From the Earth to the Moon*)						
	Airmont	CL182	1968		50¢	R

Author and Title	Publisher	Serial	Date	Pp.	Price	Type
The Secret of Wilhelm Storitz						
	Panther	1784	1965	191	3/6	R
To the Sun & Off on a Comet						
	Dover	T634	1960	462	$1.75	C,R
Twenty Thousand Leagues Under the Sea						
	Fontana	52	1955	315	2/6	R
	Bantam	F2458	1962	371	50¢	R
	Bantam	HP84	1965	371	60¢	R
	Bantam	H4448	1968	371	60¢	R
	Airmont	CL12	1963	288	50¢	R
	Washington	RE709	1966	387	50¢	R
	Scholastic	T430	1962	406	50¢	R
	Scholastic	T430	1967	406	50¢	R
	Lancer	14-608	1968		75¢	R
The Village in the Treetops	Ace	H-67	1968	190	60¢	R
Yesterday and Tomorrow	Ace	H-52	1968	189	60¢	C,R
VERNER, GERALD						
Prince of Darkness	Pedigree		1960	192	3/6	A
VERNES, HENRI						
City of a Thousand Drums	Corgi	GN7521	1966	126	3/6	
The Dinosaur Hunters	Corgi	GS7522	1966	126	3/6	
The White Gorilla	Corgi	GN7643	1967	128	3/6	
The Yellow Shadow	Corgi	GN7523	1966	127	3/6	
VERNON, ROGER LEE						
The Space Frontiers	Signet	1224	1955	152	25¢	C
VERRALL, C. S.						
Rocket Genius	Scholastic	TX752	1965	76	35¢	N
VERRILL, A. HYATT (1871−1954)						
The Strange Story of Our Earth						
	Premier	s24	1956	157	35¢	N,R
When the Moon Ran Wild [unauthorised revision, as Ray Ainsbury]						
	Consul	1197	1962	158	2/6	M
VIARD, HENRY [as Henry Ward]						
The Green Suns	Panther	1594	1963	127	2/6	R
Hell's Above Us	Panther	1505	1963	219	3/6	R
VIDAL, GORE (1925−)						
Messiah	Ballantine	94	1954	201	35¢	R
	Ballantine	484K	1961	201	35¢	R
	Ballantine	U5022	1965	244	60¢	R
	Ballantine	72006	1968	244	75¢	R
	FSB	1533	1966	221	5/-	R
Visit to a Small Planet	Signet	S1788	1960	127	35¢	R
VIERECK, G(EORGE) S(YLVESTER) (1884−1962) [with P. Eldridge]						
My First Two Thousand Years						
	Crest	s148	1956	287	35¢	R
	Crest	d425	1961	287	50¢	R
	FSB	752	1962	512	5/-	R
Salome	Ace	D-43	1954	320	35¢	R
	FSB	801	1963	416	5/-	R
VINCENT, HARL (pseud) See SCHOEPFLIN, H.						
VOLTA, ORNELLA						
The Vampire	Tandem	T25	1965	159	3/6	N
The Vampire [with Valeria Riva]						
	Pan	M112	1965	316	5/-	A,R
VOLTAIRE, (FRANÇOIS MARIE) (1694−1778)						
See also HALDEMAN-JULIUS CO., page 790.						
Candide	Penguin	L4	1947	144	3/6	R

Author and Title	Publisher	Serial	Date	Pp.	Price	Type
VON BRAUN, WERNHER (1912−1977)						
Project Mars [with W. Ley] (originally *The Exploration of Mars*)						
	Badger	SS4	1962	184	2/6	N,R
VON HARBOU, THEA (1888−1954)						
Metropolis	Ace	F-246	1963	222	40¢	R
VONNEGUT, KURT (1922−)						
Canary in a Cat House	Gold Medal	s1153	1961	160	35¢	C
Cat's Cradle	Dell	Delta 1149	1964	231	$1.65	R
	Dell	1149	1965	191	60¢	R
	Penguin	2308	1965	179	3/6	R
God Bless You, Mr. Rosewater						
	Dell	2929	1966	190	75¢	R
	Panther	2279	1967	222	6/-	R
Player Piano (also titled *Utopia 14*)						
	Mayflower	A19	1962	288	3/6	R
	Avon	NS16	1967	320	95¢	R
The Sirens of Titan	Dell	B138	1959	319	35¢	
	Dell	7948	1966	319	75¢	R
	Corgi	GS1452	1964	222	3/6	R
	Hodder	02876	1967	224	3/6	R
Utopia 14 (originally *Player Piano*)						
	Bantam	A1262	1954	312	35¢	R

W

Author and Title	Publisher	Serial	Date	Pp.	Price	Type
WADD, CHANNY						
Nymphos, Nymphets and Satyrs						
	Bee-Line (UK)	114	1968			
WADE, ROBERT See MASTERTON, W. (pseud, with B. Miller)						
WADE, TOM						
The Voice From Baru	Digit	R661	1963	157	2/6	
The World of Theda	Digit	R610	1962	155	2/6	
WADEY, VICTOR						
A Planet Named Terra	Digit	R588	1962	160	2/6	
The United Planets	Digit	R590	1962	160	2/6	
WAKEFIELD, H(ERBERT) R. (1888−1965)						
Stories From The Clock Strikes Twelve						
	Ballantine	531	1961	159	35¢	C,R
WALKER, DAVID (HARRY) (1911−)						
Winter of Madness	Pocket Bks	50176	1965	218	50¢	R
WALKER, KENNETH M(ACFARLANE) (1882−1966) [with G. Boumphrey]						
The Log of the Ark	Puffin	PS154	1963	159	3/-	J
WALL, JOHN W. (1910−) [as Sarban]						
The Doll Maker	Ballantine	431K	1960	144	35¢	R
	Ballantine	U2849	1967	144	50¢	R
	Consul	1143	1962	158	2/6	R
Ringstones	Ballantine	498K	1961	139	35¢	R
The Sound of His Horn	Ballantine	377K	1960	125	35¢	R
WALL, MERVYN (1908−)						
The Unfortunate Fursey	Helicon		1965	241	10/-	R

Author and Title	Publisher	Serial	Date	Pp.	Price	Type
WALL STREET JOURNAL						
Here Comes Tomorrow!	Dow Jones		1967	196	$1.85	N,R
WALLACE, C. H.						
Witchcraft in the World Today						
	Award	A269S	1967	191	75¢	N
	Tandem	T170	1967	191	5/-	N
WALLACE, EDGAR (1875—1932)						
Captain of Souls	Long	260	1952	256	2/-	R
Green Rust	Ward Lock		1956	191	2/-	R
King Kong [with M. C. Cooper] [novelization by D. W. Lovelace]						
	Bantam	F3093	1965	152	50¢	R
	Corgi	GN7461	1966	152	3/6	R
WALLACE, F(LOYD) L.						
Address: Centauri	Galaxy Nov	32	1958	191	35¢	R
Worlds in Balance	Atlas	SFL4	1955	114	2/-	C
WALLACE, IAN (pseud) See PRITCHARD, J. W.						
WALLACE, IRVING (1916—)						
The Man	Crest	m841	1965	768	95¢	R
WALLACE, ROBERT						
The Beast-King Murders	Corinth	CR103	1965	160	60¢	M
The Broadway Murders	Corinth	CR105	1965	160	60¢	M
The Corpse Parade	Corinth	CR139	1966	159	60¢	M
The Curio Murders	Corinth	CR113	1966	159	60¢	M
The Daggers of Kali	Corinth	CR106	1965	160	60¢	M
The Dancing Doll Murders	Corinth	CR102	1965	160	60¢	M
Death Glow	Corinth	CR117	1966	159	60¢	M
Death Under Contract	Corinth	CR135	1966	160	60¢	M
Fangs of Murder	Corinth	CR112	1966	159	60¢	M
The Forty Thieves	Corinth	CR131	1966	160	60¢	M
The Green Glare Murders	Corinth	CR111	1966	159	60¢	M
The Melody Murders	Corinth	CR123	1966	160	60¢	M
Murder Money	Corinth	CR115	1966	159	60¢	M
Murder Stalks a Billion	Corinth	CR114	1966	159	60¢	M
Murder Trail	Corinth	CR110	1965	159	60¢	M
Murder Under the Big Top	Corinth	CR107	1965	159	60¢	M
Stones of Satan	Corinth	CR119	1966	159	60¢	M
The Trail to Death	Corinth	CR108	1965	159	60¢	M
Tycoon of Crime	Corinth	CR104	1965	159	60¢	M
The Uniformed Killers	Corinth	CR127	1966	160	60¢	M
The Vampire Murders	Corinth	CR101	1965	159	60¢	M
Yellow Shadows of Death	Corinth	CR109	1965	159	60¢	M
WALLER, LESLIE (1923—) [as C. S. Cody]						
The Witching Night	Dell	670	1953	256	25¢	R
	Corgi	T27	1953	280	2/-	R
	Corgi	GN1282	1963	254	3/6	R
	Lancer	73-720	1968	286	60¢	R
WALLIS, DAVE						
Only Lovers Left Alive	Bantam	H3029	1965	185	60¢	R
	Pan	X464	1966	190	3/6	R
WALLIS, G. McDONALD (1925—)						
Legend of Lost Earth	Ace	F-187*	1963	133	40¢	
The Light of Lilith	Ace	F-108*	1961	123	40¢	
WALLOP, DOUGLAS (1920—)						
The Year the Yankees Lost the Pennant						
	Cardinal	C328	1958	186	35¢	R
	American Sports					
		F115	1965	159	2/6	R
WALPOLE, HORACE (1717—1797)						
The Castle of Otranto	Collier	HS57	1963	128	65¢	R

Author and Title	Publisher	Serial	Date	Pp.	Price	Type
WALPOLE, HUGH (1884—1941)						
Portrait of a Man With Red Hair						
	Avon	204	1949	188	25¢	R
	Paperback	53-409	1967	223	60¢	R
WALSH, J(AMES) M(ORGAN) (1897—1952)						
Vanguard to Neptune	Kemsley	CT410	1952	190	1/6	M
WALTER, ELIZABETH						
Snowfall and Other Chilling Events						
	Fontana	1706	1968	160	3/6	C,R
WALTERS, HUGH (pseud) See HUGHES, W. L.						
WALTON, EVANGELINE						
Witch House	Monarch	264	1962	159	35¢	R
WALTON, STEPHEN						
No Transfer	Signet	P3376	1968	160	60¢	R
WANDREI, DONALD (1908—)						
The Web of Easter Island	Consul	HS1035	1961	174	2/6	R
WARD, DON (1911—)						
Black Magic: 13 Chilling Tales						
	Dell	0627	1967	252	60¢	A
WARD, HAROLD [as Zorro]						
The Gray Creatures	Corinth	CR121	1966	159	60¢	M
The Shriveling Murders	Corinth	CR125	1966	159	60¢	M
12 Must Die	Corinth	CR118	1966	159	60¢	M
WARD, HENRY (pseud) See VIARD, HENRI						
WARREN, ROY (pseud) See CAMRA, ROY						
WATER, SILAS (pseud) See LOOMIS, N.						
WATKIN, LAWRENCE EDWARD						
Darby O'Gill and the Little People						
	Dell	A181	1959	159	25¢	
On Borrowed Time	Armed	779	nd	223	np	R
WATKINS, PETER						
The War Game	Avon	NS23			95¢	R
WATKINS-PITCHFORD, DENYS JAMES (1905—) [as 'B.B.']						
Little Grey Men, The	Puffin	PS160	1963	255	4/-	J,R
WAUGH, MICHAEL						
The Abominable Snowman (*The Mystery of the Abominable Snowman*						
on cover)	Cleveland		1954	32	9d	
Back From the Dead	Cleveland		1955	32	9d	
Fangs of the Vampire	Cleveland	*ca.*1954		34	9d	
The Living Dead	Cleveland		1955	34	9d	
WAYMAN, TONY RUSSELL (1929—)						
World of the Sleeper	Ace	H-21*	1967	184	60¢	
WEBB, JACK						
The Gilded Witch	Regency	RB111	1963	156	50¢	
WEINBAUM, STANLEY G. (1900—1935)						
The Black Flame	Harlequin	205	1953	223	35¢	R
A Martian Odyssey	Lancer	74-808	1962	159	75¢	C
	Lancer	72-146	1966	159	50¢	C,R
Parasite Planet	Whitman		1950	48	6d	M
WEINSTEIN, NATHAN WALLENSTEIN See WEST, N. (pseud)						

Author and Title	Publisher	Serial	Date	Pp.	Price	Type
WEISS, GEORGE (1898—1946) [as Francis Flagg]						
The Night People	FPCI		1947	32	25¢	
WELLARD, JAMES						
Night in Babylon	Pan	313	1954	220	2/-	R
WELLES, ORSON (1915—)						
Invasion From Mars	Dell	305	1949	191	25¢	A
WELLMAN, MANLY WADE (1905—)						
The Beasts From Beyond (originally *Strangers on the Heights*)						
	WDL	WFC	1950	160	1/6	M
The Dark Destroyers	Ace	D-443*	1960	111	35¢	R
Devil's Planet	WDL	WFC	1951	128	1/6	M
The Invading Asteroid	Stellar	SFS15	1932	24	10¢	
Romance in Black [as Gans T. Field]						
	Utopian		nd	64	6d	M
Sojarr of Titan	Crestwood	11	1949	120	25¢	M
The Solar Invasion	Popular	60-2346	1968	126	60¢	M
Twice in Time	Galaxy Nov	34	1958	191	35¢	R
Who Fears the Devil?	Ballantine	U2222	1964	186	50¢	C,R
WELLMAN, PAUL I. (1898—1966)						
The Fiery Flower	Permabks	M4192	1961	197	35¢	R
	Mayflower	2510	1963	222	3/6	R
	Mayflower	2510	1966	222	5/-	R
WELLS, BARRY						
The Day the Earth Caught Fire						
	FSB	903	1961	160	2/6	R
	FSB	903	1962	160	2/6	R
	Ballantine	F602	1962	154	50¢	R
WELLS, H(ERBERT) G(EORGE) (1866—1946)						
See also HALDEMAN-JULIUS CO., page 790.						
Best Science Fiction Stories of H. G. Wells						
	Dover	T1531	1966	303	$1.75	C
Best Stories of H. G. Wells	Ballantine	s414K	1960	320	75¢	C
	Ballantine	S742	1963	320	75¢	C,R
The Cone	Fontana	1125	1965	160	3/6	C
The Country of the Blind	Todd	Bantam	nd		6d	R
	Todd	Polybook	nd		4d	R
The Empire of the Ants	Todd	Bantam	nd		6d	R
The First Men in the Moon	Dell	201	1947	239	25¢	R
	Corgi	T225	1957	222	2/-	R
	Corgi	SS898	1960	188	2/6	R
	Fontana	433	1960	251	2/6	R
	Fontana	433	1964	255	3/6	R
	Ballantine	F687	1963	160	50¢	R
	Ballantine	U2232	1964	160	50¢	R
	Airmont	CL78	1965		50¢	R
	Berkley	F1398	1967	176	50¢	R
	Dell	2552	1967	192	60¢	R
The Food of the Gods	Armed	958	nd	320	np	R
	Ballantine	F725	1963	189	50¢	R
	Popular	SP286	1964	207	50¢	R
	Airmont	CL59	1965	190	50¢	R
	Berkley	X1407	1967	254	60¢	R
(with other titles)	Dover	T1135	1963	645	$2.00	C,R
In the Days of the Comet	Airmont	CL111	1966	192	50¢	R
	Berkley	X1440	1967	223	60¢	R
(with other titles)	Dover	T1135	1963	645	$2.00	C,R
The Inexperienced Ghost and Nine Other Stories						
	Bantam	FP81	1965	167	50¢	C
The Invisible Man	Penguin	151	1938		6d	R
	Penguin-Aust.		1945	126	1/6	R
	Dell	269	1948	142	25¢	R
	Pocket Bks	1140	1957	150	25¢	R
	Washington	RE104	1964	150	60¢	R
	Fontana	367	1959	223	2/6	R
	Fontana	1371	1966	223	3/6	R
	Fontana	1371	1968	223	3/6	R
	Chariot	CB28	1960	195	50¢	R
	Berkley	C934	1964	143	45¢	R
	Berkley	F1256	1966	143	50¢	R
	Airmont	CL40	1964	127	40¢	R
	Popular	K71	1964	125	40¢	R
	Scholastic	T540	1964	220	40¢	R
The Invisible Man and The War of the Worlds						
	Washington	W276	1962	329	45¢	C,R
The Island of Dr. Moreau	Armed	698	nd		np	R
	Penguin	571	1946	151	1/-	R
	Penguin	571	1962	192	3/6	R
	Penguin	571	1967	192	3/6	R
	Ace	D-309	1958	192	35¢	R
	Ballantine	F761	1963	126	50¢	R
	Berkley	C909	1964	128	45¢	R
	Berkley	F1363	1966	128	50¢	R
	Airmont	CL110	1966	127	50¢	R
	Lancer	13-435	1968	189	60¢	R
The Land Ironclads	Todd	Bantam	nd		6d	R
The Man Who Could Work Miracles						
	Todd	Polybook	1943		4d	R
The Man Who Could Work Miracles & The Time Machine See *The Time Machine*						
A Modern Utopia	Bison	BB393	1967	393	$2.45	R
Selected Short Stories of H. G. Wells (selected from *The Short Stories of H. G. Wells*)	Penguin	1310	1958	352	4/-	C,R
The Shape of Things to Come						
[volume 1]	Hutchinson	*ca.*1935		252	6d	R
[volume 2]	Hutchinson	*ca.*1935		256	6d	R
	Corgi	ES7682	1967	446	7/6	R
The Sleeper Wakes (originally *When the Sleeper Wakes*)						
	Collins	*ca.*1930		126	6d	R
Three Prophetic Novels of H. G. Wells [edited by E. F. Bleiler]						
	Dover	T605	1960	335	$1.45	C,R
The Time Machine (also contained in *Three Prophetic Novels of H. G. Wells*)	Poynings		1943	32	1/-	R
	Armed	t-2	nd	128	np	R
	Penguin	573	1946	280	1/-	R
	Berkley	380	1957	96	25¢	R
	Berkley	G445	1960	139	35¢	R
	Berkley	Y789	1963	141	40¢	R
	Berkley	C1063	1965	141	45¢	R
	Berkley	F1361	1966	141	50¢	R
	Airmont	CL44	1964	126	40¢	R
	Everyman	1915	1964	105	4/-	R
	Bantam	FP4063	1968	115	50¢	R
The Time Machine and Other Stories						
	Scholastic	T530	1964	217	45¢	C
The Time Machine & The Man Who Could Work Miracles						
	Pan	251	1953	157	2/-	C,R
	Pan	251	1954	157	2/-	C,R
	Pan	G697	1965	123	2/6	C,R
	Pan	01697	1968	123	3/6	C,R
The Time Machine & The War of the Worlds						
	Dolphin	C304	1961	276	95¢	C,R
	Premier	T384	1968		75¢	C,R
The Truth About Pyecraft	Todd	Polybook	1943		4d	R
The Valley of the Spiders and Other Stories						
	Fontana	1035	1966	191	3/6	C
The War in the Air	Penguin	343	1941	255	np	R
	Penguin	343	1967	255	5/-	R
The War in the Air; In the Days of the Comet; The Food of the Gods						
	Dover	T1135	1963	645	$2.00	C,R
The War of the Worlds	Dell		1938	48	10¢	R
	Armed	745	nd	256	np	R
	Armed	1091	nd	256	np	R
	Penguin	570	1946	208	1/-	R
	Penguin	570	1954	192	2/-	R

Author and Title	Publisher	Serial	Date	Pp.	Price	Type
	Penguin	570	1959	192	2/6	R
	Penguin	570	1962	192	2/6	R
	Penguin	570	1964	192	3/6	R
	Penguin	570	1967	192	3/6	R
	Pocket Bks	947	1953	180	25¢	R
	Popular	SP170	1962	189	50¢	R
	Berkley	C922	1964	173	45¢	R
	Berkley	F1255	1966	173	50¢	R
	Lancer	13-410	1967	253	60¢	R
The War of the Worlds & The Time Machine						
	Dolphin	C304	1961	276	95¢	C,R
The War of the Worlds & The Invisible Man						
	Washington	W276	1962	329	45¢	C,R
	Washington	W276	1964	329	45¢	C,R

When the Sleeper Wakes (also titled *The Sleeper Wakes*) (also contained in *Three Prophetic Novels of H. G. Wells*)

Author and Title	Publisher	Serial	Date	Pp.	Price	Type
	Ace	D-388	1959	288	35¢	R
	Ace	F-240	1963	288	40¢	R

WERNER, GEORGE
Author and Title	Publisher	Serial	Date	Pp.	Price	Type
One Helluva Below	Gold Star	IL7-27	1964	126	40¢	

WERPER, BARTON (pseud) See SCOTT, PETER

WEST, JESSAMYN (1907—)
The Chilekings (as "Little Men" in *Star Short Novels*, Pohl, 1954)
Author and Title	Publisher	Serial	Date	Pp.	Price	Type
	Ballantine	U2845	1967	123	50¢	R

WEST, MORRIS
Author and Title	Publisher	Serial	Date	Pp.	Price	Type
The Shoes of the Fisherman						
	Pan	X305	1964	256	3/6	R
	Pan	X305	1965	256	3/6	R
	Pan	10305	1968	256	5/-	R
	Dell	7833	1968	288	95¢	R

WEST, NATHANAEL (pseud of Nathan Wallenstein Weinstein [1903—1940])
A Cool Million & The Dream Life of Balso Snell
Author and Title	Publisher	Serial	Date	Pp.	Price	Type
	Avon	SS6	1965	158	60¢	R

WEST, WALLACE (1900—1980)
Author and Title	Publisher	Serial	Date	Pp.	Price	Type
The Bird of Time	Ace	F-114	1961	224	40¢	R
Lords of Atlantis	Airmont	SF3	1963	128	40¢	R
The Memory Bank	Airmont	SF1	1962	127	35¢	R

WESTLAKE, DONALD E.
Author and Title	Publisher	Serial	Date	Pp.	Price	Type
Anarchaos [as Curt Clark]	Ace	F-421	1967	143	40¢	

WESTON, GEORGE (1880—1965)
Author and Title	Publisher	Serial	Date	Pp.	Price	Type
His First Million Women	Avon	396	1952	220	25¢	R

WESTWARD, ELTON
Author and Title	Publisher	Serial	Date	Pp.	Price	Type
Return to Mars	Brown-Wat.		1954	111	1/6	

WESTWOOD, ALVIN
Author and Title	Publisher	Serial	Date	Pp.	Price	Type
Sinister Forces	Brown-Wat.		1953	105	1/6	

WHEATLEY, DENNIS (1897—1977)
Author and Title	Publisher	Serial	Date	Pp.	Price	Type
Black August	Arrow	560	1960	320	2/-	R
	Arrow	560	1963	320	2/6	R
The Black Baroness	Arrow	558	1960	376	3/6	R
The Devil Rides Out	Arrow	345H	1954	245	2/-	R
	Arrow	345H	1958	245	2/6	R
	Arrow	345	1961	245	2/6	R
	Arrow	345	1965	245	3/6	R
	Bantam	S3549	1967	310	75¢	R
The Fabulous Valley	Arrow	284H	1953	286	2/-	R
	Arrow	284H	1958	286	2/6	R
	Arrow	284	1963	286	2/6	R

Author and Title	Publisher	Serial	Date	Pp.	Price	Type
Gunmen, Gallants and Ghosts						
	Arrow	691	1963	318	3/6	C,R
The Haunting of Toby Jugg	Arrow	543	1959	352	3/6	R
	Arrow	543	1961	352	3/6	R
	Arrow	543	1964	352	3/6	R
	Arrow	543	1966	352	3/6	R
The Ka of Gifford Hillary	Arrow	583	1961	400	3/6	R
	Arrow	583	1963	400	3/6	R
	Arrow	583	1964	400	3/6	R
	Arrow	583	1965	400	5/-	R
The Man Who Missed the War						
	Arrow	534	1966	384	5/-	R
Quiver of Horror	Arrow	759	1964	288	3/6	A,R
The Satanist	Arrow	653	1962	448	5/-	R
	Arrow	653	1963	448	5/-	R
	Bantam	S3550	1967	440	75¢	R
The Secret War	Arrow	336H	1953	288	2/6	R
	Arrow	336H	1958	288	2/6	R
	Arrow	336	1964	288	3/6	R
Shafts of Fear	Arrow	760	1964	288	3/6	A,R
Sixty Days to Live	Arrow	559	1960	351	3/6	R
Star of Ill-Omen	Arrow	378H	1954	288	2/-	R
	Arrow	378	1962	288	2/6	R
	Arrow	378	1963	288	3/6	R
Strange Conflict	Arrow	549	1960	291	2/6	R
	Arrow	549	1965	291	3/6	R
Such Power Is Dangerous	Hutchinson	235	*ca.*1935	285	2/-	R
	Arrow	628	1962	256	2/6	R
They Found Atlantis	Arrow	335H	1953	256	2/-	R
	Arrow	335H	1958	256	2/6	R
	Arrow	335	1961	256	2/6	R
They Used Dark Forces	Arrow	891	1966	511	5/-	R
To the Devil—A Daughter	Arrow	412H	1957	384	3/6	R
	Arrow	412H	1960	384	3/6	R
	Arrow	412	1961	384	3/6	R
	Arrow	412	1963	384	5/-	R
	Arrow	412	1964	384	5/-	R
	Arrow	412	1965	384	5/-	R
	Arrow	412	1968	384	5/-	R
	Bantam	S3764	1968	329	75¢	R
Uncharted Seas	Arrow	580	1960	288	2/6	R

WHEELER, J(OHN) HARVEY (1918—) See BURDICK, E. L. (co-author)

WHITAKER, DAVID (1930—)
Doctor Who in an Exciting Adventure With the Daleks
Author and Title	Publisher	Serial	Date	Pp.	Price	Type
	Avon	G1322	1967	144	50¢	

WHITE, JAMES (1928—)
Author and Title	Publisher	Serial	Date	Pp.	Price	Type
Deadly Litter	Ballantine	U2224	1964	175	50¢	C
	Corgi	08052	1968	157	3/6	C,R
The Escape Orbit (also titled *Open Prison*)						
	Ace	F-317	1965	188	40¢	M
Hospital Station	Ballantine	F595	1962	191	50¢	C,M
	Corgi	GS7651	1967	191	3/6	C,R
Open Prison (also titled *The Escape Orbit*)						
	FSB	1228	1965	158	3/6	R
Second Ending	Ace	F-173*	1962	100	40¢	M
The Secret Visitors	Ace	D-237*	1957	155	35¢	M
	Ace	G-675	1967	155	50¢	R
	Digit	D479	1961	160	2/6	R
	Digit	R725	1963	158	2/6	R
Star Surgeon	Ballantine	F709	1963	159	50¢	M
	Ballantine	U2866	1968	159	50¢	R
	Corgi	GS7702	1967	156	3/6	R
The Watch Below	Ballantine	U2285	1966	189	50¢	
	Corgi	GS7759	1967	174	3/6	R

Author and Title	Publisher	Serial	Date	Pp.	Price	Type
WHITE, T(ERENCE) H(ANBURY) (1906—1964)						
See also MONTREAL STAR, page 790.						
Camelot (originally *The Once and Future King*)						
	Berkley	D1662	1968	639	$1.25	C,R
The Master	Peacock	PK43	1964	217	4/6	R
	Avon	ZS118	1967	175	60¢	R
Mistress Masham's Repose						
	Capricorn	CAP39	1960	257	$1.35	R
	Peacock	PK20	1963	204	4/-	R
The Once and Future King (also titled *Camelot*)						
	Dell	Y001	1960	639	95¢	C,R
	Dell	6612	1964	639	95¢	C,R
	Fontana	609L	1962	638	6/-	C,R
	Berkley	N1320	1966	639	95¢	C,R
	Berkley	N1320	1968	639	95¢	C,R
The Sword in the Stone (part of *The Once and Future King*)						
	Fontana	898	1963	286	3/6	R
	Dell	8445	1964	288	50¢	R
WHITE, TED E. (1938—)						
Android Avenger	Ace	M-123*	1965	113	45¢	
Captain America: The Great Gold Steal See *The Great Gold Steal*						
The Great Gold Steal	Bantam	F3780	1968	118	50¢	
Invasion From 2500 [as Norman Edwards (joint pseud. with Terry Carr)]						
	Monarch	453	1964	126	40¢	
The Jewels of Elsewhen	Belmont	B50-751	1967	172	50¢	
Lost in Space [as Ron Archer, with D. Van Arnam]						
	Pyramid	X1679	1967	157	60¢	
Phoenix Prime	Lancer	73-476	1966	189	60¢	
Sideslip [with D. Van Arnam]						
	Pyramid	X1787	1968	188	60¢	
The Sorceress of Qar	Lancer	73-528	1966	191	60¢	
The Spawn of the Death Machine						
	Paperback	53-680	1968	175	60¢	
WHITE, WILLIAM ANTHONY PARKER See BOUCHER, A. (pseud)						
WHITE, WILLIAM CHAPMAN (1903—1955)						
The Pale Blonde of Sands Street						
	Popular	EB8	1954	128	25¢	R
WHITFIELD, STEPHEN E.						
The Making of Star Trek [with G. Roddenberry]						
	Ballantine	73004	1968	414	95¢	N
WHITLEY, REID See BOY'S FRIEND LIBRARY, page 789.						
WHITMAN, S. H. See HALDEMAN-JULIUS CO., page 790.						
WHITTEN, LESLIE H(UNTER) (1928—)						
Progeny of the Adder	Ace	H-53	1968	189	60¢	R
WHITTINGTON, HARRY						
The Doomsday Affair	Ace	G-560	1965	159	50¢	
WHRITENOUR, JEAN See STEIGER, B. (co-author)						
WIBBERLEY, LEONARD (1915—)						
See also MONTREAL STAR, page 790.						
A Feast of Freedom	Bantam	F2983	1965	120	50¢	R
The Mouse on the Moon	Bantam	F2641	1963	124	50¢	R
	Bantam	FP104	1965	124	50¢	R
The Mouse That Roared	Bantam	A1982	1959	152	35¢	R
	Bantam	J2457	1962	152	40¢	R
	Bantam	EP80	1964	152	45¢	R
	Bantam	FP80	1968	152	50¢	R
	Corgi	723	1959	188	2/6	R
WILDE, OSCAR (1854—1900)						
See also HALDEMAN-JULIUS CO., page 790.						
The Happy Prince and Other Stories						
	Puffin	PS164	1968	186		C,R
The Picture of Dorian Grey	Penguin	616	1949	256	2/-	R
	Penguin	616	1961	248	2/6	R
	Penguin	616	1966	248	3/6	R
	Dell	681	1953	224	25¢	R
	Dell	D167	1956	224	35¢	R
	Dell	LB145	1960	224	35¢	R
	Dell	6914	1964	224	50¢	R
	Digit	G394	1961	316	3/6	R
	Pyramid	G584	1960		35¢	R
	Airmont	CL39	1964	221	50¢	R
The Picture of Dorian Grey and Other Selected Stories						
	Signet	CP115	1962	304	60¢	C,R
WILDING, PHILIP [as John R. Haynes]						
Scream From Outer Space	Panther	852	1958	160	2/6	R
WILHELM, KATE (1928—)						
The Clone [with T. L. Thomas]						
	Berkley	F1169	1965	143	50¢	
The Mile-Long Spaceship						
(also titled *Andover and the Android*)						
	Berkley	F862	1963	160	50¢	C
WILK, MAX						
Yellow Submarine	Signet	Q3632	1968	128	95¢	
WILKINS, HAROLD T. (1891—)						
Flying Saucers on the Attack						
	Ace	A-11	1967	319	75¢	N,R
Flying Saucers Uncensored	Pyramid	T1651	1967	270	75¢	N,R
Mysteries (originally *Strange Mysteries of Time and Space*)						
	Elek	Bestseller	1961	207	3/6	N,R
Strange Mysteries of Time and Space (also titled *Mysteries*)						
	Ace	H-12	1965	318	60¢	N,R
WILLEFORD, CHARLES (1918—)						
The Machine in Ward Eleven						
	Belmont	90-286	1963	141	40¢	C
	Consul	1309	1964	138	2/6	C,R
WILLIAMS, CHARLES (1886—1945)						
All Hallow's Eve	Noonday	247	1963	273	$1.75	R
Descent Into Hell	Eerdmans		1964	222	$1.95	R
The Greater Trumps	Noonday	N228	1962	268	$1.75	R
Many Dimensions	Penguin	884	1952	254	2/-	R
	Faber		1963	269	6/6	R
	Eerdmans		1965	269	$1.95	R
The Place of the Lion	Faber		1965	206	6/6	R
	Eerdmans		1965	206	$1.95	R
Shadows of Ecstasy	Eerdmans		1965	224	$1.95	R
	Faber		1965	224	7/6	R
War in Heaven	Faber		1962	256	6/-	R
	Eerdmans		1964	256	$1.95	R
Witchcraft	Meridian	M62	1959	316	$1.45	N,R
WILLIAMS, HERBERT (1914—)						
Avon Ghost Reader	Avon	90	1946	258	25¢	A
Terror at Night	Avon	110	1947	194	25¢	A
WILLIAMS, ISLWYN						
Newbury in Orm	Gryphon		1954	191	2/-	J,R
WILLIAMS, J. X. (pseud)						
Her	Leisure	LB1218	1967	160	60¢	
The Sex Pill See OFFUTT, A. J.						
Witch in Heat	Leisure	LB1206	1967		60¢	

Author and Title	Publisher	Serial	Date	Pp.	Price	Type
WILLIAMS, JAMES						
Objective Venus	Badger	SF4	1958	158	2/-	
WILLIAMS, JAY (1914—1978)						
Danny Dunn and the Anti-Gravity Paint [with Raymond Abrashkin]						
	Scholastic	TX158	1958	113		J,R
Danny Dunn and the Homework Machine [with Raymond Abrashkin]						
	Scholastic	TX303	1963	122	35¢	J,R
The Witches	Bantam	A1937	1959	276	35¢	R
	Panther	1549	1963	254	3/6	R
WILLIAMS, NICK BODDIE (1906—)						
Atom Curtain	Ace	D-139*	1956	168	35¢	
WILLIAMS, PAT [with D. Hill]						
The Supernatural	Signet	Q3256	1967	240	95¢	N
WILLIAMS, ROBERT MOORE (1907—1977)						
The Bell From Infinity	Lancer	73-766	1968	189	60¢	
The Blue Atom	Ace	D-322*	1958	124	35¢	
The Chaos Fighters	Ace	S-90	1955	160	25¢	
Conquest of the Space Sea	Ace	D-99*	1955	151	35¢	
The Darkness Before Tomorrow						
	Ace	F-141*	1962	118	40¢	
The Day They H-Bombed Los Angeles						
	Ace	D-530	1961	128	35¢	
Doomsday Eve	Ace	D-215*	1957	148	35¢	
Flight From Yesterday	Ace	F-223*	1963	120	40¢	
King of the Fourth Planet	Ace	F-149*	1962	120	40¢	
The Lunar Eye	Ace	F-261*	1964	115	40¢	
The Second Atlantis	Ace	F-335	1965	123	40¢	
The Star Wasps	Ace	F-177*	1963	126	40¢	
To the End of Time and Other Stories						
	Ace	D-427*	1960	108	35¢	C
Vigilante 21st Century	Lancer	73-644	1967	189	60¢	
The Void Beyond and Other Stories						
	Ace	D-322*	1958	130	35¢	C
World of the Masterminds	Ace	D-427*	1960	148	35¢	
Zanthar at Moon's Madness						
	Lancer	73-805	1968	189	60¢	
Zanthar at the Edge of Never						
	Lancer	74-941	1968	285	75¢	
Zanthar of the Many Worlds						
	Lancer	73-694	1967	192	60¢	
WILLIAMS, URSULA MORAY (1911—)						
The Moonball	Scholastic	TX1229	1968	159	50¢	J,R
WILLIAMSON, JACK [JOHN STEWART] (1908—)						
After World's End	Digit	R538	1961	156	2/6	R
	Digit	R671	1963	159	2/6	R
	Magabook	2*	1963	160	50¢	R
Bright New Universe	Ace	G-641	1967	158	50¢	
The Cometeers	Pyramid	X1634	1967	157	60¢	R
Darker Than You Think	Lancer	73-421	1963	223	60¢	R
Dome Around America	Ace	D-118*	1955	133	35¢	M
Dragon's Island (also titled *The Not-Men*)						
	Popular	447	1952	224	25¢	R
	Tower	43-531	1965	222	60¢	R
The Girl From Mars [with M. J. Breuer]						
	Stellar	SFS1	1929	24	10¢	
Golden Blood	Lancer	72-740	1964	157	50¢	M
	Lancer	73-630	1967	285	60¢	R
The Green Girl	Avon	FN2	1950	125	25¢	M
The Humanoids	Galaxy Nov	21	1954	128	35¢	R
	Lancer	74-812	1963	178	75¢	R
	Lancer	72-129	1966	178	50¢	R
Lady in Danger	Utopian	AF nn	nd	36	1/-	A
The Legion of Space	Galaxy Nov	2	1950	158	25¢	R
	Pyramid	X1576	1967	189	60¢	R

Author and Title	Publisher	Serial	Date	Pp.	Price	Type
The Legion of Time	Digit	R522	1961	156	2/6	R
	Digit	R703	1963	160	2/6	R
	Pyramid	X1586	1967	204	60¢	R
	Magabook	2*	1963	160	50¢	R
The Not-Men (originally *Dragon's Island*)						
	Tower	43957	1968	222	60¢	R
One Against the Legion	Pyramid	X1657	1967	220	60¢	C,R
The Reefs of Space [with F. Pohl]						
	Ballantine	U2172	1964	188	50¢	M
The Reign of Wizardry	Lancer	72-761	1964	142	50¢	M
	Lancer	73-748	1968	264	60¢	R
Seetee Ship [hardcover ed. under pseud. Will Stewart]						
	Lancer	73-732	1968	222	60¢	R
Seetee Shock [hardcover ed. under pseud. Will Stewart]						
	Lancer	73-733	1968	223	60¢	R
Star Bridge [with J. E. Gunn]						
	Ace	D-169	1956	255	35¢	R
	Ace	F-241	1963	255	50¢	R
Starchild [with F. Pohl]	Ballantine	U2176	1965	191	50¢	M
Trapped in Space	Semaphore	22484	1968	144	$1.75	R
The Trial of Terra	Ace	D-555	1962	159	35¢	
WILLSON, W. See BOY'S FRIEND LIBRARY, page 789.						
WILSON, ANGUS (1913—)						
The Old Men at the Zoo	Penguin	2079	1964	345	5/-	R
WILSON, COLIN (1931—)						
The Mind Parasites	Bantam	F3905	1968	197	50¢	R
WILSON, G. M.						
Nightmare Cottage	Digit	R834	1964	160	2/6	
Shadows on the Landing	Digit	R763	1963	160	2/6	
Witchwater	Digit	R722	1963	160	2/6	
WILSON, JOHN BURGESS (1917—) [as Anthony Burgess]						
A Clockwork Orange	Norton	N224	1963	184	95¢	R
	Ballantine	U5032	1965	191	60¢	R
	Pan	X321	1964	189	3/6	R
The Wanting Seed	Ballantine	U5030	1964	223	60¢	R
	Pan	X384	1965	206	3/6	R
WILSON, RAYMOND See BARTER, A. F. (co-anthologist)						
WILSON, RICHARD (1920—)						
And Then the Town Took Off						
	Ace	D-437*	1960	123	35¢	M
The Girls From Planet 5	Ballantine	117	1955	184	35¢	
(identical hardcover edition $2.00)						
	Lancer	73-550	1967	223	60¢	R
30-Day Wonder	Ballantine	434K	1960	158	35¢	
	Icon	SF2	1963	158	3/6	R
Those Idiots From Earth	Ballantine	237	1957	160	35¢	C
Time Out for Tomorrow	Ballantine	F658	1962	159	50¢	C
	Mayflower	8914	1967	141	3/6	C,R
WINFIELD, DICK (pseud of Dick Perry [1922—])						
Up-Tight	Paperback	52-605	1967	176	50¢	R
WINSOR, FREDERICK (1900—1958)						
The Space Child's Mother Goose						
	Simon & Schuster		1958	45	$1.45	R
WINSOR, KATHLEEN						
The Lovers	Signet		1955	320	50¢	R
	Corgi	711	1959	384	3/6	R
WINSTON, D.						
Sinister Stone	Paperback	52-975	1966	159	50¢	
The Wakefield Witches	Award	185X	1966	176	60¢	

Author and Title	Publisher	Serial	Date	Pp.	Price	Type
WINTERBOTHAM, R(USSELL) R(OBERT) (1904—1971)						
The Man From Arcturus	Consul	1418	1965	172	3/6	R
The Other World [as J. Harvey Bond]						
	Mayflower	6746	1964	127	2/6	R
Planet Big Zero [as Franklin Hadley]						
	Monarch	431	1964	126	40¢	
The Red Planet	Monarch	270	1962	140	35¢	
The Space Egg	Monarch	252	1962	140	35¢	R
WISE, HERBERT A. (1893?—1961) [with Phyllis Fraser]						
Great Tales of Terror and the Supernatural						
	Omnibook		ca.1945			A,R
WISE, ROBERT A.						
Twelve to the Moon	Badger	SF59	1961	158	2/6	
WOBIG, ELLEN (1911—)						
The Youth Monopoly	Ace	H-48*	1968	114	60¢	
WOLFE, BERNARD (1915—)						
Limbo (also titled *Limbo 90*)	Ace	A-3	1963	413	75¢	R
Limbo 90 [abr.] (originally *Limbo*)						
	Penguin	1647	1961	367	5/-	R
WOLLHEIM, DONALD A. (1914—)						
Across Time [as David Grinnell]						
	Ace	D-286*	1958	150	35¢	R
	Ace	G-728	1968	150	50¢	R
Adventures in the Far Future						
	Ace	D-73*	1954	177	35¢	A
Adventures on Other Planets						
	Ace	S-133	1955	160	25¢	A
	Ace	D-490	1961	160	35¢	A,R
Destination: Saturn [as David Grinnell, with Lin Carter]						
	Ace	H-85*	1968	107	60¢	R
Destiny's Orbit [as David Grinnell]						
	Ace	F-161*	1962	114	40¢	R
The Earth in Peril	Ace	D-205*	1957	158	35¢	A
The Edge of Time [as David Grinnell]						
	Ace	D-362*	1959	145	35¢	R
	Ace	M-162	1967	143	45¢	R
The End of the World	Ace	S-183	1956	159	25¢	A
Flight Into Space	Kemsley	CT403	1951	190	1/6	A,R
The Girl With the Hungry Eyes and Other Stories						
	Avon	184	1949	127	25¢	A
The Hidden Planet	Ace	D-354	1959	190	35¢	A
The Macabre Reader	Ace	D-353	1959	223	35¢	A
	Digit	D362	1960	188	2/-	A,R
The Martian Missile [as David Grinnell]						
	Ace	D-465*	1960	127	35¢	R
Men on the Moon	Ace	D-277*	1958	137	35¢	A
Mike Mars and the Mystery Satellite						
	Paperback	56-369	1966	128	45¢	J,R
Mike Mars Around the Moon						
	Paperback	56-383	1966	125	45¢	J,R
Mike Mars, Astronaut	Paperback	56-968	1966	128	45¢	J,R
Mike Mars at Cape Kennedy						
	Paperback	56-981	1966	128	45¢	J,R
Mike Mars Flies the Dyna-Soar						
	Paperback	56-340	1966	128	45¢	J,R
Mike Mars Flies the X-15	Paperback	56-972	1966	125	45¢	J,R
Mike Mars in Orbit	Paperback	56-998	1966	127	45¢	J,R
Mike Mars, South Pole Spaceman						
	Paperback	56-358	1966	126	45¢	J,R
More Adventures on Other Planets						
	Ace	F-178	1963	190	40¢	A
More Macabre	Ace	D-508	1961	192	35¢	A
More Terror in the Modern Vein (selections from *Terror in the Modern*						
Vein)	Digit	R508	1961	156	2/6	A,R
The Pocket Book of Science-Fiction						
	Pocket Bks	214	1943	310	25¢	A
The Secret of Saturn's Rings						
	Paperback	52-996	1966	159	50¢	J,R
The Secret of the Martian Moons						
	Tempo	T28	1963	191	50¢	J,R
The Secret of the Ninth Planet						
	Paperback	52-874	1965	154	50¢	J,R
Swordsmen in the Sky	Ace	F-311	1964	192	40¢	A
Tales of Outer Space	Ace	D-73*	1954	140	35¢	A
Terror in the Modern Vein (selections from hardcover; see also *More Terror in the Modern Vein*)	Digit	R460	1961	156	2/6	A
The Ultimate Invader and Other Science Fiction						
	Ace	D-44*	1954	139	35¢	A
World's Best Science Fiction: 1965 [with Terry Carr]						
	Ace	G-551	1965	288	50¢	A
World's Best Science Fiction: 1966 [with Terry Carr]						
	Ace	H-15	1966	287	60¢	A
World's Best Science Fiction: 1967 [with Terry Carr]						
	Ace	A-10	1967	285	75¢	A
World's Best Science Fiction: 1968 [with Terry Carr]						
	Ace	A-15	1968	319	75¢	A
WOOD, CHARLES E. S. (1852—1944)						
Heavenly Discourse	Penguin-U.S.	594	1946	252	25¢	R
WOOD, EDWARD D., Jr.						
Orgy of the Dead	Greenleaf	GC205	1966	160		
WOOD, ERIC See BOY'S FRIEND LIBRARY, page 789.						
WOODCOTT, KEITH (pseud) See BRUNNER, J.						
WOODMAN, T. E.						
Britain in the Ice Grip	Pearson		ca.1945	64	np	
WOOLF, VIRGINIA (1882—1941)						
Orlando: A Biography	Penguin	381	1942			R
	Penguin	381	1963	234	3/6	R
	Penguin-U.S.	590	1946	216	25¢	R
	Signet	CD18	1960	224	50¢	R
WOOLRICH, CORNELL (1906—1968)						
After-Dinner Story [as William Irish]						
	Armed	s-20	nd	318	np	R
Beyond the Night	Avon	T354	1959	160	35¢	C
The Doom Stone	Avon	T408	1960	159	35¢	M
The Night Has a Thousand Eyes [as George Hopley]						
	Zephyr	169	1948	278	np	R
	Dell	679	1953	288	35¢	R
Savage Bride	Gold Medal	?	nd	160	25¢	
	Gold Medal	136	1950	178	25¢	R
WORKMAN, JAMES						
Horror Tales [as James Dark]						
	Horwitz	PB138	1963	130	3/9	C
Operation Octopus [as James Dark]						
	Signet	P3303	1968	125	60¢	
Operation Scuba [as James Dark]						
	Signet		1967	125		
Shock Stories	Horwitz	PB119	1962	130	3/9	C
Terrifying Tales [as James Dark]						
	Horwitz	PB129	1962	130	3/9	C
Throne of Satan [as James Dark]						
	Signet	P3185	1967	128	60¢	
The Witch Hunters	Horwitz	PB149	1963	129	4/-	
WORMSER, RICHARD (1908—)						
Pan Satyrus	Avon	G1191	1963	144	50¢	

Author and Title	Publisher	Serial	Date	Pp.	Price	Type
WORTS, GEORGE F. (1892—)						
The Monster of the Lagoon Swan			1947	96	1/-	M
WOUK, HERMAN (1915—)						
The "Lomokome" Papers Pocket Bks		75226	1968	113	75¢	R
WRAY, REGINALD See BOY'S FRIEND LIBRARY, page 789.						
WRIGHT, AUSTIN TAPPAN (1883—1931)						
Islandia	Signet	Y2870	1966	944	$1.25	R
WRIGHT, HARRY B.						
Witness to Witchcraft	Corgi	S615	1958	221	2/6	N
	Corgi	GG1483	1964	191	3/6	N,R
WRIGHT, LAN [LIONEL] (1923—)						
Assignment Luther	Digit	R686	1963	158	2/6	M
The Creeping Shroud (originally *The Last Hope of Earth*)						
	Compact	F293	1966	190	3/6	R
Exile From Xanadu	Ace	M-103*	1964	137	45¢	M
The Last Hope of Earth (also titled *The Creeping Shroud*)						
	Ace	F-347	1965	159	40¢	
A Man Called Destiny	Ace	D-311*	1958	128	35¢	
	Digit	R514	1961	160	2/6	R
	Digit	R785	1963	160	2/6	R
The Pictures of Pavanne Ace		H-48*	1968	139	60¢	
Who Speaks of Conquest? Ace		D-205*	1957	160	35¢	M
	Digit	R490	1961	156	2/6	R
	Digit	R742	1963	159	2/6	R
WRIGHT, LEE [with Richard G. Sheehan]						
These Will Chill You	Bantam	H3206	1967	168	60¢	A
Wake Up Screaming	Bantam	H2950	1967	213	60¢	A
WRIGHT, S(YDNEY) FOWLER (1874—1965)						
The Amphibians (Part I of hardcover *The World Below*)						
	Galaxy Nov	4	1951	126	25¢	R
Deluge	Cher. Tree					R
The Dwellers (originally *The Amphibians*, Part I of *The World Below*)						
	Panther	nn	1954	127	1/6	R
The Island of Captain Sparrow						
	Penguin	507	1945	192	1/-	R
	Regal	101	1953	174	2/-	R
Power	Bay Tree	2	nd	256	6d	R
The Screaming Lake	Regal	102	1953	175	2/-	R
Two Famous Stories: Justice, The Rat						
	Books of Today	nd		36	1/-	C,R
The World Below (Part II of hardcover; see also *The Amphibians* and						
The Dwellers) Galaxy Nov		5	1951	121	25¢	R
	Panther	44	1953	160	1/6	R
WULFF, EVE See QUINN, J. L. (co-author)						
WYLIE, PHILIP (1902—1971)						
After Worlds Collide [with Edwin Balmer]						
	Paperback	52-255	1963	190	50¢	R
The Answer	Paperback	52-205	1963	91	50¢	R
The Disappearance	Cardinal	C40	1952	384	35¢	R
	Pocket Bks	75147	1966	384	75¢	R
Gladiator	Avon	216	1949	187	35¢	R
	Avon	T-155		187	35¢	R
	Lancer	72-937	1965	191	50¢	R
	Lancer	73-562	1967	191	60¢	R
The Murderer Invisible Popular		60-2209	1967	205	60¢	R
Night Unto Night	Armed	774	nd	447	np	R
	Signet	830	1950	190	25¢	R
	Popular	W1132	1964	349	75¢	R
The Savage Gentleman	Dell	85	1945	337	25¢	R
	Avon	390	1951	155	25¢	R

Author and Title	Publisher	Serial	Date	Pp.	Price	Type
Selected Short Stories of Philip Wylie						
	Armed	s-8	nd		np	C
The Smuggled Atom Bomb Avon		727	1957	126	25¢	R
	Lancer	72-916	1965	142	50¢	R
Tomorrow!	Popular	G156	1956	288	35¢	R
	Popular	PC1005	1961	288	50¢	R
	Popular	M2035	1963	288	60¢	R
Triumph	Crest	R675	1964	240	60¢	R
	Crest	R1033	1967	240	60¢	R
When Worlds Collide [with Edwin Balmer]						
	Armed	801	nd	384	np	R
	Dell	627	1953	255	25¢	R
	Paperback	52-180	1962	192	50¢	R
	Paperback	52-521	1965	192	50¢	R
WYNDHAM, JOHN (pseud) See HARRIS, J. B.						

Y,Z

Author and Title	Publisher	Serial	Date	Pp.	Price	Type
YORKE, JACQUELINE						
Brides of the Devil	Fawcett	136	1950	178	25¢	R
YORKE, PRESTON						
The Gamma Ray Murders Everybody's			nd	128	2/-	
Space-Time Task Force Hector Kelly			1953	192	1/6	
(identical hardcover edition 6/-)						
YOUD, CHRISTOPHER S. (1922—) [as John Christopher]						
Cloud on Silver (originally *Sweeney's Island*)						
	Hodder	796	1966	256	3/6	R
The Death of Grass (also titled *No Blade of Grass*)						
	Penguin	1300	1958	185	2/6	R
	Penguin	1300	1963	191	3/-	R
The Little People	Avon	V2243	1968	224	75¢	R
The Long Winter (also titled *The World in Winter*)						
	Crest	d612	1963	208	50¢	R
	Gold Medal	R2001	1968	208	60¢	R
No Blade of Grass (also titled *The Death of Grass*)						
	Pocket Bks	1183	1958	184	25¢	R
	Avon	S288	1967	190	60¢	R
Planet in Peril (originally *The Year of the Comet*)						
	Avon	T371	1959	159	35¢	M
The Possessors	Avon	S230	1966	207	60¢	R
	Hodder	812	1966	220	3/6	R
The Ragged Edge (also titled *A Wrinkle in the Skin*)						
	Signet	P3124	1967	192	60¢	R
Sweeney's Island (also titled *Cloud on Silver*)						
	Crest	R1029	1967	207	60¢	R
The Twenty-Second Century						
	Panther	1142	1960	191	2/6	C,R
	Lancer	74-811	1962	190	75¢	C,R
The World in Winter (originally *The Long Winter*)						
	Penguin	2131	1964	205	3/6	R
	Penguin	2131	1965	205	3/6	R
A Wrinkle in the Skin (originally *The Ragged Edge*)						
	Hodder	02716	1968	220	3/6	R
YOUNG, F. H. R.						
The Talking Skull	Wells Gardner		1947	128	1/-	C
YOUNG, F. W. See NUGGET LIBRARY, page 790.						

Author and Title	Publisher	Serial	Date	Pp.	Price	Type
YOUNG, M.						
The Rise of the Meritocracy 1870-2033						
	Pelican	A485	1961	190	3/6	N
YOUNG, ROBERT F. (1915—)						
The Worlds of Robert F. Young						
	Panther	024034	1968	187	5/-	C,R
ZACHERLE, JOHN C. (1919—) [as Zacherley]						
Zacherley's Midnight Snacks						
	Ballantine	370K	1960	157	35¢	A
	Ballantine	556	1961	157	35¢	A,R
Zacherley's Vulture Stew						
	Ballantine	417K	1960	160	35¢	A
	Ballantine	574	1962	160	35¢	A,R
ZACHERLEY (pseud) See ZACHERLE, J. C.						
ZAMIATIN, EUGENE (1884—1937)						
We	Everyman-Dutt.	D39	1959	218	$1.45	R

Author and Title	Publisher	Serial	Date	Pp.	Price	Type
ZEIGFREID, KURT (house pseudonym, used mostly by R. L. Fanthorpe, *q.v.*; authorship of following not known)						
Beyond the Galaxy	Spencer		1953	112	1/6	
Chaos in Arcturus	Spencer		1953	124	1/6	
Chariot Into Time	Spencer		1953	128	1/6	
ZELAZNY, ROGER (1937—)						
The Dream Master	Ace	F-403	1966	155	40¢	M
	Panther	026304	1968	157	5/-	R
Four for Tomorrow	Ace	M-155	1966	191	45¢	C
This Immortal	Ace	F-393	1966	174	40¢	M
	Panther	025316	1968	187	5/-	R
ZIM, H. S.						
Rockets and Jets	Armed	960	nd		np	N
ZORRO (pseud) See WARD, H.						
ZUGSMITH, ALBERT [with R. Hill]						
The Private Lives of Adam and Eve						
	Bantam	A2055	1960	153	35¢	

Paperback Publishers

Introduction

Each publisher's heading block gives the company's name, location, and other information. This is followed by the publisher or imprint abbreviation (as used in the *AUTHORS* section), and then the listing of titles for that imprint. Where one publisher has several imprints, they are listed in the heading block, and the titles are grouped under the appropriate imprint abbreviation. Cross-references are given for publisher and imprint abbreviations that are alphabetically different from the publisher's name.

The publisher's serial number (order code), if any, is given for each edition, where known. Some publishers (notably Ace and Belmont) have issued books containing two titles, with one serial number for the book as a whole. These are indicated by using "do" ["ditto"] for the number of the second title. (These "doubles" are indicated in the *AUTHORS* section by an asterisk [*] after the serial number of each title.)

The main *PUBLISHERS* section is followed by a brief section of *Ephemerals*: publishers' series outside the normal run. These are listed in the *TITLES* section, with the notation *Eph.*, but are not listed in the *AUTHORS* section. Instead, there are "see also" notes under each author, referring to the publisher and page number in *Ephemerals*.

A

ACE BOOKS, INC., New York, N.Y., U.S.A.

Serial number prefixes: S- 25¢; D- 35¢; T- 35¢; F- 40¢; M- 45¢; G- 50¢; K- 50¢; H- 60¢; A- 75¢; N- 95¢.

Some serial numbers in the Authors section are followed by an asterisk, e.g., D-36*; this indicates that the title is one part of an "Ace Double," consisting of two novels bound back to back and upside down with respect to each other. In effect, the "double" has two front covers and no back cover. Doubles are indicated below by "do" (ditto) instead of repeating the serial code for the second novel.

Some books use the designation 'Star' on early K- and T- series of the late 1950's.

Ace

1953

D-13	Drachman, T. S.	**Cry Plague!**
do	Edgley, L.	**The Judas Goat**
D-31	van Vogt, A. E.	**The Universe Maker**
do	van Vogt, A. E.	**The World of Null-A**
D-36	Howard, R. E.	**Conan the Conqueror**
do	Brackett, L.	**The Sword of Rhiannon**
D-43	Viereck, G. S., & Eldridge, P.	
		Salome

1954

D-44	Russell, E. F.	**Sentinels From Space** (*Sentinels of Space* on cover)
do	Wollheim, D. A.	**The Ultimate Invader**
D-53	Leinster, M.	**Gateway to Elsewhere**
do	van Vogt, A. E.	**The Weapon Shops of Isher**
D-61	de Camp, L. S.	**Cosmic Manhunt**
do	Simak, C. D.	**Ring Around the Sun**
D-69	Padgett, L., & Moore, C. L.	
		Beyond Earth's Gates
do	Norton, Andre	**Daybreak—2250 A.D.**
D-73	Wollheim, D. A.	**Adventures in the Far Future**
do	Wollheim, D. A.	**Tales of Outer Space**
D-79	Bellamy, F. R.	**Atta**
do	Leinster, M.	**The Brain Stealers**
D-84	Dee, R.	**An Earth Gone Mad**
do	Asimov, I.	**The Rebellious Stars**
S-66	Hubbard, L. R.	**Return to Tomorrow**

1955

D-94	van Vogt, A. E.	**One Against Eternity**
do	Leinster, M.	**The Other Side of Here**
D-96	Norton, Andre	**The Last Planet**
do	Nourse, A. E.	**A Man Obsessed**
D-99	Williams, R. M.	**Conquest of the Space Sea**
do	Brackett, L.	**The Galactic Breed**
D-103	Brackett, L.	**The Big Jump**
do	Dick, P. K.	**Solar Lottery**
D-110	Anderson, P.	**No World of Their Own**
do	Asimov, I.	**The 1,000-Year Plan**
D-113	McIntosh, J. T.	**One in 300**
do	Swain, D. V.	**The Transposed Man**
D-118	Williamson, J.	**Dome Around America**
do	Harness, C. L.	**The Paradox Men**
D-121	Norton, Andre	**The Stars Are Ours**
do	Merwin, S.	**Three Faces of Time**
D-125	Asimov, I.	**The Man Who Upset the Universe**
S-90	Williams, R. M.	**The Chaos Fighters**
S-133	Wollheim, D. A.	**Adventures on Other Planets**

1956

D-139	Dickson, G. R.	**Alien From Arcturus**
do	Williams, N. B.	**Atom Curtain**

D-146	Correy, L.	**Contraband Rocket**
do	Leinster, M.	**The Forgotten Planet**
D-150	St. Clair, M.	**Agent of the Unknown**
do	Dick, P. K.	**The World Jones Made**
D-155	Verne, J.	**A Journey to the Center of the Earth**
D-162	Miller, R. D., & Hunger, A.	
		The Man Who Lived Forever
do	Sohl, J.	**The Mars Monopoly**
D-164	Norton, Andre	**The Crossroads of Time**
do	Dickson, G. R.	**Mankind on the Run**
D-169	Williamson, J., & Gunn, J. E.	
		Star Bridge
D-173	Cummings, R.	**The Man Who Mastered Time**
do	Kelleam, J. E.	**Overlords From Space**
D-176	St. Clair, M.	**The Green Queen**
do	McClary, T. C.	**Three Thousand Years**
D-187	van Vogt, A. E.	**The Pawns of Null-A**
D-193	Dick, P. K.	**The Man Who Japed**
do	Tubb, E. C.	**The Space-Born**
D-199	Anderson, P.	**Planet of No Return**
do	Norton, Andre	**Star Guard**
D-200	Ruppelt, E. J.	**The Report on Unidentified Flying Objects**
S-183	Wollheim, D. A.	**The End of the World**

1957

D-205	Wollheim, D. A.	**The Earth in Peril**
do	Wright, L.	**Who Speaks of Conquest?**
D-211	Dick, P. K.	**Eye in the Sky**
D-215	Williams, R. M.	**Doomsday Eve**
do	Russell, E. F.	**Three to Conquer**
D-223	Silverberg, R.	**The 13th Immortal**
do	Gunn, J. E.	**This Fortress World**
D-227	Piper, H. B., & McGuire, J. J.	
		Crisis in 2140
do	Judd, Cyril	**Gunner Cade**
D-233	Gordon, Rex	**First on Mars**
D-237	Silverberg, R.	**Master of Life and Death**
do	White, James	**The Secret Visitors**
D-239	Stine, G. H.	**Earth Satellites and the Race for Space Superiority**
D-242	van Vogt, A. E.	**Empire of the Atom**
do	Long, F. B.	**Space Station No. 1**
D-245	Verne, J.	**Off on a Comet**
D-249	Dick, P. K.	**The Cosmic Puppets**
do	North, A.	**Sargasso of Space**
D-255	Bulmer, K.	**City Under the Sea**
do	Anderson, P.	**Star Ways**
D-261	Dick, P. K.	**The Variable Man and Other Stories**

1958

D-265	Bloch, R.	**The Shooting Star**
do	Bloch, R.	**Terror in the Night**
D-266	Tubb, E. C.	**The Mechanical Monarch**
do	Fontenay, C. L.	**Twice Upon a Time**
D-274	Maine, C. E.	**World Without Men**
D-277	Leinster, M.	**City on the Moon**
do	Wollheim, D. A.	**Men on the Moon**
D-283	Simak, C. D.	**City**
D-286	Grinnell, D.	**Across Time**
do	Silverberg, R.	**Invaders From Earth**
D-291	Knox, C. M.	**Lest We Forget Thee, Earth**
do	Gallun, R. Z.	**People Minus X**
D-295	Vance, J.	**Big Planet**
do	Vance, J.	**Slaves of the Klau**
D-299	Piper, H. B., & McGuire, J. J.	
		A Planet for Texans
do	Norton, Andre	**Star Born**
D-303	Anderson, P.	**The Snows of Ganymede**
do	Anderson, P.	**War of the Wing-Men**
D-309	Wells, H. G.	**The Island of Dr. Moreau**
D-311	Wright, L.	**A Man Called Destiny**
do	Silverberg, R.	**Stepsons of Terra**
D-315	Russell, E. F.	**Six Worlds Yonder**
do	Russell, E. F.	**The Space Willies**

D-322	Williams, R. M.	The Blue Atom
do	Williams, R. M.	The Void Beyond and Other Stories
D-324	Cummings, R.	Brigands of the Moon
D-327	Sutton, J.	First on the Moon
D-331	Cummings, R.	Beyond the Vanishing Point
do	Bulmer, K.	The Secret of ZI
1959		
D-335	Brunner, J.	Threshold of Eternity
do	Anderson, P.	The War of Two Worlds
D-339	Simak, C. D.	Ring Around the Sun
D-340	Dick, P. K.	Solar Lottery
D-345	North, A.	Plague Ship
do	North, A.	Voodoo Planet
D-350	Bryant, P.	Red Alert
D-351	Jorgenson, I.	Starhaven
do	Hamilton, E.	The Sun Smasher
D-353	Wollheim, D. A.	The Macabre Reader
D-354	Wollheim, D. A.	The Hidden Planet
D-358	Knox, C. M.	The Plot Against Earth
do	Lesser, M.	Recruit for Andromeda
D-359	Cooper, J. C.	The Haunted Strangler
D-362	Grinnell, D.	The Edge of Time
do	Brunner, J.	The 100th Millennium
D-366	Nourse, A. E., & Meyer, J. A.	
		The Invaders Are Coming
D-369	Bulmer, K.	The Changeling Worlds
do	Aldiss, B. W.	Vanguard From Alpha
D-375	Smith, G. O.	Fire in the Heavens
do	Knight, D.	Masters of Evolution
D-377	Sutton, J.	Bombs in Orbit
D-381	Sohl, J.	One Against Herculum
do	Norton, Andre	Secret of the Lost Race
D-385	Brunner, J.	Echo in the Skull
do	Nourse, A. E.	Rocket to Limbo
D-388	Wells, H. G.	When the Sleeper Wakes
D-391	van Vogt, A. E.	Siege of the Unseen
do	Brunner, J.	The World Swappers
D-397	Verne, J.	A Journey to the Center of the Earth
D-403	Leinster, M.	The Mutant Weapon
do	Leinster, M.	The Pirates of Zan
D-405	Gordon, R.	First to the Stars
D-407	Silverberg, R.	The Planet Killers
do	Anderson, P.	We Claim These Stars
D-413	Ellison, H.	The Man With Nine Lives
do	Ellison, H.	A Touch of Infinity
K-117	Edwards, K.	Stranger Than Science
1960		
D-421	Dick, P. K.	Dr. Futurity
do	Brunner, J.	Slavers of Space
D-422	Boucher, A., & McComas, J. F.	
		The Best From Fantasy and Science Fiction, Third Series
D-427	Williams, R. M.	To the End of Time and Other Stories
do	Williams, R. M.	World of the Masterminds
D-431	van Vogt, A. E.	Earth's Last Fortress
do	Smith, G. O.	Lost in Space
D-434	Verne, J.	The Purchase of the North Pole
D-437	Wilson, R.	And Then the Town Took Off
do	Norton, Andre	The Sioux Spaceman
D-443	Aldiss, B. W.	Bow Down to Nul
do	Wellman, M. W.	The Dark Destroyers
D-449	Dickson, G. R.	The Genetic General
do	Dickson, G. R.	Time to Teleport
D-453	Bulmer, K.	The Earth Gods Are Coming
do	St. Clair, M.	The Games of Neith
D-455	Boucher, A.	The Best From Fantasy and Science Fiction, Fourth Series
D-457	Brunner, J.	The Skynappers
do	Dick, P. K.	Vulcan's Hammer
D-461	Norton, Andre	The Time Traders
D-465	Brunner, J.	The Atlantic Abomination
do	Grinnell, D.	The Martian Missile
D-467	Anderson, W. C.	Five, Four, Three, Two, One—Pffff
D-468	Russell, E. F.	Sentinels of Space
D-471	Brunner, J.	Sanctuary in the Sky
do	Sharkey, J.	The Secret Martians
D-473	Taine, J.	The Greatest Adventure
D-478	Sutton, J.	Spacehive
D-479	Anderson, P.	Earthman, Go Home!
do	Tucker, W.	To the Tombaugh Station
D-482	van Vogt, A. E.	The Weapon Shops of Isher
K-110	Kirst, H. H.	The Seventh Day
K-113	Duthie, E.	Tall Short Stories
1961		
D-485	Biggle, L.	The Angry Espers
do	Lowndes, R. A. W.	The Puzzle Planet
D-490	Wollheim, D. A.	Adventures on Other Planets
D-491	Leiber, F.	The Big Time
do	Leiber, F.	The Mind Spider and Other Stories
D-497	Woodcott, K.	I Speak for Earth
do	Cummings, R.	Wandl, the Invader
D-498	Norton, Andre	Galactic Derelict
D-504	Verne, J.	Master of the World [includes *Robur the Conqueror*]
D-507	Bulmer, K.	Beyond the Silver Sky
do	Brunner, J.	Meeting at Infinity
D-508	Wollheim, D. A.	More Macabre
D-509	Norton, Andre	The Beast Master
do	Norton, Andre	Star Hunter
D-516	Kline, O. A.	The Swordsman of Mars
D-517	Chandler, A. B.	Bring Back Yesterday
do	Simak, C. D.	The Trouble With Tycho
D-525	Leinster, M.	This World Is Taboo
D-527	Norton, Andre	Star Guard
D-528	Leinster, M.	The Forgotten Planet
D-530	Williams, R. M.	The Day They H-Bombed Los Angeles
D-531	Kline, O. A.	The Outlaws of Mars
D-534	Norton, Andre	Daybreak—2250 A.D.
F-104	Anderson, P.	Mayday Orbit
do	Bulmer, K.	No Man's World
F-105	Boucher, A.	The Best From Fantasy and Science Fiction, Fifth Series
F-108	Wallis, G. McD.	The Light of Lilith
do	Knight, D.	The Sun Saboteurs
F-109	Norton, Andre	Storm Over Warlock
F-113	Fontenay, C. L.	Rebels of the Red Planet
do	McIntosh, J. T.	200 Years to Christmas
F-114	West, W.	The Bird of Time
F-117	Bradley, M. Z.	The Door Through Space
do	Chandler, A. B.	Rendezvous on a Lost World
F-119	Dickson, G. R.	Delusion World
do	Dickson, G. R.	Spacial Delivery
F-123	Silverberg, R.	Collision Course
do	Brackett, L.	Nemesis From Terra
1962		
D-535	Cummings, R.	The Shadow Girl
D-538	Asimov, I.	The 1,000-Year Plan
D-541	Nourse, A. E.	Scavengers in Space
D-542	Norton, Andre	The Last Planet
D-544	Long, F. B.	Space Station No. 1
D-546	Norton, Andre	The Crossroads of Time
D-547	Brunner, J.	The Super Barbarians
D-548	Owen, D.	The End of the World
D-550	Anderson, P.	No World of Their Own
D-553	Hodgson, W. H.	The House on the Borderland
D-555	Williamson, J.	The Trial of Terra
F-127	Bradley, M. Z.	Seven From the Stars
do	Laumer, K.	Worlds of the Imperium
F-129	Temple, W. F.	The Automated Goliath
do	Temple, W. F.	The Three Suns of Amara
F-131	Boucher, A.	The Best From Fantasy and Science Fiction, Sixth Series
F-133	Chandler, A. B.	The Rim of Space
do	Brunner, J.	Secret Agent of Terra

F-135	Brackett, L.	The Long Tomorrow
F-137	Miller, R. D.	Impossible—Yet It Happened
F-139	Anderson, P.	The Makeshift Rocket
do	Anderson, P.	Un-Man and Other Novellas
F-141	Williams, R. M.	The Darkness Before Tomorrow
do	Woodcott, K.	The Ladder in the Sky
F-145	Silverberg, R.	Next Stop the Stars
do	Silverberg, R.	The Seed of Earth
F-147	Norton, Andre	Eye of the Monster
do	Norton, Andre	Sea Siege
F-149	De Vet, C., & MacLean, K.	
		Cosmic Checkmate
do	Williams, R. M.	King of the Fourth Planet
F-153	Bradley, M. Z.	The Planet Savers
do	Bradley, M. Z.	The Sword of Aldones
F-154	van Vogt, A. E.	The Wizard of Linn
F-156	Burroughs, E. R.	At the Earth's Core
F-157	Burroughs, E. R.	The Moon Maid
F-158	Burroughs, E. R.	Pellucidar
F-159	Burroughs, E. R.	The Moon Men
F-161	Grinnell, D.	Destiny's Orbit
do	Brunner, J.	Times Without Number
F-162	Boucher, A.	The Best From Fantasy and Science Fiction, Seventh Series
F-165	Farmer, P. J.	Cache From Outer Space
do	Farmer, P. J.	The Celestial Blueprint
F-167	Norton, Andre	Catseye
F-168	Burroughs, E. R.	Thuvia, Maid of Mars
F-169	Burroughs, E. R.	Tarzan and the Lost Empire
F-170	Burroughs, E. R.	The Chessmen of Mars
F-171	Burroughs, E. R.	Tanar of Pellucidar
F-173	Delany, S. R.	The Jewels of Aptor
do	White, J.	Second Ending
F-174	Gordon, R.	First Through Time
K-144	Edwards, F.	Strangest of All
K-149	Mundy, T.	Queen Cleopatra
K-154	Stewart, G. R.	Earth Abides
K-156	Fort, C.	The Book of the Damned
K-160	Endore, G.	The Werewolf of Paris
1963		
A-3	Wolfe, B.	Limbo
D-568	Anderson, P.	Star Ways
F-177	Williams, R. M.	The Star Wasps
do	Carr, T.	Warlord of Kor
F-178	Wollheim, D. A.	More Adventures on Other Planets
F-179	Burroughs, E. R.	Pirates of Venus
F-180	Burroughs, E. R.	Tarzan at the Earth's Core
F-181	Burroughs, E. R.	Master Mind of Mars
F-182	Burroughs, E. R.	The Monster Men
F-183	Norton, Andre	The Defiant Agents
F-185	Vance, J.	The Dragon Masters
do	Vance, J.	The Five Gold Bands
F-187	Brackett, L.	Alpha Centauri or Die!
do	Wallis, G. McD.	Legend of Lost Earth
F-188	Nowlan, P.	Armageddon 2419 A.D.
F-189	Burroughs, E. R.	Tarzan the Invincible
F-190	Burroughs, E. R.	A Fighting Man of Mars
F-191	Verne, J.	A Journey to the Center of the Earth
F-192	Norton, Andre	Star Born
F-193	Burroughs, E. R.	Son of Tarzan
F-194	Burroughs, E. R.	Tarzan Triumphant
F-195	Temple, W. F.	Battle on Venus
do	Silverberg, R.	The Silent Invaders
F-197	Norton, Andre	Witch World
F-199	Delany, S. R.	Captives of the Flame
do	Woodcott, K.	The Psionic Menace
F-201	MacTyre, P.	Doomsday, 1999
F-203	Burroughs, E. R.	The Beasts of Tarzan
F-204	Burroughs, E. R.	Tarzan and the Jewels of Opar
F-205	Burroughs, E. R.	Tarzan and the City of Gold
F-206	Burroughs, E. R.	Jungle Tales of Tarzan
F-207	Norton, Andre	The Stars Are Ours
F-209	Anderson, P.	Let the Spacemen Beware!
do	Bulmer, K.	The Wizard of Starship Poseidon
F-210	Bryant, P.	Red Alert
F-211	Kline, O. A.	The Planet of Peril
F-212	Burroughs, E. R.	Tarzan and the Lion Man
F-213	Burroughs, E. R.	The Land That Time Forgot
F-215	Brunner, J.	Listen! The Stars!
do	Roberts, J.	The Rebellers
F-216	Asimov, I.	The Man Who Upset the Universe
F-217	Boucher, A.	The Best From Fantasy and Science Fiction, Eighth Series
F-218	Churchill, A.	They Never Came Back
F-220	Burroughs, E. R.	The People That Time Forgot
F-221	Burroughs, E. R.	Lost on Venus
F-222	Sutton, J.	First on the Moon
F-223	Laumer, K.	Envoy to New Worlds
do	Williams, R. M.	Flight From Yesterday
F-225	Piper, H. B.	Space Viking
F-226	Norton, Andre	Huon of the Horn
F-227	Brunner, J.	The Astronauts Must Not Land
do	Brunner, J.	The Space-Time Juggler
F-231	Norton, Andre	Star Gate
F-232	Burroughs, E. R.	The Land of Hidden Men
F-233	Burroughs, E. R.	Out of Time's Abyss
F-234	Burroughs, E. R.	The Eternal Savage
F-235	Burroughs, E. R.	The Lost Continent
F-236	Norton, Andre	The Time Traders
F-237	Chandler, A. B.	Beyond the Galactic Rim
do	Chandler, A. B.	The Ship From Outside
F-239	Simak, C. B.	Time and Again
F-240	Wells, H. G.	When the Sleeper Wakes
F-241	Williamson, J., & Gunn, J. E.	
		Star Bridge
F-242	Brunner, J.	Castaway's World
do	Brunner, J.	The Rites of Ohe
F-243	Norton, Andre	Lord of Thunder
F-245	Burroughs, E. R.	Back to the Stone Age
F-246	Von Harbou, T.	Metropolis
F-247	Burroughs, E. R.	Carson of Venus
F-248	Cummings, R.	Beyond the Stars
F-249	de Camp, L. S.	The Hand of Zei
do	de Camp, L. S.	The Search for Zei
F-251	Dick, P. K.	The Game-Players of Titan
F-253	Knox, C. M.	One of Our Asteroids Is Missing
do	van Vogt, A. E.	The Twisted Men
F-255	High, P. E.	The Prodigal Sun
F-256	Burroughs, E. R.	Land of Terror
F-257	Pratt, F.	Alien Planet
K-163	Furneaux, R.	The World's Strangest Stories
K-165	Eyre, K. W.	The Lute and the Glove
K-166	Jackson, S.	The Sundial
K-167	Andrezel, P.	The Angelic Avengers
K-168	Miller, R. D.	Stranger Than Life
1964		
F-258	Burroughs, E. R.	The Cave Girl
F-259	Kline, O. A.	The Prince of Peril
F-261	Williams, R. M.	The Lunar Eye
do	Delany, S. R.	The Towers of Toron
F-263	Norton, A.	Web of the Witch World
F-265	Vance, J.	The Houses of Iszm
do	Vance, J.	Son of the Tree
F-267	Mills, R. P.	The Best From Fantasy and Science Fiction, Ninth Series
F-268	Burroughs, E. R.	Escape on Venus
F-269	Rosny, J. H.	Quest of the Dawn Man
F-270	Burroughs, E. R.	The Mad King
F-271	Hamilton, E.	Outside the Universe
F-273	Bradley, M. Z.	The Dark Intruder
do	Bradley, M. Z.	Falcons of Narabedla
F-274	Piper, H. B.	The Cosmic Computer
F-275	Leinster, M.	The Duplicators
do	High, P. E.	No Truce With Terra

F-277	Brunner, J.	**To Conquer Chaos**
F-279	North, A.	**Sargasso of Space**
F-280	Burroughs, E. R.	**Savage Pellucidar**
F-281	Benoit, P.	**Atlantida**
F-282	Burroughs, E. R.	**Beyond the Farthest Star**
F-283	Rohmer, S.	**The Day the World Ended**
F-285	Bulmer, K.	**The Million Year Hunt**
do	Leiber, F.	**Ships to the Stars**
F-287	Norton, Andre	**Key out of Time**
F-289	Bulmer, K.	**Demons' World**
do	Purdom, T.	**I Want the Stars**
F-291	North, A.	**Plague Ship**
F-293	Tubb, E. C.	**Moon Base**
F-294	Kline, O. A.	**The Port of Peril**
F-295	van Vogt, A. E.	**The World of Null-A**
F-296	Arnold, E. L.	**Gulliver of Mars**
F-297	Kuttner, H.	**Valley of the Flame**
F-299	Fox, G. F.	**The Arsenal of Miracles**
do	Brunner, J.	**Endless Shadow**
F-301	Dick, P. K.	**The Simulacra**
F-303	Bradley, M. Z.	**The Bloody Sun**
F-304	Farley, R. M.	**The Radio Beasts**
F-305	Howard, R. E.	**Almuric**
F-306	Moore, C. L., & Kuttner, H.	
		Earth's Last Citadel
F-307	Fox, G. F.	**Warrior of Llarn**
F-308	Norton, Andre	**Judgment on Janus**
F-309	Dick, P. K.	**Clans of the Alphane Moon**
F-310	Norton, Andre	**Galactic Derelict**
F-311	Wollheim, D. A.	**Swordsmen in the Sky**
F-312	Farley, R. M.	**The Radio Planet**
F-313	Cummings, R.	**A Brand New World**
F-314	Schmitz, J. H.	**The Universe Against Her**
F-315	Norton, Andre	**The Beast Master**
F-317	White, J.	**The Escape Orbit**
F-318	Hall, A.	**The Spot of Life**
G-537	Ruppelt, E. J.	**The Report on Unidentified Flying Objects**
G-547	Hall, A., & Flint, H. E.	
		The Blind Spot
K-185	Jackson, S.	**Hangsaman**
K-199	O'Brien, B.	**Operators and Things**
K-206	Edwards, F.	**Strange World**
K-210	Holzer, H.	**Ghost Hunter**
M-101	Brackett, L.	**People of the Talisman**
do	Brackett, L.	**The Secret of Sinharat**
M-103	Wright, L.	**Exile From Xanadu**
do	Saberhagen, F.	**The Golden People**
M-105	St. Clair, M.	**Message From the Eocene**
do	St. Clair, M.	**Three Worlds to Futurity**
M-107	Chandler, A. B.	**The Coils of Time**
do	Chandler, A. B.	**Into the Alternate Universe**
1965		
A-4	Tolkien, J. R. R.	**The Fellowship of the Ring**
A-5	Tolkien, J. R. R.	**The Two Towers**
A-6	Tolkien, J. R. R.	**The Return of the King**
D-110	Asimov, I.	**The 1,000-Year Plan**
F-319	Hamilton, E.	**Crashing Suns**
F-320	Woodcott, K.	**The Martian Sphinx**
F-321	Kline, O. A.	**Maza of the Moon**
F-322	Delany, S. R.	**City of a Thousand Suns**
F-323	Norton, Andre	**Daybreak—2250 A.D.**
F-325	Norton, Andre	**Ordeal in Otherwhere**
F-326	Carter, Lin	**The Wizard of Lemuria**
F-327	Kuttner, H.	**The Dark World**
F-328	Smith, Edward E.	**The Galaxy Primes**
F-329	Norton, Andre	**Storm Over Warlock**
F-330	Davidson, A.	**What Strange Stars and Skies**
F-332	Norton, Andre	**Three Against the Witch World**
F-333	de Camp, L. S.	**Rogue Queen**
F-334	Levie, R.	**The Insect Warriors**
F-335	Williams, R. M.	**The Second Atlantis**
F-337	Dick, P. K.	**Dr. Bloodmoney**

F-342	Piper, H. B.	**Lord Kalvan of Otherwhen**
F-343	Cummings, R.	**The Exile of Time**
F-344	Kuttner, H.	**The Well of the Worlds**
F-345	Flint, H. E.	**The Lord of Death and The Queen of Life**
F-346	Campbell, J. W.	**The Black Star Passes**
F-347	Wright, L.	**The Last Hope of Earth**
F-350	Bradley, M. Z.	**Star of Danger**
F-353	Davidson, A.	**Rogue Dragon**
F-354	Fox, G. F.	**The Hunter out of Time**
F-355	Flint, H. E.	**The Devolutionist and The Emancipatrix**
F-356	Kuttner, H.	**The Time Axis**
F-357	Norton, Andre	**Year of the Unicorn**
F-361	Brunner, J.	**The Day of the Star Cities**
F-363	Cummings, R.	**Tama of the Light Country**
F-364	Campbell, J. W.	**The Mightiest Machine**
F-365	Norton, Andre	**Night of Masks**
F-366	Norton, Andre	**The Last Planet**
F-367	Farmer, P. J.	**The Maker of Universes**
G-551	Wollheim, D. A., & Carr, T.	
		World's Best Science Fiction: 1965
G-553	Avallone, M.	**The Thousand Coffins Affair**
G-560	Whittington, H.	**The Doomsday Affair**
G-564	Oram, J.	**The Copenhagen Affair**
G-566	Charles, T.	**Lady in the Mist**
G-571	McDaniel, D.	**The Dagger Affair**
H-12	Wilkins, H. T.	**Strange Mysteries of Time and Space**
H-13	Soule, G.	**The Mystery Monsters**
H-14	Gaddis, V.	**Invisible Horizons**
K-217	Fort, C.	**Lo!**
M-109	Edmondson, G. C.	**The Ship That Sailed the Time Stream**
do	Edmondson, G. C.	**Stranger Than You Think**
M-111	Hamilton, E.	**Fugitive of the Stars**
do	Bulmer, K.	**Land Beyond the Map**
M-113	Knight, D.	**Off Center**
do	Knight, D.	**The Rithian Terror**
M-115	Brunner, J.	**Enigma From Tantalus**
do	Brunner, J.	**The Repairmen of Cyclops**
M-116	Mills, R. P.	**The Best From Fantasy and Science Fiction, Tenth Series**
M-117	Ronald, B. W.	**Our Man in Space**
do	Sharkey, J.	**Ultimatum in 2050 A.D.**
M-119	Verne, J.	**A Journey to the Center of the Earth**
M-121	Petaja, E.	**Alpha Yes, Terra No!**
do	Delany, S. R.	**The Ballad of Beta-2**
M-123	Brunner, J.	**The Altar on Asconel**
do	White, Ted	**Android Avenger**
M-125	Vance, J.	**Monsters in Orbit**
do	Vance, J.	**The World Between and Other Stories**
M-127	Saberhagen, F.	**The Water of Thought**
do	Rackham, J.	**We, the Venusians**
M-129	Chandler, A. B.	**The Alternate Martians**
do	Chandler, A. B.	**Empress of Outer Space**
M-131	Bulmer, K.	**Behold the Stars**
do	Reynolds, M.	**Planetary Agent X**
M-132	Chambers, R. W.	**The King in Yellow**
M-133	Petaja, E.	**The Caves of Mars**
do	Chandler, A. B.	**Space Mercenaries**
1966		
A-8	Myers, J. M.	**Silverlock**
F-372	Smith, Edward E.	**Spacehounds of IPC**
F-373	Cory, H. L.	**The Sword of Lankor**
F-374	Sutton, J.	**The Atom Conspiracy**
F-375	Heinlein, R. A.	**The Worlds of Robert A. Heinlein**
F-377	Dick, P. K.	**The Crack in Space**
F-379	Herbert, F.	**The Green Brain**
F-382	Aldiss, B. W.	**Bow Down to Nul**
F-383	Carter, Lin	**Thongor of Lemuria**
F-386	Norton, Andre	**The Time Traders**
F-388	Delany, S. R	**Babel-17**
F-390	Vance, J.	**The Languages of Pao**
F-391	Norton, Andre	**The Crossroads of Time**
F-392	Petaja, E.	**Saga of Lost Earths**

F-393	Zelazny, R.	This Immortal
F-396	Bulmer, K.	Worlds for the Taking
F-398	Russell, E. F.	Somewhere a Voice
F-399	Fox, G. F.	The Thief of Llarn
F-400	Kline, O. A.	Jan of the Jungle
F-402	Smith, Cordwainer	Quest of the Three Worlds
F-403	Zelazny, R.	The Dream Master
F-406	Cummings, R.	Tama, Princess of Mercury
F-407	Swann, T. B.	Day of the Minotaur
F-408	Norton, Andre	The Sioux Spaceman
F-412	Farmer, P. J.	The Gates of Creation
F-414	Petaja, E.	The Star Mill
F-416	Gordon, R.	Utopia Minus X
G-570	Garner, A.	The Weirdstone of Brisingamen
G-574	LeGuin, U.	Rocannon's World
do	Davidson, A.	The Kar-Chee Reign
G-576	Rackham, J.	Danger From Vega
do	Davidson, A.	Clash of Star-Kings
G-580	Reynolds, M.	Dawnman Planet
do	Nunes, C.	Inherit the Earth
G-581	Phillifent, J. T.	The Mad Scientist Affair
G-582	Verne, J.	A Journey to the Center of the Earth
G-585	Campbell, J. W.	The Planeteers
do	Campbell, J. W.	The Ultimate Weapon
G-586	Chester, W. L.	Hawk of the Wilderness
G-588	Baxter, J.	The Off-Worlders
do	Carter, L.	The Star Magicians
G-590	McDaniel, D.	The Vampire Affair
G-592	Rackham	The Beasts of Kohl
do	Brunner, J.	A Planet of Your Own
G-595	Norton, Andre	Quest Crosstime
G-597	Disch, T. M.	Mankind Under the Leash
do	LeGuin, U.	Planet of Exile
G-599	Norton, Andre	Star Guard
G-600	Leslie, P.	The Radioactive Camel Affair
G-602	Cory, H. L.	The Mind Monsters
do	Dick, P. K.	The Unteleported Man
G-605	Maddock, L.	The Flying Saucer Gambit
G-606	Carter, L.	The Man Without a Planet
do	Rackham, J.	Time to Live
H-15	Wollheim, D. A., & Carr, T.	
		World's Best Science Fiction: 1966
H-16	Holzer, H.	Ghosts I've Met
H-17	Vallee, J.	Anatomy of a Phenomenon
K-229	Miller, R. D.	Impossible—Yet It Happened
K-241	Steiger, B.	Strange Guests
K-244	Singer, K.	The Gothic Reader
M-135	High, P. E.	The Mad Metropolis
do	Leinster, M.	Space Captain
M-137	Mills, R. P.	The Best From Fantasy and Science Fic-tion, Eleventh Series
M-139	Delany, S. R.	Empire Star
do	Purdom, T.	The Tree Lord of Imeten
M-141	Vance, J.	The Brains of Earth
do	Vance, J.	The Many Worlds of Magnus Ridolph
M-142	Heard, G.	The Doppelgangers
M-143	Campbell, J. W.	Islands of Space
M-147	Norton, Andre	The Stars Are Ours
M-148	Norton, Andre	Star Born
M-149	Vance, J.	The Eyes of the Overworld
M-150	Norton, Andre	The Defiant Agents
M-151	Norton, Andre	The Last Planet
M-152	Munn, H. W.	King of the World's Edge
M-153	van Vogt, A. E.	The Weapon Makers
M-154	Campbell, J. W.	Invaders From the Infinite
M-155	Zelazny, R.	Four for Tomorrow
M-156	Norton, Andre	Key out of Time
M-157	Norton, Andre	Star Gate
M-162	Grinnell, D.	Edge of Time

1967

A-10	Wollheim, D. A., & Carr, T.	
		World's Best Science Fiction: 1967

A-11	Wilkins, H. T.	Flying Saucers on the Attack
A-12	Carr, T.	New Worlds of Fantasy
F-420	Jones, N. R.	The Planet of the Double Sun
F-421	Clark, C.	Anarchaos
F-422	Brackett, L.	The Sword of Rhiannon
F-425	Anderson, P.	World Without Stars
F-426	Dickson, G. R.	The Genetic General
F-427	Delany, S. R.	The Einstein Intersection
F-429	Dick, P. K.	The World Jones Made
G-609	Chandler, A. B.	Contraband From Otherspace
do	High, P. E.	Reality Forbidden
G-611	Davidson, A.	The Best From Fantasy and Science Fic-tion, Twelfth Series
G-613	McDaniel, D.	The Monster Wheel Affair
G-614	Shaw, F. L.	Envoy to the Dog Star
do	Richmond, W. & L.	Shock Wave
G-617	Leslie, P.	The Diving Dames Affair
G-618	Munn, H. W.	The Ship From Atlantis
do	Petaja, E.	The Stolen Sun
G-620	Maddock, L.	The Golden Goddess Gambit
G-623	Rackham, J.	The Double Invaders
do	High, P. E.	These Savage Futurians
G-625	Bulmer, K.	To Outrun Doomsday
G-626	LeGuin, U.	City of Illusions
G-627	Leiber, F.	The Big Time
G-630	Norton, Andre	Warlock of the Witch World
G-631	Jones, N. R.	The Sunless World
G-632	Chandler, A. B.	Nebula Alert
do	Reynolds, M.	The Rival Rigellians
G-634	Anderson, P.	War of the Wing-Men
G-636	Holly, J. H.	The Assassination Affair
G-637	Dick, P. K., & Nelson, R.	
		The Ganymede Takeover
G-639	Hamilton, E.	The Weapon From Beyond
G-640	Swann, T. B.	The Weirwoods
G-641	Williamson, J.	Bright New Universe
G-644	Maddock, L	The Emerald Elephant Gambit
G-645	Stratton, T.	The Invisibility Affair
G-646	Norton, Andre	The X Factor
G-647	Leinster, M.	S.O.S. From Three Worlds
G-649	Brunner, J.	The World Swappers
G-650	Jones, N. R.	Space War
G-654	Norton, Andre	Catseye
G-656	Jakes, J.	When the Star Kings Die
G-660	van Vogt, A. E.	The Universe Maker
G-661	Vance, J.	Big Planet
G-663	Stratton, T.	The Mind Twisters Affair
G-664	Brunner, J.	Born Under Mars
G-667	McDaniel, D.	Arsenal out of Time
G-669	Brackett, L.	The Coming of the Terrans
G-670	McDaniel, D.	The Rainbow Affair
G-673	Geston, M.	Lords of the Starship
G-675	White, J.	The Secret Visitors
G-677	Knight, D.	Turning On
G-680	Bulmer, K.	Cycle of Nemesis
G-681	Jones, N. R.	Twin Worlds
G-683	Brackett, L.	The Big Jump
G-690	Norton, Andre	The Beast Master
G-691	Norton, Andre	Lord of Thunder
G-692	Kline, O. A.	The Swordsman of Mars
G-693	Kline, O. A.	Outlaws of Mars
H-18	Sutton, J.	H-Bomb Over America
H-19	Pohl, F.	The If Reader of Science Fiction
H-20	Bulmer, K.	The Key to Irunium
do	Schwartz, A.	The Wandering Tellurian
H-21	Vance, J.	The Last Castle
do	Wayman, T. R.	World of the Sleeper
H-22	Petaja, E.	Lord of the Green Planet
do	Purdom, T.	Five Against Arlane
H-24	Fort, C.	The Book of the Damned
H-26	Davidson, A.	The Best From Fantasy and Science Fic-tion, 13th Series

H-27	Coulson, J.	**Crisis on Cheiron**
do	Tubb, E. C.	**The Winds of Gath**
H-28	Vallee, J. & J.	**Challenge to Science—The UFO Enigma**
H-29	Richmond, W. & L.	**The Lost Millennium**
do	Chandler, A. B.	**The Road to the Rim**
H-30	Simak, C. B.	**City**
H-33	Norton, Andre	**Moon of Three Rings**
H-34	Reynolds, M.	**Computer War**
do	Tubb, E. C.	**Death Is a Dream**
H-36	Petaja	**Tramontane**
do	Moorcock, M.	**The Wrecks of Time**
K-259	Hervey, M.	**Strange Happenings**
K-272	Holzer, H.	**Yankee Ghosts**
K-276	Hurwood, B. J.	**Strange Talents**
K-291	Steiger, B.	**We Have Lived Before**
M-165	Laumer, K.	**Worlds of the Imperium**
N-3	Herbert, F.	**Dune**

1968

A-13	Schmitz, J. H.	**The Witches of Karres**
A-15	Wollheim, D. A., & Carr, T.	
		World's Best Science Fiction: 1968
A-16	Panshin, A.	**Rite of Passage**
A-17	Davidson, A.	**The Best From Fantasy and Science Fiction, Fourteenth Series**
A-19	Anthony, P., & Margroff, R.	
		The Ring
A-27	Harmon, J.	**The Great Radio Heroes**
A-29	Blish, J., & Knight, N. L.	
		A Torrent of Faces
G-688	Vance, J.	**City of the Chasch**
G-689	Davies, F.	**The Cross of Gold Affair**
G-694	Swann, T. B.	**The Dolphin and the Deep**
G-697	Anderson, P.	**We Claim These Stars**
G-701	Hamilton, E.	**The Closed Worlds**
G-702	Johnston, W.	**Miracle at San Tanco**
G-703	Norton, Andre	**Victory on Janus**
G-706	Delany, S. R.	**The Jewels of Aptor**
G-709	Brunner, J.	**Bedlam Planet**
G-712	Boucher, A., & McComas, J. F.	
		The Best From Fantasy and Science Fiction, Third Series
G-713	Boucher, A.	**The Best From Fantasy and Science Fiction, Fourth Series**
G-714	Boucher, A.	**The Best From Fantasy and Science Fiction, Fifth Series**
G-715	Boucher, A.	**The Best From Fantasy and Science Fiction, Sixth Series**
G-716	Norton, Andre	**Web of the Witchworld**
G-717	Norton, Andre	**Daybreak—2250 A.D.**
G-718	Dick, P. K.	**Solar Lottery**
G-719	Jones, N. R.	**Doomsday on Ajiat**
G-723	Norton, Andre	**Star Hunter & Voodoo Planet**
G-724	Farmer, P. J.	**A Private Cosmos**
G-728	Grinnell, D.	**Across Time**
G-729	McDaniel, D.	**The Utopia Affair**
G-730	Nourse, A. E.	**Psi High and Others**
G-733	Burroughs, E. R.	**At the Earth's Core**
G-734	Burroughs, E. R.	**Pellucidar**
G-735	Burroughs, E. R.	**Tanar of Pellucidar**
G-736	Burroughs, E. R.	**Tarzan at the Earth's Core**
G-737	Burroughs, E. R.	**Back to the Stone Age**
G-738	Burroughs, E. R.	**Land of Terror**
G-739	Burroughs, E. R.	**Savage Pellucidar**
G-740	Saberhagen, F.	**The Broken Lands**
G-745	Burroughs, E. R.	**The Moon Maid**
G-748	Burroughs, E. R.	**The Moon Men**
G-752	Leslie, P.	**The Splintered Sunglasses Affair**
G-753	Garner, A.	**Moon of Gomrath**
G-756	Panshin, A.	**Star Well**
G-758	Swann, T. B.	**Moondust**
G-761	Brunner, J.	**Catch a Falling Star**
G-762	Panshin, A.	**The Thurb Revolution**

G-766	Hamilton, E.	**World of the Starwolves**
H-38	Leiber, F.	**The Swords of Lankhmar**
H-39	Dick, P. K.	**Eye in the Sky**
H-40	Rackham, J.	**Alien Sea**
do	Tubb, E. C.	**C.O.D. Mars**
H-41	Verne, J.	**Into the Niger Bend**
H-42	Simak, C. D.	**Why Call Them Back From Heaven?**
H-43	Verne, J.	**The City in the Sahara**
H-47	Holzer, H.	**Lively Ghosts of Ireland**
H-48	Wright, L.	**The Pictures of Pavanne**
do	Wobig, E.	**The Youth Monopoly**
H-49	Verne, J.	**The Begum's Fortune**
H-51	Faucette, J. M.	**Crown of Infinity**
do	Petaja, E.	**The Prism**
H-52	Verne, J.	**Yesterday and Tomorrow**
H-53	Whitten, L. H.	**Progeny of the Adder**
H-54	Lafferty, R. A.	**Past Master**
H-55	Ley, W.	**On Earth and in the Sky**
H-56	Hill, E.	**Pity About Earth**
do	Lafferty, R. A.	**Space Chantey**
H-58	Friedberg, G.	**The Revolving Boy**
H-59	Trimble, L. E.	**Anthropol**
do	High, P. E.	**The Time Mercenaries**
H-60	Verne, J.	**Carpathian Castle**
H-62	Tucker, W.	**The Lincoln Hunters**
H-64	Trench, B. Le P.	**The Flying Saucer Story**
H-65	Bulmer, K.	**The Key to Venudine**
do	Reynolds, M.	**Mercenary From Tomorrow**
H-67	Verne, J.	**The Village in the Treetops**
H-70	Petaja, E.	**Doom of the Green Planet**
do	Koontz, D. R.	**Star Quest**
H-72	Russ, J.	**Picnic on Paradise**
H-73	Leiber, F.	**Swords Against Wizardry**
H-74	Fort, C.	**New Lands**
H-77	Tubb, E. C.	**Derai**
do	Coulson, J.	**The Singing Stones**
H-78	Verne, J.	**The Hunt for the Meteor**
H-79	Shaw, B.	**The Two-Timers**
H-83	Hurwood, B. J.	**Vampires, Werewolves and Ghouls**
H-84	Norton, Andre	**Sorceress of the Witch World**
H-85	Grinnell, D., & Carter, L.	
		Destination: Saturn
do	High, P. E.	**Invader on My Back**
H-86	Compton, D.	**Synthajoy**
H-88	Fort, C.	**Wild Talents**
H-90	Leiber, F.	**Swords in the Mist**
H-91	Rackham, J.	**The Proxima Project**
do	Janifer, L. M., & Treibich, J.	
		Target: Terra
H-92	van Vogt, A. E.	**The Far-Out Worlds of A. E. van Vogt**
H-95	Sutton, J.	**The Man Who Saw Tomorrow**
do	Simak, C. D.	**So Bright the Vision**
H-96	Jackson, S.	**The Sundial**
H-100	Holzer, H.	**ESP and You**
H-102	Smith, Edward E.	**Subspace Explorers**
H-103	Faucette, J. M.	**The Age of Ruin**
do	Reynolds, M.	**Code Duello**
H-105	Schmitz, J. H.	**The Demon Breed**
N-4	Asimov, I.	**Is Anyone There?**
N-6	Lupoff, R. A.	**Edgar Rice Burroughs: Master of Adventure**
?	Johnston, W.	**The Littlest Rebels**

Ace (Brit.) See NEW ENGLISH LIBRARY LTD.

ACORN. No further information.

Acorn

1963

AB18	Hepper, E.	**Palace Under the Sea**

ADVENT:PUBLISHERS, INC., Chicago, Illinois, U.S.A.
Advent
1960
—	Knight, D.	**In Search of Wonder**

1962
—	Bloch, R.	**The Eighth Stage of Fandom**

1963
—	Kemp, E.	**Proceedings of the 20th World Science Fiction Convention—Chicon III**

1964
—	Eshbach, L.	**Of Worlds Beyond**
—	Symposium	**The Science Fiction Novel**

1965
—	Eney, R.	**Proceedings of the 21st World Science Fiction Convention: Discon**

1966
—	Eney, R.	**Proceedings of the 21st World Science Fiction Convention: Discon**
—	Kemp, E.	**Proceedings of the 20th World Science Fiction Convention—Chicon III**

1967
—	Rogers, A.	**A Requiem for Astounding**
—	Atheling, W. Jr.	**The Issue at Hand**

1968
—	Knight, D.	**In Search of Wonder** (revised)
—	Ellik, R., & Evans, B.	
		The Universes of E. E. Smith

AIRMONT BOOKS, New York, N.Y., U.S.A.
Airmont
1962
SF1	West, W.	**The Memory Bank**

1963
CL12	Verne, J.	**Twenty Thousand Leagues Under the Sea**
CL15	Swift, J.	**Gulliver's Travels**
CL19	Shelley, M. W.	**Frankenstein**
SF2	de Camp, L. S.	**The Tower of Zanid**
SF3	West, W.	**Lords of Atlantis**

1964
CL44	Wells, H. G.	**The Time Machine**
CL39	Wilde, O.	**The Picture of Dorian Grey**
CL40	Wells, H. G.	**The Invisible Man**
CL47	Stevenson, R. L.	**Dr. Jekyll and Mr. Hyde**
CL50	Irving, W.	**The Legend of Sleepy Hollow**
SF4	Pratt, F.	**Invaders From Rigel**
SF5	del Rey, L.	**Day of the Giants**
SF6	Coblentz, S. A.	**Hidden World**
SF7	Banister, M.	**Conquest of Earth**
SF8	Blish, J., & Lowndes, R.A.W.	
		The Duplicated Man

1965
CL59	Wells, H. G.	**The Food of the Gods**
CL60	Verne, J.	**A Journey to the Center of the Earth**
CL66	Hawthorne, N.	**Twice-Told Tales**
CL69	Baum, L. F.	**The Wonderful Wizard of Oz**
CL72	Stoker, B.	**Dracula**
CL73	Verne, J.	**Master of the World**
CL76	Collins, W. W.	**The Moonstone**
CL77	Verne, J.	**The Mysterious Island**
CL78	Wells, H. G.	**The First Men in the Moon**
CL87	Hudson, W. H.	**Green Mansions**

1966
CL100	MacDonald, G.	**At the Back of the North Wind**
CL110	Wells, H. G.	**The Island of Dr. Moreau**
CL111	Wells, H. G.	**In the Days of the Comet**

1967
CL130	Butler, S.	**Erewhon**
CL142	Verne, J.	**From the Earth to the Moon**
CL146	Haggard, H. R.	**She**
CL155	James, H.	**The Turn of the Screw**

1968
CL172	Plato	**The Republic**

CL175	Hawthorne, N.	**Tanglewood Tales**
CL181	Baum, L. F.	**The Land of Oz**
CL182	Verne, J.	**Round the Moon**

Aldine See DENT, J. M., & SONS LTD.

ALL-SAINTS PRESS, U.S.A.
All-Saints
1963
AS-230	Hughes, R.	**The Hills Were Liars**

ALL STAR. U.S.A. publisher.
All Star
1962
518	Farmer, A.	**The Nymph and the Satyr**

ALLEN & UNWIN, London, England.
Allen Unwin
1964
54	Tolkien, J. R. R.	**Tree and Leaf**

1968
65	Tolkien, J. R. R.	**The Hobbit**
87.1	Tolkien, J. R. R.	**The Lord of the Rings**

ALLIANCE PRESS, London, England.
[World War II publishers.]
Alliance
1945
—	Fox, L. H.	**The Vampire and 16 Other Stories**

AMERICAN ART ENTERPRISES INC. North Hollywood, California, U.S.A. Imprints include **Brandon House** and **Essex House**.
Brandon
1964
625	Bixby, J.	**The Devil's Scrapbook**

1967
1070	Geis, R. E.	**The Sex Machine**

1968
2061	Geis, R. E.	**The Endless Orgy**

Essex House
1968
0102	Meltzer, D.	**The Agency**
0104	Meltzer, D.	**The Agent**
0107	Meltzer, D.	**How Many Blocks in the Pile?**
0108	Farmer, P. J.	**Image of the Beast**
0109	Perkins, M.	**Evil Companions**
0112	Stine, H.	**Season of the Witch**

AMERICAN SPORTS LIBRARY. No further information
American Sports Library
1965
F-115	Wallop, D.	**The Year the Yankees Lost the Pennant**

Anchor See DOUBLEDAY & CO.

ANGUS & ROBERTSON LTD., Sydney, N.S.W., Australia.
Pacific
1968
92	Baxter, J. M.	**The Pacific Book of Australian Science Fiction**
101	Cusack, F.	**True Australian Ghost Stories**

Apollo See MORROW

ARC PRESS, London, England.
Arc
1954
1	Haley, C.	**Beyond the Solar System**

ARCHER PRESS, London, England.
Archer
1952
—	Fysh, G.	**Planetary War**

ARKHAM HOUSE, Sauk City, Wisconsin, U.S.A.
Arkham
1959
| — | Derleth, A. | **Some Notes on H. P. Lovecraft** |

Armada See COLLINS SONS LTD.

ARMED SERVICES EDITIONS; published by Editions for the Armed Services Inc., U.S.A., during World War II (1942-1945). Most were not dated, and none were priced, as they were distributed free to servicemen and not offered on the civilian market. Those marked * were special selections, not reprints. The following listing gives titles of possible fantasy interest.
Armed

801	Balmer, E., & Wylie, P.	
		When Worlds Collide
710	Benefield, B.	**Eddie and the Archangel Mike**
c-67	Beerbohm, M.	**Seven Men**
c-77	Benét, S. V.	**Short Stories***
1258	Beymer, W. G.	**The Middle of Midnight**
s-26	Blackwood, A.	**Selected Short Stories of Algernon Blackwood***
i244	Bradford, R.	**Ol' Man Adam an' His Chillun**
D103	Bryan, G. S.	**Mystery Ship**
m-16	Burroughs, E. R.	**Tarzan of the Apes**
o-22	Burroughs, E. R.	**The Return of Tarzan**
984	Chesterton, G. K.	**The Man Who Was Thursday**
871	Collier, J.	**Green Thoughts***
j-273	Conrad, J.	**The Shadow Line**
r-7	Corwin, N.	**Selected Radio Plays***
s-4	Cozzens, J. G.	**Castaway**
r-33	Derleth, A.	**Sleep No More**
687	Dinesen, I.	**Seven Gothic Tales**
802	Dinesen, I.	**Winter's Tales**
713	Fisher, V.	**The Golden Rooms**
1217	Frank, P.	**Mr. Adam**
p-1	Garnett, D.	**Lady Into Fox**
795	Haggard, H. R.	**King Solomon's Mines**
881	Haggard, H. R.	**She**
f-179	Hall, J. N.	**Dr. Dogbody's Leg**
f-162	Harte, B.	**Selected Short Stories of Bret Harte***
863	Hawthorne, J.	**The Gray Champion***
921	Hecht, B.	**Concerning a Woman in Sin and Other Stories***
?	Hilton, J.	**Lost Horizon**
925	Homer [Trans.—T. E. Shaw]	
		Odyssey
c-71	Hudson, W. H.	**Green Mansions**
G-196	Hudson, W. H.	**A Crystal Age**
828	Hughes, Dorothy	**The Delicate Ape**
926	Huxley, A.	**The Gioconda Smile and Other Weird Stories***
s-20	Irish, W.	**After-Dinner Story**
o-28	James, M. R.	**Selected Ghost Stories of M. R. James***
g-187	Knight, E.	**Sam Small Flies Again**
685	Laing, A.	**The Cadaver of Gideon Wyck**
899	Lawson, R.	**Mr. Wilmer**
730	Lovecraft, H. P.	**The Dunwich Horror***
656	Lowther, G.	**Adventures of Superman**
b-51	Macardle, D.	**The Uninvited**
1185	Macardle, D.	**The Unforeseen**
940	Machen, A.	**The Great God Pan and Other Stories***
1223	Margolies, J. A.	**Strange and Fantastic Stories**
655	Nathan, R.	**Portrait of Jenny**
737	Nathan, R.	**The Enchanted Voyage**
800	Nathan, R.	**The Bishop's Wife***
j-297	Poe, E. A.	**Selected Short Stories of Edgar Allan Poe***
767	Poe, E. A.	**Selected Short Stories of Edgar Allan Poe***
t-22	Rame, D.	**Tunnel From Calais**
O-20	Russell, J.	**Selected Short Stories of John Russell***
1042	Russell, J.	**Selected Short Stories of John Russell***
m-3 (?)	Saki	**Selected Short Stories of Saki***

s-7	Sale, R.	**Not Too Narrow, Not Too Deep**
t-12	Sharp, M.	**The Stone of Chastity**
909	Shelley, M.	**Frankenstein**
o-9	Siodmak, C.	**Donovan's Brain**
b-40	Sloane, W.	**To Walk the Night**
t-23	Sloane, W.	**The Edge of Running Water**
1169	Sloane, W.	**The Edge of Running Water**
g181	Smith, T.	**The Glorious Pool**
h-230	Smith, T.	**The Bishop's Jaegers**
J-284	Smith, T.	**Skin and Bones**
k-15	Smith, T.	**The Stray Lamb**
l-17	Smith, T.	**Turnabout**
q-13	Smith, T.	**The Passionate Witch**
s-28	Smith, T.	**The Night Life of the Gods**
671	Smith, T.	**The Glorious Pool**
922	Smith, T.	**Rain in the Doorway**
953	Smith, T.	**The Passionate Witch**
l-4	Stephens, J.	**Etched in Moonlight**
N-5	Stephens, J.	**The Crock of Gold**
1121	Stephens, J.	**The Crock of Gold**
1228	Stern, D.	**Francis**
885	Stevenson, R. L.	**Dr. Jekyll and Mr. Hyde***
l-25	Stoker, B.	**Dracula**
851	Stoker, B.	**Dracula**
e-139	Twain, M.	**A Connecticut Yankee in King Arthur's Court**
n-1	Twain, M.	**The Mysterious Stranger**
m-3 (?)	Twain, M.	**Selected Short Stories of Mark Twain***
779	Watkin, L.	**On Borrowed Time**
t-2	Wells, H. G.	**The Time Machine**
698	Wells, H. G.	**The Island of Dr. Moreau**
745	Wells, H. G.	**The War of the Worlds**
1091	Wells, H. G.	**The War of the Worlds**
958	Wells, H. G.	**The Food of the Gods**
s-8	Wylie, P.	**Selected Short Stories of Philip Wylie***
774	Wylie, P.	**Night Unto Night**
960	Zim, H. S.	**Rockets and Jets**

Arrow See HUTCHINSON & CO.

ART & EDUCATIONAL PUBLISHERS LTD., Glasgow, Scotland.
Art & Educ.
1945 (approx.)
—	Hardie, J. L.	**Another Seven Strange Stories**
—	Hardie, J. L.	**Seven More Strange Stories**
—	Hardie, J. L.	**Seven Strange Stories**
—	Hardie, J. L.	**Strange Stories—The Last Seven**

ART ENTERPRISES, INC., Los Angeles, Calif., U.S.A. Imprints include **Epic**, **Heart**, **Moonlight Reader**, and **Ram**.
Epic
1961
| 103 | Smith, G. H. | **1976—The Year of Terror** |
| 110 | Smith, G. H. | **Scourge of the Blood Cult** |
1962
| 144 | Camra, R. | **Assault** |
Heart
Undated
| 105 | Camra, R. | **Space Sex** |
Moonlight Reader
Undated
| 103 | Anon. [G. H. Smith] | **The Year of Love** |
Ram
Undated
| 104 | Camra, R. | **Sex Machine** |

Assoc G P See TRANSPORT PUBLISHING CO.

ATLANTIC BOOK CO., London, England.
Atlantic
1954
| — | Bradford, M. | **Invasion From Space** |

ATLANTIC BOOK PUBLISHING CO. LTD., London, England.
Dragon (adapted for readers 12-15 years old)
1967

D-42	Burroughs, E. R.	**Tarzan of the Apes**
D-43	Burroughs, E. R.	**The Return of Tarzan**
D-44	Burroughs, E. R.	**The Beasts of Tarzan**
D-45	Burroughs, E. R.	**The Son of Tarzan**
D-62	Burroughs, E. R.	**Tarzan and the Jewels of Opar I**
D-63	Burroughs, E. R.	**Tarzan and the Jewels of Opar II**
D-64	Burroughs, E. R.	**Tarzan and the Ant Men**
D-65	Burroughs, E. R.	**Tarzan's Quest**

1968

D-76	Burroughs, E. R.	**A Princess of Mars**
D-77	Burroughs, E. R.	**The Gods of Mars**
D-88	Clarke, A. C.	**Dolphin Island**
D-105	Burroughs, E. R.	**The Warlord of Mars**
D-106	Burroughs, E. R.	**Thuvia, Maid of Mars**

ATLAS PUBLICATIONS PTY LTD., Melbourne, Victoria, Australia.
SFL = Science Fiction Library (not dated).
Atlas
1955

SFL1	Burke, J. F.	**The Echoing Worlds**
SFL2	Tubb, E. C.	**The World at Bay**
SFL3	Berry, B.	**From What Far Star?**
SFL4	Wallace, F. L.	**Worlds in Balance**

1956

SFL5	Campbell, H. J.	**Another Space, Another Time**
SFL6	Bulmer, K.	**The Stars Are Ours**
SFL7	Berry, B.	**And the Stars Remain**
SFL8	Phillips, R.	**Time Trap**

AUSTRALIAN SCIENCE FICTION ASSOCIATION, Canberra, Australia.
Australian SF Assn
1968

—	Stone, G. B.	**Australian Science Fiction Index 1925-1967**

Authentic See PANTHER BOOKS LTD.

AVON BOOK DIVISION, The Hearst Corporation, New York, N.Y., U.S.A.

Avon began about 1941 and was bought out by Hearst in May 1959.

Special series codes include: MM = Avon Murder Mystery Monthly Series; FN = Fantasy Novel. Prices up to 1954 were generally 25¢; serial price codes since then are: T- 35¢; G- 50¢; S- 60¢; ZS- 60¢; V- 75¢; N- 95¢; NS- 95¢.

See also ETON BOOKS, understood to be another division of Avon.

Avon
1941

6	Anonymous	**The Haunted Hotel and 25 Other Ghost Stories**

1942

26	Merritt, A.	**Seven Footprints to Satan**
MM1	Merritt, A.	**Seven Footprints to Satan**
MM5	Merritt, A.	**Burn, Witch, Burn!**
MM11	Merritt, A.	**Creep, Shadow, Creep!**

1943

6	Anonymous	**25 Great Ghost Stories**
43	Merritt, A.	**Burn, Witch, Burn!**

1944

MM18	Merritt, A.	**The Moon Pool**
MM24	Merritt, A.	**Dwellers in the Mirage**

1945

69	Smith, T.	**The Stray Lamb**
MM29	Merritt, A.	**The Face in the Abyss**
MM34	Merritt, A.	**The Ship of Ishtar**

1946

90	Williams, H.	**The Avon Ghost Reader**
108	Heard, H. F.	**A Taste for Honey**
113	Louys, P.	**Aphrodite**

MM41	Merritt, A.	**The Metal Monster**
MM43	Merritt, A.	**Burn, Witch, Burn!**
MM47	Merritt, A.	**Creep, Shadow, Creep!**

1947

110	Williams, H.	**Terror at Night**
117	Merritt, A.	**Creep, Shadow, Creep!**
136	Lovecraft, H. P.	**The Lurking Fear**

1948

165	Sharp, M.	**The Stone of Chastity**
171	de Bibiena, J. G.	**Amorous Philandre**

1949

184	Wollheim, D. A.	**The Girl With the Hungry Eyes**
189	Rohmer, S.	**Daughter of Fu Manchu**
195	Lewis, C. S.	**Out of the Silent Planet**
204	Walpole, H.	**Portrait of a Man With Red Hair**
211	Bloch, R.	**The Scarf of Passion**
214	Merritt, A.	**The Fox Woman**
216	Wylie, P.	**Gladiator**
235	Merritt, A.	**Seven Footprints to Satan**

1950

249	Davies, V.	**It Happens Every Spring**
277	Lewis, C. S.	**Perelandra**
281	Coblentz	**Into Plutonian Depths**
285	Farley, R. M.	**An Earthman on Venus**
FN1	Cummings, R.	**The Princess of the Atom**
FN2	Williamson, J.	**The Green Girl**

1951

315	Merritt, A.	**The Metal Monster**
323	Endore, G.	**The Furies in Her Body**
324	Merritt, A.	**The Ship of Ishtar**
327	Thayer, T.	**One-Man Show**
339	Kennerley, J.	**The Terror of the Leopard Men**
354	Endore, G.	**The Werewolf of Paris**
370	Merritt, A.	**The Moon Pool**
388	Huxley, A.	**After Many a Summer Dies the Swan**
389	Fles, B.	**The Saturday Evening Post Fantasy Stories**
390	Wylie, P.	**The Savage Gentleman**
392	Merritt, A.	**Burn, Witch, Burn!**

1952

396	Weston, G.	**His First Million Women**
413	Merritt, A.	**Dwellers in the Mirage**
AT435	Huxley, A.	**After Many a Summer Dies the Swan**
494	Bloch, R.	**The Scarf**

1953

548	van Vogt, A. E.	**Away and Beyond**

1954

628	Bierce, A.	**The Monk and the Hangman's Daughter**
T75	Huxley, A.	**After Many a Summer Dies the Swan**
T80	Bond, N. S.	**No Time Like the Future**

1955

624	Sharp, M.	**The Stone of Chastity**
630	Anonymous	**20 Great Ghost Stories**
T115	Merritt, A.	**Seven Footprints to Satan**

1956

T127	Lewis, C. S.	**Out of the Silent Planet**
T135	Merritt, A.	**The Moon Pool**
T146	Herbert, F.	**21st Century Sub**
T152	Merritt, A.	**The Ship of Ishtar**
T155	Wylie, P.	**Gladiator**

1957

727	Wylie, P.	**The Smuggled Atom Bomb**
T157	Lewis, C. S.	**Perelandra**
T161	Merritt, A.	**The Face in the Abyss**
T168	Tucker, W.	**Tomorrow Plus X**
T172	Merritt, A.	**The Metal Monster**
T175	Clement, H.	**From Outer Space**
T180	Smith, G. O.	**Space Plague**
T186	Sohl, J.	**The Time Dissolver**
T193	Blish, J.	**Year 2018!**
T202	Leinster, M.	**The Planet Explorer**
T208	Merritt, A.	**Seven Footprints to Satan**

1958

808	Heard, H. F.	**A Taste for Murder**
T211	Lewis, C. S.	**The Tortured Planet**
T221	Shiras, W. H.	**Children of the Atom**
T225	Blish, J.	**Earthman, Come Home**
T232	Asimov, I.	**Second Foundation**
T238	Blish, J.	**VOR**
T249	McIntosh, J. T.	**Worlds Apart**
T252	van Vogt, A. E.	**The Mind Cage**
T261	Heinlein, R. A.	**Waldo: Genius in Orbit**
T268	Blish, J.	**ESP-er**
T275	Kuttner, H.	**Destination: Infinity**
T279	Blish, J.	**The Triumph of Time**
T284	Lovecraft, H. P.	**Cry Horror!**

1959

T289	Conklin, G.	**Br-r-r!**
T297	Moore, C. L.	**Doomsday Morning**
T304	Sturgeon, T.	**Aliens 4**
T345	Leinster, M.	**Monsters and Such**
T354	Woolrich, C.	**Beyond the Night**

1960

G2001	Huxley, A.	**After Many a Summer Dies the Swan**
T360	Noel, S.	**We Who Survived**
T362	Lyndon, J., & Sangster, J.	
		The Man Who Could Cheat Death
T371	Christopher, J.	**Planet in Peril**
T389	Leinster, M.	**Twists in Time**
T408	Woolrich, C.	**The Doom Stone**
T410	Lewis, C. S.	**Out of the Silent Planet**
T439	Sturgeon, T.	**Beyond**
T449	Jackson, S.	**The Lottery**

1961

G1003	Louys, P.	**The Collected Works of Pierre Louys**
G1090	Potocki, J.	**The Saragossa Manuscript**
G1092	Herbert, F.	**21st Century Sub**
G1096	Simak, C. D.	**The Worlds of Clifford Simak**
G1134	Kirk, R.	**Old House of Fear**
T483	Leinster, M.	**The Wailing Asteroid**
T524	Maine, C. E.	**He Owned the World**

1962

F118	Piper, H. B.	**Little Fuzzy**
F122	Blish, J.	**The Star Dwellers**
G1120	Leinster, M.	**Talents, Incorporated**
G1124	Simak, C. D.	**The Other Worlds of Clifford Simak**
G1127	Anderson, P.	**Three Hearts and Three Lions**
G1129	Mead, S.	**The Big Ball of Wax**
G1143	MacLean, K.	**The Diploids**
G1170	Raven, S.	**Doctors Wear Scarlet**
V2056	Heinlein, R. A.	**Stranger in a Strange Land**

1963

G1132	Taylor, R. L.	**Adrift in a Boneyard**
G1154	Smith, G. O.	**Space Plague**
G1166	Aylesworth, J.	**Fee, Fei, Fo, Fum!**
G1168	Clement, H.	**From Outer Space**
G1178	Collins, C. M.	**Fright**
G1185	Henderson, Z.	**Pilgrimage**
G1191	Wormser, R.	**Pan Satyrus**
H102	Dutourd, J.	**A Dog's Head**
H107	Blish, J.	**A Life for the Stars**
S127	Asimov, I.	**The Hugo Winners**
S135	Brinton, H.	**Purple 6**

1964

G1192	Merritt, A.	**Seven Footprints to Satan**
G1211	Heinlein, R. A.	**Podkayne of Mars**
G1220	Piper, H. B.	**The Other Human Race**
G1227	Lewis, I.	**The Day They Invaded New York**
G1231	Holly, J. H.	**The Time Twisters**
G1237	Cooper, M.	**The Munsters**
G1248	Asimov, I.	**Second Foundation**
V2075	Graves, R.	**Watch the North Wind Rise**
V2102	Heinlein, R. A.	**Glory Road**
VS1	Huxley, A.	**After Many a Summer Dies the Swan**

VS7	Cabell, J. B.	**Jurgen**

1965

G1254	Karloff, B.	**Boris Karloff's Favourite Horror Stories**
G1262	Kirk, R.	**Old House of Fear**
G1268	Blish, J.	**The Star Dwellers**
G1278	Nolan, W. F.	**Man Against Tomorrow**
S197	Jackson, S.	**The Lottery**
SS4	Grahame, K.	**The Wind in the Willows**
SS6	West, N.	**A Cool Million & The Dream Life of Balso Snell**

1966

G1280	Blish, J.	**A Life for the Stars**
G1299	Rios, Tere	**The Fifteenth Pelican**
G1301	Tucker, W.	**Wild Talent**
G1306	Leinster, M.	**The Wailing Asteroid**
S208	Knowler, J.	**The Trap**
S210	Blish, J.	**They Shall Have Stars**
S212	Masterson, W.	**The Dark Fantastic**
S218	Blish, J.	**Earthman, Come Home**
S221	Blish, J.	**The Triumph of Time**
S224	Asimov, I.	**Foundation**
S229	Merritt, A.	**The Ship of Ishtar**
S230	Christopher, J.	**The Possessors**
S231	Merritt, A.	**The Metal Monster**
S234	Asimov, I.	**Foundation and Empire**
S237	Asimov, I.	**Second Foundation**
S243	Henderson, Z.	**Pilgrimage**
V2102	Heinlein, R. A.	**Glory Road**
ZS103	Milne, A. A.	**Once on a Time**

1967

G1310	Leinster, M.	**Miners in the Sky**
G1315	Lewis, I.	**The Day New York Trembled**
G1318	Leinster, M.	**Space Gypsies**
G1322	Whitaker, D.	**Dr. Who in an Exciting Adventure With the Daleks**
N161	Taylor, G.	**Court of Honor**
NS16	Vonnegut, K.	**Player Piano**
S255	Clement, H.	**Needle**
S270	Simak, C. D.	**Ring Around the Sun**
S271	Merritt, A.	**The Dwellers in the Mirage**
S277	Collins, C. M.	**A Feast of Blood**
S288	Christopher, J.	**No Blade of Grass**
S290	Herbert, F.	**The Dragon in the Sea**
S298	Guin, W.	**Living Way Out**
S301	Trevor, E.	**The Shoot**
S303	Mundy, T.	**Tros**
S304	Burke, J. F.	**Privilege**
S309	Mundy, T.	**Helma**
S313	Blish, J.	**VOR**
S316	Mundy, T.	**Liafail**
S318	Mundy, T.	**Helene**
V2166	Goldston, R.	**The Last of Lazarus**
V2191	Heinlein, R. A.	**Stranger in a Strange Land**
V2202	Heinlein, R. A.	**Glory Road**
V2212	Mundy, T.	**Om: The Secret of Ahbor Valley**
V2216	Blish, J.	**They Shall Have Stars**
ZS118	White, T. H.	**The Master**
ZS122	Baum, L. F.	**The Wizard of Oz**

1968

G1280	Blish, J.	**A Life for the Stars**
N179	Tregaskis, R.	**China Bomb**
N189	Southwell, S. B.	**If All the Rebels Die**
N191	Lurie, A.	**Imaginary Friends**
N192	Pauwels, L., & Bergier, J.	
		The Morning of the Magicians
NS23	Watkins, P.	**The War Game**
S218	Blish, J.	**Earthman, Come Home**
S221	Blish, J.	**The Triumph of Time**
S237	Asimov, I.	**Second Foundation**
S280	Merritt, A.	**Seven Footprints to Satan**
S319	Herbert, F.	**The Heaven Makers**
S323	Brunner, J.	**Now Then!**

S328	Henderson, Z.	**The People: No Different Flesh**
S329	Silverberg, R.	**Master of Life and Death**
S335	Heinlein, R. A.	**Podkayne of Mars**
S336	Nolan, W. F.	**3 to the Highest Power**
S337	Blish, J.	**Jack of Eagles**
S347	McIntosh, J. T.	**Snow White and the Giants**
S349	Sohl, J.	**Costigan's Needle**
S351	Moorcock, M.	**The Final Programme**
S355	Pohl, F.	**The Expert Dreamers**
S363	Jakes, J.	**Brak the Barbarian**
S365	Silverberg, R.	**Invaders From Earth**
S368	Hoffe, A.	**Something Evil**
S372	Silverberg, R.	**The Time Hoppers**
S376	Lanning, G.	**The Pedestal**
S377	Neill, R.	**Witch Bane**
S378	Moore, C. L.	**Doomsday Morning**
V2220	Mundy, T.	**Jimgrim**
V2230	Mundy, T.	**The Devil's Guard**
V2236	Asimov, I.	**Foundation and Empire**
V2242	Mundy, T.	**The Nine Unknown**
V2243	Christopher, J.	**The Little People**
V2248	Asimov, I.	**Foundation**
V2249	Boardman, T.	**An ABC of Science Fiction**
ZS127	Follett, B. N.	**The House Without Windows**
ZS136	Harrison, H.	**The Man From P.I.G.**
ZS139	Alexander, L.	**Time Cat**
ZS146	Hunter, M.	**The Kelpie's Pearls**
ZV147	Baum, L. F.	**The Land of Oz**

Award See UNIVERSAL PUBLISHING & DISTRIBUTING CORP.

B

BACKGROUND BOOKS LTD., London, England.
Background
1948
—		Scott-Moncrieff, D. **Not for the Squeamish**

Badger See (JOHN) SPENCER & CO.

STANLEY BAKER (PUB) LTD., Brighton, Sussex, England.
  Serial code FST = Fantastic Science Thriller.
Baker
1953
FST1	Querry, S.	**Adventures on the Planets**
FST2	Causett, W.	**Pirates in Space**
FST3	Mois, J.	**A Spot on the Sun**
FST4	Marfax, C.	**Planets of Peril**
FST5	Collins, E.	**Conquerors of Space**

BALLANTINE BOOKS, INC., New York, N.Y., U.S.A.
  This publisher initially issued simultaneous paperback and hardcover editions for many titles, as noted in the Authors section. Hardcover prices commenced at $1.50 in 1953, but rose to $2.75 (with some exceptions) before hardcover editions were abandoned in 1958. A few titles (denoted †) had hardcover editions from other publishers.

  Not all cartoon (comic book) works such as the *Mad* Readers are covered, nor are associational items by noted authors.

  Paperback pricing began at 35¢. Later serial codes are: F- 50¢; S- 75¢; U2000 series, 50¢; U5000, 60¢; U7000, 95¢; 70000, 50¢; 72000, 75¢; 73000, 95¢.
Ballantine
1953
16	Pohl, F.	**Star Science Fiction Stories**

21	Kornbluth, C. M., & Pohl, F.	
		The Space Merchants
25	Pratt, F.	**The Undying Fire**
28	Kersh, G.	**The Secret Masters**
30	Kuttner, H.	**Ahead of Time**
33	Clarke, A. C.	**Childhood's End**
38	Moore, W.	**Bring the Jubilee**
41	Bradbury R.	**Fahrenheit 451**
46	Sturgeon, T.	**More Than Human**
50	Wyndham, J.	**Out of the Deeps**
52	Clarke, A. C.	**Expedition to Earth**
55	Pohl, F.	**Star Science Fiction Stories No. 2**
1954		
56	Duncan, D.	**Dark Dominion**
58	Siodmak, C.	**Riders to the Stars**
61	Kornbluth, C. M., & Pohl, F.	
		Search the Sky
68	Clarke, A. C.	**Prelude to Space†**
71	Crane, R.	**Hero's Walk**
73	Sheckley, R.	**Untouched by Human Hands**
80	Anderson, P.	**Brain Wave**
86	Kornbluth, C. M.	**The Explorers**
89	Pohl, F.	**Star Short Novels**
91	Oliver, C.	**Shadows in the Sun**
94	Vidal, G.	**Messiah†**
96	Pohl, F.	**Star Science Fiction Stories No. 3**
1955		
97	Clarke, A. C.	**Earthlight**
99	Tenn, W.	**Of All Possible Worlds**
102	Duncan, D.	**Beyond Eden**
104	Wyndham, J.	**Re-Birth**
107	Kornbluth, C. M., & Pohl, F.	
		Gladiator-at-Law
109	Boucher, A.	**Far and Away**
113	Oliver, C.	**Another Kind**
117	Wilson, R.	**The Girls From Planet 5**
119	Sturgeon, T.	**Caviar**
122	Kuttner, H., & Moore, C. L.	
		No Boundaries
126	Sheckley, R.	**Citizen in Space**
1956		
130	Pohl, F.	**Alternating Currents**
135	Clarke, A. C.	**Reach for Tomorrow**
F139	Bradbury, R.	**The October Country**
147	Mead, H.	**The Bright Phoenix**
151	del Rey, L.	**Nerves**
159	Tenn, W.	**The Human Angle**
167	Vance, J.	**To Live Forever**
174	Mead, S.	**The Big Ball of Wax**
179	Sturgeon, T.	**E Pluribus Unicorn**
182	Wyndham, J.	**Tales of Gooseflesh and Laughter**
1957		
186	Clarke, A. C.	**Tales From the White Hart**
192	Pohl, F.	**Slave Ship**
197	Blish, J.	**The Frozen Year**
200	Clement, H.	**Cycle of Fire**
206	Pohl, F.	**The Case Against Tomorrow**
210	Farmer, P. J.	**The Green Odyssey**
215	Anonymous	**Sometime, Never**
218	Maine, C. E.	**High Vacuum**
230	Duncan, D.	**Occam's Razor**
237	Wilson, R.	**Those Idiots From Earth**
1958		
243	Budrys, A.	**Man of Earth**
246	del Rey, L.	**Robots and Changelings**
249	Clarke, A. C.	**Earthlight**
256	Blish, J.	**A Case of Conscience**
257	Conklin, G.	**The Graveyard Reader**
260	Cooper, E.	**Deadly Image**
268	Kersh, G.	**On an Odd Note**
272K	Pohl, F.	**Star Science Fiction Stories No. 4**
273K	Dornberger, W.	**V-2**

279K	Cooper, E.	**Tomorrow's Gift**

1959

284K	Bowen, J.	**After the Rain**
290K	Maine, C. E.	**The Tide Went Out**
299K	Wyndham, J.	**The Midwich Cuckoos**
303K	Kornbluth, C. M.	**The Marching Morons**
308K	Pohl, F.	**Star Science Fiction Stories No. 5**
316K	Smith, G. O.	**The Fourth "R"**
325K	Pohl, F.	**Tomorrow Times Seven**
326K	Davenport, B.	**Deals With the Devil**
327	Cooper, E.	**Seed of Light**
329K	Harvey, F.	**Air Force!**
335K	Kornbluth, C. M., & Pohl, F.	
		Wolfbane
341K	Wyndham, J., & Parkes, L.	
		The Outward Urge
345K	Appel, B.	**The Funhouse**
353K	Pohl, F.	**Star Science Fiction No. 6**

1960

360K	Maine, C. E.	**Fire Past the Future**
365K	Oliver, C.	**Unearthly Neighbors**
370K	Zacherley	**Zacherley's Midnight Snacks**
377K	Sarban	**The Sound of His Horn**
380K	Davenport, B.	**Horror Stories From Tales To Be Told in the Dark**
381K	Kornbluth, C. M., & Pohl, F.	
		The Space Merchants
382K	Bradbury, R.	**Fahrenheit 451**
388K	Budrys, A.	**The Unexpected Dimension**
391K	Farmer, P. J.	**Strange Relations**
393K	Anderson, P.	**Brain Wave**
397K	Pohl, F.	**The Man Who Ate the World**
398K	Clarke, A. C.	**Childhood's End**
401K	Davenport, B.	**Invisible Men**
406K	Livingston, H.	**The Climacticon**
407K	Tenn, W.	**Of All Possible Worlds**
S414K	Wells, H. G.	**Best Stories of H. G. Wells**
417K	Zacherley	**Zacherley's Vulture Stew**
422K	Anderson, P.	**Guardians of Time**
423K	Wyndham, J.	**Re-Birth**
431K	Sarban	**The Doll Maker**
434K	Wilson, R.	**30-Day Wonder**
437K	Sheckley, R.	**Untouched by Human Hands**
439K	Pohl, F.	**Drunkard's Walk**
441K	Laski, M.	**The Victorian Chaise-Longue**
F446K	Gardner, M.	**Fads and Fallacies in the Name of Science**
449K	Wyndham, J.	**Trouble With Lichen**
453K	Wyndham, J.	**Village of the Damned**
462K	Sturgeon, T.	**More Than Human**

1961

458K	Sturgeon, T.	**Some of Your Blood**
465K	Blish, J.	**So Close to Home**
466K	Burnett, W. & H.	**Things With Claws**
472K	Clarke, A. C.	**Expedition to Earth**
476K	Pohl, F.	**Turn Left at Thursday**
479K	Amis, K.	**New Maps of Hell**
480K	Cross, J. K.	**The Other Passenger**
483K	Anderson, P.	**Strangers From Earth**
484K	Vidal, G.	**Messiah**
497K	Kuttner, H.	**Bypass to Otherness**
498K	Sarban	**Ringstones**
506K	Sturgeon, T.	**Not Without Sorcery**
507K	Farmer, P. J.	**The Lovers**
508K	Leiber, F.	**Night's Black Agents**
511K	van Vogt, A. E.	**Slan**
519K	Clingerman, M.	**A Cupful of Space**
521K	Pohl, F.	**Star Science Fiction Stories No. 1**
522K	Congdon, D.	**Tales of Love and Horror**
527	Moore, W.	**Greener Than You Think**
F528	Clarke, A. C.	**The Challenge of the Space Ship**
531	Wakefield, H. R.	**Stories From The Clock Strikes 12**
539	Clarke, A. C.	**Tales From the White Hart**

540	Russell, R.	**Sardonicus**
542	Derleth, A.	**Not Long for This World**
F543	King-Hall, S.	**Moment of No Return**
545	Wyndham, J.	**Out of the Deeps**
546	Wyndham, J.	**The Infinite Moment**
552	del Rey, L.	**. . . And Some Were Human**
F555	Aldiss, B. W.	**The Primal Urge**
556	Zacherley	**Zacherley's Midnight Snacks**
F561	Leiber, F.	**The Silver Eggheads**
563	Congdon, M. & D.	**Alone by Night**

1962

F562	Sturgeon, T.	**Caviar**
F570	Kornbluth, C. M., & Pohl, F.	
		Gladiator-at-Law
F571	Gillon, D. & M.	**The Unsleeep**
574	Zacherley	**Zacherley's Vulture Stew**
577	Leiber, F.	**Shadows With Eyes**
579	Anderson, P.	**After Doomsday**
F580	Bradbury, R.	**The October Country**
F581	Golston, R. C.	**Satan's Disciples**
587	Brennan, J. P.	**Nine Horrors and a Dream**
F588	Bester, A.	**The Alley God**
F595	White, J.	**Hospital Station**
597	Pohl, F.	**The Man Who Ate the World**
F602	Wells, B.	**The Day the Earth Caught Fire**
F609	Sellings, A.	**Telepath**
612	Pohl, F.	**Star Science Fiction Stories No. 2**
F619	Kuttner, H.	**Return to Otherness**
F626	Miller, W. M.	**Conditionally Human**
629	Lovecraft, H. P.	**The Survivor and Others**
632	Blish, J.	**So Close to Home**
F638	Kornbluth, C. M., & Pohl, F.	
		The Wonder Effect
F639	Clifton, M.	**Eight Keys to Eden**
F641	Beaumont, C.	**The Fiend in You**
F647	Blish, J.	**The Night Shapes**
F648	Sheckley, R.	**Citizen in Space**
F657	Anonymous	**Sometime, Never**
F658	Wilson, R.	**Time Out for Tomorrow**
F675	Pohl, F.	**Star Science Fiction Stories No. 3**
F676	Bradbury, R.	**Fahrenheit 451**
F680	Beck, C.	**The Frankenstein Reader**

1963

F685	Pohl, F.	**The Abominable Earthman**
F687	Wells, H. G.	**The First Men in the Moon**
F698	Clarke, A. C.	**Earthlight**
F701	Burroughs, E. R.	**A Princess of Mars**
F702	Burroughs, E. R.	**The Gods of Mars**
F703	Brown, R. G.	**A Handful of Time**
F708	Kornbluth, C. M.	**The Explorers**
F709	White, J.	**Star Surgeon**
F711	Burroughs, E. R.	**The Warlord of Mars**
F722	Patrick, Q.	**The Grindle Nightmare**
F724	Kuttner, H.	**Mutant**
F725	Wells, H. G.	**The Food of the Gods**
F728	Burroughs, E. R.	**The Swords of Mars**
F730	Pohl, F.	**Star Short Novels**
X733	Haggard, H. R.	**King Solomon's Mines**
F738	Kornbluth, C. M., & Pohl, F.	
		Search the Sky
F739	Burroughs, E. R.	**Synthetic Men of Mars**
S742	Wells, H. G.	**Best Stories of H. G. Wells**
X743	Haggard, H. R.	**Allan Quatermain**
F745	Burroughs, E. R.	**Tarzan of the Apes**
F746	Burroughs, E. R.	**The Return of Tarzan**
F747	Burroughs, E. R.	**The Beasts of Tarzan**
F748	Burroughs, E. R.	**The Son of Tarzan**
F749	Burroughs, E. R.	**Tarzan and the Jewels of Opar**
F750	Burroughs, E. R.	**Jungle Tales of Tarzan**
F751	Burroughs, E. R.	**Tarzan the Untamed**
F752	Burroughs, E. R.	**Tarzan the Terrible**
F753	Burroughs, E. R.	**Tarzan and the Golden Lion**

F754	Burroughs, E. R.	**Tarzan and the Ant-Men**
F760	Kornbluth, C. M.	**The Marching Morons**
F761	Wells, H. G.	**The Island of Dr. Moreau**
F762	Burroughs, E. R.	**Llana of Gathol**
F770	Burroughs, E. R.	**Thuvia, Maid of Mars**
F772	Burroughs, E. R.	**Tarzan, Lord of the Jungle**
F776	Burroughs, E. R.	**The Chessmen of Mars**
F777	Burroughs, E. R.	**Tarzan and the Lost Empire**
U2001	Burroughs, E. R.	**Tarzan of the Apes**
U2002	Burroughs, E. R.	**The Return of Tarzan**
U2003	Burroughs, E. R.	**The Beasts of Tarzan**
U2004	Burroughs, E. R.	**The Son of Tarzan**
U2005	Burroughs, E. R.	**Tarzan and the Jewels of Opar**
U2006	Burroughs, E. R.	**Jungle Tales of Tarzan**
U2007	Burroughs, E. R.	**Tarzan the Untamed**
U2008	Burroughs, E. R.	**Tarzan the Terrible**
U2009	Burroughs, E. R.	**Tarzan and the Golden Lion**
U2010	Burroughs, E. R.	**Tarzan and the Ant-Men**
U2011	Burroughs, E. R.	**Tarzan, Lord of the Jungle**
U2012	Burroughs, E. R.	**Tarzan and the Lost Empire**
U2031	Burroughs, E. R.	**A Princess of Mars**
U2032	Burroughs, E. R.	**The Gods of Mars**
U2036	Burroughs, E. R.	**The Master Mind of Mars**
U2037	Burroughs, E. R.	**A Fighting Man of Mars**
U2110	Clarke, A. C.	**Reach for Tomorrow**
U2111	Clarke, A. C.	**Childhood's End**
U2138	Bradbury, R.	**Fahrenheit 451**

1964

U2013	Burroughs, E. R.	**Tarzan at the Earth's Core**
U2014	Burroughs, E. R.	**Tarzan the Invincible**
U2015	Burroughs, E. R.	**Tarzan Triumphant**
U2016	Burroughs, E. R.	**Tarzan and the City of Gold**
U2017	Burroughs, E. R.	**Tarzan and the Lion Man**
U2018	Burroughs, E. R.	**Tarzan and the Leopard Men**
U2019	Burroughs, E. R.	**Tarzan's Quest**
U2020	Burroughs, E. R.	**Tarzan and the Forbidden City**
U2021	Burroughs, E. R.	**Tarzan the Magnificent**
U2022	Burroughs, E. R.	**Tarzan and the "Foreign Legion"**
U2048	Burroughs, E. R.	**The Lad and the Lion**
U2171	Pohl, F.	**Star of Stars**
U2172	Pohl, F., & Williamson, J.	
		The Reefs of Space
U2173	Kornbluth, C. M., & Pohl, F.	
		The Space Merchants
U2190	Tenn, W.	**The Human Angle**
U2191	Dick, P. K.	**Martian Time-Slip**
U2192	Farmer, P. J.	**Inside Outside**
U2203	Bixby, J.	**Space by the Tale**
U2213	Conquest, R.	**A World of Difference**
U2214	Vance, J.	**Future Tense**
U2215	Clement, H.	**Close to Critical**
U2216	Leiber, F.	**A Pail of Air**
U2219	Brunner, J.	**The Whole Man**
U2220	Ferman, J. W.	**No Limits**
U2222	Wellman, M. W.	**Who Fears the Devil?**
U2224	White, J.	**Deadly Litter**
U2232	Wells, H. G.	**The First Men in the Moon**
U5004	Shute, N.	**In the Wet**
U5030	Burgess, A.	**The Wanting Seed**
U6010	Leiber, F.	**The Wanderer**
U6018	Pangborn, E.	**Davy**

1965

U2023	Burroughs, E. R.	**Tarzan and the Madman**
U2024	Burroughs, E. R.	**Tarzan and the Castaways**
U2033	Burroughs, E. R.	**The Warlord of Mars**
U2034	Burroughs, E. R.	**Thuvia, Maid of Mars**
U2038	Burroughs, E. R.	**The Swords of Mars**
U2039	Burroughs, E. R.	**Synthetic Men of Mars**
U2040	Burroughs, E. R.	**Llana of Gathol**
U2041	Burroughs, E. R.	**John Carter of Mars**
U2106	Anonymous	**Tales From the Crypt**
U2107	Anonymous	**The Vault of Horror**

U2112	Clarke, A. C.	**Expedition to Earth**
U2139	Bradbury, R.	**The October Country**
U2140	Anonymous	**Tales of the Incredible**
U2141	Bradbury, R.	**The Autumn People**
U2174	Pohl, F.	**A Plague of Pythons**
U2175	Pohl, F.	**The Case Against Tomorrow**
U2176	Pohl, F., & Williamson, J.	
		Starchild
U2193	Farmer, P. J.	**Dare**
U2212	Miller, W. M.	**View From the Stars**
U2231	Sturgeon, T.	**More Than Human**
U2232	Wells, H. G.	**The First Men in the Moon**
U2233	Green, J. L.	**The Loafers of Refuge**
U2235	Clement, H.	**Natives of Space**
U2236	del Rey, L.	**Mortals and Monsters**
U2247	Sturgeon, T.	**E Pluribus Unicorn**
U2248	Bowen, J.	**After the Rain**
U2807	Davenport, B.	**Horror Stories From Tales To Be Told in the Dark**
U2809	Wyndham, J., & Parkes, J.	
		The Outward Urge
U2814	Wyndham, J.	**Out of the Deeps**
U2816	Burnett, W. & H.	**Things With Claws**
U2820	Wyndham, J.	**Re-Birth**
U2822	Conklin, G.	**The Graveyard Reader**
U2824	Clarke, A. C.	**Earthlight**
U5022	Vidal, G.	**Messiah**
U5032	Burgess, A.	**A Clockwork Orange**
U5050	Sheckley, R.	**The 10th Victim**
U6035	Brunner, J.	**The Squares of the City**
U7039	Tolkien, J. R. R.	**The Hobbit**
U7040	Tolkien, J. R. R.	**The Fellowship of the Ring**
U7041	Tolkien, J. R. R.	**The Two Towers**
U7042	Tolkien, J. R. R.	**The Return of the King**

1966

U2001	Burroughs, E. R.	**Tarzan of the Apes**
U2113	Clarke, A. C.	**Tales From the White Hart**
U2142	Bradbury, R.	**Tomorrow Midnight**
U2169	Vance, J.	**The Blue World**
U2177	Pohl, F.	**Slave Ship**
U2178	Pohl, F.	**Digits and Dastards**
U2251	Blish, J.	**A Case of Conscience**
U2253	Sturgeon, T.	**Some of Your Blood**
U2254	Leiber, F.	**The Night of the Wolf**
U2271	Stoker, B.	**Dracula**
U2285	White, J.	**The Watch Below**
U2328	Niven, L.	**World of Ptavvs**
U2329	Brunner, J.	**The Long Result**
U2330	Silverberg, R.	**Needle in a Timestack**
U2331	Blish, J.	**New Dreams This Morning**
U2341	Kuttner, H.	**Ahead of Time**
U2342	Anderson, P.	**Brain Wave**
U2344	del Rey, L.	**Nerves**
U2345	Farmer, P. J.	**The Green Odyssey**
U2346	Vance, J.	**To Live Forever**
U2828	Davenport, B.	**Deals With the Devil**
U2832	Wyndham, J.	**Tales of Gooseflesh and Laughter**
U2840	Wyndham, J.	**The Midwich Cuckoos**
U2842	Davenport, B.	**Invisible Men**
U6039	Burroughs, E. R.	**The Mucker**
U6049	Hodder-Williams, C.	**The Main Experiment**
U6071	Norman, J.	**Tarnsman of Gor**
U6125	Leiber, F.	**Tarzan and the Valley of Gold**
U7038	Tolkien, J. R. R.	**The Tolkien Reader**

1967

U2002	Burroughs, E. R.	**The Return of Tarzan**
U2343	Kornbluth, C. M., & Pohl, F.	
		Gladiator-at-Law
U2843	Bradbury, R.	**Fahrenheit 451**
U2845	West, J.	**The Chilekings**
U2849	Sarban	**The Dollmaker**
U2852	Congdon, M. & D.	**Alone by Night**

U2853	Anonymous	**Sometime, Never**
U2855	Sheckley, R.	**Untouched by Human Hands**
U5060	Bradbury, R.	**Fahrenheit 451**
U5063	Saberhagen, F.	**Berserker**
U5064	Brunner, J.	**Out of My Mind**
U5066	Clarke, A. C.	**Childhood's End**
U6072	Norman, J.	**Outlaw of Gor**
U6085	Burroughs, J. C.	**Treasure of the Black Falcon**
U6092	Maine, C. E.	**B.E.A.S.T.**
U6093	Silverberg, R.	**To Open the Sky**
U6097	Silverberg, R.	**Thorns**
U6099	Anderson, C.	**The Butterfly Revolution**
U6100	Meyers, R.	**Dolphin Boy**
U6107	Anthony, P.	**Chthon**
U6108	McCaffrey, A.	**Restoree**
U6112	Howard, H.	**The Eskimo Invasion**
U6114	Amis, K.	**The Anti-Death League**
U7061	Eddison, E. R.	**The Worm Ouroboros**
U7063	Eddison, E. R.	**Mistress of Mistresses**
U7083	Moskowitz, S.	**Seekers of Tomorrow**
1968		
U2220	Ferman, J. W.	**No Limits**
U2857	Oliver, C.	**Shadows in the Sun**
U2859	Kuttner, H.	**Mutant**
U2862	Sheckley, R.	**Citizen in Space**
U2866	White, J.	**Star Surgeon**
U6115	Thomas, D.	**The Seed**
U6120	Niven, L.	**Neutron Star**
U6121	Silverberg, R.	**The Masks of Time**
U6124	McCaffrey, A.	**Dragonflight**
U6131	Tenn, W.	**Of Men and Monsters**
U6132	Tenn, W.	**The Square Root of Man**
U6133	Tenn, W.	**The Wooden Star**
U6134	Tenn, W.	**The Seven Sexes**
U6135	Tenn, W.	**The Human Angle**
U6136	Tenn, W.	**Of All Possible Worlds**
U6199	Wyndham, J.	**Chocky**
U7064	Eddison, E. R.	**A Fish Dinner in Memison**
70002	Bradbury, R.	**Fahrenheit 451**
70005	Laski, M.	**The Victorian Chaise-Longue**
70007	Clement, H.	**Cycle of Fire**
72001	Meyers, R.	**Daughters of the Dolphin**
72006	Vidal, G.	**Messiah**
72008	Biggers, W. W.	**The Man Inside**
72009	Sturgeon, T.	**More Than Human**
72014	Anthony, P.	**Omnivore**
72015	Norman, J.	**The Priest-Kings of Gor**
72113	Niven, L.	**A Gift From Earth**
72138	Bradbury, R.	**The October Country**
73004	Whitfield, S. E., & Roddenberry, G.	
		The Making of Star Trek
73007	Peake, M.	**Titus Groan**
73008	Peake, M.	**Gormenghast**
73009	Peake, M.	**Titus Alone**
73010	Lindsay, D.	**A Voyage to Arcturus**

Banner See HEARST CORP.

BANTAM. Understood to be a U.S. West Coast publisher (not to be confused with Bantam Books, Inc.).
Bant.
1940

—	Burroughs, E. R.	**Tarzan in the Forbidden City**

BANTAM BOOKS, INC., New York, N.Y., U.S.A.
Prices began at 25¢. Serial codes are: A- 35¢; J- 40¢; E- 45¢; F- 50¢; FP- 50¢; H- 60¢; HP- 60¢; S- 75¢; N- 95¢; NC- 95¢.
Prefix "P" denotes Pennant Books imprint.
Bantam
1946

37	Addams, C.	**Drawn and Quartered**
63	Hudson, W. H.	**Green Mansions**

1947		
90	Macardle, D.	**The Uninvited**
1948		
410	Malcolm-Smith, G.	**The Grass Is Always Greener**
502	Cerf, B.	**The Unexpected**
1950		
751	Merril, J.	**Shot in the Dark**
819	Siodmak, C.	**Donovan's Brain**
835	Brown, F.	**What Mad Universe**
1951		
886	Bradbury, R.	**The Martian Chronicles**
915	Macardle, D.	**The Unforeseen**
1952		
A944	Bradbury, R.	**Timeless Stories for Today and Tomorrow**
991	Bradbury, R.	**The Illustrated Man**
1007	Cozzens, J. G.	**Castaway**
A1009	Carr, J. D.	**The Devil in Velvet**
1953		
P15	Kornbluth, C. M.	**Takeoff**
A1071	Huxley, A.	**Brave New World**
1077	Brown, F.	**Space on My Hands**
1079	Heard, G.	**Is Another World Watching?**
A1106	Collier, J.	**Fancies and Goodnights**
1954		
P44	Healy, R. J., & McComas, J. F.	
		Adventures in Time and Space
P55	O'Farrell, W.	**Repeat Performance**
P56	Merril, J.	**(Selections From) Beyond Human Ken**
P75	Sohl, J.	**The Altered Ego**
1207	Carr, J. D.	**The Burning Court**
A1241	Bradbury, R.	**Golden Apples of the Sun**
1251	Padgett, L.	**Line to Tomorrow**
1253	Brown, F.	**What Mad Universe**
1261	Bradbury, R.	**The Martian Chronicles**
A1262	Vonnegut, K.	**Utopia 14**
1278	Sohl, J.	**Costigan's Needle**
1282	Bradbury, R.	**The Illustrated Man**
1955		
1285	Brown, F.	**The Lights in the Sky Are Stars**
A1292	Capek, K.	**War With the Newts**
1294	Matheson, R.	**Third From the Sun**
1310	Healy, R. J., & McComas, J. F.	
		More Adventures in Time and Space
1317	Kornbluth, C. M.	**The Syndic**
1328	Bleiler, E. F., & Dikty, T. E.	
		Frontiers in Space
1343	Tucker, W.	**The Man From Tomorrow**
1352	Conklin, G.	**Science Fiction Thinking Machines**
1362	Russell, E. F.	**Deep Space**
A1369	Huxley, A.	**Brave New World**
A1374	Jessup, M. K.	**The Case for the UFO**
1400	Tucker, W.	**Time: X**
1956		
1423	Brown, F.	**Star Shine**
F1441	Cartmell, V. H., & Grayson, C.	
		The Golden Argosy
A1443	Stuart, W. J.	**Forbidden Planet**
A1470	Maine, C. E.	**Timeliner**
A1492	Kornbluth, C. M.	**Not This August**
1507	Miller, R. D.	**Reincarnation: The Whole Startling Story**
A1519	Bradbury, R.	**The Circus of Dr. Lao**
1541	Smith, H. A.	**The Age of the Tail**
A1546	Brown, F.	**Martians, Go Home**
1957		
A1550	Burnett, W. & H.	**19 Tales of Terror**
A1553	Frank, P.	**Forbidden Area**
A1571	Matheson, R.	**The Shores of Space**
A1593	Robinson, F. M.	**The Power**
A1615	Reynolds, M., & Brown, F.	
		Science Fiction Carnival
A1646	Asimov, I.	**Pebble in the Sky**
A1672	Sheckley, R.	**Pilgrimage to Earth**

| A1701 | Brown, F. | Rogue in Space |
| F1703 | Collier, J. | Fancies and Goodnights |

1958

A1731	Asimov, I.	The Naked Sun
A1753	Steinbeck, J.	The Short Reign of Pippin IV
A1759	Beaumont, C.	Yonder
A1766	Castle, J. L.	Satellite E One
A1786	Tenn, W.	Time in Advance
A1793	Huxley, A.	Ape and Essence
A1812	Brown, F.	Honeymoon in Hell
A1825	Gunn, J. E.	Station in Space
A1842	Van Druten, J.	Bell, Book and Candle
A1847	Carr, J. D.	Fire, Burn!
A1860	Ehrlich, M.	The Big Eye
FC13	France, A.	Penguin Island

1959

F1878	Hudson, W. H.	Green Mansions
A1885	Bradbury, R.	The Martian Chronicles
A1917	Beaumont, C.	Hunger
A1922	Bradbury, R.	Dandelion Wine
A1937	Williams, J.	The Witches
A1952	Sohl, J.	Point Ultimate
A1971	Sohl, J.	The Transcendent Man
A1978	Asimov, I.	Earth Is Room Enough
A1982	Wibberley, L.	The Mouse That Roared
A1991	Sheckley, R.	Immortality, Inc.
A2000	Dickson, C.	Fear Is the Same
AC1	Huxley, A.	Brave New World
FC46	Capek, K.	War With the Newts

1960

A2003	Sheckley, R.	Notions: Unlimited
A2046	Serling, R.	Stories From the Twilight Zone
A2048	Bahnson, A.	The Stars Are Too High
F2052	Carr, J. D.	The Devil in Velvet
F2054	Frank, P.	Alas, Babylon
A2055	Zugsmith, A., & Hill, R.	
		The Private Lives of Adam and Eve
A2069	Bradbury, R.	A Medicine for Melancholy
A2087	Beaumont, C.	Night Ride and Other Journeys
A2121	Asimov, I.	Nine Tomorrows
F2124	Huxley, A.	Brave New World Revisited
A2160	Harrison, H.	Deathworld
A2170	Sheckley, R.	The Store of Infinity

1961

A2187	Brown, F.	The Mind Thing
F2212	Miller, W. M.	A Canticle for Leibowitz
A2219	Gunn, J. T.	The Joy Makers
A2227	Serling, R.	More Stories From the Twilight Zone
A2241	Kantor, M.	If the South Had Won the Civil War
A2254	Fast, H.	The Edge of Tomorrow
F2255	Fitzgibbon, C.	When the Kissing Had to Stop
J2266	Galouye, D. F.	Dark Universe
H2290	Hersey, J.	The Child Buyer
J2296	Brown, F.	Nightmares and Geezenstacks
J2306	Bradbury, R.	Golden Apples of the Sun
F2329	Richter, C.	The Waters of Kronos
H2343	Bradbury, R.	Timeless Stories for Today and Tomorrow

1962

FC85	Huxley, A.	Brave New World
FC189	Huxley, A.	Brave New World
J2316	Harrison, H.	Planet of the Damned
J2363	Bone, J. F.	The Lani People
A2412	Serling, R.	New Stories From the Twilight Zone
F2438	Bradbury, R.	The Martian Chronicles
J2443	Sheckley, R.	Shards of Space
J2457	Wibberley, L.	The Mouse That Roared
F2458	Verne, J.	Twenty Thousand Leagues Under the Sea
J2467	Matheson, R.	Third From the Sun
J2484	Gunn, J.	The Immortals
S2526	Hailey, A.	In High Places

1963

| FP30 | Cerf, B. | Stories Selected From The Unexpected |

FC46	Capek, K.	War With the Newts
NC171	Spector, R. D.	7 Masterpieces of Gothic Horror
J2530	Brooks, W.	The Original Mr. Ed
J2555	Galouye, D. F.	Lords of the Psychon
J2578	Brown, F.	The Lights in the Sky Are Stars
F2588	Bradbury, R.	The Illustrated Man
J2617	St. Clair, M.	Sign of the Labrys
H2618	Miller, W. M.	A Canticle for Leibowitz
J2623	Serling, R.	Rod Serling's Triple W: Witches, Warlocks and Werewolves
H2630	Bradbury, R.	Something Wicked This Way Comes
F2637	Bradbury, R.	A Medicine for Melancholy
N2640	Knebel, F., & Bailey, C. W.	
		Seven Days in May
F2641	Wibberley, L.	The Mouse on the Moon
J2650	Brown, F.	Honeymoon in Hell
J2686	Charbonneau, L.	The Sentinel Stars
J2693	Serling, R.	Stories From the Twilight Zone
S2695	Huxley, A.	Island
F2697	Manvell, R.	The Dreamers
J2706	Carr, J. D.	The Burning Court
J2717	Gunn, J. E.	Future Imperfect

1964

EP47	Asimov, I.	Pebble in the Sky
FP55	Bradbury, R.	Dandelion Wine
FP58	Poe, E. A.	Great Tales of Horror
EP63	Conklin, G.	(Selections From) Science Fiction Thinking Machines
HP70	Frank, P.	Alas, Babylon
EP80	Wibberley, L.	The Mouse That Roared
EP89	Serling, R.	Stories From The Twilight Zone
SC91	Collier, J.	Fancies and Goodnights
SC165	Swift, J.	Gulliver's Travels
HC206	Huxley, A.	Brave New World
HC262	Huxley, A.	Ape and Essence
F2679	George, P.	Dr. Strangelove
J2717	Gunn, J. E.	Future Imperfect
H2728	Trew, A.	Two Hours to Darkness
H2734	Clarke, A. C.	Profiles of the Future
J2744	Matheson, R.	I Am Legend
J2753	Engle, E.	Countdown for Cindy
F2755	Finney, C. G.	The Circus of Dr. Lao
J2797	Galouye, D. F.	Simulacron-3
F2812	Sheckley, R.	Pilgrimage to Earth
F2838	Harrison, H.	Deathworld 2
E2853	Robeson, K.	The Man of Bronze
E2854	Robeson, K.	The Thousand-Headed Man
E2855	Robeson, K.	Meteor Menace
J2872	Serling, R.	New Stories From The Twilight Zone
J2880	Serling, R.	More Stories From The Twilight Zone

1965

FP81	Wells, H. G.	The Inexperienced Ghost and Nine Other Stories
HP84	Verne, J.	Twenty Thousand Leagues Under the Sea
HP103	Hudson, W. H.	Green Mansions
FP104	Wibberley, L.	The Mouse on the Moon
EP121	Serling, R.	New Stories From The Twilight Zone
FP127	Bradbury, R.	The Illustrated Man
SC247	France, A.	Penguin Island
QC250	Capek, K.	War With the Newts
F2817	Knight, D.	13 French Science-Fiction Stories
F2915	Bradbury, R.	R Is for Rocket
H2917	Southern, T.	The Magic Christian
F2929	Charbonneau, L.	Psychedelic-40
F2941	Dickson, G. R.	The Alien Way
S2965	Caidin, M.	Marooned
S2973	Miller, W. M.	A Canticle for Leibowitz
F2980	Serling, R.	Rod Serling's Triple W: Witches, Warlocks and Werewolves
F2983	Wibberley, L.	A Feast of Freedom
H2988	Bradbury, R.	The Machineries of Joy
E3015	Robeson, K.	The Polar Treasure

E3016	Robeson, K.	**The Brand of the Werewolf**
E3017	Robeson, K.	**The Lost Oasis**
E3029	Wallis, D.	**Only Lovers Left Alive**
E3033	Robeson, K.	**The Monsters**
E3042	Robeson, K.	**The Land of Terror**
F3093	Wallace, E., & Cooper, M. C.	
		King Kong
E3115	Robeson, K.	**The Mystic Mullah**

1966

EP169	Serling, R.	**More Stories From The Twilight Zone**
E3047	Robeson, K.	**The Phantom City**
Q3095	Hersey, J.	**White Lotus**
F3102	Healy, R. J., & McComas, J. F.	
		Adventures in Time and Space
E3110	Robeson, K.	**The Quest of Qui**
E3146	Robeson, K.	**Fear Cay**
H3148	Macardle, D.	**The Uninvited**
H3152	Knebel, F., & Bailey, C. W.	
		Night of Camp David
H3177	Asimov, I.	**Fantastic Voyage**
H3202	Robeson, K.	**The Land of Always-Night**
H3211	Macardle, D.	**The Unforeseen**
F3245	Carnell, E. J.	**New Writings in SF 1**
F3261	Healy, R. J., & McComas, J. F.	
		More Adventures in Time and Space
S3267	Gordon, M. & G.	**Power Play**
E3269	Robeson, K.	**The Fantastic Island**
F3309	Fast, H.	**The Edge of Tomorrow**
S3339	Keyes, D.	**Flowers for Algernon**
F3379	Carnell, E. J.	**New Writings in SF 2**

1967

SA2	Holmes, D. C.	**The Search for Life on Other Worlds**
HP55	Bradbury, R.	**Dandelion Wine**
FP161	Verne, J.	**From the Earth to the Moon**
FP164	Bradbury, R.	**R Is for Rocket**
FP165	Shelley, M. W.	**Frankenstein**
FP166	Stevenson, R. L.	**Dr. Jekyll and Mr. Hyde**
S1404	Capek, K.	**War With the Newts**
H2950	Wright, L., & Sheehan, R. G.	
		Wake Up Screaming
F3047	Robeson, K.	**The Phantom City**
E3150	Serling, R.	**More Stories From The Twilight Zone**
H3206	Wright, L., & Sheehan, R. G.	
		These Will Chill You
H3243	Bradbury, R.	**The Martian Chronicles**
F3296	Robeson, K.	**Murder Melody**
H3324	Serling, R.	**Rod Serling's Devils and Demons**
H3329	Macardle, D.	**Dark Enchantment**
S3339	Keyes, D.	**Flowers for Algernon**
F3340	Robeson, K.	**The Spook Legion**
H3357	Bradbury, R.	**The Golden Apples of the Sun**
H3358	Bradbury, R.	**Timeless Stories for Today and Tomorrow**
S3378	Edwards, F.	**Flying Saucers—Serious Business**
F3380	Carnell, E. J.	**New Writings in SF 3**
F3381	Sheckley, R.	**Time Limit**
F3387	Robeson, K.	**The Red Skull**
H3398	Bradbury, R.	**A Medicine for Melancholy**
N3400	Hersey, J.	**Too Far To Walk**
S3408	Bradbury, R.	**Something Wicked This Way Comes**
H3425	Derleth, A.	**Stories From Sleep No More**
H3426	Sloane, W.	**To Walk the Night**
H3427	Sloane, W.	**The Edge of Running Water**
H3428	Russell, R.	**Unholy Trinity**
F3441	Robeson, K.	**The Sargasso Ogre**
F3442	Charbonneau, L.	**Down to Earth**
F3455	Robeson, K.	**Fear Cay**
F3456	Robeson, K.	**The Quest of Qui**
F3459	Blish, J.	**Star Trek**
F3464	Robeson, K.	**The Mystic Mullah**
H3469	Edwards, F.	**Stranger Than Science**
H3484	Bradbury, R.	**The Illustrated Man**
F3486	Robeson, K.	**The Pirate of the Pacific**

H3493	Serling, R.	**Rod Serling's Triple W: Witches, Warlocks and Werewolves**
H3494	Manvell, R.	**The Dreamers**
F3496	Robeson, K.	**The Man of Bronze**
F3498	Robeson, K.	**The Lost Oasis**
F3499	Robeson, K.	**The Monsters**
F3520	Robeson, K.	**The Land of Always-Night**
F3533	Robeson, K.	**The Secret in the Sky**
S3549	Wheatley, D.	**The Devil Rides Out**
S3550	Wheatley, D.	**The Satanist**
F3569	Binder, O.	**The Avengers Battle the Earth-Wrecker**
F3573	Robeson, K.	**The Brand of the Werewolf**
K3656	Cicellis, K.	**The Day the Fish Came Out**
N5764	Pynchon, T.	**The Crying of Lot 49**

1968

FP47	Asimov, I.	**Pebble in the Sky**
FP80	Wibberley, L.	**The Mouse That Roared**
S3339	Keyes, D.	**Flowers for Algernon**
F3439	Blish, J.	**Star Trek 2**
N3481	Huxley, A.	**Island**
S3578	Boileau, P., & Narcejac, T.	
		Choice Cuts
F3584	Robeson, K.	**Cold Death**
F3585	Galouye, D. F.	**A Scourge of Screamers**
S3631	Edwards, D.	**Flying Saucers—Here and Now**
S3637	Carr, J. D.	**The Devil in Velvet**
S3638	Carr, J. D.	**Fire, Burn!**
F3640	Harrison, H.	**Plague From Space**
H3656	Cicellis, K.	**The Day the Fish Came Out**
F3667	Robeson, K.	**The Czar of Fear**
N3687	Rimmer, R. H.	**The Zolotov Affair**
F3716	Robeson, K.	**The Fortress of Solitude**
F3722	Harrison, H.	**Two Tales and Eight Tomorrows**
F3755	Robeson, K.	**The Mystery Under the Sea**
H3759	Charbonneau, L.	**The Sensitives**
F3763	Carnell, E. J.	**New Writings in SF 4**
S3764	Wheatley, D.	**To the Devil—A Daughter**
F3780	White, Ted	**Captain America: The Great Gold Steal**
F3782	Robeson, K.	**The Green Eagle**
F3805	Robeson, K.	**Death in Silver**
F3839	Robeson, K.	**The Deadly Dwarf**
F3841	Robeson, K.	**The Devil's Playground**
F3850	Sheckley, R.	**Notions: Unlimited**
S3851	Serling, R.	**The Season To Be Wary**
S3856	George, P.	**Dr. Strangelove**
S3875	Shute, N.	**On the Beach**
F3877	Robeson, K.	**The Other World**
F3885	Robeson, K.	**The Annihilist**
F3897	Robeson, K.	**The Flaming Falcons**
F3905	Wilson, C.	**The Mind Parasites**
H3915	Gunn, J.	**The Immortals**
FP4063	Wells, H. G.	**The Time Machine**
FP4078	Bradbury, R.	**R Is for Rocket**
FP4094	Serling, R.	**Stories From The Twilight Zone**
SY4172	Huxley, A.	**Brave New World**
HP4197	Bradbury, R.	**Dandelion Wine**
S4323	Edwards, F.	**Stranger Than Science**
HP4448	Verne, J.	**Twenty Thousand Leagues Under the Sea**

ARTHUR BARKER LTD., London, England.
Prefix "D" denotes Dragon Books imprint.
Barker
1958

D20	Bull, R. C.	**Perturbed Spirits**

1959

D40	Hartley, L. P.	**The Travelling Grave and Other Stories**

A. S. BARNES & CO. See ZWEMMER, A.

BARRINGTON GRAY LTD., Leigh-on-Sea, Essex, England.
Barrington
1954 (approx.)

—	Marquis, R.	**The Moon Monsters**

1955

—	Elliott, R. C.	**Sabotage**

BARTHOLOMEW HOUSE INC., New York, N.Y., U.S.A.
Bart House
1944

4	Lovecraft, H. P.	**The Weird Shadow Over Innsmouth**
6	McClary, T. C.	**Rebirth**
9	Maxon, P. B.	**The Waltz of Death**

1945

12	Lovecraft, H. P.	**The Dunwich Horror**

Bay Tree See WITHY GROVE PRESS LTD.

Beac (Gal) See GALAXY PUB. CORP.

Beac (Odh) See ODHAMS PRESS LTD.

BEACON PRESS, Boston, Mass., U.S.A.
Beac (Prs)
1967

BP251	Manuel, F. E.	**Utopias and Utopian Thought**

BEACON PUBLICATIONS CORP., New York, N.Y., U.S.A.
Beac (Pub)
1945 (approx.)

105	Mundy, T.	**King of the Khyber Rifles**

BEAR HUDSON LTD., London, England
Bear
1946 (approx.)

—	Pragnell, F.	**The Terror of Timorkal**

Not dated

—	Firth, N. W.	**Spawn of the Vampire***

1957

538	Firth, N. W.	**Spawn of the Vampire***

* Both editions apparently also contained "All Set for Murder," Frank
  Griffin, not s.f.

A. W. BEARNE
Bearne
1968

—	Bearne, A. W.	**Flying Saucers Over the West**

BEE-LINE, New York.
Bee-Line
1966

118	Savage, H.	**Jetman Meets the Mad Madam**
133	Earle, R.	**Forever Ember**
145	Carnelle, I.	**The Girl From B.U.S.T.**

1967

194	Carnelle, I.	**Joy Ride**

1968

307N	Key, D.	**The Sex Machine**
313N	Pendleton, D.	**Revolt!**

BEE-LINE, United Kingdom.
Bee-Line (UK)
1968

114	Wadd, C.	**Nymphos, Nymphets and Satyrs**

BELMONT PRODUCTIONS INC., New York, N.Y., U.S.A.
  Some books contain two novels; these are indicated by "do" (ditto)
instead of repeating the serial code for the second novel.
Belmont
1961

230	Hammett, D.	**Creeps by Night**
233	Bloch, R.	**Nightmares**
239	Hammett, D.	**The Red Brain**

1962

L92-527	Bloch, R.	**Yours Truly, Jack the Ripper**

L92-530	Bloch, R.	**More Nightmares**
L92-535	Conklin, G.	**Twisted**
L92-541	Gold, H. L.	**The Weird Ones**

1963

90-277	Long, F. B.	**It Was the Day of the Robot**
90-275	Bloch, R.	**Horror-7**
90-286	Willeford, C.	**The Machine in Ward Eleven**
90-297	Avallone, M.	**Tales of the Frightened**
90-298	Gibson, W. B.	**The Return of the Shadow**
L92-557	Howard, I.	**Rare Science Fiction**
L92-564	Howard, I.	**6 and the Silent Scream**
L92-567	Howard, I.	**Novelets of Science Fiction**
L92-569	Long, F. B.	**The Hounds of Tindalos**
L92-571	Howard, I.	**Escape to Earth**

1964

L92-575	Howard, I.	**Way Out**
L92-579	Long, F. B.	**The Dark Beasts**
L92-582	Howard, I.	**Things**
L92-584	Simak, C. D.	**Worlds Without End**
L92-588	Jones, R. F.	**The NonStatistical Man**
L92-591	Silverberg, R.	**Godling, Go Home**
L92-594	Derleth, A.	**Mr. George and Other Odd Persons**
L92-600	Long, F. B.	**Odd Science Fiction**
92-602	Grant, M.	**The Shadow Strikes Back**
92-603	Dick, P. K.	**The Penultimate Truth**
92-606	Anonymous	**Masters of Science Fiction**
92-611	Neville, K.	**The Unearth People**

1965

90297	Avallone, M.	**Tales of the Frightened**
92-612	Anonymous	**A Pair From Space**
92-615	Grant, M.	**Shadow Beware**
92-617	Lovecraft, H. P.	**The Case of Charles Dexter Ward**
92-618	Dick, P. K.	**Time out of Joint**
92-621	Lesser, M.	**Secret of the Black Planet**
92-622	Singer, K.	**The Unearthly**
92-624	Grant, M.	**Cry Shadow!**
92-625	Leinster, M.	**Space Platform**
B50-627	Binder, E.	**Anton York, Immortal**
B50-632	Leinster, M.	**Space Tug**
B50-633	Rathbone, B.	**Strange Tales**
B50-642	Sarac, R.	**The Throwbacks**
B50-643	Schmitz, J. H.	**A Tale of Two Clocks**
B50-646	Anonymous	**Now and Beyond**
B50-647	Grant, M.	**The Shadow's Revenge**

1966

B50-657	Hamilton, E.	**Doomstar**
B50-663	Long, F. B.	**This Strange Tomorrow**
B50-676	Leinster, M.	**Get Off My World**
B50-680	Reynolds, M.	**Of Godlike Power**
B50-682	del Rey, L.	**The Scheme of Things**
B50-683	Grant, M.	**The Mark of the Shadow**
B50-692	Tralins, R.	**The Cosmozoids**
B50-699	Smith, G. H.	**The Four Day Weekend**
B50-708	Jones, R. F.	**The Alien**
B50-709	Grant, M.	**Shadow—Go Mad!**
B50-717	Farmer, P. J.	**The Gate of Time**
B50-725	Grant, M.	**The Night of the Shadow**
B50-726	Long, F. B.	**Lest Earth Be Conquered**
B50-730	Neville, K.	**The Mutants**
B50-761	Stanton, L. J.	**Flying Saucers—Hoax or Reality?**

1967

B50-735	Hurwood, B. J.	**Monsters and Nightmares**
B50-736	Avallone, M.	**Tales of the Frightened**
B50-737	Grant, M.	**Destination: Moon**
B50-739	Spinrad, N.	**Agent of Chaos**
B50-745	Tralins, B.	**The Ring-a-Ding UFO's**
B50-751	White, Ted	**The Jewels of Elsewhen**
B50-757	Long, F. B.	**Journey Into Darkness**
B50-759	Carter, L.	**The Flame of Iridar**
do	Neville, K.	**Peril of the Starmen**
B50-770	Howard, I.	**Novelets of Science Fiction**
B50-771	Conklin, G.	**Twisted**

B50-779	Ellison, H.	Doomsman
do	Hoffman, L	Telepower
B50-781	Anonymous	Time Untamed
B50-787	Bloch, R.	The Living Demons
B50-788	Neville, K.	Special Delivery
do	Van Arnam, D.	Star Gladiator
B50-791	Simak, C. D.	Worlds Without End
B50-795	Reynolds, M.	After Some Tomorrow
B50-797	Kelley, L. P.	The Counterfeits
B60-069	Ellison, H.	From the Land of Fear
1968		
B50-809	Long, F. B.	. . . And Others Shall Be Born
do	Carter, L.	The Thief of Thoth
B50-810	Janifer, L. M.	Impossible?
B50-811	Janifer, L. M.	A Piece of Martin Cann
B50-813	Anonymous	A Pair From Space
B50-819	Elliott, B.	Asylum Earth
B50-820	Jones, R. F.	The Non-Statistical Man
B50-826	Reynolds, M.	Earth Unaware
B50-839	Rathbone, B.	Strange Tales
B50-840	Cogswell, T. R.	The Third Eye
B50-843	Neville, K.	The Unearth People
B50-845	Kelley, L. P.	Odyssey to Earthdeath
B50-846	Leinster, M.	Space Tug
B50-849	Jorgenson, I.	Whom the Gods Would Slay
B60-077	Tenn, W.	A Lamp for Medusa
do	Van Arnam, D.	The Players of Hell
B60-080	Bloch, R.	This Crowded Earth & Ladies' Day
B60-081	Brunner, J.	Father of Lies
do	Duncan, B.	Mirror Image
B60-082	Knight, D.	The Metal Smile
B60-085	Kelley, L. P.	Odyssey to Earthdeath
B75-215	Crossen, K. F.	Adventures in Tomorrow
B75-218	Binder, O. O.	Flying Saucers Are Watching Us
00804	Carter, L.	The Tower at the End of Time

ERNEST BENN LTD., London, England.
Benn
1958

—	Anonymous	Benn's Bedside Book

BERKLEY PUBLISHING CORP., New York, N.Y., U.S.A.
  Price code prefixes: none, 25¢; G- 35¢; Y- 40¢; C- 45¢; F- 50¢; X- 60¢; S- 75¢; N- 95¢; D- $1.25. In the 1960's "Medallion" was often included in series naming.
Berkley
1955

111	Mirbeau, O.	Torture Garden
344	van Vogt, A. E.	Mission to the Stars
G3	Conklin, G.	Possible Worlds of Science Fiction
1956		
G31	Conklin, G.	Science Fiction Omnibus
G36	Bromfield, L.	The Strange Case of Miss Annie Spragg
G39	Mirbeau, O.	Torture Garden
G41	Campbell, J. W.	The Astounding Science Fiction Anthology
1957		
380	Wells, H. G.	The Time Machine
G47	Campbell, J. W.	Astounding Tales of Space and Time
G53	Conklin, G.	The Big Book of Science Fiction
G63	Conklin, G.	The Treasury of Science Fiction
G71	Simak, C. D.	Strangers in the Universe
G77	Derleth, A.	Beachheads in Space
1958		
G104	Derleth, A.	Beyond Time and Space
G116	Derleth, A.	The Outer Reaches
G119	Cheever, J.	The Enormous Radio
G131	Derleth, A.	Strange Ports of Call
G148	Russell, E. F.	Men, Martians and Machines
G163	Derleth, A.	Worlds of Tomorrow
G189	Derleth, A.	Time to Come
1959		
G215	van Vogt, A. E.	Away and Beyond

G233	Bleiler, E. F., & Dikty, T. E.	
		Imagination Unlimited
G249	Derleth, A.	The Other Side of the Moon
G280	Sturgeon, T.	A Touch of Strange
G289	Anderson, P.	The Enemy Stars
1960		
G410	Leinster, M.	The Aliens
G445	Wells, H. G.	The Time Machine
G461	Leinster, M.	Men Into Space
G466	Hadley, A. T.	The Joy Wagon
G471	Conklin, G.	Possible Worlds of Science Fiction
1961		
G495	Hoyle, F.	Ossian's Ride
BG500	Southern, T.	The Magic Christian
G507	Blish, J.	Titans' Daughter
G518	Kerr, G.	Under the Influence
G536	de Camp, L. S., & Miller, P. S.	
		Genus Homo
G549	Leinster, M.	Creatures of the Abyss
F563	Stapledon, O.	Star Maker
Y582	Gantz, K. F.	Not in Solitude
1962		
F600	Ballard, J. G.	The Wind From Nowhere
F607	Ballard, J. G.	The Voices of Time
F616	Knight, D.	Far Out
F621	Leiber, F.	Conjure Wife
F634	Aymé, M.	The Walker-Through-Walls
F639	Davidson, A.	Or All the Seas With Oysters
F647	Knight, D.	The Analogue Men
F655	Ballard, J. G.	The Drowned World
F666	Cantor, H.	Ghosts and Things
F667	Ballard, J. G.	Billenium
F679	Leiber, F.	Gather, Darkness!
F694	Leinster, M.	Operation Terror
F704	van Vogt, A. E.	Mission to the Stars
1963		
F712	Anonymous	Beyond
F733	Amis, K., & Conquest, R.	
		Spectrum
F743	Anderson, P.	Shield
F760	Knight, D.	In Deep
F780	Laumer, K.	A Trace of Memory
Y789	Wells, H. G.	The Time Machine
F799	Budrys, A.	Budrys' Inferno
F812	van Vogt, A. E.	Away and Beyond
F823	Ballard, J. G.	Passport to Eternity
X834	Huxley, A.	Time Must Have a Stop
F835	Simak, C. D.	Strangers in the Universe
F851	Conklin, G.	Science Fiction Omnibus
F862	Wilhelm, K.	The Mile-Long Spaceship
F875	Campbell, J. W.	The Astounding Science Fiction Anthology
1964		
F883	Carnell, E. J.	Lambda 1 and Other Stories
F893	van Vogt, A. E.	Destination Universe
F905	Vance, J.	The Star King
C909	Wells, H. G.	The Island of Dr. Moreau
F918	Leinster, M.	The Other Side of Nowhere
C922	Wells, H. G.	The War of the Worlds
F928	Ballard, J. G.	Terminal Beach
C934	Wells, H. G.	The Invisible Man
F950	Amis, K., & Conquest, R.	
		Spectrum II
F951	Campbell, J. W.	Astounding Tales of Space and Time
F961	Ballard, J. G.	The Burning World
F974	Kapp, C.	Transfinite Man
F975	Conklin, G.	The Big Book of Science Fiction
F987	Moudy, W.	No Man on Earth
F1003	Vance, J.	The Killing Machine
F1014	Sharp, M.	Miss Bianca
F1022	Leinster, M.	Invaders of Space
1965		
F1032	Kornbluth, C. M.	The Syndic

F1047	Conklin, G.	**A Treasury of Science Fiction**
F1053	Conklin, G.	**Science Fiction Adventures in Dimension**
F1058	Sturgeon, T.	**A Touch of Strange**
C1063	Wells, H. G.	**The Time Machine**
F1071	Ray, J.	**Ghouls in My Grave**
F1086	Laumer, K.	**A Plague of Demons**
F1088	Russell, E. F.	**Men, Martians and Machines**
F1096	Conklin, G.	**Science Fiction Adventures in Mutation**
X1108	Amis, K., & Conquest, R.	
		Spectrum 3
F1112	Anderson, P.	**The Enemy Stars**
F1128	Stapledon, O.	**Odd John**
F1129	Laumer, K.	**The Other Side of Time**
F1136	Knight, D.	**A for Anything**
F1139	Leinster, M.	**The Aliens**
X1144	Sharp, M.	**The Stone of Chastity**
F1146	Davidson, A.	**Rork!**
F1147	Dickson, G. R.	**Mission to Universe**
F1160	Knight, D.	**Mind Switch**
F1162	Doyle, A. C.	**The Lost World**
F1169	Thomas, T. L., & Wilhelm, K.	
		The Clone
F1170	Disch, T. M.	**The Genocides**

1966

F1163	Blish, J.	**Titans' Daughter**
F1175	Addams, C.	**Dear Dead Days**
F1177	Roberts, K.	**The Furies**
F1185	Laumer, K.	**The Time Bender**
F1186	Harrison, H.	**Bill, the Galactic Hero**
F1195	van Vogt, A. E.	**The Players of Null-A**
F1198	Ballard, J. G.	**The Wind From Nowhere**
F1203	Doyle, A. C.	**The Poison Belt**
F1204	Ballard, J. G.	**The Impossible Man**
X1240	Laumer, K.	**Galactic Diplomat**
F1243	Ballard, J. G.	**The Voices of Time**
F1248	Farmer, P. J.	**Night of Light**
F1249	Herbert, F.	**Destination: Void**
F1255	Wells, H. G.	**The War of the Worlds**
F1256	Wells, H. G.	**The Invisible Man**
F1263	Leinster, M.	**Checkpoint Lambda**
F1266	Ballard, J. G.	**The Drowned World**
S1272	Amis, K., & Conquest, R.	
		Spectrum 4
F1273	Laumer, K.	**Catastrophe Planet**
F1283	Herbert, F.	**The Eyes of Heisenberg**
F1284	Anderson, P.	**Trader to the Stars**
F1291	Knight, D.	**Orbit 1**
F1292	van Vogt, A. E.	**Rogue Ship**
S1311	Conklin, G.	**Science Fiction Oddities**
X1312	Simak, C. D.	**All Flesh Is Grass**
S1315	Household, G.	**The Spanish Cave**
N1320	White, T. H.	**The Once and Future King**
X1340	Laumer, K.	**The Monitors**
X1341	Davidson, A.	**The Enemy of My Enemy**
F1361	Wells, H. G.	**The Time Machine**
F1363	Wells, H. G.	**The Island of Dr. Moreau**

1967

X1349	Disch, T. N.	**Echo Round His Bones**
X1350	Sellings, A.	**The Quy Effect**
S1354	Fuller, J. G.	**Incident at Exeter**
X1371	Dickson, G. R.	**The Space Swimmers**
X1372	Dick, P. K.	**Counter-Clock World**
X1379	Sellings, A.	**The Uncensored Man**
X1380	Ballard, J. G.	**The Crystal World**
X1393	Biggle, L.	**The Fury out of Time**
X1394	Raphael, R.	**Code Three**
F1398	Wells, H. G.	**The First Men in the Moon**
X1401	Gardner, A.	**Six Day Week**
X1403	van Vogt, A. E., & Hull, E. M.	
		The Winged Man
S1404	Capek, K.	**The War With the Newts**
X1407	Wells, H. G.	**The Food of the Gods**

X1408	Sternberg, J.	**Sexualis '95**
X1414	Norton, Alden H.	**Horror Times Ten**
X1416	Harrison, H.	**Make Room! Make Room!**
X1417	Anderson, P.	**The Trouble Twisters**
S1426	Heinlein, R. A.	**Tomorrow, the Stars**
S1427	Laumer, K.	**Retief's War**
S1435	Raven, S.	**Doctors Wear Scarlet**
S1437	Nolan, W. F.	**The Pseudo-People**
X1438	Coleman, J. N.	**Seeker From the Stars**
X1440	Wells, H. G.	**In the Days of the Comet**
X1447	Laumer, K.	**Galactic Odyssey**
S1448	Knight, D.	**Orbit 2**
X1451	Amis, K., & Conquest, R.	
		Spectrum II
X1454	Vance, J.	**The Palace of Love**
X1455	Jones, D. F.	**Colossus**
S1464	Denis, A.	**Taboo**
X1469	Cooper, E.	**All Fools' Day**
X1470	Platt, C.	**Garbage World**
X1490	Campbell, J. W.	**The Astounding Science Fiction Anthology**
X1491	Daventry, L.	**A Man of Double Deed**

1968

N1320	White, T. H.	**The Once and Future King**
X1426	McCutchan, P.	**Skyprobe**
S1463	Simak, C. D.	**The Werewolf Principle**
F1495	Clarke, A. C.	**Dolphin Island**
X1497	Norton, Alden H.	**Masters of Horror**
X1503	Brown, R. G.	**Galactic Sibyl Sue Blue**
X1506	Hoyle, F.	**Ossian's Ride**
X1513	Moorcock, M.	**The Best Science Fiction Stories From**
		New Worlds
X1514	Laumer, K.	**Greylorn**
X1526	McCutchan, P.	**Skyprobe**
X1528	Lafferty, R. A.	**The Reefs of Earth**
S1529	Harrison, H., & Aldiss, B. W.	
		Best SF: 1967
X1543	van Vogt, A. E.	**Slan**
S1544	Laumer, K., & Brown, R. G.	
		Earthblood
X1558	van Thal, H.	**Lie Ten Nights Awake**
S1560	Heinlein, R. A.	**Starship Troopers**
S1561	Conklin, G.	**Elsewhere and Elsewhen**
S1567	Harrison, H.	**SF: Authors' Choice**
N1571	Heinlein, R. A.	**Stranger in a Strange Land**
X1588	Laumer, K., & Dickson, G. R.	
		Planet Run
X1589	Simak, C. D.	**Strangers in the Universe**
S1595	Amis, K., & Conquest, R.	
		Spectrum 5
X1596	Laumer, K.	**Assignment in Nowhere**
N1601	Heinlein, R. A.	**The Moon Is a Harsh Mistress**
X1607	Cooper, E.	**A Far Sunset**
S1608	Knight, D.	**Orbit 3**
N1610	Tapsell, R. F.	**The Year of the Horsetails**
X1613	Creasey, J.	**The Depths**
S1615	Herbert, F.	**The Santaroga Barrier**
X1616	Wallace, Ian	**Croyd**
X1627	Creasey, J.	**The Inferno**
X1630	Harness, C. L.	**The Ring of Ritornel**
X1633	Conklin, G.	**Possible Worlds of Science Fiction**
X1639	Creasey, J.	**The Terror**
X1640	Harrison, H.	**The Technicolor Time Machine**
X1641	Laumer, K.	**It's a Mad, Mad, Mad Galaxy**
D1662	White, T. H.	**Camelot**

BERNARDO AMALGAMATED INDUSTRIES LTD., England.
Bernardo
Early 1940's

—	Horan, K.	**The Squid**

Bestseller Library See ELEK LTD.

E. BIDDLE, London, England.
Biddle
Early 1940's
—   "Edward"   **The Laboratory Medium**

Bison See UNIVERSITY OF NEBRASKA

BLACKIE. Publisher in London, England. Imprint "Blackie Star Classic."
Blackie
1967
1   Verne, J.   **A Journey to the Centre of the Earth**

BLUE STAR. British publisher.
Blue Star
1945 (approx.)
—   Delray, C.   **Realm of the Alien**

J. V. BOARDMAN & CO. LTD., London, England.
Boardman
1954
140   Carnell, E. J.   **No Place Like Earth**
149   Ehrlich, M.   **The Big Eye**
154   Brown, F.   **What Mad Universe**
159   Ashton, F.   **The Wrong Side of the Moon**
1955
163   Carnell, E. J.   **The Best From New Worlds Science Fiction**

Bonanza See CROWN PUBLISHERS

BOND-CHARTERIS PUBS., Hollywood, California, U.S.A.
Bond-Charteris
1945
—   Charteris, L.   **The Saint's Choice of Impossible Crime**
—   Jameson, M.   **Atomic Bomb**

BOOK COMPANY OF AMERICA, Beverly Hills, California, U.S.A.
Book Amer.
1965
013   Mendelsohn, F.   **Club Tycoon Sends Man to Moon**
014   van Vogt, A. E., & Hull, E. M.
                             Planets for Sale
015   Nuetzel, C.   **If This Goes On**

BOOKS OF TODAY LTD., London, England
Books of Today
No date
—   Wright, S. F.   **Two Famous Stories: Justice, The Rat**

BOUDOIR BOOKS. No information; probably U.S.
Boudoir
1963
1027   Jason, J.   **Sexodus**

Brandon See AMERICAN ART ENTERPRISES INC.

BRITISH PUBLISHERS GUILD LTD., London, England.
Guild
1941
4   Harvey, W. F.   **The Beast With Five Fingers**
13   Brown, D., & Serpell, S.
                             If Hitler Comes
104   Sale, R.   **Not Too Narrow, Not Too Deep**
1945
       Knight, E.   **Sam Small Flies Again**
1950
420   Hudson, W. H.   **Green Mansions**
423   Saki   **The Best of Saki**
1952
?   Carr, J. D.   **The Burning Court**

1953
—   Rohmer, S.   **The Mystery of Dr. Fu Manchu**
05   Tucker, W.   **The Long Loud Silence**
07   Laski, M.   **The Victorian Chaise-Longue**
465   Bell, N.   **Life Comes to Seathorpe**

BROWN-WATSON LTD., Willesden, London, England.
    From 1956 to 1965 most titles were under the **Digit** imprint, listed below following the Brown-Watson titles.
Brown-Wat.
1953
—   Westwood, A.   **Sinister Forces**
1954
—   Rogersohn, W.   **North Dimension**
—   Westward, E.   **Return to Mars**
107   Rogersohn, W.   **Amiro**
1960
—   McKenzie, N.   **Day of Judgment**
1965
R888   McIntosh, J. T.   **Out of Chaos**
R895   Capon, P.   **Into the Tenth Millennium**
R904   Jones, R. F.   **The Non-Statistical Man**
R907   Long, F. B.   **The Horror From the Hills**
R913   Stuart, S., & Bloch, R.
                            The Night Walker
R920   Hallums, J. R.   **They Came, They Saw**
1966
R965   Long, F. B.   **This Strange Tomorrow**
R968   Haining, P.   **Summoned From the Tomb**
Digit
1956
—   Gribble, L.   **Atomic Murder**
1957
—   Trevor, E.   **Dream of Death**
—   Kornbluth, C. M.   **Christmas Eve**
—   Bounds, S. J.   **The Robot Brains**
—   Boland, J.   **White August**
1958
—   Bounds, S. J.   **The Moon Raiders**
D157   Kornbluth, C. M., & Pohl, F.
                            Gladiator-at-Law
D164   Asimov, I.   **I, Robot**
D173   Brown, F.   **Project Jupiter**
D192   Asimov, I.   **Second Foundation**
R214   Cooper, J. C.   **The Grip of the Strangler**
D217   Verne, J.   **From the Earth to the Moon**
1959
D235   Heinlein, R. A.   **Revolt in 2100**
D248   Barr, T. C.   **The Split Worlds**
D266   Smith, Edward E.   **The Skylark of Space**
D280   Cooper, E.   **Tomorrow's Gift**
1960
D315   Leslie, D.   **The Amazing Mr. Lutterworth**
D327   Pohl, F., & Kornbluth, C. M.
                            The Space Merchants
R335   Verne, J.   **A Journey to the Center of the Earth**
D343   van Vogt, A. E.   **Mission to the Stars**
D349   Cooper, E.   **Voices in the Dark**
D350   Poe, E. A.   **The Gold Bug**
D352   Pohl, F., & Kornbluth, C. M.
                            Search the Sky
D361   van Vogt, A. E.   **The House That Stood Still**
D362   Wollheim, D. A.   **The Macabre Reader**
D368   Heinlein, R. A.   **Assignment in Eternity**
D377   van Vogt, A. E.   **The Pawns of Null-A**
D386   Heinlein, R. A.   **Lost Legacy**
R396   Aldiss, B. W.   **Non-Stop**
R413   Kuttner, H.   **Fury**
1961
G394   Wilde, O.   **The Picture of Dorian Gray**
R437   Dickson, G. R.   **The Genetic General**
R449   Tubb, E. C.   **The Space-Born**

R454	van Vogt, A. E.	The Weapon Makers		R673	Grant, Matthew	Hyper-Drive
R460	Wollheim, D. A.	Terror in the Modern Vein		R674	Savage, R.	When the Moon Die
R461	Poe, E. A.	The Fall of the House of Usher		R676	Bredeson, L.	More From One Step Beyond
D466	Bulmer, K.	The Changeling Worlds		R681	Bulmer, K.	Of Earth Foretold
R468	Bredeson, L.	One Step Beyond		R683	Roberts, C.	Nuclear Subtraction
D478	Ash, A.	Conditioned for Space		R686	Wright, L.	Assignment Luther
D479	White, J.	The Secret Visitors		R695	Aldiss, B. W.	Equator
R486	Burke, T.	Limehouse Nights		R696	Dagmar, P.	The Sands of Time
R487	Gibbs, J. W.	Late Final		R703	Williamson, J.	The Legion of Time
R490	Wright, L.	Who Speaks of Conquest?		R704	Casewit, C.	The Peacemakers
R499	Pohl, F., & Kornbluth, C. M.			R715	MacGregor, R.	Horror in the Night
		The Space Merchants		R717	Ranzetta, L.	The Night of the Death Rain
R505	Bulmer, K.	City Under the Sea		R721	Foster, G. C.	The Change
R506	Aldiss, B. W.	The Interpreter		R722	Wilson, G. M.	Witchwater
R508	Wollheim, D. A.	More Terror in the Modern Vein		R725	White, J.	The Secret Visitors
R512	Poe, E. A.	Descent Into the Maelstrom		R727	Hansen, V.	The Twisters
R514	Wright, L.	A Man Called Destiny		R728	de Rouen, R.	Split Image
R515	Bulmer, K.	The Secret of ZI		R730	Newman, B.	The Blue Ants
R521	Bounds, S. J.	The Robot Brains		R734	Low, A. M.	Satellite in Space
R522	Williamson, J.	The Legion of Time		R735	Ray, Rene	The Strange World of Planet X
T532	Morgan, D.	The Uninhibited		R740	de Timms, G.	Three Quarters
R533	Aldiss, B. W.	Equator		R742	Wright, L.	Who Speaks of Conquest?
R538	Williamson, J.	After World's End		R745	O'Donnell, E.	Ghosts With a Purpose
R539	Bulmer, K.	Of Earth Foretold		R746	Dagmar, P.	Once in Time
R549	Ellis, D. E.	A Thousand Ages		R747	Newton, J. P.	The Forgotten Race
R550	Clarke, Alfred G. C.	Into the Darkness		R750	O'Donnell, E.	Phantoms of the Night
1962				R753	Charbonneau, L.	Corpus Earthling
R468	Bredeson, L.	One Step Beyond		R754	Ash, A.	Conditioned for Space
R552	Bredeson, L.	More From One Step Beyond		R757	Ellis, D. E.	A Thousand Ages
R553	Veheyne, C.	Horror		R758	Bulmer, K.	The Changeling Worlds
R557	Ranzetta, L.	The Uncharted Planet		R760	Danforth, M.	From Outer Space
R558	Barr, D. N.	The Man With Only One Head		R763	Wilson, G. M.	Shadows on the Landing
R560	Sangster, J.	The Terror of the Tongs		R766	Aldiss, B. W.	The Interpreter
R562	Conklin, G.	Invaders of the Earth		R768	MacGregor, R.	The Creeping Plague
R563	Barr, T. C.	Split Worlds		R770	Chilton, C.	The Red Planet
R565	Poe, E. A.	The Pit and the Pendulum		R771	Morgan, D.	The Uninhibited
R572	Bulmer, K.	Earth's Long Shadow		R780	Hansen, V.	Creatures of the Mist
R577	Conklin, G.	Enemies in Space		R781	O'Donnell, E.	Haunted People
R581	Stevenson, R. L.	Dr. Jekyll and Mr. Hyde		R782	Charkin, P.	The Living Gem
R583	Heinlein, R. A.	The Green Hills of Earth		R785	Wright, L.	A Man Called Destiny
R584	Haile, T.	Space Train		R792	O'Donnell, E.	Shadows of Evil
R587	Rafcam, N.	The Troglodytes		R796	Edgar, P.	Cities of the Dead
R588	Wadey, V.	A Planet Named Terra		R807	de Timms, G.	Split
R590	Wadey, V.	The United Planets		R808	Maine, C. E.	World Without Men
R597	Bulmer, K.	The Fatal Fire		R811	Chilton, C.	Journey Into Space
R605	Dagmar, P.	Alien Skies		**1964**		
R606	Ranzetta, L.	The Maru Invasion		R802	Clarke, A. C.	Islands in the Sky
R607	Bulmer, K.	The Wind of Liberty		R803	Hansen, V.	Claws of the Night
R609	Dagmar, P.	Spykos 4		R819	Bounds, S. J.	The Robot Brains
R610	Wade, T.	The World of Theda		R824	Rohmer, S.	The Moon Is Red
R612	Burke, J.	Pursuit Through Time		R828	Brown, F.	Project Jupiter
R613	Buchan, J.	The Watcher by the Threshold		R834	Wilson, G. M.	Nightmare Cottage
R616	Carr, C.	Salamander War		R835	Rohmer, S.	The Sins of Sumuru
R617	Carr, C.	Colonists of Space		R836	Ranzetta, L.	Yellow Inferno
R618	Ranzetta, L.	The World in Reverse		R840	Hansen, V.	The Grip of Fear
R623	van Vogt, A. E.	The House That Stood Still		R842	Capon, P.	Down to Earth
R628	MacGregor, R.	The Day a Village Died		R843	Rohmer, S.	Sand and Satin
R636	Heinlein, R. A.	Assignment in Eternity		R846	Blackburn, J.	A Scent of New-Mown Hay
R637	van Vogt, A. E.	Mission to the Stars		R851	Rayer, F. G.	Cardinal of the Stars
R638	Reed, C. C.	Martian Enterprise		R854	Bateman, R.	When the Whites Went
R649	Mair, G. B.	The Day Khrushchev Panicked		R856	MacGregor, R.	The Deadly Sun
R651	Merwin, S.	Killer to Come		R860	Rayer, F. G.	The Iron and the Anger
R652	Haile, T.	Galaxies Ahead		R862	Smith, G. H.	The Coming of the Rats
R654	Clarke, Alfred G. C.	The Mind Master		R863	Capon, P.	The World at Bay
1963				R864	Thomas, M.	Beyond the Spectrum
R658	Rackham, J.	The Touch of Evil		R876	Ray, Robert	No Stars for Us
R661	Wade, T.	The Voice From Baru		R877	Livesey, E. M.	The Desolate Land
R662	Pohl, F., & Kornbluth, C. M.			R882	McIntosh, J. T.	The Noman Way
		Search the Sky		R883	Conklin, G.	Enemies in Space
R663	Cooper, E.	Voices in the Dark		R885	Bounds, S. J.	The World Wrecker
R666	Bulmer, K.	Defiance		R887	Capon, P.	Phobos, the Robot Planet
R671	Williamson, J.	After World's End				
R672	Bulmer, K.	City Under the Sea				

Series numbers continued under Brown-Watson imprint; see above.

BURKE, London, England.
  JP = Junior Pacemaker.
Burke
1964
JP   Moore, P.   **Raiders of Mars**
JP   MacVicar, A.   **Red Fire on Lost Planet**

C

CALVERT PUBLISHING CO. PTY. LTD., Sydney, N.S.W., Australia.
Calvert
1964
—   Janes, G.   **Come and Go Mad**

Candid Reader See GREENLEAF CLASSICS

(JONATHAN) CAPE, London.
Cape
1966
—   Fleming, H.   **Blast-Off Into Space**

CAPRICORN BOOKS, New York, N.Y., U.S.A.
Capricorn
1959
CAP14   Golding, W.   **The Lord of the Flies**
CAP18   Coates, R. M.   **The Eater of Darkness**
1960
CAP27   Chesterton, G. K.   **The Man Who Was Thursday**
CAP39   White, T. H.   **Mistress Masham's Repose**
1963 (approx.)
CAP14   Golding, W.   **The Lord of the Flies**
1966
273   Ley, W.   **Exotic Zoology**
1967 (approx.)
CAP14   Golding, W.   **The Lord of the Flies**
Giant 295
        Clarens, C.   **An Illustrated History of the Horror Film**
Undated
66   Golding, W.   **Pincher Martin**

CARAVELLE BOOK INC., New York, N.Y., U.S.A.
Flagship
1967
00715   Carpenter, E. J.   **Moonspin**
1968
00840   Olemy, P. T.   **The Clones**
00864   Cummings, M. A. **Exile and Other Tales of Fantasy**

Cardinal See POCKET BOOKS INC.

Cavalcade See DELTA LIBRARY

CAXTON PRESS, Swansea, England.
Caxton
1946
—   Richmond, C.   **A Step Into Infinity**

Cedar See WORLD'S WORK

CENTURY PUBLISHERS, Chicago, Illinois, U.S.A.
Century
1946
104   Sherman, H. M.   **The Green Man**
1949
116   Phillips, R.   **Time Trap**

1950
124   Phillips, R.   **Worlds Within**
B10   Smith, G. O.   **Operation Interstellar**
1951
B13   Phillips, R.   **World of If**

CHANCERY BOOKS, London, England.
Chancery
1941
—   Lynn, G.   **The Return of Karl Marx**

CHARIOT, London, England.
Chariot (Brit.)
1952
6   Haggard, H. R.   **Benita**

CHARIOT BOOKS, U.S.A.
Chariot
1960
CB28   Wells, H. G.   **The Invisible Man**
CB123   Long, F. B.   **Woman From Another Planet**
CB150   Barr, T. C.   **The Last 14**
1961
CB162   Long, F. B.   **Mating Center**

Cher. Tree See WITHY GROVE PRESS LTD.

Cherry Tree See KEMSLEY NEWSPAPERS LTD.

CHICAGO PAPERBACK NOVELS INC., Chicago, Illinois, U.S.A.
Chicago
1962
A107   Taylor, F.   **Court of Honor**
A108   Kemper, W. E.   **Another Man's Hell**

CITADEL PRESS, New York, N.Y., U.S.A.
Citadel
1959
—   Hearn, L.   **Selected Writings of Lafcadio Hearn**
1960
—   Bredeson, L.   **One Step Beyond**
1961
—   Bredeson, L.   **More From One Step Beyond**
1963
—   Bierce, A.   **Collected Writings of Ambrose Bierce**
1967
C89   Michelet, J.   **Satanism and Witchcraft**

CLEVELAND PUBLISHING CO., Sydney, N.S.W., Australia.
Cleveland
1954-55
—   Waugh, M.   **The Abominable Snowman**
—   Waugh, M.   **Back From the Dead**
—   Waugh, M.   **Fangs of the Vampire**
—   Waugh, M.   **The Living Dead**

Cobra See (JOHN) SPENCER & CO.

LLOYD COLE, Worthing, England [later London, England].
Cole
Early 1940's
—   Burton, E.   **In Quest of the Golden Orchid**
—   Burton, E.   **The Radium King**
—   Herbert, B.   **The Red-Haired Girl**
—   Herbert, B.   **Strange Romance**
—   Herbert, B.   **Hand of Glory**
—   Herbert, B., & Pragnell, F.
                         Thieves of the Air

Collier See CROWELL-COLLIER

(WILLIAM) COLLINS SONS & CO. LTD., Glasgow, Scotland.
  Imprints include **Collins, Armada, Black-Out Thriller, Fontana,** and **Spitfire** (see below). "Armada" was first published by ARMADA, London, then taken over by COLLINS in the late 1960's as a juvenile paperback series.

Collins
1930 (approx.)

	Wells, H. G.	**The Sleeper Wakes**

1939 (approx.)

505	Southwold, S.	**The Gas War of 1940**

1945

215	Sharp, M.	**The Stone of Chastity**

1952

205c	Farjeon, J. J.	**The Death of a World**

Armada [all juvenile]
1965

C107	Richards, F.	**Bunter and the Phantom of the Towers**
C131	Theydon, J.	**Stingray**

1966

C141	Theydon, J.	**Thunderbirds**
C144	Theydon, J.	**Calling Thunderbirds**
C148	Theydon, J.	**Stingray and the Monster**
C161	Theydon, J.	**Thunderbirds' Ring of Fire**
C162	Anderson, G. & S.	**Thunderbirds Are Go**

1967

C163	Theydon, J.	**Lady Penelope: The Albanian Affair**
C197	Bernard, C.	**The Armada Ghost Book**
C201	Theydon, J.	**Captain Scarlet and the Mysterians**
C202	Theydon, J.	**Captain Scarlet and the Silent Saboteur**

1968

C209	Theydon, J.	**The Angels and the Creeping Enemy**
C253	Bernard, C.	**The Second Armada Ghost Book**

Black-Out Thriller
Undated

15	Darlington, W. A.	**Alf's Button**

Fontana
1952

52	Verne, J.	**Twenty Thousand Leagues Under the Sea**

1955

49B	Lewis, C. S.	**The Screwtape Letters**

1956

—	Sharp, M.	**The Stone of Chastity**

1959

367	Wells, H. G.	**The Invisible Man**

1960

433	Wells, H. G.	**The First Men in the Moon**

1961

532	Sharp, M.	**The Stone of Chastity**
561	Kneale, N.	**Tomato Cain**
603	Halifax, Lord	**Lord Halifax's Ghost Book**

1962

—	Symonds, J.	**The 31st of February**
609L	White, T. H.	**The Once and Future King**
681	Barzman, B.	**Out of This World**
742R	Marshall, B.	**Father Malachy's Miracle**

1963

898	White, T. H.	**The Sword in the Stone**
917	Stuart, I.	**The Satan Bug**

1964

433	Wells, H. G.	**The First Men in the Moon**
603	Halifax, Lord	**Lord Halifax's Ghost Book**
981	Aickman, R.	**Dark Entries**

1965

1055	Aickman, R.	**The Fontana Book of Great Ghost Stories**
1125	Wells, H. G.	**The Cone**
1173	MacLean, A.	**The Satan Bug**

1966

970	Christie, A.	**The Hound of Death and Other Stories**
1035	Wells, H. G.	**The Valley of the Spiders and Other Stories**
1227	Aickman, R.	**The Second Fontana Book of Great Ghost Stories**
1232	Bernard, C.	**The Fontana Book of Great Horror Stories**
1324	Douglas, B.	**Great Stories of Mystery and Imagination**
1371	Wells, H. G.	**The Invisible Man**
1419	Frayn, M.	**The Tin Men**
1465	Aickman, R.	**The Third Fontana Book of Great Ghost Stories**

1967

1484	Hadfield, J.	**A Chamber of Horrors**
1599	Fleming, J.	**The Chill and the Kill**
1610	Bardens, D.	**Ghosts and Hauntings**
1635	Aickman, R.	**The Fourth Fontana Book of Great Ghost Stories**
1702	Bernard, C.	**The Third Fontana Book of Great Horror Stories**

1968

1371	Wells, H. G.	**The Invisible Man**
1706	Walter, E.	**Snowfall and Other Chilling Events**
1748	Bernard, C.	**The Fontana Book of Great Horror Stories**
1827	Aickman, R.	**Powers of Darkness**
1852	Strating, J. J.	**European Tales of Terror**
1856	Halifax, Lord	**Lord Halifax's Ghost Book**

Spitfire [juvenile fiction]
1967

—	Deakin, B.	**The Menace of Mask**
—	Johnson, E.	**Strangers in Space**

COLUMBIA PUBLICATIONS, New York, N.Y., U.S.A.
SFC = Science Fiction Classics. DAB = Double Action Books.
Columbia
Undated (approx. 1941-1942)

SFC1	Coleridge, J.	**Martian Martyrs**
SFC2	Clive, D.	**Valley of Pretenders**
SFC3	Callahan, W.	**The Machine That Thought**
SFC4	Coleridge, J.	**The New Life**
SFC5	Clive, D.	**The Voice Commands**
SFC6	Olsen, B.	**Rhythm Rides the Rocket**

1955

DAB	Loomis, N.	**City of Glass**

Comet See SANDPIPER PRESS

Compact See ROBERTS & VINTER LTD.

Compass See VIKING PRESS

COMYNS (PUBLISHERS) LTD., London, England.
Comyns
1953-1954

	Tubb, E. C.	**Venusian Adventure**
	Maras, K.	**Zhorani**

1955

	Maras, K.	**Peril From Space**

CONSOLIDATED PRESS LTD., Sydney, N.S.W., Australia
Condor
Undated (approx. 1965)

1	Poe, E. A.	**The Murders in the Rue Morgue**

Consul See WORLD DISTRIBUTORS (MANCHESTER) LTD.

CONTINENTAL BOOK COMPANY AB, Stockholm, Sweden.
  The Zephyr books are in English, marked not for sale in the British Empire or U.S.A.
Zephyr
1947 (approx.)

70	Swift, J.	**Gulliver's Travels**
129	Stevenson, R. L.	**Dr. Jekyll and Mr. Hyde**
159	James, H.	**The Turn of the Screw**

1948

169	Hopley, G.	**The Night Has a Thousand Eyes**

Corgi See TRANSWORLD PUBLISHERS

CORINTH PUBLICATIONS, U.S.A.

The 1965-1966 titles were reprints from the following magazines: *The Phantom Detective* (PD), *Operator 5* (OF), *Doctor Death* (DD), *Secret Agent X* (SA), *Dusty Ayres and His Battle Aces* (DA), and *Terror Tales* (TT). The magazine abbreviation and issue whole number follows each title.

This publisher also was associated with GREENLEAF CLASSICS and related imprints.

Corinth
1965

CR101	Wallace, R.	**The Vampire Murders** (PD1)
CR102	Wallace, R.	**The Dancing Doll Murders** (PD2)
CR103	Wallace, R.	**The Beast-King Murders** (PD3)
CR104	Wallace, R.	**Tycoon of Crime** (PD4)
CR105	Wallace, R.	**The Broadway Murders** (PD5)
CR106	Wallace, R.	**The Daggers of Kali** (PD6)
CR107	Wallace, R.	**Murder Under the Big Top** (PD7)
CR108	Wallace, R.	**The Trail to Death** (PD8)
CR109	Wallace, R.	**Yellow Shadows of Death** (PD9)
CR110	Wallace, R.	**Murder Trail** (PD10)

1966

CR111	Wallace, R.	**The Green Glare Murders** (PD11)
CR112	Wallace, R.	**Fangs of Murder** (PD12)
CR113	Wallace, R.	**The Curio Murders** (PD13)
CR114	Wallace, R.	**Murder Stalks a Billion** (PD14)
CR115	Wallace, R.	**Murder Money** (PD15)
CR116	Steele, C.	**Legions of the Death Master** (OF1)
CR117	Wallace, R.	**Death Glow** (PD16)
CR118	Zorro	**12 Must Die** (DD1)
CR119	Wallace, R.	**Stones of Satan** (PD17)
CR120	Steele, C.	**The Army of the Dead** (OF2)
CR121	Zorro	**The Gray Creatures** (DD2)
CR122	House, B.	**The Torture Trust** (SA1)
CR123	Wallace, R.	**The Melody Murders** (PD18)
CR124	Steele, C.	**The Invisible Empire** (OF3)
CR125	Zorro	**The Shriveling Murders** (DD3)
CR126	House, B.	**Servants of the Skull** (SA2)
CR127	Wallace, R.	**The Uniformed Killers** (PD19)
CR128	Steele, C.	**Master of Broken Men** (OF4)
CR129	Hanlon, J.	**Stories From Doctor Death and Other Terror Tales** (DD4)
CR130	House, B.	**Curse of the Mandarin's Fan** (SA3)
CR131	Wallace, R.	**The Forty Thieves** (PD20)
CR132	Steele, C.	**Hosts of the Flaming Death** (OF5)
CR133	Bowen, R. S.	**Black Lightning** (DA1)
CR134	House, B.	**City of Living Dead** (SA4)
CR135	Wallace, R.	**Death Under Contract** (PD21)
CR136	Steele, C.	**Blood Reign of the Dictator** (OF6)
CR137	Bowen, R. S.	**Crimson Doom** (DA2)
CR138	House, B.	**The Death-Torch Terror** (SA5)
CR139	Wallace, R.	**The Corpse Parade** (PD22)
CR140	Steele, C.	**March of the Flame Marauders** (OF7)
CR141	Bowen, R. S.	**Purple Tornado** (DA3)
CR142	House, B.	**Octopus of Crime** (SA6)
CR143	Hanlon, J.	**The House of Living Death and Other Terror Tales** (TT1)
CR144	Steele, C.	**Invasion of the Yellow Warlords** (OF8)
CR145	Bowen, R. S.	**The Telsa Raiders** (DA4)
CR146	House, B.	**The Sinister Scourge** (SA7)
CR147	Hanlon, J.	**Death's Loving Arms and Other Terror Tales** (TT2)
CR148	Bowen, R. S.	**Black Invaders vs. the Battle Birds** (DA5)

CORNELL UNIVERSITY PRESS, Ithaca, N.Y., U.S.A.
Great Seal imprint.

Cornell
1956

—	Nicolson, M. H.	**Science and Imagination**

Coronet See HODDER & STOUGHTON

CRAWFORD PUBLISHING CO. INC., Los Angeles, California, U.S.A.
Crawford
1946

—	Simak, C. D.	**The Creator**
—	Crawford, W.	**The Garden of Fear**

Crest See FAWCETT

Cresta See JARROLDS

CRESTWOOD PUBLISHING CO. INC., New York, N.Y., U.S.A.
Prize = Prize Science Fiction Novels
Crestwood
1949

Prize 10	Leinster, M.	**Fight for Life**
Prize 11	Wellman, M. W.	**Sojarr of Titan**

CROWELL-COLLIER PUB. CO., New York, N.Y., U.S.A.
Imprints: **Apollo**; **Collier**.

Apollo
1968

A-184	Burger, D.	**Sphereland: A Fantasy . . . .**

Collier
1961

HS3V	Shelley, M. W.	**Frankenstein**
HS7	Swift, J.	**Gulliver's Travels**
HS16	Butler, S.	**Erewhon**
AS34X	Merritt, A.	**The Face in the Abyss**
BS58V	Lewis, C. S.	**That Hideous Strength**

1962

HS51V	Haggard, H. R.	**King Solomon's Mines**
AS103X	Merritt, A.	**The Moon Pool**
AS109X	Shiel, M. P.	**How the Old Woman Got Home**
AS144	Innes, H.	**The Survivors**
AS183	Lewis, C. S.	**Perelandra**
AS207V	Lewis, C. S.	**Out of the Silent Planet**
AS218	Conklin, G.	**Great Science Fiction by Scientists**
AS257X	Laing, A.	**The Cadaver of Gideon Wyck**
AS279V	Anonymous	**Soviet Science Fiction**
AS295V	Anonymous	**More Soviet Science Fiction**
AS392X	Conklin, G. & L.	**The Supernatural Reader**
AS481	Tallant, R.	**Voodoo in New Orleans**

1963

AS516	Asimov, I., & Conklin, G.	**Fifty Short Science Fiction Tales**
AS518	Conklin, G., & Fabricant, D.	**Great Science Fiction About Doctors**
AS528V	Perutz, L.	**The Master of the Day of Judgment**
AS548	Moskowitz, S.	**The Coming of the Robots**
AS551	Moskowitz, S.	**Exploring Other Worlds**
AS567	DeGraeff, A.	**Human and Other Beings**
HS3V	Shelley, M. W.	**Frankenstein**
HS57	Walpole, H.	**The Castle of Otranto**

1965

AS279V	Anonymous	**Soviet Science Fiction**
01895	Conklin, G., & Fabricant, D.	**Great Science Fiction About Doctors**

1966

01639	Asimov, I., & Conklin, G.	**Fifty Short Science Fiction Tales**
01895	Conklin, G., & Fabricant, D.	**Great Science Fiction About Doctors**
01903	Conklin, G.	**Great Science Fiction by Scientists**
01911	Conklin, G. & L.	**The Supernatural Reader**
02287	Merritt, A.	**The Moon Pool**
02311	Moskowitz, S.	**Exploring Other Worlds**
02527	Shelley, M. W.	**Frankenstein**

1967

01647	Anonymous	**More Soviet Science Fiction**
01655	Anonymous	**Soviet Science Fiction**
02279	Merritt, A.	**The Face in the Abyss**
02551	Stephens, J.	**The Crock of Gold**

| 02623 | Verne, J. | A Journey to the Center of the Earth |
| 09676 | Tallant, R. | Voodoo in New Orleans |

1968

AS183V	Lewis, C. S.	Perelandra
01625	Anderson, P.	Is There Life on Other Worlds?
01911	Conklin, G. & L.	The Supernatural Reader
02886	Hole, C.	Witchcraft in England

CROWN PUBLISHERS INC., New York, N.Y., U.S.A.
Imprints: **Bonanza**; **Xanadu Library**.

Bonanza

1963

| — | Conklin, G. | The Best of Science Fiction |

Xanadu

1962

—	Cabell, J. B.	Jurgen
—	Bramah, E.	Kai Lung's Golden Hours
—	Shiel, M. P.	The Lord of the Sea
—	Churchward, J.	The Lost Continent of Mu
—	Mundy, T.	Om
—	France, A.	Revolt of the Angels
X5	Eddison, E. R.	The Worm Ouroboros

1963

| — | Donnelly, I. | Atlantis |

CURRAWONG PUB. CO., Sydney, N.S.W., Australia.

Currawong

1940

| — | Heming, J. W. | The Living Dead |
| — | Heming, J. W. | Subterranean City |

1941

—	Heming, J. W.	King of the Underseas
—	Heming, J. W.	From Earth to Mars
—	Heming, J. W.	Other Worlds

1942

| — | Heming, J. W. | In Aztec Hands |
| — | De Wreder, P. | Time Marches Off |

1943

—	Healy, D.	A Voyage to Venus
—	Molesworth, V.	Ape of God
—	Molesworth, V.	Monster at Large
—	Saunders, P. I.	Scorched Earth

1944

| — | Molesworth, V. | Prelude for Death |
| — | Molesworth, V. | Satan's Understudy |

1945

—	Connell, A.	Lords of Serpent Land
—	Connell, A.	Prisoners of Serpent Land
—	Connell, A.	Warriors of Serpent Land

CURTIS WARREN LTD., London, England.
Titles by Marco Garron are listed under 1952, but the dates are not certain.

Curtis War.

1950

—	Hughes, D.	Murder by Telecopter
—	Hughes, D.	The Earth Invasion Battalion
—	Hughes, D.	Formula 695
—	Hughes, D.	War Lords of Space
—	Shaw, D.	Laboratory "X"
—	Shaw, D.	Planet Federation

1951

—	Anonymous	Suspense Stories
—	Hughes, D.	Moon War
—	Hunt, G.	Planet X
—	Hunt, G.	Hostile Worlds
—	Hunt, G.	Elektron Union
—	Hunt, G.	Space Flight
—	Hunt, G.	Vega
—	Hunt, G.	Spatial Ray
—	Hunt, G.	Galactic Storm
—	Hunt, G.	Planet Fall

—	Lang, K.	Task Flight
—	Lang, K.	Astro Race
—	Lang, K.	Gyrator Control
—	Lang, K.	Rocket Invasion
—	Lang, K.	Projectile War
—	Lang, K.	Saturn Patrol
—	Shaw, D.	Space Men

1952

—	Barry, R.	Death Dimension
—	Barry, R.	Ominous Folly
—	Barry, R.	Blue Peril
—	Barry, R.	Gamma Product
—	Barry, R.	Humanoid Puppets
—	Cameron, B.	Destination Alpha
—	Cameron, B.	Photomesis
—	Cameron, B.	Black Infinity
—	Cameron, B.	Cosmic Echelon
—	Cameron, B.	Sphero Nova
—	Carter, D.	Blue Cordon
—	Charles, N.	Para-Robot
—	Charles, N.	Titan's Moon
—	Charles, N.	Twenty-Four Hours
—	Charles, N.	The Land of Esa
—	Elliot, L.	Bio-Muton
—	Garron, M.	Jungle Fever
—	Garron, M.	King Hunters
—	Garron, M.	The Lost City
—	Garron, M.	The Missing Safari
—	Garron, M.	Tribal War
—	Garron, M.	White Fangs
—	Garron, M.	Black Fury
—	Garron, M.	Black Sport
—	Garron, M.	Bush Claws
—	Garron, M.	Jungle Allies
—	Garron, M.	Leopard God
—	Garron, M.	Silent River
—	Garron, M.	Snake Valley
—	Garron, M.	Veldt Warriors
—	Hunt, G.	Fission
—	Hunt, G.	Zero Field
—	Hunt, G.	Station 7
—	Kent, B.	Catalyst
—	Kent, B.	The Fatal Law
—	Kent, B.	Biology "A"
—	Kent, B.	Out of the Silent Places
—	Lane, J.	Maid of Thuro
—	Lang, K.	Terra!
—	Lang, K.	Space Line
—	Lang, K.	Trans-Mercurian
—	Le Page, R.	"A" Men
—	Le Page, R.	Satellite B.C.
—	Le Page, R.	War of Argos
—	Le Page, R.	Blue Asp
—	Le Page, R.	Time and Space
—	Le Page, R.	Zero Point
—	Le Page, R.	Beyond These Suns
—	Lorraine, P.	Two Worlds
—	Luna, K.	Stellar Radium Discharge
—	Reed, V.	House of Many Changes
—	Rey, R.	The Queen People
—	Shaw, Brian	Argentis
—	Shaw, Brian	Ships of Vero
—	Storm, B.	Red Storm

1953

—	Ashton, M.	People of Asa
—	Blair, A.	Cosmic Conquest
—	Cameron, B.	Lost Aeons
—	Cameron, B.	Solar Gravita
—	Carter, D.	Chloroplasm
—	Carter, D.	Purple Islands
—	Charles, N.	Planet Tha
—	Charles, N.	Beyond Zoaster

—	Charles, N.	**Pre-Gargantua**
—	Charles, N.	**World of Gol**
—	Charles, N.	**Research Opta**
—	Elliot, L.	**Overlord New York**
—	Elliot, L.	**The Third Mutant**
—	Ford, K.	**Prototype P.Z.642**
—	Ford, K.	**Sky Fighters**
—	Gruen, V.	**The Mortals of Reni**
—	Kellar, V.	**Tri-Planet**
—	Kellar, V.	**Ionic Barrier**
—	Lane, J.	**Mammalia**
—	Le Page, R.	**Asteroid Forma**
—	Lorraine, P.	**Two Worlds**
—	Lorraine, P.	**Zenith-D**
—	Lorraine, P.	**Dark Boundaries**
—	Luna, K.	**Operation Orbit**
—	Reed, V.	**Dwellers in Space**
—	Rey, R.	**Valley of Terror**
—	Romilus, A.	**Brain Palaeo**
—	Romilus, A.	**Beyond Geo**
—	Shaw, Brian	**Z Formations**
—	Shaw, Brian	**Lost World**

1954

—	Bulmer, H. K.	**Challenge**
—	Casson, M.	**Time Drug**
—	Fenton, C.	**The Seeing Knife**
—	Kinley, G.	**Ferry Rocket**
—	Luna, K.	**Operation Orbit**
—	Melde, G. R.	**Pacific Advance**
—	Romilus, A.	**Organic Destiny**
—	Royce, E. R.	**Experiment in Telepathy**

D

DELL PUBLISHING CO. INC., New York, N.Y., U.S.A.

The prefix *Alfred Hitchcock Presents:* is omitted from many Hitchcock titles (see Volume 1).

Additional imprint: **Delta** (quality paperbacks), see below.

Dell

1938

—	Wells, H. G.	**The War of the Worlds**

1943

—	Boucher, A.	**Rocket to the Morgue**

1945

85	Wylie, P.	**The Savage Gentleman**
92	Hitchcock, A.	**Suspense**

1946

125	Karlova, I.	**Dreadful Hollow**
143	Hitchcock, A.	**Bar the Doors!**

1947

201	Wells, H. G.	**The First Men in the Moon**
206	Hitchcock, A.	**Hold Your Breath!**

1948

264	Hitchcock, A.	**Fear and Trembling**
269	Wells, H. G.	**The Invisible Man**

1949

305	Welles, O.	**Invasion From Mars**
320	Burroughs, E. R.	**The Cave Girl**
339	Haggard, H. R.	**She**
367	Hitchcock, A.	**Suspense Stories**

1950

415	Kummer, F. A.	**Ladies in Hades**
433	Haggard, H. R.	**King Solomon's Mines**
507	Stern, J. D.	**Francis**

1951

36	Heinlein, R. A.	**Universe**
536	Burroughs, E. R.	**Tarzan and the Lost Empire**

1952

591	Boucher, A.	**Rocket to the Morgue**
600	de Camp, L. S.	**Rogue Queen**

1953

627	Wylie, P., & Balmer, E.	
		When Worlds Collide
670	Cody, C. S.	**The Witching Night**
679	Hopley, G.	**The Night Has a Thousand Eyes**
680	Simak, C. D.	**First He Died**
681	Wilde, O.	**The Picture of Dorian Grey**
695	Turney, C.	**The Other One**
696	van Vogt, A. E.	**Slan**

1954

—	Fitzgerald, F. S.	**This Side of Paradise**
D9	Conklin, G.	**6 Great Short Novels of Science Fiction**
32	Crossen, K. F.	**Year of Consent**
760	Judd, C.	**Outpost Mars**
781	Carr, R. S.	**Beyond Infinity**
791	Tucker, W.	**The Long Loud Silence**
797	Barnard, A.	**The Harlot Killer**
800	James, H.	**The Turn of the Screw**

1955

42	Finney, J.	**The Body Snatchers**
D150	Campbell, J. W.	**Who Goes There?**
856	Sloane, W.	**To Walk the Night**

1956

B103	Merril, J.	**SF: The Year's Greatest Science-Fiction and Fantasy**
D167	Wilde, O.	**The Picture of Dorian Grey**
D178	Schneider, J.	**The Golden Kazoo**
D181	James, H.	**The Turn of the Screw**
D183	Endore, G.	**Nightmare**
928	Sloane, W.	**The Unquiet Corpse**

1957

B107	Congdon, D.	**Stories for the Dead of Night**
B110	Merril, J.	**SF: The Year's Greatest Science-Fiction and Fantasy: Second Annual Volume**
D191	Dinesen, I.	**A Winter's Tales**

1958

B119	Merril, J.	**SF: The Year's Greatest Science-Fiction and Fantasy: Third Annual Volume**
B120	Sturgeon, T.	**The Cosmic Rape**
D231	Hitchcock, A.	**12 Stories They Wouldn't Let Me Use on TV**
D246	Pangborn, E.	**A Mirror for Observers**

1959

LB126	Bennett, G.	**Great Tales of Action and Adventure**
B129	Merril, J.	**SF: The Year's Greatest Science-Fiction and Fantasy: Fourth Annual Volume**
B138	Vonnegut, K.	**The Sirens of Titan**
A181	Watkin, L. E.	**Darby O'Gill and the Little People**
D274	Finney, J.	**The Third Level**
D281	Hitchcock, A.	**13 More Stories They Wouldn't Let Me Do on TV**

1960

Y001	White, T. H.	**The Once and Future King**
C111	Conklin, G.	**Six Great Short Science Fiction Novels**
F124	Searls, H.	**The Big X**
F125	Hitchcock, A.	**14 of My Favourites in Suspense**
LB145	Wilde, O.	**The Picture of Dorian Grey**
1013	Bohle, E.	**The Man Who Disappeared**
1339	Haggard, H. R.	**She**

1961

F118	Merril, J.	**The Year's Best S-F: 5th Annual Edition**
F128	Dahl, R.	**Kiss, Kiss**
F130	Hitchcock, A.	**More of My Favourites in Suspense**
F139	Dahl, R.	**Someone Like You**
LC164	Swift, J.	**Gulliver's Travels**
LC172	Haggard, H. R.	**King Solomon's Mines**

B195	Matheson, R.	**Shock!**
B204	Finney, J.	**The Body Snatchers**
F206	Hitchcock, A.	**12 Stories They Wouldn't Let Me Do on TV**
1962		
X12	Mills, R. P.	**A Decade of Fantasy and Science Fiction**
R114	McCann, E.	**Preferred Risk**
F166	Hitchcock, A.	**Bar the Doors**
3428	Hitchcock, A.	**A Hangman's Dozen**
3645	Hitchcock, A.	**12 Stories They Wouldn't Let Me Do on TV**
5815	Hitchcock, A.	**More Stories for Late at Night**
9178	Hitchcock, A.	**12 Stories for Late at Night**
9772	Merril, J.	**The Year's Best S-F: 6th Annual Edition**
1963		
0241	Faraday, R.	**The Anytime Rings**
1157	Knight, D.	**A Century of Science Fiction**
2459	Burdick, E., & Wheeler, H.	
		Fail-Safe
2463	Clarke, A. C.	**A Fall of Moondust**
2495	Hitchcock, A.	**Fear and Trembling**
2876	Sinclair, D.	**The Gilead Bomb**
3160	Smith, C. T.	**Great Science Fiction Stories**
3626	Hitchcock, A.	**A Baker's Dozen of Suspense Stories**
3658	Hitchcock, A.	**Hold Your Breath**
6809	Holton, L.	**A Pact With Satan**
7746	Conklin, G.	**17 X Infinity**
8011	Hitchcock, A.	**16 Skeletons From My Closet**
8466	Benedict, S. H.	**Tales of Terror and Suspense**
9773	Merril, J.	**The Year's Best S-F: 7th Annual Edition**
1964		
1155	Schoonover, L.	**Central Passage**
2923	Albert, M. H.	**Goodbye Charlie**
3620	Hitchcock, A.	**More of My Favourites in Suspense**
3632	Hitchcock, A.	**14 Suspense Stories to Play Russian Roulette By**
6612	White, T. H.	**The Once and Future King**
6622	Hitchcock, A.	**Once Upon a Dreadful Time**
6914	Wilde, O.	**The Picture of Dorian Grey**
7829	Matheson, R.	**Shock II**
8445	White, T. H.	**The Sword in the Stone**
8467	Clarke, A. C.	**Tales of Ten Worlds**
9774	Merril, J.	**The Year's Best S-F: 8th Annual Edition**
1965		
0436	Hitchcock, A.	**Bar the Door**
0551	Hine, A.	**Bewitched**
1149	Vonnegut, K.	**Cat's Cradle**
1158	Knight, D.	**A Century of Great Short Science Fiction Novels**
2148	Stoker, B.	**Dracula**
2717	Shelley, M. W.	**Frankenstein**
4572	Dahl, R.	**Kiss, Kiss**
4794	Savage, M.	**A Likeness to Voices**
5816	Hitchcock, A.	**More Stories My Mother Never Told Me**
8116	Dahl, R.	**Someone Like You**
8290	Hitchcock, A.	**Stories My Mother Never Told Me**
8741	Conklin, G.	**12 Above the Night**
9613	Hitchcock, A.	**Alfred Hitchcock's Witches' Brew**
9700	Irving, W.	**The World of Washington Irving**
9775	Merril, J.	**The Year's Best S-F: 9th Annual Edition**
1966		
1430	George, P.	**Commander-1**
2929	Vonnegut, K.	**God Bless You, Mr. Rosewater**
3231	Friend, E.	**The Green Hornet in the Infernal Light**
3308	Swift, J.	**Gulliver's Travels**
3946	Malamud, B.	**Idiots First**
4031	Saki	**Incredible Tales**
5613	Malamud, B.	**The Magic Barrel**
5816	Hitchcock, A.	**More Stories My Mother Never Told Me**
6873	Gray, A.	**The Penetrators**

7828	Matheson, R.	**Shock!**
7830	Matheson, R.	**Shock 3**
7948	Vonnegut, K.	**The Sirens of Titan**
8288	Hitchcock, A.	**Stories Not for the Nervous**
8611	Merril, J.	**The Year's Best S-F: 10th Annual Edition**
8922	Silverberg, R.	**The Time of the Great Freeze**
9442	Pangborn, E.	**West of the Sun**
1967		
0627	Ward, D.	**Black Magic: 13 Chilling Tales**
0674	Finney, J.	**The Body Snatchers**
1307	Savage, M.	**The Coach Draws Near**
2079	St. Clair, M.	**The Dolphins of Altair**
2227	Poe, E. A.	**18 Best Stories by Edgar Allan Poe**
2241	Merril, J.	**The Year's Best S-F: 11th Annual Edition**
2552	Wells, H. G.	**The First Men in the Moon**
4068	Fuller, J. G.	**The Interrupted Journey**
4292	Pangborn, E.	**The Judgment of Eve**
4748	Adler, B.	**Letters to the Air Force on UFO's**
5643	Sheckley, R.	**Mindswap**
5815	Hitchcock, A.	**More Stories for Late at Night**
8090	Dickson, G. R.	**Soldier, Ask Not**
8184	Hoopes, N.	**Speak of the Devil**
8246	Heinlein, R. A.	**Starman Jones**
8295	Congdon, D.	**Stories for the Dead of Night**
8925	Clarke, A. C.	**Time Probe**
9312	Shapley, H.	**The View From a Distant Star**
9702	Velikovsky, I.	**Worlds in Collision**
1968		
0085	Aldiss, B. W.	**All About Venus**
0508	Merril, J.	**S-F: The Best of the Best**
1031	Drury, A.	**Capable of Honor**
1456	Silverberg, R.	**Conquerors From the Darkness**
1512	Sturgeon, T.	**The Cosmic Rape**
1849	Harrison, H.	**Deathworld 3**
1940	Sheckley, R.	**Dimension of Miracles**
2203	Velikovsky, I.	**Earth in Upheaval**
2206	Silverberg, R.	**Earthmen and Strangers**
2518	Heinlein, R. A.	**Farmer in the Sky**
2769	Curtis, R.	**Future Tense**
3308	Swift, J.	**Gulliver's Travels**
5797	Arthur, R.	**Monster Mix**
5915	Asturias, M. A.	**Mulata**
6244	Gaddis, V. H.	**Mysterious Fires and Lights**
6762	Baker, R.	**Our Next President**
6862	Anonymous	**Path Into the Unknown**
6881	Sheckley, R.	**The People Trap**
7102	Serling, R. J.	**The President's Plane Is Missing**
7509	Levin, I.	**Rosemary's Baby**
7833	West, M.	**The Shoes of the Fisherman**
8249	Sheckley, R.	**The Status Civilization**
8911	Petaja, E.	**The Time Twister**
?	Brautigan, R.	**In Watermelon Sugar**
Delta		
1960		
2530	Beagle, P. S.	**A Fine and Private Place**
1964		
1149	Vonnegut, K.	**Cat's Cradle**
1965		
2203	Velikovsky, I.	**Earth in Upheaval**
9702	Velikovsky, I.	**Worlds in Collision**

DELTA LIBRARY INC., New York, N.Y., U.S.A.
Cavalcade
No date

2	Livingston, A.	**Magic for Murder**

J. DENNETT, Sydney, N.S.W., Australia.
Dennett
1944 (approx.)

—	Molesworth, V.	**Wolfblood**

J. M. DENT & SONS LTD., London, England.
    Series imprints: **Aldine**; **Everyman**.
Aldine
1962
10   Harvey, W. F.   **The Beast With Five Fingers**
1964
33   Norton, M.   **The Borrowers Aloft**
Everyman
1960
1060   Swift, J.   **Gulliver's Travels**
1961
P616   Shelley, M. W.   **Frankenstein**
952   Hampden, J.   **Ghost Stories**
1963
1779   Verne, J.   **Five Weeks in a Balloon** (with *Around the World in 80 Days* [not sf])
1964
1767   Stevenson, R. L.   **The Strange Case of Dr. Jekyll and Mr. Hyde**
1912   James, H.   **The Turn of the Screw** (with *The Aspern Papers* [not sf])
1915   Wells, H. G.   **The Time Machine**

Digit See BROWN-WATSON

DIVERSEY PERIODICALS INC., Chicago, Illinois, U.S.A.
Diversey
1949
4   Prince, D.   **Tom's Temptations**

Dolphin See DOUBLEDAY & CO.

DOUBLEDAY & CO. INC., Garden City, N.Y., U.S.A.
    Imprints: **Anchor**; **Dolphin**; **Permabooks** [sold in 1954 to POCKET BOOKS, *q.v.*].
Anchor
1963
A212   Murray, M.   **The God of the Witches**
1965
470   Barthelme, D.   **Come Back, Dr. Caligari**
Dolphin
Dating not known
C50   Poe, E. A.   **Tales of the Grotesque and Arabesque**
C55   Bellamy, E.   **Looking Backward**
C130   Wyndham, J.   **The Day of the Triffids**
1960
C26   Marquis, D.   **Archy and Mehitabel**
1961
C304   Wells, H. G.   **The War of the Worlds & The Time Machine**
1962
C320   Brown, C. B.   **Wieland, or The Transformation**
C351   Anderson, P.   **The High Crusade**

DOVER PUBLICATIONS INC., New York, N.Y., U.S.A.
Dover
1952
—   Abbott, E. A.   **Flatland**
1955
—   Abbott, E. A.   **Flatland**
1960
T605   Wells, H. G.   **Three Prophetic Novels of H. G. Wells**
T633   Verne, J.   **From the Earth to the Moon & All Around the Moon**
T634   Verne, J.   **To the Sun & Off on a Comet**
T691   Baum, L. F.   **The Wonderful Wizard of Oz**
1961
T692   Baum, L. F.   **The Marvelous Land of Oz**
1962
T39   Burroughs, E. R.   **Three Martian Novels**

1963
T358   Burroughs, E. E.   **The Land That Time Forgot & The Moon Maid**
T376   Chappell, G. S.   **Through the Alimentary Canal With Gun and Camera**
T768   Bierce, A.   **The Sardonic Humour of Ambrose Bierce**
T1051   Burroughs, E. R.   **Three Science Fiction Novels**
T1053   Burroughs, E. R.   **Pirates of Venus & Lost on Venus**
T1135   Wells, H. G.   **The War in the Air; In the Days of the Comet; The Food of the Gods**
1964
T415   Le Fanu, J. S.   **The Best Ghost Stories of Sheridan Le Fanu**
T767   Bierce, A.   **The Ghost and Horror Stories of Ambrose Bierce**
T1140   Burroughs, E. R.   **A Princess of Mars & A Fighting Man of Mars**
T1180   Taine, J.   **Three Science Fiction Novels: The Time Stream; The Greatest Adventure; The Purple Sapphire**
1966
T1232   Bleiler, E. F.   **Three Gothic Novels**
T1531   Wells, H. G.   **The Best Science Fiction Stories of H. G. Wells**
T1626   Taine, J.   **Seeds of Life & The White Lily**
1967
T767   Bierce, A.   **The Ghost and Horror Stories of Ambrose Bierce**
T1715   Le Fanu, J. S.   **Uncle Silas**
21793   Hoffmann, E. T. A.   **The Best Tales of Hoffmann**
1968
T1892   Baum, L. F.   **The Surprising Adventures of the Magical Monarch of Mo**
T1879   Pyle, H.   **Twilight Land**
T1962   Stapledon, O.   **The Last and First Men & Star Maker**
T2191   Todd, R.   **The Lost Traveller**
21901.1   Hearn, L.   **Kwaidan**

DOW JONES, New York, N.Y., U.S.A.
Dow Jones
1967
—   Wall Street Journal   **Here Comes Tomorrow!**

Dragon See ATLANTIC BOOK PUBLISHING CO.

DRAGON PUBLICATIONS LTD., England.
    This firm was essentially a continuation of Scion Ltd.
Dragon Pub.
1954
—   Statten, V.   **1,000-Year Voyage**
—   Statten, V.   **Creature From the Black Lagoon**
1955
—   Statten, V.   **Earth 2**

DUCHESS PRINTING & PUBLISHING CO. LTD., Toronto, Ontario, Canada.
Duchess
1944 (approx.)
—   Campbell, J. W. [wrongly credited; should be R. Cummings] **Brigands of the Moon**
—   Rud, A.   **The Stuffed Men**

(GERALD) DUCKWORTH, London, England.
Paperduck
1966
9   Hudson, W. H.   **Green Mansions**

E. P. DUTTON & COMPANY INC., New York, N.Y., U.S.A.
    Imprints: **Dutton** and **Everyman-Dutton**.
Dutton
1954
—   Henderson, P.   **Shorter Novels of the 18th Century**

Everyman-Dutt.
1959
D39   Zamiatin, E.   **We**
1965
D166   Blackwood, A.   **Tales of Terror and the Unknown**

E, F

E. L. PUBLISHING CO., New York, U.S.A.
E.L. Pub. Co.
1968
L-21   Raymond, B.   **The Miracle of the Foomtra**

WILLIAM B. EERDMANS PUBLISHING CO., Grand Rapids, Michigan, U.S.A.
Eerdmans
1964
—   Williams, C.   **Descent Into Hell**
—   Williams, C.   **War in Heaven**
—   MacDonald, G.   **Phantastes & Lilith**
—   Lewis, C. S.   **Till We Have Faces**
1965
—   Williams, C.   **Many Dimensions**
—   Williams, C.   **The Place of the Lion**
—   Williams, C.   **Shadows of Ecstasy**

PAUL ELEK LTD., London, England.
All titles listed are in "Bestseller" series.
Elek
1960
—   Lewis, M. G.   **The Monk**
1961
—   Anonymous   **Horror Stories**
—   Wilkins, H. T.   **Mysteries**
1962
—   Lee, E.   **More Horror Stories**

Epic See ART ENTERPRISES INC.

Essex House See ART ENTERPRISES INC.

ETON BOOKS, New York, U.S.A.
(Understood to have been a division of Avon Books.)
Eton
1952
E119   Noel, S.   **I Killed Stalin**

Evergreen See GROVE PRESS

EVERYBODY'S BOOKS, England.
Publisher during World War II.
Everybody's
Not dated (early 1940's)
—   Anonymous   **Tales of Murder and Mystery**
—   Anonymous   **Tales of Mystery and Surprises**
—   Anonymous   **Third Finger—Left Hand and Other Thrilling Stories**
—   Anonymous   **More Tales of Terror and Surprise**
—   Yorke, P.   **The Gamma Ray Murders**
1944
—   Anonymous   **Tales of Terror and the Unknown**
—   Ascher, E.   **The Grim Caretaker**
—   Ascher, E.   **Uncanny Adventures**
—   Atholl, J.   **The Grey Beast**

—   Atholl, J.   **Land of Hidden Death**
—   Hervey, M.   **Queer-Looking Box: Seven Gripping Stories**

Everyman See DENT

Everyman-Dutt. See DUTTON

EXPORT PUBLISHING ENTERPRISES LTD., Toronto, Ontario, Canada.
Export
1946
—   Kelley, T. P.   **I Found Cleopatra**
1949
60   Hughes, C.   **He Dared Not Look Behind!**
1950
KN18A   Fischer, L.   **Let out the Beast**
122   Kelley, T. P.   **The Gorilla's Daughter**
141   Jenkins, W. F.   **Destroy the U.S.A.**
MDS142 Phillips, R.   **Worlds Within**

FABER AND FABER LTD., London, England.
All titles are paperback reprints of hardcover titles.
Faber
1958
—   Crispin, E.   **Best SF**
—   Golding, W.   **Lord of the Flies**
1960
—   Crispin, E.   **Best SF Two**
—   Ridler, A.   **Best Ghost Stories**
—   Golding, W.   **Pincher Martin**
1962
—   Cross, J. K.   **Best Horror Stories**
—   Crispin, E.   **Best SF Three**
—   Tutuola, A.   **The Palm-Wine Drinkard**
—   de la Mare, W. J.   **Some Stories**
—   Williams, C.   **War in Heaven**
1963
—   Cross, J. K.   **Best Black Magic Stories**
—   Davenport, B.   **Ghostly Tales To Be Told**
—   Golding, W.   **Lord of the Flies**
—   Williams, C.   **Many Dimensions**
1964
—   Golding, W.   **The Inheritors**
1965
—   Crispin, E.   **Best SF Four**
—   Walters, H.   **Blast Off at Woomera**
—   Aldiss, B. W.   **NonStop**
—   Williams, C.   **The Place of the Lion**
—   Williams, C.   **Shadows of Ecstasy**
1966
—   Crispin, E.   **Best Tales of Terror**
1967
—   Aldiss, B. W.   **Introducing Science Fiction**
—   Golding, W.   **Lord of the Flies**
—   Davenport, B.   **Tales To Be Told in the Dark**
1968
—   Crispin, E.   **The Stars and Under**
34   Eliot, T. S.   **The Family Reunion** [play]

FANTASY PRESS, Reading, Pennsylvania, U.S.A.
Titles in "Golden Science Fiction Library" series.
Fantasy
1956
1   Smith, Edward E.   **Galactic Patrol**
2   Campbell, J. W.   **The Moon Is Hell**
3   Leinster, M.   **Operation: Outer Space**

FANTASY PUBLISHING CO. INC., Los Angeles, Calif., U.S.A.
FPCI
1947
—   Flagg, F.   **The Night People**

FAWCETT HODDER LTD., London, England.

Coronet began as an imprint by Fawcett Hodder, but later became an imprint of Hodder & Stoughton, *q.v.*

FAWCETT PUBLICATIONS, New York, N.Y. U.S.A.; or Greenwich, Connecticut, U.S.A.

Imprints: **Crest** (usually published for Fawcett World Library); **Fawcett** (usually popular magazine size); **Gold Medal**; **Premier** (usually nonfiction).

Crest
1956
s145	Sherman, H.	**You Live After Death**
s148	Viereck, G. S., & Eldridge, P.	
		My First 2,000 Years
150	McIntosh, J. T.	**The Rule of the Pagbeasts**

1957
s184	Hamilton, E.	**City at World's End**
s197	Dikty, T. E.	**5 Tales From Tomorrow**

1958
s209	Mantley, J.	**The 27th Day**
s216	Verne, J.	**From the Earth to the Moon & A Trip Around It**
s226	Gernsback, H.	**Ralph 124C 41 +**
s245	Margulies, L., & Friend, O. J.	
		Race to the Stars
s258	Dikty, T. E.	**6 From Worlds Beyond**

1959
s282	Margulies, L.	**3 From Out There**
s308	Matheson, R.	**A Stir of Echoes**
s329	Hamilton, E.	**The Star of Life**
s342	Charbonneau, L.	**No Place on Earth**

1960
s362	Margulies, L.	**Get out of My Sky**
s395	Baum, L. F.	**The Wizard of Oz**

1961
d425	Viereck, G. S., & Eldridge, P.	
		My First 2,000 Years
s494	Hamilton, E.	**The City at World's End**

1962
s518	Blaisdell, A.	**Nightmare**
d531	Wyndham, J.	**The Day of the Triffids**
d547	Simak, C. D.	**Time Is the Simplest Thing**
d557	Alexander, D.	**Tales for a Rainy Night**

1963
d586	Vercors	**Sylva**
d595	Cunningham, E. V.	**Phyllis**
d597	Dikty, T. E.	**5 Tales From Tomorrow**
d612	Christopher, J.	**The Long Winter**
K674	Baum, L. F.	**The Wizard of Oz**

1964
R675	Wylie, P.	**Triumph**
R682	Updike, J.	**The Centaur**
m713	Sutcliff, R.	**Sword at Sunset**
L728	Margulies, L.	**Get Out of My Sky**
d741	Wyndham, J.	**The Day of the Triffids**
d752	Simak, C. D.	**Time Is the Simplest Thing**
L758	Hamilton, E.	**The City at World's End**
d773	Hoyle, F., & Elliot, J.	
		A for Andromeda

1965
k781	McShane, M.	**Seance on a Wet Afternoon**
R793	Miller, Warren	**Looking for the General**
R798	Searls, H.	**The Pilgrim Project**
d812	Hoyle, F. & G.	**The Fifth Planet**
d814	Grubb, D.	**Twelve Tales of Suspense and the Supernatural**
R833	Miller, Warren	**The Siege of Harlem**
R836	Saul, G. B.	**Owls' Watch**
m841	Wallace, Irving	**The Man**

1966
R897	Lind, J.	**Soul of Wood and Other Stories**

1967
D996	Dikty, T. E.	**5 Tales From Tomorrow**
R1029	Christopher, J.	**Sweeney's Island**
R1033	Wylie, P.	**Triumph**
R1049	Wyndham, J.	**The Day of the Triffids**
R1050	Updike, J.	**The Centaur**
P1052	Barth, J.	**Giles Goat-Boy**
R1080	Hoyle, F., & Elliot, J.	
		Andromeda Breakthrough

1968
R1155	Hoyle, F.	**October the First Is Too Late**
R1166	Stern, P. Van D.	**Strange Beasts and Unnatural Monsters**
R1205	Hoyle, F., & Elliot, J.	
		A for Andromeda

Fawcett
1948
—	Keyhoe, D. E.	**The Flying Saucers Are Real**

1950
136	Yorke, J.	**Brides of the Devil**

Gold Medal
Undated
?	Woolrich, C.	**Savage Bride**

1950
105	Rohmer, S.	**Nude in Mink**
107	Keyhoe, D. E.	**The Flying Saucers Are Real**
136	Woolrich, C.	**Savage Bride**

1951
199	Rohmer, S.	**Sumuru**

1952
273	Rosmanith, O.	**Unholy Flame**
283	Rohmer, S.	**The Fire Goddess**

1953
321	Rohmer, S.	**Nude in Mink**

1954
408	Rohmer, S.	**The Return of Sumuru**
417	Matheson, R.	**I Am Legend**
498	Brennan, F. H.	**One of Our H-Bombs Is Missing**

1956
555	Rohmer, S.	**Sinister Madonna**
s577	Matheson, R.	**The Shrinking Man**

1957
s684	Rohmer, S.	**Re-Enter Fu Manchu**

1958
s726	Margulies, L.	**Three Times Infinity**
s751	Leinster, M.	**War With the Gizmos**
s757	Rohmer, S.	**Sumuru**

1959
s832	Leinster, M.	**Monster From Earth's End**
s853	Foster, R.	**The Rest Must Die**
868	Rohmer, S.	**The Return of Sumuru**
s929	Rohmer, S.	**Emperor Fu Manchu**
s937	Leinster, M.	**Four From Planet 5**

1960
s975	Keene, D., & Pruyn, L.	
		World Without Women
s989	Coppel, A.	**Dark December**
s997	Conklin, G.	**13 Great Stories of Science Fiction**
s1057	Budrys, A.	**Rogue Moon**

1961
s1153	Vonnegut, K.	**Canary in a Cat House**

1962
d1203	Matheson, R.	**The Shrinking Man**
s1231	Bloch, R.	**Atoms and Evil**
k1243	Conklin, G.	**13 Great Stories of Science Fiction**
s1259	MacDonald, J. D.	**The Girl, the Gold Watch and Everything**

1963
k1276	Tevis, W.	**The Man Who Fell to Earth**
d1324	Margulies, L.	**Three Times Infinity**
d1366	Conklin, G.	**12 Great Classics of Science Fiction**

1964
K1397	Leinster, M.	**Four From Planet 5**
d1428	Knight, D.	**Tomorrow X 4**
d1444	Conklin, G.	**13 Great Stories of Science Fiction**
k1446	Einstein, C.	**The Day New York Went Dry**

k1458	Rohmer, S.	**Re-Enter Fu Manchu**
K1474	Budrys, A.	**Rogue Moon**
k1488	Gotlieb, P.	**Sunburst**
L1494	Kastle, H.	**The Reassembled Man**

1965

L1504	Keene, D., & Pruyn, L.	
		World Without Women
K1513	MacDonald, J. D.	**The Girl, the Gold Watch and Everything**
d1544	Hurwood, B. J.	**Monsters Galaore**
d1549	Conklin, G.	**5 Unearthly Visions**
d1561	Sohl, J.	**Night Slaves**
d1586	Beaumont, C.	**The Magic Man**

1966

d1628	Conklin, G.	**Another Part of the Galaxy**
d1669	Conklin, G.	**12 Great Classics of Science Fiction**
d1680	Margulies, L.	**Three Times Infinity**
d1693	Van Thal, H.	**The Pan Book of Horror Stories**
d1719	Keel, J. A.	**The Fickle Finger of Fate**
d1752	Conklin, G.	**Seven Come Infinity**

1967

d1727	Bloch, R.	**The Scarf**
d1783	Chamberlain, W.	**China Strike**
d1792	MacDonald, J. D.	**The Girl, the Gold Watch and Everything**
d1852	Budrys, A.	**The Amsirs and the Iron Thorn**
D1868	Conklin, G.	**5 Unearthly Visions**
?	Binder, O.	**What We Really Know About Flying Saucers**

1968

d1883	Baum, L. F.	**The Wizard of Oz**
d1887	Kersh, G.	**Nightshade and Damnations**
R1918	Maine, C. E.	**Survival Margin**
R1924	Conklin, G.	**Seven Trips Through Time and Space**
R1942	Knight, D.	**Worlds to Come**
R1993	MacDonald, J. D.	**Ballroom of the Skies**
R1994	MacDonald, J. D.	**Wine of the Dreamers**
R2001	Christopher, J.	**The Long Winter**

Premier

1956

| s24 | Verrill, A. H. | **The Strange Story of Our Earth** |

1959

| d83 | Gatland, K. W., & Dempster, D. D. | |
| | | **The Inhabited Universe** |

1960

| d93 | del Rey, L. | **Rockets Through Space** |

1961

| d102 | Clarke, A. C. | **The Exploration of Space** |

1964

| R228 | Clarke, A. C. | **The Exploration of Space** |

1968

| T384 | Wells, H. G. | **The Time Machine** |

FEATURE BOOKS LTD., London, England.
Feature

| — | Borgia, A. | **Beyond This Life** |

Flagship See CARAVELLE BOOK INC.

FLPH See FOREIGN LANGUAGES PUBLISHING HOUSE

Fontana See (WILLIAM) COLLINS SONS & CO. LTD.

FOREIGN LANGUAGES PUBLISHING HOUSE, Moscow, U.S.S.R.
FLPH
1960's

—	Dixon, R.	**Destination: Amaltheia**
—	Anonymous	**The Heart of the Serpent**
—	Anonymous	**A Visitor From Outer Space**

FORWARD PUBLISHING CO., Toronto, Ontario, Canada.
Forward
1944

| — | Lowe, A. | **Death of the Last Taxpayer** |

W. FOULSHAM & CO. LTD., Slough, Bucks, England
Foulsham
1950

| — | Stoker, B. | **The Lair of the White Worm** |

Four Square Books See NEW ENGLISH LIBRARY

FPCI See FANTASY PUBLISHING CO.

FRANCE, U.S.A.
France
1962

| F14 | Olin, R. | **Lust Planet** |

1963

| — | Deer, M. J. | **Flames of Desire** |
| — | Deer, M. J. | **A Place Named Hell** |

SAMUEL FRENCH, New York, U.S.A.
French
Late 1940's

—	Bond, N. S.	**Mr. Mergenthwirker's Lobblies**
—	Deane, H., & Balderston, J. L.	
		Dracula
—	Masters, R. & L.	**The Mystery of the Ming Tree**

FSB (Four Square Books) See NEW ENGLISH LIBRARY

FUNK & WAGNALLS, New York, N.Y., U.S.A.
Funk Wagnalls
1968

| F47 | Carr, T. | **Science Fiction for People Who Hate Science Fiction** |

FUTURIAN PRESS, Sydney, N.S.W., Australia.
  Australian amateur press, now defunct, producing limited editions of 200 copies (or less) at 6/-.
Futurian
1950

| — | Larnach, S. L. | **A Checklist of Australian Fantasy** |

1951

| — | Molesworth, V. | **Blinded They Fly** |

1952

—	Stone, G. B. (& Williams, R.)	
		Zero Equals Nothing
—	Molesworth, V.	**Let There Be Monsters**
—	Molesworth, V.	**An Outline History of Australian Fandom (Part 1)**

G

GALAXY PUBLISHING CORP., New York, N.Y., U.S.A.
  Galaxy Novels Nos. 1 through 7 were published by World Editions, New York; Galaxy Publishing Corp. took over with No. 8. Effective with No. 36, the series appeared under the Beacon Distributing Co. imprint (though the publisher was still the Guin Co., New York). These editions are noted **Beac (Gal)** in the AUTHORS section. Beacon used a different serial code, though occasionally the Galaxy Novel number (shown below following the title) was given inside the book. The Beacon editions showed a bias to sex which is rather mild by later standards. Galaxy Novels began as companions to *Galaxy* magazine, and were the same digest-magazine size through No. 31; thereafter they became the regular newsstand paperback size.

An additional imprint is **Magabook**, which published two novels or novellas in each book.

Galaxy Nov
1950
1	Russell, E. F.	**Sinister Barrier**
2	Williamson, J.	**The Legion of Space**

1951
3	Clarke, A. C.	**Prelude to Space**
4	Wright, S. F.	**The Amphibians**
5	Wright, S. F.	**The World Below**
6	Jones, R. R.	**The Alien**
7	Simak, C. D.	**Empire**

1952
8	Stapledon, O.	**Odd John**
9	Temple, W. F.	**Four-Sided Triangle**
10	Franklin, J.	**The Rat Race**
11	Tucker, W.	**The City in the Sea**
12	Merwin, S.	**The House of Many Worlds**

1953
13	Taine, J.	**Seeds of Life**
14	Asimov, I.	**Pebble in the Sky**
15	Mitchell, J. L.	**Three Go Back**
16	Blish, J.	**The Warriors of Day**
17	Padgett, L.	**The Well of the Worlds**
18	Hamilton, E.	**The City at World's End**

1954
19	Blish, J.	**Jack of Eagles**
20	Leinster, M.	**The Black Galaxy**
21	Williamson, J.	**The Humanoids**
22	Merwin, S.	**Killer to Come**

1955
23	Reed, D. V.	**Murder in Space**
24	de Camp, L. S.	**Lest Darkness Fall**
25	Leinster, M.	**The Last Space Ship**

1956
26	Padgett, L.	**Chessboard Planet**
27	Jameson, M.	**Tarnished Utopia**

1957
28	Leiber, F.	**Destiny Times Three**
29	Hubbard, L. R.	**Fear**
30	Pratt, F.	**Double Jeopardy**
31	Moore, C. L.	**Shambleau**

Change to newsstand paperback size
32	Wallace, F. L.	**Address: Centauri**
33	Clement, H.	**Mission of Gravity**
34	Wellman, M. W.	**Twice in Time**

1959
35	Clifton, M., & Riley, F.	
		The Forever Machine

Change to Beacon imprint and serial code
Beac (Gal)
1959
236	Stapledon, O.	**Odd John** (GN36)
242	Jones, R. F.	**The Deviates** (GN37)
256	Smith, G. O.	**Troubled Star** (GN38)
263	Garrett, R., & Harris, L. M.	
		Pagan Passions (GN39)

1960
270	Anderson, P.	**Virgin Planet** (GN40)
277	Farmer, P. J.	**Flesh** (GN41)
284	Merwin, S.	**The Sex War** (GN42)
291	Farmer, P. J.	**A Woman a Day** (GN43)
298	van Vogt, A. E.	**The Mating Cry** (GN44)

1961
305	Aldiss, B. W.	**The Male Response** (GN45)
312	Judd, C.	**Sin in Space** (GN46)

Magabook
1963
1	del Rey, L.	**The Sky Is Falling & Badge of Infamy**
2	Williamson, J.	**The Legion of Time & After World's End**

1965
3	Sturgeon, T.	**And My Fear Is Great & Baby Is Three**

GANNET PRESS, London, England.
Gannet
1953
1	Mistral, B.	**Pirates of Cerelius**
2	Mistral, B.	**Space Flight 139**
3	Brack, V.	**Odyssey in Space**
4	Mistral, B.	**The Brains of Helle**
5	Brack, V.	**Castaway From Space**
6	Vallance, K.	**Global Blackout**
7	Amper, D.	**Far Beyond the Blue**
8	Brack, V.	**The "X" People**
9	Beemish, C.	**Worlds Away**

1954
10	Steel, M.	**Trouble Planet**

GAYWOOD PRESS LTD., London, England.
See also PALADIN PRESS, operated from same address.
Gaywood
1951-1952
—	del Martia, A.	**Dawn of Darkness**
—	del Martia, A.	**Interstellar Espionage**
—	del Martia, A.	**The Space Pirates**
—	del Martia, A.	**The Trembling World**
—	Finn, R. L.	**Captive on the Flying Saucer**
—	Finn, R. L.	**Freaks Against Superman**

GNOME PRESS, New York, N.Y., U.S.A.
Paper-covered editions of hardcover titles, for distribution to U.S. military forces overseas; some came on the commercial market.
Gnome
1949
—	Asimov, I.	**I, Robot**
—	Bond, N. S.	**The 31st of February**
—	Simak, C. D.	**Cosmic Engineers**
—	Smith, G. O.	**Pattern for Conquest**

Gold Medal See FAWCETT PUBLICATIONS

Gold Star See MONARCH BOOKS

(MARK) GOULDEN LTD., London, England.
Imprints: **Goulden** until about 1953; thereafter **Pinnacle**. All titles were noted as distributed by W. H. Allen, London.
Goulden
1949 (approx.)
—	Home-Gall, E. R.	**The Human Bat**
—	Home-Gall, E. R.	**The Human Bat v. the Robot Gangster**
—	de Camp, L. S.	**Rogue Queen**
—	Burroughs, E. R.	**Tarzan and the Lost Empire**
—	Burroughs, E. R.	**Tarzan, Lord of the Jungle**
—	Burroughs, E. R.	**Tarzan the Invincible**
—	Burroughs, E. R.	**Tarzan at the Earth's Core**
—	Burroughs, E. R.	**Tarzan's Quest**
—	Burroughs, E. R.	**A Princess of Mars**

1950
1	Burroughs, E. R.	**Tarzan and the Lost Empire**
7	Burroughs, E. R.	**Tarzan and the Lion Man**
8	Burroughs, E. R.	**Tarzan and the Forbidden City**
9	Burroughs, E. R.	**Carson of Venus**
10	Burroughs, E. R.	**Tarzan and the Leopard Men**
11	Burroughs, E. R.	**Tarzan and the City of Gold**
12	Burroughs, E. R.	**Tarzan Triumphant**
13	Burroughs, E. R.	**Tarzan and the Foreign Legion**
14	Burroughs, E. R.	**Tarzan the Magnificent**

1951
1	Burroughs, E. R.	**Tarzan and the Lost Empire**
4	Burroughs, E. R.	**Tarzan at the Earth's Core**
11	Burroughs, E. R.	**Tarzan and the City of Gold**
15	Burroughs, E. R.	**Tarzan of the Apes**
16	Burroughs, E. R.	**Tarzan the Untamed**
17	Burroughs, E. R.	**Tarzan and the Jewels of Opar**
18	Burroughs, E. R.	**The Beasts of Tarzan**

19	Burroughs, E. R.	The Return of Tarzan

1952

1	Burroughs, E. R.	Tarzan and the Lost Empire
3	Burroughs, E. R.	Tarzan the Invincible
4	Burroughs, E. R.	Tarzan at the Earth's Core
5	Burroughs, E. R.	Tarzan's Quest
8	Burroughs, E. R.	Tarzan and the Forbidden City
9	Burroughs, E. R.	Carson of Venus
10	Burroughs, E. R.	Tarzan and the Leopard Men
11	Burroughs, E. R.	Tarzan and the City of Gold
12	Burroughs, E. R.	Tarzan Triumphant
13	Burroughs, E. R.	Tarzan and the Foreign Legion
14	Burroughs, E. R.	Tarzan the Magnificent
15	Burroughs, E. R.	Tarzan of the Apes
16	Burroughs, E. R.	Tarzan the Untamed

Pinnacle

1953

2	Burroughs, E. R.	Tarzan, Lord of the Jungle
20	Burroughs, E. R.	Tarzan and the Golden Lion
21	Burroughs, E. R.	The Son of Tarzan
22	Burroughs, E. R.	Tarzan the Terrible
23	Burroughs, E. R.	Lost on Venus
24	Burroughs, E. R.	Tarzan and the Ant Men
25	Burroughs, E. R.	Thuvia, Maid of Mars
26	Burroughs, E. R.	The Warlord of Mars
27	Burroughs, E. R.	The Outlaw of Torn [not sf]
28	Burroughs, E. R.	The Eternal Lover
29	Burroughs, E. R.	Tanar of Pellucidar
30	Burroughs, E. R.	The Gods of Mars
31	Burroughs, E. R.	The Bandit of Hell's Bend [not sf]

1954

32	Burroughs, E. R.	Jungle Tales of Tarzan
33	Burroughs, E. R.	A Fighting Man of Mars
34	Burroughs, E. R.	Pirates of Venus
35	Burroughs, E. R.	The Cave Girl
36	Burroughs, E. R.	The Chessmen of Mars
37	Burroughs, E. R.	The Girl From Hollywood [not sf]

1955

33	Burroughs, E. R.	A Fighting Man of Mars
38	Burroughs, E. R.	The Master Mind of Mars
39	Burroughs, E. R.	Pellucidar
nn	de Camp, L. S.	Rogue Queen

1958

—	Burroughs, E. R.	Tarzan and the Lost Empire
—	Burroughs, E. R.	Tarzan, Lord of the Jungle
—	Burroughs, E. R.	Tarzan the Invincible
—	Burroughs, E. R.	Tarzan and the Foreign Legion

GRAFTON PUBLICATIONS, Dublin, Eire.
Grafton
Mid-1940's

—	O'Donnell, E.	Caravan of Crime
—	O'Donnell, E.	Haunted and Hunted
—	O'Donnell, E.	Hell Ships of Many Waters
—	Delray, C.	Realm of the Alien

GRAPHIC PUBLISHING CO. INC., Hasbrouck Heights, N.Y., U.S.A.
Graphic
1956

G216	Erskine, J.	The Private Life of Helen of Troy
504	Rohmer, S.	Hangover House

GREENLEAF CLASSICS, San Diego, California, U.S.A.
Imprints by this publisher include **Adult Books, Candid Reader, Ember Library, Greenleaf, Idle Hour Books, Leisure Books, Nightstand Books**, and **Pleasure Reader**. Most titles are pornographic in nature.
Adult
1967

AB404	Holliday, D.	Three on a Broomstick
AB417	Dale, C.	Chief Sexecutive

Candid Reader
1967

CA901	Allison, C.	The Sin Funnel
CA909	Hudson, D.	The N.U.D.E. Caper

1968

CA930	Allison, C.	The Desert Damsels
CA940	Bellmore, D.	Sin Seance

Greenleaf
1966

GC205	Wood, E. D., Jr.	Orgy of the Dead
GC206	Nuetzel, C.	Queen of Blood

1967

GC218	Kalnen, R.	The Love Box
GC220	Hudson, J.	Those Sexy Saucer People

Idle Hour
1966

IH576	Hudson, D.	Dreamlover

Ember Library
1965

EL301	Allison, C.	Our Man From Sadisto
EL303	Hudson, D.	Nightmare Clinic
EL305	Allison, C.	Our Girl From Mephisto
EL309	Allison, C.	Nautipuss

1966

EL313	Allison, C.	Go-Go Sadisto
EL321	Allison, C.	Gamefinger
EL323	Dexter, John	Garden of Shame
EL325	Allison, C.	Sadisto Royale
EL329	Allison, C.	For Your Sighs Only
EL333	Allison, C.	The Lost Bomb
?	Allison, C.	The Desdamona Affair

1967

EL365	Allison, C.	The Ice Maiden

Leisure
1965

LB1106	Dexter, John	The Sinners of Hwang

1966

LB1140	Allison, C.	0008 Meets Gnatman
LB1152	Dexter, John	The Sin Veldt
LB1159	Allison, C.	The Merciless Mermaids
LB1160	Allison, C.	Mondo Sadisto
LB1165	Dexter, John	Carnaby Consort
LB1169	Allison, C.	0008 Meets Modesta Blaze
LB1174	Allison, C.	The Sex Ray
LB1176	Allison, C.	Roburta the Conqueress
?	Allison, C.	From Rapture to Love

1967

LB1206	Williams, J. X.	Witch in Heat
LB1207	Lynn, D.	Zardoc, Warrior Stud
LB1218	Williams, J. X.	Her

Nightstand
1968

NB1864	Bellmore, D.	Leopard Lust
NB1877	Allison, C.	Platypussy
NB1883	Cross, G.	Nude in Orbit
NB1889	Kalnen, R.	The Day the Universe Came
NB1910	Lynn, D.	Cybro Sex

Pleasure Reader
1968

PR172	Williams, J. X.	The Sex Pill
PR180	Bellmore, D.	By Lust Possessed

Grey Arrow See HUTCHINSON & CO.

GROSSET & DUNLAP INC., New York, N.Y., U.S.A.
Imprints: **Tempo** and **Universal Library** [Univ. Lib.].
Tempo
1962

T6	Conklin, G.	Invaders of Earth
T9	Coombs, C.	The Mystery of Satellite 7
T13	Walters, H.	First on the Moon

1963
T28	Wollheim, D.	**The Secret of the Martian Moons**
T39	Conklin, G.	**Great Stories of Space Travel**

1965
T89	Serling, R.	**Chilling Stories From Rod Serling's The Twilight Zone**
—	Johnston, W.	**Get Smart!**

1966
T111	Conklin, G.	**Giants Unleashed**
T112	Sinclair, U.	**The Gnomobile**
—	Johnston, W.	**Get Smart Once Again!**
—	Johnston, W.	**Max Smart and the Perilous Pellets**
—	Johnston, W.	**Sorry, Chief**

1967
T151	Brink, C. M.	**Andy Buckram's Tin Men**
T158	Johnston, W.	**Captain Nice**
—	Johnston, W.	**And Loving It**
—	Johnston, W.	**Missed It By That Much!**
4789	Serling, R.	**Twilight Zone**
4851	Brink, C. M.	**Andy Buckram's Tin Men**
7171	Serling, R.	**Rod Serling's Twilight Zone Revisited**

1968
—	Johnston, W.	**Max Smart Loses Control**
—	Johnston, W.	**Max Smart—The Spy Who Went Out to the Cold**
T182	Skelton, R.	**Red Skelton's Favorite Ghost Stories**
T190	Parish, A.	**Floating Island**

Univ. Lib.
1957
UL19	Graves, R.	**Hercules, My Shipmate**

1962
UL126	Karp, D.	**One**

1963
UL161	James, H.	**The Ghostly Tales of Henry James**

1964
UL172	Forster, E. M.	**The Eternal Moment**

GROVE PRESS INC., New York, U.S.A.
   Additional imprint: **Evergreen Black Cat Books**.
Grove
1953
E15	Tutuola, A.	**The Palm-Wine Drinkard**

1954
E13	Lee, V.	**The Snake Lady**

1968
GS2	Forest, J. P.	**Barbarella**

Evergreen
1959
E147	Hoffmann, E.T.A.	**Tales of Hoffmann**
E160	Kerouac, J.	**Doctor Sax**
E163	Lewis, M. G.	**The Monk**

1962
E368	Borges, J. L.	**Ficciones**

1965
BC102	Burroughs, W. S.	**The Nova Express**

1967
BC131	Burroughs, W. S.	**The Soft Machine**

1968
B164	Burroughs, W. S.	**The Ticket That Exploded**

GRYPHON, England.
Gryphon
1954
—	Williams, I.	**Newbury in Orm**

Guild See BRITISH PUBLISHERS GUILD LTD.

GULLIVER BOOKS LTD., Lower Chelston, England.
Gulliver
Not dated (early 1940's)
—	Anonymous	**Thrilling Tales of Unusual Interest**
—	Bachelor, G. C.	**True Ghost Stories**
—	Hervey, M.	**Thrilling Tales**

H

H. J. SERVICE, London, England.
H.J. Service
1943
—	Frater Om	**The Mongolian Master and His Disciple**

HAFNER PUBLISHING CO., New York and London.
Hafner
1958
17	Brown, C. B.	**Wieland**

1962
24	Brown, C. B.	**Ormond**

ROBERT HALE LTD., London, England.
Hale
1955
—	Divine, D.	**Atom at Spithead**

A. HALLE, London, England.
Halle
1945 (approx.)
—	Tulip, J.	**The Moon Goddess**

HAMILTON & CO. (STAFFORD) LTD.
   British publisher of the Authentic and Panther series (as well as some not so designated). About 1964 the firm became PANTHER BOOKS LTD., *q.v.*

HAMPTON PRESS, Essex, England.
Hampton
Not dated (1941-1945)
—	Hervey, M.	**Horror Medley**
—	Hervey, M.	**Creeps Medley**

HARBOROUGH PUBLISHING CO., Stoke-on-Trent, England.
Harborough
1951
—	King, J.	**Shuna and the Lost Tribe**
—	King, J.	**Shuna, White Queen of the Jungle**

Harbrace See HARCOURT, BRACE & WORLD

HARCOURT, BRACE & WORLD, New York, U.S.A.
   Other imprints: **Harbrace** and **Voyager**.
Harcourt
1963
—	Golding, W.	**The Inheritors**

1965
—	Golding, W.	**The Spire**

Harbrace
1966
HPL1	Clarke, A. C.	**The City and the Stars**

1968
HPL25	Clarke, A. C.	**The Other Side of the Sky**

Voyager
1966
AVB43	Kendall, C.	**The Gammage Cup**

HARLEQUIN BOOKS, Toronto and Winnipeg, Canada.
Harlequin
1950
79	Sale, R.	**Lazarus Number Seven**

1952
177	van Vogt, A. E.	**The House That Stood Still**

1953

205	Weinbaum, S. G.	**The Black Flame**
218	Fearn, J. R.	**The Golden Amazon**
238	Doyle, A. C.	**The Lost World** [in association with Pan Books]

1954

320	Fearn, J. R.	**The Deathless Amazon**

1958

421	Fearn, J. R.	**The Golden Amazon's Triumph**

HARPER & ROW PUBLISHERS, New York, N.Y., U.S.A.
  Additional imprints: **Perennial** and **Torchbook**.
Harper
1965

P60A	Hoyle, F.	**Ossian's Ride**

Perennial
Date unknown

P23	Huxley, A.	**Brave New World Revisited**
P37	Hoyle, F.	**The Black Cloud**

1965

P3018	Swift, J.	**Gulliver's Travels**

1966

P99B	Shute, N.	**On the Beach**

1967

P3029	Collins, W. W.	**The Moonstone**

Torchbook
1966

TB1282	Cantril, H.	**The Invasion From Mars**

HART PUBLISHING CO. INC., New York, N.Y., U.S.A.
Hart
1965

—	Morris, R.	**Masterpieces of Mystery and Detection**

1966

—	Morris, R.	**Masterpieces of Horror**
—	Morris, R.	**Masterpieces of Suspense**
—	Monahan, J. L.	**Masterpieces of Surprise**

HEADLINE BOOKS, U.S.A.
Headline
Mid1960's

105	Sellers, C.	**Red Rape**

HEALTH RESEARCH, Mokelumne Hill, California, U.S.A.
Health Research
1965

—	Emerson, W. G.	**The Smoky God**

THE HEARST CORPORATION, New York, N.Y., U.S.A.
  See also AVON BOOKS.
Banner
1967

B50-105	Milton, H. A.	**The President Is Missing!**
B50-113	Karp, D.	**The Brotherhood of Velvet**
B50-117	Luther, R.	**Intermind**
B60-110	Shaw, B.	**Night Walk**

HEART BOOKS, U.S.A.
Heart
Mid-1960's

HV105	Warren, R.	**Space Sex**

Hector Kelly See KELLY

HELICON, Dublin, Eire.
Helicon
1965

—	Wall, M.	**The Unfortunate Fursey**

HILLMAN PERIODICALS. New York, U.S.A.
  TNC = Thriller Novel Classic
Hillman
1950

41	Vance, J.	**The Dying Earth**

1950's?

TNC4	Rohmer, S.	**The Insidious Dr. Fu-Manchu**
TNC5	Horler, S.	**Land of Terror**
TNC9	Rohmer, S.	**The Golden Scorpion**
TNC10	Franklin, G.	**The White Wolf**
TNC13	Chambers, W.	**Invasion**

HODDER & STOUGHTON LTD., London, England.
  Additional imprint: **Coronet** (see below). The Coronet imprint was first used by FAWCETT HODDER LTD., London; in 1968 it became the imprint for Hodder & Stoughton paperbacks.
Hodder
1949

119	Haggard, H. R.	**She**

1951

C118	Haggard, H. R.	**Allan Quatermain**

1952

C10	Seamark	**The Avenging Ray**

1953

—	Mason, A.E.W.	**The Prisoner in the Opal**
C119	Haggard, H. R.	**She**

1955

C215	Horler, S.	**The Curse of Doone**

1958

C118	Haggard, H. R.	**Allan Quatermain**
C350	Creasey, J.	**The Flood**

1959

360	Jones, H. S.	**Life on Other Worlds**

1961

—	Hodder-Williams, C.	**Final Approach**
119	Haggard, H. R.	**She**
485	Hodder-Williams, C.	**Chain Reaction**

1962

511	Maine, C. E.	**Subterfuge**
542	Creasey, J.	**The Plague of Silence**

1963

620	Haggard, H. R.	**Cleopatra**

1964

?	Gordon, D.	**Star Raker**

1965

119	Haggard, H. R.	**She**
737	Lymington, J.	**The Star Witches**
738	Lymington, J.	**Night of the Big Heat**
746	Gordon, D.	**Flight of the Bat**
753	Lymington, J.	**The Giant Stumbles**

1966

118	Haggard, H. R.	**Allan Quatermain**
772	Creasey, J.	**The Terror**
779	Eden, D.	**Cat's Prey**
780	Eden, D.	**The Voice of the Dolls**
796	Christopher, J.	**Cloud on Silver**
812	Christopher, J.	**The Possessors**

1967

818	Lymington, J.	**Froomb!**
2485	Creasey, J.	**The Depths**
2790	Creasey, J.	**The Inferno**
02860	Cooper, E.	**All Fools' Day**
02876	Vonnegut, K.	**The Sirens of Titan**
04364	Cooper, E.	**A Far Sunset**

1968

1808	Haggard, H. R.	**She**
02716	L'Engle, M.	**A Wrinkle in the Skin**
4362	Peters, L.	**Riot '71**
04455	Budrys, A.	**Rogue Moon**

Coronet
1966

F109	Beaumont, C.	**The Magic Man**

F117	Gotlieb, P.	**Sunburst**
1967		
F124	Knight, D.	**Tomorrow X 4**
2482	Conklin, G.	**13 Great Stories of Science Fiction**
2690	Van Thal, H.	**Lie Ten Nights Awake**
02860	Cooper, E.	**All Fools' Day**
02863	Maine, C. E.	**B.E.A.S.T.**
02880	Conklin, G.	**Seven Come Infinity**
1968		
02679	MacDonald, J. D.	**The Girl, the Gold Watch and Everything**

HOGBIN, POOLE, Sydney, N.S.W., Australia.
Hogbin, Poole
1944

—	Foster, L. B.	**The Hocus Root**

HOLT, RINEHART & WINSTON, New York, U.S.A.
Holt
1962

N112	Brown, C. B.	**Arthur Mervyn**

HORROR CLUB, England.
Horror Club
195?

—	Scott-Moncrieff, D.	**The Vaivaisukko's Bride**

HORWITZ PUBLICATIONS PTY. LTD., Sydney, N.S.W., Australia.
   Many titles reprinted under license from Penguin Books Ltd., England.
Horwitz
1959

NA13	Mars, A.	**Arctic Submarine**
NA14	Mars, A.	**Atomic Submarine**
1961		
FH15	Foley, J.	**The Man in the Moon**
PB82	Higham, C.	**Weird Stories**
PB93	Higham, C.	**Tales of Terror**
FH116	Burroughs, E. R.	**Tarzan the Magnificent**
H993	Wyndham, J.	**The Day of the Triffids**
H1308	Wyndham, J.	**The Chrysalids**
H1385	Wyndham, J.	**The Seeds of Time**
1962		
FH22	Searls, H.	**The Big X**
FH24	Bateman, R.	**The Hands of Orlac**
FH28	George, B.	**Atom of Doubt**
PB98	Higham, C.	**Spine-Tingling Tales**
PB104	Higham, C.	**Tales of Horror**
PB111	Higham, C.	**The Curse of Dracula and Other Terrifying Tales**
PB117	Higham, C.	**Nightmare Stories**
PB119	Workman, J.	**Shock Stories**
PB129	Dark, J.	**Terrifying Tales**
1963		
PB149	Workman, J.	**The Witch Hunters**
PB153	Conklin, G.	**Twisted!**
PB138	Dark, J.	**Horror Tales**
PB160	Bloch, R.	**Horror-7**
1965		
36	Holledge, J.	**Flying Saucers Over Australia**
PB216	Broderick, D.	**A Man Returned**
PB233	Burke, J.	**Pattern of Shadows**
PB238	Burke, J.	**Exodus From Elysium**
246	Scott, J.	**The Death Dealer**
1966		
PB265	Castle, J.	**The 7th Fury**
1967		
PB364	Fagan, J.	**Jules Verne's Rocket to the Moon**
1968		
PB345	Baxter, J.	**The God Killers**
PB374	Chandler, A. B.	**False Fatherland**

HOUGHTON MIFFLIN, New York, N.Y., U.S.A.
Sentry
1963

29	Forbes, A.	**A Mirror for Witches**

HOUSE OF GREYSTOKE, U.S.A.
House of Greystoke
1964

—	Burroughs, E. R.	**Tarzan and the Jewels of Opar**

HULTON.
Hulton
1967

—	McCullagh, S. K.	**The Kingdom Under the Sea**

Humorbooks See (URE) SMITH PTY. LTD.

HUTCHINSON & CO. (PUBLISHERS), London, England.
   Additional imprints (see below): **Arrow; Grey Arrow.**
Hutchinson
Not dated

9d Lib	Marsh, R.	**The Beetle**
1935 (approx.)		
235	Wheatley, D.	**Such Power Is Dangerous**
303	Haggard, H. R.	**Wisdom's Daughter**
359	Benoit, P.	**The Queen of Atlantis**
—	Wells, H. G.	**The Shape of Things To Come, Vol. 1**
—	Wells, H. G.	**The Shape of Things To Come, Vol. 2**
1945 (approx.)		
123	Asquith, C.	**The Ghost Book**
?	Asquith, C.	**The Black Cap**

Arrow   Arrow Books Ltd., London, England.
      An imprint of the Hutchinson Group. Many titles have been reprinted with the original "H" omitted from the serial code, and are not necessarily listed again; this includes some Dennis Wheatley titles.

1950		
?	Keyhoe, D. E.	**The Flying Saucers Are Real**
1953		
284H	Wheatley, D.	**The Fabulous Valley**
335H	Wheatley, D.	**They Found Atlantis**
336H	Wheatley, D.	**The Secret War**
1954		
345H	Wheatley, D.	**The Devil Rides Out**
378H	Wheatley, D.	**Star of Ill-Omen**
1955		
402H	Keyhoe, D. E.	**Flying Saucers From Outer Space**
1957		
412H	Wheatley, D.	**To the Devil—A Daughter**
370	Stoker, B.	**Dracula**
1958		
284H	Wheatley, D.	**The Fabulous Valley**
335H	Wheatley, D.	**They Found Atlantis**
336H	Wheatley, D.	**The Secret War**
345H	Wheatley, D.	**The Devil Rides Out**
505	Boileau, P., & Narcejac, T. N.	
		The Living and the Dead
1959		
543	Wheatley, D.	**The Haunting of Toby Jugg**
1960		
412H	Wheatley, D.	**To the Devil—A Daughter**
543	Wheatley, D.	**The Haunting of Toby Jugg**
549	Wheatley, D.	**Strange Conflict**
558	Wheatley, D.	**The Black Baroness**
559	Wheatley, D.	**Sixty Days to Live**
560	Wheatley, D.	**Black August**
580	Wheatley, D.	**Uncharted Seas**
583	Wheatley, D.	**The Ka of Gifford Hiliary**
585	Stoker, B.	**The Lair of the White Worm**
586	Thomson, C. C.	**Not at Night**
587	Haggard, H. R.	**She and Allan**

1961

335	Wheatley, D.	**They Found Atlantis**
345	Wheatley, D.	**The Devil Rides Out**
412	Wheatley, D.	**To the Devil — A Daughter**
543	Wheatley, D.	**The Haunting of Toby Jugg**
583	Wheatley, D.	**The Ka of Gifford Hillary**
608	Thomson, C. C.	**More Not at Night**
628	Wheatley, D.	**Such Power Is Dangerous**

1962

378	Wheatley, D.	**Star of Ill-Omen**
628	Wheatley, D.	**Such Power Is Dangerous**
630	Stoker, B.	**The Jewel of Seven Stars**
644	Stoker, B.	**The Lady of the Shroud**
653	Wheatley, D.	**The Satanist**
671	Thomson, C. C.	**Still Not at Night**
685	Slaughter, F. G.	**Epidemic!**

1963

284	Wheatley, D.	**The Fabulous Valley**
378	Wheatley, D.	**Star of Ill-Omen**
412	Wheatley, D.	**To the Devil — A Daughter**
560	Wheatley, D.	**Black August**
583	Wheatley, D.	**The Ka of Gifford Hillary**
585	Stoker, B.	**The Lair of the White Worm**
653	Wheatley, D.	**The Satanist**
679	Asquith, C.	**When Churchyards Yawn**
691	Wheatley, D.	**Gunmen, Gallants and Ghosts**
693	Bennett, G.	**This Creeping Evil**
699	Creasey, J.	**The Sons of Satan**
701	Brinton, H.	**Purple-6**
705	Taine, J.	**G.O.G. 666**
717	Creasey, J.	**League of Light**
718	Creasey, J.	**The Man Who Shook the World**

1964

336	Wheatley, D.	**The Secret War**
412	Wheatley, D.	**To the Devil — A Daughter**
543	Wheatley, D.	**The Haunting of Toby Jugg**
583	Wheatley, D.	**The Ka of Gifford Hillary**
759	Wheatley, D.	**Quiver of Horror**
760	Wheatley, D.	**Shafts of Fear**
779	Creasey, J.	**The Dark Peril**
780	Creasey, J.	**The Peril Ahead**
784	O'Donnell, E.	**The Dead Riders**
785	Summers, M.	**Witchcraft and Black Magic**
795	Water, S.	**The Man With Absolute Motion**

1965

345	Wheatley, D.	**The Devil Rides Out**
412	Wheatley, D.	**To the Devil — A Daughter**
505	Boileau, P., & Narcejac, T. N.	
		The Living and the Dead
543	Wheatley, D.	**The Haunting of Toby Jugg**
549	Wheatley, D.	**Strange Conflict**
583	Wheatley, D.	**The Ka of Gifford Hillary**
789	Rhodes, H.T.F.	**The Satanic Mass**
800	Anonymous	**The Second Arrow Book of Horror**
838	Ludlam, H.	**The Coming of Jonathan Smith**

1966

534	Wheatley, D.	**The Man Who Missed the War**
543	Wheatley, D.	**The Haunting of Toby Jugg**
795	Water, S.	**The Man With Absolute Motion**
862	Creasey, J.	**The Perilous Country**
891	Wheatley, D.	**They Used Dark Forces**
924	Ahmed, R.	**The Black Art**
926	Gardner, G. B.	**Witchcraft Today**

1967

630	Stoker, B.	**The Jewel of Seven Stars**
644	Stoker, B.	**The Lady of the Shroud**
916	Stoker, B.	**Dracula's Guest**
925	Grubb, D.	**One Foot in the Grave**

1968

127	Pinner, D.	**Ritual**
153	Clarke, A. C.	**2001: A Space Odyssey**
412	Wheatley, D.	**To the Devil — A Daughter**

Grey Arrow
1960

G40	Carrington, R.	**Mermaids and Mastodons**

1961

G65	Saki	**The Best of Saki**
G89	Hawkes, J.	**Providence Island**

I, J, K

ICON BOOKS LTD., London, England.
Icon
1962

SF1	Rayer, F. G.	**Tomorrow Sometimes Comes**

1963

SF2	Wilson, R.	**30-Day Wonder**
SF3	Leiber, F.	**The Green Millennium**

1964

F14	Haggard, H. R.	**Ayesha: The Return of She**

Inspired Novels See PALMER PUBLICATIONS

International See LIVERPOLITAN LTD.

IVOR NICHOLSON & WATSON LTD., London, England.
Ivor Nich.
1948

—	Poe, E. A.	**The Pit and the Pendulum**
—	Poe, E. A.	**Descent Into the Maelstrom**

JACKDAW LIBRARY, England.
Jackdaw
1937

10	Newman, B.	**Armoured Doves**

JADE BOOKS, Hollywood, California, U.S.A.
Jade
1963

211	O'Neill, S.	**Martian Sexpot**

JARROLDS PUBLISHERS (LONDON) LTD., London, England.
 Imprint: **Cresta.**
Cresta
Not dated

—	Dunsany, Lord	**The Fourth Book of Jorkens**
—	Thorndike, R.	**The Master of the Macabre**

JAY BOOKS, London, England.
Jay Books
1958

31	Creasey, J.	**The Children of Despair**

JONES, U.S.A.
Jones
1958

—	Jones, F. E.	**The Big-Ball**

JUBILEE PUBLICATIONS PTY. LTD., North Sydney, N.S.W.,
Australia.
Satellite
1958

211	Anonymous	**Beyond the Stars and Other Stories**
212	Anonymous	**Space Station 42 and Other Stories**
213	Anonymous	**The Sands of Mars and Other Stories**
214	Anonymous	**The Planet of Doom and Other Stories**

215   Miller, R. D., & Hunger, A.
      Year 3097
216   Sohl, J.   **The Mars Monopoly**

JUDD, Sydney, Australia.
Judd
1932
—   Bellamy, E.   **Looking Backward**

JUNIPER, New York, U.S.A.
Juniper
1959
—   Eenhoorn, M.   **An Omnibus of American Mysteries**
3   Le Fanu, J. S.   **The Diabolical Genius**
1963
7   Radcliffe, A.   **The Mysteries of Udolpho**
Not dated
VI   Machen, A.   **The Strange World of Arthur Machen**

JUPITER BOOKS, published by John Calder (Publishers) Ltd., London, England.
Jupiter
1965
J7   Borges, J. L.   **Fictions**
1966
J8   Lewis, W.   **The Childermass**
J12   Lewis, W.   **Monstre Gai**
J16   Lewis, W.   **Malign Fiesta**

KANER PUB. CO., Llandudno, Wales.
Kaner
Mid-1940's
—   Fearn, J. R.   **Slaves of Ijax**
—   Kaner, H.   **Ape-Man's Offering**
—   Kaner, H.   **The Cynic's Desperate Mission**
—   Kaner, H.   **Squaring the Triangle and Other Short Stories**
—   Kaner, H.   **Hot Swag**
1944
—   Kaner, H.   **Fire Watcher's Night**

KANGAROO. Might be Australian.
Kangaroo
Not dated
1   Stevenson, R. L.   **Dr. Jekyll and Mr. Hyde**

KAYE PUBLICATIONS, London, England. [Distributed by Gaywood Press.]
Kaye
Not dated (early 1950's)
—   Lederman, F.   **Tremor**

(HECTOR) KELLY LTD., London, England.
Hector Kelly
1953
—   Yorke, P.   **Space-Time Task Force**
1954
—   Vandel, J. G.   **Enemy Beyond Pluto**

KEMSLEY NEWSPAPERS LTD., London, England.
    CT = Cherry Tree (Fantasy Books) titles; not dated.
Kemsley
1951
CT400   Long, F. B.   **John Carstairs: Space Detective**
CT401   Friend, O. J.   **The Kid From Mars**
CT402   Coblentz, S. A.   **The Sunken World**
CT403   Wollheim, D. A.   **Flight Into Space**
1952
CT404   Leinster, M.   **The Last Space Ship**
CT405   Tweed, T. F.   **Gabriel Over the White House**
CT406   Gernsback, H.   **Ralph 124C 41 +**
CT407   Russell, E. F.   **Sinister Barrier**

CT408   Campbell, J. W.   **The Thing and Other Stories**
CT409   Hubbard, L. R.   **Typewriter in the Sky**
CT410   Walsh, J. M.   **Vanguard to Neptune**
CT411   Du Bois, T.   **Solution t-25**

KOZY BOOKS. U.S. publisher.
Kozy
1961
K136   Lewis, P.   **Father of the Amazon**

L

LANCER BOOKS INC., New York, N.Y., U.S.A.
    The term "Magnum" was used on "Easy Eye" books of the late 1960's.
    Price serial codes: 13- 60¢; 14- 75¢; 70- 40¢; 71- 35¢; 72- 50¢; 73- 60¢; 74- 75¢; 75- 95¢.
Lancer
1961
71-303   Poe, E. A.   **The Pit and the Pendulum**
72-610   Clarke, A. C.   **Master of Space**
72-614   Haggard, H. R.   **She**
1962
71-313   Poe, E. A.   **Premature Burial**
71-325   Poe, E. A.   **Poe's Tales of Terror**
72-645   Shute, N.   **An Old Captivity**
74-807   Vance, J.   **The Dying Earth**
74-808   Weinbaum, S. G.   **A Martian Odyssey**
74-810   Silverberg, R.   **Recalled to Life**
74-811   Christopher, J.   **The Twenty-Second Century**
1963
70-034   Poe, E. A.   **The Raven**
70-052   Sudak, E.   **X**
73-421   Williamson, J.   **Darker Than You Think**
72-656   Hurwood, B. J.   **Terror by Night**
72-672   Knight, D.   **First Flight**
72-679   Smith, Evelyn E.   **The Perfect Planet**
72-697   Shaw, L. T.   **Great Science Fiction Adventures**
72-702   Lovecraft, H. P.   **The Dunwich Horror**
74-812   Williamson, J.   **The Humanoids**
74-815   Asimov, I.   **The Stars, Like Dust**
74-816   Asimov, I.   **The Currents of Space**
74-818   Asimov, I.   **The End of Eternity**
74-819   Russell, E. F.   **Dreadful Sanctuary**
1964
70-067   Lee, E.   **Comedy of Terrors**
73-425   Lovecraft, H. P.   **The Colour out of Space**
73-432   Shute, N.   **An Old Captivity**
72-701   Harris, J. B.   **The Secret People**
72-721   Hamilton, E.   **The Valley of Creation**
72-725   Poe, E. A.   **The Masque of the Red Death**
72-740   Williamson, J.   **Golden Blood**
72-752   Heard, G.   **A Taste for Honey**
72-753   Asimov, I.   **The Naked Sun**
72-754   Heard, G.   **Reply Paid**
72-758   Cooper, E.   **Transit**
72-761   Williamson, J.   **The Reign of Wizardry**
72-768   de Camp, L. S.   **Divide and Rule**
1965
73-441   McLaughlin, D.   **The Man Who Wanted Stars**
72-789   Janifer, L. M.   **You Sane Men**
74-840   Mirbeau, O.   **The Torture Garden**
72-916   Wylie, P.   **The Smuggled Atom Bomb**
72-925   Haggard, H. R.   **She**
72-937   Wylie, P.   **Gladiator**

72-942 Russell, E. F.   The Mindwarpers
1966
72-103 Asimov, I.   **The Stars, Like Dust**
72-104 Asimov, I.   **The Currents of Space**
72-106 Long, F. B.   **So Dark a Heritage**
72-107 Asimov, I.   **The End of Eternity**
72-108 Asimov, I.   **The Naked Sun**
72-118 Bradbury, E. P.   **Warriors of Mars**
72-122 Bradbury, E. P.   **Blades of Mars**
72-127 Bradbury, E. P.   **Barbarians of Mars**
72-129 Williamson, J.   **The Humanoids**
72-139 Shaw, L. T.   **Terror!**
72-140 Haggard, H. R.   **She**
72-145 Knight, D.   **First Flight**
72-146 Weinbaum, S. G.   **A Martian Odyssey**
73-468 del Rey, L.   **Siege Perilous**
73-476 White, Ted   **Phoenix Prime**
73-505 Anderson, P.   **The Corridors of Time**
73-509 Blackburn, J.   **The Reluctant Spy**
72-526 Howard, R. E., & de Camp, L. S.
                            Conan the Adventurer
72-528 White, Ted   **The Sorceress of Qar**
73-540 Loraine, P.   **13**
1967
72-149 Russell, E. F.   **Dreadful Sanctuary**
72-155 Harris, J. B.   **The Secret People**
72-156 Silverberg, R.   **Recalled to Life**
72-159 Nourse, A. E.   **Trouble on Titan**
12-404 Grahame, K.   **The Wind in the Willows**
13-404 Poe, E. A.   **Poe's Tales of Mystery and Terror**
13-409 Verne, J.   **A Journey to the Center of the Earth**
13-410 Wells, H. G.   **The War of the Worlds**
73-545 Moorcock, M.   **The Stealer of Souls**
73-549 Howard, R. E., & de Camp, L. S.
                            Conan the Warrior
73-550 Wilson, R.   **The Girls From Planet 5**
73-562 Wylie, P.   **Gladiator**
73-566 Sinstadt, G.   **Ship of Spies**
73-572 Howard, R. E.   **Conan the Conqueror**
73-573 Hubbard, L. R.   **Slaves of Sleep**
73-577 Hamilton, E.   **The Valley of Creation**
73-579 Moorcock, M.   **Stormbringer**
73-580 Blish, J.   **Warriors of Day**
73-599 Howard, R. E., & de Camp, L. S.
                            Conan the Usurper
73-600 Heath, P.   **The Mind Brothers**
73-608 Lovecraft, H. P.   **The Color out of Space**
73-615 Bloch, R.   **Firebug**
73-624 Greenfield, I. A.   **UFO Report**
73-630 Williamson, J.   **Golden Blood**
73-631 Heath, P.   **Assassins From Tomorrow**
73-636 Smith, G. O.   **Highways in Hiding**
73-644 Williams, R. M.   **Vigilante 21st Century**
73-647 Heard, G.   **A Taste for Honey**
73-650 Howard, R. E., & Carter, L.
                            King Kull
73-653 Blaisdell, A.   **Nightmare**
73-660 Thomas, M.   **Hand of Cain**
73-662 de Camp, L. S., & Pratt, F.
                            The Carnelian Cube
73-672 Greenfield, I. A.   **The Waters of Death**
73-677 Anderson, P.   **Ensign Flandry**
73-685 Howard, R. E.; de Camp, L. S.; & Carter, L.
                            Conan
73-688 Moorcock, M.   **The Jewel in the Skull**
73-690 Cooper, E.   **Transit**
73-691 Knight, D.   **Science Fiction Inventions**
73-694 Williams, R. M.   **Zanthar of the Many Worlds**
74-892 Lupoff, R.   **One Million Centuries**
74-899 Haggard, H. R.   **The Return of She**
74-905 Fairman, P. W.   **Rest in Agony**
74-911 Pratt, F.   **The Well of the Unicorn**

1968
75-020 Quayne, J.   **The Jasper Gate**
75-038 Seabrook, W.   **Magic Island**
13-425 Verne, J.   **Master of the World**
13-433 James, H.   **The Turn of the Screw & Daisy Miller**
13-435 Wells, H. G.   **The Island of Dr. Moreau**
13-440 Bellamy, E.   **Looking Backward**
13-445 Butler, S.   **Erewhon**
13-448 Collodi, C.   **The Adventures of Pinocchio**
13-452 Hawthorne, N.   **A Wonder Book**
13-453 Irving, W.   **The Legend of Sleepy Hollow**
74-603 Swift, J.   **Gulliver's Travels**
14-608 Verne, J.   **Twenty Thousand Leagues Under the Sea**
73-701 Asimov, I.   **The End of Eternity**
73-702 Asimov, I.   **The Naked Sun**
73-703 Asimov, I.   **The Currents of Space**
73-704 Asimov, I.   **The Stars, Like Dust**
73-706 Nile, D.   **The Vampire Cameo**
73-707 Moorcock, M.   **Sorcerer's Amulet**
73-714 Saxon, P.   **Through the Dark Curtain**
73-715 Farmer, P. J.   **The Day of Timestop**
73-720 Cody, C. S.   **The Witching Night**
73-721 Howard, R. E.   **Wolfshead**
73-727 Brown, F.   **Daymares**
73-732 Williamson, J.   **Seetee Ship**
73-733 Williamson, J.   **Seetee Shock**
73-735 Fairman, P. W.   **I, the Machine**
73-740 Shaw, L. T.   **Great Science Fiction Adventures**
73-746 Paul, H.   **Master of the Undead**
73-748 Williamson, J.   **The Reign of Wizardry**
73-750 Saxon, P.   **The Curse of Rathlaw**
73-752 Janifer, L. M.   **Bloodworld**
73-754 Paul, F. W.   **The Orgy at Madame Dracula's**
73-759 Paul, F. W.   **Sock It to Me, Zombie!**
73-761 Moorcock, M.   **Sword of the Dawn**
73-766 Williams, R. M.   **The Bell From Infinity**
73-780 Howard, R. E.; Nyberg, B.; & de Camp, L. S.
                            Conan the Avenger
73-783 Heath, P.   **Men Who Die Twice**
73-784 Saxon, P.   **Satan's Child**
73-797 Brunner, J.   **Into the Slave Nebula**
73-800 de Camp, L. S., & Carter, L.
                            Conan of the Isles
73-805 Williams, R. M.   **Zanthar at Moon's Madness**
73-809 Jackson, N.   **The Daring Adventures of Captain Sex**
73-810 Budrys, A.   **Who?**
74-924 Seabrook, W.   **Witchcraft**
74-936 Smith, G. O.   **The Brain Machine**
74-941 Williams, R. M.   **Zanthar at the Edge of Never**
74-942 Avallone, M.   **The Coffin Things**
74-944 Shaw, L. T.   **Great Science Fiction Adventures**
74-949 McLaughlin, D.   **The Man Who Wanted Stars**
74-953 Santesson, H.   **Flying Saucers in Fact and Fiction**
74-958 Howard, R. E.; de Camp, L. S.; & Carter, L.
                            Conan
74-963 Howard, R. E., & de Camp, L. S.
                            Conan the Freebooter
74-976 Howard, R. E.; de Camp, L. S.; & Carter, L.
                            Conan the Wanderer

LANDSBOROUGH PUBLICATIONS, former publisher of Four Square Books (later published by NEW ENGLISH LIBRARY LTD., *q.v.*).

Lantern See POCKET BOOKS INC.

T. WERNER LAURIE LTD., London, England.
Laurie
1948
—   Sinclair, U.   **A Giant's Strength**

Leisure See GREENLEAF CLASSICS

LION LIBRARY EDITIONS, New York, N.Y., U.S.A.
Lion
1950

14	Jackson, S.	The Lottery
1953		
118	Sohl, J.	The Haploids
146	Shelley, M.	Frankenstein
148	Scott, W.	Doomsday
1954		
LL3	Frazee, S.	The Sky Block
LL7	Leiber, F.	The Green Millennium
179	Leiber, F.	Conjure Wife
196	Dutourd, J.	A Dog's Head
205	Merril, J.	Human?
214	Fessier, M.	Fully Dressed and in His Right Mind
230	Budrys, A.	False Night
1955		
LL10	Karp, D.	Escape to Nowhere
LL13	Knight, D.	Hell's Pavement
LL25	Merril, J.	Galaxy of Ghouls
LL31	Greene, G.	Nineteen Stories
233	Leonardo da Vinci & Payne, R.	
		The Deluge

LIVERPOLITAN LTD., Birkenhead, Cheshire, England.
    Imprint: **International Storyteller Omnibus.**
International
1964

3	Anonymous	Science Fiction

JOHN LONG, London, England.
Long
1938

2	Tweedale, V.	Phantoms of the Dawn
1952		
260	Wallace, E.	Captain of Souls

(JOHN W.) LUCE, Boston, U.S.A.
Luce
Not dated (1916?)

—	Dunsany, L.	Carcassonne

M

MacDONALD & CO., London, England
MacDonald
1965

—	Magee, B.	Towards 2000

MacFADDEN-BARTELL CORP., New York, N.Y., U.S.A.
    First two digits of serial number indicate price: 40- = 40¢, etc.
Macfadden
1962

40-100	Kornbluth, C. M.	A Mile Beyond the Moon
1963		
40-105	Clifton, M.	When They Come From Space
60-140	Michael, S.	Journey Into Limbo
60-146	van Vogt, A. E.	The Voyage of the Space Beagle
50-156	Sayers, D.	Human and Inhuman Stories
50-165	Simak, C. D.	All the Traps of Earth
50-170	Sayers, D.	Stories of the Supernatural
50-179	Dickson, G. R.	No Room for Man

50-183	Mair, G. B.	The Day Khrushchev Panicked
50-184	Simak, C. D.	They Walked Like Men
1964		
75-126	Caldwell, T.	The Devil's Advocate
75-152	Stearn, J.	The Door to the Future
60-169	van Vogt, A. E.	The Beast
60-198	Simak, C. D.	Way Station
50-199	Nourse, A. E.	Tiger by the Tail
50-211	Anderson, P.	The High Crusade
50-224	Leinster, M.	The Greks Bring Gifts
1965		
60-206	Anderson, P.	Time and Stars
50-234	Knight, D.	Beyond the Barrier
50-244	Anonymous	The 6 Fingers of Time and Other Stories
1966		
60-229	Anonymous	The Frozen Planet
60-240	Dick, P. K.	The Three Stigmata of Palmer Eldritch
60-267	van Vogt, A. E.	Empire of the Atom
50-288	Kornbluth, C. M.	A Mile Beyond the Moon
50-311	Moskowitz, S.	Doorway Into Time
50-329	Dickson, G. R.	No Room for Man
75-166	Ettinger, R. C. W.	The Prospect of Immortality
1967		
75-175	Allingham, M.	The Mind Readers
75-183	Knight, D.	Cities of Wonder
75-184	Caldwell, T.	The Devil's Advocate
60-239	Temple, W. F.	Shoot at the Moon
60-277	North, E.	The Ant Men
60-287	Lymington, J.	Froomb!
60-291	Holly, J. H.	The Mind Traders
60-298	Sayers, D.	Human and Inhuman Stories
50-300	Sayers, D.	Stories of the Supernatural
50-334	van Vogt, A. E.	Masters of Time
50-335	van Vogt, A. E.	The Changeling
50-341	Clifton, M.	When They Come From Space
50-381	Simak, C. D.	They Walked Like Men
50-388	Simak, C. D.	All the Traps of Earth
1968		
60-309	Nourse, A. E.	Tiger by the Tail
60-318	van Vogt, A. E.	The Voyage of the Space Beagle
60-321	Casewit, C.	The Peacemakers
60-325	Smith, Edward E.	The Vortex Blaster
60-335	Moskowitz, S.	Microcosmic God and Other Stories
60-343	van Vogt, A. E.	The Beast
60-349	Anderson, P.	The High Crusade
60-352	Dick, P. K.	Now Wait for Last Year
60-366	van Vogt, A. E.	The Wizard of Linn
50-418	Leinster, M.	The Greks Bring Gifts

MACMILLAN & CO., London, England.
Papermac
1966

—	Barter, A. F., & Wilson, R.	
		Untravelled Worlds
1967		
P76	Kipling, R.	Puck of Pook's Hill

MACMILLAN PAPERBACKS, New York, N.Y., U.S.A.
Macmillan
1960

—	Lewis, C. S.	The Screwtape Letters
MP7	Nicolson, M. H.	Voyages to the Moon
1964		
115	Skinner, B. F.	Walden Two
1965		
08688	Lewis, C. S.	Out of the Silent Planet
—	Lewis, C. S.	Perelandra
08692	Lewis, C. S.	That Hideous Strength
1966		
08686	Lewis, C. S.	The Screwtape Letters
1968		
08678	Lewis, C. S.	The Great Divorce

Magabook See GALAXY PUBLISHING CORP.

Magnum See LANCER BOOKS INC.

MALIAN PRESS PTY. LTD., Sydney, N.S.W., Australia.
For *American Science Fiction (Magazine)* and *Selected Science Fiction*, see *MAGAZINES* section.

MASTERPIECE LIBRARY, England. Soft cover series.
Masterpiece Lib
1896
—   Haggard, H. R.   **She**

MAY FAIR BOOKS LTD., London, England.
May Fair
1961
1	Laski, M.	**The Offshore Island**
9	Smith, T.	**The Stray Lamb**
22	Smith, T.	**The Jovial Ghosts**
31	Smith, T.	**The Passionate Witch**

1962
43	Smith, T.	**The Glorious Pool**
50	Smith, T.	**Skin and Bones**
57	Smith, T.	**Rain in the Doorway**
66	Smith, T.	**Turnabout**

MAYFLOWER BOOKS LTD., London, England.
Mayflower
1961
B12	Koestler, A.	**The Age of Longing**

1962
A14	Russell, E. F.	**Next of Kin**
A19	Vonnegut, K.	**Player Piano**
B27	Kuttner, H.	**Mutant**
B32	Russell, E. F.	**Great World Mysteries**
B35	Mead, S.	**The Big Ball of Wax**
A36	Heinlein, R. A.	**The Day After Tomorrow**
B57	Brackett, L.	**The Long Tomorrow**

1963
0238	Langart, D. T.	**Anything You Can Do**
0436	Hitchcock, A.	**Bar the Doors**
0480	Hamilton, E.	**Battle for the Stars**
0543	Merril, J.	**The Best of Sci-Fi**
0799	Dickson, G.	**Necromancer**
1655	Derleth, A.	**Dark Mind, Dark Heart**
2205	Blish, J.	**Earthman, Come Home**
2510	Wellman, P. I.	**The Fiery Flower**
2779	Kuttner, H.	**Fury**
6458	Boland, J.	**No Refuge**
6532	Tenn, W.	**Of All Possible Worlds**
7166	Hesky, O.	**The Purple Armchair**
7881	Randall, R.	**The Shrouded Planet**
9220	Garrett, R.	**Unwise Child**
9514	Boland, J.	**White August**

1964
0045	Schmitz, J. H.	**Agent of Vega**
0244	Sutton, J.	**Apollo at Go**
1678	Randall, R.	**The Dawning Light**
3160	Smith, C. T.	**The Best of Sci-Fi 3**
3255	Holly, J. H.	**The Grey Aliens**
3428	Hitchcock, A.	**A Hangman's Dozen**
3569	Smith, G. O.	**Hellflower**
3632	Hitchcock, A.	**14 Suspense Stories to Play Russian Roulette By**
3658	Hitchcock, A.	**Hold Your Breath**
3985	Bleiler, E. F., & Dikty, T. E.	**Imagination Unlimited**
4120	Sambrot, W.	**Island of Fear**
6746	Bond, J. H.	**The Other World**
7746	Conklin, G.	**17 X Infinity**
8011	Hitchcock, A.	**16 Skeletons From My Closet**
8014	Frazee, S.	**The Sky Block**

8103	Budrys, A.	**Some Will Not Die**
8345	Anderson, P.	**Strangers From Earth**
8474	Avallone, M.	**Tales of the Frightened**
9773	Merril, J.	**The Best of Sci-Fi 2**

1965
0544	Merril, J.	**The Best of Sci-Fi 4**
0547	Kuttner, H.	**The Best of Kuttner 1**
0551	Hine, A.	**Bewitched**
0765	Anderson, P.	**Brain Wave**
2450	Aymé, M.	**The Fable and the Flesh**
3720	Bentlif, S.	**Horror Anthology**
4128	Lewis, S.	**It Can't Happen Here**
4622	Thomas, M.	**Laird of Evil**
6500	Brunner, J.	**Now Then!**
6705	Heinlein, R. A.	**Orphans of the Sky**
7401	Kuttner, H.	**Return to Otherness**
7764	Reid, D.	**Let My People Be**
7815	Howard, I.	**Things**
9438	Aickman, R., & Howard, E. J.	**We Are for the Dark**

1966
0529	Bulmer, K.	**Behold the Stars**
0531	Merril, J.	**The Best of Sci-Fi 5**
0547	Kuttner, H.	**The Best of Kuttner 2**
1655	Derleth, A.	**Dark Mind, Dark Heart**
1657	Kuttner, H.	**Dark World**
1659	Saxon, P.	**The Darkest Night**
1678	Randall, R.	**The Dawning Light**
1947	Saxon, P.	**The Disorientated Man**
2153	Ballinger, W. A.	**Drums of the Dark Gods**
2510	Wellman, P. I.	**The Fiery Flower**
2779	Kuttner, H.	**Fury**
3425	Thomas, M.	**The Hands of Cain**
6532	Tenn, W.	**Of All Possible Worlds**
6740	Derleth, A.	**The Other Side of the Moon**
6917	Searls, H.	**The Pilgrim Project**
8156	Martin, T.	**Sorcerers of Set**
8604	Sheckley, R.	**The 10th Victim**
8873	Anderson, P.	**Three Worlds to Conquer**
8967	Saxon, P.	**The Torturer**
9336	Anderson, P.	**Virgin Planet**
9504	Haining, P.	**Where Nightmares Are**

1967
1885	Chandler, A. B.	**The Deep Reaches of Space**
2627	Edwards, F.	**Flying Saucers—Serious Business**
3230	Russell, E. F.	**Great World Mysteries**
5810	Tubb, E. C.	**Moon Base**
6840	Davies, L. P.	**The Paper Dolls**
7172	Nolan, W. F.	**The Pseudo-People**
7175	Davies, L. P.	**Pyschogeist**
8022	Reid, D.	**The Slave Brain**
8611	Merril, J.	**The Year's Best Science Fiction 10th**
8914	Wilson, R.	**Time Out for Tomorrow**
9775	Merril, J.	**The Year's Best Science Fiction 9th**

1968
1168	Knight, D.	**A Century of Great Short Science Fiction Novels**
5644	Sheckley, R.	**Mindswap**
6304	Cooper, E.	**News From Elsewhere**
8474	Avallone, M.	**Tales of the Frightened**
112145	Saxon, P.	**Black Honey**
112250	Kornbluth, M.	**Science Fiction Showcase**
112625	Davies, L. P.	**Man out of Nowhere**
113036	Gibbons, S.	**Cold Comfort Farm**
113087	Davies, L. P.	**The Artificial Man**
11329X	Laumer, K.	**A Trace of Memory**
113435	Moorcock, M.	**Stormbringer**
113443	Moorcock, M.	**The Stealer of Souls**

Mentor See NEW AMERICAN LIBRARY

MERCURY BOOKS, New York, N.Y., U.S.A.
Mercury
Not dated

—	Flannigan, R.	**County Court**
99	Shearing, D.	**The Spectral Bride**

Meridian See WORLD PUBLISHING CO.

MERIT. U.S. publisher.
Merit
1960

503	Paul, A.	**The Love Machine**

1964

GM417	Goff, J. M.	**Fantastic Seducer**

1965

GM490	Steiger, B.	**Monsters, Maidens and Mayhem**

MERLIN, London, England.
Merlin
1967

M8	Saville, M.	**Saucers Over the Moor**
M18	Crompton, R.	**Richard and the Space Animal**

1968

M37	Crompton, R.	**Richard and the Moon Rocket**
M39	Eliott, E. C.	**Kemlo and the Space Lanes**
M40	Eliott, E. C.	**Kemlo and the Star Men**

METHUEN & CO., London, England.
Methuen
1942

—	Morton, H. V.	**I, James Blunt**

1961

—	Grahame, K.	**The Wind in the Willows**

1964

—	Herbert, A. P.	**Watch This Space**

MILESTONE PUBLICATIONS LTD., London, England.
Milestone
1953

1019	Gridban, V.	**Planetoid Disposals Ltd.**
1044	Grey, C.	**The Wall**
1062	Grey, C.	**Dynasty of Doom**
1066	Grey, C.	**Tormented City**
—	Grey, C.	**I Fight for Mars**
—	Grey, C.	**Space Hunger**
—	Gridban, V.	**Fugitive of Time**

1954

—	Grey, C.	**The Extra Man**
—	Grey, C.	**Enterprise 2115**
—	Grey, C.	**The Hand of Havoc**

MILITARY SERVICE PUB. CO., Harrisburg, Pa., U.S.A. Imprints include **Military** and **Superior**.
Military
1944

M638	Bradford, R.	**Ol' Man Adam an' His Chillun**

1945

143	Saki	**The She-Wolf**

Superior
1945

M656	Saki	**A Saki Sampler**

MILLER. British publisher.
"Banner" series.
Miller
1958

59	Knight, D.	**Hell's Pavement**

MITRE PRESS, London, England.
Mitre
1941

—	Carroll, L.	**You Can't Hang the Dead**

1944

—	Atholl, J.	**The Oasis of Sleep**
—	Atholl, J.	**The Man Who Tilted the Earth**
—	Ascher, E.	**There Were No Asper Ladies**
—	Hopkins, R. T.	**Uncanny Tales**

1945

—	Atholl, J.	**Death in the Green Fields**
—	Bachelor, G. C.	**Uncanny**
—	Hopkins, R. T.	**Weird and Uncanny Stories**

1946

—	Hervey, M.	**Death at My Heels**
—	Hopkins, R. T.	**Horror Parade**

MODERN LIBRARY PAPERBACKS, U.S.A.
Modern Library
1957

P17	Cozzens, J. G.	**Castaway**

1963

P21	Cerf, B.	**Famous Ghost Stories**

MONARCH BOOKS, Derby, Connecticut, U.S.A.; New York, N.Y., U.S.A.
    Additional imprint: **Gold Star** (see below).
Monarch
1960

MM602	Owen, D.	**Brides of Dracula**
MM603	Bingham, C.	**Gorgo**
MM604	Owen, D.	**Konga**

1961

MM605	Owen, D.	**Reptilicus**
213	Holly, J. H.	**The Green Planet**

1962

240	Holly, J. H.	**Encounter**
252	Winterbotham, R.	**The Space Egg**
260	Holly, J. H.	**The Flying Eyes**
264	Walton, E.	**Witch House**
270	Winterbotham, R. R.	**The Red Planet**

1963

297	Jorgenson, I.	**Ten From Infinity**
342	Holly, J. H.	**The Running Man**
354	Hatch, G.	**The Day the Earth Froze**
362	Jorgensen, I.	**Rest in Agony**
368	Bradley, M. Z.	**The Colors of Space**
388	Smith, G. H.	**The Doomsday Wing**
390	Chandler, A. B.	**The Hamelin Plague**

1964

414	Millard, J. J.	**The Gods Hate Kansas**
431	Hadley, F. T.	**Planet Big Zero**
443	Fontenay, C. L.	**The Day the Oceans Overflowed**
453	Edwards, N.	**Invasion From 2500**
464	Smith, G. H.	**The Unending Night**
471	Fairman, P. W.	**The World Grabbers**
478	Anvil, C.	**The Day the Machines Stopped**

Gold Star
1964

IL7-27	Werner, G.	**One Helluva Below**
IL7-42	Werper, B.	**Tarzan and the Silver Globe**
IL7-49	Werper, B.	**Tarzan and the Cave City**
IL7-54	Werper, B.	**Tarzan and the Snake People**
IL7-60	Werper, B.	**Tarzan and the Abominable Snowmen**

1965

IL7-65	Werper, B.	**Tarzan and the Winged Invaders**

MOODY PRESS, Chicago, Illinois, U.S.A.
Moody
Not dated
Colportage Library 200

	Albertson, G. V.	**A Visit to Mars**

1967

?	Palmer, B.	**Jim Dunlap and the Strange Dr. Brockton**

1968

34-196	Palmer, B.	**Jim Dunlap and the Mysterious Orbiting Rocket**
?	Palmer, B.	**Jim Dunlap and the Secret Rocket Formula**
?	Palmer, B.	**Jim Dunlap and the Wingless Plane**

(ALEX) MORING, England.
Moring
Not dated

	Janson, H.	**The Unseen Assassin**

1955

	Janson, H.	**Tomorrow and a Day**

MORROW, New York, U.S.A.
   Apollo series.
Morrow
1963

A75	Bradbury, R.	**The Anthem Sprinters**

1964

A97	Shute, N.	**On the Beach**

FREDERICK MULLER LTD., London, England.
   GM = Gold Medal (most reprinted from U.S. original, with Muller being agent for Fawcett Publications).
Muller
1956

GM156	Caldwell, T.	**Your Sins and Mine**

1958

GM259	Matheson, R.	**The Shrinking Man**

1960

GM368	Leinster, M.	**War With the Gizmos**
GM433	Leinster, M.	**The Monster From Earth's End**
GM462	Foster, R.	**The Rest Must Die**

1961

GM531	Keene, D., & Pruyn, L.	
		World Without Women

1962

GM540	Budrys, A.	**Rogue Moon**

1963

GM638	Bloch, R.	**Atoms and Evil**

1964

GM694	MacDonald, J. D.	**The Girl, the Gold Watch and Everything**

Not dated (*ca.*1965)

—	Caldwell, T.	**Your Sins and Mine**
—	Keene, D., & Pruyn, L.	
		World Without Women
—	Leinster, M.	**War With the Gizmos**
—	Matheson, R.	**The Shrinking Man**

JOHN MURRAY (PUBLISHERS) LTD., London, England.
Murray
1961

—	Doyle, A. C.	**The Lost World**
—	Doyle, A. C.	**The Maracot Deep**

1968

—	Doyle, A. C.	**The Maracot Deep**
—	Doyle, A. C.	**When the World Screamed**
—	Doyle, A. C.	**Tales of Terror and Mystery**

N

NEGRAM, c/o The Hereford Times Ltd., Hereford, England.
Negram
1959

—	Godwin, F.	**The Man in the Moone**

NEL See NEW ENGLISH LIBRARY

THOMAS NELSON & SONS LTD., Edinburgh, Scotland; London, England.
   Imprints: **Junior** and **Panther**.
Nelson (Junior)
1959

—	Eliott, E. C.	**Kemlo and the Martian Ghosts**
—	Eliott, E. C.	**Kemlo and the Space Lanes**
—	Eliott, E. C.	**Kemlo and the Zones of Silence**

Nelson (Panther)
1960 (approx.)

—	Eliott, E. C.	**Tas and the Postal Rocket**
—	Eliott, E. C.	**Tas and the Space Machine**

NEW AMERICAN LIBRARY OF WORLD LITERATURE INC., New York, N.Y., U.S.A.
   Imprints: **Mentor** (nonfiction); **Signet**.
Mentor
1949

M39	Jones, H. S.	**Life on Other Worlds**

1956

MD144	Jones, H. S.	**Life on Other Worlds**

1957

MD200	Hoyle, F.	**The Frontiers of Astronomy**

1962

MP440	Jones, H. S.	**Life on Other Worlds**

1965

MT625	Drucker, P. F.	**The Future of Industrial Man**

Signet
Price codes: No prefix, 25¢; S- 35¢; KS- 35¢; D- 50¢; CD- 50¢; P- 60¢; CP- 60¢; T- 75¢; Q- 95¢. CD and CP denote "Signet Classic" series.
1950

778	McHugh, V.	**I Am Thinking of My Darling**
798	Orwell, G.	**1984**
812	Hamilton, E.	**Beyond the Moon**
830	Wylie, P.	**Night Unto Night**

1951

847	Heinlein, R. A.	**The Man Who Sold the Moon**
882	Heinlein, R. A.	**The Day After Tomorrow**

1952

914	van Vogt, A. E.	**Mission Interplanetary**
943	Heinlein, R. A.	**The Green Hills of Earth**
980	Heinlein, R. A.	**The Puppet Masters**

1953

1007	van Vogt, A. E.	**Destination: Universe**
1044	Heinlein, R. A.	**Tomorrow, the Stars**
1082	Asimov, I.	**The Currents of Space**

1954

1105	Bester, A.	**The Demolished Man**
1127	Tucker, W.	**The Time Masters**
1161	Heinlein, R. A.	**Assignment in Eternity**
?	Hoyle, F.	**The Nature of the Universe**

1955

1194	Heinlein, R. A.	**Revolt in 2100**
S1215	McInnes, G.	**The Lost Island**
1224	Vernon, R. L.	**The Space Frontiers**
S1240	Asimov, I.	**The Caves of Steel**
	Winsor, K.	**The Lovers**

1956

Ks336	Dingwall, E., & Langdon-Davies, J.	
		The Unknown—Is It Nearer?
S798	Orwell, G.	**1984**
S1282	Asimov, I.	**I, Robot**
1289	Orwell, G.	**Animal Farm**
1296	Bowles, P.	**The Delicate Prey and Other Stories**

1957

S1346	Leinster, M.	**Operation: Outer Space**
S1389	Bester, A.	**The Stars My Destination**
S1433	Asimov, I.	**The Martian Way**
S1444	Heinlein, R. A.	**Double Star**
S1464	Clarke, A. C.	**The City and the Stars**
?	Jackson, S.	**Lizzie**

1958

Ks352	Soule, G.	**The Shape of Tomorrow**
KS360	Ley, W.	**Satellites, Rockets and Outer Space**
S1493	Asimov, I.	**The End of Eternity**
S1524	Bester, A.	**Starburst**
S1534	Coon, H.	**43,000 Years Later**
S1537	Heinlein, R. A.	**The Green Hills of Earth**
S1544	Heinlein, R. A.	**The Puppet Masters**
S1558	van Vogt, A. E.	**Destination: Universe**
D1562	Shute, N.	**On the Beach**
S1577	Heinlein, R. A.	**The Day After Tomorrow**
S1583	Clarke, A. C.	**The Deep Range**
S1593	Bester, A.	**The Demolished Man**
D1615	Orwell, G.	**Animal Farm**

1959

S1622	Blish, J.	**The Seedling Stars**
S1639	Heinlein, R. A.	**The Door Into Summer**
D1640	Orwell, G.	**1984**
S1644	Heinlein, R. A.	**The Man Who Sold the Moon**
S1673	Hoyle, F.	**The Black Cloud**
S1683	Aldiss, B. W.	**No Time Like Tomorrow**
S1699	Heinlein, R. A.	**Revolt in 2100**
Q1702	Rand, A.	**Atlas Shrugged**
S1719	Blish, J.	**Galactic Cluster**
S1729	Clarke, A. C.	**The Other Side of the Sky**

1960

CD18	Woolf, V.	**Orlando: A Biography**
CD26	Bellamy, E.	**Looking Backward**
CD29	Poe, E. A.	**The Fall of the House of Usher**
S1752	Heinlein, R. A.	**Methuselah's Children**
S1769	Clarke, A. C.	**Islands in the Sky**
S1779	Aldiss, B. W.	**Starship**
S1788	Vidal, G.	**Visit to a Small Planet**
S1815	Aldiss, B. W.	**Galaxies Like Grains of Sand**
T1826	Condon, R.	**The Manchurian Candidate**
S1840	Sheckley, R.	**The Status Civilization**
S1850	Fleming, I.	**Moonraker**
D1858	Clarke, A. C.	**The City and the Stars**
S1891	Heinlein, R. A.	**Beyond This Horizon**

1961

CD14	Swift, J.	**Gulliver's Travels**
CD41	Butler, S.	**Erewhon**
CD60	Bierce, A.	**In the Midst of Life**
CP100	Orwell, G.	**1984**
S1885	Asimov, I.	**I, Robot**
S1931	Bester, A.	**The Stars My Destination**
S1939	Siodmak, C.	**Skyport**
D1956	Roshwald, M.	**Level 7**
D1985	Rand, A.	**Anthem**
S1987	Heinlein, R. A.	**Starship Troopers**

1962

CP115	Wilde, O.	**The Picture of Dorian Grey**
CP121	Orwell, G.	**Animal Farm**
CP132	Tolstoy, L.	**Fables and Fairy Tales**
D2018	Aldiss, B. W.	**The Long Afternoon of Earth**
D2077	Sillitoe, A.	**The General**
D2105	Heinlein, R. A.	**The Menace From Earth**
D2150	Orkow, B.	**When Time Stood Still**
D2191	Heinlein, R. A.	**Methuselah's Children**
D2202	Hoyle, F.	**The Black Cloud**
D2223	Sheckley, R.	**Journey Beyond Tomorrow**

1963

CP153	Hawthorne, N.	**The Celestial Railroad and Other Stories**
CD158	Twain, M.	**A Connecticut Yankee in King Arthur's Court**
D1985	Rand, A.	**Anthem**
D2053	Fleming, I.	**Moonraker**
D2271	Aldiss, B. W.	**Starship**
T2309	Hoyle, F.	**Frontiers of Astronomy**
P2331	Hoyle, F.	**The Nature of the Universe**
D2348	Heinlein, R. A.	**The Green Hills of Earth**
D2358	Heinlein, R. A.	**The Man Who Sold the Moon**

D2366	Heinlein, R. A.	**The Puppet Masters**
D2381	Heinlein, R. A.	**Starship Troopers**

1964

CP215	Ibsen, H.	**Peer Gynt**
D2105	Heinlein, R. A.	**The Menace From Earth**
D2411	Aldiss, B. W.	**Starswarm**
D2414	Montelheit, H.	**Return From the Ashes**
D2419	Heinlein, R. A.	**Double Star**
P2431	Dennis, N.	**Cards of Identity**
D2433	Clarke, A. C.	**The Other Side of the Sky**
D2443	Heinlein, R. A.	**The Door Into Summer**
P2445	Ley, W.	**Missiles, Moonprobes and Megaparsecs**
P2450	Huxley, A.	**Tomorrow and Tomorrow and Tomorrow**
D2458	Asimov, I.	**I, Robot**
D2474	Bester, A.	**The Dark Side of Earth**
D2497	Aldiss, B. W.	**The Dark Light-Years**
T2503	Scaevola, P.	**'68—A Novel of Presidential Politics**
D2507	Ely, D.	**Seconds**
P2515	Kennaway, J.	**The Mind Benders**
D2428	Clarke, A. C.	**The Deep Range**
D2539	Heinlein, R. A.	**Beyond This Horizon**
D2547	Boulle, P.	**Planet of the Apes**
D2549	Blish, J.	**The Seedling Stars**

1965

KD510	Clarke, A. C.	**Islands in the Sky**
D2414	Montelheit, H.	**Return From the Ashes**
D2587	Heinlein, R. A.	**Assignment in Eternity**
D2618	Heinlein, R. A.	**Orphans of the Sky**
D2621	Heinlein, R. A.	**Methuselah's Children**
D2638	Heinlein, R. A.	**Revolt in 2100**
D2649	Heinlein, R. A.	**The Day After Tomorrow**
D2659	Roshwald, M.	**Level 7**
D2672	Bester, A.	**Starburst**
P2677	New Republic	**America Tomorrow**
D2679	Bester, A.	**The Demolished Man**
P2689	Aldiss, B. W.	**Greybeard**
T2704	Heinlein, R. A.	**Farnham's Freehold**
D2773	Haggard, W.	**Slow Burner**
D2790	Blish, J.	**Galactic Cluster**
P2793	Stoker, B.	**Dracula**
D2806	Ellin, S.	**Quiet Horror**
P2888	Pincher, C.	**Not With a Bang**

1966

CT304	Orwell, G.	**Animal Farm**
CT311	Orwell, G.	**1984**
D2805	Ellin, S.	**The Blessington Method**
P2809	Rand, A.	**Anthem**
T2835	Chopping, R.	**The Fly**
P2863	Heinlein, R. A.	**The Puppet Masters**
Y2870	Wright, A. T.	**Islandia**
T2872	Sullivan, W.	**We Are Not Alone**
P2888	Pincher, C.	**Not With a Bang**
P2920	Anderson, P.	**The Star Fox**
P2923	Meyer, B.	**Ultimatum**
D2940	Lyon, W.	**Batman vs. Three Villains of Doom**
D2995	Lyon, W.	**Batman vs. the Fearsome Foursome**
P3027	Davies, L. P.	**The Paper Dolls**
P3031	Boulle, P.	**The Garden on the Moon**
T3058	Lorenzen, C. E.	**Flying Saucers: The Startling Evidence of the Invasion From Outer Space**
D3062	Farr, C.	**House of Tombs**
P3116	Aldiss, B. W.	**Earthworks**
—	Avallone, M.	**The Birds-of-Feather Affair**
—	Avallone, M.	**The Blazing Affair**

1967

P3113	Brunner, J.	**The Productions of Time**
P3124	Christopher, J.	**The Ragged Edge**
P3160	Silverberg, R.	**Those Who Watch**
P3163	Heinlein, R. A.	**Assignment in Eternity**
P3183	Javor, F. A.	**The RimWorld Legacy**
P3185	Dark, J.	**Throne of Satan**
T3193	Heinlein, R. A.	**The Green Hills of Earth**

T3205	Lorenzen, C.	**Flying Saucer Occupants**
Q3256	Hill, D., & Williams, P.	
		The Supernatural
T3278	David, J.	**The Flying Saucer Reader**
P3311	Aldiss, B. W.	**Who Can Replace a Man?**
Q3397	Bulgakov, M.	**The Master and Margarita**
—	Dark, J.	**Operation Scuba**

1968

T2704	Heinlein, R. A.	**Farnham's Freehold**
P3303	Dark, J.	**Operation Octopus**
P3344	Heinlein, R. A.	**Orphans of the Sky**
P3349	Anderson, P.	**The Horn of Time**
P3376	Walton, S.	**No Transfer**
P3384	Hoyle, F.	**The Black Cloud**
P3399	Boulle, P.	**Planet of the Apes**
T3423	Boulle, P.	**Planet of the Apes**
P3429	Clarke, A. C.	**The City and the Stars**
P3463	Hoyle, F.	**Element 79**
T3484	Bach, M.	**Strange Altars**
T3513	Lorenzen, J. & C.	**UFO's Over the Americas**
P3540	Asimov, I.	**I, Robot**
P3563	Heinlein, R. A.	**Revolt in 2100**
Q3580	Clarke, A. C.	**2001: A Space Odyssey**
T3617	Galbraith, J. K.	**The McLandress Dimension**
Q3632	Wilk, M.	**Yellow Submarine**
T3690	Heinlein, R. A.	**Waldo & Magic, Inc.**
T3705	Fleming, I.	**Chitty-Chitty-Bang-Bang**
P3774	Meade, R.	**The Sword of Morning Star**

NEW COLLECTORS, New York, U.S.A.
New Collectors
1948

—	Mullen, S.	**The Sphinx Child**

1949

—	Long, F. B.	**The Goblin Tower**

NEW DIRECTIONS PUBLISHING CORP., New York, N.Y., U.S.A.
New Direc.
1964

NDP186	Borges, J. L.	**Labyrinths**

1966

NDP208	Read, H.	**The Green Child**

NEW ENGLISH LIBRARY LTD., London, England.

This publisher issued Ace Books [denoted **Ace (Brit.)** to avoid confusion with the U.S. publisher of similar name]. Around 1962 New English Library acquired Four Square Books [denoted **FSB**], which had been published by Landsborough Publications; FSB titles from both publishers are listed below. Around mid-1968 the FSB imprint was dropped and replaced by New English Library [denoted by **NEL**].

Ace (Brit.)
1959

H278	Aymé, M.	**The Grand Seduction**
H280	Sansom, J.	**The Man Who Could Cheat Death**

1960

H380	Aymé, M.	**Across Paris and Other Stories**

1961

H422	Bradbury, R.	**The October Country**
H457	Bowen, E.	**Encounters**
H489	Glaskin, G. M.	**A Change of Mind**
H497	Roshwald, M.	**Level 7**

1962

H521	Bradbury, R.	**The Small Assassin**

FSB
1957

1	Priestley, J. B.	**The Magicians**

1958

11	Grant, J.	**Winged Pharaoh**

1959

87	Burroughs, E. R.	**Tarzan of the Apes**
93	Burroughs, E. R.	**The Return of Tarzan**
137	Frankau, P.	**The Bridge**

152	Burroughs, E. R.	**Tarzan the Magnificent**
168	Burroughs, E. R.	**Tarzan at the Earth's Core**
183	Burroughs, E. R.	**The Son of Tarzan**
184	Burroughs, E. R.	**Tarzan and the Jewels of Opar**
185	Burroughs, E. R.	**Tarzan the Untamed**
186	Burroughs, E. R.	**Tarzan and the Ant-Men**

1960

93	Burroughs, E. R.	**The Return of Tarzan**
152	Burroughs, E. R.	**Tarzan the Magnificent**
184	Burroughs, E. R.	**Tarzan and the Jewels of Opar**
240	Burroughs, E. R.	**The Beasts of Tarzan**
254	Burroughs, E. R.	**Tarzan the Terrible**
261	Burroughs, E. R.	**Tarzan and the Golden Lion**
266	Burroughs, E. R.	**Tarzan's Quest**
271	Foley, J.	**The Man in the Moon**
274	Searls, H.	**The Big X**
289	Bateman, R.	**The Hands of Orlac**

1961

87	Burroughs, E. R.	**Tarzan of the Apes**
93	Burroughs, E. R.	**The Return of Tarzan**
196	George, B.	**Atom of Doubt**
254	Burroughs, E. R.	**Tarzan the Terrible**
261	Burroughs, E. R.	**Tarzan and the Golden Lion**
284	Burroughs, E. R.	**Tarzan's Jungle Tales**
299	Heinlein, R. A.	**Starship Troopers**
306	Burroughs, E. R.	**A Princess of Mars**
317	Hoyle, F.	**Ossian's Ride**
319	Burroughs, E. R.	**Tarzan the Invincible**
328	Valentine, V.	**A Cure for Death**
339	Burroughs, E. R.	**Tarzan Triumphant**
340	Blish, J.	**Fallen Star**
349	Boileau, P., & Narcejac, T.	
		The Evil Eye
353	Burroughs, E. R.	**The Gods of Mars**
358	Burroughs, E. R.	**Tarzan and the City of Gold**
363	Mantley, J.	**The 27th Day**
367	Burroughs, E. R.	**The Warlord of Mars**
371	Kuttner, H.	**Ahead of Time**
380	Burroughs, E. R.	**Tarzan and the Leopard Men**
382	Knight, D.	**A for Anything**
759	O'Brien, F.	**At Swim-Two-Birds**
903	Wells, B.	**The Day the Earth Caught Fire**

1962

168	Burroughs, E. R.	**Tarzan at the Earth's Core**
183	Burroughs, E. R.	**The Son of Tarzan**
184	Burroughs, E. R.	**Tarzan and the Jewels of Opar**
266	Burroughs, E. R.	**Tarzan's Quest**
306	Burroughs, E. R.	**A Princess of Mars**
353	Burroughs, E. R.	**The Gods of Mars**
613	Burroughs, E. R.	**Thuvia, Maid of Mars**
646	Duncan, D.	**Occam's Razor**
661	Burroughs, E. R.	**The Chessmen of Mars**
687	Cayrol, J.	**All in a Night**
697	Stanton, P.	**Village of Stars**
709	Brown, F.	**Angels and Spaceships**
730	Wyndham, J.	**Jizzle**
751	Burroughs, E. R.	**The Mastermind of Mars**
752	Viereck, G. S., & Eldridge, P.	
		My First 2,000 Years
755	Clarke, A. C.	**Prelude to Space**
903	Wells, B.	**The Day the Earth Caught Fire**

1963

H422	Bradbury, R.	**The October Country**
730	Wyndham, J.	**Jizzle**
758	Raven, S.	**Doctors Wear Scarlet**
794	Derleth, A.	**Worlds of Tomorrow**
801	Viereck, G. S., & Eldridge, P.	
		Salome
811	Gillon, D. & M.	**The Unsleep**
820	Burroughs, E. R.	**Pirates of Venus**
821	Aldiss, B. W.	**The Canopy of Time**
842	Derleth, A.	**New Worlds for Old**

848	Jackson, S.	The Haunting of Hill House
857	Pohl, F.	Slave Ship
863	Amis, K.	New Maps of Hell
868	Creasey, J.	The Mists of Fear
873	Iggulden, J.	Breakthrough
889	Blish, J.	Galactic Cluster
912	Blish, J.	Titans' Daughter
929	Simak, C. D.	Aliens for Neighbours
932	Munby, A. N. L.	The Alabaster Hand
933	Burroughs, E. R.	Tarzan, Lord of the Jungle
942	Blish, J.	The Night Shapes
943	Derleth, A.	The Sleeping and the Dead
1964		
93	Burroughs, E. R.	The Return of Tarzan
152	Burroughs, E. R.	Tarzan the Magnificent
240	Burroughs, E. R.	The Beasts of Tarzan
371	Kuttner, H.	Ahead of Time
613	Burroughs, E. R.	Thuvia, Maid of Mars
661	Burroughs, E. R.	The Chessmen of Mars
886	Rohmer, S.	Sinister Madonna
954	Blish, J.	Year 2018
971	Burroughs, E. R.	Tarzan and the Lost Empire
982	Derleth, A.	The Unquiet Grave
984	Burroughs, E. R.	Tarzan the Terrible
990	Sellwood, A. V.	Children of the Damned
993	Simak, C. D.	All the Traps of Earth
996	Burroughs, E. R.	Tarzan and the Foreign Legion
997	Burroughs, E. R.	Tarzan of the Apes
1040	Simak, C. D.	Night of the Puudly
1043	Burroughs, E. R.	Tarzan the Invincible
1044	Burroughs, E. R.	Tarzan's Quest
1059	Burroughs, E. R.	Tarzan and the Ant Men
1060	Burroughs, E. R.	Tarzan and the City of Gold
1061	Burroughs, E. R.	Tarzan at the Earth's Core
1062	Burroughs, E. R.	The Son of Tarzan
1073	Derleth, A.	Beachheads in Space
1077	Burroughs, E. R.	Tarzan Triumphant
1078	Aldiss, B. W.	The Canopy of Time
1090	Mitchison, N.	The Memoirs of a Spacewoman
1094	Burroughs, E. R.	Tarzan the Untamed
1095	Burroughs, E. R.	Tarzan and the Golden Lion
1097	Clarke, A. C.	Prelude to Space
1107	Derleth, A.	From Other Worlds
1111	Burroughs, E. R.	Tarzan and the Jewels of Opar
1128	Clifton, M.	When They Come From Space
1129	Langelaan, G.	Out of Time
1132	Burroughs, E. R.	Tarzan and the Leopard Men
1133	Burroughs, E. R.	Tarzan's Jungle Tales
1147	Aldiss, B. W.	Hothouse
1150	Leslie, S.	Shane Leslie's Ghost Book
1153	Burroughs, E. R.	Synthetic Men of Mars
1162	Mantley, J.	The 27th Day
1166	Campbell, J. W.	The First Astounding Science Fiction Anthology
1196	Bloch, R.	Horror-7
1199	Burroughs, E. R.	The Gods of Mars
1216	Burroughs, E. R.	The Master Mind of Mars
1217	Burroughs, E. R.	The Pirates of Venus
1965		
1040	Simak, C. D.	Night of the Puudly
1177	Oliver, C.	Shadows in the Sun
1181	Burroughs, E. R.	Tarzan and the Forbidden City
1195	Reynolds, M.	The Earth War
1199	Burroughs, E. R.	The Gods of Mars
1211	Campbell, J. W.	The Second Astounding Science Fiction Anthology
1215	Burroughs, E. R.	Lost on Venus
1216	Burroughs, E. R.	The Master Mind of Mars
1217	Burroughs, E. R.	Pirates of Venus
1228	White, J.	Open Prison
1229	Dahl, R.	Someone Like You
1232	Burroughs, E. R.	The Warlord of Mars
1233	Bradbury, R.	The October Country
1234	Bradbury, R.	The Small Assassin
1250	Simak, C. D.	City
1253	Burroughs, E. R.	Tarzan and the Lion Man
1267	Leiber, F.	The Big Time
1282	Heinlein, R. A.	Stranger in a Strange Land
1283	Asquith, C.	What Dreams May Come
1290	Ely, D.	Seconds
1300	Heinlein, R. A.	Glory Road
1305	Blish, J.	The Night Shapes
1306	Blish, J.	Year 2018!
1307	Blish, J.	Titans' Daughter
1308	Wyndham, J.	Jizzle
1325	Aldiss, B. W.	The Airs of Earth
1328	Hammett, D.	The Red Brain
1347	Boardman, T.	The Unfriendly Future
1378	Moore, W.	Bring the Jubilee
1379	Conklin, G.	Twisted
1391	Cooper, E.	Transit
1399	Burroughs, E. R.	Tarzan the Magnificent
1401	Burroughs, E. R.	A Princess of Mars
1402	Burroughs, E. R.	Thuvia, Maid of Mars
1403	Burroughs, E. R.	The Chessmen of Mars
1404	Burroughs, E. R.	Tarzan, Lord of the Jungle
1405	Burroughs, E. R.	Tarzan and the Lost Empire
1423	Haining, P.	The Hell of Mirrors
1966		
1418	Roshwald, M.	A Small Armageddon
1422	Burroughs, E. R.	Tarzan and the Madman
1437	Aldiss, B. W.	The Dark Light Years
1438	Hammett, D.	Creeps by Night
1459	Reynolds, M.	Time Gladiator
1471	Hitchcock, A.	Alfred Hitchcock's Haunted Household
1478	O'Rourke, F.	Instant Gold
1496	Aldiss, B. W.	Space, Time and Nathaniel
1516	Gary, R.	Hissing Tales
1533	Vidal, G.	Messiah
1548	Leiber, F.	Gather, Darkness
1552	Burroughs, E. R.	Tarzan and the Castaways
1559	Chapela, E. S.	Naked in Piccadilly
1561	Maturin, C.	Melmoth the Wanderer
1564	Duke, M.	Claret, Sandwiches and Sin
1575	Beckford, W.	Vathek
1576	Ainsworth, W. H.	The Elixir of Life
1577	Marryat, F.	The Phantom Ship
1578	Godwin, W.	Caleb Williams
1585	Judd, C.	Outpost Mars
1605	Harrison, H.	The Stainless Steel Rat
1606	Roth, H.	The Mask of Glass
1608	O'Donnell, E.	The Screaming Skull and Other Ghost Stories
1623	Aldiss, B. W.	The Male Response
1627	Trevor, E.	The Shoot
1629	Leiber, F.	The Silver Eggheads
1634	Haining, P.	Beyond the Curtain of Dark
1638	Burroughs, E. R.	A Fighting Man of Mars
1652	Boardman, T.	An ABC of Science Fiction
1656	Hitchcock, A.	Guaranteed Rest in Peace
1657	Derleth, A.	The Night Side
1660	Burroughs, E. R.	Escape on Venus
1671	Reynolds, M.	Space Pioneer
1676	Burroughs, E. R.	Swords of Mars
1678	Haining, F.	The Craft of Terror
1719	Russell, E. F.	Dreadful Sanctuary
1726	Burroughs, E. R.	Carson of Venus
1741	Aldiss, B. W.	Earthworks

1746	Burroughs, E. R.	**Llana of Gathol**
1769	Harness, C. L.	**The Paradox Men**
—	Leslie, P.	**The Finger in the Sky Affair**
—	Leslie, P.	**The Radioactive Camel Affair**
1967		
1043	Burroughs, E. R.	**Tarzan the Invincible**
1044	Burroughs, E. R.	**Tarzan's Quest**
1059	Burroughs, E. R.	**Tarzan and the Ant Men**
1060	Burroughs, E. R.	**Tarzan and the City of Gold**
1061	Burroughs, E. R.	**Tarzan at the Earth's Core**
1132	Burroughs, E. R.	**Tarzan and the Leopard Men**
1133	Burroughs, E. R.	**Tarzan's Jungle Tales**
1196	Bloch, R.	**Horror-7**
1399	Burroughs, E. R.	**Tarzan the Magnificent**
1552	Burroughs, E. R.	**Tarzan and the Castaways**
1723	Hitchcock, A.	**This Day's Evil**
1729	Topor, R.	**The Tenant**
1734	Pincher, C.	**Not With a Bang**
1769	Harness, C. L.	**The Paradox Men**
1773	Hitchcock, A.	**Behind the Locked Door**
1797	Dinesen, I.	**Last Tales**
1803	Heinlein, R. A.	**Starship Troopers**
1804	Sheckley, R.	**Untouched by Human Hands**
1845	Copper, B.	**Not After Nightfall**
1866	Asimov, I.	**Through a Glass, Clearly**
1869	Hitchcock, A.	**Meet Death at Night**
1873	Sheckley, R.	**The Status Civilization**
1894	Maugham, R.	**The Man With Two Shadows**
1954	O'Donnell, E.	**The Midnight Hearse**
1959	Neal, J. H.	**Jungle Magic**
1961	Singer, K.	**Ghost Omnibus**
1970	Aldiss, B. W.	**The Interpreter**
1971	Simak, C. D.	**Ring Around the Sun**
1979	Hitchcock	**The Late Unlamented**
1982	Singer, K.	**The Second Ghost Omnibus**
1986	Pohl, F.	**Slave Ship**
1990	Kuttner, H.	**Ahead of Time**
1995	Burroughs, E. R.	**Tarzan of the Apes**
2051	Hoyle, F.	**Ossian's Ride**
2085	Sinclair, U.	**The Gnomobile**
—	Leslie, P.	**The Cornish Pixie Affair**
—	Leslie, P.	**The Diving Dames Affair**
—	Latter, S.	**The Global Globules Affair**
—	Latter, S.	**The Golden Boats of Taradata Affair**
—	Phillifent, J. T.	**The Corfu Affair**
—	Phillifent, J. T.	**The Power Cube Affair**
—	Bernard, J.	**The Thinking Machine Affair**
1968 [became NEL about halfway through year]		
1040	Simak, C. D.	**Night of the Puudly**
1111	Burroughs, E. R.	**Tarzan and the Jewels of Opar**
1181	Burroughs, E. R.	**Tarzan and the Forbidden City**
1422	Burroughs, E. R.	**Tarzan and the Madman**
1729	Topor, R.	**The Tenant**
1758	Burroughs, E. R.	**John Carter of Mars**
1784	Hammett, D.	**Breakdown**
2056	Blackburn, J.	**A Scent of New-Mown Hay**
2094	Haining, P.	**Legends for the Dark**
2102	Brunner, J.	**Out of My Mind**
2124	Heinlein, R. A.	**Stranger in a Strange Land**
2138	Brunner, J.	**Not Before Time**
2147	Clarke, A. C.	**Prelude to Space**
2176	Herbert, F.	**Dune**
2229	Blish, J.	**Galactic Cluster**
2250	Heinlein, R. A.	**Glory Road**
—	Leslie, P.	**The Splintered Sunglasses Affair**
—	Leslie, P.	**The Unfair Fare Affair**
NEL		
1968		
2281	Hitchcock, A.	**The Graveyard Man**
2303	Blish, J.	**They Shall Have Stars**

NEW ERA LIBRARY, Racine, Wisconsin, U.S.A.
New Era
Early 1940's?

22	Anonymous	**Great Ghost Stories**

NEW SOUTH WALES BOOKSTALL See N.S.W. BOOKSTALL CO.

NEWNES LTD., London, England.
Newnes
1899

—	Haggard, H. R.	**She**
—	Chambers, R. W.	**The Tracer of Lost Persons**

Newsstand See EXPORT PUBLISHING ENTERPRISES

(IVOR) NICHOLSON & WATSON LTD. See under IVOR, etc.

NITE-TIME, Hollywood, California, U.S.A.
Nite-Time
1964

96	Stopeck, F.	**Promiscuous Philbert**
116	Taylor, A.	**Door of Desire**

NOBLE, New York, U.S.A.
Noble
1968

F227	Allen, V. F.	**Times 4**

(WILLIAM F.) NOLAN, San Diego, California, U.S.A.
Nolan
1952

—	Nolan, W. F.	**Ray Bradbury Review**

NOONDAY, U.S.A.
Noonday
1960

204	Juenger, E.	**The Glass Bees**
1962		
N228	Williams, C.	**The Greater Trumps**
1963		
247	Williams, C.	**All Hallow's Eve**

W. W. NORTON & CO., New York, U.S.A.
Norton
1963

N224	Burgess, A.	**A Clockwork Orange**

NOVA PUBLICATIONS, London, England.
  Imprint: **Nova Novels** (changed format after first issue).
Nova
1953

1	Beynon, J.	**Stowaway to Mars**
1954		
NS1	van Vogt, A. E.	**The Weapon Shops of Isher**
NS2	Tucker, W.	**The City in the Sea**
1955		
NS3	Sturgeon, T.	**The Dreaming Jewels**
NS4	Blish, J.	**Jack of Eagles**

NOVEL BOOKS INC., U.S.A.
  Additional imprint: **Three Star Books**.
Novel Books
1963

6081	Sellers, C.	**F.S.C.**
Three Star		
1965		
102	Licata, T.	**Great Science Fiction**

N.S.W. BOOKSTALL CO. PTY. LTD., Sydney, N.S.W., Australia.
N.S.W. Bookstall
Not dated

—	Martin, A. E.	**The Shudder Show**

O,P

ODHAMS PRESS LTD., London, England.
    Imprints: **Beacon** [denoted **Beac (Odh)**] and **Odhams.**
Beac (Odh)
1957
B17   Blair, C.   **The Atomic Submarine**
—   Finney, J.   **The Body Snatchers**
1958
B26   Mantley, J.   **The 27th Day**

OLYMPIA PRESS, New York, N.Y.
    Imprints: **Olympia; Ophelia; Traveller's Companion.**
Olympia
1967
TC206 Homer and Associates
                             A Bedside Odyssey
Ophelia
1968
OPS-132 Grimm, B.   **Conception of the Beast**
OPH-112 Van Heller, M.   **The Ring**
Traveller's Comp.
1968
TC432 Kainen, R.   **A Sea of Thighs**
TC2227 Martin, E.   **Busy Bodies**

OLYMPIC FOTO READERS. U.S.A.
Olympic
1968
F-111   Meiter, W.   **The Deadly Organ**

OMNIBOOK, New York, N.Y., U.S.A.
Omnibook
1945 (approx.)
—   Wise, H., & Fraser, P.
                             Great Tales of Terror and the Supernatural

Ophelia See OLYMPIA PRESS

ORGAN (DOUGLAS), London, England.
Organ
Early 1940's
—   Titterton, W. R.   **Death Ray Dictator and Other Stories**

OXFORD UNIVERSITY PRESS, Oxford, England, and New York, N.Y., U.S.A..
Oxford
1954
—   Gallant, J.   **Stories of Scientific Imagination**
1961
34   Capek, K. & J.   **R.U.R. & The Insects**
PB34   Capek, K. & J.   **R.U.R. & The Insects**
1962
53   Murray, M. A.   **The Witch-Cult in Western Europe**
1968
GB261 Franklin, H. B.   **Future Perfect**

Pacific See ANGUS & ROBERTSON LTD.

PALADIN PRESS, London, England.
    See also GAYWOOD PRESS.
Paladin
1954
—   Maras, K.   **The Plant From Infinity**

1956
—   Tubb, E. C.   **Alien Life**

PALMER PUBLICATIONS, Amherst, Wisconsin, U.S.A.
    Imprint: **Inspired Novels.**
Inspired Nov.
1962
A3   Lloyd, John U.   **Etidorhpa**
1965
D3   Emerson, W. G.   **The Smoky God**
D4   Reeve, B. & H.   **Flying Saucer Pilgrimage**

PAN BOOKS LTD., London, England.
Pan
1947
2   Hilton, J.   **Lost Horizon**
7   Priestley, J. B.   **Three Time Plays**
22   Anonymous   **Tales of the Supernatural**
1948
60   Russell, J.   **Where the Pavement Ends**
1949
2   Hilton, J.   **Lost Horizon**
7   Priestley, J. B.   **Three Time Plays**
100   Doyle, A. C.   **The Lost World**
109   Priestley, J. B.   **The Doomsday Men**
1950
2   Hilton, J.   **Lost Horizon**
100   Doyle, A. C.   **The Lost World** [2 eds.]
152   Van Thal, H.   **Told in the Dark**
1951
22   Anonymous   **Tales of the Supernatural**
163   Haggard, H. R.   **King Solomon's Mines**
1952
100   Doyle, A. C.   **The Lost World**
152   Van Thal, H.   **Told in the Dark**
207   Marshall, B.   **Father Malachy's Miracle**
213   Lewis, C. S.   **Out of the Silent Planet**
GP13   Priestley, J. B.   **Three Time Plays**
1953
2   Hilton, J.   **Lost Horizon**
100   Doyle, A. C.   **The Lost World**
251   Wells, H. G.   **The Time Machine & The Man Who Could Work Miracles**
246   Sharp, M.   **The Stone of Chastity**
253   Lewis, C. S.   **Voyage to Venus**
262   Stephens, J.   **The Crock of Gold**
266   James, M. R.   **Ghost Stories of an Antiquary**
1954
2   Hilton, J.   **Lost Horizon**
251   Wells, H. G.   **The Time Machine & The Man Who Could Work Miracles**
270   De La Mare, W. J.   **The Return**
297   Maine, C. E.   **Spaceways**
301   Clarke, A. C.   **Prelude to Space**
313   Wellard, J.   **Night in Babylon**
315   Van Thal, H.   **A Book of Strange Stories**
1955
100   Doyle, A. C.   **The Lost World**
253   Lewis, C. S.   **Voyage to Venus**
213   Lewis, C. S.   **Out of the Silent Planet**
321   Lewis, C. S.   **That Hideous Strength**
327   Heinlein, R. A.   **The Man Who Sold the Moon**
359   James, M. R.   **More Ghost Stories of an Antiquary**
1956
213   Lewis, C. S.   **Out of the Silent Planet**
253   Lewis, C. S.   **Voyage to Venus**
321   Lewis, C. S.   **That Hideous Strength**
369   Clarke, A. C.   **Childhood's End**
377   Heinlein, R. A.   **The Green Hills of Earth**
392   Fleming, I.   **Moonraker**
393   Asquith, C.   **The Second Ghost Book**

1957		
2	Hilton, J.	**Lost Horizon**
420	Clarke, A. C.	**Earthlight**
GP86	Asquith, C.	**The Third Ghost Book**
1958		
437	Chilton, C.	**Journey Into Space**
G138	Kerr, G.	**Under the Influence**
G186	Sherriff, R. C.	**The Cataclysm**
1959		
G216	Fleming, I.	**Moonraker**
G252	Steinbeck, J.	**The Short Reign of Pippin IV**
G255	Frank, P.	**Seven Days to Never**
G315	Asquith, C.	**The Second Ghost Book**
X45	Van Thal, H.	**The Pan Book of Horror Stories**
1960		
G274	Chilton, C.	**The Red Planet**
G321	Poe, E. A.	**Tales of Mystery and Imagination**
G330	Hilton, J.	**Lost Horizon**
G377	Christie, A.	**The Hound of Death**
G403	Lewis, C. S.	**Out of the Silent Planet**
G404	Lewis, C. S.	**Voyage to Venus**
G421	Lewis, C. S.	**That Hideous Strength**
X67	Van Thal, H.	**The Second Pan Book of Horror Stories**
X71	Hitchcock, A.	**Alfred Hitchcock Presents: Stories They Wouldn't Let Me Do on TV**
GP86	Asquith, C.	**The Third Ghost Book**
1961		
G315	Asquith, C.	**The Second Ghost Book**
G403	Lewis, C. S.	**Out of the Silent Planet**
G404	Lewis, C. S.	**Voyage to Venus**
G463	Clarke, A. C.	**Childhood's End**
X105	Frank, P.	**Alas, Babylon**
1962		
G330	Hilton, J.	**Lost Horizon**
G403	Lewis, C. S.	**Out of the Silent Planet**
G404	Lewis, C. S.	**Voyage to Venus**
G421	Lewis, C. S.	**That Hideous Strength**
G543	Fitzgibbon, C.	**When the Kissing Had to Stop**
G561	Buck, P. S.	**Command the Morning**
G579	Chilton, C.	**The World in Peril**
X156	Condon, R.	**The Manchurian Candidate**
X161	Van Thal, H.	**The Third Pan Book of Horror Stories**
X177	Hitchcock, A.	**Alfred Hitchcock Presents: My Favourites in Suspense**
1963		
G315	Asquith, C.	**The Second Ghost Book**
G463	Clarke, A. C.	**Childhood's End**
G608	McShane, M.	**Seance on a Wet Afternoon**
G632	Kennaway, J.	**The Mind Benders**
G641	Clarke, A. C.	**Earthlight**
G645	Blackwood, A.	**The Dance of Death**
X156	Condon, R.	**The Manchurian Candidate**
X186	Fitzgibbon, C.	**When the Kissing Had to Stop**
X208	Dickson, C.	**The Department of Queer Complaints**
X224	Shute, N.	**No Highway**
X227	Heinlein, R. A.	**The Man Who Sold the Moon**
X234	Fleming, I.	**Moonraker**
X252	Edwards, F.	**Stranger Than Science**
X261	Van Thal, H.	**The Fourth Pan Book of Horror Stories**
X266	Lewis, C. S.	**That Hideous Strength**
X268	Lewis, C. S.	**Voyage to Venus**
X270	Lewis, C. S.	**Out of the Silent Planet**
X271	Hitchcock, A.	**My Favourites in Suspense Pt II**
GP86	Asquith, C.	**The Third Ghost Book**
1964		
?	Cunningham, E. V.	**Phyllis**
G503	Ustinov, P.	**And a Dash of Pity**
G561	Buck, P. S.	**Command the Morning**
G660	Anderson, P.	**Guardians of Time**
X224	Shute, N.	**No Highway**
X280	Clarke, A. C.	**A Fall of Moondust** [2 eds.]
X281	Clarke, A. C.	**The Sands of Mars** [2 eds.]

X305	West, M.	**The Shoes of the Fisherman**
X321	Burgess, A.	**A Clockwork Orange**
X331	Van Thal, H.	**The Fifth Pan Book of Horror Stories**
X340	Simak, C. D.	**Time Is the Simplest Thing**
X344	Hitchcock, A.	**Stories for Late at Night Pt I**
XP54	Clarke, A. C.	**Profiles of the Future**
M61	Amis, K., & Conquest, R.	
		Spectrum 1
1965		
G692	Burke, J.	**Dr. Terror's House of Horrors**
G694	Monsarrat, N.	**The Time Before This**
G697	Wells, H. G.	**The Time Machine**
G698	Barron, D. G.	**The Zilov Bombs**
M75	Amis, K., & Conquest, R.	
		Spectrum 2
M112	Volta, O., & Riva, A.	
		The Vampire
X224	Shute, N.	**No Highway**
X266	Lewis, C. S.	**That Hideous Strength**
X268	Lewis, C. S.	**Voyage to Venus**
X270	Lewis, C. S.	**Out of the Silent Planet**
X305	West, M. L.	**The Shoes of the Fisherman**
X353	Clifton, M.	**Eight Keys to Eden**
X361	Stephens, J.	**The Crock of Gold**
X373	Maple, E.	**The Dark World of Witches**
X380	Shute, N.	**What Happened to the Corbetts**
X384	Burgess, A.	**The Wanting Seed**
X388	Burdick, E. L., & Wheeler, H.	
		Fail Safe
X405	Russell, R.	**The Case Against Satan**
X424	Clarke, A. C.	**Tales of Ten Worlds**
X425	Simak, C. D.	**They Walked Like Men**
X447	Van Thal, H.	**The Sixth Pan Book of Horror Stories**
X457	Hitchcock, A.	**Stories for Late at Night Pt II**
1966		
X156	Condon, R.	**The Manchurian Candidate**
X224	Shute, N.	**No Highway**
X380	Shute, N.	**What Happened to the Corbetts**
X462	Clarke, A. C.	**Expedition to Earth**
X463	Pohl, F.	**The Expert Dreamers**
X464	Wallis, D.	**Only Lovers Left Alive**
X482	Burke, J.	**Tales of Unease**
X484	Edwards, F.	**Strange People**
X520	Burke, J.	**The Hammer Horror Omnibus**
X524	George, P.	**Commander-1**
X526	Heinlein, R. A.	**Methuselah's Children**
X555	Van Thal, H.	**The Seventh Pan Book of Horror Stories**
X570	Shute, N.	**On the Beach**
X571	Kornbluth, C. M., & Pohl, F.	
		Gladiator-at-Law
X572	Simak, C. D.	**Way Station**
X573	Clarke, A. C.	**Childhood's End**
X574	Clarke, A. C.	**Earthlight**
X581	Hitchcock, A.	**Stories My Mother Never Told Me**
X588	Hilton, J.	**Lost Horizon**
X591	Curtis, P.	**The Witches**
M113	Amis, K., & Conquest, R.	
		Spectrum 3
M144	Gallico, P.	**Too Many Ghosts**
M171	Asimov, I.	**Nine Tomorrows**
M172	Heinlein, R. A.	**Revolt in 2100**
T19	Knight, D.	**A Century of Science Fiction**
23102	Heywood, R.	**The Infinite Hive**
1967		
X156	Condon, R.	**The Manchurian Candidate**
X380	Shute, N.	**What Happened to the Corbetts**
X570	Shute, N.	**On the Beach**
X625	Braddon, R.	**The Years of the Angry Rabbit**
X650	Daventry, L.	**A Man of Double Deed**
X651	Green, J.	**The Loafers of Refuge**
X679	Heinlein, R. A.	**The Green Hills of Earth**
X699	Van Thal, H.	**The Eighth Pan Book of Horror Stories**

X712	Heinlein, R. A.	**The Red Planet**
X713	Heinlein, R. A.	**Farmer in the Sky**
M192	Pohl, F.	**The Seventh Galaxy Reader**
M193	Amis, K., & Conquest, R.	
		Spectrum 4
M219	Maple, E.	**The Realm of Ghosts**
M223	Burke, J.	**The Second Hammer Horror Film Omnibus**
M224	Buck, P. S.	**Command the Morning**
M228	Chopping, R.	**The Fly**
M250	Hitchcock, A.	**Stories My Mother Never Told Me Pt II**
M251	Hitchcock, A.	**Stories They Wouldn't Let Me Do on TV**

1968

X699	Van Thal, H.	**The Eighth Pan Book of Horror Stories**
X741	Poe, E. A.	**Tales of Mystery and Imagination**
01697	Wells, H. G.	**The Time Machine**
02121	Finney, J.	**I Love Galesburg in the Springtime**
02028	Heinlein, R. A.	**Time for the Stars**
02029	Heinlein, R. A.	**Tunnel in the Sky**
02042	Simak, C. D.	**All Flesh Is Grass**
02043	Pohl, F.	**Star Fourteen**
02050	Turner, J.	**The Fourth Ghost Book**
02061	Asquith, C.	**The Third Ghost Book**
02072	Shute, N.	**No Highway**
02094	Keyes, D.	**Flowers for Algernon**
02109	Pohl, F.	**The Eighth Galaxy Reader**
02110	Jones, D. F.	**Colossus**
02115X	Levin, I.	**Rosemary's Baby**
02144	Van Thal, H.	**The Ninth Pan Book of Horror**
02170	Lewis, C. S.	**That Hideous Strength**
02171	Lewis, C. S.	**Voyage to Venus**
02172	Lewis, C. S.	**Out of the Silent Planet**
02194	Gallico, P.	**The Man Who Was Magic**
02195	Hitchcock, A.	**Stories Not for the Nervous Pt I**
02231	Maple, E.	**The Domain of Devils**
10271	Hitchcock, A.	**My Favourites in Suspense Pt II**
10305	West, M. L.	**The Shoes of the Fisherman**
30044	Irving, C.	**The Thirty-Eighth Floor**

PANTHER BOOKS LTD., London, England.

This series was originally published by HAMILTON & CO. (STAFFORD) LTD.; the firm changed to the Panther name about 1964, still using the same address.

Hamilton issued some titles before starting the **Authentic** and **Panther** series (see below). Most Hamilton titles were not dated (Harbottle gives the Fearn novels as 1950).

Hamilton
1946 (approx.)
—	Hervey, M.	**Strange Hunger**

1950
—	Fearn, J. R.	**Emperor of Mars**
—	Fearn, J. R.	**Goddess of Mars**
—	Fearn, J. R.	**Red Men of Mars**
—	Fearn, J. R.	**Warrior of Mars**

Not dated (1950's)
—	Firth, N. W.	**The Terror Strikes**
—	Hay, G.	**Flight of the "Hesper"**
—	Hay, G.	**This Planet for Sale**
—	MacCartney, C.	**Dark Side of Venus**
—	Robb, J.	**Space Beam**

1952
—	Flackes, B.	**Duel in Nightmare Worlds**
—	Sheldon, R.	**The Mammoth Man**
—	Sheldon, R.	**Moment out of Time**

Authentic

This title covers the "novel" issues, embracing title changes as follows: *Authentic Science Fiction Series*: No. 1; *Authentic* [small letters] *Science Fiction Fortnightly*: Nos. 2-8; *Authentic Science Fiction Monthly*: Nos. 9-12; *Authentic Science Fiction*: Nos. 13-28. The publication then became more of a true magazine and is so reviewed in the *Magazines* section.

1951
1	Stanton, L.	**Mushroom Men of Mars**
2	Deegan, J. J.	**Reconnoitre Krelling II**
3	Sheldon, R.	**Gold Men of Aureus**
4	Deegan, J. J.	**Old Growler**
5	Stanton, L.	**Seven to the Moon**
6	Sheldon, R.	**Phantom Moon**
7	Sheldon, R.	**Energy Alive**
8	Campbell, H. J.	**The World in a Test Tube**
9	Deegan, J. J.	**Old Growler and Orbis**
10	Hay, G.	**Man, Woman and Android**
11	Campbell, H. J.	**The Last Mutation**
12	MacCartney, C.	**Ten Years to Oblivion**
13	Sheldon, R.	**Beam of Malice**
14	Deegan, J. J.	**Planet of Power**
15	Stanton, L.	**Report From Mandazo**
16	Campbell, H. J.	**The Moon Is Heaven**

1952
17	Rayer, F. G.	**Coming of the Darakua**
18	Campbell, H. J.	**Chaos in Miniature**
19	Sheldon, R.	**Space Warp**
20	Rayer, F. G.	**Earth Our New Eden**
21	Tubb, E. C.	**Alien Impact**
22	Campbell, H. J.	**Mice or Machines**
23	Deegan, J. J.	**The Singing Spheres**
24	Berry, B.	**Aftermath**
25	Sheldon, R.	**The Plastic Peril**
26	Conroy, R.	**Martians in a Frozen World**
27	Sheldon, R.	**Star of Death**
28	Rayer, F. G.	**We Cast No Shadow**

Panther

This imprint began about 1951; the first few were unnumbered and some were not noted as "Panther" but had the characteristic cover style. Many of the titles around 1953 also had hardcover editions, and are so noted in the *Author* listing.

1951
—	Sheldon, R.	**Two Days of Terror**

1952
—	Berry, B.	**And the Stars Remain**
—	Berry, B.	**Born in Captivity**
—	Berry, B.	**Return to Earth**
—	Clarke, A. V., & Bulmer, H. K.	
		Cybernetic Controller
—	Clarke, A. V., & Bulmer, H. K.	
—		**Space Treason**
—	Conroy, R.	**Mission From Mars**
—	Tubb, E. C.	**Atom-War on Mars**
16	Sheldon, R.	**The Menacing Sleep**
17	Deegan, J. J.	**Underworld of Zello**
28	Berry, B.	**Dread Visitor**
29	Bulmer, K.	**Encounter in Space**

1953
—	Campbell, H. J.	**Beyond the Visible**
32	Deegan, J. J.	**Amateurs in Alchemy**
37	Bulmer, K.	**Space Salvage**
38	Tubb, E. C.	**The Mutants Rebel**
39	Deegan, J. J.	**Antro the Life-Giver**
40	Berry, B.	**From What Far Star?**
44	Wright, S. F.	**The World Below**
47	Sheldon, R.	**Atoms in Action**
48	Bulmer, K.	**The Stars Are Ours**
57	Berry, B.	**The Venom Seekers**
58	Deegan, J. J.	**The Great Ones**
59	Sheldon, R.	**House of Entropy**
60	Bulmer, K.	**Galactic Intrigue**
67	Campbell, H. J.	**Another Space—Another Time**
68	Garner, R.	**Resurgent Dust**
69	Bulmer, K.	**Empire of Chaos**
70	Bounds, S. J.	**Dimension of Horror**
77	Campbell, H. J.	**The Red Planet**
78	Garner, R.	**The Immortals**
85	Deegan, J. J.	**The Corridors of Time**

| 86 | Campbell, H. J. | Brain Ultimate |
| 92 | de Camp, L. S. | Sprague de Camp's New Anthology of Science Fiction |

1954

94	Burke, J.	The Dark Gateway
95	Merak, A. J.	Dark Andromeda
96	Deegan, J. J.	Beyond the Fourth Door
101	Campbell, H. J.	Tomorrow's Universe
103	Burke, J.	The Echoing Worlds
104	Garner, R.	The Indestructible
109	Sheldon, R.	The Metal Eater
110	Tubb, E. C.	The World at Bay
—	Wright, S. F.	The Dwellers
117	Deegan, J. J.	Exiles of Time
118	Burke, J.	Twilight of Reason
135	Burke, J.	Hotel Cosmos
136	Falkner, J.	Untrodden Streets of Time
159	Bulmer, K.	World Aflame
160	Campbell, H. J.	Once Upon a Space

1955

—	Schwartz, B.	Crimson Clay
181	Morgan, D.	Cee-Tee Man
182	Burke, J.	Deep Freeze
192	Burke, J.	Revolt of the Humans
193	Falkner, J.	Overlords of Andromeda

1957

663	Adamski, G., & Leslie, D.	
		The Flying Saucers Have Landed
688	Frank, P.	Mr. Adam
692	Hubbard, L. R.	Return to Tomorrow
696	Swain, D. V.	The Transposed Man

1958

747	Dornberger, W.	V-2
755	Bridgman, B.	The Lonely Sky
763	de Rouen, R.	Split Image
784	Taine, J.	Seeds of Life
785	Dick, P. K.	The World of Chance
786	Makepeace-Lott, S.	Escape to Venus
824	Asimov, I.	The Currents of Space
835	Asimov, I.	The Caves of Steel
839	Sangster, J.	The Revenge of Frankenstein
852	Haynes, J. R.	The Scream From Outer Space
863	Asimov, I.	The Stars, Like Dust

1959

881	Asimov, I.	The End of Eternity
933	Bester, A.	The Demolished Man
973	Bester, A.	The Stars My Destination
975	Coon, H.	43,000 Years Later
988	Cooper, E.	Deadly Image
990	van Vogt, A. E.	The Voyage of the Space Beagle

1960

1001	Heinlein, R. A.	The Puppet Masters
1016	Asimov, I.	The Naked Sun
1021	Heinlein, R. A.	The Door Into Summer
1024	Masters, D.	The Accident
1041	Owen, T.	Circus of Horrors
1042	Asimov, I.	Earth Is Room Enough
1057	Margulies, L.	3 From Out There
1060	Rohmer, S.	Shadow of Fu Manchu
1063	van Vogt, A. E.	Destination: Universe
1074	Rohmer, S.	Slaves of Sumuru
1080	Asimov, I.	Foundation
1084	Rohmer, S.	Re-Enter Fu Manchu
1094	Cooper, E.	Seed of Light
1112	van Vogt, A. E.	The Mind Cage
1116	Chase, J. H.	Miss Shumway Waves a Hand
1120	Heinlein, R. A.	Double Star
1123	Rohmer, S.	Emperor Fu Manchu
1132	van Vogt, A. E.	Slan
1142	Christopher, J.	The Twenty-Second Century

1961

| 1168 | van Vogt, A. E. | The War Against the Rull |

1183	Sturgeon, T.	E Pluribus Unicorn
1193	Finney, J.	The Clock of Time
1252	Carnell, E. J.	No Place Like Earth
1276	Crisp, F.	The Night Callers

1962

1287	Bennett, J.	Catacombs
1288	Bell, N.	Who Walk in Fear?
1332	Simak, C. D.	Strangers in the Universe
1349	Sissons, M.	In the Dead of Night
1355	Asimov, I.	Foundation and Empire
1379	Sissons, M.	Asleep in Armageddon
1397	Anonymous	Tales of the Supernatural
1414	Santesson, H. S.	The Fantastic Universe Omnibus
1426	Van Thal, H.	Great Ghost Stories
1454	Anonymous	Tales of the Uncanny

1963

990	van Vogt, A. E.	The Voyage of the Space Beagle
1112	van Vogt, A. E.	The Mind Cage
1120	Heinlein, R. A.	Double Star
1460	Carnell, E. J.	Gateway to Tomorrow
1474	Lovecraft, H. P.	The Haunter of the Dark
1475	Anonymous	Bedside Tales of Mystery and Suspense
1487	Russell, E. F.	Wasp
1489	Bull, R. C.	Great Tales of Terror
1483	Pape, R.	And So Ends the World
1502	Hopkins, R. T.	Cavalcade of Ghosts
1505	Ward, H.	Hell's Above Us
1511	Cooper, E.	Tomorrow Came
1513	Lovecraft, H. P.	The Case of Charles Dexter Ward
1537	Machen, A.	Tales of Horror and the Supernatural
1541	Derleth, A.	The Other Side of the Moon
1549	Williams, J.	The Witches
1555	Endore, G.	The Werewolf of Paris
1569	van Vogt, A. E.	Away and Beyond
1570	Lipsky, E.	The Scientists
1575	Verne, J.	Carpathian Castle
1594	Ward, H.	The Green Suns
1599	Russell, E. F.	Dark Tides

1964

824	Asimov, I.	The Currents of Space
835	Asimov, I.	The Caves of Steel
863	Asimov, I.	The Stars, Like Dust
881	Asimov, I.	The End of Eternity
990	van Vogt, A. E.	The Voyage of the Space Beagle
1016	Asimov, I.	The Naked Sun
1057	Margulies, L.	3 From Out There
1063	van Vogt, A. E.	Destination: Universe
1080	Asimov, I.	Foundation
1355	Asimov, I.	Foundation and Empire
1474	Lovecraft, H. P.	The Haunter of the Dark
1610	Maine, C. E.	The Man Who Owned the World
1625	Russell, E. F.	The Great Explosion
1627	Algren, N.	The Book of Lonesome Monsters
1634	Masson, L.	The Barbed Wire Fence
1635	Baker, F.	The Birds
1649	Budrys, A.	The Unexpected Dimension
1671	Poe, E. A., & Verne, J.	
		The Mystery of Arthur Gordon Pym
1676	Anderson, P.	Twilight World
1691	Russell, E. F.	Far Stars
1700	Maine, C. E.	The Mind of Mr. Soames
1713	Asimov, I.	Second Foundation
1729	Verne, J.	Black Diamonds
1731	Verne, J.	Five Weeks in a Balloon
1738	Mills, R.	The Best From Fantasy and Science Fiction, Ninth Series
1743	Pauwels, L., & Bergier, J.	
		The Dawn of Magic
1755	Sissons, M.	The Masque of the Red Death
1757	Cooper, G.	The Other Man
1759	Lovecraft, H. P.	The Lurking Fear and Other Stories
1767	Beaumont, C.	Shadow Play

1768	O'Grady, R.	**Pippin's Journal**
1769	Derleth, A.	**Who Knocks?**
1770	Derleth, A.	**Sleep No More**
1965		
863	Asimov, I.	**The Stars, Like Dust**
881	Asimov, I.	**The End of Eternity**
1016	Asimov, I.	**The Naked Sun**
1080	Asimov, I.	**Foundation**
1355	Asimov, I.	**Foundation and Empire**
1474	Lovecraft, H. P.	**The Haunter of the Dark**
1713	Asimov, I.	**Second Foundation**
1770	Derleth, A.	**Sleep No More**
1779	Maine, C. E.	**The Darkest of Nights**
1783	Verne, J.	**Propellor Island**
1784	Verne, J.	**The Secret of Wilhelm Storitz**
1787	Sellings, A.	**The Silent Speakers**
1798	Anderson, P.	**After Doomsday**
1799	Asimov, I.	**The Martian Way**
1840	Brunner, J.	**No Future in It**
1861	Singer, K.	**The World's Greatest Stories of the Occult**
1890	Russell, E. F.	**Men, Martians and Machines**
1921	Gordon, R.	**The Time Factor**
1954	London, J.	**The Chldren of the Frost**
1956	Rampton, A.	**The First Panther Book of Horror**
1957	Sloane, W.	**The Edge of Running Water**
1958	Sloane, W.	**To Walk the Night**
1959	Baker, F.	**Miss Hargreaves**
1960	Pizer, L.	**Stories Strange and Sinister**
1961	Symonds, J.	**In the Astral Light**
1971	Henderson, Z.	**Pilgrimage**
1966		
1080	Asimov, I.	**Foundation**
1649	Budrys, A.	**The Unexpected Dimension**
1983	Matheson, H.	**Balance of Fear**
1989	Miller, W. M.	**Conditionally Human**
1991	Raven, S.	**Doctors Wear Scarlet**
2019	Budrys, A.	**The Furious Future**
2037	Tenn, W.	**Time in Advance**
2052	Mills, R.	**The Best From Fantasy and Science Fiction No. 11**
2077	Abel, R. C., & Barren, C.	
		Trivana I
2092	Farmer, P. J.	**Strange Relations**
2108	Dick, P. K.	**A Handful of Darkness**
2109	Anderson, P.	**Time and Stars**
2112	Reynolds, S.	**Better Dead Than Red**
2124	Mills, R. P.	**Worlds of Science Fiction**
2142	Ray, D.	**End of the Fourth Reich**
2149	Hill, D.	**The Way of the Werewolf**
2150	Birkin, C.	**My Name Is Death and Other New Tales of Horror**
2151	Beaumont, C.	**The Edge**
2152	Evans, I. O.	**Science Fiction Through the Ages 1**
2158	Singer, K.	**Horror Omnibus**
2159	Evans, I. O.	**Science Fiction Through the Ages 2**
1967		
824	Asimov, I.	**The Currents of Space**
835	Asimov, I.	**The Caves of Steel**
1016	Asimov, I.	**The Naked Sun**
1042	Asimov, I.	**Earth Is Room Enough**
1743	Pauwels, L., & Bergier, J.	
		The Dawn of Magic
1799	Asimov, I.	**The Martian Way**
1991	Raven, S.	**Doctors Wear Scarlet**
2186	Vance, J.	**The Dragon Masters**
2199	Summers, M.	**The Supernatural Omnibus I**
2214	Anderson, P.	**Trader to the Stars**
2228	Summers, M.	**The Supernatural Omnibus II**
2234	Gilliatt, P.	**One by One**
2241	Bowen, J.	**After the Rain**
2242	Andrzeyevski, G.	**The Gates of Paradise**
2234	Gilliatt, P.	**One by One**

2243	Moorcock, M.	**Best Science Fiction Stories From New Worlds**
2254	Campbell, J. W.	**Analog 2**
2255	Campbell, J. W.	**Prologue to Analog**
2256	Campbell, J. W.	**Analog 1**
2275	Davidson, A.	**The Best From Fantasy and Science Fiction, Twelfth Series**
2279	Vonnegut, K.	**God Bless You, Mr. Rosewater**
2286	Butler, W.	**The Butterfly Revolution**
2290	Tindall, G.	**A Handbook on Witches**
2298	Temple, W. F.	**Shoot at the Moon**
2306	Poe, E. A.	**Bizarre and Arabesque**
2307	Ballard, J. G.	**The Day of Forever**
2311	Kressing, H.	**The Cook**
2325	Knight, D.	**Orbit 1**
2333	Pizer, L. N.	**More Stories Strange and Sinister**
2334	Pizer, L. N.	**Great Psychological Stories**
2335	Van Thal, H.	**Famous Tales of the Fantastic**
2336	Ballard, J. G.	**The Overloaded Man**
17135	Asimov, I.	**Second Foundation**
23488	Heinlein, R. A.	**Beyond This Horizon**
1968		
01487X	Russell, E. F.	**Wasp**
02476X	Vance, J.	**The Star King**
011129	van Vogt, A. E.	**The Mind Cage**
011838	Sturgeon, T.	**E Pluribus Unicorn**
018905	Russell, E. F.	**Men, Martians and Machines**
023690	Moorcock, M.	**Best Stories From New Worlds II**
023704	Burkett, W. R.	**Sleeping Planet**
023771	Burroughs, W. S.	**The Nova Express**
023852	Miller, W. M.	**The View From the Stars**
023879	Brown, P. C.	**Smallcreeps Day**
024026	Raphael, R.	**The Thirst Quenchers**
024034	Young, R. F.	**The Worlds of Robert F. Young**
024190	Ballard, J. G.	**The Crystal World**
024204	Disch, T. M.	**The Genocides**
024379	van Vogt, A. E.	**Away and Beyond**
024387	van Vogt, A. E.	**Slan**
024395	van Vogt, A. E.	**The Voyage of the Space Beagle**
024409	Asimov, I.	**The End of Eternity**
024417	Asimov, I.	**The Stars, Like Dust**
024603	Aldiss, B. W.	**Greybeard**
024689	Blackburn, J.	**Children of the Night**
024700	Boileau, P., & Narcejac, T.	
		Choice Cuts
024840	van Vogt, A. E.	**Destination Universe**
024956	Moorcock, M.	**Best Science Fiction Stories From New Worlds 3**
025022	Heinlein, R. A.	**Double Star**
025316	Zelazny, R.	**This Immortal**
025324	Asimov, I.	**I, Robot**
025650	Peterkiewicz, J.	**Inner Circle**
025693	Anderson, P.	**The Corridors of Time**
025707	Raphael, R.	**Code Three**
025847	Sissons, M.	**In the Dead of Night**
025855	Rampton, A.	**The Panther Book of Horror**
025944	Asimov, I.	**The Rest of the Robots**
025952	Campbell, J. W.	**Analog 3**
025960	Lovecraft, H. P.	**At the Mountains of Madness**
026037	Kressing H.	**The Cook**
026177	Platt, C.	**Garbage World**
026185	Davidson, A.	**The Best From Fantasy and Science Fiction, 13th Series**
026304	Zelazny, R.	**The Dream Master**
026312	Anderson, P.	**The Star Fox**

PAPERBACK LIBRARY INC., New York. Originally an independent publisher, but now a division of Coronet Communications Inc., New York, N.Y., U.S.A.

Paperback

1962

52-127	Kersh, G.	**Men Without Bones**

52-130	Barzman, B.	Echo X
52-142	Merritt, A.	Dwellers in the Mirage
52-149	Ellison, H.	Ellison Wonderland
52-180	Balmer, E., & Wylie, P.	
		When Worlds Collide

1963

52-201	Smith, T.	Turnabout
52-205	Wylie, P.	The Answer
52-210	Russell, R.	The Case Against Satan
52-211	Keyes, N.	Contact!
52-232	Shiel, M. P.	The Purple Cloud
52-250	Nolan, W. F.	Impact-20
52-255	Balmer, E., & Wylie, P.	
		After Worlds Collide

1964

52-273	Fox, G. F.	Escape Across the Cosmos
52-287	Russell, E. F.	Sinister Barrier
52-290	Ackerman, F. J.	The Best From Famous Monsters of Film-land
52-293	Campbell, J. W.	Analog 1
52-304	van Vogt, A. E.	Two Hundred Million A.D.
52-311	Hamilton, E.	Battle for the Stars
52-316	Kirk, R.	The Surly Sullen Bell
52-320	Elwood, R.	Alien Worlds
52-329	Barzman, B.	Echo X
52-501	Chamberlain, W.	Red January
52-502	deFord, M. A.	Space, Time and Crime
52-506	Simak, C. D.	Cosmic Engineers
52-508	Ellison, H.	Earthman, Go Home

1965

52-504	Ackerman, F. J.	The Son of Famous Monsters of Filmland
52-509	Campbell, J. W.	Analog 2
52-514	Biggle, L.	All the Colors of Darkness
52-515	van Vogt, A. E.	Monsters
52-516	Merritt, A.	Dwellers in the Mirage
52-519	Elwood, R.	Invasion of the Robots
52-521	Balmer, E., & Wylie, P.	
		When Worlds Collide
53-603	Smith, T.	Turnabout
52-804	Bond, N. S.	Exiles of Time
52-811	Vale, R.	Beyond the Sealed World
52-813	Ackerman, F. J.	Famous Monsters of Filmland Strike Back
54-819	Mills, R. P.	The Worlds of Science Fiction
54-830	Cleary, J.	A Flight of Chariots
52-837	Keyes, N.	Contact!
52-847	Binder, E.	Adam Link, Robot
52-848	Somers, B.	Beyond the Black Enigma
53-860	Karlova, I.	Dreadful Hollow
52-863	Moore, C. L.	Judgment Night
52-873	van Vogt, A. E.	The House That Stood Still
52-874	Wollheim, D. A.	Secret of the Ninth Planet

1966

52-334	La Spina, Greye	Shadow of Evil
52-338	Dexter, W.	World in Eclipse
56-340	Wollheim, D. A.	Mike Mars Flies the Dynasoar
52-357	Dexter, W.	Children of the Void
56-358	Wollheim, D. A.	Mike Mars, South Pole Spaceman
52-364	Lloyd, S.	Graveswood
52-365	Kirk, R.	The Surly Sullen Bell
52-368	Moorcock, M.	The Sundered Worlds
56-369	Wollheim, D. A.	Mike Mars and the Mystery Satellite
52-376	Morrison, R.	Tree of Evil
56-383	Wollheim, D. A.	Mike Mars Around the Moon
52-384	Russell, E. F.	Sinister Barrier
52-386	Ross, M.	Dark Shadows
53-931	Horler, S.	The Curse of Doone
52-941	Adler, A.	Terror on Planet Ionus
52-944	Shiel, M. P.	The Purple Cloud
53-946	Stoker, B.	The Garden of Evil
52-955	del Rey, L.	Step to the Stars
54-960	Collins, W. W.	The Moonstone

54-962	Stoker, B.	The Lady of the Shroud
56-968	Wollheim, D. A.	Mike Mars, Astronaut
52-971	Nolan, W. F.	Impact-20
56-972	Wollheim, D. A.	Mike Mars Flies the X-15
52-975	Winston, D.	Sinister Stone
53-976	Nicolson, J. U.	Fingers of Fear
56-981	Wollheim, D. A.	Mike Mars at Cape Kennedy
52-985	Spinrad, N.	The Solarians
52-996	Wollheim, D. A.	Secret of Saturn's Rings
56-998	Wollheim, D. A.	Mike Mars in Orbit

1967

50-335	van Vogt, A. E.	The Changeling
54-390	Le Fanu, J. S.	Uncle Silas
52-392	High, P. E.	Twin Planets
52-406	van Vogt, A. E.	Two Hundred Million A.D.
53-409	Walpole, H.	Portrait of a Man With Red Hair
52-415	del Rey, L.	Marooned on Mars
52-421	Ross, M.	Victoria Winters
53-428	Adamski, G.	Inside the Flying Saucers
52-430	Somers, B.	Abandon Galaxy
53-439	Adamski, G.	Behind the Flying Saucer Mystery
54-445	Burkett, W. R.	Sleeping Planet
52-452	Ross, M.	The Mystery of Fury Castle
52-462	Nourse, A. E.	The Universe Between
52-468	Birkin, C.	The Witch Baiter
52-469	Saxon, P.	The Torturer
52-472	Birkin, C.	The Haunted Dancers
52-475	Moorcock, M.	The Fireclown
53-487	Reynolds, J.	Ghosts in American Houses
52-488	Majors, S.	The Druid Stone
52-498	Simak, C. D.	Cosmic Engineers
52-527	Blackstock, C.	Witches' Sabbath
53-538	Hamilton, E.	The Star Kings
52-543	Ross, M.	Strangers at Collins House
52-554	Thomas, M.	Beyond the Spectrum
52-555	van Vogt, A. E.	Science Fiction Monsters
52-562	Saxon, P.	The Darkest Night
53-567	O'Donnell, E.	The Dead Riders
52-572	Stuart, W. J.	Forbidden Planet
53-577	Mills, R.	The Worlds of Science Fiction
52-584	Ballinger, W. A.	Drums of the Dark Gods
53-585	Gibbons, G.	On Board the Flying Saucers
52-586	Carter, L.	Thongor Against the Gods
52-598	Saxon, P.	Scream and Scream Again
52-599	Mason, D. R.	Eight Against Utopia
52-605	Winfield, D.	Up-Tight
52-609	Hamilton, E.	Battle for the Stars

1968

63-368	Ross, M.	The Curse of Collinwood
52-610	Ross, M.	The Mystery of Collinwood
54-616	Churchward, J.	The Lost Continent of Mu
54-617	Ahmed, R.	The Black Art
53-618	de Camp, L. S.	The Tritonian Ring
52-622	deFord, M. A.	Space, Time and Crime
54-629	Ford, A.	Nothing So Strange
54-633	Santesson, H. S.	The Fantastic Universe Omnibus
52-635	Fox, G. F.	Escape Across the Cosmos
54-639	Churchward, J.	The Children of Mu
53-640	Taylor, R. W.	Doomsday Square
52-649	MacApp, C. C.	Omha Abides
52-651	Vale, R.	Beyond the Sealed World
54-662	Turney, C.	Possessed
54-663	Churchward, J.	The Sacred Symbols of Mu
53-665	Carter, L.	Thongor in the City of Magicians
53-667	Elwood, R.	Alien Worlds
53-677	Giles, R.	Night of the Warlock
54-678	Churchward, J.	The Cosmic Forces of Mu
53-680	White, Ted	The Spawn of the Death Machine
54-684	Barzman, B.	Echo X
52-687	Resnick, M.	The Goddess of Ganymede
53-689	Shulman, S.	The Daughters of Astaroth
54-691	Reynolds, J.	Ghosts in Irish Houses

55-693	Gaskell, J.	**The Serpent**
53-727	Ellison, H.	**Earthman, Go Home**
55-738	Gaskell, J.	**Atlan**
53-746	Biggle, L.	**All the Colors of Darkness**
55-752	Treece, H.	**The Green Man**
54-754	Churchward, J.	**The Second Book of the Cosmic Forces of Mu**
52-760	Resnick, M.	**Pursuit on Ganymede**
53-763	Binder, E.	**Adam Link, Robot**
53-780	Carter, L.	**Thongor at the End of Time**
53-785	Somers, B.	**Beyond the Black Enigma**
62-001	Ross, M.	**Barnabas Collins**
64-006	Reynolds, J.	**More Ghosts in Irish Houses**
63-016	van Vogt, A. E.	**The House That Stood Still**
64-019	Gaskell, J.	**The City**

Paperduck See DUCKWORTH

Papermac See MACMILLAN & CO.

PARADOX PRESS, U.S.A. [R. Bretnor]
Paradox
1962

—	Bretnor, R.	**Through Time and Space With Ferdinand Feghoot**

Peacock See PENGUIN BOOKS

C. ARTHUR PEARSON LTD., London, England.
All titles noted as T-B (Tit-Bits Science Fiction Library).
Pearson
1945 (approx.)

—	Woodman, T. E.	**Britain in the Ice Grip**
1953		
(Sep)	Rose, L. F.	**The Hell Fruit**
(Oct)	Holt, C.	**Cosmic Exodus**
(Nov)	Future, S.	**Doomed Nation of the Skies**
(Dec)	Rayer, F. G.	**The Star Seekers**
1954		
(Jan)	Reisen, M.	**Before the Beginning**
—	Anonymous	**The Dome of Survival**
—	Condray, B. G.	**The Dissentizens**
—	Condray, B. G.	**Exile From Jupiter**
—	Future, S.	**Slave Traders of the Sky**
—	Heine, I.	**Dimension of Illion**
—	Kent, P.	**Home Is the Martian**
—	Kent, P.	**Mission to the Stars**
—	Kent, P.	**Slaves of the Spectrum**
—	Kent, P.	**Vassals of Venus**
—	Maddox, C.	**Menace From the Past**
—	Maddox, C.	**The Living World**
—	Rackham, J.	**Alien Virus**
—	Rackham, J.	**Jupiter Equilateral**
—	Rackham, J.	**The Master Weed**
—	Rackham, J.	**Space Puppet**

PEC Giant See PUBLISHERS EXPORT CO.

Pedigree See (EDWIN) SELF & CO. LTD.

Pelican See PENGUIN BOOKS LTD.

PENDULUM PUBLICATIONS LTD., London, England.
See additional coverage under *GENERAL*.
Pendulum
1946 (approx.)

ST1	Arnold, F. E.	**Wings Across Time**
—	Carnell, J.	**Jinn and Jitters**
—	Cross, P.	**Other Eyes Watching**

PENGUIN BOOKS LTD., Harmondshire, Middlesex, England.
Imprints: **Penguin** [prefix "L" denotes Penguin Classics]; **Peacock**; **Pelican**; **Puffin**. See also PENGUIN-AUST below.
Penguin

1935		
19	Bromfield, L.	**The Strange Case of Miss Annie Spragg**
1936		
20	Butler, S.	**Erewhon**
38	de la Mare, W. J.	**The Return**
39	Bramah, E.	**The Wallet of Kai Lung**
1937		
73	Powys, T. F.	**Mr. Weston's Good Wine**
91	James, M. R.	**Ghost Stories of an Antiquary**
92	Beresford, J. D.	**The Hampdenshire Wonder**
95	Chesterton, G. K.	**The Man Who Was Thursday**
108	Bramah, E.	**Kai Lung Unrolls His Mat** [2nd ed.]
1938		
C10	Swift, J.	**Gulliver's Travels**
140	Gibbons, S.	**Cold Comfort Farm**
151	Wells, H. G.	**The Invisible Man**
157	Rohmer, S.	**The Mystery of Dr. Fu Manchu**
166	Blackwood, A.	**The Centaur**
174	Bramah, E.	**Kai Lung's Golden Hours**
1939		
108	Bramah, E.	**Kai Lung Unrolls His Mat**
186	Garnett, R.	**Twilight of the Gods**
199	Bierce, A.	**In the Midst of Life**
222	Onions, O.	**Widdershins**
1940		
95	Chesterton, G. K.	**The Man Who Was Thursday**
184	Munro, H. H.	**Selected Short Stories of Saki**
268	Cabell, J. B.	**Jurgen** [2nd ed.]
1941		
108	Bramah, E.	**Kai Lung Unrolls His Mat**
343	Wells, H. G.	**The War in the Air**
1942		
381	Woolf, V.	**Orlando: A Biography**
393	Blackwood, A.	**Selected Tales of Algernon Blackwood**
1944		
475	Golding, L.	**The Miracle Boy**
1945		
461	London, J.	**The Iron Heel**
487	Falkner, J.	**The Lost Stradivarius**
507	Wright, S. F.	**The Island of Captain Sparrow**
1946		
526	Machen, A.	**Holy Terrors**
542	Anstey, F.	**The Brass Bottle**
550	Chesterton, G. K.	**The Napoleon of Notting Hill**
570	Wells, H. G.	**The War of the Worlds**
571	Wells, H. G.	**The Island of Dr. Moreau**
573	Wells, H. G.	**The Time Machine**
582	Connington, J. J.	**Nordenholt's Million**
595	Coppard, A. E.	**Adam and Eve and Pinch Me**
?	James, H.	**The Turn of the Screw**
1947		
L4	Voltaire, F.	**Candide**
586	Garnett, R.	**Twilight of the Gods**
—	Le Fanu, J. S.	**Uncle Silas**
1948		
393	Blackwood, A.	**Selected Tales of Algernon Blackwood**
617	France, A.	**Penguin Island**
1949		
174	Bramah, E.	**Kai Lung's Golden Hours**
616	Wilde, O.	**The Picture of Dorian Grey**
1950		
783	Baker, F.	**Miss Hargreaves**
1951		
838	Orwell, G.	**Animal Farm**
140	Gibbons, S.	**Cold Comfort Farm**

1952
884 Williams, C. **Many Dimensions**
1953
907 Kafka, F. **The Trial**
1954
20 Butler, S. **Erewhon**
570 Wells, H. G. **The War of the Worlds**
838 Orwell, G. **Animal Farm**
901 Rice, E. **A Voyage to Purilia**
972 Orwell, G. **1984**
993 Wyndham, J. **The Day of the Triffids**
1010 Beerbohm, M. **Seven Men and Two Others**
1031 Forester, C. S. **Collected Short Stories**
1955
972 Orwell, G. **1984**
1049 Huxley, A. **After Many a Summer Dies the Swan**
1052 Huxley, A. **Brave New World**
1072 Collins, W. W. **The Moonstone**
1075 Wyndham, J. **The Kraken Wakes**
1956
140 Gibbons, S. **Cold Comfort Farm**
1031 Forster, E. M. **Collected Short Stories**
1075 Wyndham, J. **The Kraken Wakes**
1109 Poe, E. A. **Selected Tales of Edgar Allan Poe**
1957
L76 Green, R. L. **Two Satyr Plays**
1215 Menen, A. **The Prevalence of Witches**
1218 Smith, T. **The Night Life of the Gods**
1219 Smith, T. **Topper Takes a Trip**
1235 Kafka, F. **The Castle**
1237 Roth, H. **Mask of Glass**
1242 Carr, J. D. **The Devil in Velvet**
1958
95 Chesterton, G. K. **The Man Who Was Thursday**
570 Wells, H. G. **The War of the Worlds**
993 Wyndham, J. **The Day of the Triffids**
1052 Huxley, A. **Brave New World**
1219 Smith, T. **Topper Takes a Trip**
1300 Christopher, J. **The Death of Grass**
1308 Wyndham, J. **The Chrysalids**
1310 Wells, H. G. **Selected Short Stories of H. G. Wells**
1338 Chesterton, G. K. **The Flying Inn**
1959
19 Bromfield, L. **The Strange Case of Miss Annie Spragg**
91 James, M. R. **Ghost Stories of an Antiquary**
570 Wells, H. G. **The War of the Worlds**
838 Orwell, G. **Animal Farm**
972 Orwell, G. **1984**
1049 Huxley, A. **After Many a Summer Dies the Swan**
1347 James, M. R. **More Ghost Stories of an Antiquary**
1385 Wyndham, J. **The Seeds of Time**
1421 Kneale, N. **The Quatermass Experiment**
1960
91 James, M. R. **Ghost Stories of an Antiquary**
1440 Wyndham, J. **The Midwich Cuckoos**
1448 Kneale, N. **Quatermass II**
1449 Kneale, N. **Quatermass and the Pit**
1459 Karp, D. **One**
1466 Hoyle, F. **The Black Cloud**
1468 Dennis, N. **Cards of Identity**
1471 Golding, W. **Lord of the Flies**
1961
S195 Vassiliev, M., & Gouschev, S. **Life in the Twenty-First Century**
616 Wilde, O. **The Picture of Dorian Grey**
1031 Forster, E. M. **Collected Short Stories**
1049 Huxley, A. **After Many a Summer Dies the Swan**
1075 Wyndham, J. **The Kraken Wakes**
1308 Wyndham, J. **The Chrysalids**
1385 Wyndham, J. **The Seeds of Time**
1516 Aymé, M. **The Green Mare**
1615 Blackburn, J. **A Scent of New-Mown Hay**

1622 Carr, J. D. **Fire, Burn!**
1624 Heard, G. **A Taste for Honey**
1634 Bowen, J. **After the Rain**
1638 Aldiss, B. W. **Penguin Science Fiction**
1645 Russell, B. **Satan in the Suburbs**
1647 Wolfe, B. **Limbo 90**
1962
95 Chesterton, G. K. **The Man Who Was Thursday**
570 Wells, H. G. **The War of the Worlds**
571 Wells, H. G. **The Island of Dr. Moreau**
838 Orwell, G. **Animal Farm**
972 Orwell, G. **1984**
1235 Kafka, F. **The Castle**
1347 James, M. R. **More Ghost Stories of an Antiquary**
1544 Wyndham, J., & Parkes, L. **The Outward Urge**
1686 Golding, W. **Pincher Martin**
1832 Dahl, R. **Kiss, Kiss**
1835 Laski, M. **The Victorian Chaise-Longue**
1858 Russell, B. **Nightmares of Eminent Persons**
1963
381 Woolf, V. **Orlando: A Biography**
1300 Christopher, J. **The Death of Grass**
1466 Hoyle, F. **The Black Cloud**
1809 Blish, J. **A Case of Conscience**
1867 Fitzgerald, F. S. **This Side of Paradise**
1875 Stapledon, O. **The Last and First Men**
1878 Bradbury, R. **The Day It Rained Forever**
1886 Herbert, F. **The Dragon in the Sea**
1912 Spark, M. **The Go-Away Bird**
1928 Menen, A. **The Fig Tree**
1952 Dinesen, I. **Seven Gothic Tales**
1963 Aldiss, B. W. **More Penguin Science Fiction**
1978 Clement, H. **Mission of Gravity**
1986 Wyndham, J. **Trouble With Lichen**
2005 Russell, E. F. **Three to Conquer**
1964
570 Wells, H. G. **The War of the Worlds**
1075 Wyndham, J. **The Kraken Wakes**
1905 Asimov, I. **The Hugo Winners**
1963 Aldiss, B. W. **More Penguin Science Fiction**
1999 Stapledon, O. **Sirius**
2004 Lewis, R. **The Evolution Man**
2079 Wilson, A. **The Old Men in the Zoo**
2095 Harrison, H. **Deathworld**
2131 Christopher, J. **The World in Winter**
2135 Capote, T. **Other Voices, Other Rooms**
2189 Aldiss, B. W. **Yet More Penguin Science Fiction**
2193 Huxley, A. **Island**
2217 Budrys, A. **Who?**
2223 Boardman, T. **Connoisseur's Science Fiction**
1965
1049 Huxley, A. **After Many a Summer Dies the Swan**
C1622 Carr, J. D. **Fire, Burn!**
1986 Wyndham, J. **Trouble With Lichen**
2131 Christopher, J. **The World in Winter**
2152 Hersey, J. **The Child Buyer**
2223 Boardman, T. **Connoisseur's Science Fiction**
2224 Kornbluth, C. M., & Pohl, F. **The Space Merchants**
2229 Ballard, J. G. **The Drowned World**
2231 Wyndham, J. **Consider Her Ways**
2233 Haggard, W. **Slow Burner**
2244 Hoyle, F. & G. **The Fifth Planet**
2265 Verne, J. **A Journey to the Centre of the Earth**
2275 Carnell, J. **Lambda 1 and Other Stories**
2308 Vonnegut, K. **Cat's Cradle**
2309 Sturgeon, T. **More Than Human**
2345 Ballard, J. G. **The Four-Dimensional Nightmare**
2358 Russell, E. F. **With a Strange Device**
2376 Dick, P. K. **The Man in the High Castle**

1966

EL14	Collins, W. W.	The Moonstone
616	Wilde, O.	The Picture of Dorian Grey
907	Kafka, F.	The Trial
1052	Huxley, A.	Brave New World
1075	Wyndham, J.	The Kraken Wakes
1638	Aldiss, B. W.	Penguin Science Fiction
1832	Dahl, R.	Kiss, Kiss
1875	Stapledon, O.	The Last and First Men
2095	Harrison, H.	Deathworld
2189	Aldiss, B. W.	Yet More Penguin Science Fiction
2193	Huxley, A.	Island
2223	Boardman, T.	Connoisseur's Science Fiction
2387	Biggle, L.	All the Colors of Darkness
2401	Boulle, P.	Monkey Planet
2452	Pohl, F.	Alternating Currents
2454	Pangborn, E.	A Mirror for Observers
2455	Hartley, L. P.	Facial Justice
2460	Judd, C.	Gunner Cade
2491	Cooper, S.	Mandrake
2499	Ballard, J. G.	Terminal Beach
2510	Heinlein, R. A.	The Unpleasant Profession of Jonathan Hoag
2521	Pohl, F.	Drunkard's Walk
2527	Blackwood, A.	The Insanity of Jones and Other Tales
2537	Finney, C. G.	The Circus of Dr. Lao

1967

EL28	Poe, E. A.	Selected Writings of Edgar Allan Poe
95	Chesterton, G. K.	The Man Who Was Thursday
343	Wells, H. G.	The War in the Air
570	Wells, H. G.	The War of the Worlds
571	Wells, H. G.	The Island of Dr. Moreau
972	Orwell, G.	1984
1308	Wyndham, J.	The Chrysalids
1440	Wyndham, J.	The Midwich Cuckoos
2376	Dick, P. K.	The Man in the High Castle
2536	Bester, A.	The Demolished Man
2561	Kornbluth, C. M., & Pohl, F.	Wolfbane
2591	Ballard, J. G.	The Wind From Nowhere
2596	Simak, C. D.	Time and Again
2620	Bester, A.	Tiger! Tiger!
2636	O'Brien, F.	At Swim-Two-Birds
2662	Deighton, L.	Billion Dollar Brain
2664	Harrison, H.	Make Room! Make Room!
2689	Herbert, F.	Destination: Void
2698	Laumer, K.	A Plague of Demons
2702	Sturgeon, T.	The Joyous Invasions
2728	Barth, J.	Giles Goat-Boy
2755	Gallico, P.	Adventures of Hiram Holliday

1968

EL22	Swift, J.	Gulliver's Travels
EL36	Fairclough, P.	Three Gothic Novels
838	Orwell, G.	Animal Farm
993	Wyndham, J.	The Day of the Triffids
1052	Huxley, A.	Brave New World
1308	Wyndham, J.	The Chrysalids
1466	Hoyle, F.	The Black Cloud
1572	Kafka, F.	The Metamorphosis and Other Stories
1905	Asimov, I.	The Hugo Winners
2193	Huxley, A.	Island
2265	Verne, J.	A Journey to the Centre of the Earth
2560	Brophy, B.	Hackenfeller's Ape
2700	Phelps, G.	The Winter People
2702	Sturgeon, T.	The Joyous Invasions
2715	Brunner, J.	Telepathist
2722	Russell, E. F.	Somewhere a Voice
2734	Petty, J.	The Last Refuge
2753	Ballard, J. G.	The Drought
2762	Peake, M.	Titus Groan
C2779	Allingham, M.	The Mind Readers
2803	Amis, K.	The Anti-Death League

2804	Brunner, J.	The Long Result
2886	Hoyle, F.	October the First Is Too Late
2904	Blackwood, A.	Ancient Sorceries

Peacock

1963

PK20	White, T. H.	Mistress Masham's Repose

1964

PK43	White, T. H.	The Master

1968

PK61	Norton, Andre	The Beast Master
PK62	Norton, Andre	Lord of Thunder
PK63	Ball, B. N.	Tales of Science Fiction

Pelican

1938

PSA3	Stapledon, O.	The Last and First Men

1958

A434	Clarke, A. C.	The Exploration of Space

1961

A485	Young, M.	The Rise of the Meritocracy 1870-2033

1964

A663	Gabor, D.	Inventing the Future

1965

A745	Hughes, P.	Witchcraft

Puffin [juvenile fiction]

1946

PS33	Hunter, N.	The Incredible Adventures of Professor Branestawm

1948

PS16	Haldane, J. B. S.	My Friend Mr. Leaky

1950

PS33	Hunter, N.	The Incredible Adventures of Professor Branestawm

1952

PS57	Hughes, J.	Ditta's Tree

1957

PS107	Greener, L.	Moon Ahead!
PS111	Haggard, H. R.	King Solomon's Mines

1959

PS33	Hunter, N.	The Incredible Adventures of Professor Branestawm
PS128	Nesbit, E.	Five Children and It
PS132	Lewis, C. S.	The Lion, the Witch, and the Wardrobe

1961

PS128	Nesbit, E.	Five Children and It
PS161	Tolkien, J. R. R.	The Hobbit

1962

PS173	Lewis, C. S.	Prince Caspian
PS177	Severn, D.	The Future Took Us
PS180	Thurber, J.	The 13 Clocks and The Wonderful O

1963

PS154	Walker, K., & Boumphrey, G.	The Log of the Ark
PS160	B.B.	The Little Grey Men
PS161	Tolkien, J. R. R.	The Hobbit
PS173	Lewis, C. S.	Prince Caspian
PS184	Saint-Exupéry, A. de	The Little Prince
PS187	Masefield, J.	The Midnight Folk
PS192	Lewis, C. S.	The Magician's Nephew
PS193	Garner, A.	The Weirdstone of Brisingamen

1964

PS205	Lewis, C. S.	The Last Battle
PS220	MacDonald, G.	The Princess and the Goblin
PS223	Thackeray, W.	The Rose and the Ring

1965

PS128	Nesbit, E.	Five Children and It
PS130	Nesbit, E.	The Story of the Amulet
PS182	Travers, P. L.	Mary Poppins
PS229	Lewis, C. S.	The Voyage of the "Dawn Treader"
PS234	Masefield, J.	The Box of Delights
PS236	Juster, N.	The Phantom Tollbooth
PS240	Lewis, C. S.	The Silver Chair

PS242	Garner, A.	**Moon of Gomrath**
PS244	Lewis, C. S.	**The Horse and His Boy**

1966

PS111	Haggard, H. R.	**King Solomon's Mines**
PS220	MacDonald, G.	**The Princess and the Goblin**
PS260	MacDonald, G.	**The Princess and Curdie**
PS267	Heinlein, R. A.	**Starman Jones**
PS275	Hunter, N.	**Professor Branestawm's Treasure Hunt**

1967

PS129	Nesbit, E.	**The Phoenix and the Carpet**
PS155	Sleigh, B.	**Carbonel**
PS288	L'Engle, M.	**A Wrinkle in Time**
PS297	Manning, R.	**Green Smoke**
PS315	Norton, Andre	**Catseye**
PS317	Garner, A.	**Elidor**
PS319	Hitchcock, A.	**Ghostly Gallery**

1968

PS57	Hughes, J.	**Ditta's Tree**
PS111	Haggard, H. R.	**King Solomon's Mines**
PS164	Wilde, O.	**The Happy Prince**
PS177	Severn, D.	**The Future Took Us**
PS362	Cooper, S.	**Over Sea, Under Stone**
PS377	Milne, A. A.	**Once on a Time**
PS378	Sinclair-Stevenson, C.	
		A Book of Princes

Penguin-Aust
   Penguin Books printed by Australian Lothian Pub. Co., Sydney.
1946 (approx.)

	Wells, H. G.	**The Invisible Man**

PENGUIN BOOKS INC., New York, N.Y., U.S.A.
Penguin-US
1944

—	Benét, S. V.	**O'Halloran's Luck**
S37	Morley, C.	**Thunder on the Left**
537	Fast, J.	**Out of This World**
550	Sloane, W.	**To Walk the Night**

1945

554	Defoe, D.	**Tales of Piracy, Crimes and Ghosts**

1946

582	Morley, C.	**Thunder on the Left**
590	Woolf, V.	**Orlando: A Biography**
594	Wood, C. E. S.	**Heaveny Discourse**
601	Cabell, J. B.	**Jurgen**
615	Garnett, D.	**Lady Into Fox**

1947

638	Nathan, R.	**Portrait of Jennie**

1953

?	Anstey, F.	**The Brass Bottle**

Pennant See BANTAM BOOKS

Perennial See HARPER

PERGAMON PRESS LTD., Oxford, England.
Pergamon
1967

103349	Mansfield, R.	**The Starlit Corridor** [Teacher's ed.]
103370	Mansfield, R.	**The Starlit Corridor** [Student's ed.]

Permabks PERMABOOKS; see POCKET BOOKS INC.

PHAROS BOOKS, Colwyn Bay, North Wales.
Pharos
1946

—	Bennett, A. G.	**Whom the Gods Destroy**

PICTORIAL ART LTD., London, England.
Pictorial
Mid-1940's

—	Anonymous	**Imperial Overture and Other Stories**

PIKE BOOKS, Van Nuys, California, U.S.A.
Pike
Early 1960's

101	Rivere, A.	**Lost City of the Damned**
203	Smith, G. H.	**The Coming of the Rats**

1961

205	Hudson, J.	**Love Cult**

PILLAR PUBLISHING CO., Dublin, Ireland.
Pillar
Mid-1940's

	O'Donnell, E.	**Dread of Night**

Pinnacle See (MARK) GOULDEN LTD.

PINNACLE PRESS, Sydney, N.S.W., Australia.
Pinnacle (Sydney)
1941

	Batt, L.	**Formula for Power**

PITT AND BOND TRADING PTY. LTD., Sydney, N.S.W., Australia.
Pitt & Bond
1963

PB512	Muller, J. E.	**Orbit One**
PB516	Muller, J. E.	**Edge of Eternity**

PLAYBOY PRESS, Chicago, Illinois, U.S.A.
Playboy
1968

BAO115	Anonymous [Russell, R.]	
		The Playboy Book of Science Fiction and Fantasy
BAO119	Anonymous [Russell, R.]	
		The Playboy Book of Horror and Supernatural

Pleasure Pleasure Books; see GREENLEAF CLASSICS

POCKET BOOKS INC., New York, N.Y., U.S.A.
   Other imprints: **Cardinal, Lantern, Permabooks, Washington Square Press.**
Pocket Bks
1939

1	Hilton, J.	**Lost Horizon**
16	Hudson, W. H.	**Green Mansions**
34	Swift, J.	**Gulliver's Travels**

1940

39	Poe, E. A.	**Great Tales and Poems of Edgar Allan Poe**

1941

97	Endore, G.	**The Werewolf of Paris**
123	Stevenson, R. L.	**The Strange Case of Dr. Jekyll and Mr. Hyde**

1943

1	Hilton, J.	**Lost Horizon**
4	Smith, T.	**Topper**
209	Smith, T.	**Topper Takes a Trip**
214	Wollheim, D. A.	**The Pocket Book of Science Fiction**

1945

209	Smith, T.	**Topper Takes a Trip**
314	Smith, T.	**The Bishop's Jaegers**

1946

360	Benét, S. V.	**The Stephen Vincent Benét Pocket Book**
401	Smith, T.	**The Passionate Witch**
408	Russell, J.	**The Lost God and Other Adventure Stories**
409	Smith, T.	**The Glorious Pool**

1947

384	Stern, P. Van D.	**The Pocket Book of Ghost Stories**
428	Smith, T.	**The Night Life of the Gods**
435	Marshall, B.	**Father Malachy's Miracle**
447	Smith, T.	**Turnabout**
452	Stoker, B.	**Dracula**

1948

490	Smith, T.	**Skin and Bones**
493	Knight, E.	**The Flying Yorkshireman**
497	Twain, M.	**A Connecticut Yankee in King Arthur's Court**
498	Frank, P.	**Mr. Adam**
503	Jones, G. P. & C. B.	**Peabody's Mermaid**
518	Smith, T.	**The Stray Lamb**

1949

546	Smith, T.	**Rain in the Doorway**

1950

695	Smith, H. A.	**Rhubarb**

1952

1	Hilton, J.	**Lost Horizon**
903	Davies, V.	**Miracle on 34th Street**
908	Healy, R. J.	**New Tales of Space and Time**

1953

920	Leinster, M.	**Space Platform**
943	MacDonald, J. D.	**The Planet of the Dreamers**
947	Wells, H. G.	**The War of the Worlds**

1954

989	Clarke, A. C.	**The Sands of Mars**
1007	Margulies, L., & Friend, O. J.	
		My Best Science Fiction Story
PL14	Stevenson, R. L.	**Great Short Stories of Robert Louis Stevenson**

1955

1037	Leinster, M.	**Space Tug**
1038	Vercors	**You Shall Know Them**
1045	Conklin, G.	**Science Fiction Terror Tales**
1074	Conklin, G.	**Invaders of Earth**
2209	Smith, T.	**Topper Takes a Trip**
2428	Smith, T.	**The Night Life of the Gods**
2498	Frank, P.	**Mr. Adam**

1956

1	Hilton, J.	**Lost Horizon**
GC37	Bernstein, M.	**The Search for Bridey Murphy**
PL46	Poe, E. A.	**Great Tales and Poems**

1957

1140	Wells, H. G.	**The Invisible Man**

1958

—	Maugham, W. S.	**The Magician**
1183	Christopher, J.	**No Blade of Grass**
1206	Vercors	**Murder of the Missing Link**

1959

1	Hilton, J.	**Lost Horizon**
1222	Oliver, C.	**The Winds of Time**
2498	Frank, P.	**Mr. Adam**

1961

GC952	Drury, A.	**Advise and Consent**

1962

6093	Searls, H.	**The Astronaut**

1963

GC165	Priestley, J.	**Saturn Over the Water**
GC961	Drury, A.	**A Shade of Difference**
6163	Gold, H. L.	**The Fifth Galaxy Reader**
6189	Smith, T.	**The Glorious Pool**
6207	Smith, T.	**The Passionate Witch**
7025	Haggard, H. R.	**Cleopatra**

1964

GC789	Rascovich, M.	**The Bedford Incident**
50003	Barrett, W. E.	**The Fools of Time**
50007	Hilton, J.	**Lost Horizon**

1965

10063	Riefe, A.	**Tales of Horror**
50126	Anderson, W. C.	**Penelope**
50156	Laumer, K.	**The Great Time Machine Hoax**
50176	Walker, D.	**Winter of Madness**

1966

10130	Brewster, D.	**I Dream of Jeannie**
50499	Monserrat, N.	**The Time Before This**
75147	Wylie, P.	**The Disappearance**

1967

50532	Pohl, F.	**The Ninth Galaxy Reader**
75174	Wylie, P.	**The Disappearance**
75275	Knight, D.	**Nebula Award Stories**

1968

55052	McCall, A.	**Holocaust**
75114	Aldiss, B. W., & Harrison, H.	
		Nebula Award Stories 2
75226	Wouk, H.	**The "Lomokome" Papers**
75287	Smith, H. A.	**Rhubarb**

Cardinal

1952

C40	Wylie, P.	**The Disappearance**
C45	Poe, E. A.	**Great Tales and Poems**

1954

C107	Twain, M.	**A Connecticut Yankee in King Arthur's Court**
C135	Clarke, A. C.	**The Exploration of Space**
C156	Stern, P. Van D.	**Great Tales of Fantasy and Imagination**

1956

C207	Goodwin, H. L.	**The Science Book of Space Travel**
C215	Griffith, M.	**The Gadget Maker**

1958

C319	Healy, R. J.	**New Tales of Space and Time**
C328	Wallop, D.	**The Year the Yankees Lost the Pennant**

1961

C426	Gallico, P.	**Too Many Ghosts**

1964

GC787	Golding, W.	**The Inheritors**

1966

75169	Golding, W.	**The Inheritors**

Lantern

1964

50092	Furman, A. L.	**Ghost Stories**
50096	Elam, R. M.	**Science Fiction Stories**

1965

50260	Furman, A. L.	**Outer Space Stories**

1967

50526	Elam, R. M.	**Super Science Stories**

1968

50593	Furman, A. L.	**More Ghost Stories**

Permabks

PERMABOOKS was a division of Doubleday Book Co. from 1948 to mid-1954, and was then purchased by Pocket Books Inc. Titles under both ownerships are listed below.

1950

P67	Conklin, G.	**The Science Fiction Galaxy**
P94	Holland, B.	**The Permabook of Ghost Stories**

1951

P117	Conklin, G.	**In the Grip of Terror**

1952

P145	Pohl, F.	**Beyond the End of Time**

1953

P236	Pohl, F.	**Shadow of Tomorrow**
P254	Conklin, G.	**Crossroads in Time**

1954

264	Simak, C. D.	**City**
279	Doyle, A. C.	**The Lost World**
P291	Tenn, W.	**Outsiders: Children of Wonder**
297	Keyhoe, D. E.	**Flying Saucers From Outer Space**
310	Clarke, A. C.	**Against the Fall of Night**

1955

M4022	Conklin, G.	**Operation Future**

1956

M3027	McIntosh, J. T.	**World out of Mind**
M3034	Holden, R.	**Snow Fury**

1957

M3070	Fleming, I.	**Too Hot to Handle**
M4088	Stoker, B.	**Dracula**
M4095	Shute, N.	**In the Wet**

1958

M4088	Stoker, B.	**Dracula**

1959

M4120	Russell, E. F.	Wasp
M4149	Clarke, A. C.	The Sands of Mars
M4161	Verne, J.	A Journey to the Center of the Earth

1960

M4158	Gold, H. L.	Five Galaxy Short Novels
M4172	Gold, H. L.	The Third Galaxy Reader
M4184	Gold, H. L.	The Fourth Galaxy Reader
M4185	Buckner, R.	Starfire

1961

M4192	Wellman, P. I.	The Fiery Flower
M4197	Gold, H. L.	The World that Couldn't Be
M6002	Verne, J.	The Mysterious Island

1962

M4230	Stanton, P.	Village of Stars
M4241	Buckner, R.	Moon Pilot
M4242	Schmitz, J. H.	Agent of Vega
M4252	Gold, H. L.	Bodyguard and Four Other Short Novels From Galaxy
M4263	van Vogt, A. E.	The War Against the Rull
M5044	Slaughter, F. G.	Epidemic!

1963

M4278	Sambrot, W.	The Island of Fear
M4279	Fuller, R.	The Son of Flubber
M4287	Gold, H. L.	Mind Partner

Washington

1959

W601	Shapley, H.	Of Stars and Men

1960

W150	Twain, M.	A Connecticut Yankee in King Arthur's Court
W246	Poe, E. A.	Great Tales and Poems
W251	Swift, J.	Gulliver's Travels

1961

W580	Hawthorne, N.	Twice Told Tales

1962

W276	Wells, H. G.	The War of the Worlds & The Invisible Man
W581	Irving, W.	The Legend of Sleepy Hollow
W592	Stern, P. Van D.	Great Ghost Stories

1964

RE104	Wells, H. G.	The Invisible Man
RE108	Hilton, J.	Lost Horizon
W253	Bunyan, J.	The Pilgrim's Progress
W276	Wells, H. G.	The War of the Worlds & The Invisible Man
RE301	Twain, M.	A Connecticut Yankee in King Arthur's Court

1965

W704	Stern, P. Van D.	Great Tales of Fantasy and Imagination

1966

RE709	Verne, J.	Twenty Thousand Leagues Under the Sea
W924	Haber, H.	Stars, Men and Atoms

1967

?	Stern, P. Van D.	Great Ghost Stories

1968

29013	Benét, S. V.	The Devil and Daniel Webster

POPULAR LIBRARY INC., New York, N.Y., U.S.A.

Popular

1943

130	Furman, A. L.	The Mystery Companion

1944

—	Carr, J. D.	The Burning Court

1948

147	Erskine, J.	The Private Life of Helen of Troy
200	Matson, N.	Bats in the Belfry

1949

228	Mead, S.	The Sex Machine

1950

217	Rohmer, S.	Tales of Chinatown
273	Ehrlich, M.	The Big Eye

1951

326	Scully, F.	Behind the Flying Saucers

1952

411	Wyndham, J.	Revolt of the Triffids
447	Williamson, J.	Dragon's Island

1953

544	Gerard, F.	The Mark of the Moon

1954

EB8	White, W. C.	The Pale Blonde of James Street

1955

686	Schafer, R.	The Naked and the Damned

1956

G156	Wylie, P.	Tomorrow!

1957

G156X	Wylie, P.	Tomorrow!

1961

G556	Caldwell, T.	Your Sins and Mine
G560	Siodmak, C.	Donovan's Brain
PC1005	Wylie, P.	Tomorrow!
W1110	Marshall, E.	Earth Giant

1962

K6	Jackson, S.	The Haunting of Hill House
SP170	Wells, H. G.	The War of the Worlds
SP195	Priestley, J. B.	The Doomsday Men

1963

K6	Jackson, S.	The Haunting of Hill House
K18	Bloch, R.	Blood Runs Cold
K38	Harris, K.	Jane Arden: Space Nurse
K64	Stevenson, R. L.	Dr. Jekyll and Mr. Hyde
SP214	Fleischman, T.	Double Exposure
SP231	Martin, I.	The Satan Bug
SP232	Priestley, J. B.	The Shapes of Sleep
M2035	Wylie, P.	Tomorrow!

1964

K71	Wells, H. G.	The Invisible Man
SP250	Dick, P. K.	The Man in the High Castle
SP286	Wells, H. G.	The Food of the Gods
SP305	Sutton, J.	Apollo at Go
SP329	Pinckney, J.	Great Mischief
SP331	Saturday Evening Post	The Saturday Evening Post Reader of Fantasy and Science Fiction
W1132	Wylie, P.	Night Unto Night

1965

SP351	Karp, M. A., & Settel, I.	Suddenly!
SP352	Knight, D.	The Shape of Things
SP375	Allen, M. C.	Shock!
SP385	Colby, C. B.	The Weirdest People in the World
SP397	Peck, I.	A Treasury of Great Ghost Stories
SP405	Karp, M. A.	The Unhumans
PC1046	Edwards, F.	Strange People

1966

60-2195	Nichols, B.	The Powers That Be

1967

60-2202	Vercors	You Shall Know Them
60-2209	Wylie, P.	The Murderer Invisible
60-2223	Green, G.	Let's Face the Facts About Flying Saucers

1968

75-1260	Goldston, R.	The Catafalque
60-2121	Jackson, S.	The Haunting of Hill House
60-2289	Dick, P. K.	The Man in the High Castle
60-2335	Sterling, B.	Danger Planet
60-2346	Wellman, M. W.	The Solar Invasion
60-2348	Denham, A.	The Ghost and Mrs. Muir
60-2355	Kuttner, H.	The Creature From Beyond Infinity
60-2376	Hamilton, E.	Outlaw World
60-8059	Robinson, F. M.	The Power

POPULAR PUBLICATIONS, Toronto, Canada.

Popular Pub

1947

—	Daly, C. J.	The Legion of the Living Dead

| — | Farley, R. M. | **The Immortals** |
| — | Roscoe, T. | **A Grave Must Be Deep** |

POYNINGS PRESS LTD., Wineham, England.
Poynings
Early 1940's
| — | Wells, H. G. | **The Time Machine** |
1944
| — | Golding, L. | **The Call of the Hand and Other Stories** |

Premier See FAWCETT PUBLICATIONS

PUBLISHERS EXPORT CO., San Diego, California, U.S.A.
PEC Giant
1966
| G-1117 | Kahler, J. | **Rubber Dolly** |
1968
| G-1130 | Flair, T. | **Psychic Passion** |

Puffin See PENGUIN BOOKS LTD.

G. PUTNAM'S SONS, London, England.
G. Putnam's
1930
| — | Britton, L. | **Brain** |

PYRAMID PUBLICATIONS INC., New York, N.Y., U.S.A.
Serial codes: G- 35¢; F- 40¢; R- 50¢; X- 60¢; T- 75¢.
Pyramid
1950
| 19 | Collins, W. W. | **The Moonstone** |
1953
| G88 | Collins, W. W. | **The Moonstone** |
1956
| G184 | Sturgeon, T. | **A Way Home** |
| G214 | Hunter, E. | **Tomorrow and Tomorrow** |
1957
G234	Greenberg, M.	**Men Against the Stars**
G247	Sturgeon, T.	**The Synthetic Man**
R290	Shelley, M. W.	**Frankenstein**
G298	Smith, G. O.	**Hellflower**
1958
PR11	Collins, W. W.	**The Moonstone**
PG13	Frazee, S.	**The Sky Block**
G332	Smith, Edward E.	**The Skylark of Space**
G339	Budrys, A.	**Who?**
1959
PR15	Doyle, A. C.	**The Lost World**
G397	Merril, J.	**Off the Beaten Orbit**
G416	Budrys, A.	**The Falling Torch**
R419	Fisher, V.	**The Divine Passion**
G434	Conklin, G.	**Four for the Future**
G438	Nathan, R.	**So Love Returns**
G458	Evans, E. E.	**Man of Many Minds**
1960
R472	Fisher, V.	**The Golden Rooms**
G480	Godwin, T.	**Space Prison**
G499	Merril, J.	**Out of Bounds**
G502	Merril, J.	**The Tomorrow People**
G514	Doyle, A. C.	**The Lost World**
R527	Fisher, V.	**The Darkness and the Deep**
G530	de Camp, L. S., & Pratt, F.	
		The Incomplete Enchanter
G544	Sturgeon, T.	**Venus Plus X**
G554	Clarke, A. C.	**Against the Fall of Night**
G584	Wilde, O.	**The Picture of Dorian Grey**
1961
G579	Rohmer, S.	**The Insidious Dr. Fu Manchu**
G590	Margulies, L.	**The Unexpected**
G615	Anderson, P.	**Orbit Unlimited**
G622	Sturgeon, T.	**Voyage to the Bottom of the Sea**
G624	Tabori, P.	**The Green Rain**

R628	Fisher, V.	**The Divine Passion**
R630	Smith, T.	**The Night Life of the Gods**
G636	Sturgeon, T.	**The Synthetic Man**
G641	Rohmer, S.	**The Return of Dr. Fu Manchu**
G642	Heinlein, R. A.	**6 X H**
R654	Hunter, E.	**Tomorrow and Tomorrow**
R657	Fisher, V.	**The Intimations of Eve**
G658	Gallun, R. Z.	**The Planet Strappers**
G665	Margulies, L.	**The Ghoul Keepers**
F672	Harrison, H.	**The Stainless Steel Rat**
F673	Sturgeon, T.	**A Way Home**
R677	Fisher, V.	**Adam and the Serpent**
F682	Dickson, G. R.	**Naked to the Stars**
F683	Merril, J.	**Off the Beaten Orbit**
F688	Rohmer, S.	**The Hand of Fu Manchu**
F693	Budrys, A.	**The Falling Torch**
1962
X696	Fisher, V.	**The Golden Rooms**
F698	Hamilton, E.	**The Haunted Stars**
F703	Cogswell, T. R.	**The Wall Around the World**
F713	Doyle, A. C.	**The Lost World**
F722	de Camp, L. S., & Pratt, F.	
		The Castle of Iron
F723	de Camp, L. S., & Pratt, F.	
		The Incomplete Enchanter
F728	Smith, T.	**Topper Takes a Trip**
F732	Sturgeon, T.	**Venus Plus X**
F733	Conklin, G.	**Worlds of When**
R738	Fisher, V.	**Darkness and the Deep**
F740	Rohmer, S.	**The Mask of Fu Manchu**
F742	Long, F. B.	**Mars Is My Destination**
F743	Conklin, G.	**Four for the Future**
F753	Verne, J.	**Five Weeks in a Balloon**
F754	Clarke, A. C.	**Against the Fall of Night**
F761	Rohmer, S.	**The Bride of Fu Manchu**
F763	McLaughlin, D.	**Dome World**
F764	Smith, Edward E.	**The Skylark of Space**
F771	Harrison, H.	**The War With the Robots**
R772	Nathan, R.	**So Love Returns**
F774	Godwin, T.	**Space Prison**
F783	Phillips, M.	**Brain Twister**
F784	Asimov, I.	**The Caves of Steel**
F786	Clement, H.	**Mission of Gravity**
F794	Fyfe, H. B.	**D-99**
F795	Margulies, L.	**The Unexpected**
F804	Rohmer, S.	**The Drums of Fu Manchu**
F805	Moore, W., & Davidson, A.	
		Joyleg
F806	Merril, J.	**The Tomorrow People**
1963
F817	de Camp, L. S.	**Lest Darkness Fall**
F818	Anderson, P.	**Orbit Unlimited**
F829	Brunner, J.	**The Dreaming Earth**
F830	Merril, J.	**Out of Bounds**
F837	Rohmer, S.	**Shadow of Fu Manchu**
F839	Bloch, R.	**Bogey Men**
F840	Janifer, L. M.	**Slave Planet**
X845	Fisher, V.	**The Divine Passion**
F851	Benson, D. R.	**The Unknown**
F852	Greenberg, M.	**Men Against the Stars**
F856	Pratt, T.	**The White God**
F858	Rohmer, S.	**The Island of Fu Manchu**
F859	Heinlein, R. A.	**Waldo and Magic Inc.**
F862	Russell, E. F.	**The Great Explosion**
F875	Phillips, M.	**The Impossibles**
F886	Reynolds, M.	**The Earth War**
F898	McIntosh, J. T.	**The Million Cities**
F899	Margulies, L.	**Three in One**
F908	Rohmer, S.	**The Insidious Dr. Fu-Manchu**
F909	Phillips, M.	**Supermind**
F910	Heinlein, R. A.	**6 X H**
F923	McLaughlin, D.	**The Fury From Earth**

F924	Smith, Edward E.	Skylark Three
F933	Nourse, A. E.	Raiders From the Rings
F941	Jones, R. F.	Man of Two Worlds
F946	Rohmer, S.	President Fu-Manchu
F948	Smith, Edward E.	Skylark of Valeron
F950	de Camp, L. S.	Swords and Sorcery
R950	de Camp, L. S.	Swords and Sorcery
1964		
R962	Benson, D. R.	The Unknown Five
F963	Janifer, L. M.	The Wonder War
R963	Janifer, L. M.	The Wonder War
F973	Conklin, G.	Dimension 4
F974	Sturgeon, T.	Sturgeon in Orbit
F986	Silverberg, R.	Regan's Planet
F987	Leinster, M.	Doctor to the Stars
R993	Godwin, T.	The Space Barbarians
R994	Anderson, P.	Three Worlds to Conquer
R1003	Rohmer, S.	The Trail of Fu Manchu
X1005	Conrad, E.	The Premier
F1015	Anderson, C., & Kurland, M.	
		Ten Years to Doomsday
R1015	Anderson, C., & Kurland, M.	
		Ten Years to Doomsday
F1028	Budrys, A.	The Falling Torch
R1028	Budrys, A.	The Falling Torch
R1029	Margulies, L.	Weird Tales
R1032	Rohmer, S.	Daughter of Fu Manchu
R1042	Finney, C. G.	The Ghosts of Manacle
R1043	Leinster, M.	Time Tunnel
R1055	Farmer, P. J.	Tongues of the Moon
R1056	Conklin, G.	Five—Odd
R1068	Sturgeon, T.	Voyage to the Bottom of the Sea
R1069	Davidson, A.	Mutiny in Space
R1084	Smith, Cordwainer	The Planet Buyer
F1101	Hirsch, P.	Ghoul Days
R1103	Smith, Edward E.	Galactic Patrol
R1114	Smith, Edward E.	First Lensman
1965		
WS3	Nourse, A. E.	Nine Planets
R738	Fisher, V.	Darkness and the Deep
R883	Fisher, V.	The Intimations of Eve
R1125	Margulies, L.	Worlds of Weird
R1126	Sturgeon, T.	The Synthetic Man
R1139	Bloch, R.	Tales in a Jugular Vein
R1140	Vance, J.	Space Opera
R1152	Tabori, P.	The Green Rain
R1162	Fairman, P. W.	City Under the Sea
R1170	Hunter, E.	Tomorrow and Tomorrow
R1183	Smith, Cordwainer	Space Lords
R1190	Daniels, N. A.	Spy Ghost
R1192	de Camp, L. S.	The Spell of Seven
R1208	Davidson, A.	Masters of the Maze
R1210	Margulies, L.	The Ghoul Keepers
R1212	Shelley, M. W.	Frankenstein
R1213	Stoker, B.	Dracula
T1215	Kirst, H. H.	The Seventh Day
R1222	Smith, Edward E.	Triplanetary
R1227	Santesson, H. S.	Rulers of Men
R1229	Sharkey, J.	The Addams Family
R1245	Smith, Edward E.	Gray Lensman
X1245	Smith, Edward E.	Gray Lensman
R1247	Bloch, R.	The Skull of the Marquis de Sade
R1262	Smith, Edward E.	Second Stage Lensmen
R1270	Ellison, H.	Paingod and Other Delusions
R1301	Rohmer, S.	The Insidious Dr. Fu-Manchu
R1302	Rohmer, S.	The Return of Dr. Fu Manchu
1966		
R1283	Asimov, I.	The Rest of the Robots
X1286	Heinlein, R. A.	Waldo and Magic Inc.
X1294	Smith, Edward E.	Children of the Lens
R1299	Phillips, M.	The Impossibles
R1303	Rohmer, S.	The Mask of Fu Manchu
R1304	Rohmer, S.	Shadow of Dr. Fu Manchu
R1305	Rohmer, S.	The Island of Fu Manchu
R1306	Rohmer, S.	The Hand of Fu Manchu
R1307	Rohmer, S.	The Drums of Fu Manchu
R1308	Rohmer, S.	The Trail of Fu Manchu
R1310	Rohmer, S.	Emperor Fu Manchu
R1313	Rohmer, S.	The Quest of the Sacred Slipper
R1314	Rohmer, S.	Brood of the Witch Queen
R1315	Rohmer, S.	The Golden Scorpion
R1316	Rohmer, S.	The Dream Detective
R1317	Rohmer, S.	The Yellow Claw
S1346	Graves, R.	Hercules, My Shipmate
X1350	Smith, Edward E.	The Skylark of Space
R1401	Haggard, H. R.	King Solomon's Mines
X1402	Collins, W. W.	The Moonstone
X1403	Haggard, H. R.	She
X1455	Smith, Edward E.	Triplanetary
X1456	Smith, Edward E.	First Lensman
X1457	Smith, Edward E.	Galactic Patrol
X1458	Smith, Edward E.	Skylark of Valeron
X1459	Smith, Edward E.	Skylark Three
R1498	Lee, C.	Christopher's Lee Treasury of Terror
X1539	Smith, Edward E.	Skylark DuQuesne
X1543	Sturgeon, T.	Starshine
1967		
R1068	Sturgeon, T.	Voyage to the Bottom of the Sea
X1245	Smith, Edward E.	Gray Lensman
X1262	Smith, Edward E.	Second Stage Lensmen
X1294	Smith, Edward E.	Children of the Lens
X1456	Smith, Edward E.	First Lensman
X1457	Smith, Edward E.	Galactic Patrol
R1522	Leinster, M.	Time Tunnel
R1569	Dick, P. K.	The Zap Gun
X1576	Williamson, J.	The Legion of Space
X1586	Williamson, J.	The Legion of Time
X1611	Ellison, H.	I Have No Mouth and I Must Scream
R1621	de Camp, L. S.	The Fantastic Swordsmen
T1630	Menger, H.	From Outer Space
X1634	Williamson, J.	The Cometeers
T1647	Michel, A.	The Truth About Flying Saucers
T1651	Wilkins, H. T.	Flying Saucers Uncensored
X1657	Williamson, J.	One Against the Legion
R1664	Laumer, K.	The Invaders
X1679	Van Arnam, D., & Archer, R.	
		Lost in Space
R1680	Leinster, M.	Timeslip!
X1681	Boucher, A.	Rocket to the Morgue
X1689	Laumer, K.	Enemies From Beyond
X1691	Sturgeon, T.	The Synthetic Man
T1692	Sanderson, I. T.	Things
X1693	Runyon, P.	Commando X
X1698	Stout, R.	The President Vanishes
X1703	Clarke, A. C.	Against the Fall of Night
R1711	Bernard, R.	Army of the Undead
T1724	Smith, G. O.	Venus Equilateral
X1728	Tabori, P.	The Invisible Eye
X1730	Anderson, C.	The Butterfly Kid
1968		
X1262	Smith, Edward E.	Second Stage Lensmen
X1350	Smith, Edward E.	The Skylark of Space
X1739	Sturgeon, T.	A Way Home
X1758	Heinlein, R. A.	Waldo and Magic Inc.
X1773	Sturgeon, T.	Venus Plus X
X1774	Rohmer, S.	Re-Enter Fu Manchu
R1783	Asimov, I.	The Rest of the Robots
X1787	White, T., & Van Arnam, D.	
		Sideslip
X1798	Thom, R.	Wild in the Streets
X1802	Merril, J.	The Tomorrow People
X1818	Finney, C. G.	The Unholy City & Magician out of Manchuria
X1824	Asimov, I.	The Caves of Steel

X1837	Budrys, A.	**The Falling Torch**
X1846	Leinster, M.	**Land of the Giants**
X1851	Smith, Edward E.	**Masters of the Vortex**
X1875	Anderson, P.	**Three Worlds to Conquer**
T1887	Kirst, H. H.	**The Seventh Day**
X1890	Anthony, P.	**Sos, the Rope**
X1891	Evans, E. E.	**Man of Many Minds**
X1898	Harrison, H.	**War With the Robots**
X1910	Smith, Cordwainer	**The Underpeople**
X1911	Smith, Cordwainer	**Space Lords**
T1927	de Camp, L. S.	**The Goblin Tower**
X1928	de Camp, L. S., & Pratt, F.	
		The Incomplete Enchanter
X1937	Crispin, E.	**Buried for Pleasure**
X1976	Kurland, M.	**Mission: Tank War**

Q,R

QUINN PUB. CO. INC., Kingston, N.Y., U.S.A.
H = HandiBook Mystery.
Quinn
1943

H13	Sale, R.	**Lazarus Number Seven**

1945

H34	Chambers, D.	**The Last Secret**

1947

H62	Jenkins, W. F.	**The Murder of the U.S.A.**

1957

nn	Quinn, J. L.	**The First World of If**

1958

nn	Quinn, J. L.	**The Second World of If**

RANDOM HOUSE, New York, U.S.A.
Imprints: **Vintage Books**, a division of Random House, also co-published by Alfred A. Knopf, New York, another division of Random House; **College**: Modern Library College Editions.
Vintage
1958

K56	Graves, R.	**The White Goddess**

1959

K79	Bowen, E.	**Stories by Elizabeth Bowen**

1960

V140	Cerf, B.	**Famous Ghost Stories**

1965

V294	Bradbury, R.	**The Vintage Bradbury**

1966

V326	Cerf, C.	**The Vintage Anthology of Science Fantasy**

College
1968

T92	Swift, J.	**Gulliver's Travels**
T96	Johnson, J. W.	**Utopian Literature: A Selection**

C. A. RANSOM, London, England.
Ransom
1929

—	Burroughs, E. R.	**Son of Tarzan**

READERS' LIBRARY PUBLISHING CO. LTD., London, England.
Readers' Library
1946?

—	Houghton, C.	**The Passing of the Third Floor Back**

REGAL BOOKS, Manchester, England.
Regal
1953

101	Wright, S. F.	**The Island of Captain Sparrow**
102	Wright, S. F.	**The Screaming Lake**

REGENCY BOOKS, Evanston, Illinois, U.S.A. The publisher, W. L. Hamling, later moved to San Diego and established GREENLEAF CLASSICS, *q.v.*
Regency
1961

RB101	Bloch, R.	**Firebug**
RB110	Budrys, A.	**Some Will Not Die**
RB113	del Rey, L.	**The Eleventh Commandment**

1963

RB309	Smith, Cordwainer	**You Will Never Be the Same**
RB311	Webb, J.	**The Gilded Witch**

REGENCY PRESS, London, England.
Regency (Brit.)
1950's?

—	T., M.	**Venus Speaks**
	Howard, D.	**My Flight to Venus**

REGULAR PUBLICATIONS, England.
Regular
Not dated

	Borodin, G.	**Threatened People**

RIDER, London, England.
Rider
1954

	Stoker, B.	**Dracula**

ROBERTS & VINTER LTD., London, England.
Compact
1965

F266	Moorcock, M.	**The Sundered Worlds**
F273	High, P. E.	**The Prodigal Sun**
F275	Bradbury, E. P.	**Warriors of Mars**
F277	Bulmer, K.	**The Demons**
F279	Bradbury, E. P.	**Blades of Mars**
F281	Moorcock, M.	**The Fireclown**
H287	Moorcock, M.	**The Best of New Worlds**
F291	Bradbury, E. P.	**Barbarians of Mars**

1966

F293	Wright, L.	**The Creeping Shroud**
F295	Harness, C. L.	**The Rose**
F299	Morgan, D.	**The Richest Corpse in Show Business**
F302	Sellings, A.	**Time Transfer**
F305	Colvin, J.	**The Deep Fix**
F308	Harker, K.	**The Symmetrians**
F311	de Camp, L. S.	**A Planet Named Krishna**
F313	Moorcock, M.	**The Twilight Man**
F317	Brunner, J.	**No Other Gods But Me**
F321	de Camp, L. S.	**The Floating Continent**
H324	Moorcock, M.	**SF Reprise 2**
H325	Bonfiglioli, K.	**SF Reprise 3**
F325	Merril, J.	**Shadow on the Hearth**

1967

H326	Bonfiglioli, K.	**SF Reprise 4**
F327	Disch, T. M.	**One Hundred and Two H-Bombs**
H329	Moorcock, M.	**SF Reprise 5**
H331	Bonfiglioli, K.	**SF Reprise 6**

ROBERTSON & MULLEN, Melbourne, Victoria, Australia.
Robertson & Mullen
1939

—	Cox, E.	**Fool's Harvest**

GEORGE ROUTLEDGE & SONS, England.
Routledge
1904
—   Bellamy, E.   **Looking Backward**

ROWE, PETERSEN & CO., Evanston, Illinois, U.S.A.
Rowe
Not dated
—   Parker, B. M.   **Beyond the Solar System**

Royal Giant See UNIVERSAL PUBLISHING

S

SAGAMORE, U.S.A.
Sagamore
1957
S16   Howells, W. D.   **A Traveler From Altruria**

SAINT ENTERPRISES, U.S.A.
Saint Enterprises
1946
22   Kline, O. A.   **The Man Who Limped**

SANDPIPER PRESS, New York, N.Y., U.S.A.
Comet
1948
12   Household, G.   **The Spanish Cave**

Satellite See JUBILEE PUBLICATIONS

SCHOCKEN, U.S.A.
Schocken
1968
Sb172   Kafka, F.   **The Metamorphosis**

SCHOLASTIC LIBRARY EDITION, U.S.A.
Scholastic
1958
TX158   Williams, J., & Abrashkin, R.
         Danny Dunn and the Anti-Gravity Paint
1960
TX232   Kramer, N.   **The Arrow Book of Ghost Stories**
1961
TX101   MacGregor, E.   **Miss Pickerell Goes to Mars**
T250   Verne, J.   **The Mysterious Island**
T290   Poe, E. A.   **Eight Tales of Terror**
TX306   Butterworth, O.   **The Enormous Egg**
1962
T210   Poe, E. A.   **Ten Great Mysteries**
TX235   Lang, A.   **Tales From the Red Fairy Book**
TX409   Lampman, E. S.   **The Shy Stegosaurus of Cricket Creek**
T430   Verne, J.   **Twenty Thousand Leagues Under the Sea**
1963
TX303   Williams, J., & Abrashkin, R.
         Danny Dunn and the Homework Machine
T487   Anonymous   **Stories of Suspense**
TX519   Cockrell, M.   **Shadow Castle**
T550   Stevenson, R. L.   **Dr. Jekyll and Mr. Hyde**
1964
TX301   MacGregor, E.   **Miss Pickerell Goes Undersea**
TX331   Preston, E. M.   **The Arrow Book of Spooky Stories**
TX517   Gunther, J.   **Jason and the Golden Fleece**
T530   Wells, H. G.   **The Time Machine and Other Stories**
TX535   Silverberg, R.   **Lost Race of Mars**

T540   Wells, H. G.   **The Invisible Man**
T625   Nourse, A. E.   **Star Surgeon**
1965
T599   Saki   **Humor, Horror and the Supernatural**
TX752   Verrall, T. S.   **Rocket Genius**
1966
TX250   Verne, J.   **The Mysterious Island**
T388   Kjelgaard, J.   **Fire-Hunter**
TX533   Emerson, C. D.   **The Magic Tunnel**
T573   Hurley, R. J.   **Beyond Belief**
T618   Verne, J.   **A Journey to the Center of the Earth**
T619   Verne, J.   **From the Earth to the Moon**
TX863   del Rey, L.   **The Runaway Robot**
TX875   Littledale, F.   **13 Ghostly Tales**
TX913   Cameron, E.   **The Wonderful Flight to the Mushroom Planet**
TX959   Dickson, G. R.   **Secret Under the Sea**
1967
TX219   Coolidge, O. E.   **Hercules and Other Tales From Greek Myths**
TX250   Verne, J.   **The Mysterious Island**
T430   Verne, J.   **Twenty Thousand Leagues Under the Sea**
TK650   James, H.   **The Turn of the Screw**
TX757   Asimov, I.   **Environments Out There**
T896   Owen, B. M.   **Stories of the Supernatural**
TX918   Norton, Andre   **Gray Magic**
T941   Nourse, A. E.   **The Counterfeit Man**
TX1001   Little, J.   **Spook**
TX1065   del Rey, L.   **Tunnel Through Time**
TX1111   Griffen, E. L.   **The Shaggy Dog**
T1112   Snyder, Z. K.   **Black and Blue Magic**
TW1145   Rinkoff, B.   **The Dragon's Handbook**
TW1158   Peterson, J.   **The Littles**
1968
TX163   Baum, L. F.   **The Wizard of Oz**
TK700   Hawthorne, N.   **The Birthmark and Other Stories**
TX791   Key, A.   **The Forgotten Door**
T838   Born, F.   **Jules Verne: The Man Who Invented the Future**
TK1056   Brondfield, J.   **Night in Funland**
TK1115   Stahl, B.   **Blackbeard's Ghost**
TX1119   Kassirer, N.   **Magic Elizabeth**
TK1172   Shute, N.   **On the Beach**
TX1229   Williams, U. M.   **The Moonball**
TK1248   Davies, L. P.   **The Artificial Man**
TX1276   Rinkoff, B.   **Elbert the Mind Reader**
TX1308   Kedabra, A.   **Nine Witch Tales**

SCION LTD., London, England.
    Understood to have gone bankrupt and been briefly succeeded by DRAGON PRESS, *q.v.*
    The titles by Vargo Statten are given below in order of appearance.
Scion
1949
—   Fearn, J. R.   **Operation Venus**
1950
—   Statten, V.   **Annihilation!**
—   Statten, V.   **The Micro Men**
—   Statten, V.   **Wanderer of Space**
—   Statten, V.   **2000 Years On**
—   Statten, V.   **Inferno!**
—   Statten, V.   **The Cosmic Flame**
—   Statten, V.   **Nebula X**
—   Statten, V.   **The Sun Makers**
1951
—   Brede, A.   **Sister Earth**
—   Norwood, V.   **The Caves of Death**
—   Norwood, V.   **The Skull of Kanaima**
—   Norwood, V.   **The Temple of the Dead**
—   Norwood, V.   **The Untamed**
—   Statten, V.   **The Avenging Martian**
—   Statten, V.   **Cataclysm**

—	Statten, V.	**The Red Insects**
—	Statten, V.	**Deadline to Pluto**
—	Statten, V.	**The Petrified Planet**
—	Statten, V.	**Born of Luna**
—	Statten, V.	**The Devouring Fire**
—	Statten, V.	**The New Satellite**
—	Statten, V.	**The Catalyst**
—	Titan, E.	**The Gold of Akada**
—	Titan, E.	**Anjani the Mighty**

1952

—	Harkon, F.	**Spawn of Space**
—	Gridban, V.	**Alien Universe**
—	Gridban, V.	**Reverse Universe**
—	Norwood, V.	**The Island of Creeping Death**
—	Statten, V.	**The Renegade Star**
—	Statten, V.	**The Inner Cosmos**
—	Statten, V.	**Man From Tomorrow**
—	Statten, V.	**The Space Warp**
—	Statten, V.	**The Eclipse Express**
—	Statten, V.	**The G-Bomb**
—	Statten, V.	**The Time Bridge**
—	Statten, V.	**Laughter in Space**
—	Statten, V.	**Across the Ages**
—	Statten, V.	**Decreation**
—	Statten, V.	**The Last Martian**
—	Statten, V.	**Worlds to Conquer**
—	Statten, V.	**The Time Trap**
—	Statten, V.	**Science Metropolis**
—	Statten, V.	**To the Ultimate**

1953

—	Gridban, V.	**De Bracy's Drug**
—	Gridban, V.	**Moons for Sale**
—	Gridban, V.	**A Thing of the Past**
—	Gridban, V.	**The Dyno-Depressant**
—	Gridban, V.	**Magnetic Brain**
—	Gridban, V.	**Exit Life**
—	Gridban, V.	**Scourge of the Atom**
—	Gridban, V.	**The Purple Wizard**
—	Gridban, V.	**The Master Must Die**
—	Magroon, V.	**The Burning Void**
—	Norwood, V.	**Cry of the Beast**
—	Norwood, V.	**Drums Along the Amazon**
—	Statten, V.	**Ultra Spectrum**
—	Statten, V.	**Black-Wing of Mars**
—	Statten, V.	**The Dust Destroyer**
—	Statten, V.	**The Lie Destroyer**
—	Statten, V.	**Man in Duplicate**
—	Statten, V.	**Zero Hour**
—	Statten, V.	**The Black Avengers**
—	Statten, V.	**The Interloper**
—	Statten, V.	**Odyssey of Nine**
—	Statten, V.	**Pioneer 1990**
—	Statten, V.	**Black Bargain**
—	Statten, V.	**Man of Two Worlds**
—	Statten, V.	**The Grand Illusion**

1954

—	Gridban, V.	**The Genial Dinosaur**
—	Gridban, V.	**The Frozen Limit**
—	Gridban, V.	**The Lonely Astronomer**
—	Gridban, V.	**I Came—I Saw—I Wondered**
—	Statten, V.	**Wealth of the Void**
—	Statten, V.	**A Time Appointed**
—	Statten, V.	**The Multi-Man**
—	Statten, V.	**I Spy**
—	Tubb, E. C.	**City of No Return**
—	Tubb, E. C.	**Journey to Mars**
—	Tubb, E. C.	**Hell Planet**
—	Tubb, E. C.	**The Resurrected Man**
—	Tubb, E. C.	**The Stellar Legion**

SCORPION BOOKS, U.S.A.
Scorpion
1964

104	English, C.	**Lovers: 2075**

Scottie See TRANSWORLD PUBLISHERS

CHARLES SCRIBNER'S SONS, New York, N.Y., U.S.A.
Scribner
1962

SL67	Heinlein, R. A.	**Between Planets**

1964

SL100	Heinlein, R. A.	**The Red Planet**

SCRIPTS PTY. LTD., North Sydney, N.S.W., Australia.
Scripts
1967

PB40	Holledge, J.	**Black Magic**
PB316	Tambling, R.	**Flying Saucers: Where Do They Come From?**

1968

PB366	Macaulay, K.	**The Nuclear Nazis**
PB376	Berkley, T.	**Legend of the Holocaust**

(EDWIN) SELF & CO. LTD., London, England.
Additional imprint: **Pedigree**.
Edw. Self
1952

—	Browne, G. S.	**Destination Mars**
—	Browne, G. S.	**The Planetoid Peril**
—	Kennedy, E. R.	**The Mystery Planet**

Not dated (1952-53)

7	Kennedy, E. R.	**Conquerors of Venus**
—	Van Loden, E.	**Curse of Planet Kuz**

1954

—	Browne, G. S.	**The Yellow Planet**
—	Van Loden, E.	**Voyage Into Space**

Pedigree
1957

—	Merritt, A.	**Burn, Witch, Burn!**

1958

—	Michelet, J.	**Satanism and Witchcraft**

1959

—	Stevenson, R. L.	**Dr. Jekyll and Mr. Hyde**
—	Verissimo, E.	**Night**

1960

—	Rhodes, H. T. F.	**The Satanic Mass**
—	Gardner, G. B.	**Witchcraft Today**
—	Hole, C.	**A Mirror of Witchcraft**
—	Verner, G.	**Prince of Darkness**

SEMAPHORE. U.S. publisher.
Semaphore
1968

22484	Williamson, J.	**Trapped in Space**

SENTINEL PUBLICATIONS, London, England.
Sentinel
1947

—	Miller, S.	**H for Horrific**

Sentry See HOUGHTON MIFFLIN CO.

SEVEN SEAS BOOKS, Berlin, Germany.
Books in English.
Seven Seas
1959

—	Lieber, M.	**Ghosts, Ghouls and Other Nuisances**

1966

—	Pankey, K.	**Spooks in Your Cupboard**

SEXTON BLAKE LIBRARY. British series.
Sexton Blake Lib.
1960
457   Reid, D.   **The World Shakers**

SHROUD PUBLISHERS, Buffalo, New York, U.S.A.
Shroud
1954
—   Chambers, R. W.   **The Maker of Dreams**
—   Burks, A. J.   **Look Behind You**
1955
—   Lovecraft, H. P.   **The Dream Quest of Unknown Kadath**
—   McDougle, W.   **The Female Demon**
1965
—   Kinross, A.   **The Fearsome Island**

Signet See NEW AMERICAN LIBRARY

SIMON & SCHUSTER, New York, N.Y., U.S.A.
    This firm also published Walt Kelly's *Pogo* series [not listed].
Simon Schuster
1930
—   Moxley, F. W.   **Red Snow**
1958
—   Winsor, F.   **The Space Child's Mother Goose**
1961
—   Szilard, L.   **The Voice of the Dolphins and Other Stories**
1962
—   Fadiman, C.   **Fantasia Mathematica**
1963
—   Fadiman, C.   **The Mathematical Magpie**
1968
—   Hoyle, F.   **Encounter With the Future**

(URE) SMITH PTY. LTD., Sydney, N.S.W., Australia.
Humorbooks
1966
H29   Smith, K.   **Ogf**
1968
H47   Saki   **The Best of Saki**

Softcover See UNIVERSAL PUBLISHING CO.

SPACE AGE PRESS, Fort Worth, Texas, U.S.A.
Space Age
1967
—   Dring, N.   **The Earth Is Your Spaceship**

JOHN SPENCER & CO. (PUBLISHERS) LTD., London, England.
    Other imprints: **Badger SF** (fiction); **Badger SS** (Science Series, non-fiction); **Badger SN** (Supernatural); **Cobra** [see under **Badger SF**, 1957]. All Badger information copyright Robert Reginald.
Spencer
1953
—   La Salle, V.   **After the Atom**
—   La Salle, V.   **Assault From Infinity**
—   La Salle, V.   **The Black Sphere**
—   La Salle, V.   **Dawn of the Half-Gods**
—   La Salle, V.   **The Seventh Dimension**
—   La Salle, V.   **Suns in Duo**
—   Zeigfreid, K.   **Beyond the Galaxy**
—   Zeigfreid, K.   **Chaos in Arcturus**
—   Zeigfreid, K.   **Chariot Into Time**
—   Zeigfreid, K.   **The Uranium Seekers**
1954
—   La Salle, V.   **Menace From Mercury**
—   La Salle, V.   **Twilight Zone**
—   Zeigfreid, K.   **Dark Centauri**

Badger SF
1957
SS1   Bowers, R. L.   **This Second Earth**
    [Labelled "Science Series No. 1" and the only book in the SF series to bear the Cobra imprint.]
1958
SF1   Fanthorpe, R. L.   **The Waiting World**
SF2   Maxwell, J. C.   **The World Makers**
SF3   Fear, W. H.   **The Ultimate**
SF4   Williams, James   **Objective Venus**
SF5   Fear, W. H.   **Operation Satellite**
SF6   Dexter, J. B.   **The Time Kings**
SF7   Fear, W. H.   **Lunar Flight**
    [No SF8]
SF9   Fear, W. H.   **Return to Space**
SF10   Elton, James   **Quest of the Seeker**
SF11   Manning, P. L.   **The Destroyers**
1959
SF12   Charkin, P.   **Light of Mars**
SF13   La Salle, V.   **Twilight Zone**
SF14   Kenton, L. P.   **Destination Moon**
SF15   Fanthorpe, R. L.   **Alien From the Stars**
SF16   Merak, A. J.   **No Dawn and No Horizon**
SF17   Fanthorpe, R. L.   **Hyperspace**
SF18   Roberts, L.   **Dawn of the Mutants**
SF19   Merak, A. J.   **The Dark Millennium**
SF20   Fanthorpe, R. L.   **Space-Borne**
SF21   Chetwynd-Hayes, R. **The Man From the Bomb**
SF22   Fanthorpe, R. L.   **Fiends**
SF23   Roberts, L.   **Time Echo**
1960
SF24   Charkin, P.   **The Other Side of Night**
SF25   Fanthorpe, R. L.   **Doomed World**
SF26   Roberts, L.   **Cyclops in the Sky**
SF27   Fanthorpe, R. L.   **Satellite**
SF28   Budrys, A.   **Who?**
SF29   Merwin, S., Jr.   **Three Faces of Time**
SF30   Merak, A. J.   **Barrier Unknown**
SF31   Adam, J.   **When the Gods Came**
SF32   Powers, J. L.   **Black Abyss**
SF33   Leinster, M.   **The Brain Stealers**
SF34   Muller, J. E.   **Space Void**
SF35   Fanthorpe, R. L.   **Asteroid Man**
SF36   Merak, A. J.   **Hydrosphere**
SF37   Roberts, L.   **The In-World**
SF38   Thorpe, T.   **Lightning World**
SF39   Roberts, L.   **The Face of X**
SF40   Brett, L.   **Exit Humanity**
SF41   Fane, B.   **Juggernaut**
SF42   Torro, P.   **Frozen Planet**
SF43   Brett, L.   **The Microscopic Ones**
SF44   Fanthorpe, R. L.   **Hand of Doom**
SF45   Torro, P.   **World of the Gods**
SF46   Fane, B.   **Last Man on Earth**
SF47   Brett, L.   **The Faceless Planet**
1961
SF48   Muller, J. E.   **Search the Dark Stars**
SF49   Fanthorpe, R. L.   **Flame Mass**
SF50   Muller, J. E.   **A 1,000 Years On**
SF51   Muller, J. E.   **Day of the Beasts**
SF52   Roberts, L.   **The Synthetic Ones**
SF53   Brett, L.   **March of the Robots**
SF54   Brett, L.   **Mind Force**
SF55   Fane, B.   **Rodent Mutation**
SF56   Muller, J. E.   **The Ultimate Man**
SF57   Muller, J. E.   **The Uninvited**
SF58   Muller, J. E.   **The Mind Makers**
SF59   Wise, R. A.   **12 to the Moon**
SF60   Muller, J. E.   **Crimson Planet**
SF61   Muller, J. E.   **Alien**
SF62   Muller, J. E.   **The Venus Venture**
SF63   Muller, J. E.   **Forbidden Planet**

1962

SF64	Norwood, V.	**Night of the Black Horror**
SF65	Muller, J. E.	**Edge of Eternity**
SF66	Muller, J. E.	**Perilous Galaxy**
SF67	Muller, J. E.	**Uranium 235**
SF68	Muller, J. E.	**The Man Who Conquered Time**
SF69	Muller, J. E.	**Orbit One**
SF70	Muller, J. E.	**Micro Infinity**
SF71	Muller, J. E.	**Beyond Time**
SF72	Muller, J. E.	**Infinity Machine**
SF73	Muller, J. E.	**The Day the World Died**
SF74	Muller, J. E.	**The X-Machine**
SF75	Muller, J. E.	**Night of the Big Fire**
SF76	Muller, J. E.	**In the Beginning**
SF77	Fanthorpe, R. L.	**Space Fury**
SF78	Zeigfreid, K.	**Walk Through To-morrow**
SF79	Zeigfreid, K.	**Android**
SF80	Zeigfreid, K.	**Atomic Nemesis**
SF81	Zeigfreid, K.	**Zero Minus X**

1963

SF82	Zeigfreid, K.	**Escape to Infinity**
SF83	Zeigfreid, K.	**Radar Alert**
SF84	Zeigfreid, K.	**World of Tomorrow**
SF85	Zeigfreid, K.	**The World That Never Was**
SF86	Torro, P.	**Galaxy 666**
SF87	Torro, P.	**Formula 29X**
SF88	Fanthorpe, R. L.	**Negative Minus**
SF89	Fane, B.	**The Intruders**
SF90	Glynn, A. A.	**Plan for Conquest**
SF91	Torro, P.	**Through the Barrier**
SF92	Fane, B.	**Somewhere Out There**
SF93	Torro, P.	**The Last Astronaut**
SF94	Brett, L.	**The Alien Ones**
SF95	Brett, L.	**Power Sphere**
SF96	Muller, J. E.	**Reactor XK9**
SF97	Muller, J. E.	**Special Mission**

1964

SF98	Bell, T.	**Space Trap**
SF99	Barton, E.	**The Planet Seekers**
SF100	Fane, B.	**Nemesis**
SF101	Torro, P.	**The Return**
SF102	Fane, B.	**Suspension**
SF103	Zeigfreid, K.	**Projection Infinity**
SF104	Muller, J. E.	**Dark Continuum**
SF105	Muller, J. E.	**Mark of the Beast**
SF106	Torro, P.	**Space No Barrier**
SF107	Zeigfreid, K.	**No Way Back**

1965

SF108	Fanthorpe, R. L.	**Neuron World**
SF109	Muller, J. E.	**The Negative Ones**
SF110	Torro, P.	**Force 97X**
SF111	Muller, J. E.	**The Man From Beyond**
SF112	Muller, J. E.	**Beyond the Void**
SF113	Zeigfreid, K.	**Barrier 346**
SF114	Zeigfreid, K.	**Girl From Tomorrow**
SF115	Fane, B.	**U.F.O. 517**

1966

SF116	Muller, J. E.	**Phenomena X**
SF117	Muller, J. E.	**Survival Project**
SF118	Fanthorpe, R. L.	**Watching World**

Badger SS [Science Series, nonfiction]

1959

SS1	Vassiliev, M., & Dobronravow, V. V.	
		Sputnik Into Space
SS2	Coombs, C. I.	**Survival in the Sky**

1960

SS3	Barker, G.	**The Unidentified**

1962

SS4	Ley, W., & Von Braun, W.	
		Project Mars

Badger Supernatural

[Only the "novel" issues are listed in the *Author* and *Title* sections. Titles below in quotation marks are the principal story in the "magazine" issues. The "novel" issues began at No. 29, and were the even-numbered from No. 40. This series is considered as a magazine and is listed in the *Magazines* section.]

1954

SN1	Conway, R.	**"The Gods of Fear"**
SN2	Roberts, L.	**"The Incredulist"**
SN3	Cormic, R.	**"Something From the Sea"**
SN4	Merak, A. J.	**"House of Unreason"**

1955

SN5	Merak, A. J.	**"My Name Is Satan"**
SN6	Hamilton, M.	**"Voice of the Drum"**
SN7	Merak, A. J.	**"Moonbeast"**
SN8	Cosmic, R.	**"The Golden Scarab"**

1956

SN9	Stanton, J. S., & Richards, E. [credited to Stanton on cover, to Edwards within] **"The Devil's Dictionary"**	

1957 [First two may be 1956]

SN10	Conway, R.	**"Nightmare"**
SN11	Hamilton, M.	**"The Night Creatures"**
SN12	Fanthorpe, R. L.	**"Resurgam"**
SN13	Fanthorpe, R. L.	**"Secret of the Snows"**

1958

SN14	Fanthorpe, R. L.	**"The Flight of the Valkyries"**
SN15	Fanthorpe, R. L.	**"Watchers of the Forest"**
SN16	Roberts, L.	**"Guardians of the Tomb"**
SN17	Fanthorpe, R. L.	**"Call of the Werwolf"**
SN18	Merak, A. J.	**"The Chalice of Circe"**
SN19	Roberts, L.	**"The Golden Warrior"**
SN20	Fanthorpe, R. L.	**"The Death Note"**
SN21	Thorpe, T.	**"The Haunted Pool"**

1959

SN22	Conway, R.	**"Out of the Shadows"**
SN23	Fanthorpe, R. L.	**"Mermaid Reef"**
SN24	Brett, L.	**"The Druid"**
SN25	Brett, L.	**"The Return"**
SN26	Conway, R.	**"The Shadow of Terror"**
SN27	Fanthorpe, R. L.	**"The Ghost Rider"**
SN28	Hansby, J. J.	**"The Creature From the Depths"**
SN29	Merak, A. J.	**Dark Conflict**

1960

SN30	Fane, B.	**"The Crawling Fiend"**
SN31	Merak, A. J.	**"The Sorcerers of Bast"**
SN32	Thorpe, T.	**Five Faces of Fear**
SN33	Fanthorpe, R. L.	**"The Man Who Couldn't Die"**
SN34	Morton, J.	**"The Sea Thing"**
SN35	Fanthorpe, R. L.	**Out of the Darkness**
SN36	Fanthorpe, R. L.	**"Face of Evil"**
SN37	Fanthorpe, R. L.	**"Werewolf at Large"**
SN38	Fanthorpe, R. L.	**"Whirlwind of Death"**

1961

SN39	Thorpe, T.	**"Voodoo Hell Drums"**
SN40	Roberts, L.	**The Last Valkyrie**
SN41	Fanthorpe, R. L.	**"Fingers of Darkness"**
SN42	Muller, J. E.	**The Unpossessed**
SN43	Fanthorpe, R. L.	**"Face in the Dark"**
SN44	Brett, L.	**Black Infinity**
SN45	Merak, A. J.	**"Something About Spiders"**
SN46	Roberts, L.	**Flame Goddess**
SN47	Fanthorpe, R. L.	**"Devil From the Depths"**
SN48	Torro, P.	**The Phantom Ones**
SN49	Fanthorpe, R. L.	**"Centurion's Vengeance"**
SN50	Fanthorpe, R. L.	**The Golden Chalice**
SN51	Fanthorpe, R. L.	**"The Grip of Fear"**

1962

SN52	Muller, J. E.	**The Return of Zeus**
SN53	Fanthorpe, R. L.	**"Chariot of Apollo"**
SN54	Brett, L.	**Nightmare**
SN55	Fane, B.	**"Storm God's Fury"**
SN56	Muller, J. E.	**The Eye of Karnak**

SN57	Fanthorpe, R. L.	"Hell Has Wings"
SN58	Brett, L.	Face in the Night
SN59	Fanthorpe, R. L.	"Graveyard of the Damned"
SN60	Muller, J. E.	Vengeance of Siva
SN61	Fanthorpe, R. L.	"The Darker Drink"
SN62	Brett, L.	The Immortals
SN63	Merak, A. J.	"The Lonely Shadows"
SN64	Zeigfreid, K.	Gods of Darkness
SN65	Fanthorpe, R. L.	"Curse of the Totem"
SN66	Torro, P.	Legion of the Lost
SN67	Brett, L.	"The Frozen Tomb"

1963

SN68	Brett, L.	They Never Come Back
SN69	Fanthorpe, R. L.	"Goddess of the Night"
SN70	Torro, P.	The Strange Ones
SN71	Fanthorpe, R. L.	"Twilight Ancestor"
SN72	Brett, L.	The Forbidden
SN73	Fanthorpe, R. L.	"Sands of Eternity"
SN74	Brett, L.	From Realms Beyond
SN75	Brett, L.	"Phantom Crusader"
SN76	Torro, P.	The Timeless Ones
SN77	Fanthorpe, R. L.	"Moon Wolf"
SN78	Barton, L.	The Unseen
SN79	Merak, A. J.	"Howl at the Moon"
SN80	Fane, B.	Softly by Moonlight
SN81	Fane, B.	"The Thing From Sheol"
SN82	Torro, P.	The Face of Fear
SN83	Trent, O.	"Roman Twilight"

1964

SN84	Fane, B.	Unknown Destiny
SN85	Fanthorpe, R. L.	"Avenging Goddess"
SN86	Thanet, N.	Beyond the Veil
SN87	Fanthorpe, R. L.	"Death Has Two Faces"
SN88	Thanet, N.	The Man Who Came Back
SN89	Fanthorpe, R. L.	"The Shrouded Abbot"
SN90	Fane, B.	The Macabre Ones
SN91	Novel, P.	"The Hand From Gehenna"
SN92	Bell, T.	Chaos
SN93	Fane, B.	"The Walking Shadow"

1965

SN94	Muller, J. E.	The Exorcists
SN95	Fanthorpe, R. L.	"Bitter Reflection"
SN96	Fanthorpe, R. L.	The Triple Man
SN97	Fanthorpe, R. L.	"Call of the Wild"
SN98	Muller, J. E.	Spectre of Darkness
SN99	Fanthorpe, R. L.	"Vision of the Damned"
SN100	Muller, J. E.	Out of the Night
SN101	Fanthorpe, R. L.	"The Sealed Sarcophagus"

1966

SN102	Fanthorpe, R. L.	The Unconfined
SN103	Fanthorpe, R. L.	"Stranger in the Shadow"
SN104	Barton, L.	The Shadow Man
SN105	Fanthorpe, R. L.	"Curse of the Khan"
SN106	[Never issued]	
SN107	Conway, R.	"Body and Soul"

SPHERE BOOKS LIMITED, London, England.
Sphere
1966

| 37818 | Gaskell, J. | Atlan |

1967

10820	Aldiss, B. W.	The Primal Urge
28924	Derleth, A.	Far Boundaries
37435	Galouye, D. F.	Dark Universe
37818	Gaskell, J.	Atlan
37826	Gaskell, J.	The City
37834	Gaskell, J.	The Serpent
53031	Knight, D.	The Analogue Men
78417	Silverberg, R.	Needle in a Timestack
80098	Sohl, J.	The Odious Ones
80101	Sohl, J.	The Time Dissolver
82335	Sturgeon, T.	Some of Your Blood

| 83208 | Szilard, L. | The Voice of the Dolphins and Other Stories |

1968

10839	Aldiss, B. W.	The Saliva Tree
16071	Bester, A.	Starburst
16519	Biggle, L.	The Fury out of Time
19564	Dick, P. K.	Counter-Clock World
23973	Clarke, A. C.	Expedition to Earth
24562	Saxon, P.	Corruption
28835	Delany, S. R.	Out of the Dead City
28843	Delany, S. R.	The Towers of Toron
29564	Dick, P. K.	Counter-Clock World
37818	Gaskell, J.	Atlan
37826	Gaskell, J.	The City
43311	Harrison, H., & Aldiss, B. W.	Year's Best Science Fiction
45179	Herbert, F.	The Eyes of Heisenberg
53171	Kornbluth, C. M.	The Syndic
54798	Leinster, M.	Space Gypsies
54801	Leinster, M.	The Wailing Asteroid
54828	Leinster, M.	Miners in the Sky
74160	Robinson, F. M.	The Power
82244	Sturgeon, T.	Caviar
84425	Thom, R.	Wild in the Streets
86061	Tubb, E. C.	Ten From Tomorrow

SSSR PUBLICATIONS, Tonawanda, N.Y., U.S.A.
SSSR Pubs
1953

| — | Briney, R. E. | Shanadu |

STAPLES & STAPLES LTD., London, England.
Staples
1944

| — | Kersh, G. | The Battle of the Singing Men |

STELLAR PUBLISHING CORPORATION, New York, N.Y., U.S.A.

SFS = Science Fiction Series. SFC = Science Fiction Classic. Booklets 6 x 8 in., 24 pp., 10¢. Some have two stories; the second is denoted by "do" (ditto) instead of repeating the serial number.

Stellar
1929 (approx.)

| SFC1 | Smith, Garret | Between Worlds |

1929

SFS1	Williamson, J., & Breuer, M. J.	The Girl From Mars
SFS2	Keller, D. H.	The Thought Projector
SFS3	Michelmore, R.	An Adventure in Venus
SFS4	Stone, L. F.	When the Sun Went Out
SFS5	Lorraine, L.	The Brain of the Planet
SFS6	Colladay, M.	When the Moon Fell

1930

SFS7	Bourne, F.	The Thought Stealer
do	Long, A. R.	The Mechanical Man
SFS8	Bradley, J.	The Torch of Ra
SFS9	Eberle, M.	The Thought Translator
do	Mitchell, M.	The Creation
SFS10	Higginson, H. W.	The Elixir
SFS11	Black, P. E.	The Valley of the Great Ray
SFS12	Farrar, C.	The Life Vapor
do	Sharp, D. D.	Thirty Miles Down

1932

SFS13	Black, P. E.	The Men From the Meteor
SFS14	Renard, M.	The Flight of the Aerofix
SFS15	Wellman, M. W.	The Invading Asteroid
SFS16	Smith, C. A.	The Immortals of Mercury
SFS17	Mack, T.	The Spectre Bullet
do	Sprissler, A.	The Avenging Note
SFS18	Patzer, S.	The Ship From Nowhere
do	Gallun, R. Z.	The Moon Mirage

STREAMLINE PUBLICATIONS. No further information, but probably English.
Streamline
1950 (approx.)
| 1 | Desmond, H. | **A Pact With the Devil** |

STROTHERS. British publisher during World War II.
Strothers
Not dated
| — | Anonymous | **Third Finger—Left Hand and Other Thrilling Stories** |

Superior See MILITARY SERVICE PUBLISHING CO.

SUSPENSE. British publisher.
Suspense
1958
| J32 | Creasey, J. | **The Man Who Shook the World** |

GERALD G. SWAN, Marylebone, England.
Swan
Mid-1940's
—	Anonymous	**Occult: A Collection of the Supernatural**
—	Anonymous	**Occult Shorts: Second Selection**
—	Anonymous	**Weird Shorts: First Selection**
—	Anonymous	**The Moon Conquerors**
—	Cockcroft, W. P.	**They Come From Mars**
—	Elliott, G.	**The Case of the Missing Airman**
—	Hammond, K.	**The Dark City**
19	Hardy, P.	**Smith Minor on the Moon**
	(Schoolboys' Pocket Library series)	
26	Hardy, P.	**The Buried Country**
	(Schoolboys' Pocket Library series)	
1947
| — | Worts, G. F. | **The Monster of the Lagoon** |
1948
| — | Anonymous | **Four in One Weird and Occult Shorts** |
1952
| — | Burks, A. J. | **The Great Mirror** |
| — | Cummings, R. | **The Men on the Meteor** |
1960
| — | Anonymous | **Weird and Occult Miscellany** |

T

TAB BOOKS, affiliate of SCHOLASTIC MAGAZINES, New York, N.Y., U.S.A.
TAB
1959
| TX137 | Silverberg, R. | **Revolt on Alpha C** |
1960
| T210 | Poe, E. A. | **Ten Great Mysteries of Edgar Allan Poe** |
1962
| T210 | Poe, E. A. | **Ten Great Mysteries of Edgar Allan Poe** |
1963
| TX137 | Silverberg, R. | **Revolt on Alpha C** |

TANDEM BOOKS LTD., London, England.
Tandem
1964
| T2 | Birkin, C. | **The Kiss of Death** |
1965
T19	Bloch, R.	**The House of the Hatchet**
T25	Volta, O.	**The Vampire**
T28	Birkin, C.	**The Smell of Evil**
T30	Derleth, A.	**When Graveyards Yawn**
T35	Daraul, A.	**Witches and Sorcerers**
T47	Smith, T.	**The Jovial Ghosts**
T49	Birkin, C.	**The Tandem Book of Horror Stories**
T52	Birkin, C.	**The Tandem Book of Ghost Stories**
1966
T54	Smith, T.	**Turnabout**
T55	Burroughs, W. S.	**Dead Finger Talk**
T56	Lloyd, J.	**Tales From the Beyond**
T75	Campbell, J. W.	**The Thing From Outer Space**
T80	Birkin, C.	**Where Terror Stalked**
T93	Smith, T.	**The Passionate Witch**
1967
T2	Birkin, C.	**The Kiss of Death**
T88	del Rey, L.	**Mortals and Monsters**
T97	Smith, T.	**The Stray Lamb**
T107	Gordon, R.	**The Paw of God**
T114	Hurkos, P.	**Psychic**
T118	Anonymous	**The Mindworm**
T130	Santesson, H. S.	**Gods for Tomorrow**
T131	Gordon, F.	**Flight of the Bamboo Saucer**
T134	Steiger, B., & Whritenour, J.	
		Flying Saucers Are Hostile
T170	Wallace, C. H.	**Witchcraft in the World Today**
1968
T169	Boggon, M.	**The Inevitable Hour**
T182	B. Steiger	**Real Ghosts, Restless Spirits and Haunted Minds**
T198	Davis, R.	**Tandem Horror 2**
T199	Birkin, C.	**Dark Menace**
T200	Leinster, M.	**Operation Terror**
T201	Leinster, M.	**Invaders of Space**
T230	Steiger, B., & Whritenour, J.	
		New UFO Breakthrough
PB380	Janifer, L. M.	**Master's Choice 1**
PB381	Janifer, L. M.	**Master's Choice 2**
3455	Tabori, P.	**The Doomsday Brain**

TEMPEST PUB. CO., England.
Tempest
1950
| — | Rayer, F. G. | **Worlds at War** |

Tempo See GROSSET & DUNLAP

3-Star See (FREDERICK) WARNE & CO.

Three Star See NOVEL BOOKS INC.

THRILLER CLASSIC. English publisher.
Thriller Classic
1930's
| 4 | Rohmer, S. | **The Insidious Doctor Fu Manchu** |

Thriller Novel Classics (TNC) See HILLMAN BOOKS

TIME INCORPORATED, New York, N.Y., U.S.A.
Time Inc.
1963
| — | Bradbury, R. | **The Martian Chronicles** |
1964
| — | Marcellin, P. & P. T. | **The Beast of the Haitian Hills** |

Tit-Bits Science Fiction Library See PEARSON

TOBY PRESS, New York, U.S.A.
Toby
1953
| — | Vance, J. | **The Space Pirate** |

TODD PUBLISHING CO., London, England.
  Polybook and **Bantam** series.
Todd [Polybook]
Early 1940's

	Farjeon, J. J.	**The Invisible Companion**
	Le Fanu, J. S.	**Green Tea**
	Anonymous	**Peter Rugg, the Missing Man**
	Houghton, C.	**Three Fantastic Tales**
	Wells, H. G.	**The Country of the Blind**
	Wells, H. G.	**The Man Who Could Work Miracles**
	Wells, H. G.	**The Truth About Pyecraft**

Todd [Bantam]

	Houghton, C.	**The Man Who Could Still Laugh**
	Poe, E. A.	**The Black Cat**
	Wells, H. G.	**The Country of the Blind**
	Wells, H. G.	**The Empire of the Ants**
	Wells, H. G.	**The Land Ironclads**

TOP FICTION. No further information, but probably English.
Top Fiction
1953

1	Janson, H.	**The Unseen Assassin**

TOPLINER. English publisher.
Topliner
1968

02047	Chilton, I.	**String of Time**

TOWER PUBLICATIONS INC., New York, N.Y., U.S.A.
Tower
1965

	Jackson, S.	**The Bird's Nest**
43-461	Derleth, A.	**Time to Come**
43-503	van Vogt, A. E.	**The Mind Cage**
43-528	Moore, P.	**Once Upon a Friday**
43-531	Williamson, J.	**Dragon's Island**
43-571	Sinclair, D.	**The Project**

1966

43-620	Keel, J.	**Jadoo**
42-621	Vincent, H.	**The Doomsday Planet**

1967

43-762	Elg, S.	**Beyond Belief**
44-775	Jackson, S.	**The Bird's Nest**
43-776	van Vogt, A. E.	**The Mind Cage**
43-817	Barker, G.	**They Knew Too Much About Flying Saucers**
43-906	Moskowitz, S., & Elwood, R.	
		The Human Zero

1968

43-892	Tyler, S.	**Are the Invaders Coming?**
42-947	Vincent, H.	**The Doomsday Planet**
43-957	Williamson, J.	**The Not-Men**
43-970	Stoker, B.	**Dracula's Curse & The Jewel of Seven Stars**
43-986	Moskowitz, S., & Elwood, R.	
		The Time Curve
44-115	Davies, L. P.	**Psychogeist**

TRANSPORT PUBLISHING CO. PTY. LTD., Sydney, N.S.W., Australia. The firm absorbed Associated General Publications (which issued the two 1948 titles).
  Series: RR = Radio Record (last three had volume and number); ST = Scientific Thriller (unnumbered, issued monthly beginning Nov. 1948).
Transport
1942 (approx.)

RR	Russell, A.	**Crocodile City**

1943

RR5/64	Molesworth, V.	**Stratosphere Patrol**
RR6/18	Molesworth, V.	**Spaceward Ho!**

1944

RR6/37	Molesworth, V.	**The Three Rocketeers**

1948

—	Karlson, H.	**Atomic Death**
—	Ludwig, B.	**Jaws of Doom**

1949

ST	Valdez, P.	**Hypnotic Death**
ST	Hoffman, K.	**Blackmarket Brains**
ST	Kensch, O.	**Death Is a Habit**
ST	Herscholt, W.	**X-Ray Menace**
ST	Ludwig, B.	**The Whistle of Doom**
ST	Luigi, B.	**Death Has No Weight**
ST	Herscholt, W.	**Magnetic Peril**
ST	Kensch, O.	**Murder Has Wings**
ST	Luigi, B.	**Cosmic Calamity**
ST	Luigi, B.	**Lightning Crime**
ST	Herscholt, W.	**The Curse of Blood**
ST	Kensch, O.	**Time Has a Door**

1950

ST	Luigi, B.	**The Mummy Walks**
ST	Heinkel, S.	**King Rat**
ST	Luigi, B.	**Toppling Terror**
ST	Luigi, B.	**The Glowing Globe**
ST	Kensch, O.	**Image of Death**
ST	Luigi, B.	**Crime Flies**
ST	Kensch, O.	**Sleep Is Death**
ST	Luigi, B.	**The Master-Mind Menace**
ST	Luigi, B.	**The Curse of the Mummy**
ST	Luigi, B.	**Depths of Death**
ST	Valdez, P.	**The Fatal Focus**
ST	Luigi, B.	**The Lost Underworld**

1951

ST	Valdez, P.	**The Time Thief**
ST	Luigi, B.	**The Freezing Peril Strikes**
ST	Valdez, P.	**Flight Into Horror**
ST	Valdez, P.	**Murder Gives Notice**
ST	Glenning, R.	**Seven for Murder**
ST	Glenning, R.	**The Corpse Sat Up**
ST	Valdez, P.	**Killer by Night**
ST	Valdez, P.	**Ghosts Don't Kill**
ST	Valdez, P.	**Satan's Sabbath**
ST	Valdez, P.	**You Can't Keep Murder Out**
ST	Valdez, P.	**Kill Him Gently**
ST	Valdez, P.	**Celluloid Suicide**

1952

ST	Valdez, P.	**The Murder I Don't Remember**
ST	Valdez, P.	**There's No Future in Murder**
ST	Valdez, P.	**The Crook Who Wasn't There** [titled **The Killer** on cover]
ST	Valdez, P.	**Maniac Murders**
ST	Valdez, P.	**Feline Frame-Up**

TRANSWORLD PUBLISHERS LTD., London, England.
  Up to the mid-1950's many books were identical reprints of U.S. originals from Bantam Books Inc., for whom Transworld has often been the English distributor.
  Imprints: **Corgi**; **Scottie** [juvenile].
  Corgi serial price codes: T- 2/; SS- 2/6; SN- 2/6; YS- 3/; GN- 3/6; GS- 3/6.
Corgi
1952

819	Siodmak, C.	**Donovan's Brain**
1007	Cozzens, J. G.	**Castaway**

1953

915	Macardle, D.	**The Unforeseen**
1077	Brown, F.	**Space on My Hands**
T27	Cody, C. S.	**The Witching Night**

1954

T43	Clarke, A. C.	**The Sands of Mars**
T58	Hamilton, E.	**The City at World's End**

1955

1282	Bradbury, R.	**The Illustrated Man**

1956

886	Bradbury, R.	**The Silver Locusts**

1241	Bradbury, R.	**Golden Apples of the Sun**
1443	Stuart, W. J.	**Forbidden Planet**
G184	Stewart, G. R.	**Earth Abides**
T197	Matheson, R.	**I Am Legend**
1957		
T225	Wells, H. G.	**The First Men in the Moon**
T389	Bradbury, R.	**Fahrenheit 451**
S424	Russell, E. F.	**Men, Martians and Machines**
G443	Clarke, A. C.	**The City and the Stars**
S486	Dye, C.	**Prisoner in the Skull**
1958		
S520	Maine, C. E.	**Crisis 2000**
S554	Maine, C. E.	**Timeliner**
S564	Clarke, A. C.	**The Sands of Mars**
S569	Gordon, R.	**No Man Friday**
S576	Michel, A.	**The Truth About Flying Saucers**
S583	Asimov, I.	**Pebble in the Sky**
S596	Russell, E. F.	**Three to Conquer**
S606	Mittelhölzer, E.	**My Bones and My Flute**
S614	Matheson, R.	**The Shores of Space**
S615	Wright, H. B.	**Witness to Witchcraft**
1959		
S631	Maine, C. E.	**The Isotope Man**
S650	Clarke, A. C.	**Expedition to Earth**
S658	Robinson, F. M.	**The Power**
S669	Haggard, W.	**Slow Burner**
S681	Blish, J.	**VOR**
711	Winsor, K.	**The Lovers**
SS714	Maine, C. E.	**High Vacuum**
723	Wibberley, L.	**The Mouse That Roared**
GH736	Leacock, S.	**Laugh With Leacock**
SS746	Sheckley, R.	**Pilgrimage to Earth**
1960		
GS784	Mead, H.	**The Bright Phoenix**
SS818	Bradbury, R.	**The Illustrated Man**
SS819	Bradbury, R.	**The Silver Locusts**
SS820	Bradbury, R.	**Golden Apples of the Sun**
SS821	Bradbury, R.	**Fahrenheit 451**
SS844	Ehrlich, M.	**The Big Eye**
SS853	Siodmak, C.	**Donovan's Brain**
SS854	Matheson, R.	**I Am Legend**
SS873	Maine, C. E.	**The Tide Went Out**
SS886	Matheson, R.	**A Stir of Echoes**
SS898	Wells, H. G.	**The First Men in the Moon**
GS933	Clarke, A. C.	**The City and the Stars**
1961		
SS960	McIntosh, J. T.	**One in 300**
SS971	Maine, C. E.	**Countdown**
SS982	Lymington, J.	**The Night of the Big Heat**
SS995	McIntosh, J. T.	**World out of Mind**
GN1021	Hunter, E.	**The Last Spin**
SS1027	Matheson, R.	**Third From the Sun**
SS1051	McIntosh, J. T.	**The Fittest**
SS1063	Lymington, J.	**The Giant Stumbles**
SS1083	McIntosh, J. T.	**Born Leader**
SN1091	Bryant, P.	**Two Hours to Doom**
GS1095	Stewart, G. R.	**Earth Abides**
1962		
SS1107	Fast, H.	**The Edge of Tomorrow**
SS1118	Maine, C. E.	**Calculated Risk**
GG1137	Lindner, R.	**The Fifty-Minute Hour**
SS1143	MacDonald, J. D.	**Planet of the Dreamers**
SN1161	Calder-Marshall, A.	**The Scarlet Boy**
SN1163	Lee, V.	**The Virgin of the Seven Daggers**
SS1167	Brown, F.	**Nightmares and Geezenstacks**
SN1180	Matheson, R.	**Shock!**
SS1213	Matheson, R.	**I Am Legend**
SS1227	Lymington, J.	**The Grey Ones**
SN1229	Lee, V.	**Ravenna and Her Ghosts**
SC1238	Creasey, J.	**The Black Spiders**
EN1239	Drury, A.	**Advise and Consent**
YS1252	Sheckley, R.	**Shards of Space**

1963		
SN1181	Bone, J. F.	**The Lani People**
YS1267	Lymington, J.	**The Coming of the Strangers**
GN1273	Beagle, P. S.	**A Fine and Private Place**
GN1282	Cody, C. S.	**The Witching Night**
YS1289	Clarke, A. C.	**The Other Side of the Sky**
YS1300	Hoyle, F., & Elliot, J.	
		A for Andromeda
SS1334	Lymington, J.	**A Sword Above the Night**
FN1339	Hailey, A.	**In High Places**
SN1343	Merritt, A.	**Burn, Witch, Burn!**
YS1349	Bradbury, R.	**The Illustrated Man**
YS1350	Bradbury, R.	**The Silver Locusts**
YS1367	Bradbury, R.	**Fahrenheit 451**
YS1383	Clement, H.	**Needle**
SN1388	Priestley, J. B.	**The 31st of June**
SN1390	Priestley, J. B.	**The Other Place**
GN1392	Priestley, J. B.	**The Doomsday Men**
GS1401	Miller, W. M.	**A Canticle for Leibowitz**
SN1404	Anonymous	**The Haunters and the Haunted**
YS1423	St. Clair, M.	**Sign of the Labrys**
SN1431	Priestley, J. B.	**The Magicians**
GS1439	Knight, D.	**Far Out**
1964		
GS1452	Vonnegut, K.	**The Sirens of Titan**
SN1453	George, P.	**Dr. Strangelove**
FN1455	Knebel, F., & Bailey, C. W.	
		Seven Days in May
GS1480	Charbonneau, L.	**The Sentinel Stars**
GG1483	Wright, H. B.	**Witness to Witchcraft**
GS1497	Pickersgill, F.	**And Graves Give Up Their Dead**
GS1512	Maine, C. E.	**Timeliner**
GN1519	Priestley, J. B.	**The Shapes of Sleep**
GS1526	Nourse, A. E.	**Beyond Infinity**
GS1540	Lymington, J.	**The Night Spiders**
GN7012	Manvell, R.	**The Dreamers**
GN7020	Blaisdell, A.	**Nightmare**
SC7021	Bloch, R.	**Blood Runs Cold**
GS7027	Maine, C. E.	**Countdown**
FS7028	Mills, R. P.	**A Decade of Fantasy and Science Fiction**
GS7043	Galouye, D. F.	**The Last Leap**
GN7048	Shelley, M. W.	**Frankenstein**
SN7049	Stevenson, R. L.	**Dr. Jekyll and Mr. Hyde**
SN7050	Pickersgill, F.	**No Such Thing as a Vampire**
GS7066	Lymington, J.	**The Sleep Eaters**
GS7083	Carnell, J.	**New Writings in SF 1**
GS7084	Sellwood, A. V., & Haining, P.	
		Devil Worship in Britain
GS7130	Bradbury, R.	**Golden Apples of the Sun**
1965		
GS7097	Matheson, R.	**A Stir of Echoes**
GN7103	Sale, R.	**Not Too Narrow, Not Too Deep**
GN7107	Derleth, A.	**When Evil Wakes**
GN7114	Bradbury, R.	**Something Wicked This Way Comes**
GS7125	Carnell, J.	**New Writings in SF 2**
FS7126	Collier, J.	**Of Demons and Darkness**
GS7142	Lymington, J.	**The Screaming Face**
GS7143	Nourse, A. E.	**The Counterfeit Man**
FS7160	Kapp, C.	**The Dark Mind**
GS7184	Bradbury, R.	**The Illustrated Man**
GS7185	Bradbury, R.	**The Silver Locusts**
GS7186	Bradbury, R.	**Fahrenheit 451**
GS7199	Carnell, J.	**New Writings in SF 3**
GS7208	Carnell, J.	**Weird Shadows From Beyond**
FN7217	Caidin, M.	**Marooned**
GS7230	Matheson, R.	**The Shores of Space**
GN7240	Bradbury, R.	**Dandelion Wine**
GS7262	Carnell, J.	**New Writings in SF 4**
FS7263	Stewart, G. R.	**Earth Abides**
GN7268	Friedman, B. J.	**Black Humour**
GN7269	Machen, A.	**The Novel of the Black Seal**
GN7270	Machen, A.	**The Novel of the White Powder**

GS7271	Pickersgill, F.	**Horror-7**
GN7272	Anonymous	**Black Tales**
GN7289	Matheson, R.	**Shock 2**
FS7295	Clarke, A. C.	**The City and the Stars**
GS7312	Knight, D.	**13 French Science Fiction Stories**
GN7357	Nolan, W. F.	**Impact-20**
1966		
GS7130	Bradbury, R.	**Golden Apples of the Sun**
GS7329	Carnell, J.	**New Writings in SF 5**
GS7347	Hoyle, F., & Elliot, J.	
		Andromeda Breakthrough
GS7348	Hoyle, F., & Elliot, J.	
		A for Andromeda
GN7357	Nolan, W. F.	**Impact-20**
GS7365	Sheckley, R.	**Journey Beyond Tomorrow**
GS7366	Asimov, I.	**Fantastic Voyage**
GN7373	Mittelholzer, E.	**My Bones and My Flute**
GS7383	Carnell, J.	**New Writings in SF 6**
GN7390	HodderWilliams, C.	
		The Main Experiment
GN7392	Machen, A.	**Black Crusade**
GS7399	Knight, D.	**In Deep**
GS7417	Clement, H.	**Cycle of Fire**
ZR7435	Macardle, D.	**The Unforeseen**
GS7450	Saturday Evening Post	**The Post Reader of Fantasy and Science Fiction**
GS7451	Ball, B.	**Sundog**
ZR7453	Macardle, D.	**The Uninvited**
GN7461	Wallace, E., & Cooper, M. C.	
		King Kong
GS7469	Carnell, J.	**New Writings in SF 7**
GS7484	Hodder-Williams, C.	
		Chain Reaction
GN7489	Bradbury, R.	**The Machineries of Joy**
GS7502	Knight, D.	**Beyond the Barrier**
GS7503	Sheckley, R.	**Shards of Space**
FN7506	Le Fanu, J. S.	**Uncle Silas**
GN7507	Speed, D.	**My Blood Ran Cold**
GN7508	Hamilton, A.	**The Cold Embrace**
GN7509	Anonymous	**The Premature Burial**
GS7521	Vernes, H.	**City of a Thousand Drums**
GS7522	Vernes, H.	**The Dinosaur Hunters**
GN7523	Vernes, H.	**The Yellow Shadow**
GS7531	Clarke, A. C.	**The Other Side of the Sky**
GS7564	Carnell, J.	**New Writings in SF 8**
1967		
EN7568	Hersey, J.	**White Lotus**
FS7577	Heinlein, R. A.	**Farnham's Freehold**
GC7587	Rohmer, S.	**The Mystery of Dr. Fu Manchu**
GC7588	Rohmer, S.	**The Devil Doctor**
GS7589	Rohmer, S.	**The Si-Fan Mysteries**
GS7592	Gold, H. L.	**The Weird Ones**
GS7598	Moudy, W.	**No Man on Earth**
GN7621	Karloff, B.	**The Boris Karloff Horror Anthology**
GC7624	Rohmer, S.	**Daughter of Fu Manchu**
GS7630	Morgan, D.	**The New Minds**
GN7643	Vernes, H.	**The White Gorilla**
GS7650	Carnell, J.	**New Writings in SF 9**
GS7651	White, J.	**Hospital Station**
GS7654	Bradbury, R.	**Fahrenheit 451**
GC7664	Rohmer, S.	**The Mask of Fu-Manchu**
GN7676	Singer, K.	**I Can't Sleep at Night**
ES7682	Wells, H. G.	**The Shape of Things to Come**
GN7694	Matheson, R.	**Shock 3**
GC7698	Rohmer, S.	**The Bride of Fu Manchu**
GC7702	White, J.	**Star Surgeon**
GN7712	Machen, A.	**The Hill of Dreams**
GS7722	Carnell, J.	**New Writings in SF 10**
GN7732	Gates, T.	**I Was Walking Down Below**
GC7738	Rohmer, S.	**President Fu Manchu**
GS7742	Bernard, R.	**The Halo Highway**
GS7759	White, J.	**The Watch Below**

GC7784	Rohmer, S.	**Re-Enter Fu Manchu**
GS7788	Knight, D.	**The Dark Side**
FN7792	Gordons, The	**Power Play**
GS7803	Carnell, J.	**New Writings in SF 12**
1968		
GN7812	Hamilton, A.	**Beam of Malice**
GC7814	Rohmer, S.	**The Trail of Fu Manchu**
GS7819	Galouye, D. F.	**The Lost Perception**
GS7836	Lebaron, A.	**The Meteor Men**
07860	Heinlein, R. A.	**The Menace From Earth**
07874	Rohmer, S.	**The Island of Dr. Fu Manchu**
07878	Carnell, J.	**New Writings in SF 12**
07879	Leslie, P.	**Night of the Trilobites**
07915	Clement, H.	**Close to Critical**
07924.3	Forest, J. C.	**Barbarella**
07945	Rohmer, S.	**The Drums of Fu Manchu**
07979	Rankine, J.	**Interstellar Two-Five**
07994	Knight, D.	**The Other Foot**
08032	Cooney, M.	**Doomsday England**
08037	Carnell, J.	**New Writings in SF 13**
08052	White, J.	**Deadly Litter**
Scottie [juvenile series]		
1955		
J7	Suddaby, D.	**The Star Raiders**
1956		
J11	Verne, J.	**A Journey to the Centre of the Earth**
J48	Verne, J.	**The Clipper of the Clouds**
1957		
JS7	Clarke, A. C.	**The Scottie Book of Space Travel**

Traveller's Comp. See OLYMPIA PRESS

U,V

FREDERICK UNGER, New York, U.S.A.
Unger
1964

2139	Meyrink, G.	**The Golem**

Univ. Lib. (series *ca.* 1957) See GROSSET & DUNLAP

UNIVERSAL PUBLISHING & DISTRIBUTING CORP., New York, U.S.A.
    Additional imprints: **Award; Royal Giant; Softcover.**
Universal
1952 (approx.)

15	Reed, D. V.	**The Thing That Made Love**
Award		
1964		
A124F	Stuart, S., & Bloch, R.	
		The Night Walker
1966		
A171X	Steiger, B.	**Strangers From the Skies**
A181X	Norton, Alden H.	**Award Science Fiction Reader**
A185X	Winston, D.	**The Wakefield Witches**
A817X	Bloch, R.	**Chamber of Horrors**
1967		
—	Knight, M. T.	**The Dozen Deadly Dragons of Joy**
—	Knight, M. T.	**The Million Missing Maidens**
—	Knight, M. T.	**The Terrible Ten**
A244XK	Gordon, F.	**Flight of the Bamboo Saucer**
A199X	Noone, E.	**Edwina Noone's Gothic Sampler**
A234X	Steiger, B., & Whritenour, J.	
		Flying Saucers Are Hostile
A240X	Santesson, H. S.	**Gods for Tomorrow**

| A269S | Wallace, C. H. | **Witchcraft in the World Today** |
| A287X | Knight, M. T. | **The Dirty Rotten Depriving Ray** |

1968

—	Knight, M. T.	**The Malignant Metaphysical Menace**
—	Knight, M. T.	**Tsimmis in Tangier**
295X	Carter, N.	**Operation Moon Rocket**
A339S	Steiger, B., & Whritenour, J.	
		New UFO Breakthrough
A341X	Leiber, F.	**Conjure Wife**
A346SK	Hurwood, B. J.	**The First Occult Review Reader**
A351S	Kerruish, J. D.	**The Undying Monster**
A352X	Comer, R.	**The Witchfinders**
A398?	Boggon, M.	**The Inevitable Hour**

Royal Giant
1953

G-5	Leiber, F.	**The Sinful Ones**
do	Williams, D.	**Bulls, Blood and Passion** [not sf]
G-9	MacArthur, A.	**Aphrodite's Lover**
G-12	Mundy, T.	**Jimgrim Sahib**
G-15	Reed, D. V.	**The Thing That Made Love**
G-18	Haggard, H. R.	**Allan Quatermain & King Solomon's Mines**
?	Twain, M.	**A Connecticut Yankee in King Arthur's Court**
19	Mundy, T.	**Trek East (The Ivory Trail)**
20	Mundy, T.	**Full Moon**

Softcover
1966

| B924X | Camp, L. | **The Experiment** |
| B953X | Nathan, R. | **The Love Pill** |

UNIVERSITY OF NEBRASKA, U.S.A.
Bison
1961

| BB102 | Holberg, L. | **Journey of Niels Klim to the World Underground** |

1963

| ? | Maturin, C. | **Melmoth the Wanderer** |

1965

| BB323 | Shelley, M. W. | **The Last Man** |

1967

| BB393 | Wells, H. G. | **A Modern Utopia** |

Unwin See ALLEN & UNWIN LTD., London, England.

UPTOWN BOOKS. U.S. publisher.
Uptown
1962

| 703 | Knerr, M. | **The Sex Life of the Gods** |

UTB. British publisher, during World War II.
UTB
Not dated (1941-45)

| — | Burton, E. | **Peril of Creation** |

UTOPIAN PUBLICATIONS LTD., London, England.

AF = American Fiction. Although titles are listed in the *Paperbacks* section, this is essentially a magazine and is fully listed in the *Magazines* section. Other titles not in this series are given below.

Utopian
Mid-1940's

—	Anonymous	**Strange Love Stories**
—	Anonymous	**Thrilling Stories—Romance, Adventure**
	Farley, R. M.	**Dangerous Love**
	Field, G. T.	**Romance in Black**
	Marlowe, C.	**Chez Robert and Other Romances**
—	Lafond	**Diane**

VAN DER ELST PRESS LTD., London, England.
Van der Elst
1945

1	Van der Elst, V.	**Death of the Vampire Baroness**
2	Van der Elst, V.	Not known, but could be **The Sadistic Vampire**
3	Van der Elst, V.	**The Strange Doctor & Other Mystic Stories**
4	Van der Elst, V.	**The Mummy Comes to Life**

1946 (approx.)

5	Van der Elst, V.	**The Satanic Power**
6	Van der Elst, V.	**The Brain Master**
—	Van der Elst, V.	**The Secret Power**

D. VAN NOSTRAND CO., U.S.A.
Van Nostrand
1967

| — | Goodwin, H. L. | **Space Frontier Unlimited** |

VEGA, Los Angeles, U.S.A.

All titles below except the last two are reprints from Spencer Badger series.

Vega
1963

VSF-1	Zeigfreid, K.	**Walk Through To-morrow**
VSF-2	Fanthorpe, R. L.	**Space Fury**
VSF-3	Muller, J. E.	**The Day the World Died**
VSF-4	Zeigfreid, K.	**Radar Alert**

1964

VSF-5	Glynn, A. A.	**Plan for Conquest**
VSF-6	Muller, J. E.	**In the Beginning**
VSF-7	Barton, E.	**The Planet Seekers**
VSF-8	Muller, J. E.	**Special Mission**
VSF-9	Fane, B.	**Suspension**
VSF-10	Torro, P.	**The Return**

1965

| VSF-11 | Muller, J. E. | **The Venus Venture** |
| VSF-12 | Zeigfreid, K. | **Projection Infinity** |

1966

| VSF-13 | Becher, D. | **A Ticket to Nowhere** |
| VSF-14 | Crumley, T. W. | **Star Trail** |

VIKING BOOKS, London, England.
Viking
1957

| SF228 | MacDonald, J. D. | **Planet of the Dreamers** |

VIKING PRESS, New York, N.Y., U.S.A.
Viking Press
1959

| P12 | Poe, E. A. | **The Portable Edgar Allan Poe** |

Compass
1961

| C82 | Finney, C. G. | **The Circus of Dr. Lao** |

1967

| — | O'Brien, F. | **At Swim-Two-Birds** |

Vintage See RANDOM HOUSE

Voyager See HARCOURT, BRACE & WORLD

WAR FACTS PRESS, London, England.
War Facts
1943

| — | Maugham, R. | **The 1946 Ms.** |

WARD LOCK & CO. LTD., London, England.
Ward Lock
1955
25	Carr, C.	**Colonists of Space**
26	Bernard, R.	**The Wheel in the Sky**
33	Boothby, G.	**Dr. Nikola**

1956
—	Wallace, E.	**Green Rust**
37	Elton, J.	**The Green Plantations**
38	Ash, A.	**Conditioned for Space**

1957
| 54 | Savage, R. | **When the Moon Died** |
| 59 | Sieveking, L. | **A Private Volcano** |

FREDERICK WARNE & CO. LTD., London, England.
3-Star
Not dated
| — | Heming, J. | **The Lost World of the Colorado** |

1953
| — | George, S. C. | **The Blue Ray** |

Washington See POCKET BOOKS

WDL See WORLD DISTRIBUTORS (MANCHESTER) LTD.

WELLS, GARDNER, DARTON & CO. LTD., Redhill, Surrey, England.
Wells Gardner
1947
| — | Young, F. H. R. | **The Talking Skull and Other Stories** |

WHITMAN PRESS, Sydney, N.S.W., Australia.
Whitman
1949
| — | Binder, E. | **The Three Eternals** |

1950
—	Weinbaum, S. G.	**Parasite Planet**
—	Binder, E.	**Where Eternity Ends**
—	Binder, E.	**Adam Link in the Past**
—	Friend, O. J.	**The Roar of the Rocket**
—	Anonymous	**The Molecule Monsters**

WISDOM HOUSE, U.S.A.
Wisdom
1961
| G-1 | Moore, I. | **The Day the Communists Took Over America** |

WITHY GROVE PRESS LTD., London & Manchester, England.
Imprints: **Bay Tree; Cherry Tree.**
Bay Tree
Late 1940's
| 2 | Wright, S. F. | **Power** |
Cher. Tree
1949 (approx.)
| — | Wright, S. F. | **Deluge** |

WOLFE, London, England.
Wolfe
1967
| 1 | Thomas, J. | **Witches Stay Away From My Door** |

WONDER.
Wonder
1964
| 2046 | Anonymous | **Stories About Giants, Witches and Dragons To Be Read Aloud** |

WORLD DISTRIBUTORS (MANCHESTER) LTD., London, England.
Imprints: **WDL** (WFC = World Fantasy Classic); **Consul.**
WDL
1950-1951
—	Brackett, L.	**Shadow Over Mars**
—	Hamilton, E.	**The Monsters of Juntonheim**
—	Hamilton, E.	**Tharkol, Lord of the Unknown**

—	Luigi, B.	**The Master-Mind Menace**
—	Luigi, B.	**The Metal Monster**
—	Mannheim, K.	**Vampire of Venus**
—	Mannheim, K.	**When the Earth Died**
—	Reed, D. V.	**The Whispering Gorilla**
—	Wellman, M. W.	**The Beasts From Beyond**
—	Wellman, M. W.	**Devil's Planet**

1957
| s248 | Rein, H. | **Few Were Left** |

1958
GC294	Shelley, M. W.	**Frankenstein**
W419	Hough, S. B.	**Extinction Bomber**
M706	Conklin, G. & L.	**The Supernatural Reader**

1959
GC833	Marsh, R.	**The Beetle**
M839	Ascher, E.	**To Kill a Corpse**
HN847	Dickson, C.	**Fear Is the Same**
HS853	Lovecraft, H. P.	**Cry Horror!**

1960
SF881	Simak, C. D.	**Ring Around the Sun**
M905	Rohmer, S.	**The Mystery of Fu Manchu**
M913	Rohmer, S.	**Daughter of Fu Manchu**
M924	Rohmer, S.	**The Mask of Fu Manchu**
W937	James, H.	**The Turn of the Screw**
H947	Chesterton, G. K.	**The Napoleon of Notting Hill**
N961	Kirst, H.	**No One Will Escape**
SF963	Moore, C. L.	**Doomsday Morning**
HH970	Stern, P. Van D.	**The Midnight Reader**
SF973	Levene, P., & Morrissey, J. L.	**The City of Hidden Eyes**
SF975	Kersh, G.	**Men Without Bones**
HH981	Stern, P. Van D.	**The Moonlight Traveller**

Consul
1961
SF1007	Sohl, J.	**The Odious Ones**
SF1009	Moore, C. L.	**Shambleau**
N1018	Conklin, G.	**Four for the Future**
SF1021	Duncan, D.	**Dark Dominion**
M1023	Rohmer, S.	**The Devil Doctor**
M1024	Rohmer, S.	**The Si-Fan Mysteries**
SF1025	Kuttner, H., & Moore, C. L.	**No Boundaries**
HS1035	Wandrei, D.	**The Web of Easter Island**
HS1036	Derleth, A.	**The Mask of Cthulhu**
GS1043	O'Donnell, E.	**Ghosts**
SF1050	Gordon, R.	**The World of Eclos**
SF1053	Gordon, R.	**Utopia 239**
1093	Rohmer, S.	**President Fu Manchu**
1094	Rohmer, S.	**The Bride of Fu Manchu**

1962
1140	Castle, J. L.	**Satellite E One**
1143	Sarban	**The Doll Maker**
1167	Lawrence, H. L.	**Children of Light**
1174	O'Donnell, E.	**Dangerous Ghosts**
1192	Dexter, W.	**World in Eclipse**
1197	Ainsbury, R.	**When the Moon Ran Wild**

1963
1198	Sully, K.	**Skrine**
1207	Lukens, A.	**Sons of the Wolf**
1212	Doyle, A. C.	**The Land of Mist**
1214	Paine, L.	**This Time Tomorrow**
1220	Dexter, W.	**Children of the Void**
1227	Rohmer, S.	**The Trail of Fu Manchu**
1234	Rohmer, S.	**The Island of Fu Manchu**
1239	Derleth, A.	**Time to Come**
1241	O'Donnell, E.	**Haunted Britain**
1246	Rohmer, S.	**The Drums of Fu Manchu**
1265	Padgett, L.	**Tomorrow and Tomorrow**
1266	Padgett, L.	**The Far Reality**
1267	Derleth, A.	**The Outer Reaches**
1268	Derleth, A.	**The Time of Infinity**
1269	Kuttner, H.	**Bypass to Otherness**

1270	Blow, E. J.	**Appointment in Space**
1964		
788	Counselman, M.	**Half in Shadow**
1290	Dell, J.	**News for Heaven**
1292	Saxon, R.	**The Stars Came Down**
1298	Howard, I.	**6 and the Silent Scream**
1308	Saxon, R.	**The Hour of the Phoenix**
1309	Willeford, C.	**The Machine in Ward 11**
1335	Saxon, R.	**The Cosmic Crusade**
1338	Tabori, P.	**The Survivors**
1344	Saxon, R.	**Future for Sale**
1965		
1368	Derleth, A.	**Night's Yawning Peal**
1375	Verne, J.	**A Journey to the Centre of the Earth**
1378	Marsh, R.	**The Beetle**
1392	O'Donnell, E.	**Family Ghosts**
1411	Gardner, A.	**The Escalator**
1418	Winterbotham, R.	**The Man From Arcturus**
1425	Verne, J.	**The City in the Sahara**
1433	Ascher, E.	**To Kill a Corpse**
1443	Derleth, A.	**Far Boundaries**
1966		
1481	Cummings, R.	**Brigands of the Moon**

WORLD EDITIONS, New York, N.Y., U.S.A.
   Published the first seven of the Galaxy Science Fiction Novel series; see coverage under GALAXY PUB. CORP.

WORLD PUBLISHING CO., Cleveland and New York, U.S.A.
Meridian
1959

M62	Williams, C.	**Witchcraft**
1966		
M202	Moskowitz, S.	**Explorers of the Infinite**

WORLD WIDE PRESS, London (?), England.
World Wide
1948

—	Safroni-Middleton, A.	
		The Dreaming Skull

WORLD'S WORK, Kingswood, Surrey, England.
Cedar
1958

57	Hopkins, R. T.	**The World's Strangest Ghost Stories**

WREN BOOKS, London, England.
Wren
1941

—	Gilson, Major C.	**The Lost City**
22	Burroughs, E. R.	**Tarzan at the Earth's Core**

X,Y,Z

Xanadu Library See CROWN PUBLISHERS

YATES & MANN, Sydney, N.S.W., Australia.
Yates & Mann
1924

—	Carey, G. H.	**Road to the Moon**

ZENITH, London, England.
Zenith (UK)
1965

1	Gibson, T.	**Breaking in the Future**

ZENITH BOOKS INC., Rockville Center, N.Y., U.S.A.
Zenith
1959

ZB-14	Knight, D.	**The People Maker**
1960		
ZB-40	Charbonneau, L.	**Corpus Earthling**

Zephyr See CONTINENTAL

A. ZWEMMER LTD., London, England, and A. S. BARNES & CO., New York, U.S.A.
Zwemmer/Barnes
1967

—	Butler, I.	**The Horror Film**

Ephemerals

This supplement lists publishers' series of possible interest, including many ephemerals in the popular pre-World War II British field, as well as certain newspaper supplements.

While these works are not individually listed in the *AUTHORS* section, a reference note is given for each author. Every title is listed in the *TITLES* section.

ADVENTURE LIBRARY. Published by Street & Smith Corp., New York, U.S.A. Every book was written by William Wallace Cook.

1925	4	Cook, W. W.	A Round Trip to the Year 2000	
	9	Cook, W. W.	Marooned in 1492	309 pp., 15¢
	14	Cook, W. W.	The Eighth Wonder	318 pp., 15¢
	15	Cook, W. W.	Adrift in the Unknown	
1926	4	Cook, W. W.	Cast Away at the Pole	318 pp., ?

ALDINE ROMANCE OF INVENTION, TRAVEL AND ADVENTURE LIBRARY. Considered as a magazine; see *MAGAZINES* section.

APRILL, EDWARD M., Jr., Ann Arbor, Michigan, U.S.A. (deceased 1972).

1964	1	Nowlan, P.	Buck Rogers in the 25th Century (Great Classic Newspaper Comic Strips, No. 1)
1964	2	Nowlan, P.	Buck Rogers in the 25th Century (Great Classic Newspaper Comic Strips, No. 2)
1967	3	Nowlan, P.	Buck Rogers in the 25th Century (Great Classic Newspaper Comic Strips, No. 7)
1968	4	Nowlan, P.	Buck Rogers in the 25th Century (Great Classic Newspaper Comic Strips, No. 8)

BIZARRE SERIES. Pamphlets published by Richard Frank, Pennsylvania, U.S.A.

1936	1	Merritt, A.	Three Lines of Old French	
1940	2	Keller, D. H.	The Thing in the Cellar	32 pp.
1941	3	Binder, E.	The Cancer Machine	30 pp.

[Also listed in the *GENERAL* section]

BLACKWOOD, England.

1907	—	Ashmead-Bartlett, F.	The Immortals and the Channel Tunnel	62 pp., 1/-

BOY'S FRIEND LIBRARY. The First Series of 764 titles ran from Sep 1906 to May 1925. It included many works by such writers as Sidney Drew (pseud. of Edgar J. Murray), Cecil Hayter, John Tregellis, Fenton Ash, Alfred Armitage, and even Jules Verne. Some titles are:

1913	226	Wray, R.	Deep Sea Gold	120 pp., 3d
1920?	516	Ash, F.	By Airship to Ophir	64 pp., 9d
1921?	549	Hayward, D.	The Secret of Silent City	
1922	607	Burton, E.	The Silence	
1923	675	Whitley, R.	The Valley of Surprise	
1923?	688	Aubrey, F.	The Devil Tree of El Dorado	
1924	723	Bidston, L.	The Space Destroyer	

The Second Series ran from June 1925 to June 1940. Some titles are given below. [Titles noted (CJ) are in the "Captain Justice" series, about a millionaire adventurer with a host of fantastic inventions produced by his tame mad scientist.]

1927	107	Bidston, L.	The Crimson Claw	64 pp., 4d
1928	132	Beresford, L.	The Iron Clad Army	64 pp., 4d

1928	139	Wood, Eric	The Jungle Men	
1928	162	Day, L.	The Buried World	64 pp., 4d
1929	212	Willson, W.	Kings of the Amazon	64 pp., 4d
1930	222	Whitley, R.	The Master of Dwarf Island	65 pp., 4d
1930	230	Bidston, L.	Queen of the Skies	64 pp., 4d
1930	235	Dunn, J. A.	The Island of the Dead	64 pp., 4d
1930	256	Blake, S.	The Isle of Peril	64 pp., 4d
1931	271	Allingham, H. J.	The Robot Man	64 pp., 4d
1931	287	Edgar, Alfred	Invaders From Mars	
1931	292	Hardy, A. S.	Azar the Mighty	65 pp., 4d
1931	311	Beresford, L.	The Flying Fish	65 pp., 4d
1932	330	Lincoln, M.	The Man From Space	96 pp., 4d
1935	465	Roberts, M.	The Earthquake Maker	96 pp., 4d
1935	477	Roberts, M.	The Rocketeers	98 pp., 4d
1935	485	Roberts, M.	The Secret Kingdom	98 pp., 4d
1935	499	Gregory, D.	Lord of the Incas	98 pp., 4d
1935	505	Roberts, M.	The World in Darkness (CJ)	98 pp., 4d
1935	507	Martin, S.	When the Great Apes Came	98 pp., 4d
1936	518	Bredon, J.	The Great Disaster	98 pp., 4d
1936	529	Roberts, M.	Captain Justice Versus the Sea Eagles (CJ)	
1936	533	Roberts, M.	Jungle Castaways (CJ)	
1936	537	Rochester, G. E.	The Sea Spider	
1936	541	Roberts, M.	The Weed Men (CJ?)	98 pp., 4d
1936	549	Roberts, M.	The Hidden Land (CJ?)	48 pp., 4d
1936	554	Murdoch, T.	Vull the Invisible	98 pp., 4d
1937	561	Rochester, G. E.	The Black Mole	96 pp., 4d
1937	565	Roberts, M.	Captain Justice on Secret Service (CJ)	
1937	570	Roberts, M.	Captain Justice at Bay (CJ)	
1937	573	Roberts, M.	Raiders of Robot City (CJ)	96 pp., 4d
1937	574	Edgar, A.	The Insect Men	98 pp., 4d
1937	584	Edgar, A.	The White Knight Rides Again	
1938	608	Gordon, R.	Oom the Terrible	
1938	622	Roberts, M.	Captain Justice on Thunder Mountain (CJ)	
1938	626	Roberts, M.	The Gold Raiders (CJ)	
1938	629	Roberts, M.	The Ocean Robot (CJ)	
1938	633	Roberts, M.	The Rival Robots (CJ)	96 pp., 4d
1938	636	Rochester, G. E.	The Lost Squadron	96 pp., 4d
1938	637	Roberts, M.	Captain Justice's Airway (CJ)	
1938	641	Roberts, M.	The Mystery Planet (CJ)	98 pp., 4d
1939	659	Edgar, A.	Earthquake	
1939	663	Roberts, M.	The Flying Globes (CJ)	
1939	665	Roberts, M.	The Outlaw Raiders (CJ)	
1939	679	Fowey, R.	The Lion at Bay	
1939	684	Fowey, R.	The Lion's Revenge [sequel to 679]	
1939	689	Roberts, M.	The City of Secrets (CJ)	
1939	697	Roberts, M.	Captain Justice in the Land of Monsters (CJ)	
1939	700	Hawke, Capt. Robert	The Human Shadow	

BURNLEY, COUNTY BOROUGH OF, England.

1957	—	Bennett, W.	The Pendle Witches [nonfiction] 32 pp.

CHAMPION LIBRARY. Papercovered booklets of the 1930's.

1933	102	Dane, D.	Trail Blazers of the Polar Underseas	64pp., 4d
1935	150	Belfield, H. Wedgwood	When the World Crashed	64 pp., 4d
1935	154	Dunkee, D.	Cave Boy Evek	
1936	167	Dane, D.	The Robot Ju Ju	64 pp., 4d
1936	188	Belfield, H. W.	Piston Payne's Jungle Submortank	64 pp., 4d
1937	193	Maxwell, J.	Terror From the Stratosphere	

DAILY MAIL 6d Novels, England.

nd	97	Anstey, F.	The Giant's Robe	194 pp., 6d

EDITORIAL TECNICA E ARTISTICA, Lisbon, Portugal.

1963	—	Kopf, Seymour	Spoilers of the Moon	57 pp.

A. M. GARDNER, London.
1910? —   Hume, Fergus   **The Devil Stick**   108 pp., 6d

G.C.N.C.S. Great Classic Newspaper Comic Strips; see APRILL, E. M.

HALDEMAN-JULIUS COMPANY, Girard, Kansas, U.S.A.
Little Blue Book series: 3½ x 5 in., around 64 pages. Most editions had plain board covers printed with the title, etc., though the second editions of at least two (Nos. 1160 and 1162) had illustrated covers and handwritten titles. Early issues had ''Ten Cent Pocket Series No. —'' on the title page. Apparently the series ran from the 1930's to the early 1940's. None were dated (of ten or so examined) and even the original copyright dates were omitted. The series covered many other fields besides fiction.

12	Poe, E. A.	**Tales of Mystery**
38	Stevenson, R. L.	**Dr. Jekyll and Mr. Hyde**
40	Bulwer-Lytton, E.	**The House and the Brain**
41	Dickens, C.	**A Christmas Carol**
57	Irving, W.	**Rip Van Winkle & The Legend of Sleepy Hollow**
107	Collins, W. W.	**The Dream Woman**
108	Poe, E. A.	**The Fall of the House of Usher**
144	Whitman, S. H.	**Was Poe Immortal?**
145	Haldeman-Julius, E.	**Great Ghost Stories** (2 stories, 1 article)
161	Wells, H. G.	**The Country of the Blind** (+ 2 stories)
162	Poe, E. A.	**Ms. Found in a Bottle & The Murders in the Rue Morgue**
222	Kipling, R.	**The Vampire and Other Poems**
225	Komroff, M.	**Strange Loves**
279	Stevenson, R. L.	**Markheim**
280	Wilde, O.	**The Happy Prince and Other Tales**
290	Poe, E. A.	**The Gold Bug**
336	Kipling, R.	**The Mark of the Beast**
482	Verne, J.	**Five Weeks in a Balloon**
485	Verne, J.	**A Voyage to the Moon**
557	Shipley, M.	**Is the Moon a Dead World?** (nonfiction)
607	Shipley, M.	**Solving the Mystery of the Comets** (nonfiction)
609	Shipley, M.	**Are the Planets Inhabited** (nonfiction)
739	Smith, L. E.	**Tales in Verse of Terror and Wonder**
844	Swift, J.	**A Voyage to Lilliput**
925	Wells, H. G.	**The Empire of the Ants**
926	Wells, H. G.	**The Obliterated Man**
927	Wells, H. G.	**The Stolen Bacillus**
939	Poe, E. A.	**Tales of Imaginative Science**
940	Poe, E. A.	**Tales Grotesque and Weird**
941	Poe, E. A.	**Tales Psychological and Gruesome**
943	Haldeman-Julius, E.	**Masterpieces of Mystery**
968	Crane, S.	**The Upturned Face and Other Stories**
969	Machen, A.	**Tales of the Strange and Supernatural**
1054	Bierce, A.	**An Occurrence at Owl Creek Bridge and Other Stories**
1055	Bierce, A.	**The Horseman in the Sky and Other Stories**
1075	Bierce, A.	**Tales of Ghouls and Ghosts**
1080	Bierce, A.	**Tales of Haunted Houses**
1081	Bierce, A.	**Fantastic Debunking Fables**
1086	Bierce, A.	**My Friend the Murderer and Other Stories**
1132	McCabe, J.	**New Light on Witchcraft** (nonfiction)
1151	Hawthorne, N.	**Book of Mysterious and Fateful Stories**
1152	Hawthorne, N.	**The Seven Vagabonds and Other Queer Tales**
1153	Hawthorne, N.	**The Haunted Mind and Other Strange Tales**
1154	Poe, E. A.	**Tales of Hypnotism and Revenge**
1155	O'Brien, F.-J.	**Two Great Mystery Stories**
1156	Haldeman-Julius, E.	**Extraordinary Mystery Stories**
1158	Haldeman-Julius, E.	**Mysterious Tales of the Sea**
1160	Benson, E. F.	**Two Masterly Ghost Stories**
1160 [2nd ed.]	Mathews, B.	**Two Gripping Ghost Stories**
1161	Haldeman-Julius, E.	**Tales of the Mysterious and Weird**
1162	Haldeman-Julius, E.	**Mystery Tales of Ghosts and Villains**
1326	Shipley, M.	**Is the Moon a Dead World?**
1661	Wells, H. G.	**The Man Who Could Work Miracles**
1663	Wells, H. G.	**The Treasure in the Forest**
1664	Wells, H. G.	**A Slip Under the Microscope**
1671	James, H.	**Queer People and A Damning Passion**
nn	Voltaire	**Zadig, or Destiny**

LIPPSIUS & TISCHER, Kiel, Germany.
1949 — Collins, W. W. **The Black Cottage**   iv + 39 pp., 1.20DM

LONG ISLAND SUNDAY PRESS, Long Island, N.Y., U.S.A. Newspaper supplement.
1952 1 June Fearn, J. R.   **Daughter of the Amazon**

MASTERPIECE LIBRARY, London, England.
1896   Haggard, H. R. **She**

MONTREAL STAR, Montreal, P.Q., Canada. Newspaper supplements (12 pages).
1957	21 Sep	White, T. H.	**The Master**
1957	28 Sep	Carr, J. D.	**Fire, Burn**
1957	14 Dec	Wibberley, L.	**Take Me to Your President**
1959	7 Mar	Wibberley, L.	**Beware of the Mouse**
1959	26 Dec	Bawden, N.	**Devil by the Sea**

NEWSPAPERS PUBLICITY CO., England.
1915? — Shirley, R. **The Angel Warrior of Mons** 15 pp., 1d

NUGGET LIBRARY. Pre-World War II English boys' library.
nd	299	Rowe, J. G.	**Tuffy and the Man of Wonders**
nd	316	Young, F. W.	**The Grey Witch**

OPIUM BOOKS, Hong Kong.
1968 — Severance, F. **The Time Machine That Never Got Past First Base**   152 pp.
1968 — Boys of Ying Wa College **Queer Adventures in a Magic World**

STAR WEEKLY, Toronto, Ont., Canada. Popular weekly which published the majority of J. R. Fearn's ''Golden Amazon'' series [denoted below as (GA)]. All were 16 pages.
1944		Fearn, J. R.	**The Golden Amazon** (GA)
1945	3 Nov	Fearn, J. R.	**The Golden Amazon Returns** (GA)
1946	27 Apr	Fearn, J. R.	**The Golden Amazon's Triumph** (GA)
1947	16 Mar	Fearn, J. R.	**Diamond Quest** (GA)
1948	21 Feb	Fearn, J. R.	**The Amazon Strikes Again** (GA)
1948	13 Nov	Fearn, J. R.	**Twin of the Amazon** (GA)
1949	2 Apr	Fearn, J. R.	**Conquest of the Amazon** (GA)
1949	8 Oct	Fearn, J. R.	**Lord of Atlantis** (GA)
1950	13 May	Fearn, J. R.	**Triangle of Power** (GA)
1950	2 Sep	Fearn, J. R.	**Stranger in Our Midst** (GA)
1951	3 Mar	Fearn, J. R.	**The Amethyst City** (GA)
1951	1 Dec	Fearn, J. R.	**Daughter of the Amazon** (GA)
1952	2 Feb	Fearn, J. R.	**Glimpse**
1952	25 Oct	Fearn, J. R.	**Quorne Returns** (GA)
1952	13 Dec	Fearn, J. R.	**Deadline**
1953	23 May	Fearn, J. R.	**Winged Pestilence**
1953	22 Aug	Fearn, J. R.	**The Central Intelligence** (GA)
1954	10 July	Fearn, J. R.	**The Voice of the Conqueror**
1955	2 Feb	Fearn, J. R.	**The Cosmic Crusaders** (GA)
1955	2 Apr	Fearn, J. R.	**Here and Now**
1955	27 Aug	Fearn, J. R.	**Parasite Planet** (GA)
1956	17 Nov	Fearn, J. R.	**World out of Step** (GA)
1957	6 Apr	Fearn, J. R.	**The Shadow People** (GA)
1957	19 Oct	Fearn, J. R.	**Kingpin Planet** (GA)
1957	14 Dec	Fearn, J. R.	**Robbery Without Violence**
1958	26 Apr	Fearn, J. R.	**The World in Reverse** (GA)
1958	7 June	Fearn, J. R.	**Manton's World**
1958	29 Nov	Fearn, J. R.	**Dwellers in Darkness** (GA)
1959	21 Mar	Fearn, J. R.	**Climate Incorporated**
1959	16 May	Fearn, J. R.	**World in Duplicate** (GA)

1959	15 Aug	Hamilton, E.	**The Man Who Missed the Moon**
1960	26 Mar	Fearn, J. R.	**Standstill Planet** (GA)
1960	17 Dec	Fearn, J. R.	**Ghost World** (GA)
1961	24 June	Fearn, J. R.	**Earth Divided** (GA)
1961	12 Aug	Clarke, A. C.	**Buried Alive in the Moon**
1964	7 Nov	Chandler, A. B.	**The Coils of Time**

SUNDAY STAR LEDGER. Canadian newspaper with supplement.

| 1947 | 16 Mar | Fearn, J. R. | **Diamond Quest** (Golden Amazon) |

SUNDAY TELEGRAPH. Sydney, N.S.W., Australia. Newspaper supplement, about 24 pages; also called "Consol Free Books."

1950	9 Apr	Long, F. B.	**John Carstairs—Space Detective**
1950	16 Apr	Bond, N. S.	**The Adventures of Lancelot Biggs**
1954	2 June	Sherriff, R. C.	**The Hopkins Manuscript** [Part 1]
1954	9 June	Sherriff, R. C.	**The Hopkins Manuscript** [Part 2]

THEOSOPHICAL SOCIETY, U.S.A. and England.

| 1892 | — | Blavatsky, H. P. | **Nightmare Tales** | 133 pp., 1/- |

Paperback Titles

A

A for Andromeda .... Hoyle, F., & Elliot, J.
A for Anything .... Knight, D.
"A" Men .... Le Page, R. (pseud), see Holloway, B.
Abandon Galaxy .... Somers, B. (pseud), see Fox, G. F.
ABC of Science Fiction, An [A] .... Boardman, T.
Abominable Earthman, The [C] .... Pohl, F.
Abominable Snowman, The .... Waugh, M.
Accident, The .... Masters, D.
Across Paris and Other Stories [C] .... Aymé, M.
Across the Ages .... Statten, V. (pseud), see Fearn, J. R.
Across Time .... Grinnell, D. (pseud), see Wollheim, D. A.
Adam and Eve and Pinch Me .... [C] Coppard, A. E.
Adam and the Serpent .... Fisher, V.
Adam Link in the Past .... Binder, E. (pseud), see Binder, E. & O.
Adam Link, Robot .... Binder, E. (pseud), see Binder, E. & O.
Addams Family, The .... Sharkey, J.
Address: Centauri .... Wallace, F. L.
Adrift in a Boneyard .... Taylor, R. L.
Adrift in the Unknown .... Cook, W. W. [Eph., see page 789]
Adventure in Venus, An .... Michelmore, R.
Adventures in the Far Future [A] .... Wollheim, D. A.
Adventures in Time and Space [A] . Healy, R. J., & McComas, J. F.
Adventures in Tomorrow [A] .... Crossen, K. F.
Adventures of Hiram Holliday .... Gallico, P.
Adventures of Lancelot Biggs, The Bond, N. S. [Eph., see page 791]
Adventures of Pinocchio, The .... Collodi, C.
Adventures of Superman .... Lowther, G.
Adventures on Other Planets [A] .... Wollheim, D. A.
Adventures on the Planets .... Querry, S.
Advise and Consent .... Drury, A.
After-Dinner Story .... Irish, W. (pseud), see Woolrich, C.
After Doomsday .... Anderson, P.
After Many a Summer Dies the Swan .... Huxley, A.
After Some Tomorrow .... Reynolds, M.
After the Atom .... La Salle, V.
After the Rain .... Bowen, J.
After Worlds Collide .... Wylie, P., & Balmer, E.
After World's End .... Williamson, J.
Aftermath .... Berry, B.
Against the Fall of Night .... Clarke, Arthur C.
Age of Longing, The .... Koestler, A.
Age of Ruin, The .... Faucette, J. M.
Age of the Tail, The .... Smith, H. A.
Agency, The .... Meltzer, D.
Agent, The .... Meltzer, D.
Agent of Chaos .... Spinrad, N.
Agent of the Unknown .... St. Clair, M.
Agent of Vega [C] .... Schmitz, J. H.
Ahead of Time [C] .... Kuttner, H.
Air Force! .... Harvey, F.
Airs of Earth, The [C] .... Aldiss, B. W.
Alabaster Hand, The [C] .... Munby, A. N. L.
Alas, Babylon .... Frank, P.
Alfred Hitchcock Presents: See under main part of title
Alfred Hitchcock's Ghostly Gallery [A] .... Hitchcock, A.
Alfred Hitchcock's Haunted Household [A] .... Hitchcock, A.
Alfred Hitchcock's Witches' Brew [A] .... Hitchcock, A.
Alf's Button .... Darlington, W. A.
Alien, The .... Jones, R. F.
Alien .... Muller, J. E. (pseud), see Glasby, J. S.
Alien From Arcturus .... Dickson, G. R.
Alien From the Stars .... Fanthorpe, R. L.
Alien Impact .... Tubb, E. C.
Alien Life .... Tubb, E. C.
Alien Ones, The .... Brett, L. (pseud), see Fanthorpe, R. L.
Alien Planet .... Pratt, F.
Alien Sea .... Rackham, J. (pseud), see Phillifent, J. T.
Alien Skies .... Dagmar, P.

Alien Universe .... Gridban, V. (pseud), see Tubb, E. C.
Alien Virus .... Rackham, J. (pseud), see Phillifent, J. T.
Alien Way, The .... Dickson, G. R.
Alien Worlds [A] .... Elwood, R.
Aliens, The [C] .... Leinster, M. (pseud), see Jenkins, W. F.
Aliens for Neighbours [C] .... Simak, C. D.
Aliens 4 [C] .... Sturgeon, T.
All About Venus [A] .... Aldiss, B. W.
All Around the Moon .... Verne, J.
All Flesh Is Grass .... Simak, C. D.
All Fools' Day .... Cooper, E.
All Hallow's Eve .... Williams, C.
All in a Night .... Cayrol, J.
All the Colors of Darkness .... Biggle, L.
All the Traps of Earth [C] .... Simak, C. D.
Allan Quatermain .... Haggard, H. R.
Alley God, The [C] .... Farmer, P. J.
Almuric .... Howard, R. E.
Alone by Night [A] .... Congdon, M. & D.
Alpha Centauri—or Die! .... Brackett, L.
Alpha Yes, Terra No! .... Petaja, E.
Altar on Asconel, The .... Brunner, J.
Altered Ego, The .... Sohl, J.
Alternate Martians, The .... Chandler, A. B.
Alternating Currents [C] .... Pohl, F.
Amateurs in Alchemy .... Deegan, J. J. (pseud), see Sharp, R.
Amazing Mr. Lutterworth, The .... Leslie, D.
Amazon Strikes Again, The ...... Fearn, J. R. [Eph., see page 790]
America Tomorrow [nonfiction] .... New Republic, The
Amethyst City, The .... Fearn, J. R. [Eph., see page 790]
Amiro .... Rogersohn, W.
Amorous Philandre .... de Bibiena, J. G.
Amphibians, The .... Wright, S. F.
Amsirs and the Iron Thorn, The .... Budrys, A.
Analog 1 [A] .... Campbell, J. W.
Analog 2 [A] .... Campbell, J. W.
Analog 3 [A] .... Campbell, J. W.
Analogue Men .... Knight, D.
Anarchaos .... Clark, C. (pseud), see Westlake, D. E.
Anatomy of a Phenomenon [nonfiction] .... Vallee, J.
Ancient Sorceries and Other Stories [C] .... Blackwood, A.
And a Dash of Pity [C] .... Ustinov, P.
And Graves Give Up Their Dead [A] .... Pickersgill, F.
And Loving It .... Johnstone, W.
... And My Fear Is Great .... Sturgeon, T.
... And Others Shall Be Born .... Long, F. B.
And So Ends the World .... Pape, R.
... And Some Were Human [C] .... del Rey, L.
And the Stars Remain .... Berry, B.
And Then the Town Took Off .... Wilson, R.
Android .... Zeigfreid, K. (pseud), see Fanthorpe, R. L.
Android Avenger .... White, Ted
Andromeda Breakthrough .... Hoyle, F., & Elliot, J.
Andy Buckram's Tin Men .... Brink, C. R.
Angel Warrior of Mons, The ...... Shirley, R. [Eph., see page 790]
Angelic Avengers, The .... Andrezel, P. (pseud), see Blixen, K.
Angels and Spaceships [C] .... Brown, F.
Angels and the Creeping Enemy, The .... Theydon, J.
Angry Espers, The .... Biggle, L.
Animal Farm .... Orwell, G. (pseud), see Blair, E.
Anjani the Mighty .... Titan, E. (pseud), see Fearn, J. R.
Annihilation .... Statten V. (pseud), see Fearn, J. R.
Annihilist, The .... Robeson, K. (pseud), see Dent, L.
Another Kind [C] .... Oliver, C.
Another Man's Hell .... Kemper, W. E. Jr.
Another Part of the Galaxy [A] .... Conklin, G.
Another Seven Strange Stories [A] .... Hardie, J. L.
Another Space—Another Time .... Campbell, H. J.
Answer, The .... Wylie, P.
Ant Men, The .... North, E. (pseud), see Cronin, B. C.
Anthem .... Rand, A.
Anthem Sprinters, The [C] .... Bradbury, R.

B

Blast Off at Woomera ..... Walters, H. (pseud), see Hughes, W. L.
Blast-Off Into Space................. (pseud), see Bird, W. H. F.
Blazing Affair, The................................ Avallone, M.
Blessington Method, The [C] .... Ellin, S.
Blind Spot, The.................... Hall, A., & Flint, H. E.
Blinded They Fly .... Molesworth, V.
Blood Reign of the Dictator .... Steele, C.
Blood Runs Cold [C] .... Bloch, R.
Bloodworld .... Janifer, L. M.
Bloody Sun, The .... Bradley, M. Z.
Blue Ants, The .... Newman, B.
Blue Asp, The .... Le Page, R. (pseud), see O'Brien, D.
Blue Atom, The.......................... Williams, R. M.
Blue Cordon .... Carter, D. (pseud), see Hughes, Den
Blue Peril .... Barry, R. (pseud), see Hughes, Den
Blue Ray, The .... George, S. C.
Blue World, The .... Vance, J.
Body Snatchers, The .... Finney, J.
Bodyguard and Four Other Short Science Fiction Novels From
  Galaxy [A] .... Gold, H. L.
Bogey Men [C] .... Bloch, R.
Bombs in Orbit .... Sutton, J.
Book of Lonesome Monsters, A. [A]................. Algren, N.
Book of Mysterious and Fateful Stories [C] ....
.... Hawthorne, N. [Eph., see page 790]
Book of Princes, A [A] .... Sinclair-Stevenson, C.
Book of Strange Stories, A [A] .... Van Thal, H.
Book of the Damned, The [nonfiction] .... Fort, C.
Boris Karloff Horror Anthology, The [A] ....
.... Karloff, B. (pseud), see Pratt, W. H.
Boris Karloff's Favourite Horror Stories [A] ....
.... Karloff, B. (pseud), see Pratt, W. H.
Born in Captivity .... Berry, B.
Born Leader .... McIntosh, J. T. (pseud), see McGregor, J. M.
Born of Luna .... Statten, V. (pseud), see Fearn, J. R.
Born Under Mars .... Brunner, J.
Borrowers Aloft, The .... Norton, Mary
Bow Down to Nul .... Aldiss, B. W.
Box of Delights, The .... Masefield, J.
Brain (A Play of the Whole Earth) .... Britton, L.
Brain Machine, The......................... Smith, George O.
Brain Master, The [C] .... Van der Elset, V.
Brain of the Planet, The........................ Lorraine, L.
Brain Palaeo .... Romilus, A.
Brain Stealers, The ...... Leinster, M. (pseud), see Jenkins, W. F.
Brain Twister Phillips, M. (pseud), see Garrett, R., & Janifer, L. M.
Brain Ultimate .... Campbell, H. J.
Brain Wave...................................... Anderson, P.
Brains of Earth, The .... Vance, J.
Brains of Helle, The .... Mistral, B.
Brak the Barbarian .... Jakes, J.
Brand New World, A .... Cummings, R.
Brand of the Werewolf........ Robeson, K. (pseud), see Dent, L.
Brass Bottle, The .... Anstey, F. (pseud), see Guthrie, T. A.
Brave New World .... Huxley, A.
Brave New World Revisited [nonfiction]............. Huxley, A.
Breakdown [A] .... Hammett, D.
Breaking in the Future [nonfiction] .... Gibson, T.
Breakthrough.................................. Iggulden, J. M.
Bride of Fu Manchu, The....................... Rohmer, S.
Brides of Dracula, The ... Owen, D. (pseud), see McGaughy, D. D.
Brides of the Devil .... Yorke, J.
Bridge, The...................................... Frankau, P.
Brigands of the Moon .... Cummings, R.
Bright New Universe .... Williamson, J.
Bright Phoenix, The .... Mead, H.
Bring Back Yesterday .... Chandler, A. B.
Bring the Jubilee .... Moore, W.
Britain in the Ice Grip .... Woodman, T. E.
Broadway Murders, The......................... Wallace, R.
Broken Lands, The........................... Saberhagen, F.
Brood of the Witch Queen .... Rohmer, S.

Brotherhood of Velvet, The .... Karp, D.
Br-r-r! [A] .... Conklin, G.
Buck Rogers in the 25th Century .. Nowlan, P. [Eph., see page 789]
Budrys' Inferno [C] .... Budrys, A.
Bunter and the Phantom of the Towers .... Richards, F.
Buried Alive in the Moon....... Clarke, A. C. [Eph., see page 791]
Buried Country, The .... Hardy, P.
Buried for Pleasure.... Crispin, E. (pseud), see Montgomery, R. B.
Buried World, The .... Day, L. [Eph., see page 789]
Burn, Witch, Burn! .... Merritt, A.
Burning Court, The .... Carr, J. D.
Burning Void, The .... Magroon, V.
Burning World, The.............................. Ballard, J. G.
Bush Claws .... Garron, M.
Busy Bodies .... Martin, E.
Butterfly Kid, The .... Anderson, C.
Butterfly Revolution, The......................... Butler, W.
By Airship to Ophir............ Ash, F. [Eph., see page 789]
By Lust Possessed .... Bellmore, D.
Bypass to Otherness [C]........................... Kuttner, H.

C

Cache From Outer Space........................... Farmer, P. J.
Cadaver of Gideon Wyck, The...................... Laing, A.
Calculated Risk.......... Maine, C. E. (pseud), see McIlwain, D.
Caleb Williams .... Godwin, W.
Call of the Hand and Other Stories, The [C] .... Golding, L.
Calling Thunderbirds............................ Theydon, J.
Camelot .... White, T. H.
Canary in a Cat House [C] .... Vonnegut, K.
Cancer Machine, The .... Binder, E. [Eph., see page 789]
Candide... Voltaire, F.
Canopy of Time, The [C] .... Aldiss, B. W.
Canticle for Leibowitz, A .... Miller, W. M. Jr.
Capable of Honor .... Drury, A.
Captain America: The Great Gold Steal.............. White, Ted
Captain Justice at Bay .... Roberts, M. [Eph., see page 789]
Captain Justice in the Land of Monsters....................
.... Roberts, M. [Eph., see page 789]
Captain Justice on Secret Service. Roberts, M. [Eph., see page 789]
Captain Justice on Thunder Mountain....................
.... Roberts, M. [Eph., see page 789]
Captain Justice Versus the Sea Eagles....................
.... Roberts, M. [Eph., see page 789]
Captain Justice's Airway .... Roberts, M. [Eph., see page 789]
Captain Nice .... Johnstone, W.
Captain of Souls .... Wallace, E.
Captain Scarlet and the Mysterons .... Theydon, J.
Captain Scarlet and the Silent Saboteur............. Theydon, J.
Captive on the Flying Saucer....................... Finn, R. L.
Captives of the Flame .... Delany, S. R.
Caravan of Crime [C] .... O'Donnell, E.
Carbonel .... Sleigh, B.
Carcassonne.................................. Dunsany, Lord
Cardinal of the Stars .... Rayer, F. G.
Cards of Identity.............................. Dennis, N.
Carnaby Consort .... Dexter, John
Carnelian Cube, The .... de Camp, L. S., & Pratt, F.
Carpathian Castle................................ Verne, J.
Carson of Venus .... Burroughs, E. R.
Case Against Satan, The .... Russell, R.
Case Against Tomorrow, The [C].................... Pohl, F.
Case for the UFO, The [nonfiction] .... Jessup, M. K.
Case of Charles Dexter Ward, The................ Lovecraft, H. P.
Case of Conscience, A .... Blish, J.
Case of the Missing Airman, The .... Elliott, G.
Cast Away at the Pole......... Cook, W. W. [Eph., see page 789]
Castaway....................................... Cozzens, J. G.
Castaway From Space .... Brack, V.
Castaway's World.............................. Brunner, J.

Coming of the Rats, The........................ Smith, George H.
Coming of the Robots, The [A].................. Moskowitz, S.
Coming of the Strangers, The................... Lymington, J.
Coming of the Terrans, The [C]................ Brackett, L.
Command the Morning........................... Buck, P. S.
Commander-1................................... George, P.
Commando X.................................... Runyon, P.
Computer War.................................. Reynolds, M.
Conan [C]........... Howard, R. E., de Camp, L. S., & Carter, L.
Conan of the Isles.................. de Camp, L. S., & Carter, L.
Conan the Adventurer [C]....... Howard, R. E., & de Camp, L. S.
Conan the Avenger............ Nyberg, B., & de Camp, L. S.
Conan the Conqueror........................... Howard, R. E.
Conan the Freebooter [C]....... Howard, R. E., & de Camp, L. S.
Conan the Usurper [C]......... Howard, R. E., & de Camp, L. S.
Conan the Wanderer [C] Howard, R. E., de Camp, L. S., & Carter, L.
Conan the Warrior [C].......... Howard, R. E., & de Camp, L. S.
Conception of the Beast......................... Grimm, B.
Concerning a Woman in Sin and Other Stories [C]..... Hecht, B.
Conditionally Human [C]..................... Miller, W. M. Jr.
Conditioned for Space............................... Ash, A.
Cone, The [C].................................. Wells, H. G.
Conjure Wife.................................. Leiber, F.
Connecticut Yankee in King Arthur's Court, A..................
.... Twain, M. (pseud), see Clemens, S. L.
Connoisseur's Science Fiction [A].................. Boardman, T.
Conquerors From the Darkness.................. Silverberg, R.
Conquerors of Space............................. Collins, E.
Conquerors of Venus........................... Kennedy, E. R.
Conquest of Earth............................. Banister, M.
Conquest of the Amazon........ Fearn, J. R. [Eph., see page 790]
Conquest of the Space Sea..................... Williams, R. M.
Consider Her Ways and Others [C]..........................
.... Wyndham, J. (pseud), see Harris, J. B.
Contact! [A]............. Keyes, N. (pseud), see Keightley, D. N.
Contraband From Otherspace.................... Chandler, A. B.
Contraband Rocket.......... Correy, L. (pseud), see Stine, G. H.
Cook, The..................................... Kressing, H.
Cool Million, A..................................... West, N.
Copenhagen Affair, The......................... Oram, J.
Corfu Affair, The........ Rackham, J. (pseud), see Phillifent, J. T.
Cornish Pixie Affair, The........................ Leslie, P.
Corpse Parade, The............................. Wallace, R.
Corpse Sat Up, The............................. Glenning, R.
Corpus Earthling............................. Charbonneau, L.
Corridors of Time, The........................ Anderson, P.
Corridors of Time........... Deegan, J. J. (pseud), see Sharp, R.
Corruption .... Saxon, P.
Cosmic Calamity............................... Luigi, B.
Cosmic Checkmate............... De Vet, C. V., & MacLean, K.
Cosmic Computer, The.......................... Piper, H. B.
Cosmic Conquest........... Blair, A. (pseud), see Bird, W. H. F.
Cosmic Crusade................................ Saxon, R.
Cosmic Crusaders, The........... Fearn, J. R. [Eph., see page 790]
Cosmic Echelon........... Cameron, B. (pseud), see Glasby, J. S.
Cosmic Engineers.............................. Simak, C. D.
Cosmic Exodus......... Holt, C. G. (pseud), see Fearn, J. R.
Cosmic Flame, The.......... Statten, V. (pseud), see Fearn, J. R.
Cosmic Forces of Mu, The [nonfiction].......... Churchward, J.
Cosmic Manhunt............................. de Camp, L. S.
Cosmic Puppets, The........................... Dick, P. K.
Cosmic Rape, The.............................. Sturgeon, T.
Cosmozoids, The................................ Tralins, R.
Costigan's Needle................................ Sohl, J.
Countdown........... Maine, C. E. (pseud), see McIlwain, D.
Countdown for Cindy............................. Engle, E.
Counter-Clock World............................ Dick, P. K.
Counterfeit Man, The [C]...................... Nourse, A. E.
Counterfeits, The .... Kelley, L. P.
Country of the Blind, The Wells, H. G. [also in Eph., see page 790]
County Court.................................. Flannigan, R.
Court of Honor .... Taylor, G.

Crack in Space, The............................ Dick, P. K.
Craft of Terror, The [A]......................... Haining, P.
Crashing Suns [C]............................ Hamilton, E.
Creation, The................................ Mitchell, M.
Creator, The.................................. Simak, C. D.
Creature From Beyond Infinity, The............. Kuttner, H.
Creature From the Black Lagoon, The...........................
.... Statten, V. (pseud), see Fearn, J. R.
Creatures of the Abyss ... Leinster, M. (pseud), see Jenkins, W. F.
Creatures of the Mist.......................... Hansen, V.
Creep, Shadow, Creep!........................... Merritt, A.
Creeping Plague, The......................... MacGregor, R.
Creeping Shroud, The........................... Wright, Lan
Creeps by Night [A]........................... Hammett, D.
Creeps Medley [C]............................. Hervey, M.
Crime Flies.................................... Luigi, B.
Crimson Claw, The .... Bidston, L. [Eph., see page 789]
Crimson Clay.................................. Schwartz, B.
Crimson Doom................................. Bowen, R. S.
Crimson Planet........ Muller, J. E. (pseud), see Fanthorpe, R. L.
Crisis in 2140........... Piper, H. B., & McGuire, J. J.
Crisis on Cheiron .... Coulson, J.
Crisis 2000 .... Maine, C. E. (pseud), see McIlwain, D.
Crock of Gold, The............................ Stephens, J.
Crocodile City................................. Russell, A.
Crook (Killer) Who Wasn't There, The........... Valdez, P.
Cross of Gold Affair, The......... Davies, F. (pseud), see Ellik R.
Crossroads in Time [A]......................... Conklin, G.
Crossroads of Time, The. Norton, Andre (pseud), see Norton, Alice
Crown of Infinity .... Faucette, J. M.
Croyd... Wallace, Ian
Cry Horror! [C]............................. Lovecraft, H. P.
Cry of the Beast .... Norwood, V.
Cry Plague! .... Drachman, T. S.
Cry Shadow!............... Grant, M. (pseud), see Gibson, W. B.
Crying of Lot 49, The .... Pynchon, T.
Crystal Age, A................................ Hudson, W. H.
Crystal World, The............................ Ballard, J. G.
Cupful of Space, A [C] .... Clingerman, M.
Cure for Death, A............................. Valentine, V.
Curio Murders, The .... Wallace, R.
Currents of Space, The .... Asimov, I.
Curse of Blood, The .... Herscholt, V.
Curse of Collinwood .... Ross, M. (pseud), see Ross, W.
Curse of Doone, The .... Horler, S.
Curse of Dracula and Other Terrifying Tales, The [A] . Higham, C.
Curse of Planet Kuz........................... Van Loden, E.
Curse of Rathlaw, The .... Saxon, R. (pseud), see Martin, T.
Curse of the Mandarin's Fan . House, B. (pseud), see Chadwick, P.
Curse of the Mummy, The....................... Luigi, B.
Cybernetic Controller............ Clarke, A. V., & Bulmer, K.
Cybro Sex .... Lynn, D.
Cycle of Fire .... Clement, H. (pseud), see Stubbs, H. C.
Cycle of Nemesis.............................. Bulmer, K.
Cyclops in the Sky ...... Roberts, L. (pseud), see Fanthorpe, R. L.
Cynic's Desperate Mission........................ Kaner, H.
Czar of Fear, The .... Robeson, K. (pseud), see Dent, L.

D

D-99 .... Fyfe, H. B.
Dagger Affair, The .... McDaniel, D.
Daggers of Kali, The .... Wallace, R.
Damning Passion, A........ James, H. [Eph., see page 790]
Dance of Death, The [C]....................... Blackwood, A.
Dancing Doll Murders, The..................... Wallace, R.
Dandelion Wine [C]........................... Bradbury, R.
Danger From Vega .... Rackham, J. (pseud), see Phillifent, J. T.
Danger Planet .... Sterling, B. (pseud), see Hamilton, E.
Dangerous Ghosts [nonfiction] .... O'Donnell, E.
Dangerous Love [C] .... Farley, R. M. (pseud), see Hoar, R. S.

F

G

H

I

J

K

L

M

N

O

Possible Worlds of Science Fiction [A] .... Conklin, G.
Post Reader of Fantasy and Science Fiction, The [A]............
.... Saturday Evening Post
Power, The................................... Robinson, F. M.
Power.. Wright, S. F.
Power Cube Affair, The... Rackham, J. (pseud), see Phillifent, J. T.
Power Play .... Gordon, M. & G.
Power Sphere .... Brett, L. (pseud), see Fanthorpe, R. L.
Powers of Darkness [C] .... Aickman, R.
Powers That Be, The............................. Nichols, B.
Pre-Gargantua.................................... Charles, N.
Preferred Risk .... McCann, E. (pseud), see Pohl, F., & del Rey, L.
Prelude for Death .... Molesworth, V.
Prelude to Space .... Clarke, Arthur C.
Premature Burial .... Poe, E. A.
Premature Burial and Other Tales of Horror, The [A]. Anonymous
Premier, The .... Conrad, E.
President Fu Manchu .... Rohmer, S.
President Is Missing, The! .... Milton, H. A.
President Vanishes, The........................... Stout, J.
President's Plane Is Missing, The............. Serling, Robert J.
Prevalence of Witches, The .... Menen, A.
Priest-Kings of Gor .... Norman, J. (pseud), see Lange, J. F.
Primal Urge, The .... Aldiss, B. W.
Prince Caspian .... Lewis, C. S.
Prince of Darkness [A] .... Verner, G.
Prince of Peril .... Kline, O. A.
Princess and Curdie, The...................... MacDonald, G.
Princess and the Goblin, The .... MacDonald, G.
Princess of Mars, A........................... Burroughs, E. R.
Princess of the Atom, The .... Cummings, R.
Prism, The .... Petaja, E.
Prisoner in the Opal, The....................... Mason, A. E. W.
Prisoner in the Skull .... Dye, C.
Prisoners of Serpent Land .... Connell, A.
Private Cosmos, A .... Farmer, P. J.
Private Life of Helen of Troy, The.................. Erskine, J.
Private Lives of Adam and Eve, The...... Zugsmith, A., & Hill, R.
Private Volcano, A .... Sieveking, L.
Privilege .... Burke, J.
Proceedings of the 20th World Science Fiction Convention—Chicon
    III [nonfiction]............................... Kemp, E.
Proceedings of the 21st World Science Fiction Convention: Discon
    [nonfiction] .... Eney, R.
Prodigal Sun, The............................... High, P. E.
Productions of Time, the .... Brunner, J.
Professor Branestawm's Treasure Hunt [C] .... Hunter, N.
Profiles of the Future [nonfiction].............. Clarke, Arthur C.
Progeny of the Adder .... Whitten, L. H.
Project, The .... Sinclair, D.
Project Jupiter .... Brown, F.
Project Mars [nonfiction] .... Ley, W., & Von Braun, W.
Projectile War .... Lang, K.
Projection Infinity ..... Zeigfreid, K. (pseud), see Fanthorpe, R. L.
Prologue to Analog [A] .... Campbell, J. W.
Promiscuous Philbert............................ Stopeck, P.
Propellor Island................................. Verne, J.
Prospect of Immortality, The [nonfiction] ...... Ettinger, R. C. W.
Prototype P.Z.642............................... Ford, K.
Providence Island .... Hawkes, J.
Proxima Project, The..... Rackham, J. (pseud), see Phillifent, J. T.
Pseudo-People, The [A] .... Nolan, W.
Psi High and Others [C] .... Nourse, A. E.
Psionic Menace, The .... Woodcott, K. (pseud), see Brunner, J.
Psychedelic-40................................ Charbonneau, L.
Psychic [nonfiction] .... Hurkos, P.
Psychic Passion .... Flair, T.
Psychogeist...................................... Davies, L. P.
Puck of Pook's Hill [C] .... Kipling, R.
Puppet Masters, The .... Heinlein, R. A.
Purchase of the North Pole, The .... Verne, J.
Purple Armchair, The .... Hesky, O.

Purple Cloud, The .... Shiel, M. P.
Purple Islands .... Carter, D. (pseud), see Hughes, Den
Purple Sapphire, The........... Taine, J. (pseud), see Bell, E. T.
Purple-6.. Brinton, H.
Purple Tornado .... Bowen, R. S.
Purple Wizard, The .... Gridban, V. (pseud), see Fearn, J. R.
Pursuit on Ganymede .... Resnick, M.
Pursuit Through Time............................ Burke, J.
Puzzle Planet, The.......................... Lowndes, R. A. W.

Q

Quatermass and the Pit .... Kneale, N.
Quatermass Experiment, The .... Kneale, N.
Quatermass II................................... Kneale, N.
Queen Cleopatra .... Mundy, T.
Queen of Atlantis, The.......................... Benoit, P.
Queen of Blood .... Nuetzel, C.
Queen of Life, The.............................. Flint, H. E.
Queen of the Skies .... Bidston, L. [Eph., see page 789]
Queen People, The .... Rey, R. (pseud), see Hughes, Den
Queer Adventures in a Magic World ....
.... Boys of Ying Wa College [Eph., see page 790]
Queer-Looking Box: Seven Gripping Mystery Stories [C] Hervey, M.
Queer People and A Damning Passion James, H. [Eph., see page 790]
Quest Crosstime .... Norton, Andre (pseud), see Norton, Alice
Quest of Qui................. Robeson, K. (pseud), see Dent, L.
Quest of the Dawn Man .... Rosny, J. H.
Quest of the Sacred Slipper, The .... Rohmer, S.
Quest of the Seeker, The .... Elton, J.
Quest of the Three Worlds [C] Smith, C. (pseud), see Linebarger, P.
Quiet Horror [C] .... Ellin, S.
Quiver of Horror [A] .... Wheatley, D.
Quorne Returns............... Fearn, J. R. [Eph., see page 790]
Quy Effect, The............. Sellings, A. (pseud), see Ley, R. A.

R

R Is for Rocket [C] .... Bradbury, R.
Race to the Stars [A] .... Margulies, L., & Friend, O. J.
Radar Alert .... Zeigfreid, K. (pseud), see Fanthorpe, R. L.
Radio Beasts, The .... Farley, R. M. (pseud), see Hoar, R. S.
Radio Planet, The......... Farley, R. M. (pseud), see Hoar, R. S.
Radioactive Camel Affair, The .... Leslie, P.
Radium King, The .... Burton, E.
Ragged Edge, The........ Christopher, J. (pseud), See Youd, C. S.
Raiders From the Rings .... Nourse, A. E.
Raiders of Mars .... Moore, P. A.
Raiders of Robot City .... Roberts, M. [Eph., see page 789]
Rain in the Doorway .... Smith, T.
Rainbow Affair, The .... McDaniel, D.
Ralph 124C 41 + ... Gernsback, H.
Rare Science Fiction [A]......................... Howard, I.
Rat Race .... Franklin, J. (pseud), see Carter, J. F.
Raven, The...................... Poe, E. A. (& Sudak, E.)
Ravenna and Her Ghosts [C] ...... Lee, V. (pseud), see Paget, V.
Ray Bradbury Review [nonfiction] .... Nolan, W. F.
Re-Birth .... Wyndham, J. (pseud), see Harris, J. B.
Re-Enter Fu Manchu............................. Rohmer, S.
Reach for Tomorrow [C]...................... Clarke, Arthur C.
Reactor XK9........... Muller, J. E.(pseud), see Fanthorpe, R. L.
Real Ghosts, Restless Spirits and Haunted Minds [nonfiction]....
.... Steiger, B. (pseud), see Olson, J.
Reality Forbidden .... High, P. E.
Realm of Ghosts, The [nonfiction] .... Maple, E.
Realm of the Alien............................... Delray, C.
Reassembled Man, The........................... Kastle, H. D.
Rebellers, The .... Roberts, J.
Rebellious Stars, The .... Asimov, I.
Rebels of the Red Planet .... Fontenay, C. L.

S

Seetee Ship . . . . Williamson, J.
Seetee Shock . . . . Williamson, J.
Selected Ghost Stories of M. R. James [C] . . . . James, M. R.
Selected Radio Plays [C] . . . . Corwin, N.
Selected Short Stories of Algernon Blackwood [C] . . . Blackwood, A.
Selected Short Stories of Bret Harte [C] . . . . Harte, B.
Selected Short Stories of Edgar Allan Poe [C] . . . . Poe, E. A.
Selected Short Stories of H. G. Wells [C] . . . . Wells, H. G.
Selected Short Stories of John Russell [C] . . . . Russell, J.
Selected Short Stories of Mark Twain [C] . . . .
. . . . Twain, M. (pseud), see Clemens, S. L.
Selected Short Stories of Philip Wylie [C] . . . . Wylie, P.
Selected Short Stories of Saki [C] . Saki (pseud), see Munro, H. H.
Selected Tales of Algernon Blackwood [C] . . . . Blackwood, A.
Selected Tales of Edgar Allan Poe [C] . . . . Poe, E. A.
Selected Writings of Edgar Allan Poe [C] . . . . Poe, E. A.
Selected Writings of Lafcadio Hearn [C] . . . . Hearn, L.
Selections From Beyond Human Ken [A] . . . . Merril, J.
Sensitives, The . . . . Charbonneau, L.
Sentinel Stars, The . . . . Charbonneau, L.
Sentinels [From] of Space . . . . Russell, E. F.
Serpent, The . . . . Gaskell, J.
Servants of the Skull . . . . House, B. (pseud), see Chadwick, P.
Seven Come Infinity [A] . . . . Conklin, G.
Seven Days in May . . . . Knebel, F., & Bailey, C. W.
Seven Days to Never . . . . Frank, P.
Seven Footprints to Satan . . . . Merritt, A.
Seven for Murder . . . . Glenning, R.
Seven From the Stars . . . . Bradley, M. Z.
Seven Gothic Tales [C] . . . . Dinesen, I. (pseud), see Blixen, K.
Seven Masterpieces of Gothic Horror [A] . . . . Spector, R. D.
Seven Men (and Two Others) [C] . . . . Beerbohm, M.
Seven More Strange Stories [A] . . . . Hardie, J. L.
Seven Sexes, The [C] . . . . Tenn, W. (pseud), see Klass, P.
Seven Strange Stories [A] . . . . Hardie, J. L.
Seven to the Moon . . . . Stanton, L.
Seven Trips Through Time and Space [A] . . . . Conklin, G.
Seven Vagabonds and Other Queer Tales, The [C] . . . .
. . . . Hawthorne, N. [Eph., see page 790]
17 X Infinity [A] . . . . Conklin, G.
Seventh Day, The . . . . Kirst, H. H.
Seventh Dimension, The . . . . La Salle, V.
7th Fury, The . . . . Castle, John
Seventh Galaxy Reader, The [A] . . . . Pohl, F.
Seventh Pan Book of Horror Stories, The [A] . . . . Van Thal, H.
Sex Demon of Vangal, The . . . . Brent, L. W.
Sex Life of the Gods, The . . . . Knerr, M.
Sex Machine . . . . Camra, R.
Sex Machine, The . . . . Geis, R. E.
Sex Machine, The . . . . Key, D.
Sex Machine, The . . . . Mead, S.
Sex Pill, The . . . . Williams, J. X. (pseud), see Offutt, A. J.
Sex Ray, The . . . . Allison, C.
Sex Serum, The . . . . Dickinson, H. O.
Sex War, The . . . . Merwin, S.
Sexodus . . . . Jason, J.
Sexualis '95 . . . . Sternberg, J.
SF: Author's Choice [A] . . . . Harrison, H.
SF Reprise 2 [A] . . . . Moorcock, M.
SF Reprise 3 [A] . . . . Bonfiglioli, K.
SF Reprise 4 [A] . . . . Bonfiglioli, K.
SF Reprise 5 [A] . . . . Moorcock, M.
SF Reprise 6 [A] . . . . Bonfiglioli, K.
Shade of Difference, A . . . . Drury, A.
Shadow Beware . . . . Grant, M. (pseud), see Gibson, W. B.
Shadow Castle . . . . Cockrell, M.
Shadow Girl, The . . . . Cummings, R.
Shadow—Go Mad! . . . . Grant, M. (pseud), see Gibson, W. B.
Shadow Line, The . . . . Conrad, J.
Shadow Man . . . . Barton, L. (pseud), see Fanthorpe, R. L.
Shadow of Evil . . . . La Spina, G.
Shadow of Fu Manchu . . . . Rohmer, S.

Shadow of Tomorrow [A] . . . . Pohl, F.
Shadow on the Hearth . . . . Merril, J.
Shadow Over Mars . . . . Brackett, L.
Shadow People, The . . . . Fearn, J. R. [Eph., see page 790]
Shadow Play [C] . . . . Beaumont, C.
Shadow Strikes Back, The . . . Grant, M. (pseud), see Gibson, W. B.
Shadows in the Sun . . . . Oliver, C.
Shadows of Ecstasy . . . . Williams, C.
Shadows of Evil [nonfiction] . . . . O'Donnell, E.
Shadows on the Landing . . . . Wilson, G. M.
Shadow's Revenge, The . . . . . Grant, M. (pseud), see Gibson, W. B.
Shadows With Eyes [C] . . . . Leiber, F.
Shafts of Fear [A] . . . . Wheatley, D.
Shaggy Dog, The . . . . Griffen, E. L.
Shambleau [C] . . . . Moore, C. L.
Shanadu [A] . . . . Briney, R. E.
Shane Leslie's Ghost Book [nonfiction] [C] . . . . Leslie, S.
Shape of Things, The [A] . . . . Knight, D.
Shape of Things to Come, The . . . . Wells, H. G.
Shape of Tomorrow, The [nonfiction] . . . . Soule, George
Shapes of Sleep, The . . . . Priestley, J. B.
Shards of Space [C] . . . . Sheckley, R.
She . . . . Haggard, H. R. [also in Eph., see page 790]
She and Allan . . . . Haggard, H. R.
She-Wolf, The [C] . . . . Saki (pseud), see Munro, H. H.
Shield . . . . Anderson, P.
Ship From Atlantis, The . . . . Munn, H. W.
Ship From Nowhere, The . . . . Patzer, S.
Ship From Outside, The . . . . Chandler, A. B.
Ship of Ishtar, The . . . . Merritt, A.
Ship of Spies . . . . Sinstadt, G.
Ship That Sailed the Time Stream, The . . . . Edmondson, G. C.
Ships of Vero . . . . Shaw, Brian (pseud), see O'Brien, D.
Ships to the Stars [C] . . . . Leiber, F.
Shock! [A] . . . . Allen, M. C.
Shock [C] . . . . Matheson, R.
Shock II [C] . . . . Matheson, R.
Shock III [C] . . . . Matheson, R.
Shock Stories [C] . . . . Workman, J.
Shock Wave . . . . Richmond, W. & L.
Shoes of the Fisherman, The . . . . West, M.
Shoot, The . . . . Trevor, E.
Shoot at the Moon . . . . Temple, W. F.
Shooting Star, The . . . . Bloch, R.
Shores of Space, The [C] . . . . Matheson, R.
Short Reign of Pippin IV, The . . . . Steinbeck, J.
Short Stories of Stephen Vincent Benét [C] . . . . Benét, S. V.
Shorter Novels of the 18th Century [A] . . . . Henderson, P.
Shot in the Dark [A] . . . . Merril, J.
Shrinking Man, The . . . . Matheson, R.
Shriveling Murders, The . . . . Zorro (pseud), see Ward, Harold
Shrouded Planet, The . . . .
. . . . Randall, R. (pseud), see Silverberg, R., & Garrett, R.
Shudder Show, The [C] . . . . Martin, A. E.
Shuna and the Lost Tribe . . . . King, J.
Shuna, White Queen of the Jungle . . . . King, J.
Shy Stegosaurus of Cricket Creek, The . . . . Lampman, E. S.
Si-Fan Mysteries, The . . . . Rohmer, S.
Sideslip . . . . White, Ted, & Van Arnam, D.
Siege of Harlem, The . . . . Miller, Warren
Siege of the Unseen . . . . van Vogt, A. E.
Siege Perilous . . . . del Rey, L.
Sign of the Labrys . . . . St. Clair, M.
Silence, The . . . . Burton, E. [Eph., see page 789]
Silent Invaders, The . . . . Silverberg, R.
Silent River . . . . Garron, M.
Silent Speakers, The . . . . Sellings, A. (pseud), see Ley, R. A.
Silver Chair, The . . . . Lewis, C. S.
Silver Eggheads, The . . . . Leiber, F.
Silver Locusts, The [C] . . . . Bradbury, R.
Silverlock . . . . Myers, J. M.
Simulacra, The . . . . Dick, P. K.

T

World Between and Other Stories, The [C] .... Vance, J,
World Grabbers, The .... Fairman, P. W.
World in a Test Tube........................ Campbell, H. J.
World in Darkness, The .... Roberts, M. [Eph., see page 789]
World in Duplicate .... Fearn, J. R. [Eph., see page 790]
World in Eclipse .... Dexter, W. (pseud), see Pritchard, W. T.
World in Peril, The .... Chilton, C.
World in Reverse, The.......... Fearn, J. R. [Eph., see page 790]
World in Reverse, The........................ Ranzetta, L.
World in Winter, The ..... Christopher, J. (pseud), see Youd, C. S.
World Jones Made, The .... Dick, P. K.
World Makers, The ...... Maxwell, J. C. (pseud), see Glasby, J. S.
World of Chance .... Dick, P. K.
World of Difference, A........................... Conquest, R.
World of Gol.............................. Charles, N.
World of If .... Phillips, R. (pseud), see Graham, R. P.
World of Null-A, The .... van Vogt, A. E.
World of Ptavvs.............................. Niven, L.
World of the Gods .... Torro, P. (pseud), see Fanthorpe, R. L.
World of the Masterminds .... Williams, R. M.
World of the Sleeper........................ Wayman, T. R.
World of the Starwolves .... Hamilton, E.
World of Theda, The .... Wade, T.
World of Tomorrow..... Zeigfreid, K. (pseud), see Fanthorpe, R. L.
World of Washington Irving, The [C] .... Irving, W.
World out of Mind .. McIntosh, J. T. (pseud), see McGregor, J. M.
World out of Step .... Fearn, J. R. [Eph., see page 790]
World Shakers, The............................ Reid, D.
World Swappers, The........................ Brunner, J.
World That Couldn't Be, The [A] .... Gold, H. L.
World That Never Was, The ....
.... Zeigfreid, K. (pseud), see Fanthorpe, R. L.
World Without Men....... Maine, C. E. (pseud), see McIlwain, D.
World Without Stars .... Anderson, P.
World Without Women .... Keene, D., & Pruyn, L.
World Wrecker, The............................ Bounds, S. J.
Worlds Apart .... McIntosh, J. T. (pseud), see McGregor, J. M.
Worlds at War [A] .... Anonymous, see Rayer, F. G.
Worlds Away .... Beemish, C.
World's Best Science Fiction: 1965 [A] Wollheim, D. A., & Carr, T.
World's Best Science Fiction: 1966 [A] Wollheim, D. A., & Carr, T.
World's Best Science Fiction: 1967 [A] Wollheim, D. A., & Carr, T.
World's Best Science Fiction: 1968 [A] Wollheim, D. A., & Carr, T.
Worlds for the Taking .... Bulmer, K.
World's Greatest Stories of the Occult, The [nonfiction] . Singer, K.
Worlds in Balance .... Wallace, F. L.
Worlds in Collision [nonfiction] .... Velikovsky, I.
Worlds of Clifford Simak, The [C].............. Simak, C. D.
Worlds of Eclos .... Gordon, R. (pseud), see Hough, R. A.
Worlds of Robert A. Heinlein, The [C].......... Heinlein, R. A.
Worlds of Robert F. Young, The [C] .... Young, R. F.
Worlds of Science Fiction, The [A] .... Mills, R. P.
Worlds of the Imperium .... Laumer, K.
Worlds of Tomorrow [A] .... Derleth, A.
Worlds of Weird [A]........................ Margulies, L.
Worlds of When [A] .... Conklin, G.
World's Strangest Ghost Stories, The [C].......Hopkins, R. T.
World's Strangest Mysteries, The [nonfiction] .... Furneaux, R.
Worlds to Come [A] .... Knight, D.
Worlds to Conquer .... Statten, V. (pseud), see Fearn, J. R.
Worlds Within........... Phillips, R. (pseud), see Graham, R. P.
Worlds Without End [C]....................... Simak, C. D.
Worm Ouroboros, The........................ Eddison, E. R.
Wrecks of Time, The........................ Moorcock, M.
Wrinkle in the Skin, A .... Christopher, J. (pseud), see Youd, C. S.

Wrinkle in Time, A .... L'Engle, M.
Wrong Side of the Moon, The .... Ashton, F.

X, Y, Z

X... Sudak, E.
X Factor, The .... Norton, Andre (pseud), see Norton, Alice
X-Machine, The .... Muller, J. E. (pseud), see Fanthorpe, R. L.
X People, The .... Brack, V.
X-Ray Menace.............................. Herscholt, W.
Yankee Ghosts [nonfiction] .... Holzer, H.
Year of Consent........................... Crossen, K. F.
Year of Love, The........... Anonymous, see Smith, George H.
Year of the Angry Rabbit, The .... Braddon, R.
Year of the Horsetails, The .... Tapsell, R. F.
Year of the Unicorn ..... Norton, Andre (pseud), see Norton, Alice
Year the Yankees Lost the Pennant, The .... Wallop, D.
Year 3097 .... Miller, R. D., & Hunger, A.
Year 2018! .... Blish, J.
Year's Best S-F: 5th Annual Edition [A]............. Merril, J.
Year's Best S-F: 6th Annual Edition [A]............. Merril, J.
Year's Best S-F: 7th Annual Edition [A]............. Merril, J.
Year's Best S-F: 8th Annual Edition [A]............. Merril, J.
Year's Best S-F: 9th Annual Edition [A]............. Merril, J.
Year's Best S-F: 10th Annual Edition [A] .... Merril, J.
Year's Best S-F: 11th Annual Edition [A] .... Merril, J.
Year's Best Science Fiction [A] ..... Harrison, H., & Aldiss, B. W.
Yellow Claw, The.......................... Rohmer, S.
Yellow Inferno.............................. Ranzetta, L.
Yellow Planet, The.......................... Browne, G. S.
Yellow Shadow, The .... Vernes, H.
Yellow Shadows of Death....................... Wallace, R.
Yellow Submarine .... Wilk, M.
Yesterday and Tomorrow [C].................... Verne, J.
Yet More Penguin Science Fiction [A] .... Aldiss, B. W.
Yonder [C] .... Beaumont, C.
You Can't Hang the Dead .... Carroll, L.
You Can't Keep Murder Out .... Valdez, P.
You Live After Death [nonfiction] .... Sherman, H.
You Sane Men............................ Janifer, L. M.
You Shall Know Them .... Vercors (pseud), see Bruller, J.
You Will Never Be the Same [C] Smith, C. (pseud), see Linebarger, P.
Your Sins and Mine........................... Caldwell, T.
Yours Truly, Jack the Ripper [C] .... Bloch, R.
Youth Madness............................ Coblentz, S. A.
Youth Monopoly, The .... Wobig, E.
Z Formations.............. Shaw, Brian (pseud), see Fearn, J. R.
Zacherley's Midnight Snacks [A] Zacherley (pseud), see Zacherle, J.
Zacherley's Vulture Stew [A] .. Zacherley (pseud), see Zacherle, J.
Zadig, or Destiny .... Voltaire [Eph., see page 790]
Zanthar at Moon's Madness.................... Williams, R. M.
Zanthar at the Edge of Never .... Williams, R. M.
Zanthar of the Many Worlds.................... Williams, R. M.
Zap Gun, The .... Dick, P. K.
Zardoc, Warrior Stud........................... Lynn, D.
Zenith-D................. Lorraine, P. (pseud), see Glasby, J. S.
Zero Equals Nothing .... Stone, G. B., & Williams, R.
Zero Field .... Hunt, G. (pseud), see Jennison, J. W.
Zero Hour .... Statten, V. (pseud), see Fearn, J. R.
Zero Minus X .... Zeigfreid, K. (pseud), see Fanthorpe, R. L.
Zero Point................ Le Page, R. (pseud), see Glasby, J. S.
Zhorani .... Maras, K. (pseud), see Bulmer, K.
Zilov Bombs, The............................ Barron, D. G.
Zolotov Affair, The........................... Rimmer, R. H.

PSEUDONYMS

System and Abbreviations

This section lists the known pseudonyms of personalities who have had material published in the science-fiction, fantasy, weird or associated fields. Some current mainstream pseudonyms are also given for interest.

The first part lists by pseudonym and the second part by real name.

Most authors are covered in the *WHO'S WHO* under their real names. Some personalities, however, are better known under their pseudonyms – sometimes adopted as a legal name – and they are so indexed (for example, Anthony Boucher and Theodore Sturgeon). Some female authors are better known under their maiden names, under which their works appear, and are so listed in the *WHO'S WHO*; they are noted in the pseudonym listings by "née."

The abbreviation "(h)" denotes a *house name*, that is, a pseudonym employed at various times by different authors on stories written for one publishing house. The name belongs to the publisher rather than to any one author.

When a pseudonym is used by authors writing in collaboration, their real names are connected by "&". For example, if the real names behind a pseudonym are shown as "R. Garrett & R. Silverberg," then Garrett and Silverberg wrote the stories together. But "R. Garrett; R. Silverberg" means that some stories under the pseudonym were by Garrett and others by Silverberg.

The listing primarily covers contemporary writers, but omits many listed in the Bleiler *Checklist of Fantastic Literature* (1948), as their works have not been carried forward into the *Encyclopedia*.

The list of pseudonyms has been compiled through the accumulation of knowledge through the years, as well as a number of outside sources. These include NFFF listings of the 1950's and a list in J. Page's amateur magazine *Lore* for September 1966. Specific books in this area include:

Sciencefiction and Fantasy Pseudonyms, Barry McGhan (1976)

Who Goes There, James Rock (1979)

McGhan lists the authority for the pseudonym. Often the verification of a particular pseudonym can cause major difficulties.

Other sources have included:

Index to the Science-Fiction Magazines 1926-1950, D. B. Day (1952)

The Index of Science Fiction Magazines 1951-1965, N. Metcalf (1968)

The Hero-Pulp Index, L. McKinstry & R. Weinberg (1970)

Stella Nova, R. Reginald (1970)

Who's Who in Horror and Fantasy Fiction, M. Ashley (1977)

Twentieth Century Science Fiction Writers, C. V. Smith (1981)

We are particularly indebted to R. Reginald's *Science Fiction and Fantasy Literature* (1979) for clarifying certain points in this listing. In addition, both R. Reginald and M. Ashley have provided many of the obscure pseudonyms of the British sf field of the 1950's.

Pseudonym   *Real Name*   *Pseudonym*   *Real Name*

Pseudonyms/Real Names

A

Pseudonym	Real Name
A., D. E.	M. Dominick
A, Dr.	Isaac Asimov
A. E.	George William Russell
Abbot, Anthony	Fulton Oursler
Ack Ack, Sgt.	Forrest J Ackerman (fan pseud.)
Acre, Stephen	Frank Gruber
Acula, Dr.	Forrest J Ackerman
Adair, Hazel	H. I. Addis
Adams, Chuck	E. C. Tubb
Adams, John	John S. Glasby
Adams, Louis J. A.	Joe L. Hensley & Alexei Panshin
Addison, Hugh	Harry Collinson Owen
Adeler, Max	Charles Heber Clark
Adlard, Mark	Peter Marcus Adlard
Aghill, Gordon	R. Silverberg & R. Garrett
Ahearne, Bert	Albert Hernhuter
Ainsbury, Ray	A. Hyatt Verrill
Akers, Alan Burt	Kenneth Bulmer
Akers, Floyd	L. Frank Baum
Alan, A. J.	Leslie Harrison Lambert
Alban, Anthony	Anthony A. Thompson
Alejandro	Alejandro Canedo
Alexander, Dair	Christine Campbell Thomson
Alexander, Ed	E. A. Emshwiller
Alexander, Jay	Victor J. Banis
Allardyce, Paula	Ursula Torday
Allen, F. M.	Edmond Downey
Allison, Clyde	William Knoles
Allison, Sam	Noel M. Loomis
Allport, Arthur	Raymond Z. Gallun
Altair	Anthony Jerome Griffin
Alvarez, John	Lester del Rey
Alvarez, R.	Lester del Rey
Alzee, Grendon	Arthur L. Zagat
Ames, Clinton	Roger P. Graham
Ames, Clyde	William Knoles
Ames, Leslie	W. E. D. Ross
Amherst, Wes	Richard S. Shaver
Amory, Guy	Ray Bradbury (fan pseud.)
Anderson, Andy	William C. Anderson
Anderson, David	Raymond F. Jones
Andre, Lee	L. R. Andrus
Andrew, Stephen	Frank George Layton
Andrews, Elton V.	Frederik Pohl
Andrews, Felicia	Charles L. Grant
Andrews, Thomas	Sewell P. Wright
Andrezel, Pierre	Karen Blixen
Annixter, Paul	Howard A. Sturtzel
Ansky, S.	S. Rappaport
Anstey, F.	Thomas A. Guthrie
Anthony, C. L.	Dorothy Gladys Smith
Anthony, John	John Ciardi
Anthony, Piers	Piers Anthony Dillingham Jacob
Antoniorrobles	Antonio Robles Soler
Anvic, Frank	Jory Sherman
Anvil, Christopher	Harry C. Crosby
Appel, H. M.	Wayne Rogers
Appleton, Laurence	H. P. Lovecraft
Appleton, Victor	E. Stratemeyer (syndicate); H. R. Garis
Arch, E. L.	Rachel C. Payes
Archer, Lee (h)	H. Ellison; others
Archer, Ron	Ted White
Archette, Guy	Chester S. Geier

Pseudonym	Real Name
Arcot, Roger	Robert D. Locke
Arden, J. E. M.	Robert Conquest
Arden, Rice	Maurice A. Weakley
Arden, William	Dennis Lynds
Arlen, Michael	Dikran Kuyamjian
Armstrong, Anthony	Anthony A. Willis
Armstrong, Charlotte	Charlotte Armstrong Lewis
Armstrong, Geoffrey	John Russell Fearn
Armstrong, Warren	W. E. Bennett
Arne, Aaron	A. A. Jorgenson
Arnette, Robert (h)	C. S. Geier (?); R. Silverberg
Arnette, Stephen	Stephen A. Rynas
Arno, Elroy	Leroy Yerxa
Arnold, John	Frederick A. Kummer, Jr.
Aronin, Ben	Edna Herron
Arr, Stephen	Stephen A. Rynas
Arrow, William (h)	Don Pfeil; William Rotsler
Arthur, Peter	Arthur Porges
Arthur, Robert	R. A. Feder
Arthur, William	Wilfred McNeilly
Arzhak, Nicolai	Yuli Daniel
Ash, Fenton	Frank Atkins, Jr.
Ash, Paul	Pauline Ashwell
Ashe, Gordon	John Creasey
Ashley, Fred	Frank Atkins
Asquith, Lady Cynthia	Mary Evelyn Charteris
Atheling, William, Jr.	James Blish
Atomcracker, Buzz-Bolt	Don Wilcox
Atterley, Joseph	George Tucker
Aubrey, Frank	Frank Atkins, Jr.
August, Leo	Don Segall
Augustus, Albert, Jr.	Charles Nuetzel
Aumbry, Alan	Barrington J. Bayley
Austin, Frank	Frederick Faust
Austin, Mary	Jane Rice
Avery, Richard	Edmund Cooper
Axton, David	Dean R. Koontz
Ayes, Anthony	William Sambrot
Ayes, William	William Sambrot
Ayre, Thornton	John Russell Fearn

B

Pseudonym	Real Name
B.B.	Denys J. Watkins-Pitchford
Badger, Richard C.	Eric Temple Bell
Bagnold, Enid	Lady Jones
Bahl, Franklin (h)	Roger P. Graham; others
Bahr, Robert	Sam Moskowitz (fan pseud.)
Bain, Ted	E. C. Tubb
Baker, Martin L.	Sydney J. Bounds
Baker, W. Howard	Wilfred McNeilly
Balfort, Neil	Robert L. Fanthorpe
Ballinger, W. A. (h)	Wilfred McNeilly
Balons, Earl	Cyril Kornbluth
Banat, D. R.	Ray Bradbury
Banks, Edward	Ray Bradbury
Bannon, Mark	Albert King
Banshuck, Grego	Hugo Gernsback
Barbee, Phillips	Robert Sheckley
Barber, Antonio	Barbara Anthony
Barbet, Pierre	Claude Avice
Barclay, Alan	George B. Tait
Barclay, Bill	Michael Moorcock
Barclay, Gabriel (h)	Cyril Kornbluth; M. W. Wellman
Barclay, Lester	Berkeley Livingston
Barlay, Bennett	Kendell Foster Crossen
Barnes, Dave	Arthur K. Barnes & Norbert Davis
Baron, Othello	Robert L. Fanthorpe

Pseudonym	Real Name	Pseudonym	Real Name
Barr, Densil Neve	Douglas Norton Buttrey	Blaine, John	H. L. Goodwin & P. J. Harkins
Barretton, Grandall (or **Grandell**)		Blair, Adrian	William F. Bird
	Randall Garrett	Blake, Alan	Omar Gwinn
Barrington, E.	L. Adams Beck	Blake, Alfred	Laurence M. Janifer
Barrington, Michael	Barrington J. Bayley & Michael Moorcock	Blake, Andrew	Laurence M. Janifer
Barry, B. X.	Ray A. Giles	Blake, Anthony	E. C. Tubb
Barry, Mike	Barry N. Malzberg	Blake, Ken	Kenneth Bulmer
Barry, Ray	Dennis Hughes	Blake, Nicholas	Cecil D. Lewis
Barshofsky, Philip	M. M. Kaplan	Bland, Edith	Edith Nesbit
Bartel, Philip J.	M. M. Kaplan	Blayn, Hugo	John Russell Fearn
Bartlett, Laura	L. Frank Baum	Blayre, Christopher	E. Heron-Allen
Barton, Erle	Robert L. Fanthorpe	Blixen, Karen	Baroness Karen Christence Blixen-Finecke
Barton, Lee	Robert L. Fanthorpe	Bloodstone, John	Stuart J. Byrne
Bass, T. J.	Thomas J. Bassler	Boehm, Herb	John Varley
Bawden, Nina	Nina Mary Kark	Bohassian, Gregor	William Rotsler
Baxter, George Owen	Frederick Faust	Boisgilbert, Edmund	Ignatius Donnelly
Beal, Nick	Forrest J Ackerman	Bok, Hannes	Wayne Woodard
Beale, Anne	F. Orlin Tremaine	Boland, John	Bertram J. Boland
Bean, Normal	Edgar Rice Burroughs	Bolt, Lee	Frederick Faust
Bean, Norman	Edgar Rice Burroughs	Bond, Evelyn	Morris Hershman
Bearden, Anthony	Paul M. A. Linebarger	Bond, J. Harvey	Russell R. Winterbotham
Beaumont, Charles	Charles Nutt	Bonehill, Capt. Ralph	Edward Stratemeyer (syndicate)
Beaumont, E. J.	Charles Nutt	Boone, Barney	William Rotsler
Beck, Allen	Hugh B. Cave	Booth, Irwin	Edward D. Hoch
Beckman, Ross	Frederic V. R. Dey & Donald Fairde & Kenneth Fearing	Borodin, George	George A. Bankoff
		Boston, Charles K.	Frank Gruber
Bedford, Donald E.	Henry Bedford-Jones	Botham, R. R.	Russell R. Winterbotham
Beecher, Lee	Stanley Mullen	Boucher, Anthony	W. A. P. White
Beecher, Stanley	Stanley Mullen	Boult, S. Kye	Willam E. Cochrane
Beeding, Francis	John L. Palmer & Hilary St. G. Saunders	Bowen, Marjorie	Gabrielle M. V. Long
Belflower, James A.	Guy Fowler	Bowen, Olwen	Olwen B. Davies
Bell, Neil	Stephen Southwold	Bowers, Mrs. J. Milton	Ambrose Bierce
Bell, Thornton	Robert L. Fanthorpe	Bowers, R. L.	John S. Glasby
Bellin, Edward J. (h)	H. Kuttner; others	Box, Edgar	Gore Vidal
Bellini, Signor	Joshua Smith	Boyce, Morton	John Russell Fearn
Benedict, Lynn	Victor J. Banis	Boyd, Felix	Harry Harrison
Bennet, John	James Weakley	Boyd, John	Boyd B. Upchurch
Bennett, Elizabeth Deare	Sam Merwin, Jr.	Brack, Vektis (h)	Leslie G. Humphreys
Benson, Edwin	Real person, but used as house name by Richard S. Shaver & others.	Brackett, Leigh (née)	Mrs. Edmond Hamilton
		Brackett, Waring	William Rotsler
Benson, Stella (née)	Mrs. J. O. Anderson	Bradbury, Edward P.	Michael Moorcock
Beresford, Marcus	Marc Brandel	Bradford, Adam	Joseph Wasserburg
Berkeley, Anthony	Anthony B. Cox	Bradford, Simon	Russell R. Winterbotham
Berry, Julian	Ernesto Gastoldi	Bradley, Alice	Alice Sheldon
Bertin, Jack	Giovanni Bartignono	Brahms, Caryl	Doris C. Abrahams
Bertram, Noel	Noel Boston; Robert L. Fanthorpe	Bramah, Ernest	Ernest B. Smith
Bethlen, T. D.	Robert Silverberg	Brand, Christianna	Mary Christianna Milne Lewis
Bevan, Alistair	Keith Roberts	Brand, Hilary (h)	Hilary Bailey
Beynon, John	John B. Harris	Brand, Max	Frederick Faust
Bickerstaffe, Isaac, Jr.	H. P. Lovecraft	Brandel, Marc	Marcus Beresford
Bigly, Cantell A.	George W. Peck	Brandon, Carl	Ron Ellik; Peter Graham (fan pseud.)
Bilbo, Jack	Hugo Baruch	Brandon, Frank	Kenneth Bulmer
Binder, Eando	Earl A. Binder & Otto Binder; Otto Binder	Brendall, Eith	Eddy Bertin
Bingham, Carson	Bruce Cassiday	Brengle, William (h)	H. Browne; others
Bird, Cordwainer	Harlan Ellison	Brent, Loring	George F. Worts
Bird, Cortwainer	Harlan Ellison	Brett, Leo	Robert L. Fanthorpe
Bishop, Zealia B.	Zealia B. Reed	Briarton, Grendel	Reginald Bretnor
Black, Robert	Robert B. Holdstock	Bridge, Ann	M. D. O'Malley
Blackburn, John	J. Moldon Mott	Bridge, Frank J.	Frank J. Brueckel
Blacklin, Malcolm	Aidan Chambers	Bridger, John	Joe Gibson
Blackmon, Robert C.	Roger Howard Norton	Brisbane, Coutts	R. Coutts Armour
Blackstock, Charity	Ursula Torday	Brissard, Montague	H. Bedford-Jones
Blade, Alexander (h)	David Vern originally; then house name for Ziff-Davis (*AS* & *FA*): H. Browne; M. Cooke; R. Garrett & R. Silverberg; C. S. Geier; R. P. Graham; E. Hamilton; H. Hauser; John Jakes; B. Livingston; W. P. McGivern; D. W. O'Brien; L. H. Sampliner; R. S. Shaver; D. Wilcox; L. Yerxa; others	Bristol, John A.	Jack Speer
		Britain, Dan	Don Pendleton
		Brock, Lynn	Allister McAllister
		Brock, Stuart	Louis Trimble
		Brockley, Fenton	Donald S. Rowland
		Brogan, James	Christopher Hodder-Williams
		Bronson, L. T.	E. C. Tubb
		Brown, Carter (h)	Alan G. Yates

Pseudonym	Real Name
Brown, Douglas	Walter B. Gibson
Brown, John	Willy Ley
Brown, L. J.	Linda DuBreuil
Brown, William	Ernst H. Richter
Browning, Craig	Roger P. Graham
Browning, John S.	Robert M. Williams
Bruce, Ian	F. C. Kneller
Brunner, K. Houston	John Brunner
Bruss, B. R.	Roger Blondel
Brutsche, Alphonse	Jean-Pierre Andrevon
Bryan, Michael	Brian Moore
Bryant, Peter	Peter George
Bryusov, Valery	Valery Brussof (transliteration variation)
Buckner, Bradner	Ed Earl Repp
Bupp, Walter	Randall Garrett
Burgess, Anthony	John Burgess Wilson
Burke, Carl F.	Forrest J Ackerman
Burke, Jonathan	John F. Burke
Burke, Ralph	Randall Garrett & Robert Silverberg
Burleigh, Cecil	Lu Senarens
Burr, Aaron Ainsworth	Frederic V. R. Dey
Burton, Edmund	Edmund Burton Childs
Burton, Miles	Cecil J. C. Street
Burton, Raymond L.	E. C. Tubb
Butler, Ivan	Edward Ivan Oakley Beuttler
Butler, Joan	Robert W. Alexander
Butler, Nathan	Gerald Allan Sohl
Butler, Walter C.	Frederick Faust
Buxton, C.	Harold Hersey

C

Pseudonym	Real Name
Cabot, John York	David W. O'Brien
Cahill, Mike	William F. Nolan
Caine, Jeff	Rainer Eisfeld
Caldwell, Taylor	Janet Taylor Caldwell & Marcus Reback
Calhoun, Mary	Mary H. Wilkins
Callahan, William	Raymond Z. Gallun
Callender, Julian	Austin Lee
Calvert, Mary	Mary Danby
Cameron, Berl (h)	John Glasby; Brian Holloway; Dennis T. Hughes; David O'Brien & Arthur Roberts
Cameron, Ian	Donald G. Payne
Cameron, John	Archibald Gordon MacDonnell
Cameron, Leigh	Sewell P. Wright
Campbell, Angus	Ronald Chetwynd-Hayes
Campbell, Clyde Crane	H. L. Gold
Campbell, Margaret	Gabrielle M. V. Long
Campbell, Molly	Christine Campbell Thomson
Campbell, R. T.	Ruthven Todd
Cannon, Curt	Evan Hunter
Capella, Ray	Raul Garcia Capella
Capp, Al	A. G. Caplin
Caravan, T. P.	Charles Munoz
Carey, Julian	E. C. Tubb
Carghill, Ralph	Arthur J. Cox
Carleton, Hugh B. (h)	H. Browne; others
Carleton, S.	S. Carleton Jones
Carlsen, Chris	Robert P. Holdstock
Carlton, Roger	Donald S. Rowland
Carnac, Levin	George Chetwynd Griffith-Jones
Carne, Roger	Sydney J. Bounds
Carnell, John	Edward J. Carnell
Carpenter, Morley	E. C. Tubb
Carr, Charles	Sydney Charles Mason
Carr, Jayge	Margery Krueger
Carrel, Mark	Lauran Bosworth Paine

Pseudonym	Real Name
Carroll, Lewis	Charles L. Dodgson
Carsac, Francis	François Bordes
Carse, Shannon	William Rotsler
Carter, Bronson D.	Thomas W. Wade
Carter, Bruce	Richard A. Hough
Carter, Dee (h)	Dennis T. Hughes
Carter, Diana	Dorothy Copper
Carter, Elizabeth Eliot	Cecelia Holland
Carter, Nick (h)	Michael Avallone; Bryan Carter; William Wallace Cook; John R. Coryell; Frederick W. Davis; Frederic Dey; W. Bert Foster; Thomas W. Hanshew; Thomas C. Harbaugh; George C. Jenks; Johnston McCulley; Eugene T. Sawyer; Ormond G. Smith; John W. Whitson; R. Wormser
Carter, Philip	Paul A. Carter
Cary, Jud	E. C. Tubb
Case, Justin	Hugh B. Cave
Casey, Kent	Kenneth McIntosh
Casey, Richard (h)	Leroy Yerxa; others (Ziff-Davis magazines)
Cassaba, Carlos	Michel Parry
Castle, J.	R. C. Payner & J. W. Garrod
Castle, Robert	Edmond Hamilton
Cavendish, Peter	Sydney Horler
Caxton	W. H. Rhodes
Cecil, Henry	Henry Cecil Leon, a real person; also used as pseudonym by David H. Keller.
Cente, H. F.	Ross Rocklin
Cerra, Gerda Ann	Mrs. Dean R. Koontz
Chaber, M. E.	Kendell F. Crossen
Chain, Julian	Julian Chain May Dikty (Mrs. T. E. Dikty)
Challis, George	Frederick Faust
Chance, George	G. T. Fleming-Roberts
Chandler, Lawrence (h)	H. Browne; others
Chapman, Lee	Marion Z. Bradley
Chapman, Walter	Robert Silverberg
Charles, Neil (h)	Brian Holloway; John W. Jennison; Dennis Hughes
Chartair, Max	John S. Glasby
Charteris, Leslie	Leslie C. B. Lin (mostly); C. Cartmill; H. Harrison;
Chase, Adam	Paul W. Fairman & Milton Lesser
Chase, Alice	Georgess McHargue
Chase, Cleveland B.	H. Bedford-Jones
Chase, James Hadley	Rene Raymond
Cheiro	Louis Hamon
Cherryh, C. J.	Carolyn Janice Cherry
Chesney, Weatherby	C. J. Cutcliffe Hyne
Chinwell, Walter	Forrest J Ackerman
Chipperfield, Robert Orr	Isabel Ostrander
Christian, Colin	Chris Steinbrunner
Christopher, John	Christopher S. Youd
Churchill, Joyce	M. John Harrison
Churchward, John	W. J. Baker
Claire, Keith	Claire Andrews & Keith Andrews
Clapp, Patricia	P. C. L. Cone
Clark, Curt	Donald E. Westlake
Clark(e), Dale	Ronal Kayser
Clarke, W. B.	Norman A. Lazenby
Clarkson, J. F.	E. C. Tubb
Clarkson, W. E.	Sydney J. Bounds
Clay, Bertha M. (h)	Frederic V. R. Dey
Clement, Hal	Harry C. Stubbs
Cleve, John	Andrew J. Offutt
Clinton, Dirk	Robert Silverberg
Clinton, Jeff	Jack Miles Bickham
Clinton, Rupert	Kenneth Bulmer
Clive, Dennis	John Russell Fearn
Cloukey, Charles	Charles Cloutier

Pseudonym	Real Name
Clyde, Kit	Lu Senarens
Coburn, L. J. (h)	John Harvey; Laurence James
Cody, C. S.	Leslie Waller
Cody, John	Ed Earl Repp
Coffey, Brian	Dean R. Koontz
Cole, Burt	Thomas Dixon
Coleridge, John	Earl and Otto Binder
Coles, Manning	Adelaide Manning & Cyril Coles
Coley, Robert	Howard E. Wandrei
Collier, Harry	Harry Walton
Collins, Charles	Wilkie Collins & Charles Dickens
Collins, Clark	Dallas McCord Reynolds
Collins, Hunt	Evan Hunter
Collins, Mabel C.	Mabel C. Cook
Collins, Michael	Dennis Lynds
Collinson, Peter	Dashiell Hammett
Collodi, Carlo	Carlo Lorenzini
Colson, Bill	William V. Athanas
Colt, Winchester Remington	
	L. Ron Hubbard
Colter, Eli	Elizabeth Colter
Colvin, James	Michael Moorcock
Comer, Ralph	John Sanders
Comfort, Montgomery (h)	Ramsey Campbell
Compton, Guy	D. G. Compton
Compton, Margaret	Amelia W. Harrison
Conanight	Chester Cohen & Damon Knight
Conant, Chester B.	Chester Cohen
Condray, Bruno G.	Leslie G. Humphreys
Conn, Alan	Alan Connell
Connington, J. J.	Alfred W. Stewart
Connolly, Paul	Tom Wicker
Conrad, Gregg	Roger P. Graham
Conrad, Joseph	Teodor J. K. Korzeniowski
Conrad, Logan	William Rotsler
Conrad, Paul	Albert King
Conway, Bowen	John Michel
Conway, Hugh	Frederick John Fargus
Conway, Randall	John S. Glasby
Conway, Ritter	Damon Knight
Conway, Troy (h)	Michael Avallone; Gardner F. Fox; others
Conyers, Latham	Arthur L. Zagat
Cook, John Estes	L. Frank Baum
Cooke, Arthur	E. Balter & Cyril Kornbluth & R. Lowndes & J. Michel & D. Wollheim (jointly)
Cooke, M. E.	John Creasey
Cooke, Margaret	John Creasey
Cooper, C. Everett	M. R. Burgess
Cooper, Henry St. John	John Creasey
Cooper, Jefferson	Gardner F. Fox
Coover, Wayne	R. Eisfeld
Corbett, Chan	Nathan Schachner
Corbin, Michael	Cleve Cartmill
Cord, Barry	Peter B. Germano
Cordell, Alexander	Alexander Graber
Corelli, Marie	Mary MacKay
Corley, Ernest	Kenneth Bulmer
Corning, Kyle	Erle Stanley Gardner
Corren, Grace	Robert Hoskins
Correy, Lee	G. Harry Stine
Corvais, Anthony	Ray Bradbury (fan pseud.)
Corvo, Baron	Frederick Rolfe
Corwin, Cecil	Cyril Kornbluth
Cory, Desmond	Shaun McCarthy
Cory, Howard L.	Jack Owen Jardine & Julie Ann Jardine (former wife)
Cosmic, Ray	John S. Glasby
Cost, March	Peggy Morrison
Costello, P. F. (h)	C. S. Geier; R. P. Graham; others
Coster, Arthur	Richard DeMille

Pseudonym	Real Name
Cotton, John	John Russell Fearn
Cottrell, Harvey S.	Harold Standish Corbin
Council of Four	complex—see *WHO'S WHO*
Coupling, J. J.	John R. Pierce
Cowper, Richard	Colin Middleton Murry
Cox, Jean	Arthur J. Cox
Coxe, Kathleen Buddington	Amelia Reynolds Long & Edna McHugh
Craig, A. A.	Poul Anderson
Craig, Brian	Brian Stableford
Craig, David	Allan James Tucker
Craig, Randolph	Norvell Page
Craig, Webster	Eric F. Russell
Craigie, David	Dorothy M. Craigie
Crane, Eric	Gabriel Setterborg
Crane, Robert	Bernard Glemser
Crawford, Robert	Hugh C. Rae
Cresswell, Helen	Helen Rowe
Crispin, Edmund	Robert B. Montgomery
Cristabel	Christine Elizabeth Abrahamsen
Critchie, Estil	Arthur J. Burks
Crompton, Richmal	Richmal Crompton Lambourn
Cross, Gene	Arthur J. Cox
Cross, Polton	John Russell Fearn
Crow, Levi	Manly W. Wellman
Crowe, John	Dennis Lynds
Crowley, Aleister	Edward Alexander Crowley
Culver, Timothy J.	Donald E. Westlake
Cunningham, Cathy	Chet Cunningham
Cunningham, Cecil Claybourne	
	Ray Bradbury (fan pseud.)
Cunningham, E.	Ray Bradbury (fan pseud.)
Cunningham, E. V.	Howard M. Fast
Cunningham, J. Morgan	Donald E. Westlake
Curtis, Jean-Louis	Louis Lafitte
Curtis, Peter	Norah Lofts
Curtis, Wade	Jerry Pournelle

D

Pseudonym	Real Name
Dain, Alex	Alex Lukeman
Dale, Donald	Mary Dale Buckner
Dale, George E.	Isaac Asimov
Dale, Norman	E. C. Tubb
Dallas, Ian	Davis, Ian
Dalton, Priscilla	Michael Avallone
Daly, Hamlin	E. Hoffmann Price
Damon, Carl	Calvin W. Demmon
Dana, Rose	W. E. D. Ross
Dancer, J. B. (h)	John Harvey; Angus Wells
Dane, Clemence	Winifred Ashton
Dane, Mark	Michael Avallone
Daniels, Dorothy	Dorothy Daniels & Norman Daniels
Daniels, Gil	Gyle Davis
Daniels, Jan	W. E. D. Ross
Daniels, Louis G.	Daniel F. Galouye
Daniels, Max	Roberta Gellis
Danvers, Jack	C. A. M. Caseleyr
Danzell, George	Nelson S. Bond
Dare, Alan	George Goodchild
Dare, Howard	Stuart J. Byrne
D'Argyre, Gilles	Gerard Klein
Darlton, Clark	Walter Ernsting
Darrow, Jack	Clifford Kornoelje
Davidson, Gene A.	David Lesperance
Davidson, Hugh	Edmond Hamilton
Davies, Walter C.	Cyril Kornbluth
Davis, Elizabeth	Lou Ellen Davis
Davis, Pat	David E. Pattee

Pseudonym	Real Name	Pseudonym	Real Name
Dawson, Peter	Frederick Faust	**Dreadstone, Carl** (h)	J. Ramsey Campbell
De Casseres, Benjamin	Clark Ashton Smith	**Drew, Sheridan**	John Russell Fearn
de Castro, Adolphe	Gustaf A. de Castro Danziger	**Drexel, Jay B.**	Jerome Bixby
De Costa, Henry	Frederik Pohl (fan pseud.)	**Drummond, J.**	John N. Chance
de la Torre, Lillian	Lillian McCue	**Drummond, John Peter** (h)	Stanley Mullen; others
de Natale, Francine	Barry N. Malzberg	**Drummond, Walter**	Robert Silverberg
de Pre, Jean-Anne	Michael Avallone	**Druon, Maurice**	Maurice Kessel
De Reyna, Jorge	Diane Detzer	**Dryasdüst**	M. Y. Halidom (itself a pseud.)
D.E.A.	M. Dominick	**Duane, Andrew**	Robert E. Briney
Deane, Norman	John Creasey	**Duane, Toby**	W. Paul Ganley
Decles, Jon	Don Studebaker	**Dudley, Trevor**	Trevor Dudley-Smith
Dee, Nicholas	Joan Aiken	**Duka, Ivo**	Ivo Duchacek
Dee, Roger	Roger D. Aycock	**Dumas, Claudine**	Barry N. Malzberg
Dee, Sylvia	Josephine M. Proffitt	**Duncan, Bruce**	Irving A. Greenfield
Deegan, Jon J. (h)	H. J. Campbell	**Dunn, Saul**	Philip M. Dunn
Deeming, Richard	Richard Deming	**Dunne, John T.**	H. P. Lovecraft
Deer, M. J.	George H. Smith & M. Jane Deer	**Dunsany, Lord**	Edward J. M. D. Plunkett
deGraeff, W. B.	A. P. Blaustein & G. Conklin	**Dunstan, Andrew**	A. Bertram Chandler
Dehan, Richard	Clotilde I. M. Graves	**Dupont, Kurt**	Andre Ruellan
del Martia, Astron (h)	Stephen Frances; John R. Fearn; others	**Durham, David**	Roy Vickers
del Rey, Lester	Ramon Alvarez del Rey	**Durrant, Theo**	William Anthony Parker White
Dell, Dudley	Horace L. Gold	**Dwyer, Deanna**	Dean R. Koontz
Dell, Paul	Paul Blaisdell	**Dwyer, K. R.**	Dean R. Koontz
Demijohn, Thom	Thomas M. Disch		
DeMourant, George Souli	H. Bedford-Jones		
Dempsey, Hank	Harry Harrison		
Denholm, Mark	John Russell Fearn	**E., A.**	George William Russell
Denmark, Harrison	Roger Zelazny	**Eagle, Solomon**	Sir John Collings Squire
Dennis, Bruce	David W. O'Brien	**Earle, W. J.**	Lu Senarens
Dentinger, Stephen	Edward D. Hoch	**Earle, William**	W. E. Johns
Destiny, Archibald	Larry Shaw	**Eaton, George L.**	Harold B. Montayne; Chuck Vernal
DeWeese, Jean	Eugene DeWeese	**Eckman, J. Forrester**	Forrest J Ackerman
Dexter, Edwin	Richard S. Shaver	**Edgar, Peter**	Peter King-Scott
Dexter, J. B.	John S. Glasby	**Edmonds, Paul**	Henry Kuttner
Dexter, John	Marion Z. Bradley	**Edmondson, G. C.**	J. M. G. O. Edmondson y Cotton
Dexter, John	John Coleman	**Edson, George Alden**	Paul Ernst
Dexter, Martin	Frederick Faust	**Edwards, Dolton**	W. E. Lessing
Dexter, Peter	Richard S. Shaver	**Edwards, Gawain**	G. Edward Pendray
Dexter, William	Wm. Thomas Pritchard	**Edwards, Hamm**	Thelma Hamm Evans (Mrs. E. E. Evans)
Dey, Marmaduke	Frederic V. R. Dey	**Edwards, Norman**	Ted White & Terry Carr
di Savuto, Baroni	Greye Bragg La Spina	**Efremov, I.**	I. Yefremov (different transliterations)
Diamond, John	Barrington J. Bayley	**Egbert, H. M.**	Victor R. Emanuel
Dick, R. A.	Josephine Leslie	**Egerton, George**	Mary Chavelita Dunne Bright
Dickson, Carr	John D. Carr	**Egremont, Michael**	Michael Harrison
Dickson, Carter	John D. Carr	**Eisner, Sam**	Cyril Kornbluth
Dinesen, Isaak	Karen Blixen-Finecke	**Eisner, Simon**	Cyril Kornbluth
Diomede, John K.	George Alec Effinger	**Elclair, Mollie**	Richard S. Shaver
Diplomat	John Franklin Carter	**Eldershaw, M. Barnard**	F. S. P. Eldershaw & Marjorie F. Barnard (one sf novel by latter only)
Divine, David	Arthur D. Divine		
Doak	Hugh Rankin	**Eldon, Cleo**	Don Wilcox
Dr. A	Isaac Asimov	**Eldred, Brian**	Ray Bradbury (fan pseud.)
Doctor X	Alan E. Nourse	**Elgin, Suzette Haden**	Patricia A. Suzette Elgin
Dodd, Douglas	John Russell Fearn	**Eliott, E. C.**	R. A. Martin
Doenim, Susan	George Alec Effinger	**Ellanbee, Boyd**	Wm. C. Boyd & Lyle G. Boyd
Dogbolt, Barnaby	H. Silvette	**Ellanby, Boyd**	Wm. C. Boyd & Lyle G. Boyd
Dolbokov	Boris Dolgov & Hannes Bok (W. Woodard)	**Ellerman, Gene**	Basil Wells
Dolinsky, Mike	Meyer Dolinsky	**Elliot, Lee** (h)	William H. Bird; Dennis T. Hughes
Donne, Hamilton (h)	Norman A. Lazenby	**Elliott, William**	Ray Bradbury
Donovan, Dick	Joyce E. Preston-Muddock	**Ellis, Craig** (h)	Lee Rogow; D. Vern; others (Ziff-Davis magazines)
Dorot, Richard	Richard S. Shaver		
Doughty, Frank	Lu Senarens	**Ellis, John**	F. C. Kneller
Douglas, Jeff	Andrew J. Offutt & D. Bruce Berry	**Elstar, Dow**	Raymond Z. Gallun
Douglas, Leonard	Ray Bradbury	**Elton, John**	J. Marsh
Douglas, Michael	Michael Crichton	**Elton, Max**	John Russell Fearn
Douglas, R. M.	Douglas R. Mason	**Ely, David**	David Lilienthal, Jr.
Douglas, Theo	Mrs. H. D. Everett	**Emsh, Ed**	Ed A. Emshwiller
Downes, Quentin	Michael Harrison	**Emsler**	Ed A. Emshwiller
Doyle, John	Harlan Ellison (ghost written)	**Enfield, Hugh**	Gwilym F. Hughes
Draco, F.	Julia David	**Engelhardt, Frederick**	L. Ron Hubbard
Drake, Morgan	D. Bruce Berry		

E

Pseudonym	Real Name
English, Charles	Charles Nuetzel
English, Richard	Richard S. Shaver
Ennis, Robert D.	E. C. Tubb
Epernay, Mark	John Kenneth Galbraith
Erckmann-Chatrian	Emile Erckmann & Alexandre Chatrian
Ericson, Walter	Howard M. Fast
Erman, Jacques de Forrest	Forrest J Ackerman
Ermann, Jack	Forrest J Ackerman (fan pseud.)
Ervin, Patrick	Robert E. Howard
Esterbrook, Tom	L. Ron Hubbard
Esteven, John	Samuel Shellabarger
Estival	Ivan Leon Estival
Eustace, Robert	Eustace Rawlins
Evans, Dean	George Kull
Evans, Evan	Frederick Faust
Evans, Evin	Frederick Faust
Evans, Ian	Angus Wells
Evans, John	Howard Browne
Ewing, Frederick R.	Theodore Sturgeon & Jean Shepherd
Ex-Private X	A. M. Burrage

F

Pseudonym	Real Name
Faine, Djinn	Virginia Faine Russell
Fair, A. A.	Erle Stanley Gardner
Faire, Zabrina	Florence Stevenson
Fairfield, Henry W. A.	Harold Standish Corbin
Fairless, Michael	Margaret Barber
Falconer, Kenneth	Cyril Kornbluth
Fane, Bron	Robert L. Fanthorpe
Fanhope, Robert Lionel	Robert L. Fanthorpe
Farley, Ralph Milne	Roger S. Hoar
Farmer, Arthur	Jack Jardine
Farnsworth, Duncan	David W. O'Brien
Farr, Caroline	Alan Geoffrey Yates
Farr, John	Jack Webb
Farrell, John Wade	John D. MacDonald
Farrere, Claude	Charles Bargone
Farrow, James S.	E. C. Tubb
Fassbinder, Carlton J.	T. Bruce Yerke
Faust, Alexander	Harry Altshuler
Fawkes, Farrah	Andrew J. Offutt
Fecamps, Elise	John Creasey
Feld, Friedrich	F. Rosenfeld
Fenner, James R.	E. C. Tubb
Fenton, Bruce (h)	F. C. Kneller
Ferney, Manuel	Manly Wade Wellman
Ferrat, Jacques Jean	Sam Merwin, Jr.
Ferval, Paul	H. Bedford-Jones
Fickling, G. G.	Gloria Fickling & Forrest E. Fickling
Field, Frank Chester	Bernard Glemser
Field, Gans T.	Manly W. Wellman
Field, George Peterson	Robert L. Forward
Field, Peter	Ed Earl Repp
Finney, Jack	Walter B. Finney
Fips, Mohammed Ulysses Socrates	
	Hugo Gernsback
Fisher, Clay	Henry Allen
Fiske, Tarleton	Robert Bloch
Fitt, Mary	Kathleen Freeman
Fitzgerald, Hugh	L. Frank Baum
Fitzgerald, William	Will F. Jenkins
Flagg, Francis	George H. Weiss
Flanders, John	Raymond de Kremer
Flehr, Paul	Frederik Pohl
Fleming, Harry	William H. F. Bird
Fleming, Stuart	Damon Knight
Fletcher, George U.	Fletcher Pratt

Pseudonym	Real Name
Fletcher, John C.	Harold Standish Corbin
Fodor, Nandor	Hereward Carrington
Folke, Will	Robert Bloch
Foray, Verge	Howard L. Myers
Forbes, Colin	Raymond Harold Sawkins
Ford, Garret	William L. & Margaret Crawford
Ford, Hilary	Christopher S. Youd
Ford, Leslie	Zenith Brown
Forman, Ginny	Hugh Zachery
Forrest, David	David Eliades & Robert Forrest-Webb
Forrest, Felix C.	Paul M. A. Linebarger
Fortune, Dion	Violet Mary Firth
Fosse, Harold C.	Horace L. Gold
Foster, Richard	Kendell F. Crossen
Fowler, Sidney	S. Fowler Wright
France, Anatole	Jacques A. Thibault
Francis, Gregory	Frank Parnell, alone & with J. M. MacGregor
Francis, Jean	Anita Grace
Francis, Lee (h)	Leroy Yerxa; H. Browne
Frank, Pat	Harry Hart Frank
Franklin, Jay	John Franklin Carter
Franklin, Max	Richard Deming
Franklin, Paul	Bryce Walton
Frazee, Steve	Charles S. Frazee
Frazer, Andrew	Milton Lesser
Frazier, Arthur (h)	Kenneth Bulmer; Laurence James
Frederick, John	Frederick Faust
Fredericks, Harriet	Clyde Laurents & James Smock
French, Paul	Isaac Asimov
Frikell, Samri	Fulton Oursler
Frome, David	Zenith Brown
Frost, Frederick	Frederick Faust
Fuller, Roger	Donald Fiske Tracy
Fuqua, Robert	Joe W. Tillotson
Furey, Michael	Arthur Sarsfield Ward (Sax Rohmer)
Furth, Carlton	Joe Gibson
Fury, Nick	Michel Parry

G

Pseudonym	Real Name
Gade, Henry (h)	R. A. Palmer; others
Gage, Wilson	Mary Quintard Steele
Gaite, Francis	Adelaide F. O. Manning & C. H. Coles
Galaxan, Sol	Alfred Coppel
Gale, Floyd C.	Floyd Gold
Gallister, Michael	H. Bedford-Jones
Galt, Walter	William Lancaster Gribbon (Talbot Mundy)
Ganpat	M. L. Gompertz
Gardner, Harry J.	E. Everett Evans
Gardner, Jeffrey	Gardner F. Fox
Gardner, Miriam	Marion Z. Bradley
Gardner, Noel	Henry Kuttner
Garfield, Frances	Mrs. Manly W. Wellman
Garne, Gaston	Lu Senarens
Garner, Graham	Donald S. Rowland
Garner, Rolf	Bryan Berry
Garnet, G.	Irvin Ashkenazy
Garrett, Charles C. (h)	Laurence James; Angus Wells
Garrett, Eileen J.	Eileen J. Lyttle
Garrett, Gordon	Randall Garrett
Garron, Robert A.	Howard E. Wandrei
Garson, Clee	David W. O'Brien
Garth, Andrew	William Rotsler
Garth, Will (h)	O. Binder; A. Derleth; E. Hamilton; H. Kuttner; M. Weisinger; M. W. Wellman
Gary, Gene	J. J. Des Ormeaux
Gary, Romain	Romain Kacewgari
Gashbuck, Greno	Hugo Gernsback

Pseudonym	Real Name
Gaskell, Jane	Jane Gaskell Lynch
Gast, Kelly P.	J. M. G. O. Edmondson y Cotton
Gaul, Gilbert	James DeMille
Gawsworth, John	Terence I. F. Armstrong
Ged, Caer	Jerrold D. Friedman
General X	Roger S. Hoar
George, Daniel	D. G. Bunting
George, Edward	Jerrold D. Friedman & Bob Vardeman
Geris, Tom Erwin	Mort Weisinger
Gerrold, David	Jerrold David Friedman
Gibbon, Lewis Grassic	J. Leslie Mitchell
Gibbs, Lewis	Joseph W. Cove
Gibson, Floyd	Albert King
Gift, Theo	Dora Havers
Gilbert, Anthony	Lucy Beatrice Malleson
Giles, Baxter	Andrew J. Offutt
Giles, Douglas	James Hall
Giles, Elizabeth	John R. Holt
Giles, Geoffrey	Forrest J Ackerman & Walter Gillings (fan pseud.)
Giles, Gordon A.	Otto Binder
Giles, Raymond	John R. Holt
Gill, Patrick	John Creasey
Gilman, George G.	Terry Harknett
Gilman, Robert Cham	Alfred Coppel
Gilmer, Ann	W. E. D. Ross
Gilmore, Anthony	Harry Bates & Desmond W. Hall
Gilmore, Marian (h)	Frederic V. R. Dey
Glamis, Walter	Nathan Schachner
Godfrey, R. H.	E. C. Tubb
Godfrey, William	Christopher S. Youd
Goldthwaite, James A.	Francis James
Gonsales, Domingo	Francis Godwin
Goodrich, Clifford	Alan Hathway
Goodwin, John	Sidney F. Gowing
Gopaleen, Myles Na	Brian O Nolan
Gordon, David	Randall Garrett
Gordon, Donald	Donald G. Payne
Gordon, Fritz	F. G. Jarvis
Gordon, Millard Verne	Donald A. Wollheim
Gordon, Nathaniel	Gordon Gasko
Gordon, Rex	Stanley B. Hough
Gordon, Spike	John Russell Fearn
Gordon, Stuart	Richard Gordon
Gottesman, S. D.	Cyril Kornbluth; Kornbluth & F. Pohl; Kornbluth, Pohl & R. W. Lowndes
Gould, Arthur Lee	Arthur S. G. Lee
Graaf, Peter	Christopher S. Youd
Graey, Julian	H. L. Gold
Graham, Charles S.	E. C. Tubb
Graham, Felix	Fredric Brown
Graham, Howard W.	Howard Wandrei
Graham, Robert	Joe W. Haldeman
Granger, D. J.	Milton Lesser
Granger, Darius John	John W. Jakes
Grant, Joan	Joan Marshall Kelsey
Grant, Maxwell (h)	Walter B. Gibson (mainly); Lester Dent; Bruce Elliott; Philip José Farmer; Dennis Lynds; Theodore Tinsley
Grantland, Keith	Charles Nutt
Graves, Valerie	Marion Z. Bradley
Gray, Anthony	Ernest K. Gann
Gray, Charles	E. C. Tubb
Gray, Rod (h)	Gardner F. Fox; others
Gray, Russell	Bruno Fischer
Gray, Woody	G. L. Rapuzzi
Green,,Charles M.	Erle Stanley Gardner
Green, Peter	Kenneth Bulmer
Greener, Carl	Robert W. Lowndes
Greenwald, Sheila	Sheila Ellen Green

Pseudonym	Real Name
Greer, Richard	Robert Silverberg & Randall Garrett
Gregg, Martin	Wilfred McNeilly
Gregor, Lee	Milton A. Rothman
Gregory, John	Robert Hoskins
Grendon, Stephen	August W. Derleth
Grey, A. F.	Adeline Phyllis Neal
Grey, Carol	Robert W. Lowndes
Grey, Charles	E. C. Tubb
Grey, Judson	Jim Harmon; Harmon & Ron Haydock
Greysun, Doriac	Eddy C. Bertin
Gridban, Volsted (h)	John Russell Fearn; E. C. Tubb
Griff (h)	F. Dubrez Fawcett; John R. Fearn
Griff, Alan	Donald Suddaby
Griffith, George	George Chetwynd Griffith-Jones
Grile, Dod	Ambrose Bierce
Grindle, Carleton	Gerald W. Page
Grinnell, David	Donald A. Wollheim
Groupe, Darryl R.	David R. Bunch
Grove, Frederick Philip	Felix Paul Greve
Guernsey, H. W.	Howard Wandrei
Gulliver, Martin	Norman A. Lazenby
Gunn, Tom (h)	Frank Gruber
Gurney, David	Patrick Bair
Guthrie, Alan	E. C. Tubb
Guthrie, John	John Brodie
Gwinn, Omar	Alan Blake

H

Pseudonym	Real Name
Habergock, Gus N.	Hugo Gernsback
Hadley, Franklin T.	Russell R. Winterbotham
Haggard, William	Richard Clayton
Halibut, Edward	Richard Wilson
Hall, Cameron	Lester del Rey; Harry Harrison
Hall, James	Henry Kuttner
Hall, John Ryder	William Rotsler
Halliday, Brett	David Dresser
Halliday, Michael	John Creasey
Hamilton, Clive	C. S. Lewis
Hamilton, Michael	John S. Glasby
Hamm, T. D. (née)	Thelma Hamm Evans (Mrs. E. E. Evans)
Hammond, Keith	Henry Kuttner & C. L. Moore
Hammond, Paul	Sydney J. Bounds
Hanlon, Jon	Earl Kemp
Hannon, Ezra	Evan Hunter
Hansby, J. J.	John S. Glasby
Hansley, J. J.	John S. Glasby
Hard, Francis	Farnsworth Wright
Harding, Lee	Leo Harding
Harding, Todd	Dallas McCord Reynolds
Hardy, Adam (h)	Kenneth Bulmer; Terry Harknett
Hare, Cyril	Alfred A. G. Clark
Hargreave, Leonie	Thomas M. Disch
Harman, Jane	Terry Harknett
Harmon, H. H.	Robert M. Williams
Harris, Arthur T. (h)	Unknown, used by Ziff-Davis magazines
Harris, Kathleen	Adelaide Humphries
Harris, Larry M.	Laurence M. Janifer
Harrison, Bruce	Edgar Pangborn
Hart, Ellis	Harlan Ellison
Hartley, Christine	Christine Campbell Thomson
Hartley, Malcolm	John Russell Fearn
Hastings, Hudson	H. Kuttner & C. L. Moore
Hatch, Gerald	Dave Foley
Hawkwood, Allan	H. Bedford-Jones
Hawthorne, Rainey	Mrs. J. H. Riddell
Hayes, Timothy	John Russell Fearn
Haynes, John R.	Philip Wilding

Pseudonym	Real Name		Pseudonym	Real Name
Hazel, William	Margaret St. Clair		Hudson, Jeffrey	Michael Crichton
Hazeltine, Horace	Charles Stokes Wayne		Hughes, Colin	John Creasey
Hazzard, Wilton	Margaret St. Clair		Hughes, Elizabeth	Hugh Zachary
Head, Matthew	John Canaday		Hughes, Zach	Hugh Zachary
Heard, Gerald	Henry F. Heard		Hugi, Maurice	Real name; used by E. F. Russell (one story
Heath, Eldon (h)	August W. Derleth			in *ASF*)
Heath, Peter	Peter Fine		Hull, E. Mayne (née)	Mrs. A. E. van Vogt
Held, Peter	Jack Vance		Hull, Richard	Richard H. Sampson
Heller, Cord	William Rotsler		Hung Long Tom	Roswell Williams
Helvick, James	Claud Cockburn		Hunt, Charlotte	Doris Marjorie Hodges
Henneberg, Charles	Real name; also used by Nathalie Charles-		Hunt, Gill (h)	John Brunner; David A. Griffiths; Dennis T.
	Henneberg (wife)			Hughes; John W. Jennison; E. C. Tubb
Henry, Marion	Lester del Rey		Hunt, Kyle	John Creasey
Henry, O.	William S. Porter		Hunter, E. Waldo	Theodore Sturgeon
Henry, Will	Henry Allen		Hunter, Evan	Now legal name of former S. A. Lombino
Heritage, A. J.	Hazel I. W. Addis		Hunter, Joe	Wilfred McNeilly
Heritage, Martin	Sydney Horler		Hunter, Mollie	Maureen Mollie Hunter McIlwraith
Heron, E. & H.	H. Hesketh Prichard & Kate Prichard			
	(mother)			
Herrick, Thornecliff (h)	J. Bixby; others			
Hext, Harrington	Eden Phillpotts			
Hickey, H. B.	Herb Livingston			
Highland, Dora	Michael Avallone			
Higon, Albert	Michel Jeury & Pierre Marlson		Iles, Francis	Anthony B. Cox
Hill, H. Haverstock	J. M. Walsh		Ingoldsby, Thomas	Richard Barham
Hill, King	Bernard Glemser		Innes, Alan	E. C. Tubb
Hilliard, Latham	William Rotsler		Innes, Michael	John I. M. Stewart
Hindin, Nathan	Robert Bloch & Nathan Hindin		Irish, William	Cornell Woolrich
Hine, Muriel	Mrs. Sydney Coxon		Irwin, G. H. (h)	R. A. Palmer; R. S. Shaver
Hitchcock, Alfred	Robert Arthur Feder; Peter Haining;		Ives, Morgan	Marion Zimmer Bradley
	Harold Q. Masur (ghost editors)		Jackson, E. F.	E. C. Tubb
Hodgkins, David C.	Algis Budrys		Jackson, J. Austin	Norman A. Lazenby
Hogarth, Charles	John Creasey		James, Edwin	James E. Gunn
Holbrook, John	Jack Vance		James, Henry	Real name; L. C. Kellenberger
Holiday, Grant	Erle Stanley Gardner		James, Mack	F. C. Kneller
Holland, Linda	William Rotsler		James, Philip	Lester del Rey; James Cawthorn
Hollerbochen	Ray Bradbury (fan pseud.)		James, William M. (h)	Terry Harknett; Laurence James
Hollis, H. H.	Ben Ramey		Jameson, Storm	Mrs. Guy Chapman
Holly, J. Hunter	Joan C. Holly		Janda, N. L.	Lino Aldani
Holmes, A. R.	Harry Bates		Janifer, Laurence M. (now legal name)	
Holmes, Gordon	Louis Tracy; Tracy & M. P. Shiel			Larry Mark Harris (former name)
Holmes, H. H.	Anthony Boucher (pseud. of W. A. P.		Jans, Emerson	Jerome Bixby
	White)		Janson, Hank (h)	Michael Moorcock; Harry Hobson
Holmes, Kenyon	August W. Derleth		Janvier, Ivan	Algis J. Budrys
Holt, Conrad G.	John Russell Fearn		Janvier, Paul	Algis J. Budrys
Holt, George	E. C. Tubb		Jarvis, E. K. (h)	Robert Bloch; Robert Silverberg; R. M.
Holt, Harmony	William Rotsler			Williams; others
Holt, Victoria	Eleanor Alice Burford Hibbert		Jarvis, Lee	Albert Hernhuter
Holton, Leonard	Leonard Wibberley		Jason, Jerry	George H. Smith
Homes, Geoffrey	Daniel Woolrich		Jay, Mel	Robert L. Fanthorpe
Hope, Brian	John Creasey		Jay, Simon	Colin James Alexander
Hopley, George	Cornell Woolrich		Jefferson, Henry Lee	James Branch Cabell
Horn, Peter (h)	David Vern; H. Kuttner		Jeffries, Hugh	Geoffrey Hewelcke
Hoskins, Phillip	Robert Hoskins		Jennifer, Susan (h)	D. R. Bensen; Robert Hoskins
Houdini, Harry	H. P. Lovecraft; Ehrich Weiss; Walter B.		Jeppson, J. O.	Mrs. Isaac Asimov
	Gibson (ghost written)		Jerome, Owen Fox	Oscar J. Friend
Houghton, Claude	Claude H. Oldfield		Jessel, John	Stanley G. Weinbaum
House, Brant	Paul Chadwick		Johannesson, Olof	Hannes Alfven
House, Brian	Robert Ludlum		John, Jasper	Rosalie Muspratt
Houston, Kilian	John Brunner		Johns, Avery	Margaret Cousins
Howard, Captain	Lu Senarens		Johns, Kenneth	John Newman & Ken Bulmer
Howard, Corrie	Julie Jardine		Johns, Marston (h)	Robert L. Fanthorpe
Howard, Joan	Patricia Gordon		Johns, Willy	W. Johns Meeker
Howard, Patrick	Robert E. Howard		Johnson, Mel	Barry N. Malzberg
Howard, Paul	Henry Treat Sperry		Johnson, W. Bollingbroke	Morris Bishop
Howard, Troy	Lauran Paine		Jones, Frank	John Russell Fearn
Howard, Warren F.	Frederik Pohl		Jones, Mack	F. C. Kneller
Howell, Scott	Albert King		Jones, Plato	Lynn Hickman
Howes, Jane	Wilmar H. Shiras		Jorgensen, Ivar (also **Jorgenson**) (h)	
Hudson, Jan	George H. Smith			P. W. Fairman; R. Silverberg & R. Garrett;
				others

I, J

Pseudonym	Real Name
Josephs, Henry	R. W. Lowndes
Joslin, Sesye	Sesye J. Hine
Judd, Cyril	Cyril Kornbluth & Judith Merril

K

Pseudonym	Real Name
Kaempfert, Wade (h)	Harry Harrison; Lester del Rey
Kains, Josephine	Ron Goulart
Kalnen, Ray	Ray Kainen
Kamin, Nick	Robert J. Antonick
Kane, Pablo	Hugh Zachary
Kane, Wilson (h)	Robert Bloch; others
Kanto, Peter	John Coleman; Hugh Zachary
Karageorge, Michael	Poul Anderson
Karloff, Boris	William H. Pratt
Kastel, Warren (h)	Chester S. Geier; Robert Silverberg; others
Katcha, Vahe	Vahe Katchadourian
Kavan, Anna	Helen Edmonds
Kaye, Marx (h)	S. J. Byrne; others
Kayne, Marvin	John Russell Fearn
Kayser, Ronal	Dale Clark
Kearny, Julian	Ron Goulart
Keith, Colin	Malcolm Jameson
Keith, Donald	Donald Monroe & Keith Monroe
Keith, Leigh	H. L. Gold
Kellino, Pamela	Pamela Mason
Kemp, H.	Harold Hersey
Kendrake, Carleton	Erle Stanley Gardner
Kendricks, James	Gardner F. Fox
Kennaway, James	James E. Peebles
Kennedy, P.	Harold Hersey
Kennedy, X. J.	Joe Kennedy
Kenny, Charles J.	Erle Stanley Gardner
Kent, Brad (h)	Dennis T. Hughes; Maurice Hugi
Kent, Gordon	E. C. Tubb
Kent, Kelvin	A. K. Barnes; H. Kuttner (alone and in collaboration)
Kent, Mallory	R. W. Lowndes
Kent, Philip	Kenneth Bulmer
Kent, Richard	Roswell Williams
Kenton, Bernard J.	Jerome Siegel
Kenton, L. P.	Robert L. Fanthorpe
Kenyon, Paul	Bob Vardeman
Kenyon, Robert O.	Henry Kuttner
Kerby, Susan Alice	Elizabeth Burton
Kern, Gregory	E. C. Tubb
Kerr, M. E.	Marijane Meaker
Kerr, Michael	Robert Hoskins
Keyes, Noel	David Keightley
Keyne, Gordon	H. Bedford-Jones
Kidde, Janet	George Wolk
Kigi, Takataro	Takashi Hayashi
Kimball, Conrad	Wayne Rogers
Kimbrough, Katheryn	John Kimbro
King, Christopher	Albert King
King, Ray	Ray Cummings
King, Vincent	Rex T. Vinson
Kingsmill, Hugh	H. K. Lunn
Kingston, John	Keith Roberts
Kinney, Win	Winston K. Marks
Kinsey-Jones, Brian	Brian N. Ball
Kippax, John	John C. Hynam
Kiproy, C.	Harold Hersey
Kirby, Jack	Jack Kurtzberg
Kirk, Lawrence	Eric A. Simson
Kirk, Richard (h)	Angus Wells; Robert Holdstock
Kirkham, Milo	Garen Drussai
Kjelgaard, Jim	Real name; Robert Bloch

Pseudonym	Real Name
Klimaris, J. S.	Walter Kubilius
Klimius, Nicholas	Ludvig Holberg
Knight, Kobold	Eric C. G. Giddy
Knight, Mallory T.	Bernhardt J. Hurwood
Knox, Calvin M.	Robert Silverberg
Knye, Cassandra	Thomas M. Disch
Kofoed, J. C.	Greye La Spina
Koomoter, Zeno	Joseph Marnell
Korda, Lothar	William Rotsler
Kornbluth, C. M.	Cyril Kornbluth
Krauss, Bruno	Kenneth Bulmer
Kruse, June Millichamp	Karen Anderson
Kuppord, Skelton	J. Adams
Kyle, Sefton	Roy Vickers

L

Pseudonym	Real Name
La Salle, Victor (h)	Gerald Evans; Robert L. Fanthorpe; John S. Glasby
La Tourette, Jacqueline	Jacqueline Gibeson
Lacy, Ed	Leonard S. Zinberg
Lafayette, Rene	L. Ron Hubbard
Laing, Patrick	Amelia Long
Lambert, Arthur	Arthur L. Widner
Lambert, William J., III	Lambert Wilhelm
Lambourne, John	John Battersby Crompton Lamburn
Lamont, Duncan	E. C. Tubb
Lamplugh, Lois	Lois Carlile Davis
Lamprey, A. C.	Robert L. Fish
Lancing, George	Bluebell M. Hunter
Lancour, Gene	Gene Fisher
Lane, Arthur	F. Orlin Tremaine
Lane, Jane	Elaine Dakers
Lane, John (h)	Dennis T. Hughes; others
Lang, King (h)	David A. Griffiths; George Hay; Brian Holloway; John W. Jennison; E. C. Tubb
Lang, Simon	Darlene Hartman
Langart, Darrel T.	Randall Garrett
Lange, John	Michael Crichton; real name
Langell, Sears	Allen Glasser
Langholm, Neil (h)	Kenneth Bulmer; Laurence James
Langley, Dorothy	Mrs. Dorothy H. Kissling
Lantry, Mike	E. C. Tubb
Larrovitch	Harold Hersey
Laski, Marghanita	Marghanita Laski Howard
Lasly, Walt	Frederik Pohl
Lassez, M.	H. Bedford-Jones
Latham, Philip	Robert S. Richardson
Lathen, Emma	Martha Hennissart & Mary J. Latis
Lathrop, Francis	Fritz Leiber
Lauder, George Dick	Sir George A. Dick-Lauder
Lauler, Michael	Richard Osenburg
Laurie, Andre	Paschal Grousset
Laverty, Donald	J. Blish & D. Knight
Lavington, Hubert	Hereward Carrington
Lavond, Paul Dennis (h)	R. W. Lowndes; Lowndes & F. Pohl; Cyril Kornbluth & Pohl; Lowndes & Pohl & D. Wylie (itself a pseud.); Pohl & Wylie
Lawrence	Lawrence S. Stevens
Lawrence, Judith Ann (née)	Mrs. James Blish
Lawrence, Margery	Mrs. Arthur E. Towle
Lawrence, P.	E. C. Tubb
Lawrence, Richard	L. E. Bartle
Lawson, Chet	E. C. Tubb
Lawton, Dennis	Frederick Faust
Laynham, Peter	John S. Glasby
Le Carre, John	David Cornwell

Pseudonym	Real Name
Le Fanu, J. Sheridan	Real name; A. W. Derleth (one story in *WT*)
Le Graeme, D. A.	Dale Graham
Le Moyne, R.	Harold Hersey
Le Page, Rand (h)	William H. Bird; John Glasby; Brian Hollo- way; David O'Brien; Cyril Protheroe; Arthur Roberts
Le Sieg, Theo	Theodor Seuss Geisel
Lebaron, Anthony	Keith Laumer
Leberecht, Peter	Johann Ludwig Tieck
Lecale, Errol	Wilfred McNeilly
Lee, Charles	Roger P. Graham
Lee, Edward	E. L. Fouts
Lee, Elsie	Elsie Lee Sheridan
Lee, Howard	Ron Goulart
Lee, Matt	Sam Merwin, Jr.
Lee, Robert Eggert	Paul W. Fairman
Lee, Rosie	Joan Aiken
Lee, Steve	Michel Parry
Lee, Vernon	Violet Paget
Leighton, J. G.	John Cole
Leinster, Murray	Will F. Jenkins
Leitch, Lavinia	Lavinia Hynd
Lemke, Henry E.	Richard Tooker
Lennard, H. K.	John S. Glasby
Lennox, John	Alfred Bester
Leodhas, Sorche Nic	Leclaire Gowans Alger
Leppoc, Derfla	Alfred Coppel
LeRoyd, Raymond	T. W. Wade
Lerteth, Oben	Robert L. Fanthorpe
Leslie, Lilian	Archer Leslie Hood & Violet Lilian Perkins
Leslie, O. H.	Henry Slesar
Lesser, Derwin	Charles D. Hornig
Lester, Irvin	Fletcher Pratt
Lethbridge, Rex	Roy Meyers
Levi, Eliphas	Alphonse L. Constant
Lewis, Charles	Roger Dixon
Lewis, Clifford	John Russell Fearn (unconfirmed)
Lewis, D. B.	Jerome Bixby
Liddell, C. H.	H. Kuttner & C. L. Moore
Lightner, Alice M.	Mrs. Ernest Hopf
Linder, D. Barry	Linda DuBreuil
Lionel, Robert	Robert L. Fanthorpe
Liston, B. E.	Berkeley Livingston
Liston, E. J.	Berkeley Livingston
Littlewit, Humphrey	H. P. Lovecraft
Llewellyn, Edward	Edward Llewellyn-Thomas
Lloyd, Charles	Charles L. Birkin
Lloyd, Herbert	John Russell Fearn
Lockhard, Leonard	Theodore L. Thomas
Logan, William	Laurence M. Janifer
Lohrman, Paul (h)	R. S. Shaver; P. W. Fairman
Lombino, S. A.	Evan Hunter (now legal name)
Long, Lyda Belknap	Frank Belknap Long
Long, Wesley	George O. Smith
Longdon, George	Francis G. Rayer
Lorac, E. C. R.	Edith C. Rivett
Loraine, Philip	Robin Estridge
Loran, Martin	Ron Smith & John Baxter
Lord, Garland	Isabel Garland & Mindret Lord
Lord, Jeffrey (h)	Roland Green; R. Faraday Nelson
Lorraine, Alden	Forrest J Ackerman
Lorraine, Lilith	Mary M. Wright
Lorraine, Paul (h)	John R. Fearn; John S. Glasby; William H. Bird; Arthur Roberts
Lottman, Eileen	Maud Willis
Louvigny, Andre	Andre Ruellan
Lovecraft, Linda	Michel Parry
Lovehill, C. B.	Charles Nutt
Lovell, Marc	Mark McShane
Loxmith, John	K. Houston (John) Brunner

Pseudonym	Real Name
Lucas, George	Real name; Alan Dean Foster
Lukens, Adam	Diane Detzer
Lum, Peter	B. L. Crowe
Luna, Kris (h)	William H. Bird; David O'Brien; others
Lurgan, Lester	Mabel Winifred Knowles
Lurie, Alison	Alison Bishop
Luther, Ray	Robert Arthur Ley
Lymington, John	John Newton Chance
Lynch, Frances	David G. Compton
Lyndon, Barre	Alfred Edgar
Lyon, Lyman R.	L. Sprague de Camp
Lyons, Delphine C.	Evelyn E. Smith
Lyons, Marcus	James Blish
Lytton, Lord	E. G. Bulwer-Lytton

M

Pseudonym	Real Name
McAllister, Annie Laurie	Bruce Cassiday
MacApp, C. C.	Carroll M. Capps
MacArthur, Burke	Arthur J. Burks
McBain, Ed	Evan Hunter
McCall, Anthony	Henry Kane
McCann, Arthur	John W. Campbell, Jr.
McCann, Edson	Frederik Pohl & Lester del Rey
McCarter, Jody	Jodi DeMelikoff & Vermille McCarter
McCord, Clay	William Rotsler
McCord, Guy	Dallas McCord Reynolds
McCormack, Charlotte	W. E. D. Ross
MacCreigh, James	Frederik Pohl
McCulloch, John Tyler	Edgar Rice Burroughs
McDaniel, Charles	Charles M. Garrison
McDaniel, David	Ted Johnstone
McDermott, Dennis	Walter L. Dennis & P. McDermott; Dennis & McDermott & P. S. Miller
MacDiarmid, Hugh	Christopher Murray Grieve
MacDonald, Anson	Robert A. Heinlein
MacDougal, John	J. Blish & R. W. Lowndes
MacDuff, Andrew	Horace B. Fyfe
MacFarlane, Stephen	John K. Cross
McGowan, Inez	Roger P. Graham
McGreevey, John (h)	H. Browne; W. L. Hamling
McGregor, Ellen	Real name; S. F. Pantell
MacGregor, Mary	Malcolm Jameson
McIntosh, J. T. (also M'Intosh)	James MacGregor
McKenzie, Ray	Robert Silverberg
McLaglen, John J.	John Harvey; Laurence James
Maclean, Arthur	E. C. Tubb
McLeish, Dougal	Donald James
MacLeod, Fiona	W. Sharp
McLociard, George	Charles F. Locke
McNeill, Janet	Janet Alexander
MacPatterson, F.	Walter Ernsting
MacTyre, Paul	Robert J. Adam
Maddock, Larry	Jack Jardine
Maddock, Stephen	J. M. Walsh
Maddox, Carl	E. C. Tubb
Maddux, Rachel	R. M. Baker
Maepenn, Hugh	Henry Kuttner
Maepenn, K. K.	Henry Kuttner
Magill, Rory	Dorothea M. Faulkner
Magnus, John	Harlan Ellison (ghost written)
Maine, Charles Eric	David McIlwain
Maine, David	Claude Avice
Majors, Simon	Gardner F. Fox
Malcolm, Dan	Robert Silverberg
Malcolm, Honey	William Rotsler
Malet, Oriel	Auriel R. Vaughan

Pseudonym	Real Name	Pseudonym	Real Name
Mallory, Mark	Dallas McCord Reynolds	**Merriman, Alex**	Robert Silverberg
Malone, Sherry	Robert Bloch	**Merritt, Aime**	Forrest J Ackerman
Mand, Cyril	George R. Hahn & Richard Levin	**Metcalf, Suzanne**	L. Frank Baum
Manders, John F.	L. Sandfield	**Metcalfe, Francis**	J. K. Egerton
Mann, Abel	John Creasey	**Meyrink, Gustave**	Gustav Meyer
Mann, Charles	Roger P. Graham	**Miall, Robert**	John Frederick Burke
Mann, Jack	Charles Cannell	**Michaels, Barbara**	Barbara Mertz
Manners, Alexandra	Anne Rundle	**Michaels, Steve**	Michael Avallone
Mannes, Marya	Mrs. Richard Blow	**Miles**	Stephen Southwold
Manning, David	Frederick Faust	**Miles, Howard Scott**	William Rotsler
Manton, Peter	John Creasey	**Miles, Keith**	Robert Tralins
Maras, Karl (h)	Ken Bulmer; Peter Hawkins; others	**Miller, Benj.**	Noel Loomis
Marcellinus, Ammianus	Aaron Nadel	**Miller, Frank**	Noel Loomis
March, William	William E. M. Campbell	**Miller, Wade**	Bob Wade & Bill Miller
Marconette	Mark Marchioni	**Mingston, R. G.**	R. G. Stamp
Marin, A. C.	Alfred Coppel	**Minton, Paula**	Paul H. Little
Mariner, David	David M. Smith	**Mitchell, Clyde** (h)	R. Silverberg & R. Garrett
Mariner, Scott	Cyril Kornbluth & F. Pohl	**Mitchell, Gene**	H. O. Hoadley
Marion, Henry	Lester del Rey	**Moamrath, M. M.**	Joe Pumilia
Marius	Steve Benedict	**Mondelle, Wendayne**	Wendayne Ackerman (fan pseud.)
Mark, Ted	Ted Gottfried	**Monett, Lireve**	Everil Worrell
Markham, Hord	William Rotsler	**Monig, Christopher**	Kendell F. Crossen
Markham, Robert	Kingsley Amis	**Monroe, Lyle**	Robert A. Heinlein; Heinlein & Elma Wentz
Markham, Russ	Steve Hall		
Marlowe, Stephen	Milton Lesser	**Montague, Meryl St. John**	L. Sandfield
Marlowe, Webb	J. Francis McComas	**Moore, Catherine L.** (née)	Mrs. Henry Kuttner
Marner, Robert	Algis Budrys	**Moore, Denis**	Keith Taylor
Marric, J. J.	John Creasey	**Moore, Harris**	Arthur Moore & Alf Harris
Marryat, Capt.	Frederick Marryat	**Moore, Robert**	Robert M. Williams
Marsden, James	John Creasey	**Moore, Wallace**	Gerard F. Conway
Marshall, James Vance	Donald Gordon Payne	**More, Anthony**	Ed M. Clinton, Jr.
Marsten, Richard	Evan Hunter	**Morel, Dighton**	Kenneth L. Warner
Martens, Paul	Stephen Southwold	**Moresby, Louis**	L. Adams Beck
Martin, Anthony	A. A. Glynn	**Morgan, Scott**	Henry Kuttner
Martin, John R.	T. W. Wade	**Morland, Dick**	Reginald C. Hill
Martin, Peter	Peter M. Leckie	**Morland, Peter Henry**	Frederick Faust
Martin, Richard	John Creasey	**Morley, Brian**	Marion Z. Bradley
Martin, Stella	Georgette Heyer	**Morley, Susan**	John K. Cross
Martin, Webber	Robert Silverberg	**Morley, Wilfred Owen**	Robert W. Lowndes
Martyn, Phillip	E. C. Tubb	**Morojo**	Myrtle R. Douglas
Marvell, Andrew	Real name; Howell Davies	**Morris, G. A.**	Katherine MacLean
Mason, Ernst	Frederik Pohl	**Morrison, Richard**	Robert W. Lowndes
Mason, Ernest	Frederik Pohl	**Morrison, William**	Joseph Samachson
Mason, Gregory	Doris Meek & Adrienne Jones	**Morton, Anthony**	John Creasey
Mason, John	E. C. Tubb	**Morton, John**	John S. Glasby
Mason, Lee W.	Barry N. Malzberg	**Moulton, Carl**	E. C. Tubb
Mason, Michael	Edgar Smith	**Moykher-Sforim, Mendele**	Sholem Yankev Abramovitch
Mason, Ray (h)	F. C. Kneller	**Mudgett, Herman W.**	A. Boucher (W. A. P. White)
Mason, Tally	August W. Derleth	**Muir, James A.**	Angus Wells
Masterson, Whit	Bob Wade & Bill Miller	**Muller, John E.** (h)	Robert L. Fanthorpe; John S. Glasby; Anthony A. Glynn
Matheson, Joan	Jacob Transue		
Mathieson, Una Cooper	Amanda Melvina Thorley Gibson	**Muller, Paul**	Albert King
Mattheson, Rodney	John Creasey	**Munchausen, Baron**	Hugo Gernsback
Matthews, Kevin	Gardner F. Fox	**Mundy, Talbot**	William Lancaster Gribbon
Mavity, Hubert	Nelson S. Bond	**Munro, Duncan H.**	Eric F. Russell
Maxwell, Ann	Lee Pattinson	**Murdoch, H. J.**	James M. MacGregor
Maxwell, John C.	John S. Glasby	**Murphy, Dennis Jasper**	Charles R. Maturin
Maxwell, Joslyn	Max J. Ireland	**Murry, Colin**	John Middleton Murry
May, Jonathan	Laurence James	**Muspratt, Rosalia**	John Jasper
May, Julian C.	Judy M. Dikty		
Mayfield, M. I.	H. I. Hirshfield & G. M. Mateyko		
Maynwaring, Archibald	H. P. Lovecraft		
Meade, L. T.	Elizabeth Thomasina Meade Smith		
Meade, Richard	Benjamin Leopold Haas		
Melville, Lewis	L. S. Benjamin (& R. Hargreaves at times)	**Na Gopaleen, Myles**	B. O Nolan
Menasco, Norman	Wyman Guin	**Nadaar, Abu**	E. R. Morrough
Mencer, D. J.	F. C. Kneller	**Natale, Francine de**	Barry N. Malzberg
Merak, A. J.	John S. Glasby	**Nathan, Daniel**	Frederic Dannay
Merlini	Clayton Rawson	**Neal, Gavin**	E. C. Tubb
Merlyn, Arthur	James Blish	**Neal, Harry**	Jerome Bixby

N

Pseudonym	Real Name
Neef, Elton T.	Robert L. Fanthorpe
Neefe, Elton T.	Robert L. Fanthorpe
Neeper, Cary	Carolyn Neeper
Nesbit, Edith	Mrs. Edith Bland
Netzen, Klaus	Laurence James
Newman, Robert	Roger Howard Norton
Newton, Clark	Jim Harmon
Newton, David C.	John N. Chance
Niall, Ian	John McNeillie
Nichols, Peter	Christopher S. Youd
Nicholson, Sam	Shirley Nikolaisen
Nihil	P. Schuyler Miller
Nile, Dorothea	Michael Avallone
Nister, Der	Pinhas Kahanovitch
Nobel, Phil	Robert L. Fanthorpe
Nolan, Christopher	Laurence James
Noname	Lu Senarens; Harry Enton
Noon, Ed	Michael Avallone
Noone, Edwina	Michael Avallone
Noordung, Hermann	Captain Potocnik
Norbert, W.	Norbert Wiener
Norman, Eric	Eugene Olson
Norman, John	John F. Lange
Norman, Mick	Laurence James
North, Andrew	Alice M. Norton
North, Eric	Bernard C. Cronin
North, Jessica	Jessica N(orth) MacDonald
Northern, Leslie (h)	Frank B. Long; others
Northrop, Captain B. A.	L. Ron Hubbard
Norton, Andre	Alice M. Norton
Norvil, Manning	Kenneth Bulmer
Nostradamus	Michel de Notredame
Nye, Harold G.	Leo Harding

O

Pseudonym	Real Name
O'Brien, Clancy	George H. Smith
O'Brien, Dean D.	Earl & Otto Binder
O'Brien, Dee	Marion Z. Bradley
O'Brien, E. G.	Arthur C. Clarke
O'Brien, Flann	Brian O Nolan
O'Brien, Larry Clinton	C. Edward O'Brien
O'Brien, Robert C.	Robert L. Conly
O'Connor, Patrick	Leonard Wibberley
O'Donnell, K. M.	Barry N. Malzberg
O'Donnell, Lawrence	Catherine L. Moore; Henry Kuttner; both
O'Donnevan, Finn	Robert Sheckley
O'Flinn, Peter	Robert L. Fanthorpe
O'Flynn, Peter	Robert L. Fanthorpe
Ogden, H. B.	Isaac Asimov
O'Grady, Rohan	June O'Grady Skinner
O'Hara, Kenneth	Real name; Bryce Walton
O'Hara, Scott	John D. MacDonald
Olben, Bob (probably misprint)	
	Alfred Johannes Olsen, Jr.
Oliphant, Mrs.	Margaret Oliphant
Olsen, Bob	Alfred Johannes Olsen, Jr.
Omega	Ray Bradbury (fan pseud.)
Onions, Oliver	George Oliver
O'Quinn, Vithaldas H.	Hans S. Santesson
Oram, John	John Oram Thomas
Orchards, Theodore	Stuart Palmer
Ormond, Frederic	Frederic V. R. Dey
O'Rourke, Frank	Frank O'Malley
Orth, Bennington	Roger S. Hoar
Orwell, George	Eric Blair
Osborne, David	Robert Silverberg
Osborne, George	Robert Silverberg

Pseudonym	Real Name
O'Sullivan, Vincent	Sean O'Suilleabhain
Ouspensky, P. D.	Petr Uspenskii
Overton, Max	Don Wilcox
Owen, Dean	Dudley D. McGaughy
Owen, Frank	Roswell Williams
Owen, Hugh	Frederick Faust
Owens, A.	Harold Hersey

P

Pseudonym	Real Name
Packer, Vin	Marijane Meaker
Padgett, Lewis	Henry Kuttner & Catherine L. Moore
Page, Marco	Harry Kurnitz
Pagery, François	Gerard Klein
Paget, John	John Aiken
Paget-Lowe, H.	H. P. Lovecraft
Paget-Lowe, Henry	H. P. Lovecraft
Paine, Guthrie	F. Orlin Tremaine
Paley, Morton D.	Jerome Bixby & Sam Merwin, Jr. (fan pseud.)
Palm, Gene	Luigi Palmisano
Parabellum	Ferdinand Heinrich Grautoff
Park, Jordan	Cyril Kornbluth & F. Pohl
Parkes, Lucas	John B. Harris
Parkes, Wyndham	John B. Harris
Parnell, Francis	Festus Pragnell
Parnell, Keith	P. K. Palmer
Parr, Robert	Erle Stanley Gardner
Passante, Dom	John Russell Fearn
Pater, Roger	Dom Gilbert Roger Hudlestone
Patrick, John	Michael Avallone
Patrick, Q.	Richard Wilson Webb; Mary Louise Aswell & Webb; Webb & Hugh C. Wheeler; Webb & Martha M. Kelley
Patton, Frank (h)	R. A. Palmer; R. S. Shaver; others
Paul, F. W.	Paul W. Fairman
Paul, Hugo	Paul H. Little
Paye, Robert	Gabrielle M. V. Long
Payne, Alan	John W. Jakes
Pearson, Martin	Donald A. Wollheim
Pease, Lieut. John	Roger S. Hoar
Pedler, Kit	Christopher Magnus Howard Pedler
Peggy, Aunt	Russell R. Winterbotham
Pelkie, J. W.	Raymond A. Palmer
Pemberton, Renfrew	F. M. Busby
Pembrooke, Kenneth	Gerald W. Page
Pendarves, G. G.	Gladys G. Trenery
Pendragon, Eric	Michel Parry
Penjean, Lucian	H. Bedford-Jones
Penny, Richard	David Lasser
Pentecost, Hugh	Hugh Pentecost Philips
Peregoy, Calvin	Thomas C. McClary
Perez, Juan	Manly Wade Wellman
Peril, Milton R.	Francis A. Jones
Perkins, Grace	Grace Oursler
Perri, Leslie	Doris B. Wilson
Peterkiewicz, Jerzy	Jerzy Pietrkiewicz
Peters, Bryan	Peter George
Peters, L. T.	Jo-Ann Klainer & Albert S. Klainer
Peters, Ludovic	Peter Brent
Peyton, Green	G. Peyton Wertenbaker
Phelan, Jeremiah	C. Daly King
Phillips, Frank	Philip F. Nowlan
Phillips, Mark	R. Garrett & L. M. Janifer
Phillips, Michael	Charles Nutt
Phillips, Peter (h)	Howard Browne
Phillips, Richard	Philip K. Dick
Phillips, Rog	Roger P. Graham

Pseudonym	Real Name	Pseudonym	Real Name
Phipson, Joan	Joan M. Fitzhardinge	**Reginald, Robert R.**	M. R. Burgess
Phylos the Tibetan	Frederick S. Oliver	**Rei, Kosumi**	Takumi Shibano
Pierre, Paul	Paul Calle	**Reid, Desmond** (h)	John Newton Chance; Wilfred McNeilly; James Cawthorn & Michael Moorcock
Pike, Charles R. (h)	Kenneth Bulmer; Terry Harknett; Angus Wells		
Pike, Robert L.	Robert L. Fish	**Reilly, William K.**	John Creasey
Pilgrim, Derral	Hugh Zachary	**Remenham, John**	J. A. Vlasto
Pine, Theodore	Emil Petaja; Petaja & H. Hasse	**Renna, G.**	G. L. Rapuzzi
Planet Prince, The	J. Harvey Haggard	**Retla, Robert**	Robert Alter
Plum, Jennifer	Michael Kurland	**Rey, Russell** (h)	Dennis T. Hughes; others
Poge, N. Wooten	Norvell W. Page	**Reynolds, Adrian**	Amelia Long
Pollard, John X. (h)	H. Browne; others	**Reynolds, L. Major**	Louise Leipiar
Pong, Hoy Ping	Arthur Wilson Tucker	**Reynolds, Mack**	Dallas McCord Reynolds
Portal, Ellis	Bruce Powe	**Reynolds, Maxine**	Dallas McCord Reynolds
Powell, Sonny	Alfred Bester	**Reynolds, Peter**	Amelia Long
Powers, J. L.	John S. Glasby	**Reynolds, Ron**	Ray Bradbury
Powers, L. C.	E. C. Tubb	**Rhode, John**	Cecil J. C. Street
Powers, M. L.	E. C. Tubb	**Rice, Craig**	Evan Hunter & G. A. Randolph
Preedy, George	Gabrielle M. V. Long	**Rice, Elmer**	Elmer Reizenstein
Prescot, Dray	Kenneth Bulmer	**Rich, D. Coleman**	Darrell C. Richardson
Prospero and Caliban	Frederick Rolfe	**Richard, Kent**	Kendell Foster Crossen
Pseudoman, Akkad	Edwin F. Northrup	**Richard, Louis**	John Michel
Putnam, Isra	Greye La Spina	**Richard-Bessiere, F.**	F. Richard & R. Bessiere
Putnam, Kenneth	Philip Klass	**Richards, Clay**	Kendell Foster Crossen
		Richards, Edward	E. C. Tubb
		Richards, Frank	Charles Hamilton
		Richards, Henry	Joseph Laurence Morrissey
		Richards, Henry	Richard Saxon
		Richards, Paul	Paul Buddee

Q,R

Pseudonym	Real Name	Pseudonym	Real Name
"Q"	Sir Arthur T. Quiller-Couch	**Richardson, Flavia**	Christine C. Thomson
Queen, Ellery (h)	Avram Davidson; Paul W. Fairman	**Richardson, Francis**	L. E. Bartle & F. Parnell
Queen, Ellery, Jr.	Frederic Dannay & Manfred B. Lee; Jack Vance	**Ridgway, Jason**	Milton Lesser
		Riker, Anthony	F. Anton Reeds
Quentin, Patrick	Richard W. Webb & Hugh C. Wheeler	**Riley, Frank**	Frank Ryhlock
Quick, Dorothy	Margaret Rogers Straub	**Riley, Tex**	John Creasey
Quiller, Andrew (h)	Kenneth Bulmer	**Rios, Tere**	Maria Teresa Rios Versack
Quinton, Matthew	Harlan Ellison	**Rivere, Alec**	Charles Nuetzel
Quitman, Wallace (h)	Raymond A. Palmer	**Riverside, John**	Robert A. Heinlein
Rackham, John	John T. Phillifent	**Robbins, Tod**	Clarence A. Robbins
Ragatzy, Anton	Julian F. Parr	**Robbins, W. Wayne**	Ormond Gregory
Rainey, William B.	Wyatt Blassingame	**Roberts, James Hall**	Robert L. Duncan
Raleigh, Richard	H. P. Lovecraft	**Roberts, John**	John R. Pierce
Ramal, Walter	Walter de la Mare	**Roberts, Kenneth**	Lester Dent
Rame, David	Arthur D. Divine	**Roberts, Lionel**	Robert L. Fanthorpe
Rampa, T. Lopsang	Cyril Henry Hoskin	**Roberts, Murray**	Robert Murray Graydon
Rampo, Edogawa	Taro Hirai	**Roberts, Terence**	Ivan T. Sanderson
Randall, Clint	William Rotsler	**Robertson, E. Arnot**	Eileen Arbuthnot Robertson
Randall, Robert	R. Silverberg & R. Garrett	**Robertson, James**	F. C. Kneller
Randolph, Ellen	W. E. D. Ross	**Robertson, John**	F. C. Kneller
Randolph, Marion	Marie F. Rodell	**Robertson, Vincent**	T. W. Wade
Randolphe, Arabella	Jack Younger	**Robeson, Kenneth** (h)	Lester Dent (mainly); William Bogart; Norman A. Daniels; Harold A. Davis; Paul Ernst; Philip José Farmer; Ron Goulart; Alan Hathway; W. Ryerson Johnson; Emile Tepperman
Random, Alex	Donald S. Rowland		
Rangely, Olivia	Hugh Zachary		
Ranger, Ken	John Creasey		
Rankine, John	Douglas R. Mason		
Rawle, Henry	John Russell Fearn (unconfirmed)	**Rochdale, Thomas**	A. Hind
Ray, Jean	R. De Kremer	**Rocklynne, Ross**	Ross Rocklin
Raycraft, Stan	Richard S. Shaver	**Rockwood, Roy** (h)	Edward Stratemeyer; others (syndicate)
Raymond, E. V.	Raymond Z. Gallun	**Rodman, Eric**	Robert Silverberg
Raymond, Hugh	John Michel	**Roeder, Pat**	Harlan Ellison (ghost written)
Raymond, John	Lester del Rey	**Rogers, Don**	Claude Degler
Raymond, John (h)	Robert L. Fanthorpe	**Rogers, Doug**	Ray Bradbury (fan pseud.)
Rayner, Richard	David McIlwain	**Rogers, Melva**	Roger P. Graham
Recour, Charles	Henry Bott	**Rogers, Pat**	Arthur Porges
Rectez, Ian	Mort Weisinger	**Rohmer, Elizabeth Sax**	Rose Elizabeth Knox Ward
Reed, Allan	Rainer Eisfeld	**Rohmer, Sax**	A. S. Ward
Reed, David V.	David Vern	**Rohr, Wolf Detler**	Rainer Eisfeld
Reed, Kit	Lillian Craig Reed	**Roland, Nicholas**	Arnold R. Walmsley
Reed, Peter	John D. MacDonald	**Rolant, René**	Robert L. Fanthorpe
Reed, Van (h)	Dennis T. Hughes; others	**Rome, Alger**	A. J. Budrys & J. Bixby
		Rome, David	David Boutland

Pseudonym	*Real Name*	*Pseudonym*	*Real Name*
Ronns, Edward	Edward S. Aarons	**Schoolcraft, John**	Frederick Faust
Rose, Billy	William S. Rosenberg	**Sclanders, Doorn**	John Russell Fearn
Rose, Francis	John Russell Fearn	**Scot, Chesman**	Kenneth Bulmer
Rose, Lawrence F.	John Russell Fearn	**Scotland, Jay**	John W. Jakes
Rosny, J.-H. (Ainé)	J. H. H. Boëx	**Scott, Martin**	Richard Gehman
Ross, Clarissa	William E. D. Ross	**Scott, Mildred**	Francis G. Rayer
Ross, Dallas	Dallas McCord Reynolds	**Scott, Warwick**	Elleston Trevor
Ross, Dan	W. E. D. Ross	**Sea-Lion**	Geoffrey Martin Bennett
Ross, Ian	John F. Rossmann	**Seaborn, Capt. Adam**	J. C. Symmes
Ross, James	Sydney J. Bounds	**Seabright, Idris**	Margaret St. Clair
Ross, Joseph	Joseph Wrocz	**Seabright, John**	E. C. Tubb
Ross, Maggie	Maurine J. L. Bermange	**Seabrooke, David**	H. Bedford-Jones
Ross, Marilyn	William E. D. Ross	**Seagar, Joan**	John Russell Fearn
Ross, Ward	John Russell Fearn	**Seamark**	Austin J. Small
Rossiter, Jane	W. E. D. Ross	**Searls, Hank**	Henry H. Searls
Rossiter, Oscar	Vernon H. Skeels	**Sebastian, John**	Curtis Harrington
Rousseau, Victor	Victor R. Emanuel	**Sebastian, Lee**	Robert Silverberg
Rowley, Ames Dorrance	H. P. Lovecraft	**Sedolin, Sture**	Carl Hallstrom
Royce, Kenneth	Kenneth Royce Gandley	**Selden, George**	George Selden Thompson
Ruby, B. F.	Fletcher Pratt	**Sellings, Arthur**	Arthur Ley
Ruck, Berta	Amy Roberta Oliver	**Senectissimus, Theobaldus, Esq.**	
Ruppert, Chester	Roger P. Graham		H. P. Lovecraft
Russell, Albert	Jerome Bixby	**Sentry, John A.**	Algis J. Budrys
Russell, J.	Jerome Bixby	**Septama, Aladra**	Judson Reeves
Russell, John	John Russell Fearn	**Seriel, Jerome**	Jacques Vallee
Ryan, Tim	Lester Dent	**Seuss, Dr.**	Theodor Seuss Geisel
Ryder, Thom	John Harvey	**Severance, Felix**	March Laumer
Rye, Anthony	Christopher S. Youd	**Severence, Felix**	March Laumer
		Severn, David	David S. Unwin
		Seymour, Henry	Helmut Henry Hartmann
		Shackleton, C. C.	Brian W. Aldiss
# **S**		**Shadow, Mark**	Robert W. Sneddon
		Shannon, Fred	William S. Ruben
Sabe, Quien	N. C. Hero; H. Bates (1956)	**Sharkey, Jack**	John Michael Sharkey
Sackerman, Henry	H. S. Kahn	**Sharon, Rose**	Judith Merril
St. Clair, Eric	George A. Pflaum	**Sharpe, D. Richard**	Richard S. Shaver
St. James, Blakely	Charles Platt	**Shaw, Brian (or Bryan)** (h)	John R. Fearn; David A. Griffiths; David
St. John, David	Everett Howard Hunt, Jr.		O'Brien, E. C. Tubb
St. John, Henry	John Creasey	**Shaw, David** (h)	David A. Griffiths
St. John, Philip	Lester del Rey	**Shaw, Frank S.** (error)	Ron Goulart
St. Mars, F.	Frank Atkins, Jr.	**Shaw, Robert Sanders**	Sam Moskowitz (fan pseud.)
St. Paul, Sterner	S. P. Meek	**Shawn, Frank S.**	Ron Goulart
St. Reynard, Geoff	Robert W. Krepps	**Shearing, Joseph**	Gabrielle M. V. Long
Saki	Hector Hugh Munro	**Sheldon, John**	Robert Bloch
Sand, Warren B.	F. Orlin Tremaine	**Sheldon, Lee**	Wayne C. Lee
Sanders, George	Real name; Leigh Brackett (ghost written)	**Sheldon, Raccoona**	Alice H. Sheldon
Sanders, Winston P.	Poul Anderson	**Sheldon, Roy** (h)	Hubert J. Campbell; George Hay; E. C.
Sands, Dave (h)	Bryce Walton; others		Tubb; others
Sangerson, Margaret Love	H. Bedford-Jones	**Shelton, Miles**	Don Wilcox
Sansom, John	Barre Lyndon (pseud. of Alfred Edgar) &	**Sheridan, Lee**	Elsie Lee Sheridan
	Jimmy Sangster	**Sheridan, Thomas**	Walter Gillings
Santos, Alfred	F. Orlin Tremaine	**Sherman, Michael**	Robert W. Lowndes
Sarac, Roger	Roger A. Caras	**Sherman, Peter Michael**	Robert W. Lowndes
Sarban	John W. Wall	**Sherry, Oliver**	George Edmund Lobo
Satterfield, Charles	Frederik Pohl; Lester del Rey	**Sherwood, Nelson**	Kenneth Bulmer
Saturn, Sergeant (h)	M. Weisinger; O. J. Friend; S. Merwin, Jr.	**Shols, W. W.**	Winfried Scholz
Saunders, Caleb	Robert A. Heinlein	**Shotwell, Ray P.**	Ray Cummings
Saunders, Wes	Sydney J. Bounds	**Shubik, Irene**	Brian Hayles (ghost edited)
Sava, George	Alexis Milkomanovich Milkomane	**Shute, Nevil**	Nevil S. Norway
Savage, Blake	H. L. Goodwin	**Sidney, Stuart**	Michael Avallone
Savage, Richard	Ivan Roe	**Silent, William T.**	John William Jackson, Jr.
Sawtelle, William Carter (h)		**Silva, Joseph**	Ron Goulart
	Roger P. Graham	**Silve, Claude**	P. de Comtesse Laforest-Divonne
Saxon, Peter (h)	Thomas H. Martin; Wilfred McNeilly;	**Silver, Nicholas**	Frederick Faust
	others	**Silver, Richard** (h)	Kenneth Bulmer
Saxon, Richard	Joseph Laurence Morrissey	**Simenon, Georges**	Georges Sim
Scanlon, C. K. M. (h)	Norman Daniels; Frank Gruber	**Sinclair, Anna** (née)	Mrs. L. Moffatt
Scarff, William	Algis Budrys	**Singer, Adam**	David Karp
Schire	John Russell Fearn	**Sitty, Basil**	Norman A. Lazenby
Schofield, Paul	E. C. Tubb	**Skorpios, Antares**	James William Barlow

Pseudonym	Real Name
Sky, Kathleen (née)	Mrs. Stephen Goldin
Slate, John	John Russell Fearn
Sloan, John	T. W. Wade
Sloluck, J. Milton	Ambrose Bierce
Smith, Carmichael	Paul M. A. Linebarger
Smith, Cordwainer	Paul M. A. Linebarger
Smith, Ford	Oscar J. Friend
Smith, George Hudson	George Henry Smith
Smith, Hogan	Allen D. Morgan
Smith, Jan	George Henry Smith
Smith, Lawrence	Sydney J. Bounds
Smith, Richard E.	Richard R. Smith
Smith, Shelley	Nancy Hermione Bodington
Smith, Woodrow Wilson	Henry Kuttner
Snooks, Epaminondas T.	C. P. Mason
Softly, Edward	H. P. Lovecraft
Sohl, Jerry	Gerald Allan Sohl
Sologub, Fedor	Fedor Kuzmich Teternikov
Somers, Bart	Gardner F. Fox
Sorensen, Beverly	William Rotsler
Souli, Charles George	H. Bedford-Jones
South, Clark	Dwight V. Swain
Spalding, Neil J.	F. C. Kneller
Sparling, Ned	Lu Senarens
Spartacus, Deutero	Robert L. Fanthorpe
Spaulding, Douglas	Ray Bradbury
Spaulding, Leonard	Ray Bradbury
Spaulding, Neil J.	F. C. Kneller
Speed, Donald	Alex Hamilton
Spencer, Leonard G. (h)	R. Silverberg & R. Garrett
Spencer, Parke	Sewell P. Wright
Spie, Oliver	Joseph Slotkin
Spielberg, Stephen	Real name; Leslie Waller
Spillane, Mickey	Frank Spillane
Sprague, Carter	Sam Merwin, Jr.
Spriel, Stephen	Michael Pilotin
Sprigel, Oliver	Claude Avice
Square, A	Edwin A. Abbott
Squires, Phil	S. Omar Barker
Stacy, O'Connor	William Stacy Urann Rollins
Stafford, Peter	Paul Tabor
Stagge, Jonathan	Richard W. Webb & Hugh C. Wheeler
Stair, Virginia	Winifred Brent Russell
Standish, Robert	Digby George Gerahty
Stanley, Bennett	Stanley B. Hough
Stanley, Marge	Stanley G. Weinbaum
Stannard, Lane	James V. Taurasi, Sr.
Stanton, John	George C. Wallis
Stanton, Schuyler	L. Frank Baum
Stanton, Vance	Michael Avallone
Stark, Richard	Donald Westlake
Starke, Henderson	Kris Neville
Starr, John (h)	Roger D. Aycock; others
Starr, Mark	Gerard Klein
Starr, Roland	Donald S. Rowland
Statten, Vargo	John Russell Fearn
Steber, A. R.(h)	R. A. Palmer; R. P. Graham
Steele, Addison E.	Richard A. Lupoff
Steele, Curtis (h)	Frederick C. Davis; Emile Tepperman
Steele, Kurt	Rudolph Kagey
Steele, Morris J. (h)	R. Palmer; Berkeley Livingston
Steffanson, Con (h)	Carson Bingham; Ron Goulart; others
Steiger, Brad	Eugene E. Olson
Steiner, Kurt	Andre Ruellan
Stephens, I. M. (née)	Inga Stephens Pratt
Sterling, Brett (h)	R. Bradbury; E. Hamilton; W. Morrison; J. Samachson
Sterling, Stewart	Prentice Winchell
Stern, Paul Frederick	Paul Ernst
Stevens, Francis	Gertrude Bennett
Stevens, John	E. C. Tubb
Stewart, Wendall	Gordon Eklund
Stewart, Will	Jack Williamson
Stine, Hank	Hank Stein
Stockbridge, Grant	Norvell W. Page
Stoddard, Charles (h)	Henry Kuttner; others
Stokes, Edward	F. C. Kneller
Stone, Leslie F.	Leslie F. Rubenstein (Mrs. William Silberberg)
Storey, Richard	H. L. Gold
Storm, Brian (h)	Brian Holloway
Storm, Eric	E. C. Tubb
Storm, Harrison	Bruno Fischer
Storm, Mallory	Paul W. Fairman
Storm, Russell	Robert M. Williams
Storme, Peter	Philip Van Doren Stern
Strang, Herbert	George Herbert Ely & C. J. L'Estrange
Strange, John Stephen	Dorothy Stockbridge Tillett
Stranger, Ralph	Ralph Judson
Stratford, H. Philip	Kenneth Bulmer
Stratton, Thomas	Robert Coulson & Eugene DeWeese
Strickland, Jerome	Lan Wright
Strike, Jeremy	Thomas E. Renn
Stringer, David	Keith Roberts
Stringer, Keith	Keith Roberts
Strong, Spencer	Forrest J Ackerman
Strongi'th'arm, Charles	Charles Wicksteed Armstrong
Stroud, Albert	Algis J. Budrys
Struther, Jan	Joyce Anstruther
Stuart, Alex R.	Richard Gordon
Stuart, Don A.	John W. Campbell, Jr.
Stuart, Gordon	H. Bedford-Jones
Stuart, Ian	Alistair MacLean
Stuart, Sidney	Michael Avallone
Stumpke, Harold	Gerold Steiner
Sturgeon, Theodore (now legal name)	E. H. Waldo (former name)
Sturgis, Colin	Les Cole & Mel Sturgis
Suffling, Mark	Donald S. Rowland
Sullivan, Sean Mei	Gerald Allan Sohl
Sullivan, Vernon	Boris Vian
Summers, Diane	George H. Smith
Summers, Leo Ramon	Leo Morey
Sutton, Andrew	E. C. Tubb
Sutton, Henry	David Rytman Slavitt
Swanson, Logan	Richard Matheson
Swenson, Peggy	Richard E. Geis
Swift, Anthony	Joseph Jefferson Farjeon
Swift, August T.	H. P. Lovecraft

T

Pseudonym	Real Name
T., J.	E. T. Bell
Tabori, Paul	Paul Tabor
Taine, John	Eric T. Bell
Talbot, Hake	Henning Nelms
Tall, Stephen	Crompton N. Crook
Tara, John	John Michel
Tarne, Rosina	John Russell Fearn
Tate, Robin	Robert L. Fanthorpe
Taverel, John	Robert E. Howard
Temple, James	Eric Temple Bell
Temple, Robin	Samuel Andrew Wood
Tenn, William	Philip Klass
Tenneshaw, S. M. (h)	C. Geier; E. Hamilton; M. Lesser; R. Garrett; R. Silverberg; Garrett & Silverberg
Terridge, Ernest	Ernst H. Richter
Tertz, Abram	Andrei Donatevich Siniavskii

Pseudonym	Real Name
Thames, C. H. (h)	John Jakes; Milton Lesser
Thanet, Neil	Robert L. Fanthorpe
Thanet, Octave	Alice French
Thatcher, Julia	Robert Hoskins
Thayer, Urann	William Stacy Urann Rollins
Theobaldus	H. P. Lovecraft
Thiusen, Ismar	John Macnie
Thomas, Cogswell	Theodore Cogswell & Theodore L. Thomas
Thomas, Dan	Leonard M. Sanders, Jr.
Thomas, Doris	Doris Vancel
Thomas, K.	John Russell Fearn
Thomas, Martin	Thomas H. Martin
Thomas, Martin (h)	Wilfred McNeilly
Thomas, Paul	Paul Misraki
Thomson, Edward	E. C. Tubb
Thor, Terry	Larry T. Shaw
Thorne, Roger	Ray Russell
Thornton, Hall	Robert Silverberg
Thorpe, Trebor	Robert L. Fanthorpe
Thurston, Howard	Real name; Walter B. Gibson
Thynn, Alexander	Viscount Weymouth
Tigrina	Edythe Eide
Tillray, Les	Erle Stanley Gardner
Tilton, Alice	Phoebe Atwood Taylor
Tinker, Joseph	Randall Garrett
Tiptree, James, Jr.	Alice H. Sheldon
Titan, Earl	John Russell Fearn
Todd, Mike	Avrom Goldbogen
Tolz, Nick	Joseph Slotkin
Torley, Luke	James Blish
Torro, Pel	Robert L. Fanthorpe
Toucan, John	William Bird
Towers, Ivar (h)	Cyril Kornbluth & Richard Wilson
Towne, Stuart	Clayton Rawson
Trafford, F. G.	Mrs. J. H. Riddell
Transue, Jacob	Joan Matheson
Traven, Bernard	Traven Torsvan
Travis, Gerry	Louis Trimble
Tremaine, D. Lerium	Ray Bradbury (fan pseud.)
Trent, Clive	Victor R. Emanuel
Trent, Olaf	Robert L. Fanthorpe
Trevarthen, Hal P.	J. K. Heydon
Trevision, Torquay	H. Bedford-Jones
Trevor, Elleston (now legal name)	
	Trevor Dudley-Smith
Trevor, Glen	James Hilton
Trevor, William	William Trevor Cox
Trout, Kilgore	Philip José Farmer
Tucker, Bob	Arthur W. Tucker
Tucker, Wilson	Arthur W. Tucker
Turbojew, Alexej	Karl-Herbert Scheer
Twain, Mark	Samuel L. Clemens
Tyler, Jay	Robert W. Lowndes
Tyler, Theodore	Edward W. Ziegler
Tyson, A.	Harold Hersey

U, V

Pseudonym	Real Name
Undercliffe, Errol	Ramsey Campbell
Unofficial Observer	J. F. Carter
Uriel, Henry	Frederick Faust
Usher, Margo Seesse	Georgess McHargue
Vace, Geoffrey	Hugh B. Cave
Vaeth, Martin	Frederick Arnold Kummer, Jr.
Vaid, Sanford	Arthur W. Tucker & Dorothy Les Tina
Valding, Victor	John V. Peterson & Allan I. Benson
Van Campen, Karl	John W. Campbell, Jr.
Van Dall, Harold	Algis J. Budrys

Pseudonym	Real Name
Van Dine, S. S.	Willard H. Wright
Van Doren, Dirck	Frederic V. R. Dey
Van Dyne, Edith	L. Frank Baum
Van Heller, Marcus	John Coleman
Van Lhin, Erik	Lester del Rey
Van Loden, Earl	Lisle Willis
Van Loden, Erle	Lisle Willis
Van Lorne, Warner	Nelson Tremaine; F. O. Tremaine (1 story)
Vanardy, Varrick	Frederic V. R. Dey
Vance, Gerald (h)	P. W. Fairman; R. Garrett; C. S. Geier; R. P. Graham; R. Silverberg; Garrett & Silverberg
Vanny, Jim	E. J. Van Name
Vardon, Richard	David W. O'Brien
Vardre, Leslie	Leslie P. Davies
Vedder, John K.	Frank Gruber
Venable, Lyn	Marilyn Venable
Venning, Hugh	C. H. Van Zeller
Vercors	Jean Bruller
Vere, Margaret	Gabrielle M. V. Long
Verett, H. E.	E. E. Evans & Thelma Hamm Evans
Verlanger, Julia	Heliane Taieb
Vernon, V.	Harold Hersey
Vigan, Luc	Andre Ruellan
Vincent, Claire	Miriam Lynch
Vincent, Harl	H. V. Schoepflin
Vincent, J. Harry	James V. Taurasi, Sr.
Vincent, James	Vincent Napoli
Vincent, John	Lester del Rey
Vine, William	Christopher S. Youd
Vipont, Elfrida	Elfrida Vipont Foulds
Vivian, E. Charles	Charles Henry Cannell
Voltaire	François Marie Arouet
Von Drey, Howard	Howard Wandrei
Von Rachen, Kurt	L. Ron Hubbard
Voyant, Claire	Forrest J Ackerman (fan pseud.)

W

Pseudonym	Real Name
W. W.	William Bloom
Wade, Alan	Jack Vance
Wade, Robert	David McIlwain
Wainwright, Ken	E. C. Tubb
Waldo, E. Hunter (former name)	
	Theodore Sturgeon (now legal name)
Walker, Max	Michael Avallone
Wallace, Clifford	Sydney J. Bounds
Wallace, Doreen	Dora Eileen Agnew Rash
Wallace, Edgar	Richard E. Wallace
Wallace, Ian	John Wallace Pritchard
Wallis, G. McDonald	Hope Campbell
Walser, Sam	Robert E. Howard
Walters, Gordon	George W. Locke
Walters, Hugh	W. L. Hughes
Walters, Seldon	Walt Sheldon
Ward, Henry	Henri Viard
Ward, Peter	Frederick Faust
Ward, Robert	Robert E. Howard
Ward, Taylor	Alan Hyde
Ware, Wallace	David Karp
Wargar, Kurt	Andre Ruellan
Waring, Beth	William Rotsler
Warland, Allen	Donald A. Wollheim
Warner, Douglas	J. D. Currie & E. Warner
Washington, Berwell	James Branch Cabell
Water, Silas	Noel Loomis
Waterhouse, Arthur	John Russell Fearn
Waters, Silas	Noel Loomis

Pseudonym	Real Name
Watkins, Gerrold	Barry N. Malzberg
Watson, Billy	Theodore Sturgeon
Watson, Richard F.	Robert Silverberg
Webb, Christopher	Leonard Wibberley
Webb, Lucas	M. R. Burgess
Webster, Robert N.	Ray Palmer
Weight, Frank	E. C. Tubb
Weinbaum, Helen (née)	Helen W. Kasson
Weiner, William M.	Sam Moskowitz (fan pseud.)
Weir, Mordred	Amelia R. Long
Weldon, Rex	Duane W. Rimel
Wells, Braxton	Donald A. Wollheim
Wells, Hampton	Manly Wade Wellman
Wells, Hubert George	Forrest J Ackerman
Wells, J. Wellington	L. Sprague de Camp
Wells, John Jay	Marion Zimmer Bradley & Juanita Coulson
Wells, Wade	Manly Wade Wellman
Wellsley, Julie	Wilfred McNeilly
Wentworth, Robert	Edmond Hamilton
Wenzel, Sophie Louise	Sophie Wenzell Ellis
Werheim, John	John Russell Fearn
Werper, Barton	Peter Scott
Wesley, Art	Dean A. Grennell
Wesso, H. W.	Hans Waldemar Wessolowski
West, Douglas	E. C. Tubb
West, Michael	August W. Derleth
Westcott, Kathleen	Christine E. Abrahamsen
Westflag, Fletcher	William Rotsler
Westmacott, Mary	Agatha Christie
Weston, Allen	Alice M. Norton & Grace Allen
Westwood, N. J.	Joseph J. Millard
White, Cecil B.	William H. Christie
White, George M.	J. M. Walsh
White, Harlan	Harlan Ellison
White, Parker	W. A. P. White (i.e., A. Boucher)
Whitley, George	A. Bertram Chandler
Whitney, Elliott	H. Bedford-Jones
Whitney, Elliott	Joseph H. Dockweiler & Frederic Arnold Kummer, Jr.
Whitney, Reid	R. Coutts Armour
Whitney, Spencer	Arthur J. Burks
Whitton, Daniel	John H. Pomeroy
Wilde, Jimmy	John Creasey
Wilde, Lady	Lady Jane Francisca Speranza Wilde
Wilder, Allen	John W. Jakes
Wilder, Cherry	Cherry B. Grimm
Wilding, Eric	E. C. Tubb
Wiley, John (h)	Roger P. Graham; others
Willard, C. D.	Charles W. Diffin
Willer	Ed Emshwiller
Willey, Robert	Willy Ley
Williams, J. X. (h)	Jordan James; Andrew J. Offutt
Williams, Speedy	L. H. Smith
Williams, Tennessee	Thomas L. Williams
Willie, Albert Frederick	H. P. Lovecraft
Willis, Charles	Arthur C. Clarke
Willy the Wisp	Donald A. Wollheim (fan pseud.)
Wilson, Barbara	Laurence M. Janifer
Wilson, Gabriel	Ray Cummings & Mrs. Ray Cummings

Pseudonym	Real Name
Wilson, Sandy	A. Galbraith
Winch, John	Gabrielle M. V. Long
Winfield, Dick	Dick Perry
Wingrave, A.	S. Fowler Wright
Winiki, Ephriam	John Russell Fearn
Winnard, Frank	E. C. Tubb
Winslow, Dorian	Daoma Winston
Winter, H. G.	H. Bates & Desmond Hall
Winter, Turk	Andrew J. Offutt
Winterbottom, Russ	Russell R. Winterbotham
Winters, Rae	Raymond A. Palmer
Witherup, Anne Warrington	
	John Kendrick Bangs
Wollonover, Fred	Sam Moskowitz (fan pseud.)
Woodcott, Keith	John Brunner
Woodford, Jack	Josiah Pitts Woolfolk
Woodruff, Clyde	David Vern
Woods, Lawrence	D. Wollheim & R. W. Lowndes & J. Michel
Woods, P. F.	Barrington J. Bayley
Worcester, Roland	Francis G. Rayer
Worth, Amy	David H. Keller
Worth, Peter (h)	C. S. Geier; R. P. Graham
Wright, Kenneth	Lester del Rey
Wright, Robert	R. W. Lowndes & F. J Ackerman
Wright, Weaver	Forrest J Ackerman
Wul, Stefan	Pierre Pairault
Wurf, Karl	George Scithers
Wyatt, Lee	Jerrold D. Friedman
Wycliffe, John	H. Bedford-Jones
Wylie, Dirk	J. H. Dockweiler & Cyril Kornbluth & F. Pohl
Wyndham, John	John B. Harris

X,Y,Z

Pseudonym	Real Name
X	Donald A. Wollheim
X, Doctor	Alan E. Nourse
X, Ex-Private	A. M. Burrage
X, General	Roger S. Hoar
Xanthus, Xavier	March Laumer
York, Anton	Arthur Leo Zagat
York, Georgia	Lee Hoffman
York, Jeremy	John Creasey
York, Simon	Robert A. Heinlein
Young, Carter Travis	Louis Charbonneau
Young, Collier	Robert Bloch
Young, Raymond A.	Vernon H. Jones
Zachary, Elizabeth	Hugh Zachary
Zacherley	John Zacherle
Zambock, George	Allen Glasser
Zeigfreid, Karl (h)	Robert L. Fanthorpe; John S. Glasby; T. W. Wade
Zetford, Tully	Kenneth Bulmer
Zoilus	H. P. Lovecraft
Zorro	Harold Ward
Zweig, Allen	Frederik Pohl (fan pseud.)

Real Name	*Pseudonym*

Real Names/Pseudonyms

A

Aarons, Edward S.	Edward Ronns
Abbott, Edwin Abbott	A Square
Abrahams, Doris Caroline	Caryl Brahms
Abrahamsen, Christine Elizabeth	
	Cristabel; Kathleen Westcott
Abramovitch, Sholem Yankev	
	Mendele Moykher-Sforim
Ackerman, Forrest J	Sgt. Ack Ack (fan pseud.); Dr. Acula; Nick Beal; Carl F. Burke; Walter Chinwell; J. Forrester Eckman; Jacques de Forrest Erman; Jack Ermann (fan pseud.); Geoffrey Giles (with W. Gillings) (fan pseud.); Alden Lorraine; Aime Merritt; Spencer Strong; Claire Voyant (fan pseud.); Hubert George Wells; Robert Wright (with R. W. Lowndes); Weaver Wright
Ackerman, Wendayne	Wendayne Mondelle (fan pseud.)
Adam, Robert James	Paul MacTyre
Adams, J.	Skelton Kuppord
Addis, Hazel Iris (Wilson)	Hazel Adair; A. J. Heritage
Adlard, Peter Marcus	Mark Adlard
Aiken, Joan	Nicholas Dee; Rosie Lee
Aiken, John	John Paget
Aldani, Lino	N. L. Janda
Aldiss, Brian W.	C. C. Shackleton
Alexander, Colin James	Simon Jay
Alexander, Janet	Janet McNeill
Alexander, Robert William	Joan Butler
Alfven, Hannes	Olof Johannesson
Alger, Leclaire Gowans	Sorche Nic Leodhas
Allen, Edward Heron	*See* Heron-Allen, E.
Allen, Grace	Allen Weston (with Alice M. Norton)
Allen, Henry	Clay Fisher; Will Henry
Alter, Robert	Robert Retla
Altshuler, Harry	Alexander Faust
Amis, Kingsley	Robert Markham
Anderson, Mrs. J. O.	Stella Benson (née)
Anderson, Karen (Mrs. P. Anderson)	
	June Millichamp Kruse
Anderson, Poul	A. A. Craig; Michael Karageorge; Winston P. Sanders
Anderson, William C.	Andy Anderson
Andrevon, Jean-Pierre	Alphonse Brutsche
Andrews, Claire	Keith Claire (with Keith Andrews)
Andrews, Keith	Keith Claire (with Claire Andrews)
Andrus, L. R.	Lee Andre
Anstruther, Joyce	Jan Struther
Anthony, Barbara	Antonio Barber
Antonick, Robert J.	Nick Kamin
Armour, R. Coutts	Coutts Brisbane; Reid Whitney
Armstrong, Charles Wicksteed	
	Charles Strongi'th'arm
Armstrong, Terence Ian Fytton	
	John Gawsworth
Arouet, François Marie	Voltaire
Ashkenazy, Irvin	G. Garnet
Ashton, Winifred	Clemence Dane
Ashwell, Pauline	Paul Ash
Asimov, Isaac	Dr. A; George E. Dale; Paul French; H. B. Ogden
Asimov, Mrs. Isaac	J. O. Jeppson

Real Name	*Pseudonym*
Aswell, Mary Louise	Q. Patrick (with R. W. Webb)
Athanas, William Verne	Bill Colson
Atkins, Frank, Jr.	Fenton Ash; Fred Ashley; Frank Aubrey; F. St. Mars
Avallone, Michael	Nick Carter (h); Troy Conway (h); Priscilla Dalton; Mark Dane; Jean-Anne de Pre; Dora Highland; Steve Michaels; Dorothea Nile; Ed Noon; Edwina Noone; John Patrick; Stuart Sidney; Vance Stanton; Sidney Stuart; Max Walker
Avice, Claude	Pierre Barbet; David Maine; Oliver Sprigel
Aycock, Roger D.	Roger Dee; John Starr (h)

B

Bailey, Hilary	Hilary Brand (h)
Bair, Patrick	David Gurney
Baker, Rachel Maddux	Rachel Maddux
Baker, W. J.	John Churchward
Ball, Brian N.	Brian Kinsey-Jones
Balter, E.	Arthur Cooke (complex collaboration)
Bangs, John Kendrick	Anne Warrington Witherup
Banis, Victor J.	Jay Alexander; Lynn Benedict
Bankoff, George Alexis	George Borodin
Barber, Margaret	Michael Fairless
Bargone, Charles	Claude Farrere
Barham, Richard Harris	Thomas Ingoldsby
Barker, S. Omar	Phil Squires
Barlow, James William	Antares Skorpios
Barnard, Marjorie F.	M. Barnard Eldershaw (with F. S. Eldershaw, except on the only sf novel)
Barnes, Arthur K.	Kelvin Kent (some with H. Kuttner); Dave Barnes (with Norbert Davis)
Bartignono, Giovanni	Jack Bertin
Bartle, L. E.	Richard Lawrence; Francis Richardson (with F. Parnell)
Baruch, Hugo	Jack Bilbo
Bassler, Thomas J.	T. J. Bass
Bates, Harry	Anthony Gilmore (alone, or with D. W. Hall); A. R. Holmes; Quien Sabe (1956); H. G. Winter (with D. W. Hall)
Baum, L. Frank	Floyd Akers; Laura Bartlett; John Estes Cook; Hugh Fitzgerald; Suzanne Metcalf; Schuyler Stanton; Edith Van Dyne
Baxter, John	Martin Loran (with Ron Smith)
Bayley, Barrington J.	Alan Aumbry; Michael Barrington (with M. Moorcock); John Diamond; P. F. Woods
Beck, L. Adams	E. Barrington; Louis Moresby
Bedford-Jones, Henry	Donald Bedford; Montague Brissard; Cleveland B. Chase; George Souli DeMourant; Paul Ferval; Michael Gallister; Allan Hawkwood; Gordon Keyne; M. Lassez; Lucian Penjean; Margaret Love Sangerson; David Seabrooke; Charles George Souli; Gordon Stuart; Torquay Trevision; Elliott Whitney; John Wycliffe
Bell, Eric Temple	Richard C. Badger; J. T.; John Taine; James Temple
Benedict, Steve	Marius
Benjamin, Lewis Saul	Lewis Melville (some with R. Hargreaves)
Bennett, Geoffrey Martin	Sea-Lion
Bennett, Gertrude Barrows	Francis Stevens
Bennett, W. E.	Warren Armstrong
Bensen, D. R.	Susan Jennifer (h)
Benson, Allan Ingvald	Victor Valding (with J. V. Peterson)
Beresford, Marcus	Marc Brandel
Bermange, Maurine J. L.	Maggie Ross

Real Name	Pseudonym
Berry, Bryan	Rolf Garner
Berry, D. Bruce	Jeff Douglas (with A. J. Offutt); Morgan Drake
Bertin, Eddy C.	Edith Brendall; Doriac Greysun
Bessiere, Richard	F. Richard-Bessiere (with F. Richard)
Bester, Alfred	John Lennox; Sonny Powell
Beuttler, Edward Ivan Oakley	
	Ivan Butler
Bickham, Jack Miles	Jeff Clinton
Bierce, Ambrose	Mrs. J. Milton Bowers; Dod Grile; J. Milton Sloluck
Binder, Earl Andrew, and **Binder, Otto Oscar**	
	Eando Binder ; John Coleridge; Will Garth (h); Gordon A. Giles; Dean D. O'Brien. *Note:* From 1939 most stories by Otto only.
Binder, Otto	*See* Binder, Earl
Bingham, Carson	Con Steffanson (h)
Bird, William Henry Fleming	
	Adrian Blair; Lee Elliot (h); Harry Fleming; Rand Le Page (h); Paul Lorraine (h); Kris Luna (h); John Toucan
Birkin, Charles Lloyd	Charles Lloyd
Bishop, Alison	Alison Lurie
Bishop, Morris	W. Bollingbroke Johnson
Bixby, (Drexel) Jerome	Jay B. Drexel; Thornecliff Herrick (h); Emerson Jans; D. B. Lewis; Harry Neal; Morton D. Paley (with S. Merwin Jr.) (fan pseud.); Alger Rome (with A. J. Budrys); Albert Russell; J. Russell
Blair, Eric	George Orwell
Blaisdell, Paul	Paul Dell
Blake, Alan	Omar Gwinn
Bland, Mrs. Edith	Edith Nesbit
Blassingame, Wyatt	William B. Rainey
Blaustein, A. P.	W. B. deGraeff (with G. Conklin)
Blish, James	William Atheling, Jr.; Donald Laverty (with D. Knight); Marcus Lyons; John MacDougal (with R. W. Lowndes); Arthur Merlyn; Luke Torley
Blish, Mrs. James	Judith Ann Lawrence (née)
Blixen-Finecke, Baroness **Karen Christence**	
	Pierre Andrezel; Karen Blixen; Isaak Dinesen
Bloch, Robert	Tarleton Fiske; Will Folke; Nathan Hindin (with Nathan Hindin); E. K. Jarvis (h); Wilson Kane (h); Jim Kjelgaard (real name); Sherry Malone; John Sheldon; Collier Young
Blondel, Roger	B. R. Bruss
Bloom, William	W.W.
Blow, Mrs. Richard	Marya Mannes
Bodington, Nancy Hermione	
	Shelley Smith
Boëx, J. H. H.	J.-H. (Aîné) Rosny
Bogart, William	Kenneth Robeson (h) (a few novels)
Bok, Hannes	Dolbokov (with Boris Dolgov)
Boland, Bertram J.	John Boland
Bond, Nelson S.	George Danzell; Hubert Mavity
Bordes, François	Francis Carsac
Boston, Noel	Noel Bertram
Bott, Henry	Charles Recour
Boucher, Anthony (pseud.—see White, W. A. P.)	
	H. H. Holmes
Bounds, Sydney J.	Martin L. Baker; Roger Carne; W. E. Clarkson; Paul Hammond; James Ross; Wes Saunders; Lawrence Smith; Clifford Wallace
Boutland, David	David Rome
Boyd, Lyle G.	*See* Boyd, William C.

Real Name	Pseudonym
Boyd, William Clouser	Boyd Ellanbee; Boyd Ellanby. (Often with wife, Lyle G. Boyd)
Brackett, Leigh	George Sanders (real name) (ghost written)
Bradbury, Ray	Guy Amory (fan pseud.); D. R. Banat; Edward Banks; Anthony Corvais (fan pseud.); Cecil Claybourne Cunningham (fan pseud.); E. Cunningham (fan pseud.); Leonard Douglas; Brian Eldred (fan pseud.); William Elliott; Hollerbochen (fan pseud.); Omega (fan pseud.); Ron Reynolds; Doug Rogers (fan pseud.); Douglas Spaulding; Leonard Spaulding; Brett Sterling (h); D. Lerium Tremaine (fan pseud.)
Bradley, Marion Zimmer	Lee Chapman; John Dexter; Miriam Gardner; Morgan Ives; Brian Morley; Dee O'Brien; John Jay Wells (with Juanita Coulson)
Brandel, Marc	Marcus Beresford
Brent, Peter	Ludovic Peters
Bretnor, Reginald	Grendel Briarton
Bright, Mary Chavelita Dunne	
	George Egerton
Briney, Robert E.	Andrew Duane
Brodie, John	John Guthrie
Brown, Fredric	Felix Graham
Brown, Zenith	Leslie Ford; David Frome
Browne, Howard	Alexander Blade (h); William Brengle (h); Hugh B. Carleton (h); Lawrence Chandler (h); John Evans; Lee Francis (h); John McGreevey (h); Peter Phillips (h); John X. Pollard (h)
Brueckel, Frank J.	Frank J. Bridge
Bruller, Jean	Vercors
Brunner, John (Kilian Houston)	
	K. Houston Brunner; Kilian Houston; Gill Hunt (h); John Loxmith; Keith Woodcott
Brussof, Valery	Valery Bryusov (variant transliteration)
Buckner, Mary Dale	Donald Dale
Buddee, Paul	Paul Richards
Budrys, Algis J.	David C. Hodgkins; Ivan Janvier; Paul Janvier; Robert Marner; Alger Rome (with J. Bixby); William Scarff; John A. Sentry; Albert Stroud; Harold Van Dall
Bulmer, (H.) Kenneth	Alan Burt Akers; Ken Blake; Frank Brandon; Rupert Clinton; Ernest Corley; Arthur Frazier (h); Peter Green; Adam Hardy (h); Kenneth Johns (with J. Newman, for nonfiction); Philip Kent; Bruno Krauss; Neil Langholm (h); Karl Maras (h); Manning Norvil; Charles R. Pike (h); Dray Prescot; Andrew Quiller (h); Chesman Scot; Nelson Sherwood; Richard Silver (h); H. Philip Stratford; Tully Zetford
Bulwer-Lytton, Edward George	
	Lord Lytton
Bunch, David R.	Darryl R. Groupe
Bunting, D. G.	Daniel George
Burgess, M. R.	C. Everett Cooper; Robert R. Reginald; Lucas Webb
Burke, John Frederick	Jonathan Burke; Robert Miall
Burks, Arthur J.	Estil Critchie; Burke MacArthur; Spencer Whitney
Burrage, Alfred McClelland	
	Ex-Private X
Burroughs, Edgar Rice	Normal Bean; Norman Bean; John Tyler McCulloch
Burton, Elizabeth	Susan Alice Kerby

Real Name	Pseudonym
Busby, F. M.	Renfrew Pemberton
Buttrey, Douglas Norton	Densil Neve Barr
Byrne, Stuart J.	John Bloodstone; Howard Dare; Marx Kaye (h)

C

Real Name	Pseudonym
Cabell, James Branch	Henry Lee Jefferson; Berwell Washington
Caldwell, Janet Taylor	Taylor Caldwell (with Marcus Reback)
Calle, Paul	Paul Pierre
Campbell, Hope	G. McDonald Wallis
Campbell, Hubert J.	Jon J. Deegan (h); Roy Sheldon (h)
Campbell, John Wood, Jr.	Arthur McCann; Don A. Stuart; Karl Van Campen
Campbell, [J.] Ramsey	Montgomery Comfort (h); Carl Dreadstone (h); Errol Undercliffe
Campbell, William E. M.	William March
Canaday, John	Matthew Head
Canedo, Alejandro	Alejandro
Cannell, Charles Henry	Jack Mann; E. Charles Vivian
Capella, Raul Garcia	Ray Capella
Caplin, Alfred Gerald	Al Capp
Capps, Carroll M.	C. C. MacApp
Caras, Roger Andrew	Roger Sarac
Carnell, Edward J.	John Carnell
Carr, John Dickson	Carr Dickson; Carter Dickson
Carr, Terry	Norman Edwards (with Ted White)
Carrington, Hereward	Nandor Fodor; Hubert Lavington
Carter, Bryan	Nick Carter (h)
Carter, John Franklin	Diplomat; Jay Franklin; Unofficial Observer
Carter, Paul A.	Philip Carter
Cartmill, Cleve	Leslie Charteris; Michael Corbin
Caseleyr, C. A. M.	Jack Danvers
Cassiday, Bruce	Carson Bingham; Annie Laurie McAllister
Cave, Hugh B.	Allen Beck; Justin Case; Geoffrey Vace
Cawthorn, James	Philip James; Desmond Reid (h)
Chadwick, Paul	Brant House
Chambers, Aidan	Malcolm Blacklin
Chance, John Newton	J. Drummond; John Lymington; David C. Newton; Desmond Reid (h)
Chandler, A. Bertram	Andrew Dunstan; George Whitley
Chapman, (Mrs.) Guy	Storm Jameson
Charbonneau, Louis	Carter Travis Young
Charles-Henneberg, Nathalie	
	Charles Henneberg (real name); also used by his wife after his death
Charteris, Mary Evelyn	Lady Cynthia Asquith
Chatrian, Alexandre	Erckmann-Chatrian (with Emile Erckmann)
Cherry, Carolyn Janice	C. J. Cherryh
Chetwynd-Hayes, Ronald	Angus Campbell
Childs, Edmund Burton	Edmund Burton
Christie, Agatha	Mary Westmacott
Christie, William H.	Cecil B. White
Ciardi, John	John Anthony
Clark, Alfred Alexander Gordon	
	Cyril Hare
Clark, Charles Heber	Max Adeler
Clark, Dale	Ronal Kayser
Clarke, Arthur C.	E. G. O'Brien; Charles Willis
Clayton, Richard	William Haggard
Clemens, Samuel Langhorne	
	Mark Twain
Clinton, Ed M., Jr.,	Anthony More
Cloutier, Charles	Charles Cloukey
Cochrane, Willam E.	S. Kye Boult
Cockburn, Claud	James Helvick

Real Name	Pseudonym
Cogswell, Theodore	Cogswell Thomas (with Theodore L. Thomas)
Cohen, Chester	Conanight (with D. Knight); Chester B. Conant
Cole, John	J. G. Leighton
Cole, Les	Colin Sturgis (with Mel Sturgis)
Coleman, John	John Dexter; Peter Kanto; Marcus Van Heller
Coles, Cyril H.	Manning Coles; Francis Gaite. (Both with Adelaide F. O. Manning)
Collins, Wilkie	Charles Collins (with Charles Dickens)
Colter, Elizabeth	Eli Colter
Compton, David Guy	Guy Compton; Frances Lynch
Cone, P. C. L.	Patricia Clapp
Conklin, Groff	W. B. deGraeff (with A. P. Blaustein)
Conly, Robert L.	Robert C. O'Brien
Connell, Alan	Alan Conn
Conquest, Robert	J. E. M. Arden
Constant, Alphonse Louis	Eliphas Levi
Conway, Gerard F.	Wallace Moore
Cook, Mabel C.	Mabel C. Collins
Cook, William Wallace	Nick Carter (h)
Cooke, Millen	Alexander Blade (h)
Cooper, Edmund	Richard Avery
Coppel, Alfred	Sol Galaxan; Robert Cham Gilman; Derfla Leppoc; A. C. Marin
Copper, Dorothy	Diana Carter
Corbin, Harold Standish	Harvey S. Cottrell; Henry W. A. Fairfield; John C. Fletcher
Cornwell, David	John Le Carre
Coryell, John R.	Nick Carter (h)
Coulson, Juanita	John Jay Wells (with M. Z. Bradley)
Coulson, Robert	Thomas Stratton (with Eugene DeWeese)
Cousins, Margaret	Avery Johns
Cove, Joseph Walter	Lewis Gibbs
Cox, Anthony Berkeley	Anthony Berkeley; Francis Iles
Cox, Arthur Jean	Ralph Carghill; Jean Cox; Gene Cross
Cox, William Trevor	William Trevor
Coxon, Mrs. Sydney	Muriel Hine
Craigie, Dorothy M.	David Craigie
Crawford, Margaret	Garret Ford (with William L. Crawford [husband])
Crawford, William L.	Garret Ford (with Margaret Crawford [wife])
Creasey, John	Gordon Ashe; M. E. Cooke; Margaret Cooke; Henry St. John Cooper; Norman Deane; Elise Fecamps; Patrick Gill; Michael Halliday; Charles Hogarth; Brian Hope; Colin Hughes; Kyle Hunt; Abel Mann; Peter Manton; J. J. Marric; James Marsden; Richard Martin; Rodney Mattheson; Anthony Morton; Ken Ranger; William K. Reilly; Tex Riley; Henry St. John; Jimmy Wilde; Jeremy York
Crichton, Michael	Michael Douglas; Jeffrey Hudson; John Lange (which is also the real name of another author)
Cronin, Bernard C.	Eric North
Crook, Crompton N.	Stephen Tall
Crosby, Harry C.	Christopher Anvil
Cross, John Keir	Stephen MacFarlane; Susan Morley
Crossen, Kendell Foster	Bennett Barlay; M. E. Chaber; Richard Foster; Christopher Monig; Kent Richard; Clay Richards
Crowe, B. L.	Peter Lum
Crowley, Edward Alexander	Aleister Crowley
Cummings, Ray	Ray King; Ray P. Shotwell; Gabriel Wilson (with Mrs. Cummings))
Cummings, Mrs. Ray	Gabriel Wilson (with R. Cummings)

Real Name	Pseudonym
Cunningham, Chet	Cathy Cunningham
Currie, J. D.	Douglas Warner (with E. Warner)

D

Real Name	Pseudonym
Dakers, Elaine	Jane Lane
Danby, Mary	Mary Calvert
Daniel, Yuli	Nicolai Arzhak
Daniels, Dorothy	Dorothy Daniels (with Norman Daniels)
Daniels, Norman A.	Dorothy Daniels (with Dorothy Daniels); Kenneth Robeson (h); C. K. M. Scanlon (h)
Dannay, Frederic	Ellery Queen, Jr. (with M. Lee); Daniel Nathan
Danziger, Gustaf A. de Castro	Adolphe de Castro
David, Julia	F. Draco
Davidson, Avram	Ellery Queen (h)
Davies, Howell	Andrew Marvell (real name)
Davies, Leslie P.	Leslie Vardre
Davies, Olwen B.	Olwen Bowen
Davis, Frederick C.	Curtis Steele (h)
Davis, Frederick W.	Nick Carter (h)
Davis, Gyle	Gil Daniels
Davis, Harold A.	Kenneth Robeson (h)
Davis, Ian	Ian Dallas
Davis, Lois Carlile	Lois Lamplugh
Davis, Lou Ellen	Elizabeth Davis
Davis, Norbert	Dave Barnes (with A. K. Barnes)
de Camp, Lyon Sprague	Lyman R. Lyon; J. Wellington Wells
De Kremer, Raymond	John Flanders; Jean Ray
de la Mare, Walter	Walter Ramal
Deer, M. Jane	M. J. Deer (with G. H. Smith)
Degler, Claude	Don Rogers
del Rey, Lester	*See* del Rey, Ramon Alvarez
del Rey, Ramon Alvarez	John Alvarez; R. Alvarez; Lester del Rey (usually known name); Cameron Hall; Marion Henry; Philip James; Wade Kaempfert (h); Edson McCann (with F. Pohl); Henry Marion; John Raymond; Philip St. John; Charles Satterfield; Erik Van Lhin; John Vincent; Kenneth Wright
DeMelikoff, Jodi	Jody McCarter (with Vermille McCarter)
DeMille, James	Gilbert Gaul
DeMille, Richard	Arthur Coster
Deming, Richard	Richard Deeming; Max Franklin
Demmon, Calvin W.	Carl Damon
Dennis, Walter L.	Dennis McDermott (with P. S. Miller)
Dent, Lester	Maxwell Grant (h, some titles); Kenneth Roberts; Kenneth Robeson (h, most titles); Tim Ryan
Derleth, August W.	Will Garth (h); Stephen Grendon; Eldon Heath (h); Kenyon Holmes; J. Sheridan Le Fanu (1 story) (real name); Tally Mason; Michael West
Des Ormeaux, J. J.	Gene Gary
Detzer, Diane	Jorge De Reyna; Adam Lukens
DeWeese, Eugene	Jean DeWeese; Thomas Stratton (with Robert Coulson)
Dey, Frederic V. R.	Ross Beckman (with D. Fairde & K. Fearing); Aaron Ainsworth Burr; Nick Carter (h); Bertha M. Clay (h); Marmaduke Dey; Marian Gilmore (h); Frederic Ormond; Dirck Van Doren; Varrick Vanardy
Dick, Philip K.	Richard Phillips
Dick-Lauder, Sir George A.	George Dick Lauder

Real Name	Pseudonym
Dickens, Charles	Charles Collins (with Wilkie Collins)
Diffin, Charles W.	C. D. Willard
Dikty, Julian (Judy) Chain May (Mrs. T. E. Dikty)	Julian Chain; Julian C. May
Disch, Thomas M.	Thom Demijohn; Leonie Hargreave; Cassandra Knye
Divine, Arthur D(urham)	David Divine; David Rame
Dixon, Roger	Charles Lewis
Dixon, Thomas	Burt Cole
Dockweiler, Joseph Harold	Elliott Whitney (with F. A. Kummer, Jr.); Dirk Wylie (with others)
Dodgson, Charles L.	Lewis Carroll
Dolgov, Boris	Dolbokov (with H. Bok [W. Woodard])
Dolinsky, Meyer	Mike Dolinsky
Dominick, M.	D.E.A.
Donnelly, Ignatius	Edmund Boisgilbert
Douglas, Myrtle R.	Morojo
Downey, Edmond	F. M. Allen
Dresser, David	Brett Halliday
Drussai, Garen	Milo Kirkham
DuBreuil, Linda	L. J. Brown; D. Barry Linder
Duchacek, Ivo	Ivo Duka
Dudley-Smith, Trevor (former name)	Trevor Dudley; Elleston Trevor (new legal name)
Duncan, Robert L.	James Hall Roberts
Dunn, Philip M.	Saul Dunn

E

Real Name	Pseudonym
Edgar, Alfred	Barre Lyndon; John Sansom (with Jimmy Sangster)
Edmonds, Mrs. Helen	Anna Kavan
Edmondson y Cotton, J. M. G. O.	G. C. Edmondson; Kelly P. Gast
Effinger, George Alec	John K. Diomede; Susan Doenim
Egerton, J. K.	Francis Metcalfe
Eide, Edythe	Tigrina
Eisfeld, Rainer	Jeff Caine; Wayne Coover; Allan Reed; Wolf Detler Rohr
Eklund, Gordon	Wendall Stewart
Eldershaw, Flora S. P.	M. Barnard Eldershaw (with M. F. Barnard)
Elgin, Patricia A. Suzette	Suzette Haden Elgin
Eliades, David	David Forrest (with Robert Forrest-Webb); Robert Forrest Webb (co-author)
Ellik, Ron	Carl Brandon
Elliott, Bruce	Maxwell Grant (h)
Ellis, Sophie Wenzel	Sophie Louise Wenzel
Ellison, Harlan	Lee Archer (h); Cordwainer Bird; Cortwainer Bird; John Doyle (ghost written); Ellis Hart; John Magnus (ghost written); Matthew Quinton; Pat Roeder (ghost written); Harlan White
Ely, George Herbert	Herbert Strang (with C. J. L'Estrange)
Emanuel, Victor Rousseau	H. M. Egbert; Victor Rousseau; Clive Trent
Emshwiller, Edmund A.	Ed Alexander; Ed Emsh; Emsler; Willer Noname
Enton, Harry	
Erckmann, Emile	Erckmann-Chatrian (with Alexandre Chatrian)
Ernst, Paul	George Alden Edson; Kenneth Robeson (h); Paul Frederick Stern
Ernsting, Walter	Clark Darlton; F. MacPatterson
Estival, Ivan Leon	Estival
Estridge, Robin	Philip Loraine
Evans, Edward Everett	Harry J. Gardner; H. E. Verett (with T. H. Evans)
Evans, Gerald	Victor La Salle (h)

Real Name	Pseudonym
Evans, Thelma Hamm (Mrs. E. E. Evans)	Hamm Edwards; T. D. Hamm (née); H. E. Verett (with E. E. Evans)
Everett, Mrs. H. D.	Theo Douglas

F

Fairde, Donald	Ross Beckman (with F. V. R. Dey & K. Fearing)
Fairman, Paul W.	Adam Chase (with M. Lesser); Ivar Jorgensen (also Jorgenson) (h); Robert Eggert Lee; Paul Lohrman (h); F. W. Paul; Ellery Queen (h); Mallory Storm; Gerald Vance (h)
Fanthorpe, Robert Lionel	Neil Balfort; Othello Baron; Erle Barton; Lee Barton; Thornton Bell; Noel Bertram; Leo Brett; Bron Fane; Robert Lionel Fanhope; Mel Jay; Marston Johns (h); L. P. Kenton; Victor La Salle (h); Oben Lerteth; Robert Lionel; John E. Muller (h); Elton T. Neef; Elton T. Neefe; Phil Nobel; Peter O'Flinn; Peter O'Flynn; John Raymond (h); Lionel Roberts; René Rolant; Deutero Spartacus; Robin Tate; Neil Thanet; Trebor Thorpe; Pel Torro; Olaf Trent; Karl Zeigfreid (h)
Fargus, Frederick John	Hugh Conway
Farjeon, Joseph Jefferson	Anthony Swift
Farmer, Philip José	Maxwell Grant (h); Kenneth Robeson (h); Kilgore Trout
Fast, Howard M.	E. V. Cunningham; Walter Ericson
Faulkner, Dorothea M.	Rory Magill
Faust, Frederick	Frank Austin; George Owen Baxter; Lee Bolt; Max Brand; Walter C. Butler; George Challis; Peter Dawson; Martin Dexter; Evan Evans; Evin Evans; John Frederick; Frederick Frost; Dennis Lawton; David Manning; Peter Henry Morland; Hugh Owen; John Schoolcraft; Nicholas Silver; Henry Uriel; Peter Ward
Fawcett, F. Dubrez	Griff (h)
Fearing, Kenneth	Ross Beckman (with D. Fairde & F. V. R. Dey)
Fearn, John Russell	Geoffrey Armstrong; Thornton Ayre; Hugo Blayn (only for detective & mystery); Morton Boyce*; Dennis Clive; John Cotton; Polton Cross; Astron del Martia (h) (1 novel); Mark Denholm; Douglas Dodd*; Sheridan Drew*; Max Elton*; Spike Gordon; Volsted Gridban (h) (about half); Griff (h); Malcolm Hartley*; Timothy Hayes (only for westerns); Conrad G. Holt; Frank Jones; Marvin Kayne*; Clifford Lewis (unconfirmed); Herbert Lloyd*; Paul Lorraine (h); Dom Passante; Henry Rawle (unconfirmed); Francis Rose*; Lawrence F. Rose; Ward Ross*; John Russell; Schire; Doorn Sclanders (only for westerns); Joan Seagar (only for romances); Brian Shaw; John Slate (only for detective & mystery); Vargo Statten; Rosina Tarne; K. Thomas; Earl Titan; Arthur Waterhouse*; John Werheim; Ephriam Winiki
	* Only used in Fearn's *Vargo Statten Science Fiction Magazine* (later *British Space Fiction Magazine*)

Real Name	Pseudonym
Feder, Robert Arthur	Robert Arthur; Alfred Hitchcock (ghost editor)
Fickling, Forrest E.	G. G. Fickling (with Gloria Fickling)
Fickling, Gloria	G. G. Fickling (with Forrest E. Fickling)
Fine, Peter	Peter Heath
Finney, Walter B.	Jack Finney
Firth, Violet Mary	Dion Fortune
Fischer, Bruno	Russell Gray; Harrison Storm
Fish, Robert L.	A. C. Lamprey; Robert L. Pike
Fisher, Gene	Gene Lancour
Fitzhardinge, Joan Margaret	
	Joan Phipson
Fleming-Roberts, G. T.	George Chance
Foley, Dave	Gerald Hatch
Forrest-Webb, Robert	David Forrest (with D. Eliades)
Forward, Robert L.	George Peterson Field
Foster, Alan Dean	George Lucas (real name)
Foster, W. Bert	Nick Carter (h)
Foulds, Elfrida Vipont	Elfrida Vipont
Fouts, Edward Lee	Edward Lee
Fowler, Guy	James A. Belflower
Fox, Gardner F.	Troy Conway (h); Jefferson Cooper; Jeffrey Gardner; Rod Gray (h); James Kendricks; Simon Majors; Kevin Matthews; Bart Somers
Frances, Stephen	Astron del Martia (h)
Frank, Harry Hart	Pat Frank
Frazee, Charles S.	Steve Frazee
Freeman, Kathleen	Mary Fitt
French, Alice	Octave Thanet
Friedman, Jerrold David	Caer Ged; Edward George (with Bob Vardeman); David Gerrold; Lee Wyatt
Friend, Oscar J.	Owen Fox Jerome; Sergeant Saturn (h) (some); Ford Smith
Fyfe, Horace B.	Andrew MacDuff

G

Galbraith, A.	Sandy Wilson
Galbraith, John Kenneth	Mark Epernay
Gallun, Raymond Z.	Arthur Allport; William Callahan; Dow Elstar; E. V. Raymond
Galouye, Daniel F.	Louis G. Daniels
Gandley, Kenneth Royce	Kenneth Royce
Ganley, W. Paul	Toby Duane
Gann, Ernest K.	Anthony Gray
Gardner, Erle Stanley	Kyle Corning; A. A. Fair; Charles M. Green; Grant Holiday; Carleton Kendrake; Charles J. Kenny; Robert Parr; Les Tillray
Garis, H. R.	Victor Appleton (for Stratemeyer Syndicate)
Garland, Isabel	Garland Lord (with Mindret Lord)
Garrett, Randall	Gordon Aghill (with R. Silverberg); Grandall (or Grandell) Barretton; Alexander Blade (h) (with R. Silverberg); Walter Bupp; Ralph Burke (with R. Silverberg); Gordon Garrett; David Gordon; Richard Greer (with R. Silverberg); Ivar Jorgenson (with R. Silverberg); Darrel T. Langart; Clyde Mitchell (h) (with R. Silverberg); Mark Phillips (with L. M. Janifer); Robert Randall (with R. Silverberg); Leonard G. Spencer (h) (with R. Silverberg); S. M. Tenneshaw (h) (some with R. Silverberg); Joseph Tinker; Gerald Vance (h) (some with R. Silverberg)

Real Name	Pseudonym
Garrison, Charles M.	Charles McDaniel
Garrod, J. W.	J. Castle (with R. C. Payner)
Gasko, Gordon	Nathaniel Gordon
Gastoldi, Ernesto	Julian Berry
Gehman, Richard	Martin Scott
Geier, Chester S.	Guy Archette; Robert Arnette (?) (h); Alexander Blade (h); P. F. Costello (h); Warren Kastel (h); S. M. Tenneshaw (h); Gerald Vance (h); Peter Worth (h)
Geis, Richard	Peggy Swenson
Geisel, Theodor Seuss	Theo Le Sieg; Dr. Seuss
Gellis, Roberta	Max Daniels
George, Peter	Peter Bryant; Bryan Peters
Gerahty, Digby George	Robert Standish
Germano, Peter B.	Barry Cord
Gernsback, Hugo	Grego Banshuck; Mohammed Ulysses Socrates Fips; Greno Gashbuck; Gus N. Habergock; Baron Munchausen
Gibeson, Jacqueline	Jacqueline La Tourette
Gibson, Amanda Melvina Thorley	
	Una Cooper Mathieson
Gibson, Joe	John Bridger; Carlton Furth
Gibson, Walter B.	Douglas Brown; Maxwell Grant (h) (most titles); Harry Houdini (ghost written); Howard Thurston (real name)
Giddy, Eric Cawood Gwyddin	
	Kobold Knight
Giles, Ray A.	B. X. Barry
Gillings, Walter	Geoffrey Giles (fan pseud.) (with F. J Ackerman); Thomas Sheridan
Glasby, John S.	John Adams; R. L. Bowers; Berl Cameron (h); Max Chartair; Randall Conway; Ray Cosmic; J. B. Dexter; Michael Hamilton; J. J. Hansby; J. J. Hansley; Victor La Salle (h); Peter Laynham; Rand Le Page (h); H. K. Lennard; Paul Lorraine (h); John C. Maxwell; A. J. Merak; John Morton; John E. Muller (h); J. L. Powers; Karl Zeigfreid (h)
Glasser, Allen	Sears Langell; George Zambock
Glemser, Bernard	Robert Crane; Frank Chester Field; King Hill
Glynn, Anthony A.	Anthony Martin; John E. Muller (h)
Godwin, Francis	Domingo Gonsales
Gold, Floyd	Floyd C. Gale
Gold, Horace L.	Clyde Crane Campbell; Dudley Dell; Harold C. Fosse; Julian Graey; Leigh Keith; Richard Storey
Goldbogen, Avrom	Mike Todd
Goldin, Mrs. Stephen	Kathleen Sky
Gompertz, M. L.	Ganpat
Goodchild, George	Alan Dare
Goodwin, Harold L.	John Blaine (with P. J. Harkins); Blake Savage
Gordon, Patricia	Joan Howard
Gordon, Richard	Stuart Gordon; Alex R. Stuart
Gottfried, Ted	Ted Mark
Goulart, Ron	Josephine Kains; Julian Kearny; Howard Lee; Kenneth Robeson (h); Frank S. Shaw (error); Frank S. Shawn; Joseph Silva; Con Steffanson (h)
Gowing, Sidney F.	John Goodwin
Graber, Alexander	Alexander Cordell
Grace, Anita	Jean Francis
Graham, Dale	D. A. Le Graeme
Graham, Peter	Carl Brandon (fan pseud.)
Graham, Roger Phillips	Clinton Ames; Franklin Bahl (h); Alexander Blade (h); Craig Browning; Gregg Conrad; P. F. Costello (h); Charles Lee; Inez McGowan; Charles Mann; Rog

Real Name	Pseudonym
	Phillips; Melva Rogers; Chester Ruppert; William Carter Sawtelle (h); A. R. Steber (h); Gerald Vance (h); John Wiley (h); Peter Worth (h)
Grant, Charles L.	Felicia Andrews
Grautoff, Ferdinand Heinrich	
	Parabellum
Graves, Clotilde I. M.	Richard Dehan
Graydon, Robert Murray	Murray Roberts
Green, Roland	Jeffrey Lord (h) ("Richard Blade" series from No. 9)
Green, Sheila Ellen	Sheila Greenwald
Greenfield, Irving A.	Bruce Duncan
Gregory, Ormond	W. Wayne Robbins
Grennell, Dean A.	Art Wesley
Greve, Felix Paul	Frederick Philip Grove
Gribbon, William Lancaster	
	Walter Galt; Talbot Mundy
Grieve, Christopher Murray	
	Hugh MacDiarmid
Griffin, Anthony Jerome	Altair
Griffith-Jones, George Chetwynd	
	Levin Carnac; George Griffith
Griffiths, David Arthur	Gill Hunt (h); King Lang (h); Brian Shaw (h); David Shaw (h)
Grimm, Cherry B.	Cherry Wilder
Grousset, Paschal	Andre Laurie
Gruber, Frank	Stephen Acre; Charles K. Boston; Tom Gunn (h); C. K. M. Scanlon (h); John K. Vedder
Guin, Wyman	Norman Menasco
Gunn, James E.	Edwin James
Guthrie, Thomas Anstey	F. Anstey
Gwinn, Omar	Alan Blake

H

Haas, Benjamin Leopold	Richard Meade
Haggard, J. Harvey	The Planet Prince
Hahn, George R.	Cyril Mand (with Richard Levin)
Haining, Peter	Alfred Hitchcock (ghost editor)
Haldeman, Joe W.	Robert Graham
Halidom, M. Y. (unknown pseudonym)	
	Dryasdust
Hall, Desmond W.	Anthony Gilmore (with H. Bates); H. G. Winter (with H. Bates)
Hall, James	Douglas Giles
Hall, Steve	Russ Markham
Hallstrom, Carl	Sture Sedolin
Hamilton, Alex	Donald Speed
Hamilton, Charles	Frank Richards
Hamilton, Edmond	Alexander Blade (h); Robert Castle; Hugh Davidson; Will Garth (h); Brett Sterling (h); S. M. Tenneshaw (h); Robert Wentworth
Hamilton, Mrs. Edmond	Leigh Brackett (née)
Hamling, William L.	John McGreevey (h)
Hammett, Dashiell	Peter Collinson
Hamon, Louis	Cheiro
Hanshew, Thomas W.	Nick Carter (h)
Harbaugh, Thomas C.	Nick Carter (h)
Harding, Leo	Lee Harding; Harold G. Nye
Hargreaves, R.	Lewis Melville (with L. S. Benjamin)
Harkins, P. J.	John Blaine (with H. L. Goodwin)
Harknett, Terry	George G. Gilman; Adam Hardy (h); Jane Harman; William M. James (h); Charles R. Pike (h)
Harmon, Jim	Judson Grey (some with Ron Haydock); Clark Newton

Real Name	Pseudonym
Harrington, Curtis	John Sebastian
Harris, Alf	Harris Moore (with Arthur Moore)
Harris, John Beynon	John Beynon; Lucas Parkes; Wyndham Parkes; John Wyndham
Harris, Larry Mark (former name)	
	Laurence M. Janifer (now legal name)
Harrison, Amelia W.	Margaret Compton
Harrison, Harry	Felix Boyd; Leslie Charteris (1 novel); Hank Dempsey; Cameron Hall; Wade Kaempfert (h)
Harrison, M. John	Joyce Churchill
Harrison, Michael	Quentin Downes; Michael Egremont
Hartman, Darlene	Simon Lang
Hartmann, Helmut Henry	Henry Seymour
Harvey, John	L. J. Coburn (h); J. B. Dancer (h); John J. McLaglen; Thom Ryder
Hasse, Henry	Theodore Pine (some titles, with E. Petaja)
Hathway, Alan	Kenneth Robeson (h); Clifford Goodrich
Hauser, Heinrich	Alexander Blade (h)
Havers, Dora	Theo Gift
Hawkins, Peter	Karl Maras (h)
Hay, George (Albert)	King Lang (h); Roy Sheldon (h)
Hayashi, Takashi	Takataro Kigi
Haydock, Ron	Judson Grey (with Jim Harmon)
Hayles, Brian	Irene Shubik (ghost edited)
Heard, Henry Fitzgerald	Gerald Heard
Heinlein, Robert Anson	Anson MacDonald; Lyle Monroe (some with Elma Wentz); John Riverside; Caleb Saunders; Simon York
Hennissart, Martha	Emma Lathen (with M. J. Latis)
Hensley, Joe L.	Louis J. A. Adams (with Alexei Panshin)
Hernhuter, Albert	Bert Ahearne; Lee Jarvis
Hero, Numa C.	Quien Sabe
Heron-Allen, Edward	Christopher Blayre
Herron, Edna	Ben Aronin
Hersey, Harold	C. Buxton; H. Kemp; P. Kennedy; C. Kiproy; Larrovitch; R. Le Moyne; A. Owens; A. Tyson; V. Vernon
Hershman, Morris	Evelyn Bond
Hewelcke, Geoffrey	Hugh Jeffries
Heydon, J. K.	Hal P. Trevarthen
Heyer, Georgette	Stella Martin
Hibbert, Eleanor Alice Burford	
	Victoria Holt
Hickman, Lynn	Plato Jones
Hill, Reginald Charles	Dick Morland
Hilton, James	Glen Trevor
Hind, Alfred	Thomas Rochdale
Hindin, Nathan	Nathan Hindin (with Robert Bloch)
Hine, Sesye Joslin	Sesye Joslin
Hirai, Taro	Edogawa Rampo
Hirshfield, Henry I.	M. I. Mayfield (with G. M. Mateyko)
Hoadley, H. O.	Gene Mitchell
Hoar, Roger Sherman	Ralph Milne Farley; Bennington Orth; Lieut. John Pease; General X
Hobson, Harry	Hank Janson (h)
Hoch, Edward D.	Irwin Booth; Stephen Dentinger
Hodder-Williams, Christopher	
	James Brogan
Hodges, Doris Marjorie	Charlotte Hunt
Hoffman, Lee	Georgia York
Holberg, Ludvig	Nicholas Klimius
Holdstock, Robert	Robert Black; Chris Carlsen; Richard Kirk (h)
Holland, Cecelia (Anastasia)	
	Elizabeth Eliot Carter
Holloway, Brian	Berl Cameron (h); Neil Charles (h); King Lang (h); Rand Le Page (h); Brian Storm (h)
Holly, Joan C.	J. Hunter Holly

Real Name	Pseudonym
Holt, John Robert	Elizabeth Giles; Raymond Giles
Hood, Archer Leslie	Lilian Leslie (with V. L. Perkins)
Hopf, Mrs. Ernest	Alice M. Lightner
Horler, Sydney	Peter Cavendish; Martin Heritage
Hornig, Charles D.	Derwin Lesser
Hoskin, Cyril Henry	T. Lopsang Rampa
Hoskins, Robert	Grace Corren; John Gregory; Phillip Hoskins; Susan Jennifer (h); Michael Kerr; Julia Thatcher
Hough, Richard Alexander	Bruce Carter
Hough, Stanley Bennett	Rex Gordon; Bennett Stanley
Howard, Marghanita Laski	
	Marghanita Laski
Howard, Robert E(rvin)	Patrick Ervin; Patrick Howard; John Taverel; Sam Walser; Robert Ward
Hubbard, L(afayette) Ron	Winchester Remington Colt; Frederick Engelhardt; Tom Esterbrook; Rene Lafayette; Captain B. A. Northrop; Kurt Von Rachen
Hudlestone, Dom Gilbert Roger	
	Roger Pater
Hughes, Den(n)is Talbot	Ray Barry; Berl Cameron (h); Dee Carter (h); Neil Charles (h); Lee Elliot (h); Gill Hunt (h); Brad Kent (h); John Lane (h); Van Reed (h); Russell Rey (h)
Hughes, Gwilym Fielden	Hugh Enfield
Hughes, William Llewellyn	
	Hugh Walters
Hugi, Maurice	Brad Kent (h)
Humphreys, Leslie George	Vektis Brack (h); Bruno G. Condray
Humphries, Adelaide	Kathleen Harris
Hunt, Everett Howard, Jr.	David St. John
Hunter, Bluebell M.	George Lancing
Hunter, Evan (now legal name)	
	Curt Cannon; Hunt Collins; Ezra Hannon; S. A. Lombino (former legal name); Ed McBain; Richard Marsten; Craig Rice (with G. A. Randolph)
Hurwood, Bernhardt J(ackson)	
	Mallory T. Knight
Hyde, Alan	Taylor Ward
Hynam, John C.	John Kippax
Hynd, Lavinia	Lavinia Leitch
Hyne, C. J. Cutcliffe	Weatherby Chesney

I, J

Ireland, Max J.	Joslyn Maxwell
Jackson, John William, Jr.	William T. Silent
Jacob, Piers Anthony Dillingham	
	Piers Anthony
Jakes, John William	Alexander Blade (h); Darius John Granger; Alan Payne; Jay Scotland; C. H. Thames (h); Allen Wilder
James, Donald	Dougal McLeish
James, Francis	James A. Goldthwaite
James, Jordan	J. X. Williams (h)
James, Laurence	L. J. Coburn (h); Arthur Frazier (h); Charles C. Garrett (h); William M. James (h); Neil Langholm (h); John J. McLaglen; Jonathan May; Klaus Netzen; Christopher Nolan; Mick Norman
Jameson, Malcolm	Colin Keith; Mary MacGregor
Janifer, Laurence M. (now legal name)	
	Alfred Blake; Andrew Blake; Larry M. Harris (former name); William Logan; Mark Phillips (with R. Garrett); Barbara Wilson

Real Name	Pseudonym
Jardine, Jack Owen	Howard L. Cory (with former wife, Julie); Arthur Farmer; Larry Maddock
Jardine, Julie Ann	Howard L. Cory (with former husband, Jack); Corrie Howard
Jarvis, F. G.	Fritz Gordon
Jasper, John	Rosalia Muspratt
Jenkins, William Fitzgerald	
	William Fitzgerald; Murray Leinster
Jenks, George C.	Nick Carter (h)
Jennison, John William	Neil Charles (h); Gill Hunt (h); King Lang (h)
Jeury, Michel	Albert Higon (with Pierre Marlson)
Johns, W(illiam) E(arl)	William Earle
Johnson, W. Ryerson	Kenneth Robeson (h)
Johnstone, Ted	David McDaniel
Jones, Adrienne	Gregory Mason (with Doris Meek)
Jones, Francis A.	Milton R. Peril
Jones, Lady Roderick	Enid Bagnold
Jones, Raymond F.	David Anderson
Jones, Susan Carleton	S. Carleton
Jones, Vernon H.	Raymond A. Young
Jorgenson, Alf A.	Aaron Arne
Judson, Ralph	Ralph Stranger

K

Real Name	Pseudonym
Kacewgari, Romain	Romain Gary
Kagey, Rudolph	Kurt Steele
Kahanovitch, Pinhas	Der Nister
Kahn, H. S.	Henry Sackerman
Kainen, Ray	Ray Kalnen
Kane, Henry	Anthony McCall
Kaplan, M. M.	Philip Barshofsky; Philip J. Bartel
Kark, Nina Mary	Nina Bawden
Karp, David	Adam Singer; Wallace Ware
Kasson, Helen W.	Helen Weinbaum (née)
Katchadourian, Vahe	Vahe Katcha
Kayser, Ronal	Dale Clark(e)
Keightley, David	Noel Keyes
Kellenberger, L. C.	Henry James (who was also a real author)
Keller, David H.	Henry Cecil (also a real author); Amy Worth
Kelley, Martha M.	Q. Patrick (with R. W. Webb)
Kelsey, Joan Marshall	Joan Grant
Kemp, Earl	Jon Hanlon
Kennedy, Joe	X. J. Kennedy
Kessel, Maurice	Maurice Druon
Kimbro, John	Katheryn Kimbrough
King, Albert	Mark Bannon; Paul Conrad; Floyd Gibson; Scott Howell; Christopher King; Paul Muller
King, C. Daly	Jeremiah Phelan
King-Scott, Peter	Peter Edgar
Kissling, Mrs. Dorothy Hight	
	Dorothy Langley
Klainer, Albert S.	L. T. Peters (with Jo-Ann Klainer)
Klainer, Jo-Ann	L. T. Peters (with Albert S. Klainer)
Klass, Philip	Kenneth Putnam; William Tenn
Klein, Gerard	Gilles D'Argyre; François Pagery; Mark Starr
Kneller, F. C.	Ian Bruce; John Ellis; Bruce Fenton (h); Mack James; Mack Jones; Ray Mason (h); D. J. Mencer (h); James Robertson; John Robertson; Neil J. Spalding; Neil J. Spaulding; Edward Stokes
Knight, Damon	Conanight (with C. Cohen); Ritter Conway; Stuart Fleming; Donald Laverty (with J. Blish)

Real Name	Pseudonym
Knoles, William	Clyde Allison; Clyde Ames
Knowles, Mabel Winifred	Lester Lurgan
Koontz, Dean R.	David Axton; Brian Coffey; Deanna Dwyer; K. R. Dwyer
Koontz, Mrs. Dean R.	Gerda Ann Cerra
Kornbluth, Cyril	Earl Balons; Gabriel Barclay (h); Arthur Cooke (complex collaboration); Cecil Corwin; Walter C. Davies; Sam Eisner; Simon Eisner; Kenneth Falconer; S. D. Gottesman (alone and in collaboration); Cyril Judd (with Judith Merril); C. M. Kornbluth; Paul Dennis Lavond (h) (complex collaboration); Scott Mariner (with F. Pohl); Jordan Park (with F. Pohl); Ivar Towers (h) (with R. Wilson); Dirk Wylie (collaborations)
Kornoelje, Clifford	Jack Darrow
Korzeniowski, Teodor Josef Konrad	
	Joseph Conrad
Kremer, Raymond de	John Flanders; Jean Ray
Krepps, Robert W.	Geoff St. Reynard
Krueger, Margery	Jayge Carr
Kubilius, Walter	J. S. Klimaris
Kull, George	Dean Evans
Kummer, Frederic Arnold, Jr.	
	John Arnold; Martin Vaeth; Elliott Whitney (with J. H. Dockweiler)
Kurland, Michael	Jennifer Plum
Kurnitz, Harry	Marco Page
Kurtzberg, Jack	Jack Kirby
Kuttner, Henry	Edward J. Bellin (h); Paul Edmonds; Noel Gardner; Will Garth (h); James Hall; Keith Hammond (with wife, C. L. Moore); Hudson Hastings (with C. L. Moore); Peter Horn (h); Kelvin Kent (alone, or with A. K. Barnes); Robert O. Kenyon; C. H. Liddell (with C. L. Moore); Hugh Maepenn; K. K. Maepenn; Scott Morgan; Lawrence O'Donnell (with C. L. Moore—most by Moore); Lewis Padgett (with C. L. Moore); Woodrow Wilson Smith; Charles Stoddard (h)
Kuttner, Mrs. Henry	Catherine L. Moore (née) (see also Kuttner, Henry)
Kuyamjian, Dikran	Michael Arlen

L

Real Name	Pseudonym
La Spina, Greye Bragg	Baroni di Savuto; J. C. Kofoed; Isra Putnam
Lafitte, Louis	Jean-Louis Curtis
Laforest-Divonne, P. de Comtesse	
	Claude Silve
Lambert, Leslie Harrison	A. J. Alan
Lambourn, Richmal Crompton	
	Richmal Crompton
Lamburn, John Battersby Crompton	
	John Lambourne
Lange, John F.	John Norman
Lasser, David	Richard Penny
Latis, Mary J.	Emma Lathen (with M. Hennissart)
Laumer, Keith	Anthony Lebaron
Laumer, March	Felix Severance; Felix Severence; Xavier Xanthus
Laurents, Clyde	Harriet Fredericks (with James Smock)
Layton, Frank George	Stephen Andrew
Lazenby, Norman A.	W. B. Clarke; Hamilton Donne (h); Martin Gulliver; J. Austin Jackson; Basil Sitty

Real Name	Pseudonym
Leckie, Peter Martin	Peter Martin
Lee, Arthur Stanley Gould	Arthur Lee Gould
Lee, Austin	Julian Callender
Lee, Manfred B.	Ellery Queen, Jr. (with F. Dannay)
Lee, Wayne C.	Lee Sheldon
Leiber, Fritz	Francis Lathrop
Leipiar, Louise	L. Major Reynolds
Leon, Henry Cecil	Henry Cecil
Les Tina, Dorothy	Sanford Vaid (with A. W. Tucker)
Leslie, Josephine	R. A. Dick
Lesperance, David	Gene A. Davidson
Lesser, Milton	Adam Chase (with P. W. Fairman); Andrew Frazier; D. J. Granger; Stephen Marlowe; Jason Ridgway; S. M. Tenneshaw (h); C. H. Thames (h)
Lessing, Wilfred Edward	Dolton Edwards
L'Estrange, C. J.	Herbert Strang (with G. H. Ely)
Levin, Richard	Cyril Mand (with George R. Hahn)
Lewis, C. S.	Clive Hamilton
Lewis, Cecil Day	Nicholas Blake
Lewis, Charlotte Armstrong	
	Charlotte Armstrong
Lewis, Mary Christianna Milne	
	Christianna Brand
Ley, Robert Arthur	Ray Luther; Arthur Sellings
Ley, Willy	John Brown; Robert Willey
Lilienthal, David, Jr.	David Ely
Lin, Leslie C. B.	Leslie Charteris
Linebarger, Paul Myron Anthony	
	Anthony Bearden; Felix C. Forrest; Carmichael Smith; Cordwainer Smith
Little, Paul H.	Paula Minton; Hugo Paul
Livingston, Berkeley	Lester Barclay; Alexander Blade (h); B. E. Liston; E. J. Liston; Morris J. Steele (h)
Livingston, Herb	H. B. Hickey
Llewellyn-Thomas, Edward	Edward Llewellyn
Lobo, George Edmund	Oliver Sherry
Locke, Charles F.	George McLociard
Locke, George W.	Gordon Walters
Locke, Robert D.	Roger Arcot
Lofts, Norah	Peter Curtis
Lombino, S. A. (former name)	
	Evan Hunter (now legal name)
Long, Amelia Reynolds	Kathleen Buddington Coxe (with Edna McHugh); Patrick Laing; Adrian Reynolds; Peter Reynolds; Mordred Weir
Long, Frank Belknap	Lyda Belknap Long; Leslie Northern (h)
Long, Gabrielle M. V.	Marjorie Bowen; Margaret Campbell; Robert Paye; George Preedy; Joseph Shearing; Margaret Vere; John Winch
Loomis, Noel M.	Sam Allison; Benj. Miller; Frank Miller; Silas Water; Silas Waters
Lord, Mindret	Garland Lord (with Isabel Garland)
Lorenzini, Carlo	Carlo Collodi
Lovecraft, H. P.	Laurence Appleton; Isaac Bickerstaffe, Jr.; John T. Dunne; Harry Houdini (ghost written); Humphrey Littlewit; Archibald Maynwaring; H. Paget-Lowe; Henry Paget-Lowe; Richard Raleigh; Ames Dorrance Rowley; Theobaldus Senectissimus, Esq.; Edward Softly; August T. Swift; Theobaldus; Albert Frederick Willie; Zoilus
Lowndes, Robert (A.) W.	Arthur Cooke (complex collaborations); S. D. Gottesman (collaborations); Carl Greener; Carol Grey; Henry Josephs; Mallory Kent; Paul Dennis Lavond (h) (various collaborations); John MacDougal (with J. Blish); Wilfred Owen Morley; Richard Morrison; Michael

Real Name	Pseudonym
	Sherman; Peter Michael Sherman; Jay Tyler; Lawrence Woods (with D. A. Wollheim & J. Michel); Robert Wright (with F. J Ackerman)
Ludlum, Robert	Brian House
Lukeman, Alex	Alex Dain
Lunn, Hugh K.	Hugh Kingsmill
Lupoff, Richard A.	Addison E. Steele
Lynch, Jane Gaskell	Jane Gaskell
Lynch, Miriam	Claire Vincent
Lyndon, Barre (pseud. of Alfred Edgar)	
	John Sansom (with Jimmy Sangster)
Lynds, Dennis	William Arden; Michael Collins; John Crowe; Maxwell Grant (h)
Lyttle, Eileen Jeanette	Eileen J. Garrett

M

Real Name	Pseudonym
McAllister, Allister	Lynn Brock
McCarter, Vermille	Jody McCarter (with Jodi DeMelikoff)
McCarthy, Shaun	Desmond Cory
McClary, Thomas C.	Calvin Peregoy
McComas, J. Francis	Webb Marlowe
McCue, Lillian	Lillian de la Torre
McCulley, Johnston	Nick Carter (h)
McDermott, P.	Dennis McDermott (with W. L. Dennis, and some with P. S. Miller also)
MacDonald, Jessica N(orth)	
	Jessica North
MacDonald, John D(ann)	John Wade Farrell; Scott O'Hara; Peter Reed
MacDonnell, Archibald Gordon	
	John Cameron
McGaughy, Dudley Dean	Dean Owen
McGivern, W. P.	Alexander Blade (h)
MacGregor, James Murdoch	
	Gregory Francis (with F. Parnell); J. T. McIntosh (also M'Intosh); H. J. Murdoch
McHargue, Georgess	Alice Chase; Margo Seesse Usher
McHugh, Edna	Kathleen Buddington Coxe (with A. R. Long)
McIlwain, David	Charles Eric Maine; Richard Rayner; Robert Wade
McIlwraith, Maureen Mollie Hunter	
	Mollie Hunter
McIntosh, Kenneth	Kent Casey
MacKay, Mary	Marie Corelli
MacLean, Alistair	Ian Stuart
MacLean, Katherine	G. A. Morris
McNeillie, John	Ian Niall
McNeilly, Wilfred	William Arthur; W. A. Ballinger (h); W. Howard Baker; Martin Gregg; Joe Hunter; Errol Lecale; Desmond Reid (h); Peter Saxon (h); Martin Thomas; Julie Wellsley
Macnie, John	Ismar Thiusen
McShane, Mark	Marc Lovell
Malleson, Lucy Beatrice	Anthony Gilbert
Malzberg, Barry N.	Mike Barry; Francine de Natale; Claudine Dumas; Mel Johnson; Lee W. Mason; K. M. O'Donnell; Gerrold Watkins
Manning, Adelaide F. O.	Manning Coles (with C. H. Coles); Francis Gaite (with C. H. Coles)
Marchioni, Mark	Marconette
Marks, Winston K.	Win Kinney
Marlson, Pierre	Albert Higon (with Michel Jeury)
Marnell, Joseph	Zeno Koomoter
Marryat, Frederick	Capt. Marryat

Real Name	Pseudonym
Marsh, J.	John Elton
Martin, R. A.	E. C. Eliott
Martin, Thomas Hector	Peter Saxon (h); Martin Thomas
Mason, C. P.	Epaminondas T. Snooks
Mason, Douglas R.	R. M. Douglas; John Rankine
Mason, Pamela	Pamela Kellino
Mason, Sydney Charles	Charles Carr
Masur, Harold Q.	Alfred Hitchcock (ghost editor)
Mateyko, G. M.	M. I. Mayfield (with H. I. Hirshfield)
Matheson, Joan	Jacob Transue
Matheson, Richard	Logan Swanson
Maturin, Charles R.	Dennis Jasper Murphy
Meaker, Marijane	M. E. Kerr; Vin Packer
Meek, Doris	Gregory Mason (with Adrienne Jones)
Meek, Sterner St. P.	Sterner St. Paul
Meeker, W. Johns	Willy Johns
Merril, Judith	Cyril Judd (with Cyril Kornbluth); Rose Sharon
Mertz, Barbara	Barbara Michaels
Merwin, Sam, Jr.	Elizabeth Deare Bennett; Jacques Jean Ferrat; Matt Lee; Morton D. Paley (fan pseud.) (with Jerome Bixby); Sergeant Saturn (for a period); Carter Sprague
Meyer, Gustav	Gustave Meyrink
Meyers, Roy	Rex Lethbridge
Michel, John	Bowen Conway; Arthur Cooke (complex collaboration); Hugh Raymond; Louis Richard; John Tara; Lawrence Woods (with D. Wollheim & R. W. Lowndes)
Milkomane, Alexis Milkomanovich	
	George Sava
Millard, Joseph J.	N. J. Westwood
Miller, Bill	Whit Masterson (with Bob Wade); Wade Miller (with Bob Wade)
Miller, P. Schuyler	Dennis McDermott (collaborations); Nihil
Misraki, Paul	Paul Thomas
Mitchell, J. Leslie	Lewis Grassic Gibbon
Moffatt, Mrs. Len	Anna Sinclair
Monroe, Donald	Donald Keith (with Keith Monroe)
Monroe, Keith	Donald Keith (with Donald Monroe)
Montayne, Harold B.	George L. Eaton
Montgomery, Robert Bruce	Edmund Crispin
Moorcock, Michael	Bill Barclay; Michael Barrington (with B. J. Bayley); Edward P. Bradbury; James Colvin; Hank Janson (h); Desmond Reid (h)
Moore, Arthur	Harris Moore (with Alf Harris)
Moore, Brian	Michael Bryan
Moore, Catherine L. (Mrs. Henry Kuttner)	
	All in collaboration with husband: Hudson Hastings; C. H. Liddell; Lawrence O'Donnell; Lewis Padgett
Morey, Leo	Leo Ramon Summers
Morgan, Allen D.	Hogan Smith
Morrison, Peggy	March Cost
Morrison, William	Brett Sterling (h)
Morrissey, Joseph Laurence	
	Henry Richards; Richard Saxon
Morrough, E. R.	Abu Nadaar
Moskowitz, Sam	Robert Bahr (fan pseud.); Robert Sanders Shaw (fan pseud.); William M. Weiner (fan pseud.); Fred Wollonover (fan pseud.)
Mott, J. Moldon	John Blackburn
Mullen, Stanley	Lee Beecher; Stanley Beecher; John Peter Drummond (h)
Munoz, Charles	T. P. Caravan
Munro, Hector Hugh	Saki
Murry, Colin Middleton	Richard Cowper; Colin Murry
Muspratt, Rosalie	Jasper John
Myers, Howard L.	Verge Foray

N,O

Real Name	Pseudonym
Nadel, Aaron	Ammianus Marcellinus
Napoli, Vincent	James Vincent
Neal, Adeline Phyllis	A. F. Grey
Neeper, Carolyn	Cary Neeper
Nelms, Henning	Hake Talbot
Nelson, Ray Faraday	Jeffrey Lord (h)
Nesbit, Edith	Edith Bland
Neville, Kris	Henderson Starke
Newman, John	Kenneth Johns (with K. Bulmer—nonfiction)
Nikolaisen, Shirley	Sam Nicholson
Nolan, William F.	Mike Cahill
Northrup, Edwin F.	Akkad Pseudoman
Norton, Alice Mary	Andrew North; Andre Norton; Allen Weston (with Grace Allen)
Norton, Roger Howard	Robert C. Blackmon; Robert Newman
Norway, Nevil Shute	Nevil Shute
Notredame, Michel de	Nostradamus
Nourse, Alan E.	Doctor X
Nowlan, Philip Francis	Frank Phillips
Nuetzel, Charles	Albert Augustus, Jr.; Charles English; Alec Rivere
Nutt, Charles	Charles Beaumont; E. J. Beaumont; Keith Grantland; C. B. Lovehill; Michael Phillips
O'Brien, C. Edward	Larry Clinton O'Brien
O'Brien, David	Berl Cameron (h) (with Arthur Roberts); Rand Le Page (h); Kris Luna (h); Brian Shaw (h)
O'Brien, David Wright	Alexander Blade (h); John York Cabot; Bruce Dennis; Duncan Farnsworth; Clee Garson; Richard Vardon
Offutt, Andrew J.	John Cleve; Jeff Douglas (with D. Bruce Berry); Farrah Fawkes; Baxter Giles; J. X. Williams (h); Turk Winter
Oldfield, Claude Houghton	Claude Houghton
Oliphant, Margaret	Mrs. Oliphant
Oliver, Amy Roberta	Berta Ruck
Oliver, Frederick Spencer	Phylos the Tibetan
Oliver, George	Oliver Onions
Olsen, Alfred Johannes, Jr.	
	Bob Olben (probably misprint); Bob Olsen
Olson, Eugene E.	Eric Norman; Brad Steiger
O'Malley, Frank	Frank O'Rourke
O'Malley, Mary Dolling	Ann Bridge
O Nolan, Brian	Myles Na Gopaleen; Flann O'Brien
Osenburg, Richard	Michael Lauler
Ostrander, Isabel	Robert Orr Chipperfield
O'Suilleabhain, Sean	Vincent O'Sullivan
Oursler, (Francis) Fulton	Anthony Abbot; Samri Frikell
Oursler, Grace	Grace Perkins
Owen, Frank	Hung Long Tom
Owen, Harry Collinson	Hugh Addison

P

Real Name	Pseudonym
Page, Gerald W.	Carleton Grindle; Kenneth Pembrooke
Page, Norvell W.	Randolph Craig; N. Wooten Poge; Grant Stockbridge
Paget, Violet	Vernon Lee
Paine, Lauran Bosworth	Mark Carrel; Troy Howard
Pairault, Pierre	Stefan Wul
Palmer, John Leslie	Francis Beeding (with H. St. G. Saunders)
Palmer, P. K.	Keith Parnell

Real Name	*Pseudonym*
Palmer, Raymond A.	Henry Gade (h); G. H. Irwin (h); Frank Patton (h); J. W. Pelkie; Wallace Quitman (h); A. R. Steber (h); Morris J. Steele (h); Robert N. Webster; Rae Winters
Palmer, Stuart	Theodore Orchards
Palmisano, Luigi	Gene Palm
Pangborn, Edgar	Bruce Harrison
Panshin, Alexei	Louis J. A. Adams (with Joe L. Hensley)
Pantell, S. F.	Real name; Ellen McGregor
Parnell, Frank	Gregory Francis (alone, or with J. M. MacGregor); Francis Richardson (with L. E. Bartle)
Parr, Julian F.	Anton Ragatzy
Parry, Michel (Patrick)	Carlos Cassaba; Nick Fury; Steve Lee; Linda Lovecraft; Eric Pendragon
Pattee, David E.	Pat Davis
Pattinson, Lee	Ann Maxwell
Payes, Rachel C.	E. L. Arch
Payne, Donald Gordon	Ian Cameron; Donald Gordon; James Vance Marshall
Payner, R. C.	J. Castle (with J. W. Garrod)
Peck, George W.	Cantell A. Bigly
Pedler, Christopher Magnus Howard	Kit Pedler
Peebles, James E.	James Kennaway
Pendleton, Don	Dan Britain
Pendray, G. Edward	Gawain Edwards
Perkins, Violet Lilian	Lilian Leslie (with A. L. Hood)
Perry, Dick	Dick Winfield
Petaja, Emil	Theodore Pine (alone, or with H. Hasse)
Peterson, John Victor	Victor Valding (with A. V. Benson)
Pfeil, Donald F.	William Arrow (h)
Pflaum, George A.	Eric St. Clair
Philips, Hugh Pentecost	Hugh Pentecost
Phillifent, John T.	John Rackham
Phillpotts, Eden	Harrington Hext
Pierce, John R.	J. J. Coupling; John Roberts
Pietrkiewicz, Jerzy	Jerzy Peterkiewicz
Pilotin, Michael	Stephen Spriel
Platt, Charles	Blakely St. James
Plunkett, Edward John Moreton Drax	Lord Dunsany
Pohl, Frederik	Elton V. Andrews; Henry De Costa (fan pseud.); Paul Flehr; S. D. Gottesman (with C. Kornbluth); Warren F. Howard; Walt Lasly; Paul Dennis Lavond (h) (many in collaboration); Edson McCann (with L. del Rey); James MacCreigh; Scott Mariner (with C. Kornbluth); Ernest Mason; Ernst Mason; Jordan Park (with C. Kornbluth); Charles Satterfield (some); Dirk Wylie (some, in collaboration); Allen Zweig (fan pseud.)
Pomeroy, John H.	Daniel Whitton
Porges, Arthur	Peter Arthur; Pat Rogers
Porter, William Sydney	O. Henry
Potocnik, Captain	Hermann Noordung
Pournelle, Jerry	Wade Curtis
Powe, Bruce	Ellis Portal
Pragnell, Festus	Francis Parnell
Pratt, Fletcher	Ray Ainsbury (h); George U. Fletcher; Irvin Lester; B. F. Ruby
Pratt, Inga Stephens	I. M. Stephens
Pratt, William Henry	Boris Karloff
Preston-Muddock, Joyce E.	Dick Donovan
Price, E. Hoffmann	Hamlin Daly
Prichard, H. Hesketh	E. & H. Heron (with mother, Kate Hesketh Prichard)
Prichard, Kate Hesketh	*See* Prichard, H. Hesketh
Pritchard, John Wallace	Ian Wallace
Pritchard, William Thomas	William Dexter
Proffitt, Josephine Moore	Sylvia Dee
Protheroe, Cyril	Rand Le Page (h)
Pumilia, Joe (Joseph L.)	M. M. Moamrath

Q,R

Real Name	*Pseudonym*
Quiller-Couch, Sir Arthur T.	"Q"
Rae, Hugh C.	Robert Crawford
Ramey, Ben	H. H. Hollis
Randolph, G. A.	Craig Rice (with Evan Hunter)
Rankin, Hugh	Doak
Rappaport, S.	S. Ansky
Rapuzzi, G. L.	Woody Gray; G. Renna
Rash, Dora Eileen Agnew	Doreen Wallace
Rawlins, Eustace	Robert Eustace
Rawson, Clayton	Merlini; Stuart Towne
Rayer, Francis G.	George Longdon; Mildred Scott; Roland Worcester
Raymond, Rene	James Hadley Chase
Reback, Marcus	Taylor Caldwell (with J. T. Caldwell)
Reed, Lillian Craig	Kit Reed
Reed, Zealia Brown	Zealia B. Bishop
Reeds, F. Anton	Anthony Riker
Reeves, Judson	Aladra Septama
Reizenstein, Elmer	Elmer Rice
Renn, Thomas E.	Jeremy Strike
Repp, Ed Earl	Bradner Buckner; John Cody; Peter Field
Reynolds, Dallas McCord	Clark Collins; Todd Harding; Guy McCord; Mark Mallory; Mack Reynolds (usually known name); Maxine Reynolds; Dallas Ross
Rhodes, W. H.	Caxton
Rice, Jane	Mary Austin
Richard, François	F. Richard-Bessiere (with R. Bessiere)
Richardson, Darrell C.	D. Coleman Rich
Richardson, Robert S.	Philip Latham
Richter, Ernst H.	William Brown; Ernest Terridge
Riddell, Mrs. J. H.	Rainey Hawthorne; F. G. Trafford
Rimel, Duane W.	Rex Weldon
Rivett, Edith Caroline	E. C. R. Lorac
Robbins, Clarence A.	Tod Robbins
Roberts, Arthur	Berl Cameron (h) (with David O'Brien); Rand Le Page (h); Paul Lorraine (h)
Roberts, Keith	Alistair Bevan; John Kingston; David Stringer; Keith Stringer
Robertson, Eileen Arbuthnot	E. Arnot Robertson
Robles, Antonio	Antoniorrobles
Rocklin, Ross	Ross Rocklynne; H. F. Cente
Rodell, Marie F.	Marion Randolph
Roe, Ivan	Richard Savage
Rogers, Wayne	H. M. Appel; Conrad Kimball
Rogow, Lee	Craig Ellis (h)
Rohmer, Sax (pseud)	Michael Furey
Rolfe, Frederick	Baron Corvo; Prospero and Caliban
Rollins, William Stacy Urann	O'Connor Stacy; Urann Thayer
Rosenberg, William S.	Billy Rose
Rosenfeld, F.	Friedrich Feld
Ross, William Edward Daniel	Leslie Ames; Rose Dana; Jan Daniels; Ann Gilmer; Charlotte McCormack; Ellen Randolph; Clarissa Ross; Dan Ross; Marilyn Ross; Jane Rossiter
Rossmann, John F.	Ian Ross
Rothman, Milton A.	Lee Gregor

Real Name	Pseudonym
Rotsler, William	William Arrow (h); Gregor Bohassian; Barney Boone; Waring Brackett; Shannon Carse; Logan Conrad; Andrew Garth; John Ryder Hall; Cord Heller; Latham Hilliard; Linda Holland; Harmony Holt; Lothar Korda; Clay McCord; Honey Malcolm; Hord Markham; Howard Scott Miles; Clint Randall; Beverly Sorensen; Beth Waring; Fletcher Westflag
Rowe, Helen	Helen Cresswell
Rowland, Donald Sydney	Fenton Brockley; Roger Carlton; Graham Garner; Alex Random; Roland Starr; Mark Suffling
Ruben, William S.	Fred Shannon
Rubenstein, Leslie F. (Mrs. William Silberberg)	Leslie F. Stone)
Ruellan, Andre	Kurt Dupont; Andre Louvigny; Kurt Steiner; Luc Vigan; Kurt Wargar
Rundle, Anne	Alexandra Manners
Russell, Eric Frank	Webster Craig; Maurice Hugi (real name, used on one story); Duncan H. Munro
Russell, George William	A. E.
Russell, Ray	Roger Thorne
Russell, Virginia Faine	Djinn Faine
Russell, Winifred Brent	Virginia Stair
Ryhloch, Frank	Frank Riley
Rynas, Stephen A.	Stephen Arnette; Stephen Arr

S

Real Name	Pseudonym
St. Clair, Margaret	William Hazel; Wilton Hazzard; Idris Seabright
Samachson, Joseph	William Morrison; Brett Sterling (h)
Sambrot, William	Anthony Ayes; William Ayes
Sampliner, Louis H.	Alexander Blade (h)
Sampson, Richard Henry	Richard Hull
Sanders, John	Ralph Comer
Sanders, Leonard M., Jr.	Dan Thomas
Sanderson, Ivan T.	Terence Roberts
Sandfield, Laurence	John F. Manders; Meryl St. John Montague
Sangster, Jimmy	John Sansom (with Barre Lyndon [Alfred Edgar])
Santesson, Hans Stefan	Vithaldas H. O'Quinn
Saunders, Hilary St. G.	Francis Beeding (with J. L. Palmer)
Sawkins, Raymond Harold	Colin Forbes
Sawyer, Eugene T.	Nick Carter (h)
Saxon, Richard	Henry Richards
Schachner, Nathan	Chan Corbett; Walter Glamis
Scheer, Karl-Herbert	Alexej Turbojew
Schoepflin, Harl Vincent	Harl Vincent
Scholz, Winfried	W. W. Shols
Scithers, George	Karl Wurf
Scott, Peter	Barton Werper
Searls, Henry Hunt	Hank Searls
Segall, Don	Leo August
Senarens, Luis P. (Lu)	Cecil Burleigh; Kit Clyde; Frank Doughty; W. J. Earle; Gaston Garne; Captain Howard; Noname; Ned Sparling
Setterborg, Gabriel	Eric Crane
Sharkey, John Michael	Jack Sharkey
Sharp, William	Fiona MacLeod
Shaver, Richard S.	Wes Amherst; Edwin Benson(real & house); Alexander Blade (h); Edwin Dexter; Peter Dexter; Richard Dorot; Mollie Elclair; Richard English; G. H. Irwin (h); Paul Lohrman (h); Frank Patton (h); Stan Raycraft; D. Richard Sharpe

Real Name	Pseudonym
Shaw, Larry T.	Archibald Destiny; Terry Thor
Sheckley, Robert	Phillips Barbee; Finn O'Donnevan
Sheldon, Alice Hastings	Alice Bradley; Raccoona Sheldon; James Tiptree, Jr.
Sheldon, Walt	Seldon Walters
Shellabarger, Samuel	John Esteven
Shepherd, Jean	Frederick R. Ewing (with Theodore Sturgeon)
Sheridan, Elsie Lee	Elsie Lee; Lee Sheridan
Sherman, Jory	Frank Anvic
Shibano, Takumi	Kosumi Rei
Shiel, M(atthew) P(hipps)	Gordon Holmes (with L. Tracy)
Shiras, Wilmar H.	Jane Howes
Siegel, Jerome	Bernard J. Kenton
Silberberg, Mrs. William	Leslie F. Stone
Silverberg, Robert	Gordon Aghill (with R. Garrett); Robert Arnette (h); T. D. Bethlen; Alexander Blade (h); Ralph Burke (with R. Garrett); Walter Chapman; Dirk Clinton; Walter Drummond; Richard Greer (with R. Garrett); E. K. Jarvis (h); Ivar Jorgensen (also Jorgenson) (h) (with R. Garrett); Warren Kastel (h); Calvin M. Knox; Ray McKenzie; Dan Malcolm; Webber Martin; Alex Merriman; Clyde Mitchell (h) (with R. Garrett); David Osborne; George Osborne; Robert Randall (with R. Garrett); Eric Rodman; Lee Sebastian; Leonard G. Spencer (h) (with R. Garrett); S. M. Tenneshaw (h) (some with R. Garrett); Hall Thornton; Gerald Vance (h) (some with R. Garrett); Richard F. Watson
Silvette, Henry	Barnaby Dogbolt
Sim, Georges	Georges Simenon
Simson, Eric Andrew	Lawrence Kirk
Siniavskii, Andrei Donatevich	Abram Tertz
Skeels, Vernon H.	Oscar Rossiter
Skinner, June O'Grady	Rohan O'Grady
Slavitt, David Rytman	Henry Sutton
Slesar, Henry	O. H. Leslie
Slotkin, Joseph	Oliver Spie; Nick Tolz
Small, Austin J.	Seamark
Smith, Clark Ashton	Benjamin De Casseres
Smith, David McLeod	David Mariner
Smith, Dorothy Gladys	C. L. Anthony
Smith, Edgar	Michael Mason
Smith, Elizabeth Thomasina Meade	L. T. Meade
Smith, Ernest Bramah	Ernest Bramah
Smith, Evelyn E.	Delphine C. Lyons
Smith, George Henry	M. J. Deer (with M. Jane Deer); Jan Hudson; Jerry Jason; Clancy O'Brien; George Hudson Smith; Jan Smith; Diane Summers
Smith, George O.	Wesley Long
Smith, Joshua	Signor Bellini
Smith, L. H.	Speedy Williams
Smith, Ormond G.	Nick Carter (h)
Smith, Richard R.	Richard E. Smith
Smith, Ron	Martin Loran (with John Baxter)
Smock, James	Harriet Fredericks (with C. Laurents)
Sneddon, Robert W.	Mark Shadow
Sohl, Gerald Allan	Nathan Butler; Jerry Sohl; Sean Mei Sullivan
Soler, Antonio Robles	Antoniorrobles
Southwold, Stephen	Neil Bell; Paul Martens; Miles
Speer, Jack	John A. Bristol
Sperry, Henry Treat	Paul Howard

Real Name	Pseudonym
Spillane, Frank	Mickey Spillane
Squire, Sir John Collings	Solomon Eagle
Stableford, Brian	Brian Craig
Stamp, R. G.	R. G. Mingston
Steele, Mary Quintard	Wilson Gage
Stein, Hank	Hank Stine
Steinbrunner, Chris	Colin Christian
Steiner, Gerold	Harold Stumpke
Stern, Philip Van Doren	Peter Storme
Stevens, Lawrence Sterne	Lawrence
Stevenson, Florence	Zabrina Faire
Stewart, Alfred Walter	J. J. Connington
Stewart, John Innes Mackintosh	
	Michael Innes
Stine, G. Harry	Lee Correy
Stratemeyer, Edward (syndicate)	
	Victor Appleton; Capt. Ralph Bonehill; Roy Rockwood
Straub, Margaret Rogers	Dorothy Quick
Street, Cecil John Charles	Miles Burton; John Rhode
Stubbs, Harry Clement	Hal Clement
Studebaker, Don	Jon Decles
Sturgeon, Theodore	Frederick R. Ewing (with Jean Shepherd, on a historical novel); E. Waldo Hunter; E. Hunter Waldo; Billy Watson
Sturgis, Mel	Colin Sturgis (with Les Cole)
Sturtzel, Howard Allison	Paul Annixter
Suddaby, Donald	Alan Griff
Swain, Dwight V.	Clark South
Symmes, J. C.	Capt. Adam Seaborn

T

Real Name	Pseudonym
Tabor, Paul	Peter Stafford; Paul Tabori
Taieb, Heliane	Julia Verlanger
Tait, George B.	Alan Barclay
Taurasi, James V., Sr.	Lane Stannard; J. Harry Vincent
Taylor, Keith	Denis Moore
Taylor, Phoebe Atwood	Alice Tilton
Tepperman, Emile	Kenneth Robeson (h) (a few titles); Curtis Steele (h)
Teternikov, Fedor Kuzmich	Fedor Sologub
Thibault, Jacques Anatole	Anatole France
Thomas, John Oram	John Oram
Thomas, Theodore L.	Leonard Lockhard; Cogswell Thomas (with T. Cogswell)
Thompson, Anthony A.	Anthony Alban
Thompson, George Selden	George Selden
Thomson, Christine Campbell	
	Dair Alexander; Molly Campbell; Christine Hartley; Flavia Richardson
Tieck, Johann Ludwig	Peter Leberecht
Tillett, Dorothy Stockbridge	
	John Stephen Strange
Tillotson, Joe W.	Robert Fuqua
Tinsley, Theodore	Maxwell Grant (h)
Todd, Ruthven	R. T. Campbell
Tooker, Richard	Henry E. Lemke
Torday, Ursula	Paula Allardyce; Charity Blackstock
Torsvan, Traven	Bernard Traven
Towle, Mrs. Arthur Edward	
	Margery Lawrence
Tracy, Donald Fiske	Roger Fuller
Tracy, Louis	Gordon Holmes (some with M. P. Shiel)
Tralins, Robert	Keith Miles
Transue, Jacob	Joan Matheson
Tremaine, F. Orlin	Anne Beale; Arthur Lane; Guthrie Paine; Warren B. Sand; Alfred Santos; Warner Van Lorne (one story)

Real Name	Pseudonym
Tremaine, Nelson	Warner Van Lorne (all but one story)
Trenery, Gladys G.	G. G. Pendarves
Trevor, Elleston (formerly Trevor Dudley-Smith)	
	Warwick Scott
Trimble, Louis	Stuart Brock; Gerry Travis
Tubb, Edwin Charles	Chuck Adams; Ted Bain; Anthony Blake; L. T. Bronson; Raymond L. Burton; Julian Carey; Morley Carpenter; Jud Cary; J. F. Clarkson; Norman Dale; Robert D. Ennis; James S. Farrow; James R. Fenner; R. H. Godfrey; Charles S. Graham; Charles Gray; Charles Grey; Volsted Gridban (h) (half of the titles); Alan Guthrie; George Holt; Gill Hunt (h); Alan Innes; E. F. Jackson; Gordon Kent; Gregory Kern (h); Duncan Lamont; King Lang (h); Mike Lantry; P. Lawrence; Chet Lawson; Arthur Maclean; Carl Maddox; Phillip Martyn; John Mason; Carl Moulton; Gavin Neal; L. C. Powers; M. L. Powers; Edward Richards; Paul Schofield; John Seabright; Brian Shaw (h); Roy Sheldon (h) (one novel); John Stevens; Eric Storm; Andrew Sutton; Edward Thomson; Ken Wainwright; Frank Weight; Douglas West; Eric Wilding; Frank Winnard
Tucker, Allan James	David Craig
Tucker, Arthur Wilson	Hoy Ping Pong; Bob Tucker; Wilson Tucker; Sanford Vaid (with Dorothy Les Tina)
Tucker, George	Joseph Atterley

U,V,W

Real Name	Pseudonym
Unwin, David S.	David Severn
Upchurch, Boyd B.	John Boyd
Uspenskii, Petr	P. D. Ouspensky
Vallee, Jacques	Jerome Seriel
Van Name, E. J.	Jim Vanny
van Vogt, Mrs. A. E.	E. Mayne Hull (née)
Van Zeller, C. H.	Hugh Venning
Vance, Jack	Peter Held; John Holbrook; Ellery Queen; Alan Wade
Vancel, Doris	Doris Thomas
Vardeman, Bob	Edward George (with David E. Gerrold [J. D. Friedman]); Paul Kenyon
Varley, John	Herb Boehm
Vaughan, Auriel R.	Oriel Malet
Venable, Marilyn	Lyn Venable
Vern, David	Alexander Blade (h); Craig Ellis (h); Peter Horn (h); David V. Reed; Clyde Woodruff
Vernal, Chuck	George L. Eaton
Versack, Maria Teresa Rios	Tere Rios
Vian, Boris	Vernon Sullivan
Viard, Henri	Henry Ward
Vickers, Roy	David Durham; Sefton Kyle
Vidal, Gore	Edgar Box
Vinson, Rex T.	Vincent King
Vlasto, J. A.	John Remenham
Wade, Robert (Bob)	Whit Masterson (with Bill Miller); Wade Miller (with Bill Miller)
Wade, Thomas W.	Bronson D. Carter; Raymond LeRoyd; John R. Martin; Vincent Robertson; John Sloan; Karl Zeigfreid (h)
Waldo, E. Hunter	Theodore Sturgeon (now legal name)
Wall, John W.	Sarban
Wallace, Richard E.	Edgar Wallace

Real Name	Pseudonym
Waller, Leslie	C. S. Cody; Stephen Spielberg (real name)
Wallis, George C.	John Stanton (for comics, etc.)
Walmsley, Arnold R.	Nicholas Roland
Walsh, John M.	H. Haverstock Hill; Stephen Maddock; George M. White
Walton, Bryce	Paul Franklin; Kenneth O'Hara (real name); Dave Sands (h)
Walton, Harry	Harry Collier
Wandrei, Howard Elmer	Robert Coley; Robert A. Garron; Howard W. Graham; H. W. Guernsey; Howard Von Drey
Ward, Arthur Sarsfield	Michael Furey; Sax Rohmer
Ward, Harold	Zorro
Ward, Rose Elizabeth Knox	Elizabeth Sax Rohmer
Warner, E.	Douglas Warner (with J. D. Currie)
Warner, Kenneth Lewis	Dighton Morel
Wasserburg, Joseph	Adam Bradford
Watkins-Pitchford, Denys Jones	
	B.B.
Wayne, Charles Stokes	Horace Hazeltine
Weakley, James	John Bennet
Weakley, Maurice A.	Rice Arden
Webb, Jack	John Farr
Webb, Richard Wilson	Q. Patrick (alone, or with M. L. Aswell, or with S. Kelley, or with H. C. Wheeler); Patrick Quentin (with H. C. Wheeler); Jonathan Stagge (with H. C. Wheeler)
Webb, Robert Forrest	See Forrest-Webb, Robert
Weinbaum, Stanley G.	John Jessel; Marge Stanley
Weisinger, Mortimer	Will Garth (h); Tom Erwin Geris; Ian Rectez; Sergeant Saturn (for a time)
Weiss, Ehrich	Harry Houdini (ghost written)
Weiss, George Henry	Francis Flagg
Wellman, Manly Wade	Gabriel Barclay (h); John Cotton; Levi Crow; Manuel Ferney; Gans T. Field; Will Garth (h); Juan Perez; Hampton Wells; Wade Wells
Wellman, Mrs. Manly W.	Frances Garfield
Wells, Angus	J. B. Dancer (h); Ian Evans; Charles C. Garrett (h); Richard Kirk (h); James A. Muir; Charles R. Pike (h)
Wells, Basil	Gene Ellerman
Wentz, Elma	Lyle Monroe (with R. A. Heinlein)
Wertenbaker, G. Peyton	Green Peyton
Wessolowski, Hans Waldemar	
	H. W. Wesso
Westlake, Donald E.	Curt Clark; Timothy J. Culver; J. Morgan Cunningham; Richard Stark
Weymouth, Viscount	Alexander Thynn
Wheeler, Hugh Callingham	Q. Patrick (with R. W. Webb); Patrick Quentin (with R. W. Webb); Jonathan Stagge (with R. W. Webb)
White, Ted	Ron Archer; Norman Edwards (with T. Carr)
White, William Anthony Parker	
	Anthony Boucher; Theo Durrant; H. H. Holmes; Herman W. Mudgett; Parker White
Whitson, John W.	Nick Carter (h)
Wibberley, Leonard	Leonard Holton; Patrick O'Connor; Christopher Webb
Wicker, Tom	Paul Connolly
Widner, Arthur L.	Arthur Lambert
Wiener, Norbert	W. Norbert
Wilcox, Don	Buzz-Bolt Atomcracker; Alexander Blade (h); Cleo Eldon; Max Overton; Miles Shelton
Wilde, Lady Jane Francisca Speranza	
	Lady Wilde
Wilding, Philip	John R. Haynes

Real Name	Pseudonym
Wilhelm, Lambert	William J. Lambert, III
Wilkins, Mary H.	Mary Calhoun
Williams, Robert Moore	John S. Browning; H. H. Harmon; E. K. Jarvis (h); Robert Moore; Russell Storm
Williams, Roswell	Richard Kent; Frank Owen; Hung Long Tom (poetry)
Williams, Thomas Lanier	Tennessee Williams
Williamson, Jack (John Stewart)	
	Will Stewart
Willis, Anthony Armstrong	Anthony Armstrong
Willis, Lisle	Earl Van Loden; Erle Van Loden
Willis, Maud	Eileen Lottman
Wilson, Doris B.	Leslie Perri
Wilson, John Anthony Burgess	
	Anthony Burgess
Wilson, Richard	Edward Halibut; Ivar Towers (h) (with Cyril Kornbluth)
Winchell, Prentice	Stewart Sterling
Winston, Daoma	Dorian Winslow
Winterbotham, Russ(ell) R.	
	J. Harvey Bond; R. R. Botham; Simon Bradford; Franklin T. Hadley; Aunt Peggy; Russ Winterbottom
Wolk, George	Janet Kidde
Wollheim, Donald A.	Arthur Cooke (complex collaboration); Millard Verne Gordon; David Grinnell; Martin Pearson; Allen Warland; Braxton Wells; Willy the Wisp (fan pseud.); Lawrence Woods (with R. W. Lowndes & J. Michel); X
Wood, Samuel Andrew	Robin Temple
Woodard, Wayne	Hannes Bok; Dolbokov (with Boris Dolgov)
Woolfolk, Josiah Pitts	Jack Woodford
Woolrich, Cornell	George Hopley; William Irish
Woolrich, Daniel	Geoffrey Homes
Wormser, Richard	Nick Carter (h)
Worrell, Everil	Lireve Monett
Worts, George F.	Loring Brent
Wright, Farnsworth,	Francis Hard
Wright, Lan	Jerome Strickland
Wright, Mary M.	Lilith Lorraine
Wright, Sewell Peaslee	Thomas Andrews; Leigh Cameron; Parke Spencer
Wright, Sydney Fowler	Sidney Fowler; A. Wingrave
Wright, Willard Huntington	
	S. S. Van Dine
Wrocz, Joseph	Joseph Ross

Y, Z

Real Name	Pseudonym
Yates, Alan Geoffrey	Carter Brown (h); Caroline Farr
Yefremov, I.	I. Efremov (different transliterations)
Yerke, T. Bruce	Carlton J. Fassbinder
Yerxa, Leroy	Elroy Arno; Alexander Blade (h); Richard Casey (h); Lee Francis (h)
Youd, Christopher S.	John Christopher; Hilary Ford; William Godfrey; Peter Graaf; Peter Nichols; Anthony Rye; William Vine
Younger, Jack	Arabella Randolphe
Zachary, Hugh	Ginny Forman; Elizabeth Hughes; Zach Hughes; Pablo Kane; Peter Kanto; Derral Pilgrim; Olivia Rangely; Elizabeth Zachary
Zacherle, John	Zacherley
Zagat, Arthur Leo	Grendon Alzee; Latham Conyers; Anton York
Zelazny, Roger	Harrison Denmark
Ziegler, Edward W.	Theodore Tyler
Zinberg, Leonard S.	Ed Lacy

SERIES, CONNECTED STORIES, AND SEQUELS

Introduction

Series titles are given in bold face.

An asterisk (*) following a series title indicates that the series is listed in the given author's *WHO'S WHO* entry in Volumes 1 or 2. If two authors are given, check the *WHO'S WHO* for both.

A series title which is a person's name is alphabetized by family name. Thus, the "Hawk Carse" series is listed under C for Carse. Where there is a title or an honorific, the series is in most cases listed by family name and also by the title or honorific. Thus, "Ensign De Ruyter" is listed both under E for Ensign and D for De Ruyter, and "Dr. Fosdick" is under D for Doctor (as if spelled out) and also F for Fosdick.

When a story is listed as the first of a series, and the series has the same name as the story title, the series generally is not listed separately.

A book title in brackets at the end of a listing indicates a collection or novelization of the series.

A

AAA Ace Interplanetary Decontamination Service*—Sheckley, R.

"Abdication," *ASF*, Apr 1943; first of **Artur Blord*** series—Hull, E. M. [*Planets for Sale*]

Abercrombie, Dr. Aesop*—Carlson, E.

"Abercrombie Station," J. Vance, *TWS*, Feb 1952; "Cholwell's Chickens," Aug 1952 [*Monsters in Orbit*]

"Admiral's Inspection," *ASF*, Apr 1940; first of **Bullard*** series—Jameson, M. [*Bullard of the Space Patrol*]

"Advent," *ASF*, Jan 1948; first of **Advent*** series—Bade, W. L.

"Adventure in Lemuria," F. A. Kummer, *FA*, May 1939; "Intrigue in Lemuria," July 1939; "Volcano Slaves of Mu," Mar 1940.

"Adventure of a Snitch in Time, The," M. Reynolds & A. Derleth, *F&SF*, July 1953; "The Adventure of the Ball of Nostradamus," June 1955 [part of **Solar Pons*** series—Derleth, A.]

"After Some Tomorrow," M. Reynolds, *If*, June 1956; "Of Pot and Potter," *FU*, Jan 1958 [matriarchy]

Agent of T.E.R.R.A.*—Maddock, L. (pseud)—Jardine, J.O. [pa]

"Agent of Vega," *ASF*, July 1949; first of **Vegan Confederation*** series—Schmitz, J. H. [*Agent of Vega*]

Alak, Wing*—P. Anderson

"Alien Machine, The," R. F. Jones, *TWS*, June 1949; "The Shroud of Secrecy," Dec 1949; "The Greater Conflict," Feb 1950 [*This Island Earth*]

Allen, Dig*—Greene, J. I. [juvenile books]

Allison, James*—Howard, R. E.

"Alter Ego," A. B. Chandler, *ASF*, Mar 1945; "Special Knowledge," Feb 1946

Amberdon, Telzey*—Schmitz, J. J. [*Universe Against Her*, etc.]

"Ambidexter, The," *AS*, Apr 1931; first of **Wing Loo*** series—Keller, D. H. [the middle story was also in the **Taine*** series]

Amphibians, The; *The World Below*—Wright, S. F.

"Anachron, Inc.," M. Jameson, *ASF*, Oct 1942; "Barrius, Imp.," Jan 1943; "When Is When," Aug 1943

"Anachronistic Optics," M. Schere, *ASF*, Feb 1938; "The Brain-Storm Vibration," May 1938

Angry Planet, The; *SOS From Mars*—Cross, J. K.

"Anita," *Science-Fantasy*, Sep/Oct 1964; first of **Anita*** series—Roberts, K.

"Appendix and the Spectacles, The," M. J. Breuer, *AS*, Dec 1928; "The Captured Cross-Section," Feb 1929; "The Book of Worlds," July 1929

"Ararat," *F&SF*, Oct 1952; first of **People*** series—Henderson, Z. [*Pilgrimage*, etc.]

Arcot, Morey and Wade*—Campbell, J. W. [became books]

"Arcturus Times Three," *GSF*, Oct 1961; first of **Jerry Norcriss*** series—Sharkey, J.

"Armageddon—2419," P. Nowlan, *AS*, Aug 1929, Apr 1961; "The Airlords of Han," Mar 1929, May 1962 [*Armageddon—2419*]

"Aspect," B. Shaw, *Nebula*, Aug 1954; "Sounds in the Dawn," Jan 1956

"Aspirin Won't Help," J. Sentry, *ASF*, Sep 1955; "Psioid Charley," May 1956

"Assisted Passage," J. White, *NW*, Jan 1953; "False Alarm," July 1957

"Asteroid of Death," N. R. Jones, *WSQ*, Fall 1931; "The Moon Pirates," *AS*, sr2, Sep 1934

"Asylum," A. E. van Vogt, *ASF*, May 1942; "The Proxy Intelligence," *If*, Oct 1968

"At the Center of Gravity," *ASF*, June 1936; first of **Colbie and Deverel*** series—Rocklynne, R.

At the Earth's Core; first of **Pellucidar*** series—Burroughs, E. R.

Atlantis* trilogy—Gaskell, J.

"Atom War," R. Phillips [R. P. Graham], *AS*, May 1946; "The Mutants," July 1946; "Battle of the Gods," Sep 1946

"Attitudes," *F&SF*, Oct 1953; first of **Father John Carmody*** series—Farmer, P. J.

"Automatic Self-Serving Dining Table, The," *AS*, Apr 1927; first of **Hick's Inventions*** series—Simmons, H. H.

"Avenging Ray, The," A. R. Hilliard, *WSQ*, Spr 1931; "The Island of the Giants," *WS*, Aug 1931

B

"Bacular Clock, The," *BB*, July 1942; first of **Pat Pending*** series—Bond, N. S.

Baker, Lefty*—Phillips, R. (pseud)—Graham, R. P.

"Balance," *NW*, Spr 1951; first of **Max Larkin*** series—Christopher, J. (pseud)—Youd, C. S.

Baldy*—Padgett, L. (pseud)—Kuttner, H. [*Mutant*]

Baron Munchausen's Scientific Adventures*—Gernsback, H. See also Munchausen in the *GENERAL* section.

"Battle in the Dawn," *AS*, Jan 1939; first of **Hok*** series—Wellman, M. W.

"Battle of the Toads," *WT*, Oct 1929; first of **Overlord of Cornwall*** series—Keller, D. H.

"Beam Transmission," G. H. Scheer, *AS*, July 1934; "Another Dimension," Oct 1935; "The Crystalline Salvation," June 1937

Beast Master, The; *Lord of Thunder*—Norton, Andre

"Beast Men of Ceres, The," A. Septama, *ASQ*, Win 1929; "The Cry From the Ether," Spr 1929; "Dragons of Space," Spr 1930

"Beautiful Weed," E. R. James, *NW*, Mar 1957; "Fourth Species," May 1957 [on Mars ecology]

"Before the Universe," S. D. Gottesman, *Super Science*, July 1940; "Nova Midplane," Nov 1940

"Beginner's Luck," *Science-Fantasy*, Aug 1962; first of **Midnight Club*** series—Hall, Steve

Belov, Hek*—Mackin, E.

"Ben Gleed, King of Speed," D. Wilcox, *AS*, Dec 1939; "The Iron Men of Super City," May 1941; "The Fiend of New London," Feb 1942

Berserker*—Saberhagen, F. [*Berserker*]

"Bettyann," K. Neville, in *New Tales of Space and Time* [Healy], 1951; "Overture," in *9 Tales of Space and Time* [Healy], 1954

"Beyond Gravity," E. E. Repp, *Air Wonder*, Aug 1929; "The Annihilator Comes," *WS*, Aug 1930

Beyond the Black Enigma; *Abandon Galaxy!*—Somers, B. (pseud)—Fox, G. F. [pa]

"Beyond the Heaviside Layer," S. P. Meek, *ASF*, July 1930; "The Attack From Space," Sep 1930

"Beyond the Yellow Fog," E. McDowell, *Planet*, Spr 1947; "The Outcasts of Solar III," Spr 1948

Big Time, The, F. Leiber; "No Great Magic," *GSF*, Dec 1963

Biggs, Lancelot*—Bond, N. S. [*Lancelot Biggs: Spaceman*]

Bird, Dr.*—Meek, S. P.

"Black Cat's Paw, The," *Science-Fantasy*, Dec 1960; first of **Chappie Jones*** series—Rackham, J. (pseud)—Phillifent, J. T.

"Black Comet, The," J. Coleridge, *Science Fiction*, June 1939; "World of Illusion," *Future*, Nov 1940

"Black Destroyer," A. E. van Vogt, *ASF*, July 1939; "Discord in Scarlet," Dec 1939; "War of Nerves," *Other Worlds*, Mar 1950 [*The Voyage of the Space Beagle*]

"Black God's Kiss, The," *WT*, Oct 1934; first of **Jirel of Joiry*** series—Moore, C. L. [most in *Shambleau* and *Northwest of Earth*]

Black, Johnny*—de Camp, L. S.

"Black Spot,The," K. Bulmer, *NW*, Feb 1955; "Total Recall," Aug 1955; "Plaything," Nov 1955

Blast Off at Woomera; first of **Chris Godfrey*** series—Walter, H. (pseud)—Hughes, W. L. [juvenile books]

"Blind Man's Buff," J. U. Giesy, *FFM*, Sep/Oct 1939; "The Gravity Experiment," Nov 1939 [originally published in *Argosy*; there may be others in the series]

Blind Spot, The, A. Hall & H. E. Flint; *The Spot of Life*, A. Hall (alone)—see Hall, A.

Blord, Artur*—Hull, E. M. [*Planets for Sale*]

"Blue and Silver Brocade," *Unknown*, Oct 1939; first of **Patchwork Quilt*** series—Quick, D.

"Blue Fire," *GSF*, June 1965; first of series published as *To Open the Sky*—Silverberg, R.

Book of Three, The—first of **Prydain*** series—Alexander, L.

"Brain Stealers of Mars, The," *TWS*, Dec 1936, *WS Annual*, 1952; first of **Penton and Blake*** series—Campbell, J. W. [*The Planeteers*]

Brak the Barbarian*—Jakes, J.

Bran Mak Morn*—Howard, R. E.
Brief Candles; Happy Returns; Come and Go—see Coles, M.
Brigands of the Moon, R. Cummings, *ASF*, sr4, Mar 1930, *SFQ*, Fall 1942; *Wandl the Invader*, *ASF*, sr4, Feb 1932, *SFQ*, Spr 1943
Buckley, Joan*—Bryning, F. B.
Bullard*—Jameson, M. [*Bullard of the Space Patrol*]
Bupp, Walter*—Garrett, R.
"Bureau of Slick Tricks, The," *ASF*, Dec 1948; first of **Bureau of Slick Tricks*** series—Fyfe, H. B.
Burn Witch, Burn!; Creep, Shadow—Merritt, A.

C

Calkins, Ajax*—Pearson, M. (pseud)—Wollheim, D. A.
"Call of the Mech-Men, The," *WS*, Nov 1933; first of **Stranger Club*** series—Manning, L.
"Canticle for Leibowitz, A," W. M. Miller Jr., *F&SF*, Apr 1955; "And the Light Is Risen," Aug 1956; "The Last Canticle," Feb 1957 [*A Canticle for Leibowitz*]
"Captain Brink and the Space Marines," B. Olsen, *AS*, Nov 1932; "The Space Marines and the Slavers," Dec 1936
Captain Future*—Hamilton, E.
"Captain Future and the Space Emperor," *Captain Future*, Win 1940; first of **Captain Future*** series—Hamilton, E.
"Captain Stinky," G. Vance, *AS*, June 1942; "Captain Stinky's Luck," Sep 1942
Captives of the Flame; The Towers of Toron; City of a Thousand Suns—Delany, S. R. [**Toromon*** trilogy]
"Card Trick," *ASF*, Jan 1961; first of **Walter Bupp*** series—Garrett, R.
"Cargo: Death," T. H. Mathieu, *Future*, June 1958; "The Earthquake Remedy," Aug 1958
Carlisle, Gerry*—Barnes, A. K. [*Interplanetary Hunter*]
Carlos de la Muerte, el Tigre*—Quinn, S.
Carmichael, Amberson, apKern and Weinberg*—Quinn, S.
Carmody, Father John*—Farmer, P. J.
Cars Society*—Young, Robert F.
Carse, Hawk*—Gilmore, A. (pseud)—Bates, H. [*Space Hawk*]
Carson of Venus—see **Venusian*** series—Burroughs, E. R.
Carstairs, John*—Long, F. B. [*John Carstairs: Space Detective*]
Carter, John—see **Martian*** series—Burroughs, E. R.
Carter, Randolph*—Lovecraft, H. P.
"Case of Identity, A," *ASF*, Sep 1964; first of **Lord Darcy*** series—Garrett, R.
"Case of the Jailer's Daughter, The," *WT*, Sep 1926; first of **Surgeon of Souls*** series—Rousseau, V. (pseud)—Emanuel, V. R.
"Case of the Vanishing Cellars, The," J. S. Klimaris, *Future*, Aug 1942; "The Case of the Baby Dinosaur," Oct 1942
"Caves of Horror, The," *ASF*, Jan 1930; first of **Dr. Bird*** series—Meek, S. P.
Caves of Steel, The; The Naked Sun—Asimov, I.
Change War*—Leiber, F.
"Chestnut Beads, The," Jane Roberts, *F&SF*, Oct 1957; "The Bundu," Mar 1958
Childermass, The; Monstre Gai; Malign Fiesta; The Trial of Man—Lewis, W.
Children* tetralogy—Eager, E.
Children of the Green Knowe; first of **Green Knowe** series—Boston, L. M.
"Children of the Stars," Clifford C. Reed, *SFA* [British], July 1959; "Forgotten Knowledge," Nov 1959; "The Road Back," Feb 1960 [*Martian Enterprise*]
"Chosen People, The," *ASF*, June 1956; first of **Nidor*** series—Randall, R. (pseud)—Silverberg, R., & Garrett, R. [*The Shrouded Planet* and *The Dawning Light*]
"Chowhound," M. Reynolds, *Marvel*, Nov 1951; "Snafu in New Taos," *Venture*, Sep 1957
"Chrome Pastures," *If*, Apr 1956; first of **Cars Society*** series—Young, Robert F.
Chronicles of Narnia*—Lewis, C. S.
"Circle of Confusion," *ASF*, Mar 1944; first of **Plutonian Lens*** series—W. Long (pseud)—G. O. Smith

Cities on Other Worlds—Paul, F. R. [back cover paintings]
"City," *ASF*, May 1944; first of **City*** series—Simak, C. D. [*City*]
City of Glass, N. Loomis, *SS*, July 1942; "Iron Men," Win 1945
"City of Lost Souls," R. M. Farley & A. P. Nelson, *FA*, July 1941; "Holy City of Mars," May 1942
"City of the Living Dead, The," L. Manning & F. Pratt, *Science Wonder*, May 1930; "The City of Sleep," L. Manning, *WS*, May 1933, *SS*, July 1940
"City of the Singing Flame, The," C. A. Smith, *WS*, July 1931, *SS*, Jan 1941; "Beyond the Singing Flame," *WS*, Nov 1931, *SS*, Jan 1941; both, *Tales of Wonder*, Spr 1940
"City of the Tiger," J. Brunner, *Science-Fantasy*, Dec 1958, *FU*, Nov 1959; "The Whole Man," *Science-Fantasy*, Apr 1959 ("Curative Telepath," *FU*, Dec 1959) [*The Whole Man*; also as *Telepathist*]
"Clash by Night," L. O'Donnell, *ASF*, Mar 1943; *Fury*, sr3, May 1947 [see Kuttner, H.]
"Code Three," *ASF*, Feb 1963; first of **Thruway Patrol*** series—Raphael, R. [*Code Three*]
Colbie and Deverel*—Rocklynne, R.
"Collision Orbit," *ASF*, July 1942; first of **Seetee*** series—Stewart, W. (pseud)—Williamson, J. [*Seetee Ship* and *Seetee Shock*]
Colonists of Space; Salamander War—Carr, C.
"Colossus," D. Wandrei, *ASF*, Jan 1934; "Colossus Eternal," Dec 1934
"Coming Generation," *FU*, July 1955 ["The Gambler," *Australian Monthly*, 5 Oct 1954]; first of **Joan Buckley*** series—Bryning, F. B.
"Command, The," *ASF*, Oct 1938; first of **Johnny Black*** series—de Camp, L. S.
"Comrades of Time," E. Hamilton, *WT*, Mar 1939; "Armies From the Past," Apr 1939
Conan*—Howard, R. E. [both story and book series]
"Concealment," *ASF*, Sep 1943; first of **Dellian Robot*** series—van Vogt, A. E. [*The Mixed Men*; also as *Mission to the Stars*]
"Conquerors, The," D. H. Keller, *Science Wonder*, sr2, Dec 1929, *FSM*, Sum 1951; "The Evening Star," *Science Wonder*, sr2, Apr 1930, *FSM*, Win 1952
"Conquest of Life, The," *TWS*, Aug 1937, *SS*, May 1949; first of **Anton York*** series—Binder, E. [*Anton York—Immortal*]
Conquest of Space*—Lafayette, R. (pseud)—Hubbard, L. R.
"Conversion Factor," C. Sturgis, *F&SF*, Nov 1957; "The 24,000-Mile Field Goal," Jan 1958
"Co-operate—or Else!" A. E. van Vogt, *ASF*, Apr 1942; "The Second Solution," Oct 1942; "The Rull," May 1948 [in *The War Against the Rull*]
Corbett, Tom*—Rockwell, C. [juvenile books]
Cornelius, Jerry*—Moorcock, M. [*The Final Programme*]
Corridors of Time; Beyond the Fourth Door; Exiles of Time—Deegan, J. J. [pa]
"Cosmic Gun, The," M. Colladay, *WS*, May 1931; "The Return of the Cosmic Gun," Oct 1931
"Crazy Joey," *ASF*, Aug 1953; first of **Joey*** series—Clifton, M.
"Creatures Incorporated," L. Maddock, *NW*, June 1960; "Alien for Hire," Aug 1960; "When in Doubt," Dec 1960
Creeps Library—book series; see *WHO'S WHO* section.
"Criffle-Shaped," *Science-Fantasy*, Dec 1957; first of **Hek Belov*** series—Mackin, E.
Crossroads of Time; Quest Across Time—Norton, Andre
Cugel the Clever*—Vance, J. [*The Eyes of the Overworld*]
"Cult of the Witch Queen," R. S. Shaver, *AS*, July 1946; "The Sea People," Aug 1946; "Earth Slaves to Space," Sep 1946 [part of the **Shaver Mystery*** series]
"Cursed Be the City," H. Kuttner, *Strange Stories*, Apr 1939; "Citadel of Darkness," Aug 1939 [Prince Raynor stories]

D

"Damp Man, The," A. V. Harding, *WT*, July 1947; "The Damp Man Returns," Sep 1947; "The Damp Man Again," May 1949
Darcy, Lord*—Garrett, R.
"Dark Moon," C. W. Diffin, *ASF*, May 1931; "Brood of the Dark Moon," sr4, Aug 1931; "The Finding of Haldgren," Apr 1932

Darkness*—Rocklynne, R.

Darkness and Dawn trilogy*—England, G. A. [Darkness and Dawn, etc.]

Darkness and the Deep; first of Testament of Man* series—Fisher, V. [books, not all sf]

"Darkness on Fifth Avenue," Arg, 30 Nov 1929; first of Master of Darkness* series—Leinster, M. (pseud)—Jenkins, W. F.

Darkover*—Bradley, M. Z.

D'Artois, Pierre*—Price, E. H.

"Date Line," TWS, Oct 1948; first of Orig Prem* series—Miller, B. (pseud)—Loomis, N.

"Daughter of Darkness," H. Lawlor, FA, Apr 1943; "The Irresistible Perfume," May 1943

David Starr: Spaceranger; first of David Starr* series—French, P. (pseud)—Asimov, I. [juvenile books]

"Dawn of Flame," S. G. Weinbaum, TWS, June 1939, FSM, Spr 1952; "The Black Flame," SS, Jan 1939, FSM, Spr 1952 [both as book, The Black Flame]

Dawson, Johnny*—Rackham, J. (pseud)—Phillifent, J. T.

Dawson, Johnny*—Wright, L.

"Day of the Great Shout, The," Worlds of Tomorrow, Jan 1965; first of Riverworld* series—Farmer, P. J.

De Grandin, Jules*—Quinn S. [some in The Phantom Fighter]

De Ruyter, Ensign*—Porges, A.

"Death and Birth of the Angakok," GSF, Apr 1965; first of Eskimo Invasion* series—Howard, H.

"Death From the Stars," A. R. Hilliard, WS, Oct 1931; "The Reign of the Star Death," Apr 1932

"Death Rides at Night," L. Yerxa, AS, Aug 1942; "Phantom Transport," Feb 1943

Deathworld, ASF, sr3, Jan 1960; first of Jason dinAlt* series—H. Harrison

"Decadence," TWS, Dec 1941; first of Robot Saga*—Cummings, R.

"Defiance," K. Bulmer, NW, July 1957; "The Gentle Approach," June 1959

Dellian Robot*—van Vogt, A. E.

Deluge; Dawn—Wright, S. F.

"Derelict, The," W. J. Mathews, Planet, Fall 1946; "Space Trap at Banya Tor," Spr 1948

"Detour to the Stars," J. Blish, Infinity, Dec 1956; "Nor Iron Bars," Nov 1957

"Devil and Democracy, The," B. Cleeve, F&SF, Nov 1966; "The Devil and Jake O'Hara," Aug 1968; "The Devil in Exile," Nov 1968 [Devil and Belphagor set]

Devil Rides Out, The; Strange Conflict—Wheatley, D.

Devil's Hunting Ground, The; Cold War in Hell—Blamires, H.

"Devils in the Hills," Fantastic, May 1963; first of Brak the Barbarian* series—Jakes, J.

Dilvish the Deliverer*—Zelazny, R.

"Dimple," J. Kippax, Science-Fantasy, Dec 1954; "Special Delivery," June 1955

dinAlt, Jason*—Harrison, H.

"Disciplinary Circuit, The," TWS, Win 1956; first of Kim Rendell* series—M. Leinster (pseud)—W. F. Jenkins

Doc Methuselah*—Lafayette, R. (pseud)—Hubbard, L. R.

Doc Savage*—Robeson, K. (pseud)—see Dent, L.

Dr. Aesop Abercrombie,*—Carlson, E.

Dr. Bird*—Meek, S. P.

Dr. Doolittle*—Lofting, H. [juvenile books]

Dr. Fosdick*—Morgan, J.

"Dr. Fosdick Invents the 'Seidlitzmobile'," AS, June 1926; first of Dr. Fosdick* series—Morgan, J.

Dr. Hackensaw*—Fezandie, C.

Dr. Morgan series—see Grandon* series—Kline, O. A.

Dr. Satan*—Ernst, P.

"Doctor Universe," C. Jacobi, Planet, Fall 1944; "Double Trouble," Spr 1944-45

"Dr. Varsag's Experiment," C. Ellis, AS, Jan 1940; "Dr. Varsag's Second Experiment," Aug 1943

Dr. Von Theil and Sergeant John West*—Casey, K.

"Don Kelz of the I.S.P.," C. B. Kruse, ASF, Feb 1936; "The Drums," Mar 1936; "Flight of the Typhoon," Oct 1936

Doolittle, Dr.*—Lofting, H. [juvenile books]

"Doom Ship," R. M. Williams, FA, Feb 1950; "Three Against the Roum," June 1951

"Double-Dyed Villains, The," ASF, Sep 1949; first of Wing Alak* series—Anderson, P.

"Double Jeopardy," F. Pratt, TWS, Apr 1952; "The Square Cube Law," June 1952 [Double Jeopardy]

Draco, Manning*—Crossen, K. F. [Once Upon a Star]

Dracula; Dracula's Guest—Stoker, B.

Dragoman*—Kline, O. A. [most in The Man Who Limped]

"Dragon's Teeth," J. K. Aitken, NW, No. 3, 1947; "Cassandra," Sep 1949; "Phoenix Nest," Spr 1950

"Dreaming City," Science-Fantasy, June 1961; first of Elric* series—Moorcock, M.

Dribble, Dusty*—Tubb, E. C.

Drums of Tapajos, The, AS, Nov 1930; Troyana, sr3, Feb 1932—Meek, S. P.

Dunn, Danny*—Williams, Jay, & Abrashkin, R. [juvenile books]

Durna Rangue*—Jones, N. R.

Dusty Dribble*—Tubb, E. C.

E

Earth-Shurilala-Takkat*—Bulmer, K.

Earthguard*—Haggard, J. H.

Ebbtide Jones*—Shelton, M. (pseud)—Wilcox, D.

Eden, Jim*—Pohl, F., & Williamson, J.

Elak of Atlantis*—Kuttner, H.

"Elephas Frumenti," F&SF, Win-Spr 1950; first of Gavagan's Bar* series—de Camp, L. S., & Pratt, F. [Tales From Gavagan's Bar]

Elric*—Moorcock, M. [The Stealer of Souls; Stormbringer]

"Empire of Evil," R. Arnette, AS, Jan 1951; "Cosmic Kill," sr2, Apr 1957

Empress of Space; Space Mercenaries—Chandler, A. B. [pa]

"En Route to Pluto," W. West, ASF, Aug 1936; "The Lure of Polaris," TWS, Oct 1949; "The Bird of Time," Aug 1952; "Captive Audience," June 1953 [the latter two chronologically precede the first two] [The Bird of Time]

"Enchanted Bookshelf, The," FA, Mar 1943; first of Three Musketeers* series—McGivern, W. P.

"End of Tyme, The," A. Fedor & H. Hasse, WS, Nov 1933; "The Return of Tyme," Aug 1934

Ensign De Ruyter*—Porges, A.

Erewhon; Erewhon Revisited—Butler, S.

"Escapement," NW, Dec 1956; first of Future crowded city life*—Ballard, J. G.

Eskimo Invasion*—Howard, H.

"Eternal Man, The," D. D. Sharp, Science Wonder, Aug 1929; "The Eternal Man Revives," WSQ, Sum 1930 [combined as "The Eternal Man," SS, Jan 1939; WS Annual, 1950]

"Ether Breather," T. Sturgeon, ASF, Sep 1939; "Butyl and the Breather," Oct 1940

"Ethical Equations, The," M. Leinster [W. F. Jenkins], ASF, June 1945; "Adapter," Mar 1946

"Exit the Professor," TWS, Oct 1947; first of Hogben* series—Kuttner, H.

"Expedition Mercy," J. A. Winter, ASF, Nov 1948; "Expedition Polychrome," Jan 1949

Explorers Into Infinity, R. Cummings, WT, sr3, Apr 1927; "The Giant World," sr3, Jan 1928

"Explorers of Callisto, The," H. Vincent, AS, Feb 1930; "Callisto at War," Mar 1930

F

"Face Beyond the Veil, The," F. Bahl, FA, Apr 1950; "The Justice of Tor," Jan 1951

Face in the Abyss, The; "The Snake Mother"—Merritt, A.

"Fair Exchange," *NW*, Jan 1955; first of **Johnny Dawson*** series—Wright, L.

"Farmer," M. Reynolds, *GSF*, June 1961; "Black Man's Burden," *ASF*, sr2, Dec 1961 [set in Africa]

Father John Carmody*—Farmer, P. J.

Federation of Suns*—Hamilton, E.

Feep, Lefty*—Bloch, R.

Fellowship of the Ring, The; first of **Lord of the Rings*** trilogy—Tolkien, J. R. R.

"Fifth Dimension, The," M. Leinster [W. F. Jenkins], *ASF*, Jan 1932; "The Fifth-Dimension Tube," Jan 1933

"Fitzgerald Contraction, The," M. J. Breuer, *Science Wonder*, Jan 1930, *SS*, Jan 1942; "The Time Valve," *WS*, July 1930

"Flame Winds," N. W. Page, *Unknown*, June 1939; "Sons of the Bear God," Nov 1939 [Prester John stories]

Flandry, Dominic*—Anderson, P.

Flannigan, Michael*—Bloodstone, J. (pseud)—Byrne, S. J.

"Flareback," *ASF*, Mar 1938; first of **Dr. von Theil and Sgt. John West*** series—Casey, K.

Flying Saucer Gambit, The; first of **Agent of T.E.R.R.A.*** series—Maddock, L. (pseud)—Jardine, J. O. [pa]

"F.O.B. Venus," *FA*, Nov 1939; first of **Lancelot Biggs*** series—Bond, N.S. [*Lancelot Biggs: Spaceman*]

"For All the Night," *NW*, Apr 1958 [also as "The Troons of Space," *Fantastic*, Nov 1958]; first of **Troon*** series—Wyndham, J. (pseud)—Harris, J. B. [*The Outward Urge*]

"Forbidden Voyage," *SS*, Jan 1949; first of **Conquest of Space*** series—Lafayette, R. (pseud)—Hubbard, L. R.

"Forgotten Planet," *ASF*, July 1930; first of **John Hansen*** series—Wright, S. P.

"Fortress Ship," *If*, Jan 1963; first of **Berserker*** series—Saberhagen, F.

Fosdick, Dr.*—Morgan, J.

"Foundation," *ASF*, May 1942; first of **Foundation*** series—Asimov, I. [magazine series, then books]

Four Dimensional*—Olsen, B.

"Four Dimensional Roller Press," *AS*, June 1927; first of **Four Dimensional*** series—Olsen, B.

"Four Dimensional Space Penetrator," J. Kendig, *AS*, Jan 1930; "The Eternal Mask," Feb 1933

"Freddie Funk's Madcap Mermaid," *FA*, Jan 1943; first of **Freddie Funk*** series—Yerxa, L.

Freddy*—Brooks, W. R. [juvenile books]

"From the Ocean's Depths," S. P. Wright, *ASF*, Mar 1930; "Into Ocean's Depths," May 1930

Fu Manchu*—Rohmer, S.

Funk, Freddie*—Yerxa, L.

Future, Captain*—Hamilton, E.

Future crowded city life*—Ballard, J. G.

Future History*—Heinlein, R. A. [books]

G

Galactic Patrol, *ASF*, sr6, Sep 1937; first of **Lensman*** (magazine) series—Smith, Edward E.

Galactic Survey Team*—Markham, R.

Gale, Vivienne*—Bryning, F. B.

Gallegher, Galloway*—Padgett, L. (pseud)—Kuttner, H. [*Robots Have No Tails*]

"Garden of Fear," *Marvel Tales*, July 1934; first of **James Allison*** series—Howard, R. E.

Gavagan's Bar*—de Camp, L. S., & Pratt, F. [*Tales From Gavagan's Bar*]

Gees*—Mann, J. (pseud)—Vivian, E. C.

"Ghost of Mars," *AS*, Dec 1938; first of **Don Hargreaves*** series—Pragnell, F.

"Giants of Mogo, The," D. Wilcox, *AS*, Nov 1947; "Mad Monster of Mogo," Nov 1952

"Girl in the Golden Atom, The," first of **Matter, Space and Time*** trilogy—Cummings, R.

"Gland Superman, The," E. E. Repp, *AS*, Oct 1938; "The Deadly Paint of Harley Gale," Apr 1939

"Glory of the U.S.L., The," N. J. Westwood, *TWS*, June 1942; "Minnie of Mars," Aug 1942; "Aimless Asteroid," Feb 1943

"Gnurrs Come From the Voodvork Out, The," R. Bretnor, *F&SF*, Fall 1949; "Little Anton," in *New Tales of Space and Time* [Healy], 1954

Goddess of Ganymede; *Pursuit on Ganymede*—Resnick, M. D. [pa]

Godfrey, Chris*—Walters, H. (pseud)—Hughes, W. L.

Gods*—van Vogt, A. E. [*Empire of the Atom*; *The Wizard of Linn*]

"Gods of Bal-Sagoth, The," *WT*, Oct 1931; first of **Turlogh O'Brien*** series—Howard, R. E.

"Gods of Venus," R. S. Shaver, *AS*, Mar 1948; "Titan's Daughter," Sep 1948

"Golden Amazon, The," *FA*, July 1939; first of **Golden Amazon*** series—Fearn, J. R.

"Golden Girl of Kalendar," F. O. Tremaine, *FA*, Sep 1939; "Jalu of Radiant Valley," Mar 1940

"Golden Girl of Munan, The," H. Vincent, *AS*, June 1928; "The War of the Planets," Jan 1929

"Golden Horn, The," E. Pangborn, *F&SF*, Feb 1962; "A War of No Consequence," Mar 1962 [in *Davy*]

"Good Old Brig!" *ASF*, July 1938; first of **Kelton*** series—Casey, K.

"Goodbye, Doctor Gabriel," *NW*, Aug 1961; first of **Johnny Dawson*** series—Rackham, J. (pseud)—Phillifent, J. T.

Gor*—Norman, J. (pseud)—Lange, J. F. [pa]

Gormenghast* trilogy—Peake, M.

Grandin, Jules De*—Quinn S. [some in *The Phantom Fighter*]

Grandon, Robert*—Kline, O. A.

Gray Mouser and Fafhrd*—Leiber, F.

"Great Engine, The," A. E. van Vogt, *ASF*, July 1943; "The Beast," Nov 1943

Great Legend*—West, W. [*Lords of Atlantis*]

Gree*—MacApp, C. C. (pseud)—Capps, C. M.

Green Knowe—Boston, L. M.

Green Man, The, H. Sherman, *AS*, Oct 1946; "The Green Man Returns," Dec 1947

Gregory, Bud*—Fitzgerald, W. (pseud)—Jenkins, W. F. [*Out of This World*]

"Gregory Circle, The," *TWS*, Apr 1947; first of **Bud Gregory*** series—Fitzgerald, W. (pseud)—Jenkins, W. F. [*Out of This World*]

H

Hackensaw, Dr.*—Fezandie, C.

"Hairy Ones Shall Dance, The," *WT*, sr3, Jan 1938; first of **Judge Pursuivant*** series—Field, G. T. (pseud)—Wellman, M. W.

Hale, John*—Repp, E. E.

Hale, Leland*—Garrett, R.

"Half-Breed," I. Asimov, *Astonishing*, Feb 1940; "Half Breeds on Venus," Dec 1940

Half Magic; *Knight's Castle*; *Magic by the Lake*; *The Time Garden*—Eager, E.

Hansen, John*—Wright, S. P.

"Hard Luck Diggings," *SS*, July 1948; first of **Magnus Ridolph*** series—Vance, J. [*The Many Worlds of Magnus Ridolph*]

Hargreaves, Don*—Pragnell, F.

Harrigan, Tex*—Derleth, A.

"Hawk Carse," *ASF*, Nov 1931; first of **Hawk Carse*** series—Gilmore, A. (pseud)—Bates, H. [*Space Hawk*]

"Hawk of the Wilderness," *BB*, sr7, Apr 1935; first of **Kioga*** series—Chester, W. L.

"Heads You Win," *F&SF*, Apr 1953; first of **Dr. Aesop Abercrombie*** series—Carlson, E.

Hek Belov*—Mackin, E.

"Hell Ship," *ASF*, Aug 1938; first of **Josh McNab*** series—Burks, A. J.

"Help! I Am Dr. Morris Goldpepper," A. Davidson, *GSF*, July 1957; "Dr. Morris Goldpepper Returns," Dec 1962

"Henry Horn's Super-Solvent," *FA*, Nov 1941; first of **Henry Horn*** series—Swain, D. V.

"Heroes Are Made," *Other Worlds*, May 1951; first of **Hoka*** series—Anderson, P., & Dickson, G. R. [*Earthman's Burden*]

"Hi Diddle Diddle," C. M. Knox [R. Silverberg], *ASF*, Feb 1959; "The Calibrated Alligator," Feb 1960

Hicks' Inventions With a Kick*—Simmons, H. H.
"High Threshold," A. E. Nourse, *ASF*, Mar 1951; "The Universe Between," Sep 1951 [*The Universe Between*]
High Water at Catfish Bend; *Seven Stars for Catfish Bend*—Burman, B. L.
Hoenig, Robby*—Dickson, G. R. [juvenile books]
Hoffman Center*—Nourse, A. E.
Hogben*—Kuttner, H.
Hok*—Wellman, M. W.
Hoka*—Anderson, P., & Dickson, G. R. [*Earthman's Burden*]
"Hollywood on the Moon," *TWS*, Apr 1938, *SS*, July 1949; first of **Hollywood on the Moon*** series—Kuttner, H. [mainly about Tony Quade]
"Homing Tantalus," A. B. Chandler, *NW*, July 1960; "No Return," Aug 1960
Horn, Henry*—Swain, D. V.
Horsesense Hank*—Bond, N. S.
Hothouse*—Aldiss, B. W. [*The Long Afternoon of Earth*, or *Hothouse*]
"Hothouse Planet, The," *TWS*, Oct 1939, *SS*, Sep 1949; first of **Gerry Carlisle*** series—Barnes, A. K. [*Interplanetary Hunter*]
House of Many Worlds, The, S. Merwin, *SS*, Sep 1951; *Journey to Misenum*, Aug 1953 [*3 Faces of Time*]
Houseboat on the Styx, A; *The Pursuit of the Houseboat*—Bangs, J. K.
Hubble's Bubble; *The Hubbles and the Robot*—Horseman, E. [juvenile books]
"Hunters out of Time," [*The Little Men*], *AS*, Feb 1959; *Hunters of Space*, May 1960—Kelleam, J. E.

I

"I Remember Lemuria," R. S. Shaver, *AS*, Mar 1945; "Invasion of the Micro Men," Feb 1946; "The Return of Sathanas," Oct 1946 [part of **Shaver Mystery*** series]
"I, Robot," *AS*, Jan 1939; first of **Adam Link*** series—Binder, E. [*Adam Link—Robot*]
"Idealist, The," *ASF*, July 1940; first of **Kilkenny Cats*** series—Von Rachen, K. (pseud)—Hubbard, L. R.
"I'll Dream of You," *FA*, Jan 1947; first of **Toffee*** series—Myers, C. F.
"Improbable Profession," *ASF*, Sep 1952; first of **Patent Attorney*** series—Lockhard, L. (pseud)—Thomas, T. L.
"In Hiding," W. H. Shiras, *ASF*, Nov 1948; "Opening Doors," Mar 1949; "New Foundations," Mar 1950 [with 2 new stories—*Children of the Atom*]
"In 20,000 A.D.," A. L. Zagat & N. Schachner, *WS*, Sep 1930; "Back to 20,000 A.D.," Mar 1931
Incomplete Enchanter, The; first of **Shea*** [book] series—de Camp, L. S., & Pratt, F.
"Initiation Rites," *NW*, Apr 1962; first of **Refuge*** series—Green, J. [*The Loafers of Refuge*]
Innes, David See **Pellucidar*** series—Burroughs, E. R.
Instrumentality*—Smith, C. (pseud)—Linebarger, P.M.L.
Interstellar Patrol*—Hamilton, E. [*Crashing Suns*; *Outside the Universe*]
"Into the Darkness," *Astonishing*, June 1940; first of **Darkness*** series—Rocklynne, R.
"Into the Green Prism," A.H. Verrill, *AS*, sr2, Mar 1929; "Beyond the Green Prism," sr2, Jan 1930
"Invasion From the Microcosm," *Orbit*, No. 1, 1953; first of **Tex Harrigan*** series—Derleth, A.
"Invasion of the Planet of Love," G. P. Elliot, *F&SF*, Jan 1959; "Nothing But Love," Feb 1959
"Invisible Invaders, The," E. E. Repp, *Air Wonder*, Oct 1929; "Beyond the Aurora," Nov 1929
"Invisible Robin-Hood, The," E. Binder, *FA*, May 1939; "Land of the Shadow Dragons," May 1941

J,K

Jacko*—Barclay, A. (pseud)—Tait, G. B.
Jameson, Professor*—Jones, N. R. [*The Planet of the Double Sun* and others; pa series]

"Jameson Satellite, The," *AS*, July 1931; first of **Professor Jameson*** series—Jones, N. R.
"Jan of the Jungle" [*Call of the Savage*], O. A. Kline, *Arg*, sr6, 18 Apr 1931; "Jan in India," sr3, 12 Jan 1935
"Jay Score," E. F. Russell, *ASF*, May 1941; "Mechanistria," Jan 1942; "Symbiotica," Oct 1943 [with one new story, as *Men Martians and Machines*]
Jewel in the Skull, The; first of **Runestaff*** series—Moorcock, M. [pa]
"Jinn and Tonic," W. P. McGivern, *Fantastic*, May 1953; "Love That Potion," Feb 1955 [about Reggie]
Jirel of Joiry*—Moore, C. L.
Joey*—Clifton, M.
John the Minstrel*—Wellman, M. W. [*Who Fears the Devil?*]
Jones, Chappie*—Rackham, J. (pseud)—Phillifent, J. T. [part as *The Touch of Evil*]
Jones, Ebbtide*—Shelton, M. (pseud)—Wilcox, D.
"Jones Gets the Willies," E. Arno, *FA*, Mar 1943; "Jones Buys War Blondes," Dec 1943
Jones, Juggernaut*—McKenzie, A. R.
"Jongor of Lost Land," R. M. Williams, *FA*, Oct 1940; "The Return of Jongor," Apr 1944; "Jongor Fights Back," Dec 1951
Journey Into Space; *The Red Planet*; *The Earth in Peril*—Chilton, C.
Judge Pursuivant*—Field, G. T. (pseud)—Wellman, M. W.
Judgment on Janus; *Victory on Janus*—Norton, Andre [pa]
"Juggernaut Jones, Salesman," *AS*, May 1942; first of **Juggernaut Jones*** series—McKenzie, A. R.
Kai Lung*—Bramah, E. (pseud)—Ernest Smith [books]
Kane, Michael*—Bradbury, E. P. (pseud)—Moorcock, M. [pa]
Kane, Solomon*—Howard, R. E.
Kelton*—Casey, K.
Kemlo*—Elliott, E. C. [juvenile books]
Kennedy, Craig*—Reeves, A. D.
Kennedy, Ralph*—Clifton, M.
Kilkenny Cats*—Von Rachen, K. (pseud)—Hubbard, L. R.
King Kull*—Howard, R. E.
"King of the Dinosaurs," *FA*, Oct 1945; first of **Toka*** series—Pelkie, J. W. (pseud)—Palmer, R. A.
Kings of Space; *Return to Mars*—Johns, W. E.
"Kings of the Night," *WT*, Nov 1930; first of **Bran Mak Morn*** series—Howard, R. E.
Kioga*—Chester, W. L.
Kull, King*—Howard, R. E.
Kyben*—Ellison, H.

L

"Lady in the Tower, The," A. McCaffrey, *F&SF*, Apr 1959; "A Meeting of Minds," June 1969
"Lair of the Grimalkin," G. H. Irwin [R. S. Shaver], *FA*, Apr 1948; "Glass Woman of Venus," *Other Worlds*, Jan 1951
"Land Beyond the Lens," *AS*, Mar 1952; first of **Michael Flannigan*** series—Bloodstone, J. (pseud)—Byrne, S. J.
Landscapes on Other Worlds*—Ley, W. [articles]
Larkin, Max*—Christopher, J. (pseud)—Youd, C. S.
"Laughing Death, The," S. G. Hale, *AS*, Apr 1931; "Worlds Adrift," May 1931
Laws of Robotics*—Asimov, I.
Lefty Baker*—Phillips, R. (pseud)—Graham, R. P.
Lefty Feep*—Bloch, R.
"Legacy," N. S. Bond, *ASF*, Dec 1940; "Jessifer Rides Again," *TWS*, Oct 1942
Legion of Space, The, J. Williamson, *ASF*, sr6, Apr 1934, Galaxy SF Novel No. 2, 1950; *The Cometeers*, sr4, May 1936; "One Against the Legion," sr3, Apr 1939 [in *The Cometeers*]
Lemurian Documents*—Burtt, J. L.
Lensman*—Smith, Edward E.
"Life Hutch," H. Ellison, *If*, Apr 1954; "The Crackpots," June 1956; *A Touch of Infinity*, Ace pa [**Kyben*** series]
"Life-Line," *ASF*, Aug 1939; first of **Future History*** series—Heinlein, R. A.

*Life on Other Worlds**—Paul, F. R. [back cover paintings]

"Lilliput Revisited," A. Bradford, *Fantastic*, Dec 1963; "Return to Brobdingnag," Feb 1964; "Gulliver's Magic Island," May 1964

Liners of Time, J. R. Fearn, *AS*, sr4, May 1935; "Zagribud," sr3, Dec 1938

Link, Adam*—Binder, E. (pseud)—Binder, O. O. [*Adam Link—Robot*]

Lion, the Witch and the Wardrobe, The; first of **Chronicles of Narnia***—Lewis, C. S.

Little Fuzzy; *The Other Human Race*—Piper, H. B. [pa]

"Little Hercules," *ASF*, Sep 1936; first of **Durna Rangue*** series—Jones, N. R.

"Little Miss Ignorance," E. E. Evans, *Other Worlds*, Sep 1950; "Little Miss Martian," May 1951; "Little Miss Boss," Aug 1952

"Little People, The," E. Binder, *FA*, Mar 1940; "Wanderer of Little Land," June 1941

"Lonely Path, The," J. Ashcroft, *SFA*, Dec 1960; "No Longer Alone," June 1961

Loo, Wing*—Keller, D. H.

Lord Darcy*—Garrett, R.

Lord of the Green Planet; *Doom of the Green Planet*—Petaja, E. [pa]

"Lord of the Lightning," A. K. Barnes, *WS*, Dec 1931; "The Challenge of the Comet," Feb 1932

Lord of the Rings* trilogy—Tolkien, J.R.R.

Lost Planet*—MacVicar, A. [juvenile books]

"Lot," W. Moore, *F&SF*, May 1953; "Lot's Daughter," Oct 1954

Lovers, The, P. J. Farmer; *SS*, Aug 1952; "Moth and Rust," June 1953

"Lundstret's Invention," R. M. Williams, *AS*, June 1939; "Rockets Over Europe," Feb 1940

Lung, Kai*—Bramah, E. (pseud)—Ernest Smith [books]

"Luvium," *AS*, Nov 1931; first of **Luvium*** series—McKenzie, A. R.

M

McGhee, Squaredeal Sam*—Bond, N. S.

"Machine, The," *ASF*, Feb 1935; first of **Machine*** series—Stuart, D. A. (pseud)—Campbell, J. W.

"Machine Man of Ardathia, The," F. Flagg, *AS*, Nov 1927; "Cities of Ardathia," Mar 1932

McNab, Josh*—Burks, A. J.

Mad Friend*—Edmondson, G. C. [*Stranger Than You Think*]

"Mad Planet, The," *Arg*, 12 June 1920; first of **Burl*** series—Leinster, M. (pseud)—Jenkins, W. F.

Magic Ball From Mars, The; *Starboy*—Biemiller, C. L. [juvenile books]

Magnis Mensas*—Rayer, F. G.

Magnus, Martin*—Temple, W. F. [juvenile books]

Magnus Ridolph*—Vance, J. [*The Many Worlds of Magnus Ridolph*]

Maker of Universes, The; first of **World of Tiers*** series—Farmer, P. J. [pa]

Malone, Kenneth*—Phillips, M. (pseud)—Garrett, R., & Janifer, L. M.

"Man From Agharti, The," John & Dorothy De Courcy, *AS*, July 1948; "The Golden Mask of Agharti," Jan 1950

"Man in the Moon, The," H. E. Flint, *ASW*, 4 Oct 1919; "Out of the Moon," *Arg*, sr4, 15 Dec 1923

"Man Named Jones, A," C. B. Stilson, *ASW*, sr5, 25 Oct 1919; "Land of the Shadow People," sr5, 26 June 1920 [first is only high adventure, but second is definitely fantasy]

Man of Many Minds; *Alien Minds*—Evans, E. E.

"Man Who Awoke, The," *WS*, Mar 1933; first of **Man Who Awoke*** series—Manning, L.

"Man Who Discovered Nothing, The," *ASW*, 10 Jan 1920; first of **Tubby*** series—Cummings, R.

Man Who Mastered Time, The, R. Cummings, *Arg*, sr5, 12 July 1924; *The Shadow Girl*, sr4, 22 June 1922; "The Exile of Time," *ASF*, sr4, Apr 1931 [section of **Matter, Space and Time*** trilogy]

Man Who Rocked the Earth, The; *The Moon Maker*—Train, A., & Wood, R. W.

"Man Who Saw Two Worlds, The," T. Ayre [J. R. Fearn], *AS*, Jan 1940; "The Case of the Murdered Savants," Apr 1940; "The Case of the Mesozoic Monsters," May 1942

Man Who Sold the Moon, The; first of **Future History*** series—Heinlein, R. A. [books]

"Man Without a World, The," J. C. & H. Burroughs, *TWS*, Jan 1939; "The Lightning Men," Feb 1940

"Manape the Mighty," A. J. Burks, *ASF*, June 1931; "The Mind Masters," sr2, Jan 1932

Manderpootz, Professor*—Weinbaum, S. G.

"Manhunt," C. Walker, *New Worlds*, Spr 1951; "The Scapegoats," Aut 1951

Manx, Pete*—Kent, K. (pseud)—Kuttner, H. (with Barnes, A. K.)

"Margin of Profit," *ASF*, Sep 1956; first of **Nicholas Van Rijn*** series—Anderson, P.

"Marooned in Andromeda," C. A. Smith, *WS*, Oct 1930; "The Amazing Planet," *WSQ*, Sum 1931

"Marooned off Vesta," I. Asimov, *AS*, Mar 1939, Mar 1959; "Anniversary," Mar 1959

"Marque and Reprisal," P. Anderson, *F&SF*, Feb 1965; "Arsenal Port," Apr 1965; "Admiralty," June 1965 [*The Star Fox*]

Martian* [John Carter]—Burroughs, E. R.

"Martian Odyssey, A," S. G. Weinbaum, *WS*, July 1934, *SS*, Nov 1939; "Valley of Dreams," *WS*, Nov 1934, *SS*, May 1940 [in some collections]

Martin Magnus, Planet Rover; first of **Martin Magnus*** series—Temple, W. F.

Master of Darkness*—Leinster, M. (pseud)—Jenkins, W. F.

"Master of Mystery, The," B. Olsen, *AS*, Oct 1931; "Seven Sunstrokes," Apr 1932; "The Pool of Death," Jan 1932

"Mathematica," J. R. Fearn, *ASF*, Feb 1936; "Mathematica Plus," May 1936

"Mathematical Kid, The," R. Rocklynne, *AS*, June 1940; "Alphabetical Scoop," *Nebula*, Sep 1953, *Vortex SF*, No. 2, 1953

"Matrix," R. Phillips [R. P. Graham], *AS*, Oct 1949; "Beyond the Matrix of Time," Nov 1949

Matter, Space and Time* trilogy—Cummings, R.

Matuchek, Stephen*—Anderson, P.

Mayhem, Johnny*—Thames, C. H. (pseud)—Marlowe, S.

Med Ship*—Leinster, M. (pseud)—Jenkins, W. F.

Meg the Priestess*—Bond, N. S.

"Men With Wings," L. F. Stone, *Air Wonder*, July 1929; "Women With Wings," May 1930

"Menace, The," *ASQ*, Sum 1928; first of **Taine*** series—Keller, D. H.

"Menace From Below, The," H. Vincent, *Science Wonder*, July 1929; "The Return to Subterrania," Apr 1930

Mensas, Magnis*—Rayer, F. G.

"Merakian Miracle, The," *TWS*, Oct 1951; first of **Manning Draco*** series—Crossen, K. F.

Methuselah, Doc*—Lafayette, R. (pseud)—Hubbard, L. R.

Midnight Club*—Hall, S.

Mightiest Machine, The, J. W. Campbell, *ASF*, sr5, Dec 1934; *The Incredible Planet*

"Milk Run," *GSF*, Sep 1954; first of **AAA Ace Interplanetary*** series—Sheckley, R.

Minions of the Moon; first of **Minions*** series—Beyer, W. G.

"Misfit," *F&SF*, Feb 1959; first of **Mad Friend*** series—Edmondson, G. C. [*Stranger Than You Think*]

Miss Pickerell*—MacGregor, E. [juvenile books]

"Mission One Hundred," K. Bulmer, *NW*, Sep 1957; "Greenie Gunner," Dec 1960; "Flame in the Flux Field," Mar 1962

Mission to Mars; first of **Maurice Gray*** series—Moore, P. A. [juvenile books]

"Mr. Meek—Musketeer," C. D. Simak, *Planet*, Sum 1942; "Mr. Meek Plays Polo," Fall 1944

Mistress of Mistresses—Eddison, E. R. [see **Zimiamvian*** trilogy]

"Mistress of the Djinn," G. St. Reynard, *FA*, Nov 1950; "The Enchanted Crusade," *Imagination*, Apr 1953

"Monsters of Neptune," H. D. Juve, *WSQ*, Sum 1930; "The Struggle for Neptune," Fall 1930

"Moon Conquerors, The," R. H. Romans, *WSQ*, Win 1930, *SFQ*, Win 1941; "The War of the Planets," *WSQ*, Sum 1930

Moon Pool, The; "The Conquest of the Moon Pool"; *The Metal Monster*—Merritt, A.

"Moon Strollers, The," J. R. Ullrich, *AS*, May 1929; "The Stolen Chrysalis," July 1931

Morgan, Dr. —see **Grandon*** series—Kline, O. A.

Morks, Murchison*—Arthur, R.

Morn, Bran Mak*—Howard, R. E.

"Mother," P. J. Farmer, *TWS*, Apr 1953; "Daughter," Win 1954

Munchausen's Scientific Adventures, Baron*—Gernsback, H. See also Munchausen in the *GENERAL* section.

Mushroom Planet*—Cameron, E. [juvenile books]

My First Two Thousand Years; first of **Wandering Jew*** trilogy—Viereck, G. S., & Eldridge, P.

"My Name Is Mayhem," *AS*, Sep 1955; first of **Johnny Mayhem*** series—Thames, C. H. (pseud)—Marlowe, S.

"Mystery of the Bulawayo Diamond, The," *Amazing Detective*, June 1930; first of **Craig Kennedy*** series—Reeve, A. D.

Mythology*—Paul, F. R. [back cover paintings]

N,O

Napier, Carson—Burroughs, E. R. [see **Venusian*** series]

"Narapoia," A. Nelson, *F&SF*, Apr 1951; "The Shopdropper," Jan 1955

Narnia, the Chronicles of*—Lewis, C. S.

N'Chaka*—Brackett, L.

Nidor*—Randall, R. (pseud)—Silverberg, R., & Garrett, R.

"Nightmare Tower," J. J. Ferrat, *FU*, June/July 1953; "The White Rain Came," May 1955; "Snowstorm on Mars," June 1956

"No Future in This," R. Randall, *SFQ*, May 1956; "Deus ex Machina," Nov 1956

"No Way Out," R. Silverberg, *ASF*, Feb 1958; *Master of Life and Death* [pa]; "The Seed of Earth," *GSF*, June 1962

"Nobody Bothers Gus," P. Janvier, *ASF*, Sep 1955; "The Peasant Girl," June 1956; "And Then She Found Him," *Venture*, July 1957

Norcriss, Jerry*—Sharkey, J.

Northwest Smith*—Moore, C. L. [*Shambleau*; *Northwest of Earth*]

Not at Night series—Thomson, C. C. [book anthologies]

"Not in the Rules," M. Reynolds, *Imagination*, Apr 1951; "The Cosmic Bluff," Oct 1952

"Not So Great an Enemy," J. E. Gunn, *Venture*, July 1957; "The Immortals," *Star SF No. 4*

"Nova in Messier 33," C. Corbett, *ASF*, May 1937; "When Time Stood Still," June 1937

"Novice," *ASF*, June 1962; first of **Telzey*** series—Schmitz, J. H.

"Nuse Man, The," M. St. Clair, *GSF*, Feb 1960; "The Airy Servitor," Apr 1960

"O Ugly Bird!" *F&SF*, Dec 1951; first of **John the Minstrel*** series—Wellman, M. W. [*Who Fears the Devil?*]

O'Brien, Turlogh*—Howard, R. E.

"Okie," *ASF*, Apr 1950; first of **Okie*** series—Blish, J. [*Earthman, Come Home*]

"Old Doc Methuselah," *ASF*, Oct 1947; first of **Doc Methuselah*** series—Lafayette, R. (pseud)—Hubbard, L. R.

"Old Faithful," *ASF*, Dec 1934; first of **Old Faithful*** series—Gallun, R. Z.

"Old Fireball," N. Schachner, *ASF*, June 1941; "Jurisdiction," Aug 1941 [*Space Lawyer*]

Old Growler*—Deegan, J. J. [pa]

"On the Gem Planet," Cordwainer Smith [P. Linebarger], *GSF*, Oct 1963; "On the Storm Planet," Feb 1965; "On the Sand Planet," *AS*, Dec 1965; "Three to a Given Star," *GSF*, Oct 1965 [*Quest of the Three Worlds*]

"One Every Minute," *Authentic*, Sep 1955; first of **Dusty Dribble*** series—Tubb, E. C.

"One in Three Hundred," J. T. McIntosh [J. M. MacGregor], *F&SF*, Feb 1953; "One in a Thousand," Jan 1954; "One Too Many," Sep 1954 [*One in 300*]

"One's Got To Be Best," *BB*, Mar 1943; first of **Squaredeal Sam McGhee*** series—Bond, N. S.

"Only an Echo," *NW*, Apr 1954; first of **Jacko*** series—Barclay, A. (pseud)—Tait, G. B.

Oona*—St. Clair, M.

"Operation Afreet," *F&SF*, Sep 1956; first of **Stephen Matuchek*** series—Anderson, P.

"Operation in Free Orbit" *FU*, Feb 1955 ["Operation in Free Flight," *Australian Magazine*, Mar 1952]; first of **Vivienne Gale*** series—Bryning, F. B.

Orig Prem*—Miller, B. (pseud)—Loomis, N.

"Oscar, Detective of Mars," *FA*, Oct 1940; first of **Oscar, Detective of Mars*** series—Norman, J.

Other Side of the Sun, The; *The Other Half of the Planet*; *Down to Earth*—Capon, P.

"Our Director," J. E. Harry, *Astonishing*, Apr 1941; "Our Director Meets Trouble," Dec 1942

"Our Distant Cousins," Lord Dunsany [in some collections and anthologies]; "The Slugly Beast," *AFR* No. 7, 1948

"Out of Night," D. A. Stuart [J. W. Campbell], *ASF*, Oct 1937; "Cloak of Aesir," Mar 1939 [*Cloak of Aesir*]

Out of the Silent Planet; *Perelandra* (or *Voyage to Venus*); *That Hideous Strength* (or *The Tortured Planet*)—Lewis, C. S.

"Out of the Void," L. F. Stone, *ASF*, sr2, Aug 1929; "Across the Void," sr3, Nov 1930 [*Out of the Void*]

Overlord of Cornwall*—Keller, D. H.

"Overworld, The," *F&SF*, Dec 1965; first of **Cugel the Clever*** series—Vance, J. [*The Eyes of the Overworld*]

Oz books—Baum, L. F.

"Ozar the Aztec," Valentine Wood, *Top-Notch Mag*, Jan 1933; "Ozar and the Plumed Serpent," Feb 1933; "Ozar and the Jade Altar," Mar 1933; "The Dreams of Ozar," Apr 1933; "Ozar and the Black Skull," May 1933; "Ozar's Crown of Victory," June 1933

P

"Palos of the Dog Star Pack," *All-Story*, sr5, 13 July 1918, *FFM*, Oct 1941; first of **Palos*** trilogy—Giesy, J. U. [mag & books]

"Pandora's Planet," C. Anvil [H. C. Crosby], *ASF*, Sep 1956; "Pandora's Envoy," Apr 1961; "The Toughest Opponent," Aug 1962 [since continued]

"Paradox," C. Cloukey, *ASQ*, Sum 1929; "Paradox +," *AS*, July 1930; "Anachronism," Dec 1930

"Parasite Planet," S. G. Weinbaum, *ASF*, Feb 1935; "The Lotus Eaters," Apr 1935; "The Planet of Doubt," Oct 1935

Paratime*—Piper, H. B.

"Passage to Dilfar," *Fantastic*, Feb 1965; first of **Dilvish the Deliverer*** series—Zelazny, R.

"Past, Present and Future," *ASF*, Sep 1937; first of **Past, Present and Future*** series—Schachner, N.

Pat Pending*—Bond, N. S.

Patchwork Quilt*—Quick, D.

Patent Attorney*—Lockhard, L. (pseud)—Thomas, T. L.

"Paul Revere and the Time Machine," A. W. Bernal, *AS*, Mar 1940; "King Arthur's Knight in a Yankee Court," Apr 1941

Pavane*—Roberts, K. [*Pavane*]

Pellucidar*—Burroughs, E. R. [mainly about David Innes]

Pending, Pat*—Bond, N. S.

Penton and Blake*—Campbell, J. W. [*The Planeteers*]

People*—Henderson, Z. [*Pilgrimage*; *The People*]

PEST*—Aldiss, B. W.

"Phantom Moon," *Authentic*, No. 6, 1951; first of **Shiny Spear*** series—Sheldon, R.

"Philosophical Corps," *ASF*, Mar 1951; first of **Philosophical Corps*** series—Cole, E. B. [*The Philosophical Corps*]

Pickerell, Miss*—MacGregor, E. [juvenile books]

"Piper's Son, The," *ASF*, Feb 1945; first of **Baldy*** series—Padgett, L. (pseud)—Kuttner, H. [*Mutant*]

"Piracy Preferred," *AS*, June 1930; first of **Arcot, Morey and Wade*** series—Campbell, J. W. [also as books]

Pirates of Venus; first of **Venusian*** series—Burroughs, E. R.

"Planet of Peril, The," *Arg*, sr6, 20 July 1929; first of **Robert Grandon*** series—Kline, O. A.

Planetary Exploration*—Malcolm, D.

"Planeteer, The," H. E. Flint, *ASW*, 9 Mar 1918; "King of Conserve Island," 12 Oct 1918

"Planet's Air Master, The," E. E. Chapelow, *Air Wonder*, Aug 1929; "The Return of the Air Master," Mar 1930

"Plants Must Grow," *TWS*, Oct 1941; first of **John Carstairs*** series—Long, F. B. [*John Carstairs: Space Detective*]

"Plimsoll Line," F. G. Rayer, *Science-Fantasy*, Spr 1952; "Trader's Planet," Spr 1953; "Space Prize," May 1954

Plutonian Lens*—W. Long (pseud)—G. O. Smith

"Pocket Universes," M. Leinster, *TWS*, Fall 1946; "The End," Dec 1946

"Poetry Machine, The," *F&SF*, Fall 1950; first of **C. P. Ranson*** series—Nearing, H. [*Sinister Researches of C. P. Ransom*]

Pogo*—Kelly, W.

"Pogo Planet," *Future*, Oct 1941; first of **Ajax Calkins*** series—Pearson, M. (pseud)—Wollheim, D. A.

"Polaris of the Snows," *ASW*, sr3, 18 Dec 1915; *FFM*, July 1942; first of **Polaris*** trilogy—Stilson, C. B. [mag & books]

"Police Operation," *ASF*, July 1948; first of **Paratime*** series—Piper, H. B.

Pons, Solar*—Derleth, A. W.

Posi and Nega*—Skidmore, J. W.

"Postpaid to Paradise," *F&SF*, Win/Spr 1950 [from 15 Jan 1940 *Arg*]; first *F&SF* appearance of **Murchison Morks*** series—Arthur, R.

"Prefabrication," E. R. James, *Fantasy* (Gillings), No. 2, Apr 1957; "Advent of the Entities," *Science-Fantasy*, Sum 1950

"Preliminary Data," *NW*, Aug 1965; first of **Jerry Cornelius*** series—Moorcock, M. [*The Final Programme*]

Prem, Orig*—Miller, B. (pseud)—Loomis, N.

"Priestess Who Rebelled, The," *AS*, Oct 1939; first of **Meg the Priestess*** series—Bond, N. S.

"Prima Belladonna," J. G. Ballard, *Science-Fantasy*, Dec 1956; "Studio 5: The Stars," Jan 1961

"Prince of Arelli, The," A. Septama, *ASQ*, Sum 1930; "The Terrors of Arelli," Fall 1930

Princess of Mars, A; first of **Martian*** series—Burroughs, E. R.

Professor Jameson*—Jones, N. R. [*The Planet of the Double Sun* and others; pa series]

Professor Manderpootz*—Weinbaum, S. G.

"Project Stall," P. E. High, *NW*, May 1959; "The Martian Hunters," Nov 1961

"Prometheus II," S. J. Byrne, *AS*, Feb 1948; "Colossus," *Other Worlds*, May 1950; "Colossus II," July 1950; "Colossus III," Sep 1950; "The Golden Guardsmen," sr3, Apr 1952

"Prowler of the Wastelands," H. Vincent, *ASF*, Apr 1935; "Return of the Prowler," Nov 1938

Prydain*—Alexander, L.

"Pygmalion," *AS*, Jan 1932; first of **Lemurian Documents*** series—Burtt, J. L.

Q, R

"Q.R.M.—Interplanetary," *ASF*, Oct 1942; first of **Venus Equilateral*** series—Smith, G. O. [*Venus Equilateral*]

Quade, Tony See **Hollywood on the Moon*** series—Kuttner, H.

"Queen of the Martian Catacombs," *Planet*, Sum 1949; first of **N'Chaka*** series—Brackett, L.

Quest of the Spaceways; *World of Mists*—**Quest*** series—Moore, P. A.

"Quest of Thig," B. Wells, *Planet*, Fall 1942; "Quest's End," Spr 1944

"Q.U.R.," H. H. Holmes, *ASF*, Mar 1943; "Robinc," Sep 1943 [see A. Boucher]

"Race Through Time, A," D. Wandrei, *ASF*, Oct 1933; "Farewell to Earth," Dec 1933

"Radicalite," R. R. Murray, *AS*, Jan 1932; "Solarite," Mar 1932

Radio Man, The, *Arg*, sr4, 28 June 1924; first of **Radio Man*** series—Farley, R. M. (pseud)—Hoar, R. S.

"Raid of the Mercury, The," A. H. Johnson, *AS*, July 1931; "The Superman," Aug 1931

Ransom, C. P.*—Nearing, H.

"Ray of Hypnosis, The," M. Kaletsky, *AS*, July 1940; "Homer Higginbotham, Rain Maker," June 1941

"Rebel Soul, The," A. Hall, *ASW*, 30 June 1917, *FFM*, Aug 1940; "Into the Infinite," sr6, Apr 1919, sr4, Oct 1942

"Reckoning From Eternity," H. Annas, *Other Worlds*, Nov 1955; "Daughter of Doom," Feb 1956; "Witch of the Dark Star," Apr 1956

"Reconnoitre Krellig II," *Authentic*, No. 2, 1951; first of **Old Growler*** series—Deegan, J. J.

Red Dwarf*—Shaver, R. S.

"Red Peril, The," S. P. Meek, *AS*, Sep 1929; "The Last War," Aug 1930

"Red Shadows," *WT*, Aug 1928; first of **Soloman Kane*** series—Howard, R. E.

"Red Spot of Jupiter, The," D. McDermott, *WS*, July 1931; "The Duel on the Asteroid" [with P. S. Miller], June 1932

"Redmask of the Outlands," N. Schachner, *ASF*, Jan 1934; "The Son of Redmask," Aug 1935

Reefs of Space, The; *Starchild*—Pohl, F., & Williamson, J.

Refuge*—Green, J. L. [*The Loafers of Refuge*]

"Regulations Provide," R. F. Jones, *ASF*, Mar 1950; "Tools of the Trade," Nov 1950

Rendell, Kim*—Leinster, M. (pseud)—Jenkins, W. F. [*The Last Space Ship*]

"Rescue From Jupiter, A," G. Edwards [G. E. Pendray], *Science Wonder*, sr2, Feb 1930; "The Return From Jupiter," *WS*, sr2, Mar 1931

Resurgent Dust; *The Immortals*; *The Indestructible*—Garner, R. (pseud)—Berry, B.

Retief*—Laumer, K. [mag & books]

"Retreat From Mars," C. B. White, *AS*, Aug 1927; "The Return of the Martians," Apr 1928

"Revolt of the Scientists, The," *WS*, Apr 1933; first of **Revolt of the Scientists*** series—Schachner, N.

"Rex and Mr. Rejilla," G. R. Dickson, *GSF*, Jan 1958; "Who Dares a Bulbur Eat?" Oct 1962

"Ribbon in the Sky," *ASF*, June 1957; first of **Med Ship*** series—Leinster, M. (pseud)—Jenkins, W. F.

Ridolph, Magnus*—Vance, J. [*The Many Worlds of Magnus Ridolph*]

Riverworld*—Farmer, P. J.

"Roaring Trumpet, The," *Unknown*, May 1940; first of **Harold Shea*** series—de Camp, L. S., & Pratt, F. [check for books]

"Robin Hood's Barn," P. Anderson, *ASF*, Jan 1959; "Condemned to Die," *FU*, Oct 1959; "The Burning Bridge," *ASF*, Jan 1960 [Constitutionalists]

Robot Saga*—Cummings, R.

Robots See **Laws of Robotics*** series—Asimov, I.

"Robur the Conqueror," J. Verne, *AS*, sr2, Dec 1926; "Master of the World," sr2, Feb 1928 [also as books]

"Roman Holiday," *TWS*, Aug 1939; *SS*, Jan 1950; first of **Pete Manx*** series—Kent, K. (pseud)—Kuttner, H. [and with Barnes, A. K.]

"Romance of Posi and Nega, The," *AS*, Sep 1932; first of **Posi and Nega*** series—Skidmore, J. W.

Runestaff*—Moorcock, M. [pa]

"Ruum, The," A. Porges, *F&SF*, Oct 1953; "A Specimen for the Queen," May 1960

S

Saga of Lost Earths; *The Star Mill*—Petaja, E.

"Sandhound, The," R. Rocklynne, *Planet*, May 1943; "The Sandhound Strikes," Spr 1944/45

"Sands of Time," P. S. Miller, *ASF*, Apr 1937; "Coils of Time," May 1939

Sargasso of Space; *Plague Ship*; *Voodoo Planet*—North, A. (pseud)—Norton, Andre

Satan, Doctor*—Ernst, P.

"Satan on Holiday," Ralph Bennitt, *FU*, May 1956; "Satan and the Comrades," Sep 1956

Savage, Doc*—Robeson, K. (pseud)—see Dent, L.

"Scarlet Denial," N. Sherwood *SFA* (British), May 1962; "Scarlet Dawn," Sep 1962

"Scientific Ghost, The," *AS*, Jan 1939; first of **John Hale*** series—Repp, E. E.

"Scientific Pioneer, The," *AS*, Mar 1940; first of **Horsesense Hank***
series—Bond, N. S.

"Second Seeded," R. C. Fitzpatrick, *ASF*, Jan 1966; "There Is a Tide"
(with Leigh Richmond), Jan 1968 [Dr. Jensen series]

"Secret of the Black Planet," M. Lesser, *AS*, June 1952; "Son of the
Black Chalice," July 1952 [*Secret of the Black Planet*]

Secret Under the Sea; *Secret Under Antarctica*; *Secret Under the Carib-
bean*—Dickson, G. R.

"Sector General," *NW*, Nov 1957; first of **Sector General*** series—
White, J.

"Seed of the Arctic Ice," H. G. Winter, *ASF*, Feb 1932; "Under Arctic
Ice," Jan 1933

"Seesaw, The," *ASF*, July 1941; first of **Weapon Shops*** series—van
Vogt, A. E.

Seetee*—Stewart, W. (pseud)—Williamson, J. [*Seetee Ship*; *Seetee Shock*]

"Segregation," *NW*, July 1958; first of **PEST*** series—Aldiss, B. W.

"Septimus Spink, Circa 2021," J. Archibald, *FU*, Jan 1955; "Flight
From New Mu," May 1955; "Operation Earthworm," Sep 1955

"Sergeant Shane of the Space Marines," *AS*, Oct 1941; first of **Sergeant
Shane*** series—Cabot, J. Y. (pseud)—O'Brien, D. W.

Serpent, The; *Atlan*; *The City*—Gaskell, J.

"Seventh Stair, The," Frank Brandon, *Science-Fantasy*, Oct 1961;
"Perilous Portal," Aug 1962

Shadow, The*—Gibson, W. B. [pa]

"Shadow Kingdom, The," *WT*, Aug 1929; first of **King Kull*** series—
Howard, R. E.

"Shadow of the Sword," W. Whiteford, *SFA* (British), Jan 1959; "Distant Drum," July 1959

"Shadrach," N. S. Bond, *Planet*, Fall 1941; "The Lorelei Death," Win
1941/42

"Shambleau," *WT*, Nov 1933, *AFR*, No. 7, 1948; first of **Northwest
Smith*** series—Moore, C. L. [also as books]

Shane, Sergeant*—Cabot, J. Y. (pseud)—O'Brien, D. W.

Shaver Mystery*—Shaver, R.

Shea, Harold*—de Camp, L. S., & Pratt, F.

"Shining Land, The," E. Hamilton, *WT*, May 1945; "Lost Elysium,"
Nov 1945

Shiny Spear*—Sheldon, R.

"Shortwave Castle," C. Peregoy [T. C. McClary], *ASF*, Feb 1934; "Dr.
Conklin—Pacifist," Aug 1934; "Shortwave Experiment," Feb 1935

"Shot Into Infinity, The," O. W. Gail, *WSQ*, Fall 1929, *SFQ*, Win 1941;
"The Shot From the Moon," Spr 1930

"Signaller, The," *Impulse*, Mar 1966; first of **Pavane*** series—Roberts,
K. [*Pavane*]

"Silent Destroyer, The," H. D. Juve, *Air Wonder*, Aug 1929; "The Sky
Maniac," Oct 1929; "The Vanishing Fleet," Feb 1930

"Singing Bell, The," *F&SF*, Jan 1955; first of **Wendell Urth*** series—
Asimov, I.

Skull-Face*—Howard, R. E.

"Sky People, The," P. Anderson, *F&SF*, Mar 1959; "Progress," Jan
1962

Skylark of Space, The, *AS*, sr3, Aug 1928; first of **Skylark*** series—
Smith, Edward E.

"Slave Raiders of Mercury," D. Wilcox, *AS*, June 1940; "Battering
Rams of Space," Feb 1941; "Earth Stealers," June 1943

Slaves of Sleep, L. R. Hubbard, *Unknown*, July 1939; "The Masters of
Sleep," *FA*, Oct 1950

Smith, Northwest*—Moore, C. L. [*Shambleau*; *Northwest of Earth*]

Snakes and Spiders*—Leiber, F.

"So Shall Ye Reap," R. Phillips [R. P. Graham], *AS*, Aug 1947; "Starship From Sirius," Aug 1948

Society of Time*—Brunner, J. [*Times Without Number*]

"Soma Racks, The," *SS*, Mar 1947; first of **Oona*** series—St. Clair, M.

"Son Is Born, A," *ASF*, May 1946; first of **Gods*** series—van Vogt,
A. E. [*Empire of the Atom*; *The Wizard of Linn*]

Space Cat; first of **Space Cat*** series—Todd, R. [juvenile books]

"Space Mirror," E. Hamilton, *TWS*, Aug 1937; "Murder in the Void,"
June 1938

Space Platform; *Space Tug*; *City on the Moon*—Leinster, M. (pseud)—
Jenkins, W. F.

"Space Salvage," *TWS*, Aug 1949; first of **Space Salvage*** series—
Cartmill, C.

"Spaceship Named McGuire, A," R. Garrett, *ASF*, July 1961; "His
Master's Voice," Mar 1962

"Spacetime for Springers," F. Leiber, *Star SF*, June 1958; "Kreativity
for Kats," *GSF*, Apr 1961

Spaceward Ho!; *Stratosphere Patrol*; *The Three Rocketeers*—Molesworth, V. [pa]

"Spoil of Yesterday," *SFA* (British), Mar 1962; first of **Society of
Time*** series—Brunner, J. [*Times Without Number*]

Squaredeal Sam McGhee*—Bond, N. S.

"Stainless Steel Rat, The," H. Harrison, *ASF*, Aug 1957; "The Misplaced Battleship," Apr 1960 [*The Stainless Steel Rat*]

Stand By for Mars; first of **Tom Corbett*** series—Rockwell, C. [juvenile
books]

"Star Dwellers, The," *WT*, Feb 1929; first of **Interstellar Patrol*** series—Hamilton, E.

Star King, The; *The Killing Machine*; *The Palace of Love*—Vance, J. [pa]

"Star-Mouse, The," F. Brown, *Planet*, Spr 1942; "Mitkey Rides
Again," Nov 1950

"Star of Panadur," A. de Pina & H. Hasse, *Planet*, Mar 1943; "The Star
Guardsman" (de Pina only), Win 1943

Star Well; first of **Anthony Villiers*** series—Panshin, A [pa]

Starr, David*—French, P. (pseud)—Asimov, I. [juvenile books]

Stars Are Ours, The; *Star Born*—Norton, Andre

Starwolf*—Hamilton, E. [pa]

"Stellar Missile, The," E. E. Repp, *Science Wonder*, Nov 1929; "The
Second Missile," *AS*, Dec 1930 [*The Stellar Missiles*]

Step to the Stars; *Mission to the Moon*—del Rey, L.

Stories of the Stars*—Paul, F. R. [back cover paintings]

Storm Over Warlock; *Ordeal in Otherwhere*—Norton, Andre

"Story of Rod Cantrell, The," M. Leinster, *SS*, Jan 1949; "The Black
Galaxy," Mar 1949; *Galaxy SF Novel* No. 20

"Story of the Stone Age, A," H. G. Wells, *AS*, Nov 1927, etc.; "A
Story of the Days to Come," sr2, Apr 1927, etc.

Stowaway to Mars (or *Planet Plane*), J. Beynon [J. B. Harris]; "Sleepers
of Mars," *Tales of Wonder* No. 2, 1938

"Strange City," W. Van Lorne, *ASF*, Jan 1936; "World of the Purple
Light," Dec 1936

"Strange Voyage of Dr. Penwing, The," R. O. Lewis, *AS*, Mar 1940;
"The Incredible Theory of Dr. Penwing," Aug 1940

Stranger Club*—Manning, L.

"Strangers to Paradise," C. Anvil, *ASF*, Oct 1966; "The Dukes of Desire," June 1967; "The King's Legions," Sep 1967; "The Royal
Road," June 1968 [about Roberts, Hammell, and Morrissey]

"Strike," R. Wilson, *Future*, July 1953; "New Weapon," Nov 1953
["Dateline Mars"]

"Submicroscopic," S. P. Meek, *AS*, Aug 1931; "Awlo of Ulm," Sep
1931

"Success Story," J. Chain, *ASF*, May 1951; "Prometheus," Aug 1951;
"Cosmophyte," Apr 1952

Sumuru*—Rohmer, S.

"Sun Makers, The," W. McMorrow, *Arg*, sr3, 21 Nov 1925, *FFM*, Dec
1940; "Venus or Earth," *Arg*, 9 July 1927, *FFM*, Apr 1941

Surgeon of Souls*—Rousseau, V. (pseud)—Emanuel, V. R.

"Survival," A. J. Burks, *Marvel*, Aug 1938; "Exodus," Nov 1938

"Swap Shop," A. B. Chandler, *NW*, Dec 1957; "In the Box," May
1958

Swift, Tom*—Appleton, V. [juvenile books]

Sword in the Stone, The; *The Witch in the Wood*; *The Ill-Made Knight*—
White, T. H. [*The Once and Future King*]

T

Taine*—Keller, D. H.

"Tale of the Red Dwarf, The," *FA*, May 1947; first of **Red Dwarf***
series—Shaver, R. S.

"Tama of the Light Country," *Arg*, sr3, 13 Dec 1930; first of **Tama***
series—Cummings, R.

Tarnsman of Gor; first of **Gor*** series—Norman, J. (pseud)—Lange, J. F.

"Taste of Poison, A," C. Anvil [H. C. Crosby], *ASF*, Aug 1960; "No
Small Enemy," Nov 1961 [about Cardan]

"Tedric," Edward E. Smith, *Other Worlds*, Mar 1953; "Lord Tedric," *Universe*, Mar 1954

Telzey*—Schmitz, J. H. [*Universe Against Her*, etc.]

T.E.R.R.A., Agent of*—Maddock, L. (pseud)—Jardine, J.O. [pa]

Testament of Man*—Fisher, V. [books]

"That Sweet Little Old Lady," *ASF*, sr2, Sep 1959; first of **Kenneth Malone*** series—Phillips, M. (pseud)—Garrett, R., & Janifer, L. M.

"That's Just Like a Martian," M. W. Wellman, *TWS*, Fall 1943; "Gambler's Asteroid," Spr 1944

They Shall Have Stars [or *Year 2018!*]; *Earthman, Come Home*; *The Triumph of Time*—Blish, J.

"Thing of Venus, The," W. S. Peacock, *Planet*, Spr 1942; "Planet of No Return," Win 1942

"Things of Distinction," K. F. Crossen, *SS*, Mar 1952; "Halos Inc.," Apr 1953

"Third Cry to Legba, The," *WT*, Nov 1953; first of **John Thunstone*** series—Wellman, M. W.

Thongor*—Carter, L. [pa]

Thorinn*—Knight, D.

"Though Dreamers Die," L. del Rey, *ASF*, Feb 1944; "Robots Return," R. M. Williams, *ASF*, Sep 1938

Three Musketeers*—McGivern, W. P. [includes one story by C. McCune]

Through Space to the Planets; *Rangers of the Universe*—Law, W. [juvenile books]

"Through the Einstein Line," *WS*, Nov 1933; first of **Earthguard*** series—Haggard, J. H.

"Through the Vibrations," P. S. Miller, *AS*, May 1931; "Cleon of Yzdral," July 1931

Thruway Patrol*—Raphael, R. [*Code Three*]

"Thunder in the Dawn," *WT*, sr2, May 1938; first of **Elak of Atlantis*** series—Kuttner, H.

Thunstone, John*—Wellman, M. W.

"Thy Days Are Numbered," *Future*, May 1952; first of **Great Legend*** series—West, W. [*Lords of Atlantis*]

"Time Dweller, The," M. Moorcock, *Science-Fantasy*, Feb 1964; "Escape From Evening," Mar 1965

"Time Locker," *ASF*, Jan 1943; first of **Galloway Gallegher*** series—Padgett, L. (pseud)—Kuttner, H. [*Robots Have No Tails*]

Time Masters, The; *Time Bomb*—Tucker, W.

"Time Patrol," *F&SF*, May 1955; first of **Time Patrol*** series—Anderson, P. [*Guardians of Time*]

"Time to Rest," J. Beynon [J. B. Harris], *NW*, No. 5, 1959; "No Place Like Earth," No. 9, 1951

Time Traders, The; first of **Time Traders*** series—Norton, Andre

"Time Was," R. Goulart, *F&SF*, Feb 1961; "Please Stand By," Jan 1962; "Uncle Arly," July 1962

"Time Was," F. G. Rayer, *NW*, Win 1952; "Man's Questing Ended," July 1952 [*The Star Seekers*]

"Time Wounds All Heels," *FA*, Apr 1942; first of **Lefty Feep*** series—Bloch, R.

"Tink Takes a Hand," *FA*, Oct 1941; first of **Tink*** series—McGivern, W. P.

Titus Groan; *Gormenghast*; *Titus Alone*—Peake, M.

"To Make a Hero," *Infinity*, Oct 1957; first of **Leland Hale*** series—Garrett, R.

Toffee*—Myers, C. F.

Toka*—Pelkie, J. W. (pseud)—Palmer, R. A.

Tomorrrow*—Zagat, A. L.

"Tomorrow's Children," P. Anderson & F. N. Waldrop, *ASF*, Mar 1947; "Logic" [Anderson only], July 1947 [*Twilight World*, P. Anderson]

"Tonight the Sky Will Fall," D. F. Galouye, *Imagination*, May 1952; "The Day the Sun Died," Dec 1955

"Topaz Gate, The," J. Blish, *Future*, Aug 1941; "The Solar Comedy," June 1942

Toromon* trilogy—Delany, S. R.

"Tower of the Elephant, The," first of **Conan*** series—Howard, R. E.

"Trade Secret," R. F. Jones, *ASF*, Nov 1953; "The School," Dec 1954

"Trail of Cthulhu, The," *WT*, Mar 1944; first of **Trail of Cthulhu*** series—Derleth, A.

Transportation on Other Worlds*—Settles, J. B. [back cover paintings]

"Treasure of Asteroid X, The," F. A. Kummer, *AS*, Jan 1939; "Slaves of Vibration," Jan 1940

Troon*—Wyndham, J. (pseud)—Harris, J. B. [*The Outward Urge*]

Tros of Samothrace*—Mundy, T.

"Trouble Times Two," G. O. Smith, *ASF*, Dec 1945; "Trouble," July 1946

"Trouble With Telstar, The," J. Berryman, *ASF*, June 1963; "Stuck," June 1964 [about Mike Seaman]

"Try and Change the Past," *ASF*, Mar 1958; first of **Change War*** series—Leiber, F.

Tubby*—Cummings, R.

"Tumithak of the Corridors," *AS*, Jan 1932; first of **Tumithak*** series—Tanner, C. R.

"Twilight," D. A. Stuart [J. W. Campbell], *ASF*, Nov 1934; "Night," Oct 1935 [*Who Goes There?*]

"Two Sought Adventure," *Unknown*, Aug 1939; first of **Gray Mouser*** series—Leiber, F. [*Two Sought Adventure*, etc.]

U,V

Undersea Quest; first of **Jim Eden*** series—Pohl, F., & Williamson, J. [juvenile books]

"Undetected, The," G. O. Smith, *GSF*, Dec 1959; "The Big Fix," Dec 1959

Unfortunate Fursey, The; *The Return of Fursey*—Wall, M.

"Unhappy Man, The," J. E. Gunn, *FU*, Feb 1955; "The Naked Sky," *SS*, Fall 1955; "Name Your Pleasure," *TWS*, Win 1955 [*The Joy Makers*]

United Planets*—Reynolds, M.

"Universe," R. A. Heinlein, *ASF*, May 1941; "Common Sense," Oct 1941 [*Orphans of the Sky*]. See also **Future History*** series.

"Unnamable, The," *WT*, July 1925; first of **Randolph Carter*** series—Lovecraft, H. P.

"Unreluctant Tread, The," *NW*, Feb 1958; first of **Earth-Shurilala-Takkat*** series—Bulmer, K.

"Unwillingly to School," P. Ashwell, *ASF*, Jan 1958; "The Lost Kafoozalum," Oct 1960

"Urned Reprieve," *AS*, Oct 1964; first of **Ensign De Ruyter*** series—Porges, A.

Urth, Wendell*—Asimov, I.

"Usurpers, The," G. St. Reynard, *FA*, Jan 1950; "Beware, the Usurpers," *Imagination*, Nov 1951

"Vagabonds of Space," H. Vincent, *ASF*, Nov 1930; "Creatures of Vibration," Jan 1932

"Valley of Teeheemen, The," A. Thatcher, *WT*, sr2, Dec 1924; "The Last of the Teeheemen," sr2, Mar 1925

Van Rijn, Nicholas*—Anderson, P.

Vandals of the Void, J. M. Walsh, *WSQ*, Sum 1931, *FSM*, Spr 1951; "The Struggle for Pallas," *WSQ*, Fall 1931

"Vanishing Diamonds, The," C. R. Tanner, *AS*, June 1938; "The Stillwell Degravitator," Feb 1941

Vegan Confederation*—Schmitz, J. H. [*Agent of Vega*]

"Velocity of Escape, The," J. W. Skidmore, *AS*, Aug 1934; "Murder by Atom," June 1937

Venus Equilateral*—Smith, G. O. [*Venus Equilateral*]

"Venus Liberated," H. Vincent, *ASQ*, Sum 1929; "Faster Than Light," Fall/Win 1932

"Venus Trouble-Shooter," J. Wiley, *Other Worlds*, Nov 1949; "Venus Trouble," Oct 1950

Venusian*—Burroughs, E. R. [about Carson Napier]

"Via Etherline," *TWS*, Oct 1937; first of **Via*** series—Giles, G. A. (pseud)—Binder, E.

*Viagens Interplanetarias***—de Camp, L. S.

"Vigorish," W. Bupp [R. Garrett], *ASF*, June 1960; "Card Trick," Jan 1961; "Modus Vivendi," Sep 1961

Villiers, Anthony*—Panshin, A.

Visit From Venus, A; *Jupiter in the Chair*; *Trout's Testament*—Fraser, R.
Von Theil and Sergeant John West*—Casey, K.
Vortex Blaster*—Smith, Edward E. [*The Vortex Blaster*]
"Voyage of the Asteroid," L. Manning, *WSQ*, Sum 1932; "The Wreck of the Asteroid," *WS*, sr3, Dec 1932

W,Y,Z

"Wailing Wall," R. Dee [R. D. Aycock], *GSF*, July 1952; "Pet Farm," Feb 1954; "Control Group," *AS*, Jan 1960
Wandering Jew*—Viereck, G. S., & Eldridge, P.
Warrior of Llarn; *Thief of Llarn*—Fox, G. F. [pa]
Warrior of the Dawn, H. Browne, *AS*, sr2, Dec 1942; *The Return of Tharn*, sr3, Oct 1948
"Warriors of Eternity," C. Buchanan & A. Carr, *ASF*, Aug 1934; "Discus Men of Ekta," Feb 1935
Warriors of Mars; *Blades of Mars*; *Barbarians of Mars*—Bradbury, E. P. (pseud)—Moorcock, M.
"Way of Decision, The," M. C. Pease, *SF Stories*, No. 1, 1953; "Peace Agent," No. 2, 1954
Weapon From Beyond, The; first of **Starwolf*** series—Hamilton, E.
Weapon Shops*—van Vogt, A. E.
Werewolf of Ponkert*—Munn, H. W.
"Weyr Search," McCaffrey, A., *ASF*, Oct 1967; "Dragonrider," sr2, Dec 1967 [*Dragonflight*]
"What the Left Hand Was Doing," D. T. Langart [R. Garrett], *ASF*, Feb 1960; "Psychopath," Oct 1960; "Fifty Per Cent Prophet," Sep 1961
"What Thin Partitions," *ASF*, Sep 1953; first of **Ralph Kennedy*** series—Clifton, M.
"When Planets Clashed," M. W. Wellman, *WSQ*, Spr 1931, *SS*, Mar 1947; "The Disc-Men of Jupiter," *WS*, Sep 1931, *SS*, May 1947
"When the Atoms Failed," J. W. Campbell, *AS*, Jan 1930; "The Metal Horde," Apr 1930
"When the Earth Died," D. Wilcox, *AS*, Sep 1939; "Wives in Duplicate," Aug 1939
When Worlds Collide; *After Worlds Collide*—Balmer, E., & Wylie, P.

"Whirlpool in Space," *AS*, Nov 1939; first of **Ebbtide Jones*** series—Shelton, M. (pseud)—Wilcox, D.
"Whispering Gorilla, The," D. Wilcox, *FA*, Nov 1940; "The Return of the Whispering Gorilla," D. V. Reed, Feb 1943 [*The Whispering Gorilla*]
"Who Went Where?" *NW*, Nov 1962; first of **Galactic Survey Team*** series—Markham, R.
"Winds of Truth," *NW*, May 1960; first of **Planetary Exploration*** series—Malcolm, D.
Wing Alak*—P. Anderson
Wing Loo*—Keller, D. H.
Witch World*—Norton, Andre [pa]
"With Folded Hands . . .," J. Williamson, *ASF*, July 1947; ". . . And Searching Mind," sr3, Mar 1948 [latter also as *The Humanoids*]
"Without Bugles," *NW*, Jan 1952; see *Alien Dust*—Tubb, E. C.
Wizard of Lemuria, The; first of **Thongor*** series—Carter, L. [pa]
"World and Thorinn, The," *GSF*, Apr 1968; first of **Thorinn*** series—Knight, D.
World in Eclipse; *Children of the Void*—Dexter, W. (pseud)—Pritchard, W. T.
"World in Shadow," J. Brophy, *NW*, No. 4, 1949; "The Dawn Breaks Red," Sum 1950
World of $\overline{A}$, A. E. van Vogt, *AS*, sr3, Aug 1945; *The Players of* $\overline{A}$, sr4, Oct 1948
World of Tiers*—Farmer, P. J. [pa]
"World That Drowned, The," F. C. Painton, *Arg*, 4 May 1940; "The Golden Empress," 5 Oct 1940; "The Dawn Seekers," sr2, 19 Apr 1941
"World Without, The," B. Herbert, *WS*, Feb 1931, *SS*, Sep 1940; "The World Within," Aug 1931
"World Without Chance," P. Cross, *TWS*, Feb 1939; "Chameleon Planet," *Astonishing*, Feb 1940
"Worlds of If, The," *WS*, Aug 1935, *SS*, Mar 1941, *Fantasy* (Gillings), Dec 1946; first of **Professor Manderpootz*** series—Weinbaum, S. G.
"W62 to Mercury," *ASF*, Sep 1935; first of **W62*** series—Kruse, C. B.
Year 2018! (or *They Shall Have Stars*); *Earthman, Come Home*; *The Triumph of Time*—Blish, J.
York, Anton*—Binder, E. [*Anton York, Immortal*]
Zimiamvian* trilogy—Eddison, E. R.
Zip-Zip*—Schealer, J. M. [juvenile books]

GENERAL

Introduction

This section covers selected material important to the science fiction and fantasy fields not treated in detail elsewhere in the *Encyclopedia*.

The subjects include hardcover and paperback publishers with titled series (covering many foreign ones), films not covered in the *WHO'S WHO* author entries, the more noted amateur magazines, awards, conventions, and radio and television shows. Some aspects of fan terminology are outlined, but a far more complete and important reference work in this regard is *Fancyclopedia II* by R. Eney (1959).

A brief outline of science-fiction and fantasy publishing and other activities is given for the following countries: Argentina, Australia, Austria, Belgium, Brazil, Canada, Czechoslovakia, Denmark, France, Germany, Holland, Hungary, India, Italy, Japan, Mexico, New Zealand, Poland, Portugal, Russia, South Africa, Spain, and Sweden.

A list of the subjects follows. Many of the entries also refer to relevant books, authors, etc., mentioned in the *WHO'S WHO* sections (Volumes 1 and 2) or elsewhere in Volume 3.

Ace Books
Ace Science Fiction Specials
Advent:Publishers, Inc.
Adventures in Science Fiction
Amateur Magazines
American International Pictures
American Rocket Society
Amra
Ancient Civilizations
Animals, see Zoology
Anthem Press
Anticipation
Argentina
Arkham House
Arra Publishers
Astronomy
Atlantis, see Ancient Civilizations
Atlas Publications
Atomböck
Atomböckerna
Atomic Research
Australia
Austria
Avalon Books
Avon Publications Inc.
Barbarella
Batman
Beast From 20,000 Fathoms, The
Belgium
Bell, Book and Candle
Biblioteca Economica Mondadori
Birds, The
Bizarre
Bizarre Series
Book Clubs
Brazil
British Interplanetary Society
British Science Fiction Association
Cabinet of Dr. Caligari, The
Canada

Cartoonists
Cenit
Chamberlain Press
Classics
Classiques de la Science-Fiction, Les
Club House, The
Comics
Connoisseur's Library of Strange Fiction
Conquest of Space
Conventions (Australian)
Conventions (British)
Conventions (European)
Conventions (Swedish)
Conventions (U.S.A.)
Conventions (World)
Corgi Books
Cosmic Library
"Cosmos"
Creature From the Black Lagoon, The
Cthulhu Mythos
Cybernetics and Mechanical Brains
Czechoslovakia
Dawn Press
Day the Earth Caught Fire, The
Day the Earth Stood Still, The
Denmark
Destination Moon
Dianetics
Dr. Cyclops
Dr. Who
Doubleday Science Fiction Book Club, see Science Fiction Book Club [D'day SF B.C.]
Earth
Eastern Science Fiction Association
End of the World
ESP, see Extrasensory Perception

Espacio
Etherline
Extrasensory Perception
Extra-Terrestrial Life
Faber
Fan Magazines, see Amateur Magazines
Fandom House
Fanscient, The
Fantaciencia
Fantascienza
Fantastic Voyage
Fantastic Worlds
Fantasy Amateur Press Association
Fantasy Calendars
Fantasy Commentator
Fantasy Fan, The
Fantasy Magazine
Fantasy Press
Fantasy Publishing Company Inc.
Fantasy-Times, see *Science-Fiction Times*
Fantasy Veterans Association
Fictitious Books
Films
First Fandom
Five
5,000 Fingers of Dr. T., The
Flying Saucers, see Unidentified Flying Objects
Folk Tales
Fourth Dimension
France
Fremtidsromanen
Futile Press
Futurian Press
Futurian Society of Sydney
Galaxie Bis
Galaxy Awards
Gamma People, The

ACE BOOKS

ACE BOOKS The noted paperback series published by Ace Books Inc., New York. A. A. Wyn was president until his death in Nov 1977. Editors were D. A. Wollheim for science fiction from 1953, and T. Carr for "Science Fiction Specials" from 1968.

The series began printing science fiction and fantasy in late 1953; all are appropriately covered in the *PAPERBACK* section and, with the exception of some of only minor interest, also in the *WHO'S WHO* section.

The series was notable for the "Ace Doubles," volumes containing two novels (or collections) printed back to back and upside down with respect to each other, so that there are two "front" covers and no back cover.

ACE SCIENCE FICTION SPECIALS A high-quality paperback series published by Ace Books. It was edited by Terry Carr (assistant to D. A. Wollheim). The titles were:
1967 *Why Call Them Back From Heaven?*, Clifford D. Simak
1968 *The Witches of Karres*, James H. Schmitz
    Past Master, R. A. Lafferty
    The Revolving Boy, Gertrude Friedberg
    The Lincoln Hunters, Wilson Tucker
    Rite of Passage, Alexei Panshin
    Picnic on Paradise, Joanna Russ
    The Two Timers, Bob Shaw
    Synthajoy, D. G. Compton
    The Ring, Piers Anthony [P.A.D. Jacob] & Robert E. Margroff
    A Torrent of Faces, James Blish & Norman L. Knight
    The Demon Breed, James H. Schmitz

ADVENT:PUBLISHERS, Chicago. Formed in 1956 by five Chicago fans for publishing works about science fiction. It was originally managed by Earl Kemp, and since 1965 by George Price. Founded as a partnership, the company incorporated in 1968.

Its first work was *In Search of Wonder*, D. Knight (1956). Later titles have been *Frank Kelly Freas: A Portfolio* (1957) [artwork]; *Best Science Fiction Stories and Novels, 9th Series*, T. E. Dikty (1958); *The Science Fiction Novel* (1959) [symposium]; *The Eighth Stage of Fandom*, R. Bloch (1962); *Proceedings of the 20th World Science Fiction Convention— Chicon III*, E. Kemp (1963); *The Issue at Hand*, W. Atheling [J. Blish] (1964); *A Requiem for Astounding*, A. Rogers (1964); *Of Worlds Beyond*, L. A. Eshbach (1964; reprint); *Proceedings of the 21st World Science Fiction Convention: Discon*, R. Eney (1965); *The Universes of E. E. Smith*, R. Ellik & Bill Evans (1966); *In Search of Wonder*, D. Knight (1967; revised edition); *Heinlein in Dimension*, A. Panshin (1968).

ADVENTURES IN SCIENCE FICTION A juvenile fiction series (including one nonfiction title) edited by Cecile Matschat and Carl Carmer, published by The John C. Winston Co., Philadelphia, starting in 1952. By the 1960's the series tapered off in quantity. In 1961 Winston merged with other publishers to become Holt, Rinehart and Winston, which continued to produce occasional books more or less within the series.

At first the books were issued in groups every few months:
April 1952: *Earthbound*, M. Lesser; *Find the Feathered Serpent*, E. Hunter; *Five Against Venus*, P. Latham [R. S. Richardson]; *Marooned on Mars*, L. del Rey; *Son of the Stars*, R. F. Jones.
Fall 1952: *Islands in the Sky*, A. C. Clarke; *Mists of the Dawn*, C. Oliver; *Rocket Jockey*, P. St. John [L. del Rey]; *Sons of the Ocean Deeps*, B. Walton; *Vault of the Ages*, P. Anderson.
April 1953: *Battle on Mercury*, E. Van Lhin [L. del Rey]; *The Mysterious Planet*, K. Wright; *Mystery of the Third Mine*, R. W. Lowndes; *Rocket to Luna*, R. Marsten [E. Hunter]; *Vandals of the Void*, J. Vance.

Sep 1953: *Planet of Light*, R. F. Jones; *The Star Seekers*, M. Lesser; *Missing Men of Saturn*, P. Latham [R. S. Richardson]; *Danger: Dinosaurs*, R. Marsten [E. Hunter]; *Attack From Atlantis*, L. del Rey.
19 Apr 1954: *Trouble on Titan*, A. E. Nourse; *Rockets to Nowhere*, P. St. John [L. del Rey]; *The Secret of Saturn's Rings*, D. A. Wollheim; *The Year After Tomorrow* [anthology], L. del Rey.
6 Sep 1954: *The World at Bay*, P. Capon; *Step to the Stars*, L. del Rey.
Early 1955: *The Ant Men*, E. North [B. C. Cronin].
12 Sep 1955: *Secret of the Martian Moons*, D. A. Wollheim.
1956: *Mission to the Moon*, L. del Rey; *The Lost Planet*, P. V. Dallas.
1957: *Rockets Through Space* [nonfiction], L. del Rey.
1958: *The Year the Stardust Fell*, R. F. Jones.
1959: *The Star Conquerors*, B. Bova.
1960: *The Secret of the Ninth Planet*, D. A. Wollheim; *Lost Race of Mars*, R. Silverberg; *Stadium Beyond the Stars*, M. Lesser.

Most of the early novels were translated into Japanese and published by Ginga Shobo, Sekisen-sha, Tokyo, 1955-1956. A number were also reprinted by Hutchinson, London. Others were translated into Italian for the *Urania* series, and some into Spanish by Ed. Acmé of Buenos Aires.

AMATEUR MAGAZINES In the science fiction, fantasy and associated fields, these are popularly termed "fan" magazines or "fanzines." Many hundreds have been and are being published throughout the world. *Fanzine Index*, by Bob Pavlat and Bill Evans, listed some two thousand from the beginning to 1952; it was reissued by the late Harold P. Piser in 1965.

The following titles of note are given separate entries in this section: *Amra, Bizarre, Etherline, The Fanscient, Fantastic Worlds, Fantasy Commentator, The Fantasy Fan, Fantasy Magazine, Fantasy Times* (see *Science-Fiction Times*), *Forerunner, The Golden Atom, Inside, The Journal of Science Fiction, Leaves, New Frontiers, The New Futurian, Operation Fantast, Science Fiction, Science-Fiction Advertiser, Science-Fiction News, Science-Fiction Times, Science Fiction World, Scientifiction.*

AMERICAN INTERNATIONAL PICTURES U.S. film company begun by James H. Nicholson and Samuel Z. Arkoff. It produced a number of horror films in the mid-1950's, and in the early 1960's became particularly noted for its macabre films based on Poe, Lovecraft, etc., such as *The Masque of the Red Death* and *The Fall of the House of Usher*. One of the company's more notable directors was Roger Corman. (Check the film list in E. A. Poe *WHO'S WHO* listing.)

AMERICAN ROCKET SOCIETY Formed in 1930 as the American Interplanetary Society; the name was changed in 1934. G. Edward Pendray and David Lasser were early presidents; N. Schachner was the first secretary. Its journals *Astronautics* and *Jet Propulsion* were started around the end of World War II.

AMRA U.S. amateur magazine started in 1957, originally termed the Official Organ of the Hyborian Legion and devoted to facts and fancies relating to the author Robert E. Howard and associated material. It was noted as being published by The Terminus, Owlswick, & Ft Mudge Electrick Street Railway Gazette. Format was usually 7 x 10 in., photolith, at 25¢. The 22nd issue was July 1962; by 1968 it had around 40 issues.

Edited by George Scithers, the magazine has presented "sword and sorcery" material of interest to the fantasy enthusiast from such professional writers as F. Leiber, P. Anderson, and L. S. de Camp, as well as amateur contributors, with interesting artwork from R. Krenkel and others.

ANCIENT CIVILIZATIONS
General: *Conquest by Man*, P. Herrman (1955); *Lost Continents*, L. S. de Camp (1954); *Fair Gods and Stone Faces*, C. Irwin (1963).
America (& Aztec): *America's Ancient Civilization*, A. H. Verrill (1953).
America, Central: *The Conquest of the Maya*, J. L. Mitchell (1934); *Maya Art and Civilization*, H. J. Spinden (1913, 1957).
America, South: *Mysteries of Ancient South America* (1946) & *Secret Cities of Old South America* (1950), both by H. T. Wilkins.
Atlantis: *Atlantis: The Antediluvian World*, I. Donnelly (1882, 1949 rev.); *The Atlantis Myth*, H. S. Bellamy (1948); *Lands Beyond*, L. S.

de Camp (1954); *Atlantis—The Mystery Unravelled*, J. Spanuth (1956). There are also numerous books on this alleged continent not covered in the *Encyclopedia*; authorities include E. Sykes (who revised an edition of I. Donnelly's *Atlantis* in 1949 and H. Eichner (who has prepared a comprehensive bibliography yet to be published).

Mu: An alleged continent, belief in which was fostered by J. Churchward.

ANIMALS See **ZOOLOGY**

ANTHEM PRESS, Baltimore. Established about 1961 and operated by Jack L. Chalker for publishing nonfiction about the weird and science fiction fields. An offshoot has been the magazine *Mirage*; another imprint is Mirage Press. Early works appeared mimeographed in limited editions. There have been several items on H. P. Lovecraft, including *The New H. P. Lovecraft Bibliography*, J. L. Chalker (1962, 40 pp.) and *Mirage on Lovecraft*, J. L. Chalker (1962). Other titles include *In Memoriam: Clark Ashton Smith* (1962); *The Necronomicon—A Study*, M. Owings (1967, 32 pp., $1.95); and the important listing of specialty publishing houses *The Index to the Science-Fantasy Publishers*, M. Owings & J. L. Chalker (1966, $5.00).

ANTICIPATION French science fiction book series, published by Le Fleuve Noir, Paris, starting in Sep 1951. By the end of 1968 there were 362 issues, numbered to No. 361 (with one not numbered).

The novels have been mainly of the essentially juvenile "thrill and thunder" type. French authors to consistently appear have included F. Richard-Bessiere, J. Guieu, J. G. Gaston, B. R. Bruss, M. A. Rayjean, K. Steiner, G. d'Argyre, and S. Wul. The series has published translations of many of J. R. Fearn's novels (originally under the V. Statten and V. Gridban pseudonyms), as well as 22 titles in the German "Perry Rhodan" series (in 11 books—2 per volume). There have also been occasional moderately good translations from contemporary British and U.S writers, recently including *A for Andromeda* and *Andromeda Breakthrough*, both by F. Hoyle & J. Elliot (1967), and *Invaders of Space*, M. Leinster [W. F. Jenkins] (1967).

ARGENTINA This country has published a little sf and fantasy. Magazines have been the notable *Narraciones Terrorificas*, which began before World War II and apparently ceased in 1950, *Pistas Del Espacio*, which may still be current, and *Más Allá* (1953—1957). There is understood to have been a reprint edition of *Galaxy Science Fiction*.

Two book series existing in the early 1960's, 'Minotauro' and 'Fantaciencia,' gave Spanish translations of U.S. and British material.

In 1940 the noted anthology *Antologia de la Literatura Fantastica*, edited by S. Ocampo, A. B. Casares, and J. L. Borges, was published in Buenos Aires; it contained stories by M. Beerbohm, Lord Dunsany, H. G. Wells, F. Kafka, O. Stapledon, and others.

In recent years Jorge L. Borges, director of the Argentine National Library, has become one of the most noted literary figures in South America. His fantastic works have lately seen translation in such collections as *Ficciones* and *Labyrinths* (both 1962).

ARKHAM HOUSE, Sauk City, Wisconsin. This publishing firm was originally formed by A. Derleth and D. Wandrei in 1939 to specialise in fantasy and weird novels and collections. The first work was *The Outsider and Others*, by H. P. Lovecraft (1200 copies); this is now a rare and valuable collector's item. Later Wandrei withdrew from the venture to enter military service.

Titles were issued frequently until the early 1950's, when production slowed to one or two per year. The history of the firm is given in *Arkham House: The First 20 Years 1939—1959* (Arkham, 1959, 54 pp., pa $1.00; 900 copies). This gives the contents of all books to that time as well as the eight issues of *Arkham Sampler*. The titles generally ran to editions of 2,000 to 3,000 copies, and all issued to the mid-1950's are now rather scarce.

ARRA PUBLISHERS U.S. amateur publisher formed around 1932-33 from the staff of the amateur magazine *The Time Traveller*, comprising J. Schwartz, M. Weisinger, C. Ruppert, and A. Glasser. Three pamphlets were published: *Cavemen of Venus*, A. Glasser; *Price of Peace*,

M. Weisinger; *Through the Dragon Glass*, A. Merritt. The first two were original stories and the last a reprint.

ASTRONOMY This science has naturally not been specifically covered in the *Encyclopedia*, but the following writers have astronomical works (either general or covering particular planets) listed in their entries:

General: G. De Vaucouleurs; V. A. Firsoff; F. Hoyle; W. Ley; P. A. Moore; R. S. Richardson. Jupiter: B. M. Peek. Mars: G. De Vaucouleurs; H. Strughold; R. S. Richardson; W. Von Braun. Moon: H. P. Wilkins. Venus: P. A. Moore.

See also: EXTRA-TERRESTRIAL LIFE.

ATLANTIS See ANCIENT CIVILIZATIONS

ATLAS PUBLICATIONS, London. This British firm produced editions of *Astounding Science Fiction* [now *Analog*] and *Unknown* during World War II and for a long time afterward because of the war-time ban on importing magazines of U.S. origin. These editions did much to maintain interest in science fiction within the British Empire in the period 1939-1963.

In 1939-1940 Atlas published some issues of *Science Fiction*, and probably the one issue of *Dynamic Science Stories* that appeared. Postwar it published *Thrilling Wonder Stories* for a time, the British 2nd Series of *The Magazine of Fantasy and Science Fiction*, and more recently the British edition of *Venture Science Fiction*. The contents of all British magazines, including all the Atlas titles, have been listed in *Index to British SF Magazines*, by G. Stone.

ATOMBÖCK [Atom Book] A Swedish science fiction series published by Pingvinförlaget, Gothenburg (printed by Elanders); 22 issues 1957-1959, 128 pp., 1 kr.

The series gave translations of the poorer British paperbacks by such writers as Lee Elliot, Brian Shaw, Kris Luna, and Neil Charles. There was only one original story: No. 19, *Anfall från rymden*, by Gabriel Setterborg, written under the pseudonym Eric Crane.

An earlier series of better quality was AtombÖckerna.

ATOMBÖCKERNA [Atom Books] A Swedish science fiction series published by Lindqvist, Stockholm; 12 numbers, 1954-1956.

This was a high-class series of reprints of U.S. and British material, plus one original novel. The titles were:

The Stars, Like Dust, I. Asimov; *After Worlds Collide & When Worlds Collide*, E. Balmer & P. Wylie; *The Demolished Man*, A. Bester; *Stowaway to Mars*, J. B. Harris; *Dark Dominion*, D. Duncan; *Starman Jones*, R. A. Heinlein; *This Island Earth*, R. F. Jones; *Judgment Night*, C. L. Moore; *The Weapon Shops of Isher*, A. E. van Vogt; *Destination: Universe*, A. E. van Vogt. The original was *Alternativ Luna*, Carl Henner [pseud of Henrik Nanne].

ATOMIC RESEARCH Works directly mentioned: *The Atomic Story*, J. W. Campbell Jr.; *The Man in the Thick Lead Suit*, D. Lang.

AUSTRALIA A number of Australians have written works of interest, many of which have been published in Great Britain.

Australian-born writers who made their names as resident authors in Britain include G. Boothby, F. Hume, V. Knowles, and J. M. Walsh. Before World War II the best-known novelist resident in Australia was Erle Cox, whose *Out of the Silence* (1925) is considered a science fiction classic. The paper-covered booklet *A Checklist of Australian Fantasy*, S. L. Larnach (Futurian Press, Sydney, 1950) lists pertinent material somewhat sketchily to 1937.

Other prewar writers, essentially of science fiction, include A. Connell and B. C. Cronin [under the pseudonym E. North]. J. Heming and Vol Molesworth (a former fan) became prominent in the paperback field of the early 1940's. After the war F. Bryning, the late N. Hemming, and W. Whiteford achieved prominence in the magazine field.

Mainstream writers who have had one or two books of sf/fantasy interest include C.A.M. Caseleyr [better known as Jack Danvers], J. Cleary, G. M. Glaskin, L. Greener (originally English), J. Iggulden, W. Law (for juveniles), I. Southall (juveniles with slight sf slant), D. Stivens, E. V. Timms, and J. Workman (weird stories in paperback). British-born authors who became resident in Australia include the late

Nevil Shute [pseudonym for N. S. Norway] and A. B. Chandler, as well as C. Higham, who edited a weird fiction paperback series.

Writers in the 1960's include J. Baxter, who had a novel and an anthology and is now becoming a film reviewer, D. Broderick, and R. Braddon. F. Cusack has collected "authentic" tales in *Australian Ghost Stories* (1967).

Before World War II, U.S. and British magazines were freely imported, including both current and remaindered issues. In May 1940 U.S. magazine imports were banned, due to wartime conditions. Only a limited supply of British editions were available, so some Australian interests entered the field. The most important firm was Currawong Publishers, Sydney, who issued a number of saddle-stapled paper-covered items from late 1940, with the principal authors being Heming, Molesworth, and Connell. A few items appeared from other publishers.

After the war, but before any magazine commenced, Molesworth had an interplanetary trilogy published by Radio Record, Sydney. Then in the mid-1940's Transport Publishing Company, Sydney, issued some 40 novels in their "Scientific Thriller" series (more "thriller" than sf). Slightly later, Whitman Press, Sydney, produced six paper-covered booklets reprinting U.S. material.

The first magazine was *Thrills Incorporated*, quite juvenile in outlook, which ran for 23 issues (Mar 1950—June 1952). This was followed by the Malian Press *American Science Fiction (Magazine)* with 41 issues (June 1952—Sep 1955) and companion *Selected Science-Fiction Magazine* with 5 issues (May 1955—Sep 1955); all were undated. They reprinted novels, with shorts as fillers, generally U.S. material of good standard, and are mainly remembered for their Stanley Pitt covers.

Two magazines of more conventional type commenced around mid-1953 and ran irregularly to April 1955. These were the Frew Publications *Future Science Fiction* and *Popular Science Fiction*, each having 6 issues and reprinting U.S. sf suitable for a less sophisticated audience. [Oddly, two issues of each were reprinted in 1967.] A reprint of *Orbit Science Fiction*, in large size and not of much consequence, appeared in early 1954.

A relatively important magazine was the quarterly edition of *The Magazine of Fantasy and Science Fiction* from Consolidated Press, Sydney, which ran for 14 issues and terminated about the middle of 1958. The final and probably most important Australian magazine venture was *Science Fiction Monthly*, which appeared for 18 issues (Sep 1955—Feb 1957), not dated. It reprinted from overseas sources, but for its last six issues had a science-fiction column by G. Stone, giving club news, sf reminiscences, book reviews, etc., to interest the general reader. [Since the period under review, a further magazine *Vision* was published for a time by the late noted collector Ron Graham of Sydney.]

Australian authority G. Stone has compiled *Australian Science Fiction Index 1925-1967* (Futurian Society, Sydney, 1968), which covers all these publications. He is also progressively bringing out *An Index to the British Science-Fiction Magazines 1934-1953* in supplementary form.

Other Australian publishers have included Futurian Press, a fan operation which started in 1951. Atlas Publications issued *Science Fiction Library* in 1955 as a companion to *Science Fiction Monthly*. Then Jubilee Publications produced its "Satellite" series, numbered 211 through 216, comprising the four anthologies *Beyond the Stars*, *Space Station 42*, *The Sands of Mars*, and *Planet of Doom*, plus the novels *Year 3097*, R. D. Miller & A. Hunger, and *The Mars Monopoly*, Jerry Sohl. The anthologies were a package deal from the U.S., reprinting from Conklin's *The Best of Science Fiction* and some of the magazines of the 1950's.

In the 1960's the only publisher of interest has been Horwitz Publications, Sydney. This firm's works include many J. B. Harris titles under licence from Penguin, England, a weird anthology series compiled by C. Higham, several J. Burke reprints, and a number of single works, including one on flying saucers (over Australia!). Two titles in 1968 by J. Baxter and A. B. Chandler were supposed to start a science fiction series, but sales did not warrant its continuation. Baxter's anthology *The Pacific Book of Australian Science Fiction* (Angus & Robertson, Sydney) has proved most successful.

The ban on American imports was rescinded towards the end of 1959, and most U.S. and British science fiction and fantasy is now reasonably available. Consequently, independent Australian publishing has practically ceased.

In fan affairs there has been considerable activity at times in societies,

the production of fan magazines, and even the running of conventions. From 1938 to 1942 many groups in both Sydney and Melbourne produced publications. By the late 1940's G. Stone ran The Australian Science-Fiction Society, a loosely-knit body with contacts throughout the continent. It lapsed by the mid-1950's, but then Stone reconstituted it in early 1965 as The Australian Science Fiction Association. Its activities have continued, including bibliographic work and a monthly journal presenting book reviews, etc.

Sydney's Futurian Society ran spasmodically through the war years, and has at times lapsed, but is now quite active. The Melbourne Science-Fiction Club has been most active since the early 1950's and ran the first Australian conventions, including the "Olympicon" in 1956.

Amateur magazines of importance have included *Etherline*, *Forerunner*, and *Science Fiction News*.

AUSTRIA Dr. Herbert W. Franke is noted for important popular-science books as well as for *Der grüne Komet* (1960—65 vignettes), *Das Gedankennetz* (1960), *Der Orchideenkafig* (1961), *Die Glasfalle* (1962), *Die Stahlwüste* (1962), and *Planet der Verlorenen* (using pseudonym "Sergius Both"), all published by Goldmann, Germany. Other authors of note include Erich Dolezal, for a number of good juveniles; Manfred Langrenus (pseudonym of Prof. Dr. Friedrich Heer, an authoritative chemist); Hannelore Valcebcak, a Ph.D. in physics, for her *Die Höhlen Noahs* (1961, rewrite from earlier novel), on survival after an atomic holocaust. A. M. Lernet-Holenia has appeared in English with *Count Luna* (1956).

Two short-lived juvenile science fiction magazines were *Star-Utopia* and *Uranus*.

AVALON BOOKS, New York. An offshoot of publishers Thomas Bouregy & Co. Beginning in October 1956, books have generally appeared monthly, with some slowing down towards the late 1960's; it is one of the few specialist science fiction publishers remaining in the field. R.A.W. Lowndes has edited most of the series (except for four books in early 1958).

Although Avalon has published occasional novels of note, much has been run of the mill. Reprint novels have often been cut to fit page limits.

Authors have included L. del Rey (under pseudonym Erik van Lhin), P. Anderson, R. C. Payes (as E. L. Arch), E. Binder, S. A. Coblentz, R. Cummings, L. S. de Camp, G. A. England (titles covering the "Darkness and Dawn" trilogy), J. U. Giesy (titles in the "Palos" trilogy), J. E. Kelleam, O. A. Kline, F. B. Long, A. Lukens (pseudonym of D. Detzer), C. B. Stilson ("Polaris" trilogy), R. Sheckley, J. Vance, W. West, and R. Winterbotham.

AVON PUBLICATIONS INC. One of the first U.S. publishers of paperbacks [listed in the *PAPERBACK* section]. After about 20 years of independent operation it was purchased by the Hearst Corporation in May 1959; the name was continued as "Avon Division."

Besides paperbacks, this firm at various times published the magazines *Avon Fantasy Reader*, *Avon Science Fiction Reader*, *Avon Science Fiction and Fantasy Reader*, *Out of This World Adventures*, and *10 Story Fantasy*.

B

BARBARELLA French-Italian film, Paramount, 1967, based on the comic strip by Jean-Claude Forest. Produced by Dino de Laurentiis, directed by Roger Vadim, with Jane Fonda playing the title role.

Although suffering from the transition from comic strip to film, Jane Fonda's portrayal of a sexually emancipated space woman is considered excellent by most reviewers.

BATMAN The comic strip by Bob Kane was the basis for the two films *Batman* (1943) and *Batman and Robin* (1949); these were serials and not very fantastic. The television series consisted of 120 episodes 1966-1968. It was played as a "serious romp"—very much the comic strip acted by people. Episodes were 30 minutes, in colour, and played as two-part serials with the first episode having a cliff-hanger ending with a menacing voice of doom exhorting everyone to tune in "same bat-time, same bat-channel." The regular cast was Adam West (playing Batman/Bruce Wayne), Burt Ward (Robin/Dick Grayson), Neil Hamilton (Police Commissioner Gordon), and Stafford Repp (Chief O'Hara). Villains included Frank Gorshin (The Riddler), Cesar Romero (Joker), George Sanders (Mr. Freeze), and Burgess Meredith (Penguin).

BEAST FROM 20,000 FATHOMS, THE U.S. film, Warner Brothers, 1953, derived from a Ray Bradbury story published in *The Saturday Evening Post*, 23 June 1951.

Directed by Eugene Lourie and produced by Jack Dietz, it starred Paul Christian, Paula Raymond, and Cecil Kellaway, and had special effects by Ray Harryhausen. A rhodosaurus wakes in the arctic and goes south to New York, bringing a deadly virus.

BELGIUM Following information abridged from listing in the pamphlet *Early Bird*, 1970, M. Feron & D. de Laet:
Writers and Fans
Buyens, Frans (1924—): Dutch-speaking author of *Bora de eerste* [Bora the First] (Satiricus, Antwerp, 1956), a juvenile; *Na ons de monsters* [After Us, the Monsters] (Satiricus, 1957).
De Laet, Danny (1944—): Well-known Belgian fan in both Dutch- and French-speaking fandom. He has published numerous amateur magazines and written a history of Belgian sf.
Feron, Michel (1943—): Belgium's most important fan editor and publisher. He first collaborated with Michael Grayn on the fanzine *Atlanta*, but when this turned professional he published his own magazines covering such wide fields as comics, weird, fantasy and horror pictures, science fiction, and fandom. Some material has been published in English (in *Early Bird*). He was the first Belgian to be a member of four apas (amateur press associations).
Grayn, Michael: Pen-name of Michel Englebert and publisher of *Atlanta*, one of the first Belgian fanzines. This magazine was published by M. Feron in 1965, but Grayn's own company made it professional in 1966 (see *MAGAZINES* section). Grayn has translated B. Stoker's *Dracula* as well as Dutch and German novels and short stories. His first anthology was *Comme une odeur de soufre* [Like a Smell of Sulphur] (Assoc. Européenne de Littérature Parallèle, Moxhe, 1967).
Muet, Theo (1890—1969): Flemish popular writer of dime novels and some detective fiction; he was considered to have been influenced by the American pulp magazines. He wrote what was probably the first Belgian science fiction novel: *De Vrede-mensch van't jaar 3000* [The Peacemaker of Year 3000] (? , Antwerp, 1933), war between the United States of Europe and the U.S.A.
Jacobs, Edgar P.: Acclaimed as one of the more important European comic strip artists, most of his work is in science fiction. Starting in 1941 he produced a strip in the vein of Alex Raymond's *Flash Gordon* when that became no longer available during the war. He has developed his own style—no superheroes, but a scientist (Prof. Mortimer) and an English officer (Capt. Blake, by Jove!) who are always involved in amazing adventures such as discovering Atlantis or using an out-of-order time machine. These books include *Le rayon U* [The U Ray] (CABD, Brussels, 1966, reprint); *Le secret de l'Espadon* [The Secret of the Swordfish] (Brussels, 2 parts, 1950, 1953); *L'énigme de l'Atlantide* [The Mystery of Atlantis] (Lombard, Brussels, 1957); *Le piège diabolique* [The Evil Trap] (Lombard, Brussels, 19??).
Kremer, Raymond de (1887—1964): Belgium's most important writer of fantasy and weird fiction. See *WHO'S WHO* listing.
Lampo, Hubert (1920): Dutch-speaking author and also one of the greatest Flemish writers. Most of his works are influenced by a kind of fantasy called "magical realism." Books of interest include *De komst van Joachim Stiller* [The Arrival of Joachim Stiller] (Meulenhoff, Amsterdam, 1961), parallel worlds and Jungian archetype theories; *Dochters van Lemurie* [Daughters of Lemuria] (Meulenhoff, Amsterdam, 1964), an anthology of sf and fantasy.
Owen, Thomas (1910—): A writer in the style of Jean Ray [Raymond

de Kremer] and an important figure in horror, fantasy and weird fiction. He writes in French and has stories published in magazines. His books, all anthologies, are *Les chemins étranges* [Strange Roads] (? , Brussels, 1943); *La cave aux crapauds* [Toads' Cave] (La Boetie, Brussels, 1945); *Cérémonial nocturne* [Night Ceremony] (Marabout, Verviers, 1966). The first two were republished together in 1963 by Marabout.
Proumen, Henri-Jacques (1879—1961?): Noted as a scientist, he wrote some mainstream material, including many juveniles. He introduced the mutant theme to science fiction in *Le sceptre vole aux hommes* [The Scepter Stolen From Mankind] (Renaissance du Livre, Paris, 1930). Other books of interest were *Sur le chemin de dieux* [On the Gods' Way] (Renaissance, Paris, 1928), and *L'homme qui a été mangè* [The Man Who Has Eaten] (Office de Publicite, 1950), an anthology.
Thiry, Marcel (1897—): Noted writer of French poetry and prose, with some fiction of interest, including *Echec du temps* [To Defeat the Time] (Nouvelle France, Paris, 1946)—time travellers try to interfere at Waterloo so Napoleon can win (written in 1938); *Nouvelles du Grand Possible* [Tales of the Great Possible] (Marabout, Verviers, 1967)—anthology of fantasy stories.
Van Hageland, Albert (1919—): Considered to be "Mr. Science Fiction in Belgium," a promoter of sf like F. J Ackerman, editor of *Utopia* magazine, and writer of sf short stories. His wife, A. M. Lamend, has also written several sf juveniles.
Van Herck, Paul (1938—): Dutch-writing sf author, born in Antwerp. He is one of today's best Belgian sf writers, with short stories published in *Atlanta* and other magazines. Books include *De cirkels* [The Circles] (Kentaur, Antwerp, 1965)—short stories, and *Sam* [Meulenhoff, Amsterdam, 1968].
Van Limbergen, Jos (1902—): Belgian editor of *Weetlust*, a science magazine, and later publisher and editor of *Natuurwereld*, Belgium's most popular science magazine. Interested in the better science fiction, he often makes sarcastic comments on UFO's in his magazine. A nonfiction work of interest is *De rode Mars* [Red Mars] (Janssens, Antwerp, 1956?).
Van Offel, Horace (1878—1944): French-writing Flemish author who devoted most of his works to fantasy and science fiction, never writing pure weird or horror. These include *La brèche de Bréda* [The Breda Breach] (in *Cassandre*, serial, 1935, Brussels); *La terreur fauve* [The Animal Terror] (Albin-Michel, Paris, 1922)—group become masters of world by collective hypnotism; *Le capitaine du vaisseau fantome* [Captain of the Ghost Ship] (Toison d'Or, Brussels, 19?)—witch lives two lives and seduces soldier in World War I.
Vermeiren, Leopold (1914—): Considered by some to be the Belgian Jules Verne, this author wrote many sf juveniles, mostly on space and underground travel; he now writes medieval novels for the young. His works include the "Justa I" series (1948+); *Naar Mars* [To Mars] (Norbertus, Tongerlo, 19?); and *Vliegende mensen* [Flying People] (Davidsfonds, Leuven, 1956).
Fandom
Fan associations have included:
Club Alpha: Founded and operated by Jan Jansen of Antwerp during the 1950's.
The Association Européenne de Littérature Parallèle: Founded in 1966 by Michael Grayn. A serious but not stodgy organization which operated the magazine *Atlanta*, ran two story contests, and published three fantasy books.
Club Cosmorama: Organised in Liège during 1968 by Claude Dumont, but ceased when he moved to France.
The Sfan Club: The newest group, formed in 1969 by Julien C. Raasveld in Antwerp.
Amateur Magazines
A survey has shown over 60 former or current magazines. Michel Feron has prepared a bibliography, and also edits a considerable number. Other editors include Julien C. Raasveld, D. De Laet, Claude Dumont, Andre Leborgne, Marc Schelfhout, and Alain Feron.
Professional Magazines [check the *MAGAZINES* section for these]
Anticipations: 14 issues (Sep 1945—May 1946).
Atlanta: 12 issues (Jan/Feb 1966—Nov/Dec 1967).
Utopia: 24 issues (1961—May 1963); a pulp magazine presenting some science fiction.

BELL, BOOK AND CANDLE U.S. film, Columbia, 1958, in colour, produced by Julian Blaustein, directed by Richard Quine, with screenplay by Daniel Taradash derived from the play by John Van Druten. It starred James Stewart, Kim Novak, and Jack Lemmon. A comedy of a modern-day witch and a love spell that gets out of hand.

BIBLIOTECA ECONOMICA MONDADORI Italian book series, with the same editor, Giorgio Monicelli, as *I Romanzi di Urania* (or *Urania*). It presented mainstream literature in the late 1950's, but included some science fiction: *Seeds of Life*, T. Taine [E. T. Bell]; *The Martian Chronicles*, R. Bradbury; *Zero Hour*, V. Statten [J. R. Fearn]; *Mutant*, H. Kuttner; *The Long Loud Silence*, W. Tucker; *The Currents of Space*, I. Asimov; *Childhood's End*, A. C. Clarke; *A Mirror for Observers*, E. Pangborn.

BIRDS, THE U.S. film, Universal, 1963, directed by A. Hitchcock, screenplay by E. Hunter based on a story by Daphne Du Maurier, and starring Rod Taylor and Tippi Hedren. A love story, but with progressively more violent attacks by the birds on the people in a particular area.

BIZARRE U.S. amateur magazine, of which one printed issue, Jan 1941, is of note. Edited by Jack C. Leponen and Walter E. Marconette, with cover by H. Bok, this had 22 pp. and cost 20¢. It presented "The Thing in the Moonlight," H. P. Lovecraft, and the missing ending of *The Dwellers in the Mirage*, A. Merritt (which was not accepted for all published versions, rewriting being required). Articles were by J. W. Campbell, E. E. Smith, and H. Bok.

BIZARRE SERIES U.S. pamphlets edited by Richard Frank and published at Millheim, Pennsylvania. These were: No. 1, *Three Lines of Old French*, A. Merritt (1936); No. 2, *The Thing in the Cellar*, D. H. Keller (1940) (including "An Essay on Fear," biography and interview, and two poems); No. 3, *The Cancer Machine*, E. Binder (undated, *ca.* 1941, 30 pp., 6 x 4½ in.).

BOOK CLUBS Those covered in this section are: (Doubleday) Science Fiction Book Club, New Collector's Group, Pick-a-Book, Reader's Service Book Club, Science Fiction Book Club (Sidgwick & Jackson, London), and Transgalaxis (German).

BRAZIL Some science fiction has been translated into Portuguese and published in Brazil. There were many Verne novels early in the century, followed by H. G. Wells works in the 1930's; some were book club selections. Around this time an important adventure series, "Terramarear," appeared with Burroughs' "Tarzan" series, the pirate stories of Emilio Salgari, and the space novels of J. Aragon and Gustave Le Rouge.

In the 1950's Mario da Silva Brito edited an anthology, *Wonders of Science Fiction*, using such American authors as Bradbury, Heinlein, van Vogt, Bester, and Leinster.

Following this, the "Coleçao Argonauta" series began, and now has over 120 paperback titles, including most of the novels of Heinlein, Asimov, Clarke, Simak, and Leinster, and collections of Bradbury. The 100th volume was an anthology of selected sf stories. Other paperback series have followed; translations include *A Canticle for Leibowitz*, *A Case of Conscience*, and *The Space Merchants*. The Russian author Beliaev has had a special series. French writers include Maurice Lima, Richard Bessiere, Jimmy Guieu (including his prize winning *Project Dinosaur*), and J. G. Vandel.

The publishing houses with series or anthologies in the field are Cia. Editora Nacional, Gertrum Carbeiro, Edameris, GRD, Edart, Von Schmidt, Brasiliense, Saraiva, and 4 Artes.

Brazilian writers include: Fausto Cunha, a literary critic and journalist, with many stories (some collected as *The Martian Nights*); Dinah Silveira de Queiroz, with sociological satires; Nilson Martello and Clovis Garcia, each with works in the vein of R. Bradbury (Martello also had *The Thousand Shadows of the New Moon*, a collection of stories of Earth after an atomic war); Jeronimo Monteiro, a general writer of mystery and detective novels, radio serializations, etc., who was the first to start sf in Brazil, around 30 years ago—his noted novels are *3 Months in the 81st Century*, *Escape to Nowhere*, and *The Lost City*.

The first magazine to be published was *Galaxia 2000*, appearing in 1968, although sf stories had of course been in general magazines before then.

Fandom as become more organized since the newspaper *A Naçao* ran the First Brazilian Science Fiction Convention in 1965; the Second Convention was held in Sep 1968.

(Summary of "São Paulo Letter," by Walter Martins, *Amazing*, Sep 1968.)

BRITISH INTERPLANETARY SOCIETY Formed in 1933 by P. E. Cleator, with Leslie J. Johnson as Secretary. Over the years members have included A. M. Low and A. C. Clarke (each having been president), W. F. Temple (one-time editor of the *Journal*), Mary Patchett, and P. A. Moore. Amongst its many projects it drew up plans for a spaceship before World War II. Technical articles on all aspects of spaceflight are published in the *Journal of the British Interplanetary Society*.

L. J. Carter, secretary in the mid-1960's, edits the *Journal* and has also edited a comprehensive nonfiction work on spaceflight. In the 1950's the BIS founded the popular magazine *Spaceflight* to cater to public interest in the field; in its initial years it was edited by P. A. Moore.

BRITISH SCIENCE FICTION ASSOCIATION Founded at the informal convention held at Kettering, Easter 1958. Initiated by A. Vincent Clarke, it was successfully inaugurated by David J. Newman. The first secretary was Eric Bentcliffe. B. W. Aldiss was president for a number of years.

The Association has an open membership, runs a library, and also regularly publishes the club organ *Vector*, and in 1961 published an index to *Galaxy Science Fiction* (60 pp., 3/6). It also organises the British SF Conventions.

C

CABINET OF DR. CALIGARI, THE Noted German fantasy film made in 1919 by Decla-Bioscop. It starred Conrad Veidt and was directed by Robert Wiene. The story begins in an insane asylum with a patient narrating: a man is supposedly kept in suspended animation (actually hypnotised?), and his master sends him out at night to do murder. The sets are quite fantastic in the German expressionist style.

CANADA Most Canadian authors specialising in the field write for the U.S. magazines. Two such writers prewar were T. P. Kelley and R. Vaughan. Writers with books of interest include L. Fischer, A. Hailey, S. B. Leacock, J. Mantley, and C.G.D. Roberts. A. E. van Vogt was born in Canada but emigrated to the U.S.A.; J. Buchan spent the last years of his life in Canada. More recent Canadians include Phyllis Gotlieb and the supernatural author D. Hill. The fan A. Cameron produced the *Fantasy Classification System*, one of the more notable efforts to classify the sf/fantasy field. (All the above writers are covered in the *WHO'S WHO* section.)

Canadian publishers are often affiliated with U.S. and/or British publishers, so that many U.S. and British books have identical Canadian editions; most of these are mentioned in the appropriate title entries.

Original Canadian magazines have been *Les Adventures Futuristes* (10 issues, 1949), *Eerie Tales* (1 issue, 1941), *Uncanny Tales* (21 issues, 1940-1943); there have also been a number of Canadian editions of U.S. originals. One of the latter, *Super Science Stories*, is of particular interest as it reprinted from the Munsey *Famous Fantastic Mysteries*, etc., in its latter issues.

The weekly newspaper magazines *Star Weekly* (Toronto) and *Montreal Star* have at times published science fiction and fantasy in their novel sections. The *Star Weekly* printed a considerable number of novels by J. R. Fearn, including his book-length "Golden Amazon" series. The titles known are listed in the *PAPERBACK PUBLISHERS* section.

CARTOONISTS The *WHO'S WHO* covers the following artists who have produced cartoons and drawings of a weird/fantasy flavour: C. S. Addams, Al Capp, J. Charlot, W. Kelly, H. Kley, H. Kurtzman, R. Searle, and G. Wilson. Wilson has had a cartoon in each issue of *F&SF* since early 1965.

CENIT Spanish science fiction paperback book series, published in Barcelona. It had 72 titles, early 1960 to mid-1964, and was priced at 32 pesetas (about 50¢ U.S.).

It presented many high-class U.S. authors, and some French and British; these included P. K. Dick, I. Asimov, M. Leinster [W. F. Jenkins], P. Anderson, G. O. Smith, J. Williamson, J. Brunner, J. Blish, F. Richard-Bessiere, and R. L. Fanthorpe (under some of his pseudonyms). There was only about one original Spanish work.

CHAMBERLAIN PRESS U.S. specialty science fiction and fantasy book publisher, formed in 1953. A. E. Nourse was executive vice-president. It published only one book, *Born of Man and Woman*, R. Matheson.

CLASSICS Although the aim of the *Encyclopedia* has been to cover only works published since 1945, many older classics have been reprinted and have therefore been given comprehensive coverage. Among other sources, S. Moskowitz's works and J. O. Bailey's *Pilgrims Through Space and Time* cover such older material.

Titles include *Voyages to the Moon and the Sun*, Cyrano de Bergerac (1657); *The Man in the Moon*, F. Godwin (1638); *The Brick Moon*, E. E. Hale (1869); *Journey of Niels Klim*, L. Holberg (1741). *Gulliver's Travels*, J. Swift (1726), is briefly mentioned.

See also GOTHIC STORIES; SCIENCE FICTION; UTOPIAS.

CLASSIQUES DE LA SCIENCE-FICTION, LES French hardcover book series from Ed. Opta, Paris; limited editions of 3,000 to 4,000 copies. These omnibus volumes are very well produced and illustrated.

1965 1. I. Asimov: *Foundation*; *Foundation and Empire**; *Second Foundation**
    2. A. E. van Vogt: *The Weapon Shops of Isher*; *The Weapons Makers**
1966 3. C. D. Simak: *City*; *The Fisherman**
    4. A. E. van Vogt: *World of Null-A*; *The Players of Null-A*
    5. C. L. Moore: *Judgment Night**; *Doomsday Morning**
    6. E. R. Burroughs: *At the Earth's Core*; *Pellucidar*
1967 7. I. Asimov: *I, Robot**; *The Rest of the Robots*
    8. C. S. Lewis: *Out of the Silent Planet*; *Perelandra**; *That Hideous Strength*
    9. E. R. Burroughs: *Tanar of Pellucidar**; *Tarzan at the Earth's Core**
    10. R. A. Heinlein: *The Man Who Sold the Moon*; *The Green Hills of Earth**
1968 11. A. E. van Vogt: *Empire of the Atom**; *The Wizard of Linn**
    12. E. Hamilton: *The Star Kings*; *Retour aux etoiles** [latter was first book appearance (from short stories), later issued as U.S. paperback]
    13. P. J. Farmer: *The Lovers**; *Inside Outside**
    14. A. E. van Vogt: *Slan*; *The Voyage of the Space Beagle*
* First French translation.

CLUB HOUSE, THE The noted fan department run by Rog Phillips [R. P. Graham], giving frank and sincere comments on fan magazines and associated matters. It began in *Amazing Stories*, Jan 1948, missed a few of issues at first, and then became continuous to Mar 1953. It was continued in *Universe* from July 1954, and finally in *Other Worlds* May 1955—Feb 1956.

COMICS No attempt has been made to cover this field in the *Encyclopedia*, though occasional references are made. An early figure in the field was M. Weisinger, whose connection with *Superman* has been covered by S. Moskowitz in *Seekers of Tomorrow*. A book of interest is *The Great Comic Book Heroes*, J. Feiffer (1965).

CONNOISSEUR'S LIBRARY OF STRANGE FICTION A reprint series of quality material published by Gollancz, London, 1946-1947

(most also later reprinted): 1. *A Voyage to Arcturus*, D. Lindsay; 2. *The Haunted Woman*, D. Lindsay; 3. *Medusa*, E. H. Visiak; 4. *Confession of a Justified Sinner*, J. Hogg; 5. *The Place of the Lions*, C. Williams.

CONQUEST OF SPACE U.S. film, Paramount, 1955, in Technicolour; produced by George Pal, directed by Byron Haskin, with main roles played by Walter Brooke and Eric Fleming; astronomical backdrops by C. Bonestell.

Derived from the book of the same title by W. Ley and C. Bonestell (and also from *Project Mars*, W. Von Braun), it had good special effects but the plot was overly dramatic.

CONVENTIONS (AUSTRALIAN)
1. Sydney, 22 March 1952
2. Sydney, 1-3 May 1953
3. Sydney, 17-19 April 1954
4. Sydney, 19-20 March 1955
5. Melbourne, 8-9 December 1956 ("Olympicon")
6. Melbourne, 5-6 April 1958
7. Melbourne, Easter, 1966
Several local conferences were held prior to the above.

CONVENTIONS (BRITISH) Since 1958 these have been held on the Easter weekend.
    1937 Leeds
    1938 London
    1941 London ("Bombcon")
    1944 Birmingham
1. 1948 London ("Whitcon")
2. 1949 London (Lord Raglan Hotel)
3. 1951 London (Royal Hotel); 1st International Convention; started the International Fantasy Award.
4. 1952 London (Royal Hotel)
5. 1953 London (Bonnington Hotel), ("Coroncon") (23-24 May)
6. 1954 Manchester ("Supermancon") (5-6 June)
7. 1955 Kettering ("Cytricon I")
8. 1956 Kettering ("Cytricon II")
— 1957 London (World Convention) ("Loncon I")
9. 1958 Kettering ("Cytricon III")
10. 1959 Birmingham (Imperial Hotel)
11. 1960 London
12. 1961 Gloucester ("Lexicon")
13. 1962 Harrogate
14. 1963 Peterborough (Bull Hotel)
15. 1964 Peterborough ("Repetercon")
16. 1965 Birmingham (Midland Hotel) ("Brumcon I")
— 1965 London (World Convention) (Mount Royal Hotel) ("Loncon II")
17. 1966 Yarmouth (Royal Hotel) ("Yarcon")
18. 1967 Bristol (Hawthorns Hotel)
19. 1968 Buxton (St. Anne's Hotel) ("Thirdmancon")

CONVENTIONS (EUROPEAN) The first was organised by S-F Club Europa, 22-23 August 1959 at Zürich, Switzerland. The German equivalent of the Hugo was awarded, and the Kurd Lasswitz Literary Achievement Award was given for the first time.

CONVENTIONS (SWEDISH)
1956 18-19 August, Lund ("Luncon")
1957 23-24 August, Stockholm ("Stocon")
1958 22-24 August, Stockholm ("Stocon II")
1959 19-21 June, Malmö ("Malcon")
1960 22-23 August, Halmstad ("Halmcon")
1961 25 February, Stockholm ("Stocon III")
1962 September, Stockholm [no further information]

CONVENTIONS (U.S.A.) Besides the World SF Convention (which is not always held in the U.S.A.), there are a number of annual regional conventions, among the oldest of which are Midwestcon (in Cincinnati) and Westercon (West Coast). While the Fan-Vets group was in operation it held its own conventions.

The Westercon began in 1948. It is held at centres on the U.S. West

Coast, with Los Angeles the most frequent host and running the event when no other group bids for it. From 1951 it has had a noted personality as Guest of Honour. The 7th Westercon, in San Francisco in 1954, was combined with the 12th World Convention, and the 11th, in Los Angeles in 1958, was combined with the 16th Worldcon.

CONVENTIONS (WORLD) The forerunner of these was the first inter-city fan meeting at Philadelphia in 1936. The "catchnames" are not now used as much as formerly. The sponsoring body is usually the local science fiction society at the place where the particular convention is held. All are called "World Science Fiction Convention," but there is no formal continuing organisation (though there have been several attempts to establish one, with indifferent success). The members of each Worldcon vote to choose the site of the next one (more recently, 2 years in advance). A rotation plan is generally followed, placing the Worldcon in the Western U.S. or Canada, then the Midwest, then the East, except when it goes outside the U.S. or Canada. The first and the third through sixth Worldcons were held on the Fourth of July weekend; all others through 1968 have been on the Labor Day weekend (usually the first weekend in September). The Hugo Awards (see separate listing) were initiated at the 1953 convention, omitted in 1954, and given each year since.

		Chairman	Guest of Honour
1.	1939 New York ("Nycon")	S. Moskowitz	F. R. Paul
2.	1940 Chicago ("Chicon")	M. Reinsberg	E. E. Smith
3.	1941 Denver ("Denvention")	O. F. Wiggins	R. A. Heinlein
4.	1946 Los Angeles ("Pacificon")	W. J. Daugherty	A. E. van Vogt & E. M. Hull
5.	1947 Philadelphia ("Philcon")	M. A. Rothman	J. W. Campbell Jr.
6.	1948 Toronto ("Torcon")	N. McKeown	R. Bloch
7.	1949 Cincinnati ("Cinvention")	D. E. Ford	L. A. Eshbach
8.	1950 Portland, Oregon ("Norwescon")	D. B. Day	A. Boucher
9.	1951 New Orleans ("Nolacon")	H. B. Moore	F. Leiber
10.	1952 Chicago ("Chicon II")	Julian May	H. Gernsback
11.	1953 Philadelphia ("Philcon II")	M. A. Rothman	W. Ley
12.	1954 San Francisco ("SFCon")	Les & Es Cole	J. W. Campbell Jr.
13.	1955 Cleveland ("Clevention")	Nick & Noreen Falasca	I. Asimov
14.	1956 New York ("Nycon II")	D. Kyle	A. C. Clarke
15.	1957 London ("Loncon")	E. J. Carnell	J. W. Campbell Jr.
16.	1958 Los Angeles ("Solacon")	A. S. Moffatt	R. Matheson
17.	1959 Detroit ("Detention")	R. Sims & F. Prophet	P. Anderson
18.	1960 Pittsburgh ("Pittcon")	D. S. Archer	J. Blish
19.	1961 Seattle ("Seacon")	W. Weber	R. A. Heinlein
20.	1962 Chicago ("Chicon III")	E. Kemp	T. Sturgeon

[*Proceedings* edited by E. Kemp, published by Advent.]

21.	1963 Washington ("Discon")	G. H. Scithers	W. F. Jenkins

[*Proceedings* edited by R. Eney, published by Advent.]

22.	1964 Oakland, California ("Pacificon II")	A. Halevy & J. B. Stark	E. Hamilton & L. Brackett
23.	1965 London ("Loncon II")	E. Parker	B. W. Aldiss
24.	1966 Cleveland ("Tricon")	B. Jason	L. S. de Camp
25.	1967 New York ("Nycon 3")	T. White & D. Van Arnam	L. del Rey
26.	1968 Berkeley, Cal. ("Baycon")	B. Donaho, J. B. Stark, A. Rogers	P. J. Farmer

CORGI BOOKS British paperbacks published by Transworld Publishers, a subsidiary of Bantam Books, New York.

The first work was *Donovan's Brain*, C. Siodmak, in 1952, a facsimile reprint of the Bantam edition. Thereafter the editorship was taken over by Michael Legat. The art director was John Richards, who did the majority of the covers to the end of 1962. There are over 100 titles of direct interest (see the publisher's entry in the *PAPERBACKS* section).

COSMIC LIBRARY U.S. amateur publications from J. Taurasi and

Associates (offshoot of *Science-Fiction Times*): No. 1, "The Magician of Space," J. Taurasi (1944, 6 pp.); No. 2, "Science Fiction Market Survey 1956," S. Moskowitz (1960); No. 3, the photo-offset issue of *Science-Fiction Times* in 1958.

"COSMOS" The famous "round robin" serial which appeared in the amateur magazine *Science Fiction Digest* (later *Fantasy Magazine*) for 17 installments, each by a different and noted science fiction writer.

It began in July 1933, with each chapter printed on smaller pages in a partly bound-in supplement with its own pagination. The authors were: R. M. Farley, D. H. Keller, A. J. Burks, B. Olsen, F. Flagg, J. W. Campbell Jr., Rae Winters [R. A. Palmer], O. A. Kline, E. H. Price, A. J. Gelula, A. Merritt, J. H. Haggard, E. E. Smith, P. S. Miller, L. A. Eshbach, E. Binder, and E. Hamilton.

CREATURE FROM THE BLACK LAGOON, THE U.S. film, Universal, 1954; starring Richard Carlson, Julia Adams, and Ben Chapman; screenplay by Harry Essex.

A devil fish-man menaces an expedition. The story was later novelized as a British paperback by Vargo Statten [J. R. Fearn].

Film sequels were *Revenge of the Creature* (1955), with John Agar, and *The Creature Walks Among Us* (Universal, 1956), starring Jeff Morrow, Rex Reason, and Leigh Snowden.

CTHULHU MYTHOS A setting developed by H. P. Lovecraft centering around the exile to Earth of the Great Old Ones who had rebelled against the Elder Gods. The (fictitious) *Necronomicon* of Abdul Alhazred, the mad Arab, is supposedly the source of much of this knowledge. A number of other writers at times based stories on this theme, including A. Derleth with a series. See R. Eney's *Fancyclopedia* (1959).

CYBERNETICS AND MECHANICAL BRAINS For nonfiction aspects, check authors W. R. Ashby, W. G. Walter, and N. Wiener. The theme is often used in fiction; a recent novel was *The Cybernetic Brains*, R. F. Jones.

CZECHOSLOVAKIA Authors covered in the *WHO'S WHO* are K. Capek and J. Nesvadba.

D

DAWN PRESS U.S. amateur publishing house operated by Fran and Ken Krueger. In 1958 they published the lost classic *The Moon Maker*, A. Train & R. W. Wood.

DAY THE EARTH CAUGHT FIRE, THE British film by J. Arthur Rank (Val Guest Production), released in 1962; starring Janet Munro, Leo McKern, and Edward Judd.

America and Russia simultaneously explode big bombs in the Arctic and Antarctic, and the world's weather begins to change. It is first thought that the Earth's axis has tilted 11° but later found that the planet is out of its orbit and falling into the Sun. Centred around the London *Daily Express*, the film has sparkling dialogue, mounting tension, and first-class camera work and acting.

The screenplay by V. Guest and W. Mankowitz was novelized by Barry Wells (FSB: 903, 1961, pa 2/6; Ballantine: F602, 1962, 154 pp., pa 50¢).

DAY THE EARTH STOOD STILL, THE U.S. film, 20th Century Fox, 1951; directed by Robert Wise; starring Michael Rennie and Patricia Neal.

Based on the novelette "Farewell to the Master," H. Bates (*ASF*, Oct 1940)—an interstellar visitor with a robot tries to bring world peace.

DENMARK Probably the historically most noted fantasy writer for this country before Hans Christian Andersen was L. Holberg (1684—1754), whose *Journey of Niels Klim to the World Underground* is a famous classic. Other writers mentioned in the *WHO'S WHO* are J. Lie and V. Sorenson. A contemporary writer of fantasy interest, not covered, is Niels E. Nielsen.

In the magazine field there was only a short-lived edition of *Astounding Science Fiction* titled *Planet-Magasinet*. Skrifola Publishers, Copenhagen, had several book series that have since ceased: "Fremtidsromanen," "Planetbögerne," and "Lommeromanen" [the last being a general series with some sf].

DESTINATION MOON U.S. film, released in 1950 by Eagle-Lion; produced by George Pal, directed by Irving Pichel; with John Archer, Warner Anderson, and Tom Powers.

Though very loosely based on *Rocket Ship Galileo*, by R. A. Heinlein, who also advised on the film, the plot is not strong. C. Bonestell was the technical adviser and painted the lunar landscapes. (Written up by W. Ley, *ASF*, July 1950.)

DIANETICS The alleged science elaborated by L. Ron Hubbard for healing and improving the human mind. Hubbard revealed it in a long article in *Astounding Science Fiction* (May 1950), simultaneously with the publication of his book *Dianetics* (Hermitage, New York, 1950, xxvii+452 pp., $4.00; McLeod, Toronto, $5.25; Derricke Ridgway, London, 1951, 30/-), which gives the working technique of dianetic therapy. Hubbard has written many later works on the subject. A foundation was soon formed, which Hubbard left and later returned to. He later coined the term "scientology" as a continuation and successor to dianetics, and scientology groups have now spread world-wide. A. E. van Vogt has been connected with the Los Angeles section. The pros and cons of the early days of this "science" are covered by J. A. Winter in his book *A Doctor's Report on Dianetics* (Julian, New York, 1951, 220 pp. + appendix, $3.50). Scientology has been converted into a church, and has practically gone underground in some parts of the world. Hubbard has allegedly become a very rich man.

DR. CYCLOPS U.S. film, Paramount, 1939; starring Albert Dekker and Janice Logan.

The story of a "mad scientist" making people into midgets, and their fight against him. It was written as a novelette by H. Kuttner for *Thrilling Wonder Stories*, June 1940; the book version appeared under the pseudonym of Will Garth.

DR. WHO The British TV series which started around 1964, about an eccentric scientist-adventurer who travels through time and space with a girl companion. There have been four different actors starring as the Doctor. The serials had episodes of about 25 minutes, and varied in number of installments. Most of the William Hartnell stories had a different name for each episode and no collective title. The following listing is by courtesy of the Australasian Dr. Who Fan Club, *Zerinza-2*, edited by A. Howe.

Stories with **William Hartnell** as Dr. Who:

(Unearthly Child): 1. Unearthly Child; 2. The Cave of Skulls; 3. The Forest of Fear; 4. The Firemaker. Story had no collective name. Four episodes by Anthony Coburn, an Australian. Susan is taken home by Ian and Barbara; Ian operates the Tardis (a machine).

(The Dead Planet): 1. The Dead Planet; 2. The Survivors; 3. The Escape; 4. The Ambush; 5. The Expedition; 6. The Ordeal; 7. The Rescue. Story had no collective name. Working title was "The Mutants"; story by Terry Nation. Amicus Productions made this into the film *Dr. Who and the Daleks*; the novel of the same title was by David Whitaker.

(The Edge of Destruction): 1. The Edge of Destruction; 2. The Brink of Disaster. No collective title; by David Whitaker. The Tardis passes through a new galaxy during its formation.

Marco Polo: 1. The Roof of the World; 2. The Singing Sands; 3. Five Hundred Eyes; 4. The Wall of Lies; 5. Rider From Shanghai; 6. Mighty Kublai Khan; 7. Assassin at Peking. Title used by the *Dr. Who Special* and which is incorrect. By John Lucarotti.

The Keys of Marinus: 1. The Sea of Death; 2. The Silver Web; 3. The Screaming Jungle; 4. The Snows of Terror; 5. Sentence of Death; 6. The Keys of Marinus. Story by Terry Nation.

The Aztecs: 1. The Temple of Evil; 2. The Warriors of Death; 3. The Bridge of Sacrifice; 4. The Day of Darkness. Story by John Lucarotti.

The Sensorites: 1. Strangers in Space; 2. The Unwilling Warriors; 3. Hidden Danger; 4. A Race Against Death; 5. Kidnap; 6. A Desperate Venture. Story by Peter Newman

The French Revolution: 1. A Land of Fear; 2. Guests of Mme. Guillotine; 3. A Change of Identity; 4. The Tyrant of France; 5. A Bargain of Necessity; 6. Prisoners of the Conciergerie. Story by Dennis Spooner. Has been incorrectly titled *Reign of Terror*.

Planet of Giants: 1. Planet of Giants; 2. Dangerous Journey; 3. Crisis. Story by Louis Marks.

The Dalek Invasion of Earth: 1. World's End; 2. The Daleks; 3. Day of Reckoning; 4. The End of Tomorrow; 5. The Waking Ally; 6. Flashpoint. Story by Terry Nation. Susan leaves the series after this group. Amicus Productions made this as *Daleks—Invasion Earth, 2150 A.D.*

The Rescue: 1. The Powerful Enemy; 2. Desperate Measures. Story by David Whitaker. Vikki begins travelling with the Doctor.

The Slave Traders: 1. The Slave Traders; 2. All Roads Lead to Rome; 3. Conspiracy; 4. Inferno. Story by D. Spooner.

The Web Planet: 1. The Web Planet; 2. The Zarbi; 3. Escape to Danger; 4. Crater of Needles; 5. Invasion; 6. The Centre. TV and book, *The Zarbi*, by Bill Strutton.

The Lionheart: 1. The Lion; 2. The Knight of Jaffa; 3. Wheel of Fortune; 4. The Warlords. Book title *The Crusaders*; TV and book by David Whitaker.

The Space Museum: 1. The Space Museum; 2. The Dimensions of Time; 3. The Search; 4. The Final Phase. Story by Glyn Jones.

The Chase: 1. The Executioners; 2. The Death of Time; 3. Flight Through Eternity; 4. Journey Into Terror; 5. The Death of Dr. Who; 6. Planet of Decision. Story by Terry Nation. The third Dalek story, in which they discover how to move in time. Ian and Barbara leave after this series, with Steven Taylor beginning. Final episode was made into a record.

The Time Meddler: 1. The Watcher; 2. The Meddling Monk; 3. A Battle of Wits; 4. Checkmate. Story by Dennis Spooner. Another time traveller like the Doctor tries to change history. A Time Lord???

Galaxy Four: 1. 400 Dawns; 2. Trap of Steel; 3. Airlock; 4. The Exploding Planet. Story by William Emms.

(No title): 1. Mission to the Unknown. Story by Terry Nation. Single episode build-up to *The Dalek Master-Plan*. Dr. Who is not in it.

The Mythmakers: 1. Temple of Secrets; 2. Small Prophet, Quick Return; 3. Death of a Spy; 4. Horse of Destruction. Story by Donald Cotton. Steven is wounded at the end, Vikki stays in Troy, a Trojan helps Steven into the Tardis and stays with the Doctor.

The Dalek Master-Plan: 1. The Nightmare Begins; 2. Day of Armageddon; 3. Devil's Planet; 4. The Traitors; 5. Counter-Plot; 6. Coronas of the Sun; 7. The Feast of Steven; 8. Volcano; 9. Golden Death; 10. Escape Switch; 11. Abandoned Planet; 12. Destruction of Time. Fourth Dalek story; by Terry Nation and Dennis Spooner. (Classed as "horror" by the censors in Australia!) In episode 4, Katarina is killed and replaced by Space Agent Sara Kingdom, who is killed in 12 when the Time Destructor is operated. Episode 7 was a special Christmas programme without Daleks.

The Massacre: 1. War of God; 2. The Sea Beggar; 3. Priest of Death; 4. Bell of Doom. Story by John Lucarotti. At the end of episode 4, Dodo enters the Tardis to call police, and is taken into the future.

The Ark: 1. The Steel Sky; 2. The Plague; 3. The Return; 4. The Bomb. Story by Paul Erickson & Lesley Scott.

The Celestial Toymaker: 1. The Celestial Toyroom; 2. The Hall of Dolls; 3. The Dancing Floor; 4. The Final Test. Story by Brian Hayles.

The Gunfighters: 1. A Holiday for the Doctor; 2. Don't Shoot the Pianist; 3. Johnny Ringo; 4. O.K. Corral. Story by Donald Cotton.

[From here on the stories have only one overall title.]

The Savages (4 episodes), by Ian Stuart Black. At the end of episode 4, Steven leaves the Doctor.

The War Machines (4 episodes), by Ian S. Black. Polly and Ben enter the story in episode 1, Dodo is not seen after 3 and officially leaves in 4, with Polly and Ben taking her place.

The Smugglers (4 episodes), by Brian Hayles.

The Tenth Planet (4 episodes), by Kit Pedler & Gerry Davis. Book of same title by G. Davis. The first Cyberman story. Doctor Who, worn out, collapses in the Tardis, and his appearance changes.

Stories with **Patrick Troughton** as Dr. Who:

The Power of the Daleks (6 episodes), by David Whitaker. The fifth Dalek story.

The Highlanders (4 episodes), by Elwyn Jones & Gerry Davis. The Doctor meets Jamie in episode 1, and after adventures Jamie stays.

The Underwater Menace (4 episodes), by Geoffrey Orme.

The Moonbase (4 episodes), by Kit Pedler. Novel *The Cybermen*, Gerry Davis. The second Cyberman story.

The Macra Terror (4 episodes), by Ian Stuart Black.

The Faceless Ones (6 episodes), by David Elis & Malcolm Hulke. At the end Polly and Ben leave the Doctor and the Tardis is stolen.

The Evil of the Daleks (7 episodes), by D. Whitaker. The sixth Dalek story. Victoria escapes from Skaro with the Doctor.

The Tomb of the Cybermen (episodes), by Kit Pedler & Gerry Davis. The third Cyberman story.

The Abominable Snowmen (6 episodes), by Mervyn Haisman & Henry Lincoln. Book of same title by T. Dicks. The first Great Intelligence story.

The Ice Warriors (6 episodes); TV and book of same title by B. Hayles. First Ice Warrior story.

The Enemy of the World (6 episodes), by David Whitaker.

The Web of Fear (6 episodes), by M. Haisman & H. Lincoln. Book of same title by T. Dicks. The second Great Intelligence story.

Fury From the Deep (6 episodes), by Victor Pemberton. At the end Victoria decides to stay on Earth.

The Wheel in Space (6 episodes), by D. Whitaker. In the last episode Zoe begins travels with the Doctor and Jamie.

The Dominators (5 episodes), by Norman Ashby.

The Mind Robber (5 episodes), by Peter Ling.

The Invasion (8 episodes), by Derrick Sherwin. The fifth Cyberman story. U.N.I.T. helps the Doctor for the first time.

The Krotons (4 episodes), by Robert Holmes.

The Seeds of Death (6 episodes), by Brian Hayles. The second Ice Warrior story.

The Space Pirates (6 episodes), by R. Holmes.

The War Games (10 episodes), by Terrance Dicks & Malcolm Hulke. A renegade Time Lord appears; he and the Doctor are captured by the Time Lords. Jamie and Zoe are returned to their correct times at the end. The Time Lords then exile the Doctor to Earth and change his appearance.

Stories with **Jon Pertwee** as Dr. Who:

Spearhead From Space (4 episodes), by R. Holmes; book *The Auton Invasion*, Terrance Dicks. The first Auton story. Liz Shaw becomes the Doctor's assistant.

Doctor Who and the Silurians (7 episodes); TV and book, *The Cave Monsters*, by M. Hulke.

The Ambassadors of Death (7 episodes), by D. Whitaker.

Inferno (7 episodes), by Don Houghton.

The Terror of the Autons (4 episodes), by R. Holmes. Book of same title by T. Dicks. The first Master story and second Auton story. Jo Grant replaces Liz Shaw in the first episode.

The Mind of Evil (6 episodes), by D. Houghton. The second Master story.

The Claws of Axos (4 episodes), by Dave Martin & Bob Baker. The third Master story.

Colony in Space (5 episodes), by Guy Leopold; book of same title by M. Hulke. The fourth Master story.

The Daemons (5 episodes), by Guy Leopold; book of same title by Barry Letts. The fifth Master story.

The Day of the Daleks (4 episodes), by Louis Marks; book of same title by T. Dicks. The seventh Dalek story.

The Curse of Peladon (4 episodes); TV and book of same title by B. Hayles. The first Peladon story and third Ice Warrior story.

The Sea Devils (6 episodes); TV and book of same title by M. Hulke. The sixth Master story.

The Mutants (6 episodes), by D. Martin & B. Baker.

The Time Monster (6 episodes), by Robert Sloman. The seventh Master story.

The Three Doctors (4 episodes), by D. Martin & B. Baker; book of same title by T. Dicks.

The Carnival of Monsters (4 episodes), by R. Holmes.

Frontier in Space (6 episodes); TV and book, *The Space War*, by M. Hulke. The eighth Master story.

Planet of the Daleks (6 episodes), by Terry Nation; book of same title by T. Dicks. The eighth Dalek story.

The Green Death (6 episodes), by R. Sloman; book of same title by M. Hulke. Jo gets married and goes to the Amazon in the last episode.

The Time Warrior (4 episodes), by R. Holmes. Sarah Jane Smith, a journalist, becomes the Doctor's new assistant.

Invasion of the Dinosaurs (6 episodes); TV and book of same title by M. Hulke.

Death to the Daleks (4 episodes), by T. Nation. Ninth Dalek story.

The Monster of Peladon (6 episodes), by Brian Hayles. The fourth Ice Warrior story and second Peladon story.

The Planet of the Spiders (6 episodes), by Robert Sloman; book of same title by T. Dicks. Over-exposed to radiation, the Doctor collapses; his body rejuvenates, changing his appearance again. The series continues with **Tom Baker** as Doctor Who.

DOUBLEDAY SCIENCE FICTION BOOK CLUB See SCIENCE FICTION BOOK CLUB [D'day SF B.C.]

E

EARTH

The Future: Trends in population, inventions, etc. (but not covering the recent spate of books on overpopulation and the resulting ills): *It's Bound To Happen*, A. M. Low (1950); *The Next Million Years*, C. G. Darwin (1952); *The Robots Are Among Us*, R. Strehl (1952); *The Challenge of Man's Future*, H. S. Brown (1954); *Utopia 1976*, M. Ernst (1955); *The Foreseeable Future*, G. P. Thomson (1955); *1999: Our Hopeful Future*, V. Cohn (1956); *The Fabulous Future*, Fortune (magazine) (1956); *The Next Hundred Years*, H. S. Brown (1957); *You and the World to Come*, M. Droke (1959); *The Future of Man*, P. Medawar (1960); *Can Man Be Modified?*, J. Rostand (1960); *Life in the 21st Century*, M. Vassiliev & S. Gouschev (1960); *The Prospect of Immortality*, R.C.W. Ettinger (1964); *The Cold War in Biology*, C. C. Lindegren (1966); *Famine 1975!*, W. & P. Paddock (1966); *Crisis in Abundance*, D. Stenhouse (1966); *The Dynamics of Change*, D. Fabun (1967); *Yesterday's Tomorrows*, W. H. Armytage (1968); *The Year 2000*, H. Kahn & A. J. Weiner (1968).

Earth's End: *The End of the World* [fiction], G. Dennis (1930); *Creation's Doom*, D. Papp (1932); *The End of the World*, K. Heuer (1953).

The Past: *Mankind So Far*, W. Howells (1944); *The Strange Story of Our Earth*, A. H. Verrill (1952); *Evolution in Action*, J. Huxley (1953); *The Story of Man*, C. S. Coon (1954); *Back of History*, W. Howells (1954); *Man's Emerging Mind*, N. J. Berrill (1954); *A Million Years of Progress*, I. D. Cardiff (1954); *The Living Past*, I. Lissner (1957); *Brave New World Revisited*, A. Huxley (1958); *The Firmament of Time*, L. Eiseley (1960); *African Genesis*, R. Ardrey (1961).

As Seen by Other Eyes: *View From Orbit Two*, A. Avenel (1957); *Is There Intelligent Life on Earth?*, A. Dunn (1960); *Take Me to Your Leader*, L. Waller (1961); *View From a Distant Star*, H. Shapley (1963).

Mysteries (see also SUPERNATURAL; C. Fort): *The Last Secrets of the Earth*, B. Busson (1955); *The Inexplicable Sky*, A. Constance (1956); *The Hollow Earth*, R. Bernard (1964).

Legends (the truth behind): *Myth or Legend?*, G. E. Daniel (1955).

EASTERN SCIENCE FICTION ASSOCIATION [ESFA] Founded by S. Moskowitz and some other enthusiasts in 1946 to organise fandom in the New York City area. Members have included J. V. Taurasi, Belle

Dietz (the first woman president of the club), and the late T. S. Gardner. In many years it has run an annual open meeting with noted speakers. The Tenth Anniversary was celebrated on 4 March 1956. The group also sponsored the 14th World Science Fiction Convention in 1956.

END OF THE WORLD U.S. film, American-International, 1962; starring Ray Milland, with Jean Hagen and Frankie Avalon; screenplay by John Morton & Jay Simms.

Survival after an atomic war. The story was novelized by D. Owen as an Ace paperback.

ESP See EXTRASENSORY PERCEPTION

ESPACIO Spanish paperback book series; 25 titles published 1962-1963 by Editorial Toray at 15 pesetas (about 25¢)—cheaper than most others and of lower quality. The first was a translation of *Conditioned for Space*, A. Ash. The titles of British origin were mainly translations from the "Badger SF" series; one other was R. Winterbotham's *The Red Planet*. There were several translations from French as well as some works by Spanish authors. The companion "Espacio Extra" series published material by Spanish pulp writers.

ETHERLINE Australian amateur magazine with 101 issues (Mar 1953—Sep 1958), edited by I. J. Crozier for Amateur Fantasy Publications of Australia and published in Melbourne. It was duplicated foolscap folded in half and centre stapled. Quite regular for most of its life, it appeared every two or three weeks until the last issues.

It presented book reviews, various articles, book news, Australian fan news, etc., and a continuous bibliographic series of authors' story listings. Special issues were published in the same format to cover conventions.

A second series was begun by another fan in the late 1960's, but ceased after about three issues.

EXTRASENSORY PERCEPTION (ESP) **& PSYCHIC PHENOMENA**

See authors M. Bernstein, H. Carrington, E. J. Dingwall, E. J. Garrett, R. Heywood, R. Lindner, A. Pukarich, J. B. Rhine, and S. G. Soal.

A London symposium was *ESP—Extrasensory Perception*, Ciba Foundation (Little Brown, Boston, 1956, 240+ix pp., $6.00). Others include *ESP and Personality Patterns*, G. R. Schmeidler & R. A. McConnell (Yale Univ., 1958, 136 pp., $4.00)—data-packed progress report full of statistics and proving little; *Parapsychology: An Insider's View of ESP*, J. Gaither Pratt (Doubleday, New York, 1964, 300 pp., $4.95)—professor at Duke Univ., more anecdotal than J. B. Rhine but covering same type of ground; *Parapsychology: Frontier Science of the Mind*, J. B. Rhine, J. G. Pratt, & C. C. Thomas (published in Springfield [Illinois], mid-1960's) is a sort of textbook on the subject.

EXTRA-TERRESTRIAL LIFE There was a series of 14 short articles by Ben Bova in *Amazing Stories* from June 1962. F. R. Paul had a series of back cover paintings of "Life on Other Worlds" in *Fantastic Adventures* May 1939—May 1940.

Books covered in the *Encyclopedia* are: *Life on Other Worlds*, H. S. Jones (1940); *Men of Other Planets*, K. Heuer (1951); *There Is Life on Mars*, A.F.J.H. Nelson (1955); *Of Stars and Men*, H. Shapley (1958); *Is There Life on Other Worlds?*, P. Anderson (1963); *We Are Not Alone*, W. Sullivan (1964); *Habitable Planets for Man*, S. H. Dole (1964); *The Quest—A Report on Extraterrestrial Life*, T. B. Allen (1965); *Other Worlds Than Ours*, C. M. Cade (1966); *Intelligent Life in the Universe*, I. S. Shklovskii & C. Sagan (1966).

F

FABER British publisher, London. Faber has published a number of the better quality sf titles and also many anthologies, such as the *Best SF*

series by Edmund Crispin [R. B. Montgomery]. Some titles have softcover editions.

FAN MAGAZINES See AMATEUR MAGAZINES

FANDOM HOUSE The name used by J. V. Taurasi and partners for publishing *Fantasy Times* (later *Science-Fiction Times*) and other amateur publications from Fall 1948 to Jan 1958. Random House Inc. became unhappy with this name, and so it became Science-Fiction Times Inc. from 10 March 1958.

FANSCIENT, THE U.S. amateur magazine, 13 issues Fall 1947 to Spr/Sum 1951. It was edited by the late D. B. Day first for the Portland [Oregon] Science-Fantasy Society, and without this sponsorship from No. 10. It began duplicated and lithographed at 5⅛ x 8 in., then completely litho in "vest pocket" size (4¼ x 5¼ in.), mainly 32 pp. except Nos. 9 and 13/14 at 64 pp.

The magazine featured fiction and articles of high standard by such collectors as Thyril Ladd, S. Moskowitz, and D. C. Richardson. Each issue also ran an "Author, Author" section in which a noted author wrote an autobiographical sketch, to which his bibliography was added: No. 1 (unknown); 2, E. Hamilton; 3, E. E. Smith; 4, J. Williamson; 5, D. H. Keller; 6, R. Bradbury; 7, M. Leinster; 8, R. Bloch; 9, R. A. Heinlein; 10, G. O. Smith; 11, T. Sturgeon; 12, A. Boucher; 13/14, L. S. de Camp.

FANTACIENCIA Argentine paperback book series published by Jacobo Muchnik. It presented six issues in 1956 and six in 1957, mostly Spanish translations of high-quality U.S. science fiction. Authors included C. M. Kornbluth, W. Tucker, J. Sohl, H. Clement, C. Oliver, J. Mantley, J. Williamson, and A. Norton.

FANTASCIENZA, gli esploratori dello spazio. Italian paperback book series, published every two months by Editrice Romana Periodici at 200 lire. There were 11 titles Dec 1961—Feb 1963, with translations of medium-quality U.S. science fiction.

FANTASTIC VOYAGE U.S. film, 1966, 20th Century Fox, directed by Richard Fleischer; screenplay by Harry Kleiner based on a story by Otto Klement and Jerome Bixby; featuring Stephen Boyd, Arthur Kennedy, Donald Pleasance, William Redfield, and Raquel Welch.

The noted journey into a human body by miniaturisation. It was novelized by I. Asimov for *The Saturday Evening Post* (sr2, 20 Feb 1966), and then enlarged and published as a book in several editions. It also appeared as a single comic book.

FANTASTIC WORLDS U.S. amateur magazine; 8 issues, Summer 1952—Fall 1954. First edited by E. W. Ludwig, then by S. Sackett; photolith, quarterly, 30¢, 40 pp.

This magazine printed high-class fiction by such authors as D. H. Keller and A. B. Chandler, as well as nonfiction such as "The Arkham House Story," A. Derleth (first issue) and "Fielding, Writer of Fantasy," S. Sackett (Fall 1954). It also gave comprehensive book reviews.

FANTASY AMATEUR PRESS ASSOCIATION [FAPA] The oldest of the amateur press associations, operating since 1937. This type of organization has its members send their amateur publications to an Official Editor who then redistributes them to members in identical bundles, so that each member gets the publications of all the other members. A member must produce a publication at least once a year, or have material printed in two different magazines in two different cities. FAPA always has a waiting list of prospective members.

FANTASY CALENDARS Although information on this specialised medium is sketchy, the following are known:

Gnome Press has produced: 1949—12 months, with 6 by H. Bok, 5 by E. Cartier, and 1 by F. R. Paul; 1950, 5 by Bok, 5 by Cartier, 2 by Paul; 1951, not known; 1952, four quarters (Winter, Spring, Summer, Autumn), all by Cartier.

A set for 1960 is known, with 6 drawings by G. Baer; this was probably English.

FANTASY COMMENTATOR U.S. amateur magazine, 26 issues, Dec 1943—Spr/Sum 1952. Edited by A. Langley Searles; duplicated, quarto, approximately quarterly.

One of the finest magazines of its type ever produced, this presented comprehensive book review, articles on such writers as W. H. Hodgson, H. P. Lovecraft, J. Taine, and D. H. Keller, and also listings of fantasy in the older general magazines. It serialised *The Immortal Storm*, S. Moskowitz's fan history.

FANTASY FAN, THE U.S. amateur magazine, one of the earliest; 18 issues, Sep 1933—Feb 1935. It was started by C. D. Hornig as a general magazine on sf, etc., but later championed the special cause of weird fiction. Contributors included such professionals as H. P. Lovecraft (with the first appearance of his essay *Supernatural Horror in Literature*), C. A. Smith, R. E. Howard, and A. Derleth. It was printed by C. H. Ruppert.

It is understood that H. Gernsback appointed Hornig as managing editor of *Wonder Stories* in 1934 because of his outstanding editorship of *The Fantasy Fan*.

FANTASY MAGAZINE U.S. amateur magazine, formerly *Science Fiction Digest*; it incorporated Allen Glasser's *The Time Traveller* in October 1932. Edited by M. Weisinger, it gave reviews, news on films, science fiction celebrities, etc., and ran a collector's department. It was printed by C. H. Ruppert to Sep 1935 and then by W. H. Crawford, and terminated with the 39th issue (Jan 1937).

The leading amateur magazine of the mid-1930's, this published some fiction by prominent authors, the most notable of which were the serials "Cosmos" [see separate entry] and "Alice in Blunderland," P. S. Miller's devastating satire originally under the pseudonym "Nihil."

It was supposedly continued as *Science-Fantasy Correspondent* (3 issues, Nov/Dec 1936—Mar/Apr 1937) and then as *Amateur Corrrespondent* (3 issues to Nov/Dec 1937).

FANTASY PRESS U.S. specialist science fiction publishing house, Reading, Pennsylvania, one of the first such presses to be formed. It was founded in 1946 by L. A. Eshbach, with partners A. J. Donnell as commercial artist, G. H. MacGregor as sales manager, and L. H. Houck as accountant.

The first Fantasy Press book was *Spacehounds of IPC*, E. E. Smith (1946). Later titles included all of Smith's "Lensman" series and many others.

In 1950 Eshbach bought out his partners and ran the company alone; he later established the companion imprint "Polaris Press." Its publishing output slowed in the mid-1950's, and it had virtually ceased operations before being bought out by M. Greenberg around 1959. Greenberg acquired the book stock, both bound and unbound (later cheaply bound), and all became available in his "Pick-A-Book" scheme in conjunction with Gnome Press.

FANTASY PUBLISHING COMPANY INC. The first specialist publisher in the science fiction and fantasy fields; operated by W. L. Crawford in Los Angeles. In the early 1930's it published the fantasy magazines *Marvel Tales* and *Unusual Stories*. After some pamphlets, Crawford then published *Mars Mountain*, by E. G. Key, a collection of three stories, bound in boards and with a dust-jacket; it cost 35¢ but sold poorly. Then followed the clothbound *Shadow Over Innsmouth*, H. P. Lovecraft. Crawford's editions usually were 400 copies for books and 1,000 copies for magazines. Several other fantasy titles were announced, but due to the discouraging reception of previous titles, were not printed.

After World War II Crawford returned to the field as Fantasy Publishing Co. Inc. [FPCI], Los Angeles. Titles by J. Taine [E. T. Bell], O. Stapledon, R. M. Farley [R. S. Hoar], A. Hall, A. E. van Vogt, S. A. Coblentz, L. R. Hubbard, E. E. Repp and others were published, as well as the magazines *Fantasy Book* and *Spaceways (Science Fiction)*.

Around 1959 some titles were bought by M. Greenberg, and these FPCI books, often rebound, became part of the Pick-A-Book scheme associated with Gnome Press. Since 1969 a number have been rebound and reissued as paper-covered books.

FANTASY-TIMES See *SCIENCE-FICTION TIMES*

FANTASY VETERANS ASSOCIATION [Fan-Vets] An American organization formed by J. V. Taurasi and R. Van Houten after the start of the Korean campaign. Composed of science fiction fans who had been (or still were) servicemen, it acted as an agency for sending sf to fans and readers in uniform overseas. For a time it held an annual convention, the first being 22 April 1951. Taurasi published its amateur magazines *Fan-Vet*. The association disappeared in the mid-1950's.

FICTITIOUS BOOKS A number of fantasy authors have at times invented books which they then used as reference sources within their own writings. The better-known ones are: *The Necronomicon*, H. P. Lovecraft (basis for the Cthulhu Mythos); *The Book of Eibon*, C. A. Smith; *Unaussprechlichen Kulten*, R. E. Howard. R. Bloch was the inventor of titles by "Ludwig Prinn," *De Vernis Mysteriis* and *Cultes des Goules*. [Adapted from *Astonishing Stories*, Dec 1942.]

FILMS The *Encyclopedia* briefly covers only films which are pertinent to a particular author's works [described in the author's *WHO'S WHO* entry] or which are particularly noteworthy in their own right [covered by title in this section of the *Encyclopedia*]. The poor science fiction films and general run-of-the-mill "horror" films are not covered.

Reference works include: *Science-Fiction and Fantasy Film Checklist*, W. Lee (Summer 1958); *Film Index*, published by A. Dodd & R. Ringdall (1960); *Monsters, Maidens and Mayhem*, B. Steiger (1965, pa); *Fantasy Films and Their Fiends*, J. Jones (1964); *Horror!*, D. Drake (1966); *An Illustrated History of the Horror Film*, C. Clarens (1967). The first two are amateur publications generally unobtainable today. The others are all of interest, with the last-named the most important. [Since the period under review, J. Baxter of Sydney has come to the fore as a film authority, and W. Lee has issued a major work, *Reference Guide to Fantastic Films* (3 vols., 1972-1974)].

Film producers of interest include H. Koch, G. Melies (French), N. Nayfack, A. Oboler, and G. Pal. F. J Ackerman has edited several of movie magazines for a number of years; the most important are *Famous Monsters of Filmland* for horror and weird films, and *Spacemen* (ceased) for science fiction—both have featured stills from the films discussed. There have also been several other monster film magazines (see MONSTER MAGAZINES in the *MAGAZINES* section).

Titles Covered (those in this *GENERAL* section are marked *; for others check the author in the *WHO'S WHO*):

Alice in Wonderland (L. Carroll); *Animal Farm* (E. Blair); *Around the World in Eighty Days* (J. Verne); *Atlantis* (see G. Pal).

Barbarella (J. C. Forest); *Batman**; *The Beast From 20,000 Fathoms**; *The Beast With Five Fingers* (W. F. Harvey); *Bell, Book and Candle**; *The Black Cat* (E. A. Poe); *The Body Snatcher* (R. L. Stevenson); *(Invasion of) The Body Snatchers* (J. Finney).

The Cabinet of Dr. Caligari*; *The Canterville Ghost* (O. Wilde); *A Connecticut Yankee in King Arthur's Court* (S. L. Clemens); *The Conquest of Space**; *Creature From the Black Lagoon** (and others); *The Creeping Unknown* (see *The Quatermass Experiment*, N. Kneale); *Curse of the Demon* (M. R. James).

The Day the Earth Caught Fire*; *The Day the Earth Stood Still**; *Deluge* (S. F. Wright); *Destination Moon**; *The Devil Commands* (see *Edge of Running Water*, W. M. Sloane); *The Devil Doll* (see *Burn, Witch, Burn!*, A. Merritt); *Dr. Cyclops**; *Dr. Jekyll and Mr. Hyde* (R. L. Stevenson); *Donovan's Brain* (C. Siodmak); *Dracula* (and others) (B. Stoker); *The Dream Machine* (see *Escapement*, D. McIlwain).

End of the World*; *Enemy From Space* (see *Quatermass II*, N. Kneale).

F.P. 1 Does Not Reply (C. Siodmak); *The Fall of the House of Usher* (E. A. Poe); *Fiend Without a Face* (A. R. Long); *Five**; *The 5,000 Fingers of Dr. T.**; *The Fly* (G. Langelaan); *Forbidden Planet* (W. J. Stuart); *Four-Sided Triangle* (W. F. Temple); *Frankenstein* (and others) (M. W. Shelley); *From the Earth to the Moon* (J. Verne); *Fu Manchu series* (see S. Rohmer).

Gabriel Over the White House (T. F. Tweed); *The Gamma People**; *The Girl in the Moon* (T. Von Harbou); *The Gladiator* (P. Wylie); *Godzilla, King of the Monsters**; *Gog**; *Green Mansions* (W. H. Hudson); *Gulliver's Travels* (J. Swift).

Hands of Orlac (M. Renard).

I Married a Witch (see *The Passionate Witch*, T. Smith); *The Incredible Shrinking Man* (see *The Shrinking Man*, R. Matheson); *The Innocents* (see *The Turn of the Screw*, H. James); *Invasion of the Body Snatchers* (see *The Body Snatchers*, above); *Invasion of the Saucer Men* (see P. W. Fairman); *The Invisible Boy* (see E. Cooper); *The Invisble Man* (H. G. Wells); *The Island of Lost Souls* (see *The Island of Dr. Moreau*, H. G. Wells); *It Came From Outer Space*.

King Kong*; *King Solomon's Mines* (H. R. Haggard).

The Lady and the Monster (see *Donovan's Brain*, C. Siodmak); *Lord of the Flies* (W. Golding); *Lost Horizon* (J. Hilton); *Lost World* (A. C. Doyle).

Mad Love (see *The Hands of Orlac*, M. Renard); *The Magnetic Monster**; *The Man Who Could Work Miracles* (H. G. Wells); *Metropolis* (T. Von Harbou); *Mr. Peabody and the Mermaid* (see *Peabody's Mermaid*, G. & C. Jones); *Mothra**; *The Mysterians**; *The Mysterious Dr. Fu Manchu* (see S. Rohmer); *Mysterious Island* (J. Verne).

Naked Jungle*; *No Highway (in the Sky)* (N. S. Norway); *1984* (E. Blair).

On the Beach (N. S. Norway); *One Million B.C.**

Peter Pan (J. M. Barrie); *The Picture of Dorian Grey* (O. Wilde).

The Quatermass Experiment (N. Kneale).

Riders to the Stars (C. Siodmak); *Robinson Crusoe on Mars**; *The Rocket Man**; *Rodan**; *R.U.R.* (K. Capek).

Sadko*; *Sardonicus* (R. Russell); *Seven Faces of Dr. Lao* (see *The Circus of Dr. Lao*, C. G. Finney); *Seven Footprints to Satan* (A. Merritt); *She* (H. R. Haggard); *The She-Devil* (see S. G. Weinbaum); *Siren of Atlantis* (see *L'Atlantide*, P. Benoit); *Stairway to Heaven**.

Target—Earth!*; *The Tenth Victim* (R. Sheckley); *Them**; *The Thing**; *Things to Come* (H. G. Wells); *This Island Earth* (R. F. Jones); *The Three Worlds of Gulliver* (see J. Swift); *Timeslip* (see *The Isotope Man*, D. McIlwain); *Topper* (and others) (see T. Smith); *The Twonky* (see H. Kuttner); *Transatlantic Tunnel**; *2001: A Space Odyssey* (A. C. Clarke); *Turnabout* (T. Smith); *20,000 Leagues Under the Sea* (J. Verne).

The Undying Monster (J. D. Kerruish); *The Unholy Three* (C. A. Robbins); *The Uninvited* (D. Macardle).

The Village of the Damned (see *The Midwich Cuckoos*, J. B. Harris); *Voyage to the Bottom of the Sea* (T. Sturgeon).

War of the Worlds (H. G. Wells); *When Worlds Collide* (E. Balmer); *The Wizard of Oz* (L. F. Baum).

X (E. Sudak).

You Know What Sailors Are (see *Sylvester*, E. S. Hyams).

FIRST FANDOM A club restricted to fans active in 1938 or before. Founded in mid-1959 by Bob Madle, C. L. Barrett, Don Ford, Lou Tabakow, and Dale and Lynn Hickman, it is still active.

FIVE U.S. film, Columbia, 1951, directed by Arch Oboler.

This was one of the first films about the last small group of people on Earth. It was well acted by a comparatively unknown cast.

5,000 FINGERS OF DR. T., THE U.S. film, Columbia, 1953, directed by Sterling Kramer; with Peter Lind Hayes and Mary Healy. Superb Technicolor and choreography; very good orchestration and presentation.

A boy hates his music teacher and dreams up the fantastic world of Dr. Terwhillicher, a villain forcing 500 boys (hence 5,000 fingers) to play on a huge piano. The film pokes fun at numerous musical classics and has a good humorous background.

FLYING SAUCERS See UNIDENTIFIED FLYING OBJECTS

FOLK TALES Books covered in the *Encyclopedia*:
General: *Spoor of Spooks*, B. B. Evans (1954); *Spooks in the Valley*, L. C. Jones (1948); *Things That Go Bump in the Night*, L. C. Jones (1959).
Charleston: *The Doctor to the Dead*, J. Bennett (1946).
Ozarks: See works of V. Randolph.
Truth behind legends: *Myth or Legend*, G. Daniel (1955).
Review: *The American Imagination at Work*, B. C. Clough (1947).

FOURTH DIMENSION A field much used by science fiction writers, especially in the early days of magazine sf. One such early author was B. Olsen, with the "Four Dimensional" series starting in *Amazing Stories*, June 1927. Disagreeing with Olsen's line of attack, M. J. Breuer wrote a series beginning with "The Appendix and the Spectacles," *AS*, Dec

1928. See both series in the *SERIES* section and under each author. Since then many other writers have extrapolated plots about spatial dimensions beyond the three that we know.

FRANCE A historical survey of the whole French field would show many firsts in science fiction concepts and techniques; however, as with old science fiction and utopian literature in English, this is beyond the scope of the *Encyclopedia*.

Encyclopedia Coverage: The more contemporary authors covered in the *WHO'S WHO* are G. Apollinaire, M. Aymé, R. Barjavel, P. Benoit, P. Berna, P. Boulle, Y. Berger, B. R. Bruss, Cyrano de Bergerac, J.-L. Curtis, R. Daumal, G. de Maupassant, C. de Richter, A. Dumas, Erckmann-Chatrian, C. Farrere, T. Gautier, Y. Gandon, J. Guieu, S. S. Held, C. Henneberg, M. Level, F. Marceau, A. Maurois, A. Michel, O. Mirbeau, I. Perret, M.-A. Rayjean, P. Reynolds, F. Richards-Bessiere, J. H. Rosny, J. Rostand, C. Seignolle, J. G. Vandel, H. Ward, S. Wul, and C. Yelnick. Most of these have been translated into English, and are prominent because of their novels. D. Knight, the anthologist, has translated much French fantasy material, primarily for *F&SF*; his selection of works by essentially short-story writers has appeared as *13 French Science-Fiction Stories* (1965, pa). Naturally Jules Verne has a comprehensive entry.

Other personalities covered include J. Bergier, R. Caillois (for an anthology), R. Messac, G. H. Gallet, P. Versins, S. Spriel, and G. Melies.

Magazines have included *Satellite*, now defunct, and *Fiction* and *Galaxie*, both still current. Publishers have been Hachette and Gallimard with "Le Rayon Fantastique" series (now ceased), Le Fleuve Noire with the "Anticipation" series, and Denoël with the "Presence Du Futur" series. Since 1965, Ed. Opta, Paris, has produced "Les Classiques de la Science-Fiction" series in hardcover and the "Galaxie Bis" paperback series.

Jules Verne Prize

First Series (published in *Lectures pour Tous* magazine, then as books):
1927 *La petite-fille de Michel Strogoff*, Octave Beliard [about TV]
1928 *Le secret des sables, roman du Transsaharian*, J. L. Gaston [first railways in the Sahara]
1929 *L'Ether-Alpha*, Albert Bailly [spaceship to the Moon finds radiant inhabitants]
1930 *L'ile au sable vert Tancrède*, Vallerey ['copters and subterranean journey]
1931 *L'étrange menace du professeur Louchkoff*, Herve du Peslouan [giant super-plane]
1932 A western.
1933 *Les vaisseaux en flammes*, Jean-Toussaint Samat [a new apparatus for extinguishing fires in ships] [only in *Lectures pour Tous*, Aug & Sep 1936]
Second Series:
1958 *L'adieu aux astres*, Serge Martel
1959 *Surface de la planète*, Daniel Drode
1960 *La Machine du pouvoir*, Albert Higon
1961 *Le sub-espace*, Jérôme Sériel
1962 *Le ressac de l'espace*, Philippe Curval
No further information.

France is rich in original material not translated into English. Following is a list compiled by the noted French bibliographer P. Versins.

As Introduction:

Martin, Charles-Noël: *Les vingts sens de l'homme devant l'inconnu* (Gallimard "Aux Frontières de la Science," 1958).

Pauwels, Louis, & Bergier, Jacques: *Le matin des magiciens* (Gallimard, 1960) [see author entry for English translation].

Science Fiction—Philosophical (social, religious, historic, etc.):

Arnyvelde, Andre: *L'Arche* (Société Mutuelle d'Edition, Paris, 1920; Club Futopia "Aldébarane No. 2," 1961).

Balzac, Honoré de: *Louis Lambert* (1833; numerous reissues).

Bopp, Léon: *Liaisons du monde* (4 vols. 1938-1944; Gallimard, 2 vols., 1948).

Coeurderoy, Ernest: *Hurrah!!! ou la Révolution par les Cosaques* (Londres, 1854).

Drode, Daniel: *Surface de la planète* (Hachette Le RF, 1959) [Jules Verne Prize; introduction of future language].

Geoffroy, Louis: *Napoléon apocryphe* (1836; Librairie Illustrée, 1896).

Jackson, Ben [pseud. of Jean-Marie Gerbault]: *L'âge Alpha ou la marche du temps* (Rodez "Ed. du Méridien," 1941).

Maurois, Andre: *Deux fragments d'une Histoire Universelle* [see author entry].

Mercier, Louis-Sebastien: *L'an 2440, rêve s'il en fut jamais* (chez Van-Harrevelt, London & Amsterdam, 1771).

Randau, Robert: *L'Oeil du Monde* (Les Ed. du Monde Moderne, 1927).

Roussel, Raymond: *Locus Solus* (Lemerre, 1914; part reprinted, 1918).

Saint-Martin, Louis Claude de: *Le crocodile ou la guerre du bien et du mal* (Impr.-Libr. du Cercle-Social an VII, Triades Editions, 1962).

Science Fiction—Scientific:

Jullien, Jean: *Enquête sur le monde futur* (Fasquelle, 1909).

Langlais, Xavier de: *L'île sous cloche* (first published in Gaelic [Breton] as "Enez ar Rod," 1944; translated by author, Aux Portes du Large, Nantes, 1946).

Moreux, Abbé Th.: *Le miroir sombre* (Lethielleux, 1911).

Pawlowski, Gaston de: *Voyage au pays de la quatrième dimension* (Fasquelle, 1912, 1923; La Boétie, Bruxelles, 1945, illus.).

Perochon, Ernest: *Les hommes frénétiques* (Plon, 1925).

Richepin, Jean: *L'aile* (Lafitte, 1911).

Robida, Albert: *Le 20e siecle* (Descaux, 1883; numerous pa reissues).

Rosny, Snr., J. H.; *La guerre du feu*; *La force mystérieuse*; *La mort de la terre* [see author entry].

Verne, Jules: *Face au drapeau* [see *For the Flag*, author entry].

Science Fiction—Entertaining:

Allorge, Henri: *Ciel contre Terre* (Hachette "Bibliotheque de la Jeunesse," 1924).

Barjavel, René: *Le voyageur imprudent* (Denoël, 1944; PF, 1958?).

Couvreur, Andre: *L'androgyne* (Oeuvres Libres No. 7, Fayard, Jan 1922; Albin Michel, 1923).

Giffard, Pierre: *La guerre infernale* (Mericant, 1908; "Les drames de l'air," 8 vols.).

La Hire, Jean de: *Le mystère des XV* (in *Le Matin* [daily newspaper], 1911; Ferenczi, 1922—Les Romans d'Aventures, Nos. 8 & 9).

Laurie, Andre: *Les exiles de la Terre* (Hetzel, nd [1887], 2 vols., not illus.; Hachette, nd [1887], 1 vol., 8-p. introduction., illus.).

Leblanc, Maurice: *Les trois yeux* (Lafitte, 1920; Lafitte-Hachette "Le Point d'Interrogation No. 40," 1935; also Canadian ed. in French).

Leonard, François: *Le triomphe de l'homme* (Lamberty, Bruxelles, nd [1911]; Kemplen, nd).

Le Rouge, Gustave: *Le prisonnier de la planète Mars—La guerre des vampires* (Mericant, nd [1908-09], 2 vols., illus.; *Le naufrage de l'espace—L'astre d'épouante*, Mericant, nd [1912-13], & Larousse "Contes et Romans Pour Tous," serie, beige, Nos. 4 & 7, 1928?).

Nizerolles, R. M. de: *Les aventuriers du ciel* (Ferenczi, 1935-37, abr. 1950-51).

Renard, Maurice: *Le peril bleu* (Louis Michaud, 1912; Cres, *ca.* 1933; Tallandier, 1954 [incomplete], 1958).

Souvestre, Emile: *Le monde tel qu'il sera* (Coquebert, 1845; Lévy, 1871).

Spitz, Jacques: *La guerre des mouches* (Gallimard, 1938).

Thebault, Eugene: *Le deux reines du Pole Sud* (Tallandier, 1932).

FREMTIDSROMANEN Danish science fiction paperback book series, 16 titles, June 1957—Sep 1958. Published by Skrifola, Copenhagen; edited by J. Lademan for first three, then L. I. Madsen. Most titles were about 120 pp. (No. 13, 144 pp.) at 1.75 Danish kroner.

These were considered by one authority as one of the best sf series from Scandinavia. Most had inside illustrations and all used full-colour front covers, mostly by the Italian artist C. Caesar; these were apparently from the Italian *Urania* series.

Translations were presented from such U.S. and British writers as R. Bradbury (*The Martian Chronicles*, abr.), J. Wyndham [J. B. Harris], M. Leinster [W. F. Jenkins], and P. Anderson. There was one collection of 8 original stories by Niels E. Nielsen, and some material of French origin.

FUTILE PRESS U.S. fan press operated by Claire P. Beck in 1937-38. The title published were *Hammer and Tongs* (reprinting articles from Beck's amateur magazine *Science Fiction Critic*), 25¢; *Nero and Other Poems*, C. A. Smith, 25¢; *Notes and Commonplace Book*, H. P. Lovecraft, $1.00, 75 copies (later published in *Beyond the Wall of Sleep*).

FUTURIAN PRESS Australian private press, Sydney, publishing some science fiction in limited editions of 200 (or less) at 6/-. It began with a bibliography of science fiction and fantasy published in Australia to 1937, then presented some original sf and fantasy, and also some poetry. Titles: *A Checklist of Australian Fantasy*, S. L. Larnach (Mar 1951); *Blinded They Fly*, V. Molesworth (Mar 1951); *Zero Equals Nothing*, G. B. Stone & R. Williams (Nov 1951); *Let There Be Monsters*, V. Molesworth (Nov 1951).

FUTURIAN SOCIETY OF SYDNEY This Australian society was inaugurated on 5 Nov 1939; it held its 20th Anniversary on 5 Nov 1959, though regular meetings had not been held since 1955. The group has flourished at times, running a postal library and sponsoring various publications. Noted Australian fans who have been associated with it include the late V. Molesworth, G. B. Stone, and the late Norma Hemming.

G

GALAXIE BIS French paperback series published by Ed. Opta, Paris (publishers of *Galaxie* magazine). Specializing in translations of prominent U.S. authors, it started in late 1965 with *Gladiator-at-Law*, F. Pohl & C. M. Kornbluth. There were 8 titles by mid-1968. These paperbacks bear the number of the current *Galaxie* magazine, plus "Bis" and the number in this series.

GALAXY AWARDS These were begun in 1968 by the publishers of *Galaxy Science Fiction* and *(Worlds of) If*; the "awards" were in effect premium payments above the customary rates for authors.

"Goblin Reservation," C. D. Simak, $1000 (*GSF*, sr2, Apr 1968); "Slowboat Cargo," L. Niven, $250 (*If*, sr3, Feb 1968); "The Man in the Maze," R. Silverberg, $100 (*If*, sr2, Apr 1968); "Getting Through University," P. Anthony, $100 (*If*, n'te, Aug 1968); "The Time Trawlers," Burt F. Filer, $100 (*GSF*, short, Aug 1968).

GAMMA PEOPLE, THE U.S. film, Warwick-Columbia, 1956. The accidental visit of an American newspaperman (Paul Douglas) and an English photographer (Leslie Phillips) to a mythical state in the Alps where a mad scientist (Walter Rilla) experiments with gamma rays to change people to geniuses (or goons!).

GERMAN ROCKET SOCIETY In 1927 Max Valier formed the Verein für Raumschiffahrt—literally the Society for Spaceship Travel, but usually translated as the German Rocket Society. At one time H. Oberth was president; others members included Johannes Winkler, A. B. Shershevsky, Rudolf Nebel, and W. Ley. The Society did considerable experimentation on rocketry in the early 1930's; Max Valier was killed in a test. Some members also advised on the film *The Girl in the Moon* [see T. Von Harbou in *WHO'S WHO*]. The late W. Ley gives highlights of this society in his article "Eight Days in the Story of Rocketry" (*TWS*, Dec 1937) and also in his *Rockets, Missiles and Space Travel*.

GERMANY This country has a rich heritage of utopian and associated literature. The Transgalaxis *Katalog der deutschsprachigen utopisch-phantastischen Literatur*, H. Bingenheimer, 1960, attempts to list most material—even the magazine series—but further research has shown many omissions; these are being assembled by J. Bleymehl and other bibliographers.

Authors who have made a name outside their own country include J. Andreae (1586-1654) for his *Christianopolis*, H. H. Ewers (1871-1943), H. Hesse (1867-1962), G. Hauptman (1862-1945), E.T.A. Hoffmann (1776-1822), E. Juenger (1895—), R. Jungk for his nonfiction *Brighter Than a Thousand Suns*. Others of importance, but not available in translation, include H. Dominik (1872-1945), Richard Koch, K. Lasswitz (1848-1910), and F. Van Holk.

Robert Kraft (1870-1916) was probably the best of the unheralded pulp writers.

Perhaps the best contemporary writer is Dr. Robert W. Franke, born in Vienna (14 May 1927—). After studying physics, mathematics, and chemistry, he became a successful popular-science writer. His science fiction includes *Der Grüne Komet* (1960) (The Green Comet [C]), *Das Gedankennetz* (1961) (The Thought Net), *Der Orchideenkafig* (1961) (Cage of Orchids), *Die Glasfalle* (1962) (The Glass Trap), *Die Stahl-wüste* (1962) (The Steel Desert), *Planet der Verlorenen* (1963, under pseud. "Sergius Both") (Planet of Lost Men), and *Der Elfenbeinturm* (1965) (The Ivory Tower)—all published by Goldmann. He has been translated into Japanese, French, and Hungarian.

Many of the above-mentioned writers are covered in the *WHO'S WHO*. Also covered, because of works translated into English, are the following:

(1) Authors in U.S. magazines (pre-war) edited by H. Gernsback: L. Anton, B. H. Burgel, F. Freksa, O. W. Gail, and O. Von Hanstein.

(2) Author in post-war magazine: H. Hauser.

(3) Fiction translated: I. Aichinger, H. H. Kirst, W. Jens, T. Von Harbou (in late 1920's), K. Siodmak (resident in the U.S. for many years).

(4) Nonfiction translated: W. Buedeler, W. Dornberger, H. Gart-mann, I. Lissner, D. Papp; plus the following who emigrated to the U.S.: G. Gunther, H. Haber, H. Strughold, W. Von Braun, and W. Ley.

Some works of particular note, but not in translation, include *Alle Macht den Frauen*, Paul Frechter (matriarchy of 1980); the trilogy *Die Arche*, Stefan Andres (modern psychological sf novel); *Der Schwarze Stern*, Croixelles [pseud] (3rd world war); *Die Affen Gottes*, Walter von Molo (historical writer with satire about a modern Noah's Ark); *Gott und das Gewurn*, Anton van de Velde (vision of a new Ragnarok); *Die Eroberung der Welt*, Oscar Maria Graf (civilization after 3rd world war).

A book listing besides Bingenheimer's Transgalaxis catalogue was *The Future in Books* (German SF Club, 1955). The Science-Fiction Club Europa was serialising a listing in its journal *Blick in die Zukunft* in the 1950's. A serious treatise on the sf field was *Vom Staatsroman zur Science Fiction*, Dr. M. Schwonke (Enke, Stuttgart, 1957).

The more important contemporary personalities involved mainly in the German magazine and magazine series field include W. Ernsting, editor, translator, and writer (under pseudonym "Clark Darlton"); Gunther Schelwokat, former editor of the *Terra* series and still editor for the Heyne paperback books; K. H. Scheer, writer; and the late E. Richter, writer.

The magazine and magazine series field has changed considerably in recent years, so that at the turn of the Seventies the only current ones are *Perry Rhodan*, *Atlan*, *Terra Nova*, and *Zauberkreis SF*.

An early magazine which published material of interest was *Captain Mors*, about 180 issues, 1908-1914. No other magazines of direct interest are known until the emergence after World War II of the various *Utopia* series commencing with *Utopia-Kleinband* in 1953. This became *Utopia-Zukunftsromane*, ending in 1968 after 591 issues. Other titles were *Utopia-Grossband*, *Utopia-Kriminal*, and *Utopia-Magazin*, which all ceased some years earlier.

Strictly speaking, the only real magazines were *Utopia-Magazin* and *Galaxis* (a short-lived edition of the U.S. *Galaxy Magazine*); the others were more like paperback books issued on a regular schedule. The Moe-wig group of *Terra*, *Terra Extra*, and *Terra Sonderband* (later *Sonder-reihe*) had many numbers and appeared within the period 1957-1968. There were a number of magazines appearing for brief times, including two Austrian ones: *Star-Utopia* and *Uranus*.

Practically all novels in the magazine series were abridged and generally the translations were poor. They covered a wide range of the U.S. magazine field, presenting material at some time or another from practically all the regular authors. Only "novella" type stories were uncut, e.g., "Symbiotica," E. F. Russell. Occasional stories were "pad-ded"—three new chapters were added to "Non-Stop," B. W. Aldiss (without his knowledge). Few of the series bought much from German writers, and in 1961 a group of these combined to produce the *Perry Rhodan* series. This magazine was at its 368th issue in 1968, and was selling 200,000 copies weekly. There is also a hardcover series, and overseas translations include those from Ace Books, New York.

The first organised fan activities stemmed from Julian Parr, an Englishman residing in Germany in the early post-war years. Later Ernsting did much to organise German fandom. There have been a number of smaller German groups, with the biggest club being SFCG (Science Fiction Club Germany). The first German SF Convention was held at Bad Homburg, near Frankfurt, 14-16 September 1957. S-F Club Europa (since ceased) organised the First European Convention at Zürich, Switzerland, 23-23 August 1959; at this the German Hugo and the Kurd Lasswitz Literary Achievement Award were given.

Films:

The most noted German film is *The Cabinet of Dr. Caligari* (see separate entry), while F. Lang's *Metropolis* and *The Girl in the Moon* are of considerable importance to the history of sf films.

Anthologies [translated from the English]:

General:

Gespenster, Mary Hottinger (Diogenes, Zürich, 1956, 373 pp.)

Introduction by the compiler, and the following stories: "The Apparition of Mrs. Veal," D. Defoe; "The Haunters and the Haunted," E. Bulwer-Lytton; "The Dream Woman," W. W. Collins; "The Monkey's Paw," W. W. Jacobs; "On the Brighton Road," R. Middleton; "The Face," E. F. Benson; "Across the Moors," W. F. Harvey; "The Amorous Ghost," Enid Bagnold; "The Adventure in Norfolk," A. J. Alan; "The Ring," Mary Hottinger; "The Demon Lover," Elizabeth Bowen; "The Doll," A. Blackwood; "The Apple Tree," Daphne du Maurier; "Oh! Whistle and I'll Come to You, My Lad," M. R. James.

Nur ein Mareweib, Anonymous [translator—Leopold Voelker] (Ull-stein: 248, Berlin, 1959, 192 pp., pa)

Sf, 9 stories, selected from *Best SF* and *Best SF, Two*, E. Crispin [R. B. Montgomery]: "Nur ein Marsweib" ("Dumb Martian"), J. Wynd-ham; "Die neun Milliarden Namen Gottes" ("The Nine Billion Names of God"), A. C. Clarke; "First Lady" (same), J. T. McIntosh; "Una" (same), J. Wyndham; "Stunde Null" ("Zero Hour"), R. Bradbury; "Bilder lügen nicht" ("Pictures Don't Lie"), K. MacLean; "Keine Frau ward je geboren" ("No Woman Born"), C. L. Moore; "Das Prott" ("Prott"), M. St. Clair; "Der Ruum" ("The Ruum"), A. Porges.

Panik, Mary Hottinger (Diogenes, Zürich, 1961, 449 pp.)

Weird, with Introduction, "Apologia Horroris," M. Hottinger, and the following stories: "The Voyage of the Marie Celeste," Mary Hottinger; "The Masque of the Red Death," E. A. Poe; "The Cosy Room," A. Machen; "The Signal-Man," C. Dickens; "The Watcher by the Dead," A. Bierce; "A Matter of Fact," R. Kipling; "Our Feathered Friends," P. MacDonald; "Markheim," R. L. Stevenson; "A Room in the Tower," E. F. Benson; "The Beckoning Fair One," O. Onions; "They," R. Kipling; "Sredni Vashtar," Saki; "Lost Proper-ty," R. H. Mottram; "The Pipe-Smoker," Martin Armstrong; "The Man Who Liked Dickens," E. Waugh; "August Heat," W. F. Harvey; "The Lottery," Shirley Jackson; "The Waxwork," A. M. Burrage; "The Killers," E. Hemingway; "Funeral March of a Marionette," J. Metcalfe; "Bella Fleace Gave a Party," E. Waugh; "The Ghost Ship," R. Middleton.

Roboter, Peter Naujack [compiler & translator] (Diogenes, Zürich, 1962, 383 pp., illus.)

Sf, 12 stories and final article: "Logik" ("Reason"), I. Asimov; "Marionetten, e.V." ("Marionettes, Inc."), R. Bradbury; "In fremder Gewalt" ("Command Performance"), W. M. Miller Jr.; "Die Coffin-Kur" ("The Coffin Cure"), A. E. Nourse; "Heimkehr" ("The New Wine"), J. Christopher; "Nennt mich Joe" ("Call Me Joe"), P. Anderson; "Der Stern" ("The Star"), A. C. Clarke; "Wonnen der Einsamkeit" ("The Bliss of Solitude" ["Hallucination Orbit"]), J. T. McIntosh; "Im Kreis" ("By His Bootstraps"), R. A. Heinlein; "An der Grenze" ("Limiting Factor"), C. D. Simak; "Die Falle" ("The Box"), J. Blish; "Science Fiction—eine neue Literaturgattung?" ("Science Fiction—A New Genre of Literature?"), P. Naujack.

Überwindung von Raum und Zeit, G. Gunther. See author in *WHO'S WHO*.

Issued by Heyne Publishers, München:

1. A large-size paperback series selected from *The Magazine of Fantasy and Science Fiction* (U.S.) under the general title *Fantasy und Science Fiction*. The price was 2.20 DM initially. Each was numbered Band 1, Band 2, etc., with changing sub-titles:

1963 1. *Saturn im Morgenlicht*
  2. *Das letzte Element*
  3. *Heimkehr zu den Sternen*
  4. *Signale vom Pluto*
  5. *Die Esper greifen ein*
1964 6. *Die Überlebenden*
  7. *Musik aus dem All*
  8. *Irrtum der Maschinen*
  9. *Die Kristallwelt*
  10. *Wanderer durch Raum und Zeit*
  11. *Roboter auf dem Kriegspfad*
1965 12. *Die letzte Stadt der Erde*
  13. *Expedition nach Chronos*
  14. *Im Dschungel der Urzeit*
1966 15. *Die Maulwurfe von Manhattan*
  16. *Die Menschenfarm*
1967 17. *Grenzgänger zwischen den Welten*
  18. *Die Kolonie auf dem 3. Planeten*
  19. *Welt der Illusionen*
1968 20. *Mord in der Raumstation*
  21. *Flucht in die Vergangenheit*

The first few of these selections were anonymously translated and edited. Then W. Ernsting did most of the work to from Nos. 10 to 14; from No. 15, W. H. Bergner has made the selections and translations.
2. A similar paperback series selected from *Galaxy Science Fiction* by W. Ernsting, with no subtitles. These ran: 1965, Nos. 1 to 4; 1966, Nos. 5 to 9; 1968, No. 10
3. A number of original anthologies edited by H. W. Mommers and Arnulf Krauss:

10 Science Fiction Kriminal Stories (1965, 300 pp.) [Heyne Anthologien 11]
   "The Last Witness," E. F. Russell; "Two-Handed Engine," C. L. Moore & H. Kuttner; "Private Eye," H. Kuttner; "Judas Danced," B. W. Aldiss; "Mother Hitton's Littul Kittons," Cordwainer Smith; "The Undetected," G. O. Smith; "The Seven Deadly Virtues," F. Pohl; "The Pliable," D. F. Galouye; "Wenn trügerisch Besuch kommt," H. W. Mommers & E. Vlcek; "No Place for Crime," B. W. Aldiss.
7 Science Fiction Stories (1966, 296 pp.) [Heyne Anthologien 17]
   Foreword; "Tranquility, or Else!" F. Leiber; "Descent Into the Maelstrom," D. F. Galouye; "Android," H. Kuttner; "Design for Great-Day," E. F. Russell; "Psyclops," B. W. Aldiss; "The Silkie," A. E. van Vogt; "Nightfall," I. Asimov.
7 Science Fiction Stories [2nd Series] (1966, 316 pp.) [Heyne Anthologien 20]
   Foreword; "Immigrant," C. D. Simak; "Frost and Fire," R. Bradbury; "Wherever You May Be," J. E. Gunn; "The Midas Plague," F. Pohl; "The Education of Drusilla Strange," T. Sturgeon; "The Night of Light," P. J. Farmer; "Hobson's Choice," A. Bester.
8 Science Fiction Stories (1967, 301 pp.) [Heyne Anthologien 23]
   Foreword; "The Real People," A. Budrys; "Foster, You're Dead," P. K. Dick; "Consider Her Ways," J. Wyndham; "Carrier," R. Sheckley; "Death and the Senator," A. C. Clarke; "Common Time," J. Blish; "Jerry Is a Man," R. A. Heinlein; "The Darfsteller," W. M. Miller Jr.
[The above three books were billed as "Anthologies of the Famous," and were supposed to contain the best stories of the most important sf authors. The selectors originally planned on 7 stories per number, but because they were unable to have Sheckley's long "Mindswap" in the last one, it had to have 8 stories to fill out the assigned space.]
22 Horror Stories (1966, 293 pp.) [Heyne Anthologien 16]
   "Bianca's Hands," T. Sturgeon; "The Little Girl Later," Septimus Dale; "Legion of Plotters," R. Matheson; "The Hunger," C. Beaumont; "Butcher," R. S. Prather; "Lucy Comes to Stay," T. Fiske; "Second Honeymoon," R. Deming; "Schizo-Jimmy," F. Leiber; "The Rats in the Walls," H. P. Lovecraft; "Behind the Yellow Door," Flavia Richardson; "The Small Assassin," R. Bradbury; "De Mortuis," J. Collier; "The Gloating Place," R. Bloch; "The House of Horror," S. Quinn; "The Graveyard Rats," H. Kuttner; "The Importance of Remaining Ernest," M. S. Waddell; "Jizzle," J. Wyndham; "Boomerang," Oscar Cook; "Night Drive," W. F. Jenkins; "Wolfsrachen," H. W. Mommers & E. Vlcek; "Dulcie," Hugh Reid; "Miss Gentilbelle," C. Beaumont.

21 Grusel-Stories (1966, 301 pp.) [Heyne Anthologien 21]
   "The Skull of the Marquis de Sade," R. Bloch; "Wolves Don't Cry," B. Elliott; "Perchance to Dream," C. Beaumont; "Slime," J. P. Brennan; "Masquerade," H. Kuttner; "Evening Primrose," J. Collier; "The Witch in the Fog," H. Altshuler; "The Pond," N. Kneale; "Doll for the End of the Day," D. R. Bunch; "The Horror in the Museum," H. Heald; "The Kill," P. Fleming; "The Final Ingredient," J. Sharkey; "The Ocean Leech," F. B. Long; "Over the River," P. Schuyler Miller; "Augen," H. W. Mommers; "More Spinned Against," J. Wyndham; "It," T. Sturgeon; "Crickets," R. Matheson; "The Eyes of the Mummy," T. Fiske; "The Hound," F. Leiber; "Skeleton," R. Bradbury.
22 Horror Stories (1967, 295 pp.) [Heyne Anthologien 26]
   "Into the Lion's Den," W. F. Nolan; "No Such Thing as a Vampire," R. Matheson; "My Little Man," A. Ridley; "Taboo," G. Household; "The Touch of Nutmeg Makes It," J. Collier; "Fear in the Night," R. Sheckley; "The Unforgiven," S. Dale; "A Real Need," W. Samson; "Rosie," W. Martin; "The Whole Town's Sleeping," R. Bradbury; "Die, Maestro, Die!" T. Sturgeon; "The New People," C. Beaumont; "All the Sounds of Fear," H. Ellison; "Rhyme Never Pays," R. Bloch; "Side Bet," W. F. Jenkins; "Choice of Weapons," R. Aickman; "The Girl With Love," R. Cardwell; "Preyin' to Satan," Hogarth Brown; "State of Mind," E. C. Tubb; "Piece-Meal," Oscar Cook; "Man Skin," M. S. Waddell; "The Masterpiece," T. Fiske.
Die Nacht der zehn Milliarden Lichter (1967, 160 pp.) [Heyne: 3106]
   "Christmas Present," G. R. Dickson; "Christmas Tree," J. Christopher; "The Night of the Meek," R. Serling; "Christmas on Ganymede," I. Asimov; "Christmas Treason," J. White; "Christmas on Mars," I. E. Cox Jr.; "Happy Birthday, Dear Jesus," F. Pohl; "The Gift," R. Bradbury; "A Little Girl's Xmas in Modernia," David R. Bunch.
4. As an adjunct to the anthologies from *The Magazine of Fantasy and Science Fiction*, there were several edited by A. Boucher: *16 Science Fiction Stories* (1964); *20 Science Fiction Stories*.

Anthologies in the German magazine series:

Terra-Sonderband: No. 50, *Die Roboter und wir*, M. Greenberg (abridged from U.S. original); No. 56, *Sternenstaub*, D. A. Wollheim (*Adventures in the Far Future*); No. 62, *Die Rätsel der Venus* (*The Hidden Planet*).
Terra: No. 271, *Der letzte Mensch*, D. A. Wollheim (*The End of the World*); 344, *Auf fernen Planeten*, D. A. Wollheim (*Adventures on Other Planets*); 356, *Die Erde in Gefahr*, D. A. Wollheim (*The Earth in Peril*); 452, *Flucht zur Erde*, I. Howard (*Escape to Earth*); 551, *Der Mensch und das Universum*, I. Howard (*Novelets of Science Fiction*).
Utopia Zukunftsromane. Though not directly derived from U.S. originals, the following issues are known to be anthologies: Nos. 403, 415, 421, 424, 427, 430, 432, 435 [SF-Cocktail 1], 436 [SF-Cocktail 2], 437 [SF-Cocktail 3], 440, 449, 461, 463, 466, 474, 485, 492, 499, 506, 521, 526, 534, 543, 565, 575.

Publishers:

In 1968 the most important German sf publishers were Bewin, Goldmann, Heyne, Moewig, Ullstein, Rowohl, and Zimmerman. Some with occasional titles were Diogenes, Insel, Hanser, Moos, and Schünemann.

GHOSTS [see also FOLK TALES and SUPERNATURAL PHENOMENA]

A coverage of this field is *Ghost Story Index*, F. Siemon (1967), covering 2,200 stories from 190 books (presumably fiction).
   Writers of nonfiction on the subject include D. Bardens, J. Braddock, J. Canning, E. J. Dingwall, C.L.W. Halifax, T. H. Hall, J. Harden, H. Holzer, R. T. Hopkins, B. J. Hurwood, L. C. Jones, C. J. Laughlin, T. C. Lethbridge, M. DuP. Lee, M. R. Martin, L. O'Donnell, J. Reynolds, S. Leslie, W. O. Stevens, and D. Walker.

GNOME PRESS, New York. One of the specialist science fiction presses. Starting in 1949 it produced over 50 books before it ceased in the early 1960's. Executives included David Kyle, with M. Greenberg operating it for the later years, in conjunction with his "Pick-A-Book" scheme.
   Four of the early books—*Pattern for Conquest*, G. O. Smith, *The 31st of February*, N. S. Bond, *Cosmic Engineers*, C. D. Simak, and *I, Robot*, I.

Asimov—saw simultaneous hard and soft cover editions, with the latter for distribution by the U.S. armed forces; some of those paperbacks became available to the public through other channels. Other books included *The Porcelain Magician*, F. Owen, the Conan stories (book series) of R. E. Howard, and novels by R. A. Heinlein.

GODZILLA, KING OF THE MONSTERS Japanese film, Jewel Enterprises Toho, 1956; directed by Terry Morse; with Raymond Burr.
One of the more noted Japanese monster films. A sequel was *Godzilla Raids Again* (1957).

GOG U.S. film, United Artists, 1954; produced by Ivan Tors; starring Richard Egan as a security agent. Investigating mysterious deaths in an underground super-laboratory, he finds that Novac, the giant computer, has been tampered with.

GOLDEN ATOM U.S. amateur magazine, published by Larry B. Farsace; 10 issues (Oct 1939—Win 1943) plus one "annual" (1954/55, 100 pp., $1.00).
The annual was an interesting publication, printed quite expensively. It contained a long resumé on science fiction, the first part of "Looking Backward Into the Future," H. Hersey (on the beginnings of *Thrill Book* and other early magazines), and some general interest (not sf) material.

GOLDEN SCIENCE FICTION LIBRARY Cheap editions from Fantasy Press, beginning Dec 1956, at $1.00: No. 1, *Galactic Patrol*, E. E. Smith; No. 2, *The Moon Is Hell*, J. W. Campbell Jr.; No. 3, *Operation: Outer Space*, M. Leinster [W. F. Jenkins].

GOTHIC STORIES This encyclopedia is not designed to cover this phase of literature—the forerunner of present-day weird fiction—but where a Gothic novel has been of importance and has been reprinted in recent years, a full entry is given. These are: *The Monk*, M. G. Lewis (1796); *Melmoth the Wanderer*, C. Maturin (1820); *The Castle of Otranto*, H. Walpole (*ca.* 1764-65).
M. Summers was the most noted authority in this field, and his *A Gothic Bibliography* (Fortune, London, 1940; Columbia Univ, Press, 1941; Russell & Russell, London, 1964) is the most important source. A more recent work is *Gothic Flame*, D. P. Varma (1957).

GRANDON COMPANY U.S. science fiction and fantasy publisher; organised by Don Grant after he purchased Hadley Publishing Company. The first book with the Grandon imprint was *Port of Peril*, O. A. Kline, in 1949. Others have included *The Return of Tharn*, H. Browne (1957); *The Werewolf of Ponkert*, H. W. Munn (1958); and *333*, J. H. Crawford (1953). By the late 1960's Grant was still publishing but no longer using this imprint.

GRIFFIN PUBLISHING COMPANY U.S. specialist imprint, an offshoot of Fantasy Publishing Co. Inc., Los Angeles, operated by W. Crawford. It published *The Machine God Laughs*, F. Pragnell. Another work was Griffin Science Fantasy Booklet No. 1, *ca.* 1959, 35¢, containing "The Gifts of Asti," A. North, and "The Empire of the Dust," B. Wells.

H

HACHETTE, Paris. One of France's largest publishers. Hachette coöperated with Gallimard Publishers in the production of the science fiction series *Le Rayon Fantastique*, issuing some 120 titles before ceasing late in 1963. G. H. Gallet was the Hachette editor; he concentrated on reprinting the simple, straightforward type of sf translated from English.

HADLEY PUBLISHING COMPANY, Providence, Rhode Island. A U.S. science fiction press, originally named Buffalo Book Co., formed by a group of science fiction enthusiasts. From 1946 it published *The Time Stream*, J. Taine [E. T. Bell], *The Skylark of Space*, E. E. Smith, and *The Weapon Makers*, A. E. van Vogt. After the change to Hadley, it issued *The Mightiest Machine*, J. W. Campbell, and *Final Blackout*, L. R. Hubbard. The company was bought out by Don Grant and reorganised as The Grandon Company.

HAMMER FILMS British film company which from 1958 has made a number of the better horror films. These often starred Peter Cushing and Christopher Lee, with stories written by J. Sangster and directed by Terence Fisher. Films have included *Frankenstein*, *The Horror of Dracula*, *The Hound of the Baskervilles*, *The Man Who Cheated Death* (published as a paperback), and *The Mummy*.

HAYAKAWA POCKET FANTASY BOOKS The main Japanese series in the sf field, it began at the end of 1957, published by Hayakawa Shobo, Tokyo. As sales increased the title changed to Hayakawa Science Fiction Series; by the end of 1968, 205 titles had appeared. Most books are translations of U.S. and British works, but a few Russian and German stories have been included, as well as some 20 original Japanese novels and collections.

HEARST CORPORATION U.S. publishing group. It entered the sf publishing field upon the purchase of Avon Publicaions, Inc., around May 1959. Avon was one of the first paperback publishers and had been in business 20 years. The name has continued as the Avon Book Division within the Hearst Corporation.

HOLLAND Some original novels have been *Uranium-koorts* [Uranium Fever], Koert de Haan & Hans van Assumburg; *Redder der Aarde* [Saviour of Earth], Edward Multon. There have also been some translations of R. A. Heinlein, A. C. Clarke, etc. An author covered in the *Encyclopedia* is D. Burger, with *Sphereland*.
Ben Abbas edited the now-extinct *Fantasie en Wetenschap*, and N. Osterbaan the one issue of *Planeet Science Fiction*. *Space Fiction* was a further magazine.
A reference work of importance is *100 Jaar SF in Nederland*, D. Scheepstra (published by the compiler, Harlingen, 1968); lists sf as published by the year, and also by author.

"HORLA, THE" A short story by Guy de Maupassant, considered by many to be one of the greatest old short weird horror stories. A translation from the French, by G. A. England, appeared in *The Scrap Book*, June 1911, and was reprinted in *FFM*, Sep 1942. The story has also been published in many anthologies, such as *Tales of the Supernatural*, Anonymous (1947, pa).

HUGO AWARDS These noted science fiction awards were named to honour the work in sf of the late Hugo Gernsback, founder of *Amazing Stories*, the first magazine devoted to sf. The awards were initiated at the World Science Fiction Convention of 1953 in Philadelphia. None were given at San Francisco the following year, but since 1955 they have been a feature of each World SF Convention. The rules of selection were somewhat indefinite in the early years, but were finally stabilized for the 1961 convention (though they still change slightly from time to time).
The shorter fiction for the period 1955-1961 was later anthologised as *The Hugo Winners*, I. Asimov, in 1962.
1953 (Philadelphia)
Novel: *The Demolished Man*, A. Bester [from *GSF*]
Professional Magazine: *Galaxy SF* and *Astounding SF* (tie)
Cover Artist: Ed Emshwiller (i.e., Emsh) & H. Bok (tie)
Interior Illustrator: Virgil Finlay
Fact Articles: Willy Ley
New SF Author or Artist: Philip José Farmer
No. 1 Fan Personality: Forrest J Ackerman (who declined and gave it to Ken Slater).
1954 (San Francisco)
No awards.

1955 (Cleveland)
Novel: *They'd Rather Be Right*, M. Clifton & F. Riley [*ASF*]
Novelette: "The Darfsteller," W. M. Miller Jr. [*ASF*]
Short Story: "Allamagoosa," E. F. Russell [*ASF*]
Professional Magazine: *Astounding Science Fiction*
Illustrator: Frank Kelly Freas
Fan Magazine: *Fantasy-Times*
1956 (New York)
Novel: *Double Star*, R. A. Heinlein [*ASF*]
Novelette: "Exploration Team," M. Leinster [W. F. Jenkins] [*ASF*]
Short Story: "The Star," Arthur C. Clarke [*Infinity*]
Professional Magazine: *Astounding Science Fiction*
Artist: Frank Kelly Freas
Feature Writer: Willy Ley
Fan Magazine: *Inside*
Most Promising New Author: Robert Silverberg
Book Reviewer: Damon Knight
1957 (London)
American Professional Magazine: *Astounding Science Fiction*
British Professional Magazine: *New Worlds*
Fan Magazine: *Science-Fiction Times*
See INTERNATIONAL FANTASY AWARD, 1957.
1958 (Los Angeles)
Novel or Novelette: *The Big Time*, F. Leiber [*GSF*]
Short Story: "Or All the Seas With Oysters," Avram Davidson [*GSF*]
Professional Magazine: *Fantasy and Science Fiction*
Artist: Frank Kelly Freas
Movie: *The Incredible Shrinking Man*
"Acti-Fan": Walter A. Willis
1959 (Detroit)
Novel: *A Case of Conscience*, J. Blish
Novelette: "The Big Front Yard," Clifford D. Simak [*ASF*]
Short Story: "That Hell-Bound Train," Robert Bloch [*F&SF*]
Professional Magazine: *Fantasy & Science Fiction*
Artist: Frank Kelly Freas
Movie: No Award
Amateur Magazine: *Fanac*
New Author: B. W. Aldiss
1960 (Pittsburgh)
Novel: *Starship Troopers*, R. A. Heinlein
Novelette or Short Story: "Flowers for Algernon," D. Keyes [*F&SF*]
Professional Magazine: *Fantasy & Science Fiction*
Fan Magazine: *Cry of the Nameless*
Artist: E. Emsh(willer)
Dramatic Presentation: *Twilight Zone*, Rod Serling [TV series]
Special Hugo: Hugo Gernsback
1961 (Seattle)
Novel: *A Canticle for Leibowitz*, Walter M. Miller Jr.
Short Fiction: "The Longest Voyage," P. Anderson [*ASF*]
Professional Magazine: *Analog* [i.e., *ASF*]
Professional Artist: Ed Emsh(willer)
Amateur Publication: *Who Killed Science Fiction?*, edited by Earl Kemp
Dramatic Presentation: *Twilight Zone*, R. Serling
1962 (Chicago)
Novel: *Stranger in a Strange Land*, R. A. Heinlein
Short Fiction: The "Hothouse" series, Brian W. Aldiss
Professional Magazine: *Analog*
Professional Artist: Ed Emsh(willer)
Dramatic Presentation: *Twilight Zone*, R. Serling
Amateur Magazine: *Warhoon*, edited by Richard Bergeron
1963 (Washington)
Novel: *The Man in the High Castle*, P. K. Dick
Short Fiction: "The Dragon Masters," J. Vance [*GSF*]
Professional Magazine: *Fantasy & Science Fiction*
Artist: Roy Krenkel
Dramatic Presentation: No Award
Amateur Magazine: *Xero*, edited by Dick Lupoff
Special Award: P. Schuyler Miller for The Reference Library in *ASF*
1964 (Oakland, Calif.)
Novel: *Way Station*, Clifford D. Simak [*GSF*]
Short Fiction: "No Truce With Kings," P. Anderson [*F&SF*]
Professional Magazine: *Analog*

Artist: Ed Emsh(willer)
Amateur Magazine: *Amra*, edited by George Scithers
Book Publisher: Ace Books
1965 (London)
Novel: *The Wanderer*, F. Leiber
Short Fiction: "Soldier, Ask Not," G. R. Dickson
Professional Magazine: *Analog*
Artist: John Schoenherr
Dramatic Presentation: *Dr. Strangelove*
Amateur Magazine: *Yandro*, edited by Robert & Juanita Coulson
1966 (Cleveland)
Novel: *Dune*, F. Herbert [*ASF*] tieing with "And Call Me Conrad" [*F&SF*] [*This Immortal*]
Short Fiction: "Repent, Harlequin! Said the Ticktockman," H. Ellison [*GSF*]
Professional Magazine: *If*
Artist: F. Frazetta
Best All-Time Series: "Foundation" series, I. Asimov
Amateur Magazine: *ERB-Dom*, edited by C. Cazedessus Jr.
1967 (New York)
Novel: *The Moon Is a Harsh Mistress*, R. A. Heinlein [*If*]
Novelette: "The Last Castle," J. Vance [*GSF*]
Short Story: "Neutron Star," L. Niven [*If*]
Professional Magazine: *If*
Artist: J. Gaughan
Dramatic Presentation: "The Menagerie" [one episode of TV's *Star Trek*]
Amateur Magazine: *Niekus*, E. Meskys
Fan Writer: Alexei Panshin
1968 (Oakland/Berkeley, Calif.)
Novel: *Lord of Light*, R. Zelazny
Novella: "Weyr Search," A. McCaffrey tieing with "Riders of the Purple Wage," P. J. Farmer
Novelette: "Gonna Roll the Bones," F. Leiber
Short Story: "I Have No Mouth and I Must Scream," H. Ellison
Professional Magazine: *If*
Professional Artist: J. Gaughan
Dramatic Presentation: "City on the Edge of Forever" [one episode of TV's *Star Trek*]
Amateur Magazine: *Amra*, edited by G. Scithers.
Fan Writer: Ted White
Fan Artist: George Barr

HUGO AWARDS (GERMAN) This trophy, in the form of a document signed by Hugo Gernsback, was first awarded at the Biggercon in 1957, covering 1955 and 1956; the second was in 1958 [neither recipient known]. The third was in 1959 at the First European Convention, Zürich, to K.-H. Scheer for the novel *Oktavian III*.

HUNGARY An author in the *Encyclopedia* is F. Karinthy. Noted works from Hungary include *The Prophet of World's End*, Kaurus Jokai (very rare); *Voyage to Capillaria*, *Voyage to Faremide*, *The Land of Thousand-Faced Souls*, all by F. Karinthy; *The Voyage to Kazzolinia*, Eugen Szatmary

I

INDIA The first original science fiction serial in Hindi literature was "Khagras" [Full Eclipse], Acharya Chatursen Shastri, in *Dharmyug* [weekly magazine published by *The Times of India*] beginning 30 Aug 1959. It told of the first landing on the Moon by Russians.

INSIDE (SCIENCE FICTION) U.S. amateur magazine, edited by Ron Smith. It was noted for its review articles, excellent fan fiction, and at times its trading section. It started in 1953 as *Inside*; from No. 6 (Nov

1954) it incorporated *Science Fiction Advertiser*, and from No. 12 (Nov 1955), *Kaymar Trader*.

The magazine was photolithographed, 5¼ x 8½ in., usually bimonthly, with pages varying up to 72. The publication frequency stretched out for its last few issues: No. 17 was Mar 1957; 18 was Oct 1957, and 19 was Sep 1958. The last two ran detailed parodies of *ASF* and *F&SF*. A revival by Jon White in Oct 1962 was short-lived, and was transmuted into *Riverside Quarterly*, which still continues.

INTERNATIONAL FANTASY AWARD [IFA] An award originated by the four British science fiction personalities J. B. Harris (better known as J. Wyndham), Frank A. Cooper, G. Ken Chapman, and Leslie Flood for the 1951 British Convention. For the first three years this group financed the scheme without outside support. They also were the judges for the initial award. Later, up to 15 sf personalities selected worldwide acted as judges. By 1955 the Award was financed by the "Science Fiction Luncheon Club," a loosely-knit group of London publishing firms. However, interest waned so much that there was no award in 1956, the remaining members largely financed the 1957 award, and the Club virtually ceased by 1958.

Awards were given around June to cover the fiction of the previous year; there was also a nonfiction award until 1954.

1951: *Earth Abides*, G. R. Stewart. Nonfiction: *The Conquest of Space*, W. Ley & C. Bonestell

1952: *Fancies and Goodnights*, J. Collier. Nonfiction: *The Exploration of Space*, A. C. Clarke

1953: *City*, C. D. Simak. Nonfiction: *Lands Beyond*, W. Ley & L. S. de Camp

1954: *More Than Human*, T. Sturgeon

1955: *A Mirror for Observers*, E. Pangborn

1956: No award

1957: *Lord of the Rings* Trilogy, J.R.R. Tolkien

INTERNATIONAL SCIENCE-FICTION FILM FESTIVAL Held annually at Trieste, Italy, with awards by an International Jury of film critics and spectators.

First (6 to 14 July 1963):

Gold Asteroid: *Ikaria XB1* (Czech; released in U.S.A. by American-International as *Voyage to the End of the Universe*); *The Runway* (France)

Silver Asteroid: *The Man With the X-Ray Eyes* (American-International, 1963); *The Amphibious Man* (U.S.S.R.)

Second (9 to 18 July 1964):

Gold Asteroid: *The Damned* (Great Britain; released in the U.S.A. as *These Are the Damned*; based on book *Children of the Light*, H. L. Lawrence)

Silver Seal: *The First Pavilion* (Poland)

No further information.

INVADERS, THE U.S. television series, ABC network; 43 episodes, 1967-68; a Quinn Martin production, starring Roy Thinnes as David Vincent. Sixty-minute colour episodes, based on the theme of "they" are among us. The first season, 1967, was 17 episodes, "Beach Head" to "The Condemned." The second season, 1967-68, ran "Condition Red" through to "Inquisition."

Offshoots from the TV series were several paperbacks and a quarterly comic book. The paperbacks were:

The Invaders, K. Laumer (3 stories) (Pyramid: R-1664, 1967; also titled as *The Meteor Men*, Anthony Lebaron [pseud], Corgi: GS7836, 1968)

Enemies From Beyond, K. Laumer (4 stories) (Pyramid: X-1689, 1967)

Army of the Undead, R. Bernard (Pyramid: R-1711, 1967; also titled as *The Halo Highway*, Corgi: GS7742, 1967)

Dam of Death, Jack Pearl (Whitman, 1967)

Alien Missile Threat, Paul S. Newman (Whitman, 1967)

It is understood that the last two are very juvenile; they are not listed in the *PAPERBACKS* section.

IT CAME FROM OUTER SPACE U.S. film, Universal-International, 1953; script adapted by R. Bradbury; starring Richard Carlson and Barbara Rush; three-dimensional.

Strange things happen when an invisible extra-terrestrial lands.

ITALY This country apparently has little or no heritage of science fiction or fantasy writers. However, Jules Verne and H. G. Wells have seen translation. Science fiction literature made its first official appearance in April 1952 with the initial issue of the magazine *Scienza Fantastica*. However, this lasted only seven issues. Probably the most important Italian magazine has been *I Romanzi di Urania* [later titled *Urania*], which began in October 1952 and was approaching 500 issues by the end of 1968.

The most informative publication on Italian science fiction is *Catalogo Generale della Fantascienza*, Alfio Bertoni & Gianluigi Missiaja (Centro Cultori SF, Venezia, 1968, duplicated, foolscap), which briefly lists all the magazine series, some amateur material, and then gives 307 pages of authors' works: novels and shorter material, both Italian writers and others.

There have been many short-lived magazines. Among the longer-running ones were *I Romanzi del Cosmo* (202 issues, 1957-1967), *Cronache del Futuro* (24 issues, 1957-1958), *Oltre il Cielo* (148 issues, 1957-1967), *Gamma* (27 issues, 1965-1968), and an edition of *Galaxy SF* had 72 issues (1958-1964). *Galassia* started in 1961 and seems to be the main surviving magazine besides *Urania*. The more important of all these magazines presented translations of U.S. and British writers, and at times French and German authors of lesser reputation; there seems to be little original Italian fiction in this field. There is also little critical work on sf, though Mrs. Robert Rambelli has commented on some errors.

The few authors of direct interest include Dino Buzzati, who has some stories in translation. Other writers listed in the *Encyclopedia* are I. Calvino, Leonardo da Vinci (for a literary curiosity), U. Malagati, and D. Vare. The mainstream writer Giovanni Papini has some fantasy aspects in *Gog*, his most famous book.

The pulp volume *Superfantascienza* (1955, 350 pp.) printed three sf novels, including "Il Signore dei Mondi," N. Muhanof, translated from Russian.

J, K

JAPAN Although science fiction has been popular in Japan since around 1880, it was principally the works of Jules Verne that saw translation before World War I. Then between the two wars there appeared several writers of interest, including Mushitarō Oguri (mainly adventure romance) and Fuboku Kosakai and Ikujirō Ran (for scientific fiction). Juza Unno (deceased 1949) was probably the most popular and capable, introducing the attitudes of the newly developing sf of H. Gernsback for the first time in the 1930's; he appealed mainly to young readers and was not at all esteemed in the field of general literature.

In the same period Takatorō Kigi and Komatsi Kitamura (respectively mystery and mainstream writers) also wrote some good science fiction. Some novels of H. G. Wells were also translated, but E. R. Burroughs' novels were practically neglected.

After World War II a flood of sf paperbacks, discarded by Allied military personnel, filled the shelves of the second-hand book shops in the big cities. This stimulated some ambitious publishers to attempt translations of this new type of literature. Most trials failed because of limited sales.

Books

Most of the noted weird classics have seen translation from various publishers, starting with *Frankenstein* in 1948.

A series of selections from *Amazing Stories* and *Fantastic Adventures* by Seibundo-Shinkosha Company appeared, and folded after seven books in 1950. Muromachi-Shobo published *The Currents of Space*, I. Asimov, and *Sands of Mars*, A. C. Clarke (both abridged), in 1955 in a projected series which, however, did not continue. Later Gengen-sha published 18 books in a series begun in April 1956 and terminating in Feb 1957 (numbered 1 to 17, and 19, with No. 18 to have been issued later); these were translations of high-grade U.S. material. The same publisher, in conjunction with Tokyo-Life-Sha then presented two anthologies (abridged) in a Space Science Fiction series: *Science Fiction Terror Tales*, G. Conklin, and *Adventures in Time and Space*, R. J. Healy & J. F. McComas.

The only series still running, the Hayakawa Pocket Fantasy Books, began in Dec 1957 at No. 3001; they were slightly changed in title to Hayakawa Science Fiction Series with No. 3032, and were at No. 3205 by the end of 1968. Most of the books in this series are translations of U.S. and British stories, with a few German and Russian stories included, as well as some twenty original Japanese novels and collections.

Other anthologies include an abridged edition of *Fantasia Mathematica*, C. Fadiman, in 1959, and *Science Fiction: Best 10* (Arechi Shuppan-sha, 1961), selected from *S-F Magazine*.

Hayakawa-Shobo started a new series of original Japanese novels in 1964 and had published 12 by the end of 1968. A few competitors have now appeared; Tokyo-Sogensha Company established an sf section of the Sogen Mystery series in 1964 which has reached some 70 titles. These are understood to have been profitable, as they include semi-classics by E. R. Burroughs and E. E. Smith.

Magazines

The first sf magazine was *Seiun*, appearing in Dec 1954 with four translations and three original stories in its only issue. Then the mystery magazine *Hôseki* had two special sf issues in Feb and Aug 1955; the former had four translations, including "Strange Playfellow," I. Asimov, and the latter had three translations, including "The Yehudi Principle," F. Brown. The only regular magazine at present is *S-F Magazine*, which began in Feb 1960 as an edition of *The Magazine of Fantasy and Science Fiction*; by Jan 1962 it had dissolved the contract with Mercury Press. Since then it has printed stories from the various U.S. magazines as well as many by Japanese writers. It reached No. 115 by the end of 1968.

Personalities

Masami Fukushima (1929—): He is regarded as the leading character in Japanese sf pro-dom, having founded both the Hayakawa SF series and *S-F Magazine*. He has helped gain serious consideration of sf in the literary and journalistic fields, and has also written some juvenile sf and translated U.S. and British works.

Sakyō Komatsu (1931—): An active and skillful story-teller of wide interests, he is also an opinion shaper in Japanese futurology. He writes mainly in the social sciences and has had nearly 20 books, the most noted being *The Day of Rebirth* (1964) and *At the End of Endless Stream* (1966).

Shin'ichi Hoshi (1926—): Mainly a short story writer with an elegant sense of fable criticism; of about ten books, *A Manmade Beauty* is considered the best. He worked with Takumi Shibano on the early *Uchujin* (amateur magazine) and helped popularize the name "SF" in the early days of Japanese science fiction.

Kōbō Abe (1925—): Essentially a mainstream writer of social critiques, he is noted for *The Invention of R62 & Other Stories* (1956) and *The Leaden Egg & Other Stories*, as well as *The Fourth Interglacier Period* (1959), a great achievement of modern Japanese sf.

Yukio Mishima: A mainstream writer; *Beautiful Planet* is of interest.

Yasutaka Tsutsui: He began as a professional writer after folding his amateur magazine *Null*; he is noted for *Viet-Nam Sight-Seeing Co.* (1967).

Ryū Mitsuse (1928—): Prefers the hard-science type, with his best being *A Return in Twilight* (1964).

Taku Mayumura (1934—): He is considered one of the more serious writers; he uses the near future for novels such as *Expo '87* (1968).

Masao Segawa (1931—): One of the "big three" of the juvenile sf world, and noted for the scientific research he puts into his work; his best is *61-Cygni* (1960).

Tetsu Yano (1923—): He and Masao Segawa and Masami Fukushima are considered the "big three" of juvenile sf. He was famous as the first Science Fiction Fan in Japan. He is now a professional translator as well as a juvenile sf writer.

Aritsune Toyota (1938—): Noted for *Afterglow of Mongol* (1968).

Kazumasa Hirai (1938—): Noted for *"Tiger" in Megaropolis* (1968).

Alan Kiodomari (1912—): A fantasy writer in the general literary field who gradually worked into sf; most noted for *Tower of the Light* (1962).

Others

Shigeru Kayama, Jojiro Okami, Michio Tsuzuki, Yo Sano, Kyo Takikawa, Ichiro Kano (1928—), and Tadashi Hirose (1924—) are mystery or fantasy writers who at times write science fiction. Fujio Ishihara (*Highway Planet*, 1967) and Koichi Yamano (*Take the X-Train*, 1965) are also of interest. Takashi Ishikawa (1930—) is a both a critic of mystery fiction and the only professional critic of science fiction.

In the field of sf comics Osamu Tezula (1926—) was the top name for many years; he produced *Astroboy*, the first animated TV film series in Japan. Among many other artists, Shotaro Ishimori (1938—) is the most important.

Takumi Shibano, Koichiro Noda, and Norio Itoh are recognised as among the most noted fans—Shibano visited the West Coast of the U.S.A. in 1968 as a guest of American fandom and stayed for over a month.

Among the many professional translators, Noriyoshi Saito (1935—) and Hisashi Asakura (1930—) are the specialists in sf.

Fan Activities

The history of Japanese fandom began with Uchujin, a club for fans and writers. Its fanzine *Uchujin* first appeared in May 1957; generally appearing monthly, it attained its 129th issue in Dec 1968. This is an important magazine with a circulation of over 500 and has made its editor, Takumi Shibano, a major name in fandom. More than half of the writers who now work in the Japanese sf field have grown up in the Uchujin Club or been associated with it.

Following this club's formation, several fan groups began to appear in 1960. Null-Club in Osaka published *Null* for 11 issues before folding in 1964. SFM-Fan Club—with its fanzine *Uchu-Kiryu* (meaning "space current")—started in Tokyo in 1962; this is now reputed to be the largest fan group in Japan (apart from the subscription group to *Uchujin*), with over 100 members.

The number of fan groups and fanzines increased rapidly to 50 or more in 1965 and 1966, though most were groups of juveniles. The Federation of S-F Fan Groups of Japan was started with 9 groups in 1965 and consisted of 14 late in 1968.

Conventions (annually beginning in 1962):

1. 1962 "Meg-Con" One day in Tokyo; sponsored by Uchujin Club; 200 attendees; SFM-Club announced its founding.
2. 1963 "Tokon" Two-day programme—movies, art, banquet, etc.
3. 1964 "Daicon" Held in Osaka; promoted by Null Club, chairman Yasutaka Tsutsui.
4. 1965 "Tokon-2" Sponsored by Uchujin, Uchu-Kiryu, and SF Art-Club (established 1963); 350 attending.
5. 1966 "Meicon" Held in Nagoya; sponsored by the Mutants Club, a local group started by Den Yoshimitsu.
6. 1967 "Tokon-3" Serious symposium; 180 attending.
7. 1968 "Tokon-4" 250 attending.

JOURNAL OF SCIENCE FICTION, THE U.S. amateur magazine; 4 issues (Fall 1951-1953); edited by Charles Freudenthal, with Edward Wood as Co-Editor from 2nd issue. Photolithographed, 32 pp., 25¢ (last issue 80 pp., 50¢).

A notable publication presenting reviews on H. L. Gold, R. Bradbury, *Amazing Stories* 1926-1951; articles such as S. Moskowitz's "The Case Against Modern Science Fiction" and a reply; K. F. Slater on British paperback publishing; a listing of articles on science fiction in the last issue. The third and fourth issues presented story listings for the sf magazines of 1951 and 1952 respectively.

JUPITER PRESS U.S. press organised by Jack Corder and Vernell Coriell and supposed to start in mid-1954. Apparently, poor support for the proposed book, *Beware Malobra*, Hannes Bok, caused these plans to lapse.

KING KONG U.S. film, RKO, 1933. The classic giant ape film; directed by Ernest B. Schoedsack; starring Fay Wray and Robert Armstrong. The story was novelized by E. Wallace and M. C. Cooper (1932), with illustrations from the film.

A giant ape captured in Africa breaks free in New York, terrorizes the city, and combats U.S. fighter planes from the top of the Empire State

Building. The movie grossed over $2 million when first played, and was reshown in the early 1950's and said to have grossed $8 million.

Less successful films in the same vein have been *The Son of Kong* (1933) and the comparatively recent *Mighty Joe Young* (1949; also released as *Mr. Joseph Young of Africa*).

L

LAND OF THE GIANTS U.S. television series, ABC network; 51 episodes (60 minutes, in colour), 1968-1970. An Irwin Allen production for 20th Century Fox. Humans in a spaceship pass through a mysterious cloud and land on a world of fantastic proportions, with giant people, cats, automobiles, etc. Several adventures were written in paperback by Murray Leinster [W. F. Jenkins].

LEAVES U.S. amateur magazine; two issues, 1937 and 1938, about 50 pp., mimeo. It is considered one of the finest in the fan field.

R. H. Barlow published the first issue, and prepared the stencils for the second, which Claire Beck (of Futile Press) duplicated. The first issue had 100 copies and the second had 60; both are now extremely rare. The contents included:

No. 1: "People of the Pit," A. Merritt; letters by H. P. Lovecraft under pseudonym Lewis Theobold Jr.; "Third Episode of Vathek," C. A. Smith (completion of a fragment by W. Beckford); "Red Brain," D. Wandrei (with hitherto unpublished ending and sequel).

No. 2: "Werewoman," C. L. Moore (an original "Northwest Smith" story); "The Tree-Man," H. S. Whitehead, and a listing by Barlow of Whitehead's stories; other contributions by Lovecraft, etc.

LOMMEROMANEN Danish paperback book series published by Skrifola Pubs., Copenhagen. A general series appearing weekly, in 1959 it published six sf titles originally scheduled for the "Planetbogerne" series: *The 27th Day*, J. Mantley; *Space Station No. 1*, F. B. Long; *The Puppet Masters*, R. A. Heinlein; *Twice Upon a Time*, C. L. Fontenay; *First He Died*, C. D. Simak; *Prelude to Space*, A. C. Clarke.

LOS ANGELES SCIENCE FANTASY SOCIETY [LASFS] The oldest surviving fan club, founded in 1934. Two of the original members are still with it: F. J Ackerman and R. J. Hodgkins. Its membership over the years has included many professionals, such as Ray Bradbury.

The one thousandth meeting was held 26 Oct 1956, and the 1125th meeting (special oldtimers evening) on 5 March 1959. This society sponsored the 1946 and 1958 World SF Conventions, and it also runs the annual Westercon whenever no other group bids for it.

LOST IN SPACE U.S. television series, CBS network; 83 episodes, 1965-1968. An Irwin Allen production for 20th Century Fox. In 1997 the Robinson family blasts off to settle another planet, but becomes lost through the villainy of stowaway Dr. Zachary Smith. The regular cast included Guy Williams (as Prof. John Robinson), June Lockhart (Maureen Robinson), Billy Mumy (Will Robinson), Mark Goddard (Don West), Marta Kristen (Judy Robinson), Angela Cartwright (Penny Robinson), and Jonathan Harris (Dr. Z. Smith). In the pilot episode the family robot is a heavy, but it soon developed into a good guy and became one of the most popular characters.

M

MACMILLAN'S LIBRARY OF SCIENCE FICTION CLASSICS U.S. publisher's 1963 series: *Before Adam*, J. London; *The Star Rover*, J. London; *The Weigher of Souls* & *The Earth Dwellers*, A. Maurois; *Dr.*

Ox's Experiment, J. Verne; *The Hopkins Manuscript*, R. C. Sherriff; *A Voyage to Arcturus*, D. Lindsay.

MAGNETIC MONSTER, THE U.S. film, Tors-Siodmak-Carlson Enterprise, 1953; released through United Artists; directed by C. Siodmak; starring Richard Carlson.

A radioactive element of prolific growth and powerful magnetic flux field threatens to destroy Earth. The working title was "The A-Men."

MALIAN PRESS Australian publisher, Sydney, N.S.W., which issued science fiction in a regular paper-covered series from 1952 to 1955. Reprints, mostly of U.S. magazine fiction, became known by their cover story titles, but were in the *American Science Fiction (Magazine)* series (41 issues) and the later companion *Selected Science Fiction* (5 issues).

MASTER SCIENCE FICTION SERIES A book series published by World's Work, Tadsworth, England. Nos. 1, 3, 4, and 5 were novels in the "Golden Amazon" series [see J. R. FEARN in the *WHO'S WHO*]; NO. 2 was *David Starr: Spaceranger*, P. French [see I. ASIMOV]; and No. 6 was *Seetee Shock*, W. Stewart [see J. WILLIAMSON].

MEXICO There have been the following magazines, all now defunct: *Antologia de Cuentos Fantasticos*, *Ciencia y Fantasia* [an edition of *F&SF*], *Los Cuentos Fantasticos*, *Enigmas*, and *Fantasias del Futuro*.

Editorial Novaro-Mexico, publisher of *Ciencia y Fantasia*, also published translations of *The War of the Worlds*, H. G. Wells; *The World in Danger*, E. C. Tubb; *The World in Flames*, H. K. Bulmer; and *Another Space—Another Time*, *The Red Planet*, and *Brain Ultimate*, all by H. J. Campbell.

Editora Sol S.A. published for some years the comic *Fantastico* (reprinting from U.S. comic magazines) and also a paperback *Coleccion Aventuras* (Adventure Collection) series, including many reprints of J. Verne; some 90 volumes have appeared.

Mexico now has no science-fiction magazines. Apart from the intelligentsia, most literate Mexicans prefer comic books, and consequently these sell very well.

MINOTAURO Argentine series of books, mostly very good translations, though there were also many original Spanish titles. Editions were fine, but not hard bound. The series apparently ceased in 1962. Titles include:

1955 *The Martian Chronicles*, R. Bradbury; *More Than Human*, T. Sturgeon; *The Space Merchants*, F. Pohl & C. M. Kornbluth; *The Illustrated Man*, R. Bradbury

1956 *Childhood's End*, A. C. Clarke; *The Demolished Man*, A. Bester; *The Day of the Triffids*, J. Wyndham [J. B. Harris]

1957 *The Colour out of Space*, H. P. Lovecraft (includes "The Call of Cthulhu"; "The Whisperer in Darkness"; "At the Mountains of Madness"); *City*, C. D. Simak

1958 *Odd John*, O. Stapledon; *Fahrenheit 451*, R. Bradbury; *The World Below*, S. F. Wright (with *The Amphibians*)

1959 None

1960 *I Am Legend*, R. Matheson; *To Walk the Night*, W. Sloane; *Sirius*, O. Stapledon

1961 *The Dreaming Jewels*, T. Sturgeon; *The Golden Apples of the Sun*, R. Bradbury (omits "The Wilderness" & "A Sound of Thunder")

1962 *Earth Abides*, G. R. Stewart

MOON Books covering theories of the Moon's formation, etc., include *The Moon Puzzle*, N. O. Bergquist (1954) and *Moon Travellers*, P. Leighton (1960). Fictional aspects are covered in *Voyages to the Moon*, M. H. Nicholson (1949) as well as *Pilgrims Through Space and Time*, J. O. Bailey (1947).

The Moon Hoax—this can be termed a classic hoax. It originated as a serial article in *The New York Sun* in the last week of August 1835. Written by Richard Adams Locke, it described the inhabitants of the Moon as seen through a giant telescope built in South Africa. The article has been reprinted in booklet form, in *Sky* magazine (now *Sky and Telescope*), and in *Amazing Stories*, Sep 1926 with other newspaper comments of the time.

There was a contest story "The Moon Doom" in *Wonder Stories*, Feb to June 1933, with each part written by a different author (none of note).

H. Oberth's *Moon Car* (1959) describes a vehicle for Lunar use.

MOTHRA Noted Japanese monster film, 1962; directed by Inoshiro Honda for Toho Productions.

A giant caterpillar destroys Tokyo in retribution for the kidnapping of two tiny "magic ladies."

MUNCHAUSEN, BARON A character who actually lived (1720—1797); he served with the Russians against the Turks, but has come down through history as a figure of folklore.

Rudolph Erich Raspe, after escaping to England from one of the German states where he was wanted for theft and embezzlement, wrote the Munchausen stories with the implication that they had been told to him by the Baron. The Baron was very angry, but as the book had been published anonymously he was unable to impose retribution. Raspe never claimed the authorship, but it was discovered after his death.

Other writers have used this character through the years. In sf and fantasy there are the books by J. K. Bangs—*The Enchanted Typewriter* and *Mr. Munchausen*—and the magazine series by H. Gernsback originally in *The Electrical Experimenter* and later reprinted in *Amazing Stories* [see H. GERNSBACK in the *WHO'S WHO*].

MYSTERIANS, THE Japanese film, 1958, in colour; released through M.G.M with English dubbed voices.

Invaders from the destroyed fifth planet set up a base in Japan to control the world.

N

NAKED JUNGLE, THE U.S. film, Paramount, 1954; produced by George Pal, directed by Byron Haskin; starring Charlton Heston and Eleanor Parker; based on C. Stephenson's short story "Leiningen Versus the Ants."

NATIONAL FANTASY FAN FEDERATION [NFFF] The most important of the loosely-knit world-wide fan organizations. Based in the U.S.A., it has been going since about April 1941. It publishes news sheets, amateur magazines, etc., and at times various information booklets for members. The NFFF (often called the N3F) is primarily for young and new fans and helps ease their entry into the more esoteric reaches of fandom.

NEBULA AWARDS The awards presented annually by the Science Fiction Writers of America [SFWA], chosen by vote of the membership.

1965
Novel: *Dune*, F. Herbert
Novella: Tie: "The Saliva Tree," B. W. Aldiss; "He Who Shapes," R. Zelazny
Novelette: "The Doors of His Face, the Lamps of His Mouth," R. Zelazny
Short Story: " 'Repent, Harlequin!' Said the Ticktockman," H. Ellison
All stories except the novel, but including the runners-up, published as *Nebula Award Stories 1965* (or No. 1), D. Knight (1966).

1966
Novel: Tie: *Flowers for Algernon*, D. Keyes; *Babel-17*, S. R. Delany
Novella: "The Last Castle," J. Vance
Novelette: "Call Him Lord," G. R. Dickson
Short Story: "The Secret Place," R. M. McKenna
Published as *Nebula Award Stories 1967*, B. W. Aldiss & H. Harrison (1967).

1967
Novel: *The Einstein Intersection*, S. R. Delany
Novella: "Behold the Man," M. Moorcock
Novelette: "Gonna Roll the Bones," F. Leiber
Short Story: "Aye and Gomorrah," S. R. Delany
Published as *Nebula Award Stories No. 3*, R. Zelazny (1968).

1968
Novel: *Rite of Passage*, A. Panshin
Novella: "Dragonrider," A. McCaffrey
Novelette: "Mother to the World," Richard Wilson
Short Story: "The Planners," Kate Wilhelm

NEBULAE Spanish science fiction paperback book series, published by EDHASA, Barcelona, at 30 pesetas (about 50¢). The best sf in the Spanish field, and very well edited, these presented translations of many major novels and collections by contemporary U.S. and British writers.

Starting Feb 1955 with *The Puppet Masters*, R. A. Heinlein, the series ceased in late 1965 at No. 114 with the same writer's *Beyond This Horizon*. Other authors included P. Anderson, I. Asimov, A. C. Clarke, E. Hamilton, R. F. Jones, M. Leinster [W. F. Jenkins], R. Silverberg, C. Simak, G. O. Smith, A. E. van Vogt, J. Williamson, and J. Wyndham [J. B. Harris].

NETHERLANDS See HOLLAND

NEW COLLECTORS' GROUP A U.S. fantasy book club founded in 1947 with the aim of publishing original works of well-known authors in special collector's editions. The president was Paul O'Connor.

It produced the two A. Merritt works that had been completed by H. Bok: *The Black Wheel* and *The Fox Woman and the Blue Pagoda*. The third and fourth books promoted, but which never appeared, were *The Eternal Conflict and Other Weird Tales*, D. H. Keller [title story later published by Prime Press] and *The Outlawed World*, N. R. Jones.

NEW ERA PUBLISHING COMPANY U.S. specialist book publisher begun by the veteran Philadelphia fantasy fans Robert Madle and Jack Agnew. The only title produced was *The Solitary Hunters and The Abyss*, D. H. Keller (1948).

NEW FUTURIAN, THE British amateur magazine, published by the late Michael Rosenblum; 8 issues (Spr 1954—1958); quarto, duplicated, 40 pp.; began quarterly, then became irregular.

This was Rosenblum's return to the amateur publishing field after World War II (he had previously published *The Futurian*, 1938-1940, and *Futurian War Digest*). *The New Futurian* presented articles on various phases of science fiction, reviewed noted "older" books, and serialised the late Walter Gillings' story of British science fiction fandom, which more recently appeared in revised form as "The Impatient Dreamers" (*Visions of Tomorrow* 1969-1970).

NEW ZEALAND This country is similar to Australia with regard to importing British and U.S. material, though monetary exchange with the U.S. was for some years easier than in Australia.

Organised fandom is said to have started in 1951 with the formation of the Auckland SF Club. Later groups were the Christchurch SF Club, the Wellington SF Circle, and the Auckland Space Club. Nothing is known of activity in the late 1960's.

A New Zealand author is Bee Baldwin, noted for her *The Red Dust*. The Utopian writer S. Butler lived in this country for a period. Thomas G. L. Cockcroft is a noted bibliographer in the weird fiction field.

NOVA PUBLICATIONS A British publishing house formed in 1949, with the backing of British fandom, to revive the magazine *New Worlds*. Later *Science-Fantasy* was produced. A third magazine was *Science Fiction Adventures*, first begun as a reprint of a U.S. magazine of the same title, and then continued with original stories. Two attempts were made to start a paperback book series: Nova SF Novels.

Originally E. J. Carnell edited *New Worlds* and W. Gillings edited *Science-Fantasy*. Gillings soon left, and Carnell remained as the responsible editor until Nova ceased in 1964.

O

ONE MILLION B.C. U.S. film, United Artists, 1940; directed by Hal Roach Sr. & Jr. and D. W. Griffith; starring Victor Mature and Carole Landis.

One of the prehistoric-type films, based on photographing lizards and spiders on miniature sets. It did convey some sense of the past.

It was remade by Hammer in 1966 as *One Million Years B.C.*, with identical script, effects by Ray Harryhausen, and starring the voluptuous Raquel Welch.

ONE STEP BEYOND U.S. television series, ABC network, 1959-1961, 94 episodes (30 minutes, black & white). It was hosted by John Newland, who also directed and acted. The series gave stories of the supernatural, and was generally highly regarded. Some of the stories appeared in paperbacks edited by L. Bredeson.

OPERATION FANTAST The non-profit trading organization operated by British fan Capt. Kenneth Slater in the post-war years until 1955. World-wide in scope, it mainly covered magazine swapping but also had many other activities. *Operation Fantast* was also the organization's amateur magazine (duplicated 1947-1949, then printed photolith for 18 issues, July 1949-May 1955). Other publications included *Operation Fantast Handbook*, which gave data on many aspects of science fiction and fantasy.

After leaving the British Army, Slater was forced to run Operation Fantast on more strictly business lines, and its trading section was incorporated as Fantast (Medway) Ltd., a book and magazine dealership which is still operating in Wisbech, England.

OPIUM BOOKS Hong Kong, founded by March Laumer.
1965 No. 1. *Horace, Boris, Norris, Morris and Doris*, Felix Severance (vi+97 pp.)—reminiscences of a soldier (not sf).
1966 No. 2?. *John Dough and the Cherub*, L. F. Baum.
1967 No. 3?. *Trolls! Trolls! Trolls!*, Boys at Ying Wa College, Hong Kong (98 pp., pa $7.00)—juvenile fantasy.
1968 No. 4. *Queer Adventures in a Magic World*, Boys at Ying Wa College (193 pp., $10.00, 15/-)—juvenile fantasy.
   No. 5. *The Time Machine That Never Got Past First Base*, F. Severance [M. Laumer] (iv+152 pp., *ca.* P1).
   No. ?. *Woosooloo the Saviour*, Boys at Ying Wa College (170 pp., $10.00)—juvenile fantasy.
1969 *Queen Zixi of Ix*, L. F. Baum
   Mr. Flint in Oz, R. Powell
   Wooden Soldiers of Oz, A. M. Volkov
   Aillinn o' My Dreams, M. Laumer
   The Tides in the Bay of Fundy, Xavier Xanthus [M. Laumer]
This publisher then apparently ceased.

OUT OF THE UNKNOWN One of the best British television series to be produced so far (to 1968). It was based on noted science fiction short stories. Titles included "Time in Advance," W. Tenn; "No Place Like Earth," J. Wyndham; "Sucker Bait," I. Asimov; "Lambda 1," Colin Kapp; "The Midas Plague," F. Pohl; "The Fox and the Forest," Ray Bradbury; "Andover and the Android," Kate Wilhelm; "Thirteen to Centaurus," J. G. Ballard.

OUTER LIMITS, THE U.S. television series, ABC network; 49 episodes (60 minutes, black & white), 1963-1965; a Daystar-Ville di Stefano production for United Artists.

A dramatic sf series, with each show having some type of monster. H. Ellison wrote some of the scripts. Leslie Stevens was executive producer; Joseph Stefano was producer for the first season, and Ben Brady was producer for the second season. The episodes were:

First Season (Sep 1963—May 1964)
The Galaxy Being (writer: Leslie Stevens). A radio engineer experimenting with a 3-D TV receiver tunes in a being from Andromeda.
The One Hundred Days of the Dragon (A. Balter). A winning Presidential candidate is impersonated by an Oriental despot's agent who can alter his skin appearance.
The Architects of Fear (M. Dolinsky). A group of scientists create a fake being from another planet to force the nations into peaceful co-existence. Starring Robert Culp.
The Man With the Power (J. Ross). A meek college instructor acquires incredible and uncontrollable mental powers after an experiment.
The Sixth Finger (E. St. Joseph). A geneticist uses a willing miner to advance his experiments in evolution. Starring David McCallum.
The Man Who Was Never Born (A. Lawrence). An astronaut passes through a time warp and finds the Earth of 2148 barren and populated by grotesque humanoids. Cast includes Martin Landau.
O.B.I.T. (M. Dolinksy). A senatorial investigation reveals the existence of an electronic surveillance device planted by beings from another world.
The Human Factor (D. Duncan). At a military base in Greenland the brains of two men are accidentally exchanged.
Corpus Earthling (O. Borstein, from the story by L. Charbonneau). The metal plate in a doctor's head enables him to hear two crystalline rocks planning to take over Earth. Cast includes Robert Culp.
Nightmare (J. Stefano). Aliens from the planet Ebon attack Earth and capture some people who undergo alien interrogation. Cast includes Ed Nelson.
It Crawled out of the Woodwork (J. Stefano). A ball of black dust sucked into a vacuum cleaner feeds on the motor's energy and grows uncontrollably.
The Borderland (L. Stevens). A team of scientists financed by a wealthy man hoping to contact his dead son propel themselves into the fourth dimension, where everything is a mirror image of itself.
Tourist Attraction (D. Riesner). A tycoon on a fishing cruise off South America captures a supposedly extinct "lizard-fish."
The Zanti Misfits (J. Stefano). Incapable of executing their criminals, the rulers of the planet Zanti send them to Earth.
The Mice (B. S. Ballinger & J. Stefano, from a story by Ballinger & L. Morheim). As an alternative to prison, a man volunteers for the "inhabitant exchange" programme with the planet Chromo.
Controlled Experiment (L. Stevens). Two Martians investigate Earth's quaint custom of homicide, using a machine that can replay a murder. Cast includes B. Morse.
Don't Open Till Doomsday (J. Stefano). Eloping teenagers spend their wedding night in a suite unoccupied since 1929—and a box in the room contains a creature from another planet.
Z-Z-Z-Z-Z (M. Dolinsky). A queen bee assumes human form to lure an entomologist into her world to make him a human drone.
The Invisibles (J. Stefano). Intelligence agent infiltrates the strange society known as the "Invisibles," which hopes to conquer man by attaching parasitic creatures to human spinal cords.
The Bellero Shield (J. Stefano). A scientist accidentally captures a space creature with an impenetrable protective shield. Cast includes M. Landau.
Children of Spider County (A. Lawrence). Five geniuses vanish; their father, an alien from a distant world, returns to claim them.
Specimen: Unknown (S. Lord). Space station crewmen encounter mushroomlike organisms that emit lethal gas and multiply rapidly.
Second Chance (also titled *Joy Ride*) (L. Morheim & Lin Dane). A group of people board an amusement-park space ship only to find it is the real thing.
Moonstone (W. Bast, based on story by L. Morheim & J. Stefano). Military and scientific staff on the Moon discover a strange object that is round, smooth—and alive.
The Mutant (A. Balter & R. Mintz, from a story by Jerome B. Thomas). Caught in a strange silver downpour on another planet, a scientist turns into a telepathic killer.
The Guests (D. S. Sanford). A drifter comes across a strange house where time stands still and the occupants are captive to a weird and unearthly creature.
Fun and Games (R. Specht & J. Stefano). On satellite Arena creatures from many worlds battle, with the losers forfeiting the lives of every-

one on their particular planets.

The Special One (O. Crawford). An agent from the planet Xenon tutors the brilliant children of Earth for a special project—the conquest of Earth.

A Feasibility Study (J. Stefano). Six city blocks are transferred to another galaxy.

Production and Decay of Strange Particles (L. Stevens). A nuclear reactor goes out of control and its radiation is released as near-human creatures.

The Chameleon (R. Towne, J. Stefano & L. Morheim). An intelligence agent disguises himself to infiltrate a party of creatures from another planet.

The Form of Things Unknown (J. Stefano). An elusive madman devises a machine that can "tilt" time to bring the dead back to life.

Second Season (Sep 1964—Jan 1965)

Soldier (H. Ellison). Caught in a "laser light," a soldier of the future is catapulted back into our time. Cast includes Lloyd Nolan and Michael Ansara.

Cold Hands, Warm Heart (D. Ulman & M. Krims). An astronaut returns from a successful flight around the scorching planet Venus, and then finds he can't keep himself warm. Cast includes William Shatner.

Behold, Eck! (J. Mantley, from a story by W. Cox). An eye specialist fashions several pairs of glasses which enable the wearers to see a friendly but dangerous monster.

Expanding Human (F. Cockrell). A university professor experiments with a drug that expands human consciousness.

Demon With a Glass Hand (H. Ellison). A suspenseful chase drama with the last man on Earth returning to the 20th Century to find why he was a survivor of an alien attack. Cast includes Robert Culp.

City of Silence (L. Charbonneau). A couple are stalked by animated tumbleweeds possessed by an alien intelligence. Cast includes Eddie Albert and June Havoc.

The Invisible Enemy (J. Sohl). An expedition to Mars is menaced by horde of monsters who dwell in a sea of sand.

Wolf 359 (S. Lester & R. Landau). A professor reproduces a distant planet in miniature and watches speeded-up evolution.

I, Robot (O. Binder). An almost-human robot is put on trial for murdering its creator.

The Inheritors (2 parts; by S. Newman, S. Lester & E. Adamson). After a meteorite crashes, bullets molded from its metal find their way into battle and strike down four men who then become powerful alien intelligences. In Part 2 they become involved in a mysterious project involving a number of children.

Keeper of the Purple Twilight (M. Krims). An alien scientist makes a deal to exchange his intellect for an Earth scientist's emotions, and then falls in love with the Earthman's wife.

The Duplicate Man (R. Dennis, from a story by C. Simak). To recapture a murderous space creature an anthropologist creates a duplicate of himself. Starring Ron Randell.

Counterweight (M. Krims). Six people and an extraordinary patch of light board a simulated flight to another planet, and the flight turns out to be real.

The Brain of Colonel Barham (R. C. Dennis). Scientists decide that the ideal instrument for space exploration would be a computer activated by a human brain.

The Premonition (S. Rocca & I. Melchior). Test pilot and his wife are saved from sudden death by an equally sudden suspension of time.

The Probe (S. Lester, from a story by Sam Neuman). The survivors of a Pacific plane crash find themselves sitting motionless on a seemingly solid sea.

P

PEARSON LTD., London. General British publisher. In 1934 Pearson published *Scoops*; after the war it published the SF paperback series "Tit-Bits Science Fiction Library."

PENDULUM PUBLICATIONS LTD., London. The British firm which published the first three issues of *New Worlds*. Soon after the release of the first *NW* around late 1946, a brochure announced planned publications:

"Spacetime Series" (Editor: F. E. Arnold): *Wings Across Time*, F. E. Arnold; *Other Eyes Watching*, P. Cross [J. R. Fearn]; *Green Man of Kilsona*, F. Pragnell. [Only the first two appeared.]

"Science Series" (Editor: A. M. Low): *Six Scientific Years*, A. M. Low. [Presumably appeared.]

"Fantasy Series" (Editor: E. J. Carnell): *Jinn and Jitters*, E. J. Carnell (A); *Lost Legacy*, L. Monroe [R. A. Heinlein]. [Only the first appeared.]

"Weird Series" (Editor: E. J. Carnell): *Devil Dog and Others; Ghoul's Gallows.* [Apparently neither appeared.]

PHILADELPHIA SCIENCE FICTION SOCIETY [PSFS] This began in Dec 1934 as Chapter 11 of the Science Fiction League, with M. A. Rothman and others. Slightly later J. V. Baltadonis, J. Agnew, H. Greenblatt, and R. A. Madle, who had their own group, joined; the reorganisation meeting was Oct 1935. Oswald Train was another early member. The Society has continued to the present day, sponsoring its own annual convention; it also sponsored the 1947 and 1953 World SF Conventions.

PICK-A-BOOK The reduced-price book purchasing scheme initiated by M. Greenberg around 1958. Besides his own Gnome Press books, he offered Fantasy Press and Fantasy Publishing Co. Inc. books which he had bought, and also Avalon books from 1959. The price was $1.20. The plan lapsed in the early 1960's.

PLANETBÖGERNE Danish science fiction paperback book series; 14 issues (15 Oct 1957—Nov 1958); edited by L. I. Madsen; published by Skrifola, Copenhagen; normal paperback size, 2.50 Danish kroner.

This was a companion series to "Fremtidsromanen," but more expensively produced, with covers and illustrations mainly from the Italian *Urania* series.

Translations were published of such authors as R. Bradbury (*The Illustrated Man*, abridged), W. Moore, D. Wandrei, J. R. Fearn, W. Tucker, B. Glemser, A. C. Clarke, S. Merwin, C. M. Kornbluth, I. Asimov, J. Boland, and M. Leinster [W. F. Jenkins].

Two titles were reissued in combined format similar to an Ace Double at 3.75 kr in an attempt to sell remainders.

POLAND Stanislaw Lem (1921—) is one of the most noted contemporary writers now appearing in translation into English. Also covered in the *Encyclopedia* is J. Potocki (1761—1815). Not covered, but of some interest, is Nobel Prize winner W. St. Reymont, with two novels *The Revolt* and *The Vampire*.

POLARIS PRESS U.S. imprint, an offshoot of L. A. Eshbach's Fantasy Press. It printed lesser-known classics of interest to collectors in limited editions of 1,500 and not sold through regular channels. Titles were: *The Heads of Cerberus*, F. Stevens [G. Bennett]; *The Abyss of Wonders*, P. P. Sheehan.

PORTFOLIOS—ART The magazines *Famous Fantastic Mysteries* and *Fantastic Novels* published the following portfolios, containing illustrations used in their pages: V. Finlay (No. 1), 1941, 8 drawings, 60¢; (2) 1953, 8, 60¢; (3) 1949, 8, 75¢. Lawrence (No. 1), 1945, 8, 75¢; (2) 1949, 8, 75¢. Many other portfolios have appeared from private sources. The Bokanalia Foundation has produced 3 folders on Hannes Bok and a special edition of *And Flights of Angels*. Advent:Publishers issued an F. K. Freas portfolio in 1957.

PORTUGAL An association of mystery and fantasy fans was the Clube de Literatura Policiaria, which intended to publish the magazine *XYZ* in 1957, with Lima da Costa as editor.

Portuguese editions include *A Cidade no Tempo* (*City*), C. D. Simak; *A Uniao dos Universes* (*Ceux de Nulle Part*), Francis Carsac; *1984*, G. Orwell [E. Blair]; *Admiravel Mundo Novo* (*Brave New World*), A. Huxley; *Homem cu Vampire* (*Dracula*), B. Stoker; *Recordações Fantasticas* (*Fantastic Memories*), M. Sandoz; *Os Mortos Podem Voltar* (*The Case of*

C. D. Ward), H. P. Lovecraft; as well as two ghost-detective novels by Igor Maslowski and Olivier Sechan in collaboration. [Information up to 1957 only.]

PRESENCE DU FUTUR French science fiction and fantasy book series published by Denoël, Paris. It began in March 1954 and by the end of 1968 had issued 102 books (109 numbers, as some double books had two numbers).

Titles have included most of R. Bradbury's collections, a number of collections of H. P. Lovecraft's short stories, and works by such authors as F. Brown, J. W. Campbell, A. Bester, R. Matheson, C. Oliver, A. E. van Vogt, J. Blish, B. W. Aldiss, I. Asimov, and J. Vance, plus several by the Polish writer S. Lem, and some by other foreign authors.

PRIME PRESS U.S. science fiction and fantasy publisher, one of the specialist houses which ran for a period after World War II. Headed by James Williams and Oswald Train, it was situated in Philadelphia.

Prime Press began with *The Mislaid Charm*, A. M. Phillips, and then issued notable collections by L. del Rey and T. Sturgeon, as well as novels by L. S. de Camp, D. Keller, G. O. Smith, and N. S. Bond.

It also began a reprint series of American Utopias, of which *Equality, or, A History of Lithconia*, Anon., and *Three Hundred Years Hence*, Mary Griffiths, appeared.

PRISONER, THE U.S. television series, CBS network; 17 episodes (60 minutes, colour), 1968; created by main actor Patrick McGoohan; produced by David Tomblin. The enigmatic trials of a newly resigned intelligence agent who finds himself in an village from which there is no escape. The episodes were:

Arrival. Opening to series, with our protagonist in "The Village."

The Chimes of Big Ben. The Prisoner seemingly makes a successful escape, but . . .

A, B, & C. Intrigue with dreams and a mysterious resignation.

Free for All. The Prisoner becomes a contender for the post of Number Two.

The Schizoid Man. A double is used to convince him he's someone else.

The General. The Prisoner tries to thwart an instant knowledge system.

Many Happy Returns. When the Village appears abandoned he attempts to escape.

Dance of Death. He attempts to smuggle out a plea for help in a corpse.

Do Not Forsake Me Oh My Darling. A strange procedure puts the Prisoner's mind in another man's body.

It's Your Funeral. The Prisoner is fed misinformation to prevent him foiling Their plans.

Checkmate. He becomes a pawn in a life-sized chess game.

A Change of Mind. The Village leaders use an electronic method for transforming human mental processes.

Hammer Into Anvil. To avenge the murder of a young girl the Prisoner tries to trick Number Two.

The Girl Who Was Death. The Prisoner faces a lethal struggle with a young woman who introduces herself as "Death."

Once Upon a Time. The Prisoner and Number Two face a deadly conflict of wills with a dangerous electronic mind probe.

Fall Out. He finally wins the right not to be called by number but to be an individual, but he can't escape the prison of himself.

Living in Harmony. The Prisoner finds himself sheriff of a western town and undergoes mental conflict. This episode was never aired on the network but appeared in syndication.

Two paperbacks based on the series appeared in 1969.

PSYCHIC PHENOMENA See EXTRASENSORY PERCEPTION

PUBLISHERS The following list contains companies covered in this *GENERAL* section as well as individuals, noted with an asterisk (*), who should be looked up in the *WHO'S WHO*. It includes some whose plans were never carried out.

Advent:Publishers; Arkham House [also see A. Derleth*]; Arra Publishers; Atlas Publications; Avalon Books; Avon Publications.

I. Ballantine*.

Chamberlain Press; W. P. Cook*; W. L. Crawford*.

Dawn Press.

Fandom House; Fantasy Press; Fantasy Publishing Co. Inc.; J. W.

Ferman*; Futile Press; Futurian Press.

W. M. Gaines*; Gnome Press; Grandon Company; D. M. Grant*; Griffin Publishing Co.; R. M. Guinn*.

Hachette; Hadley Publishing Co.; P. Hamilton*; W. L. Hamling*; Hearst Corporation; B. Herbert*; H. Hersey*.

Jupiter Press.

Malian Press.

New Era Publishing Co.; Nova Publications.

R. A. Palmer*; Pearsons Ltd.; Pendulum Publications; Polaris Press; Prime Press.

Renown Books; C. H. Ruppert*.

Scientific American; Shasta Publishers; Shroud Publishers; L. Silberkleit*; Stellar Publishing Co.; Strato Publications; Swan Limited.

Utopian Publications.

J. Warren*; J. A. Williams*; World's Work,

W. B. Ziff*.

The Associated Fantasy Publishers, a trade association formed in 1948, had as members: Arkham House, Fantasy Press, Prime Press, Shasta Publishers, Gnome Press, Fantasy Publishing Co., Hadley Publishing Co., and New Era Publishing Co.

Published Series [in English, including amateur]: Adventures in Science Fiction (juvenile books); Bizarre; Connoisseur's Library of Strange Fiction; Cosmic Library; Golden Science Fiction Library; Master Science Fiction Series.

Published Series [pocket-book or paper-covered]: Full lists are given in each publisher's entry in the *PAPERBACK* section; this *GENERAL* section includes further information on only the following:

Ace Books; Corgi Books; Satellite Series; Science Fiction Classics; Science Fiction Library; Science Fiction Series; Tit-Bits Science Fiction Library; Xanadu Library.

Published Series [foreign]: Many magazine series, e.g., the German *Utopia* and *Terra* series are covered in *MAGAZINES*. This *GENERAL* section covers the following:

Argentine: Fantaciencia, Minotauro.

Danish: Fremtidsromanen, Lommeromanen, Planetbogerne.

French: Anticipation, Presence du Futur, Le Rayon Fantastique.

Italian: Biblioteca Economica Mondadori, Fantascienza.

Japanese: Hayakawa.

Spanish: Cenit, Espacio, Nebulae.

Swedish: Atombök, Atomböckerna, Rymdböckerna.

R

RADIO Since World War II numerous novels and short stories have seen radio (and TV) presentation, while some originally written for radio have also had book publication.

Historically, the most important radio broadcast was Orson Welles' dramatic 1938 presentation of H. G. Wells' *The War of the Worlds*. Around 1954 the BBC serialised Wells' *The First Men in the Moon*. Others have included C. Chilton's "Jet Morgan" trilogy [see *WHO'S WHO*] and several John Wyndham [J. B. Harris] novels. About 1960 "Orbiter X," produced by B. T. Maxwell with story by B. D. Chapman, appeared.

A reference work in this field is *The Great Radio Heroes*, J. Harmon (1967; Ace, 1968 pa).

RAYON FANTASTIQUE, LE French science fiction book series published by Hachette (editor: G. H. Gallet) and Gallimard (editor: Stephen Spriel). There were about 120 titles from 1951 to early 1964; paperback, 4½ x 7 in.

At first the books were not numbered; they became numbered early in 1960. Up to about 1958 about three quarters of the titles were translations of the better books in English; thereafter a higher percentage of original French material was used. Sales generally averaged 12,000 copies, with a few reaching 25,000 or 30,000. The books were actually printed in Poland.

The two editors were quite dissimilar in their choices. Gallet used adventure stories so that French readers could become used to the sf idiom in easy stages; Spriel, who had discovered sf in its postwar state, was enthusiastic over the intellectual aspect, which he thought would appeal to sophisticated readers. This caused dissatisfaction among the readers. Towards the end of the series relations also became strained between the two publishers, and Hachette produced practically all of the last titles.

The series published each Jules Verne Prize novel from 1958. See the appropriate author entry in the *WHO'S WHO* for translations. Authors included M. Leinster [W. F. Jenkins], E. Hamilton, L. S. de Camp, T. Sturgeon, E. F. Russell, C. S. Lewis, O. Stapledon, A. E. van Vogt, I. Asimov, R. A. Heinlein, R. Wilson, and C. D. Simak. French writers included S. Martel, C. Henneberg, and F. Carsac.

READERS' SERVICE BOOK CLUB A dealer who sold science fiction about 1952, operated from San Jose, California, by Lloyd Cheney. The books had "Book Club Edition" stamped on the dust wrapper, and were special editions of Fantasy Publishing Co. Inc. works.

The titles included: *The Kingslayer*, L. R. Hubbard ($1.98); *Out of the Unknown*, A. E. van Vogt & E. M. Hull ($2.19); *Drome*, J. M. Leahy ($1.98); *The Hidden Universe*, R. M. Farley ($1.39); *The Dark Other*, S. G. Weinbaum (pa 98¢); *Worlds of Wonder*, O. Stapledon ($1.98); *Green Fire*, J. Taine ($1.98); *The Radium Pool*, E. E. Repp ($1.98); *The Toy-maker*, R. F. Jones ($1.98); *The Sunken World*, S. A. Coblentz (pa 98¢); *The Undesired Princess*, L. S. de Camp ($1.98); *People of the Comet*, A. Hall ($1.39); *The Iron Star*, J. Taine ($1.98); *Planets of Adventure*, B. Wells (pa 98¢); *Doorways to Space*, B. Wells ($1.69).

RECORDINGS A complete listing is impossible, but this entry summarizes the most important, noted from an Australian enthusiast of the early 1960's, giving an idea of the types available.
Associational: "Music in 2061: A view of musical life 100 years in the future," Edward Cole and Bernard Seeman (1961).
Films (theme music): Walt Disney's fantasies, including *Fantasia*, *Alice in Wonderland*, and *The Absent-Minded Professor*; *Bell, Book and Candle*; *Destination Moon*; *On the Beach*; C. Chaplin's *Modern Times*.
Operas and Musicals: *Aniara*, composed by H. Martinson (recorded by Columbia, 1959); *The Transposed Heads*, composed by Peggy Glanville-Hocks; *The Turn of the Screw*, composed by Benjamin Britten from the H. James story; *The Devil and Daniel Webster* (folk opera), composed by D. Moore from the S. V. Benét story; *Brigadoon*; *Camelot* (from *The Once and Future King*, T. H. White).
Plays: *The Cocktail Party*, written by T. S. Eliot, starring Alec Guinness; *The Investigator*, Reuben Ship with John Drainie; *Peter Pan*, J. Barrie, starring Jean Arthur and Boris Karloff; *Drop Dead*, written and directed by Arch Oboler (7 stories, with cast of 17 players).
Readings (separate recordings for each reader listed): *A Christmas Carol*, C. Dickens—read by C. Laughton, F. Pettingell, R. Richardson, and others; *The Pied Piper*, R. Browning—read by B. Karloff; certain stories of Hans Christian Anderson, by M. Redgrave, B. Karloff; certain stories of E. A. Poe, by J. Mason, B. Rathbone, R. Taylor, Marvin Miller, M. Olmstead, and others; *Dr. Jekyll and Mr. Hyde*, R. L. Stevenson—by G. Lockhard; certain stories of N. Hawthorne, by B. Rathbone; H. P. Lovecraft stories, by R. McDowell; R. Bradbury stories, by B. Meredith; Brothers Grimm stories, by J. Schildkraut; *Terror Tales*, R. P. Hamilton, by Martha Wentworth; *Sleep No More*; *Famous Ghost and Horror Stories*, read by N. Olmstead; J. Swift selections, by A. Guinness, D. Johnston; W. de la Mare reading some of his own stories; C. Dickens stories, by E. Williams; Orson Welles with his original 1938 version of *The War of the Worlds*; O. Wilde stories, read by B. Rathbone, F. Pettingell; John Zacherle also has made reading records.
Space, Imaginative: *Adventures in Sound and Space*, C. E. Crumpacker (1959); *Fantasy in Space*; *Journey to Infinity*, written by C. T. Reece and narrated by W. E. Sickles.
Space, Realistic or Discussions: *Colonel John Glenn in Orbit* (1962); *Conquest of Space*, conversation between W. Von Braun and W. Ley; *Rockets, Missiles and Space Travel* (1959), written and directed by W. Ley with voices of W. Von Braun, W. Dornberger, K. Ehricke and Yates.
Other: *Sounds of Science Fiction*, conceived and recorded by Mel Kaiser

(1959); *Music To Be Murdered By*, presented by A. Hitchcock.

Many of the above have pressings in both Great Britain and the U.S.A.

RENOWN BOOKS U.S. book publishing house founded by L. Margulies with intention of publishing four books every two months, one at least to be science fiction. No sf books appeared, although *Mission to a Star*, F. B. Long [enlarged from *Satellite SF*, Feb 1958] was originally planned in Aug 1959.

ROBINSON CRUSOE ON MARS U.S. film, Paramount, 1964; directed by Byron Haskin, with screenplay by Ib Melchior & John C. Higgins; based on the Daniel Defoe novel *Robinson Crusoe*.

Astronaut Paul Mantee struggles to survive on a desolate Mars; first he is plagued by the ghost of his dead friend Adam West, later he rescues a humanoid from an alien race.

ROCKET MAN, THE U.S. film, 20th Century Fox, 1954; panoramic screen; produced by Leonard Goldstein, directed by Oscar Rudolph, from a story by G. W. George & G. F. Slevin; starring Charles Coburn, Spring Byington, George Winslow, Anne Francis, and John Agar.

A space opera fan is given a futuristic space gun with magic powers; the plot develops into a warm comedy with a touch of fantasy.

ROCKETRY The *Encyclopedia* does not deal with this subject comprehensively, though a number of early books are covered under SPACE TRAVEL (which see).

RODAN Japanese film, Toho, 1956; released by Distributors Corp. of America, late 1957; directed by Inoshiro Honda; screenplay based on a story by Takashi Kuronuma.

Nuclear tests release prehistoric beasts—gigantic insects and pteranodons, etc.—which terrorise the world and are only vanquished by an erupting volcano. Technical effects are good but dialogue is poor, even allowing for dubbing.

RUSSIA Only in comparatively recent years has any quantity of Russian science fiction and fantasy appeared in translation outside the U.S.S.R.; much of it is now being published by the Foreign Languages Publishing House, Moscow.

Most of the fiction is old-fashioned in theme and writing. Isaac Asimov covers the state of the field in the early 1960's in his introductions to both *Soviet Science Fiction* (a retitling of *A Visitor From Space*) and *More Soviet Science Fiction* (*The Heart of the Serpent*) in 1962. The contents of these are covered as ANONYMOUS ANTHOLOGIES in the *WHO'S WHO*. Another of the same period, *Destination: Amaltheia*, is covered under DIXON, R.

More recent anthologies have included *Last Door to Aiya*, M. Ginsburg (1968), and the two *Russian Science Fiction* selections by R. Magidoff (1963, 1968).

Most of the FLPH editions were available in the 1960's through Cross World Publishers, U.S.A.; they have also been available at times from book stores handling Soviet propaganda.

Russian authors covered in the *Encyclopedia* are: A. Belayev, M. A. Bulgakov, V. A. Obruchev, A. Tertz (or A. D. Siniavskii), A. Tolstoi (for a pre-war novel), K. Tsiolkovsky (the "father" of Russian space fiction), I. A. Yefremov (or Efremov; the first author to be translated after World War II), and E. Zamiatin.

Shortly after World War II, an article on science fiction as viewed by Russian eyes was "The World of Night-Mare Fantasies," Viktor Bolkhovitinov & Vassilij Zakhartchenko, in *Literaturnaya Gazyeta*. This was reviewed in *ASF*, June 1959, and commented upon in the amateur magazine *Fantasy Review*, Dec/Jan 1949. A Russian view of science fiction is given by Julius Kagarlitsky in *International SF*, Nov 1967; he considers the best writing at present to be done by the teams of Mikhail Emtsov & E. Parnov, and Arcady & Boris Strugatsky.

There is not much information on the magazine field, though the late W. Ley knew of a magazine similar to the American *Argosy*, using some science fiction, which originated in 1907 and may have run for a considerable period. *The Pathfinder of the Oural* was a magazine which began around 1958 or 1959.

Since the first Sputnik quite an amount of Russian popular science and space travel work has been published in English; two writers in this field are M. Vassiliev and K. Gilzin. Ari Sternfeld (not covered in the *Encyclopedia*) had two books, *Internplanetary Travel* (1958) and *Soviet Space Science* (Basic Books, 1959; Hutchinson, 1959); the latter was important and gave a general coverage; of course both are now out of date. A popularisation of Russian space science back to Tsiolkovsky in 1903 was *Soviet Writings on Earth Satellites and Space Travel* (MacGibbon & Kee, London, 1959; Citadel, New York, 1959). A number of paper-covered booklets were also published in London in 1959, such as *Soviet Moon Rockets* and *Soviet Planet Into Space*.

The interesting work *Intelligent Life in the Universe* (1966) was a collaboration between I. S. Shklovskii and the U.S. scientist C. Sagan.

Notable figures born in Russia but later resident elsewhere include the artist B. Artzybasheff, the writers I. Asimov and R. Bretnor, the late scientist G. Gamow, and the late political philosopher Ayn Rand.

RYMDBÖCKERNA (The Space Books) Swedish science fiction book series; 20 issues, 1957-1959; edited by Höjering; published by Wennerberg, Stockholm. The first eight were the U.S. newsstand paperback size; the remainder were slightly larger. Prices: first 8, 1.75 kr; 9 to 18, 1.95 kr.; 19-20, 2.25 kr.

This printed a number of the better U.S. juveniles and other fiction, by such authors as L. R. Hubbard, P. Capon, R. F. Jones, R. S. Richardson, L. del Rey, D. A. Wollheim, J. Williamson, F. Pratt, C. D. Simak, F. B. Long, C. Fontenay, F. Brown, J. D. MacDonald, P. Anderson, W. Tucker, and R. Silverberg.

S

SADKO A U.S.S.R. film, Sovexportfilm; in special Sovacolor; directed by A. Pkuskilo; starring S. Stolyarov as Sadko and A. Laroonova as Lyuboda.

An exquisite film based on a musical fantasy by Rimsky-Korsakov.

SATELLITE SERIES Australian paper-covered sf series; 6 issues (Nos. 211-216), 1958, not dated. The first four were saddle-stapled, 5½ x 7 in., about Apr 1958; other two were 4½ x 6½ in., about Oct. They were issued by Jubilee Publications Pty. Ltd., Sydney (now defunct).

The first four were anthologies apparently prepared in the U.S.; they were selections from *Orbit SF* Nos. 2, 4, & 5, and the G. Conklin anthology *Possible Worlds of Science Fiction*. The titles were, respectively, *Beyond the Stars and Other Stories; Space Station 42 and Other Stories; The Sands of Mars and Other Stories;* and *Planet of Doom and Other Stories.* (Fully listed under ANONYMOUS ANTHOLOGIES, Satellite Series, in the *WHO'S WHO.*)

Nos. 215 and 216 were reprints of Ace Double D-162, 1956: *Year 3097,* R. D. Miller & A. Hunger [retitling of *The Man Who Lived Forever*], and *The Mars Monopoly,* J. Sohl.

SCIENCE Authors with books of a general nature covered or mentioned in the *WHO'S WHO* are I. Asimov, with several volumes of essays; J. Bronowski, *The Common Sense of Science* (1953); R. Gallant, popular writer for juveniles; G. Gamow; M. Gardner, *Fads and Fallacies in the Name of Science* (1957); I. J. Good, *The Scientist Speculates* (1962); J. Newman (with K. Bulmer), many articles in *New Worlds* from 1953 to 1964; I. Velikovsky.

SCIENCE CORRESPONDENCE CLUB [SCC] Founded in 1930 by Walter L. Dennis, it flourished for a period. In its early stage M. J. Breuer was adviser; other members included Jack Williamson and David M. Speaker. R. A. Palmer was very active as secretary, and Dennis was treasurer. The journal *Cosmology* was published.

Off-shoot associations were The Scienceers in the New York area and the East Bay Scientific Association in the San Francisco area. The group also inspired the formation of the junior "Boys Scientifiction Club."

When the SCC became the International Scientific Association in 1932, the junior body became the Junior Scientific Association. Palmer was publicity director of the SCC in its latter years.

At one stage in the early 1930's the club talked of giving a Jules Verne Prize for Science Fiction, but this never bore fruit. Around 1935 the SCC organ was *The International Observer*. The group organised the first science fiction convention in Philadelphia.

SCIENCE FICTION Works discussing or indexing science fiction. (See also CLASSICS and UTOPIAS.)
Books (lists, bibliographies, etc.):
The Checklist of Fantastic Literature, E. F. Bleiler (1947); *The Tale of the Future,* I. F. Clarke (1961); *Voices Prophesying War 1763-1984,* I. F. Clarke (1966); *Checklist of Science Fiction Anthologies,* W. R. Cole (1964); *The Supplemental Checklist of Fantastic Literature,* B. M. Day (1963); *Index to the Science-Fantasy Publishers,* M. Owings & J. Chalker (1966).

A suggested basic science fiction library (as of the late 1940's) was summarised from a symposium and given in *Arkham Sampler* (Winter 1949): Seven Famous Novels, H. G. Wells; *The Short Stories of H. G. Wells; Last and First Men, Sirius,* and *Star Maker,* all by O. Stapledon; *Brave New World,* A. Huxley; *Adventures in Time and Space,* ed. R. J. Healy & J. F. McComas; *The World Below,* S. F. Wright; *Slan,* A. E. van Vogt; *Strange Ports of Call,* ed. A. Derleth; *To Walk the Night,* W. Sloane; *The Lost World,* Sir A. C. Doyle; *Gladiator,* P. Wylie; *Before the Dawn,* J. Taine [E. T. Bell]; *Who Goes There? & Other Stories,* J. W. Campbell; *The Best of Science Fiction,* ed. G. Conklin; *Out of the Silence,* E. Cox.

A similar survey in the categories "Development of Science Fiction" and "The Basic Library" was conducted by P. S. Miller and listed in *ASF,* Jan 1953. He also conducted similar surveys later.

Foreign listings include:
France: *Les Marges,* P. Versins (1960) (only Part 1 appeared).
Germany: *Katalog der deutschsprachigen utopisch-phantastischen Literatur,* H. Bingenheimer (1960).
Holland: *100 Jaar SF in Nederland,* D. Scheepstra (1968).
Italy: *Catalogo Generale Della Fantascienza,* A. Bertoni & G. Missiaja (1968).
Sweden: *Bibliografi över Science Fiction och Fantasy,* S. J. Lundwall (1962, 1964).

Writing:
Science Fiction Handbook, L. S. de Camp (1953); *Of Worlds Beyond,* L. A. Eshbach (1947; reprinted 1964).
Reviews and Critiques (on books):
New Maps of Hell, K. Amis (1960); *The Issue at Hand,* W. Atheling Jr. [J. Blish] (1964); *Pilgrims Through Space and Time,* J. O. Bailey (1947); *Modern Science Fiction,* R. Bretnor (1953); *Inquiry Into Science Fiction,* B. Davenport (1955); *Future Perfect,* H. B. Franklin (1966); *The Imaginary Voyage in Prose Fiction,* P. B. Gove (1961); *Into Other Worlds,* R. L. Green (1957); *The Future as Nightmare,* M. R. Hillegas (1967); *American Science Fiction 1926-50,* W. Kirsch [doctoral dissertation]; *In Search of Wonder,* D. Knight (1956; revised 1967); *Science and Fiction,* P. A. Moore (1957); *Explorers of the Infinite* (1963) and *Seekers of Tomorrow* (1966), both by S. Moskowitz [profiles of authors]; *Voyages to the Moon,* M. H. Nicholson (1949); *The Fabulators,* R. Scholes (1967); *Vom Staatsroman zur Science Fiction,* M. Schwonke (1957) [German, not translated]; *The Science Fiction Novel,* Symposia (1959).

J. Blish had articles in the magazines, notably "Science in Science Fiction" (*SFQ,* sr4, May 1951 to May 1952); J. E. Gunn gave a critical analysis (his master's thesis) in *Dynamic SF* (sr4, Mar 1953 to Jan 1954).

There are also a number of books studying individual authors, including A. Panshin's *Heinlein in Dimension* (1968) and R. Ellik's and Bill Evans' concordance *The Universes of E. E. Smith* (1966). *The Magazine of Fantasy and Science Fiction* has had several issues devoted to celebrating the work of a particular author.
Magazines (indexes and listings):
Issues checklist:
The Complete Checklist of Science-Fiction Magazines, B. M. Day (1961).
Contents:
Index to the Science-Fiction Magazines: 1926-1950, D. B. Day (1952).
Index to the S-F Magazines, 1951-1965, E. R. Strauss (1966).

Index of Science Fiction Magazines 1951-1965, N. Metcalf (1968).

The Strauss index is a computer-sorted printout. The Metcalf is considered to be the better arranged, but exists in two editions, one from J. Ben Stark, Berkeley, Calif., and the other a corrected version from Metcalf.

Non-sf magazines:

Index to the Weird Fiction Magazines, T.G.L. Cockcroft (1962).

Index on the Weird and Fantastica in Magazines, B. M. Day (1953).

Science Fiction by Gaslight, S. Moskowitz (1968) [a history of the popular magazines around the turn of the 20th Century].

Australian Science Fiction Index 1925-1967, G. B. Stone (1968) [essentially covers the magazine and paper-covered field].

There have also been indexes for individual magazines, such as *Galaxy Science Fiction* and *Unknown (Worlds)*; these have been amateur publications. Fan ventures have also included a series of yearbooks indexing the sf published in any one year; Al Lewis did some for 1961, 1962, and 1963.

Classification:

Fantasy Classification System, A. Cameron (1952).

Fandom:

General: *The Eighth Stage of Fandom*, R. Bloch (1962).
Terminology: *Fancyclopedia II*, R. H. Eney (1959).
History (U.S.): *The Immortal Storm*, S. Moskowitz (1954).
Who's Who: *Who's Who in Science Fiction Fandom*, L. D. Broyles (1961).
Amateur Publications: *Fanzine Index*, B. Pavlat & B. Evans (1952-59; reprinted, H. P. Piser, 1965).

SCIENCE FICTION U.S. amateur magazine, edited by J. Siegel and J. Shuster for 5 issues from Oct 1932. This was the first fanzine to use the title *Science Fiction*, although a previous fan publication had used the words in its title: *Science Fiction Digest*.

The fourth issue began a 2-part story, "Dimension Drug," R. A. Palmer, one of this writer's early pieces. The sixth issue, which never appeared, was scheduled to have "The Living Machine," D. H. Keller; this later appeared in *Wonder Stories*, May 1935 [see S. Moskowitz, *Future SF*, June 1958].

SCIENCE FICTION ADVERTISER U.S. amateur magazine. Gus Wilmorth began it as *Fantasy Advertiser* in April 1946, and later changed the name; Roy Squires assumed control from Jan 1950.

This was one of the best magazines of its type, featuring book reviews, articles on various aspects of science fiction, etc., and also (as its name implies) acting as a sales medium. Much notable artwork was done by M. S. Dollens. The magazine was incorporated into the amateur magazine *Inside* from Nov 1954.

SCIENCE FICTION BOOK CLUB [D'day SF B.C.] U.S. book club, started in 1953 and operated as a subsidiary of the Doubleday publishing group. Books were first priced at $1.00 to members, then $1.15 in 1954, $1.20 from July 1958, and $1.70 from Jan 1967 (with a number at higher prices and so noted). The jackets state "Book Club Edition," with no price given, and there is no First Edition noted with the copyright data.

Some of the titles in the early 1960's were technically the only editions, as copies were shipped to dealers with the Book Club label snipped off and the full list price marked on. These include *A Tale of Two Clocks*, J. H. Schmitz; *Triangle*, I. Asimov; *Treasury of Great Science Fiction*, A. Boucher.

The initial selections in early 1953 were special purchases of trade editions: *The Astounding Science Fiction Anthology*, J. W. Campbell ($1.90); *The Stars Like Dust*, I. Asimov; *The Puppet Masters*, R. A. Heinlein; *Takeoff*, C. M. Kornbluth; *The Sands of Mars*, A. C. Clarke; *The Illustrated Man*, R. Bradbury; *The Mixed Men*, A. E. van Vogt; *Omnibus of Science Fiction*, G. Conklin ($1.90); *The House of Many Worlds*, S. Merwin; *The White Widows*, S. Merwin; *Lancelot Biggs, Spaceman*, N. S. Bond; *The Sinister Researches of C. P. Ransom*, H. Nearing; *The Shadow of Fu Manchu*, S. Rohmer; *Double Jeopardy*, F. Pratt; *The Martian Chronicles*, R. Bradbury; *Day of the Triffids*, J. Wyndham [J. B. Harris]; *Needle*, H. Clement [H. C. Stubbs]; *Rogue Queen*, L. S. de Camp; *Solution t-25*, T. Du Bois; *Double in Space*, F. Pratt.

The SF Book Club then began its own editions:

1953
Mar *The Currents of Space*, I. Asimov
Apr *West of the Sun*, E. Pangborn
May *The Long, Loud Silence*, W. Tucker
Jun *Player Piano*, K. Vonnegut Jr.
Jul *Children of Wonder* [A], Wm. Tenn [P. Klass]
Aug *World out of Mind*, J. T. McIntosh [J. M. MacGregor]
Sep *This Island Earth*, R. F. Jones
Oct *Ring Around the Sun*, C. D. Simak
Nov *Second Foundation*, I. Asimov
Dec *The Syndic*, C. M. Kornbluth

1954
Jan *Costigan's Needle*, J. Sohl
Feb *The Lights in the Sky Are Stars*, F. Brown
Mar *Born Leader*, J. T. McIntosh [J. M. MacGregor]
Apr *Wild Talent*, W. Tucker
May *The Caves of Steel*, I. Asimov
Jun *Mission of Gravity*, H. Clement [H. C. Stubbs]
Jul *A Mirror for Observers*, E. Pangborn
Aug *Best From Fantasy and Science Fiction, Third Series*, A. Boucher
Sep *The Altered Ego*, J. Sohl
Oct *One in 300*, J. T. McIntosh [J. M. MacGregor]
Nov *Assignment in Tomorrow*, F. Pohl
Dec *Satellite E One*, J. L. Castle
Others: *Across the Space Frontier*, C. Ryan [nonfiction]; *Children of Wonder*, W. Tenn [P. Klass]; *Second Foundation*, I. Asimov; *Treasury of Science Fiction Classics*, H. Kuebler [$1.65].

1955
Jan *Portals of Tomorrow*, A. Derleth
Feb *Angels and Spaceships*, F. Brown
Mar *Beyond the Barriers of Space and Time*, J. Merril
Apr *Best From Fantasy and Science Fiction, Fourth Series*, A. Boucher
May *Timeliner*, C. E. Maine [D. McIlwain]
Jun *Snow Fury*, R. C. Holden
Jul *The Fittest*, J. T. McIntosh [J. M. MacGregor]
Aug *The Martian Way*, I. Asimov
Sep *Point Ultimate*, J. Sohl
Oct *The Demolished Man*, A. Bester
Nov *Edge of Running Water*, Wm. Sloane
Dec *Martians, Go Home!*, F. Brown
Other: *Exploring Mars*, R. S. Richardson [nonfiction].

1956
Jan *Time Bomb*, W. Tucker
Feb *The Long Tomorrow*, L. Brackett
Mar *Best From Fantasy and Science Fiction, Fifth Series*, A. Boucher
Apr *Not This August*, C. M. Kornbluth
May *The End of Eternity*, I. Asimov
Jun *The Dragon in the Sea*, F. Herbert
Jul *Earthman, Come Home*, J. Blish
Aug *Report on Unidentified Flying Objects*, E. J. Ruppelt [nonfiction]
Sep *The Power*, F. M. Robinson
Oct *The City and the Stars*, A. C. Clarke
Nov *Best Science Fiction Stories and Novels 1956*, T. E. Dikty
Dec *Double Star*, R. A. Heinlein
Other: *The Viking Rocket Story*, M. Rosen [nonfiction].

1957
Feb *Empire of the Atom*, A. E. van Vogt
Mar *Best From Fantasy and Science Fiction, Sixth Series*, A. Boucher
Apr *The Naked Sun*, I. Asimov
May *Strangers in the Universe*, C. D. Simak
Jun *The Twenty-Seventh Day*, J. Mantley
Jul *Time for the Stars*, R. A. Heinlein
Aug *The Winds of Time*, C. Oliver
Sep *The Isotope Man*, C. E. Maine [D. McIlwain]
Oct *Earth Is Room Enough*, I. Asimov
Nov *Vanguard to Venus*, J. L. Castle
Dec *The Third Level*, J. Finney

1958
Jan *The Door Into Summer*, R. A. Heinlein
Feb *Doomsday Morning*, C. L. Moore
Mar *Best Science Fiction Stories and Novels, 9th Series*, T. E. Dikty

Apr *The Mind Cage*, A. E. van Vogt
May *Best From Fantasy and Science Fiction, Seventh Series*, A. Boucher [$1.65]
Jun *No Blade of Grass*, J. Christopher [C. S. Youd]
Jul *The Black Cloud*, F. Hoyle
Aug *The Man Who Couldn't Sleep*, C. E. Maine [D. McIlwain]
Sep *The Lincoln Hunters*, W. Tucker
Oct *A Touch of Strange*, T. Sturgeon
Nov *Spacepower*, D. Cox & I. M. Stocks [$1.90] [nonfiction]
Dec *The Third Galaxy Reader*, H. L. Gold

1959

Jan *No Place on Earth*, L. Charbonneau
Feb *A Mile Beyond the Moon*, C. M. Kornbluth
Mar *Best From Fantasy and Science Fiction, Eighth Series*, A. Boucher
Apr *The Star of Life*, E. Hamilton
May *Triad*, A. E. van Vogt
Jun *Nine Tomorrows*, I. Asimov
Jul *Not in Solitude*, K. Gantz
Aug *The Enemy Stars*, P. Anderson
Sep *The Fourth Galaxy Reader*, H. L. Gold
Oct *Ossian's Ride*, F. Hoyle
Nov *Across the Sea of Stars*, A. C. Clarke [$1.90]
Dec *The War Against the Rull*, A. E. van Vogt
Others: *The Report on Unidentified Flying Objects*, E. J. Ruppelt [$1.90, rev. ed., nonfiction]; alternative for April: *A Treasury of Great Mysteries*, H. Haycraft & J. Beecroft [detective].

1960

Jan *A Journey to the Center of the Earth*, J. Verne
Feb *A Treasury of Great Science Fiction*, A. Boucher [2 vols., $2.25]
Mar *The Haunted Stars*, E. Hamilton
Apr *Science Fiction Showcase*, Mary Kornbluth
May *Best From Fantasy and Science Fiction, Ninth Series*, R. P. Mills
Jun *Eight Keys to Eden*, M. Clifton
Jul *Level Seven*, M. Roshwald
Aug *The Worlds of Clifford Simak*, C. D. Simak
Sep *Twinkle, Twinkle, Little Star*, B. Barzman
Oct *The Fantastic Universe Omnibus*, H. Santesson
Nov *Bodyguard*, H. L. Gold
Dec *Flying Saucers: Top Secret*, D. E. Keyhoe

1961

Jan *Star of Stars*, F. Pohl
Feb *Twilight World*, P. Anderson
Mar *A Decade of Fantasy and Science Fiction*, R. P. Mills
Apr *Facial Justice*, L. P. Hartley
May *Triangle*, I. Asimov
Jun *Far Out*, D. Knight
Jul *Stranger in a Strange Land*, R. A. Heinlein
Aug *Three Hearts and Three Lions*, P. Anderson
Sep *The Fifth Galaxy Reader*, H. L. Gold
Oct *Tiger by the Tail*, A. E. Nourse
Nov *Time Is the Simplest Thing*, C. D. Simak
Dec *Battle for the Stars*, E. Hamilton

1962

Jan *From the Ocean, From the Stars*, A. C. Clarke
Feb *When They Come From Space*, M. Clifton
Mar *Prologue to Analog*, J. W. Campbell
Apr *A Tale of Two Clocks*, J. H. Schmitz
May *All the Traps of Earth*, C. D. Simak
Jun *Necromancer*, G. R. Dickson
Jul *A Century of Science Fiction*, D. Knight
Aug *Central Passage*, L. Schoonover
Sep *Unwise Child*, R. Garrett
Oct *The Great Explosion*, E. F. Russell
     Best From Fantasy and Science Fiction, Eleventh Series, R. P. Mills [$1.69]
Fall *A for Andromeda*, F. Hoyle & J. Elliott
     The Sixth Galaxy Reader, H. L. Gold
Nov *The Man in the High Castle*, P. K. Dick
Dec *The Long Winter*, J. Christopher [C. S. Youd]
Other: *The Hugo Winners*, I. Asimov.

1963

Jan *They Walked Like Men*, C. D. Simak

Feb *Analog I*, J. W. Campbell
Mar *Anything You Can Do . . .*, D. T. Langart [R. Garrett]
Apr *Cat's Cradle*, K. Vonnegut
May *The Beast*, A. E. van Vogt
Jun *Best From Fantasy and Science Fiction, 12th Series*, A. Davidson
Jul *The World of Flying Saucers*, D. Menzel & L. G. Boyd [nonfiction]
Aug *I, Robot*, I. Asimov
Sep *Glory Road*, R. A. Heinlein
Oct *The Foundation Trilogy*, I. Asimov
Nov *Way Station*, C. D. Simak
Dec *Apollo at Go*, J. Sutton

1964

Jan *Beyond the Barrier*, D. Knight
Feb *Analog II*, J. W. Campbell
Winter: *Fifth Planet*, F. & G. Hoyle
Mar *All the Colors of Darkness*, L. Biggle
Apr *Time and Stars*, P. Anderson
May *Orphans of the Sky*, R. A. Heinlein
Jun *The Hopkins Manuscript*, R. C. Sherriff [$1.90]
Jul *Best From Fantasy and Science Fiction, 13th Series*, A. Davidson
Aug *Instant Gold*, F. O'Rourke
Sep *Trader to the Stars*, P. Anderson
Oct *The Seventh Galaxy Reader*, F. Pohl
Nov *Farnham's Freehold*, R. A. Heinlein
Dec *The Rest of the Robots*, I. Asimov [$1.90]
Others: *Post Reader of Fantasy and Science Fiction*, The Saturday Evening Post [$1.90]; *From The Twilight Zone*, R. Serling [$2.20].

1965

Jan *The Three Stigmata of Palmer Eldritch*, P. K. Dick
Feb *The Dark Side*, D. Knight
Mar *The Drowned World & The Wind From Nowhere*, J. G. Ballard
Apr *The Year's Best S-F: 9th Annual Edition*, J. Merril [$1.90]
May *Andromeda Breakthrough*, F. Hoyle & J. Elliot
Spring #1: *The Main Experiment*, C. Hodder-Williams
Spring #2: *The Possessors*, J. Christopher [C. S. Youd]
Jun *Not With A Bang*, C. Pincher
Jul *The Star Fox*, P. Anderson
Aug *Prelude to Mars*, A. C. Clarke [$1.90]
Sep *Best From Fantasy and Science Fiction, 14th Series*, A. Davidson
Oct *Rogue Ship*, A. E. van Vogt
Nov *The Corridors of Time*, P. Anderson
Dec *Three by Heinlein*, R. A. Heinlein [$1.90]

1966

Jan *A Man of Double Deed*, L. Daventry
Feb *Froomb!*, J. Lymington
Mar *Twice Twenty-Two*, R. Bradbury [$1.90]
Apr *The Ragged Edge*, J. Christopher [C. S. Youd]
May *Mindswap*, R. Sheckley
Jun *The Year's Best S-F: 10th Annual Edition*, J. Merril [$1.90]
Jul *Earthworks*, B. W. Aldiss
Summer: *The Crystal World*, J. G. Ballard
Aug *Fantastic Voyage*, I. Asimov
Sep *Shoot at the Moon*, W. F. Temple
Oct *Nebula Award Stories*, D. Knight
Nov *October the First Is Too Late*, F. Hoyle
Dec *Watchers of the Dark*, L. Biggle

1967

Jan *Earthblood*, K. Laumer & R. G. Brown [$1.70]
Feb *The Artificial Man*, L. P. Davies
     From hereon regular price is $1.70.
Mar *The Little People*, J. Christopher [C. S. Youd]
Apr *The Past Through Tomorrow*, R. A. Heinlein [$2.30]
May *Fahrenheit 451*, R. Bradbury
Jun *The Killer Thing*, K. Wilhelm
Jul *Colossus*, D. F. Jones
Summer: *Three Novels*, D. Knight
Aug *The Time Hoppers*, R. Silverberg
Sep *Psychogeist*, L. P. Davies
Oct *Element 79*, F. Hoyle
Nov *The Egg-Shaped Thing*, C. Hodder-Williams
Dec *Dangerous Visions*, H. Ellison [$2.80]
Others: *The Flying Saucer Reader*, Jay David [$1.95]; *The Interrupted*

Journey, J. G. Fuller [$2.30]. Also sold trade editions at reduced prices: *Analog 3*, J. W. Campbell [$1.70]; *Plague From Space*, H. Harrison [$1.95]; *Sibyl Sue Blue*, R. G. Brown [$1.95].

1968
Jan *Lord of Light*, R. Zelazny
Feb *A Torrent of Faces*, J. Blish & N. L. Knight
Mar *Quicksand*, J. Brunner
Apr *Asimov's Mysteries*, I. Asimov
May *Cryptozoic!*, B. W. Aldiss
Jun *Pendulum*, J. Christopher [C. S. Youd]
Jul *Implosion*, D. F. Jones
Summer: *The Werewolf Principle*, C. D. Simak
Aug *Hauser's Memory*, C. Siodmak
Sep *2001—A Space Odyssey*, A. C. Clarke
Oct *Twilight Journey*, L. P. Davies
Nov *The Last Starship From Earth*, J. Boyd [B. B. Upchurch]
Dec *Chocky*, J. Wyndham [J. B. Harris]
Also sold trade editions at reduced prices: *Now Wait for Last Year*, P. K. Dick [$1.95]; *Three Stories*, S. Moskowitz [$1.95]; *The Men in the Jungle*, N. Spinrad [$1.95].

SCIENCE FICTION BOOK CLUB [SF B.C. [S.J.]] The book club sponsored by the publishers Sidgwick & Jackson, London. The original selection panel in 1953 was A. C. Clarke, J. G. Porter, E. Shanks, and E. J. Carnell. Around 1958 Herbert Jones replaced Shanks; by 1961 the panel was Carnell, Porter, and Kingsley Amis.

Titles were initially priced at 6/-, but soon dropped to 4/6; by 1958 they became 5/6, and then 5/9 in 1962. Around Sep 1963 they became 6/-, and by mid-1968 were 8/-. Specials were priced higher. Selections were made bimonthly to start, but have been monthly since 1961.

1953
Mar-Apr 1. *Earth Abides*, G. R. Stewart
May-Jun 2. *The Martian Chronicles*, R. Bradbury
Jul-Aug 3. *Last and First Men*, O. Stapledon
Sep-Oct 4. *Tomorrow Sometimes Comes*, F. G. Rayer
Nov-Dec 5. *Minimum Man*, A. Marvel
1954
Jan-Feb 6. *No Place Like Earth*, E. J. Carnell [A]
Mar-Apr 7. *I, Robot*, I. Asimov [C]
May-Jun 8. *The Voyage of the Space Beagle*, A. E. van Vogt
Jul-Aug 9. *Player Piano*, K. Vonnegut
Sep-Oct 10. *Odd John*, O. Stapledon
Nov-Dec 11. *The Demolished Man*, A. Bester
1955
Jan-Feb 12. *Great Stories of Science Fiction*, M. Leinster [A]
Mar-Apr 13. *The Kraken Wakes*, J. Wyndham
May-Jun 14. *Fahrenheit 451*, R. Bradbury
Jul-Aug 15. *Childhood's End*, A. C. Clarke
Sep-Oct 16. *More Than Human*, T. Sturgeon
Nov-Dec 17. *Fury*, H. Kuttner
1956
Jan-Feb 18. *The Caves of Steel*, I. Asimov
Mar-Apr 19. *Moment Without Time*, S. Mines [A]
May-Jun 20. *Wild Talent*, W. Tucker
Jul-Aug 21. *Alien Dust*, E. C. Tubb
Sep-Oct 22. *A Mirror for Observers*, E. Pangborn
Nov-Dec 23. *One in 300*, J. T. McIntosh
1957
Jan-Feb 24. *Beyond the Barriers of Space and Time*, J. Merril [A]
Mar-Apr 25. *The Long Way Back*, M. Bennett
May-Jun 26. *World of Chance*, P. K. Dick
Jul-Aug 27. *The Death of Grass*, J. Christopher
Sep-Oct 28. *The Twenty-Seventh Day*, J. Mantley
Nov-Dec 29. *Further Outlook*, W. G. Walter
1958
Jan-Feb 30. *Earthman, Come Home*, J. Blish
Mar-Apr 31. *Tiger! Tiger!*, A. Bester
May-Jun 32. *Christmas Eve*, C. M. Kornbluth
Jul-Aug 33. *Robert Heinlein Omnibus*, R. A. Heinlein [C]
Sep-Oct 34. *Best SF, Two*, E. Crispin [A]
Nov-Dec 35. *Science and Fiction*, P. A. Moore [nonfiction]

1959
Jan-Feb 36. *The Naked Sun*, I. Asimov
Mar-Apr 37. *Children of the Atom*, W. H. Shiras
May-Jun 38. *Strangers in the Universe*, C. D. Simak [C]
Jul-Aug 39. *Occam's Razor*, D. Duncan
Sep-Oct 40. *The Tide Went Out*, C. E. Maine
Nov-Dec 41. *Double Star*, R. A. Heinlein
1960
Jan-Feb 42. *The Clock of Time*, J. Finney [C]
Mar-Apr 43. *Non-Stop*, B. W. Aldiss
May-Jun 44. *The Day It Rained Forever*, R. Bradbury [C]
Jul-Aug 45. *A Case of Conscience*, J. Blish
Sep-Oct 46. *Best SF, Three*, E. Crispin [A]
Nov-Dec 47. *The Deep Range*, A. C. Clarke
Extra: Jan *The Neon Halo*, J. L. Curtis
Extra: Dec *Lord of the Rings*, J.R.R. Tolkien [trilogy]
1961
Jan 48. *The Lincoln Hunters*, W. Tucker
Feb 49. *Wasp*, E. F. Russell
Mar 50. *The Outward Urge*, J. Wyndham
May 51. *The Canopy of Time*, B. W. Aldiss [C]
Jul 52. *A Canticle for Leibowitz*, W. M. Miller Jr.
Sep 53. *The Dragon in the Sea*, F. Herbert
Oct 54. *Time out of Joint*, P. K. Dick
Nov 55. *City*, C. D. Simak
Dec 56. *Galactic Cluster*, J. Blish [C]
Extra: Oct *Jizzle*, J. Wyndham
Extra: Dec *Lord of the Rings*, Tolkien (3 vols., 36/-)
1962
Jan 57. *Mutant*, H. Kuttner
Feb 58. *The Trouble With Lichen*, J. Wyndham
Mar 59. *Wolfbane*, C. M. Kornbluth & F. Pohl
Apr 60. *The Other Side of the Sky*, A. C. Clarke [C]
May 61. *New Maps of Hell*, K. Amis [nonfiction]
Jun 62. *The Stars Are Too High*, A. H. Bahnson
Jul 63. *Best SF, Four*, E. Crispin [A]
Aug 64. *Slave Ship*, F. Pohl
Sep 65. *Needle*, H. Clement
Oct 66. *Guardians of Time*, P. Anderson
Nov 67. *Aliens for Neighbours*, C. D. Simak [C]
Dec 68. *Spectrum*, K. Amis & R. Conquest [A]
1963
Jan 69. *Drunkard's Walk*, F. Pohl
Feb 70. *The Unexpected Dimension*, A. Budrys [C]
Mar 71. *The Great Explosion*, E. F. Russell
Apr 72. *Time Is the Simplest Thing*, C. D. Simak
May 73. *A Fall of Moondust*, A. C. Clarke
Jun 74. *Twilight World*, P. Anderson
Jul 75. *Pilgrimage*, Z. Henderson
Aug 76. *Last Men in London*, O. Stapledon
Sep 77. *Tiger by the Tail*, A. E. Nourse [C]
Oct 78. *Best From Fantasy and Science Fiction, Ninth Series*, R. Mills [A]
Nov 79. *Hothouse*, B. W. Aldiss
Dec 80. *Dark Universe*, D. F. Galouye
Extra: Feb *Eight Keys to Eden*, M. Clifton (8/6)
Extra: Dec *Spectrum II*, K. Amis & R. Conquest [A] (11/6)
1964
Jan 81. *No Future in It*, J. Brunner [C]
Feb 82. *The Drowned World*, J. G. Ballard
Mar 83. *The Darkest of Nights*, C. E. Maine
Apr 84. *Time in Advance*, W. Tenn [C]
May 85. *Orphans of the Sky*, R. A. Heinlein
Jun 86. *Tales of Ten Worlds*, A. C. Clarke
Jul 87. *The Four-Dimensional Nightmare*, J. G. Ballard [C]
Aug 88. *The Expert Dreamers*, F. Pohl [A]
Sep 89. *Methuselah's Children*, R. A. Heinlein
Oct 90. *The Joy Makers*, J. T. Gunn
Nov 91. *Conditionally Human*, W. Miller Jr. [C]
Dec 92. *Nine Tomorrows*, I. Asimov [C]
Extra: Sep *Spectrum III*, K. Amis & R. Conquest [A] (10/6)

1965

Jan 93. *The Airs of Earth*, B. W. Aldiss [C]
Feb 94. *Gladiator-at-Law*, F. Pohl & C. M. Kornbluth
Mar 95. *Doppelgangers*, G. Heard
Apr 96. *In Deep*, D. Knight [C]
May 97. *Way Station*, C. D. Simak
Jun 98. *Counterfeit World*, D. F. Galouye
Jul 99. *Revolt in 2100*, R. A. Heinlein
Aug 100. *All the Colours of Darkness*, L. Biggle
Sep 101. *Time and Stars*, P. Anderson [C]
Oct 102. *Gunner Cade*, C. Judd
Nov 103. *The Uncensored Man*, A. Sellings
Dec 104. *Greybeard*, B. W. Aldiss
Extra: Aug *The Unpleasant Profession of Jonathan Hoag*, R. A. Heinlein

1966

Jan 105. *A Man of Double Deed*, L. Daventry
Feb 106. *Space Born*, L. Wright
Mar 107. *The Paradox Men*, C. Harness
Apr 108. *The Seventh Galaxy Reader*, F. Pohl [A]
May 109. *The Syndic*, C. M. Kornbluth
Jun 110. *The Joyous Invasions*, T. Sturgeon [C]
Jul 111. *Telepathist*, J. Brunner
Aug 112. *The Thirst Quenchers*, R. Raphael [C]
Sep 113. *The Specials*, L. Charbonneau
Oct 114. *Sleeping Planet*, W. R. Burkett
Nov 115. *The Lost Perception*, D. F. Galouye
Dec 116. *The Worlds of Robert F. Young* [C]

1967

Jan 117. *The Eighth Seal*, A. MacLeod
Feb 118. *All Flesh Is Grass*, C. D. Simak
Mar 119. *The Anything Box*, Z. Henderson [C]
Apr 120. *Shield*, P. Anderson
May 121. *The Star Fox*, P. Anderson
Jun 122. *The Saliva Tree and Other Strange Growths*, B. W. Aldiss [C]
Jul 123. *A Plague of Pythons*, F. Pohl
Aug 124. *Interstellar Two-Five*, J. Rankine
Sep 125. *Spectrum 5*, K. Amis & R. Conquest [A]
Oct 126. *October the First Is Too Late*, F. Hoyle
Nov 127. *The Corridors of Time*, P. Anderson
Dec 128. *Mindswap*, R. Sheckley
Extra: *Voices From the Sky*, A. C. Clarke [nonfiction] (14/-)

1968

Jan 129. *The Quy Effect*, A. Sellings
Feb 130. *Why Call Them Back From Heaven?*, C. D. Simak
Mar 131. *Path Into the Unknown—The Best Soviet SF*, Anon. [A]
Apr 132. *The Mind Parasites*, C. Wilson
May 133. *Antic Earth*, L. Charbonneau
Jun 134. *Twilight Journey*, L. P. Davies
Jul 135. *The Killing Machine*, J. Vance
Aug 136. *Breakthrough*, R. Cowper
Sep 137. *The Hole in the Zero*, M. K. Joseph
Oct 138. *War With the Robots*, H. Harrison
Nov 139. *Three Novels*, D. Knight [C]
Dec 140. *Babel-17*, S. R. Delany

SCIENCE FICTION CLASSICS U.S. paper-covered series published about 1942 by Columbia Publications, New York. There were six, reprints of stories in early issues of *Science Fiction*. They are listed under the publisher in the *PAPERBACK* section.

SCIENCE FICTION LEAGUE The association begun by H. Gernsback and announced in *Wonder Stories*, Apr 1934. It was designed to broaden the scope and popularize the art of science fiction in all countries and act as parent for all local sf clubs throughout the world. Space was allotted in *Wonder Stories* to give club news, etc. The granting of Science Fiction Degrees was instituted with the Jan 1935 issue; three exams were held (before *WS* was sold), and many fans passed.

When *Wonder* changed to *Thrilling Wonder Stories* the League was less fostered by the magazine, and gradually it dwindled until it ceased altogether around the mid-1940's. Nevertheless it played an important part in the formation of fandom, and its effect on the growth of science fiction cannot be calculated.

SCIENCE FICTION LIBRARY Australian paper-covered series published by Atlas Publications, Melbourne, for 8 issues, 1955-56. It reprinted mainly from the British publisher Hamilton's "Panther" series. Titles are listed under the publisher in the *PAPERBACK* section.

SCIENCE FICTION NEWS Australian amateur magazine, 24 issues (Jan 1953—Aug 1959); edited by G. B. Stone, Sydney. Quite regular (bimonthly) in its early issues, it was photolithed for the first 6 and then printed by letterpress. Normally it was 8 pp., 6¾ x 9½ in. To No. 15 it was 12 issues for 6/-, then 7/6 (i.e., 75¢ Aust.).

This magazine gave news of Australian and overseas sf plus critical reviews of books and fan magazines.

SCIENCE FICTION SERIES U.S. paper-covered booklets published by Stellar Corp., New York (H. Gernsback) as an offshoot to *Science Wonder Stories*, etc.; 18 issues (1929-1932). The titles are listed under the publisher in the *PAPERBACK* section; they are now scarce.

SCIENCE-FICTION TIMES U.S. science fiction and fantasy amateur magazine; 465 issues (Sep 1941 to Apr 1969). It was probably the longest lived of any amateur general circulation publication.

Founded by J. V. Taurasi as *Fantasy-Times*, it ran as such until the second April 1957 issue. For a considerable time it had two issues per month; it was monthly from 1962 until it ceased except for a hiatus of about a year. James Ashe became editor from Jan 1967, then Ann F. Dietz took over in 1968. Taurasi's last issue was apparently Dec 1965 (No. 434), still an amazing achievement in length of editorship. Frank R. Prieto became publisher in 1965. The magazine was photolithographed for some periods, and at some other times mimeoed quarto size.

S. Moskowitz was co-editor with Taurasi in the early years. The late Raymond Van Houten was also a staff member for a number of years. J. Blish ran a book review column 1956-57. The late T. S. Gardner gave an annual review of all pro magazines for the years to 1957; this feature was then handled by Edward Wood. F. J Ackerman and others had columns at times.

From the very beginning *S-F Times* was slanted to the reporting of professional rather than fan events (though it capably covered many a world sf convention). Besides publishing news, it kept a continuing record of the magazines, books, and paperbacks in the field, not to mention its reviewing of comics and films, etc. It often had offshoot publications on various subjects. The history of sf was recorded in the pages of *Science-Fiction Times*.

SCIENCE-FICTION WORLD, THE U.S. amateur magazine published by Gnome Press; edited by Robert Bloch and Bob Tucker; 5 issues (1955—Spr 1957); printed, folio size, 4 pp., 10¢.

This reviewed books, etc., covered fan activities, and advertised Gnome Press items.

SCIENCE FICTION WRITERS OF AMERICA [SFWA] This was formed in 1965 as a professional society aiming primarily to assist writers in their dealings with publishers. For the first two years D. Knight and L. Biggle did much to get the group on its feet. Knight was the first president; in 1967 R. Silverberg was president and R. Zelazny was secretary-treasurer.

SFWA has its own awards for best fiction in the sf field—the annual Nebula Awards (which see). The shorter fiction is usually reprinted as an annual anthology.

SCIENCE FICTIONEERS U.S. fan society announced in the first issue of *Super Science Stories*, Mar 1940. It was intended to take the place of the Science Fiction League, which had not been receiving much attention in *Thrilling Wonder Stories*. The organization soon disappeared.

SCIENTIFICTION British amateur magazine, edited by W. Gillings, 1937-38. It printed material suited to the British scene, though perhaps dated by U.S. standards. It included a column by Julius Schwartz and ran an autobiography of O. Stapledon. Professionally printed, the issues were: No. 1, Jan 1937; 2, Apr 1937; 3, June 1937; 4, Aug 1937; 5, Oct 1937; 6, Jan 1938; 7, Mar 1938; then incorporated with *Tomorrow*, Vol. 2 No. 1 (Spr 1938), 2 (Sum 1938), 3 (Aut 1938).

SHASTA PUBLISHERS, Chicago. Specialty publishing firm begun by the fans Erle Korshak and T. E. Dikty. The first book from this press was *The Checklist of Fantastic Literature*, edited by E. F. Bleiler (1948). A number of others followed, including *Slaves of Sleep*, L. R. Hubbard; *Who Goes There?*, J. W. Campbell; and the first three books in R. A. Heinlein's "Future History" series. The last book was *Empire of the Atom*, A. E. van Vogt (1957).

SHAVER MYSTERY CLUB U.S. club formed by C. S. Geier in 1947 when R. A. Palmer ceased printing the "Shaver Mystery" stories in *Amazing*. The club organ, *Shaver Mystery Magazine*, was edited by Geier; it printed Shaver's "Mandark," the story of a christ.

SHROUD PUBLISHERS, Buffalo, N.Y. Publishing group, including K. J. Kreuger, formed in 1954. Its first work was a reissue of the novelette *The Maker of Moons*, R. W. Chambers; this was followed by *Look Behind You*, A. J. Burks [C], *The Female Demon*, W. McDougle [C][verse], and *The Dream Quest of Unknown Kadath*, H. P. Lovecraft. Although a number of further books were projected from late 1955, the press did not continue.

SMALLNESS Journeys into the atom, people shrinking into midgets, etc. R. Cummings originated this type of story in the modern sf field, notably his *The Girl in the Golden Atom* and sequels [see *CONNECTED STORIES* section]. Other stories of interest include "He Who Shrank," H. Hasse (*AS*, Aug 1936); "The Man Who Fought a Fly," L. F. Stone (*AS*, Oct 1932); "It's a Small World," R. Bloch (*AS*, Mar 1944); *The Green Man of Graypec*, F. Pragnell.

Films in this category have included *Dr. Cyclops* and *The Incredible Shrinking Man* [see R. Matheson in the *WHO'S WHO*]. A television series was *Land of the Giants*, which also appeared as a comic and in paperback.

SOCIETIES, FAN Covered in this *GENERAL* section: British Science Fiction Association; Eastern Science Fiction Association; Fantasy Amateur Press Association; Fantasy Veterans Association; First Fandom; Futurian Society of Sydney; Los Angeles Science Fantasy Society; National Fantasy Fan Federation; Philadelphia Science Fiction Society; Science Correspondence Club; Science Fiction League; Science Fictioneers; Shaver Mystery Club.

SOCIETIES, LEARNED American Rocket Society; British Interplanetary Society; German Rocket Society.

SOUTH AFRICA This country appears to have published no original science fiction or fantasy. South African writers who have been published outside their country in these fields include E. J. Blow, H. A. Fagan, C. C. Reed, and, before World War II, W. Rose.

SPACE TRAVEL (AND ROCKETRY) The *Encyclopedia* does not cover the works published in this field in entirety. Certain authors who have written predominantly in a popular mode plus others with works of particular note or who normally write fiction have such works briefly covered. From the fan viewpoint the master reference to this field is *Rockets, Missiles and Men in Space*, W. Ley (1968), which has been often revised.

Authors covered (including rocketry both before and after World War II) are: E. R. Bergaust, F. M. Branley, W. Buedeler, E. Burgess, M. Caidin, A. C. Clarke, P. E. Cleator, C. I. Coombs, D. I. Cox, W. Dornberger, F. J. Field, R. Freedman, H. Gartmann, K. W. Gatland, H. Haber, D. Lasser, I. M. Levitt, W. Ley, L. Mallan, T. Maloney, J. Marbarger, P. A. Moore, H. Oberth, G. E. Pendray, P. Ritner, N. P. Ruzic, C. Ryan, F. Tinsley, W. Von Braun, and B. Williams.

The biographical "Men of Space" series edited by S. Thomas began in 1965. G. Harry Stine has had occasional articles on Russian progress and other space subjects in *ASF*.

SPAIN The Spanish authors who have written in the fantasy/sf field include Jesus de Aragon, who in the early 1930's wrote adventure novels, some of which had elements of science fiction, such as *Los piratas del aire, 40,000 km a bordo del aeroplano fantasma*, and *De noche sobre la ciudad prohibida*. His *Una extraña aventura de amor en la Luna*

was straight sf, involving travel to the Moon and adventures there in the mood of E. R. Burroughs. Gustavo Adolfo Becquer (1836—1870), one of the best romantic poets and authors of Spain, wrote many legends with a strong fantasy element, such as "Maese Perez el organista" [translated and published in many weird anthologies], "Los ojos verdes," "El caudillo de las manos rojas," etc. Early this century Enrique de Benito wrote *El hijo del Capitan Nemo*, a sequel to Verne's *20,000 Leagues Under the Sea*, and Dr. Lazaro Clendobius published *Elois y Morlocks* (1909), a continuation to H. G. Wells' *The Time Machine*, but neither are particularly important.

José de Elola (1859— ?), soldier and scientist, inventor and fine tactician, wrote much sf with sound descriptions of planets, atomic energy, interplanetary travel, etc.; his main book, *Viajes Interplanetarios en el siglo XXII* has 8 volumes. Although a genius, his works are rather dull; nevertheless he warrants more attention as a pioneer in the field.

Tomas Salvador, one of the best contemporary mainstream writers, has a short sf story "Los estandartes humullados." His *La Nave* (Ed. Destino, 1959) tells the story of people after generations in a very long voyage (like Heinlein's "Universe") and deserves more attention than it received—the last third is in the form of a poem in prose.

Other authors listed in the *WHO'S WHO* are M. A. Asturias, E. S. Chapela, F. M. Florez, J. M. Gironella, and A. Robles.

Translations into Spanish include E. R. Burroughs' *Carson of Venus* (serialised in a magazine in the 1930's, then as a book in the 1940's) and *John Carter of Mars* (1950); Elliot's "Kemlo" series [see R. A. Martin] (1957+); R. Cummings' *Tarrano the Conqueror* (1931); Lord Dunsany's *Dreamer's Tales* (1945); O. Stapledon's *First and Last Men* (1931); Bulwer-Lytton's *The Coming Race* (1954); L. de Wohl's *Second Conquest* (1956).

In the magazine field, it is understood that one issue of a pirated edition of *Astounding Science Fiction* appeared in 1948. In the same year the magazine *Fantastica* had 19 issues. Three regular space-opera magazines printing Spanish pulp writers are *Espacio, el mundo futuro*; *Luchadores del Espacio*; and *S.I.P.*; the last has ceased, and the others may have. A magazine of somewhat better quality was *Futuro, novelas de ciencia y fantasia*, which appeared for 34 issues in 1954.

In pocket books, the principal series was "Nebula"; this began in Feb 1955 and ceased in late 1965 after 114 titles. It reprinted some good material and gave some originals. The "Cenit" series begun in 1960 presented a somewhat "faster-paced" type of material (like the U.S. Ace Books from which a number of novels have been translated), while the "Espacio" series, begun in 1962, presents somewhat lower-quality material—reprints from the British "Badger" series, etc.—and the "Espacio Extra" series covers Spanish pulp writers.

SPWSSTFM The acronym coined by Bob Tucker in letters in *ASF* (Nov 1934) and *Wonder Stories* (Feb 1935), standing for "Society for the Prevention of Wire Staples in Scientifiction Magazines." This was the forerunner of all such abbreviations as BEM or GAFIA, which are so much a part of a fan's vocabulary.

STAIRWAY TO HEAVEN English film, Universal, 1946; partly in colour; director, Michael Powell; starring David Niven, Roger Livesey, Raymond Massey, and Kim Hunter.

Noted fantasy in which the messenger for Heaven misses taking an R.A.F. pilot "up there" after a war-time mission; later a case in the "higher" court becomes necessary. It has been retitled *A Matter of Life and Death* for TV runs.

STAR TREK U.S. television series, NBC network; 79 episodes, 1966-1969; creator and executive producer, Gene Roddenberry; story consultants S. Carabatsos & D. C. Fontana; 60 minute episodes, in colour. The regular cast included William Shatner as Capt. James T. Kirk, Leonard Nimoy as Mr. Spock, DeForest Kelley as Dr. Leonard "Bones" McCoy, Nichelle Nichols as Lt. Uhura, George Takei as Lt. Sulu, Jimmy Doohan as Chief Engineer Scott, Majel Barrett as Nurse Christine Chapel, Walter Koenig as Ensign Chekov (from second season), and Grace Lee Whitney as Yeoman Janice Rand (first season only).

First Season (8 Sep 1966—13 Apr 1967):
Man Trap (story by George Clayton Johnson). A kind of vampire transforms itself into Dr. McCoy's former flame.

Charlie X (D.C. Fontana, from a story by G. Roddenberry). Reared on an alien planet, a teen-aged boy threatens the *Enterprise* with his unearthly powers.

Where No Man Has Gone Before (Sam Peeples). After journeying through a strange barrier at the edge of the galaxy, two crew members develop god-like powers.

The Naked Time (John D. F. Black). A virus strips the *Enterprise* crew of their mental and emotional control as the ship spirals towards destruction.

The Enemy Within (Richard Matheson). A transporter malfunction transforms Kirk into two people—one meek and the other violent.

Mudd's Women (S. Kandel, from a story by G. Roddenberry). A space captain has a Venus drug to hypnotise people into believing that any woman is beautiful and uses it for lithium trading with miners.

What Are Little Girls Made Of? (Robert Bloch). Nurse Chapel's fiancé is readying a race of androids for conquest, and makes one as a double for Kirk.

Miri (Adian Spies). The *Enterprise* finds a planet inhabited by "children" over 300 years old.

Dagger of the Mind (Shimon Wincelberg). Kirk investigates the "advanced" reformatory methods of a penologist, who has a machine that can empty the brain.

Corbomite Maneuver (Jerry Sohl). Kirk uses a tactical bluff to save the *Enterprise* and make a cultural exchange.

Menagerie (2 parts, Gene Roddenberry). Spock "hijacks" the ship and sets out for Talos IV following the kidnapping of his former commanding officer. In Part II he goes on trial and tells the story of Pike's bizarre experience on Talos IV. [This pair of episodes used footage from *The Cage*, the original *Star Trek* pilot film.]

Conscience of the King (Barry Trivers). Intrigue with a planetary governor killing half his population to save the remainder from a plague.

Balance of Terror (Paul Schneider). Kirk engages in a battle of wits with the commander of a Romulan ship.

Shore Leave (Theodore Sturgeon). Checking a planet for shore leave becomes a frightening adventure with a computer that can take things from the mind.

The Galileo Seven (Oliver Crawford). Sent to investigate a quasar, Spock and his companions crash on a planet with gorilla-like inhabitants.

Squire of Gothos (Paul Schneider). Kirk plays a game of death with a maniacal alien who plans to use the ship as a toy.

Arena (Gene Coon, from a story by Fredric Brown). Kirk fights Gorm, an ugly monster, on an Earth outpost.

Tomorrow Is Yesterday (D. C. Fontana). The *Enterprise* catapults back in time to an Earth of the 1960's, where it is thought to be a UFO.

Court Martial (D. Mankiewicz & S. W. Carabatsos). Kirk goes on trial after the *Enterprise* computer accuses him of murdering a fellow officer.

The Return of the Archons (B. Sobelman, from a story by G. Roddenberry). Kirk must cause Landru, the computer ruler of an alien planet, to self-destruct to save the population.

Space Seed (G. L. Coon & C. Wilbur). The *Enterprise* resuscitates a group in a space ship, and finds they are tyrannical supermen.

A Taste of Armageddon (R. Jamnor & G. L. Coon, from a story by R. Jamnor). Kirk and Spock become involved in the computer war of two planets.

This Side of Paradise (D. C. Fontana, from a story by N. Butler & D. C. Fontana). Alien spores lull the crew into tranquility, but Spock reacts differently.

The Devil in the Dark (G. L. Coon & J. Prohaska). In a mining colony Kirk and Spock battle the Horta, a creature able to tunnel through rock.

Errand of Mercy (G. L. Coon). Kirk and Spock try to persuade the Organians to forge a treaty with the Klingons.

The Alternative Factor (Don Ingalls). An uncharted planet is investigated and a man named "Lazarus" from an alternative universe is encountered.

The City on the Edge of Forever (H. Ellison). Kirk and Spock follow a sick McCoy to Chicago of the 1930's, where Kirk falls in love with a woman he must let die.

Operation Annihilate (S. W. Carabatsos). The *Enterprise* endeavours to save the inhabitants of Deneva, where Kirk's brother and sister-in-law die from parasites that enter their bodies.

Second Season (15 Sep 1967—29 Mar 1968):

Amok Time (T. Sturgeon). Spock is overwhelmed by the Vulcan mating drive, and Kirk must fight him in the Vulcan fashion.

Who Mourns for Adonis? (G. Ralston & G. L. Coon, from a story by Ralston). An alien named Apollo who claims he is the last of his race, once hailed on Earth as gods, seeks to keep part of the crew as worshippers.

The Changeling (John M. Lucas). The *Enterprise* faces destruction by Nomad, an ancient robot probe.

Mirror, Mirror (Jerome Bixby). During an ion storm Kirk and some others are beamed to a duplicated *Enterprise* in which their counterparts are cruel and vicious.

The Apple (M. Ehrlich & G. Coon). The *Enterprise* encounters a primitive culture ruled by a powerful "god" machine.

The Doomsday Machine (Norman Spinrad). A "doomsday machine" rampaging through space nearly destroys the *Enterprise*.

Catspaw (Robert Bloch & D. C. Fontana). Kirk and his top aides are captured by two weird creatures who can assume magical forms.

I, Mudd (Stephen Kandel). A sophisticated android delivers the starship to Harry Mudd, who controls 2,000 beautiful androids.

Metamorphosis (Gene L. Coon). A space pioneer is kept alive by a cloudlike alien life form.

Journey to Babel (D. C. Fontana). Kirk encounters many crises transporting delegates, including Spock's parents, to a meeting on the planet Babel.

The Deadly Years (David P. Harmon). Members of a landing party, including Kirk and Spock, begin to age at an astonishing rate after visiting the planet Gamma Hydra IV.

Obsession (Art Wallace). Kirk re-encounters a gaseous creature that he couldn't kill 13 years earlier.

Wolf in the Fold (Robert Bloch). Scotty is suspected of murdering three women until Kirk discovers the historical villain Jack the Ripper is responsible.

The Trouble With Tribbles (David Gerrold). Kirk has his hands full with tiny purring creatures that multiply at an alarming rate.

The Gamesters of Triskelion (Margaret Armen). Kirk and the crew visit a planet where some of the residents perform in "games" for the amusement of their masters.

A Piece of the Action (D. L. Harmon & G. L. Coon). The *Enterprise* discovers a planet running alone the lines of the gangster organisations of the 1920's.

The Immunity Syndrome (Robert Sabaroff). The *Enterprise* must destroy a giant amoeba-like creature which threatens to engulf the galaxy.

A Private Little War (G. Roddenberry). When natives of a primitive planet receive advanced weapons, Kirk must furnish the rival tribes with guns to maintain the balance of power.

Return to Tomorrow (John Kingsbridge). Three alien minds take over Kirk, Spock, and Dr. Ann Mulhall, and plan to build robot bodies so their minds can live on.

Patterns of Force (John M. Lucas). Kirk and Spock alight on a planet run by a Nazi-like regime

By Any Other Name (D. C. Fontana). The *Enterprise* is hijacked by entities that turn the crew into geometrical solids.

Omega Glory (G. Roddenberry). A starship captain mistakenly believes he has found the secret of immortality on the planet Omega.

The Ultimate Computer (D. C. Fontana). The *Enterprise* is a guinea pig in an experiment to prove a multitronic computer can run a space ship more efficiently than humans.

Bread and Circuses (G. Roddenberry & G. L. Coon, from a story by John Kneubel). People from the *Enterprise* find themselves in a society like ancient Rome, complete with gladiators and arena games.

Friday's Child (D. C. Fontana). Kirk violates a tribal taboo and is forced to take to the hills with the Chief's wife.

Assignment Earth (Art Wallace, from a story by G. Roddenberry & A. Wallace). *The Enterprise* beams aboard a human raised by aliens who hopes to save mankind from itself.

Third Season (1968—1969, chronological order not known):

Spock's Brain (Lee Cronin). A beautiful and mysterious woman materialises aboard the *Enterprise* and kidnaps Mr. Spock's brain.

The Enterprise Incident (D. C. Fontana). Kirk and Spock use intrigue as they seek a cloaking device of the Romulans.

The Paradise Syndrome (Margaret Armen). Kirk, suffering from amnesia, marries a beautiful alien woman but is oblivious to the impending destruction of her planet.

And the Small Children Shall Lead (Edward J. Lasko). Children under the spell of an alien villain play on the secret fears of crew members in an attempt to conquer the *Enterprise*.

Is There No Truth in Beauty? (Jean L. Aroeste). Spock gazes on a Medusan and is doomed to death by madness unless Kirk can persuade a woman to save him.

Spectre of the Gun (Lee Cronin). After violating Melkotian space, Kirk, Spock, and McCoy are trapped in a bizarre reconstruction of the gunfight at the O.K. Corral.

Day of the Dove (Jerome Bixby). Klingons and *Enterprise* officers clash as a monster feeds on their hatred.

For the World Is Hollow and I Have Touched the Sky (Rik Vollaerts). The queen of a hollow world camouflaged as an asteroid enslaves a dying Dr. McCoy.

The Tholian Web (Judy Burns & Chet Richards). With Kirk trapped in hyperspace, the Tholians seek to trap the *Enterprise* with their powerful web.

Plato's Stepchildren (M. Dolinsky). The *Enterprise* responds to a distress call from Platonius, and crew members become slaves to creatures with advanced telepathic powers.

Wink of an Eye (Lee Cronin). A group who move so fast they cannot be seen take over the *Enterprise*, and one chooses Kirk as a temporary mate.

The Empath (Joyce Muskat). A mute girl with the gift of sensing emotion and transferring pain learns compassion.

Elaan of Troyius (John M. Lucas). Kirk falls prey to the tears of an alien woman who must wed for the cause of peace.

Whom the Gods Destroy (Lee Irwin). An insane star captain tries to take over the *Enterprise*.

Let That Be Your Last Battlefield (Oliver Crawford, from a story by Lee Cronin). Two aliens attempt to transform the *Enterprise* into a battlefield to end a 50,000-year struggle.

Mark of Gideon (George F. Slavin & Stanley Adams). Kirk is lured onto a fake *Enterprise* on the planet Gideon, and Spock has to play diplomat.

That Which Survives (D. C. Fontana). The *Enterprise* encounters a menacing android, the last of her race, and is hurled a thousand light years, leaving Kirk, Sulu and McCoy stranded on the planet.

Requiem for Methuselah (Jerome Bixby). A powerful alien claims to have lived on Earth as Methuselah and others.

The Way to Eden (Arthur Heineimann, from a story by M. Richards & Heinemann). An explorer disillusioned with modern technology leads a group of space hippies to take over the *Enterprise*.

The Lights of Zetar (Jeremy Tarcher & Shari Lewis). A living electrical storm endangers Lt. Mira and Chief Engineer Scott, who has fallen in love with her.

The Cloud Minders (Margaret Armen, from a story by David Gerrold & Oliver Crawford). The *Enterprise* responds to an emergency call and is caught in a slave rebellion.

The Savage Curtain (Arthur Heinemann & G. Roddenberry). Historical figures aid Kirk and his crew in a bizarre battle against evil.

All Our Yesterdays (Jean L. Aroeste). A strange machine on a doomed planet hurtles Kirk, Spock, and McCoy into different eras of Earth's past.

Turnabout Intruder (Arthur Singer, from a story by G. Roddenberry). The mind of Kirk is imprisoned in the body of Dr. Janice Lester while she takes over the *Enterprise* as Kirk.

A book on the series is *The Making of Star Trek*, Stephen E. Whitfield & Gene Roddenberry (Ballantine: 73004, 1968, 413 pp., pa 95¢). It contains diagrams, photos, portions of scripts, and casts of all shows through to March 1968.

James Blish has revised many of the script stories into a series of paperbacks, as *Star Trek*, *Star Trek Two*, etc.

The episodes *Menagerie* and *City on the Edge of Forever* won the Hugo Award for drama for 1967 and 1968 respectively. The high standard of the series tapered off towards the end of its third and final season.

STELLAR PUBLISHING CORPORATION, New York. The company formed by H. Gernsback after he was forced to leave Experimenter Publishing Co. in 1929 (where he had published *Amazing Stories* and *Amazing Stories Quarterly*.). Stellar published the "Wonder Magazines"—*Air Wonder Stories* and *Science Wonder Stories* (later to be combined)—and also issued the paper-covered "Science Fiction" series. There was also one book in a planned "Science Fiction Classics" series: No. 1, *Between Worlds*, Garret Smith.

STRATO PUBLICATIONS LTD. The publishers who produced British editions of *Galaxy*, *Science Fiction Stories*, and *Future Science Fiction*.

SUPERMAN The cartoon strip worked out by Jerome Siegel and drawn by Joseph Shuster in the mid-1930's. They tried for years to sell the idea to publishers, and it was accepted in 1938 for use in *Action Comics* (which had been started to keep a New Jersey printer's presses busy during the depths of the Depression). The strip caught on immediately.

Siegel and Shuster did not retain any rights in the Superman comic group and nowadays have nothing at all to do with the strip. M. Weisinger was head of the Superman comic group in the mid-1950's [see S. Moskowitz, *Future SF*, June 1958, p. 120].

A film based on the cartoon strip, *Superman and the Mole Men*, was released in 1951. Then the U.S. television series, ABC network, ran for six seasons 1953-1957, with 104 episodes (30 minutes, black & white for first two seasons, then colour). George Reeves portrayed Superman (and his "alter ego" Clark Kent), with Phyllis Coates as Lois Lane (later replaced by Noel Neill), and Jack Larson as the naive and bumbling cub reporter Jimmy.

SUPERMEN Of the many tales of such beings, four novels are considered classics in their own right: *Gladiator*, P. Wylie; *The New Adam*, S. G. Weinbaum; *Odd John*, O. Stapledon; *Slan*, A. E. van Vogt.

SUPERNATURAL PHENOMENA [see also GHOSTS]
Literary Aspects: *The Supernatural in Fiction*, P. Penzoldt (1952); *Supernatural Horror in Literature*, H. P. Lovecraft (originally 1934, in collection 1939, book 1945); *The Supernatural in Modern English Fiction*, D. Scarborough (1917); *King Arthur Today*, N. C. Starr (1954).
Recorded Phenomena, etc.: See authors P. Andreas, A. G. Bennett, H. Carrington, C. B. Colby, A. David-Neel, E. J. Dingwall, F. Edwards, C. Fort, V. H. Gaddis, B. House, D. Mahoney, R. D. Miller, I. J. Nebel, E. F. Russell, I. Sanderson, E. R. Snow, G.N.M. Tyrrell, H. T. Wilkins, and also *Fate* (in WHO'S WHO).

SWAN LIMITED, London. British publisher issuing occasional items of science fiction and fantasy since the early 1940's. These include:
Ca. 1943: Two more or less complete reprints of *Science Fiction Quarterly* titled *Into the Fourth Dimension* and *The Moon Conquerors*; both 1/-.
Not dated: *The Dark City*, Kay Hammond, Weird Pocket Library No. 1 (no more appearing).
Not dated: *Weird Shorts: First Selection*, original short stories by W. P. Cockcroft, J. O. Evans, etc. A volume of crime stories also appeared under the *Weird Shorts* title.
Not dated: *The Case of the Missing Airman*, G. Elliott—one of the "Martin Speed, Detective" series.
1945: *Occult: A Collection of Stories of the Supernatural*, 7 original short stories by Henry Rawle, W. P. Cockcroft, and John C. Craig and others.
Not dated: *They Came From Mars*, W. P. Cockcroft.
Magazines: *Weird Story Magazine*; *Swan American Magazine*; *Swan Yankee Magazine*; 3 issues of *Weird Tales* (British edition); *Weird and Occult 1/- Library*; *Science Fiction 1/- Library*.

SWEDEN Claes Lundin, a well-known journalist, wrote the first real Swedish science fiction novel, *Oxygen och Aromasia—Bilder fran ar 2378* [Oxygen and Aromasia—Pictures From Year 2378] (J. Seligmann, Stockholm, 1878). But the names of the central characters and most of the story were derived from Kurd Lasswitz's *Bilder aus der Zukunft*, published in Breslau, Germany, earlier that year. Nevertheless it is of interest. Other old works of interest are *Ny Upptäckt av Landet Catacombe* [New Discovery of the Country Catacomb], by P. O. Fredell (Stockholm, 1780), and *Ormus och Ariman* [Ormouz and Ariman], by Carl Jonas Love Almqvist (1930).

A recent survey shows that there are around a thousand original Swedish works in sf, fantasy, etc., and some three thousand translations, of which more than a quarter were published in the boom of 1890 to 1910. Probably the most noted original Swedish novel is *Kallocain*, Karin Boye; other works include the famous poem *Lycksalighetens Ö* [Island of Happiness], Per Atterbom, and *Katastrofen* [The Catastrophe], Gustaf Jansson (1914).

More recently Nils Parling's *Korset* [The Cross], Ann-Margret Dahlquist-Ljungberg's *Stralen* [The Ray], and Harry Martinson's poem *Aniara* have achieved prominence. Others authors of note are Henning Berger, Henrik Nanne [as Carl Henner], Gustav Sandgren [as Gabriel Linde]. S. Lönnerstrand and B. Nyberg have entries in the *WHO'S WHO*.

Quite a large amount of English and American science fiction has been translated. Much of it is in the following publishers' series: Eklunds Bokförlag, with Eklunds SF-Serie, the first real sf series (1953-1955); Pingvinförlaget with Atomböcken; Lindqvist with Atombökckerna and Lindqvist LP Pocket; and Wennerberg with Rymdböckerna. All have ceased except Lindqvist LP Pocket, a series of inferior quality.

One of the first magazines that can be considered science fiction was published in Sweden: *Hugin*, 1916-1920, with Otto Witt as editor and publisher. The excellent fan-financed *Häpna* started in 1954, and its existence helped organise Swedish sf fandom; it ceased with the January 1966 issue. Plans have been reported for it to start again under the title *Tidskrift för Science Fiction* [Magazine of Science Fiction], with Sam J. Lundwall as editor. Other magazines have included *Jules Verne Magasinet*, 1940-1948, and a Swedish edition of *Galaxy*, 1958-1960. Yet another, *Alpha*, reached the printing stage but never appeared.

Sweden also had an early popular-science magazine, *Vetenskapen och Livet* [Science and Life], apparently very similar to H. Gernsback's *Science and Invention*, from which it took much of its material. Edited by E. Thall and published by Gebers Bokförlag, it was to have begun in 1914, but was delayed by World War I, and finally appeared in mid-1916. It ran bimonthly to the end of 1922, then monthly until it ceased at the end of 1928. *Vetenskapen och Livet* was pulp size, averaging 70 to 80 pages per issue, and sold for 2.50 kr (a high price at that time, equivalent to a three-course dinner!). It covered rockets, future towns, etc., was richly illustrated with photographs and drawings, and its colour covers were prominent for their quality. There was a French edition, *La Science et la Vie*, from 1918, and also a Finnish edition, *Tiede ja Elämä*.

Swedish fandom is quite strong and thriving, and many amateur magazines have been produced since the first appeared in 1952. The "Alvar" award is presented to persons who have contributed in some way to the field of science fiction.

Personalities include illustrators Hans Arnold (who has done work for *The Magazine of F&SF*), Eugen Semitjov, Björn Karlström, and Sven O. Emilsson (mainly fan work); Kjell Ekström (editor and translator); Sam J. Lundwall (author, translator, and bibliographer of Swedish books); Roland Adlerberth (translator and reviewer). In the fan field there are Denis Lindbohm, Bo Stenfors, and Ingvar Svensson.

Anthologies [covering translated stories]:

Kalla karar, Olle Strandberg (Raben & Sjögren, 1956, 349 pp., illus.—Arnold, 8 kr, 12.50 kr)

"Oh Whistle, and I'll Come to You, My Lad," M. R. James; "Alexander Perk's Ghost," R. D. Frisbie; "The Inexperienced Ghost," H. G. Wells; "Man Overboard," F. M. Crawford; "On the Brighton Road," R. Middleton; "The Occupant of the Room," A. Blackwood; "Faith, Hope and Love," I. S. Cobb; "The Derelict," W. H. Hodgson; "The Spider," H. H. Ewers; "The Open Window," Saki; "The Facts in the Case of M. Valdemar," E. A. Poe; "Silver Mask," H. Walpole; "The Rat," A. Sandemose [Scandinavian author]; "The Price on a Head," J. Russel; "Moonlight Music," A. Woolcott; "The Glass Eye," J. K. Cross; "A Modest Proposal," J. Swift; "A Problem for Emmy," R. S. Townes.

Stors Skräckboken [The Big Horror Book], Torsten Jungstedt (Rabén & Sjögren, 1959, 438 pp., illus.—Arnold, 24 kr, 29 kr)

"The Poet's Cat," Mally Dixon; "How I Silence Katubi," J. Torrend; "Mr. Loveday's Little Outing," E. Waugh; "Amédée ou Comment s'en Débarasser," E. Ionesco; "Helping the Fairies," Lord Dunsany; "The Caterpillar," Ramp; "Bezdna," I. Andrejev; "Morgan," F. Nilsson-Piraten [Scandinavian]; "The Renegade," S. Jackson; "The Public Hating," S. Allen; "Christ in Concrete," P. di Donato; "Exami-

nation Day," H. Slesar; "The Wheel-Barrow Boy," R. Parker; "It's a Good Life," J. Bixby; "Sentry," F. Brown; "The New Sound," C. Beaumont; "The Luckiest Man in the World," R. Sheckley; "In the Vault," H. P. Lovecraft; "The Screaming Woman," R. Bradbury; "The Color out of Space," H. P. Lovecraft; "The Man Upstairs," R. Bradbury; "Thus I Refute Beelzy," J. Collier; "Little Memento," J. Colliers; "Minuke," N. Kneale; "Chains," N. Kneale; "The Dead Woman," D. H. Keller; "A Piece of Linoleum," D. H. Keller; "The Yellow Wallpaper," C. Perkins; "The Music," T. Sturgeon; "The Night Side," R. Bloch; "My Last Book," C. & M. Lipman; "The Graveyard Rats," H. Kuttner; "The Loved Dead," C. M. Eddy; "A Note for the Milkman," S. Carroll; "The Happiest Man on Earth," A. Maltz; "Min Son Skall Förklara" [My Son Will Explain], T. Jungstedt [Scandinavian].

Raketmännen Fran Jorden [Rocket Men From Earth], Anonymous (Saxon & Lindström, Stockholm, 1956, 223 pp., pa 2.70 kr)

"Rocket Men From Earth," M. Lesser; "The God's Image," A. E. Nourse; "Why Skeets Malloy Had Two Heads," R. Shaver; "The Dog Hair," C. Beaumont; "The Paradox," M. Reynolds; "Animal in the House," M. Shaara; "The Thinker and the Thought," A. Derleth; "My Friend Bobby," A. E. Nourse; "Last Night of Summer," A. Coppel; "Cargo," D. J. Moffat; "The Bee Man," G. R. Dickson; "Never More the Stars," I. E. Cox; "The Ungrateful House," Anon.

T

TARGET—EARTH! U.S. film, United Artists, 1954; produced by Herman Cohen; starring Richard Denning, Virginia Grey, Richard Reeves, and Kathleen Crowley.

Based on the story "Deadly City" by P. W. Fairman (*If*, Mar 1953).

TELEVISION Among the earliest series was *Superman*, first appearing on TV in 1953, though its origin was of course many years earlier in comic books. The most noted of the U.S. television series is undoubtedly *Star Trek*, interest in which has continued in certain fan circles for a decade since it was produced.

Rod Serling's *Twilight Zone* is probably the next most noted, up to 1968; it won some Hugo awards. Paralleling it was *One Step Beyond*, dealing more with psychic phenomena. A further series of interest was *Thriller*, hosted by Boris Karloff.

The first television science fiction of any note appeared in 1963: *The Outer Limits*, which had a science line and also an element of terror. A group of sf-adventure series were the Irwin Allen productions *Voyage to the Bottom of the Sea* (adventures with a super-sub), *Lost in Space* (trials of an American space family), *The Time Tunnel* (adventure in many historical situations), and *Land of the Giants* (humans in a world of huge dimensions). The exaggerated comic-style *Batman* with its menacing background voice of doom and cliff-hanger episode in every two-part serial was also quite successful. The "aliens are among us" theme was covered in *The Invaders*, while one of the most thoughtful and bizarre series was *The Prisoner*.

Other U.S. series were *The Addams Family*, the long-running *Alfred Hitchcock Presents* (or *Hour*), *Bewitched*, *Dark Shadows*, *The Flying Nun*, *The Ghost and Mrs. Muir*, and *I Dream of Jeannie*, as well as a number of relatively minor ones.

On British television there have been the *Quatermass* series (see N. Kneale in *WHO'S WHO*), and F. Hoyle's *A for Andromeda* and *Andromeda Breakthrough*—all highly considered. Boris Karloff introduced an *Out of This World* series; *Out of the Unknown* was quite high class also. The Gerry Anderson puppet series—*Fireball XL*, *Stingray*, *Super-Car*, and *Thunderbirds*—are all juveniles with sf overtones. The long-running *Dr. Who* also has its followers and is responsible for the "Dalek" phenomenon.

THEM! U.S. film, Warner Brothers, 1954; starring James Whitmore, Edmund Gwenn, and Joan Weldon; from a story by George W. Yates.

After atomic explosions, intelligent giant ants escape, are hunted, and finally wiped out by flame throwers; suspenseful and well acted.

THING, THE U.S. film, RKO, 1951; produced by Howard Hawks; starring Kenneth Tobey and James Young.

Adapted from the novella "Who Goes There?" J. W. Campbell (*ASF*, Aug 1938), this is well acted and quite suspenseful. Unfortunately, it doesn't follow the Campbell story at all.

THRILLER U.S. television series, NBC network, 67 episodes, 1960-1962; a Hubbell Robinson production for Revue (Universal); 60-minute episodes, black & white.

A mystery-suspense series which began poorly but later built up in interest. It included Boris Karloff as host and occasional star.

THUNDERBIRDS British television series, 1966; produced by Gerry & Sylvia Anderson; probably the best of their puppet fantasy series. Set in the 21st Century, it featured the adventures of space age heroes. The format was a half-hour cliffhanger followed by a half-hour solution. Filmed in Super Marionation.

TIME Books about time are *An Experiment With Time*, J. W. Dunne (1927); *The Voices of Time*, J. T. Fraser (1966); *The Conquest of Time*, H. Horwood (1959); *Man in the Universe*, F. Hoyle (1966).

TIME CAPSULE The first was "The Westinghouse Time Record," which was lowered into the earth at the New York World's Fair on 23 Sep 1938, to be opened in 5,000 years. The write-up in *Amazing Stories*, Jan 1939, mentioned that the Oct 1938 issue had been put on microfilm and included in the capsule's contents.

TIME TUNNEL, THE U.S. television series, ABC network, 30 episodes, 1966; an Irwin Allen production for 20th Century Fox; 60-minute episodes in colour. The regular cast was James Darren (as Dr. Tony Newman), Robert Colbert (Dr. Doug Phillips), Whit Bissell (Lt. Gen. Heywood Kirk), John Zaremba (Dr. Raymond Swain), Wesley Lau (Army Master Sgt. Jiggs).

The use of a time machine lands the two protagonists in many dangerous situations in both the future and past of Earth's history.

TRANS-ATLANTIC FAN FUND [TAFF] The science fiction fan organisation to collect money to pay expenses for a member of fandom (either from North America or Europe) to attend a convention on the opposite side of the Atlantic. The "TAFF Delegate" is chosen by vote of those who donate. The collection is taken up on both sides of the Atlantic, with the collector being usually the previous winner.

TRANSATLANTIC TUNNEL Gaumont film, 1935; starring Richard Dix and Madge Evans; screenplay by C. Siodmak. Covering the drilling of a tunnel from England to the U.S.A., it was quite dramatic and was generally recommended.

TRANSGALAXIS German book club founded in 1959 and operated by H. Bingenheimer, and then by his widow. It produced a German book catalogue, and for a period issued regular leaflets informing of new publications.

TWILIGHT ZONE, THE U.S. television series, CBS network; 151 episodes in five seasons, 1959-1964; a Cayuga production filmed at MGM. Rod Serling hosted the series and produced it with Buck Houghton. All but the fourth season were 30-minute episodes in black & white; the fourth was 60 minutes.

This was a top-notch series of stories often having a twist at the end. Some plots were sf but there was no set formula. Serling wrote most episodes, but Richard Matheson and Charles Beaumont also wrote a number. Many anthologies have been selected from the series [see SERLING, R.].

U,V

UNIDENTIFIED FLYING OBJECTS [UFO's] [or FLYING SAUCERS] Books of nonfiction—or at least purporting to be nonfiction—covered in the *WHO's WHO* are listed below. A review of this material in the early 1960's for U.S. libraries commented that Menzel was considered the best, followed by Keyhoe, Heard, and Scully.

1950 *The Flying Saucers Are Real*, D. E. Keyhoe; *Behind the Flying Saucers*, F. Scully; *Riddle of the Flying Saucers*, G. Heard.

1952 *The Coming of the Saucers*, K. Arnold.

1953 *Flying Saucers*, D. Menzel; *Flying Saucers From Outer Space*, D. E. Keyhoe; *The Flying Saucers Have Landed*, G. Adamski.

1954 *Flying Saucers on the Attack (British ed.: Flying Saucers on the Moon)*, H. T. Wilkins; *Flying Saucers From Mars*, G. Allingham; *Space, Gravity and the Flying Saucer*, L. Cramp; *The Saucers Speak*, G. H. Williamson.

1955 *The Case for the Unidentified Flying Objects*, M. K. Jessup; *The Flying Saucer Conspiracy*, D. E. Keyhoe; *Flying Saucers Uncensored*, H. T. Wilkins; *The Secret of the Saucers*, O. Angelucci; *Flying Saucers and Common Sense*, W. Girvan; *Inside the Space Ships*, G. Adamski.

1956 *Report on Unidentifed Flying Objects*, E. J. Ruppelt; *Flying Saucers From Another World*, A. Michel; *They Knew Too Much About Flying Saucers*, G. Barker; *UFO and the Bible*, M. K. Jessup; *UFO Annual*, M. K. Jessup; *The Truth About Flying Saucers*, A. Michel.

1957 *The Coming of the Space-Ships*, G. Gibbons; *The Expanding Case for the UFO*, M. K. Jessup; *Other Tongues—Other Flesh*, G. H. Williamson; *They Rode in Spaceships*, G. Gibbons; *Saucer People*, R. G. Garver.

1958 *I Doubted Flying Saucers*, S. Layne; *Flying Saucers and the Straight-Line Mystery*, A. Michel; *UFOs Confidential*, G. H. Williamson.

1961 *Flying Saucers Farewell*, G. Adamski.

1962 *The Great Flying Saucer Hoax*, C. F. Lorenzen.

1963 *World of Flying Saucers*, D. Menzel & L. G. Boyd.

1965 *Anatomy of a Phenomenon*, J. Vallee; *Flying Saucers Over Australia*, J. Holledge.

1966 *The Reference for Outstanding UFO Sighting Reports*, UFO Information Retrieval Center.

1967 *Behind the Flying Saucer Mystery*, G. Adamski; *What We Really Know About Flying Saucers*, O. Binder; *On Board the Flying Saucers*, C. Gibbons; *The UFO Report*, I. A. Greenfield.

1968 *UFO's—Identified*, P. Klass; *Flying Saucers in Fact and Fiction*, H. Santesson.

Many magazines, both professional and amateur, have concerned themselves with the UFO phenomena. *Flying Saucer Review* was a British magazine begun May 1955, quoted as a quarterly at 21/- per year; it apparently became bimonthly soon after. Numerous articles were published in *Fantastic Universe* from 1957; *Amazing Stories* had a special saucer issue, Oct 1957.

R. A. Palmer changed the policy of *Other Worlds* in 1957 and made it *Flying Saucers From Other Worlds*; Palmer also made up a comprehensive list of flying saucer material which was published in *Amazing*, Nov 1957.

U.S.S.R. See RUSSIA

UTOPIAN PUBLICATIONS LTD. Formed by Benson Herbert early in the 1940's, this firm produced science fiction and fantasy in a paper-covered form. For several years W. Gillings was on the editorial staff. Most of the publications are now quite scarce because of the flimsiness of the booklets and the small editions. The most important items were the *American Fiction* series and the magazine *Strange Tales of the Mysterious and Supernatural*.

UTOPIAS
Literary Studies: *Journey Through Utopia*, M. L. Berneri (1950); *The Quest for Utopia*, G. Negley (1952); *Utopian Fantasy*, R. Gerber (1955);

American Dreams, A Study of American Utopias, V. Parrington (1947). **Collections:** *Famous Utopias*, C. M. Andrews (1901); *Ideal Commonwealths*, H. Morley (1895).

The first American Utopia is considered to be *Equality*, Anonymous (1802); this and *Three Hundred Years Hence*, Mary Griffiths (1836) were reprinted in 1947 and 1950, respectively, by Prime Press.

Other utopian (or dystopian) "classics" covered in the *Encyclopedia* include *Looking Backward*, E. Bellamy (1888); *1984*, G. Orwell [E. Blair] (1949); *Erewhon*, S. Butler (1972); *Caesar's Column*, I. Donnelly (1890); *A Description of the Famous Kingdom of Macaria*, S. Hartlib (1641); *Journey of Nils Klim Underground*, L. Holberg (1741); *A Crystal Age*, W. H. Hudson (1887); *Brave New World*, A. Huxley (1932); *We*, E. Zamiatin (1920).

VOYAGE TO THE BOTTOM OF THE SEA Film, Irwin Allen, 1961; with Walter Pidgeon as an admiral blowing out a fire in the Van Allen Belt. The submarine was used in the ensuing television series of the same name: 110 episodes, 1964-1968. The first season was in black & white, then it was made in colour, with 60-minute episodes. It starred Richard Basehart as Admiral Harrington Nelson.

VOYAGE TO THE END OF THE WORLD, THE This anonymous work is said to be the first science fiction story; it appeared in manuscript about 1540. Circulation reached either six or sixteen copies, until it was banned by the Vatican. It is mentioned in Hartmann's *German Literature of the 15th and 16th Centuries* [see *Amazing Stories*, Nov 1940, p. 123].

W,Y,Z

WITCHCRAFT Works covered in the *WHO'S WHO*: *The Black Art*, R. Ahmed (1936, 1968); *Devils, Monsters and Nightmares*, H. Daniel (1964); *Witches and Sorcerers*, A. Daraul (1965, pa); *Here Are Ghosts and Witches*, J. W. Day (1954); *Man Into Wolf*, R. Eisler (1951); *Witchcraft Today*, G. B. Gardner (1954); *Satan's Disciples*, R. C. Goldston (1962, pa); *Pictorial Anthology of Witchcraft, Magic and Alchemy*, E. Grillot de Givry (1931); *Picture Museum of Sorcery, Magic and Alchemy*, E. Grillot de Givry (1963); The Supernatural, D. Hill [with P. Williams] (1965); *A Mirror of Witchcraft*, C. Hole (1957); *Witchcraft*, P. Hughes (1965, pa); *Malleus Malificarium*, H. Institoris (1489) (considered a classic); *Diary of a Witch*, S. Leek (1968); *The Dark World of Witches*, E. Maple (1962); *The Realm of Ghosts*, E. Maple (1964); *The God of the Witches*, M. A. Murray (1962); *Witch-Cult in Western Europe*, M. A. Murray (1963); *Witchcraft: European and African*, G. Parrinder (1965); *The Dawn of Magic*, L. Pauwels [with J. Bergier] (1963); *The Satanic Mass*, H. T. Rhodes (1954); *The Magic Island*, W. B. Seabrook (1929); *Witchcraft*, W. B. Seabrook (1940); *Devil Worship in Britain*, A. V. Sellwood [with P. Haining] (1964); many works by M. Summers; *A Treasury of Witchcraft*, H. E. Wedeck (1961).

An anthology of both fiction and nonfiction on witchcraft is *Prince of Darkness*, G. Verner (1946).

WORLD OF TOMORROW, THE Set of 50 cards issued in England by Mitchell's Cigarettes in the 1930's. This included such items as a scene from the film *Things to Come* and the F. R. Paul illustration from "The World at Bay" (*AS*, 1927). No full sets are known. Interest in the set was created by comment in *Spacemen* magazine [see No. 5].

WORLD'S WORK, Tadsworth, England. British publisher who before World War II produced the *Master Thriller* series (a very involved range of magazines of all types, some of which became regular publications—see entry in *MAGAZINES* section) and *Tales of Wonder* (not usually considered part of the series).

The firm continued at least into the mid-1950's, with the first book edition of *Sinister Barrier*, E. Russell (1943), and the *Master Science Fiction* series, which included some titles in J. R. Fearn's *Golden Amazon* novels as late as 1954.

YANDRO Noted U.S. amateur magazine, edited by Buck and Juanita Coulson of Indiana. Normally mimeographed, it runs articles and reviews; the April 1966 issue was the 150th, in its 13th year of publication. It won the 1965 Hugo for amateur publications. It is still being published as of 1980.

ZARNAK The U.S. comic strip which began in *Thrilling Wonder Stories*, running from Aug 1936 to Oct 1937 (8 parts), but was dropped in the middle of a sequence; it was continued in various comic books.

ZOOLOGY Works in the *WHO'S WHO* concerning animals, real or otherwise: *Animal Legends*, M. Burton (1955); *Mermaids and Mastodons*, R. Carrington (1957); *Unnatural History: An Illustrated Bestiary*, C. Clair (1967); *Prehistoric Animals*, S. Epstein (1957); *Monsters of the Deep*, T. Helm (1962); *On the Track of Unknown Animals*, B. Heuvelmans (1959); *Exotic Zoology* (and others), W. Ley; *Fabulous Beasts*, P. Lum (1951); *Mystery Monsters*, G. Soule (1965); *The Snouters*, H. Stumpke (1967).